World History of Design

Volume 2

2 World History of Design

World War I to World War II

Victor Margolin

Bloomsbury Academic
An imprint of Bloomsbury
Publishing Plc

B L O O M S B U R Y

LONDON · OXFORD · NEW YORK · NEW DELHI · SYDNEY

Bloomsbury Academic

An imprint of Bloomsbury Publishing Plc

50 Bedford Square	1385 Broadway
London	New York
WC1B 3DP	NY 10018
UK	USA

www.bloomsbury.com

BLOOMSBURY and the Diana logo are trademarks of Bloomsbury Publishing Plc

First published 2015

Hardback reprinted 2017
Paperback edition first published 2017

British Library Cataloguing-in-Publication Data
A catalogue record for this book is available from the British Library.

ISBN: HB: 978-1-4725-6651-5
2-Volume Set: 978-1-4725-6928-8
PB: 978-1-3500-1273-8
2-Volume Set (PB): 978-1-3500-1845-7

Library of Congress Cataloging-in-Publication Data
A catalog record for this book is available from the Library of Congress.

Cover design: Louise Dugdale

Typeset by Fakenham Prepress Solutions, Fakenham, Norfolk NR21 8NN
Printed and bound in India

Contents

List of Illustrations

Figures

Acknowledgments

As with Volume 1 of this history, colleagues continued to be helpful in ways similar to the first volume: reading chapter drafts, recommending or providing books and additional reference material, helping with translations, or simply offering an opportunity to talk over some of my thoughts. For this volume in particular, many colleagues were helpful in locating and in some cases providing images to complement the text. Those who helped with the volume include Huda Smitshuizen Abefares, Esra Aksan, Jenny Aland, Ralph Austen, Tevfik Balcioglu, Helena Barbosa, Noemi Bitterman, Gui Bnsiepe, Zhou Bo, Michael Bogle, Geoffrey Caban, Irina Carabas, Pedro Alvarez Caselli, Eduardo Castillo, Rosa Chiesa, David Crowley, Mic Czerwinski, Sigal Davidi-Kunda, Rafael Denis, Veronica Devalle, Luz Carmen de Vilchis Esquivel, Marina Emmanouil, Gökhan Ersan, Kjetil Fallan, Lucilla Fernandez, Haruhiko Fujita, Howard Garfinkel, Marina Garone, Paul Gehl, John Green, Jørn Guldberg, Mor Halimi, Steven Heller, Richard Hollis, Ken Isaacs, Nasim Jafarinaimi, A. Bou Jawdeh, Beni Kadar, Sadik Karamustafa, Nurith Kenaan-Kadar, Yassaman Khodadadeh, Yuko Kikuchi, Pekka Korvenma, Jackie Kwok, Soojin Lee, Cathy Leff, Elliott Lefkovitz, Dimitrios Legakos, Zeina Maasri, Klimis Mastoridis, Peter McNeil, Jeff Meikle, Pepe Menendez, Marcello Montore, Josef Mrozek, Maria Nicholas, Márton Orosz, Vanni Pasca, Raquel Pelta, Jiri Pelzl, César Augusto Peña, Alton Purvis, Martin Racine, Roger Remington, Jacinto Salcedo, Marlis Saleh, Paul Shaw, Miryam Sommerfeld, Adi Stern, Paul Stiff, Ittai Joseph Tamari, David Tartakover, Sarah Teasley, Christopher Thompson, Oscar Traversa, Jilly Treganou, Giovani Tronconi, Humberto Valdivieso, Anna Valtonen, Fedja Vukić, Gennifer Weisenfeld, Kerstin Wichman, Artemis Yagou, Yun Wang, Jerry Zbiral, and Larry Zeman.

To produce two books as large and complicated as volumes 1 and 2 of *A World History of Design* required a dedicated staff. I have been fortunate to work with a group of excellent professionals who have managed the myriad details of this project with aplomb. Tristan Palmer was the editor who first brought the books to Bloomsbury (then Berg). It was a pleasure to work with him and then with his successors, Simon Cowell, followed by Rebecca Barden. Abbie Sharman has kept track of the many administrative details on the editorial side. Ken Bruce and Joanne Murphy have been in charge of production, while Clare Turner has contributed design expertise. Kim Storry as Project Manager has kept track of all the many drafts, proofs, and changes. Working with her were Ronnie Hanna, copy editor and proofreader, Tristan Defew, typesetter, and Martin Hargreaves, who did the index. I am particularly grateful to my colleague John Massey and his associate Matthew Terdich for their superb cover and layout designs.

Introduction to Volume 2

This volume begins with the Russian Revolution, which transformed a nation that was oppressed by a czar and a self-serving aristocratic class into an unprecedented society of centralized planning and Communist Party rule. The ideals of the revolution spread across Europe even as they were undermined by actual events in what became the Soviet Union.

After Germany's defeat in World War I, three nations—France, Great Britain, and the United States, the leading Allied victors—emerged as the world's Great Powers. All had strong economies before the war and expected to improve their economic competitiveness, now that the war had ended.

The ambition of the Great Powers was to shape a better world in the wake of Germany's defeat, but the alliance among them soon began to disintegrate. Woodrow Wilson, the American president, proposed Fourteen Points for the reconstruction of Europe which urged the creation of an international body that would encompass the principles of collective security and prevent another destructive world conflict. Known as the League of Nations, it was formulated and subscribed to at the Paris Peace Conference in 1919. However, the U.S. Congress did not ratify the necessary treaties or support United States participation in the League. Adopting an isolationist position, the Republican-dominated Congress effectively ensured that the United States would have a diminished influence on future European affairs.

Although Germany faced severe economic dislocation at the end of the war, by 1924, the United States had stepped in with short-term loans that helped the Germans restore their economy to prewar strength and beyond. Of all the nations in Europe, Germany most actively embraced mass-production as the best strategy for economic development. In France, the government continued to support French supremacy in the production of luxury goods, while in Britain, which had once been the industrial powerhouse of the world, many British factories were hesitant to install sophisticated machinery, apply efficiency methods of organization, or adopt a machine aesthetic for the design of their products.

Other countries in Europe were in a lesser position to exploit the economic potential of mass-production than France, Britain, and Germany. Following the war's end, the Hapsburg monarchy collapsed, resulting in the formation of the successor states of Austria, Hungary, and Czechoslovakia, and the distribution of the rest of its territories to already existing nations—a process that seriously destabilized East and Central Europe. By 1923, Poland had emerged once again as an independent nation after several treaties had mandated the redrawing of its borders. However, the economies of all these countries were predominantly agricultural or were otherwise based on the extraction of resources. Only Czechoslovakia was able to develop a balanced economy.

In the north, Finland became independent of Russia after the Bolsheviks came to power in 1917, and along with her Scandinavian neighbors—Denmark, Sweden, and Norway—sought to establish a culture that was firmly based on an equitable use of resources for a predominantly middle-class population. This endured until Russia invaded Finland in 1939. Smaller European countries such as Belgium, the Netherlands, and Switzerland also fostered domestic growth for a middle-class market. Throughout the 1920s and early 1930s Spain experienced nearly continuous political turmoil, which led to the Spanish Civil War. It began in 1936, resulted in the dictatorship of General Francisco Franco, and served as a staging ground for World War

II. The Portuguese government was equally unstable until António de Oliveira Salazar assumed the role of dictator in 1926. Like the Scandinavians, none of these countries was in a position to build a major industrial economy, although many of them had one or several prominent manufacturers who embraced the machine and the tenets of mass-production.

Thus modernity was a spotty enterprise in Europe during the 1920s and 1930s. Germany, the defeated power, embraced it more enthusiastically and aggressively than did any other country except the United States, therefore setting an example of how design could contribute to the making of a modern nation. German innovations in design such as the manufacture of furniture from tubular steel, the modern working-class housing estates, and the New Typography of Jan Tschichold were adopted cautiously and sporadically across Europe and faced greater overall resistance than enthusiasm. While the association of modernity with German revitalization was problematic for some countries, the new German design and architecture were also seen by many as a direct threat to traditional values, whether the preservation of a pronounced class structure as was the case in countries like France, Austria, and Britain, or else the nostalgic retention of styles and iconography that had strong nationalist connotations.

The United States was hit hard by the Great Depression that followed from the crash of the American stock market in 1929. Though the 1930s were difficult for many Americans, as they were for people in Europe, industrial designers sought to create a language of product streamlining to bring the American populace out of the doldrums and create an optimistic atmosphere that would encourage more consumption.

During the period covered in this volume, a handful of countries controlled the lives of millions of people in their colonies. Though colonialism had been integrated into the world order in the late 19th century, it was celebrated in the first part of the 20th with large colonial exhibitions in Britain and France. Much of Africa was under colonial rule during this period as were parts of Asia including India. The same was true for large sections of the Middle East as a consequence of the Ottoman Empire's collapse after World War I and the subsequent occupation of parts of its former territory by Britain and France.

In Asia, China slowly began to engage with a culture of modernity, particularly in Shanghai, which became a model for how modern Western ideas could be adapted to an Asian population that aspired to embrace them. Japan continued its ambition to become a modern secular society as well as Asia's foremost colonial power. With its invasion of Manchuria in 1931, Japan initiated an expansionist phase that led to war with China in 1937, its attack on the United States at the end of 1941, and a subsequent war with a host of Allied forces in the Pacific theater.

Latin American nations were trading actively with Europe until World War I cut off channels of communication. This led to various degrees of import substitution and an opportunity for the United States to expand its business activities throughout the region. Modernity for the Latin Americans was refracted through the sensibilities of the region's financial and cultural elites for whom France was a more potent model to emulate than Germany or the United States.

In Europe, Benito Mussolini came to power in 1922. Coupled with the Bolshevik Revolution in Russia and Lenin's early ambition to spread communism to other European countries, Mussolini's dictatorship in Italy and the rise of the Nazi Party in Germany posed a challenge to the idealistic peace plans of the League of Nations and created uneasiness among Europe's democracies. This uneasiness grew in the 1930s when the Nazis under Adolf Hitler came to power in Germany, facing off against the Soviet Union in the Spanish Civil War. The German Army then began to march eastward where it occupied Austria and Czechoslovakia in 1938 and Poland in 1939. Hitler signed a peace pact with the Soviet Union in 1939 but betrayed it when the German Army invaded that country in 1941. Once a number of allied countries declared war on Germany and World War II began, Germany continued her European conquests and attacks on Great Britain until her final defeat in 1945. Italy and Japan were also defeated, thus preparing for a post-war world of nations that aspired for the first time to a state of global unity and universal human rights even as colonialism still persisted in some parts of the world.

Chapter 20: Design in the Soviet Union 1905–1928

The Revolution of 1905

At the beginning of the 20th century, the discontent of Russia's factory workers and peasants began to coalesce into a rebellious movement against Czar Nicholas

Fig. 20.01: Anon., *Gadfly*, 1906. Institute of Modern Russian Culture and Digital Library, University of Southern California.

II, who had little interest in giving up his autocratic control of the country. Sparked by an incident known as "Bloody Sunday," in January 1905, when protesting workers marched to the czar's residence and were fired upon by his soldiers, a mass movement opposed to the czar began to grow.

The movement was supported by the editors and artists of close to 400 satirical journals with militant names like *Machine-Gun*, *Arrow*, *Sting*, *Whip*, *Hell-Post*, and *Gadfly* that began to appear late in the year (Fig. 20.01). Throughout the 19th century, the czars had kept a tight clamp on the oppositional press and the few critical journals that were published had to operate underground. By 1905, however, a large cadre of writers and artists joined forces to attack the czarist regime.

Many of the cartoonists for the Russian periodicals were trained at art schools by established artists such as Ilya Repin (1844–1930) in St. Petersburg and Valentin Serov (1865–1911) in Moscow. A few had been members of the *World of Art* group as was Serov himself. The cartoonists were stimulated by journals abroad such as Munich's humor magazine *Simplicissimus* whose cartoonists, including Olaf Gulbrannson (1873–1958) and Bruno Paul (1874–1968), lampooned Kaiser Wilhelm and the foibles of the German bourgeoisie. Other sources included the French satirical paper *L'Assiette au Beurre*. For the Russians, however, the political stakes were higher than they were in Germany or France and the artists drew as well on traditions of political satire and caricature that stretched back to the French Revolution.

Allegory and caricature were two of the main techniques of the Russian cartoonists. They represented the Russian people as a woman hanging in a noose or a virile male peasant, both of whom were victimized by the czar's military. The latter were portrayed as bats, monsters, or other distasteful creatures. As with many of the satirical journals, the masthead lettering was done by hand with the intent of being emotionally dramatic rather than typographically tasteful. On many of the covers, red was the dominant color, which more often than not depicted the blood of victims. Sadly, by 1907 most of these journals had either been suppressed or brought under government control and thus rendered less controversial.

Among the *World of Art* painters who drew cartoons and caricatures for the satirical journals were Boris Anisfeld (1879–1973), Ivan Bilibin (1876–1942), Mstislav Dobuzhinsky (1875–1957), Yevgeny Lancere (1875–1946), and Boris Kustodiev (1878–1927). Not all of these artists were active following the Bolshevik Revolution of 1917 but some were. Kustodiev, for example, became a prominent poster designer, who also won a contest to design the Red Army headdress and overcoat.

The October Revolution and the Civil War

Although Czar Nicholas was able to remain in power after the demonstrations and protests of 1905, the uprisings created a state of unrest that eventually led to his abdication in February 1917. In October the Provisional Government collapsed and the Bolshevik Party, headed by Vladimir Ilyich Lenin, seized power. However, it would not be until the spring of 1921, after a bloody Civil War in which the Red Army of the Bolsheviks was pitted against an array of forces including commanders and soldiers once loyal to the czar as well as the armies of several foreign governments, that the Communist Party, the organization through which the Bolsheviks exercised power, would be able to fully take control of the country.

By the beginning of 1918, the Bolsheviks had begun to establish a number of government departments, including the People's Commissariat of Enlightenment (or Ministry of Education) and the Supreme Council of the National Economy (VSNKh or Vesenkha). The period of War Communism, during which the Civil War was fought, was a difficult one for the Bolsheviks. The factories, which the Communists began to nationalize, lacked raw materials and the transport system had just about collapsed. Illiteracy was widespread and hunger was rampant. In order to maintain control, Lenin eliminated all non-Bolshevik newspapers and introduced a widespread propaganda campaign to secure support for the Bolshevik regime and the Red Army.

The Bolsheviks devised various means of propaganda including public art, a massive poster campaign, and public festivals to commemorate their victory, and they created propaganda trains and ships that traveled throughout the country. On of the Bolsheviks' first propaganda acts was to devise a set of official symbols for the new regime. In July 1918, the first Soviet constitution of the RSFSR (Russian Soviet Federal Socialist Republic) displayed the hammer and sickle, which symbolized a union of workers and peasants—industry and agriculture—as the new state symbol. The RSFSR remained an independent socialist state until it became one republic of the larger U.S.S.R. (Union of Soviet Socialist Republics). In 1924, the first constitution of the USSR added a five-pointed red star to the hammer and sickle. The red star had been approved in April 1918 as a symbol for the recently formed Red Army. It was displayed with a crossed hammer and plow on it to symbolize the workers and peasants who were supposed to be the army's principal source of support (Fig. 20.02).

At the time the Bolsheviks took power, Lenin had no sense of what a new Bolshevik art might look like. He therefore relied on the established bourgeois realist tradition of the 19th century. The Plan for Monumental Propaganda, which he inaugurated in April 1918, proposed that the monuments that had been erected to commemorate the czars and their respective regimes be removed and replaced by statues of revolutionary heroes such as Karl Marx and Friedrich Engels, the authors of the *Communist Manifesto*, as well as heroes of the French Revolution, including Danton and Robespierre, and Russian cultural figures like Andrei Rublev, the Russian icon painter, and the writer Fyodor Dostoyevsky.

More direct and widespread than the erection

Fig. 20.02: Dmitry Moor, Proletarians of all countries, unite!, poster, 1919. © ITAR-TASS Photo Agency/Alamy.

was often portrayed as a blacksmith pounding a piece of metal on an anvil. For the most part these figures were men, although one rare poster depicted a woman worker with a heavy hammer gesturing towards a group of buildings including a library, cafeteria, workers club, and a house for mother and children. The text states, "This is what the October Revolution has given to the working and peasant women."

Realism was far more prevalent than allegory in these posters. Whereas artists working for the satirical journals in 1905–1906 tended to portray the Russian people as a single oppressed woman or peasant, the Bolshevik artists relied more on social types including the fat capitalist in top hat and tails. They also, on occasion, represented capitalism as a fierce dragon being slain by a brave Russian worker with a sword or hammer. Due to the high degree of illiteracy in Russia, the posters tended to feature dramatic images rather than texts. One important precedent for these images was the *lubok*, an illustrated woodcut or broadside that had circulated among the peasantry since the early 17th century. Combining pictures with text, the *lubok* featured stories or fables whose subject matter included religion and folklore, as well as political issues. Another source was the religious icon painting that graced the homes of many Russians and sometimes appropriated theological subjects for political purposes.

The poster styles fell generally into two categories: heroic and satirical. The heroic posters featured a realistic style and portrayed workers, peasants, and soldiers engaged in characteristic activities. Perhaps the leading representative of this style was the Latvian Alexander Apsit (1880–1944), who had worked previously as a successful illustrator and poster artist. His first poster for the Bolsheviks showed a worker and peasant standing on the broken chains and artifacts of the imperial past (Plate 01). Other posters of his depicted soldiers and sailors in battle; the czar, Church, and pre-revolutionary aristocracy oppressing the poor Russian peasants; and a heroic worker doing battle with a hydra-headed monster who represented the political

of new monuments was the poster campaign, which resulted in over 3,600 different designs between 1918 and 1921. The artists who produced these posters had for the most part been trained in Russia's art schools before the revolution. However, some were self-taught. Many had worked as illustrators of books, magazines, and newspapers. Poster production was spread among a number of agencies and there was no overall coordination, although a body of common imagery eventually emerged. Central icons were the new social types, the worker and peasant, as well as the Red Army soldier. The soldier could be seen ramming his bayonet into an enemy or a corpulent capitalist, while the worker types of Russian imperialism. One of Apsit's best-known posters promoted the building of village reading rooms to help the peasants overcome their illiteracy.

Another artist working actively in the realist style was Dmitry Moor (1883–1946), who, besides creating posters, painted propaganda trains and contributed satirical drawings to numerous periodicals. Like Apsit, Moor employed color lithography for his designs. His poster *Have You Enrolled as a Volunteer?* depicts a soldier with a smoking factory chimney behind him, pointing his finger at the viewer and calling him to enlist in the Red Army (Fig. 20.03). The figure recalls both British artist Alfred Leete's World War I recruiting poster and James Montgomery Flagg's appropriation of it to recruit for the United States Army.

The leading artist in the satirical style was Viktor Deni, who specialized in ridiculing czarists and capitalists alike. His images were actually more akin to newspaper cartoons than posters, although their reproduction in the poster format ensured a wide circulation. Deni's poster criticizing the League of Nations showed three fat old men with swelling paunches that look like moneybags. Representing France, America, and Britain, they are seated above a sea of emaciated figures, who are ostensibly crushed by their policies. Another of Deni's posters, which included a text by the poet Demyan Bedni, depicted the capitalist as a paunchy figure in a combined top hat and crown wallowing in a sea of gold coins.

One of the more successful poster campaigns during the Civil War years was conducted by the ROSTA Telegraph Agency. Beginning in late 1919, the campaign consisted of posters that were originally created as single colored drawings but were subsequently produced in multiple copies, either from cardboard stencils or linoleum blocks. The posters were displayed in the windows of the agency's offices and other public places, mostly in Moscow but also in other cities where the agency had bureaus. Known as ROSTA Windows, they depicted the events of the day in a cartoon or comic style. The idea for the ROSTA Windows originated with artist Mikhail Cheremnykh (1890–1962), who conceived them as a sequence of panels, much like a comic strip, that depicted political fables and current events with stereotypical characters. The poet Vladimir Mayakovsky (1893–1930), who had trained as an artist before the revolution, publicized the form most widely. Mayakovsky wrote most of the short rhyming texts for the posters and he produced the drawings for many of them as well. The clearest precedent for these windows was the *lubok* woodcuts, which also relied heavily on drawings to tell

Fig. 20.03: Dmitry Moor, Have You Enrolled as a Volunteer?, poster, 1920. © Heritage Image Partnership Ltd/Alamy.

their story to a largely illiterate audience. In ROSTA window no. 132, Mayakovsky depicted Uncle Sam and a soldier from the White Army in the top panels. They persuade people with money and lies. In the last two panels, he urged the viewers to open their eyes and recognize that rifles are the Communists' weapons (Fig. 20.04). Besides Cheremnykh and Mayakovsky, other ROSTA artists in Moscow included the stage designer and cartoonist Ivan A. Malyutin (1889–1932). At the ROSTA studio in Petrograd, where linocuts were a principal medium for many of the posters, the leading artists were Vladimir Kozlinsky (1881–1967) and Vladimir Lebedev (1891–1967).

Fig. 20.04: Vladimir Mayakovsky, ROSTA window no. 132, 1920. © INTERFOTO/Alamy.

One way the Bolsheviks sought to consolidate their power after the revolution was through the creation of public rituals such as commemorating the anniversaries of the revolution and the Red Army and by re-enacting significant events like the storming of the Winter Place, which forced the abdication of the czar. For the first anniversary celebration of the revolution in Petrograd, artists decorated buildings and monuments with banners and colored panels. They also festooned bridges with bright flags and painted posters, while in Moscow the architects Viktor (1882–1950) and Alexander Vesnin (1883–1959) decorated the Kremlin building with great swaths of red fabric.

One of the more inventive propaganda activities of the Civil War years was the propaganda train, an idea that originated with the military (Fig. 20.05). Initially the army sent printed materials to soldiers at the front. This generated the idea that agitators or propagandists might be sent along to speak directly with people in order to gain support for the Red Army and the Bolsheviks. The first agitational train or "agit train" was the *V. I. Lenin*, which visited small towns in remote areas. Based on its success, others were added. The trains also carried film projectors and printing presses so they could show newsreels, frequently to peasants who had never seen a film before, and print their own newspapers and leaflets. Artists were called upon to paint the trains whose exteriors served as moving billboards for the Bolshevik cause. Some of the earlier designs were based on abstract or avant-garde forms but these were quickly found to be ineffective and more realistic depictions of political subjects became the norm. The Bolsheviks also equipped a ship, the *Red Star*, which made several long trips, particularly to regions where Russian was not the first language. Film with subtitles thus proved to be a more effective propaganda tool than live agitators, and the *Red Star* pulled a floating cinema on a barge that could accommodate between 600 and 800 people. Similar to the trains, artists also painted the front and sides of the ship with revolutionary images.

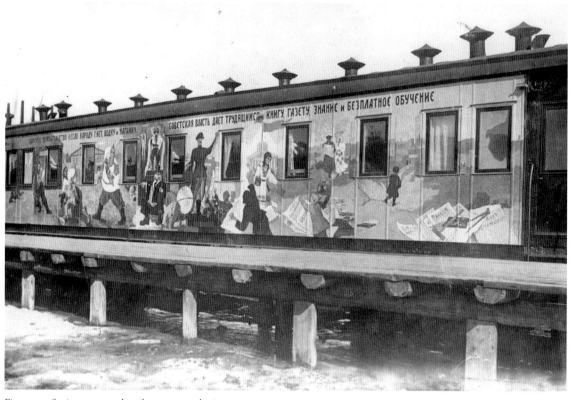

Fig. 20.05: Soviet propaganda railcar, c. 1922. akg-images.

Besides trains and ships, artists also painted such images on porcelain. "Agit-porcelain," as the ceramicware adorned with hammers and sickles or portraits of Lenin was called, had no precedent in the history of decorative art. Sergei Chekhonin (1878–1936) headed the Art Section at Petrograd's Lomonosov Factory, formerly the Imperial Porcelain Factory, where the agit-porcelain was produced. Under him were artists who worked in many different styles from the more traditional *World of Art* to the avant-garde Suprematists. Chekhonin's own designs ranged from revolutionary slogans such as "The reign of the workers and peasants will never end," to images of hammers and sickles on a ground of delicately drawn flowers and fruit.

The battle for public support during the Civil War made clear to the Bolsheviks the importance of coordinating their propaganda efforts. In August 1920, the Central Committee of the Communist Party established a section for agitation and propaganda, two activities subsequently referred to by the single word "agitprop." Around the same time, the People's Commissariat of Enlightenment also established a propaganda committee, which it called Glavpolitprosvet. These two organizations were central to the structure of a propaganda apparatus that remained in place until the political climate changed significantly at the beginning of the first Five-Year Plan in 1928.

Following the Civil War, the Bolsheviks defined two major tasks for propaganda, which they characterized as "political education." Not only did they need to identify the most ardent supporters of the revolution, whom they might bring into the Communist Party, but they also had to promote new concepts to the populace, namely the construction of a society with an entirely new economic and social basis and the creation of a new socialist individual who would find and assume his or her place in this society. This involved the establishment of state agencies for producing films, publishing books, magazines, and newspapers, and promoting literacy among a population that was still largely illiterate. Such tasks were to engage the efforts of Soviet filmmakers, authors, artists, and designers during the years following the Civil War, known as the time of the New Economic Policy (NEP), which lasted until the inauguration of the First Five-Year Plan. This was an open time when avant-garde artists and designers were able to explore inventive formal languages that they hoped might better express the new political reality than the tired realism of the 19th century.

The Vitebsk Art Institute

After the revolution, Lenin applied the term "Futurist" to all avant-garde artists, not just those associated with the pre-war Russian Futurist group. He had little taste for avant-garde art, favoring instead the 19th-century European realist tradition of art and literature. Nonetheless, avant-garde artists were active in government ministries, art schools, and cultural organizations, where they sought to formulate a new visual language to express their political ideals. Two important centers of avant-garde practice during the Civil War years were the Vitebsk Art Institute in the Pale of Settlement, a largely Jewish region, and the Art Section (IZO) within the People's Commissariat of Enlightenment.

At the Vitebsk Institute the dominant figure was the painter Kazimir Malevich (1878–1935), who had launched the Suprematist movement in 1915. The quintessential Suprematist painting was his *Black Square* of 1913, a rectilinear shape on a white ground. For Malevich, the black square represented "the zero degree of painting," a state of pure feeling rather than the visualization of nature or the social world.

Suprematism was for him a language of abstract colored shapes that he combined together in formal patterns held together in a state of tension.

In Vitebsk, Malevich was joined by El Lissitzky (1890–1941), who had studied architecture in Darmstadt, Germany, before the war. Some time after his return to Russia, Lissitzky, a Jew, became active in the movement to create a secular Yiddish culture. In 1919 he adopted a modified Cubist style to illustrate the traditional Passover story *Had Gadya* (*The Goat Kid*), and other Jewish children's books. In Vitebsk, where the artist Marc Chagall brought him in to head an architecture and graphic arts workshop, Lissitzky created a new form of abstract painting, which he called Proun, an acronym that meant "Project for a New Art."

Lissitzky joined the group called Unovis, which Malevich started. As stated in its manifesto, the aim of the group was to "construct the forms of life and projects," rather than to paint pictures. Malevich and his students adopted his formal language to design book covers, speakers' tribunes, and even the sides of a public tram in Vitebsk. In nearby Smolensk, where there was an outpost of the ROSTA Telegraph Agency, Malevich's Suprematist form language was applied to an army recruiting poster, which bore the text *What have you done for the front?*. Lissitzky adopted a more literal variant of Suprematist language for his poster of 1920, *Beat the Whites with the Red Wedge* (Fig. 20.06). Although the poster can be read as a metaphor—the wedge of the Red Army piercing the circle of their opponents known as the Whites—it is highly unlikely that it communicated effectively with a mass audience that was more attuned to realistic imagery.

Lissitzky also designed a children's book, *About Two Squares*, which used Malevich's forms—the red and black square (Plate 02). He prepared it in Vitebsk in 1920, but the book did not appear until 1922 when Gosizdat, the Soviet publishing house, brought it out in Berlin. In Lissitzky's tale, the two squares come to earth and witness a storm where everything flies apart. After the storm, a three-dimensional red structure is implanted on a black ground. In the last panel, the black square flies away from the earth, leaving a red square covering the structure. While the red square might stand for communism and the black one for Suprematism, there is no indication that this is the case. In fact, the red square might also represent Suprematism.

Although the meaning of the story is ambiguous, Lissitzky's design of the book presented a different graphic syntax from the traditional line-by-line text and ancillary illustrations. His bold typographic layout with its mix of type sizes and weights and its diagonal settings parallels the visual elements and moves the reader rapidly along to the end. One of Lissitzky's objectives was to quicken the absorption of information by eliminating visual redundancy; thus, he frequently used a common letter in several words. *About Two Squares* was Lissitzky's first demonstration of his "simultaneous" book of the future that would forge the word and image into a new unity.

Fig. 20.06: El Lissitzky, Beat the Whites with the Red Wedge, poster, 1920. © Image Asset Management Ltd/Alamy.

The Fine Art Department (IZO), People's Commissariat of Enlightenment (Narkompros)

The People's Commissariat of Enlightenment was one of the government departments the Bolsheviks established shortly after they took power. Within its broad responsibility for educational matters, a Fine Art Department was created. The department's role included the organization of art exhibitions and the founding of new museums, as well as responsibility for the applied arts. One of its subsections commissioned more than 1,200 posters for the anniversary of the revolution and almost 2,000 for the campaign to abolish illiteracy. Olga Rozanova (1886–1918), who was previously associated with the Russian Futurists, headed the Art and Production Subsection. She was assisted by Alexander Rodchenko (1891–1956), who was to become a central figure in the Constructivist movement. One of their accomplishments was to restore some of the craft workshops that had become inactive during the Civil War and create new ones. Another was to organize the First All-Russian Conference on Art and Production, which was held in 1919.

A principal objective of IZO was to develop a strategy to prepare artists for work in industry. Compared to Germany, where this was the central concern of the Deutscher Werkbund from its inception in 1907, there had been little discussion of this question in Russia. In 1905, P. S. Strakhov (dates unconfirmed) had raised the issue in a lecture entitled "Technology and the Beauty of Life," which he gave in St. Petersburg. He later published an expanded version as a book entitled *The Aesthetic Tasks of Technology* in which he argued that artists needed more technical training, while engineers required additional education in aesthetics.

During the Civil War, Russia's factories were either weakened by the pressure to shift from private ownership to a centralized economy or else the Red Army commandeered them for the production of war materiel. Nonetheless, theorists within IZO, notably Osip Brik (1888–1945), Boris Arvatov (1896–1940),

Boris Kushner (1888–1937), and Mikhail Tarabukin (1889–1956) initiated an intensive debate about the characteristics of "production art" and the role of the "artist-constructor" in the production process.

The center of the debate was IZO's Institute for Artistic Culture (INKhUK), which was established in March 1920. Initially, the painter Wassily Kandinsky (1866–1944), whose interest was in the psychological effects of artistic forms, strongly influenced its program but younger artists in the group soon rejected it. Consequently INKhUK adopted a more objective approach to the study of forms and materials and their qualities including texture, color, volume, space, and construction. In March 1921, the First Working Group of Constructivists was formed within INKhUK. Initially it consisted of Alexander Rodchenko, his wife Varvara Stepanova (1894–1958), and Alexei Gan (1889–1940), although several other artists joined them including the brothers Vladimir (1889–1982) and Gyorgy Stenberg (1900–1933). The Working Group introduced Constructivism as a way to think about the organization of materials and the role of the artist in production. The members were vehemently against art for its own sake and were strong advocates of the artist as a producer of communist forms that satisfied contemporary social demands. Their ideas were codified a year later in Gan's manifesto, *Constructivism*, which repeatedly called for the death of art and "the communist expression of material productions" (Fig. 20.07). The spare graphic style of the cover, which Rodchenko most likely designed, reflects the Constructivist aesthetic, which derived from an analytic conception of form and space. The letters were conceived as two-dimensional volumes that were organized in a structural relationship on a spatial ground.

At the end of 1921 the theorist Osip Brik proposed that the artists working in INKhUK reject easel painting and begin to work in production. As a consequence, 25 artists espoused production art and declared Constructivism to be its only form of

Fig. 20.07: Alexei Gan, *Constructivism*, cover, 1922. Collection Merrill C. Berman. Photo: Jim Frank and Joelle Jensen.

expression. Although Christina Lodder has pointed out the difficulty of identifying the signatories to Brik's document, they most likely included Alexander Rodchenko, Varvara Stepanova, Liubov Popova (1889–1924), Alexei Gan, Vladimir and Gyorgy Stenberg, and Anton Lavinsky (1893–1968), all of whom became active Constructivist designers during the 1920s.

Besides developing an argument for production art, theorists and artists in IZO were also interested in exploring the forms that buildings and monuments in the new socialist state might take. In May 1919, several sculptors and architects created a group called Sinskul'ptarkh (Sculptural and Architectural Synthesis) to work on projects that synthesized several art forms. A few months later, two painters, including Rodchenko, joined and the name was changed to Zhivskul'ptarkh (Painterly, Sculptural, and Architectural Synthesis). The group chose projects that represented new social functions such as communal housing and the dissemination of propaganda. The participants relied principally on the formal language of avant-garde art, notably

Fig. 20.08: Vladimir Tatlin, Monument to the Third International, 1920. © Heritage Image Partnership Ltd/Alamy.

lines and planes. One of Rodchenko's projects was a kiosk, which he depicted as a dynamic information and publicity center that combined different services—a clock, a billboard, a speaker's platform, a poster hoarding, and a space for the sale of books and newspapers.

Far more ambitious than the drawings of the artists and architects in Zhivskul'ptarkh was the Monument to the Third International that Vladimir Tatlin (1885–1953), an IZO artist, created. IZO commissioned it to commemorate the Comintern or Third International, the organization the party had set up to foment revolution around the world. The monument, which Tatlin produced as a model, received wide attention when it was exhibited at the Eighth Congress of the Communist Party in December 1920. Working with several assistants, Tatlin created a structure of wood that combined a spiral form with a straight angular spine. Inside the structure were three forms whose exteriors were to consist of glass. The monument was to include a motor that would enable the forms to rotate at different speeds.

The bottom form, a cube, was intended for large meetings of legislative assemblies and was to complete one revolution per year. The middle form, a pyramid, was to rotate once a month and would be used for smaller administrative meetings, while the top form, a cylinder, would rotate once a day and would house propaganda services such as preparing newspapers as well as proclamations, pamphlets, and manifestoes (Fig. 20.08). Tatlin intended the monument to be taller than the Eiffel Tower but he endowed it with so much structural complexity that it could not possibly have been built.

Nonetheless, it became a powerful symbol of revolutionary aspirations, not only in the Soviet Union, but among avant-garde artists' groups in Western Europe as well. It demonstrated that new forms could be conceived to represent unprecedented revolutionary ideals and it provided encouragement for other artists, designers, and architects in the Soviet Union to invent their own forms rather than rely on the West for their artistic and architectural inspiration. The description of Tatlin's monument provides a fitting coda to the discussion of design during the period of War Communism. The revolution began with a search for appropriate symbols to represent the new Soviet state and ended with a project whose ambitions far exceeded the state's ability to make it a reality.

New Economic Policy (NEP) 1921–1928

At the end of the Civil War, the Russian economy was in a shambles. To facilitate recovery, Lenin introduced the New Economic Policy (NEP), which allowed a limited return of capitalism in order to get the economy moving again. The policy was most evident in the sphere of agriculture, where the peasants were allowed to work their own land and keep the profits. In addition, small traders and merchants called Nepmen provided consumer goods for the peasants and others who could pay for them.

Agriculture recovered far more quickly than industry, which continued to struggle with problems of coordination and management. The leadership foresaw the need for a master plan to guide the economy and the first one, GOELRO, was drawn up to introduce widespread electrification. It was not until the beginning of the First Five-Year Plan in 1928, however, that a process was in place to coordinate the nation's thousands of factories and other enterprises.

During the NEP, Vesenkha (Supreme Council of the National Economy) created a series of administrative bodies called glavki or "trusts" to manage entire industries. By 1922, there were 430 of them. To work effectively, the glavki system required sophistication and discipline, both of which were in short supply. Nonetheless, the trusts provided the impetus for industrial development in sectors that ranged from automobiles to baby pacifiers.

Because the Soviet state had to compensate for the high percentage of goods that had been imported under the czars but were no longer available, the NEP period was one of industrial experiment and a certain degree of openness. Though the economy gradually recovered during the course of the 1920s, consumer goods comparable to those found in the West were in short supply and thus there was limited work for designers in this field. At the same time, the state initiated the first production of automobiles and the design and production of aircraft, both of which were to achieve significant success by the 1930s.

Vkhutemas

On November 29, 1920, Lenin signed a State Decree establishing the Vkhutemas (Higher State Artistic and Technical Workshops), a new school that was intended to provide master artists and designers for industry. The Vkhutemas was set up on the basis of the first and second Free Art Studios (SVOMAS), which had been created in 1918 by merging the two major art schools under the czars – the Moscow School of Painting, Sculpture, and Architecture and the Stroganov School of Applied Art.

The Vkhutemas curriculum comprised a Basic Course and a number of departments including painting; sculpture; textiles; ceramics; printing, typography, and illustration; also woodwork, metalwork, and architecture. In the Basic Course, students learned the rudiments of line, plane, color, volume, and space, while receiving instruction as well in science, languages, and the history of art. They then spent the next three years in one of the departments. Joined to the school was a Workers' Faculty or Rabfak to accommodate workers who had trouble with the more advanced curriculum in the departments. A worker could study in the Rabfak and then apply for admission to one of the departments.

The Vkhutemas faculty had representatives of all the different artistic tendencies in the Soviet Union. In the early years, however, the Constructivists based in INKhUK had considerable influence, particularly in the design of the Basic Course. Each of the school's three successive rectors had a somewhat different orientation, thus the school experienced substantial changes over

its ten-year history. Under the first rector, Efim Ravdel (dates unconfirmed), the emphasis was on exploration and experiment. The second rector, Vladimir Favorsky (1886–1964), was a woodcut artist who specialized in traditional techniques. He taught in the printing, typography, and illustration department and trained his students to follow his own conservative style. Favorsky had little interest in the design departments, namely the woodwork and metalwork studios, and tried to marginalize them. This direction was contradictory to the school's main purpose and was reversed in the final phase by the third rector, Pavel Novitsky (1888–1971), a critic and sociologist who strengthened the design concentration, which he believed was central to the school's mission. Under Novitsky, the woodwork and metalwork studios were merged into a single department known as the Dermetfak. The new, narrower, focus on technical training resulted in the reduction of the Basic Course from two years to one semester and a change in the school's name to Vkhutein (Higher Art Technical Institute).

Rodchenko headed the Metalwork Department, or Metfak, and also taught on the Basic Course. As a supporter of Gan's Constructivist manifesto, he believed that appropriate design problems and the way of solving them could provide evidence of communist character. He did not see design as a matter of aesthetics; rather, he emphasized the combination of purpose, technique, and material. Trained as an artist, Rodchenko devised the first industrial design curriculum in the Soviet Union. He taught his students to make precision drawings and he then had them build prototypes, particularly of experimental furniture. Objects with multiple functions were of particular interest to him. The Metfak also had an engineer who taught the technical aspects of production and introduced the students to problems of engineering.

Rodchenko treated the Metfak as an experimental laboratory where he and his students conceived new types of objects according to production specifications that might be suitable for industry. Among the projects his students devised were flexible beds, chairs, desks, and storage cases. One of the most practical was Zakhar Bykov's book kiosk, which could be easily disassembled and packed up in a box. A perfect example of Constructivist design, it had a strong structural form, used materials efficiently, and avoided excess elements.

A similar approach to furniture design was also evident in a project of Rodchenko's, the model Workers' Club he designed for the Soviet pavilion at the 1925 Exposition Internationale des Arts Décoratifs et Industriel Modernes in Paris (Fig. 20.09). The club interior was a space where workers could relax and study. It had areas for games, reading, viewing films, and listening to talks. Polemically, it offered a stark contrast to the luxurious pavilions of the French designers. The reading table functioned as a single axis that cut directly through the room, while the curved and linear elements of the chairs offered a more rhythmic balance. The room exuded rigor, which was a defining characteristic of Rodchenko's designs. It concentrated on essentials and conveyed a sense of communism's discipline, even if that was not always the case in reality.

Because the Metalwork and Woodwork curricula

Fig. 20.09: Alexander Rodchenko, Workers' Club, 1925. © 2014. Digital image, The Museum of Modern Art, New York/Scala, Florence. © Rodchenko & Stepanova Archive, DACS, RAO, 2017.

were experimental and the profession of industrial design was relatively unknown in Russia, few students entered either department and none graduated until 1927 when three students from the Woodwork Department were granted the title "artist-engineer." According to the Russian scholar Selim Khan-Magomedov, they were the first Soviet designers. By the time the school closed in 1930, only about 20 students had graduated with design degrees

When the Woodwork Department was first set up, the curriculum was based on craft traditions rather than the design of objects for mass production. In the furniture program, attention was initially given to the decoration of surfaces and to furniture styles. The concentration on wooden architecture featured the design of wooden pavilions for exhibitions and for rural reading rooms, while the carving concentration emphasized the design of decorative panels, reliefs, and architecture details. The program began to change after the initial phase when several new professors, including Anton Lavinsky from INKhUK, joined the faculty. The emphasis then shifted to training artist-constructors for the wood industry. A focus was placed on organizing the interiors of workers' clubs, libraries, and hostels and designing interiors for transport vehicles and stations.

Around the time the Woodwork and Metalwork Departments were combined, El Lissitzky joined the Woodwork Department, as did Vladimir Tatlin. While Lissitzky's thrust was towards mass-produced products such as the folding chair that his student B. Zemlyanitsyn designed, Tatlin's inclination was towards more poetic objects. A chair he created with his student Rogozhin consisted of springy bentwood strips that were tied together to support a cantilevered seat. Tatlin's interests extended beyond furniture to clothing and ceramics. In the Ceramics Department, he produced a nursing cup for children. Its soft curved form and the mouthpiece shaped like a nipple suggested a woman's breast and exemplified Tatlin's emphasis on organic forms, which sharply contrasted with the rectilinear structures of Rodchenko and other Constructivist designers.

In the same department, Alexei Filippov (dates unconfirmed) was the most influential teacher. Though Filippov had trained at the old Stroganov School of Applied Art, he rejected decoration in favor of clean simple forms. The Textile Department was rather conservative, despite the brief Constructivist influence of Varvara Stepanova. Among the student textile designs were a number that featured illustrative political iconography such as the hammer and sickle as decorative motifs. The Graphic Arts Department was dominated in its early years by Vladimir Favorsky who taught book printing, specializing in woodcut illustrations combined with traditional typography for the design of books and journals. Another professor, Nikolai Kuprianov (1894–1933), was sympathetic to the innovative graphic style of the Constructivists and introduced a more experimental approach to typography and publication design. As a result, a few graduates from the department such as Solomon Telingater (1903–1969) and Nikolai Prusakov (1900–1952) later gained prominence as designers of books and posters.

By the time the school closed in 1930, the Soviet Union was well into the First Five-Year Plan, whose thrust was the development of large-scale industrial enterprises rather than consumer industries for which the Vkhutemas designers were being trained. Various departments became separate entities such as the Moscow Graphics Institute and the Higher Architectural-building Institute, while others were joined to existing organizations.

Fashion, Furniture, and Ceramics

As in most industries immediately following the revolution, the textile industry was short of materials and had to rely largely on cheap fabrics. Designers rejected the decorative flower patterns of pre-revolutionary textiles and sought designs that would be more expressive of the new Soviet state. In 1923, once the industry had stabilized, the Communist Party newspaper, *Pravda*, published an appeal for artists to work in the textile factories. Varvara Stepanova and Liubov Popova, both participants in the Constructivist debates in INKhUK, answered the call and established a design workshop in the First State Textile Print Factory in Moscow. Their interest in fabric design sprang from the decision in INKhUK to reject painting and work instead for industry.

Both Stepanova and Popova introduced patterns that came from an entirely new source: the experimental forms of the Constructivists and their theoretical approach to materials. The women created dynamic formal patterns, which usually featured two strong colors and occasionally black. Stepanova produced more than 150 designs of which about two dozen were put into production. In an article of 1923 entitled "Present Day Dress—Production Clothing," Stepanova discussed the design of clothing as if it were an industrial product. Not only did she espouse mass production rather than garments sewn by hand, but she also rejected the idea of clothing as adornment and decoration, promoting instead the appropriate garments for particular functions. She devised two main categories of clothing: *prozodezhda* (production clothing) for working, and *sportodezhda* (sports clothing) for relaxing (Plate 03). Popova also proposed garments that would incorporate her and Stepanova's geometric fabrics, but her designs were less rigid in their typology than Stepanova's and put more emphasis on elegance and graceful lines.

Stepanova and Popova came to fashion design directly from avant-garde art, but Nedezda Lamanova (1861–1941), who set up a Workshop on Contemporary Dress in 1918, had been a famous couturier and owner of a fashion house before the revolution. Lamanova took up the challenge to make functional and attractive clothing for the working class. Working with flimsy fabrics that were badly dyed with dull colors, she designed clothing with a clean cut and simple line that could be easily and inexpensively manufactured.

Besides the geometric textile designs of Stepnova and Popova, fabric designers, many of whom were graduates of the Vkhutemas, tended towards repeat patterns of pictorial images, although these varied in their degrees of abstraction or realism. Among the designers who favored abstraction was Ludmilla Mayakovskaya (1884–1963), sister of the poet Vladimir Mayakovsky. Mayakovskaya studied textile design before the revolution at the Stroganov School of Applied Art and subsequently worked in a silk factory where she learned a spray-gun technique. Though her style of the 1920s was inspired by Constructivist geometry, her designs could also feature flowers or lightning as well as dynamic abstract patterns that were filled with bursts of light and energy. A dominant tendency of Soviet textile design in the 1920s and 1930s, however, was to create patterns with revolutionary icons of modernity such as airplanes or cars, factory workers, machine parts, or Red Army soldiers.

The inability of Constructivist designs to transform the fashion or textile industry was equally true in the furniture field. After nationalization following the revolution, furniture factories and workshops reverted to private ownership with the inauguration of the NEP in 1921. Historian John Bowlt writes that as late as 1929 only one quarter of the furniture industry was controlled by state trusts such as Mosdrev, the Moscow wood trust, which had commissioned some designs for workers' club furniture from the Vkhutemas Derfak. In general, commercial furniture designers in the 1920s produced little that was innovative or distinctive, despite the groundbreaking prototypes that were created at the Vkhutemas.

This is in sharp contrast to the radical new designs for buildings by Soviet architects such as Konstantin Melnikov (1890–1974), Nikolai Ladovsky (1881–1941), and Moisei Ginzburg (1892–1946). Although there were highly respectable precedents for commercial furniture before the revolution, the Arts and Crafts movement that centered on Sasha Mamontov's estate, Abramtsevo, and the estate of Princess Tenisheva at Talashkino had resulted in heavily decorated wooden furniture that derived from a romantic view of peasant life. Consequently, neither the forms nor the intensive labor process were appropriate for a society that was striving to reinvent itself as a modern industrial state. Instead, factories tended to rely more on a pre-revolutionary modern style that had been produced for a bourgeois market but was nonetheless easier to manufacture and more likely to sell than romanticized peasant-inspired pieces. Despite the many good ideas that were generated at the Vhkutemas, the production of inexpensive furniture on a mass scale would have to wait until the 1930s when it was driven by the need to support the massive worker-housing projects of the Five-Year Plans.

In ceramics, the Lomonosov Porcelain Factory in Leningrad (formerly Petrograd), where Sergei Chekhonin (1878–1936) had inaugurated an agitational style of chinaware following the revolution, remained a center of innovation in the early 1920s. In 1923, two of Kazimir Malevich's students from the Vitebsk Art Institute, Nikolai Suetin (1897–1954) and Ilya Chashnik (1902–1929), followed their teacher to Leningrad and began to work at the factory. There they applied Suprematist designs to existing forms for teapots, cups, and saucers, adapting them to the curved surfaces of the objects (Fig. 20.10). Malevich designed an experimental teapot and several cups but the forms were awkward and the objects were not produced. Chashnik left in 1924, but Suetin continued to work at the factory. In 1932 he became chief artist, a position he held until 1954.

The same year Suetin was promoted, the Hungarian ceramist Eva Stricker (1906–2011) arrived in the Soviet Union and took a position in the Lomonosov Factory. She worked under Suetin, who applied Suprematist ornaments to some of her forms. A former Bauhaus student, Stricker subsequently gained international renown as Eva Zeisel. In 1934 she moved to a large ceramics factory in Moscow and shortly thereafter she was appointed Artistic Director for the Soviet Union's entire glass and china industry. She was

Fig. 20.10: Nikolai Suetin, Suprematist teapot, c. 1925. © Heritage Image Partnership Ltd/Alamy. © DACS 2017.

imprisoned in 1936 because of a growing suspicion of foreigners and after her release in 1938 she left the Soviet Union for Britain and then the United States.

Film, Theater, and Exhibitions

Lenin was well aware of film as a propaganda tool and during the Civil War, it was an integral part of the political education campaign that was conducted by train, boat, and in public squares. An early director of newsreel films was Dziga Vertov (1896–1954), who was also one of the Soviet Union's most important film theoreticians. He was as an editor for the first Soviet newsreel in 1917, later producing his own monthly news film, *Kino Pravda* (*Film Truth*) between 1922 and 1925. Vertov believed that the camera could reveal the world in a way that the human eye could not. In his seminal manifesto "We," published in 1923, he wrote of the camera eye: "I cut into a crowd in full speed. I run in front of running soldiers. I turn over on my

back. I soar with an aeroplane … This is I, the machine, manoeuvering in the chaotic movements, recording one movement after another in the most complex combinations." Starting with the 13th installment of Vertov's *Kino Pravda*, Rodchenko designed titles that were conceived as a dynamic part of each film. Vertov, who considered animation to be "an essential arm in the struggle against the artistic film," introduced the technique to Rodchenko, suggesting it as a means to create titles whose movements could be integrated with the photographic images. Rodchenko designed the titles for quick apprehension, using simple shapes, large letters and graphic devices such as arrows to give the forms a sense of motion that was continuous with the moving image. This was perhaps the first time that animation was used for film titles, which, until the arrival of sound, usually consisted of static lines of text on a plain background. Rodchenko also designed a poster for Vertov's film *Kino Glaz* (*Film Eye*) of 1924. Since Vertov's films did not follow a conventional narrative format, Rodchenko emphasized the concept of the cine-eye by featuring a large eye at the peak of a triangular structure that moves from the human eye at the bottom through the camera to the culmination of the cinematic vision in the cine-eye at the top (Fig. 20.11).

Vertov's ambition to move beyond the conventions of the traditional film was shared by the theater director Vsevolod Meyerhold (1874–1940), who wished to replace the theater of illusion in which the actors pretended to be characters and the illustrative scenery suggested a specific time and place. Instead he invented an acting technique called "biomechanics," which was based on Frederick Winslow Taylor's attempts to improve the efficiency of factory workers. Meyerhold devised a specific vocabulary of gestures that the actors combined to portray the movements and feelings of their characters. Instead of a painted backdrop and real furniture or other objects on stage, he preferred a more abstract three-dimensional structure that could also become part of the action.

Fig. 20.11: Alexander Rodchenko, *Kino Glaz*, poster, 1924. © Heritage Image Partnership Ltd/Alamy. © Rodchenko & Stepanova Archive, DACS, RAO, 2017.

Meyerhold's radical theories of acting and stagecraft fit perfectly with the Constructivists' views of sculpture as material that was organized by the artist to produce a formal structure. For Meyerhold's production of *The Magnanimous Cuckold*, a farce by the Belgian playwright Fernand Crommelynk about a man who believes his wife is cheating on him, Liubov Popova designed a Constructivist set consisting of a platform with two revolving doors and several large circular objects whose movement became part of the drama (Fig. 20.12). Popova conceived the set as a utilitarian object whose purpose was to facilitate the action of the play.

Varvara Stepanova did something comparable with her sets for another play that Meyerhold directed, *The Death of Tarelkin* by the Russian author Alexander Sukhovo-Kobylin. Rather than design a single object, Stepanova filled the stage with multiple structures that the actors could move around and interact with, thus enabling the gymnastic movements in the biomechanics repertoire. Both Popova and Stepanova designed costumes that foreshadowed Stepanova's theory of *prozodezhda* or work clothes. Popova's actors wore blue overalls and her actresses blue overall skirts. Props such as black leather caps or aprons distinguished the different characters. Stepanova's actors wore loose-fitting costumes that foreshadowed her *sportodezhda* designs—long tunics with colored stripes, coveralls with strongly divided areas of solid colors, colored caps, and boots. As she was to write two years later, the aim of the costumes was to facilitate movement not to function as a static representation of a social type.

Throughout the 1920s, Meyerhold and other directors worked with designers who produced their

Fig. 20.12: Liubov Popova, *The Magnanimous Cuckold*, stage set drawing, 1922. Tretyakov Gallery, Moscow, Russia/Getty Images.

own versions of Constructivist sets. Liubov Popova's second collaboration with Meyerhold, *The Earth in Turmoil*, resulted in a set that functioned like a huge three-dimensional collage. Within a multi-tiered frame of red slats, authentic military items appeared—carts, rifles, machine guns, and even a real army truck was driven onto the stage. Behind the movement of actors and objects, illuminated slogans and captions flashed on a screen.

For Alexander Tairov's Kamerny Theater, the architect Alexander Vesnin (1883–1959) designed a cumbersome wooden structure for the stage version of G. K. Chesterton's English novel, *The Man who Was Thursday*. To simulate an urban scene, Vesnin added numerous props and multicolored lights to the structure which, unfortunately, took over the stage and left little room for the actors to move about. More experimental than any of these plays, however, was Vladimir Tatlin's 1923 staging of *Zangezi*, which was based on the writings of the Russian Futurist poet Velomir Khlebnikov. Tatlin's set consisted of an arrangement of large abstract wooden shapes, which he intended to parallel Khlebnikov's definition of words as building blocks of meaning.

The elaborate Constructivist sets that were characteristic of the avant-garde theater at the beginning of the NEP also served as a prelude to the exhibition designs that would become more prevalent at home and abroad, particularly during the First Five-Year Plan. The first major exhibition that significantly engaged the talents of artists and architects was the All-Union Agricultural Exhibition of 1923. For this event, the artist Alexandra Ekster (1882–1949) played a leading role. She collaborated on the external decoration of various pavilions including the design of one sponsored by the Soviet newspaper *Izvestia*, whose cacophonous structure resulted in its critique as a failure.

More successful was El Lissitzky's design for the All-Union Polygraphic Exhibition that was held in Moscow in 1927. Lissitzky was trained as an architect but worked extensively as a painter and publication designer. He had already created several noteworthy three-dimensional spaces in Europe, notably his 1923 Proun Room in Berlin, and he was able to effectively integrate lettering, printed texts, and three-dimensional structures. However, the Polygraphic Exhibition, which presented a survey of printing and publishing in the Soviet Union, provided only a modest opportunity for Lissitzky. The exhibit itself consisted primarily of printed pieces attached to flat panels. The entrance signage, which was comprised of large cut-out letters on a series of panels, was more dramatic, but the most impressive component of the design was the catalog that Lissitzky created together with Simon Telingater, a former Vkhutemas student. Rather than a single volume, it was a folder that contained a group of separate documents, all integrated with a common visual identity. Within several years, Lissitzky would be recognized as the Soviet Union's premier exhibition designer, after having undertaken the direction of three large state displays that were presented abroad.

Transportation

While the Western countries were competing fiercely at the beginning of the century to develop automobiles and airplanes, the czarist government remained on the sidelines. The Putilov Factory was a major producer of railroad engines and military equipment but the czars had not fostered a culture of invention and continued to rely extensively on imported goods of all kinds. One exception to this policy was Igor Sikorsky (1889–1972), an engineer who built his first experimental helicopter with a twin-blade rotor in 1909. After it and a second model failed, Sikorsky concentrated on fixed-wing aircraft and in 1911 he constructed the S-5, which proved to be faster than foreign aircraft in the Russian service. This led to his appointment as Chief Engineer of the aircraft subsidiary of the Russian Baltic Railroad Car Factory, which approved Sikorsky's proposal for the first four-engine airplane. Named the S-21, it made its first flight in May 1913, following which Sikorsky designed a larger plane, the S-22, also known as the

Ilya Muromets, after a Russian folk hero. Featuring an enclosed cabin, a toilet, upholstered chairs, and an exterior catwalk above the fuselage where passengers could take a turn in the fresh air, the S-22 began carrying passengers in December 1913. Subsequently a bomber version was produced for the Imperial Air Force and more than 70 were used during World War I. Sikorsky left Russia at the time of the revolution and soon thereafter emigrated to the United States, where he eventually produced the first successful helicopter in 1939.

After the revolution, Andrei Tupolev (1889–1972) became the leading Soviet aircraft designer. Following his studies with Nikolai Zhukovsky (1847–1921), a pioneer in aeronautics, Tupolev held several academic positions before he was appointed Chief of the Aircraft Design Bureau of the Central Aero-Hydrodynamic Institute in 1922. He built the Bureau into the major center of Soviet aircraft design, its distinction coming in large part from the talented staff he assembled. The staff included engineers, who designed the planes, as well as a crew of patternmakers, metalworkers, mechanics, and carpenters, who assembled the full-scale mock-ups and then built the working aircraft.

The team's first plane was the ANT-1, a single-seat monoplane of combined wood and metal construction, which was completed in 1923 and took its name from Tupolev's initials. The second aircraft, ANT-2, was the first all-metal plane produced in the Soviet Union. Whereas the ANT-1 was a prototype, the ANT-2 went into production as did seven other aircraft that Tupolev's team designed during the 1920s. After the ANT-2, the others were all military aircraft except the ANT-9, which was the Soviet Union's first domestically designed passenger airliner, aside from Sikorsky's successful design before the revolution. With a capacity of nine passengers, the ANT-9 flew domestic routes as well as international ones.

Ground transport developed more slowly. Several rudimentary automobiles, trucks, and tractors were manufactured during the NEP, but the further development and mass production of such vehicles had to await the construction of large factories after the inauguration of the First Five-Year Plan. Nonetheless, the AMO factory, which was established in 1916, did produce a truck between 1924 and 1931, the AMO F-15, which was particularly useful for transporting agricultural products.

A more distinctive Russian design was the icebreaker, a ship whose bow was strong enough to cut through frozen masses of Artic ice. Its design dates from around 1870 and its continued development resulted in vessels that opened up the Arctic to military, scientific, and commercial traffic. One of the first true icebreakers, the *Yermak*, was constructed by Stepan Makarov (1848–1904), an admiral in the Imperial Navy. It made its maiden voyage in 1899. Other ships were built during the 1920s and 1930s to carry out exploration of the Arctic Ocean as well as adjacent seas and waterways. The public followed these expeditions with interest and they resulted in some important discoveries.

Advertising and Packaging

Before the revolution, much advertising directed at Russians was produced abroad, particularly the posters that promoted foreign-made goods. Consequently, Russian commercial art and typography could hardly compare with foreign developments. The Bolsheviks rapidly became adept at political propaganda but had no comparable strategy for commodity advertising.

During the NEP, the trusts and other state enterprises hired artists to advertise their products, since these organizations were competing with private entrepreneurs. The trusts manufactured everything from cigarettes and chocolates to baby pacifiers, beer, and galoshes, while other state enterprises including the GUM Department Store and Gosizdat, the state publisher of newspapers, books, and journals also offered items for sale.

As there had been no prior training for Russian commercial artists nor was there a tradition of advertising, Russian and Soviet designers had to invent their own practice. Rodchenko and Mayakovsky played an important role in this process. Mayakovsky understood advertising for Soviet enterprises to be another form of agitprop. In a manifesto, "Agitation and Advertising," he wrote: "Advertising is industrial commercialized agitation. Not a single business, especially not the steadiest, runs without advertising. It is the weapon that mows down the competition." In 1923, Mayakovsky joined with Rodchenko to form an advertising agency to work for the government trusts and enterprises. They called themselves "advertisement constructors." Mayakovsky wrote the copy just as he had done for the ROSTA posters, while Rodchenko, assisted by several of his students, designed and painted the posters and other graphic materials. Many of the posters were used as single signs in store windows while others were reproduced in multiples by lithography or offset printing. Clients included Rezinotrest, a state trust that marketed light industrial products; GUM, the large Moscow department store; Gosizdat, the state publishing house; and Mosselprom, the large state distribution agency for agricultural products. The goods that Mayakovsky and Rodchenko promoted included cigarettes, candy, biscuits, rubbers, baby pacifiers, light bulbs, macaroni, books, and butter. In addition, Rodchenko did posters for films by Dziga Vertov and Sergei Eisenstein as well as trademarks for Dobrolet, the state agency that was promoting investment in Soviet aviation. Rodchenko was perhaps the first Soviet designer to conceive of the trademark as an abstract form rather than a narrative emblem like the hammer and sickle.

Mosselprom was one of Rodchenko's and Mayakovsky's largest clients. Konstantin Yuon (1875–1958), a realist painter who headed Mosselprom's Central Art Bureau, was responsible for all of the company's graphics. He hired many different artists and sought intuitively to create an identity program that ranged from an emblem picturing a farm worker holding a cornucopia of goods to posters, packaging,

and pricelists, as well as colored smocks for the trust's tobacco salespeople. While the Mosselprom advertising was tasteful, much of it was traditional and quite bland. Nineteenth-century color lithography was a principal source as can be seen in M. Bulanov's 1927 poster, which depicted the star of a popular silent film called *The Cigarette Girl from Mosselprom* (Plate 04).

Mayakovsky and Rodchenko brought a more aggressive advertising sensibility to their work for Mosselprom. Mayakovsky wrote a copy slogan, "Nowhere but in Mosselprom," which was used on much of the organization's advertising, gaining particular prominence through its repetition in the supergraphic advertisement Rodchenko designed to cover an entire side of Mosselprom's six-story headquarters building in central Moscow. The slogan was also integrated into the logo that Rodchenko created, featuring a photograph of the Moselprom building framed by two red arrows on top and a curved section below (Fig. 20.13). Rodchenko integrated the slogan as well into a series of eye-catching advertisements for Mosselprom's sales kiosks. They featured repetitive product images, combined with Mayakovsky's copy lines in bold text and flanked by large exclamation points.

Besides posters and signs, Rodchenko and Mayakovsky specialized in political candy wrappers such as the brand called Proletarskaia (Proletarian), which featured portraits of Bolshevik political figures, and Mayakovsky's designs for the inexpensive Red Army Star caramels whose cartoon figures were a continuation of his ROSTA Windows. To complement the cartoon-like drawings for the wrappers, Mayakovsky wrote short numbered texts that, when put together in a sequence, told the story of the Red Army's victory over the Whites.

The declarative visual and verbal style of these promotional posters and packages established a new agitational tone in Soviet commercial advertising, one that only a few other artists followed. It was a tone that transferred the excitement of political change and the active engagement of the spectator,

Fig. 20.13: Alexander Rodchenko, Nowhere but in Mosselprom, Mosselprom logo, 1924. © Heritage Image Partnership Ltd/Alamy. © Rodchenko & Stepanova Archive, DACS, RAO, 2017.

reminiscent of the Civil War posters, to the purchase of goods. The agit style was evident in Rodchenko's poster for Gosizdat, the state publishing house, which depicted a woman announcing with a shout that books were available in all fields of knowledge. Other Constructivists also contributed to Gosizdat's design program. Anton Lavinsky designed a street kiosk for the sale of books, while Stepanova designed special caps and berets for the salesmen and saleswomen at the Gosizdat bookstore

In contrast to this style of agitational advertising, some artists took their ideas from earlier American and European designers and illustrators such as J. C. Leyendecker, Ludwig Hohlwein, and French fashion illustrators. The French influence was evident in the packaging for talcum powder, soaps, and perfume produced by the Leningrad Fats Trust, whose containers featured flowers or women with bobbed hair and

dimples, images that would soon be replaced by women workers in overalls once the First Five-Year Plan began.

Besides promoting commercial goods, the other area in which advertising played an important role during the NEP was publicizing films. During the Civil War the commercial film industry was destroyed. Studios were idle and most film production was devoted to newsreels and propaganda. By late 1921, film activity began to revive and in 1922 the government established a state film agency, Goskino, which was renamed Sovkino in 1926. Throughout the 1920s, Soviet-made films competed with foreign thrillers or comedies, though most of the domestic films had a political theme. Dziga Vertov, Sergei Eisenstein, Vsevolod Pudovkin, and Lev Kuleshov, the leading Soviet directors, pioneered many innovative techniques that included theories of editing or montage, as well as new approaches to acting and cinematography.

Film posters flourished in the years between 1925 and 1929, before the government began to call for a more ideological approach to public iconography. Reklam Film, a department of Sovkino headed by Yakov Ruklevsky (1884–1965), a self-taught graphic artist and poster designer, oversaw the design and production of all posters for Soviet and imported films. Ruklevsky hired a staff that included Gyorgy and Vladimir Stenberg, Anatoly Belsky (1896–1970), Mikhail Dlugach (1893–1989), and three Vkhutemas graduates: Nikolai Prusakov (1900–1952), Grigori Borisov (1899–1942), and Alexander Naumov (1899–1928).

Compared to the techniques of agitational advertising, the designers of film posters sought to capture the mood or style of a film. Color lithography was their main medium of reproduction, although they sometimes incorporated photographs or photo fragments into their compositions. The Stenbergs, who had been part of the Constructivist group at INKhUK in the early 1920s, defined the style and approach that most of the other designers followed. They invented a projector that could enlarge, reduce, or distort a photograph, which they would then render as a drawing. Although their posters featured figurative images, they almost always depicted the figures within dynamic compositions that derived from the Constructivist aesthetic. In their poster for *Gossip*, a film by the Soviet director Ivan Perestiani that explored the consequences of careless talk, the Stenbergs combined close-up and mid-range views of two actors whom they framed in a composition of flat planes and linear elements that suggested the outline of a streetcar (Fig. 20.14). The

design is typical of most film posters from this period, which combined a dynamic organization of formal elements with an emotional content achieved through the facial expressions of the actors and their dramatic role in the composition.

Books and Magazines

Despite mass illiteracy, Russia at the start of World War I published more books annually than any other country except Germany. Following the revolution, the Bolsheviks were thus able to profit from a well-established printing and distribution network, although economic problems created by the war resulted in huge paper shortages as well as the breakdown of printing presses for which spare parts were no longer available.

In 1919, the government established a state publishing house, Gosizdat, which eventually took over much of the publishing that had been handled by private firms. Gosizdat introduced departments for propaganda, science, and pedagogy, while also republishing many classics of Soviet literature as well as fostering new writers. During the 1920s, Gosizdat imposed few restrictions on fiction writers, resulting in a period when numerous literary schools and approaches flourished. The nation's literacy rate also improved drastically with 50 million adults becoming literate in the years between 1920 and 1940.

Despite the large production of books under the czars, little had been achieved in Russian typography. The salient influence of Arts and Crafts printing, which had strongly influenced the design of type in Europe and America, passed the Russians by. Consequently, the Bolsheviks inherited a collection of undistinguished fonts, and Gosizdat had to base the appeal of its books primarily on the covers, which frequently functioned like mini-posters to announce the books' contents.

While much of Gosizdat's output, particularly the vast number of textbooks and propaganda tracts, was graphically mundane, the avant-garde produced designs for publications that strongly challenged prior conventions of what a book or journal should look like.

Fig. 20.14: Vladimir and Gyorgy Stenberg, *Gossip*, poster, 1928. © 2014. Digital image, The Museum of Modern Art, New York/Scala, Florence. © DACS 2017.

Fig. 20.15: Alexander Rodchenko, *Lef* 3, cover, 1923. Collection Merrill C. Berman. Photo: Jim Frank & Joelle Jensen. © Rodchenko & Stepanova Archive, DACS, RAO, 2017.

As with the design of textiles, theater sets, and film posters, the disciplined composition of Constructivist aesthetics was central. Rodchenko, in particular, defined the book and periodical cover as a poster-like announcement of the contents. He was perhaps the first Soviet designer to consider the consistency of a publication's visual format from one issue to the next. For the Constructivist film journal *Kino-fot*, one of his first publication designs, he devised a cover format that emphasized the title in bold letters and included

an enlarged issue number as an important design element. In 1923, he became the art director of *Lef*, a cultural journal that Vladimir Mayakovsky edited. Of all the literary and artistic groups during the NEP, *Lef* was the most insistent on applying avant-garde ideas to literature and the design of everyday objects. Rodchenko established a format for the *Lef* covers, using large drawn squared letters. As colors, he chose strong contrasting tones—black and red, black and orange, red and blue. The covers looked like small posters, a move by Rodchenko to amplify the visual impact of the journal with the devices of a more dynamic medium (Fig. 20.15). Alexei Gan, the former editor of *Kino-fot*, adopted a similar approach for the cover design of the Constructivist architectural journal *CA: Contemporary Architecture* in 1927.

Rodchenko also chose a similar poster-like format for his book covers. Some were for editions of Mayakovsky's poems, while others contained writings by different authors in the *Lef* circle such as Nikolai Aseev and Sergei Tretiakov. Rodchenko's cover for *Mayakovsky Smiles, Mayakovsky Laughs, Mayakovsky Jeers* contained the single words of the title on separate lines that alternated between green and red. His design for Aseev's edited volume, *Flight: Aviation Verse*, featured a flat drawing of an airplane in black, which he combined with a powerful typographic composition.

In 1923, Rodchenko designed *Pro Eto* (*About It*), a poem that Mayakovsky wrote, which detailed the tensions between the poet and his lover, Lili Brik (Figs. 20.16 and 20.17). The book was one of the first to feature a photographic cover. It also included eight photomontage illustrations, consisting of photographic fragments that Rodchenko cut from magazines as well as photos of Mayakovsky and his actual lover Lili Brik that were made explicitly for the project. Working with photomontage stimulated Rodchenko's interest in photography, which led to its further use on other book and journal covers and to his becoming a prominent photographer himself. During 1927–1928,

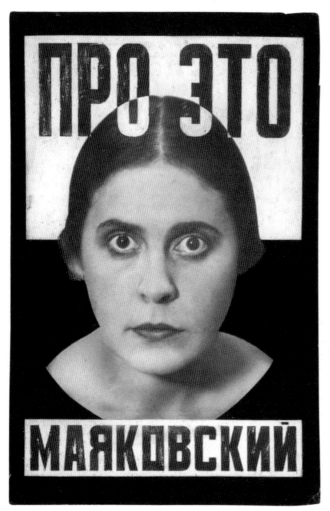

Fig. 20.16: Alexander Rodchenko, *About It*, cover, 1923. © Heritage Image Partnership Ltd/Alamy. © Rodchenko & Stepanova Archive, DACS, RAO, 2017.

as art director for *Novyi Lef* (*New Left*), the journal that Mayakovsky edited after *Lef* ceased publication in 1925, Rodchenko created a series of covers with his own photographs.

Besides Rodchenko, Gustav Klutsis (1895–1944), a former student and teacher at the Vkhutemas, began early in his career to use photomontage extensively. Claiming to have invented photomontage in the Soviet Union, Klutsis dedicated most of his efforts to propaganda, working frequently with Sergei Senkin

(1894–1963), another former Vkhutemas student. Among other projects, the two collaborated with Rodchenko on a special issue of the journal *Molodaya gwardya* (*Young Guard*) devoted to Lenin.

Whereas Rodchenko emphasized the covers of his publications, and in the case of *Pro Eto* the photomontage illustrations, El Lissitzky, who had previously been associated with Malevich rather than the Constructivists, was more concerned with the overall reading experience. He therefore envisioned an entirely new use of typography to express the inner content of a text, writing in 1923 that "the idea should be given form through the letters." While living in Berlin, he designed a book of Mayakovsky's poems entitled *Dlia golosa* (*For the Voice*) with a separate tab and graphic mark for each poem. The manager of Gosizdat found a small German printer who was able to obtain a collection of varied Russian fonts that enabled Lissitzky to achieve the book's special typographic effects, which included introducing each poem on a two-page spread where it was preceded by a graphic image constructed from typographic elements (Fig. 20.18).

Another active publication designer in the 1920s was Solomon Telingater. Between 1925 and 1927 he worked on the design of the printing industry journal *Polografcheskoe Proizvodstvo* (Polygraphic Production) and was on the organizing committe of the All-Union Polygraphic Exhibition. In fact, he designed the index for the exhibition's cata;pg. Telingater, in fact, designed the index for the All-Union Polygraphic Exhibition catalog. Between 1925 and 1927 he worked on the design of the printing industry journal *Poligraficheskoe Proizvodstvo* (*Polygraphic Production*) and was on the organizing committee of the All-Union Polygraphic Exhibition. Like Lissitzky, Telingater took a special interest in typography and concerned himself as much with the design of the book itself as with its covers. Telingater's skill as a typographer is evident in his cover design for Semen Kirsanov's book of poems, *Kirsanov Has the "Right of Word,"* where he mixes together a large number of different typefaces, combing them

Fig. 20.17: Alexander Rodchenko, *About It*, photomontage, 1923. © 2014. Photo Scala, Florence. © Rodchenko & Stepanova Archive, DACS, RAO, 2017.

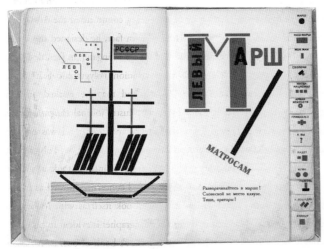

Fig. 20.18: El Lissitzky, *For the Voice*, page spread, 1923. Beinecke Rare Book and Manuscript Library, Yale University.

with other elements including a witty depiction of the poet himself.

Besides the great variety of books that were published for adults, many were also published for children. The earliest children's books included those published by the Kultur Lige, which promoted a modern Jewish culture. Among El Lissitzky's first publication designs were a number of Yiddish children's books including *Chad Gadya*.

In February 1924, the Communist Party issued a decree announcing a plan to develop a special kind of literature for children. The subject matter was to be the contemporary world rather than the world of fairy tales and folk stories that had characterized children's literature before the revolution. In 1923 a group of writers and graphic artists came together around a journal called *Sparrow*, which led to the establishment in 1925 of a Children's Publishing Department, known as Detgiz, in the State Publishing House. The directors of this department were the writer and translator Samuil Marshak (1887–1964), who collaborated with various illustrators, and Vladimir Lebedev, who had produced posters for the ROSTA Telegraph Agency in Leningrad during the Civil War. To make linocut posters, Lebedev had developed a simple style, which was well suited to children's books. Besides his own stories, he illustrated a number by Marshak including *The Circus*, *Ice Cream*, and *Yesterday and Today*. All featured relatively short texts combined with lively illustrations. *The Circus*, which showed the clowns and other performers in action, became a model for Soviet illustrators, in part because Lebedev's illustrations were so simple to reproduce. Like the ROSTA Windows, they consisted of flat colors on a white ground and had a minimum of detail.

The Soviet government also began to promote a special genre of children's books that was intended to get children enthused about science and technology. Among the first of these was a series of about 20 on objects of daily life. These were published between 1923 and 1929 by Galena (1891–1967) and Olga

(1892–1956) Chichagova, two sisters who had studied at the Vkhutemas. The aim of the series was to get children to look at the world rationally. In contrast to most children's book illustrators, the sisters favored a Constructivist aesthetic that featured bold typography, flat silhouettes, and strong contrasting colors. These qualities are evident in their design for N. G. Smirnov's *Otkuda posuda?* (*Where Do Dishes Come From?*), which told the story of how ceramicware was made. Other subjects in the series included utensils, newspapers, and travel.

Bibliography
Bibliographic essay

General political and economic histories of Russia and the Soviet Union include Donald Treadgold and Herbert J. Ellison, *Twentieth Century Russia*; Peter Kenez, *A History of the Soviet Union from the Beginning to the End*; and Alec Nove, *An Economic History of the USSR, 1917–1991.* William Blackwell focuses on the development of industry in *The Industrialization of Russia: An Historical Perspective,* and related to it is Raymond Hutchings, *Soviet Science, Technology, Design: Interaction and Convergence.* The literature on the Russian avant-garde is extensive, going back to the 1960s. I have used a selection of catalogs of comprehensive exhibitions as well as numerous monographs on individual artists. General exhibition catalogs and monographs include Stephanie Barron and Maurice Tuchman, *The Avant-Garde in Russia: New Perspectives*; Magdalena Dabrowski, Leah Dickerman, and Peter Galassi, *Aleksandr Rodchenko*; Selim Khan-Magomedov, *Rodchenko: The Complete Work* and *Alexander Vesnin and Russian Constructivism*; Alexander Lavrentiev, *Varvara Stepanova: The Complete Work*; Sophie Lissitzky-Küppers, *El Lissitzky: Life, Letters, Texts*; John Milner, *Vladimir Tatlin and the Russian Avant-Garde*; Margarita Tupitsyn, *Rodchenko & Popova; Defining Constructivism*; and Larissa Zhadova, *Malevich: Suprematism and Revolution in Russian Art, 1910–1930.* I discuss the work of Rodchenko and Lissitzky, including

a chapter on their designs for *USSR in Construction* in my book *The Struggle for Utopia: Rodchenko, Lissitzky, Moholy-Nagy, 1917–1946.* Christina Lodder's thorough *Russian Constructivism* is still the definitive book on this movement. Ruth Apter-Gabriel covers the work of avant-garde Jewish artists in *Tradition and Revolution: The Jewish Renaissance in Russian Avant-Garde Art* and the work of Jewish book artists is discussed in *Futur Antérieur: L'Avant-Garde et Le Livre Yiddish.* Gail Harrison Roman and Virginia Hagelstein Marquardt explore a range of topics related to the connections between Russian artists and art movements in the West in their edited volume *Avant-Garde Frontier: Russia Meets the West, 1910–1930.* Among the included essays is Christina Lodder's comparison of the Vkhutemas and the Bauhaus.

Peter Kenez, *The Birth of the Propaganda State: Soviet Methods of Mass Mobilization, 1917–1929* provides valuable background material for understanding the social role of graphic design during this period. On graphic design in general, see Mikhail Anikst, *Soviet Commercial Design of the Twenties*; Szymon Bojko, *New Graphic Design in Revolutionary Russia*; Leah Dickerman, ed., *Building the Collective: Soviet Graphic Design, 1917–1937: Selections from the Merrill C. Berman Collection*, and Alla Rosenfeld, ed., *Defining Russian Graphic Arts, 1898–1934: From Diaghilev to Stalin.* On Russian and Soviet posters in general, see Klaus Waschik and Nina Baburina, *Werbe für die Utopie: Russische Plakatkunst des 20. Jahrhundert.* Steven White, *The Bolshevik Poster* focuses on the period around the Civil War, while Susan Pack, *Film Posters of the Russian Avant-Garde* and Christopher Mount, *Stenberg Brothers: Constructing a Revolution in Soviet Design* concentrate on film posters. Victoria E. Bonnell, *Iconography of Power: Soviet Political Posters under Lenin and Stalin* provides an analysis of poster iconography that deals specifically with gender and class.

Susan Compton, *Russian Avant-Garde Books, 1917–1934* and Margit Rowell and Deborah Wye, *The Russian Avant-Garde Book, 1910–1934* cover the design of avant-garde books, while David King and Cathy Porter, *Images of Revolution; Graphic art from 1905 Russia*, offers an account of the little magazines that sprang up at the time of the 1905 revolution and provides extensive illustrations of their covers. Konstantin Rudnitzky discusses the design of theater sets in *Russian and Soviet Theater, 1905–1932* and Lidia Zaletova and her collaborators address the issue of dress in *Revolutionary Costume: Soviet Clothing and Textiles of the 1920s*. Mikhail Guerman, *Art of the October Revolution* is a collection of imagery with a brief text that ranges from paintings, prints, and posters to painted ceramics and figurines. Alexander Lavrentiev and Yuri V. Nasarov offer an overview of Soviet design in *Russian Design: Traditions and Experiment, 1920–1960*. Selim Khan-Magomedov's two-volume *Vhutemas, Moscou, 1920–1930* is an exhaustive study of this important design school.

Books

Anikst, Mikhail, ed. *Soviet Commercial Design of the Twenties*. Introduction and Texts by Elena Chernevich. New York: Abbeville Press, 1987.

Apter-Gabriel, Ruth. *Tradition and Revolution: The Jewish Renaissance in Russian Avant-Garde Art*. Jerusalem: The Israel Museum, 1987.

Barron, Stephanie and Maurice Tuchman. *The Avant-Garde in Russia: New Perspectives*. Los Angeles: Los Angeles County Museum of Art, 1980.

Blackwell, William L. *The Industrialization of Russia: An Historical Perspective*. New York: Thomas Y. Crowell, 1970.

Bojko, Szymon. *New Graphic Design in Revolutionary Russia*. New York and Washington: Praeger, 1972.

Bonnell, Victoria E. *Iconography of Power: Soviet Political Posters under Lenin and Stalin*. Berkeley, Los Angeles, and London: University of California Press, 1997.

Compton, Susan. *Russian Avant-Garde Books, 1917–1934*. Cambridge, MA: MIT Press, 1993.

Dabrowski, Magdalena, Leah Dickerman, and Peter Galassi. *Aleksandr Rodchenko*. With essays by Aleksandr Lavrent'ev and Varvara Rodchenko. New York: The Museum of Modern Art, 1998.

Dickerman, Leah, ed. *Building the Collective: Soviet Graphic Design, 1917–1937: Selections from the Merrill C. Berman Collection*. New York: Princeton Architectural Press, 1996.

Futur Antérieur; L'Avant-Garde et Le Livre Yiddish. Paris: Musée d'art et d'histoire de Judaisme and Skira/Flammarion, 2009.

Guerman, Mikhail, compiler and editor. *Art of the October Revolution*. New York: Harry N. Abrams, 1979.

Hutchings, Raymond. *Soviet Science, Technology, Design: Interaction and Convergence*. London, New York, and Toronto: Oxford University Press, 1976.

Kenez, Peter. *The Birth of the Propaganda State: Soviet Methods of Mass Mobilization, 1917–1929*. Cambridge: Cambridge University Press, 1985.

—*A History of the Soviet Union from the Beginning to the End*. Cambridge: Cambridge University Press, 1999.

Khan-Magomedov, Selim. *Alexander Vesnin and Russian Constructivism*. New York: Rizzoli, 1986.

—*Rodchenko: The Complete Work*. Introduced and edited by Vieri Quilici. Cambridge, MA: MIT Press, 1987 (c. 1986).

—*Vhutemas, Moscou, 1920–1930*. Paris: Éditions du Regard, 1990.

King, David and Cathy Porter. *Images of Revolution: Graphic Art from 1905 Russia*. New York: Pantheon Books, 1983.

Lavrientiev, Alexander. *Varvara Stepanova: The Complete Work*. Edited by John Bowlt. Cambridge, MA: MIT Press, 1988.

Lavrentiev, Alexander and Yuri V. Nasarov. *Russian Design: Traditions and Experiment, 1920–1960*. London: Academy Editions, 1995.

Lissitzky-Küppers, Sophie. *El Lissitzky: Life, Letters, Texts*. London: Thames and Hudson, 1968.

Lodder, Christina. *Russian Constructivism*. New Haven and London: Yale University Press, 1983.

Margolin, Victor. *The Struggle for Utopia: Rodchenko,*

Lissitzky, Moholy-Nagy, 1917–1946. Chicago and London: University of Chicago Press, 1997.

Milner, John. *Vladimir Tatlin and the Russian Avant-Garde.* New Haven and London: Yale University Press, 1983.

—*A Dictionary of Russian and Soviet Artists, 1420–1970.* Woodbridge: Antique Collectors' Club, 1993.

Mitchell, Mairin. *The Maritime History of Russia, 848–1948,* London: Sidgwick and Jackson, 1949.

Mount, Christopher. *Stenberg Brothers: Constructing a Revolution in Soviet Design.* Essay by Peter Kenez. New York: Museum of Modern Art, 1997.

Nove, Alec. *An Economic History of the USSR, 1917–1991.* London: Penguin Books, 1992.

Pack, Susan. *Film Posters of the Russian Avant-Garde.* Cologne: Taschen, 1995.

Roman, Gail Harrison and Virginia Hagelstein Marquardt, eds. *Avant-Garde Frontier: Russia Meets the West, 1910–1930.* Gainsville: University Press of Florida, 1992.

Rosenfeld, Alla, ed. *Defining Russian Graphic Arts, 1898–1934: From Diaghilev to Stalin.* New Brunswick: Rutgers University Press and the Jane Voorhees Zimmerli Art Museum, 1999.

Rowell, Margit and Deborah Wye. *The Russian Avant-Garde Book, 1910–1934.* With essays by Jared Ash, Nina Gurianova, Gerald Janecek, Margit Rowell, and Deborah Wye. New York: The Museum of Modern Art, 2002.

Rudnitzky, Konstantin. *Russian and Soviet Theater, 1905–1932.* Translation from the Russian by Roxane Parmer. New York: Harry N. Abrams, 1988.

Treadgold, Donald W. and Herbert J. Ellison. *Twentieth Century Russia.* Boulder: Westview Press, 2000.

Tupitsyn, Margarita. *Rodchenko & Popova; Defining Constructivism.* London: Tate Publishing, 2009.

Waschik, Klaus and Nina Baburina. *Werbe für die Utopie: Russische Plakatkunst des 20. Jahrhundert.* Bietigheim-Bissingen: Editions Tertium, 2003

White, Stephen. *The Bolshevik Poster.* New Haven and London: Yale University Press, 1988.

Woodward, David. *The Russians at Sea: A History of the Russian Navy.* New York and Washington: Praeger, 1965.

Zaletova, Lidya, Fabio Ciofi degli Atti, Franco Panzini, and Tatyana Strizenova. *Revolutionary Costume: Soviet Clothing and Textiles of the 1920s.* New York: Rizzoli, 1989.

Zhadova, Larissa A. *Malevich: Suprematism and Revolution in Russian Art, 1910–1930.* London: Thames and Hudson, 1982.

Chapter 21: Weimar Germany 1918–1933

Introduction

At the time of Germany's defeat in World War I, Kaiser Wilhelm II fled to Holland, thus ending two generations of imperial rule that had begun when Germany became a nation in 1871. The power breach was quickly filled by the Social Democratic Party, which, on November 9, 1918, declared Germany a republic. The Social Democrats first attempted to employ the regular army to quell an uprising in Berlin by the far left-wing Spartacus League and to quash a nascent Soviet-style republic in Bavaria, but they soon had to resort to the use of vigilantes known as the Freikorps to repress the revolutionaries. With order more or less secured, the Social Democrats conducted elections for a National Assembly to write a new constitution. Hoping for a large turnout, they commissioned posters from some of the leading Expressionist artists such as Cesar Klein (1879–1940), Heinz Fuchs (1886–1961), and Max Pechstein (1881–1955). The overall intent of the poster campaign was to unite the disparate groups of Germans in support of the Assembly's work. However, response to the posters was uneven and the workers were particularly critical. Either they found the Expressionists' drawings lacking in realism or else they thought the portrayal of the working class was too bleak. One poster that may have had a more positive effect was Max Pechstein's *Do not strangle the newborn freedom through disorder and killing your brothers. Your children could go hungry.* Though the poster stressed dire consequences for supporting the Socialists, it presented a child clutching a flag as a hopeful symbol for the new republic.

Even though some posters failed, the electorate still supported the Social Democrats, making them the largest party in the National Assembly. For safety's sake, the Assembly decided to convene in Weimar, a small town, where the great German literary figures Goethe and Schiller once lived. There, the delegates wrote the new constitution, which was the most liberal in Europe, giving women the right to vote.

Despite the Socialist victory, however, the Weimar Republic was replete with extremist groups on both the left and right. During the 14 years of its existence, the republic was rife with the tension of conflicting values, which were as readily manifest in the realms of art, architecture, design, literature, and music as they were in partisan politics. The left was most prominently represented by the Communist Party, founded in 1919, while the extreme right rallied around the National Socialist German Workers' Party whose leader was Adolf Hitler. More moderate factions on the right yearned for a return to the imperial regime of Kaiser Wilhelm II, during which Germany had enjoyed economic prosperity and international respect.

Until 1923, Germany faced severe shortages of food and fuel, harsh demands for reparations by the victors in World War I, and runaway inflation which, at its worst, could multiply the price of a loaf of bread 40 or 50 times within the span of a few hours. The stabilization of the currency in 1924, the easing of Germany's debt payment schedule (Dawes Plan), and large short-term loans from investors in the United States helped the economy considerably and by 1927 German production had regained its impressive 1913 level. The American stock market crash in 1929 and its ensuing affect on Germany, however, resulted in the recall of loans and reintroduced a period of economic and then political chaos. The National Socialist or Nazi Party rose to power on this misery, desperation, and anger. Hitler, a dedicated opponent of democracy, became the last chancellor of the republic on January 30, 1933.

The Werkbund, Arbeitsrat für Kunst, and the Novembergruppe

Germany's defeat in World War I was a setback to the promotion of its commercial goods abroad. Not only had World War I caused damage to prominent German industries, but also the nation's products were less welcome in foreign markets. During its Cologne exhibition in 1914, the Werkbund had initiated an intense debate about the future of industrial production that set Herman Muthesius's espousal of standardized product types against Henry van de Velde's claim that the individual artist was still the best person to develop new ideas for industrial goods. The debate was interrupted by the war, which, if anything, strengthened the mechanization of German industry, thus posing a challenge to those who supported *Handwerk* or craft.

When the Werkbund reconvened after the war, its members remained divided in their attitudes towards the crafts. At the organization's meeting in September 1919, Hans Poelzig (1869–1936), one of Germany's leading architects, urged in a keynote speech that a line be drawn between the world of industry and the world of art and craft. Poelzig equated industry with soulless profit-seeking materialism, while art and craft, he said, were based on the value of work for its own sake. Only artists and craftsmen, he argued, could create objects of lasting value. Though Poelzig's talk garnered some enthusiasts, many Werkbund members remained skeptical of his moral distinction between industrial production and craft. Among those who disagreed with him, Robert Bosch (1861–1942), a manufacturer of well-designed automotive products, was incensed at Poelzig's dismissal of the automobile as ephemeral art and his denigration of industrial design in comparison to art and architecture.

Poelzig's identification of industrial design with soulless capitalism helps explain why members of left-wing cultural movements that arose after the war such as the Arbeitsrat für Kunst (Workers' Council for Art), a left-wing association of artists and architects, and the Novembergruppe (November Group), a

radical artists' organization, expressed such antipathy to industry and adopted instead the pre-industrial community as their embodiment of utopia.

The espousal of Arbeitsrat ideals by Walter Gropius (1883–1969), who became director of the Bauhaus in April 1919 and was also a member of the Werkbund, is an interesting case in point. Before the war, Gropius worked briefly in the office of Peter Behrens, the former design director for the AEG, and designed the bodywork of a locomotive and the interior of a sleeping car for the railway factory in Königsberg. With Adolf Meyer, he also designed the Fagus shoe-last factory, one of the early buildings in Germany with a glass curtain wall. Gropius's shift from an architecture and design practice embedded in industrial culture to a pre-industrial vision of craftsmanship and communitarian life has never been explained and one can only speculate as to why it occurred. As a member of the Arbeitsrat, Gropius may have been influenced by the war's destruction to turn away from big business and embrace instead the vision of a simpler past where *Handwerk* and community spirit represented the moral high ground. He incorporated many of the Arbeitsrat pronouncements into the founding manifesto of the Bauhaus, among which was the claim that all the crafts should be united under the wing of a great architecture.

Gropius collaborated in the Arbeitsrat with the architect Bruno Taut (1880–1938), one of its founders. In 1919 and 1920, Taut, who was also a member of the Werkbund, published two books, *Alpine Architecture* (Plate 05) and *The Dissolution of Cities*, in which he called for a return to the land and the creation of small communities based on craft production and farming. In these communities, Taut envisioned temples of glass, following the mystical theories of glass architecture espoused by the poet and novelist Paul Scheerbart.

Within the Werkbund, Taut and Gropius were part of a radical faction that continued to challenge the organization's traditional ideals. However, by 1921 the Werkbund began to return gradually to its pre-war concern with the quality of Germany's manufactured goods. That year it sponsored a Haus Werkbund (Werkbund House) at the new Frankfurt fair, which was intended to demonstrate its concern for well-made products as pre-war exhibitions had done. However, the exhibit featured luxury items made primarily for export rather than less expensive goods for the impoverished German consumers who were beset by food shortages and inflation. The Haus Werkbund was yet to find a suitable mission in the new post-war environment. Flanked on one side by the utopian visionaries of the Arbeitsrat and the early Bauhaus and on the other by the proponents of standardization who sought to adapt Frederick Winslow Taylor's principles of scientific management to German industrial production, the Werkbund in the early 1920s was in search of a place in the new industrial order.

The Avant-Garde: Dada and Constructivism

Although Gropius and Taut, as members of the Arbeitsrat, were critical of industrial capitalism in a broad sense, they did not attack the new German republic directly as did members of the Dada group in Berlin between 1917 and 1920. In Zurich, Dada was associated with the disruptive performances of the Cabaret Voltaire, which had no specific political agenda, but in Berlin, the Dadaists initially focused their artistic enmity on the ruling class that had brought Germany into World War I, and then, after the war, they attacked the new Weimar Republic itself.

Richard Huelsenbeck brought the name "Dada" with him when he returned to Berlin from Zurich in early 1917. Around the same time, independently of Huelsenbeck, Wieland Herzfelde (1896–1988) started a left-wing publishing venture, the Malik-Verlag, whose first publication was the political newspaper *Neue Jugend* (*New Youth*). It lasted for two issues before the censors closed it down. *Neue Jugend* was designed by Wieland's brother, Helmut Herzfelde (1891–1968), who exchanged his German name for an English one, John Heartfield, as a protest against German nationalism. Heartfield

had studied commercial art at the Kunstgewerbeschule (School of Applied Art) in Munich and as a young student he is said to have admired the posters of Ludwig Hohlwein. After moving to Berlin, however, he adopted a sober approach to layout, while substituting roman fonts for the traditional German Fraktur type. When he did use a Fraktur face, he always did so selectively and ironically.

In 1918, Huelsenbeck joined with Heartfield and other artists and writers, including Raoul Hausmann (1886–1971), Hannah Hoch (1889–1978), Johannes Baader (1875–1955), Franz Jung (1888–1961), and George Grosz (1893–1959), to present a series of performances and readings at various galleries and theaters under the title Club Dada. Hausmann's prospectus design for a new periodical with that name featured a rough Expressionist woodcut combining a jagged abstract form with the jumbled letters of the title (Fig. 21.01). For the text, he mixed typefaces as the Futurists did and broke up words into separate fragments. Like Hugo Ball, Hausmann wrote and performed poems composed of sounds without meaning and in his typography he mixed words and different letter sizes and weights to give his text a sonic quality. Although Hausmann adopted the techniques of the Expressionists and the Futurists in his design for the *Club Dada* prospectus, his typographic composition took on a new meaning because it represented his and the other Dadaists' intent to subvert the forms and content of public discourse. This was as evident in the three issues of the periodical *Der Dada* that Hausmann designed in 1919 as it was in the layouts that John Heartfield and George Grosz did for *Dadaco*, an unpublished anthology of Dada writings.

Though Dada typography could be disruptive, another technique, photomontage, more forcefully expressed the Dadaists' opposition to current Weimar politics and cultural values. For the Dadaists, photomontage was a collection of photographic fragments that were arranged in a composition to yield a new meaning. The composition could either be a one-off

Fig. 21.01: Raoul Hausmann, *Club Dada*, prospectus, 1918. Collection Merrill C. Berman. Photo: Jim Frank & Joelle Jensen. © ADAGP, Paris and DACS, London 2017.

original or it could be rephotographed and produced as a poster, a magazine cover, or an illustration. For the Dadaists, photomontage was an oppositional technique. The sources of their images were primarily the bourgeois press—daily newspapers and illustrated weekly magazines such as the *Berliner Illustrirte Zeitung*. The point of Dada photomontage was to extract these photographic images from their original context and give them an oppositional meaning by reorganizing them into new compositions. Heartfield, Hausmann, and Hoch were the principal creators of photomontage among the Berlin Dadaists.

Heartfield developed photomontage as a means

of political agitation. For him, it was always related to mass media rather than art. In fact, he called himself a *monteur* or mechanic rather than an artist. He first began working with photographic fragments in *Jedermann sein eigner Fussball* (*Every man his own football*), a political newspaper whose single issue the Malik-Verlag published in 1919. For the cover, Heartfield cut out photographs of Germany's prominent politicians and military leaders and pasted them on a drawing of a woman's fan above which he placed the ironic question in Fraktur type, "Who is the best-looking?" as if the leaders were competing in a beauty contest (Fig. 21.02). Although this display was not strictly a photomontage, Heartfield did produce one of his early photomontages elsewhere on the cover, an image of himself inside a huge soccer ball, which illustrated the nonsensical title of the newspaper.

In contrast to Heartfield, Hausmann approached photomontage as an artist rather than a designer. His composition of 1920, *Tatlin at Home*, depicts a man with a machine part for a brain and though he names this figure Tatlin after the Russian artist who created the Monument to the Third International, he does not implicate him in any revolutionary activity. Instead, he constructs a curious landscape that suggests a greater interest in exploring the unconscious than in making an explicit political statement (Fig. 21.03). Other photomontages of his such as *Dada siegt* (*Dada conquers*) and *Dada Cino* (*Dada cinema*) of 1920 have a comparable enigmatic quality.

Hannah Hoch, who had studied calligraphy and book design, shared Hausmann's interest in ambiguous imagery, though she also worked occasionally with photographs of well-known political figures to produce oppositional statements about Weimar culture. Her complex photomontage *Schnitt mit dem Küchenmesser Dada durch die Letzte Weimarer Bierbauchkuluturepoche Deutschlands* (*Cut with the Kitchen Knife Dada through the Last Weimar Beer-Belly Cultural Epoch of Germany*) combines images of politicians from Kaiser Wilhelm II's regime, military leaders, and figures from the new

By the summer of 1920, Dada in Berlin had run its course. Its climax was an exhibition called the First International Dada Fair, where the public was provoked with an array of paintings, objects, and signs that urged them to take Dada seriously while also declaring the end of art. Suspended from the ceiling was Rudolf Schlichter's figure with a pig's head and an army uniform, which juxtaposed disparate elements, as did photomontage artists, to ridicule the military.

For a brief period, the Berlin Dadaists joined together in opposing the political, military, and cultural establishments of the new Weimar Republic. While they shared the name "Dada," they had different concerns ranging from the partisan politics of Heartfield and Grosz, both of whom were among the first to join the German Communist Party (KPD), to Hannah Hoch's questioning of cultural mores and Raul Hausmann's attack on the prevailing conventions of art (Plate 06).

Fig. 21.02: John Heartfield, *Jedermann sein eigner Fussball*, cover, 1919. Photobibliothek.ch © The Heartfield Community of Heirs/VG Bild-Kunst, Bonn and DACS, London 2017.

Weimar Republic with communists, dancers, athletes, and even some fellow Dadaists, Raoul Hausmann and Johannes Baader. Photographs of crowds make reference to urban life while images of ball bearings and gear wheels signify industrial culture. Among the many figures in Hoch's photomontage are some with mixed parts of men's and women's bodies. This was an early instance of her interest in gender identity, which she was to develop in subsequent photomontages for many years afterwards.

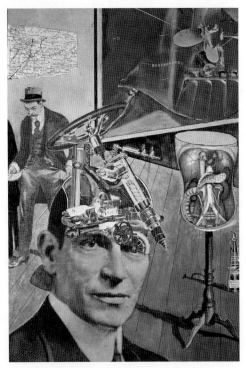

Fig. 21.03: Raoul Hausmann, *Tatlin at Home*, photomontage, 1920. Moderna Museet, Stockholm, Sweden/Bridgeman Images.

Fig. 21.04: El Lissitzky, *Veshch*, cover, 1922.© Image Asset Management Ltd/Alamy.

After the First International Dada Fair, the group's legacy of opposition was continued in the vitriolic drawings and paintings of George Grosz and in the photomontages that Heartfield began to contribute to the publications of the Communists and other left-wing organizations, including his brother's own Malik-Verlag.

Whereas the Expressionists promoted a spiritual renewal through art and architecture and the Dadaists mounted a critique of Weimar culture and politics, the Constructivists in Germany called for a language of objectivity that would manifest itself in art, architecture, and design. None of Constructivism's leading proponents were German. Theo van Doesburg (1883–1931), who founded the *De Stijl* movement, was Dutch; El Lissitzky was Russian; and László Moholy-Nagy was

Hungarian. These artists were attracted to Germany by its cosmopolitan atmosphere, particularly in Berlin. The German Constructivists, who were active in 1922 and 1923, were not part of the Russian movement, nor did they adopt a political agenda as the Constructivists in Russia did.

Although the German Constructivists mainly created paintings and sculptures, both Lissitzky and van Doesburg also produced book covers and journal designs that embodied Constructivist values. With the Russian writer Ilya Ehrenburg, Lissitzky edited two issues of a cultural magazine, *Veshch* (*Object*), that was intended to create a bridge between artists in Europe and Russia. In their initial editorial, the two editors used the term "constructive art," declaring that its mission was "not, after all, to embellish life but to organize it." Lissitzky's cover design and opening page layouts for *Veshch* were good examples of what they meant by organization.

Lissitzky was trained as an architect rather than a commercial artist. Thus, he thought of his publication designs as structural compositions rather than conventional layouts. For the two *Veshch* covers, he created a dynamic composition by contrasting a striking black diagonal with the horizontal title and issue number (Fig. 21.04). Lissitzky was a strong advocate of visual economy and demonstrated it in his cover design by reversing the French and German translations of the Russian title out of the black diagonal shape. His architectural approach to graphic composition is also evident in his cover for the First Russian Exhibition that was held at Berlin's Van Diemen Galerie in 1922. Here Lissitzky treated the letters as compositional elements and played with varying letter scales within the individual words to create a strong design. By endowing letters and abstract shapes with equivalent plastic value, Lissitzky produced typographic compositions that departed radically from the traditional conventions of commercial art, thus introducing an entirely new approach to page layout.

Though van Doesburg, was the founder

of *De Stijl* and the principal organizer of German Constructivism, he also adopted a Dada identity and expressed it through *Mécano*, a small publication he published for four issues in 1922 and 1923. However, his notion of Dada was eclectic and he was not affiliated with any existing Dada groups in Berlin, Paris, or elsewhere. The first three issues of *Mécano* were actually broadsheets that folded down into 16-page editions. One side of each sheet was printed successively in the *De Stijl* colors, blue, yellow, and red. Van Doesburg mixed photographs of sculptures by Raoul Hausmann, paintings by Moholy-Nagy, and poems by Tristan Tzara with his own short texts written under his Dada pseudonym, I. K. Bonset. Van Doesburg's combination

of discipline and playfulness was evident in his layouts as well as his cover design where he separated the letters of the title and arranged them in a rectilinear frame with rules between them.

One artist whose work van Doesburg published in *Mécano* was Kurt Schwitters (1887–1949), perhaps best known for his tightly organized collages composed of scrap paper, packaging labels, street car tickets, and other ephemera. In Hanover, Schwitters started a one-man movement called Merz, which was actually the last four letters of the German word "Commerz" (commerce). Like van Doesburg, he was also a sometime Dadaist and actually participated in a series of Dada performances on a tour through the Netherlands with van Doesburg and his wife Nellie.

Schwitters became interested in typography through his contact with van Doesburg, Lissitzky, and Moholy-Nagy and in 1923 he began to publish an irregular magazine of limited circulation called *Merz* after his movement. As with many little magazines of the period, its typography and content were innovative. Schwitters printed his own writings (he was also a poet) as well as avant-garde art and writing by his friends. In the fourth issue he presented El Lissitzky's short manifesto "Topography of Typography," in which the Russian argued for economical typographic expression and a close relation between typography and the content it expressed.

Fig. 21.05: Kurt Schwitters, *Merz* 11, cover, 1924. © 2014. Photo Scala, Florence/BPK, Bildagentur fuer Kunst, Kultur und Geschichte, Berlin. © DACS 2017.

Besides making art, Schwitters also worked as a graphic designer, operating through his own agency, Merz Werbezentrale (Merz Advertising Center). His clients included various businesses such as Günther Wagner, a Hanover company that produced Pelikan inks and related products, as well as the municipality of Hanover and the Dammerstock housing exhibition in Karlsruhe for which Schwitters designed all the promotional materials. One of the purposes of *Merz* was to present new ideas for advertising as Schwitters did in the 11th issue, where he proposed a series of new designs for Pelikan products (Fig. 21.05). Schwitters also collaborated with both Constructivists and Dadaists.

Fig. 21.06: El Lissitzky, *Merz Matineen*, poster, 1923. © INTERFOTO/Alamy.

He presented a series of Dada performances on tour with van Doesburg and his wife and invited Lissitzky to design a poster for two performances he was presenting, one with Raoul Hausmann, in Hanover. Lissitzky's poster was a complex typographic diagram that combined shapes, text, and arrows to guide the reader in several directions through the announcements (Fig. 21.06).

Although the Dadaists and Constructivists were only active for a brief period, their publications were soon to exert a major influence on working designers and art directors. With few exceptions, they were trained as artists rather than designers and thus brought a more open attitude to photography and typography as means of communication. By blurring the traditional distinctions between art and design, they applied numerous discoveries of the artistic avant-garde to the design of graphics for mass circulation.

The Bauhaus in Weimar

In early 1919, while still active in the Arbeitsrat and the Werkbund, Walter Gropius became the director of the Bauhaus in Weimar. The school inhabited the building that Henry van de Velde designed for the Weimar School of Applied Art and also inherited some of its faculty members. Although the Bauhaus curriculum was based on a workshop model that was similar to other applied arts schools in Germany, Gropius staffed each workshop with an artist or Form Master as well as a craftsman or Workshop Master. In this way, he sought to invent a new role for the artist in the design process. His emphasis on craft workshops rather than design for mechanized production was consistent with the prevailing ideas in the Arbeitsrat, as well as the beliefs of some in the Werkbund. Drawing more on the Arbeitsrat ideology than the Werkbund philosophy, however, Gropius sought to establish an idealistic community of creative teachers and students to produce artifacts for a new world.

His utopian ambitions were expressed in the founding manifesto. The woodcut image of a cathedral

Fig. 21.08: Oskar Schlemmer, Bauhaus logo, 1922. Bauhaus-Archiv, Berlin.

Fig. 21.07: Lyonel Feininger, "Bauhaus Manifesto", illustration, 1919. Beinecke Rare Book and Manuscript Library, Yale University. © DACS 2017.

of socialism on its cover was created by the Expressionist artist Lyonel Feininger (1871–1956), who was also a Bauhaus faculty member (Fig. 21.07). For Gropius, the cathedral represented the power of architecture to unite the different crafts within the common purpose of building. To foster a creative community, he attempted to break down the hierarchy between the artist and the craftsman and he reduced the aura of the professor by eliminating academic titles. In 1922, Oskar Schlemmer's depiction of a human profile ringed by the name of the school was adopted as the Bauhaus identity mark and was used throughout the school's duration (Fig. 21.08).

Essential to the Bauhaus curriculum was the foundation course, which prepared students for the specialized workshops. To teach the course, Gropius hired the Swiss artist Johannes Itten (1888–1967), who had a special interest in how children expressed their artistic abilities. Itten cultivated the creativity of each student, addressing the whole person through exercises that fostered the students' spontaneity, while also strengthening their powers of observation and analysis.

The foundation course centered on Itten's theory of contrasts, which permeated many of the exercises. Students carved wooden blocks into different textures, explored the relation of contrasting colors, and made

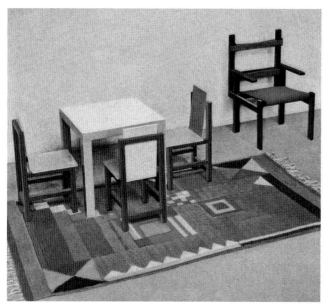

Fig. 21.09: Benita Koch Otte, rug for a child's room, 1923. akg-images.

sculptures from unusual materials that included feathers, woven cane, and even string. In addition, they learned to draw from nature and analyze the structure of famous paintings. As a result, they entered the workshops with well-developed visual vocabularies that enabled them to produce richly textured designs. For example, students in the weaving workshop, such as Benita Otte (1892–1976), created hand-woven wall hangings whose intricate patterns consisted of contrasting and complementary fibers, colors, shapes, and textures (Fig. 21.09).

The Bauhaus workshops were, with few exceptions similar to those in other schools of applied art. A major difference was the role played by the Form Masters to introduce new formal ideas. As in other schools, students learned to make furniture, pottery, wall hangings, stained glass, and metalware. The contrasting backgrounds of the Form Masters and the Workshop Masters created a number of tensions, however, although the distinctions did produce some successful results such as the pottery by students who worked under the Expressionist sculptor Gerhard Marcks (1889–1981).

Other artists who joined the faculty included the Germans Oskar Schlemmer (1888–1943) and Georg Muche (1895–1986); the Swiss painter Paul Klee (1879–1940), who taught a course in elementary design that supplemented Itten's foundation course; and the Russian artist Wassily Kandinsky (1866–1944). Schlemmer worked briefly in the wall painting and sculpture workshops before taking over the school's theater workshop in 1923. Muche was the Form Master in the weaving workshop. He also assisted Itten in the foundation course, which may account for Itten's strong influence on the tapestry designs. Both Klee and Kandinsky mainly taught outside the workshops, although their theories did have some influence on workshop production.

Until László Moholy-Nagy joined the faculty in 1923, the artists came primarily from the Expressionist milieu. Consequently the Bauhaus experienced little influence from other avant-garde movements such as Dada or Constructivism. Moholy-Nagy replaced Itten whose influence on the school did not support Gropius's ambitions for its future. Itten was trained as an art educator rather than as a craftsman and seemed to have little concern for applied arts training. He belonged to a spiritual movement called Mazdaznan and sought to recruit students for it as well as influence the school's culture by, for example, pressing the canteen to serve only vegetarian food.

Moholy-Nagy took over Itten's foundation course, while also becoming the Form Master in the metal workshop. He was the first faculty member with an interest in industrial design and he was instrumental in bringing about a cultural change at the Bauhaus that led to more prototypes for industrial production. Moholy brought a highly developed visual vocabulary to the Bauhaus and shifted the emphasis to simpler and more functional forms in the metal workshop. Soon Marianne Brandt (1893–1983), the only woman in the workshop, along with other students, was incorporating the circles, hemispheres, and related geometric forms of Moholy's Constructivist paintings and sculptures into designs for teapots, pitchers, and fruit dishes.

Fig. 21.10: Karl Jacob Jucker and Wilhelm Wagenfeld, table lamp, 1924. © V&A Images/Alamy. © DACS 2017.

Moholy also encouraged his students to produce designs for lighting, bringing them directly into the sphere of industrial design. Karl Jacob Jucker (1902–1997) explored designs for lamps with moveable positions, while he and Wilhelm Wagenfeld (1889–1949) designed a table lamp whose circular metal base, tubular glass stem, and rounded glass shade incorporated Moholy's geometric design vocabulary just as the teapots and other metal artifacts did (Fig. 21.10).

Although Gropius had called for uniting the crafts under the wing of a great architecture, he was not able to organize an architectural department until 1927 after the school had moved to Dessau. To compensate for the lack of architectural instruction, he used his professional commissions to foster cooperation among the workshops. His design of a house for the Berlin timber merchant Adolf Sommerfeld in 1921 incorporated woodcarving, stained glass, and furniture design. The primitive appearance of the house was due largely to the necessity of building it from teak timbers that Sommerfeld had reclaimed. The carved exterior beams and interior doors and walls by Joost Schmidt (1893–1948), the densely patterned stained glass designs by Josef Albers (1888–1976), and the ponderous hall furniture by Marcel Breuer (1902–1981) gave the house the feeling of a primitive community hall rather than a modern dwelling. At the time, however, this look was still compatible with the craft aesthetic that dominated the Bauhaus.

The initial furniture of Breuer, a Hungarian student in the cabinetmaking workshop, drew heavily on African forms and Hungarian folk art but he soon became interested in the spare designs of the Dutch furnituremaker, Gerrit Rietveld. This is evident in a seminal cherry wood chair of 1922, which follows Rietveld's idea of a linear frame, but Breuer chose fabric for the seat and the backrest rather than the wooden planks that Rietveld used (Fig. 21.11). The cabinet-making workshop fulfilled a number of successful commissions, providing furniture for the Sommerfeld House, an experimental children's home, and the Haus am Horn that was designed and built for the Bauhaus Exhibition in 1923.

Fig. 21.11: Marcel Breuer, chair, 1922. akg-images.

By 1923, Gropius was under pressure from the state government of Thuringia, which provided funds to the school, to demonstrate what had been accomplished in the four years since it opened. Marshaling all the workshops to show student projects, Gropius created an exhibition that became a public-relations triumph. During the exhibition, he gave a speech in which he proclaimed his belief in a new unity between art and technology. This was less evident in the workshop projects than in the Haus am Horn, a prototype for inexpensive mass-produced housing.

Designed by the artist Georg Muche (1895–1987) with the help of Adolph Meyer, Gropius's architectural partner, the house was constructed with the latest materials and had the most up-to-date kitchen equipment in Germany. Far more than the Sommerfeld house, it was furnished by many of the workshops. Marcel Breuer and Erich Dieckmann (1896–1944) from the cabinetmaking workshop produced furniture in a contemporary style, while Moholy-Nagy designed the lighting, which consisted of fluorescent tubes. The house also included specially designed carpets, tiles, radiators, and ceramic containers for the kitchen.

Alma Buscher (1899–1944), the only female student in the cabinetmaking workshop, concentrated on wooden furniture and toys for children, and her children's room for the Haus am Horn avoided the conventional adult furniture in miniature, introducing instead a modular container system that allowed the child's imagination free play. This system was later marketed by the Bauhaus.

Another example of Gropius's shift away from the craft romanticism of the school's first years was the exhibition catalog, whose cover was by a student, Herbert Bayer (1900–1985). The Bauhaus had no commercial art course until it moved to Dessau, thus all graphic material, which consisted mainly of postcards and prints that the Masters designed, was produced in the school's print shop. Other graphics such as announcements for Bauhaus events displayed Expressionist graphics consisting of hand-drawn letters

of questionable proportions. Itten's theory of contrasts was evident in Joost Schmidt's poster for the 1923 exhibition, which strove for a synthesis of diverse elements—differences of shape, texture, scale, and tone (Plate 07). The eclectic lettering was done by hand, yet it was tightly integrated into Schmidt's extremely formal composition. The poster was, however, a transitional design between a craftsman's approach to graphic form and a striving to adopt a tightly ordered composition that neatly integrated all the poster's elements.

By comparison, Bayer created a distinctly modern cover with the title displayed in large san serif letters whose colors alternated in sections of blue and red (Plate 8). Moholy-Nagy designed the interior layout in a style that recalled the rational approach to page design of van Doesburg and Lissitzky. He also published an essay in the catalog called "The New Typography," in which he espoused "unequivocal clarity in all typographic communication," and asserted that "[t]he new poster relies on photography," which he called the "new story-telling device of civilization." This was a direct challenge to the entire profession of commercial art in Germany, which was based on the artist's ability to draw both images and letters. It was also the first clarion call for a new modern approach to graphic design, a call that would shortly be heeded by the young typographer Jan Tschichold, who visited the Bauhaus exhibition and was highly stimulated by what he saw there.

Despite the new direction that the 1923 exhibition heralded, the Bauhaus nonetheless had its enemies, particularly among members of several right-wing parties who were elected to the Thuringian parliament in 1924. For them, the Bauhaus was too cosmopolitan. Its faculty was international as was its student body. And Gropius's new technological thrust angered local craftsmen. For these and other reasons, the parliament curtailed the school's funds and it had to close in 1924, only to reopen a year later in Dessau, whose mayor, Fritz Hesse, clearly understood how the presence of the Bauhaus could contribute to his vision of a modern industrial city.

Rationalization and Renewed Productivity

In 1924, the German economy began to move again, fueled by a huge loan from the United States under the Dawes Plan. That year the Werkbund organized *Form ohne Ornament* (*Form without Ornament*), an exhibition featuring unornamented objects that were both machine-made and hand-crafted. Even though not all the objects were made by machine, by emphasizing simple forms as the ideal for production, the exhibition signaled the Werkbund's move away from the Expressionist idealism of the immediate post-war years and marked its support of the more rational aesthetic of *Neue Sachlichkeit* or New Objectivity. This was the style that characterized progressive art, design, and architecture in the years between the Dawes Plan of 1924 and the stock market crash of 1929. *Form ohne Ornament* raised again the question of standardized forms for industrial production that had been central to earlier debates but the Werkbund in the 1920s was unable to promote quality design to the large companies that produced the bulk of Germany's consumer goods to the same degree that it had before the war.

The AEG, for example, one of Germany's largest manufacturers of electrical products, did not build on the accomplishments of its pre-war design director Peter Behrens. In the 1920s, the AEG manufactured many different products from hanging lamps and hair dryers to vacuum cleaners and radios but none achieved the aesthetic distinction their products had before the war. The lack of notable design was also true at Siemens & Halske, which started in the telephone business but later expanded to compete with the AEG in the manufacture of electric appliances for the consumer market. The company established a line called "Protos," which included electric cooking ranges, vacuum cleaners, toasters, electric water heaters, washing machines, and electric irons. Without a design

director of Behrens' caliber to give some character to these products, they were straightforward and practical but had no exceptional formal qualities.

One reason why design may not have seemed as important to large German companies in the 1920s as it did to the AEG before the war was the interest in Frederick Winslow Taylor's theories of scientific management. Managers in the 1920s were more concerned with increasing organizational efficiency at all levels than with addressing the questions of product form that interested the Werkbund. Within the large corporations, support for rationalization methods, which meant efficiency and standardization, spread from the production system to physical distribution and marketing as well. The rationalization movement was led by the Deutscher Normen Ausschuss (German Standards Board), which promoted efficiency methods and standards throughout Germany. The board had been founded in 1916 to standardize the production of military equipment and then continued to establish specifications for parts and procedures that covered all manufacturing sectors. It published a series of industrial standards called Deutsche Industrie Normen (German Industrial Standards) or DIN. These standards had a particular effect on graphic design through the standardized paper sizes that were based on a single unit that could be multiplied to produce sheets of varying dimensions.

Domestic Goods

As a consequence of the emphasis on scientific management and standardization in large companies, including the AEG and Siemens & Halske, designers made a greater impact on smaller firms, particularly those that produced modern versions of traditional applied arts such as glassware and ceramics. For the Jenaer Glaswerke (Jena Glass Works), Gerhard Marcks (1889–1981), the Form Master in the Bauhaus pottery workshop, and Wilhelm Wagenfeld (1900–1990), a student of Moholy-Nagy's in the metal workshop, designed a glass coffeemaker whose sculpted modern

Fig. 21.12: Gerhard Marcks and Wilhelm Wagenfeld, Sintrax coffeemaker, early 1930s. © 2014. Digital image, The Museum of Modern Art, New York/Scala, Florence. © DACS 2017.

shape recalled the ceramic forms created by some of Marcks' students (Fig. 21.12). Wagenfeld was to continue designing glassware for Schott, producing a glass tea service and a wire holder with three cups for boiling eggs among other objects.

Fig. 21.13: Marguerite Friedlander-Wildenhain and Trude Petri, Halle service, 1930. The Wolfsonian–Florida International University, Miami Beach, Florida, The Mitchell Wolfson Jr. Collection, TD1994.177.1-3. Photo: Bruce White.

In ceramics, the designs of Marguerite Friedlander-Wildenhain (1896–1985) and Trude Petri (1906–1989) for the Staatliche Porzellan-Manufaktur, Berlin (KPM), helped make that company a leader in the production of modern ceramicware. The design director for the KPM beginning in 1929 was Günther von Pechmann (1882–d.o.d. unconfirmed), a leading figure in the pre-war Werkbund and author of a 1924 book on quality production. Under von Pechmann, Friedlander-Wildenhain produced her Halle service, consisting of several white unadorned tea and coffee pots, along with tea and coffee cups with concentric gold bands that Petri designed (Fig. 21.13). The commitment to simple ceramic forms began for Friedlander-Wildenhain and Petri when they were students at the Bauhaus. Friedlander-Wildenhain was particularly active in the pottery workshop when Gerhard Marcks was the Form Master and she continued to work with Marcks when both joined the faculty of the applied arts school known as Burg Giebichenstein in Halle after they left the Bauhaus. Petri's Urbino glazed porcelain dinner service of 1930–1932 was perhaps the purest example of the new KPM ceramicware. The tops of the coffee pot and sugar bowl fit seamlessly with the rest of the object so that their separation was barely noticeable, while the cups, saucers, and plates were cut low and wide to achieve graceful curves. Among the other notable ceramic services produced during this period was the simple Functionalist dinner service, Form 1382, that Herman Gretsch (1895–1950) designed for the porcelain manufacturer Arzberg in 1931.

Automobiles

The German automobile companies Daimler and Benz were the first to design internal combustion engines but neither envisioned the car as a mass-produced product as did Henry Ford, whose adoption of the assembly line for making inexpensive vehicles revolutionized the automobile industry. Instead, German manufacturers produced custom-made vehicles for the nobility and the newly rich. Initially designers played no role in their production. Opel was perhaps the first automobile company to take design seriously. Besides the poster they commissioned from the Berlin *sachplakat* artist, Hans Rudi Erdt, an early attempt to involve a designer was their 1907 commission of a drawing for an auto body from the Austrian Secession architect Joseph Olbrich, although the design was never put into production.

The first passenger cars had closed box-like compartments, which were generally constructed with wooden frames that had flat sheet metal applied over them. The leading car designer in the early years of the German automobile industry was Ernst Neumann-Neander, who had set up a studio in Berlin to design posters, advertising, and car bodies. He worked as a consultant for several well-known coachbuilders and completed his first auto body prototypes in 1910 and in 1911. In 1912 he designed the Opel 13/30, an early attempt at a streamlined car that eventually became known as the Opel Egg. The streamline theme was pushed further by the Viennese aeronautical engineer Edmund Rumpler (1872–1940), who presented his Tropfen Auto, or teardrop car, at a Berlin auto show in 1921. Rumpler based his aerodynamic body on the precedents of his airplane designs although he

attempted to combine the aerodynamic bullet shape with a more conventional curved-box cabin. Benz tried unsuccessfully to market the car as a passenger vehicle, though the company eventually incorporated Rumpler's ideas into a racing car in 1923.

Opel took its first steps towards an affordable automobile with its Doktorwagen (Doctor's Car) in 1909. In 1924 the company began to produce a popular two-seater called the Laubfrosch (Tree Frog) because of its green body paint (Fig. 21.14). The Laubfrosch was an open car with a canvas top. As one author noted, instead of being big and black it was small and green. Modeled on a French Citroën, the Laubfrosch was the first car in Germany to be produced on an assembly line like the Ford. It was also the first German car that was accessible to a wide public. Though relatively inexpensive to begin with, its price dropped by more than half within six years after 100,000 had been produced. Opel continued to manufacture for a mass market after General Motors purchased the company in 1929. Among the new mass-oriented vehicles was the Opel Kadett of 1932, whose cab with rounded corners and arched grill followed the form of GM's Plymouth.

The best-known firms that produced larger, more expensive cars were Mercedes-Benz, BMW, Audi, Horch, and Adler. At the beginning of 1900, the Daimler Motoren Gesellschaft (DMG) developed a lighter, smaller, racing car called the Mercedes, which featured numerous innovations such as a low center of gravity, a pressed-steel frame, and a honeycomb radiator. The car, designed by Daimler engineer Wilhelm Maybach (1846–1929), was a big success. After World War I, however, German automobile manufacturing was at a low point due to the high inflation and the devastation that the war brought about. Both Daimler and its strongest rival, Benz, were producing very few cars and decided to merge in order to strengthen their operations. Following their merger in 1926, the company was called Mercedes-Benz and it adopted as its symbol a three-pointed star, which initially symbolized the

Fig. 21.14: LaubFrosch (Tree Frog), Opel, 1924. © INTERFOTO/Alamy.

Fig. 21.15: Mercedes-Benz Grosser, 1930s. Daimler AG.

Daimler engines on land, sea, and air. Rather than producing inexpensive popular cars like Opel, however, Mercedes-Benz focused on more expensive models such as the Stuttgart and the Mannheim and then in the late 1930s the company launched the Grosser, whose extended body, large rounded fenders and curved hood signified the ultimate in luxury (Fig. 21.15).

Horch, founded in 1899, produced cars for the luxury class and often had exclusive bodywork created by famous coachbuilders such as Glaser and Neuss. In 1928, the company commissioned automobile designs from the well-known commercial artist O. W. H. Hadank and shortly thereafter created its own design team. The firm's founder, August Horch, also established a second company, Audi, which produced its own automobiles until 1932 when Audi and Horch merged with two other companies under the Audi name.

BMW, the acronym for Bayrische Motoren Werke (Bavarian Motor Works), was founded in 1928, considerably later than the other leading automobile manufacturers of the 1920s, and began to produce its most significant cars in the late 1930s, when it established its own department of design headed by Wilhelm Meyerhuber (1888–1978), the chief stylist.

Like Horch, Adler also started at the beginning of the century though it produced bicycles, typewriters, and motorcycles as well as automobiles. Around 1930, the company commissioned Walter Gropius, the former Bauhaus director, to design an auto body, which it manufactured in two versions, the Standard 6 and the Standard 8. Gropius created a design that had strong horizontal and vertical lines and plain surfaces without decoration. Though Adler sought to capitalize on the name of the well-known architect, his designs made a more potent reference to modern architecture than to automobile design. Consequently they contributed little to the development of the automobile and few of the cars were sold.

In 1922 there were over 100 automobile manufacturers in Germany. Most of the cars they produced such as the Freia, the Gridi, the Libelle, and the Szawe were in production for short periods and are now mainly forgotten. What is important to note, however, is that the Weimar Republic had an active automobile culture that has received little attention to date. By 1929, when the American stock market crashed, many of automobile firms had gone out of business, others merged, and a few were bought by foreign companies. By 1933, only 16 manufacturers remained.

The Bauhaus in Dessau and Berlin

The Gropius years

The cathedral was the building type that framed the organization of the Bauhaus workshops in Weimar, but in Dessau it was the modern home to which Bauhaus production was directed. "The Bauhaus wants to serve the development of present-day housing," wrote Gropius in 1926, "from the simplest household appliances to the finished dwelling." To achieve this end, he defined the workshops as "laboratories in which prototypes of products suitable for mass production and typical of our time are carefully developed and constantly improved."

The number of workshops in Dessau was reduced. The pottery, a local Weimar enterprise, remained behind and the stained glass workshop, which did not translate easily into objects for mass production, was discontinued. Some of the Weimar teachers took other jobs, leading Gropius to promote several of the former students to the position of Workshop Master. Of these, Marcel Breuer (1902–1981) headed the cabinetmaking workshop; Gunta Stötzl (1897–1983) assisted Georg Muche in the weaving workshop; Herbert Bayer (1900–1985) transformed the printing workshop into a workshop for advertising, exhibition design, and typography; and Hinnerk Scheper (1897–1957) was in charge of the wallpainting workshop. Moholy-Nagy and former student Joseph Albers (1888–1976) shared the Foundation course, while Moholy continued to head the metal workshop until his resignation in 1928. In 1927, Gropius hired the Swiss architect Hannes Meyer (1889–1954) to head up a

Fig. 21.16: Walter Gropius, Bauhaus building, Dessau, 1926. Getty Images.

department of architecture, the first in the school's brief history. As a complement to the architecture program, Oskar Schlemmer continued to receive support for a theater workshop even though it was not directly related to the school's new emphasis on industrial production.

As with the Haus Sommerfeld and the Haus am Horn, Gropius involved all the workshops in furnishing the Bauhaus building, which was completed in 1926 and whose construction was funded by the city of Dessau. The building's plan exemplified the new rationalism of the fledgling modern movement. Functions were divided into separate wings, which were connected by corridors or walkways. Gropius preserved the sense of community that he originally desired for the school by incorporating all the functions within a single building—the student dormitory, the canteen, the auditorium, the gymnasium, and the glass-enclosed workshop wing.

Much of the work on the interior was done in the cabinetmaking workshop. Breuer designed a range of chairs and tables that were constructed with tubular steel frames. These included his seating for the auditorium—chairs with cloth seats and backs that were made of polished steel—along with chairs and tables for the canteen. Other furnishings for

Fig. 21.17: Marcel Breuer, Wassily chair, 1925. © Arcaid Images/Alamy.

the building included the tubular fluorescent lighting that Moholy-Nagy's metal workshop produced for the auditorium. Hinnerk Scheper created the color scheme for the walls, while Herbert Bayer designed huge letters spelling out "Bauhaus," which were attached to the outside of the building (Fig. 21.16).

One of the more influential objects produced in the early Dessau period was Marcel Breuer's Wassily chair of 1925, which he originally constructed of bent nickel-plated tubular steel and combined with a fabric seat and back although the chairs were later produced with leather instead of fabric. (Fig. 21.17). Breuer supposedly got the idea for the chair from the tubular steel handlebars of a bicycle. He called the chair Wassily because he designed it for the house of his colleague, the painter Wassily Kandinsky. The chair did not originate in the Bauhaus furniture workshop and Breuer sought to market it himself through a company called Standard-Möbel, which he set up with a partner in Berlin.

With funding from the timber merchant Adolf Sommerfeld, the Bauhaus established a company to market its designs to industry. Among the most successful products created at the school while Gropius was still director were the lamps that Marianne Brandt and other students designed in the metal workshop. Moholy-Nagy must be given much of the credit for this direction, which moved the school away from the craft typologies that Gropius originally envisioned. The firm Körting & Matthiesen in Leipzig produced Brandt's well-known Kandem bedside table lamp. It came in two stem lengths and like many lamps to follow, had a swivel joint between the shade and the stem, which made it possible to change the angle of the light (Fig. 21.18). All the lamps produced in the metal workshop had clean forms and no ornament. These included hanging lamps with metal shades, ceiling lamps with frosted glass globes, and wall mounted lamps with moveable arms. One of the most innovative ideas was the construction of lighting fixtures consisting of shallow glass dishes that were attached directly to the

Fig. 21.18: Marianne Brandt, Kandem table lamp, 1928. © 2014. Digital image, The Museum of Modern Art, New York/Scala, Florence. © DACS 2017.

ceiling. Almost all of these prototypes were brought to market by firms in various parts of Germany.

Due to differences with the students, Muche resigned as head of the weaving workshop in early 1927 and Gunta Stötzl replaced him. Under her guidance, students began to experiment with new

materials for machine production and these soon came to the attention of the textile industry. Leading textile manufacturers bought patterns from the Bauhaus and they became widely accepted by the public. Significant results were achieved particularly in the production of slipcover fabrics and drapery. The new textile designs were complemented by Hinnerk Scheper's innovative approach to wall decoration. Scheper was interested in covering walls with large areas of flat colors, which could vary from wall to wall. He also preferred either solid colors or subtle patterns for wallpaper because he believed that such designs would not compete with the architecture.

Herbert Bayer transformed the printing workshop into a modern studio for the design of posters, advertising stands, and promotional literature. He also assumed responsibility for the design of all Bauhaus promotional graphics including stationery, brochures, and schedules. Bayer derived his clean page organization, use of white space, and preference

Fig. 21.19: Herbert Bayer, Universal alphabet, 1925. Bauhaus-Archiv Berlin. © DACS 2017.

for san serif type from the principles of the New Typography that Moholy-Nagy had enunciated in the 1923 Bauhaus catalog and the typographer Jan Tschichold had begun to codify in a special issue of the German printing magazine *Typographische Mitteilungen* in October 1925. Bayer also adopted the argument of Dr. Walter Portsmann, an engineer who argued in his book *Sprach und Schrift* (*Speech and Writing*) of 1920 that capital letters were inefficient. Bayer began to use "kleinschreibung" or writing with small letters, to support the argument for efficiency in communication that Moholy-Nagy had also promoted in his Bauhaus catalog essay of 1923.

Bayer's interest in efficiency was the basis for his design of an alphabet he called "universal," which had no capital letters. In the spirit of modernity, Bayer rejected the tradition of roman alphabets and instead constructed his own letters from several basic elements, notably circles and arcs (Fig. 21.19). While this created some unity between letters based on similar shapes, it also left other letters outside the system, hence the alphabet lacked the consistency that was a traditional hallmark of typographic quality.

Bayer's alphabet was not picked up by a type foundry and thus it served a polemical aim rather than a functional one. Others at the Bauhaus also experimented with modular alphabets. Joseph Albers created his "kombinationschrift" (combination writing), which was based on ten modular shapes. It was an interesting experiment but had no practical application since a typesetter would have had to build letters out of modular elements rather than use already formed letters to compose lines of type.

Before the Bauhaus moved to Dessau, Gropius had asked Moholy-Nagy to co-edit a series of Bauhaus books that would publicize work being done at the Bauhaus, present the ideas of the Bauhaus teachers, and sum up the major modern movements in art and architecture. The first books appeared in 1925 and by 1929, when the series ended, 14 books had been published, although about 50 were planned. The published books

included Paul Klee's *Pedagogical Sketchbook*, Wassily Kandinsky's *Point and Line to Plane*, Kazimir Malevich's *The Non-Objective World*, and Moholy-Nagy's *Painting Photography Film*. Moholy-Nagy designed most of the books according to the principles of the New Typography that he had promoted. He organized the covers with heavy geometric elements and used photographs or photograms (cameraless photographs) in some instances. Moholy drew his design aesthetic from his own Constructivist paintings and though he was somewhat heavy handed in his designs, the Bauhaus books contrasted sharply with the conventions of book design, especially the design of covers, that prevailed in Germany at the time. The Bauhaus books helped to publicize the school widely as did the photographs of Bauhaus projects and school life that circulated widely in articles and promotional literature. Many of these photographs were taken by Moholy's first wife Lucia, who was actively documenting events at the school while he taught there.

In early 1928, Gropius decided to resign, most likely because he wanted to devote time to his architectural practice but also because he had consumed a great deal of energy defending the school against numerous critics. However, he was leaving the Bauhaus in a strong position. The facilities were excellent and the school had begun to increase its contacts with industry as was originally intended. Bayer, Moholy-Nagy, and Breuer decided to resign at the same time, which left the school with a considerable gap to fill.

The Meyer years

The new director was Hannes Meyer, the Swiss architect whom Gropius hired in 1927 to head up the first architecture department. Meyer could not have been more different from Gropius. Politically, he was considerably to the left of Gropius's moderate socialism and architecturally he promoted a rational approach to building that was based more on sociological and economic research than on design. Under Meyer, the architecture department supported a major project of

Gropius's in Dessau, the Törten housing estate, which was built with standardized components. Though there were some problems with the construction, the project pioneered new methods of low-cost efficient building that gradually began to spread within the German construction industry.

Though Meyer's emphasis on science and technology and his extreme left-wing politics antagonized some of his colleagues and some students, he did accomplish a lot at the Bauhaus and these contributions should be recognized. First, Meyer brought in a series of lecturers with knowledge of science, engineering, and the social sciences to speak about theoretical issues that might have a bearing on the curriculum. Second, he shifted the emphasis in the cabinetmaking workshop, now combined with the metal workshop, towards low-cost furniture for the working class. Compared to the more widely recognized icons of modern furniture such as Breuer's Wassily chair and his cantilevered tubular steel Cesca chair, the furniture produced under Meyer is less well known. Made primarily of wood, it featured a folding table and chair by Gustav Hassenpflug (1907–1997), a chair made of modular parts that Josef Albers designed, and a folding chair of tubular steel and plywood that Hin Bredendieck (1904–1995) created. Meyer publicized this populist approach to furniture design in several exhibitions, first in Leipzig in 1929, where the living room, bedroom, and kitchen of a Bauhaus Volkswohnung (People's Apartment) was on display, and then the following year in Moscow where he sent an exhibit that summed up Bauhaus achievements between 1928 and 1930.

Under Meyer, Joost Schmidt, a former Bauhaus student and head of the sculpture workshop, replaced Bayer in the workshop for advertising, commercial art, and typography. Schmidt worked out a successful pedagogical method for teaching students visual fundamentals, while also adding an emphasis on exhibition design. His department also designed exhibition stands for the Junkers airplane factory in Dessau and won a contract to do all the newspaper advertising for the large chemical factory, I. G. Farben. Schmidt's advertising and typography workshop was supported by a new photography workshop that was established in 1929. It was headed by Walter Pederhans (1897–1960), an industrial and portrait photographer before going to the Bauhaus, who specialized in close-ups of objects, an approach that lent itself particularly to advertising photography. Meyer's biggest commercial success was the Bauhaus wallpapers that were designed in the wall painting workshop under Hinerk Scheper. Commissioned by a wallpaper manufacturer, Emil Rasch, their subtle textures and patterns were unlike anything else on the market and four and a half million rolls were sold in the first year alone.

During his tenure as director, Gropius had sought to keep the Bauhaus politically neutral. Meyer, however, allowed the formation of a communist cell at the school, while also establishing closer ties with his counterparts in Moscow. By 1930, his political activities prompted the Dessau City Council to demand his resignation. He then took some students with him to the Soviet Union where, as the Bauhaus Brigade, they sought an engagement with the ambitious building program of Stalin's First Five-Year Plan.

The Mies years

Meyer was replaced by the architect Mies van der Rohe (1886–1969), who moved the school in its final phase towards an architectural program. He combined the furniture, metal, and wallpainting workshops into a single department for interior design, which was headed by the interior architect Lilly Reich (1885–1947), beginning in 1932. Reich was also in charge of the weaving workshop.

Mies divided the school into two main areas: architecture and interior design. His principal interest during his period as director was in single-family residences, which was a major shift from the radical social agenda of Hannes Meyer. The focus in the interior design seminar, headed first by Alfred Arndt

(1896–1976), a former student, and then by Lilly Reich, was on reasonably priced furniture for the home. Students learned to make precision construction drawings and several won prizes in a 1931 Werkbund competition for standardized home furnishings. In late 1932, the Dessau parliament, which now had a large number of Nazi members, closed the Bauhaus. Mies moved the school to Berlin, where it briefly occupied a vacant telephone factory until he finally shut it down in August 1933. Clearly the Bauhaus values, whether socialist, communist, or simply modernist, were out of step with the new Nazi regime.

Other Design Schools

Despite all its accomplishments, however, the Bauhaus engaged in only a limited segment of the modern industrial production that was emerging in Europe. Its constraints were framed by the initial emphasis on architecture and its related arts rather than the broader array of industrial products including automobiles, airplanes, radios, and other goods that formed a growing part of Germany's industrial culture. In general, the constraints of the Bauhaus were typical of other applied arts schools in Germany during the 1920s. In Frankfurt, Christian Dell (1893–1974), who had been the technical instructor in the Bauhaus metal workshop, headed up a comparable program, and in Stuttgart, the art academy, headed by Bernhard Pankok (1872–1943), the former *Jugendstil* designer, developed strong programs in furniture design and typography.

The school that had the most direct relation to the Bauhaus was Burg Giebichenstein in Halle. It was established in 1915 by the architect Paul Thiersch (1879–1928), who sought to realize the Werkbund ideals with a strong art program and complementary workshops that could produce prototypes for industry. When the Bauhaus moved from Weimar to Dessau, Gerhard Marcks, who had directed the pottery workshop in Weimar, went to teach at Burg Giebichenstein and in 1928 he became the school's director. Between 1925 and 1930, while at the Halle school, Marcks along with

Wilhelm Wagenfeld designed his well-known Sintrax coffee percolator for the Jena Glass Company.

Several former Bauhaus students—Benita Otte (1892–1976), Erich Dieckmann (1896–1944), and Marguerite Friedlander-Wildenhain—joined Marcks at Burg Giebichenstein. Otte took over the weaving workshop, where her course was more open to artistic experiment than the growing tendency towards machine production in Dessau. Dieckmann, who headed the furniture workshop, designed both wooden furniture and furniture made of cantilevered steel. In ceramics, Marguerite Friedlander-Wildenhain achieved great success with her previously mentioned Halle service for the Staatliche Porzellan-Manufaktur, Berlin, while one of the prominent graduates of the metal workshop, Wolfgang Tümpel (1903–1978), gained recognition as a designer of lamps, bowls, teapots, and other metalwork.

Besides the applied arts schools in Frankfurt, Stuttgart, Halle, and other cities, a number of private art schools offered successful design programs. Among the leading ones were the Itten-Schule and the Riemann-Schule. In 1926, Johannes Itten, who left the Bauhaus in 1923, opened his own school in Berlin. It provided basic art education for aspiring artists, architects, photographers, advertising artists, designers of fashion, and other types of designers. Among the faculty were George Muche, who had assisted Itten in the Bauhaus Foundation course and also headed the weaving workshop. Other teachers included former Bauhaus students Gyula Pap (1899–1983), who had studied in the metal workshop with Moholy-Nagy, and Umbo (a.k.a Otto Umbehr) (1902–1980), who became a well-known photojournalist. Lucia Moholy (1894–1989), Moholy-Nagy's first wife, also taught photography there. The curriculum featured classes based on Itten's Bauhaus foundation course. In the morning, students had a gymnastic session that included singing and humming to harmonize the body and spirit. Itten also made contact with several Japanese artists, and around 1932 the school offered classes in Japanese brush painting.

Another Berlin school, the Riemann-Schule, was established by Albert and Klara Riemann in 1902. It offered courses in the practical arts, including fashion, poster design, metalworking, stage design, textile design, film animation, and portrait photography. One of its specialties was window display, which achieved a high level of distinction during the Weimar years. By the late 1920s, up to 1,000 students, many from abroad, might have been studying at the school each year. The Riemann-Schule did not have its origin in the crafts as did the Bauhaus and other applied arts schools. Consequently it developed numerous programs that were not part of the traditional applied arts curriculum. However, the school was closely associated with the Werkbund and student projects were published regularly in the Werkbund yearbooks.

Architecture and the New Interior

The conflict between modernity and tradition was nowhere more evident in Weimar Germany than in the ambitious building programs that were instituted in many cities following the Dawes Plan in 1924. Although the architectural styles varied from one city to another, several cities, notably Berlin, Frankfurt-am-Main, and Stuttgart, became showcases for a modern style known as the *Neues Bauen* (New Building) that was based on rational efficient design. The large building programs also provided the impetus for the design of new furniture and interiors that supported the ambitions of architects and planners to create low-cost housing for large numbers of people.

In Berlin, Bruno Taut transformed his Expressionist yearning for community into the large Britz housing project, which featured a horseshoe-shaped ring of apartments that surrounded an open communal green space. The Britz housing was financed by the GEHAG, a socialist building society, and featured modest low-cost apartments and town houses for the working class.

In Frankfurt, the building program was directed to similar ends though it was considerably larger. The architect Ernst May (1904–2005) was in charge of the

entire project, which consisted of various large housing estates around the periphery of the city and several developments that were closer to the center.

May formed a multidisciplinary design team for the *Neue Frankfurt* or "The New Frankfurt," that included architects, planners, furniture designers, and graphic designers. Faced with such a massive project, he devised cost-cutting techniques that included establishing standards for doors, windows, and other building components, fixing a set number of floor plans, and producing modular pre-cast foamed concrete wall slabs on site. A hallmark of the housing designs was the flat roof, which the Nazis were later to equate with a racist Mediterranean style.

As part of his comprehensive plan, May was concerned with the design of standardized low-cost furniture that would fit comfortably in the new flats. To address this problem, he brought the architect Ferdinand Kramer (1898–1985) into the municipal building department. Kramer and the designer Franz Schuster (1892–1972), an Austrian who briefly directed the architecture class at the Frankfurt applied art school, created inexpensive *typenmöbel* or standardized chairs, tables, cupboards, and other furniture pieces. Primarily rectilinear in form, the designs were manufactured by Hausrat, a non-profit enterprise the city set up to sell furniture to the new tenants at a reasonable price. Another function Hausrat served was to provide work for unemployed carpenters and cabinetmakers. Kramer also created standardized children's furniture at a smaller scale for the city's kindergartens and in 1926 he designed an inexpensive cast iron heater called the Kramer-Ofen (Kramer heater) that was produced by the firm of Hugo Buderus, which specialized in heating devices.

An additional source of furniture was the *Frankfurt Register*, a catalog published by the city on a regular basis. It included lamps and light fittings as well as chairs, tables, beds, and other conventional items. Residents were strongly encouraged to furnish their apartments with the modern furniture that was either sold by the city or featured in the *Register*.

The apartments featured the Frankfurt kitchen, designed by the Polish architect Grete Schütte-Lihotzky (1897–2000), who had been inspired by May's social vision and came to Frankfurt to work with him. Schütte-Lihotzky's design was based on the same desire for household efficiency that had stimulated the Americans Catherine Beecher as well as Christine Frederick. The latter's book *The New Housekeeping: Efficiency Studies in Home Management* was translated into German in 1922 and her espousal of rationalization in the home found numerous supporters in Germany. Similar to the ideas of Frederick, Shütte-Lihotsky's kitchen was conceived like a ship's galley with continuous counter space that included a cutting

Fig. 21.20: Grete Schütte-Lihotzky, Frankfurt kitchen, 1926. akg-images/ ullstein bild.

board with its own waste bin. Besides the cabinets, an array of metal drawers was built in for the storage of basic provisions (Fig. 21.20). Shütte-Lihotsky designed the layout to reduce excess motion and facilitate the transition from one function to another. The Frankfurt kitchen challenged the traditional idea of the kitchen as a comfortable hearth and defined it instead as a space for productive work. On the manufacturing side, its most radical feature was its design as a single factory-assembled unit that could be delivered to a building site and easily integrated into the existing construction.

Das Neue Frankfurt was conceived as a total environment that included advertising, graphics, and public signage as part of the overall urban design. Walter Dexel (1890–1973), a graphic designer and gallery curator, was a consultant to the city on advertising and he introduced designs for illuminated outdoor advertising that were installed at various locations in the city. The artist Karl Peter Rohl (1890–1975), a former Bauhaus student who was teaching at the Frankfurt applied art school, devised a system of standardized signage to delineate different specialties within the medical profession, while another artist, Robert Michel (1897–1983), painted large outdoor advertising signs in a Constructivist style. Hans Leistikow (1880–1962) was the city's graphic designer whose responsibilities included the supervision of all printed designs from posters to book covers, the redesign of the city's coat of arms, and the design of *Das Neue Frankfurt*, a cultural magazine published by the city that promoted modernity in all its forms from automobile design and architecture to typography, film, and exhibition design. Between 1925 and 1930, the year Ernst May led a design team to the Soviet Union to participate in the construction of the new industrial city of Magnitogorsk in the Ural Mountains, *Das Neue Frankfurt* was an exceptional experiment in social planning that invited many architects and designers to apply the most advanced forms of modern design to a progressive social end.

By 1926, the Werkbund had shifted its attention from the problems of craft and machine production to the question of architecture. Meeting in 1926, the organization decided to sponsor a major housing exhibition the following year in Stuttgart. Directed by the architect Mies van der Rohe, the Weissenhof exhibition, as it was known, was intended to showcase the most advanced thinking in architectural design. Its set piece was an apartment building by Mies, which was joined by separate homes and small groups of row houses by Europe's leading architects including Walter Gropius, Peter Behrens, Le Corbusier, Hans Scharoun (1893–1972), and Victor Bourgeois (1897–1972). Unlike the *Neue Frankfurt*, the exhibition did not have a social agenda although some of the entries, notably the row houses by the Dutch architects Mart Stam (1899–1986) and J. J. P. Oud (1890–1963) were designed for residents with lower incomes.

The furnishings of the various houses and apartments in the exhibition highlighted two strong developments in Weimar furniture design—the inexpensive standardized wooden pieces designed for working-class flats and the higher-end tubular steel furniture that Marcel Breuer pioneered at the Bauhaus and was then developed by Mart Stam, Mies van der Rohe, and other architects and designers. Besides Ferdinand Kramer and Franz Schuster in Frankfurt, other leaders in the design of low-cost furniture were Adolf Schneck (1883–1971), a professor at the Stuttgart applied arts school, and Max Hoene (1884–1965), who designed a line of mass-production furniture for the Bayerische Hausrathilfe in south Germany.

Schneck believed that only necessary pieces of furniture should be produced in standardized forms. "Any item of furniture that is not an absolute necessity," he wrote, "is a luxury article. And a luxury article that is standardized is what we call kitsch." He created a line of inexpensive furniture for the Deutsche Werkstätten für Handwerkskunst (German Workshops for Arts and Crafts) in Hellerau, one of the firms that had started during the *Jugendstil* period. By 1927, the Werkstätten had become one of the leading manufacturers of standardized furniture and had adopted machine production.

Hoene's designs featured basic units including cupboards, that could be modified with add-on elements such as glazed cabinets or small bookcases. The intent was to encourage a sense of individuality for people who could not afford to commission custom furnishings. The firm held down costs by using plywood and rationalizing the machine production by working with a standardized frame and panel system.

Though Marcel Breuer can be credited with designing perhaps the first chair made of tubular steel, the Dutch architect Mart Stam was the first to design a cantilever chair whose suspended seat was enabled by the strength of the metal tubing that made up its frame. Stam's design was constructed with gas pipes that were held together with elbow joints. Though the design, which consisted of a single line of tubing, was potentially elegant, Stam's initial iteration was awkward. He subsequently refined the design in later models, but it was Mies van der Rohe, after learning of the idea from Stam at a planning meeting for the Weissenhof exhibition, who refined the cantilever concept and produced its most elegant versions in chromed tubular steel. These were the MR10, a simple linear form with the seat and back made either of black leather or wicker (Fig. 21.21), and the MR20, the same chair with tubular steel arms. During the planning for the Weissenhof exhibition, Mies had made no secret of

Fig. 21.21: Mies van der Rohe, MR10 tubular steel chair, 1927. © Arcaid Images/Alamy. © DACS 2017.

his dissatisfaction with the low-cost wooden furniture, which he thought had a look of poverty. As he once told a colleague, he was building homes not tin cans. In 1928, Marcel Breuer produced his own version of the cantilever form, the Cesca chair, which differed from both Stam's and Mies's designs by its combination of a partial tubular steel structure and black wooden frames for the back and seat. Caning was stretched over the frames. For the Weissenhof exhibition, tubular steel furniture was on display in a number of the dwellings and Breuer's earlier pieces, combined with lighting from the Bauhaus metal workshop, were exhibited in the two houses by Walter Gropius. They served as examples of what Breuer believed to be a "styleless" modern room that avoided "any preconceived notion of the psyches of its users."

For Mies, architecture continued to be the stimulus for the further design of modern furniture. In 1929, when he designed the German Pavilion for the International Exhibition in Barcelona, he created two chairs made of chromed flat steel frames which supported leather cushioned seats and backs. The chairs came with matching footstools and a solid glass coffee table that rested on a chromed steel cross-frame. Shortly thereafter Mies returned to the cantilever concept with his chairs for the Tugendhat house in Brno, Czechoslovakia. The padded leather back and seat of the Brno chair were exquisitely suspended in mid-air, supported by a frame of flat chromed steel strips.

Neither Stam, Breuer, nor others who designed tubular steel furniture shared Mies's preoccupation with formal elegance, believing instead that tubular steel furnishings exemplified a modern way of living that was accessible to large numbers of people. The widespread display of tubular steel furniture at the Weissenhof exhibition most likely contributed to the belief of a few furniture manufacturers such as the Austrian firm Thonet that a viable market existed for the new designs. Thonet purchased its first tubular steel designs from Marcel Breuer who had unsuccessfully tried to market his initial pieces through his own company, Standard

Möbel. Thonet took over all Breuer's designs from the Standard Möbel catalog and began to market 19 different pieces. Although tubular steel furniture was more expensive than the low-priced designs in wood by Kramer, Schneck, and others, Thonet's mass production of it lowered the price substantially. Beginning in 1932, Thonet also began to manufacture some pieces by Mies, including his two Weissenhof chairs. Other architects who produced tubular steel pieces for Thonet were the Swiss Le Corbusier, the Frenchman Andre Lurçat (1894–1970), and the supposed French architect Béwé, who was most likely a fictional character devised by the company.

Thonet was the first furniture company to introduce tubular steel furniture to a mass market. By the late 1930s, the firm had commissioned and produced several hundred designs, exploiting the material to the limit as it had previously with its bentwood chairs. But then, Thonet ceased to produce tubular steel furnishings, perhaps because so many of its designs were copied by other furniture companies both in Germany and abroad. Tubular steel had become as common as wood and when produced in sufficient amounts it was even as economical if not more so.

Capitalist Advertising, Mass Media, and Communist Propaganda

During the 1920s, advertising, typography, commercial art, mass media, and political propaganda in Germany were as diverse and complex as the economic and political situation of the nation itself. Before World War I, German poster design and advertising art as well as typography and printing had all developed to a high degree. After the war both the Dada and Constructivist avant-gardes adopted new forms of visual rhetoric that contrasted strongly with these developments. While Constructivism stimulated the emergence of the New Typography on the one hand, Dada contributed to the rise of a working-class press and print culture on the other. Weimar Germany also fostered the growth of the picture-laden photo magazines, which provided work for many photographers, introduced the new role of picture editor, and redefined the function of the art director.

To some degree, the different design practices influenced each other but they frequently clashed. Jan Tschichold's New Typography, for example, posed a powerful challenge to the conventional methods of commercial artists, both in terms of technique and style. The photograph, argued Tschichold (following Moholy-Nagy), should replace the drawing while san serif type should be used exclusively. For Tschichold, hand lettering, which most commercial artists practiced, was passé. Likewise, avant-garde designers challenged the tradition of book design and proposed new book formats that accommodated the photograph as much as or more so than the text. In many ways, the techniques of left-wing designers like John Heartfield were similar to the tenets of the New Typography and the visual strategies of the mainstream picture magazines, but as oppositional practitioners, left-wing designers always incorporated an element of criticism or irony that influenced the pictorial forms and accompanying texts of their posters and publications.

Perhaps the biggest conflict, which mirrored that of Weimar itself, was between the modern and the traditional, a clash that was echoed in other fields of design as well. Photography was central to the modern vision and its growing incorporation into book design, advertising, the picture press, and political propaganda signaled an espousal of the modern that transcended both left and right. The Modernist incursion into all aspects of graphic design did not occur without resentment and once the Nazis came to power in 1933, there was a new celebration of German black-letter typefaces aimed at replacing internationalist modernism with nationalist tradition.

Commercial art

Most commercial artists in Weimar were generalists. Some were trained as artists while others had studied poster design or taken courses in lettering and other aspects of commercial design. Many were members of the Bund der Deutschen Gebrauchsgraphiker (Association of German Commercial Artists), which was founded in 1919. The term "Gebrauchsgraphik" (literally, useful graphics) was more widely used than "Reklamekunst" (advertising art) or "Werbekunst" (publicity art) as it could be applied to a broader range of activities. It was also the name of an important commercial art magazine that began publication in 1926 and brought to the design community news of commercial art activities throughout Germany and in a number of other countries.

The clients for commercial art were predominantly small and medium-sized businesses, which made it possible for the artists to operate independently or with modest support. Among the commissions they

Fig. 21.22: Ludwig Hohlwein, Summer in Germany, poster, c. 1930. © INTERFOTO/Alamy. © DACS 2017.

undertook were the design of shop windows and retail spaces, posters, letterheads and business cards, lettering, calendars and prospectuses, newspaper ads, packaging, and company trademarks. Some also did magazine titles and covers. Book design was considered a separate art, more akin to typography. Berlin and Munich were the principal centers of graphic design activity, although commercial artists were working in most German cities.

The leading poster artist was Ludwig Hohlwein, who had already established himself as a prominent designer in Munich before the war. When he began his career, he specialized in posters that were built up with flat colors, but during the 1920s, as his fame grew, he began to model his figures in more detail. He specialized in portrayals of the German upper class—self-confident men and women who dressed elegantly, ate well, and traveled widely (Fig. 21.22). His clients included haberdashers and clothiers, makers of perfume, cigarettes, and fine foods, and manufacturers of sewing machines, typewriters, and bicycles. As well, Hohlwein created movie posters and magazine covers. He had a colonial mentality and portrayed a full array of exotic natives from all continents to promote tea, cocoa, and other goods. Hohlwein, like many commercial artists, was also a versatile lettering man who could vary his lettering style from delicate French curves to strong blocky shapes.

Other commercial artists in Munich included Valentin Zietara (1883–1935) and Otto Ottler (1891–1965). Though Ottler had his own style, he occasionally drew heavily on Hohlwein's depictions of upper-class men and women, as did another Munich poster artist, J. V. Engehard (dates unconfirmed). The artist and illustrator Walter Schnackenberg (1880–1961) developed an illustrative style that referenced French cabaret posters of the 1890s, although he depicted more daring sexual behavior including beautiful women tantalizing both young and old men.

In Berlin, Fritz Rosen (1856–1935) managed Lucian Bernhard's studio after Bernhard moved to New York in 1922, but Bernhard continued to collaborate with Rosen and the two men signed some commissions jointly. Although the focus on the single object, which characterized the *sachplakat* before the war, had declined as a visual technique, Bernhard and Rosen continued to create posters in that style but they varied it with designs that were strong on lettering or the depiction of objects from unusual angles. Among the other prominent poster and advertising artists in Berlin were the Viennese Julius Klinger (1876–1920), who frequently gave his images a humorous twist, and his student Willy Willrab (dates unconfirmed), who specialized in posters featuring architectural constructions of a product name in large three-dimensional letters; Otto Arpke (1886–1943), whose clients included the steamship company Norddeutscher Lloyd; Jupp Wiertz (1888–1939), whose drawings frequently reflected the elongated figures of French fashion illustrators; and Max Bittrof (1890–1972), whose work had a more abstract tendency, occasionally influenced by Cubism.

Though most commercial artists were men, a few women were also active. Perhaps the most prominent was Dora Mönkmeyer Corty (1890–1973), who lived in Dresden. Primarily a poster artist, she designed numerous trademarks as well. Her work often conveyed a sly wit as evidenced in her poster of a man tilted forward on his seat reading the Dresden newspaper, *Die Anzeiger*.

Fritz Hellmut Ehmcke holds an unusual place among German commercial artists of the 1920s. He had a strong background in typography and book design as well as teaching. Ehmcke was an active Werkbund member and designed the poster for the 1914 Werkbund exhibition in Cologne (see Chapter 17). Though he did many commercial jobs including posters, trademarks, colophons, and packaging, he continued to run his own press, the Rupprecht-Presse in Munich, from 1913 to 1934. He printed more than 50 books by hand, all set in his own typefaces, which reinterpreted traditional forms including Fraktur, Schwabacher, Antiqua, Rustica, and their related italics. Historian

Jeremy Anysley characterized Ehmcke as a "modern conservative." A critic of both the Bauhaus and the New Typography, Ehmcke continued to combine traditional and modern elements in his commercial work. He oversaw the graphic design and publicity for the gigantic Pressa exhibition that was held in Cologne in 1928. For that event, he designed a poster that featured a large roman letter P topped by three small crowns as the exhibition logo. The logo, combined with a color scheme of yellow, red, and black, established an identity for the exhibition and was applied to everything from cigarette packaging to postage stamps.

Fig. 21.23: Wilhelm Deffke, *Der Zuker*, poster, 1925. Collection Merrill C. Berman. Photo: Jim Frank and Joelle Jensen.

Other materials designed under Ehmcke's supervision included a souvenir booklet, a publicity leaflet, maps, and signage for visitors.

Though most commercial artists accepted a range of commissions, a few specialized in particular activities. Karl Schulpig (1884–1948), for example, was known for his trademarks, which often featured small comic figures. Another prominent trademark designer was Wilhelm Deffke, who took a more analytic approach to trademarks, basing most of his designs on combinations of letters or the creation of abstract symbols (see Chapter 17) (Fig. 21.23). O. H. W. Hadank was known for his trademarks and his packaging. What characterized both was his exquisite calligraphy, which varied according to the commission. Hadank did a great deal of work for companies that made cigarettes and produced wines and spirits (see Chapter 17). He established long-term relationships with several firms including Haus Neuerburg, a manufacturer of cigarettes, and Kaloderma, a company that made cold cream.

The commercial art scene in Germany gained an international identity from the publication of *Gebrauchsgraphik*, a magazine that published illustrated articles on German designers and their counterparts abroad. It first appeared in 1924. The editor H. K. Frenzel was an active promoter of German commercial art and gave many German designers wide exposure by inviting them to do covers in their own style. He had a special predilection for the posters of Ludwig Hohlwein and helped to make Hohlwein's reputation by featuring him prominently in the magazine. Frenzel was also a proponent of American advertising and frequently ran articles that described the more analytic American approach to selling goods and services. As he noted in a special American issue of 1926, "Advertising is the literature of the Americans."

Though commercial art was more highly developed and widely accepted in Germany than in other countries during the 1920s, there was still something insular about it. Many artists clung too strongly to tradition. They were slow to adopt new styles of modern lettering, for example, and, with some exceptions, the images they used to promote goods, services, and events were often naive or too cute. Consequently, few German commercial artists attracted international attention.

Type design

The situation was different for type designers. Germany produced a spate of modern typefaces during the 1920s and several of these became widely used abroad. Following the early German san serif face Akzidenz Grotesk, which was cut at the end of the 19th century,

Fig. 21.24: Paul Renner, Futura, promotional material, c. 1929. Collection Merrill C. Berman. Photo: Jim Frank & Joelle Jensen. © DACS 2017.

the first modern geometric san serif in Germany was Erbar, designed by Jacob Erbar (1878–1935) in 1926. The designer had taken classes with Anna Simons, a former student of Edward Johnston, and created his first san serif, Feder-Grotesk, in 1908, well before Johnston designed his typeface for the London Underground. Though Erbar possessed subtle traces of calligraphy, it had a consistency and repetition of elements that qualified it as a modern typeface.

Paul Renner (1878–1956), an early Werkbund supporter and admirer of the Arts and Crafts movement, was first exposed to Functional design when he taught for a year at the applied arts school in Frankfurt. Arriving there in 1925, he encountered, among others, Ferdinand Kramer, the architect and furniture designer, whose san serif capital letters, designed to be used for signage, provide an interesting parallel to his own san serif typeface, Futura (Fig. 21.24). In 1926, Renner left Frankfurt for Munich where he became director of the Graphische Berufsschule, a school for the printing trades, and then in 1927 he was named the first head of the Meisterschule für Deutschlands Buckdrucker (Master School for German Book Printers), which opened that year. At the Meisterschule, Renner forged a new curriculum for printers and hired the typographer Jan Tschichold, the leading proponent of the New Typography, to join the faculty.

The Bauer Foundry released Futura in 1927 and it soon became the preferred typeface for advertising and setting modern texts. Its strong geometric forms did have some relation to Herbert Bayer's Universal typeface, but Renner, an experienced typographer, refined his alphabet to work successfully as a text face in smaller point sizes as well as for larger-format advertising. Other foundries quickly recognized the need to have a modern typeface of their own. The Klingspor Foundry commissioned Rudolf Koch (1876–1934), its in-house type designer, to design Kabel. Koch based his typefaces strongly on the calligraphic tradition and some idiosyncrasies of that tradition, notably the extended height of particular letters and the disproportionate size of the upper case letters in relation to the lower case. These gave Kabel a more decorative than standardized quality. The decorative aspect of the typeface was also accentuated by Klingspor's release of Koch's Zeppelin, an inline companion to Kabel in 1929, and a striated version called Prisma in 1931.

In 1923, several years before he designed Kabel, Koch created a thick san serif black letter alphabet called Neuland for which he cut the punches himself. The rough shapes of the letters recall the irregular lines of medieval woodcuts, a reference that is suggested when the letters form a block of text. Unexpectedly, Neuland became a popular advertising typeface and found a welcome reception in Britain and the United States. The heavy black letters assumed a racial overtone when the British Monotype Corporation named its own version of the typeface Othello, after the dark-skinned lead character in Shakespeare's play of the same name. In Germany, the Bauer Foundry made an even more overt racial reference when it called a similar face, designed by Lucian Bernhard, Negro. Other novel faces that were used primarily for advertising purposes were Beton, a heavy neo-Egyptian alphabet designed by Heinrich Jost (1889–1949), typographic director of the Bauer Foundry, and Georg Trump's City, of 1931, an eccentric interpretation of a rectilinear Egyptian style.

Trump (1896–1985) studied with F. H. Ernst Schneidler (1882–1956), who taught lettering at the art academy in Stuttgart. He was one of Schneidler's most successful students, who also included the typographers Imre Reiner (1900–1987) and Walter Brudi (1907–1987). Schneidler, who had studied with Peter Behrens and F. H. Ehmcke in Düsseldorf, taught at the art academy from 1921 to 1949 and is said to have created a "Stuttgart school" of typography. Central to his teaching was the idea that typographers should study graphic disciplines besides calligraphy and that each discipline should influence the others. This is evident in the variety of typefaces created by his former students. Trump, for example, ranged from City to a black letter of 1935 called Deutsch, a three-dimensional Egyptian

face called Shadow of 1937–1945, and a condensed serif with an inordinately high x-height called Signum that he designed in 1955. Between 1929 and 1934, Imre Reiner, who moved to Switzerland in 1931, designed Corvinus, which he derived from 19th-century modern faces, as well as other faces that were based on script lettering.

The New Typography

Jan Tschichold (1902–1974) was the chief promoter of the New Typography (die neue typographie), a set of principles and rules for modern graphic design. Tschichold studied calligraphy and classical typography in Leipzig at the Staatliche Akademie der Graphischen Künste (State Academy for the Graphic Arts), whose director was the typographer and book designer Walter Tiemann (1876–1951). In 1923, Tschichold visited the previously mentioned Bauhaus exhibition in Weimar and was transformed by the modern design he saw there. A strong influence was Moholy-Nagy's essay on the New Typography in which Moholy declared clarity to be the principal aim of typography, designated photography as the most precise means of illustration, and urged the liberation of the typographic line. The innovative books that the Russian artist El Lissitzky published in Berlin, *About Two Squares* and *For the Voice*, also influenced Tschichold. Like Lissitzky, whose typographic innovations were related to his multi-directional *Proun* paintings, Moholy derived his own typographic principles from his work as a Constructivist artist. Tschichold cited both Lissitzky and Moholy-Nagy as precedents for his principles of *elementare typographie* (elementary typography) that he first enunciated in a special issue of the German printing journal *Typographische Mitteilungen* (*Typographic Communication*) in October 1925. Tschichold's ten principles echo Moholy-Nagy's claims that the New Typography should be purposeful, but Tschichold then added specific rules that forbade the use of ornament and mandated that all type should be san serif and composed in asymmetrical arrangements. To support his principles he presented examples by various avant-garde artists and designers including Lissitzky, Moholy-Nagy, Kurt Schwitters, Herbert Bayer, and Max Burchartz.

Paul Renner invited Tschichold to Munich in 1927 to teach calligraphy and typography at the Master School for German Book Printers, and Tschichold remained there until 1933. Among the design commissions he undertook in Munich was a series of film posters for the movie theater Phoebus Palast in 1927. His poster for Georg Jacoby's *Die Frau ohne Namen* (*The Woman without a Name*) makes use of angular lines and stills from the film, growing larger as they

Fig. 21.25: *Gefesselter Blick*, cover, 1930. Collection Merrill C. Berman. Photo: Jim Frank and Joelle Jensen.

advance from a vanishing point to convey a sense of movement and drama (Plate 09). Like the Soviet avant-garde designers, Tschichold limited his color pallet mainly to black, red, and white and made use of photographs rather than illustrations, which set him apart from most German graphic designers at the time.

In 1928, Tschichold published his most important book *Die Neue Typographie* (*The New Typography*), in which he explained in detail how his principles could be applied to all forms of graphic design including letterheads, posters, envelopes, bills, business cards, and logotypes. Typography played a much more important role for him than it did for other commercial artists, and the New Typography, which replaced "elementary typography," strongly challenged the heavy reliance on drawn images that German commercial artists preferred.

Tschichold presented the New Typography as a total method for graphic design, although his own emphasis on typographic rather than pictorial solutions derived from his training as a typographer rather than as a painter or illustrator. He functioned as a mediator between the avant-garde artists who inspired his thinking and the wider professions of typography, book design, and commercial art that were exposed to his ideas through the mainstream printing journals and design magazines. Tschichold's principles were controversial and were questioned or opposed by many practitioners.

There was, however, a cadre of designers, many of them artists, who embraced the New Typography and applied it in their own practices. These included Max Burchartz (1887–1961), Johannes Canis (1895–1977), Walter Dexel, Johannes Mohlzahn (1892–1965), Willi Baumeister (1889–1955), César Domela (1900–1992), Kurt Schwitters, and Anton Stankowski (1906–1998), In 1924, Burchartz, a former painter who was influenced by Constructivism and *De Stijl*, and Canis founded werbebau, Germany's first studio for modern graphic design. Located in Bochum, a town in the industrial Ruhr area of Germany, they worked extensively

for firms involved in heavy industry, particularly the Bochumer Verein für Bergbau und Gussstahlfabikation (Bochum Association for Mining and Cast Iron Manufacture), a firm specializing in metal parts of all kinds. For this client, Burchartz and Canis designed catalogs that used photographic product fragments and photomontage to present the range of parts the company produced. Burchartz moved to Essen in 1927 to develop courses in modern graphic design, photography, and advertising at the Folkwangschule, a school of applied arts. One of his outstanding students was Anton Stankowski, who relocated to Switzerland in 1929, where he became a founder of the Swiss style of "constructive" graphic design.

In 1928, Kurt Schwitters founded the ring neuer werbegestalter (circle of new advertising designers), a group of designers who adopted the New Typography and techniques of the new advertising, particularly photomontage. From its founding until 1931, the "ring" actively promoted modern graphic design through numerous exhibitions that circulated widely in Germany and occasionally abroad. The members also organized the publication of *Gefesselter Blick* (*Focused Gaze*), the most important survey of new advertising design to be published in the Weimar period (Fig. 21.25).

When the Nazis came to power, they associated the New Typography and advertising with left-wing internationalism. Tschichold was branded a cultural Bolshevik and managed to emigrate to Switzerland, where he continued to teach and work as a freelance designer. The New Typography spread to other countries, notably the Netherlands, Switzerland, and Czechoslovakia, where it continued to develop during the 1930s.

The illustrated press

During the 1920s, the mass media in Weimar grew at an exceptional pace and Germany had more illustrated newspapers and magazines than any other country in the world. By 1928, photography had replaced drawings as the principal means of illustration in these publications. The first of the illustrated magazines was the *Berliner Illustrirte Zeitung*, which was founded in 1892, while its chief competitor, the *Münchner Illustrierte Presse*, did not appear until 1923. Soon other imitators followed: *Die Kölnische Illustrierte*, *Die Hamburger Illustrierte*, *Die Stuttgarter Illustrirte*, and the *Illustrierte Blatt* in Frankfurt. The *Berliner Illustrirte Zeitung* or BIZ, as it was popularly known, had a circulation of 1,600,000 in 1928. It belonged to the Ullstein publishing empire, which also published more specialized illustrated journals such as *Uhu*, a sophisticated culture magazine, and *Die Dame*, a monthly magazine of women's fashions. Other publications featuring diverse specialized interests included the short-lived sports magazine *Arena*, whose art director was John Heartfield.

During the 1920s, Kurt Korff (dates unconfirmed) was the editor of the *Berliner Illustrirte*. He sensed the potential of photo reportage early on and began to cultivate a cadre of talented photojournalists who roamed the world in search of human-interest stories. Korff was motivated to feature photo stories by his awareness that the accelerating pace of modern life made it necessary for the weekly magazines to create "a keener and more succinct form of pictorial representation that has an effect on readers even if they just skim through the pages."

The photojournalists, who worked for Korff as well as other magazines, included Eric Salomon (1886–1944), Tim (1900–1996) and George Gidal (dates unconfirmed), Felix Man (1893–1985), Umbo (a.k.a. Otto Umbehr), and Wolfgang Weber (dates unconfirmed). Instead of the heavy plate cameras of their predecessors, they adopted the portable Leica, invented in 1913 by Oskar Barnack (1879–1936), and the Ermanox, which arrived on the market in 1925. Both cameras used 35mm roll film with multiple exposures, while the Ermanox had a light-sensitive lense that made indoor photography possible without a flash.

Korff's chief rival as an editor was Stefan Lorant (1901–1997), who headed the Berlin office of the *Münchner Illustrierte*. Korff developed techniques to dramatize the photographs such as printing them as full pages, but Lorant, who worked previously as a film cameraman and director, invented the layout format that displayed the photographs to best advantage. This was the double-page spread with one key photograph shown larger than the others. Perhaps because his earlier background was in film, Lorant was particularly sensitive to the dramatic aspect of a story, which he enhanced by the organization, scale, and juxtaposition of the photographs. His approach stood out from the layouts of his rivals, which were based on more mundane combinations of text, captions, and photographs. More than any other editor in the late 1920s, Lorant became the model of a magazine art director who was skilled at organizing photographs into exciting visual narratives. The heyday of photo reportage in Germany began in 1928 and lasted until Hitler came to power in 1933. At that time, most of the photojournalists left Germany and emigrated to countries where they contributed to or helped found illustrated magazines on the German model such as *Vu* in France, *Picture Post* in Britain, and *LIFE* in the United States.

Graphics on the left

Left-wing graphics in the Weimar Republic were at first closely intertwined with the Dada movement. Early publications critical of the government were the newspapers *Neue Jugend* and *Jederman sein eigener Fussball*, both designed by John Heartfield and published by Wieland Herzfelde's Malik-Verlag. During the years of Berlin Dada until 1923, the Malik-Verlag published several short-lived cultural-political journals, *Die Pleite* (*The Failure*), and *Der Gegner* (*The Antagonist*) as well as a portfolio of anti-war prints by George Grosz. Heartfield subsequently did considerable design work for the Communist Party.

Between 1922 and 1933, the Malik-Verlag published several series of fiction and non-fiction books. Some were by authors with broad left-wing views while others directly supported the politics of

Fig. 21.26: John Heartfield, *Oil*, front and back covers, 1927. Collection Merrill C. Berman. Photo: Jim Frank & Joelle Jensen. © The Heartfield Community of Heirs/VG Bild-Kunst, Bonn and DACS, London 2017.

the Soviet Union. Heartfield was the art director for the press and designed all its book covers. A few were typographic or featured drawings, but most consisted of photomontages. Heartfield would use both the front and back covers as complementary images while applying bold typography to the spines. As part of his Rote Roman-Serie (Red Novel Series), Herzfelde published four novels by the left-wing American author Upton Sinclair. For the translation of Sinclair's novel *Oil* of 1927, Heartfield juxtaposed portraits of a rich oil developer and a Hollywood film star on whose faces he superimposed oil wells and dollar signs (Fig. 21.26). Photomontage was particularly suited to the Malik-Verlag covers because the documentary quality of the photographic fragments emphasized the real-world social concerns of the authors. Heartfield's photomontage covers were unique in the German publishing world during the 1920s, prompting the writer Kurt Tucholsky to exclaim, "if I weren't Tucholsky, I'd like to be a book jacket for the Malik-Verlag."

Several other left-oriented publishing groups sought to provide inexpensive books for a wide public. The Büchergilde Gutenberg and the Bücherkreis were both founded in 1924. Bruno Dressler, a member of the Bildungsverband der Deutschen Buchdrucker (Association of German Book Printers), established the first, while the second was linked to the Social Democratic Party (SPD). Jan Tschichold designed covers for both groups. He created a series of strong typographic covers for the Bücherkreis, each of which featured a logo on the spine depicting a male figure holding an open book. Just as Heartfield's Malik-Verlag covers conveyed a documentary sense through the use of photomontage, so did Tschichold's Bücherkreis designs suggest a sense of immediacy through bold typography and short explanatory texts that were integrated into the cover layouts. For these covers, Tschichold broadened his typographic repertoire to adopt unusual fonts such as Georg Trump's City and Signum. The strategy behind his typographic choices was to establish a visual identity that distinguished the Bücherkreis volumes from the more classical look of earlier book series.

The politics of the two book guilds were sharply differentiated from the hard-core ideology of the German communists and other dedicated believers in the Soviet Union. The major propagandist for the Soviets was Willi Münzenberg (1889–1940), a member of the German Communist Party, who founded a series of front organizations that had as their principal

ADOLF – DER ÜBERMENSCH

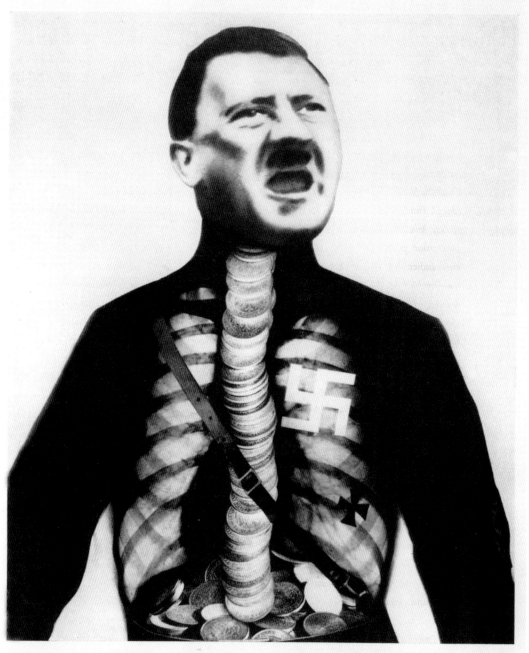

SCHLUCKT GOLD UND REDET BLECH

Fig. 21.27: John Heartfield, Adolf the Superman, *AIZ* photomontage, 1932. © 2014. Photo Scala, Florence/BPK, Bildagentur fuer Kunst, Kultur und Geschichte, Berlin. © The Heartfield Community of Heirs/VG Bild-Kunst, Bonn and DACS, London 2017.

purpose to increase Soviet influence on the communist movement within Germany. In 1921, Lenin requested Münzenberg to organize an international support effort to aid victims of the famine that had spread across Russia. Münzenberg subsequently founded the Internationale Arbeiterhilfe (International Worker Relief), which rallied supporters from across the German left. This organization attracted large numbers of participants and built a cadre of supporters for Münzenberg's other propaganda efforts, which included a publishing house, a film company, and various magazines and journals. Münzenberg's publishing venture was the Neue Deutsche Verlag (New German Press), whose projects ranged from a leftist book club to the illustrated weekly *Arbeiter Illustrierte Zeitung* (*AIZ*), which began publication in 1924 and was intended for a working-class audience just as the *Berliner llustrirte Zeitung* and the *Münchner Illustrierte Presse* served the middle class. The precursor of *AIZ* was *Sowjetrussland im Bild* (*Soviet Russia in Pictures*), a left-wing pictorial magazine that Münzenberg had founded three years earlier. For *AIZ*, Münzenberg copied the format of the bourgeois illustrated weeklies but filled his magazine with propaganda articles that were critical of capitalist society. To provide photographs, he organized classes to train working-class photographers and then created a Union of Working Class Photographers with its own journal, *Der Arbeiterfotograpf* (*The Worker Photographer*).

Münzenberg's strategy as a propagandist was to establish a broad leftist front while at the same time supporting the policies of the Soviet Comintern and the German Communist Party. Heartfield, though he was art director of the Malik-Verlag, worked more directly with the communists. In 1923 he became the editor and designer of the KPD satirical magazine *Der Knüppel* (*The Cudgel*) and the party's newspaper, *Die Rote Fahne* (*The Red Flag*). He also designed photographic covers for a related magazine, *Das Neue Russland* (*The New Russia*). For these publications, Heartfield's designs were more constrained than his iconoclastic Dada layouts and photomontages. This

was most likely due to a more conservative KPD policy on visual propaganda. However, Heartfield's ability to juxtapose images against a related text was evident in a cover for *Die Rote Fahne* related to the 1928 election. It displayed a grasping hand with an adjoining text that stated, "The hand has five fingers. Beat the enemy with five. Vote List 5," the list of KPD candidates. The image then reached a wider audience as a political poster for the election itself.

In 1930, Heartfield started to work regularly for the *AIZ*, which at one point had a circulation of 450,000. He created photomontages with related texts that were used both as covers and as separate back-page features. By 1932, he was ridiculing Hitler and the Nazi Party with a regular series of pungent photomontages that made fun of the Nazi leader while also strongly criticizing the Nazi Party and its actions. In a photomontage entitled *Adolf the Superman. Swallows gold and spouts tin*, Heartfield depicted Hitler with a weak spine consisting of gold coins (Fig. 21.27). His text inverted the idea of the medieval alchemists who claimed the ability to turn cheap metals such as tin into gold, suggesting that Hitler accepted donations from rich benefactors and turned them into a program of little value. Once Hitler came to power, the *AIZ* moved to Prague and Heartfield continued to attack the Nazis with more topical photomontages. The magazines were smuggled into Germany where they contributed to an underground resistance to Hitler. However, the *AIZ* had ceased publication by 1939, the year the Nazis invaded Czechoslovakia.

Bibliography
Bibliographic essay

John Willett, *Art and Politics in the Weimar Period: The New Sobriety, 1917–1933* is an overview of Weimar culture that draws together many of its facets including art, architecture, design, literature, theater, and music. Tilmann Buddensieg's edited volume *Berlin 1900–1933: Architecture and Design* has a more limited focus. Gert Selle discusses product design specifically in *Design*

– *Geschichte in Deutschland: Produktkultur als Entwurf und Erfahrung. Twentieth-Century Furniture Design* by Klaus Jürgen Sembach, Gabriele Leuthäuser, and Peter Gössel is a good reference for German furniture design during this period. Matilda McQuaid's exhibition catalog *Lilly Reich: Designer and Architect* adds to the limited literature on German women as designers during the Weimar years. Heinz Hirdina, *Neues Bauen, Neues Gestalten: Das Neue Frankfurt/Die Neue Stadt. Eine Zeitschrift zwischen 1926 und 1933* and Karin Kirsch, *The Weissenhofsiedlung: Experimental Housing Built for the Deutscher Werkbund* both look at the design of furniture and goods for domestic use within the context of the ambitious Weimar building program. The German interest in scientific management and efficiency is discussed in Judith A. Merkle, *Management and Ideology: The Legacy of the International Scientific Management Movement.* Joan Campbell, *The German Werkbund: The Politics of Reform in the Applied Arts* devotes considerable attention to the later activities of the organization in the Weimar period.

The Bauhaus literature is vast and I only used a few general surveys. Hans Wingler, *Bauhaus: Weimar, Dessau, Berlin, Chicago* is encyclopedic in its inclusion of photographs and documents, while Frank Whitford, *Bauhaus* is a good short summary although its emphasis on the Weimar period as opposed to Dessau is somewhat out of balance. *Bauhaus and Bauhaus People*, edited by Eckhard Neumann, has first-hand accounts by Bauhaus professors and others related to one or another incarnation of the Bauhaus. See also, Winfried Nerdinger, *Bauhaus-Moderne im Nationalsozialismus: Zwischen Anbiederung und Verfolgung.* Much more research is needed on other design schools in the Weimar Republic. Two excellent studies are Wilhelm Nauhaus, *Die Burg Giebichenstein: Geschichte einer Deutschen Kunstschule, 1915–1933* and Albert Reimann, *Die Reimann-Schule in Berlin.*

For the study of graphic design in the Weimar Republic, the pioneering book on this topic is Eckhard Neumann, *Functional Graphic Design in the 20's.* Jeremy Aynsley, *Graphic Design in Germany, 1890–1945* provides a broad overview, while Leslie Cabarga, *Progressive German Graphics 1900–1937* and Steven Heller and Louise Fili, *German Modern: Graphic Design from Wilhelm to Weimar* are most valuable as visual compilations of German advertising graphics. Both H. K. Frenzel, *Ludwig Hohlwein* and the volume edited by Christian Schneegass, *Ludwig Hohlwein: Plakate der Jahre 1906–1940* document primarily the many advertising posters that Hohlwein did for his commercial clients. Jaroslav Andel, *Avant-Garde Page Design, 1900–1950* and Steven Heller, *Merz to Emigre and Beyond: Avant-Garde Magazine Design of the Twentieth Century* are both excellent references for avant-garde design in Weimar. On Berlin Dada and design, see Stephen Foster and Rudolf Kuenzli, eds., *Dada Spectrum: The Dialectics of Revolt* and Sherwin Simmons' excellent article, "Advertising Seizes Control of Life: Berlin Dada and the Power of Advertising," *Oxford Art Journal* 22, no. 1 (1999). Simmons has also written about the contentiousness of Weimar political graphics in two important articles, "Grimaces on the Walls: Anti-Bolshevist Posters and the Debate about Kitsch,' *Design Issues* 14, no. 2 (Summer 1998) and "'Hand to the Friend, Fist to the Foe': The Struggle of Signs in the Weimar Republic," *Journal of Design History* 13, no. 4 (2000). I discuss German Constructivism, especially the involvement of Moholy-Nagy and Lissitzky, and its contribution to avant-garde design in *The Struggle for Utopia: Rodchenko, Lissitzky, Moholy-Nagy, 1917–1946.* Werner Schmalenbach makes some mention of Kurt Schwitters' graphic design within the larger context of his art activity but one volume of the exhaustive four-volume exhibition catalog, *"Typographie kann unter Umständen Kunst sein,"* edited by Volker Rattmeyer, Dietrich Helms, and Konrad Matschke, is dedicated solely to Schwitters' graphic design, while two others focus on the ring neue werbegestalter of which Schwitters was a central figure.

Sebastian Carter includes chapters on typographers Rudolf Koch, Georg Trump, and Jan Tschichold in *Twentieth Century Type Designers*, while Christopher Burke, *Paul Renner: The Art of Typography*; Gerald Cinamon, *Rudolf Koch: Letterer, Type Designer, Teacher*; Ruari McLean, *Jan Tschichold: Typographer*; and Werner Klemke's edited volume, *Leben und Werk des Typographen Jan Tschichold* discuss their subjects in greater depth. Left-wing political design, especially the work of John Heartfield, is covered in Peter Pachnicke and Klaus Honef, eds, *John Heartfield* and in the small catalog of an exhibit on the Malik-Verlag edited by James Fraser, *Malik-Verlag, 1916–1947: Berlin, Prague, New York*. Gisèle Freund, *Photography and Society* and Tim N. Gidal, *Modern Photojournalism: Origin and Evolution, 1910–1933* are excellent sources of material on popular illustrated magazines and photojournalism in the Weimar period.

Books

Andel, Jaroslav. *Avant-Garde Page Design, 1900–1950*. New York: Delano Greenidge Editions, 2002.

Aynsley, Jeremy. *Graphic Design in Germany, 1890–1945*. London and New York: Thames and Hudson, 2000.

Buddensieg, Tilmann, ed. *Berlin 1900–1933: Architecture and Design*. New York: Cooper-Hewitt Museum, and Berlin: Gebrüder Mann Verlag, 1987.

Burke, Christopher. *Paul Renner: The Art of Typography*. New York: Princeton Architectural Press, 1998.

Cabarga, Leslie. *Progressive German Graphics 1900–1937*. San Francisco: Chronicle Books, 1994.

Campbell, Joan. *The German Werkbund: The Politics of Reform in the Applied Arts*. Princeton NJ: Princeton University Press, 1978.

Carter, Sebastian. *Twentieth Century Type Designers*. London: Trefoil, 1987.

Cinamon, Gerald. *Rudolf Koch: Letterer, Type Designer, Teacher*. New Castle: Oak Knoll Press, and London: The British Library, 2000.

Conrads, Ulrich, ed. *Programs and Manifestoes on 20th-Century Architecture*. Cambridge, MA: MIT Press, 1975.

Foster, Stephen and Rudolf Kuenzli, eds. *Dada Spectrum: The Dialectics of Revolt*. Madison, WI: Coda Press, and Iowa City: University of Iowa, 1979.

Fraser, James, ed. *Malik-Verlag, 1916–1947: Berlin, Prague, New York*. New York: Goethe House, 1984.

Frenzel, H. K. *Ludwig Hohlwein*. Berlin: Phönix Illustrationsdruck und Verlag, 1926.

Freund, Gisèle. *Photography and Society*. Boston: David R. Godine, 1980.

Gidal, Tim N. *Modern Photojournalism: Origin and Evolution, 1910–1933*. New York: Macmillan, 1973.

Heller, Steven. *Merz to Emigre and Beyond: Avant-Garde Magazine Design of the Twentieth Century*. London and New York: Phaidon, 2003.

Heller, Steven and Louise Fili. *German Modern: Graphic Design from Wilhelm to Weimar*. San Francisco: Chronicle Books, 1998.

Hirdina, Heinz. *Neues Bauen, Neues Gestalten: Das Neue Frankfurt/Die Neue Stadt. Eine Zeitschrift zwischen 1926 und 1933*. Berlin: Elefanten Press, 1984.

Kirsch, Karin. *The Weissenhofsiedlung: Experimental Housing Built for the Deutscher Werkbund, Stuttgart, 1927*. New York: Rizzoli, 1989.

Klemke, Werner, ed. *Leben und Werk des Typographen Jan Tschichold*. Dresden: VEB Verlag der Kunst, 1977.

Margolin, Victor. *The Struggle for Utopia: Rodchenko, Lissitzky, Moholy-Nagy, 1917–1946*. Chicago and London: University of Chicago Press, 1997.

McLean, Ruari. *Jan Tschichold: Typographer*. Boston: David R. Godine, 1975.

McQuaid, Matilda, *Lilly Reich: Designer and Architect*. With an essay by Magdalena Droste. New York: The Museum of Modern Art, 1996.

Merkle, Judith A. *Management and Ideology: The Legacy of the International Scientific Management Movement*. Berkeley, Los Angeles, and London: University of California Press, 1980.

Nauhaus, Wilhelm. *Die Burg Giebichenstein: Geschichte einer Deutschen Kunstschule, 1915–1933*. Leipzig: E.A. Seeman, 1981.

Nerdinger, Winfried, ed. *Bauhaus-Moderne im*

Nationalsozialismus: Zwischen Anbiederung und Verfolgung. Munich: Prestel, 1993.

Neumann, Eckhard, *Functional Graphic Design in the 20's.* New York: Reinhard Publishing Co., 1967.

Neumann, Eckhard, ed. *Bauhaus and Bauhaus People; Personal Opinions and Recollections of Former Bauhaus Members and their Contemporaries.* Translation by Eva Richter and Alba Lorman. New York: Van Nostrand Publishing, 1970.

Pachnicke, Peter and Klaus Honef, eds. *John Heartfield.* New York: Harry N. Abrams, 1992.

Rattmeyer, Volker, Dietrich Helms, and Konrad Matschke, eds. *"Typographie kann unter Umständen Kunst sein,"* 4 vols.: *Friedrich Vordemberge-Gildewart: Typographie und Werbegestaltung; Kurt Schwitters: Typographie und Werbegestaltung; Ring 'neue werbegestalter' 1928–1933: Ein Überblick;* and *Ring 'neue werbegestalter': Amsterdamer Ausstelling von 1931.*

Reimann, Albert. *Die Reimann-Schule in Berlin.* Berlin: Verlag Bruno Hessling, 1966.

Schmalenbach, Werner. *Kurt Schwitters.* New York: Harry N. Abrams, 1967.

Schneegass, Christian, ed. *Ludwig Hohlwein: Plakate der Jahre 1906–1940.* Stuttgart: Staatsgalerie, 1985.

Selle, Gert. *Design – Geschichte in Deutschland: Produktkultur als Entwurf und Erfahrung.* Cologne: DuMont Buchverlag, 1987.

Sembach, Klaus-Jürgen, Gabriele Leuthäuser, and Peter Gössel. *Twentieth-Century Furniture Design.* Cologne: Taschen, 2002.

Whitford, Frank. *Bauhaus.* London: Thames and Hudson, 1984.

Willett, John. *Art and Politics in the Weimar Period: The New Sobriety, 1917–1933.* New York: Da Capo Press, 1996 (c. 1978).

Wingler, Hans. *Bauhaus: Weimar, Dessau, Berlin, Chicago.* Cambridge, MA: MIT Press, 1969.

Articles

Aynsley, Jeremy, "'Gebrauchsgraphik' as an Early Graphic Design Journal, 1924–1938," *Journal of Design History* 5, no. 1 (1992).

Simmons, Sherwin, "Grimaces on the Walls: Anti-Bolshevist Posters and the Debate about Kitsch,' *Design Issues* 14, no. 2 (Summer 1998).

—"Advertising Seizes Control of Life: Berlin Dada and the Power of Advertising," *Oxford Art Journal* 22, no. 1 (1999).

—"'Hand to the Friend, Fist to the Foe': The Struggle of Signs in the Weimar Republic," *Journal of Design History* 13, no. 4 (2000).

Chapter 22: France 1918–1939

Introduction

With the end of World War I. France, as one of the three Great Powers, sought to exact huge reparations payments from Germany to recoup some of her material losses and make it impossible for Germany to practice aggression in the future. Rather than support France in her demand for harsh terms against the Germans, the British looked away from Europe towards their colonies whose resources and productive capacity they counted on as the basis for their continued economic growth. This left France to enforce the Treaty of Versailles, which dealt a heavy blow to Germany but also justified the Germans' delaying tactics in the fulfillment of their financial obligations to the French.

The French government continued to support national supremacy in the production of luxury goods, rather than encourage the mass production of less expensive products for the national market and sale abroad. The slowness to take up mass production, in fact, put France at a disadvantage in the race among the leading industrial nations to become a major force in the world economy. Though France and England were slow to realize it, the key to gaining post-war economic supremacy was the development of a modern economy based on the machine and the new methods of management to use it productively. Though Britain remained more committed to an "economy of empire" than France, the French government nonetheless still believed that pre-World War supremacy in the global luxury markets would help ensure that France would not fall behind the other industrial nations in global competitiveness. Due to the recent war, the French remained wary of German efficiency, but they also viewed with caution the mass society that was developing rapidly in the United States.

The Society of Artist-Decorators and the 1925 Exposition Internationale des Arts Décoratifs et Industriels Modernes

In the French aesthetic hierarchy, the fine arts had always ranked higher than the arts of decoration and design. With the founding of the Society of Artist-Decorators (SAD) in 1901, French decorative artists sought an identity that was independent of this hierarchy. Members of the SAD created their own annual salon where the best designs for furniture, ceramics, and glass could be displayed without existing in the shadow of the fine arts. As early as 1911, the Society of Artist-Decorators initiated plans for an international exhibition of decorative arts to be held in Paris. The plan was stimulated by the furniture displays of the Munich Workshops at the 1910 Salon d'Automne, where the French saw for the first time the presentation of furniture in ensembles rather than as single pieces. Concerned about German competition, they intended their exhibition to survey the entire range of French decorative arts and architecture. Aiming to hold it in 1915, they had to postpone it when World War I began. The group took up the project again after the war and it was finally scheduled for 1925. The initial proposal declared that all the exhibits had to be modern and that no copy or pastiche of old styles would be admitted. However, when the exhibition was finally held, this mandate was widely ignored.

Whereas the Deutscher Werkbund promoted design for mass production, the French government supported the creation of luxury products as the principal sector of French manufacturing, largely because France could not compete easily with Germany and Britain in the production of inexpensive mass-produced goods. Consequently, the Society of Artist-Decorators gave little attention to mass production in its exhibitions.

Nor did they embrace modernity to the degree the Germans did. Various critics recognized the need for a modern style but in general French decorators sought to ally this style with an adherence to national traditions. This was manifested in a *retour a l'ordre* (return to order), which countered the elaborate ornamentation of Art Nouveau by celebrating more restrained qualities derived from classicism and rationalism that many thought constituted the core of French identity.

Though much of what the members of the SAD presented at their salons was for the luxury market, the 1919 salon, the first since 1914, featured displays of inexpensive furniture. Only a few designers responded to this challenge but some of those who did worked with factories that were gearing up for peacetime manufacturing. Among those who exhibited were the team of Louis Süe (1875–1968) and André Mare (1885–1932), who designed inexpensive ensembles of furniture made of lacquered gray poplar wood. Mass-produced by Borel and Savary, an aviation company that had been a wartime supplier, the furniture could be ordered from the catalog of Süe and Mare's recently founded La Compagnie des Arts Français (The Company of French Arts). Following the example of Samuel Bing's Art Nouveau workshop and Paul Poiret's Atelier Martine, members of La Compagnie des Arts Français worked in all the decorative arts including furniture, textiles, and small objects. They designed shop facades as well as domestic interiors for individual clients. The company included the painter and illustrator Maurice Boutet de Monvel (1851–1913); the architect Gustave-Louis Jaulmes (1873–1959), who specialized in murals, tapestries, and upholstery fabrics; Paul Véra (1882–1954), a painter, sculptor, and wood engraver; Maurice Marinot (1882–1960), a former Fauve painter and glassmaker; and André Marty (1882–1974), whose drawings graced the covers of Paris's top fashion magazines but who also designed vases, bowls, and jewelry. After creating their line of low-cost furniture, Süe, an architect, and Mare, a painter, shifted to expensive one of a kind pieces, as is evident in a screen based on Fauve painting (Plate 10).

For many of their pieces, they used exotic materials imported from the French colonies and they specialized in inlay work, creating decorative designs with pieces of colored wood that were glued into a frame on the furniture surface. Other private studios established around the same time were D.I.M. (Décoration Intérieur Moderne or Modern Interior Decoration), whose directors were René Joubert (d.o.b. uncon-firmed–1931) and Phillipe Petit (1900–1945). D.I.M. carried out a wide variety of commissions ranging from furniture and lighting to fabrics and rugs. The firm was among the first to design airplane interiors and also created metal and wood furniture that was installed on the ocean liner *l'Atlantique* in 1931. A third studio with an equally diverse range of projects was Dominique, founded in 1922 by André Domin (1883–1962) and Marcel Genévrière (1885–1967).

Similar to the private studios were those affiliated with the large Parisian department stores. Headed by well-known decorative artists and active in the Society of Artist-Decorators, they provided interior design services and limited edition furniture to a middle-class market. Primavera, the applied arts workshop of the department store Le Printemps, was founded by René Guilleré (1878–1931), a former president of the Society of Artist-Decorators, who appointed his wife Charlotte Chaucet-Guilleré (1878–1964) as artistic director. Trained as a painter, Chaucet-Guilleré designed a full range of dining room and bedroom ensembles for Le Printemps. Maurice Dufrène (1876–1955) headed La Mâitrise, the workshop of the Galeries Lafayette, while Paul Follot (1877–1941) was in charge of Pomone, the workshop of the Bon Marché. Dufrène had managed Julius Meier-Graefe's La Maison Moderne in the 1890s, while Follot designed bronzes, jewelry, and fabrics for Meier-Graefe. Both were versatile designers though neither had a distinctive style. Other department store studios included Studium, which was affiliated with the Grands Magazins du Louvre and was headed by two young designers: Étienne Kohlmann (1903–1988) and Maurice Matet (1903–1989). The department store studios exhibited regularly at the SAD salons, usually presenting a series of decorated rooms that were themed by function. They were in such demand that they could afford to design and build their own pavilions for the 1925 Exposition Internationale des Arts Décoratifs.

The exposition is associated with a style known today as Art Deco, although the term was not coined until the 1960s. While the style is not easy to define, it can nonetheless be set off on the one hand from the heavy decoration of both historicism and Art Nouveau and on the other from the extreme minimalism and geometry that had originated with *De Stijl* and Constructivism. It was most widely applied in the 1920s, particularly in France but also in other countries.

In its earliest form, the Deco style reflected the influence of French modern art forms, notably the intense colors of Fauvism and the analytical lines of Cubism. It could also embrace the strong forms of African art, the opulence of Orientalist design as evidenced in the sets and costumes of the Ballets Russes, and the motifs of pre-Columbian Mayan or Aztec architecture. Whereas historicism made reference to prior architectural styles in the Western tradition and Art Nouveau drew heavily on forms from nature, Art Deco adopted motifs from all the world's cultures, while for some designers it signified a relation to the restrained forms of French 18th-century cabinetmakers. Originally the style was evident in the decorative arts rather than mass-produced objects, but by the 1930s it became identified with industrial materials such as steel, concrete, and glass and was associated with a "look" that could be seen in architecture, furniture, and consumer products. The style connoted modernity without the minimalism, moral righteousness, or social idealism of the avant-garde inspired modern movement.

As previously mentioned, the organizing committee for the 1925 exhibition did not strictly enforce the rule that all entries had to be in a modern style, hence traditional designs for interiors and furniture were widely displayed. If there had been a glimmer of social concern at the SAD exhibition

in 1919, when several designs for inexpensive mass-produced furniture were presented, there was none among the French pavilions at the 1925 exhibition, which reveled in the display of luxurious interiors. By its own choice, the United States did not participate, nor was Germany allowed to construct a pavilion because of the lingering French resentment due to the war. By contrast, the design studios of the Parisian department stores all had their own buildings, thus contributing to the array of expensive goods that dominated the fair. The one major challenge to this image was Konstantin Melnikov's Soviet pavilion with its Workers' Club designed by Alexander Rodchenko (see Chapter 20). This was the Soviet Union's first contribution to an international exhibition and it highlighted the extreme differences between the Soviet vision of society and that of the French.

As their contribution to the exhibition, the Society of Artist-Decorators created a French Embassy, which contained 25 lavishly decorated rooms arranged around a three-sided courtyard. The rooms provided a panoramic display of work by the most celebrated members of the society. Responding to this and other displays of luxury, the critic Waldemar George chastised the architects and designers for "their devotion to the 'power of money'" and "their lack of understanding of the needs imposed by modern life."

Actually, the French Embassy was an eclectic mixture of tendencies, some of which were in opposition to each other. On the side of traditional French luxury was a bedroom for the ambassador's wife, designed by André Groult (1884–1967). His furniture evoked the traditions of French 18th-century cabinetmakers, although, like Süe and Mare, he preferred more rounded forms. Though he was not one of the foremost French furniture designers, the chest of drawers he designed for the woman's bedroom, covered in sharkskin and detailed with ivory accessories, exemplifies the softer side of the 1920s decorative style (Fig. 22.01).

Leaning towards more functional design was Francis Jourdain's Smoking Room with its built-in

Fig. 22.01: André Groult, sharkskin cabinet, 1925. © Les Arts Décoratifs, Paris/Jean Tholance/akg-images. © ADAGP, Paris and DACS, London 2017.

bookcases, cabinets, and seats, while the influence of Cubism could be seen in the black lacquer Smoking Room that Jean Dunand (1877–1942) designed. Geometrical in composition, the room had a stepped silver ceiling with red accents. Angular black lacquered panels surrounded a square lacquered table and four armchairs whose upholstery had a geometric pattern. Originally trained as a sculptor, Swiss-born Dunand studied lacquer techniques in Paris with the Japanese lacquer artist Sugawara Seizo (1884–1937). He then set up his own workshop where he produced lacquer screens and furniture. Some of his designs such as a screen comprised of angular elements exemplify the more geometric manifestations of the 1920s Deco style. Dunand also developed special techniques for lacquering copper-plated vases, notably one for embedding crushed eggshells in the lacquer to create decorative patterns (Fig. 22.02).

The epitome of luxury among the exhibition' pavilions was Pierre Patout's and Jacques-Émile Ruhlmann's L'Hôtel du Collectionneur (House of a Collector). Patout (1879–1965) designed the building whose balance of curved and rectilinear volumes was a perfect example of the call to order that replaced Art Nouveau, although the stepped rectangular elements, which recalled an Aztec temple, were an odd addition to an otherwise sober structure (Fig. 22.03). The pavilion was the most acclaimed display of the exhibition. Ruhlmann created a suite of rooms for a wealthy discerning collector. The pavilion's focal point was the Grand Salon, whose theme was music. The set piece of the room was a piano, which Ruhlmann designed. The rotunda featured paintings by his friend the artist Louis Rigal (1880–1955) depicting themes from Beethoven's symphonies, while another friend, Jean Dupas (1882–1964), did the large erotic painting called *The Parakeets* that hung over the fireplace. Besides displaying his own work, which included the rich damask wall covering, Ruhlmann brought together many leading craftsmen, artists, and decorators to create the Salon's sumptuous décor.

Ruhlmann (1879–1933) is generally considered to be the greatest French furniture craftsman working in the Deco style. More than anyone else, he adhered to the classicism of the 18th century and was known for

Fig. 22.02: Jean Dunand, egg-shell lacquer vase, c. 1923–1924. © The Art Archive/Alamy.

Fig. 22.03: Pierre Patout, L'Hôtel du Collectionneur, 1925. Sculpture by Joseph Bernard. Roger Viollet/Getty Images.

the elegant forms of his pieces, whose volumes were delicately balanced on thin tapered legs. Ruhlmann's craftsmanship was superb and his taste was elegant. Both are evident in a sideboard he showed at the Salon d'Automne in 1919 (Fig. 22.04). Here we see a trapezoidal cabinet with a rich veneer of ebony in which are embedded small pieces of ivory that form a thin outline along the top of the sideboard. A cartouche of ebony dots also frames an inlaid ivory image of a Greek charioteer. Établissements Ruhlmann et Laurent,

which Ruhlmann launched shortly after World War I, became France's most prestigious decorating firm although it was never profitable and was funded from a family business. Ruhlmann favored exotic woods and rich materials, stating quite openly that he preferred to design for the rich because they had the best taste and could afford to indulge it.

In France, there was a close relation between the decorative arts and fashion. In fact, some of the principal patrons of the artist-decorators were from the fashion milieu. Among them, the couturier Jacques Doucet (1853–1929) was perhaps the most active. He hired the young Irish designer Eileen Gray (1879–1976) to design several furniture pieces for him and she finished her first commission, a lacquer screen, in 1914. Having amassed an exceptional collection of 18th-century art, he sold it and began to collect modern painting and sculpture and at one point he owned Picasso's *Demoiselles d'Avignon*. Doucet was a major patron of Pierre Legrain (1889–1929), whom he hired to design furniture inspired by African stools and headrests to complement his collection of African art. Working mainly in wood, Legrain created chairs, benches, and stools that were heavily influenced by

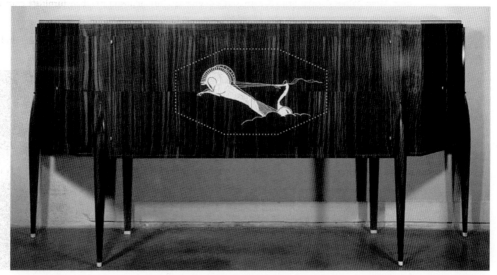

Fig. 22.04: Jacques-Émile Ruhlmann, chariot sideboard, 1919. Photo © RMN-Grand Palais (musée du Louvre)/ Les frères Chuzeville.

comparable pieces made by Ashanti, Ngombe, and Mangbetu carvers and those from other West and Central African tribes. Legrain also experimented with novel materials, often in unusual contrasts, as can be seen in his armchair veneered in burr maple with a seat, back, and decorative cubes of sharkskin.

Before working for Doucet, Eileen Gray undertook an intensive study of lacquering technique with Sugawara Seizo before Dunand studied with him. During the period that she was involved with the design of luxury furniture, her most extensive commission was for Mme. Suzanne Talbot, owner of a famous salon where expensive women's hats were sold. Rather than design individual pieces as she had for Doucet, Gray designed the entire Talbot apartment as a unified interior, a project that took approximately four years. She filled the entrance hall with lacquer panels, and for the salon, she created a lacquer and tortoise shell Pirogue sofa, known also as a lit-de-bateau or boat bed in which a person could recline.

Without the need to create prototypes for mass production, designers could be as imaginative and lavish as their clients desired. Following the lead of Jacques Doucet and perhaps recognizing the publicity that Mme. Talbot derived from Eileen Gray's dramatic interiors, other fashion designers commissioned furniture and complete interiors from decorative artists. The couturière Madeleine Vionnet (1876–1975), a pioneer in the design of draped form-conscious clothing, and the milliner Madame Agnès (dates unconfirmed) commissioned numerous furniture pieces from Jean Dunand. Armand-Albert Rateau (1882–1938), a lesser-known but active designer of furniture, interiors, and decorative objects, furnished the apartment of Jeanne Lanvin (1867–1946), the first couturière to dress men, women, and children. Rateau's workshop included cabinetmakers, carpenters, sculptors, painters, gilders, ironworkers, and other craftspersons. For Lanvin's apartment, he created bronze furniture in a Pompeian style and also designed a spherical perfume bottle for his client. It was imprinted with Paul Iribe's logo depicting Lanvin and her daughter. In addition Rateau designed the interior of Lanvin's fashion house and subsequently became the manager of Lanvin-Décoration, the company's department of interior design.

The Avant-Garde in France
De Stijl

After founding the *De Stijl* movement in the Netherlands and then spending three years in Germany, where he was the central figure in the German Constructivist movement and an adversary of the Bauhaus in Weimar, Theo van Doesburg moved to Paris in 1923. That year he participated in a show of *De Stijl* architectural projects, notably for private residences, at the Paris gallery of French art dealer Leonce Rosenberg. Among the models in the exhibition was a House for an Artist, which van Doesburg designed in collaboration with the Dutch architect Cor van Eesteren (1897–1988). The model consisted of intersecting cubic volumes with the exposed surfaces painted in black, white, and the primary colors. In a statement published in the *De Stijl* journal around the time of the exhibition, van Doesburg and van Eesteren called for objective laws for architecture that were based on fixed principles. It is "not the relationship between things themselves" that is important, they declared, "but the relationship between their qualities." Nothing could have been farther from the celebration of individual creativity that animated the exhibitions of the Society of Artist-Decorators. Van Doesburg and van Eesteren sharply criticized this attitude when they wrote that "[t]he new spirit which already governs almost all modern life is opposed to animal spontaneity (lyricism), to the domination of nature, to complicated hair styles and elaborate cooking." No wonder that their 1923 exhibition was ignored by many French critics and architects, although even those publications which stated that French architects could learn something from *De Stijl* still criticized the exhibition's drawings and models for being too reductive, too rectilinear, and lacking in softer curves. *De Stijl*, which had originated in Holland, was also excluded from the Dutch pavilion at the 1925 Exposition des Arts Décoratifs. By this time, the movement had lost its force in the Netherlands and the pavilion was dominated by more expressive architects and designers who were grouped around the journal *Wendingen* (*Turnings*). One person who did pay attention to the exhibition at the Rosenberg gallery was the Swiss architect Le Corbusier, who was quick to adopt some of the *De Stijl* geometry to his own designs as well as to begin using the axonometric projections of van Doesburg and van Eesteren, which emphasized a building's volume rather than its facade.

During the late 1920s, van Doesburg worked on several architectural projects in Holland and Germany as a color consultant and designer. He also participated in a large French commission—the interior design of the Aubette cafe and dance hall in Strasbourg. The project was offered to Hans Arp, the Dada artist, who invited van Doesburg to collaborate with him and his wife Sophie Tauber-Arp. Van Doesburg took charge of the project and designed all the equipment and small objects ranging from electrical fuse-boards to ashtrays and dishes. As lettering for the signage as well as the Aubette identity on the crockery, Van Doesburg adopted the rectilinear *De Stijl* alphabet he had designed in 1918–1919.

Sophie Tauber-Arp designed the pastry shop and tea room as well as the intimate Aubette Bar, while Hans Arp decorated the walls of the basement American bar and cellar dance hall in a free organic style. Van Doesburg designed the main rooms on the ground floor and first floor. He made his most dramatic statement in the Grand Salle, which was used for film screenings and dancing. Here he created an enormous mural that consisted of colored planes that were divided by diagonal lines. These, he contrasted with a composition of rectangles behind the film screen and rectangular panels on the ceiling (Plate 11). The lighting consisted of rows of lamps pointed towards the ceiling so that the light was reflected down onto

the dance floor. As strong a statement as the Café Aubette made, the French architectural press ignored it, although it was well received in the local papers. However, patrons did not like the decor and the proprietors began to alter it almost as soon as it was completed. By the time the Aubette had celebrated its 10th anniversary, almost all the work Van Doesburg and the Arps did had disappeared.

L'Esprit Nouveau and Purism

In November 1917, Guillaume Apollinaire gave a lecture, "L'Esprit Nouveau et les Poètes" ("The New Spirit and the Poets") in which he equated the new spirit with the "solid good sense" of classicism. "France is repulsed by disorder," Apollinaire stated. "People welcome principles and are horrified by chaos … The new spirit refers above all to the great classical qualities—order and duty—in which the French spirit is proudly manifest." Three years later an architect, Charles-Édouard Jeanneret known as Le Corbusier (1887–1965), a painter, Amédée Ozenfant (1886–1966), and a poet, Paul Dermée (1886–1951), founded a journal *L'Esprit Nouveau* in whose first issue they echoed Apollinaire's abhorrence of chaos and celebrated the beauty of pure forms—cubes, cones, spheres, cylinders, and pyramids. They also argued that the airplane and the automobile characterized the style of their time. In the fourth issue, Le Corbusier and Ozenfant published an essay entitled "Purism" in which they promoted an art that would "address itself above all to the universal properties of the senses and the mind." Although they envisioned the philosophy of Purism as embracing not only the arts but also architecture and design, the initial examples they produced were paintings—still life subjects that were influenced by Cubism and resulted in compositions of volumes rather than fragments. In architecture, Le Corbusier had begun to develop a standardized housing unit, the Maison Citrohan, which he exhibited at the Salon d'Automne in 1922, along with his Ville Contemporaine, an urban plan for a city of 3 million inhabitants based on rows of tower blocks separated by green space and high-speed throughways for automobiles.

L'Esprit Nouveau's unhappiness with chaos was consistent with the more widespread call to order that pervaded the decorative arts in France after the war, but the editors' espousal of a spare geometry as a remedy for it set them apart from the Society of Artist-Decorators as did their promulgation of a machine aesthetic. Le Corbusier was Swiss and shared neither the SAD's nor the French government's interest in a national style based on tradition. He continued his polemic for a machine aesthetic in *Vers une Architecture* (*Towards an Architecture*), which he published under his own name in 1923, even though it was based on articles that he had published with Ozenfant in *L'Esprit Nouveau*. His most salient point is that the machine was the ideal model for design. "A house is a machine for living in," he wrote, while "[a]n armchair is a machine for sitting in and so

forth." For Le Corbusier the typewriter, the telephone, the safety razor, the office desk, the steamship, the automobile, and the airplane were the objects that characterized contemporary life. The decorative arts, as most members of the SAD practiced them, were, in Le Corbusier's view, "the intolerable witnesses to a dead spirit."

Despite Le Corbusier's antipathy to the traditional decorative arts, the organizers of the 1925 Exposition des Arts Décoratifs nonetheless invited him to submit a design for an architect's house. Instead, Le Corbusier designed a populist "house for everybody" (Fig. 22.05). The organizers disliked the design and did everything they could to diminish the impact of the house. Called the Pavilion de l'Esprit Nouveau (Pavilion of the New Spirit), it was given a space on the periphery of the exhibition site. The pavilion received funding from Gabriel Voisin, a pioneer

Fig. 22.05: Le Corbusier, Pavillon de l'Esprit Nouveau, interior, 1925. Fondation Le Corbusier. Fondation Le Corbusier. © FLC/ADAGP, Paris and DACS, London 2017.

airplane designer and manufacturer who had shifted to automobile design after the war. Like other wartime manufacturers looking for peacetime projects, Voisin was interested in entering the French housing market with mass-produced dwellings. Thus, Le Corbusier's pavilion, a unit made with standardized elements, represented Voisin's interests as did the more developed version of Le Corbusier's Ville Contemporaine plan of 1922, the Plan Voisin of Paris, which was also on display in the pavilion.

Le Corbusier's idea of furniture design was close to the theory of types that Hermann Muthesius espoused in the Werkbund debates of 1914. He furnished his pavilion with "object-types," which he thought represented ideal furniture forms. These included bentwood chairs from Vienna, and English-style club chairs. The walls were hung with his own Purist paintings and paintings by Fernand Léger.

The Pavilion de l'Esprit Nouveau gained Le Corbusier his first public recognition and led to important commissions in the next few years: the workers' housing project at Pessac near Bordeaux, the Villa Stein in Garches, and the Villa Savoye outside Paris. While his pavilion gained far less attention at the time than Patout's and Ruhlmann's Hôtel du Collectioneur, in the long run it had a far greater impact on other designers as interest in and support for the luxury market in furnishings and interiors began to decline, particularly after the Great Depression of 1929.

Dada

After the poet Guillaume Apollinaire died in the influenza epidemic of 1918, he was succeeded by a group of young writers—André Breton, Paul Éluard, Phillipe Soupault, and Louis Aragon among them—who wanted to continue his experiments with literature. They had followed the Dada activities of Marcel Duchamp, Man Ray, and Francis Picabia in New York, and Tristan Tzara in Zurich. By 1920, all these artists were welcomed in Paris, where Picabia continued to publish his avant-garde newspaper *391* and Tzara launched a program

of Dada publications. Under Tzara's direction, two new journals came out: *Bulletin Dada* and *Dadaphone.* Picabia designed several witty covers for *Littérature,* the magazine edited by Aragon, Breton, and Soupault. For the cover of *Littérature 7* he made a pun on the title, breaking it up into *Lits et Ratures (Beds and Failures),* a joke he supported with drawings of one pair each of men's and women's shoe soles that suggested a man lying on top of a woman in bed.

But Dada in Paris had no political program and the best it could do was attempt to shock its audience with audacious language and provocative antics. By 1922, Breton, who had emerged as the strong force in the literary group that succeeded Apollinaire, was already speaking of the end of Dada. Tzara tried to save the movement with the establishment of a new journal, *Le Coeur à Barbe (The Bearded Heart),* whose only issue appeared in April 1922. The cover design was playful rather than political (Fig. 22.06). Tzara chose 19th-century Egyptian letters for the title and combined them in a witty way with a variety of printer's cuts that had no particular meaning. When he organized an Evening of the Bearded Heart the following year, the poster the Russian Ilia Zdanevich (1894–1975) adopted all the Dada tricks, notably a mix of type sizes and fonts, a clever use of printers' cuts, and a cacophonous sequence of words. However, the layout had no connection with the content, signifying only an anarchic relation to the conventions of print rather than a truly subversive relation to language itself. As it turned out, the event, which included a performance of Tzara's play, *Coeur à Gaz,* was disrupted by several fist fights and a physical attack on Tzara by Paul Éluard, thus effectively ending any further French interest in Dada. The following year, Breton wrote the "First Surrealist Manifesto", thereby inaugurating a new avant-garde movement with a much greater stake in exploring the psychological and political meaning of human action.

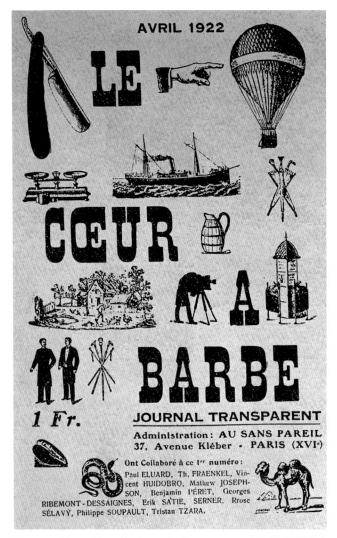

Fig. 22.06: Tristan Tzara, *Le Coeur à Barbe*, cover, 1922. © INTERFOTO/ Alamy.

The Society of Artist-Decorators and the Union des Artistes Modernes

While the 1925 Exposition was considered a success both nationally and internationally, it was also criticized for its emphasis on luxury goods for the wealthy rather than designs for ordinary people. In a speech following the exhibition, its Chief Commissioner, Fernand David, defended it, arguing that without a collection of extraordinary objects, even if they were directed at the luxury trade, the exhibition might

not have attracted a large audience. He urged the members of the SAD to turn their attention in their future exhibitions to the needs of the "average French person," However, this did not happen. Designers such as Paul Follot and Maurice Dufrène continued to create luxury interiors with a heavy emphasis on craftsmanship and tradition. What did change, however, was a greater interest among some of the society's designers in modern forms and more simplified interiors.

In 1922, the architect Robert Mallet-Stevens (1886–1945) published a portfolio of architectural prints that domesticated the spare geometric forms the editors of *l'Esprit Nouveau* had advocated. Drawing his inspiration from the architecture of Charles Rennie Mackintosh and Joseph Hoffmann, Mallet-Stevens proposed an adaptable modernism whose basic forms were graced with modest decorative touches. The following year, he collaborated with Fernand Léger and several others to design the modernistic sets for Marcel L'Herbier's film *L'Inhumaine* (*The Inhuman Woman*). Mallet-Stevens's combination of geometry and ornament, created for a popular audience, helped to define the look of the Deco style. He was active as a designer for the 1925 Exposition des Arts Décoratifs as was Georges Djo-Bourgeois (1898–1937), who had studied under him at the École Spéciale d'Architecture. For many years, Djo-Bourgeois worked for Studium, the decorating studio at the Grands Magazins du Louvre, where he designed furniture and interiors. His furniture designs were austere and geometric and sometimes incorporated innovative materials such as rubber. After 1926 he sometimes used aluminum or steel tubing as well. When placed in interiors, his pieces were enlivened by the colorful curtains and rugs that his wife Elise Djo-Bourgeois (d.o.b. unconfirmed-1986) designed and the fabrics with strong colors and abstract patterns of Hélène Henry (1891–1965), a textile designer committed to the *style moderne* or modern style. Henry was also one of the first designers to combine artificial yarns with wool and cotton. In fashion, Sonia Delaunay (1885–1979), who had produced colorful

Fig. 22.07: Sonia Delaunay, dress design with matching car body, 1925. Private Collection/Bridgeman Images.

abstract paintings in a geometric style called Orphism or simultaneism with her husband Robert Delaunay (1885–1941), applied these ideas to the decorative arts, first to the experimental book she produced with the writer Blaise Cendrars (see Chapter 18) and then to theater sets and costumes, fashion, textile designs, and interiors. In 1925, she even painted an automobile with simultaneous color patterns to promote her matching dress designs (Fig. 22.07).

Another practitioner of the modern style was the silversmith Jean Puiforcat (1897–1945), a sculptor as well as a silversmith, who introduced new geometric forms for pitchers, tea and coffee sets, and other domestic objects, often combining the silver forms with other materials such as crystal, ivory, or precious stones (Fig. 22.08). Among the pieces he designed in the early 1920s were Cubist-inspired centerpieces and tea sets with angular forms. By 1930 he began to incorporate mathematical ratios such as the Golden Section into his designs, thus bringing to the conception of modest decorative objects the discipline that was otherwise applied to the design of buildings by architects such as Le Corbusier.

At the time of the 1925 Exposition des Arts

Décoratifs, Le Corbusier published *L'Art Décoratif d'Aujourd'hui* (*The Decorative Art of Today*), a collection of previously published articles from *L'Esprit Nouveau*. The articles extended his architectural polemic into the realm of furniture and product design. He called for furniture design to be accountable to human needs and he celebrated conventional office furniture such as file cabinets and roll-top desks as examples of efficient tools. Sounding much like Adolf Loos, who contrasted straightforward English design, with the overwrought products of his fellow Viennese, Le Corbusier praised the elegant yet functional leather goods of the French luxury manufacturer Hermès.

Le Corbusier's attention to function, along with the new tubular steel furniture that was being designed in Holland and in Germany at the Bauhaus and for the Weissenhof exhibition, had an influence on some designers in France such as Eileen Gray who stopped creating lacquer furniture around 1926 and began to make prototypes largely with modern materials such as tubular steel and glass. Between 1926 and 1929, Gray designed a range of furniture pieces for her own seaside house at Roquebrune-Cap Martin. The basis of her designs was convenience and comfort. Flexibility

Fig. 22.08: Jean Puiforcat, silver tea set, c. 1925. Private Collection/Photo © Christie's Images/Bridgeman Images. © ADAGP, Paris and DACS, London 2017.

and collapsibility were key features, whether the pieces were built in or free standing. Among the built-in pieces were a writing desk concealed in a cabinet, a cupboard with rounded pivoting drawers, and a cantilevered bedside reading table with pivoting arms and an adjustable reading stand. Among the free-standing pieces were a round glass bedside table made of steel tubing, which could be raised and lowered to bring it to the desired height; a tea table with a cork surface that could be folded and stored flat; and a dining room table also with a cork surface as well as chromed steel legs, and two supports covered in leather at the end of the table to hold up a serving tray. Gray's furniture had a flexibility and inventiveness that was similar to the pieces designed by Rodchenko's students at the Vkhutemas in Moscow around the same time. She was among the first designers to work with tubular steel and one of the few to explore the idea of flexible furniture rather than fixed sculptural forms. Gray liked to mix hard and soft materials as in her Bibendum chair, which had a padded seat and two fabric-covered rolls of filling, mimicking the rounded layered body of the Michelin tire man, the company's trademark figure who goes by the name Bibendum. While many of Gray's pieces might have gone into mass production, she did not promote her designs and some of them were mass-produced only at the end of her long life when interest in her work had revived.

The shift in furniture design that Eileen Gray underwent from luxury pieces made of exotic or lacquered woods to less expensive pieces of tubular steel became manifest at the 1928 Salon of the Artists-Decorators when a number of designers introduced furniture of tubular steel, no doubt influenced by the furniture that had been on display in the model apartments and villas at the Weissenhof exhibition in Stuttgart the year before. Even the design studios of the department stores such as La Maîtrise and Studium were quick to join the trend. The most successful tubular steel furnishings could be seen in a model apartment by Djo-Bourgeois, the architect René Herbst (1891–1982), and Charlotte Perriand (1903–1999).

Perriand had studied with Maurice Dufrène at La Maîtrise before joining the studio of Le Corbusier and Pierre Jeanneret, where she was responsible, in collaboration with Le Corbusier and Jeanneret, for developing the firm's furniture designs. For the most part, the pieces were designed for architectural commissions, but Thonet acquired several for their catalog of tubular steel furniture. The chairs and the chaise

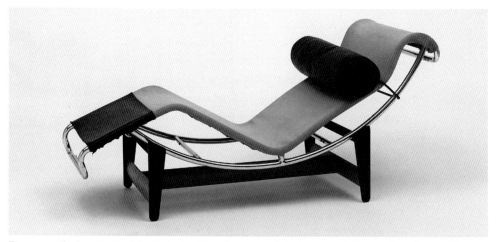

Fig. 22.09: Charlotte Perriand, Le Corbusier, Pierre Jeanneret, *chaise longue*, 1928. © 2014. Digital image, The Museum of Modern Art, New York/Scala, Florence. © ADAGP, Paris and DACS, London./© FLC/ADAGP, Paris and DACS, London 2017.

longue consist of architectonic frames that support padded leather supports. The armchair of 1928 encloses a padded leather seat with raised side arms in a chrome steel frame, while a second version has much softer leather cushions in a similar frame. The chaise longue is perhaps the most graceful piece, consisting of a wooden support and a curved tubular steel frame holding up the flat reclining surface that supports the body (Fig. 22.09). Other designers who created furniture made of metal around the same time include Jean Prouvé (1901–1984) and René Herbst, whose nickel-plated steel tube side chair includes flexible bungee cords as seat and back supports.

When the jury for the 1929 SAD exhibition rejected a proposal for a sizeable exhibition of modern furniture, a number of members left the organization and formed the Union des Artistes Modernes (Union of Modern Artists). Others joined so as to incorporate artists, designers, architects, sculptors, and graphic designers. Founding members who were architects or furniture designers included Robert Mallet-Stevens, Francis Jourdain, René Herbst, Pierre Chareau (1883–1950), Hélène Henry, Charlotte Perriand, Eileen Gray, and Le Corbusier, who had long been espousing modernist tendencies. Among the graphic designers who became members were A. M. Cassandre, Jean Carlu, and Paul Colin. The membership also counted luxury craftsmen, goldsmiths, jewelers, and bookbinders, hence it was not possible to create a unified position towards either mass housing as the Congrès International d'Architecture Moderne (CIAM) had begun to do at its annual meetings or towards mass production. In fact the Union was unable to move in its own exhibitions away from individual displays towards more collective projects and it made no more progress than the SAD towards designing for industry.

By 1928, relations between France and Germany had improved sufficiently for the Society of Artist-Decorators to invite the Deutscher Werkbund to exhibit at its 1930 salon. It was the first time a group of German designers had exhibited in Paris since 1910. Walter Gropius, the first director of the Bauhaus and who had been active in the Werkbund since its beginning, was selected as director of the Werkbund's display and he chose a group of former Bauhaus colleagues—Marcel Breuer, Herbert Bayer, and László Moholy-Nagy—to work with him. The theme of the exhibit was the design and furnishing of a ten-story hotel/boarding house that would demonstrate the possibilities of collective living through an integration of public and private space under one roof. Gropius did the plan for the steel-framed structure, which contained five rooms that housed a model apartment as well as spaces for the display of furniture and photographs. The communal space that Gropius designed featured a coffee bar and a gallery/library with separate spaces for individual activities such as reading and listening to music. The communal area was divided from the apartments by a steel bridge that enabled visitors to view the exhibit from above. The exhibit, which featured tubular steel furniture almost exclusively, included photographs displayed at angles for easier viewing, and presented a bold dramatic narrative about how people might share common space, could not have been more different from the SAD's own French Embassy of five years before. Not only did the earlier project feature luxury goods rather than mass-produced furniture, but it also presented a narrative of how the privileged elite lived. Before the 1930 Werkbund exhibit opened, Gropius told a French journalist that it would draw attention to the "standardized production of beautiful forms," while also applying the latest technical discoveries to domestic architecture and demonstrating the possibilities of community within a shared space.

The Salon des Arts Ménagers

The establishment of the annual Salon des Arts Ménagers (Salon of Household Arts) in 1923 as an organization completely independent of the Society of Artist-Decorators makes clear how fragmented the idea of design was in France between the wars. Whereas the SAD concentrated primarily on luxury furniture and decor that craftsmen produced in limited editions, the Salon des Arts Ménagers was established to display a wide range of mass-produced appliances for the home. Its founder was Jules-Louis Breton (1872–1940), the creator and first director of France's National Office of Scientific and Industrial Research and Inventions. Breton intended the salon to showcase the inventors of the best home appliances and to bring them into relation with the new consumer class that was emerging in France. As the historian Martine Segalen has shown, the principal target of the annual exhibitions was the housewife who was introduced to labor-saving devices as well as to methods of efficiency and criteria of good taste. Breton's aims to improve the efficiency

and quality of household work were paralleled by the Institut d'Organisation Menagère (Institute for Household Organization) that Paulette Bernège (dates unconfirmed) founded in 1926 and which played a role in the household efficiency movement similar to that of Christine Fredericks in the United States and others elsewhere.

Breton himself strongly advocated the role of the inventor in the creation of new household appliances, more so in fact than the majority of French industrialists. Within the salons, he organized numerous competitions that brought together consumers, engineers, designers, and others who had a stake in the quality of household life. By establishing a forum in which everyone involved in the creation of a domestic sphere could meet and discuss issues, the Salon des Arts Ménagers gave a strong impulse to the invention of new domestic appliances. After the expensive appliances that were shown in the early salons, often accompanied by uniformed maids, later salons featured smaller and less costly ones. The salons also encouraged manufacturers to adapt machines originally created for institutions such as hospitals, schools, and prisons, to home use. In this sense, the Salon des Arts Ménagers performed a function similar to the Deutscher Werkbund by serving as an intermediary between manufacturers and consumers.

As the salons developed, they came to embrace the design of the entire household rather than just individual appliances. At the 1930 salon, a competition for the furnishing of a family house was set up, while the 1936 and 1937 salons featured apartments for the French family that were highly appealing to the working class. As an example of how influential the salons were in transforming the design of the home and its interior, one can cite the French kitchen which, according to Martine Segalen, was reinvented as a separate space where specialized functions were coordinated, according to the principles of Scientific Management, into coherent ensembles of equipment.

After several years, the organizers began to promote the Salon with an annual poster designed by

Fig. 22.10: Francis Bernard, 7th Salon des Arts Ménagers, poster, 1930. © Swim Ink 2, LLC/CORBIS/Getty Images.

an established graphic artist such as Francis Bernard (1900–1979), Jacques Nathan-Garamond (1910–2001), or Jean Carlu (1900–1997). For the 1930 exhibition poster, Bernard created a logo for the salon, a woman with gear wheels inside her. Known as Marie Méchanique (Mechanical Marie), she symbolized the replacement of a weak domestic effort by mechanical household appliances (Fig. 22.10).

The only cross-over the Salon had with designers who had been active in the exhibitions of the Society of Artist-Decorators occurred in 1934 when the Union des Artistes Modernes, comprised largely of designers who had resigned from the SAD, organized a special display of their work at the Salon, but the more artistic interests of the UAM designers, coupled with the Salon organizers' suspicion that the SAD designs might be too expensive, mitigated against fruitful collaboration in the future.

Trains, Automobiles and Planes

One of the rare comprehensive design programs in France during the interwar years was initiated by Raoul Dautry (1880–1951) in the late 1920s for the French national railroad. An engineer by training, Dautry commissioned the architect and designer Henri Pacon (1882–1946) in 1929 to oversee the design of the railroad's locomotives and passenger cars as well as a number of the railway stations. As part of their effort to work out a comprehensive design policy for the railroads, Dautry and Pacon hired prominent poster designers including A. M. Cassandre, Pierre Fix-Masseau (1869–1967) and J. P. Junot (dates unconfirmed) to promote the railroad. Cassandre's seminal posters for specific trains and train lines such as the Nord Express, the Étoile du Nord (North Star), and the Oiseau Bleu (Blue Bird) were central to this effort. Pacon redesigned a locomotive, the 241-101 Etat of 1931–1932, which became a model for the railroad though he stopped considerably short of streamlining the locomotive as the American designer Norman Bel Geddes was to advocate only a year later in his seminal book *Horizons*.

The role that Dautry and Pacon played for the French railroad was similar to the one that Frank Pick created in Britain for the London Underground. Pacon also designed low-cost housing for railway workers as well as several stations in Paris, Le Havre, and Chartres to which he gave a modern look by using reinforced concrete and a stripped classical style. The design program for the railroad continued vigorously until World War II interrupted it. Sadly, it was not pursued with comparable dedication in the post-war years. While the program was active, the French railroad was considered by many to be the best in Europe.

France was a leader in the early design of automobiles and this activity continued in the 1920s and 1930s. The major manufacturers were Peugeot, Renault, and Citroën, with other firms such as Voisin producing cars for more specialized clienteles. Before introducing a steam-driven three-wheeled vehicle at the 1889 World's Fair in Paris in conjunction with Léon Serpollet (1858–1907), an early French automobile designer, the Peugeot family had built a successful business as ironmongers, manufacturing coffee grinders, umbrella frames, and bicycles. After the 1889 Exposition, Armand Peugeot urged a switch to the Daimler internal combustion engine and by 1900 Peugeot had become a leading manufacturer of automobiles in France. The company excelled in part by its ambitious use of outside designers among whom the Italian Ettore Bugatti (1881–1947) was one of the earliest. The Bébé (Baby), whose first version following Bugatti's design was completed in 1905. It was a small two-seater with a canvas top and a gracefully curved body. After World War I, Peugeot introduced a successor to the Bébé, the Quadrillette, of which 100,000 were to be built in the years that followed. This car was more significant for its front-wheel brakes and six-cylinder engine than for its staid body design.

By the beginning of the 1930s, however, Peugeot led the French automobile industry in introducing more dynamic body designs. A breakthrough for the company was the introduction of the 401 Eclipse

Fig. 22.11: Marcel Pourtout, Peugeot 401, 1934. © Peugeot Archives.

in 1934 (Fig. 22.11). With a body design by Marcel Pourtout (1894–1979), head designer of the Carrosserie Pourtout, a French custom coachbuilder, the Eclipse featured the world's first retractable hardtop roof, which could be stored in the trunk, thus converting the car from a coupe to a convertible. The roof was invented by Georges Paulin (1902–1942), a dental technician who patented his design in 1932. Following the success of the Eclipse, Paulin joined forces with Pourtout and between 1934 and 1938 they created a series of signature vehicles for different automobile companies. Their firm also produced custom auto bodies for wealthy clients, who would provide them with a chassis from an established manufacturer. Another well-known coachbuilder was Joseph Figoni (1894–d.o.d. unconfirmed), who was born in Italy but whose family moved to France when he was a boy. Known for his sensuous forms, Figoni's hallmark design signatures included sweeping dorsal tail fins, decorative chrome strips, low windshields, and elegant instrumental panels. Known as the "Great Couturier of the Automobile," Figoni designed custom bodies for chassis produced by all the major French auto manufacturers.

In 1935, Peugeot introduced its first aerodynamic body design on the 402, a car designed by Henri Thomas (dates unconfirmed), who had worked for a number of custom coachbuilders before joining a new design department at Peugeot, and Jean Andreau (1890–1953), a French engineer who specialized in aerodynamic forms and collaborated with various automobile manufacturers during the 1930s. Though Andreau was more a theorist, his ideas fueled an entire movement of aerodynamic vehicles that were produced by major manufacturers such as Peugeot and Citroën and smaller ones such as Delahaye, Delage, and Talbot-Lago.

The Peugeot 402 featured fluid lines and a rounded shield-shaped grill that protected the headlights. A strong influence on Thomas was more than likely the 1934 Chrysler Airflow, which had a similarly rounded front end, although the Airflow was far less popular in America than the 402 and subsequent aerodynamic cars were in Europe. Another source for Thomas was probably the drawings by George Hamel (1900–1972), known as Geo Ham, whose dynamic depictions of vehicles in motion graced the posters for automobile and motorcycle races in Europe for many years. The 402 was the first model in Peugeot's Fuseau Socheaux or "Socheaux rocket" line, a series of aerodynamic cars named after the Socheaux factory where they were assembled. In 1937, Peugeot produced a light body sports car called the Darl'Mat after a Paris

Peugeot dealer. Four models were available: a roadster, a convertible, a coupe, and a racing car. Georges Paulin designed the aluminum body and Maurice Pourtout was responsible for the car's production.

In 1899, a decade after Peugeot presented its first steam-powered vehicle in Paris, Louis Renault introduced two models of his new car at the Paris Auto Show. By 1904, Renault had a network of 120 dealers, and during World War I the company contributed to the war effort with its Marne taxis, which helped transport French soldiers to the front. Renault also produced military airplanes and tanks. By 1925, the company had gained a reputation for durable cars. The Renault NN, with its curved hood, was known as the car that never broke down. Other models of the 1920s were the Monasix, Renault's first mid-sized vehicle to be powered by a six-cylinder engine. The modest design featured a slightly swept back hood and a clean-lined body. The car's rugged quality and economic fuel consumption made it attractive as a taxi and more than 5,000 were in service in France in the late 1920s.

Other models that Renault produced during the 1930s—the Nervastella, Monaquatre, Celtaquatre, and the Juvaquatre—were all more conservatively designed than the aerodynamic Peugeots. Nonetheless, they did adopt some streamlined elements such as swept back hood designs. The Nervastella, which was launched in 1930, had elegant curved fenders connected by a flat dashboard, but the cab was nonetheless rather boxy. The Juvaquatre, launched in the late 1930s, adopted some modest chrome strips and featured a more rounded hood and cab similar to the earlier Chrysler Airflow. During the 1930s, Renault adopted aerodynamic elements cautiously, preferring to maintain a more pragmatic and less flamboyant stance than Peugeot. In 1938, Louis Renault visited Berlin and saw the prototype for the Volkswagen Kraft durch Freude or KdF Wagen, a people's car that was to be produced by the Nazis. When he returned to Paris, he began work on a comparable small inexpensive car. He managed to complete a prototype, which he called the 4CV, in 1942,

but it did not go into production until 1946, after the war had ended.

Of the three major automobile manufacturers, Citroën followed the mass-production methods of Henry Ford most closely. André Citroën (1878–1935), a mechanical engineer, visited Ford's American plants in 1912 and then in 1919 he introduced his own Type A automobile, whose name followed Ford's Model A. The Type A may well have been the first European car to be built on the assembly line, following the practice initiated by Henry Ford. In late 1921, Citroën launched the Model C, a small two-seater that was designed by Edmond Moyet (1884–1961) working under the engineer Jules Salomon (1873–1963). Both were part of Citroën's in-house design center. The marketing of the Model C was aimed primarily at women, who were an untapped market for automobile sales. The selling point was that the car was particularly easy to drive. It came in three body types, all with fold-down hoods. In the beginning, the Model C touring cars were painted bright yellow only, thus prompting the nickname of "Le Petit Citron," a pun on the word "lemon" and the company's name, Citroën. It was also referred to as the "Cul de Poule," or hen's rear end, due to the pointed shape of the rear bodywork (Fig. 22.12).

For the subsequent version of the Model C, the C2, Citroën added a third seat. Rather than have the driver and passenger seats side by side, the passenger seat was in the rear with a collapsible seat next to the driver. The next model, the C3, became an actual three-seater, with two seats in the front and one in the back, forming a shape that gave the car its name, the Cloverleaf. To accommodate the extra seat, the pointed shape of the Model C was rounded out. The C models eventually went out of production but not before they were adapted as small pickup vehicles for the farming community. Some also had special bodies installed that made them suitable as delivery vehicles. The C2 served as a model for the small Opel, known as the aforementioned "Tree Frog," which was perhaps the first German

Fig. 22.12: Citroën 5CV, Type C, roadster, 1924. Shannons Auctions Ltd.

automobile to be produced in relatively large numbers. In 1925, Citroën was the first manufacturer in Europe to introduce all-steel bodies, which replaced nailing sheet metal to a wooden frame.

During the 1920s, Citroëns were purchased primarily for their performance quality and, in the case of the Model C series, their novelty. At the beginning of the 1930s, the company needed to compete with Peugeot, which had gone heavily into aerodynamic body design with the introduction of the 401 and then the 402 the following year. By this time both Salomon and Moyet had left the company and Citroën engaged André Lefèbvre (1894–1964) as the project engineer for a new more streamlined car, the Type 7, which was designed by an Italian, Flaminio Bertoni (1903–1964), who had moved to France in 1931 and joined Citroën's staff. Also known as the Traction Avant or "front-wheel drive," the sleek sedan featured hydraulic brakes, rubber

motor mounts for the engine, and no dashboard. The all-metal body made it lighter than the partially wooden cars that most manufacturers produced and its mass was evenly distributed, thus reducing wind resistance and increasing its speed. Though Bertoni made numerous drawings for the vehicle, he is said to have produced the final body shape by modeling it in clay one evening.

Although the Type 7 was a revolutionary vehicle and many were produced, its development bankrupted André Citroën and a few months after its launch, his company was taken over by Michelin, the tire manufacturer. Pierre Jules Boulanger, the Michelin executive who took charge of the company and ran it after André Citroën died in 1935, chose as his first project the development of a TPV or Trés Petit Voiture ("very small car"). He envisioned this car as competition for the small Volkswagen vehicle that the Germans had commissioned Ferdinand Porsche to design. Known as the 2CV or "Deux Cheveaux" ("two horse power"), the Citroën's lean linear styling by Bertoni could not have been more different from the more ample curves of his Traction Avant. The shape was inspired in part by the aircraft from which its engineer André Lefèbvre (1894–1964) took many of his ideas for the vehicle. Because of the onset of World War II, however, the car remained a prototype only until it was brought to market in 1948.

In August 1933, five French airlines joined together to form Air France, which became France's national passenger airline a few years later. Among them, the five lines had controlled routes throughout Europe and to other parts of the world, particularly Africa, where France had numerous colonies. While Douglas, Boeing, and other airplane manufacturers abroad took a lead in designing and selling commercial aircraft in the interwar years, France had its own pioneer airplane designers and manufacturers who were less successful internationally than the American firms but were nonetheless active in producing both military and commercial airplanes.

The French government requested Marcel Bloch (1892–1986), an aeronautical engineer, to oversee the construction of the Caudron G3 aircraft. When asked to design a new rudder for the plane, Bloch produced a vastly improved propeller, which he called the "Éclair." Joined by a collaborator, Henri Potez (1891–1981), an engineer with similar training, the two set up a company to market the Éclair propeller, which they did successfully. Subsequently they, along with Louis Coroller (1893–1988), created an innovative two-seater plane called the SAE 4. When the French military canceled a large order after the end of World War I, Bloch retired temporarily from aircraft design while Potez went on to found his own company in 1919. Among the planes his firm designed were the Potez 25 biplane that was used on the Andes route between Argentina and Chile; the Potez 36 and 60, both light aircraft; and the four-engine Potez 661, the fastest civil aircraft of the time, which had its first flight in 1937. Only one was produced.

Following the establishment of the French Air Ministry in 1928, Marcel Bloch returned to aviation design, hiring several young engineers and setting up a new company, the Société des Avions Marcel Bloch. At the end of 1931, the company took orders from the government for the single-engine MB 80, a plane used especially for medical evacuations, and the MB 120, a three-engine 10-passenger commercial aircraft. Following these were a prototype for new civil aircraft, the MB 220, as well as various military planes.

A third figure of significance to French aircraft design was Louis-Charles Bréguet (1880–1955), an electrical engineer who built his first airplane in 1909. Before that he designed a gyroplane, which was a proto helicopter, in 1907, and then a hydroplane in 1912. During World War I, the French Air Force mass-produced Bréguet's design for a reconnaissance plane and in 1919 he created a commercial airline company, the Compagnie de Messageries Aériennes, which eventually became part of Air France. In 1933, one of his planes made a 4,500-mile flight across the Atlantic, the longest non-stop transatlantic flight up to that time. Around 1934, Bréguet returned to his gyroplane designs, working with the engineer René Dorand (dates unconfirmed). He called their first collaborative effort a Gyroplane Laboratory, to acknowledge its experimental status. By the time World War II began, Bréguet had created a helicopter that could lift off the ground and manage short flights, but it was far from perfected and he shelved the project in order to concentrate on the design of military bombers,

The International Colonial Exhibition

The trajectory of SAD exhibitions during the 1920s gave little evidence of France's vast colonial empire except indirectly through the use of exotic woods that were imported from the colonies and incorporated into the expensive furniture pieces by André Groult, Pierre Le Grain, Süe et Mare, and other designers. The purpose of the Exposition Coloniale et Internationale (International Colonial Exhibition) in 1931, which was preceded by several others in Marseilles in 1906 and 1922, was to bring representatives of this extensive empire to Paris and reinforce for the French people the importance of their colonies (Plate 12). Underlying the exhibition and France's general attitude towards her colonies was the *mission civilisatrice* or civilizing mission that the government adopted in order to turn all those denizens of the empire into good Frenchmen, provided they were capable of it.

Though the French government invited many countries to exhibit in Paris, some declined and others

Fig. 22.13: Jean-Victor Desmeures, Exposition Coloniale Internationale, poster, 1931. Bibliotheque Historique de la Ville de Paris, Paris, France/ Archives Charmet/Bridgeman Images.

like Britain provided only modest displays. Center stage belonged to France, which constructed an array of pavilions that represented the indigenous architecture of peoples living in Africa, the Near East, the Far East, and Oceania. French companies controlled much of the agriculture and extraction of raw materials in the colonies, while the native occupations ranged primarily from forced laborers to craftsmen and traders. On display at the exhibition were various native crafts, particularly the carpets, ornamental brass work, and hand-tooled leather of North Africa.

The West African pavilions reinforced the stereotype of primitivism. Designed by French architects, they were large wooden structures that were draped with bulky thatch. Inside, the public could see native handiwork and dioramas that narrated the history of French civilizing influences. To reinforce the impression of authenticity, no Africans or any other colonial denizens could wear European clothing on the fairgrounds. The exhibition's poster by the artist Jean-Victor Desmeures (dates unconfirmed) reinforced the Orientalist view of the colonies as exotic places that were united by a shared allegiance to France. The poster depicted an Arab Berber with a characteristic head covering, a black African with a bare torso, an Asian wearing a coolie's hat, and a fourth figure who appears to be an American Indian, perhaps reminiscent of former French colonial adventures in North America (Fig. 22.13).

Of all the French colonial pavilions, the most impressive was the faithful replica of Cambodia's Temple of Angor Wat, built by the French architectural firm of Charles and Gabriel Blanche. According to one critic, the pavilion did not symbolize the grand legacy of contemporary Cambodia as much as it did a civilization that had been diminished by native violence and which the French were now attempting to revive. Overall, the exhibition, with its multifarious displays of native architecture and culture and its plethora of statistics about improvements in health and welfare, sought to confirm for the French public the significance of the colonies as the basis for France's identity as an empire and a nation. It demonstrated, through the presence of optimistic charts, diagrams, and dioramas as well as performances and presentations by natives themselves that France's civilizing mission was working and merited the continuing support of the French population. To convey this impression, design had an important role to play in reproducing the comforting stereotypes of native life across the diverse cultural milieus of France's empire.

The Great Ocean Liners

As the 1930s began and France started to experience the effects of the Great Depression, craftsmen and decorative artists found it difficult to earn a living. Currency devaluations in Britain, Germany, and the United States had begun to affect exports, and the luxury industries were hit particularly hard. In 1931 the artist and designer Paul Iribe (1883–1935), who had illustrated the fashions of Paul Poiret 20 years earlier, published an article entitled "Profits and Losses" in which he denounced machines for ruining the French decorative arts as well as Western civilization. In a curious echo of the Bauhaus manifesto of 1919, Iribe called for a return to the crafts and the execution of manual skills. For him, the choice lay between "Standardization and individuality." In a subsequent speech he criticized the deleterious effects of German and Swiss ideas on French decoration, notably those of the Werkbund and Le Corbusier, lamenting that France had abandoned the exclusivity of its "exceptional products," which were more likely to bring economic success to the nation than standardized goods. Surprisingly, Iribe's views were widely seconded by the French press, which believed that a return to French craft expertise would protect French artisans from the current economic crisis. Such arguments favored the continuation of policies that had been in place for many years and effectively delayed the active development of a culture of mass production that had served the other major powers well since the beginning of the Industrial Revolution.

A great patron of the decorative arts in the late 1920s and the 1930s was the Compagnie Générale Transatlantique, which was responsible for France's fleet of passenger ships. Created under another name in 1855, the Compagnie had been responsible for opening up tourist routes throughout the world and building France's great ocean liners. Influenced by the 1925 exhibition of decorative arts, John Dal Piaz, President of the Compagnie Générale Transatlantique, decided to create a new ship, the *Île-de-France*, whose decor would break radically with the tradition of historic interiors that had previously dominated the design of ocean liners. German designers such as Bruno Paul, influenced by the *Jugendstil*, had made similar attempts on several ships of the North German Lloyd and Hamburg-Amerika lines a few years earlier but no shipping line had so thoroughly committed to creating a total ship's interior in a modern style.

The *Île de France* was launched in 1927. Besides an abundance of molded glass and lacquer, the designers used sheets of wood veneer extensively. Brass beds were replaced in the cabins by partial bunk beds that were decorated with elaborate marquetry or inlaid wood designs. The bar extended for 27 feet, the longest on an Atlantic liner thus far. The Atelier Martine, Süe et Mare, and the studio of Jacques-Émile Ruhlmann were among those who fulfilled commissions for the ship, which remained in service for three decades.

Following the *Île de France,* the Compagnie Générale Transatlantique built the *Normandie*, which was its crowning glory. Work on the ship began in 1931, but its outfitting, including all the machinery as well as the interior decoration, was not completed until early 1935, when the *Normandie* made its maiden voyage. Due to the hard times resulting from the stock market crash in the United States, the Compagnie Générale Transatlantique had to ask the French government for funds to assist in the construction of the ship. Structurally, the *Normandie* displayed many innovations, particularly the narrow hull at both ends and the bulbous bow below the water line designed by

Vladimir Yourkevitch (1885–1964), a Russian émigré naval architect who had previously worked on Russian battleships and became known as the developer of the modern ship hull. Yourkevitch also enclosed all the deck machinery so that there was an unobstructed vista along the length of the deck, an aesthetic touch that set the style for the ships that followed. The ship's elegant form was featured on the promotional poster that A. M. Cassandre designed.

Created for the luxury trade, the *Normandie* incorporated the talents of France's leading Art Deco architects and decorative artists. The massive funds the government spent on the interior design provided employment for hundreds of designers and craftsman. The project functioned in its own way like the Works Projects Administration that President Franklin Delano Roosevelt established in the United States, which employed large numbers of artists to undertake a variety of projects from painting murals in post offices to producing an inventory of American folk art.

The ship's interiors were all done in the Art Deco or *moderne* style. The architect Roger-Henri Expert (1882–1955) designed the main salon, which featured black and gold tapestries and silver-gilt glass panels by Jean Dupas (Fig. 22.14). It also displayed Jean Dunand's gilt and lacquered panels on the theme of Games and the Joys of Man. The elegant departure hall, whose walls were sheathed in marble, was designed by Pierre Patout and Henri Pacon, the chief designer for the French national railroad. The breathtaking dining room had a height equivalent to three decks with no intervening balcony. It was simply an enormous chamber that conveyed a sense of grandeur. Publicists for the Compagnie Générale Transatlantique liked to point out that the dining room was slightly longer than the Hall of Mirrors at Versailles. Lighting for it was provided by

Fig. 22.14: Roger-Henri Expert, *Normandie* grand salon, 1935. Decorative panels by Jean Dupas, pewter vase by Maurice Daurat, and furniture by Jean M. Rothschild. © Bettmann/CORBIS/Getty Images.

a dozen large glass cascades, which were lit from within, thus continuing the use of indirect lighting that had originated with the design of the *Île de France*.

The amount of money the government spent on the *Normandie* provoked considerable controversy but resulted in the most lavish sailing vessel ever created. Though trends in the future design of passenger ships would eventually lead towards more democratic than aristocratic layouts and interiors, the *Normandie* set a high standard for the design of a ship's interior, one against which all future designs would have to be measured. After the fall of France in 1940, the United States Navy seized the ship when it was docked in New York harbor and began to convert it into a troop carrier. During the conversion, a fire started and neither the navy personnel nor the contractors knew how to turn on the fire extinguishing system. Water pouring onto the ship from fireboats caused it to turn over and when it was finally set upright the cost of restoration was deemed too great. In 1946 the Compagnie Générale Transatlantique decided to scrap the *Normandie*.

The Paris Exhibition of 1937

When planning for the 1937 exhibition began in 1929, few could envision that by the time of its inauguration, Europe would be edging towards another world war. The French government put on a brilliant display of national accomplishments in an array of pavilions that ranged from the *style moderne* to monumental classicism. Due to the Depression, the government played a major financial role in the exhibition in contrast to the predominantly private funds that supported the exhibition of 1925. Both exhibitions sought to promote France's superiority in the creation of luxury goods and the 1937 exhibition continued this aim with a multitude of pavilions dedicated to materials such as wood and metal as well as to furniture, ceramics, aeronautics, and railroads. There was even a pavilion devoted to fashion, jewelry, and perfumes. The Society of Artist-Decorators had its own building, where it continued its traditional display of full-scale specialty rooms for the wealthy. For the first time, the Union des Artistes Modernes (UAM) had its own building, but the contents, primarily separate displays by the Union's members, were hardly innovative. Notably absent was a pavilion to recognize the design accomplishments of French industry. Despite the Salon des Arts Ménager's successful promotion of industrial products for the home, the idea of industrial design had still not entered French consciousness, consequently it did not exist as the raison d'être for a separate pavilion devoted to industrial products.

The exhibition had an unusual number of foreign pavilions, more than 40. Of these, the Russian and German ones were the most striking and faced each other ominously across the exhibition grounds. The Russian Pavilion, designed by the architect Boris Iofan (1891–1976), was topped by Vera Mukhina's gigantic sculpture, "Worker and Collective Farm Girl," while the German pavilion, created by Hitler's chief architect, Albert Speer, conveyed the Nazi's ideals through its towering Neo-Classical facade topped by an eagle perched on a swastika. This symbolic confrontation of powerful ideologies portended badly for Europe's immediate future even though the French government's ambitious building program and optimistic displays would have led one to believe otherwise. In fact, Germany invaded Czechoslovakia in March 1939, and by September, World War II had begun.

Graphic Design
Magazines and advertising

After World War I, the *Gazette du Bon Ton, Jardin des Modes,* and other leading pre-war fashion magazines in Paris continued as major sources for established illustrators like George Barbier (1882–1932), George Lepape (1887–1971), André Marty (1886–1956), and Charles Martin (1884–1934). New magazines like *Art, Goût, Beauté* (*Art, Taste, Beauty*), known for its hand-colored illustrations, and *La Femme Chic* (*The Chic Woman*) also provided sources for these illustrators. The influence of Cubism on illustration and commercial art spread after the war. It is evident in the drawings of Martin, which make obvious reference to paintings by Picasso and Modigliani. The mixture of thin curves and angular lines in Martin's illustrations and the swaths of color that suggest volumes contribute to the lightness of feeling that resonated with the French post-war sensibility. His style is evident in the drawings that Lucien Vogel commissioned for a deluxe edition of composer Eric Satie's piano compositions, *Sports et Divertissements* (*Sports and Diversions*), which was published in 1923 (Plate 13).

Lucien Vogel's *Gazette du Bon Ton* ceased publication in 1925 after the American publisher Condé Nast acquired it and merged it with his own fashion magazine, *Vogue*. Condé Nast introduced a French edition of *Vogue* in 1920 and some of the *Gazette*'s illustrators began to draw for it. George Lepape had already been contributing to *Vogue*'s New York and London editions and he then continued to draw covers for the French version until 1939. His style gradually changed to reflect the more spare Cubist aesthetic of the 1920s and his subjects became the tall slim figures sporting short hair styles and chic garments that were created by a new breed of French designers, all women, including Coco Chanel, Jeanne Lanvin, and Madeleine Vionnet. Other illustrators who specialized in depicting the suave men and stylish women of the new smart set were Leon Benigni (1892–1948), Edouard Halouze (1900–d.o.d. unconfirmed), Guy Arnoux (1886–1951), and the Spaniard Edouard Garcia Benito (1891–1981).

After 1925, photography gradually began to replace fashion illustration, although fashion editors at *Vogue* and other magazines continued to use illustrators such as Erté (1892–1990), Christian Bérard (1902–1949), René Bouét-Willaumez (1900–1979), Drian (1885–1961), and René Bouché (1906–1963) to highlight the creations of famous couturiers. The leading fashion photographers included Man Ray (1890–1976), a former collaborator with Marcel Duchamp and the French Dadaists, Horst P. Horst (1906–1999), and George Hoyningen-Heune (1900–1968). The trend

towards photography could also be seen in advertising, particularly by the beginning of the 1930s. However, there were no polemical advocates to replace advertising illustration with photography as there were in Germany, where the use of photographs in all forms of commercial art became a fundamental tenet of the New Typography.

The illustrated magazines in Germany—the *Berliner Illustrirte Zeitung*, the *Münchner Illustrierte Zeitung*, and others—had become examples of new ways to view the world and they stimulated the creation of comparable publications elsewhere. In 1928, Lucien Vogel founded *Vu*, a weekly news magazine that relied almost exclusively on photographs and was the first magazine of its kind in France (Fig. 22.15).

By the late 1920s, a number of photographers had begun to do extended feature reportages for *Vu* as well as other magazines, along with creating formally sophisticated advertising spreads. René Zuber (1902–1979) was initially intrigued with the German photographer Albert Renger-Patzsch's sharply outlined pictures of objects lined up in series, but in the 1930s he formed a partnership with Pierre Boucher (1908–2000) and began to do more reportage. Boucher had a particular interest in the Constructivist photographs of Alexander Rodchenko and the "new vision" of Bauhaus instructor László Moholy-Nagy. He produced photographic covers for the graphic design magazine *Arts et Métiers Graphique* and also published in *Vu*.

Boucher put great store in photographic manipulation and took a particular interest in several experimental techniques; photomontage, solarization, and superimposing one image on another. He was much in demand for advertising photographs and he applied his experimental techniques to these as well as to his personal work. Like Boucher, François Kollar (1904–1979) specialized in commercial and industrial photography, counting among his clients manufacturers of luxury items like the glassware firm Christophle, the manufacturer of leather goods Hermès, and the perfume maker Coty. He did fashion photography

Fig. 22.15: He has Won!, *Vu*, cover, 1933. © Photos 12/Alamy.

mixture. He presented the single shoe as a mysterious object that provokes the imagination, while placing it on a grid of black and white squares that regulates the composition and communicates a sense of order.

Posters

By the early 1920s, traces of Jules Chéret's influence lingered on in a few posters by well-known fashion illustrators but these were relatively weak efforts and had little influence on the future of the medium in France. More significant were the lively posters of Leonetto Capiello that had graced Paris billboards since the beginning of the century. In particular, it was Capiello's ability to create a single figure in action to represent a product or event, while omitting the background details, that influenced the following generation of French poster designers. A few artists such as Jean d'Ylen (1886–1938) and Henri Le Monnier (1893–1978) simply continued in Capiello's style, but others, notably A. M. Cassandre (1901–1968), Jean Carlu (1900–1997), Paul Colin (1892–1985), and Charles Loupot (1892–1962) departed significantly from it. For the latter group, Cubism was a strong influence, particularly the creation of compositions with fragments of objects, as well as the emphasis on line to suggest something that would otherwise be depicted as a volume. The stripped down Purist compositions of Le Corbusier and Ozenfant were also important sources for these designers. They rejected Capiello's emphasis on the visual anecdote, preferring instead to communicate with more formal compositions and complex narratives.

Cassandre's groundbreaking poster of 1925 for the Parisian newspaper *L'Intransigeant* exemplifies this new direction (Fig. 22.16). To represent the speed with which the newspaper transmitted the news, he chose the head of a man with telegraph wires connected to his ear. The composition consists simply of the head, the telegraph poles, the wires, and enough of the paper's title to make it intelligible to the viewer.

Cassandre's poster was seminal in the creation of an entirely new poster language based on fragments of

for *Harper's Bazaar* as well as for specific couturiers—Schiaparelli and Chanel—and also counted illustrated magazines such as *Vu*, *Voilá*, and *Plaisir de France* among his clients. Other photographers who did advertising work, particularly for companies who advertised in the illustrated magazines like *Vu*, included Roger Parry (1905–1977); Florence Henri (1893–1982), a former student of Moholy-Nagy's at the Bauhaus; Maurice Tabard (1897–1984); and André Vigneau (1892–1968).

French advertising photography was characterized by a mixture of influences from the German New Objectivity, as well as Surrealism, which often added a strange or poetic element to the pictures. André Vigneau's advertisement for Perugia shoes suggests this

Fig. 22.16: A. M. Cassandre, *L'Intransigeant*, poster, 1925. © MOURON. CASSANDRE. Lic 2016-23-11-04 www. cassandre.fr.

images and texts. These were combined into statements that forced the viewer to fill in the missing elements just as Braque and Picasso had done with their earlier Cubist still lifes. This new language was liberating for the artist for several reasons. First, it made possible more direct statements by eliminating extraneous detail. Second, statements were also more economical since parts could represent whole objects or words. Third, rhetorical devices such as hyperbole or exaggeration could be employed to dramatize a statement as in Cassandre's poster where the telegraph line emphasizes the speed with which the *L'Intransigeant* gets the news out.

In other posters, Cassandre continued to focus on single objects or object parts in order to achieve dramatic effects. His poster for the French railroad, *Nord Express* (1927), features an angular depiction of a train in motion, while *Étoile du Nord* depicts

the dynamic curves and angles of the tracks, which converge at a vanishing point, signifying the speed of a train that has already disappeared beyond the horizon (Fig. 22.17). Though many of Cassandre's posters were lithographs, he was also a master of the airbrush and occasionally introduced photographic collage fragments as in his poster for the French railroad's bar car, which he represented with a photograph of a train wheel overpainted with airbrush images of a seltzer bottle, a loaf of bread, and a bottle of wine. Cassandre, unlike Chéret or Capiello, was a meticulous letterer and carefully integrated his hand-drawn letters into his compositions. For the most part, he preferred thick san serif letters, which do not add any extraneous decorative elements to his compositions.

Jean Carlu and the Swiss artist Charles Loupot also drew on Cubist technique, although neither

Fig. 22.17: A. M. Cassandre, *Étoile du Nord*, poster, 1927. © MOURON. CASSANDRE. Lic 2016-23-11-04 www.cassandre.fr.

produced posters that were as dynamic as Cassandre's. Carlu's poster for the Monaco Aquarium featured several interlocking fishes on a dark background, while his placard of 1929 for Odéon Disques (Odeon Records) consists of several circular forms. One is a record and the other is the O of Odéon that doubles as the record's label. In 1932, Carlu founded l'Office de Propagande Graphique pour la Paix (Office of Graphic Propaganda for Peace) to produce political posters. His 1932 poster, *Pour le Désarmament des Nations* (*For the Disarmament of Nations*), featured part of a photograph by André Vigneau that depicted the heads of an anguished mother and child screaming as a bomb drops on them.

Loupot is best remembered for the series of posters he did for St. Raphael, a producer of quinine water (Fig. 22.18). Beginning in 1937, he created posters that featured redesigned versions of the company's trademark, the little red and white waiters, one short and rotund and the other tall and thin. Loupot's figures exemplified the French preference for trademarks and logotypes that were anecdotal rather than abstract. This phenomenon was evident as well in the little mustached man that Cassandre created as a logo for Dubonnet Aperitifs.

While the posters of Cassandre, Carlu, and Loupot were geared primarily to commerce, Paul Colin depicted performers in the music halls and cabarets, just as Toulouse Lautrec had done at the end of the previous century. By 1925 the rage of the Parisian music halls was the black American dancer and singer Josephine Baker, whom Colin portrayed along with several accompanying musicians (Plate 14). The features of the black performers are unflattering, suggesting Colin's lack of familiarity with the physiognomy of black Americans and his equating them with the French tradition of depicting colonial Africans as caricatures. Besides his portrayals of Josephine Baker, Colin did many other posters for music hall performers including Lisa Duncan, Damia, and the clown Grock. Among the French singers, Mistinguett was one of the most popular and was depicted in many posters by Charles Gesmar (1900–1928), who also designed her sets and costumes.

Though Cassandre was primarily a poster artist, he also designed catalogs, brochures, and even typefaces. Jean Carlu was named director of publicity for the 1937 Paris Exposition Internationale and he supervised the creation of all the graphics for that event. Colin worked primarily as a poster artist and also opened a school, where several thousand aspiring poster designers were trained. These included many such as Bernard Villemot (1911–1989) and the Swiss Herbert Leupin (1916–1999), who were among the leading poster artists of the following generation. Cassandre also ran a much smaller school for several years in the 1930s, and several

Fig. 22.18: Charles Loupot, St. Raphael Quinquina, poster, 1937. © 2014. BI, ADAGP, Paris/Scala, Florence. © ADAGP, Paris and DACS, London 2017.

of his students such as Raymond Savignac (1907–2002) established successful careers as well.

Trademarks and logotypes

The Michelin man, whose body looks like a stack of tires, was one of the earliest French trademarks. A whimsical figure who embodies characteristics of the product, he became a precedent for character trademarks that also possessed a touch of humor. Among the artists who designed such marks in the 1920s and 1930s, many were trained as decorative artists and simply adapted their drawing skills to this new enterprise. As opposed to the poster designers, most worked anonymously. The French had no theorists of trademark and logo design like the German Wilhelm Deffke, who specialized in this art and assiduously studied its history. Thus, French marks derived more from vernacular culture than from the graphic manipulation of letters or abstract shapes.

Some of the best-known marks were humans or animals, which became closely associated with a product over time. Since 1921, a laughing cow with earrings made of small cheeses has been the trademark of the cheese company known by the same name, La vache qui rit. The mark was created by Benjamin Rabier (1864–1939), a prolific illustrator who combined a successful career as an advertising artist with that of a children's book illustrator and caricaturist (Fig. 22.19). Among Rabier's many other trademarks, the lively whale that advertises *La Baleine* salt is perhaps the best known.

French trademarks depicted a variety of figures from stylish models wearing bathing suits or stockings to bearded Arabs promoting Arabian coffee. As in most Western countries during the 1920s and 1930s, the French seemed indifferent to the frequently derogatory depictions of non-whites, especially black natives who served as trademarks for many products imported from the colonies. The preponderance of human and animal trademarks, rather than abstract marks, might be seen

Fig. 22.19: Benjamin Rabier, La vache qui rit, poster with trademark, c. 1921. © Hemis/Alamy.

as a consequence of France's strong poster tradition, which had long associated distinctive figures by Chéret, Cappiello, and other designers with particular products.

Graphic design and typography

In 1923, two major type firms merged to form Deberny and Peignot, which became France's leading typefoundry during the 1920s and 1930s. Earlier, in the 1890s, the Peignot foundry, then headed by Georges Peignot (1872–1915), produced the best-known Art Nouveau types including Grasset and Auriol. Charles Peignot

(1897–1983), Georges' son, who headed the new foundry after the merger, continued the tradition of commissioning typefaces from prominent artists and designers. Peignot felt strongly that his foundry should create modern types rather than rely on designs from the past. After completing work on several typefaces that his father had initiated, he introduced his own experimental typeface, Sphinx, which had the characteristics of a 19th-century roman Fat Face, although Peignot added a few curlicues to give it a decorative quality.

The turning point for him was his visit to the 1925 Exposition des Arts Décoratifs, where he could see the new *style moderne* exemplified in furniture, interior designs, and architecture. Several years later, he began to collaborate with A. M. Cassandre, whose first poster, *Au Boucheron*, done for a furniture company, won a prize at the exposition. Cassandre designed Deberny and Peignot's most radical typeface, Bifur, which eventually became a leading Art Deco face after its release in 1929 (Plate 15). Though it was not widely adopted when it first appeared, the geometric shapes of its letters and its combination of thick and thin lines aligned it with the Cubist-derived aesthetic that characterized the arts in France, whether fashion, furniture design, or silver, during the later 1920s and 1930s. Bifur was used primarily for advertising where it contributed to the feeling of modernity that the ad or brochure was intended to display. Cassandre envisioned it as a practical typeface whose function, he said, was as clear-cut as a railway signal.

In 1930, Charles Peignot joined the Union des Artistes Modernes where he continued a working relationship with Cassandre who was also a member. That year, Cassandre designed a second typeface for Deberney and Peignot, Acier (Steel), an alphabet of thick san serif upper-case letters that were colored in combinations of black, white, and gray. Around 1933 or 1934, Cassandre began working on a third typeface for the foundry, which was named Peignot when it was released in 1937. He conceived it as a book face as well as a type for display purposes. Similar to the half-uncials of early alphabets, many of the letters were the same in upper and lower case, which gave texts set in Peignot an imposing quality that was complemented by the elegance of the thick and thin strokes of the letters as well as the exceptional lengths of the strokes that extended above and below the type line. Chosen as the official typeface of the 1937 Paris Exposition Internationale, Peignot was launched with great fanfare and came to define a particularly French typographic elegance associated with the 1930s.

Though Charles Peignot was immediately successful with Peignot and eventually did well with Bifur, his choice of other typefaces was uneven. Banjo, a face the firm brought out in 1932, consisted of thin capital letters that made it suitable for fashion advertising, but its extreme contrasts of extended and condensed letters disrupted the balance that would have given the face a delicate and unobtrusive quality. Éclair, which Deberny and Peignot released several years later, was a novelty face, introducing serrated lines to an otherwise nondescript roman face. More successful was the 1934 typeface Film, comprised of three-dimensional letters by the graphic designer Marcel Jacno (1904–1989). Peignot had no modern san serif face to compare with Paul Renner's Futura or Monotype's Gill Sans so he bought the French rights to Futura and marketed it in France under the name Europa. Besides Deberny and Peignot, other foundries produced advertising typefaces in the Deco style and promoted them internationally with expensive catalogs and specimen sheets.

But Charles Peignot was more than a type founder. Through various activities, he helped to create a culture of modern typography and graphic design in France. In 1927, he launched a new design magazine, *Arts et Métiers Graphique*, which he continued to publish until 1939. Though probably influenced by its German predecessor, *Gebrauchsgraphik, Arts et Métiers Graphique* took a broader cultural approach to typography and design, focusing less on the portfolios of contemporary graphic designers and more on articles related to printing history, reviews of limited-edition books, and issues related to type, although Peignot also published features on successful artists and graphic designers. As well, the journal editors devoted special issues to photography and advertising, which provided overviews of contemporary trends in those fields. The overall editorial thrust of the magazine came from Peignot's desire to relate typography and layout more closely to the fine arts. The magazine's typefaces were all from the Deberny and Peignot catalog and became familiar to readers through their use in the innovative layouts.

Peignot also collaborated with the typographer, art director, and critic Maximilian Vox (1894–1974), who produced a stunning series of specimen books for the foundry's types under the title *Les Divertissements Typographiques* (*Typographic Divertisements*). Intended as an inspiration for printers, each one sought to capture the spirit of a typeface, relying not only on novel forms of visual presentation but also literary texts by established authors such as Jean Cocteau. As a further means to broaden the appeal of his typefaces, Peignot established a graphic design studio whose designers used them in commissions for advertising and other forms of publicity.

In 1931, Alexander Tolmer, a French printer and design critic, published an important book entitled *Mis en Page: The Theory and Practice of Layout*. Although it appeared in English with a French summary, the book's ideas were fully in accord with Charles Peignot's desire to position modern typography and layout as part of a larger artistic culture whose roots extended far back in time. The design was lavish, combining photographs and art with expensive papers and printing techniques to demonstrate Tolmer's ideas about modern layout, which, he believed, could be enriched by knowledge of art from the past. Although Tolmer argued firmly for a modern style, his approach could not have been more different from Jan Tschichold and the German proponents of the New Typography, who posited a clean break with the past in order to create a thoroughly modern approach to graphic communication. As a German critic wrote of Tolmer's book in *Gebrauchsgraphik*, "Some of his lay-outs are so playful or so crazy that they do not appeal to the German taste."

However, it was playfulness and a relation to modern art that characterized the best French graphic design in the 1920s and 1930s. Among its leading practitioners were two émigrés, Dr. Mehemed Fehmy Agha (1896–1978), a Turk born in the Ukraine, and Alexey Brodovitch (1898–1971), a Russian refugee from the Bolshevik Revolution. Agha, a talented cartoonist and illustrator who briefly attended art school in Kiev, came to Paris to study Oriental languages, but after receiving his diploma, he ended up working for the Dorland Agency, a large international advertising firm. There he helped to modernize the advertising section of *Vogue*'s French edition by combining the elegant style of France's fashion illustrators with the new decorative modernity of French typography. His work impressed Condé Nast, the publisher of *Vogue*, who hired him in 1928 to move to Berlin as art director of *Vogue*'s German edition, following which he went to work for Condé Nast in New York.

After winning a poster contest for an artist's ball in 1924, Alexey Brodovitch earned five medals for the design of textiles, silver, china, and jewelry at the 1925 Exposition des Arts Décoratifs. With this recognition, he received numerous commissions, including posters for the French department stores Le Printemps and Bon Marché, and an opportunity to create decorative wall panels for a seafood restaurant, Prunier. In 1928, Brodovitch was hired by the Parisian department store Aux Trois Quartiers to work in its new design studio, which was named Athélia. The work of the studio ranged from interior design and exhibitions to publicity and advertising. Brodovitch's projects included the design and illustration of catalogs and advertisements for the store's luxury men's boutique, Madélios, and the decoration of the main store's temporary facade, which was widely publicized in European design magazines.

Like Cassandre, whose posters he admired,

Brodovitch was influenced by Cubism and the Purist paintings of Le Corbusier and Ozenfant. As well, he was taken with Surrealism whose emphasis on ambiguous subject matter would play a large role in the work he did later in his career. His cover for the Madélios catalog of 1928 brought together the Cubist use of fragments, in this case the classical facade of the Church of the Madeleine near where the Madélios store was located, with expressive tree branches in the background, and a geometric division of the surface that approximates the Golden Section. To create an overall visual structure, Brodovitch integrated the lines of the letters with other lines in the composition that frame the church as well as additional text. Like Cassandre, he used an airbrush to create subtle transitions of tone, which infused a dreamy quality into an otherwise geometric design. The combination of geometry with a more vague sense of mood was characteristic of Brodovitch's work for Aux Trois Quartiers and exemplifies a particularly French approach to advertising and graphic design during the interwar years.

Bibliography
Bibliographic essay

General histories of modern design with material about France in this period are numerous. They include *History of Industrial Design, 1919–1990: The Domain of Design*; Wendy Kaplan, ed., *Designing Modernity: The Arts of Reform and Persuasion, 1885–1945*; Paul Greenhalgh, ed., *Modernism in Design*; Giulia Veronesi, *Style and Design, 1919–1929*; Klaus-Jürgen Sembach, Gabriele Leuthäuser, and Peter Gössel, *Twentieth-Century Furniture Design*; and the conference proceedings edited by Victor Margolin, Anty Pansera, and Frederick Wildhagen, *Tradizione e Modernismo: Design 1918–1940/Tradition and Modernism: Design between the Wars*. There are also books that specialize in decorative art of the period and Art Deco. Among them are two by Martin Battersby, *The Decorative Twenties* and *The Decorative Thirties*; Yvonne Brunhammer, *The Nineteen Twenties*

Style; and the books edited by Charlotte and Peter Fiell, which consist mainly of pictures; *20s Decorative Art* and *30s/40s Decorative Art*. Books that treat Art Deco exclusively are Alain Lesieutre, *The Spirit and Splendour of Art Deco*; and Jean-Paul Bouillon, *Art Deco, 1893–1940*. Nancy Troy, *Modernism and the Decorative Arts in France: Art Nouveau to Le Corbusier* is an excellent scholarly study of how decorative art and design developed in France from the end of the 19th century to the 1930s. *French Decorative Art: The Societé des Artistes Decorateurs, 1900–1942* by Yvonne Brunhammer and Suzanne Tice recounts the history of the Society of Artist Decorators. Paul Overy, *De Stijl* includes material on van Doesburg's activity in Paris, while Carol S. Eliel, *L'Esprit Nouveau: Purism in Paris, 1918–1925* with essays by Françoise Ducros and Tag Gronberg concentrates on the development of Purism. Michel Sanouillet, *Dada in Paris* is the major source on that subject. Monographs on individual designers include Emmanuel Bréon and Rosalind Pepall, eds., *Ruhlmann: Genius of Art Deco*; Renato De Fusco, *Le Corbusier, Designer: Furniture, 1929*; Peter Adam, *Eileen Gray: Architect/Designer*; and Marietta Andres, Rosamund Diamond, and Brooke Hodge, eds., *Eileen Gray: An Architect for All Senses*. Two seminal books by Le Corbusier have been reprinted as *Towards a New Architecture* and *The Decorative Art of Today*. Books on the important Paris exhibitions of the 1920s and 1930s are Frank Scarlett and Marjorie Townley, *Arts Décoratifs 1925: A Personal Recollection of the Paris Exhibition* and *Paris 1937: Cinquantenaire de l'Exposition Internationale des Arts et des Techniques dans la Vie Moderne*.

General books on Art Deco graphics include Steven Heller and Louise Fili, *Deco Type: Stylish Alphabets of the '20s and '30s* and *Euro Deco*; Jean Delhaye, *Art Deco Posters and Graphics*; and Julian Robinson, *The Golden Age of Style: Art Deco Fashion Illustration*. John Mendenhall's *French Trademarks: The Art Deco Era* provides images of many French trademarks along with a brief text. Monographs on French graphic designers include Henri Mouron, *A.M.*

Cassandre; Robert K. Brown and Susan Reinhold, *The Poster Art of A.M. Cassandre*; Alain Weill and Jack Rennert, *Paul Colin: Affichiste*; and Andy Grundberg, *Brodovitch*.

Books

Adam, Peter. *Eileen Gray: Architect/Designer*. New York: Harry N. Abrams, 1987.

Andres, Marietta, Rosamund Diamond, and Brooke Hodge, eds. *Eileen Gray: An Architect for All Senses*. Tübingen and Berlin: Wasmuth, 1996.

Battersby, Martin. *The Decorative Twenties*. London: Studio Vista, 1969.

—*The Decorative Thirties*. London: Studio Vista, 1971.

Bouillon, Jean-Paul. *Art Deco, 1893–1940*. New York: Rizzoli, 1989.

Bréon, Emmanuel and Rosalind Pepall, eds. *Ruhlmann: Genius of Art Deco*. Paris: Somogy Éditions d'Art, 2004.

Brown, Robert K. and Susan Reinhold. *The Poster Art of A.M. Cassandre*. New York: E. P. Dutton, 1979.

Brunhammer, Yvonne. *The Nineteen Twenties Style*. London and New York: Paul Hamlyn, 1969.

Brunhammer, Yvonne and Suzanne Tice. *French Decorative Art: The Societé des Artistes Decorateurs, 1900–1942*. Paris: Flammarion, 1990.

DeFusco, Renato. *Le Corbusier, Designer: Furniture, 1929*. Woodbury, NY: Barron's, 1977.

Delhaye, Jean. *Art Deco Posters and Graphics*. New York: Rizzoli, 1977.

Eliel, Carol S. *L'Esprit Nouveau: Purism in Paris, 1918–1925*. With essays by Françoise Ducros and Tag Gronberg. New York: Harry N. Abrams, 2001.

Fiell, Charlotte and Peter, eds. *20s Decorative Art*. Cologne: Taschen, 2000.

—eds. *30s/40s Decorative Art*. Cologne: Taschen, 2000.

Greenhalgh, Paul, ed. *Modernism in Design*. London: Reaktion Books, 1990.

Grundberg, Andy. *Brodovitch*. New York: Harry N. Abrams, 1989.

Heller, Steven and Louise Fili. *Deco Type: Stylish*

Alphabets of the '20s and '30s. San Francisco: Chronicle Books, 1997.

—*Euro Deco.* San Francisco: Chronicle Books, 2005.

History of Industrial Design, 1919–1990: The Domain of Design. Milan: Electa, 1991.

Kaplan, Wendy, ed. *Designing Modernity: The Arts of Reform and Persuasion, 1885–1945.* London and New York: Thames and Hudson, 1995.

Le Corbusier. *Towards a New Architecture.* Translated from the French by Frederick Etchells. New York and Washington: Praeger, 1970 (c. 1927).

—*The Decorative Art of Today.* Translated and introduced by James I. Dunnett. London: The Architectural Press, 1987.

Lesieutre, Alain. *The Spirit and Splendour of Art Deco.* Secaucus, NJ: Castle Books, 1978.

Lichtheim, George. *Europe in the Twentieth Century.* New York and Washington: Praeger, 1972.

Margolin, Victor, Anty Pansera, and Frederick Wildhagen, eds. *Tradizione e Modernismo: Design 1918–1940/Tradition and Modernism: Design between the Wars.* Milan: l'Arca Edizioni, 1988.

Mendenhall, John. *French Trademarks: The Art Deco Era.* San Francisco: Chronicle Books, 1991.

Mouron, Henri. *A.M. Cassandre.* New York: Rizzoli, 1985.

Overy, Paul. *De Stijl.* London: Thames and Hudson, 1991.

Paris 1937: Cinquantenaire de l'Exposition Internationale des Arts et des Techniques dans la Vie Moderne. Paris: Institut Français d'Architecture/Paris-Musées, 1987. Exhibition catalog.

Robinson, Julian. *The Golden Age of Style: Art Deco Fashion Illustration.* London: Orbin Publishing, 1976.

Sanouillet, Michel. *Dada in Paris.* Revised and expanded by Anne Sanouillet. Translated by Sharmila Ganguly. Cambridge, MA: MIT Press, 2009.

Scarlett, Frank and Marjorie Townley. *Arts Décoratifs 1925: A Personal Recollection of the Paris Exhibition.* London: Academy Editions and New York: St. Martin's Press, 1975.

Sembach, Klaus-Jürgen, Gabriele Leuthäuser, and Peter Gössel. *Twentieth-Century Furniture Design.* Cologne: Taschen, 2002.

Sontag, Raymond. *A Broken World, 1919–1939.* New York: Harper & Row, 1971.

Sparke, Penny. *A Century of Car Design.* Hauppauge, NY: Barron's, 2002.

Troy, Nancy. *Modernism and the Decorative Arts in France: Art Nouveau to Le Corbusier.* New Haven and London: Yale University Press, 1991.

Veronesi, Giulia. *Style and Design, 1919–1929.* New York: George Braziller, 1968.

Weill, Alain, *The Poster.* Boston: G. J. K. Hall, 1985.

Weill, Alain and Jack Rennert. *Paul Colin: Affichiste.* Paris: Denoël, 1989.

Chapter 23: Great Britain 1918–1939

Introduction

The British populace was ambivalent about the machine culture that some on the continent and in America espoused. They were equally skeptical of France's emphasis on luxury goods, which the French produced in their own version of a modern style. Politically, Britain was less inclined to build relations with other European nations than to strengthen the ties within its own empire. Manufacturers could foster a notion of Englishness because they perceived it to be a marketable value, not only at home but among the nation's colonies, protectorates, and commonwealth partners as well.

Englishness as a design idea took two forms. First was a reliance on icons of the English past, particularly period styles in furniture and architecture. Much of the period furniture was produced cheaply with poor materials and questionable workmanship. A popular style in the 1920s was mock Tudor, although furnishings in the Georgian and Queen Anne styles were also sought after. Tudor was adopted for domestic architecture as well as for teashops that conveyed an atmosphere of "Ye Olde England." The most blatant example of mock-Tudor architecture was the new building for Liberty's, the department store that popularized decorative objects connected to the Aesthetic and Arts and Crafts movements.

The second notion of Englishness, which proved more fruitful as a source of new designs, was the Design and Industry Association's adoption of Arts and Crafts values. These they epitomized in the phrase "Fitness

for purpose." Since it's founding in 1915, the DIA had sought to apply traditional values of craftsmanship and truth to materials to modern design practice. The organization opposed the cheap reproductions of period design, espousing instead quality workmanship and simpler forms. The DIA respected traditional values of design but not historic styles. The result was a brand of modernism that defended the adaptation of craft techniques to serial production but stopped short of turning production over to a machine. Active and influential in the 1920s and early 1930s, the DIA was involved in many efforts to promote good design. These ranged from publications and exhibitions to support for government committees. DIA influence started to wane in the 1930s, however, as interest in machine-made goods began to spread. Though not always explicit, DIA values predominated among British design reformers, whether they were in government or the private sector.

In 1920, the Federation of British Industries formed an Industrial Art Committee with a vague mandate to consider the question of industrial design, while the government supported the establishment of the British Institute of Industrial Art (BIIA) the same year. The BIIA's mandate was twofold: to raise the standards of British industrial design and to simultaneously elevate the level of public taste. To that end, it opened an exhibition gallery in London, where it displayed examples of well-designed products, although it tended to support a handicraft-inspired aesthetic as promoted by the DIA. That same year the DIA organized its own Exhibition of Household Things and issued a report that discussed the necessary equipment for a labor-saving home. Here the organization was trying to serve as a broker between consumers and manufacturers, arguing for standardized products that could be sold at lower prices. Neither the exhibitions of the British Institute of Industrial Art nor the activities of the Design and Industry Association significantly improved consumer taste or induced manufacturers to hire designers. The British public was much more inclined towards traditional styles and production methods as well as low prices.

The British Empire Exhibition and the Empire Marketing Board

Britain's first major post-war exhibition, which opened at Wembley in north London in 1924 and closed the next year, celebrated the commercial activity and ambition of its empire. Its intent was to make the public aware of what was being produced in the colonies and dominions, thereby encouraging an expansion of trade within the empire itself. Three main areas were dedicated respectively to the exhibits of the various British ministries, including the Department of Overseas Trade; the industrial and agricultural products of the empire, which were displayed in an array of exotic pavilions; and lastly the fruits of British industry, engineering, and art. Frank Pick (1878–1941), then serving as publicity officer for the London Underground, consulted on the graphics. J. C. Herrick (dates unconfirmed) drew the crest for the exhibition, a proud lion that represented the empire. Two artists who created posters were R. T. Cooper (dates unconfirmed) and Gerald Spencer Pryse (1880–1956), the latter an artist who had also designed posters for the British government during World War I and had worked for the London Underground as well. For the exhibition poster series entitled "Scenes of Empire," Pryse completed a group of paintings that were combined with text to show industrious natives engaged in productive activity. Their intention, like the larger aim of the exhibition, was to promote opportunities for economic exchange within the empire (Plate 16).

Goods from the colonies were presented in two forms: as raw materials that British manufacturers could purchase and as handicrafts that could be sold abroad or that might inspire designs in the more developed parts of the empire. Design historian Jonathan Woodham has examined the particular case of Britain's West African colonies—Nigeria, the Gold Coast, and Sierra Leone—which exhibited a great variety of craft items at Wembley. The colonies also organized workshops manned by African craftsmen and women—known as "industrial natives"—who demonstrated techniques for producing a variety of arts and crafts.

What may have distinguished these workshops from more exotic displays of native life at past exhibitions was the Wembley exhibition's emphasis on economic development and trade. This would have given the workshops a meaning as sites of production rather than as showcases of native customs. In the Nigerian pavilion, one could see furniture for a bank office, a dining room, and a bedroom, all designed by a London firm, Messrs. Howard & Sons, and made of African woods—mahogany, teak, opepe, and walnut.

The Empire Exhibition, though widely attended, exposed a large gap in the British public's knowledge about the colonies. It was important to remedy this so that consumers would purchase more colonial goods and thereby help foster colonial trade. To this end, the Dominions Office established the Empire Marketing Board (EMB), which existed between 1926 and 1933. The EMB's campaign to promote the consumption of food, raw materials, and manufactured goods from the colonies made use of diverse media—newspaper advertisements, shop window display materials, radio broadcasts, exhibitions, films, lectures, and large numbers of posters that were designed for special outdoor display frames or hoardings. The overall media campaign was directed by EMB Secretary Stephen Tallents (1884–1958), who some consider to be the founder of public relations in Great Britain. Besides supervising the extensive poster campaign that resulted in more than 600 posters, which were displayed on 2,000 hoardings throughout Britain, Tallents founded the EMB Film Unit, headed by John Grierson, which created a new type of documentary film to promote civic aims.

Consultants to the EMB included Sir William Crawford (1840–1922), founder of one of Britain's leading advertising agencies, who chaired the Publicity

Committee, and Frank Pick, head of the Poster Sub-Committee. The poster campaign of the EMB had the hallmarks of the earlier campaign that Pick had initiated for the London Underground as well as the poster series he consulted on for the British Empire Exhibition. As large images on the hoardings in more than 500 British towns and cities, the EMB posters were widely seen. In a reduced format, they were also distributed to schools in Britain and overseas.

The figurative style of the posters was less expressive than many of the Underground placards. For the most part, the EMB poster artists were traditional painters and illustrators though some did adopt the flat color patterns of the Beggarstaff Brothers. The artists included Gerald Spencer Pryse, Fred Taylor (1875–1963), Frank Newbould (1887–1951), Charles Pears (1873–1958), E. Barnard Lintott (1875–1951), Kenneth D. Shoesmith (1890–1939), Adrian Allinson (1890–1959), Edgar Ainsworth (1906–1975), F. C. Herrick (1887–1970), who also designed the official typeface for the exhibition, and MacDonald Gill (1884–1957), already well known for his designs of early London Underground maps. The only one among the artists with a modernist bent was E. McKnight Kauffer (1890–1954), who muted his style to conform to EMB policy. The images of the colonies that the public received from these posters reinforced the managerial role of the British administrators who oversaw a workforce of natives that was efficiently mining or harvesting colonial resources.

The underlying strategy of many EMB posters was the representation of "complementary economies," which showed colonials preparing raw materials for export, thus illustrating the policy whereby the colonies and dominions sent raw material to Britain in exchange for finished goods. The British had been pursuing this policy since they began exporting textiles to India in the 19th century. A side effect of the EMB poster campaign was the reinforcement of racial and ethnic stereotypes—slightly dressed female rice growers in India, female tea-pickers in Ceylon, and black cotton pickers in Uganda, Tanganyika, Rhodesia, and Nyasaland.

The State of Domestic Design

In the concluding section of *An Enquiry into Industrial Art in England*, a study that was published in 1937, Nikolaus Pevsner (1902–1983) summed up his two years of research into the state of British design and manufacturing with the dramatic declaration that "90% of English industrial products are artistically objectionable." This statement must be tempered somewhat by the fact that Pevsner, a German art historian who emigrated to Britain in 1934, had a very high standard for good design, one that privileged the purist modernism associated with the architects and designers of the German Modern Movement. Nonetheless, the extremity of Pevsner's dissatisfaction is due in part to the slowness of British industrialists to recognize the value of design and designers, despite the fact that Britain in the 19th century had pioneered the idea of good design through the work of Christopher Dresser, Bruce Talbert, and of course William Morris. Pevsner found that design in most British firms happened casually, based on suggestions from salesmen, managers, shop assistants or others without formal design training. He cited as well low salaries for designers, a prevalence of jobs in provincial towns that lacked artistic sophistication, and the interference of sales departments. Though Pevsner concentrated on the British Midlands, there is little evidence that his findings were not equally true for Britain as a whole.

Various attempts were made to counter the conditions that Pevsner described. Each attempt in its own way contributed to a greater awareness of design and how it could enhance the quality of manufactured goods. In 1930, eight designers founded the Society of Industrial Artists (SIA). Their aim was to combat the indifference of manufacturers by promoting the idea of design as an established profession. A founding member and long-time activist in the SIA was Milner Gray (1899–1997), who also co-founded what may have been the first multi-purpose design office in Britain, Bassett-Gray. Established in 1921, the office initially concentrated on book jackets, illustration, and advertising but then expanded into packaging, and china for the pottery industry. In 1935, Bassett-Gray was reformed under the name Industrial Design Partnership, and Misha Black (1910–1977), an industrial designer, joined the firm as a partner around that time.

In the early promotional literature for the new firm, Gray emphasized research as a service that designers could provide. For him this meant finding out what the customer wanted and he developed pioneering techniques for addressing this question. Although the firm undertook many types of projects, illustration and decoration remained important services. Gray's designs for E. Brain & Co.'s Mayfair tea service consisted of drawings of traditional British figures and scenes that were applied to plates, bowls, and other pieces of the service. The firm was also well-known in the 1930s for its packaging such as that for Bryanston Biscuits, which included a tasteful logo and typography that varied in size and color on different packages. In addition, the studio produced designs for fabrics and carpets, as well as for selected industrial products such as radio cabinets and room heaters. They also designed commercial interiors and exhibitions. The Industrial Design Partnership was extremely important as a new type of design studio in Britain, perhaps the only one that paralleled the multi-service offices of the American consultant designers that were being established in New York around the same time.

Like Milner Gray, the Design and Industries Association also opposed the British manufacturer's indifference to design. The DIA promoted good design through occasional exhibitions and publications including several short-lived design magazines, but its influence was most effective through the activities of its individual members. Among the most successful was Gordon Russell (1892–1980), who began to design furniture around 1923 and founded Gordon Russell Ltd in 1929. His initial inspiration was a rustic Arts and Crafts style that he admired in the work of the Cotswold designer Ernst Gimson (1864–1919), but

gradually he began to simplify his pieces so they could serve as prototypes for limited machine production (Fig. 23.01).

By the early 1930s, Russell's firm was turning out modern cabinets, bookshelves, and other domestic furniture with clean lines and surfaces. This work served as an antidote to the plethora of poorly manufactured furniture in period styles that dominated the British market. Like William Morris's firm, Gordon Russell Ltd combined the serial production of furniture with contract work for clients who wanted custom designs. Whereas Morris and his associates often designed rooms whose decor harkened back to earlier times, Gordon Russell was associated with a modern look preferred by a small circle of architects and interior designers.

The most widely-disseminated designs of Gordon Russell Ltd were the wooden radio cabinets that R. D. Russell (1903–1981), Gordon's brother, designed for Murphy Radio Ltd beginning in 1930. Similar to the simple unornamented furniture the firm was producing, the radio cabinets for the most part had plain surfaces with geometric shapes cut in them for the speakers. They came in a variety of forms from table models to full consoles (Fig. 23.02).

The DIA member who had the greatest influence on British design in the interwar years was Frank Pick. His early career with the London Underground

Fig. 23.01: Gordon Russell, bookcase, 1930s. Private Collection/Photo © The Fine Art Society, London, UK/Bridgeman Images.

Fig. 23.02: R. D. Russell, Murphy Radio cabinet, c. 1930. © mark follon/Alamy.

shows how he used metaphor rather than conventional narrative to make his point. He depicted a rippling forearm and huge fist extending out of a whirling disk and grasping bolts of lightning. The artist reinforced the idea of power by adding a stylized depiction of a factory and lettering that supported the circular motion of the disk (Fig. 23.03).

Pick also hired other artists from abroad including the French *moderne* painter Jean Dupas, the Hungarian artist László Moholy-Nagy (1895–1946), the German designer Hans Schleger (1898–1976), and the American photographer Man Ray, who produced the Underground's most experimental poster, a photograph of the planet Saturn whirling in orbit together with a three-dimensional model of the Underground logo (Fig. 23.04).

began in 1909 (see Chapter 17). During the 1920s, Pick continued as publicity officer for the Underground and then became the Managing Director of the London Passenger Transport Board, which was established in 1933 to combine all of London's transport companies—railways, tramways, and bus companies. As a patron of poster artists, Pick continued to maintain a high standard for the London Underground posters. His principal strategy was to continue with the imagery of destinations such as the zoo, theaters, parks, concert halls, the surrounding countryside, and special events such as the Olympia Motor Show and the British Industries Fair. These scenes were depicted primarily by artists and illustrators, including C. R. W. Nevinson (1889–1946), Charles Pears (1873–1958), Dorothy Burroughes (c. 1895–1963), Rex Whistler (1905–1944), Dorothy Paton (dates unconfirmed), Horace Taylor (1881–1934), and Margaret Calkin James (1895–1985). As early as 1921, Pick had begun to feature posters by the American modernist graphic designer E. McKnight Kauffer and he continued to do so while Kauffer lived in London during the interwar years. Kauffer's poster of 1931, *Power, the nerve center of London's Underground,*

Fig. 23.03: E. McKnight Kauffer, London Underground poster, 1930. Getty Images.

Fig. 23.04: Man Ray, London Underground poster, 1939. © 2014. Christie's Images, London/Scala, Florence. © Man Ray Trust/ADAGP, Paris and DACS, London 2017.

Besides his patronage of poster artists, Pick's awareness of every component of design, no matter how small, distinguished him as a man with an extremely broad vision of how design could improve society. During the 1920s and 1930s the Underground underwent a massive expansion. As part of this process, many new stations were built while a large number of others were modernized. To develop many of these stations, Pick hired the architect Charles Holden (1875–1960), who produced a series of bold modern designs that contrasted sharply with the contemporary revival of an 18th-century style for public buildings. Pick and Holden admired and visited the modern architecture that was being built in northern Europe, embracing the geometric styles and exposed brickwork

they found on the continent. Sudbury Town station, which opened in 1931, exemplified the new style with its clean brick facade and interspersed glass sections. To complement each building design, Pick decreed that all the other elements that were part of the station—the ticket kiosks, the street furniture, the clocks, the waste baskets, and the placement of all signage—should be specially designed or considered. He continued this policy with all future construction, establishing an unprecedented attention to design detail in a public transport system.

Pick was equally concerned with the design of the Underground passenger cars. In 1924, he replaced the antiquated rolling stock with new modern cars that featured many elements to abet passenger comfort—more cross seats, arm rests, new light fittings with glass shades, and special features to reduce noise. A significant feature of the early cars was their new sliding double doors, which facilitated the entrance to and exit from the cars. In the 1930s, after the formation of the London Passenger Transport Board, Pick determined to maintain the same high design standards that he had established for the London Underground. As one example, he commissioned bold upholstery fabrics for the new system's trains and buses from leading textile designers such as Marion Dorn (1896–1964), Enid Marx (1902–1998), Paul Nash (1889–1946), and Marianne Straub (1909–1992).

A landmark achievement of the Underground administration was the design of a new map by Henry Beck (1903–1974). By the early 1930s, the existing map was a tangle of lines and stations that was impossible to read. In 1931, when Beck began work on his version of the map, he was employed by the Underground as an engineering draftsman. His design had two important innovations: he ignored the real geographic distances between stations, making the spaces between them more similar so their relations could be easily visualized; he also substituted a system of horizontals, verticals, and diagonals to indicate the route lines rather than charting their actual meandering courses

(Plate 17). After the map was successfully introduced to the public in 1933, Beck continued to suggest changes for subsequent versions. Some were accepted, while others made changes to the map as well. In 1938, Beck produced a comprehensive diagram of the entire London Transport system but it was never published because the Transport Board believed that it contained too much information.

Frank Pick's credo that art was an essential component of civilized life paralleled the earlier beliefs of William Morris, whose influence on Pick was confirmed by the extensive extracts from Morris's writings that he copied in his diary. Similarly, Pick's abiding concern with the quality of passenger amenities and services in London's transport system not only exemplified the DIA's principles in the best sense but also established a precedent for the design of public services that has hardly been matched since.

The Beginnings of British Modernism

Unlike Germany or Scandinavia, modern design in Britain did not become a pervasive force. On the continent, socialist or progressive governments saw in modernism an exemplification of democratic social values. By contrast, this democratic modernist approach was to be distinguished from the more elite modernism that one could see at the Paris 1925 Exposition des Arts Décoratifs. Though both modernisms were marginally adopted in Britain, tradition remained a more powerful presence in the national consciousness.

Just over a year after the Paris exhibition, Ambrose Heal (1872–1959), whose furniture company, Heal & Sons, had early on specialized in sturdy yeoman furnishings derived from Arts and Crafts ideals, introduced a range of modern furniture in Macassar ebony for middle-class consumers. It was influenced by the luxury style of Jacques Émile Ruhlmann but the difference was that J. F. Johnson (dates unconfirmed), head of Heal's cabinet department, transformed the subtle elegance of Ruhlmann's designs into heavier pieces that were more in keeping with British taste.

More faithful interpretations of French *moderne* were introduced to Britain in 1928 by Waring & Gillow, a London furniture manufacturer that specialized in expensive furnishings for ships, hotels, embassies, and private individuals. That year, Serge Chermayeff (1900–1996), a Russian who came to England as a boy and worked previously for a British decorating firm, joined the company as head of its newly established Modern Art Studio. Together with Paul Follot (1877–1941), the French decorator who ran Waring & Gillow's Paris branch while also heading the furniture and decorative arts workshop at the Bon Marché department store, Chermayeff organized a huge Exhibition of Modern Design in 1928 at Waring & Gillow's London showrooms. Consisting of 68 rooms, the exhibition gave the British public a broad introduction to the French modern style. Among the displays was a ten-room suite of French furniture that Follot coordinated and another ten rooms with furnishings designed in Waring & Gillow's Modern Art Studio under Chermayeff. Unlike previous exhibitions of the Arts and Crafts Society, the Waring & Gillow display made no attempt to please a populist audience, featuring instead furnishings that emulated the luxurious styles of the Paris ateliers.

Of greater importance to the development of modern furniture in Britain were two other sources: the spare aesthetic of Scandinavia's furniture designers, particularly as it became known in Britain after the modernist Stockholm Exhibition of 1930; and the tubular steel furniture that was introduced to the German public at the Weissenhof Exhibition of 1927 in Stuttgart. Chermayeff, who left Waring & Gillow after a year to start his own architectural firm, was the first designer in Britain to create tubular steel furniture for domestic use.

Originally, the British public believed steel furniture to be appropriate only for hospitals or offices. A leading periodical of furniture design referred to it in 1929 as "too austere for the British public" and derided it in 1930 as "that gas pipe stuff." The same year, Chermayeff and Paul Follot designed a tubular steel chair and table that Waring & Gillow manufactured, although this furniture was directed to an upscale clientele rather than the broader market at which Thonet had aimed its own tubular steel pieces in Germany and elsewhere on the continent. However, tubular steel furniture gained a wider appeal in Britain when Thonet opened a London showroom in 1929. Shortly thereafter architect Robert Cromie (dates unconfirmed), known for his Art Deco cinema designs, furnished the restaurant of the Capitol Cinema in London with Thonet furniture and several tubular pieces appeared in the lobby of the Strand Hotel.

Around the same time, several British manufacturers began to develop a line of metal furniture for domestic consumption. The most successful was Practical Equipment Ltd, better known by its acronym P.E.L. Initially the firm hired Oliver Percy Bernard (1881–1939), a theater set designer, to propose chair designs and several were put into production during Bernard's affiliation with P.E.L. from 1931 to 1933. Initially P.E.L. sought to combine the comfort of a traditional armchair with spare steel construction. For his SP4B armchair, Bernard produced a fully upholstered seat in green rexine—a synthetic plastic material—and supported it on a tubular steel frame. Better known, however, was a more elegant chair he designed, which included a black upholstered seat and back support that refined an earlier model by the Luckhardt brothers in Germany.

P.E.L.'s most important early commission was from the British Broadcasting Corporation for its new headquarters building, Broadcasting House. Designed by George Val Myer (1883–1959), the building was completed in 1932. The BBC hired Raymond McGrath (1903–1977), a young Australian architect who had emigrated to Britain, as its "decoration consultant." He was responsible for the complete design of the interior including the equipment for the broadcast studios. To assist him, he brought in Serge Chermayeff and the architect Wells Coates (1895–1958). In 1930, the three had formed the Twentieth Century Group to promote modern architecture and design in Britain.

Their task at the BBC was to furnish the offices, which Val Myer had placed in an outer shell surrounding the studios, and then to design the layout and equipment for the studios themselves. Broadcasting House bought a large number of P.E.L.'s standard stacking chair, the RP6, and then purchased the rights from its designer, the Austrian Bruno Pollock (dates unconfirmed), so they could use it exclusively. Because the BBC decided to use only British or commonwealth goods, P.E.L. faced no competition from abroad and hired McGrath, Chermayeff, and Coates to design additional tubular steel furniture especially for Broadcasting House. It did, however, share the BBC commission with another British manufacturer of tubular steel furniture, Cox & Co.

For the many studios and offices, McGrath, Chermayeff, and Coates designed all the furniture, house telephones, signal lights, microphone stands and signage. All the interior elements had functional forms and a standardized quality. Coates, who had an engineering background, designed a control unit that could coordinate actors in up to ten different studios. He also designed several suspended microphones, one of an aluminum alloy in a swiveling wall fitting. The other, which became the standard microphone for the BBC, was suspended on a counterbalanced arm that allowed the microphone to be moved to any part of the studio. The interior of Broadcasting House—far more adventurous than its exterior—was an impressive example of modernist design that integrated formal and technical innovations. Although modernism was slow to influence the design of domestic furnishings in Britain, it proved ideal for the BBC, which sought a bold visual style to herald its entry into a new age of broadcast communication.

The Gorrell Report and its Consequences

Besides commissioning modern furnishings for its offices and studios in London and around the world, the BBC also broadcast a series of radio talks on *Design and Modern Life* in 1933. The subjects ranged from furniture and fashion to kitchen design, architecture, and planning. The DIA position, which promoted design quality rather than a particular style, dominated the series. In his summary talk, Frank Pick, then President of the DIA, reiterated the organization's "fitness for purpose" theme, which had become the foundation of subsequent government efforts to promote good design in Britain.

The year before the BBC talks, Britain's Board of Trade released a report on *The Production and Exhibition of Good Design and Articles of Everyday Use*. Produced by a committee headed by Lord Gorrell and known as the Gorrell Report, the document strongly encouraged the promotion of good design, particularly through increased exhibitions, improvements in art education, and urging manufacturers to use industrial designers. As one result of the report, the Board of Trade established a Council for Art and Industry in 1933. Chaired by Frank Pick, who was accruing considerable power as an advocate for good design, the council membership consisted of industrialists, designers, and critics, although only one was a woman. Though established by a government agency, the Council for Art and Industry received no annual funding, thus it had to request financial support on a project-by-project basis. Unlike the Deutscher Werkbund, which was independent of the German government, the Council for Art and Industry was one of the first design promotion organizations, if not *the* first, to be appointed by a government body. Through several reports it issued in the 1930s, it sought to spread the message that design should be a vital part of Britain's overseas trade policy. It also promoted the value of good design to the domestic consumer, spreading more widely a message that the DIA had been propounding since its founding in 1915.

With an impetus from the Gorrell Report, a group of dedicated promoters organized a large exhibition of British industrial art at London's Dorland Hall in 1933. The focus was on domestic arts and the exhibition was divided among examples of well-designed individual objects and a collection of rooms that were furnished by diverse architects and designers. These ranged from Oliver Hill (1887–1968), who created a display of sheet glass furniture in the French *moderne* style for the glass manufacturer Pilkington Brothers, to staunch continental modernists like Serge Chermayeff and Wells Coates. Coates's "minimum flat" was an upscale version of the simple flats that had been promoted during the 1920s in the Neue Frankfurt and other German housing projects. The extensive exhibition showed off, at least in part, the DIA philosophy of good modern design. Despite acclamations of success by proponents of modern design, however, it did not sufficiently emphasize two concerns that were paramount for the British consumer—tradition and price. Nor were these concerns adequately addressed at a subsequent exhibition, "British Art in Industry," held in London under the auspices of the Royal Academy and the Royal Society of Arts at Burlington House in 1935. Critics claimed that the work on display was exclusive and in some cases ill conceived.

The Dorland Hall Exhibition of 1933 and the Burlington House exhibition two years later spread the gospel of good design to a certain degree but were less successful in attracting large audiences than their more inclusive and commercially-oriented counterparts, the annual British Industries Fair, inaugurated in 1915, and the Ideal Home Exhibition, founded in 1908 by the *Daily Mail*. The crowds that attended both of these fairs testified to public interest in new domestic designs, while the failure of the Dorland Hall and Burlington House exhibitions to present unified and coherent displays of good design at affordable prices was indicative that modernism in the democratic continental sense of providing modern products with simple forms and modest prices was still insufficiently understood or appreciated in Britain.

The Modernist Campaign Continues

The BBC's Broadcasting House was a major success for the modernist camp in Britain, but it was an institutional project that did little to promote an interest in modernism for the domestic home furnishings market. Nonetheless, a small number of architects and critics continued to espouse modernist ideals in selected designs, attracting a loyal following albeit a modest one.

From the triumvirate of McGrath, Coates, and Chermayeff, who completed the BBC interior design so successfully, Raymond McGrath subsequently concentrated on architecture, while Serge Chermayeff and Wells Coates became active in the fields of interiors, furniture, and industrial design, though Chermayeff emigrated to the United States in 1940. Coates's major patron for modern architecture and interior design was Jack Pritchard (1899–1992), who first began to promote modern design as the marketing manager for the Venesta plywood company, where he commissioned an exhibition stand from Le Corbusier, Pierre Jeanneret, and Charlotte Perriand.

In 1933, Pritchard and Wells Coates founded an architectural firm that shortly thereafter became Isokon Ltd. Their aim was to design prototypes for standardized houses but this ambition quickly evolved into the firm's first major project, Lawn Road Flats, a four-storey block of standardized apartments in reinforced concrete. Besides the building, Coates meticulously created interiors that were designed for efficient living as participants had argued for at the CIAM (International Congress of Modern Architecture) Congress on the "existenzminimum" (minimal living) in 1929. The units contained built-in furniture and storage space as well as freestanding modern pieces, some of which Coates designed. They also had modern fittings and appliances for the kitchen and bathroom. Completed in 1934, the flats had been promoted the year before in several rooms that Coates designed for the Dorland Hall Exhibition.

While working on the Lawn Road Flats, Coates was active in two groups that promoted modern architecture and design—MARS and Unit One. MARS, which stood for Modern Architectural Research

Association, became the British branch of CIAM whose congresses Coates and others attended. Unit One was a group of painters, sculptors, and architects who joined together to promote modernism through publications and exhibitions. Among the members, besides Coates, were the painter Ben Nicholson (1894–1982), sculptors Henry Moore (1898–1986) and Barbara Hepworth (1903–1975), the critic Herbert Read (1893–1968), and the artist and designer Paul Nash.

As a furniture designer, Coates produced a tubular steel desk and day bed for P.E.L. Ltd and plywood bookcases for Isokon. His tubular steel designs consisted of plywood volumes or cushions on metal frames, while his bookcases and built-in pieces were comprised of simple rectilinear volumes. None of this furniture broke new ground, although one piece had promise—a mobile desk with a plywood frame and tubular steel supports that could be stored away in a wall unit. However, Coates never refined it to the point where it could be successful in the market.

Following Hitler's rise to power in Germany, Walter Gropius, Marcel Breuer, and László Moholy-Nagy emigrated to Britain. After the Lawn Road Flats, Pritchard, advised by Gropius, focused Isokon on the design and marketing of modern furniture. Gropius became Isokon's Controller of Design and recommended that Breuer be the chief designer. Pritchard also hired Moholy-Nagy to design the odd flyer for the company.

Through his long years of work with Venesta, Pritchard was extremely knowledgeable about plywood and commissioned Breuer to design a cantilevered plywood reclining chair that recalled Alvar Aalto's experimental furniture with cantilevered birch slats. Breuer based his chair on an aluminum model and, after a series of refinements, created an elegant piece of furniture with a plywood frame and padded cushion (Fig. 23.05). Though he designed other pieces for Isokon including plywood tables, chairs, and stools, the long chair was his most successful project and, despite its limited production and modest sales, remains one of

Fig. 23.05: Marcel Breuer, Isokon Ltd, reclining long chair, 1936. © V&A Images/Alamy.

the best pieces of modern furniture designed in Britain during the interwar years.

In 1932, Serge Chermayeff founded Plan Ltd, a company that became one of the larger retailers of modern household furnishings in Britain during its brief existence. Making use of tubular steel, plywood, and upholstery fabrics with geometric forms, Plan Ltd based its designs on German models and commissioned no distinctive pieces of its own. The company's major innovation was its marketing scheme. Other firms produced its goods: P.E.L. for tubular steel, Best for lighting, and Donald Brothers for upholstery fabrics. Plan Ltd's contribution was to join these together in a vision of a modern home. Chermayeff sold the company to a German buyer in 1938 and for various reasons it closed the same year.

Another short-lived firm that produced modern furniture in limited quantities was Makers of Simple Furniture Ltd. Founded by Gerald Summers (1899–1967) in 1929, the company specialized in plywood furniture including chairs, tables, beds, and children's furniture. Like Alvar Aalto in Finland, Summers explored the potential of bent wood, making use of plywood as Breuer was to do for Isokon, rather than Finnish birch. Summers' lounge chair of 1934 is a curvilinear tour de force cut from a single sheet of bent plywood. Though highly praised by critics, Summers' furniture is more sculptural than practical and consequently never reached a wide market in Britain.

Betty Joel (1894–1985) designed more luxurious furniture along the lines of the French decorators. She specialized in pieces made with exotic woods from the colonies, but also used chrome and glass at times. Joel also designed carpets with geometric motifs as well as radio cabinets and other related products.

One reason why British modern furniture did not achieve large sales is due to the competition from Scandinavia, particularly Finland. In 1934, the architect and critic Philip Morton Shand (1895–1960) and the critic Geoffrey Boumphrey (1894–1969), both active members of the DIA, established Finmar Ltd to distribute the furniture of the Finnish architect, Alvar Aalto, who had designed a range of modern wooden chairs, stools, and tables, including a cantilever chair that was made of bent birch wood instead of tubular steel. Britain was the largest foreign market for Aalto's furniture and Finmar was successful in part because labor costs in Finland were cheaper than in Britain and the furniture could be offered at a competitive price. Besides its popularity in the home market, it was also widely acquired for modernist public buildings such as shops, health centers, libraries, and even an airport.

Modernism and Tradition in the Industrial Arts

Similar to the furniture industry, a few companies in the ceramics, glass, silver, and textile sectors adopted the simple geometric forms of the modern movement, while others who embraced modernism preferred the French *moderne* style. There were also companies that continued with traditional forms, as the market for these was still quite large. Among the designers in these industries, Keith Murray (1892–1981) was the strongest proponent of clean forms although some of his designs retained traces of English tradition. Trained as an architect but unable to find work, Murray turned to design in the early 1930s, working in glass, metal, and ceramics. He was one of the first British freelance designers since Christopher Dresser in the late 19th century, introducing a modern style as Dresser did to a number of different companies.

Murray created decanters and wine glasses with clean simple shapes for Stevens & Williams, a Jazz Age cocktail set for Mappin and Webb, and a coffee service and line of earthenware beer mugs and a jug for Wedgwood, one of Britain's oldest manufacturers of ceramics (Fig. 23.06). Design historian Paul Greenhalgh has noted that Murray's Wedgwood mugs, while evincing the clean lines of modernism, also retain a strong reference to the Tudor past when hearty yeomen downed tankards of ale in rural taverns.

More colorful ceramicware was designed by Susie Cooper (1902–1995) and Clarice Cliff (1899–1972). Cooper set up her own pottery in 1929, creating her own shapes and producing colored surfaces with a lithographic-transfer process. Clarice Cliff began by painting French Deco designs on old stock that belonged to the Newport Pottery, a subsidiary of her employer A. J. Wilkinson. In 1928, Cliff inaugurated her own line for Newport, which she called "Bizarre Ware." Her taste ran to angular shapes and vibrant colors, both of which she first encountered at the

Fig. 23.06: Keith Murray, Wedgwood, earthenware beer mugs, c. 1934. © Decorative Arts/Alamy.

Exposition des Arts Décoratifs in Paris. To assist her, she organized a team of young artists who painted her ceramics by hand, while she hired a group of women, known as "Bizarre Girls," to promote the ceramics at trade fairs around Britain. Other lines followed Bizarre including Fantasque, Biarritz, and Crocus. In the early 1930s, Cliff became artistic director for Wilkinson and supervised the production of ceramics designed by many well-known artists, among them—Paul Nash, Duncan Grant (1885–1978), and Vanessa Bell (1879–1961), all of the Omega Workshops.

Most carpet manufacturers preferred to continue with their traditional designs rather than set up new ones on power looms and run the risk of low sales. Several firms, however, did commission modern designs, particularly geometric ones. Among the carpet designers, some were trained in that field but others were architects, artists, and even graphic designers. Marion Dorn and her husband, the graphic designer E. McKnight Kauffer, both Americans who had spent time in Paris, were among the first to introduce luxurious carpets with abstract designs in the style of the French decorators. These carpets were frequently designed for public spaces such as the lobby of Claridge's Hotel in London.

Ashley Havinden (1903–1973), the art director for Crawford's advertising agency, also created designs for modern carpets as did the architect Serge Chermayeff, the painter Francis Bacon (1909–1992), the sculptor Barbara Hepworth (1903–1975), and the designer Marian Peplar (1904–1997), who was associated with Gordon Russell Ltd. Peplar originally trained as an architect but subsequently developed her career as a designer of rugs, carpets and curtain, and upholstery fabrics.

The Wilton Royal Carpet Factory Ltd and Edinburgh Weavers were the leading firms that produced knotted carpets with abstract designs. For all the designers of modern carpets, the primary sources were the avant-garde art movements of a few years earlier—Cubism, Purism, and Synchronism, among

Fig. 23.07: Welles Coates, Ecko AD-65 Wireless Radio, 1934. The Wolfsonian–Florida International University, Miami Beach, Florida, The Mitchell Wolfson, Jr. Collection, 85.15.1.

them. In the textile industry, Marion Straub and Enid Marx designed contemporary fabrics that were used to upholster furniture. Straub created fabrics for Gordon Russell Ltd before becoming chief designer for the textile manufacturer Helios, where she later made a significant contribution to the design of contemporary fabrics on power looms. Enid Marx's projects ranged from illustrations and trademarks to textile designs. Her work as a textile designer was widely disseminated through the aforementioned upholstery fabric with abstract shapes that Frank Pick commissioned for the London Transport rolling stock.

Designers of modern home furnishings drew primarily on German and French sources but these were less obviously applied to new typologies of objects, particularly electric and gas appliances. Radios, in particular, lacked precedents and consequently the experiments of radio manufacturers with modern

designs varied widely. R. D. Russell's veneered plywood cabinets for Murphy Radio applied the DIA's traditional "fitness for purpose" philosophy to a new type of object, while the Ecko Radio Company, founded by Eric Kirkham Cole in 1921, took a bolder approach to form, materials, and production methods. Cole was the first manufacturer in Britain to establish a plastics molding plant, while also commissioning Serge Chermayeff, Wells Coates, and other modern designers to create radio housings that could be manufactured in Bakelite, a new plastic material that came to be increasingly used for such purposes. Ecko's signature radio model in the 1930s had a circular shell that Welles Coates designed. The first version, the AD65, appeared in 1934, initially in walnut or black Bakelite (Fig. 23.07). Designed to encase a circular speaker, the AD65 also resulted in a lower manufacturing cost because of the reduced number of molding tools.

Other distinctive appliances included the streamlined HMV electric iron, that Christian Barman (1898–1980) designed. Put on the market in 1935, it was the first iron to break with the traditional flat form. The heating coils were encased in a fluid porcelain body that included the handle. While ergonomic and elegant, it broke easily if dropped. One of the few British products in the 1930s to be designed in the streamline style that was popular in the United States, the HMV introduced a new design style that was quickly copied by other manufacturers of irons such as Morphy-Richards, although without the porcelain shell.

Perhaps the most influential and longest lasting of the British electric products designed in the 1930s was George Carwardine's Anglepoise lamp (Fig. 23.08). Carwardine (1887–1947) was an automotive engineer whose firm specialized in the design of automobile suspension systems. He patented the Anglepoise lamp in 1932. Originally produced by a manufacturer of springs rather than lighting, its special feature was the springs that allowed a flexible movement of the parts. Because it could be positioned according to a task,

Fig. 23.08: George Carwardine, Anglepoise lamp, 1933. © Elizabeth Whiting & Associates/Alamy.

it was widely used in offices, factories, and hospitals, though it was popular in homes as well. Due to its novel construction, it became highly influential for later generations of task-lighting design. Modern lighting was also produced by Robert Dudley Best (1892–1984), a lighting designer and manufacturer whose Bestlite table lamp of 1930 was a modified version of a German lamp, Typ K, that Christian Dell, the former Bauhaus teacher, designed the previous year.

New designs for irons, lighting, and radios were part of a larger expansion of electrical products in the 1920s and 1930s. British firms introduced a range of electrical goods for the home—heaters, toasters, vacuum cleaners, and kitchen appliances. Though most designers of electrical products were men, women like Mrs. D'Arcy Braddell (dates unconfirmed) promoted their efficient use in the home, following the theories of management experts such as the American Christine Frederick, whose book *Household Engineering: Scientific Management in the Home* was published in 1920. Mrs. D'Arcy Braddell

designed kitchens that rationalized the workflow while also creating a gas cooker for the Parkinson Stove Company in 1935. Few women found work in the male-dominated engineering professions, but they were more active in evaluating and promoting the effective use of new labor-saving electrical products. The Electrical Association for Women, motivated by the work of American efficiency experts, organized exhibitions of model kitchens and sponsored a film entitled *Motion Study in the Home*.

The Polemics of Modernism

Three issues dominated the British debates about modernism in the 1920s and 1930s: tradition versus modernity; Englishness versus internationalism; and handicraft versus machine production. For William Lethaby (1857–1931), who strongly influenced the philosophy of the Design and Industries Association in its early years, modernism was simply a style, "another sort of humbug to pass off with a shrug." Others in the DIA such as the critic John Gloag (1896–1981), a prolific writer on design and architecture, sought to reconcile a sense of Englishness with the new ideas about mass production and modernity. Another critic who tried to reconcile the craft tradition with the demands of the machine was Noel Carrington (1895–1989), also a book designer and publisher. In his 1934 book, *Design in Civilization*, Carrington characterized the artist as someone who would protect the public from the potential dullness of machine civilization. The novelist and art critic Anthony Bertram (1897–1978) also wrote about design. He gave a series of BBC radio talks on the subject in 1937, publishing a pamphlet based on them entitled *Design in Everyday Things*. This was followed by a small book simply entitled *Design* in which Bertram asserted that design was evident in all aspects of life, from town planning to packaging. Like other design critics of the time, he was concerned with the distinction between good and bad design, adhering to some degree to tenets established by Charles Eastlake and other design reformers in the 19th century that propounded an aesthetic of simplicity, fitness for use, and truth to materials.

The most enthusiastic proponent of a machine aesthetic was the poet and art critic Herbert Read (1893–1968). He argued in his book *Art and Industry* of 1934 that the abstract artist would be the best source of designs for machine-made products. For Read, abstract art had the same relationship to design that pure mathematics had to science. He was adamant in demanding that the factory must adapt itself to the abstract artist and not vice versa. Among the illustrations in his book, Read combined modern designs for British products such as Wedgwood pottery, London Transport bus stops, and an Ecko radio cabinet by Serge Chermayeff with traditional designs and recent examples from Germany such as cantilevered chairs by Mies van der Rohe and pottery by Otto Lindig from the Bauhaus pottery workshop. An admirer of the Bauhaus, Read supported the emigration of Walter Gropius and several other Bauhaus faculty members to Britain. He also asked former Bauhaus teacher Herbert Bayer to design *Art and Industry.*

The author whose polemic on modernism reached the widest public was Nicholas Pevsner, whose critique of British industrial goods in an *Enquiry into Industrial Art in England* was published in 1937. Trained as an art historian in Germany, Pevsner had earlier published *Pioneers of the Modern Movement,* in which he established a trajectory of modern design that extended from the eclectic array of goods at the Crystal Palace exhibition to the pristine modern form of Walter Gropius's and Adolf Meyer's Fagus Factory in Alfeld-an-der-Leine, Germany.

The writings of Gloag, Carrington, Read, and Pevsner did not persuade the British populace to adopt the tenets of modern design, but they did contribute to a broad public discourse on the general importance of "good design" that was supported as well by public broadcasts on the BBC and the various reports, committees, and exhibitions that the government and engaged organizations such as the DIA organized.

Transportation
Automobiles

Perhaps because the steam locomotive was invented in Britain and rail travel first expanded there, the British showed less interest in the automobile and left its initial development to the Germans, French, and Americans. Henry Ford, whose Model T was the first mass-produced car, was quick to see a market in Britain and his Ford Motor Company began to produce cars and trucks at an assembly plant he built there in 1911.

Like other countries in Europe, the British initially concentrated on luxury cars rather than mass-produced ones like the Model T. In 1907, Rolls-Royce launched its celebrated Silver Ghost. Painted silver and adorned with silver-plated accessories, the car was touted for its excellent engineering and quiet ride. Until production ceased in 1925, the Silver Ghost set the highest standard for automobile design. Among its principal rivals in the luxury market was the Bentley, which was manufactured by a firm that W. O. Bentley (1888–1971) founded in the early 1920s. Bentley's first automobile doubled as a touring car and a racer but the company soon moved into the production of saloons, which were touring cars with heavy enclosed cabs. Independent coachbuilding firms such as H. J. Mulliner, Gurney Nutting, and Vanden Plas, which did much of the work for Bentley, made the bodies. Due to Bentley's financial difficulties, Rolls Royce bought out the company in 1931.

With their elaborate bodywork and accessories, the Rolls Royce and the Bentley were typical cars of the wealthy. These vehicles were complemented by the sports car, another type of luxury vehicle that Aston Martin and Jaguar pioneered in Britain. Beginning with the design of racing cars after World War I, Aston Martin also moved into sports car design during the 1930s. The company brought in two Italian brothers, Augusto and Enrico Bertelli (dates unconfirmed), to run the company and design its vehicles. Building on the T Type of 1927, later sports cars combined the trim lines of a racing car with the fancy dashboards and rounded fenders of higher-end cars.

The sleek rounded curves of the post-war Jaguar had a different origin than the Aston Martin. Jaguar's beginnings lie in the Swallow Sidecar Company, that William Lyons (1901–1985) and William Walmsley (1892–1961) founded in 1922 to produce motorcycle sidecars. Their first design was an aluminum-clad sidecar—the Zeppelin—with a torpedo-shaped streamline form. Nine years later the company launched its first sports car, the SS 1, which it manufactured until 1936. With its elongated body, low-cut windshield and rounded back, the four-seater SS 1 displayed features that could also be seen in some streamlined American cars of the 1930s but it still retained many traces both in scale and accessories of the traditional touring car. Other cars that pushed the streamline form to a greater extreme followed the SS1. The company changed its name to SS Cars Ltd in 1933 and then to avoid any reference to the German SS troops, it became Jaguar Cars Ltd in 1945, having first used the name Jaguar in the mid-1930s.

The two companies that initially competed with Ford in the small car market were Morris and Austin. William Morris (1877–1963), not to be confused with the Arts and Crafts designer, began by making bicycles before moving up to automobile production. The first automobile manufacturer in Britain to emulate Henry Ford's emphasis on volume manufacturing and low prices, Morris worked for three years on a car he began to market in 1913 as the Oxford. Known for its rounded bull nose design, it quickly acquired a reputation for reliability and comfort, though it was only a two-seater and could not compete as a family car. Beginning in 1915, Morris produced a larger version, the Cowley, in two-seat and four-seat versions. Unlike Ford, Morris had bought his parts from suppliers, turning to Detroit for suitable parts to build the Cowley. By 1924, Morris surpassed Ford as Britain's largest car manufacturer. In 1928, the company introduced a more up-to-date small car, the Minor, to compete with the popular Austin 7. But it did not sell well because it appeared at a time

Fig. 23.09: Herbert Austin and Stanley Edge, Austin 7, 1922. © Heritage Image Partnership Ltd/Alamy.

when the public wanted vehicles with more amenities nor could it compete with the Austin in price. Only when reintroduced after World War II with a new design that combined the comforts of a larger car with the low price of a smaller one did the Minor become a success.

Morris's principal rival, Herbert Austin (1866–1941), founded his own automobile company in 1905 and gained prominence during World War I, when his firm designed and manufactured military equipment. Following the war, Austin adopted a one-model policy, creating the Austin 20, a mid-sized car that failed in the market because it ignored the growing public demand for smaller and cheaper vehicles. In 1922, the company introduced the Austin 7, that Herbert Austin and a young engineer, Stanley Edge (1903–1990), designed (Fig. 23.09). The car was considerably smaller than Ford's Model T and rivaled it throughout Europe in popularity. Designed as a touring car with a hood, a windshield, and four seats, the Austin 7 was the first car to cater to families in a low-income bracket. Through its wide appeal, it introduced masses of Britons to the open road and helped turn Britain into an automobile culture. Originally the seating was rather tight and a later version with more space was launched in 1925. The Austin 7 remained in production until 1939.

The expansion of automobiles in Britain, spurred by the large number of family cars that Ford, Morris, and Austin produced, brought with it a transformation of the countryside as paved roads made rural towns and villages accessible to masses of new drivers. Central to this emerging automobile culture was the gasoline pump. Bowser in the Midwest and Wayne-Dresser in Texas produced the earliest ones in the United States. Bowser claims to have introduced the first roadside gasoline pump in Britain in 1914. Soon several British firms entered the market, among them W. and T. Avery of Birmingham, a company that manufactured precision scales.

A major client for gasoline pumps was the Shell Oil Company, which commissioned various designs over the years. By 1929, most pumps had counters that displayed the amount of gasoline going into the tank, thus allaying the customer's concerns about being cheated. Initially, many pumps in Britain were located either on the roadside or in garages, but eventually gasoline companies such as Shell built their own stations to dispense gas and provide maintenance services as well.

Following the lead of Frank Pick at the London Underground, who commissioned travel posters from leading artists and designers, the Shell Oil Company developed a poster campaign aimed at encouraging motorists to visit the small towns and natural landscapes of rural Britain. Their advertising of the 1920s began with rather conventional campaigns to promote the virtues of Shell oil and gasoline. The company worked primarily with fine artists such as George Denholm Armour (1864–1949), known for his depictions of British sportsmen, and cartoonists like H. M. Bateman (1887–1970), who linked Shell's products to the upper middle class. Most distinctive about Shell's early advertising was the use of its delivery trucks or lorries as sites for the poster advertising. Each truck had frames on both sides and the back to display the company's posters, which were changed regularly.

By 1930, a few companies controlled the distribution of gasoline and the price and quality were similar for all brands. Shell Mex, the name that the international Shell group used in Britain, joined with

British Petroleum to market its gasoline under the name BP. The new company was now in a position to promote both brands. Design historian John Hewitt has shown that Shell in the 1930s began to shift its advertising strategy away from touting its oil and gasoline to building brand loyalty to the company itself. It aimed to attract customers because of the values it stood for, not for what it sold. In particular, it needed to counter the lobbying groups that were established to save the countryside by demonstrating that it did not despoil the environment but rather promoted its responsible use by encouraging motorists to visit Britain's cultural and natural sites.

To launch a new advertising campaign, Shell hired Jack Beddington (1893–1959), who became the company's publicity manager in 1929. Like Frank Pick, he commissioned posters from Britain's best artists, illustrators, and graphic designers, developing an aesthetic sensibility that ranged from rural landscapes in a traditional realist style to the designs of E. McKnight Kauffer, who did posters in a modernist style for both Shell and BP. Beddington introduced a series of campaigns that were intended to present Shell as a guardian of nature as well as a promoter of responsible tourism. In its "Quick-Start" series, the attributes of Shell gasoline were linked in an indirect way to the characteristics of eagles, owls, and otters. For two travel series, See Britain First on Shell, and Everywhere You Go, You Can Be Sure of Shell, Beddington commissioned artists including modernists such as Graham Sutherland (1903–1980), Paul Nash, and E. McKnight Kauffer to portray tourist landmarks like Stonehenge, the Rye Marshes, and the town square at Lavenham. These were done in an illustrative manner, while other campaigns like You Can be Sure of Shell gave artists and designers an opportunity to make more conceptual statements (Fig. 23.10). Beddington's Shell poster campaigns of the 1930s were significant records of how the British countryside changed as a result of the automobile. Like John Constable's 19th-century depictions of rural

Fig. 23.10: Edgar Ainsworth, Everywhere You Go, You Can Be Sure of Shell, poster, 1934. © 2014. Digital image, The Museum of Modern Art, New York/Scala, Florence.

England as a timeless landscape untouched by industrialization, the Shell posters portrayed a similar vision even as motorists were being invited to regard its towns and villages as tourist destinations.

Railroads

Following the Railway Act of 1921, a considerable numer of railways in Britain were consolidated into four main companies: the London, Midland, and Scottish Railway (LMS), the London and North Eastern Railway Company (LNER), the Great Western Railway (GWR), and the Southern Railway (SR). Though covering different routes, each of these companies sought to be the most modern, the most comfortable, and the fastest of Britain's rail lines. To compete with automobile and air travel, the lines invested in new engines and rolling stock, while also putting a strong emphasis on publicity. Nigel Gresley (1876–1941), Chief Mechanical Engineer of the LNER

throughout the 1920s and 1930s, designed the most notable engines. Gresley focused his attention on large express passenger locomotives, inaugurating a series in 1922 which were known as the "Pacifics." The first three locomotives in this series, the A1 to A3, were innovative primarily in terms of mechanical improvements, but the clean lines of their elongated cylindrical boilers and their low smoke stacks gave them a distinctly modern look. Gresley's streamlined design for the A4, however, departed from these earlier designs (Fig. 23.11). Its swept-back form was inspired by the aerodynamic German train, the *Fliegende Hamburger*, and to some degree by the Burlington Zephyr, considered to be one of America's first streamlined trains. However, both of these trains were considerably smaller than the A4, which could pull more cars at a comparable or greater speed. The A4 locomotive was part of a complete streamlined train that was launched in 1935 to celebrate the Silver Jubilee of King George V. Two years later,

Fig. 23.11: Nigel Gresley, A4 *Silver Jubilee* locomotive, LNER, 1936. © Science and Society/SuperStock.

the London, Midland, and Scottish Railway launched its own streamlined locomotive, the *Coronation Scot*, designed by the staff of LMS's Chief Mechanical Engineer, William Stanfield (1876–1965), to show that the LMS was also a modern railroad like the LNER.

The LNER covered a large part of Britain with trains running from London to north-east England and Scotland. Though the company operated in a more decentralized manner than the other lines, it nonetheless had an advertising manager, William Teasdale (dates unconfirmed), who sought to unify its publicity. Central to the LNER's promotional program as well as that of the other lines was the poster. The LNER inherited over 72,000 poster hoardings, where Teasdale sought to mount distinctive campaigns that encouraged people to visit interesting places on the railroad's route. Both Teasdale and Cecil Dandridge

(dates unconfirmed), who succeeded him in 1928 when the former was promoted, strove to create a distinctive LNER look by hiring commercial artists. Similar to his influence on Jack Beddington at Shell Mex, Frank Pick's employment of travel posters on the London Underground also served as a model for Teasdale and Dandridge. Many of the LNER artists had previously done posters for the London Underground. Among them were Fred Taylor, Frank Newbould, and Frank Brangwyn (1867–1956), all of whom depicted landscapes in a somewhat romantic albeit commercial style. The LNER also commissioned occasional posters from such designers as Alexander Alexeieff (1901–1982), the filmmaker and illustrator; A. M. Cassandre in Paris; and the Swiss poster artist Leo Marfurt (1894–1977). The company's most distinctive image, however, was created by the commercial artist Tom Purvis

(1888–1959), whose posters with flat colors and lack of expressive linear detail the LNER began to feature in the late 1920s. Purvis continued a technique initiated by the Beggarstaff Brothers about 30 years earlier. His figures also had some affinity with the posters of Ludwig Hohlwein in Germany but Hohlwein had already begun to move away from flat colors by adding more expressive detail to his figures. Like the posters of the Beggarstaffs, those of Purvis relied primarily on imagery rather than text. In particular, they featured the pleasures of the seaside, depicting faceless figures sitting on the beach, playing in the sand, or boating near the shore (Fig. 23.12). For the series "East Coast Joys," Purvis produced several triptychs—series of three posters that could be displayed together as a single scene or separately as was the case with the 19th-century *u-kiyoe* prints in Japan. The text on the "East Coast Joys" posters was set in Gill Sans, the typeface by Eric Gill that the Monotype Corporation had released in 1928. Dandridge adopted it for all the LNER's signs, timetables, and publicity as well a for the name plate of Nigel Gresley's A1 *Flying Scotsman* locomotive, which Gill painted by hand.

The London, Midland, and Scottish Railway took a different approach to that of the LNER for its

Fig. 23.12: Tom Purvis, East Coast by LNER, poster, 1928. akg-images.

poster advertising. Rather than work with commercial artists, the LMS chose to commission most of its posters from established painters who were associated with the Royal Academy. Instead of building a corporate identity through graphic design, the LMS sought to establish an image of distinction by associating its publicity with the best academic painters in Britain. Its approach harkened back to the 19th century when Pears purchased the right to use Sir John Millais' academic painting *Bubbles* to advertise its soap. The few modern posters the LMS commissioned from the French artist A. M. Cassandre were an exception to the dominant company philosophy and had no influence on the overall direction of its advertising. Both the Great Western and Southern railways also commissioned occasional modern posters. McKnight Kauffer did a series on Devon and Cornwall for Great Western and Austin Cooper (1890–1964) did the odd placard for Southern Railways.

Britain's large passenger ships

The Deco interiors of the French passenger ships in the later 1920s and early 1930s—the *Ile de France* and the *Normandie*—established a new standard for other passenger lines. In Britain, Cunard, which owned one of Britain's oldest passenger fleets, merged with its main rival White Star in 1934. Recognizing that its pre-World War I ships like the *Aquitania* and the *Mauretania* were outmoded, Cunard commissioned a new ship, the *Queen Mary*, which it intended to be the largest and fastest ship of its day. The *Queen Mary*, which undertook her maiden voyage in 1936, was fitted out in a refined Art Deco style, reflecting what Paul Greenhalgh has called the "English compromise," whereby designers combined aspects of modern styles with a more traditional English sensibility. The ship's design was lavish. The rich interiors, created with more than 30 different types of wood, many from Britain's colonies, exuded a sense of tradition, while also evincing inklings of the modern. The first-class cabins featured hand-carved panels

Fig. 23.13: *Queen Mary*, observation lounge and cocktail bar, 1936. Getty Images.

and Deco furniture covered with wood veneers. The first-class bathrooms were paneled in Formica, a new material at the time.

It was the *Queen Mary*'s public spaces that most characterized the modernity of the interior. This was evident in the sweeping observation lounge and cocktail bar (Fig. 23.13) as well as in the first-class ballroom, lobby, and restaurant. The latter, seating 800 people, was the largest public space ever built on a ship. Overall, the *Queen Mary*'s design defined the look of ship interiors for years to come.

Two other ships with signature modern interiors were the *Orion*, completed a year before the *Queen Mary* in 1935, and the *Orcades*, which was finished in 1937. Both ships sailed for the Orient Line, and Colin Anderson, whose family owned it, commissioned their interiors. The designer for the two ship interiors was the modernist New Zealand architect Brian O'Rorke (1901–1974), who trained at the Architectural Association in London. Both Anderson and O'Rorke agreed that they did not want to replicate a traditional ship's interior. Thus they had to find manufacturers who would produce modern designs for them. Edinburgh Weavers provided carpeting and E. McKnight Kauffer and Marion Dorn were among those they employed to do

carpet designs. O'Rorke designed the furniture himself and made extensive use of chrome and Bakelite in his interior designs. Besides designing carpets, Kauffer created a lot of the graphic ephemera connected with the ships—posters, invitations, and brochures and even luggage labels, which he designed in a starkly modern style.

The *Orion* was the first ship to be air conditioned, although the air conditioning was initially confined to the dining rooms. Unlike Cunard's *Queen Mary*, which sailed on the heavily traveled Atlantic route, the *Orion* traveled between Britain and Australia, primarily carrying emigrants to Australia. Hence, its interior decor was modern without being luxurious like the first-class accommodations on the *Queen Mary*.

Imperial Airways

Just as Britain's many railroad lines were consolidated into four major companies in 1923, so did a government committee, established the same year, recommend that the nation's few small passenger airlines, formed after World War I, be consolidated into a single company. In 1924, Imperial Airways was created. While its mission included serving Europe as the smaller airlines had done, its principal purpose was to inaugurate long-distance air routes to Africa, Asia, and the Middle East—in short, to those parts of the world where Britain maintained an imperial presence. The move to connect Britain to the far corners of its empire through air travel was consistent with the nation's objective to increase empire trade. This intent as previously described was promoted at the Wembley Exhibition of 1924 and then through the programs of the Empire Marketing Board.

Following its initial establishment of some passenger services to Europe, Imperial Airways began its Empire Services in 1927 with flights from Cairo to Basra in the Persian Gulf. In 1929 the airline introduced its first service from London to Karachi using the S8 Calcutta, a three-engine biplane that was manufactured by Short Brothers. This was the first of the airline's

Fig. 23.14: Imperial Airways, Empire Flying Boat, promenade deck, 1936. Time & Life Pictures/Getty Images.

"flying boats." Subsequent routes were opened to South Africa, Tanzania, Singapore, and Australia among other destinations. In 1937 the airline joined with the Post Office in a program to deliver mail to the colonies; within a year it had transported 100 tons of letters to Africa and India.

Short Brothers continued to improve the flying boat and by 1936 Imperial Airways was promoting a four-engine high-wing plane that was billed as "the most luxurious flying boat in the world." Known as the S23 Empire Flying Boat, it had a totally different form than the earlier S8 biplane. The hull was streamlined, following the design of the American DC-3, and it was famous for its spacious promenade saloon and smoking cabin along with its comfortable sleeping quarters (Fig. 23.14). The reclining seats with padded arm and headrests were a far cry from the wicker chairs with which earlier Imperial Airways cabins were furnished. As an added design element, the airline commissioned a line of exclusive dishes from Susie Cooper (1902–1995), one of Britain's leading ceramic artists. While Imperial Airways purchased planes from other manufacturers besides Short Brothers, it was the flying boat that dominated its promotion of luxury air travel. In 1935, a

rival airline, British Airways Ltd, was inaugurated, but by 1939 it and Imperial Airways merged to form the government-run British Overseas Airways Corporation (BOAC), making Britain the first major power to support its own national airline.

In its advertising campaigns, Imperial Airways concentrated on promoting air travel, particularly on its international routes. For travel on these routes, the airline had to compete with travel by ship, which it did in two ways: one by emphasizing the greater speed of air travel, an argument directed at Britons living abroad who could spend more leave time at home if they returned to Britain by plane; and second, by the emphasis on the luxury and comfort of air travel, particularly on the Empire Flying Boats. A poster by Edgar Ainsworth, a painter and commercial artist who also worked for Shell Mex, made use of Otto Neurath's Isotype figures to depict in graphic terms the services offered by Imperial Airways—stewards serving three meals and high tea, relatively few passengers with sufficient leg room, adequate storage for baggage, and men's and women's washrooms. Other posters featured cutaway views of plane interiors to depict the multifarious activities and services aboard. Stuart Advertising Agency Ltd, one of the larger London agencies, handled at least part of the airline's advertising campaign. Much of the advertising was through posters, although the airline also used exhibitions to promote air travel. In 1935, they hired the avant-garde artist and former Bauhaus teacher László Moholy-Nagy, who had arrived in Britain that year, to design a large exhibit entitled "The Empire's Airway." It remained on view for almost two years at various venues, the last one being a mobile railway car.

Imperial Airways did have some sense of corporate identity. It adopted a symbol, the Speedbird icon designed by Theyre Lee-Elliott (1903–1988), which it used in various ways (Fig. 23.15). The artist was strongly influenced by the work of McKnight Kauffer and he may have adapted the Speedbird from the angular birds of Kauffer's 1917 poster for the *Daily Herald.*

IMPERIAL
AIRWAYS

FLY FROM
LONDON
TO
PARIS
OR
BRUSSELS
OR
COLOGNE
IN SPEED & COMFORT

Fig. 23.15: Theyre Lee-Elliott, Imperial Airways poster, c. 1935. The Wolfsonian–Florida International University, Miami Beach, Florida, The Mitchell Wolfson, Jr. Collection, XX1992.193. Photo: Lynton Gardiner.

The styles of artists who did posters for the airline varied greatly from the abstract forms of British Constructivist painter Ben Nicholson to the illustrations of commercial designers. Posters that invited the public to travel to far-off destinations presented such places as exotic landscapes, but they could also reinforce an imperialist vision as did a poster by illustrator Hal Woolf (1902–1962) that portrayed a group of smiling Africans in native dress ostensibly waiting

to welcome the tourists arriving in the plane that was descending behind them.

Graphic Design
Typography

The appointment of Stanley Morison (1889–1967) as typographic advisor to the Monotype Corporation in 1922 enabled him to exercise a powerful influence over the development of British typography for the next four decades. During that period, Morison helped Monotype to become the major supplier of machine-produced printing types in Britain.

Unlike Jan Tschichold, the force behind the New Typography in Germany, Morison was not trained as a typographer. Before joining Monotype, he was the director of design at the Cloister Press in Manchester, which the advertising magnate Charles W. Hobson (dates unconfirmed) had set up. There Morison ordered type from other foundries and issued his own type specimens. In 1922 he became a founding member of the Fleuron Society, whose purpose was to publish machine-printed books that possessed the same quality as hand-printed ones. Among the co-founders were Oliver Simon (1895–1956), Francis Meynell (1891–1975), and Bernard Newdigate (1869–1944), all of whom were active in adapting the exceptional design and printing standards of the late 19th-century private press movement to modern commercial printing. Simon had a long association with the Curwen Press, Meynell founded the Nonesuch Press, and Newdigate managed the Shakespeare Head Press for the publisher Basil Blackwell.

Besides commissioning typeface designs for Monotype, Morison became a prominent printing historian. In 1923, he and Oliver Simon started a lavishly produced typographic journal, *The Fleuron*. It published a large number of scholarly articles until it ceased publication in 1930. At Monotype, Morison helped to move commercial printers from the traditional hand-setting of type to setting by machine. To this end, he revived a considerable number of classical

'MONOTYPE' GILL SANS: NO SERIFS, NO THICKS AND THINS:

Aa Bb Cc Dd Ee Ff Gg Hh Ii
Jj Kk Ll Mm Nn Oo Pp Qq
Rr Ss Tt Uu Vv Ww Xx &
Yy Zz 1234567890!?'
Light: Normal: **Bold: Extra B.: Ultra**
Condensed: **Bold Condensed:** TITLING

Fig. 23.16: Eric Gill, Gill Sans typeface, 1928.
Courtesy The Newberry Library, Chicago,
case_wing_z250_a5_bx24_01ra.

typefaces for machine setting, among them Baskerville, Fournier, Bembo, and Walbaum.

Though a traditionalist by nature, Morrison recognized the need for Monotype to have at least one modern typeface and he commissioned Eric Gill (1882–1940), a sculptor, engraver, and calligrapher, to design such a face. Gill had studied lettering at the Central School of Arts and Crafts with Edward Johnston, who designed the san serif typeface Railway for the London Underground. This served as an inspiration for his own san serif face, Gill Sans. The two types share many similarities but Gill Sans has a few gestural flourishes that give it a distinct character (Fig. 23.16). Gill differentiated his typeface from Johnston's with the claim that his was designed as a text face while Johnston's was more suitable for signs. Gill Sans was widely used commercially, which led Gill to create at least seven variants of different weights including the Extra Bold version, which he dubbed "Double-Elefans."

Others typefaces by Gill such as Perpetua (1929–1930) and Golden Cockerel (1929) were more directly related to roman letter sources. Perpetua was one of the first new typefaces that Morrison commissioned for Monotype, while Golden Cockerel was designed for the Golden Cockerel Press that Robert Gibbings (1889–1958) set up to print books by traditional craft methods. All the Golden Cockerel books featured wood engravings, many done by Gill himself. For a superbly

produced version of the *Four Gospels*, published in 1931, Gill engraved a set of images whose elongated figures complemented the book's foliated ornament, hand-drawn initials, and delicate typeface.

In his small book of 1936, *An Essay on Typography*, Gill declared his philosophy of two typographies, "the typography of industrialism" and "humane typography." For Gill, the former had to be absolutely plain and was only beautiful because of its efficiency. He condemned any attempt to create fancy lettering mechanically as nauseating because craftsmen did not do it. "Humane typography," according to Gill, could never achieve mechanical perfection and was destined to be "comparatively rough." Gill's polemic did not recognize the skills of the technical experts who helped to adapt his own typographical designs for machine use. His romantic espousal of the craftsman distinguished him from Morison who also revered fine printing but was not conflicted about allying it to the machine.

Throughout his career, Morison published a large number of books on aspects of printing history including *Four Centuries of Fine Printing* (1924), *First Principles of Typography* (1929), and *A Tally of Types* (1953). Though he worked primarily as a typographic advisor for Monotype, he also advised *The Times* of London and the Cambridge University Press on typographic matters. Beginning as an advisor to *The Times* in 1929, he criticized the newspaper's typography

'MONOTYPE' TIMES NEW ROMAN, A "TWENTIETH-CENTURY CLASSIC":

ABCDEFGHJKLMNPQRS
TUVW abcefghijklmn XYZ&
1234567 opqrstuvwxyz 890?!£
*abcdefghjklmnopqrstuvwxyz A
BCDEGHKMNQRSTUWY*

Fig. 23.17: Stanley Morison, Times New Roman typeface, 1932. Courtesy The Newberry Library, Chicago, case_wing_z250_a5_bx24_01ra.

and layout. This resulted in his design of a new typeface, Times New Roman (Fig. 23.17), whose design was strongly influenced by an earlier typeface, Plantin. *The Times* changed to the new face in 1932 and the Monotype Corporation made it available for wider use the following year. It sold well, satisfying the demand for a modern typeface that still had roots in the past. Though Monotype continued to feature revivals of classic types, the firm also commissioned additional modern faces to supplement the use of Gill Sans for advertising and related purposes. Among these were Ashley Crawford (1930), an upper-case only typeface derived from lettering that Ashley Havinden, art director for the William Crawford advertising agency, devised for the agency's Chrysler automobile campaign; and Ashley Script (1955), derived from Havinden's brush lettering on a poster for the Milk Marketing Board. Another typeface was Albertus (1932–1940), designed by Berthold Wolpe (1905–1989), a German émigré typographer whose widely used typeface recalled the thick black letters of Rudolph Koch's Neuland.

The activities of the Monotype Corporation were conveyed to the public through its promotional magazine, the *Monotype Recorder*, which Beatrice Warde (1900–1969), an American printing scholar, began to edit in 1927. Two years later, Warde became Publicity Manager for Monotype, continuing to write extensively on typographic matters. In her 1932 lecture, "Printing is Invisible," she likened good typography to the transparency of a crystal glass. The lecture was published some time later with the better-known title, "The Crystal Goblet."

Advertising and graphic design

British advertising throve during the 1920s and 1930s. Among the major agencies of the period were W. S. Crawford Ltd, the Stuart Advertising Agency, and Charles W. Hobson's agency in Manchester. Both Hobson and W. S. Crawford were major figures in the advertising world. Hobson brought to advertising layout the same concern for fine printing that prevailed in the private press movement. Though successful in retail advertising, William Crawford dedicated much of his activity to public campaigns. Advisor to various government ministries, he was also actively involved with the Empire Marketing Board and chaired the Buy British campaign in 1931.

Crawford maintained an office in Berlin and was thus cognizant of the latest tendencies in German advertising and design. In 1922 he hired Ashley Havinden as a young trainee. Havinden became art director of the agency in 1929 and remained with W. S. Crawford for his entire career. He worked in a team with Bingy Mills, a copywriter, and Margaret Sangster, an account executive whom he married. With Havinden handling the graphic side, the three created campaigns for Chrysler Motors, Eno's Fruit Salt, Dewar's Whiskey, Simpsons, and Kaiser Silk Stockings. Sangster (dates unconfirmed) was also put in charge of a new Women's Department that catered to clients who made products specifically for women and children.

While most agencies continued to rely on folksy illustration, Havinden drew on the imagery of modern art, design, and photography. His abstract depictions of automobiles for Chrysler Motors, whose account Crawford had for all of Europe, fell somewhere between illustration and abstraction (Fig. 23.18), while his posters and newspaper ads for Eno's Fruit Salts featured abstracted knights on horseback bearing poles with wavy copy lines instead of banners. When Simpsons, a men's clothier, planned to open a London store with the name Simpson Piccadilly, Havinden advised them on all aspects of retail identity from the development of a logo to its application on advertisements, packaging, clothing labels, and invitation cards. His logo for Simpson fused the two words of the store's name into a hierarchy with the common letter P linking them together. Havinden, who was known to clients and friends as Ashley, moved in the circles of Britain's modernist architects and designers. When Moholy-Nagy came to Britain in 1935, Ashley was able to secure work for him with Simpson Piccadilly as

Fig. 23.18: Ashley Havinden, Hats Off for the New Chrysler 65, poster (German version), 1929. The Wolfsonian–Florida International University, Miami Beach, Florida, The Mitchell Wolfson, Jr. Collection 87.1136.4.1. Photo: Willard Associates.

their designer of displays. A few years earlier, Havinden brought in E. McKnight Kauffer, who worked for W. S. Crawford between 1927 and 1929. While employed by the agency, Kauffer developed a more modernist style, drawing heavily on Russian and German examples.

Kauffer came to Britain in 1915 and, with the exception of some time abroad, remained until 1940 when he returned to the United States. While in Britain, he worked for publishers, retailers, and government bodies, producing everything from book jackets and logos to posters, theater sets, and even carpets. He gained attention early in his career with a poster for London's *Daily Herald*, which depicted a flock of birds in an angular abstract style that was influenced by the Vorticist paintings and drawings of C. R. W. Nevinson and Wyndham Lewis (Plate 18). This poster established Kauffer as a commercial artist with an interest in modernism. His reputation continued to grow through a series of posters he did for the London Underground (see Chapter 17) as well as others he created for the

Empire Marketing Board. In the 1930s, after he left W. S. Crawford, Kauffer expanded his use of photography and photomontage, becoming one of the few graphic designers in Britain to adopt these techniques. They were evident on book covers he designed for H. G. Wells's novel *The Shape of Things to Come* and Herbert Read's *Art Now* (Fig. 23.19). Other clients for whom he did more experimental work were BP, Shell, and Imperial Airways. Besides using photographs, he continued to paint some of his images and to arrange his lettering on vertical and diagonal lines as well as horizontals.

In 1932, Kauffer began an association with the printer Lund Humphries. The firm had a gallery and from 1935 he showed there while also promoting exhibitions of work by other designers. Jan Tschichold had the first exhibition of his work at the gallery in 1935 and this may have led to his eventual commissions from Lund Humphries and Allen Lane, the publisher of Penguin Books, whose covers Tschichold redesigned in the late 1940s. Other artists from the

Fig. 23.19: E. Mcknight Kauffer, *Art Now*, cover, 1936. The Wolfsonian–Florida International University, Miami Beach, Florida, The Mitchell Wolfson, Jr. Collection, 84.2.216. Photo: David Almeida.

continent who showed in the Lund Humphries gallery were the German designer Hans Schleger, known as Zero, who emigrated to Britain not long after his exhibition, and Jan Le Witt (1907–1991) and George Him (1900–1982), a team of Polish poster artists who also moved to Britain to escape the Nazi occupation of their country.

Throughout the 1920s and 1930s, Kauffer and Ashley were the most versatile of the graphic designers interested in modernism. Tom Purvis, the artist who did a large number of posters for the LNER, worked for other clients such as the London men's clothier

Austin Reed, but he remained indebted to Ludwig Hohlwein's stilted figures. Austin Cooper (1890–1964) also developed a strong pictorial poster style. Like many poster artists in Britain, he worked for the railroads and the London Underground along with other clients.

By the mid-1930s a number of graphic designers who emigrated to Britain from the continent, as well as a few local designers, began to use a modernist approach more extensively. The émigrés included Hans Schleger, the aforementioned Polish designers Jan Le Witt and George Him, who formed a partnership, Lewitt-Him; and F. H. K. Henrion (1914–1990), who came to Britain from Germany in 1939. Before arriving in Britain, Schleger worked in New York and Chicago and then in W. S. Crawford's German office, while Henrion had studied with Paul Colin in Paris. Tom Eckersley, a British designer, established a partnership in London with Eric Lombers (1914–1978) and the two began to work in a modern style for Shell Mex, London Transport, and the General Post Office (GPO). At the GPO, Stephen Tallents became public relations manager in 1933 when the Empire Marketing Board ceased operations. In his new role he commissioned posters and produced films just as he had done for the EMB. Another British designer, Abram Games (1914–1996), began to experiment with the airbrush as a young man and in his posters of the 1930s developed a more conceptual approach to making images. Other modernists include James Fitton (1899–1982), who spent much of his career as the art director for Vernon's, a small advertising agency, and Pat Keely (d.o.b. unconfirmed–1970), who designed posters for London Transport, the Southern Railway, and the GPO. His GPO poster, Night Mail, was an abstract depiction of mail delivery without representing a train at all, only a sequence of railroad signals (Plate 19). These men formed the core of a widening pool of commercial artists who were learning to think of themselves as modern graphic designers. They gained importance as propaganda designers during World War

Fig. 23.20: H. H. Harris, Bovril prevents that sinking feeling, poster, c. 1925. © Pictorial Press Ltd/Alamy.

Fig. 23.21: John Gilroy, Guinness for strength, poster, 1934. © Pictorial Press Ltd/Alamy.

II and emerged after the war as a group that charted a new direction for British graphic design.

By contrast, the majority of Britain's commercial artists thought of themselves as painters or illustrators first. Some illustrators continued the folksy anecdotal humor that John Hassall had previously introduced in his posters and book illustrations. Rex Whistler (1905–1944) did a series of witty drawings to advertise the London department store Fortnum & Mason, while H. H. Harris (dates unconfirmed) created posters for Bovril, the beef extract. One depicted a grinning pajama-clad chap clinging to a jar of the extract that was floating in the ocean. The homey copy line read "Bovril prevents that sinking feeling" (Fig. 23.20). The most sustained example of this folksy humor was the series of posters that John Gilroy (1898–1985) designed for Guinness stout. As an artist employed by S. H. Benson, the advertising agency that had the Guinness account, Gilroy created many humorous variations on the famous copy lines, "Lovely day for a Guinness," "My goodness, my Guinness." and "Guinness for strength." In a poster with the latter copy line, Gilroy, with understated wit, showed a workman effortlessly carrying a heavy steel beam after downing a glass of stout (Fig. 23.21).

Compared to the manipulative American advertisements or the design-oriented ones in Germany and other countries that were influenced by the New Typography, humor remained a staple of British product advertising throughout the 1920s and 1930s. It was less evident, however, in the large poster campaigns for the London Underground, Shell, Imperial Airways, the railroads, and the General Post Office. The publicity managers who supervised those campaigns envisioned advertising as a new form of public art that could raise the cultural profiles of their organizations and they preferred not to detract from that aspiration with folksy humor.

Bibliography
Bibliographic essay

A number of publications address British design during the 1900–1939 period. One of the earliest is Henry G. Dowling, *A Survey of British Industrial Arts*. A major contribution came from several volumes of the ground-breaking Open University course, *History of Architecture and Design, 1890–1939*, notably *A Survey of Design in Britain 1915–1939* and *The Electric Home: A Case Study of the Domestic Revolution of the Inter-War Years*. Related books, book chapters, and articles include James Peto and Donna Loveday, *Modern Britain 1929–1939*; the exhibition catalog, *Thirties: British Art and Design Before the War*; Paul Greenhalgh's essay, "The English Compromise: Modern Design and National Consciousness, 1870–1940," in the exhibition catalog that Wendy Kaplan edited, *Designing Modernity: The Arts of Reform and Persuasion, 1885–1945*; Penny Sparke, "Great Britain: Eclecticism, Empiricism, and Anti-Industrial Culture," in *History of Industrial Design 1919–1990: The Domain of Design*; and Jonathan Woodham's article, "Design and Empire: British Design in the 1920s," *Art History* 3, no. 2 (June 1980). Woodham has written other essays and articles on this period including "British Art in Industry in 1935," in *Design and Industry: The Effects of Industrialization and Technological Change on Design,* and "British Modernism Between the Wars: An Historical Survey," in Victor Margolin, Anty Pansera, and Frederick Wildhagen, eds., *Tradizione e Modernismo: Design 1918–1940/Tradition and Modernism: Design Between the Wars.* Woodham also wrote a seminal article about the British Empire Exhibitions, "Images of Africa and Design at British Empire Exhibitions Between the Wars," *Journal of Design History* 2, no. 1 (1989). The Empire Marketing Board is discussed in Stephen Constantine, *Buy and Build; the Advertising Posters of the Empire Marketing Board* and David Meredith's article, "Imperial Images: The Empire Marketing Board, 1926–32," *History Today* 37, no. 1 (January 1987). Christian Barman, *The Man Who Built London Transport: A Biography of Frank Pick* is a major account of the man who played a central role in British design during the interwar period besides heading the London Underground, while Oliver Green, *Underground Art* is a comprehensive study of the London Underground posters.

The Design Council published an excellent series of short biographies of important British designers. Books on designers active in the interwar period include Ken and Kate Baynes, *Gordon Russell*; Avril Blake, *Milner Gray* and *Misha Black*; and Mary Schoeser, *Marianne Straub*. Another valuable biography, brought

out by a different publisher, is Sherban Cantacazuno, *Wells Coates: A Monograph.* Besides the Straub volume, other studies of women designers active in this period include Christian Boydell, "Women Textile Designers in the 1920s and 1930s: Marion Dorn, a Case Study," in Judy Attfield and Pat Kirkham, eds., *A View from the Interior: Feminism, Women and Design*; Suzette Worden, "Powerful Women: Electricity in the Home, 1919–1940," and Cheryl Buckley, "A Comparative Study of Susan Vera Cooper and Millicent Jane Taplin," both in the Attfield and Kirkham volume; Suzette Worden and Jill Seddon, "Women Designers in Britain in the 1920s and 1930s: Defining the Professional and Redefining Design," *Journal of Design History* 8, no. 3 (1995); Cheryl Buckley, "The Decorated Object: Gender, Modernism and the Design of Industrial Ceramics in Britain in the 1930s," in Bridget Elliott and Janice Helland, eds., *Women Artists and the Decorative Arts, 1880–1935*; Jill Seddon, "Mentioned, but Denied Significance: Women Designers and the 'Professionalisation' of Design in Britain c. 1920–1951," *Gender & History* 12, no. 2 (July 2000); and Jill Seddon and Suzette Worden, *Women Designing: Redefining Design in Britain Between the Wars.*

Books and articles that consider various aspects of modernism in Great Britain include Julian Holder, "'Design in Everyday Things': Promoting Modernism in Britain, 1912–1944," in Paul Greenhalgh, ed., *Modernism in Design*; Gillian Naylor, "Conscience and Consumption: Art Deco in Britain," in Charlotte Benton, Tim Benton, and Ghislaine Wood, eds., *Art Deco 1910–1939,* the catalog of a large exhibition at the Victoria & Albert Museum; and J. M. Richards, "Towards a Rational Aesthetic," in Dennis Sharp, ed., *The Rationalists: Theory and Design in the Modern Movement.* Walter Gropius, *The New Architecture and the Bauhaus* is a volume that introduced tenets of the Bauhaus and the Modern Movement to a British audience. Several books and articles cover companies that manufactured or distributed modern furniture: Barbara Tilson, "Plan Furniture 1932–1938: The German

Connection," *Journal of Design History* 3, nos. 1–2 (1990); Jack Pritchard, *View from a Long Chair;* Dennis Sharp, Tim Benton, and Barbie Campbell Cole, *Pel and Tubular Steel Furniture of the Thirties*; and Kevin Davies, "Finmar and the Furniture of the Future: The Sale of Alvar Aalto's Plywood Furniture in the UK, 1934–1939," *Journal of Design History* 11, no. 2 (1998). Kenneth Richardson's *The British Motor Industry, 1896–1939* was a helpful source of information on British automobile design, and David Jeremiah's "Filling Up: The British Experience, 1896–1940," *Journal of Design History* 8, no. 2 (1995) recounts the early history of gasoline pumps and service stations in Britain.

Books by design critics are Anthony Bertram, *Design*; Noel Carrington, *Industrial Design in Britain*; John Gloag, ed., *The English Tradition in Design* and as author, *Design in Modern Life* and *Industrial Art Explained*; Nikolaus Pevsner, *An Enquiry into Industrial Art in England*; and Herbert Read, *Art & Industry: The Principles of Industrial Design.* Articles about these books include Robin Kinross, "Herbert Read's *Art and Industry*: A History," *Journal of Design History* 1, no. 1 (1988) and Pauline Madge, "An Enquiry into Pevsner's *Enquiry*," *Journal of Design History* 1, no. 2 (1988).

On British typographers during this period, Nicholas Barker's monumental biography, *Stanley Morison*, was extremely helpful as was Malcolm Yorke, *Eric Gill: Man of Flesh and Spirit.* Gill's *An Essay on Typography* is a strong statement of his own views on the subject. An excellent discussion on book design can be found in P. M. Handover, "British Book Typography," in Kenneth Day, ed., *Book Typography 1915–1965 in Europe and The United States of America*, while a number of books and articles discuss British advertising and important graphic designers. They include Michael Havinden. *Advertising and the Artist: Ashley Havinden*; Mark Haworth-Booth, *E. McKnight Kauffer: A Designer and His Public*; Pat Schleger, *Hans Schleger: A Life in Design;* and numerous articles and a book and several articles by John Hewitt. The book is *The Commercial Art of Tom Purvis* and the articles are "The 'Nature' and

'Art' of Shell Advertising in the Early 1930s," *Journal of Design History* 5, no. 2 (1992); "*East Coast Joys*: Tom Purvis and the LNER," *Journal of Design History* 8, no. 4 (1995); and "Posters of Distinction: Art Advertising and the London, Midland, and Scottish Railways," *Design Issues* 16, no. 1 (Spring 2000).

Books

Barker, Nicolas. *Stanley Morison*. Cambridge, MA: Harvard University Press, 1972.

Barman, Christian. *The Man Who Built London Transport: A Biography of Frank Pick*. Newton Abbot, London, and North Pomfret, VT: David & Charles, 1979.

Baynes, Ken and Kate. *Gordon Russell*. London: Design Council, 1981.

Bertram, Anthony. *Design*. Harmondsworth: Penguin, 1938.

Blake, Avril. *Misha Black*. London: Design Council, 1984.

—*Milner Gray*. London: Design Council, 1986.

Cantacazuno, Sherban. *Wells Coates: A Monograph*. London: Gordon Fraser, 1978.

Carrington, Noel. *Industrial Design in Britain*. London: George Allen & Unwin, 1976.

Constantine, Stephen. *Buy and Build; the Advertising Posters of the Empire Marketing Board*. London: Her Majesty's Stationery Office, 1986.

Dowling, Henry G. *A Survey of British Industrial Arts*. Benfleet: F. Lewis, 1935.

Gill, Eric. *An Essay on Typography*. With a new introduction by Christopher Skelton. Boston: David R. Godine, 1988 (c. 1936).

Gloag, John. *Industrial Art Explained*. London: George Allen & Unwin, 1934.

—*The English Tradition in Design*. London and New York: King Penguin, 1947.

—ed. *Design in Modern Life*. London: George Allen & Unwin, 1934.

Green, Oliver. *Underground Art*. 2nd ed. London: Laurence King, 2001.

Gropius, Walter. *The New Architecture and the Bauhaus.* Introduction by Frank Pick. Translated by P. Morton Shand. Cambridge, MA: MIT Press, 1965.

Havinden, Michael. *Advertising and the Artist: Ashley Havinden.* Edinburgh: National Galleries of Scotland, 2004.

Haworth-Booth, Mark. *E. McKnight Kauffer: A Designer and His Public.* London: Gordon Fraser, 1979.

Hewitt, John. *The Commercial Art of Tom Purvis.* Manchester: Manchester Metropolitan University Press, 1996.

Open University. *A Survey of Design in Britain 1915–1939,* prepared by Geoffrey Newman; and *The Electric Home; A Case Study of the Domestic Revolution of the Inter-War Years,* prepared by Adrian Forty [History of Architecture and Design, 1890–1939]. Milton Keynes: The Open University Press, 1975.

Peto, James and Donna Loveday. *Modern Britain 1929–1939.* London: The Design Museum 1999.

Pevsner, Nikolaus. *An Enquiry into Industrial Art in England.* New York: Macmillan, and Cambridge: Cambridge University Press, 1937.

Pritchard, Jack. *View from a Long Chair.* Introduction by Fiona MacCarthy. London, Boston, Melbourne, and Henley: Routledge & Kegan Paul, 1984.

Read, Herbert. *Art & Industry: The Principles of Industrial Design.* Bloomington: Indiana University Press, 1961 (c. 1934).

Richardson, Kenneth. *The British Motor Industry, 1896–1939.* London: Macmillan, 1977.

Schleger, Pat. *Hans Schleger: A Life in Design.* New York: Princeton Architectural Press, 2001.

Schoeser, Mary. *Marianne Straub.* London: Design Council, 1984.

Seddon, Jill and Suzette Worden. *Women Designing: Redefining Design in Britain Between the Wars.* Brighton: University of Brighton, 1994.

Sharp, Dennis, Tim Benton, and Barbie Campbell Cole. *Pel and Tubular Steel Furniture of the Thirties.* London: The Architectural Association, 1977.

Sparke, Penny. *A Century of Car Design.* Hauppauge, NY: Barron's, 2002.

Thirties: British Art and Design Before the War. London: Arts Council of Great Britain, 1979.

Weill, Alain, *The Poster.* Boston: G. J. K. Hall, 1985.

Yorke, Malcolm. *Eric Gill: Man of Flesh and Spirit.* New York: Universe Books, 1981.

Chapters in books

Boydell, Christine, "Women Textile Designers in the 1920s and 1930s: Marion Dorn, a Case Study," in Judy Attfield and Pat Kirkham, eds. *A View from the Interior: Feminism, Women and Design.* London: Women's Press, 1989.

Buckley, Cheryl, "A Comparative Study of Susan Vera Cooper and Millicent Jane Taplin," in Judy Attfield and Pat Kirkham, eds. *A View from the Interior: Feminism, Women and Design.* London: Women's Press, 1989.

—"The Decorated Object: Gender, Modernism and the Design of Industrial Ceramics in Britain in the 1930s," in Bridget Elliott and Janice Helland, eds. *Women Artists and the Decorative Arts, 1880–1935.* Aldershot and Burlington, VT: Ashgate, 2002.

Greenhalgh, Paul, "The English Compromise: Modern Design and National Consciousness, 1870–1940," in Wendy Kaplan, ed. *Designing Modernity: The Arts of Reform and Persuasion, 1885–1945.* New York: Thames and Hudson, 1995.

Handover, P. M. "British Book Typography," in Kenneth Day, ed. *Book Typography 1915–1965 in Europe and The United States of America.* Chicago: University of Chicago Press, 1965.

Holder, Julian, "'Design in Everyday Things': Promoting Modernism in Britain, 1912–1944," in Paul Greenhalgh, ed. *Modernism in Design.* London: Reaktion Books, 1990.

Naylor, Gillian, "Conscience and Consumption: Art Deco in Britain," in Charlotte Benton, Tim Benton, and Ghislaine Wood, eds. *Art Deco 1910–1939.*

Boston, New York, and London: Bulfinch Group, 2003.

Richards, J. M. "Towards a Rational Aesthetic," in Dennis Sharp, ed. *The Rationalists: Theory and Design in the Modern Movement.* New York: Architectural Book Publishing, 1979.

Sparke, Penny, "Great Britain: Eclecticism, Empiricism, and Anti-Industrial Culture," in *History of Industrial Design 1919–1990: The Domain of Design.* Milan: Electa, 1991.

Woodham, Jonathan, "British Art in Industry in 1935," in *Design and Industry: The Effects of Industrialization and Technological Change on Design.* London: Design Council, 1980.

—"British Modernism Between the Wars: An Historical Survey," in Victor Margolin, Anty Pansera, and Frederick Wildhagen, eds. *Tradizione e Modernismo: Design 1918–1940/Tradition and Modernism: Design Between the Wars.* Milan: l'Arca, 1988.

Worden, Suzette, "Powerful Women: Electricity in the Home, 1919–1940," in Judy Attfield and Pat Kirkham, eds. *A View from the Interior: Feminism, Women and Design.* London: Women's Press, 1989.

Articles

Davies, Kevin, "Finmar and the Furniture of the Future: The Sale of Alvar Aalto's Plywood Furniture in the UK, 1934–1939," *Journal of Design History* 11, no. 2 (1998).

Hewitt, John, "The 'Nature' and 'Art' of Shell Advertising in the Early 1930s," *Journal of Design History* 5, no. 2 (1992).

—"*East Coast Joys*: Tom Purvis and the LNER," *Journal of Design History* 8, no. 4 (1995).

—"Posters of Distinction: Art Advertising and the London, Midland, and Scottish Railways," *Design Issues* 16, no. 1 (Spring 2000).

Jeremiah, David, "Filling Up: The British Experience, 1896–1940," *Journal of Design History* 8, no. 2 (1995).

Kinross, Robin, "Herbert Read's *Art and Industry*: A History," *Journal of Design History* 1, no. 1 (1988).

Madge, Pauline, "An Enquiry into Pevsner's *Enquiry*," *Journal of Design History* 1, no. 2 (1988).

Meredith, David, "Imperial Images: The Empire Marketing Board, 1926–32," *History Today* 37, no. 1 (January 1987).

Seddon, Jill, "Mentioned, but Denied Significance: Women Designers and the 'Professionalisation' of Design in Britain c. 1920–1951," *Gender & History* 12, no. 2 (July 2000).

Tilson, Barbara, "Plan Furniture 1932–1938: The German Connection," *Journal of Design History* 3, nos. 1–2 (1990).

Woodham, Jonathan, "Design and Empire: British Design in the 1920s," *Art History* 3, no. 2 (June 1980).

—"Images of Africa and Design at British Empire Exhibitions Between the Wars," *Journal of Design History* 2, no. 1 (1989).

Worden, Suzette and Jill Seddon, "Women Designers in Britain in the 1920s and 1930s: Defining the Professional and Redefining Design," *Journal of Design History* 8, no. 3 (1995).

Chapter 24: Western and Southern Europe 1900–1939

Introduction

Aside from the Great Powers—Britain, France, and Germany—and the widespread social democracy in Scandinavia, other countries in Western Europe experienced an extremely diverse mix of political circumstances in the period after World War I. These ranged from stable democracies in the Netherlands and Switzerland, to monarchy in Belgium, and dictatorships in Spain and Portugal. The League of Nations, which was established in Geneva, had some diplomatic success in building relations among European nations but it was ultimately unable to prevent the rise of dictatorships across Europe beginning with Benito Mussolini in Italy in 1922, and followed by Antonio Salazar in Portugal in 1926, Adolf Hitler in Germany in 1933, and finally Francisco Franco in Spain in 1939.

For small democratic countries like the Netherlands and Switzerland, which had been neutral during World War I, the political order remained stable. In Belgium, the monarchy continued, although the country was governed by an elected parliament. Belgium had its own right-wing movement in the 1930s in the form of the Rexist Party, which wanted to substitute an authoritarian corporatist society for the country's democratic government.

In Spain, the intensified bid for Catalan independence after World War I contributed to a military coup, headed by Primo de Rivera, which lasted until 1930. Between then and the start of the Spanish Civil War in 1936, the country experienced a struggle between forces of the left and right with the left ultimately being defeated in 1937 by the army of General Francisco Franco, who then established a new long-lasting dictatorship.

Netherlands

As a neutral country in World War I, the Netherlands sought to strengthen its economy so as to compete successfully with larger, more industrially developed, nations when the war ended. The Vereeniging van Ambachts- en Nijverheidskunst (Association for Crafts and Industrial Art), also known as VANK, had been founded in 1904 to promote a closer relation between art and industry. VANK supported the diverse interests of Dutch artist-craftsmen who were seeking their own relation to production rather than being continually beholden to architects for commissions. Like the Arts and Crafts Society in Britain, which was also active at the time, VANK held annual exhibitions and sponsored competitions for all forms of applied art. It also published an annual yearbook. Among its founders was the furniture designer Willem Penaat (1875–1957), a leading advocate for improving the aesthetic quality of Dutch products, who served as VANK's president from 1913 to 1922.

Though VANK was primarily concerned with the needs of its members rather than the larger economy, it did encourage the founding of other organizations that were more directly engaged with the improvement of Dutch industrial products. Shortly after Penaat became president of VANK, he lent the organization's support for the founding of the Nederlandse Driebond (Dutch Triple Alliance), an organization similar to the Deutscher Werkbund that was to bring together representatives of art, industry, and commerce. The founding was delayed by the outbreak of World War I and a later attempt to bring together the appropriate parties was unsuccessful.

A more effective effort to raise the quality of Dutch manufactured goods, though not one initiated by VANK, was the establishment of the Nederlandsche Jaarbeurs (Dutch Industries Fair), which held its first exhibition in 1917. The intention of the fair's organizers was initially to make Dutch products better known to the public but after 1921 other nations were also invited to exhibit. Dutch industries were at first slow to see the fair's value but after several years participation began to grow rapidly, though few foreign companies exhibited. The fair's annual posters by well-known designers mirrored the changes in Dutch graphic style from the decorative designs of the *Nieuwe Kunst* to the more simplified designs that were influenced by modern trends (Fig. 24.01).

Fig. 24.01: Carel Adolphe Lion Cachet, Industries Fair, poster, 1917. ReclameArsenaal, www.reclamearsenaal.nl

Although there had been insufficient interest in the Driebond, another organization, the Bond voor Kunst in Industrie (Association for Art in Industry) did take up the challenge of improving the quality of Dutch products, rather than just exhibiting them. Founded in 1924 by a group of idealistic art manufacturers and known as the BKI, its emphasis was on industrial goods. The founders of the BKI wanted to create objects of beauty just as their Arts and Crafts predecessors did, but they wished to do so through machine production rather than the crafts. Despite such efforts, craft production remained strong in the Netherlands during the interwar years. Few companies could demonstrate the economic and aesthetic potential of mass production; hence most manufacturers, particularly in the furniture sector, continued to operate on the workshop model.

The Amsterdam School

The Arts and Crafts tradition was a powerful influence on the architects and designers of the Amsterdam School, who countered the rationalism that H. P. Berlage propounded at the beginning of the century with a more Expressionist and subjective decorative style. The school's leading architects were Michel De Klerk (1884–1923) and Piet Kramer (1881–1961). The philosophy of the Amsterdam School—a name introduced by the architect Jan Gratama (1877–1947) in 1916—sustained two strong principles that were associated with the Arts and Crafts movement: a belief in the unity of all the arts from architecture and sculpture to ironwork and stained glass; and an opposition to mass production.

Both principles were evident in the first example of Amsterdam School architecture and interior design—the Scheepvarthuis, a building that housed the offices of six shipping companies. De Klerk, Kramer, and Jan van der Mey (1878–1949) collaborated on its design and construction between 1912 and 1916. Rich in all forms of decoration, both inside and outside, the Scheepvarthuis supported the argument, later to be the basis of the first Bauhaus manifesto, that architecture and the crafts could be combined to create a great work of art.

The Arts and Crafts philosophy of the Amsterdam School architects was also supported by the Social Democrats on the Amsterdam City Council who believed as the architects did that the ideals of John Ruskin and William Morris could lead to a beautiful environment for everyone. As a consequence of this intersection of beliefs, De Klerk and Kramer built several low-income housing developments in Amsterdam whose Expressionist forms, brick construction, and rich ornamentation demonstrated on an urban scale ideals of beauty that had previously only been seen in large English and Scottish suburban villas such as Philip Webb's Red House, the Perrycroft House by Charles Voysey, and Charles Rennie Mackintosh's Hill House outside of Glasgow. Of the housing estates that De Klerk and Kramer designed, those at the Spaardammerplantsoen (1913–1920) in the southern part of Amsterdam are exemplary as are the expressive sculptural blocks for the De Dagaraad (The Dawn) housing association further north. The estates, as well as various schools and bridges, were embellished with stone ornaments and figures of humans and animals, sculpted largely by Hildo Krop (1884–1970). Employed by the Municipal Department of Buildings and Works, Kramer designed more than 400 bridges for the city of Amsterdam.

De Klerk and Kramer also created interiors and furniture. Kramer's interior design for the Hague department store De Bijenkorf (The Beehive), done between 1924 and 1926, turned the retail space into a fantasy landscape with densely-patterned rugs, stained glass, tapestries, and curtains, all of which displayed related elements in different colors and scales. De Klerk's furniture embodied a similar sense of Orientalist lushness. He produced abundant sketches and designed a few pieces of furniture for t'Woonhuys (The Dwelling)—a company that marketed upscale furniture—which featured the pieces in their Amsterdam showroom (Fig. 24.02).

Fig. 24.02: Michel de Klerk, dining chair with armrests, 1916. The Wolfsonian–Florida International University, Miami Beach, Florida, The Mitchell Wolfson, Jr. Collection TD1989.328.9, Photo: Bruce White.

De Klerk's furniture suites incorporated exotic woods with the carved heads of fishes and frogs, eccentric Expressionist motifs, ornaments influenced by Scandinavian folk art, and expensive fabrics or leather coverings for the chairs. All these elements ensured the impossibility of serial production. The furniture was also far too large for the modest apartments that De Klerk and Kramer had been designing for the Amsterdam municipality. Made by craftsmen largely for specific interiors, a few pieces were also produced in limited runs. Both Kramer and the sculptor Hildo Krop designed furniture as well. Krop's was as heavy and ponderous as was De Klerk's although not as ornate. The Amsterdam School was rife with contradictions, a factor that explains why it waned and soon died out after De Klerk's death in 1923. Its primary accomplishment, however, was to demonstrate that the idealistic values of Morris and Ruskin could be realistically applied to the design of low-cost housing for the working class, particularly when it was subsidized by a progressive municipality

The monthly cultural journal *Wendingen* (*Turnings*) expressed many of the Amsterdam School's

values. Founded in 1918 by the architect Hendricus Theodorus Wijdeveld (1885–1987), its focus was on architecture but it also featured articles on ornament and many other cultural topics. Edited by Wijdeveld until he resigned in 1925, it continued to appear until 1932. The format was square. Like the Amsterdam School architects, Wijdeveld did not use modern materials. The journal was printed on rice paper and was bound with raffia, as were block books in Japan. The covers had no consistent masthead and the lettering

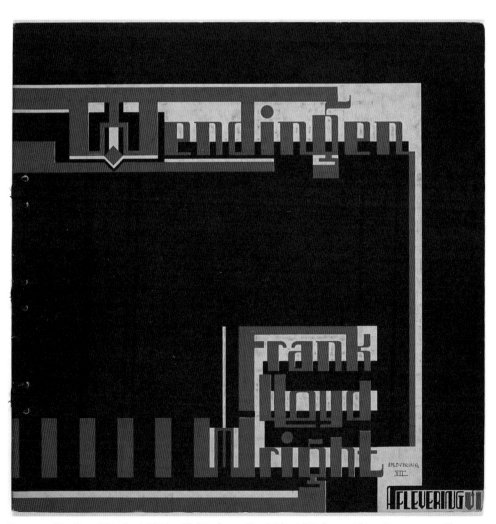

Fig. 24.03: Hendricus Theodorus Wijdeveld, *Wendingen* (Frank Lloyd Wright special issue), cover, 1925. The Wolfsonian–Florida International University, Miami Beach, Florida, The Mitchell Wolfson, Jr. Collection, XB1990.2025. Photo: David Almeida.

and design style changed from issue to issue. Widjeveld designed some of the front and back covers himself (Fig. 24.03), though he invited many artists and architects to design covers as well. Most were Dutch, but he also solicited cover designs from foreign architects and designers such as the German Expressionist Herman Finsterlin (1887–1973) and the Russian avant-garde artist and designer El Lissitzky.

Wijdeveld's own design sensibility was rooted in the dense decoration of the Dutch *Nieuwe Kunst* of the late 19th century. He also drew on the elaborate intricacy of Javanese ornament. Like De Klerk, Wijdeveld favored heavy forms. He constructed his letters from elements in the type case and crowded them together with minimal leading. This approach was also evident in the page layouts and ornaments he designed for all the issues while he was associated with the journal. Though an architect, Wijdeveld was also active as a graphic artist. Besides his work for *Wendingen*, he handled a range of commissions among which were posters, book covers and bookplates, diplomas, stationery, ornaments, and lettering assignments. His letter designs had a distinct look that came to be known as the "Wendingen style."

The Hague School

If H. P. Berlage was the architect whose rationalism the Amsterdam School rejected, he was conversely a strong influence on a group of architects and furniture designers who were called by an Amsterdam architect "de Nieuwe Haagse School" (the New Hague School). Some, like Henk Wouda (1885–1946), had trained with Berlage though they rejected the older architect's rigidity. Following his stint in Berlage's office, Wouda went to Munich where he worked for Eduard Pfeiffer (dates unconfirmed), a designer who headed the Pössenbacher Werkstätte, a studio where designers had adopted the style of the Austrian and German Secession. Back in The Hague, Wouda joined Pander, one of Holland's largest interior design firms, in 1917. Pander specialized in expensive projects for which they

provided all the work. Besides one-off interior designs for large private homes, businesses, and institutions, Pander also produced and marketed individual pieces of furniture as well as furniture suites. Much of this was in historic styles but the firm also sold a smaller number of modern pieces.

Beginning in 1911, Pander was the first furniture company in the Netherlands to hire modern designers, who were mainly employed for large projects such as furnishing ocean liners. Wouda was brought in as a designer in the modern style and shortly after joining the company he became head of the Department of Modern Interior Design. The style Wouda initially adopted was primarily based on the plain undecorated furniture of Frank Lloyd Wright. His chairs for the Villa Sevensteijn, designed in 1921, for example, strongly recall the straight-backed seating that Wright designed for the Robie House a few years earlier. Unlike Wright, however, Wouda often used exotic woods, no doubt brought from the Dutch East Indies, and he painted some of his furniture in strong colors. Pander publicized Wouda's interiors widely, featuring them in showrooms as well as their company magazine *Thuis* (*At Home*). Many of Wouda's furniture designs were single pieces or suites for wealthy clients but Pander produced cheaper versions for a wider public and featured them in their showrooms.

Designers working in Wouda's department at Pander included Cor Alons (1892–1967) and J. Brunott (1889–1951). Alons left Pander in 1921 to start his own business and in 1923 he founded an interior design firm with Frits Spanjaard (1889–1978). In the interior design projects the two undertook, they followed the example of Wouda, featuring one-off cupboards, chairs, tables, and armchairs that were lacquered pieces and designed with right angles. Besides furniture, Alons also created designs for stained glass, ceramics, and enamel kitchenware. Brunott left Pander in 1923 and, like Alons and Spanjaard, produced furniture designs on commission. For the most part all the designers who had previously worked for Pander concentrated mainly on one-off pieces, which they manufactured in small workshops.

Before joining with Alons, Spanjaard had been a designer for the idealistic LOV Furniture Factory located near The Hague. LOV was founded in 1910 by Gerrit Pelt (1864–1956), whose aim was to reform society without resorting to revolution. To do so, he sought to enhance the living standards of the working class, intending to market furniture for workers as well as set up housing organizations for them. To earn revenue, his company mainly produced luxury handcrafted furniture, at first in period styles but after 1915 in a modern idiom. These pieces were also made in inexpensive versions to suit working-class budgets. Though the company had its own showrooms and sold a limited number of pieces to furniture retailers in other cities, the managers could not create a wide enough market for the handcrafted pieces. The company folded in 1935, unable to survive the harsh economic conditions of the Depression. Though LOV did not create successful lines of low-cost furniture, Pelt did introduce major innovations in work conditions by allowing workers to have a say in company management as well as share in the company's profits. Besides paying high wages, LOV was the first furniture factory in the Netherlands to introduce the eight-hour working day. It was also one of the first to provide paid vacations for its workers.

After 1925, the Hague School designers began to add chrome strips and handles to their furniture just as designers in Paris were doing. If there was a strong influence of the French Deco style in Holland, it was in The Hague. Custom-made pieces combined exotic woods with modern designs that could just as easily have been displayed in one of the annual French decorators' salons. Clearly the Hague School designers, following Wouda's lead, had come a long way from the Prairie Style furniture of Frank Lloyd Wright.

Wouda preferred to work for individual clients where he could control not only the furniture designs but also the placement of the pieces in the interior.

In this sense, he was not so far in principle from the Amsterdam School designers who were also opposed to mass production. By 1930, however, harsh economic conditions had reduced the demand for luxury furniture and made it necessary for Dutch furniture companies to compete with the low-priced mass-produced furniture from abroad. In 1930, Wouda left his full-time position with Pander and became a freelance interior designer, concentrating as much as he could on architectural and interior design commissions. In 1933, Pander hired a Belgian designer, J. F. Semey (1891–1973), who brought in his own commissions for interior design projects in the French Deco style. Semey also worked on ship interiors including the Holland-America Line's *Nieuw Amsterdam*, which he completed between 1936 and 1938.

De Stijl

De Stijl (The Style) was an avant-garde movement founded by a Dutchman, Theo van Doesburg (1888–1931), a many-sided artist, poet, essayist, interior designer, and architect, in 1917. Whereas the Amsterdam School architects based their architecture, furniture, and decorative art on individual expression, the painters, sculptors, architects, and poets who signed the first De Stijl manifesto in 1918 were drawn together by their belief that a universal language of form could overcome the destruction of war and herald the arrival of a new spiritual consciousness. The signatories to the first De Stijl manifesto in 1918, besides van Doesburg, included artist Piet Mondrian (1872–1944), architect Robert van t'Hoff (1887–1979), artist Vilmos Huszár (1884–1960), and architect Jan Wils (1891–1972). Like *Wendingen*, which expressed the values of the Amsterdam School, van Doesburg's journal, *De Stijl*, conveyed the beliefs of his movement. The first issues carried Piet Mondrian's lengthy philosophical articles on the "nieuwe beelding" or neo-plasticism, as they referred to painting. But De Stijl ideas, in fact, had their greatest impact on the design of furniture, interiors, printed matter, and architecture.

Mondrian provided much of the visual and philosophical stimulus for De Stijl. He was influenced by the work of Dutch philosopher M. H. J. Schoenmaekers, who proclaimed the spiritual significance of the horizontal and vertical line and the three primary colors. Schoenmaekers' philosophy encouraged Mondrian to break completely with the world of nature and to create painting based on a formal system of shapes and colors that could represent the state of purity he sought. Though not an official member of De Stijl, Bart van der Leck (1876–1958) was most likely the first painter in the De Stijl milieu to limit his palette to the primary colors. Vilmos Huszár (1884–1960), who had emigrated to Holland from Hungary, followed a similar path.

In the early years of De Stijl, van Doesburg and Huszár collaborated actively with several architects including van t'Hoff and J. J. P. Oud on the design of interiors. van Doesburg did not believe that painting and sculpture belonged to a separate aesthetic realm; rather, he envisioned them as a part of life and wanted to incorporate art into the design of buildings and interiors.

Working with architect van t'Hoff in 1919, van Doesburg designed the first interior to demonstrate the principles of De Stijl. It was a remodeling project for the home of Bart de Ligt, one of Holland's leading pacifists and left-wing intellectuals. In the conservatory, the four walls and the ceiling were filled with black, green, and orange rectangles, which van Doesburg later characterized in De Stijl as demonstrating "how a painterly colour distribution is possible in a three-dimensional space."

De Ligt also commissioned chairs and a table for the conservatory from Gerrit Rietveld (1888–1964), a furniture maker who joined the De Stijl group for a brief period around 1919. Rietveld had taken evening classes in furniture design with the architect Piet Klaarhamer (1874–1954), who also taught van der Leck and Huszár, and he enrolled in industrial art classes at the Utrecht Museum of Arts and Crafts.

After working for others for some time, he opened his own furniture workshop in Utrecht in 1917. Furniture by Klaarhamer and the architect H. P. Berlage, as well as pieces by Frank Lloyd Wright and Charles Rennie Mackintosh, are likely sources for Rietveld's own designs. The armchair, later known as the Red and Blue chair, that he designed in 1918 before he was aware of the De Stijl group is a sculptural object, consisting of flat wooden panels for the back, seat, and sides, supported by a system of linear wooden braces. Rietveld never standardized the production of this chair and continued to refine it as he produced additional examples in his workshop. The initial ones were stained rather than painted and Rietveld did not create a version with the primary colors and black until 1923, several years after he encountered van Doesburg and the De Stijl journal (Plate 20).

For a beechwood sideboard of 1919, Rietveld separated the sections into a flat planar surface, linear braces, and rectangular drawers. His design exposed the sideboard's structure and emphasized its efficiency. Its open construction recalls British architect E. W. Godwin's Japanese-inspired sideboard of 1867, but Rietveld went farther than Godwin in conceiving the sideboard as an assemblage of components whose separate identities are evident in the design. Once De Stijl entered its international phase around 1921, Rietveld's furniture and his later interiors and architecture came to the attention of artists and architects abroad. His vocabulary of lines and planes was severe but it enabled him to build modestly-priced modern furniture that was accessible to middle-class consumers. Besides the furniture's affordability, its formal minimalism and rectilinear structure of lines and planes became a design ideology for several generations of architects and designers.

Rietveld further developed his aesthetic of lines and planes in the house he designed together with its client, Mrs. Truus Schröder-Schräder, in 1924–1925. Built at the end of a block of a conventional row of houses in Utrecht, the Schröder house consists of a

Fig. 24.04: Gerrit Rietveld, Schröder house, exterior, 1924–1925. © Bildarchiv Monheim GmbH/Alamy. © DACS 2017.

basic volume combined with horizontal and vertical planes and linear girders (Fig. 24.04). Following van Doesburg's ideas about integrating color into architecture, Rietveld added accents of red, yellow, and black to the exterior.

For the interior, Truss Schröder-Schräder introduced the idea of moveable panels on the second floor so that the room configurations could be changed. Rietveld continued the color accents for interior elements such as window frames, blinds, and stairway posts. He divided the floors as well into interlocking rectangular sections of gray, red, black, and white and continued to use horizontal and vertical planes for some of the built-in furniture and for various free-standing furniture pieces. One of the lighting fixtures consisted of suspended horizontal and vertical fluorescent tubes that followed a similar fixture he designed for the clinic of Dr. De Hartog in Maarssen in 1923. Though Rietveld built other houses during the 1920s, none exemplified De Stijl's strict principles of form and color as did the Schröder house.

As an avant-garde movement, De Stijl was influential in establishing a vocabulary of geometric elements that was widely adopted for furniture design, printed matter, and architecture. It challenged both the period styles that were prevalent in furniture design

and architecture as well as the expressive forms of the Amsterdam School. By 1925, the influence of the Amsterdam School had waned while the principles of De Stijl found a wider sphere of influence in the emergence of the Neue Sachlichkeit or New Objectivity in Germany, where van Doesburg lived from 1920 to 1923, and eventually back in Holland where it was known by its Dutch name, Nieuwe Zakelijkheid.

Dutch Functionalism

In response to earlier movements, Dutch Functionalism opposed both the individual expression and resistance to mechanization of the Amsterdam School while addressing in a more flexible way the potential of mass production than the De Stijl theorists did. Functionalist ideas animated the founding in 1920 of De Opbouw (Construction), an architectural club that included J. J. P. Oud, L. C. van der Vlugt (1894–1936), W. H. Gispen (1890–1981), and Mart Stam (1899–1986) as members. In 1916, Gispen had founded W. H. Gispen & Co. as a blacksmith's workshop to do custom metalwork but in 1919 his firm embraced serial production with a series of cast copper lamps. Influenced by the Functionalist ideas of De Opbouw as well as by De Stijl, Gispen began in 1926 to produce a series of modern hanging lamps covered by plain glass casings separated from the wiring by metal discs (Fig. 24.05). Sold under the trade name Giso, they were produced in sizeable runs. By standardizing many of the parts, the firm was able to produce the Giso lamp in a number of variations. In 1927, W. H. Gispen began to experiment with metal furniture and by 1929, was manufacturing tubular steel furnishings in numbers equivalent to the Giso lamp. W. H. Gispen's entry into this market was abetted by a commission from the Van Nelle tobacco, coffee and tea company to supply lighting and tubular steel furniture for their new factory, which was designed by the office of Functionalist architects Johannes Brinkman (1902–1949) and L. C. van der Vlugt (1894–1936),who were associated with the movement known as the Nieuwe Bouwen (New Building). Gispen himself also

Fig. 24.05: W. H. Gispen, Giso Lamps, poster, 1928. © PARIS PIERCE/ Alamy.

exhibition in Stuttgart, Germany, a lecturer at the Bauhaus, an architect on Ernst May's staff for the construction of the Neue Frankfurt, and a member of the team that went with May to the Soviet Union in 1930.

Stam was also the first to create a metal cantilever chair. In 1926, while collaborating with Mies van der Rohe on the plans for the Weissenhof exhibition, he designed a chair with gas-pipe tubing and elbow joints, which was then produced in an improved version with chromed tubular steel and became the prototype for similar chairs made by others (see Chapter 21). By the end of the 1920s, some Dutch designers had joined with a few manufacturers to produce tubular steel furniture for the mass market. On the one hand, it was purported to represent a new modern ideal of beauty, while on the other it embodied new attitudes towards hygiene and comfort.

Functionalism was also apparent in the glassware that a line of architects and designers created for the Leerdam Glassworks. Leerdam had been founded in 1875 and by 1919, inspired by the theosophist philosophy of the managing director P. M. Cochius, who believed that well-designed products could contribute to the spiritual advancement of humanity, the firm had already hired established artists like the architect K. P. C. de Bazel (1869–1923) and the graphic artist Jac Jongert (1883–1942) to design for them. Beginning with de Bazel, who was also a theosophist, Leerdam produced a steady stream of elegant unadorned glassware, continuing through the Normal crystalware of Cornelis de Lorm (1875–1942), done between 1923 and 1926, the Ovata service in clear and purple crystal by the architect H. P. Berlage, and Andries Dirk Copier's (1901–1991) Peer service of 1927 and his Glide crystal glassware of around 1930.

Though trained as a typographer, Copier had joined Leerdam as a designer in 1914 and supervised much of its production during the 1920s and 1930s. His Glide glassware, designed in conjunction with the Association of Dutch Wine Merchants, was based on

designed furniture for other factories as well as an armchair for the passenger ship *Nieuw Amsterdam*.

A collaborator on the Van Nelle factory was Mart Stam, who spent considerable time working in Germany, Switzerland, and the Soviet Union. Stam, who was central to the Dutch debates between formalists and Functionalists in the 1920s, pushed hard for a Functionalist position that emphasized utility and accessibility rather than aesthetics. Animated by left-wing ideas, Stam was a co-founder of the Swiss Functionalist architecture magazine *ABC*, a designer of a row of houses for the 1927 Weissenhof housing simple geometric forms whose primary purpose was utility. Copier also revealed a De Stijl influence in the set of opaque glass cactus pots in the three primary colors that he designed in 1929. Available as cubes or tall rectangles on a black base, they were modular forms with slits on their sides so they could be joined together in numerous combinations.

A functional approach was also evident in many products designed for Metz & Co. from around 1925. Metz originated in the 19th century as a draper's shop. In 1902, Joseph de Leeuw, who had become the owner around 1900, acquired the license to sell goods from the London department store Liberty's. To the Arts and Crafts-inspired products of Liberty's, de Leeuw added goods designed by Viennese, French, and Dutch industrial artists. Besides the glassware of Leerdam, Metz distributed textiles from the Weverij De Ploeg (De Ploeg Weaving Works), a cooperative enterprise that featured among its designers Otti Berger (1898–1944), who had studied and taught at the Bauhaus, and De Distel (The Thistle), which featured a broad range of ceramic products by artists, some of whom had been active in the Nieuwe Kunst.

Once Metz began its own production around 1919, Paul Bromberg (1893–1949) was hired to design furniture and advise clients on interior design. He left in 1924 to join Pander in The Hague and later went on to edit the influential interior design magazine *Binnenhuis* (*Interiors*). Bromberg was succeeded by Willem Penaat, the well-known interior architect who had been active in the early days of the VANK. Penaat's sober wooden furniture recalled the pared down designs of Henk Wouda and other designers of the Hague School, although it was made by machine rather than by craftsmen as Wouda preferred. Penaat's furniture formed the basis of Metz's department of interior furnishings, but De Leeuw had come into contact with Rietveld around 1930 and commissioned a series of experimental chairs from him. In response to the economic crisis of the early 1930s, Rietveld also designed a system of low-cost furniture in 1934 called

Krat (Crate). He intended the modular pieces for weekend houses although they were appropriate for use anywhere. The pieces were made from planks of cheap wood that could be shipped unassembled and then easily put together by the customer. The system included several different chairs and tables as well as a bookcase. One of the Rietveld Krat chairs had cushions covered in a fabric by Bart van der Leck, who also designed carpets for Metz with colored geometric elements on a light ground that recalled his earlier De Stijl-related paintings as did the fabrics. In addition, van der Leck did lettering for Metz's promotional material that also showed a De Stijl influence.

Besides Rietveld, De Leeuw invited other modern architects, notably J. J. P. Oud and Mart Stam, to design for his company. Oud worked in tubular steel while Stam experimented with bent furniture made of the plastic material Triplex. Wooden furniture was manufactured in Metz's own workshops, while tubular steel production was contracted out. From France, De Leeuw commissioned furniture from the modernist Art Deco designer Djo-Bourgeois, and fabric designs from Sonia Delaunay. The furniture production was managed by Elmar Berkovich (1897–1968), who also designed children's furniture for Metz made of aluminum tubing and wood panels.

De Leeuw followed an enlightened strategy of initially supporting small local enterprises like Weverij De Ploeg and De Distel and then commissioning small runs of avant-garde furniture and carpets from Rietveld and Van der Leck to satisfy the tastes of a limited market. He subsidized that production, which brought him considerable publicity, with the manufacture of more conservative furniture in larger runs. De Leeuw was an exemplary patron for designers and received praise from them for the considerable freedom he provided.

Allied with the Functionalist approach was the issue of efficiency, particularly as it related to the design of household appliances. Much of the concern with efficiency in design for the household centered on the kitchen. The culmination of efficiency

Fig. 24.06: Piet Zwart, Bruynzeel kitchen, 1938. Collection of the Gemeentemuseum Den Haag. © DACS 2017.

advocates Catherine Beecher and Christine Frederick was Grete Schütte-Lihotsky's Frankfurt kitchen, which was brought to The Hague by the Dutch Association of Housewives, a group dedicated to improving the working situation for women in the home. The major problem with the Frankfurt Kitchen was that it did not fit within the layout of the typical Dutch home. As a result, the association commissioned its own "Holland" kitchen in 1929. Designed by an architect, J. W. Janzen (dates unconfirmed), it embodied the results of American and German time and motion studies and became the first of a line of "scientific" kitchens to be designed over the years.

Between 1936 and 1938, Piet Zwart (1885–1997), best known as a graphic designer, designed a kitchen for Bruynzeel, a factory that specialized in tropical wood products. Based on a design that the company had commissioned from someone else, Zwart's kitchen consisted of standard modules that could be combined to fit personal preferences or available space (Fig.

24.06). The first version went on the market in 1938, but a subsequent version with more possibilities replaced it after World War II, setting the standard for the modern functional kitchen.

Other new electric products for the home included streamlined radios and vacuum cleaners by the artist Otto van Tussenbroek (1882–1957) for Van Der Heem, which marketed its products under the Erres name. Van Tussenbroek designed the firm's SZ3 vacuum cleaner in the shape of a zeppelin, which was a standard streamlined form. Though not Functionalist in appearance, the Erres vacuum cleaner was part of the move to make work in the home more efficient for the Dutch housewife. A more clearly functional form was the chrome-plated tubular steel electric heater, a modern replacement for oil and coal that Ari Verbeek (1893–1970) designed for Inventum, which produced in addition a range of electric products including foot warmers, stoves, and tea kettles. Also a designer of tubular steel furniture, Verbeek based his design for the heater on the same cantilever principle that Mart Stam used for his chair. Conforming to modern ideas of efficiency, it looked like a technical device rather than a traditional piece of furniture. The frame could accommodate from one to three detachable heating coils depending on the user's preference.

Philips and Fokker

Unlike Germany or the United States, much of the industrial production in the Netherlands during the 1920s and 1930s was by small or medium-sized firms that focused more on domestic consumption than exports. Among the exceptions was Philips, which had become a fairly large company by 1914, concentrating almost exclusively on the production of electric light bulbs. Due to Dutch neutrality in World War I, Philips increased its international marketing while its competitors in Britain and Germany were embroiled in the war effort. Anton Philips, who succeeded his brother Gerard as president in 1922, pushed the company away from heavy engineering towards consumer goods, beginning in 1918 with radio valves and continuing with loudspeakers in 1926 and finally radio receivers in 1927. Philips's first radio was so successful that the company doubled the number of its employees to 20,000 by 1929.

Initially Philips produced the radios but not their cabinets. For the latter, the company established contracts with various furniture manufacturers. Initially, the company used housings of wood as well as Bakelite, the first plastic material to be made from synthetic components. Bakelite was developed by Dr. Leo Baekeland, an American, between 1907 and 1909. Soon Philips began to manufacture its own version of the material, which it marketed as Philite. Initially the speakers and receivers of the radio sets were separate elements. After its original speaker in the shape of a saucer or dish, a form that Anton Philips championed, the company produced a seven-sided model called the Meesterzanger (Master Singer), which was available with or without legs. By 1931, Philips was combining

its receivers and speakers in single units. Throughout the 1930s, the shape, material, exterior decoration, and knob positions of the Philips radios changed frequently. A rectangular form became dominant and by 1931 the company had begun to produce less-expensive radios and other appliances, which differed little in technical terms from the more expensive models.

The diversion into other product lines accelerated. These included microphones, bicycle lamps, X-ray equipment, and televisions. The sales department pushed for the manufacture of combined radios and gramophones, resulting in the Philigraaf, which was marketed in a cabinet with a lid on top. In 1939, the company produced its first electric dry shaver, designed by the engineer Alexandre Horowitz (1904–1982), and marketed it as the Philishave. By this time the number of employees at Philips had grown to 45,000.

From around 1929, Philips had its own design bureau, which employed mostly technical draftsmen and construction experts. During the 1930s, decisions about new products were usually taken at meetings attended by heads of different departments—management, research, sales, and the design bureau among them. Louis Kalff (1897–1976), an architect trained at the Technical University in Delft, joined the company in 1925 to manage the artistic aspects of the company's advertising, products, and some of its architecture. Initially he created packaging for lamps and radio valves, including on the packaging for the latter a design with stars and waves that evolved into the company's logo. Though Kalff was responsible for a number of the company's product designs, it is likely that others were also involved in design decisions.

In late 1929, Philips established a Propaganda Center to coordinate all its services related to advertising. Kalff played a major role in this center where he led the Artistic Propaganda Section. Its tasks included the design of posters, show cards, advertisements, and brochures as well as cooperation on exhibitions such as the Brussels World's Fair of 1935 and the Paris Exposition of 1937, at both of which Philips had lavishly designed pavilions. Though most of its graphics were done in-house by Kalff and his staff, Philips also commissioned posters from well-known artists in other countries such as Marcel Baugniet in Belgium and A. M. Cassandre in France.

Another Dutch company with a strong international presence was founded by Anthony Fokker (1890–1939), an aviation pioneer who built his first airplane in 1910. Two years later he established Fokker Aeroplanbau in Berlin, where he developed the tri-plane that Germany's legendary Red Baron flew in World War I. In 1919, Fokker returned to the Netherlands and founded the country's first aircraft factory. Besides his factory in the Netherlands, he also owned three in the United States, where he first marketed the F-7, a plane with three motors known as a tri-motor. Designed for ten passengers, it had a spacious interior, upholstered seats, and walls covered with fabric. Though Fokker sold at least 100 planes to American airlines, he lost significant market share to a competitor called the Tin Goose. Funded by Henry Ford's son Edsel, the Tin Goose was almost an exact copy of Fokker's F-7 except that it was clad in metal instead of plywood, a characteristic that was more reassuring to many passengers.

After Holland's Royal Dutch Airlines (KLM) was founded in 1919, it purchased a number of Fokker's aircraft, one of which, the Fokker-7B, was the first to fly the intercontinental route from Holland to Batavia, the capital of the Dutch East Indies. Other airlines such as Sabena in Belgium and Swissair also purchased Fokker aircraft. The speed of the planes was limited, however, and by the late 1930s they were being outpaced by newer American planes, which cut seriously into Fokker's European sales.

Graphic design

The same conflicts between Arts and Crafts, modern, and avant-garde values that infused the design of furniture, household objects, and architecture during the 1920s and 1930s were also evident in the Dutch graphic arts. De Stijl introduced a rigorous system of form and primary colors that was evident in the design of its own publications and was later adapted for advertising purposes. In contrast to De Stijl's visual severity, S. H. de Roos (1877–1962), Jan van Krimpen (1892–1958), and others who specialized in typography and book design continued to draw on historic precedents even as they adapted them for modern use. De Roos, for example, considered to be the first important 20th-century book and typographic designer in the Netherlands, was as antagonistic to T. H. Wijdeveld's ornamented *Wendingen* style as he was to the architectonic layouts of Piet Zwart that derived from the New Typography in Germany.

Like Amsterdam School architecture and furniture design, to which it was closely connected, *Wendingen's* influence was most significant in the early 1920s. Around mid-decade, it was eclipsed by designers of posters and other forms of graphic art who drew on a combination of influences ranging from French Art Deco and the German *sachplakat* to De Stijl and the New Typography. By the mid-1930s, the sober rhetoric of German functional design had become a major influence on Dutch graphic designers.

De Stijl

For De Stijl members, there was less activity in the design of publications or posters than in painting, interior design, and architecture. Van Doesburg inaugurated the De Stijl journal in 1917 and continued its publication until his death in 1931. Vilmos Huszár (1884–1960) designed the original cover (Fig. 24.07). Although the woodblock shapes in the title appear to be letters spelling out "De Stijl," they are also abstract forms composed of modular sections and have no reference to typographic sources. In 1919, van Doesburg, perhaps stimulated by Huszár's earlier effort, designed an alphabet whose letters were constructed entirely of rectilinear sections. He used it only rarely, however; once for the typographic cover of his book *Klassiek Barok Modern* (*Classic, Baroque, Modern*), and

Fig. 24.07: Vilmos Huszár, *De Stijl*, cover, 1917. © DeAgostini/SuperStock. © DACS 2017.

postcards that featured the same logo with different arrangements of type.

Though Huszár and van der Leck were painters, they extended De Stijl principles to advertising design. Around 1920, the Calvé company commissioned van der Leck to create a poster for one of its products, a vegetable fat. With the precedent of Calvé's seminal Art Nouveau poster for Delft Salad Oil by Jan Toorop, van der Leck adopted the abstract visual language and primary colors of his paintings to depict a grocer behind a counter. He also composed the lettering with geometric elements that were reminiscent of Huszár's De Stijl logo. But the image was difficult to recognize and the poster was never printed.

Huszár was more successful as an advertising artist. His first major client was the woodworking company Bruynzeel, which was the most mechanized in Europe in the early 1920s. In 1917, Huszár stylized the firm's logo and in 1927 he began to produce monthly calendar blotters for advertising purposes. Around 1926 he initiated a series of advertisements for the Vittoria Egyptian Cigarette Company that promoted their Miss Blanche cigarettes. One of his first ads relied heavily on the De Stijl aesthetic, both for the figure of a woman smoking composed of flat black and white elements and the lettering that was inspired by van Doesburg's rectilinear alphabet. As Huszár's work for the company developed, he adopted more conventional advertising techniques. He modernized an older pictorial image of a woman in modern dress smoking a cigarette, which the company featured in advertisements and on its cigarette packages (Plate 21). He also experimented more with the lettering, rounding off some of the right angles and creating an additional identity for the cigarettes by combining the two words of the brand name into a single typographic composition. Both the pictorial logo and the lettering were used widely on stationary, packaging, billboards, and advertising wagons. Besides stimulating the advertising work of van der Leck and Huszár, De Stijl influenced other designers as well. It was the Netherlands' own

again on the poster he designed for the Section d'Or exhibition in 1920. In 1921, when De Stijl entered a more international phase, van Doesburg, then living in Germany, redesigned the journal's cover. It now had a horizontal shape and the lettering and type were organized as if the cover was a formal painting. The plain white background supported a composition in which the logo and issue number were delicately balanced against the single and multiple lines of type that were laid out on both horizontal and vertical axes. Van Doesburg, in collaboration with Mondrian, changed the journal's logo, this time choosing a san serif type, which was printed over large red initials that stood for Mondrian's "nieuwe beelding" (Neo-Plasticism). In addition, van Doesburg designed stationery and avant-garde movement and served as a severe formalist alternative to the more decorative graphic style of *Wendingen*.

Typography and book design

Sjoerd Hendrik de Roos (1877–1962) was the designer of *William Morris's Art and Society* in its Dutch translation (see Chapter 12). He was a socialist like Morris but not an admirer of traditional forms. His own views on typography and book design were formed by the Nieuwe Kunst, with its emphasis on the harmonious relation of typeface, text, and ornament. In 1907, de Roos joined the Lettergieterij "Amsterdam" (Type Foundry Amsterdam or TFA) as its first designer, a position he held until 1942. The TFA was one of Holland's leading foundries but neither it nor any other foundry had produced a new Dutch type for over a century. De Roos's first assignment was a series of initials embedded in squares of elaborate ornament. In 1912, the TFA released de Roos's own typeface, Hollandsche Mediaeval (Dutch Medieval), which was based on 15th-century Venetian precedents like some of the English private press types. A tasteful combination of straight lines and calligraphic curves, Hollandsche Mediaeval came to be considered as a typically Dutch typeface and replaced the printers' dependence on foreign imports. It was widely used by designers of books and publications and provided a strong impetus for the Dutch printing industry to actively engage in the design of typefaces and ornaments.

De Roos designed other typefaces throughout his career at the TFA. In 1916 the foundry released his Ella Cursief (Ella Italic), a script face. It was followed in 1923 by Erasmus Mediaeval, a lighter version of Hollandsche Mediaeval, which also appeared two years later in a bolder version called Grotius. Like their predecessor, Erasmus Medieval and Grotius were also used extensively for fine printing. Other types that de Roos created included Nobel, a san serif face produced in 1929 as the TFA's response to Futura; Egmont (1932), a more decorative face; and Libra, de Roos's least

successful effort. It was released in 1938 as a modern uncial type that combined elements of upper- and lower-case Fraktur letters in a single alphabet.

Besides designing types for the TFA, de Roos worked for other clients as a graphic artist, producing hand lettering for posters, labels, book jackets, title pages, and other printed material. As a designer of books, he had a long-term relationship with the Rotterdam publisher W. L. and J. Brusse, which was the first to use his Hollandsche Mediaeval. Besides Brusse's commitment to produce books of high quality with carefully chosen paper, type, and illustrations, the firm was inclined to publish books by socialist writers like Henriëtte Roland Holst-Van der Schalk, wife of the artist Richard Nicholas Roland Holst, who was also active in socialist politics. Between 1919 and 1932, Brusse published the yearbooks for the VANK, choosing artists as diverse as de Roos and Vilmos Huszár to design the volumes.

De Roos's greatest rival as a type and book designer was Jan van Krimpen (1892–1958). Fifteen years younger than de Roos, van Krimpen was unaffected by the *Nieuwe Kunst* as de Roos had been; neither did he share de Roos's interest in socialist ideals. He would eventually criticize de Roos's typefaces and books as being excessively decorated while de Roos complained that van Krimpen's designs were too sterile. Of the two, van Krimpen's typefaces were known and used outside the Netherlands while de Roos's were of primary interest at home.

The differences between the two designers were enhanced by the fact that they were affiliated with rival type foundries. In 1931, van Krimpen began an association with the Joh. Enschedé en Zonen type foundry in Haarlem. Enschedé was established at the beginning of the 18th century and had remained in the hands of the same family. The firm had a large collection of historic types and punches, which served as a great resource for later designs. Among its first 20th-century faces was a Javanese script that the Colonial Office used to print publications for the Dutch East Indies.

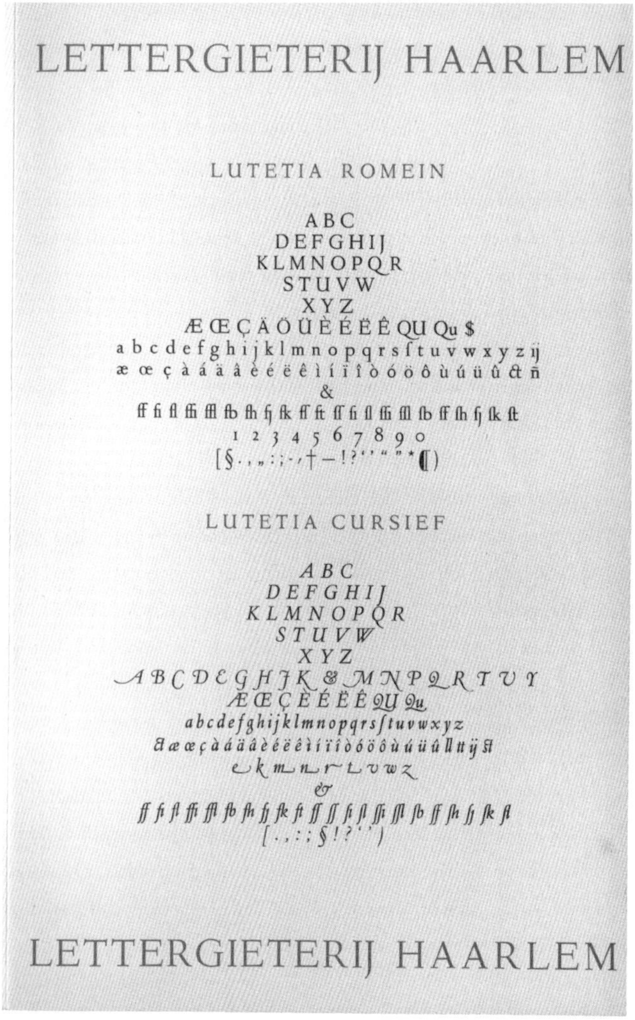

Fig. 24.08: Jan van Krimpen, Lutetia typeface, 1923–1924. Courtesy The Newberry Library, Chicago, case_wing_z250_a5_bx8_3.

The first typeface that van Krimpen designed for Enschedé, while still a freelance designer, was Lutetia, so called after the Roman name for Paris because it was used in all the official Dutch publications for the 1925 Exposition des Arts Décoratifs in that city (Fig. 24.08). Lutetia was a roman face but did not copy earlier forms as de Roos did with Hollandsche Mediaeval. It derived instead from van Krimpen's excellent sense of proportion and his superb ability as a draftsman. Lutetia came to the notice of Stanley Morison at the

Monotype Corporation in Britain and he persuaded van Krimpen to let Monotype adapt it for machine printing. This inaugurated a long relationship between van Krimpen, Morison, and Beatrice Warde. In fact, van Krimpen's aesthetic as a book designer could be characterized by the "transparent typography" that Warde espoused in her seminal essay "The Crystal Goblet."

Following the success of Lutetia, Enschedé hired van Krimpen as its first full-time art director, a role similar to that of de Roos at the TFA. Like his counterpart at the rival foundry, van Krimpen spent his entire career with Enschedé. His duties included supervising the design and printing of books, designing type specimen sheets, and creating new typefaces. As a book designer, his first obligation was to legibility and consequently his publications lacked the decorative qualities and historic references of de Roos's. After designing a Greek type, Antigone, in 1927, he produced Romulus, his most successful typeface, in 1931. A roman type, Romulus smoothed out some of the quirky elements of Lutetia. Van Krimpen, who had a great disdain for advertising, intended Romulus to be for the design of books exclusively. During the 1930s he created additions to the Romulus family, making it the first type designed for book printing to have such a range of variations.

Advertising and poster design

Many of the prominent poster artists in the Netherlands after World War I, including Jan Toorop, Chris Lebeau, Carol Adolph Lion Cachet, and Richard Nicholas Roland Holst, had previously been active in the *Nieuwe Kunst* and continued to employ its symbolism and heavy ornamentation in their later graphics. Exceptions were the painter Jan Sluijters (1881–1957), whose posters and book illustrations drew heavily on modern art movements elsewhere in Europe, particularly Fauvism and Expressionism. Sluijters' 1919 lithographic poster for the Artists' Winter Festival in The Hague depicts a woman sketchily drawn with expressive lines surrounded by loosely-applied swaths of color and accompanied by freehand lettering, while another poster that advertised a novel by Dutch author Israel Querido featured a more symbolic female figure with arms raised and eyes closed that referenced Expressionist sources. Willy Sluiters (1873–1949), Piet van der Hem (1885–1961), and the Belgian Raoul Hynckes (1893–1973) were commercial artists who were also serious painters of landscapes, portraits, or scenes of daily life. Sluiters produced a group of sober political posters in support of Dutch farmers right after World War I, although much of his commercial work—posters, magazines, and sheet music covers—had a sharp satirical edge reminiscent of the caricaturists who worked for the German humor magazine *Simplicissimus*. Van der Hem also did posters and covers for books and magazines as well as political caricatures. Hynckes, who emigrated to Holland from Belgium at the beginning of World War I, brought with him a refined drawing sensibility characteristic of Belgian Art Nouveau. Besides theater posters, he was a well-known illustrator of children's books.

The first commercial artist to collaborate closely with Dutch industry was Jac Jongert, a former assistant to Roland Holst. Jongert's earliest graphics showed strong traces of the Nieuwe Kunst aesthetic but after a visit to the 1914 Deutscher Werkbund exhibition in Cologne he began to develop a style more suited to advertising. From 1915 he worked extensively in Purmerend with a wine and spirits merchant whose head was the father of the rationalist architect J. J. P. Oud. For the firm, Jongert designed wine labels, bottles, prospectuses, and posters, which gave him excellent experience with the multiple forms of commercial graphics.

An early exponent of collaboration between art and industry, Jongert gave numerous speeches to the members of the VANK. In 1919 he undertook his first freelance commission for the large coffee, tea, and tobacco company, Van Nelle, and in 1923 he became head of the company's advertising department. He was hired by the director C. H. van der Leeuw,

Fig. 24.09: Jac Jongert, Van Nelle, poster, 1927. © PARIS PIERCE/Alamy.

whose integrated vision of a modern company included commissioning a new steel and glass factory building from Johannes Brinkman and L. C. van der Vlugt. Until he left Van Nelle in 1940, Jongert designed or supervised the design of all the company's graphics including posters, packaging, enamel street signs, advertising cards, counter displays, and even restaurant and cafe checks. While at Van Nelle, he also taught in the School of Decorative and Industrial Arts at the Rotterdam Academy, where fellow teachers included the Functionalists Piet Zwart and Gerard Kiljan.

Jongert was not averse to ornament although he favored geometric forms and straightforward lettering (Fig. 24.09). His color palette was much broader than that of the De Stijl artists and showed his preference for strong eye-catching tones. Although he employed a modern advertising rhetoric, he was not a strict Functionalist and thought that the objective style of Piet Zwart, Gerard Kiljan (1891–1968), and

Paul Schuitema (1897–1973) was too severe. Jongert continued the approach to corporate graphics that Peter Behrens initiated at the AEG in Berlin just a few years earlier. He established a graphic look for Van Nelle that was more modern than the *Wendingen* style and less objective than that espoused by adherents of the New Typography. Though he was an important figure in Dutch advertising during the 1920s and 1930s, Jongert was known primarily within the Netherlands. It was A. M. Cassandre, the French poster designer who worked for many Dutch clients including Van Nelle, the Holland-America Line, and Philips, whose posters attained the highest international standard.

The New Typography and its Dutch adherents
The New Typography was formulated by Jan Tschichold out of Germany's international avant-garde milieu. Influenced by De Stijl, Russian Constructivism, and the Bauhaus, Tschichold delineated a set of rigorous principles that called for an objective approach to typographic design and graphic layout. From the beginning, the adherents of the New Typography were as international as its sources. In the Netherlands, Piet Zwart, Paul Schuitema, and Gerard Kiljan were its leading exponents.

Zwart began as a designer of furniture and interiors before turning to graphic design around 1923. Early in his career from 1919 to 1921 he worked as a draftsman for the architect Jan Wils, a signatory to the original De Stijl manifesto. He then moved on to the architectural office of H. P. Berlage in The Hague, where he remained until 1927. In Berlage's office he worked on plans for the new municipal museum, the interior design for the Christian Science Church, and street furniture for the city. Meetings with avant-garde artists Kurt Schwitters and El Lissitzky in the Netherlands during 1923 were seminal for Zwart. His background in architecture, furniture design, and interiors paralleled Lissitzky's own architectural training to some degree, a fact that helps to explain the affinity he felt for Lissitzky' work.

Lissitzky's books *About Two Squares*, which Theo van Doesburg had published in a Dutch translation as a special issue of *De Stijl,* and *For the Voice* made a great impact on Zwart. Beginning in 1923, Lissitzky's influence could be seen in the series of several hundred black and white advertisements he designed for the Nederlandsche Kabel Fabriek (Netherlands Cable Factory or NKF). Zwart called himself a "typotekt," a term that accounts for his architectonic or structural approach to typographic layout. This is evident in his personal logo—the letter P next to a black square that represents his surname, which means "black."

Zwart specialized in advertising, which enabled him to adopt an inventive and sometimes playful approach to typography and layout. He created formal compositions with letters and printing elements, treating the letters as plastic forms that could vary in size, weight, and position. With this approach, he could produce an unending variety of arrangements. In a NKF ad of 1924, Zwart mixed varied typefaces, weights, and sizes in the same word as the Dadaists did. For one of his ads, "Hot Spots," he used the letter O as an abstract shape that belonged to two words at once, making it the center of the composition at a large scale and then as an accent at a smaller scale (Fig. 24.10).

By the mid-1920s, Zwart had started to incorporate photographs and photomontages in his NKF ads. In 1928 he began to experiment with photographic sequence and narrative in the catalog he designed for the company. Here he added photographic fragments to the stringent formal compositions that he printed in several colors. Beginning with this catalog, which attracted considerable attention, Zwart incorporated photography and photomontage in other publications he subsequently designed for the NKF, as well as for the Dutch Post Office and the publisher W. L. & J. Brusse, who published a series of monographs on international cinema for which Zwart created the photographic covers and layouts. Zwart also began to do all of

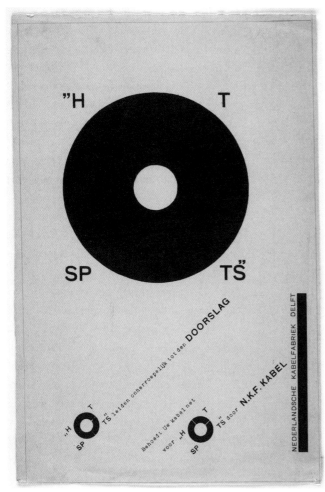

Fig. 24.10: Piet Zwart, NKF, advertisement, 1927. © 2014. Digital image, The Museum of Modern Art, New York/Scala, Florence. © DACS 2017.

strongly affected by the Russian Revolution than the earlier idealistic socialism of William Morris.

Paul Schuitema drew on many of the same sources as Zwart, though the influence of the Russian Constructivists, particularly Alexander Rodchenko, is more evident in his designs. Where Zwart was interested in the subtleties of typographic composition and enjoyed visual puns and Dada wit, Schuitema's designs confronted the viewer directly. He began his career as a commercial designer in 1924 after studying painting and drawing for six years and working briefly as an artist.

Schuitema's two most important clients were the P. Van Berkel Meat Company and the Van Berkel Patent Scale and Cutting Machine Factory. Like Jongert at the Van Nelle Factory, Schuitema was responsible for all the printed matter of both firms including advertisements, prospectuses, stationery, and labels. His logo for Berkel scales was simple—white type reversed out of a red cartouche. In fact, many pieces that Schuitema designed for Berkel as well as other clients featured red as the only color besides black and gray, just as much of the Russian Constructivist design did. By comparison with Jongert's program for Van Nelle, Schuitema's advertising strategy for Van Berkel was much more advanced. Photography and photomontage were central to the prospectuses and other advertising matter he designed for the two Van Berkel companies (Fig. 24.11). He understood the relation between modern reproduction technology and industry just as Max Burchartz and Johannis Canis did in their work for the Bochumer Verein in Germany. Schuitema sometimes created purely typographic spreads for Berkel catalog but these did not break any new ground compared to his creative use of photography, a medium he considered central to contemporary advertising. To distinguish the new advertising from the old, Schuitema characterized it as direct, succinct, and practical as opposed to the artistic, decorative, anti-social and romantic advertising of the past.

In addition to his work for industry, Schuitema designed publications and publicity material for many

Bruynzeel's advertising in 1931 after Huszár returned to painting, in part because of his dislike of photography for advertising purposes.

Zwart's approach to graphic design, like Lissitzky's, could also be applied to furniture, interiors, or buildings. In fact, he designed exhibition stands for the NKF and the Dutch Post Office and, as previously mentioned, he created a modern kitchen for Bruynzeel in the late 1930s. For Zwart, design had little to do with art. It was a social act whose aim was entirely functional. As a leftist political radical, he was more

Fig. 24.11: Paul Schuitema, Berkel scales, prospectus. © 2014. Digital image, The Museum of Modern Art, New York/Scala, Florence.

cultural and political organizations, all of them on the left though not affiliated with a particular party. He considered photography to be a weapon in the class struggle, emphasizing its ability to depict life in a matter-of-fact way. He designed covers and montages for political periodicals such as *De Wapens Neder* (*Down With Weapons*), *Nieuw Rusland* (*New Russia*), and *Links Richten* (*Left Aim*), as well as cultural magazines published by the radical film group Filmliga and De 8 en Opbouw, the progressive architectural association that resulted from a merger of two earlier architectural groups.

In 1931, Schuitema began to teach advertising design at the Royal Academy of Fine Arts at The Hague where Gerard Kiljan had established a Department of Advertising the year before. Kiljan, like Schuitema, was interested in photography and made it a central component of the curriculum. As a designer, he did much of his work for the Dutch Post Office where he produced posters, brochures, and stamps that incorporated photography and the basic principles of the New Typography. Both Schuitema and Kiljan influenced students at the Academy such as Wim Brusse (1910–1978) and Henny Cahn (1908–1999). Brusse worked for a time as Schuitema's assistant but then opened his own office where he designed book covers for the publishing firm W. L. & J. Brusse and did work for the Dutch Post Office. Henny Cahn also worked for the Post Office as well as various other organizations including the Dutch Communist Party. Like Schuitema, Cahn featured photography in many of his projects although his typographic sense was drawn more from Piet Zwart.

The visual rhetoric of the New Typography as well as the hard-hitting irony of John Heartfield's German photomontages were adopted by left-wing photographers Cas Oorthuys (1908–1975) and Mark Kolthoff (1901–1993) in the 1930s. Both men produced covers for anti-fascist publications such as *Afweerfront* (*Defense Front*) and *Links Richten*. In 1932, Oorthuis joined with the artist Jo Voskuil (1897–1972) to form a design agency, OV20 (Oorthuis-Voskuil 20), to produce political graphics rather than commercial advertising. Until they closed the agency in 1935, the two members of the Dutch Communist Party created political pamphlets, posters, book covers, and brochures for left-wing and anti-fascist organizations. Among their best-known projects after the agency closed was their poster for an exhibition that protested against the 1936 Olympic Games that were held in Nazi Germany (Fig. 24.12).

The Bauhaus influence in the Netherlands was evident in the curriculum of the Nieuwe Kunstschool, an Amsterdam art school founded in 1933 by former Bauhaus student Paul Citroen (1896–1983), a German

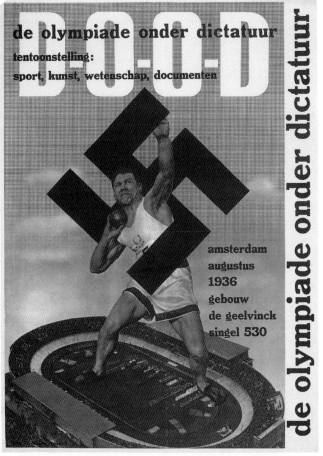

Fig. 24.12: Cas Oorthuys and Jo Voskuil, The Olympic Games under a dictator, poster, 1936. Collection Merrill C. Berman. Photo: Jim Frank and Joelle Jensen.

For a brief period after László Moholy-Nagy moved from Germany in 1933 and before he went to Britain in 1935, he brought the Bauhaus spirit of experimentation to the Netherlands. There, he worked as typographical advisor to a large printing company in Amsterdam, where he created book covers and magazine layouts and experimented with color photography. He put some of his photographic ideas into his design of a new periodical, *International Textiles*.

The Dutch Post Office (PTT)

Like Frank Pick in Great Britain, who created a unified design image for London Transport that included posters, architecture, and rolling stock, Jean François van Royen (1878–1942) performed a comparable function for the Dutch Post Office (PTT) during the 1920s and 1920s. Van Royen joined the PTT as a clerk in 1904 and by 1920 he had worked his way up to become secretary-general of the PTT's board of directors. Early in his career he had been influenced by the writings of Ruskin and Morris, which contributed to his desire to bring beauty to the public through manufactured artifacts. But he did not share Morris's suspicion of mechanization and instead embraced it as part of the modern world.

As a young man, van Royen had been apprenticed at the printing firm of Enschedé and retained a strong interest in typography and small press publishing even as his official duties at the PTT occupied much of his time. Initially van Royen was responsible for all the design projects of the PTT from the telephone directories, publicity material, and postage stamps to the telephones, phone booths, buildings, and office furnishings. For the PTT offices, he commissioned furniture from Willem Penaat, the furniture designer who was active with Metz & Co. and whom he succeeded as president of the VANK in 1922. Like Penaat, van Royen was active in the movement to improve the quality of Dutch design by strengthening the relation between art and industry. In this role, he was also a co-founder of the previously mentioned BKI (Association for Art in Industry).

who had moved to Holland. Citroen had been a disciple of Johannes Itten, the creator of the Bauhaus Foundation Course, and introduced similar principles in his school. Most of the emphasis at the school was on the applied arts including fashion, interior design, graphic design, and photography. The photographer Hajo Rose (1910–1989), also a German, taught the principles of the New Typography and the New Photography as they had been developed in Germany. He was a partner in the Amsterdam graphic design firm Co-op 2, which employed new typographic and photographic techniques in the design of posters, brochures, and book covers.

Under van Royen's leadership, the PTT began to devote more attention to advertising and public information, increasing its production of posters, booklets, instruction manuals, and related materials. New emphasis was also given to the design of mailboxes, delivery trucks, telephone booths, and buildings. Until 1927, van Royen was in charge of all the agency's design, choosing designers for stamps, brochures, and other projects, but in 1927 the agency established a new division, the PPD (Press and Propaganda Service), to produce its informational materials. It was headed by P. G. de Pater (dates unconfirmed), who would normally seek recommendations for designers from W. F. Gouwe (1977–1956), director of the Institute for Applied Arts and a co-founder of the BKI. Gouwe suggested graphic designers who worked in a broad range of styles.

For the first stamps that were designed under his leadership, van Royen turned to designers who were associated with the earlier movements of Art Nouveau and the *Nieuwe Kunst*. Jan Toorop's 1923 stamps that commemorate the Dutch Culture Fund depict stylized figures placed against heavily ornamented backgrounds that recall his dense Art Nouveau tendencies. The first stamps by Chris Lebeau (1878–1945), a *Nieuwe Kunst* designer, from 1921 also incorporate the rich ornamentation and idiosyncratic lettering of that movement, but his simpler designs for a set of lower-value stamps in 1924 embed the numbers within an abstracted image of a dove. While the lettering was still somewhat decorative, Lebeau made an effort to produce more legible forms than he had in his earlier examples. Lebeau's stamps, among the first to be produced by the offset-litho process, were the first modern Dutch stamps and remained classics of the PTT for the next 20 years. Other recognized designers who created stamps during the 1920s included P. A. H. Hofman (1885–1965), Jac Jongert, Michel de Klerk, and Sjoerd H. de Roos.

Though steeped in the British private press tradition as was his compatriot de Roos, van Royen

parted company with de Roos at the end of the 1920s when he hired Piet Zwart to design advertising materials for the PTT. Though his own taste did not run to the functional typography of Zwart, van Royen was a pragmatist who recognized the need to modernize the PTT's image. Zwart's initial commissions were brochures, advertisements and instructional sheets, which he designed with the same aesthetic of his work for the Dutch Cable Factory. In 1931, van Royen made the bold move of inviting him to design three stamps that were most likely the first anywhere to feature photography. Zwart set photographic portraits of Queen Wilhelmina against photomontage scenes of ships, planes, and industry. The simple lettering displayed one radical departure from the conventions of stamp design, the placing of the word "Nederland" on a diagonal to parallel the flight lines of two airplanes. Two years later, Zwart produced two more stamps with even more radical photomontage designs to commemorate a fund for the restoration of a church in the town of Gouda. Although they were controversial, Zwart's designs encouraged van Royen to commission additional photographic stamps from Paul Schuitema and Gerard Kiljan. Of these, Kiljan's 1931 photographic depictions of disabled children in bold colors against a white background were clearly the more striking. They established a new norm for provocative images on postage stamps and caused a considerable uproar among the press and the public.

During the 1930s, a large number of designers who espoused the principles of the New Typography worked for the PTT. Zwart's major project for the organization was *Het boek van PTT* (*The PTT Book*). He had sketched it out in 1930 but it was not published until 1938. For this publication, which was intended for schoolchildren, Zwart incorporated all the techniques he had used in his previous work and some others as well. Other designers who did designs for the PTT in the 1930s, besides Zwart, Kiljan, and Schuitema, included the students of Kiljan and Schuitema, Wim Brusse and Henny Cahn, both of whom did some of their best work for the agency. Nicolaas P. de Koo (1881–1960) had first worked for the PTT in 1918 as an interior designer, but by the 1930s he contributed to the agency as a graphic designer, having a large responsibility for the overall PTT image during those years. Among his other clients were the Rotterdam School Association, for whom he designed various printed materials including stationery and reports, and the city of Rotterdam, for which he produced a number of illustrative charts.

Other Dutch modernists

Besides the graphic designers who worked within a Functionalist framework, others were more eclectic in their approaches to typography and layout. Hendrik Nicolaas Werkman (1882–1945), an artist and a printer rather than a designer, is an excellent example. Though his work has had a strong impact on designers, Werkman does not fit easily into any camp or canon. He spent much of his life in the city of Groningen where he ran a modest printing business that had varying degrees of success until his death.

Backed by considerable experience in the design of routine printed matter—wedding and birth announcements, brochures, stationery, posters and the like—Werkman began in 1923 to publish a little magazine which had an English name, *The Next Call*. By temperament a libertarian, Werkman's typography expressed his disdain for conventions and his espousal of an individual voice. He combined blocks of linear text with expressive compositions of letters and elements from the type case, generating novel designs with his variance of letter sizes, weights, and positions. In more than 600 monotype prints, which he called *druksels*, and in the jobbing pieces he produced, Werkman experimented as well with varied textures that resulted from different inking techniques.

Though similar to Zwart's NKF ads in some ways, Werkman's layouts for *The Next Call* show less concern for a new reading syntax than an interest in artistic arrangements of type. He also emphasized the imperfections of hand printing, evincing little interest in the transparency of mechanical reproduction (Plate 22). Werkman distributed *The Next Call* to his friends and associates, using it as a forum to attack the complacency of some colleagues in the local artists' group, De Ploeg, to which he belonged.

Werkman's influence was most clearly evident in the work of Willem Sandberg (1897–1984), who acknowledged him to be his mentor. Sandberg was a professional graphic designer rather than an artist, but he always considered art to be an important component of his sensibility. He began as an art student in Amsterdam but left after a brief period and eventually studied law and the humanities. While in Vienna, where he went to study psychology around 1926, he came into contact with the system of pictorial statistics, ISOTYPE, that the sociologist Otto Neurath devised, and he undertook several projects using Neurath's system when he returned to the Netherlands at the end of the 1920s.

Sandberg became a graphic designer without any formal training. He came to understand design as a means of social betterment through his contacts with young designers in the VANK and the members of De 8 en Opbouw, the architectural group to which Paul Schuitema and other designers also belonged. His background in law, the social sciences, and philosophy, combined with his knowledge of pictorial statistics, prepared him for some of his first jobs as a designer. In 1928 he designed a chart for an exhibition on employment for the disabled at the Stedelijk Museum in Amsterdam, which was dedicated to the display of modern art, and in 1936 the museum hired him as a curator. In this position, he began to organize exhibitions of painting, sculpture, and design for which he created the catalogs and related materials. He also continued his work for other clients with an emphasis on book covers, brochures, and catalogs.

Werkman's influence was evident in Sandberg's approach to graphic design rather than in any formal similarities. Like Werkman, he considered each project with an open mind and let his ideas evolve into a distinctive form. He was not doctrinaire, and readily mixed old and new typefaces in tasteful combinations without the visual acrobatics of Zwart or his followers. Though well established by the end of the 1930s, Sandberg would become internationally recognized in the years after World War II, particularly for the expressive catalogs and posters he designed for exhibitions at the Stedelijk Museum.

The other designer known for an equally open attitude to his work was Dick Elffers (1910–1990), who had a close relation to the doctrinaire Functionalists Schuitema and Zwart but eventually went beyond their constraints. He studied at the Rotterdam Academy, where his most influential teacher was Jac Jongert. Though Elffers accepted Jongert's claim that subjectivity was essential for the graphic designer, he subsequently spent three years as an assistant to Paul Schuitema and then three more in the office of Piet Zwart, both strict devotees of an objective style. Among his early projects were advertisements and calendars that reflected the influence of both Zwart and Schuitema in their typographic layout and use of photography. He also experimented with photomontage. By 1937, Elffers had rejected the limitations of photography and the antagonism of his former teachers to drawing, a gesture that became particularly evident in the painterly posters he became known for in the 1950s and 1960s.

Belgium
Henry van de Velde

In 1926, Henry van de Velde returned to Belgium after many years abroad. Belgium's leading Art Nouveau designer at the end of the 19th century, van de Velde had gone to Germany in 1901 and remained there until 1917, when the war was near its end. In Germany, van de Velde was the founder and director of the Weimar School of Arts and Crafts, which became the Bauhaus after World War I. He was also a leading figure in the Deutscher Werkbund, defending the role of the artist

in industry during the organization's famous debate of 1914.

From Germany, van de Velde went to Switzerland and then the Netherlands before returning to Belgium. After World War I, Victor Horta, the other major figure besides van de Velde in Belgium's Art Nouveau movement, had become the director of the Académie Royale des Beaux Arts in Brussels and assumed a dominant role among Belgian architects and designers. Once an innovative architect, Horta had reverted to a conservative Neo-Classicism, which was evident in his design of the Belgian Pavilion for the 1925 Exposition des Arts Décoratifs in Paris. Initially, the Belgians planned to invite a group of young architects to design a low-cost housing project for the exhibition, but an influential group that supported Horta challenged the idea. Within the pavilion, furniture by both traditional and modern designers was displayed. A major exhibitor was De Coene Frères, Belgium's leading furniture manufacturer at the time. Earlier the firm had produced furniture influenced by the Arts and Crafts movement and Art Nouveau, including van de Velde's designs, but for the Paris exhibition De Coene Frères featured furniture in traditional historic styles.

The conservatism of Belgium's Pavilion in Paris reflected the overall attitude of the country towards design. Belgium was one of the few countries in Europe not to have an organization that promoted closer cooperation between art and industry. Traditional regionalism prevailed and there was a strong suspicion of ideas from abroad, particularly from Germany—Belgium's opponent in World War I—and the Soviet Union, where the Bolsheviks had instituted a radical new political regime.

For many in Belgium's design establishment, van de Velde was suspect because of his long association with Germany, but others still recognized him as Belgium's most famous international designer. King Albert I encouraged his return to Belgium, and Camille Huysmans, whom van de Velde had known earlier in socialist circles, offered him the opportunity to found and direct a new design school. Van de Velde had discussed plans for such a school as early as 1912 when he hoped to extend the ideas of his Weimar academy to Belgium. At the time, steps were taken to found the school but the plans did not come to fruition.

With the strong support of Huysmans, then Minister of Sciences and the Arts, and the approval of King Albert I, the Institut Supérieur des Arts Décoratifs (Higher Institute of Decorative Arts) or ISAD opened its doors in the historic Abbey of La Cambre in 1927. Van de Velde assembled a faculty consisting of artists, architects, and designers who were leaders in Belgium's progressive arts community. Among them were the architects Victor Bourgeois (1897–1962) and Huib Hoste (1881–1957), the engraver Joris Minne (1897–1987), the weaver Elizabeth De Saedeleer (1902–1972), the typographer and poster artist Lucien de Roeck (1915–2002), and the Surrealist painter Paul Delvaux (1897–1944).

Initially the workshops included design for the theater, ornamentation for the applied arts, and weaving, while architecture was added shortly thereafter. The school also had a print shop where van de Velde revived in a modern form the tradition of fine printing that the British private press movement had inspired. He considered ISAD to be third in a line of great design schools whose precedents were his own Weimar Academy and the Bauhaus. Its objective was to reinstate the values of function and social purpose that had animated van de Velde's earlier work during the Art Nouveau years in Belgium and his practice and teaching in Germany.

7 Arts

Counter to the dominant conservatism of Belgium's architecture and design community was the avant-garde movement 7 Arts, which was active between 1922 and 1929. The members of 7 Arts were painters, sculptors, architects, planners, designers, and writers who believed in a unity of the arts, hence the title of their movement and that of the French-language journal that chronicled their theories and projects. Among the leading figures were the designer and theoretician Marcel Baugniet (1896–1995), the architect Victor Bourgeois (1897–1962), his brother the poet Pierre Bourgeois (1898–1976), the architect and furniture designer Huib Hoste, the painter and designer Karl Maes (1900–1974), the painter and designer Jozef Peeters (1895–1960), and the artist and designer Victor Servranckx (1897–1965).

Unlike other avant-garde movements such as Futurism, Constructivism, and De Stijl, 7 Arts did not have a single visual style that was evident in the work of all its members. They were open to ideas from all the avant-garde movements and engaged actively with them. Compared to many of their Belgian colleagues in architecture and the applied arts, they were outspoken advocates of modern design and mass production. Their broad interest in the general environment ranged from advertising and street lighting to theater decor, furniture, architecture, and urban planning. Of these, they emphasized the significance of architecture and advocated the use of new industrial materials as well as an austere formal style that was antagonistic to ornamentation. Their views on design ran counter to the dominant Belgian emphasis on luxury goods and fine craftsmanship. Instead, they espoused standardization and design that was dictated by social needs.

Despite their interest in mass production, most of their designs were single objects, usually created for particular interiors. Marcel Baugniet, also a painter and graphic artist, created furniture in wood and occasional pieces in chrome and glass. Victor Servranckx, Huib Hoste, and the interior designer and photographer Willy Kessels (1898–1974) created a Functionalist interior for the Belgian Pavilion at the 1925 expo. Karl Maes was most engaged with furniture design. He designed dining room suites, chairs, beds, and display cabinets of wood that the Brussels furniture workshop of Victor de Cunsel manufactured. Though Maes had an active relationship with Theo van Doesburg, his furniture designs showed none of the rigor of De Stijl nor did they possess the elegance of the more industrialized furniture of Mart Stam, Marcel Breuer, or Mies van der Rohe. Conceptual projects for furniture and interior designs also appeared regularly in the journal *7 Arts*.

Design and Exhibitions in the 1930s

The founding of the Higher Institute of Decorative Arts helped restore van de Velde to a position of influence in Belgian society, although he had many detractors including Victor Horta. By the 1930s, he was again active with major industry commissions and government consultations. He designed railroad car interiors for the Belgian State Railroad and collaborated with a young engineer on the design of a packet steamer for delivering mail. Besides these projects, he continued his architectural practice and spent considerable time as a consultant to the government

on problems of architectural restoration and new construction.

During the 1930s, Belgium participated in four major exhibitions, two of which it organized itself. The first was the 1930 International Maritime and Colonial Exhibition, which commemorated a century of independence from Dutch rule. Held in Antwerp, it attracted pavilions from most countries in Europe including an enormous one from Great Britain. In 1935, Belgium hosted the first World's Fair since the 1900 exhibition in Paris. Organized by a conservative committee that excluded van de Velde for political reasons, the fair emphasized Belgium's traditions rather than its future. The pavilion of decorative arts featured fashionable luxury objects instead of mass-produced goods. Belgium's principal contribution to

Fig. 24.13: De Coene Frères, Belgian Pavilion, artisan bedroom, Paris World's Fair, 1937. The Wolfsonian–Florida International University, Miami Beach, Florida, The Mitchell Wolfson, Jr. Collection, 84.2.347. Photo: David Almeida.

the exhibition was "Old Brussels," a full-scale recreation of Brussels c. 1750.

The situation was different when Belgium began planning a pavilion for the 1937 world exhibition in Paris. Van de Velde was appointed principal designer for the project and integrated several of the Werkbund values into the plan. One was the enhancement of public taste, while another was bringing art and technics into a closer relation. The pavilion that van de Velde designed along with several assistants combined

Fig. 24.14: Jozef Peeters, "Modern Poems Recited by Germaine Michielsen," invitation, 1921. Collection Merrill C. Berman. Photo: Jim Frank and Joelle Jensen.

curved and rectilinear volumes with extensive glass walls, a far cry from Horta's regressive Neo-Classical pavilion design in 1925.

Rather than emphasizing goods for the rich, the 1937 pavilion featured rooms for the different social classes. Van de Velde and his team were careful to select products with high-quality design and a range of prices. Among the products commissioned were some designed by professors and students at van de Velde's school, which emphasized simplicity and purpose. Van de Velde also selected goods from well-established firms in the furniture, textile, and ceramics industries. Following the 1925 exhibition, De Coene Frères had begun to manufacture furniture in a modern Art Deco style that paralleled developments in France. Some of their deluxe designs were included in the pavilion as was an artisan's bedroom in a simpler style (Fig. 24.13). Overall, the pavilion presented a persuasive vision of modern design that addressed the situations of different social classes rather than a single one. Though van de Velde had filled the pavilion with objects of good taste and sound value, only a modest percentage of them were actually in production. In typical Werkbund fashion, he would have liked to raise the taste of the entire nation but had to settle instead for what he could accomplish in an exhibition pavilion rather than in society at large.

Graphic design

Just as van de Velde had played a role in improving the quality of printing and book design during the Art Nouveau years, so did he satisfy a similar aim after he became director of ISAD. One of his first actions as head of the school was to establish a print shop, where he designed a series of books by Belgian authors. The number was not large but the books exemplified the highest standards of design through the quality of their materials, layout, typography, and illustration.

Among the typefaces in the ISAD print shop was Futura, which van de Velde acquired soon after it appeared. He was one of the first designers, if not the first, in Belgium to use the typeface for setting literary texts. For him, Futura was the ideal modern typeface because it avoided any imitation of handwriting and had an international character. There was no Belgian equivalent, although van de Velde also bought several sizes and weights of Indépendent, a display type of 1930 by two Belgian commercial artists, G. Colette (dates unconfirmed) and J. Dufour (dates unconfirmed). Consisting of thick dark strokes, it was, however, more suited to headlines and titles than to blocks of text.

By contrast, the avant-garde members of 7 Arts, notably Karl Maes and Jozef Peeters, did not address

Fig. 24.15: Leo Marfurt, Belga cigarettes, package, 1925. © Wim Lanclus/ Alamy. © DACS 2017.

the functional aspects of graphic design, considering it instead to be another form of modern decorative art. Maes did occasional posters and a lot of abstract compositions that were published in the *7 Arts* magazine. Jozef Peeters was particularly active as a designer of magazine covers and posters, adopting a similar decorative attitude to his compositions. He was the co-editor with Michel Seuphor (aka Fernant Berckelaers) of the Flemish avant-garde journal *Het Overzicht* (*The Overview*), which was published between 1921 and 1925. Peeters designed some of the covers for the journal. As a graphic artist, his approach to lettering was heavy-handed. In his posters he featured dense idiosyncratic letters that derived from geometric forms (Fig. 24.14). An exception to the disregard of function by 7 Arts designers was Marcel Baugniet. He worked for a while as the director of an advertising firm, Atelier Fulgura, and it was most likely during this period that he designed one of the first modern commercial posters in Belgium albeit for a Dutch client, a promotional piece for Philips' Argenta light bulbs that he did in 1924.

Few other poster artists worked in a modern style, while many continued to produce anecdotal illustrations and even religious imagery. Leo Marfurt (1894–1977), a Swiss artist, moved to Belgium in 1921 and became the country's most widely recognized designer of modern posters. Beginning in 1923, he began a collaboration of more than 50 years with Vander Elst, the tobacco company that manufactured Belga cigarettes. During his years with the company, Marfurt did most of their advertising, which featured Miss Belga, the woman who served as the brand's well-known trademark (Fig. 24.15). Posters for Belga cigarettes incorporated the style of the German *sachplakat* (the singular object and large letters). With his ability to capture the essence of a modern object through abstracted details, Marfurt, who founded his own advertising agency, Les Créations Publicitaires, in 1927, was the perfect artist to design posters for technological products such as Remington typewriters and Chrysler automobiles that were imported from abroad. One of

Fig. 24.16: René Magritte, *The True Face of Rexism*, poster, 1939. Archives of the city of Brussels. © ADAGP, Paris and DACS, London 2017.

Besides 7 Arts, the other avant-garde movement that flourished in Belgium was Surrealism. It was centered in Paris but small groups of Surrealist artists and writers were active in other countries. René Magritte (1896–1967), the most prominent of Belgium's Surrealist artists, also worked extensively in advertising. Around 1926, when he produced his first Surrealist paintings, Magritte created illustrations for a fashion catalog that showed women with birds' heads wearing fur coats. After returning to Brussels in 1930 following a lengthy stay in Paris, Magritte and his brother formed an advertising agency, which they called Studio Dongo, and they operated it until 1935. Magrtte's paintings, such as *The Treachery of Images*, which depicted a pipe with a text beneath it that said, "This is not a pipe," expressed the ambiguities of visual and verbal language, but his posters and advertisements were more straightforward. However, some suggestion of Magritte's interest in ambiguous images can be seen in a political poster that opposes Rexism, a fascist political movement in Belgium in the late 1930s. A man looking in a mirror sees instead of his own reflection an image of Hitler (Fig. 24.16).

Switzerland

Since the mid-19th century, a number of Swiss theorists, educators, and museum officials had recognized the importance of reforming the applied arts to promote a closer relation with industry. In 1855, the German theorist Gottfried Semper, who participated in the design of the Crystal Palace exhibition of 1851, moved to Zurich where he designed the building for the new federal technical university and wrote its first architectural curriculum. In Switzerland, he also completed his seminal book *Der Stil in der technischen und tektonischen Kunsten* (*Style in the Technical and Tectonic Arts*), a theory of industrial art that arose from his analysis of the 1851 exhibition.

Besides the theories and activities of Semper, the establishment of the Schools of Design and the South Kensington Museum in Britain, along with related

his strongest designs was the post-Cubist poster for the *Flying Scotsman*, the British LNER line's signature train.

Other artists who designed posters in a modern style were August Mambour (1896–1968), a painter who spent several years as an in-house designer for the Belgian manufacturer of firearms, automobiles, and motorcycles, Fabrique Nationale or F.N.; Lucien de Roeck (1915–2002), a professor at ISAD with a strong interest in typography; and Jos Coene (dates unconfirmed), whose poster depiction of a smiling family at the Zeebrugge beach resort recalls the handsome airbrush figures of the Austrian designer Joseph Binder.

developments in Austria and elsewhere, prompted the Swiss to consider the improvement of the applied arts as a serious matter. In Lausanne, a museum of industrial art was established in 1862, while in Geneva a school of applied arts was founded in 1869. In the German-speaking section of the country, the Kunstgewerbemuseum (Applied Arts Museum), and the Kunstgewerbeschule (School of Applied Arts) in Zurich were founded in 1875 and 1878 respectively, while the Basel Allgemeine Gewerbeschule (General Trade School) was established in 1887. These institutions, along with others that were founded after them, became important pillars of Swiss design culture, particularly the schools and museums of applied arts and trades in Zurich and in Basel.

In 1903, the artist and craftsman Charles L'Eplattinier (1874–1946) became director of the School of Applied Arts in La Chaux-de-Fonds, where his most famous student was Charles Eduard Jeanneret, known as Le Corbusier. At the time, La Chaux-de-Fonds was a center of the Swiss watchmaking industry and among other objectives, L'Eplattinier trained students to design artistic watchcases. But he was also concerned that the machine might eventually replace such craftsmanship and he convinced the school to fund a study of the applied arts in Germany. In 1910 the administration commissioned Le Corbusier to undertake this project and he completed his report, *Étude sur le movement d'art decorative en Allemagne* (*A Study of the Decorative Arts Movement in Germany*), two years later. In Germany, he met all the major figures in the applied arts reform movement and subsequently wrote enthusiastically about its potential for improving the design of industrial products.

In 1913, the Swiss founded two organizations that were stimulated by the Deutscher Werkbund, L'Oeuvre (The Work), established in French-speaking Switzerland with L'Eplattinier and Le Corbusier as founding members, and a Swiss branch of the Werkbund in the German-speaking part of the country. Both organizations soon began to publish their own journals and developed parallel activities related to publishing, lectures, and exhibitions.

Following several smaller exhibitions in 1883 in Zurich, and 1896 in Geneva, the Swiss National Exhibition, held in Bern in 1914, provided a major survey of Swiss industry, including pavilions dedicated to machinery, agriculture, and the decorative and graphic arts. A feature of the exhibition, however, was a Swiss village with its church, model farm, and craft demonstrations that signified the organizers' attention to tradition as an important component of national identity. A Swiss Werkbund exhibition followed in 1918. Though dedicated to housing, it also included the applied arts. Then came the first national exhibition of applied arts in 1922 at which both the Swiss Werkbund and L'Oeuvre exhibited.

Though Switzerland did not have a mass-housing movement with concomitant furniture designers, as did Germany and Austria, there was nonetheless interest in modern home furnishings. Here, the two applied arts museums in Basel and Zurich were important in promoting modern design through a series of seminal exhibitions. A catalyst for the actual production of furniture and other objects for the modern home was Sigfried Giedion (1888–1968), a mechanical engineer who also studied art history in Germany under the Swiss art historian Heinrich Wölfflin. Giedion was active in the German Modern Movement and he became the first secretary-general of the new international architectural association CIAM that was founded in La Sarraz, Switzerland, in 1928.

With two partners, the architect Werner Moser (1896–1970) and the industrialist Rudolf Graber (dates unconfirmed), Giedion opened wohnbedarf (Home Necessities), a company with retail outlets in Zurich and Basel that sold modern home furnishings. At the time wohnbedarf was founded in 1931, the Swiss furniture market was dominated by period styles and the new company was one of the few to promote modern design. Its major suppliers were the Embru-Werke, which produced a large variety of furniture

Fig. 24.17: Compass Camera, 1937. © The Art Archive/Alamy.

in tubular steel, and Horgen-Glarus, one of Europe's oldest furniture companies, which provided chairs and tables, primarily of wood. The furniture these two companies manufactured was designed largely by Swiss architects such as Max Ernst Haefeli (1901–1976) and Werner Moser, a wohnbedarf founder. For wohnbedarf, Moser designed a folding table of tubular steel, manufactured by Embru, that could be marketed either with circular panels made of solid material or glass. With his extensive international contacts, Giedion also commissioned designs from architects and designers abroad such as Alvar Aalto in Finland and Marcel Breuer in Germany. A featured design of the company's was the "indi-leuchte," an inexpensive floor lamp that produced indirect light. Designed by Giedion and Hin Bredendieck (1904–1995) from the Bauhaus, it was produced by the lighting manufacturer BAG, located in Turgi. Perhaps Switzerland's strongest industrial sector was the manufacture of watches and other precision instruments, which were known worldwide.

In 1925, E. Paillard & Cie, a company that had been making phonographs since 1898, produced an unusual precision-made device, the Mikiphone. A miniature phonograph designed by two Hungarian brothers, Nicolas (dates unconfirmed) and Étienne Vadasz (dates unconfirmed), its metal container housed the pick-up and speaker. Paillard also created a line of other phonograph models some of which were marketed abroad under different brand names.

Another miniature product was the Compass Camera, produced in 1937 by the Geneva firm Jaeger Le Coultre. It was flat rather than bulky and could slip easily into a side pocket (Fig. 24.17). Swiss radios were manufactured by Autophon, which initiated their production in 1932. Their model 305S, however, was an almost exact replica of the people's radio designed in Germany by Walter Kesting in 1928.

Though Switzerland was not especially known for products that adopted the sweptback streamline form, the Swiss Federal Railways (SBB) chose streamlining as the preferred style for the design of several new trains in the 1930s. The first of these, the *Red Arrow*, was an electric railcar that entered service in 1935. It had a modified streamlined form, more than likely suggested by the prototype streamlined car bodies that the Hungarian engineer Paul Jaray (1899–1974) had developed earlier through his Swiss consultancy. The train was not designed to pull any cars, so it functioned like a bus or tramcar on rails. Large glass windows facilitated excellent views, particularly for skiers who rode the train on trips to the mountains.

In 1939, the Swiss government presented its first national exhibition since 1914, the Schweizerische Landesausstellung, or Landi, which was held on the banks of Lake Zurich. It was originally intended to celebrate Switzerland's industrial accomplishments, but its theme was shifted to "Spiritual Defense" in the face of the recent Nazi advances in Eastern Europe and the proximity of the Fascists in Italy. The exhibition's aim to promote a feeling of national solidarity was expressed in the official three-part poster by Pierre Gauchat

Fig. 24.18: Hans Coray, Landi chair, 1938. © Arcaid Images/Alamy.

(1902–1956) that depicted four smiling women in traditional dress, representing the different language groups of Switzerland (Plate 23).

The Landi was divided into two sections that juxtaposed modernity with tradition. Similar to its 1914 predecessor, the traditional village or "Dörfli" was a major attraction. To represent modernity, the organizers commissioned a large number of buildings as well as a piece of outdoor furniture, the Landi-Stuhl or Landi chair by Hans Coray (1906–1991), which became a signature icon of the exhibition. The chair was stackable and had a bent aluminum frame with a sheet of pressed aluminum resting on it. Large holes punched in the back and seat served as its ornamentation (Fig. 24.18).

Design was also present in other manifestations, particularly graphics. Contemporary currents in Swiss graphic design were introduced to an international audience for the first time. Around 80 designers ranging from the older generation of poster artists to the most recent modernists produced posters, exhibits, booklets, and other publicity materials. The visual set piece of the exhibition was the gigantic mural by painter and

poster designer Hans Erni (1909–d.o.d. unconfirmed) entitled *Switzerland, the World's Vacationland*. Longer than a football field and painted on the wall of a model hotel, the mural conveyed the full spectrum of Swiss life from bucolic rural activities to hydropower plants. Its optimistic depictions of active citizens was intended to shore up the nation against the dark clouds of war that were rapidly descending on Europe.

From commercial art to graphic design

Though Switzerland has long excelled in the printing industry, significant activity in commercial design did not begin until after World War I. Before that, Eugène Grasset and Théophile Steinlen, both from Lausanne in French Switzerland, were among the leading illustrators and poster artists in turn-of-the-century Paris. Grasset also designed a typeface that was widely used for printing books (see Chapter 12). The Swiss artist Ferdinand Hodler (1853–1918) produced a striking poster for a 1904 exhibition of his paintings at the Secession building in Vienna, which aroused the interest of Swiss artists who were the country's first poster designers. Among them were Cuno Amiet (1868–1961), Augusto Giacometti 1877–1947), and Émile Cardinaux (1877–1936). Posters by these artists were mainly paintings with lettering added and their themes were primarily cultural rather than commercial.

Cardinaux's poster for the 1914 Swiss National Exhibition in Bern portrayed a farmer in regional dress astride a massive green horse. It was likely inspired by Hodler's art and possibly by the colorful Expressionist paintings of the Blaue Reiter artists in Munich. The man holds a banner emblazoned with national symbols and seems, along with the horse, to embody the strength of Swiss tradition and values. But the public was bothered by the strangeness of the green horse and a new poster with a more neutral landscape image replaced Cardinaux's original image.

Though these early poster artists were primarily committed to painting, some of them continued to create posters well into the 1930s. However, they adhered to a traditional narrative format rather than adopt the flatness and solid backgrounds of the new advertising art. Burkhard Mangold (1873–1950), one of the first modern poster artists in Switzerland, featured narrative scenes but related them more closely to commercial purposes, similar to Edward Penfield, the American poster designer of the late 19th century.

Other artists such as Otto Baumberger (1889–1961), Niklaus Stoecklin (1896–1982), and Otto Morach (1887–1973) were more attentive to the new tendencies in art and advertising that were emanating from Paris, Berlin, and Munich. The lithographic printer J. E. Wolfensberger in Zurich published many of

the innovative Swiss advertising posters in the 1920s and 1930s. A breakthrough for Otto Baumberger was his 1919 poster for the Zürich hatter Baumann, which consisted simply of a black top hat on a plain background with lettering beneath it. Though the poster introduced nothing new to the international scene, it signaled a clean break with the painterly tradition of Cardinaux and others at home.

Niklaus Stoecklin had studied applied art in Munich and was later a pupil of Berthold Mangold's in Basel. He too created numerous posters with a single image accompanied by the manufacturer's name. His 1927 poster for Gaba cough drops, which depicted the black diamond-shaped lozenge dropping into the mouth of a blue silhouette figure, was one of the best Swiss examples of the German *sachplakat* approach although it was more stylized (Fig. 24.19). But Stoecklin's techniques were diverse. He could also produce more traditional illustrative posters and at

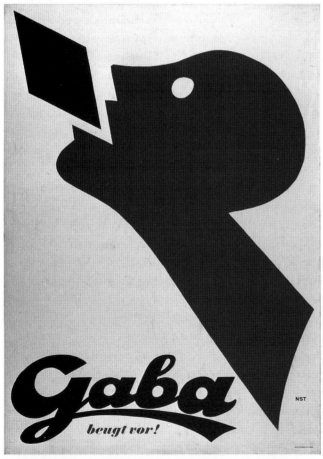

Fig. 24.19: Niklaus Stoecklin, Gaba prevents!, poster, 1927. Photograph courtesy of the Musem für Gestaltung Zürich, Poster Collection. © DACS 2017.

Fig. 24.20: Otto Baumberger, PKZ, poster, 1923. Photograph courtesy of the Musem für Gestaltung Zürich, Poster Collection. © DACS 2017.

times his imagery conveyed the mystery of Surrealism. Lesser-known designers who adopted the modern style that Baumberger and Stoecklin pioneered included Hugo Laubi (1888–1959), Carl Böckli (1889–1970), and Charles Kuhn (1903–1999).

Both Baumberger and Stoecklin were featured poster designers for Burger-Kehl & Co., the chain of men's clothing stores that marketed its own fashions under the trademark PKZ. As early as 1908, Burger-Kehl had commissioned a poster from Ludwig Hohlwein in Munich to advertise its fashions in the new German graphic style but shortly thereafter the company turned to Swiss artists. Baumberger's seminal poster of 1923, which depicted part of an overcoat with the PKZ label prominently displayed (Fig. 24.20) gained international recognition as the only Swiss example to be included in Jan Tschichold's special 1925 issue of *Typographische Mitteilungen* on "elementary typography" in Germany. In French Switzerland, the influence of Paris was stronger and artists there tended to draw more on French fashion imagery and lettering for trademarks and advertisements that featured everything from handkerchiefs to toiletries.

During the 1920s and 1930s, Burger-Kehl employed Switzerland's leading poster artists to produce a large number of posters in various styles. Unlike the posters of many manufacturers, those advertising PKZ clothing took great liberties with the viewer, counting on a basic belief in PKZ's quality to present its identity in a variety of novel images. Baumberger played with the PKZ trademark in several humorous examples, while Johann Arnhold (1891–d.o.d. unconfirmed), an Austrian designer, and Hermann Blaser (dates unconfirmed) depicted dapper men sporting elegant PKZ outfits. Besides Baumberger's overcoat, three of the company's most distinctive posters were Niklaus Stoecklin's image of a man in a bowler hat and topcoat with his back to the viewer, the depiction by Alex Diggelman (1902–1987) of a PKZ box with only a hint of a shirt showing, and the large button with the PKZ initials under it by Peter Birkhauser (1911–1976).

The European avant-gardes and the New Typography
From about 1912, several Swiss cities became leading art centers, due to the efforts of museums and private galleries to present the newest work from abroad. In Basel, the Kunsthalle was perhaps the first to present an exhibit of Picasso's art outside France, while in Zurich several private galleries featured work by Cubists, Orphists, and Futurists. In 1916, Dada began in Zurich and remained a strong force in the city until around 1919 (see Chapter 18). Its posters and publications were the first examples of avant-garde graphics in Switzerland.

Sophie Taeuber-Arp (1889–1943), who married the German-French Dada artist Hans Arp, was one of the first Swiss artists to create abstract paintings based on geometric form, which she did as early as 1918, around the same time that a group of Swiss and foreign abstract artists called Das Neue Leben (The New Life) was founded in Zurich. The manifesto of this group, which argued that artists should participate in the life of the state, most likely helped to justify the move of some members of the group into graphic design.

In 1923, the first Bauhaus exhibition was held in Zurich and within a few years several Swiss students, notably Xanti Schawinsky (1904–1979), Theo Ballmer (1902–1965), and Max Bill (1908–1994), had gone to study at the school. As art critics, Sigfried Giedion and his wife Carola Giedion-Welcker (1893–1979) promoted the Bauhaus after its move to Dessau just as they, along with Georg Schmidt (1896–1965)—an art critic and director of the Museum of Applied Art in Basel—were strong advocates of Constructivist art, particularly encouraging the interest of younger artists. In 1929, a second Bauhaus exhibition came to Switzerland, first to the Museum of Applied Arts in Basel and then to its counterpart museum in Zurich. This exhibition featured work that had been done under Hannes Meyer, the Swiss architect and member of the ABC group who became Director of the Bauhaus when Walter Gropius left in 1927. In 1938, Johannes Itten, who created the initial Preliminary Course at the Weimar Bauhaus, returned to his native Switzerland to serve as director of the Zurich Applied Arts Museum and School of Applied Arts. Back at home, he introduced elements of the Bauhaus curriculum to the School of Applied Arts and participated, though in a limited way, in the Constructivist art movement.

Early in 1924, El Lissitzky, the Russian architect and designer, came to Switzerland to recuperate from tuberculosis. Shortly after his arrival he met the Dutch architect Mart Stam, who introduced him to a group of Swiss colleagues interested in starting a magazine that would focus on radical trends in architecture. As the name of their group, they chose ABC, which also became the name of their magazine, *ABC: Beiträge zum Bauen* (*ABC: Contributions to Building*). Lissitzky's

Fig. 24.21: El Lissitzky, *Die Kunstismen*, cover, 1925. Beinecke Rare Book and Manuscript Library, Yale University.

cover design went through several iterations of which the one for Series 2 featured large bold examples of the three letters, *ABC*, arranged on a solid-colored background. The interior text was more conventional although it also included experiments with letters and words that recalled Lissitzky's layouts for avant-garde journals in Germany, notably *Veshch* and *G*. The composition of large letters on the cover of *ABC*, though not its internal layout, represented an early example of the Constructivist style that would soon come to characterize an important segment of Swiss graphic design.

More influential than *ABC* was the book *Die Kunstismen* (*The Isms of Art*) that Lissitzky wrote with the German-French artist Hans Arp. Lissitzky's cover was a tour de force of stylistic elements that he had invented for other avant-garde publications. The book was a survey of art movements between 1914 and 1924 and the cover featured the word "Kunstismen," broken up into segments so that it framed all the movements the authors discussed (Fig. 24.21). In his page layouts, Lissitzky used white space extensively, punctuating it with photographs of artists, art, and minimal titles that identified each movement. With its emphasis on visual elements to carry the narrative, *Die Kunstismen* was important for the subsequent design of Swiss posters, brochures, and other advertising materials that were based on avant-garde techniques.

Lissitzky returned to Moscow in 1925 where, several years later, he helped to organize a large "Russian Exhibition" that was sent to the Zurich Museum of Applied Art in 1929. The prominent photomontage image on the exhibition poster, which showed the heads of a male and a female Soviet youth joined together, helped to promote a use of photomontage by Swiss graphic designers, although it exemplified an emerging style of Socialist Realist propaganda rather than the graphic experimentation that had characterized Lissitzky's Swiss works just a few years earlier.

One of the first designers in Switzerland to espouse a modern graphic style was the German Walter

Fig. 24.22: Herbert Matter, Winter Holiday, Doubled Holiday, poster, 1934. Photograph courtesy of the Musem für Gestaltung Zürich, Poster Collection.

magazine *Typographische Monatsblätter* (*Typographic Monthly*) in 1933. Published by the Swiss Typographic Association, *TM*, as the journal came to be called, introduced printers to new ideas in the graphic arts both through historical and theoretical articles about design and typography and through the design of the publication itself. Cyliax was a strong proponent of the German New Photography, and the posters and brochures he designed were among the earliest to substitute photography for drawing or painting. However, they are less distinctive than the photographic work he commissioned as an art director, particularly the covers for *TM* and the publicity material for Fretz Brothers that Herbert Matter (1907–1984) designed.

Matter had initially studied art in Geneva and then in Paris with the Purist painters Fernand Léger and Amédée Ozenfant. In Paris he began to photograph and was employed by the French type foundry Debernet & Peignot as a typographer and photographer. He worked as well with the poster artist A. M. Cassandre. After Matter returned to Switzerland in 1932, the Swiss National Tourist Office hired him to design a series of posters that promoted Switzerland as a vacation spot, particularly for skiing. Using tinted photographs and photomontage, Matter created a series of posters that featured snow-capped mountains, frequently juxtaposed with the faces of handsome men and women and images of skiers or ski lifts behind them (Fig. 24.22). The photographs were overprinted with texts in the multiple languages of the neighboring European countries where the posters were displayed.

While Cyliax made use of progressive graphics as the art director of a printing firm, Max Dalang (1882–1965) did so as the founder of an advertising agency that was organized on an American model of efficiency. Dalang, a businessman, established the Atelier für Künstlerische Reklame (Agency for Artistic Advertising) in 1916. He admired the new technology and methods of industrial production in the United States and in 1919 he went there to study them. Besides gaining a greater knowledge of Frederick

Cyliax (1899–1945), who studied at the Academy of Graphic Arts in Leipzig, where Jan Tschichold had also been a student. In 1924, Cyliax became the art director for the Zurich printer Fretz Brothers, and in that capacity he helped to modernize the publications of their various clients including the Swiss Werkbund for whose monthly publication, *Das Werk* (*The Work*), he designed a strong graphic format. He was also instrumental in launching the important Swiss graphic design

Winslow Taylor's theory of scientific management and its application in Henry Ford's automobile factory, Dalang was particularly interested in the ideas of New York advertising executive J. Walter Thompson and psychologist Hugo Münsterberg's theories of "planned advertising." When he returned to Zurich, he transformed his art studio into an advertising agency based on a division of labor and a strategic program derived from Münsterbrg's theories that stressed the coordination of text and images in a particular campaign with information about the target groups to which it was directed.

Shortly before his American trip, Dalang hired Richard Paul Lohse (1902–1988) who started as an apprentice in 1918 while he was studying at the Zurich School of Applied Arts. From 1922 until 1930, Lohse continued as a staff designer at the agency, whose name Dalang changed to Max Dalang A.G. Reklame (Max Dalang A.G. Advertising). Though Lohse would eventually become one of the leading proponents of Swiss Constructivist design, the agency's advertising in the early 1920s was quite conventional, characterized by the illustrative advertisements and posters of the painter and graphic artist Alois Carigiet (1902–1985), a staff designer there. In 1927, Carigiet left the agency to open his own studio. That same year, Dalang hired Hans Neuburg (1904–1983) as a copywriter. Trained neither as an artist nor designer, Neuburg became interested in the idea of "industrial advertising," a term that Dalang had first used in 1924, perhaps in response to a group of the agency's clients in the technology and construction industries.

"Industrial advertising" first became evident in graphic design in the work of Max Burchartz and Johannes Canis for the Bochumer Verein, a large industrial firm in the German Rhineland (see Chapter 21). This was in the late 1920s when Burchartz was also teaching at the Folkwang School in Essen, which offered classes in photography in addition to the graphic arts. As previously discussed, one of his outstanding pupils was Anton Stankowski (1906–1998),

who joined the Dalang agency in 1929 after Dalang saw a presentation of Stankowski's student work at the 1928 Pressa exhibition in Cologne.

Initially Stankowski worked for Dalang as a photographer, but by 1930 he was producing photographic advertisements for Dalang's industrial clients such as Injecta Die Casting and the Thécla Iron Foundry. In fact, the Dalang agency set up a special department, separate from the main studio, to create industrial advertising. The department's aim was to emphasize the objectivity of the photograph and the rationality of the overall composition including the text. For these ads, which owe a lot to Burchartz and Canis, Stankowski combined photographs of industrial parts into arrangements that were joined by brief explanatory texts.

Though Piet Zwart had also created industrial advertisements for the Dutch Cable Company, they were predominantly typographic while Stankowski in his ads for Thécla organized the matter-of-fact photographic presentation of otherwise uninteresting injection-molded industrial parts into strong graphic compositions. In other ads, particularly those that promoted the Dalang agency in advertising periodicals, Stankowski created photomontages and made strong use of the diagonal line, a technique that gave his layouts a far more dynamic look than the photographic posters of Walter Cyliax.

We can thus recognize the Dalang agency as the principal conduit for the emergence of Constructivist advertising in Switzerland. For several years at the beginning of the 1930s, three of its leading practitioners—Stankowski, Neuburg, and Lohse—all worked there. Because Stankowski was a German citizen, he had to leave Switzerland in 1934 after the Nazis came to power, but he moved to a town on the German-Swiss border, where he continued to do freelance work for Dalang under a pseudonym. Neuburg left the agency before Stankowski to form his own studio, where he promoted "industrial graphics" through a newsletter, *Industrie–Werbung* (*Industry–Advertising*),

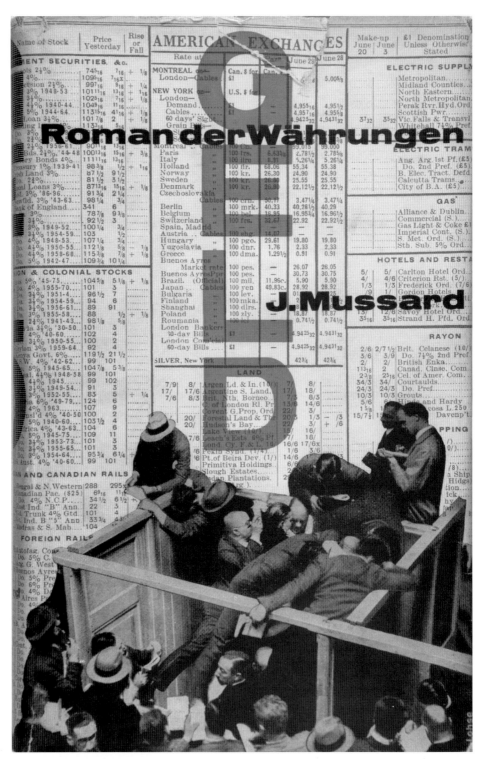

Fig. 24.23: Richard Paul Lohse, *Geld*, cover, 1938. Photobibliothek.ch © DACS 2017.

that he published from 1933 to 1937, and through many lectures and articles. Although Stankowski introduced industrial graphics to the Dalang agency, Neuburg spread the concept more widely. Collaborating with other designers, he created logotypes by distributing geometric elements within a strict partition of space. He also worked on distinctive campaigns that involved the redesign of a company's full range of advertising materials from logotypes to newspaper advertisements, posters, and detailed price lists. The campaign that he and Stankowski completed for Sulzer Brothers, an engineering firm in Winterthur, followed Stankowski's pioneering work for Dalang. They used Neuburg's favorite typeface, Akzidenz Grotesk, for the text but hand-drew the logo, which appeared at different scales and at different angles, depending on whether it was on an advertisement, a poster, or a piece of stationery. They also devised simple diagrams to depict complex processes, such as fueling a boiler, and they adopted a metaphoric use of the logo as a cloud on the cover of a brochure that described the effects of air-conditioning.

Neuburg gained additional recognition for a very different type of advertising campaign that he art-directed between 1933 and 1935 for Liebig, a producer of bouillon cubes. Instead of a geometric logo, he and Stankowski redrew the founder's signature in a flowing green script that they applied to the company's packaging as well as to its ads and posters. The seminal image of the campaign was a smiling young housewife whose photograph was broadened through distortion to create a feeling of satisfaction with the product.

Lohse left the Dalang agency in 1931 to form a studio, Atelier für Reklame-Grafik (Studio for Advertising Graphics), with Hans Trommer (1904–1989), a graphic designer who also worked briefly for Dalang. In their initial promotional literature, they declared that they could provide a full range of services using both illustration and photography. This included the design of trademarks, catalog, posters, leaflets, stationery, and exhibition stands. Though both designers had worked with Stankowski, they did not

adopt industrial graphics as their principal service the way Neuburg did. It was a part of what they offered their clients, but they also incorporated influences from De Stijl, Russian Constructivism, and the Dessau Bauhaus. With the establishment of the studios by Neuburg, Trommer, and Lohse, graphic design in Switzerland began to develop as a profession with its own theories and methods. This distinguished it from the commercial art that preceded it, which was based on a more intuitive approach.

Due to the worldwide recession of the early 1930s, Trommler's and Lohse's studio only lasted until early 1934, at which time both partners began to work on their own. Trommer moved into filmmaking, while Lohse continued to pursue a practice of Constructivist graphic design. Besides working for industrial clients, he began to design book jackets for politically progressive publishers such as the Jean Christophe-Verlag, the Europa Verlag, and the Gutenberg Book Guild. Responsive to the worsening political situation in Europe, he created politically charged jackets that combined photographs and type as John Heartfield had done for the left-wing Malik Verlag in Germany (Fig. 24.23).

Lohse had begun to consider Constructivism as an artistic method as well as a design theory. Having absorbed Max Dalang's emphasis on "planned advertising" and Stankowski's technique of industrial graphics, he started to think about painting as a form of objective planning in which the elements on the canvas were ordered according to a set of rules or principles. Beginning with images of floating curves on a solid background, after 1942 Lohse was painting canvases that consisted of colored horizontals and verticals whose hues he selected methodically. Earlier he had begun to apply his theories of modules and serial elements from painting to his graphic design layouts, and the geometrical arrangement of text and photographs became central to his design approach.

With other artists including Camille Graeser (1882–1980), Max Bill, and Verena Loewensberg (1912–1986), wife of the designer Hans Coray, Lohse became a core member of the Zürcher Konkreten (Zurich Concrete Artists) and also the co-founder with the abstract artist Leo Leuppi (1893–1972) of Allianz, an association of artists that promoted modern art through exhibitions and publications. In addition, he was a co-founder in 1933 of the Verband Unabhängiger Grafiker (Union of Independent Graphic Designers), which in 1938 became the official Swiss Verband Schweizerischer Grafiker (Union of Swiss Graphic Designers). Through his overlapping involvement with the modern art and graphic design communities in Zurich, Lohse participated in a distinctly Swiss phenomenon that contributed significantly to a style of Constructivist graphics that was grounded in sophisticated theories of visual organization, form, and color.

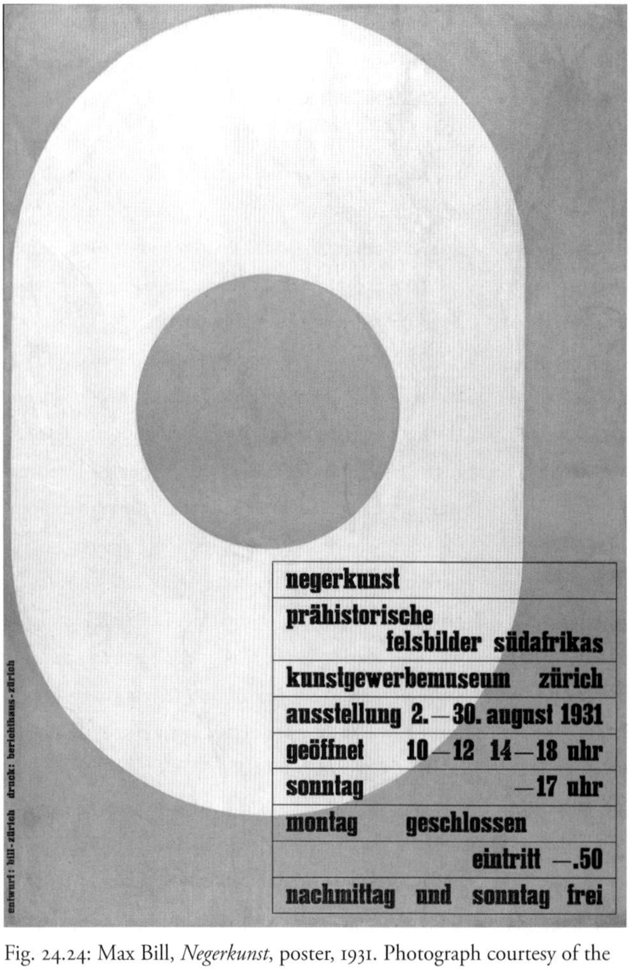

Besides Lohse, another major figure in the modern art and design communities in Zurich was Max Bill. While at the Bauhaus in 1927 and 1928, Bill studied with László Moholy-Nagy, Paul Klee, and Wassily Kandinsky. From them and other teachers, he developed a belief in the unity of the arts, and after returning to Switzerland at the end of 1928, he enjoyed a long career as a painter and sculptor, graphic designer, product designer, architect, and educator.

As an artist and sculptor, Bill was a leading figure in the Zürcher Konkreten and Allianz. In the catalog of an important exhibition of modern art and sculpture at the Zurich Kunsthaus in 1936, he published a seminal manifesto, "konkrete gestaltung" (concrete construction), where he argued that nature was no longer the source of art. Instead, art was produced through a systematic organization of forms and colors. Bill's claim was certainly aligned with the broader spirit of concrete art—a term derived from Theo van Doesburg—and it resonated as well with the aims of industrial graphics that Stankowski and Neuburg had introduced.

After his return to Switzerland, Bill earned his living primarily as a graphic designer since architectural commissions were hard to come by. Initially he called his studio bill-reklame (bill advertising). He was as much interested in the design of books and periodicals as he was in advertising and exhibitions and he worked in all those fields. An early commission was the poster and catalog for an exhibition of prehistoric rock art from South Africa at the Zurich Museum of Applied Arts. To characterize the exhibition, Bill avoided illustrative clichés and presented instead an extended white circular form on a beige ground (Fig. 24.24). The form had a primal quality that served as an abstract metaphor for the exhibition of early art. Though not the first poster to depart from the *sachplakat* poster style that was prevalent in Switzerland, Bill's design connected to a different source, the posters of Jan Tschichold, Herbert Bayer, Walter Dexel, and other modern

Fig. 24.24: Max Bill, *Negerkunst*, poster, 1931. Photograph courtesy of the Musem für Gestaltung Zürich, Poster Collection. © DACS 2017.

designers in Germany who understood typography and images—whether photographic or abstract—to be part of a unified formal order.

Given Bill's interest in architecture and modern design, it is not surprising that the founders of wohnbedarf hired him to create their graphic identity and design their advertising. His letters for the logo were expressive variants of Herbert Bayer's "Universal" alphabet of 1925, while his aim in illustrating the furnishings that wohnbedarf sold was to show them as much a possible in use, connecting them more to daily life than to formal display. Other jobs of Bill's for manufacturers of technical equipment, of which there were many in Switzerland, adopted the industrial aesthetic that had become a part of Swiss graphic design practice. A study of additional projects reveals Bill's broad interest in avant-garde precedents from Constructivism to Dada and Surrealism.

Like Lohse, he also worked closely with a number of politically progressive groups. In 1932, he began to design the socialist journal, *Information*, a project he continued for several years. Making use of the Constructivist colors of red, white, and black, he created a strong red masthead that was shaped like a triangular banner. Below it, the journal's contents were enclosed in a box but were frequently accompanied by provocative photographic images or drawings. Even before Hitler was elected chancellor of Germany, *Information* took a strong anti-Nazi position and used Nazi icons, whether photographs, symbols, or Fraktur letters, in a polemical manner.

Bill's interest in architecture no doubt led to his interest in exhibition design. Similar to Lissitzky's role in the Soviet Union, he participated in the design of various exhibitions that were sponsored by the Swiss government. Beginning with the graphics for the Swiss sections of the German Building Exhibition in Berlin and the International Exhibition for Traffic and Tourism in Poznan, Poland, he then designed a photographic display that the Swiss Tourist Board presented at the World's Fair in Brussels in 1935. Most

important was his design for the Swiss Pavilion at the 1936 Milan Triennale, where he had control of a large three-dimensional space. It was less the contents of the pavilion than Bill's inventive arrangement of objects, photographs, and sculptural shapes that led the critic for the Italian magazine *Casabella* to refer to it as exquisite. The Swiss Pavilion received the Triennale's gold medal, thus gaining recognition for Switzerland in the international design community as a country that had successfully come to terms with modernism.

Surprisingly, Bill had become more strongly committed to the tenets of the New Typography than Jan Tschichold, its founder, who had moved to Basel in 1933 to escape Nazi persecution. In Basel, Tschichold worked initially for the book publisher Benno Schwabe. Although he continued to promote the New Typography, particularly for posters and advertisements, when he returned to book design as his principal occupation he began to accede to some of its traditional techniques such as balancing the text of a page on a central axis.

Published by his employer in 1935, but only after a guaranteed subscription had been attained, Tschichold's book, *Typographische Gestaltung* (literally "Typographic forming" but translated as *Asymmetric Typography*), made clear that he was becoming less rigid about the New Typography than he had been eight years earlier when his first book appeared. This change of attitude was evident in his choice of types for the cover—Georg Trump's City for the title and an ornate script for his own name on the title page. In his discussion of type, Tschichold admitted that sans serif was no longer the best choice for all purposes. He also allowed for indented paragraphs instead of flush left settings for every line, though in a concession to modernity he continued to cite abstract art, particularly its geometric form, as a source of typographic layouts. In essence, Tschichold was rethinking the rigid typographic rules he had previously formulated, although he was not prepared to renounce them completely.

He continued to draw on the rules of the New Typography for the posters and catalogs he created for various Swiss museums in the 1930s. For example, his poster for a 1937 exhibition of European Constructivist artists at the Basel Kunsthalle, which consisted of a light brown circle on a white ground that housed the title with a vertical line of names below it, recalled Moholy-Nagy's spare *Telephone Picture* of 1922, a painting Tschichold mentioned in *Typographische Gestaltung* as a good source for graphic designers. These rules were also evident in his design for the 1938 *Penrose Annual* that was published in Britain, where two years earlier the

poster designer E. McKnight Kauffer had organized an exhibition of Tschichold's pioneering modernist work. But Tschichold's growing ambivalence about the New Typography was becoming evident in his book designs, particularly those that he did for the Basel publisher Birkhäuser after 1941. Following World War II, he would take a strong stand against the rigidity of the New Typography, a position that would garner little sympathy among a sizeable cadre of Swiss designers, particularly Max Bill, who were poised to turn their commitment to industrial advertising and avant-garde precedents into a full-blown international style.

Other graphic tendencies

Perhaps because printing was such a strong industry in Switzerland, Swiss schools of applied arts, particularly in Zurich and Basel, put a strong emphasis on the graphic arts. A seminal teacher, who trained many of Switzerland's leading graphic designers during a career of almost five decades, was Ernst Keller (1891–1968), a member of the Swiss Werkbund, who began to teach at the Zurich School of Applied Arts in 1918.

Keller did not espouse particular forms or new technologies as the proponents of industrial advertising, photography, and concrete art did. Instead he developed a pedagogical method that prepared students to analyze a problem or brief and formulate an appropriate response to it. In his own work, Keller favored hand processes, though not exclusively. He was an expert in the design of heraldic devices and official documents and he counted postage stamps among his commissions as well. His posters varied greatly in style, featuring gestural images and lettering as well as more disciplined approaches (Fig. 24.25). Keller's lettering skills were evident in the many book jackets and catalog covers he designed as well as the building signage he created for civic and commercial clients.

Many of Keller's students became prominent graphic designers during the 1920s and 1930s. Among them were Walter Käch (1901–1970), Hermann Eidenbenz (1902–1993) Gérard Miedinger (1912–1995),

Fig. 24.25: Ernst Keller, Rational Building Construction, poster, 1931. Photograph courtesy of the Musem für Gestaltung Zürich, Poster Collection.

KUNSTGEWERBE
MUSEUM
ZÜRICH

NEUES

WANDER
AUSSTELLUNG
DES DEUTSCHEN
WERKBUNDES
8. JANUAR BIS
1. FEBRUAR 1928

BAUEN

Fig. 24.26: Theo Ballmer, Neues Bauen, poster, 1928. Collection Merrill C. Berman. Photo: Jim Frank and Joelle Jensen.

Alfred Willimann (1900–1957), Heiri Steiner (1906–1983), and Walter Herdeg (1908–1995). Käch, Williman, and Steiner returned to the Zurich School of Applied Arts as teachers, while Herdeg was a founder of *Graphis*, the official journal of the Union of Swiss Graphic Designers. *Graphis*, which became known worldwide after World War II, followed the precedents of *Das Plakat* and *Gebrauchsgrafik* in Germany by publishing illustrated articles on new tendencies in graphic design in various countries.

Other teachers at the Zurich School of Applied Arts included the photographer Hans Finsler (1891–1972), who arrived from Germany in 1932 and taught at

the school for more than 30 years. Finsler inaugurated the first photography course, and many future graphic designers as well as photographers studied with him. A proponent of the New Photography, he featured detailed close-ups of objects and materials in his own work. Besides teaching, he ran a commercial studio and photographed products for many of Switzerland's leading manufacturers, particularly in the areas of furniture and textiles. In Basel, Theo Ballmer (1902–1965), a former Bauhaus student, taught photography and design at the School of Applied Arts. As his principal forms, large hand-drawn letters characterized Ballmer's posters in the late 1920s (Fig. 24.26), but several years later, when he began a poster series for the Swiss Communist Party, he also included photography, which he mixed with letterpress techniques.

Though the Swiss schools trained students who could design a poster as well as a book cover or brochure and draw faultless lettering, they did not put as much emphasis on the design of typefaces. Instead of modern types designed at home, designers relied on types such as Akzidenz Grotesk or Futura that were produced in foundries abroad. One of the few designers creating new typefaces in Switzerland during the 1920s and 1930s was the Hungarian Imre Reiner (see Chapter 21), who moved to Switzerland from Germany in 1931. Skilled in calligraphy and typography, he worked independently of the Swiss Constructivist movement as well as the approaches that were taught in the leading applied arts schools. His typefaces were produced mainly by the Bauer Foundry in Stuttgart and the Monotype Corporation in London. Reiner was an eclectic designer whose types were extremely varied. Corvinus, designed between 1929 and 1934, consisted of letters of varied thicknesses and weights with tiny thin serifs and short ascenders and descenders. The multiple versions exhibited the same curious proportions of the 19th-century modern types that served as its precedent. Other faces from the 1930s include Gotica (1933), a curious mix of traditional black letter and modern angular design; Matura

Fig. 24.27: Dora Hauth, To Protect the Young and the Weak, Yes to Women's Right to Vote, poster, 1920. Photograph courtesy of the Musem für Gestaltung Zürich, Poster Collection.

(1939), a dogged design with thick slightly rounded letters, and Symphonie (1938), an elegant script face. Due to their idiosyncrasies, these faces were most suitable for headings and titles rather than text settings, hence their limited use.

Though few Swiss women achieved prominence as graphic designers during the 1920s and 1930s, several were active in the field. Dora Hauth (1874–1957) was a painter whose illustrative posters of the 1920s addressed social causes such as alcoholism and women's right to vote (Fig. 24.27). By contrast, Frida Allenbach-Meier (1907–2002), who worked in Bern, was one of the few designers outside the main centers of Basel and Zurich to adopt the new design tendencies. In 1933 she won a competition for the exterior signs of Swiss post offices with a bold proposal that featured lower-case sans serif lettering. Helene Haasbauer-Wallrath (1885–1968), a poster artist who taught briefly at the Basel School of Applied Arts, also worked in a modern style. Her best-known poster was for an exhibition, "The Practical Kitchen," held at the Zurich Museum of Applied Arts in 1930.

Spain

Once a world power with a large empire, Spain saw its authority and influence in the world steadily decline from the 18th century on. In the 19th century the government lost control of much of Latin America due to the growing independence movements there. As a colonial power, Spain had relied more on the import and sale of raw materials from its colonies than on the development of industries at home and consequently did not participate intensively in the Industrial Revolution. By the end of World War I, Spain was still heavily agricultural. There was, however, a trajectory of industrial development in Catalonia that was celebrated at Barcelona's Universal Exhibition of 1888 and continued after that.

Catalonia remained Spain's strongest industrial region even as the Catalan people campaigned for autonomy, fueled by the foundation of the Lliga Regionalista (Regionalist League) in 1901 and the establishment of the Mancomunitat, a semi-autonomous governing body, in 1914. This campaign continued through World War I and was subsequently suppressed by General Miguel Primo de Rivera, who governed Spain as a dictator from 1923 until 1930. Primo de Rivera emphasized the completion of large public works, and his bureaucratic control of industry prevented the emergence of a diverse and independent manufacturing sector. There was a greater openness to industrial and cultural development during the brief Second Republic, which began in 1931 after Primo de

Rivera's fall from power, but it ended in 1936 with the start of the Spanish Civil War and then the beginning of General Francisco Franco's dictatorship in 1939.

Tradition and modernism

At the end of the 19th century, Catalonia experienced a renaissance in architecture and the decorative arts. The richly articulated buildings, furniture, and urban designs of Antoni Gaudí, Lluís Domènech y Montener, and Josep Puig y Catafalch, which were part of the Modernisme movement, were supported by Eusebi Güell and other enlightened industrialists and patronized by a rising middle class with progressive taste (see Chapter 12), in 1903, spurred by decorative arts reforms in Britain, Germany, and elsewhere, a group of Catalan artists, artisans, architects, and industrialists established the Fomento de las Arts Decorativas (Promotion of the Decorative Arts). Better known by its acronym FAD, the organization's aim was to advance

the cultural potential of the decorative arts as well as exploit their economic possibilities. Among FAD's activities was the organization of courses, exhibitions, and competitions—all designed to improve the quality of manufactured products. FAD, in fact, managed Spain's participation in the 1925 Exposition des Arts Décoratifs in Paris, which resulted in numerous prizes for the Spanish exhibitors.

The nation's success in Paris may have helped garner the support of the Spanish dictator Primo de Rivera for a similar exhibition at home. Planning for what became the International Exhibition of 1929 began in 1913 when a group of Spanish electrical manufacturers conceived the idea of an Exposición Universal de Industrias Eléctricas (Universal Exhibition of Electrical Industries). It was to be held in Barcelona to showcase advances in electrical products, a proposal that was broadened shortly thereafter to become a general Spanish exhibition

Fig. 24.28: Mise van der Rohe, Barcelona Pavilion, interior, 1929. © 2014. Digital image Mies van der Rohe/Gift of the Arch./MoMA/Scala. © DACS 2017.

that could replicate the success of Barcelona's earlier Universal Exhibition of 1888. As with the Paris Exposition des Arts Décoratifs, World War I delayed the project, which was not taken up again until after de Rivera became dictator in 1923. Considering the exhibition as an opportunity to promote national unity at home and pan-Hispanic unity abroad, he expanded its theme to cover industry, sport, and art. He also proposed another exhibition to run parallel to it in Seville, the Exposición Ibero-Americana, which he intended to foster new relations between Spain and the wider Spanish-speaking world.

Both exhibitions opened in 1929, although the International Exposition in Barcelona far outshone the more modest Seville event. Barcelona's architectural set piece was the National Palace of Josep Puig y Catafalch (1867–1956), which dominated the exhibition site from its commanding position atop Montjuich, a broad hill to the south of the city center. Puig y Catafalch's design, and in fact the overall design of the exhibition was based on Noucentisme, a Catalan cultural philosophy articulated by the journalist and critic Eugeni d'Ors (1881–1954) around 1906. For d'Ors, Noucentisme was a call for a return to classical ideals of order and civility, which he saw as an antidote to the spontaneity and eclecticism of modernism. While Noucentisme at the International Exhibition in Barcelona did not have a precise visual form, it exuded a sense of tradition while rejecting the technological and reductive forms of modern architecture and design that were prevalent in Germany and in other parts of Europe at the time.

The elegant minimalist German Pavilion, designed by Mies van der Rohe (Fig. 24.28), stood in high contrast to the Noucentist buildings that dominated the exhibition. For the pavilion, Mies also designed his own furniture, a chair and ottoman of curved steel with leather cushions, and a glass table with crossed chrome braces (see Chapter 21). These modern pieces stood out among the other furnishings and decorative objects at the exhibition and served as

a clarion call to Spanish architects and designers who were interested in modernism.

The introduction of modern design in Spain came from a group of rationalist architects in Barcelona who took the name GATCPAC (Grupo de Artistas y Tecnicos Catalanes para el Progreso de la Arquitectura Contemporanea/Group of Catalan Architects and Technicians for the Progress of Contemporary Architecture). The initial members of GATCPAC who came together in 1928 included among others Josep Lluís Sert (1901–1983), who had worked briefly with Le Corbusier and Pierre Jeanneret in Paris; Josep Torres Clavé (1906–1939); Raimon Duran Reynals (1895–1966); Germán Rodríguez Arias (1902–1987); and Sixt Illescas (1903–1986). By the time Primo de Rivera's dictatorship had ended, the rationalist movement had spread to other cities—San Sebastian, Bilbao, Zaragoza, as well as Madrid—where the leading rationalist architect was Fernandal García Mercadal (1896–1986), a disciple of the German architect Hans Poelzig and an admirer of Le Corbusier. In 1930, a new organization that called itself GATEPAC (Grupo de Artistas y Tecnicos Españoles para el Progreso de la Arquitectura Contemporanea/Group of Spanish Architects and Technicians for the Progress of Contemporary Architecture) was established. It took in all the groups including the Barcelona nucleus, which kept its original name.

From 1931 to 1937, GATEPAC published an important magazine, *A.C.: Documentos de Actividad Contemporánea* (*A.C.: Documents of Contemporary Activity*), which expressed the new openness of the Second Republic by promoting the latest rationalist tendencies in architecture and design. The magazine's contemporary format, featuring ample photographs and photomontages, was modeled after publications such as *Das Neue Frankfurt* in Germany that also promoted a broad modern approach to architecture, design, and urban planning.

Following German precedents as well as Le Corbusier's choice of furnishings for his Pavilion de l'Esprit Nouveau at the 1925 Exposition des Arts Décoratifs in Paris, the Barcelona architects understood the need to provide furniture conceived along rationalist lines to fill the new buildings they were designing. To that end, they established a shop called MIDVA (Muebles y Decoración para la Vivienda Actual/ Furniture and Decoration for Today's Dwelling), where they sold inexpensive furniture based on simple construction and standardized parts. And like wohnbedarf in Zurich, they also sold imported furniture by Marcel Breuer and Alvar Aalto as well as chairs manufactured by Thonet.

In Barcelona, GATEPAC architects like Sert, Rodríguez-Arias, and Torres Clavé designed furniture that was custom-manufactured in small runs for individual projects. In Madrid, the principal manufacturer of modern furniture was Rolaco-MAC, which was founded in 1932 when two companies that were set up to produce metal furniture merged. Rolaco-MAC specialized in furniture made of tubular steel and secured the rights to produce pieces by Mies van der Rohe and Marcel Breuer in Spain. The company also worked with local Madrid architects such as García Mercadal and Luiz Feduchi Ruiz (1901–1975). Rolaco-MAC made all of Feduchi Ruiz's furniture for the Art Deco Carrión Building in downtown Madrid that he designed between 1931 and 1933 with Vicente Eced (1902–1978). A multipurpose structure with 16 floors, the building included a residence hotel, a restaurant, an American bar, and the well-known Capitol Cinema.

Feduchi Ruiz's furniture, ranging from desks to bar stools and restaurant chairs, stemmed from comparable designs of the French decorators rather than those of the German Functionalists. However, the chairs' upholstered seats and backs along with metal

Fig. 24.29: Hispano-Suiza J-12, 1933. © Motoring Picture Library/Alamy.

frames included elements of both. As a result of his work with Rolaco-MAC, Feduchi Ruiz became the firm's art director, which led to his collaboration on such projects as the furniture for Madrid's Bar Chicote that combined comfortable seating with tubular steel supports. The bar was designed by another local architect, Luiz Gutiérrez Soto (1890–1977).

Though Spain was not a major manufacturer of electrical appliances or radios during the interwar years, the demands of a growing middle class stimulated the establishment of a few local firms that competed with the large volume of goods imported from abroad. Among these was Electrodomésticos Solac (Solac Household Appliances), a company founded in 1925 that specialized in small appliances such as toasters and hand irons. The designers who created its products were most likely artists, who adapted decorative elements from traditional furniture to the new metal appliances. One example is the 1930 toaster whose housing with ornamental shapes cut in the panels rests on a platform with four metal legs. A decade later, evidence of American streamlining was evident in a different company's product, the Iberia radio, whose curved form suggested modernity although the use of wood rather than metal for the housing was evidence that Iberia had not yet understood that a modern appliance need not possess the form or materials of traditional furniture.

In contrast to its modest development as a producer of modern furniture and appliances, Spain was one of the earliest European manufacturers of automobiles in Europe, with Barcelona as its center. The first Spanish car, which began production in 1898, was the little-known La Cuadra, an electric vehicle whose engine designer was the Swiss Marc Birkigt (1878–1953). Another Spanish automobile was the relatively short-lived Elizalde, a luxury car that was in production from 1914 to 1928.

In 1902, the company that had produced the La Cuadra came under new ownership and changed its name to Hispano-Suiza, although Marc Birkigt remained as the new firm's chief engineer. Positioned as luxury vehicles, early Hispano-Suizas had the look of large racing cars with elongated hoods flanked by large flat fenders. By 1911, France was proving to be a larger market for luxury cars than Spain and that year Hispano-Suiza set up a French factory. During World War I, the company became a leading manufacturer of aircraft engines, an accomplishment that would lead to more powerful engines for its automobiles after the war. Hispano-Suiza was known for its luxury cars, although it also produced buses, trucks, and ambulances. Many of the luxury bodies were designed in the Barcelona studio of the Italian stylist Emilio Basagoiti (dates unconfirmed) The heyday of the Hispano-Suiza was the 1930s when the J-12, with its powerful motor and elegant chassis with rounded fenders and arched back, became one of the world's most desirable and expensive automobiles (Fig. 24.29). Hispano-Suiza's production of cars ended with World War II, after which it concentrated on products for the aviation industry.

Commercial art, typography, and editorial design

From the beginning of the 20th century, Paris was an important center for Spanish artists. Pablo Picasso achieved notoriety there, first through the paintings of his Blue and Rose periods, then as a progenitor of Cubism. Joan Miro built his reputation in the city as did Salvador Dali, the notorious Surrealist painter. Like these men, cartoonists, illustrators, and commercial artists were also drawn to Paris. Some went there to live and work while others, who did not leave Spain, were simply attracted by the fashionable styles of French magazine illustration and poster design. Consequently, French illustration techniques and decorative lettering were influential in Spain, where Barcelona and Madrid became the leading centers of advertising art.

In Barcelona, Francesc d'Assís Galí (1880–1956) founded an important art school in 1906, Escola d'Art, where the artist Joan Miro studied. As a teacher,

Fig. 24.30: Francesc d'Assís Galí, International Exhibition Barcelona, poster, 1929. © Album/Prisma/Album/SuperStock.

funnels, which represent Catalan industry and serve as iconic images of modernity (Fig. 24.30).

French influence was stronger in the work of three leading poster designers from Madrid: Federico Ribas (1890–1952), Rafael de Penagos (1889–1954), and Salvador Bartolozzi (1882–1950), all from the generation that began as artists before moving into the world of design. Ribas had a successful career as an illustrator, caricaturist, and art director for popular magazines in Buenos Aires and Paris before returning to Spain in 1914 at the outbreak of World War I. In Madrid he spent many years as the art director for Perfumería Gal, a company that made perfumes and toiletries for women. The decorative style he adopted for the company's packaging, advertisements, and posters made strong reference to the fashion illustrations and magazine covers that Erté did for some French fashion magazines in Paris (see Chapter 22) as well as to the posters of the turn-of-the-century French artist Jules Chéret. Ribas's emphasis on decoration was also evident in the packaging and advertising of other manufacturers of perfumes and toiletries such as Perfumería Calber in San Sebastían, Myrurgia in Barcelona, where the art director was Eduardo Jenner (1882–1967), and in Madrid Perfumería Floralia, where Salvador Bartolozzi, a rival of Ribas's, created advertising and posters.

Bartolozzi (1882–1950) had done drawings for various graphic magazines in Paris before his return to Madrid in 1906. There he began to create drawings for magazines and in 1917 he became the art director for the Calleja publishing house. Winner of many poster competitions, he produced posters that were more illustrative than designed. This is evidenced by his poster for the 1929 Exposición Ibero-America in Seville that featured women in native dress from all parts of the Americas. Women in his illustrations for perfumes and toiletries possessed the delicate feminine graces of Erté's French coquettes.

Rafael de Penagos, like Ribas and Bartolozzi, also studied in Paris where his mentor was Javier Gosé (1876–1915), a Spaniard who assisted the French

Galí fostered a traditional style that had Greek and Florentine roots with a modest obeisance to Cubist form and Fauve color. During the 1920s, he spread his pedagogical method to other important Catalan art schools. He was also an active poster designer for commercial and cultural clients and his work featured strong central images that were frequently combined with contrasting background perspectives. This is evident in his prize-winning poster for Barcelona's Universal Exposition of 1929, where an ethereal woman with a dove of peace in one hand and a Catalan flag in the other floats above a mass of smokestacks and couturier Paul Poiret. After his return to Spain in 1914, Penagos developed a broad practice as an illustrator, working for magazines and publishing houses as well as creating frequent posters. The women he depicted in his advertising designs were more self-assured and aggressive than the traditional flirtatious coquette. According to some critics, his depiction of the "modern Eve," who held her own with her male counterparts as one can see in his poster for Suderal Deodorant, was a mythic figure rather than a realistic depiction of the Spanish woman.

By the 1930s, the fashion-influenced French style of illustration had been superseded by a more stream-lined and stylized Deco style that was characterized by accentuated volumes, unusual angles, and expressive lettering. France remained an important exemplar of this style, but it was now the more commercially oriented posters of Cassandre, Colin, and Carlu that set the tone. One could also argue that a Deco aesthetic spread widely from France without it being attributed to a single source. In Barcelona, Josep Morrell (1899–1949), a principal exponent of the Deco poster, had a big influence on other Spanish designers. His techniques were quite diverse. On a poster for Molfort's silk socks, he depicted with wry humor a man in his bathrobe pulling on a sock, while his many film posters for 20th Century Fox portrayed scenes with a more serious emotional content. A poster for Monopol Gasoline showed a gas pump dramatically enlarged through a worm's eye view, contrasted with the muscular head of a worker and angular lines of lettering.

Other Barcelona poster artists who worked in a Deco style were Antonio Moliné (1907–1937), Paco Ribera (dates unconfirmed), and Josep Aluma (1897–1975). Antoni Clavé (1913–2005), who studied painting and sculpture, specialized in film posters during the early 1930s, doing some for Metro-Goldwyn-Mayer as well as other producers. The juxtaposition of angular forms from Cubism and the clean shapes of Purism were strong sources for Clavé, whose work is perhaps the most original of any Spanish designer of the period. Limiting his palette to somber dramatic colors that remained subordinate to his images, he selected a singular icon or several icons to characterize each film and then presented these in dramatic combinations. Clavé brought a strong artistic culture to the popular medium of film posters and introduced a more serious and visually sophisticated representation of each film than was typical elsewhere. His poster for the 1932 horror film *Dr. Jekyll and Mr. Hyde*, for example, presented the dual personality of the protagonist in a restrained way rather than exploiting the commercial potential of a lurid drawing.

In Valencia, the important designers of commercial posters and other graphics in the early 1930s were Arturo Ballester (1892–1981) and Josep Renau (1907–1982). Both would be prominent poster designers for the Republican side during the Spanish Civil War, while Renau would be especially recognized for his radical photomontage posters and editorial illustrations. Besides designing posters, Ballester was an active collaborator with several publishing houses, notably Prometeo, founded in 1923 by the Valencian novelist Vicente Blasco Ibáñez. For seven years, until Prometeo closed, Ballester created a series of dramatic covers for its books, particularly the novels of Jack London and those of Blasco Ibáñez himself.

During the 1920s, advertising agencies flourished in Spain, promoting Spanish products such as cosmetics, food, and cigarettes, as well as films and automobiles from abroad. Helios-Publicitas and Los Tiroleses were Spanish agencies located in Madrid, while Publicidad Gala was in Barcelona. Seix i Barral was not strictly an advertising agency, but it created some of the strongest Spanish advertising of the interwar years. Founded in Barcelona in 1911 as a publishing house, it also included a printing estab-lishment and an in-house design department that produced posters, brochures, books, and other types of graphic publications. The artistic director of the department was Joan Seix (dates unconfirmed), who was also active as a painter and theatrical set designer.

Seix hired the French-Alsatian designer Franz Schuwer (dates unconfirmed), who had worked in Paris for Draeger Frères, the large French printer, publisher, and advertising agency. Schuwer introduced many new concepts from France and Germany that were absorbed by the host of young Spanish designers and illustrators whom Seix hired. These included Miguel Narro (dates unconfirmed), Martí Bas (1910–1966), Lorenzo Goñi (1911–1992), Evarist Mora (1904–1987), Ricard Giralt Miracle (1911–1994) and Nicolau Miralles (1911–d.o.d. unconfirmed), also known as "Lau."

The Milanese agency Maga opened an office in Madrid and sold Spanish clients the right to produce posters by leading Italian advertising artists. The American agency J. Walter Thompson also established a short-lived Madrid branch, particularly to service its General Motors account. Another foreign advertising agency to open an office in Madrid was Publicitas from Switzerland.

During the intellectually stimulating years of the Second Republic, several art directors and photographers in Barcelona introduced photography to the broader field of advertising. Pere Català Pic (1899–1971), a proponent of the New Photography in Germany, featured sharp close-up photographs of products, which he frequently included in expressive compositions such as his advertisement for Citronitrina tablets. Josep Sala (1896–1962) also created photographic ads with a similar use of sharply focused close-ups. Among his clients were the jeweler Roca and Myrurgia, the cosmetics company.

In the popular magazines for the middle class, the Deco style of illustration predominated. It was evident on many covers of *Nuevo Mundo* (*New World*), *Reflejos* (*Reflections*), *Blanco y Negro* (*White and Black*), and *D'Ací i d'Allà* (*From Here and There*). Published in Barcelona with striking interior illustrations and covers, *D'Ací i d'Allà* was a leader in the creative use of graphic imagery. In the early 1930s, the graphic artist Will Faber (1901–1987), who had emigrated to Spain from Germany in 1932, drew a number of covers

in a fresh light-hearted style. The popular magazines also varied their lettering from one cover to another, resulting in creative experiments with eclectic forms, all of which exemplified a new decorative style. Expressive lettering was also prominent on posters, advertisements, packaging, catalogs, metal signs, and trademarks.

In 1932, *D'Ací i d'Allà* began to incorporate photography both for its covers and its internal layouts. This occurred under the impetus of the advertising photographer Josep Sala (1896–1962), who was the magazine's art director. Comparable changes in magazine design were introduced by the Polish designer Mauricio Amster (1907–1980), who emigrated to Madrid in 1929. Amster had studied in Berlin where he was exposed to the new tendencies in typography, photomontage, and drawing, all of which he applied to his work in Spain.

A magazine known for its typography was *Arte* (*Art*), an avant-garde publication founded and edited in Lleida by Enric Crous-Vidal (1908–1987) during 1934 and 1935. Crous-Vidal established his first design studio in 1931 and undertook various commissions while also editing his magazine. He was an excellent calligrapher and published various articles in his magazine on advertising, design, and the visual aspects of typography. In 1939, when Francisco Franco came to power, Crous-Vidal emigrated to France where he worked initially for a printer. He became a successful typeface designer and a strong promoter of *grafica latina* (latin graphics), a movement that sought to counter the straightforward qualities of Anglo-Saxon and German typefaces with warmer and more decorative designs. Another Spanish proponent of a Latin typographic style was Guillermo de Mendoza (1895–1944), an industrial draftsman who came late to typography. His plan was to create a typeface for each region of Spain, a project that remained unfinished at his early death.

The Spanish Civil War

The Second Republic, which followed Primo de Rivera's dictatorship, was liberating for the Spanish people, although it unleashed strong conflicts between the right and left. A workers' revolution in October 1934 prompted the electoral victory of the leftist Popular Front, whose policies and actions provoked a military coup in July 1936 that initiated the Civil War. The coup against the Republican government was led by General Francisco Franco, whose Nationalist forces defeated the Republicans in April 1939.

Franco sought and received military aid from the Nazis in Germany and the Fascists in Italy, while the Soviet Union backed the Republicans by supporting the International Brigades that were composed of fighters from abroad. The Republicans could not match the air power or ground troops of the Nationalists, but they nonetheless fought fiercely in battles across Spain.

The Republican government, headed by Francisco Largo Caballero, was located in Madrid until late 1936, when it moved briefly to Valencia and then to Barcelona. What the Republicans lacked in materiel, they made up for in propaganda. Posters were central to their propaganda campaign and they organized diverse studios and lithographic workshops to produce them. As with posters in any war, the themes ranged from maintaining military unity to growing more food. Since the Republican government was supported by different leftist parties—Socialists, Communists, and Anarchists—posters also elicited support for these groups.

Shortly after the war began, the Republican government established a Ministry of Propaganda, which produced a large number of posters as did less official organizations such as the Junta Delegada de Defensa de Madrid (Delegated Committee for the Defense of Madrid), which had a section dedicated to propaganda and the press. In Barcelona, the Commissariat of Propaganda was an active source of posters as were related organizations in Aragon, Valencia, and other cities.

Most of Spain's poster designers, illustrators, and artists supported the Republicans and eagerly

volunteered to work for them. A number had gained considerable experience as commercial designers in the years prior to the Civil War. Among the first to join the Republican cause were a group of radical artists and designers in Barcelona who founded the Sindicat de Dibuixants Profesionals (Union of Professional Designers) in 1936. They included Helios Gómez (1905–1956), Martí Bas, Carles Fontseré (1916–2007), and Lorenzo Goñi. Goñi's 1938 poster, "And you, what have you done for victory?", was a powerful rephrasing of James Montgomery Flagg's World War I recruiting poster depicting Uncle Sam and Russian poster artist Dmitri Moor's later version done during the Russian Revolution (see Chapter 20).

Most posters were lithographed. Among the artists who produced them, besides those in the Sindicat, were Evarist Mora, Josep Bardasano (1910–1979), Josep Espert (1907–d.o.d. unconfirmed), José Briones (1905–1975), and Arturo Ballester, an admirer of the Soviet film posters by the Stenberg Brothers. Many of the artists were quite young, although Rafael de Penagos, one of the older generation of poster designers, did a number of posters for the Republican cause.

Drawing styles and themes varied. Some artists borrowed narratives from World War I posters; some adapted the heroic depictions of muscular fighters from the Bolshevik Revolution or Soviet Socialist Realism; while others reflected the smooth Deco advertising style. Even movie posters were a source of ideas and techniques.

Besides lithography, designers also used photography and photomontage. One of the most powerful posters of the Civil War featured Pere Català Pic's photograph of a peasant's foot stepping on a cracked swastika that represented fascism. Produced for the Catalan Commissariat of Propaganda and entitled "Aixafem el Feixisme" ("Smash Fascism"), it was a stark visual image of Spanish courage with no text (Fig. 24.31). Maurizio Amster also did a number of posters that combined photographs and text in the form of wall

Fig. 24.31: Pere Català Pic, Aixafem el Feixisme (Smash Fascism), c. 1936. The Wolfsonian–Florida International University, Miami Beach, Florida, The Mitchell Wolfson, Jr. Collection, TD1990.191.23.18. Photo: David Almeida.

murals, while Manuel Monleón (1904–1976) worked with photomontage like his Valencian compatriot Josep Renau.

Soviet photography and German photomontage, particularly the work of John Heartfield, were strong influences on Renau, with whom photomontage is most closely associated in Spain. A master of the airbrush as well, Renau was a prominent designer of advertising and movie posters during the 1920s and early 1930s.

He was also an active member of the Communist Party and produced photomontage covers and layouts during the 1930s for several leftist journals—*Octubre* (*October*), *Estudios* (*Studies*), and one he edited, *Nueva Culture* (*New Culture*). All were published in Valencia where he lived. During the Civil War, Renau designed powerful photomontage posters for the Communist Party in which he combined photography with airbrush techniques. He used militant symbols as in a poster to promote agriculture, where he depicted a large enemy hand stretched over a field trying to prevent a farmer from tilling it. To stop the hand he portrayed, a bayonet thrust into it (Plate 24).

When the Civil War began, Renau joined the Republican government as Director-General of Fine Arts, in which capacity he supervised the evacuation of many valuable paintings from the Prado in Madrid in order to save them from enemy aerial attacks. He also commissioned Pablo Picasso to create the large mural that depicted the German bombing of the Spanish town of Guernica.

Picasso painted the mural for the Spanish Pavilion at the 1937 World's Fair in Paris, a project that had been pushed forward by the head of the Republican government, Largo Caballero, to gain economic and political support abroad for the Republican cause. Designed by the rationalist architects Josep Lluis Sert and Luis Lacasa (1899–1966), the pavilion featured, in addition to Picasso's *Guernica* and Joan Miro's outsized mural, *Catalan Peasant in Revolt*, a large series of photo-murals by Renau. Their aim was to create a sense of Spain as a modern nation by depicting a cross-section of social and regional types engaged in productive daily activities.

When the pavilion opened, the Republicans still believed they could defeat Franco's forces. With Picasso and Miro contributing as exiles and Renau's photomurals providing a panorama of Spanish life, the pavilion exuded a sense of hope even as the clouds of war were gathering elsewhere in Europe. That hope was dashed in April 1939 when a victorious

Franco announced the end of the Civil War. For poster designers and others who created visual propaganda, the Republican struggle fostered a sense of solidarity and intense political engagement. Had the Republicans been victorious, this would have resulted in a thriving community of graphic artists. Instead, most of the active designers went into exile, either internally or abroad.

Greece

The Ottoman Empire defeated the Greek forces in the struggle over Crete in 1897, prompting the Greeks to reassess their military capabilities. Necessary to improving them was strengthening the national economy as well as the armed forces. The man to whom the Greeks looked to achieve this task was Eleuthérios Venizélos, a politician from Crete. He came to power as the result of a coup staged by a group of disaffected military officers in 1909, following the revolt of the Young Turks in the Ottoman Empire. Venizélos, credited by some as the man who created modern Greece, introduced a broad program of constitutional reform and economic development, while also attempting to reinstate the ambitious aims of the 19th-century Great Idea to unite all the Greeks in the region. He presided over the creation of the Ministry of National Economy in 1911 and subsequent labor legislation that prohibited child labor and regulated the hours of the working week. Through his diplomatic skills, Greece doubled its geographical area and population as a result of victories in the First and Second Balkan Wars in 1912–1913. Under Venizélos, Greece sided with the Allies in World War I, which expanded the nation's borders even further, thus enabling Venizélos to claim considerable success in pursuing the Great Idea.

A major event in Greece occurred in 1922 when a massive influx of refugees entered the country after the Great Fire of Smyrna (Izmir) in Turkey. The Smyrna disaster also preceded a series of turbulent political events at home over the next 20 or so years. The same year as the Smyrna fire, a military junta deposed the Greek monarchy and in 1924 the Republic of Greece was formally established. Eight years after this event, Greece signed a treaty of friendship with the Ataturk government in Turkey. However, fear of a royalist restoration prompted another military coup in 1935, which ironically resulted in the former Greek king George II being returned to the throne.

In 1936, Ioannis Metaxas, a right-wing general, became Prime Minister and persuaded the king to suspend key articles of the constitution, thus giving him dictatorial powers, which he exercised until his death in 1941. Despite his dictatorial predilection, however, Metaxas did not seek alliances with Italy and Germany, although he adopted many of the militarized characteristics for Greek society that both Mussolini and Hitler had introduced in their respective countries. Like them, he invoked values of the past, extolling the accomplishments of ancient Greece, especially the Spartans. He sought to fuse these values with those of the medieval Christian empire of Byzantium, melding them together in a new nationalist vision that he called the "Third Hellenic Civilization."

One action that followed the precedent of Mussolini and Hitler was to establish a National Youth Organization (Ethniki Organosis Neolaeas) or EON, which lasted for only four years until Metaxas' death. Like the fascist youth movements in Italy and Germany, members of EON had their own uniforms and flag whose emblem was a Greek double-headed axe with a wreath of laurels around it and a crown above it. The EON also published a photographic magazine for its members as well as posters that promoted physical fitness. During World War II, the Greeks turned back an Italian invasion but the Germans marched on Greece in 1941 and occupied the country despite acts of resistance until late 1944.

The impulse to industrialize

According to Artemis Yagou, the Smyrna disaster brought one and a half million refugees to Greece, which she sees as fueling industrialization and speeding

1933-1938

ΔΙΑΡΚΗΣ ΕΚΘΕΣΙΣ
ΕΛΛΗΝΙΚΩΝ ΠΡΟΪΟΝΤΩΝ
ΑΘΗΝΑΙ · ΖΑΠΠΕΙΟΝ

Fig. 24.32: Fokion Dimitriadis, Permanent Exhibition of Greek Products, catalog cover, 1938. Private Collection.

up the pace of capitalist expansion. She notes that the influx of refugees created a multicultural workforce with varied professional knowledge in fields such as weaving, tapestrymaking, ceramics, woodcarving, metalwork, and decorative painting. As a consequence, new industrial sectors such as carpetmaking were introduced. At the same time, many entrepreneurs from Asia Minor enriched the environment for business and entrepreneurship.

The expansion of an internal market, as Yagou notes, increased the demand for manufactured consumer goods and paved the way for more domestic production. Since many of the refugees were skilled in various applied

arts, they contributed significantly to the growth of a manufacturing sector, although one still based on craftsmanship rather than machines. Most of the manufacturing firms were small and workers were not well paid. Among the efforts that the government contributed to the country's industrial development was the Permanent Exhibition of Greek Products that occurred in Athens between 1922 and 1938 (Fig. 24.32). Besides the catalog of this exhibition, a number of companies adopted promotional techniques such as product catalogs, thus forging a market that was beginning to employ the successful sales tools of already industrialized countries.

As an example, Kosmos, a metallurgical company located in Thessaloniki, produced a bilingual catalog in Greek and French, with illustrations of its coffee and tea cups, cooking utensils, and various other household items. Comparable to this catalog were the advertising leaflets produced by another company, Thermis, which manufactured steel furniture and stoves along with additional objects for household use. Yagou notes that Thermis' metal furniture could not compete successfully with the wood furniture that dominated the domestic market. This was the case in most other countries where metal furniture was produced. As elsewhere, such furniture was successfully adopted for offices, hospitals, schools, and other public facilities.

Despite the efforts of government figures like Venizélos to promote industrialization, there was considerable debate in Greece during the interwar years about its value. One view held that greater industrialization would create a chasm that divided a small number of entrepreneurs and a large number of workers, a belief that was closely related to preserving the stability of the upper and middle classes. An agricultural Greece bereft of industrialization also served the interests of foreign governments who preferred that the country remain a market for their own products. Consequently, most government figures favored agricultural development and maintained an anti-industrial spirit.

There was little incentive for product excellence or innovation when competitiveness was sustained by high tariffs and many products were actually of poor quality. Such a situation was perpetuated by public perceptions that foreign goods were better than domestic ones in any case. Those products that were manufactured locally played to a nationalistic impulse by emphasizing their "Greekness," an intangible quality that expressed the national spirit. This was the case with the Kioutacheia potteries, which claimed that their ceramic goods were maintaining a traditional Greek art form.

Although many refugees from the Smyrna fire came with craft skills, companies that were engaged in industrial manufacturing had difficulty finding capable employees. Such was the example of Elvira, a company that was manufacturing radio sets, which required engineers, technicians, and other specialists. It was likewise so with Thermis, which had to spend many months on tests and pay high wages to foreign experts to train their staff.

One attempt to address this issue was the founding of the Sivitanidios School of Arts and Crafts in Athens in 1926, although the school did not start to operate until the 1929–1930 academic year. It's establishment was made possible by a financial legacy from the Sivitanidis brothers, two wealthy businessmen who envisioned an institution that would be comparable to France's École Nationale Supérieure d'Arts et Métiers (National School of Arts and Crafts), which had been founded in 1780. The emphasis of the Paris school was on mechanics and industrialization, which was likewise the aim of the Greek institution. Its board members included representatives from the National Technical University of Athens as well as the Federation of Greek Industrialists and Handicrafts and related organizations. The Ministry of National Economy administered the school and this provided an impetus to turn out graduates who would contribute to a national process of industrialization. The inauguration ceremony was attended by Eleuthérios Venizélos, who spoke highly of the institute's foundation.

Although the school had its ups and downs and struggled with the external perception that it was training students for jobs with low prestige, by the time World War II began, it had about 1,500 students and provided instruction in 44 different specialties. The anti-industrial perception was countered by the magazine *Erga* (*Works*), which maintained a strong but ill-fated argument for the value of technical education and manual work, encouraging its readers to cultivate in young children a zeal for such activity. In fact, despite the conditions of its original legacy, there was an attempt that was nonetheless put down by the administration of the Sivitanidios School to turn it into a School of Decorative Arts for decorators, painters, sculptors, and engravers.

As a consequence of the national ambivalence towards industrialization and the technical professions related to manufacturing, design did not develop as a practical activity in Greece during the interwar years. Artemis Yagou refers to "proto-professionalization in the margins of related, more established professions." Where design expertise was required, it was usually provided by those trained in other fields such as art—particularly in the case of commercial art—or engineering, which was more pertinent to manufacturing.

Advertising and commercial art

As Maria Nicholas has pointed out, the establishment of the Republic of Greece in 1924 brought with it openness to public communication that was a positive sign for the development of advertising agencies. There were no such agencies in Greece at the beginning of the 20th century. Newspaper staff designed and typeset their own advertisements with copy submitted directly by the client. The presence of the visual element in advertisements, however, grew to the point where in 1924, a full-page ad—the first in a Greek newspaper—for the Lambropoulos Brothers department store in Athens was published. It consisted of a large image with a copy line at the bottom.

In 1899, the first organizations were created to post bills and public declarations on building walls in an organized manner. However, outdoor advertising and billposting were generally rare before 1910. Among

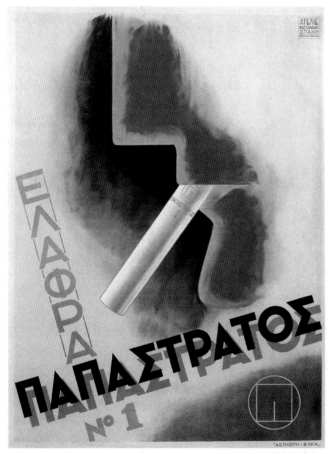

Fig. 24.33: Nikos Kastanakis and A. Sprachis, Papastratos cigarettes, poster, 1930s. E.L.I.A. Archive/M.I.E.T. (Literary and Historical Archive/National Bank of Greece Cultural Foundation).

the most prominent were the early posters for the live theater or shadow puppet theaters produced by artists who illustrated them by hand. Besides painted posters, advertisements were also printed on metal plates, which were posted on walls just as painted or printed posters were.

One of the first advertising and commercial art studios in Greece was Kastanakis-Spachis, whose principals were Nikos Kastanakis (dates unconfirmed) and A. Spachis (dates unconfirmed). The studio featured among its clients the Papastratos tobacco company for which it designed the company's first posters in various modern styles (Fig. 24.33). Compared

to the work of other advertising agencies, the work of Kastanakis-Sprachis was closest to the modern French posters that experimented with image fragments and typographical layout and the German *sachplakat* that featured large images of the advertised objects with only the company name and no copy line added. Both sources were evident in their posters for Papastratos cigarettes.

Another early advertising agency was GEO, founded in 1919 by the painter and engraver Aggelos Theodoropoulos (1883–1965), who was a graduate of the School of Fine Arts. Besides the advertising posters he produced, Theodoropoulos also worked as a cartoonist and caricaturist for Athenian newspapers. He was one of the first artists to print posters with a four-color process, a technique that only became popular in Greece after World War II.

Major clients for the advertising companies were firms that produced consumer goods such as cigarettes, beer, and wine, as well as those that distributed imported products like Kodak film and Singer sewing machines. Many of the posters were painterly, featuring attractive women in seductive garments or occasionally wearing little or nothing.

Advertising agencies continued to open throughout the 1920s and 1930s, and by 1940 there were 19 in Athens. Many functioned as commercial art ateliers, however, rather than as full-service agencies. Among those that sprang up during this period were Greka, founded in 1927 by Kostas Kotzias (dates unconfirmed); DITS, started by Theodoros Tsantilis (dates unconfirmed) the same year; Alma, founded by Tassos Bryonis (dates unconfirmed); Menetor, an agency that Takis Theofilopoulos (dates unconfirmed) and Aggelos Troianos (dates unconfirmed) inaugurated; and Minos, founded by Minos Symeonidis (dates unconfirmed), which became one of Greece's largest agencies, pioneering in product marketing, market research, and other related techniques.

Artists who created advertising posters during this period, working mainly on a freelance basis, are

Fig. 24.34: Georgios Gounaropoulos, Victory, Freedom. May the Virgin Be With Him, poster, 1940. National Historical Museum, Greece.

Panos Aravantinos (1884–1930), who was better known as a painter and set designer; Kostas Theologidis, known as Theo (dates unconfirmed); Stephanos Almaliotis (dates unconfirmed), who designed some of Greece's first film posters; and Perikles Vyzantios (1893–1972), who worked for the Greek National Lottery as well as other clients.

An important stimulus for the production of posters was the growth of the tourist industry. As a source of European civilization, Greece had been a mecca for tourists for centuries. During the 19th century, Greece was added to the route of the Grand Tour, and available services for tourists such as guides and guidebooks, transport, and hotels began to actively develop. To encourage tourism as a means of economic development, the government established the Greek National Tourism Organization within the Undersecretariat for Press and Tourism in 1927 and began to commission travel posters to attract foreign travelers. A number of prominent artists including Celest Polychroniadi (1904–1985), one of the rare women poster designers in Greece, were invited to create posters, some of which emphasized Greece's historic treasures and others that favored vacation spots (Plate 25). Other posters were produced to rally Greek resistance in World War II. These included the well-known design of 1940 by the painter Georgios Gounaropoulos (1889–1977) that featured a Greek soldier marching to war, embraced by the Virgin Mary (Fig. 24.34).

Bibliography
Bibliographic essay

Books and other writing that address design matters in Western and Southern Europe during this period usually concentrate on design in specific locales. General histories that have essays on particular countries include Philippe Garner, *Encyclopedia of the Decorative Arts, 1890–1940*; the catalog of the Wolfsonian's inaugural exhibition *Designing Modernity: The Arts of Reform and Persuasion, 1885–1945*, edited by Wendy Kaplan; two exhibition catalogs whose theme is Art Deco—Helena Dahlbäck Lutteman, *L'Art Déco en Europe: Tendances Décoratives dans les Arts Appliqués vers 1925*, and Charlotte Benton, Tim Benton, and Ghislaine Wood, eds., *Art Deco 1910–1939*; Kenneth Day, ed., *Book Typography 1815–1965 in Europe and The United States of America*; *History of Industrial Design 1919–1990: The Dominion of Design*; Victor Margolin, Anty Pansera, and Fredrik Wildhagen, eds., *Tradizione e Modernismo: Design 1918–1940/Tradition and Modernism: Design 1918–1940*; Paul Greenhalgh, ed., *Modernism in Design*; and a small book whose topic is tubular steel furniture: Barbie Campbell-Cole and Tim Benton, eds., *Tubular Steel Furniture: Conference Papers*. In *The German Werkbund: The Politics of Reform in the Applied Arts*, Joan Campbell makes some useful connections between the Werkbund organizations in Germany, Austria, and Switzerland.

There is little general literature on design in the Netherlands during the interwar period. Mieke Simon Thomas, *Dutch Design: A History* is a good introduction to the subject, while Titus M. Eliëns, Marjan Groot, and Frans Leidelmeijer, eds., *Avant-Garde Design: Dutch Decorative Arts 1880–1940* contains brief essays on the subject. A considerable amount of literature exists on *De Stijl* of which Nancy Troy, *The De Stijl Environment* remains an essential volume. Other general books on the movement include the exhibition catalog *De Stijl: 1917–1931 Visions of Utopia*; Charlotte I. Loeb and Arthur L. Loeb, eds., *De Stijl: The Formative Years, 1917–1922*; Carsten-Peter Warneke, *De Stijl 1917–1931*; and the small book by Paul Overy, *De Stijl*. Monographs on Theo van Doesburg include *Theo van Doesburg: Painter and Architect*. Wim de Wit, *The Amsterdam School: Dutch Expressionist Architecture, 1915–1930* though published some time ago remains an authoritative study, as does Martijn F. Le Coultre's *Wendingen: A Journal for the Arts, 1918–1932*. There is now ample literature on Gerrit Rietveld though one of the first books to concentrate on his design work was Daniele Baroni, *The Furniture of Gerrit Thomas Rietveld*. Dutch graphic design, both generally for this period and in monographs dedicated to individual designers, has been quite well documented in such books and essays as Kees Broos and Paul Hefting, *Grafische Formgebung in den Niederlanden: 20. Jahrhundert*, translated into English as *Dutch Graphic Design: A Century*; Alston Purvis, *Dutch Graphic Design 1918–1945*; Stephen S. Prokopoff, ed., *The Modern Dutch Poster*; G. W. Ovink, "150 Years of Book Typography in the Netherlands," in Kenneth Day, ed., *Book Typography 1815–1965 in Europe and The United States of America*; and David

Scott's "Philately and the Avant-Garde: Dutch Postage Stamp Design, 1920–1950," *The Journal of Decorative and Propaganda Arts 20* (1994). Monographs on Dutch graphic designers in this period include Flip Bool, Willem Diepraam, Adi Martis, and Anneke van Veen, eds., *Piet Zwart, 1885–1977;* Dick Maan, *Paul Schuitema: Visual Organizer;* and Alston W. Purvis, *H.N. Werkman.*

Belgium is less well documented. Henry van de Velde's autobiography, *Geschichte meines Lebens,* is the best source for material on his design activity in Belgium after his return from Germany. See also Mimi Wilms, "Henri Van de Velde and the Struggle of Belgian Modernism Between the Wars," in Paul Greenhalgh, ed., *Modernism in Design* and her essay "Belgian Design in the 1930s," in Victor Margolin, Anty Pansera, and Fredrik Wildhagen, eds., *Tradizione e Modernismo: Design 1918–1940/Tradition and Modernism: Design 1918–1940.* Serge Goyens de Heusch, *"7 Arts" Bruxelles 1922–1929: Un Front de Jeunesse pour la Révolution Artistique* is a thorough study of the 7 Arts movement, while *Les Ateliers d'Art de Courtrai De Coene Frères: 80 Ans d'Artisanat et d'Industrie Mobilier – Intérieurs – Architecture* is a history of a leading Belgian furniture manufacturer. The exhibition catalog *L'Affiche en Belgique 1880–1980* has some useful material on interwar Belgian posters.

Though much of the documentation on Swiss design is about graphic design, there are also several valuable books that discuss furniture and product design, notably Arthur Rüegg, ed., *Swiss Furniture and Interiors in the 20th Century* and the exhibition catalog *Hans Coray: Künstler und Entwerfer.* Sima Ingberman's *ABC: International Constructivist Architecture, 1922–1939* is an excellent account of the founding of that journal. Books that offer overviews of Swiss graphic design include Richard Hollis, *Swiss Graphic Design: The Origin and Growth of an International Style, 1920–1965*; Christoph Bignens, *"Swiss Style:" Die Grosse Zeit der Gebrauchsgrafik in der Schweiz 1914–1964*; and the exhibition catalog *Werbestil 1930–1940: Die Alltägliche Bildersprache Eines*

Jahrzents. The monographs on Swiss graphic designers are numerous. Among them are Christoph Bignens and Jörg Stürzebecher, eds., *Konstruktive Gebrauchsgraphik: Richard Paul Lohse*; *Ernst Keller Graphiker, 1891–1968*; *Herbert Matter: Foto-Grafiker, Sehformen der Zeit: Das Werk der Zwanziger und Dreissiger Jahre*; *Max Bill: Typografie, Reklame, Buchgestaltung*; *Niklaus Stoecklin, 1896–1982*; and *Otto Baumberger, 1889–1961*. An essential primary source is Jan Tschichold's *Asymmetric Typography.* Willy Rotzler's *Constructive Concepts: A History of Constructive Art from Cubism to the Present* contains essential background material that facilitates the comparison between Swiss Constructivist graphic design and art of the 1930s.

The huge exhibition catalog *Diseño Industrial en España* has essential material on Spanish product design, while much of the other material on Spanish design in this period emphasizes graphic design. See *La Publicidad en el Diseño Urbano*; Enric Satué, *El Diseño Gráfico en España: Historia de una Forma Comunicativa Nueva,* and John Tisa's specialist volume, *The Palette and the Flame: Posters of the Spanish Civil War.* Jordana Mendelsohn looks at several forms of graphic art in her book *Documenting Spain: Artists, Exhibition Culture and the Modern Nation, 1929–1939* and in an article written with Estrella de Diego, "Political Practice and the Arts in Spain, 1927–1936," in Virginia Hagelstein Marquardt, ed., *Art and Journals on the Political Front, 1910–1940.* The most detailed English-language book on the history of design in Greece is Artemis Yagou, *Fragile Innovation: Episodes in Greek Design History*, while Maria Nicholas's MA dissertation, *A History of Twentieth Century Greek Advertising,* was my principal source of information on Greek advertising and commercial art during this period.

Books

General

Burkhardt, Lucius, *The Werkbund: History and Ideology, 1907–1933.* Woodbury, NY: Barron's, 1977.

Campbell, Joan. *The German Werkbund: The Politics of Reform in the Applied Arts.* Princeton, NJ: Princeton University Press, 1978.

Durozoi, Gérard. *History of the Surrealist Movement.* Translated by Alison Anderson. Chicago and London: University of Chicago Press, 2004.

Hansen, E. Damsgaard. *European Economic History from Mercantilism to Maastricht and Beyond.* Copenhagen: Copenhagen Business School Press, 2001.

Netherlands

Baroni, Daniele. *The Furniture of Gerrit Thomas Rietveld.* Woodbury, NY: Barron's: 1978.

Bool, Flip, Willem Diepraam, Adi Martis, and Anneke van Veen, eds. *Piet Zwart, 1885–1977.* Essay by Kees Broos. Amsterdam: Focus Publishing, 1996 (Monografien van Nederlandse Fotografen 5).

Broos, Kees and Paul Hefting. *Grafische Formgebung in den Niederlanden: 20. Jahrhundert.* Basel: Wiese Verlag, 1993.

De Stijl: 1917–1931 Visions of Utopia. Minneapolis: Walker Art Center; New York: Abbeville Press, 1982.

de Wit, Wim, ed. *The Amsterdam School: Dutch Expressionist Architecture, 1915–1930.* New York: Cooper-Hewitt Museum; Cambridge and London: MIT Press, 1983.

Eliëns, Titus M., Marjan Groot, and Frans Leidelmeijer, eds. *Avant-Garde Design: Dutch Decorative Arts 1880–1940.* London: Philip Wilson Publishers, 1997.

Le Coultre, Martijn F. *Wendingen: A Journal for the Arts, 1918–1932.* Introduction by Ellen Lupton. Essay by Alston W. Purvis. New York: Princeton Architectural Press, 2001.

Loeb, Charlotte I. and Arthur L. Lob, Eds. *De Stijl: The Formative Years, 1917–1922.* Translated by Charlotte I. Loeb and Arthur L. Loeb. Cambridge, MA, and London: MIT Press, 1982.

Maan, Dick. *Paul Schuitema: Visual Organizer.* Rotterdam: 010 Publishers, 2006.

Overy, Paul. *De Stijl*. London: Thames and Hudson, 1991.

Piet Zwart. Introduction by Peter F. Althaus. New York: Hastings House Publishers, 1966.

Prokopoff, Stephen S., ed. *The Modern Dutch Poster*. Text by Marcel Franciscono. Urbana-Champaign; Krannert Art Museum; Cambridge, MA, and London: MIT Press, 1987.

Purvis, Alston W., *Dutch Graphic Design 1918–1945*. New York: Van Nostrand Reinhold, 1992.

—*H.N. Werkman*. London: Laurence King Publishing, 2004.

Theo van Doesburg: Painter and Architect. The Hague: SDU Publishers, 1988.

Thomas, Mieke Simon. *Dutch Design: A History*. London: Reaktion Books, 2008.

Troy, Nancy. *The De Stijl Environment*. Cambridge, MA, and London: MIT Press, 1983.

Warneke, Carsten-Peter. *De Stijl 1917–1931*. Köln: Taschen, 1991.

Belgium

L'Affiche en Belgique 1880–1980. Paris: Musée de l'Affiche, 1980.

Les Ateliers d'Art de Courtrai De Coene Frères: 80 Ans d'Artisanat et d'Industrie Mobilier – Intérieurs – Architecture. Le Livre Timperman, 2006.

Goyens de Heusch, Serge. *"7 Arts" Bruxelles 1922–1929: Un Front de Jeunesse pour la Révolution Artistique*. Bruxelles: Ministere de la Culture Française de Belgique, 1976.

van de Velde, Henry. *Geschichte meines Lebens*. München: R. Piper, 1962.

Switzerland

Bignens, Christoph. *"Swiss Style:" Die Grosse Zeit der Gebrauchsgrafik in der Schweiz 1914–1964*. Zürich: Chrosos Verlag, 2000.

Bignens, Christoph and Jörg Stürzebecher, eds. *Konstruktive Gebrauchsgraphik: Richard Paul Lohse*. Ostfildern-Ruit: Hatje Cantz Verlag, 1999.

Coray, Hans. *Hans Coray: Künstler und Entwerfer*. Zürich: Museum für Gestaltung, 1986 (Reihe Schweizer Design-Pioniere 3).

Ernst Keller Graphiker, 1891–1968 Gesamtwerk. Zürich: Kunstgewerbemuseum der Stadt Zürich, 1976.

Hans Neuburg: 50 Anni di Grafica Costrutttiva. Milan: Electa, 1982.

Herbert Matter: Foto-Grafiker, Sehformen der Zeit: Das Werk der Zwanziger und Dreissiger Jahre. Baden: Verlag Lars Muller, 1995.

Hollis, Richard. *Swiss Graphic Design: The Origin and Growth of an International Style, 1920–1965*. London: Laurence King Publishing, 2006.

Ingberman, Sima. *ABC: International Constructivist Architecture, 1922–1939*. Cambridge, MA, and London: MIT Press, 1994.

Max Bill: Typografie, Reklame, Buchgestaltung. Texts by Gerd Fleischmann, Hans Rodolf Bosshard, and Christoph Bignens. Zurich: Verlag Niggli, 1999.

Niklaus Stoecklin, 1896–1982. Zürich: Museum für Gestaltung, 1986 (Reihe Schweizer Plakatgestalter 3).

Otto Baumberger, 1889–1961. Zürich: Museum für Gestaltung, 1988 (Reihe Schweizer Plakatgestalter 4).

Rotzler, Willy. *Constructive Concepts: A History of Constructive Art from Cubism to the Present*. New York: Rizzoli, 1989.

Rüegg, Arthur, ed., *Swiss Furniture and Interiors in the 20th Century*. Basel, Boston, and Berlin: Birkhäuser, 2002.

Tschichold, Jan. *Asymmetric Typography*. Translated by Ruari McLean. New York: Reinhold Publishing Corp, and Toronto: Cooper & Beatty Ltd, 1967.

Werbestil 1930–1940: Die Alltägliche Bildersprache Eines Jahrzents. Zurich: Museum für Gestaltung, 1981.

Spain

Giralt-Miracle, Daniel, Juli Capella, and Quim Larrea, eds. *Diseño Industrial en España*. Madrid: Museo Nacional Centre de Arte Reina Sofia, 1998.

Mendelsohn, Jordana. *Documenting Spain: Artists, Exhibition Culture and the Modern Nation, 1929–1939.* University Park: Pennsylvania State University Press, 2005.

La Publicidad en el Diseño Urbano. Barcelona: Publivia, 1988.

Satué, Enric. *El Diseño Gráfico en España: Historia de una Forma Comunicativa Nueva.* Madrid: Alianza Editorial, 1997.

Tisa, John, ed. *The Palette and the Flame: Posters of the Spanish Civil War.* London and Wellingborough: Collet's Publishers Ltd, 1980.

Greece

Clogg, Richard. *A Concise History of Greece,* 2nd ed. Cambridge: Cambridge University Press, 1992.

Yagou, Artemis. *Fragile Innovation: Episodes in Greek Design History.* Copyright Artemis Yagou 2011. Printed by CreateSpace.

Chapters in books

Beckett, Jane, "WH Gispen and the Development of Tubular Steel Furniture in the Netherlands," in Barbie Campbell-Cole and Tim Benton, eds. *Tubular Steel Furniture: Conference Papers.* Introduction by Rayner Banham. London: The Art Book Company, 1979 (Art Documents 2).

Bennett, Ian, "Italy" and "Spain," in Philippe Garner, ed. *Encyclopedia of the Decorative Arts, 1890–1940.* New York: Galahad Books, 1978.

Bergvelt, Elinoor, "The Decorative Arts in Amsterdam, 1890–1930," in Wendy Kaplan, ed. *Designing Modernity: The Arts of Reform and Persuasion, 1885–1945.* New York: Thames and Hudson, 1995.

Bergvelt, Elinoor and Frans van Burkom, "Les Arts Décoratifs de l'Ecole d'Amsterdam 1910–1930;" in Helena Dahlbäck Lutteman, *L'Art Déco en Europe: Tendances Décoratives dans les Arts Appliqués vers 1925.* Bruxelles: Société des Expositions du Palais des Beaux-Arts, 1989.

Daenens, Lieven, "L'Art Déco en Belgique," in Helena

Dahlbäck Lutteman. *L'Art Déco en Europe: Tendances Décoratives dans les Arts Appliqués vers 1925.* Bruxelles: Société des Expositions du Palais des Beaux-Arts, 1989.

Garner, Philippe, "Belgium," in Philippe Garner, ed. *Encyclopedia of the Decorative Arts, 1890–1940.* New York: Galahad Books, 1978.

Liefkes, Reino, "Germany, Austria and the Netherlands," in Charlotte Benton, Tim Benton, and Ghislaine Wood, eds. *Art Deco 1910–1939.* Boston, New York, and London: Bulfinch Group, 2003.

Mendelsohn, Jordana with Estrella de Diego, "Political Practice and the Arts in Spain, 1927–1936," in Virginia Hagelstein Marquardt, ed. *Art and Journals on the Political Front, 1910–1940.* Gainsville: University Press of Florida, 1997.

Naylor, Gillian, "The Netherlands," in Philippe Garner, ed. *Encyclopedia of the Decorative Arts, 1890–1940.* New York: Galahad Books, 1978.

Ovink, G. W., "150 Years of Book Typography in the Netherlands," in Kenneth Day, ed. *Book Typography 1815–1965 in Europe and The United States of America.* Chicago: University of Chicago Press, 1965.

Ricard, André, "Catalan Creativity and the Emergence of Design," in *History of Industrial Design 1919–1990: The Dominion of Design.* Milan: Electa, 1991.

Satué, Enric, "The Period Between the Wars: Years of Apprenticeship for Spain," in Victor Margolin, Anty Pansera, and Fredrik Wildhagen, eds. *Tradizione e Modernismo: Design 1918–1940/Tradition and Modernism: Design 1918–1940.* Milan: l'Arca Edizioni, 1987.

von Moos, Stanislaw, "Switzerland: Notes for a History of Swiss Design," in *History of Industrial Design 1919–1990: The Dominion of Design.* Milan: Electa, 1991.

Wilms, Mimi, "Belgian Design in the 1930s," in Victor Margolin, Anty Pansera, and Fredrik Wildhagen, eds. *Tradizione e Modernismo: Design 1918–1940/ Tradition and Modernism: Design 1918–1940.* Milan: l'Arca Edizioni, 1987.

—"Henri Van de Velde and the Struggle of Belgian Modernism Between the Wars," in Paul Greenhalgh, ed. *Modernism in Design*. London: Reaktion Books, 1990.

Articles

Dutch Arts (July 1989). "Design in the Netherlands" (Special Issue).

Rassegna 30 (1987). "Piet Zwart: L'Opera Tipografica 1923–1933" (Special Issue).

Scott, David, "Philately and the Avant-Garde: Dutch Postage Stamp Design, 1920–1950," *The Journal of Decorative and Propaganda Arts* 20 (1994).

Weinberg-Staber, Margit, "Poster Persuasion," *The Journal of Decorative and Propaganda Arts* 19 (1993) (Swiss Theme Issue).

Dissertations and theses

Nicholas, Maria A. *A History of Twentieth Century Greek Advertising*. MA Thesis, Master of Arts in Advertising Design, Syracuse University, 2000.

Internet

Dritsas, Marguerite, "Greek Tourism: Continuities and Turning Points; 19th to 21st Century," http://www.tourismmuseum.gr/cat.php?showKat=10&lan=en (accessed March 20, 2012).

Yagou, Artemis, "Innovating by Design in Inter-War Greece," Discussion Paper 001, Entrepreneurial Discussion Papers, http:// http://www.ehdp.net/p002.html (accessed March 19, 2012).

Chapter 25: Central and Eastern Europe 1900–1939

Introduction

The end of World War I brought momentous changes in Central and Eastern Europe. With the break-up of the Austro-Hungarian, German, and Russian empires, Bohemia, Moravia, Slovakia, Ruthenia and a small part of Silesia became Czechoslovakia; Hungary restored its ancient monarchy in 1920, experienced a brief Communist coup, and was ruled by a regent after the coup collapsed, while Austria became an independent republic. Following more than a century of partition, Poland regained its national sovereignty. The South Slavs formed the fragile Kingdom of Yugoslavia in 1929, comprised of a number of disparate parts, including the former states of Serbia and Montenegro, along with Croatia, Bosnia, Herzegovina, and Slovenia, among others. Romania, an independent state since the 1870s, grew much larger as a result of diplomatic maneuvering during the war, while Bulgaria was under authoritarian rule for much of the interwar period. In the north, as a result of the Bolshevik Revolution, the Baltic states—Estonia, Latvia, and Lithuania—gained independence for a brief period until they were traded back and forth between the Soviet Union and Germany during World War II.

With the exception of Czechoslovakia, which had a strong industrial base before the war, these new nations were all predominantly agricultural and moved towards greater industrialization with difficulty. As late as 1938, Central and Eastern Europe produced only 8 percent of Europe's industrial output and at least a third of that came from Czechoslovakia. The relation between the nascent middle classes and the peasants in the region was uneasy, due in part to the peasants' ambivalence towards industrialization and suspicions regarding most features of urban life. Because of redrawn boundaries, each nation also had to devote significant energy to creating a new transportation infrastructure, while defending its national sovereignty against the menacing claims of surrounding states to restore lost territories.

Besides class distinctions, fierce differences existed among ethnic minorities—Czechs, Slovaks, and Germans in Czechoslovakia; Poles, Ukrainians, Germans, and Jews in Poland; and Bosnians, Serbs, and Croats in Yugoslavia. Hungary, severely reduced in size due to the annexation of large portions of land by its neighbors, was also weakened by ethnic conflict. Religious hatred of long standing affected relations between Christians, Jews, and Muslims. Given their histories or their lack of histories, the political arrangements of all the countries in Eastern and Central Europe proved unstable. Positioned between more powerful nations to the west and the new Soviet Union to the east and riven with ethnic, religious, and class strife, none were able to maintain democratic governments throughout the entire interwar period, although Czechoslovakia's functioned until 1938.

For each country the creation of a national identity was a top priority in order to unite its disparate minorities or dominate them. Nationalism was more important than pluralism and those groups that did not easily fall within a nationalist agenda were generally marginalized or oppressed. The creation of a national identity often meant drawing on traditional forms of culture—whether expressed in buildings, decorative arts, music, art, or literature—rather than embracing the new cultural forms of modernity. However, modernism did establish itself within small enclaves of avant-garde artists and theorists in a number of the new nations, as well as among Functionalist designers who drew their inspiration largely from the contemporary tendencies in Germany and France and to a limited degree from the Soviet vanguard. In general, Soviet culture had little influence in the region—and that little was often bitterly contested—due to the weak development and marginalization of the respective communist parties in these new nations, the widespread fears of Soviet expansionism, and the broadly based hatred of communism and all its works.

Czechoslovakia
Development of the applied arts

In the 1890s, when Art Nouveau influenced architecture and the decorative arts in what were then known as the Czech crown lands, the Czechs were still part of the Austro-Hungarian Empire and highly susceptible to influences from abroad. Alfonse Mucha, who garnered a strong reputation in Paris for his evocative posters and decorative designs, was a fervent Czech patriot and also showed his work in Prague, the center of Czech cultural life. An exhibition in 1897 presented architects and designers with works in the new style. Among those influenced by Mucha's designs and by other examples of Art Nouveau were students and professors at the School of Applied Arts, who demonstrated those influences in their contributions to the Czech display held inside the Austrian Pavilion at the 1900 Exposition Universelle in Paris. One of the strongest departments at the school was the Department of Textiles, headed by Julius Ambrose (1857–d.o.d. unconfirmed), where students worked in an eclectic style, counting floral motifs and other forms from nature among their sources, while also experimenting with new techniques of embroidery and weaving. Ceramics, glass, and metalwork were also highly developed among Prague craftspersons, many outside the school.

Cultural relations between Prague and Vienna were quite close though not particularly cordial. Nonetheless, the new Viennese tendencies in architecture and the decorative arts, notably those prompted by the Vienna Secession, made a large impact on Prague architects and designers. Perhaps the strongest Czech conveyor of the Vienna spirit was the architect

Jan Kotěra (1871–1923), a pupil of Otto Wagner from whom he learned to work in a style that rejected the historicism of the Viennese Ringstrasse. When Kotěra came back to Prague he concentrated on pragmatic architectural projects—apartment buildings, department stores, and private villas—but he also took a strong interest in the applied arts. Shortly after his return he became a professor at the School of Applied Arts where his students worked on the design of interiors for the 1900 Paris exhibition. Their adoption of the Secession approach, with its antagonism to historicism and its emphasis on stylized decorations, helped to establish a new direction for Czech interior design. Kotěra also designed glassware for a leading Czech firm.

Like Otto Wagner, Kotěra was interested in the integration of a building's exterior and interior design and gathered around him a group of collaborators to help with the production of customized furniture, carpets, curtains, glassware, and other interior elements for his buildings. When compared with the striking furniture, textiles, and decorative objects of the Vienna Secession, Kotěra's designs are not memorable but they were important because they represented a break with historicism by a designer working within the the Czech lands rather than abroad. By 1908, function had taken a priority over decoration in Kotěra's work and this was evident not only in several houses he designed but also in his designs for the interiors of municipal tram and railway carriages in Prague.

Kotěra's rejection of historicism could also be seen in the work produced by Artěl, an artists' cooperative that a group of young painters, applied artists, and architects founded in 1908. The group included the graphic artists František Kysela (1881–1941), Jaroslav Benda (1882–1970) and Vratislav Hugo Brunner (1886–1928), the ceramist Helena Johnová (1884–1962), the textile artist Marie Teinitzerová (1879–1960), and the architect Pavel Janák (1882–1956), who had studied in Vienna with Otto Wagner and then worked in Kotěra's Prague studio.

The group's credo recalled that of their likely model the Vienna Workshops—to raise the level of craftsmanship and produce useful things with beautiful forms and quality materials. Although Artěl had grand ambitions, the cooperative began with the production of small objects such as decorative glass chains and painted boxes, which it sold initially in a modest shop in the center of Prague. Eventually the Artěl designers expanded their line to include other objects made of glass, wood, and metal, along with ceramics. Their venues increased to include the 1914 Werkbund exhibition in Cologne, the 1923 exhibition of decorative arts in Monza, Italy, and finally the 1925 Exposition Internationale des Arts Décoratifs in Paris. The cooperative also published a magazine, *Drobné Uměni* (*Minor Arts*).

Though some Artěl members worked in the style of traditional folk artists, several years after its founding the cooperative also began to promote the angular ceramics of Pavel Janák, a founder and principal animator of Czech Cubism (see Chapter 18). Janák and others in the Czech Cubist group—Josef Gočár (1880–1945), Josef Chochol (1880–1956), and Vlastislav Hofman (1884–1964)—believed that objects with dynamic energy, whether ceramic coffee sets or buildings, could be created through the construction of faceted planes that cut through horizontal and vertical lines. Though Janák was the theoretician of the group, drawing heavily on theories of crystals for his ideas, he is best known for his small objects—ceramic boxes, tea sets, and vases—although he designed furniture and buildings as well. His black and white ceramic box of 1911, with its complex play of angular shapes and faceted black edges, represents his theory of form and exemplifies a class of Cubist objects and buildings that intentionally challenged Kotěra's more modest rejection of historicism. Cubist chairs, tables, and couches designed primarily by Gočár and Hofman were highly decorative and made for specific interiors rather than mass production (Fig. 25.01).

Most of the Cubist furniture was produced in the Prague Art Workshops (PUD) that Gočár and Janák founded in 1912. Their specialty was furniture production for which they had a well-equipped workshop staffed with skilled cabinetmakers. They considered each piece of furniture to be an artistic object and treated its creation as if it were a sculpture. The finished pieces, which had sharply-angled lines and planes in different configurations, were made for discerning collectors or for the designers themselves. By 1913, the workshop had expanded to include a tapestry weaving studio and a showroom that housed a permanent exhibit of its furniture as well as chandeliers, carpets, and household textiles. Perhaps their largest commission was furnishing a resort hotel that Gočár designed in the spa town of Bohdaneč, but they also did smaller interiors such as private residences.

Although the Prague Art Workshops ceased to function after World War I, during their brief existence they had become a dramatic alternative to the more staid English-inspired interiors of Kotěra and his followers. Artěl, by contrast, continued to operate well into the 1930s, changing the style of its small objects to satisfy new demands. Unlike the Prague Art Workshops, it relied on artists to produce designs in their own studios, while also contracting with several firms to make ceramics and glass objects for them.

Beginning in 1914, the strongest promoter of Czech modern interiors and design both at home and abroad was the Svaz Českého Díla (Czech Arts and Crafts Association), an association that Jan Kotěra founded. Its first major project was to organize Czech participation in the 1914 Deutscher Werkbund exhibition in Cologne. After independence, the association, whose membership included most of Prague's leading architects and applied artists, changed its name to the Svaz Československého Díla (Czechoslovak Arts and Crafts Association). Similar to the Deutscher Werkbund, which it greatly resembled, the Czechoslovak Arts and Crafts Association sought to raise the quality of Czech applied arts through numerous activities such as promoting better relations between artists and industry, organizing Czech displays at international exhibitions,

Fig. 25.01: Josef Gočár, Cubist furniture, c. 1913. © Age fotostock, Spain, S. L./Alamy.

working on shows with the Prague Museum of Applied Arts, and publishing its own journal.

Until 1925, the Czechoslovak Arts and Crafts Association supported the development of a national decorative style, an ambition that was widespread in the decorative arts after Czechoslovakia became independent in 1918. Following the war, Janák and the other Czech Cubist architects and designers substituted curves and circles for their pre-war angular designs. Their new approach, called Rondo-Cubism, was seen as a potential national style when mixed with the national colors—red, white and blue—and combined with folkloric elements.

The culmination of the style was the Czech Pavilion at the 1925 Exposition Internationale des Arts Décoratifs in Paris. Designed by Josef Gočár, the pavilion had the abstracted form of a ship, while its rich salon on the first floor, designed by Pavel Janák, resembled a medieval meeting hall. The ceiling of the salon was painted and the walls were hung with elaborate tapestries designed by the artist František

Kysela, who had previously joined the Prague Artistic Workshops as a designer of wallpapers, textiles, and carpets. The tapestries were handwoven by Marie Teinitzerová, a founder of the Artěl cooperative. The heavy oak furniture that Pavel Janák designed had an historicist cast, rejecting the earlier angled Cubist style and featuring instead crenellated frames with padded seats and backs. As in other Central and East European countries, the quest for a national style in the interwar period entailed many false starts and led to few successes. For the Czechs, the decline of Rondo-Cubism, both in architecture and furniture design, was soon replaced by a more universal Functionalism, which dominated Czech design from the late 1920s to the beginning of World War II.

Another project that had implications for a national style was that of the Slovenian architect Jože Plečnik (1872–1957). Shortly after Czech independence, the new president Tomáš Garrigue Masaryk appointed Plečnik as chief architect for the restoration of the Prague Castle, a national monument that Masaryk sought to transform from the residence of the former monarchs to that of a democratic president. Plečnik, who had replaced Jan Kotěra at Prague's School of Applied Arts in 1910 when Kotěra moved to the Academy of Fine Arts, worked on the project for 15 years from 1920 to 1935, during which time he eliminated many distasteful additions, removed restricting walls, designed elaborate gardens, and introduced monumental staircases and gateways. Remodeling the castle interior led him to draw heavily on his own extensive knowledge of how classical architects and craftsmen used stone, ceramics, and metal. Plečnik translated this knowledge into the wooden furniture he designed for the castle. His capacity to adapt classicism to a new style of design that represented Masaryk's vision of the Czech Republic was much appreciated by the nation's president and resulted in many honors along with the extensive government commissions.

Until the emergence of Functionalism in the late 1920s, the Czech cooperatives and promotional organizations paid little attention to mass production. Artěl retained a romantic idea of the crafts and neglected the consideration of mass-produced products. In fact, the organization operated more as an Arts and Crafts firm of the late 19th century. After independence, it derived much of its income from the customized furnishing of large buildings such as the interiors for some Czech diplomatic missions abroad and some commercial interiors like the Hotel Hviezdoslav in the Tatra mountains of Slovakia. In 1934, Artěl went bankrupt and was dissolved the following year.

Serial production was, however, evident in the glass and ceramics industries, most of which were located in the regions of Bohemia and Moravia. Glassmaking in Czechoslovakia goes back at least to medieval times. By the 1920s, a large number of factories produced glassware and ceramics and there were numerous schools that trained the craftsmen to work in them. The Prague Academy of Applied Arts had important departments for incising glass and making ceramics,

headed respectively by Josef Drahoňovský (1877–1938), a specialist in glass engraving, and Helena Johnová, a founder of Artěl. At the 1925 Paris exhibition, Czech glassware, including work by Professor Drahoňovský and his students, received numerous prizes.

Karel Teige and Devětsil

Despite the fact that Masaryk sought to remodel the Prague Castle in a national style that embodied traditional elements, a diverse array of cosmopolitan artists, architects, designers, and theorists as well as actors, writers, and musicians were more interested in the modernist tendencies that had begun to surface elsewhere in Europe. The strongest avant-garde movement in Czechoslovakia during the interwar years was Devětsil, an association of avant-garde artists in Prague whose founder was the artist, typographer, and theorist Karel Teige (1900–1951). For several years

Fig. 25.02: Jaromir Krejar, Jaroslav Seifert, Josef Šima, and Karel Teige, *Život*, cover, 1922. Slavic and Baltic Division, The New York Public Library, Astor, Lenox and Tilden Foundations.

Devětsil functioned without a unified theoretical foundation but, spurred by Teige, members began to develop aesthetic theories, which they spread through manifestos. The first manifesto encourages artists to look deeper for poetic qualities in ordinary objects. As a medium, a few used the picture poem which for some developed into an interest in film.

In 1922, Teige was involved with the publication of *Život* (*Life*), one of the first publications to introduce the ideas and principles of the international avant-garde to Czeshoslovakia. Inspired by Le Corbusier's and Jeanneret's journal *L'Esprit Nouveau*, *Život's* modern orientation was evident in the photomontage cover, which featured the juxtaposition of a Doric column and an automobile wheel (Fig. 25.02). The publication included articles by prominent Western architects and artists like Le Corbusier and Ozenfant, while also promulgating the experimental photography of Man Ray, contemporary film, American skyscrapers, and Russian Constructivism.

The year after *Život* appeared, Teige became the editor of the architectural magazine *Stavba* (*Building*), through which he promoted Purist and Constructivist architecture, while regularly publishing texts by Walter Gropius, Mies van der Rohe, and other architects abroad. That year he met Gropius and became familiar with the Weimar Bauhaus just as it was turning away from the expressionist tendencies of Johannes Itten. He also saw the participation of Devětsil's architects in the 1923 Bauhaus exhibition of international architecture in Weimar. Within the Devětsil groups in Prague and Brno, these architects were active in the debates that prepared the way for Czech Functionalism in the mid-1920s. Among them were Bedřich Feuerstein (1892–1936), Karel Honzik (1900–1966), and Jaromir Krejar (1895–1949), a former student of Jan Kotěra and an associate of Josef Gočár.

In 1930, Teige would feature the Bauhaus, where he lectured at the invitation of the director, Hannes Meyer, in a special issue of the journal *ReD* (*Revue Devětsil*), which he founded in 1927 and which he considered to be a "red signal of a new cultural epoch." By this time, Teige had become a strong supporter of the Soviet Union after having visited there in 1925. In 1929 he was the principal organizer of the Left Front of Cultural Workers and Intellectuals, which included a number of artists, filmmakers, photographers, writers, and architects. By the mid-1930s, however, the organization was heavily influenced by the Communist Party and no longer served as an open site for the voicing of avant-garde concerns.

Teige's views on Soviet culture became the basis for his critique of Western bourgeois housing models and his espousal of a more collective vision of public housing that involved a mix of private and public facilities. A strong believer in the liberation of women and the abolition of marriage, he advocated the elimination of individual kitchens and other features that generated household work for women. Many of his ideas were included in his book of 1932, *Nejmenší byt* (*The Minimum Dwelling*), which also promoted the tubular steel furniture designed in Czechoslovakia by Ladislav Žák and others.

Though Teige was actively engaged in many Czech architectural debates during the interwar years, he made his strongest contribution to modern culture as a theorist of typography and a designer of books and journals, not only ones he wrote or edited himself but also those by other authors.

Functionalism

Functionalism, as a basis for architecture and design, drew heavily from tendencies abroad, notably France and Germany. In France, the architecture of Le Corbusier was an influence, while in Germany, the minimalist designs of the new social housing developments and the Weissenhof Siedlung, along with the spare approach to furniture and household objects that stemmed from the Bauhaus and elsewhere provided a strong stimulus for Czech architects and designers. By the beginning of the 1930s, Functionalism, as the new movement was called in Czechoslovakia, was adopted by the well educated and internationally minded Czech middle class as its own distinctive style.

In the early 1920s, the Czech furniture industry was still extremely conservative as Czech Cubism— the boldest experimental approach to furniture until then—was limited to one-off pieces created for individual clients. But the spare wooden furniture the Thonet factories turned out in several Czech towns near Brno provided a counterpart to the decorative tendencies of Czech Cubism and stimulated interest in mass-produced pieces. In the industrial town of Brno, Jan Vaněk (1891–1962) used his experience in the production of standardized housing to create a system of serial production for modern furniture as early as 1924, when he organized UP (Industrial Arts Factories), a consortium of family manufacturing companies that produced standardized suites of furniture for a wide range of customers. The furniture consisted of variable units that emphasized maximum flexibility. One of his collaborators was Hana Kučerová Záveská (1885–1940), who promoted a line of kitchen furniture and published her Functionalist housing principles in various magazines. Vaněk complemented his manufacturing activity with the publication of a journal, *Bytová kultura* (*Housing Culture*), in 1923 and 1924. Teige also championed Vaněk's promotion of industrial production in his writings for *Stavba*.

Other furniture designers who used Functionalist rhetoric included Jindřich Halabala (1903–1978), who worked with both wood and tubular steel, designing several cantilevered chairs that more or less followed prior examples by Breuer and others; Antonin Heythum (1901–1956); and Ladislav Žak (1900–1973). Heythum, a member of Devětsil, designed interiors and exhibitions as well as furniture; in fact, he developed some of his spatial ideas for interiors as a theater set designer. Besides furniture for mass production, he also worked on designs in the late 1920s for a collapsible armchair with a pull-out foot stool as well as a collapsible couch that would convert into two beds. These projects, which were characterized by a strong sense of function, were instigated by the architectural program of minimum dwellings that Teige and others were promoting. Heythum also designed the Czech Pavilion for the 1935 Brussels World's Fair and worked on the installation for his country's pavilion at the 1939 World's Fair in New York, where he was stranded when the Germans invaded Czechoslovakia. He subsequently founded a department of industrial design at the California Institute of Technology in Pasadena and later taught at Syracuse University. Ladislav Žak was a prolific furniture designer who often used tubular steel. As an architect he adopted a Corbusian style for several private villas as well as for the furniture manufacturer Hynek Gottwald. Besides these villas, however, he participated in competitions for minimum dwellings and designed the office furniture for the Czechoslovak Ministry of Education.

The most enduring Functionalist furniture was not designed by a Czech, however; it was the steel and leather dining room chairs that Mies van der Rohe created for the Villa Tugendhat, which he completed in 1932 in Brno (Fig. 25.03). Mies constructed the cantilevered chairs from steel strips that supported a leather seat and back, drawing on a precedent of several years earlier—the chairs he designed for the Barcelona pavilion of 1929.

Functionalism in the applied arts was most prominently featured at Krásna jizba (Beautiful Household), a retail outlet for quality design that belonged to the Prague publishing house Družstevní práce (Cooperative Work). Between 1929 and 1939, the artistic director of Krásna jizba was Ladislav Sutnar (1897–1976), a graphic artist who had studied at the Prague School of Applied Arts. Politically, Sutnar espoused the liberal ideals of the Social Democrats, the party headed by President Masaryk, and as a young man he taught puppetry at the Social Democrats' Workers' Academy. In the mid-1920s his interest in education prompted him to design toys and an early successful effort was a set of blocks to construct city buildings. He followed this later with a set of wooden

Fig. 25.03: Mies van der Rohe, Villa Tugendhat, interior, 1930. © 2014. Digital image, The Museum of Modern Art, New York/Scala, Florence. © DACS 2017.

vehicles and finally in 1930 with a group of whimsical wooden animals on wheels. Artěl manufactured and marketed a number of his toys.

Sutnar's involvement with the applied arts began when he joined the Czechoslovak Arts and Crafts Association in 1924. Through his work with the association, he became involved with design for modern living, which led to his work for Krásna jizba. As the artistic director and manager of the outlet, Sutnar was able to design, commission, and distribute the kinds of furniture and household wares that he was promoting as an active member of the Arts and Crafts Association. He successfully developed a line of modern housewares by selling subscriptions for them to members of the larger publishing enterprise that owned Krásna jizba. Sutnar himself designed tea and coffee sets, cups, and wine glasses with stark geometric forms that differed significantly from the cut, engraved, and painted glass that the factories of Bohemia specialized in (Fig. 25.04). He created as well designs for soup bowls and tureens, and also porcelain cake platters. Most of his ceramicware was white although he was not averse to other colors such as solid red or blue flecks on white. In metal, Sutnar's designs ranged from cutlery to

chrome-plated egg cups, candlesticks, and canapé trays. His adoption of minimalist forms stemmed in large part from numerous trips to Germany, where he became familiar with the Bauhaus and the modern industrial aesthetic of the *Neue Sachlichkeit* or New Objectivity.

Sutnar also commissioned products from other designers. Ludvika Smrčková (1903–1991) designed a utility drinking glass that featured many of the optical properties of the material; Bohumil Južnič (1895–1963) designed everyday metal accessories made of stainless steel and silver; and Antonin Kybal (1901–1971) created modern textiles and carpet designs that featured strong colors and geometric forms. All the products that Krásna jizba sold were produced to the highest standards by leading Czech manufacturers. It is likely that Sutnar's ambitious program was an impetus to other designers such as Helena Johnová, an initial member of the Arts and Crafts Association, to adopt a more functional style. Johnová was a pioneer of modern ceramic design in Bohemia and a teacher of ceramics at the School of Applied Arts from 1919 to 1942.

Besides doing his own product designs and commissioning designs from others, Sutnar also distributed the products of various Czech companies such as the modern lamps in the Modul series that the lighting designer Miloslav Prokop (1896–1954) designed for the glass company Inwald, and he imported goods from abroad that were created by well-known architects and designers such as the glassware of Adolf Loos and the tubular-steel furniture of Marcel Breuer.

As an emporium of modern household wares, Krásna jizba can be compared with wohnbedarf in Zurich, BO in Copenhagen, and Svenskt Tenn in Stockholm, all of which were committed to bringing well-designed household goods to a middle-class public at moderate prices. In addition to designing many products and arranging the store displays, Sutnar produced all the store's advertising, collaborating with the experimental photographer Josef Sudek (1896–1976) to create photographs for brochures that presented the Krásna jizba products as abstract forms (Fig. 25.05).

Fig. 25.04: Ladislav Sutnar, glass tea set, 1931. The Museum of Decorative Arts in Prague.

Fig. 25.05: Josef Sudek, advertising photograph for Krásna jizba, The Museum of Decorative Arts in Prague.

Sutnar's comprehensive approach to design at Krásna jizba was also evident in a much larger enterprise, the Bata Shoe Works, which Tomáš Bata managed, beginning in 1895. Spurred on by a sizeable order for military shoes during World War I, Bata built his company from a small local manufacturer to an international conglomerate in three decades. Recognizing the potential efficiency of machines for large-scale production, he modeled his factory assembly line on the techniques of Henry Ford, thus enabling the company to become the largest shoe manufcturer in the world. Bata not only rationalized the production process but also the management of his workforce. He provided generous benefits that included employee canteens, medical services, and pensions. Bata followed the American model of standardized pricing for his chain stores, which enabled the company to gain a strong foothold in lower middle-class and lower-class markets.

Tomáš Bata had a long-standing interest in modern architecture and commissioned Jan Kotěra to design his personal residence in 1911 and a workers' settlement in 1918. He subsequently sought the design talents of the architect Ludvik Kysela (1893–1960) for a department store in the center of Prague to sell Bata shoes. The building, completed in 1929, was the first in Czechoslovakia to feature an all-glass facade. Between the ribbon windows on each floor were strips of white glass that were illuminated at night with advertising texts.

In 1921, Jan Kotěra, assisted by a former student, František Lydia Gahura (1891–1958), began to work with the Bata company on the plan for Zlín, its own town in southern Moravia where Bata bulit a shoe factory. The architecture in Zlín was based on standardized construction techniques and the use of modern materials such as reinforced concrete, steel, and glass. Gahura, who remained with the company until the Communist Party took it over after World War II, designed a number of the buildings in Zlín. The basic rectilinear form of the large factory building was repeated in other edifices—schools, dormitories and even the movie theater and the town's hotel. The company preferred to house workers in single family homes rather than dormitories or apartment buildings, although this was not possible for the entire labor force.

Ever mindful of public relations, Bata had its own promotional department with over 60 people who created advertising for its national network of sales outlets. In the 1920s, the company featured lithographic posters including those by the artist Fráňa Smatek (1899–1978) that showed alluring women wearing or showing off Bata shoes. After Jan Bata, the half-brother of Tomáš, took over the company when Tomáš died in a plane crash in 1932, the company hired a professional advertising photographer, Pavel Hrdlíčka (1911–1994), in 1933. He used various methods from studio compositions of shoes to arranged scenes, nature snapshots for walking and sports shoes, and photos of contemporary celebrities. In 1935, the company set up the Bata Film Studio to make advertising films and brought in several young filmmakers to staff it including Elmer Has (1910–1993), František Pilát

(1910–1987), and Alexander Hackenschmied (1907–2004), also known for his experimental photography. The studio produced a number of advertising films that incorporated avant-garde techniques and subsequently pioneered the production of educational films for schools.

The Bata Shoe Works, one of Czechoslovakia's largest enterprises during the interwar years, was a heavy consumer of design, which was applied to all aspects of the company's activity from its products to its advertising and extensive town planning and architecture program. By 1942, Bata had 105,770 employees, managed several thousand shops within Czechoslovakia, possessed factories in different parts of the world, and owned more than 60 companies that produced tires, aircraft, bicycles, and machinery, although shoes remained their primary product,

Within Czech design schools, Functionalism had the strongest presence in the School of Applied Arts in Bratislava, the center of the nation's Slovak population and a region that was far less industrialized than Bohemia or Moravia. Called by one journalist "the Bauhaus of Bratislava," the school was founded by Josef Vydra (1884–1959), a painter and art historian who may well have been influenced by the teaching of the Bahuaus professor Josef Albers, whom he heard lecture at an art education conference in Prague. The school lasted only 11 years from 1928 to 1939, when the Nazis occupied the country.

The curriculum consisted of a basic program in drawing, color, composition, and other subjects that preceded specialized work in one of the departments, which Vydra organized according to materials and functions—textiles, metal, wood, ceramics, graphic design and advertising, photography, decorative painting, and the design of shop windows. The faculty included artists who were active in the Czech avant-garde such as the painters Ludovit Fulla (1902–1980) and Mikuláš Galanda (1895–1938); the ceramist Júlia Horová (1906–1978), a member of the Devětsil group in Brno; textile designer František Malý (1900–1980);

the architect František Tröster (1904–68); the photographer Jaromír Funke (1896–1945); and the graphic designer Zdeněk Rossman (1905–1984), who had previously studied at the Bauhaus in Dessau. Prominent artists and architects from abroad including Hannes Meyer, the Bauhaus director; László Moholy-Nagy; Jan Tschichold; and Lajos Kassák also lectured at the school. Shortly before it closed, a film school was established under the direction of Karol Plicka (1894–1987).

One intention of the School of Applied Arts was to contribute to the industrial expansion of Slovakia. Beautiful carpets with modern geometric designs were produced in the textile workshop; furniture in wood and metal was created although the designs of a few wooden chairs and tables were a throwback to the Rondo-Cubist style. Julia Horová and her students also created some functional ceramic objects for mass production and pieces from the metal workshop were manufactured by several companies, notably the small objects that Bohumil Južnič created: ashtrays, book ends, ladles, serving spoons, and butter dishes among them. Some were marketed by the Sandrik Company and others by Ladislav Sutnar for Krásna jizba.

Both the graphic design and photography departments were leading contributors to Czech Functionalist design and advertising art. Zdeněk Rossman, who brought Joost Schmidt's graphic approach from the Bauhaus, headed the graphic design department, while Jaromír Funke, a leading Czech avant-garde photographer, directed the photography department. Many of Funke's students subsequently achieved distinction in the advertising industry. In other fields such as the design of interiors and theater sets, faculty and students were also distinguished. Overall, the Bratislava School of Applied Arts managed to foster a spirit of collaboration among departments and came closest of any in Czechoslovakia to implementing a Bauhaus-inspired pedagogy and a Functionalist style across a number of different artistic practices.

Czech automobiles

During the interwar period, Czechoslovakia produced two automobies of importance, the Škoda and the Tatra. The Škoda Works originally manufactured weapons, but in 1924 it acquired Laurin & Klement, a company that had been founded in 1895 to make bicyles. The firm then branched out to produce motorcycles and shortly thereafter automobiles. Based on the success of their first automobile, the Voiturette, in 1905, they expanded their automobile production and continued to make cars under their own name well into the 1920s. Laurin & Klement started making trucks just before they merged with the Škoda Works in 1925. The first car to bear the Škoda trademark was a luxury Hispano-Suiza sedan, whose license to produce it in Czechoslovakia the Škoda firm had purchased. The company made breakthroughs in the 1930s with the Škoda Popular and the Škoda Rapid, both launched in 1934. The two cars were manufactured in various models from Tudor and roadster to cabriolet and they possessed the best design features of similar cars produced elsewhere in Europe—swept back bodies, stylized grills, and rounded front fenders among them.

In 1919, the company originally titled Nesselsdorfer Wagenbau-Fabriksgesellschaft, producer of the first automobile in Central Europe, adopted the name Tatra, which was derived from the Tatra Mountains. The Austrian designer, Hans Ledwinka (1878–1967), who returned to the company after working for another automobile manufacturer, designed the Tatra 11, a small car that was the first Tatra model to adopt some of the features that would characterize later Tatra cars, especially the tubular backbone with independent suspension at the rear. The model also pioneered many basic features of modern small-car design. Following the Tatra 11 were other cars from the Tatra 12 to the Tatra 57, all of which displayed significant improvements.

Ledwinka's design of the Tatra 77, the first of a line of aerodynamic streamlined cars with rear-mounted

Fig. 25.06: Tatra 77, 1934. Tatra Archive Technical Museum.

aircooled engines was a major breakthrough when it was introduced in 1933 (Fig. 25.06). With a body designed by Paul Jaray (1889–1974), a Hungarian engineer who pioneered the development of aerodynamic auto body designs, it was a multi-passenger luxury automobile with a dorsal fin on the back as part of its design. Though produced in small numbers, it received excellent press reviews and prepared the way for several models that followed it, the Tatra 87 and 97, both produced in a larger volume with a number of improvements. Production of the streamlined Tatra 97 stopped after the Germans occupied Czechoslovakia in 1939 since Hitler thought it was too similar to the Volkswagen that he was preparing to manufacture with a design by Ferdinand Porsche. Porsche's design was possibly based on a drawing that Ledwinka is known to have shown to Hitler. It was a plan for a small air-cooled car, the Tatra V570, with a rear engine that served as a prototype for the Tatra 77 and subsequent aerodynamic models. Other Tatra patents made their way into German hands after Czechoslovakia's occupiers confiscated them.

Graphic design

The graphic arts before independence

In the late 19th century, the Czech lands experienced the same cultural influences as other countries in Europe, including symbolism, the Arts and Crafts movement, and Art Nouveau. These influences were as evident in the book arts and poster design as they were in architecture, furniture, and household goods. The Book Beautiful movement was a response to the design of mass-produced books. Among its leaders was Vojtěch Preissig (1873–1944), an artist with a strong interest in the processes of nature, including animal and plant morphology. A former student at the Prague Academy of Applied Art, Preissig had been active as a book designer and illustrator since the 1890s. He had a predilection for decorative details and featured them extensively in his designs. He based one collection

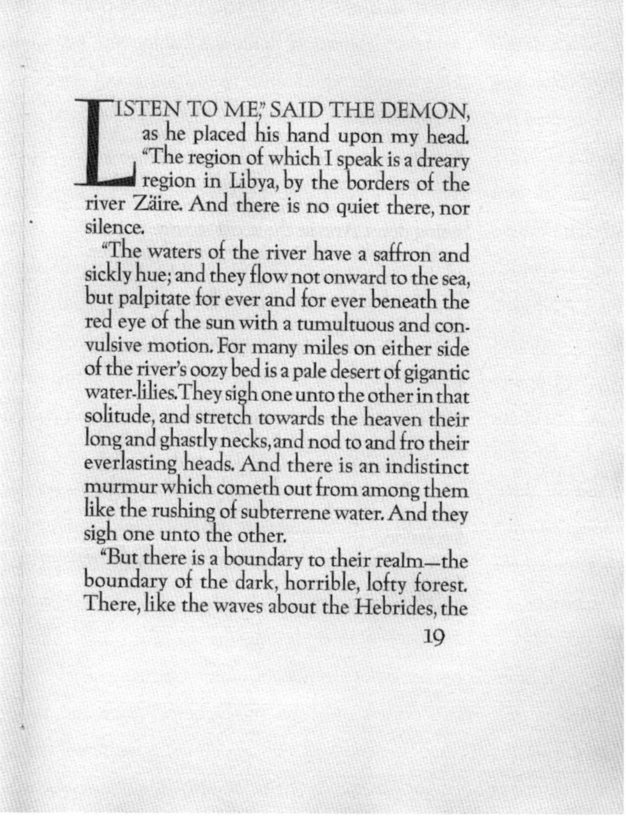

LISTEN TO ME," SAID THE DEMON, as he placed his hand upon my head. "The region of which I speak is a dreary region in Libya, by the borders of the river Zäire. And there is no quiet there, nor silence.

"The waters of the river have a saffron and sickly hue; and they flow not onward to the sea, but palpitate for ever and for ever beneath the red eye of the sun with a tumultuous and convulsive motion. For many miles on either side of the river's oozy bed is a pale desert of gigantic water-lilies. They sigh one unto the other in that solitude, and stretch towards the heaven their long and ghastly necks, and nod to and fro their everlasting heads. And there is an indistinct murmur which cometh out from among them like the rushing of subterrene water. And they sigh one unto the other.

"But there is a boundary to their realm—the boundary of the dark, horrible, lofty forest. There, like the waves about the Hebrides, the

19

Fig. 25.07: Vojtěch Preissig, Preissig Antikva typeface, c. 1914. Courtesy The Newberry Library, Chicago, wing_zp_958_s797_p19.

well. These included František Kysela, Jaroslav Benda, and Vratislav Hugo Brunner, all original members of Artěl who were designers and illustrators of books, although they also created posters, postage stamps, and other graphic forms. All were professors at the Prague School of Applied Arts in the 1920s. Kysela and Benda taught courses for graphic designers, and Brunner, who headed the department of decorative and ornamental drawing, became rector of the school in 1928.

František Kysela was one of Czechoslovakia's leading poster artists during the 1920s, working in a variety of illustrative styles, while Benda and Brunner concentrated much of their activity on book design. All emphasized lettering, and both Brunner and Benda additionally produced unpublished designs for typefaces. Benda adopted clean san serif capitals for several posters around 1913–1914, and Brunner experimented with more idiosyncratic and decorative forms. In a poster of 1914 for the Montmartre American Bar, a gathering spot for Prague's avant-garde, Brunner chose the sharp forms of Czech Cubism as a background for the angular letters he designed.

Following the precedent of the private presses abroad, some artists preferred to design and illustrate their own books and sometimes to print them as well. For František Bílak (1872–1941)—a sculptor, painter, architect, and philosopher of religion who was originally associated with Symbolism and Art Nouveau—the book was a metaphor for spiritual life. In his books he sought a unity of the written and the visual, functioning as writer, designer, illustrator, and bookbinder. In *Cesta* (*The Path*) of 1909, he enhanced his spiritual reflections on mankind's future with his expressive drawings and gothic-style lettering, recalling the lavish productions of William Morris's Kelmscott Press. Josef Váchal (1884–1969) was a painter, sculptor, woodcarver, type designer, and writer who illustrated, set, printed, and bound his own books, which he frequently wrote himself to express his tribulations as an artist.

of vignettes on multiple variations of crossed tree branches. As a designer of lettering and typography, he is said to have cut his letters from linoleum blocks. Several designs for alphabets from around 1914 show the rough angles and edges he favored in order to preserve the human touch. For many years, he continued to refine drawings for an Antique book type, which the Czech State Printing Office finally cut and released as Preissig Antikva in 1925. It became a milestone for Czech type design and a source of inspiration for later designers (Fig. 25.07).

Though Preissig derived much of his artistic inspiration from nature, he also adopted the style of abstract geometric ornament from the Vienna Secession, a practice that other designers followed as

Commercial art and typography

In 1918, two years before the new constitution was drawn up, the National Committee, which was shepherding Czechoslovakia towards full independence, invited the Art Nouveau artist Alphonse Mucha, well known as an avid Czech nationalist, to design its new postage stamps. Mucha's first series featured the Prague Castle, the most prominent symbol of national identity, which also embodied a strong sense of tradition. Following the stamps, Mucha was asked to design a series of banknotes, several of which appeared in 1919 and 1920. He drew heavily on Art Nouveau ornament and lettering, while also including symbols of Czech nationalism such as the lion, the falcon, and the dove. In addition to stamps and banknotes, he designed other state paraphernelia including an initial version of the national emblem and he even offered suggestions for police uniforms.

Mucha had returned to the Czech lands from France in 1910 and lived there following independence until his death in 1939. His major project during the years of his return was a cycle of 20 large paintings known as the *Slav Epic*. Unveiled in 1928, they were received by the Czechoslovak public with mixed emotions, particularly as many people were by this time more interested in the international iconography of modernism with its concomitant cosmpolitan character than in a series of paintings that returned them to the nation's conflicted past.

As a strong counterpart to Mucha's Art Nouveau designs, Josef Čapek (1887–1945), Jiří Dréman (1892–1946), Jiří Kroha (1893–1974), and Václav Špála (1885–1946) introduced a Cubist vocabulary to poster design between 1918 and 1920. Their posters were mainly for art exhibitions, small publications, cabarets, and theaters promoted by the Prague arts community. Čapek's lithographic poster for a small literary publication *Červen* (*June*) of 1918 depicts the head and arms of a newsboy hawking the publication against a backdrop of tall building fragments, reinforcing both the modernity of the publication as indicated by the

visual style of the poster and its contemporary urban context, depicted by buildings behind the news boy. Of particular significance in this poster is Čapek's use of partial images to stand in for entire bodies or objects, a technique of Cubist painting and collage. Čapek, who was involved in Prague literary culture as a book illustrator, cover designer, and a writer, also did a series of dramatic two-color book covers for several publishers that opened up new possibilities for this genre. His brother Karel Čapek was the author of the play *R.U.R.*, an early attempt to depict robots with human-like qualities and in fact, it was Karel Čapek who coined the term "robot."

Even though the Cubist visual vocabulary was not adopted by the mainstream advertising poster designers as it was in France, Cubist posters nonetheless created a break with the earlier naturalist and Secessionist approaches, thus clearing the way for other contemporary styles from France and Germany. There were two centers of poster production: Prague and Brno. Though Brno was not as culturally cosmopolitan as Prague, it was a major industrial city in Moravia, which had strong ties to Germany. Thus a number of the Brno poster designers were German or of German origin. Among them were Hans Jakesch (dates unconfirmed) and Eduard Milén (1891–1976), an artist who designed posters for numerous cultural events. Milén also devoted much of his time to art directing the literary magazine *Lidové noviny* (*Popular Newspaper*) for which he did layouts, illustrations, and posters in a modern style with flat colors.

Czechoslovakia in the interwar years was striving to follow the lead of France and Germany as a center for modern commerce and culture. Posters thus promoted new fashions for men and women, restaurants and night clubs, resorts, publications, and increasingly films as the young Czech film industry developed. A few artists such as Václav Klimánek (1892–d.o.d. unconfirmed) and Leo Heilbrun (dates unconfirmed) adopted the style of the French fashion illustrators, but the German style, stemming from the work of Lucian Bernhard and others, was more prevalent. Much of the poster work was done by advertising agencies such as Studio Pacold, UR Praga, Decart, Weigelt, Studio Rötter, Hofbauer-Pokorný, Heilbrun, and the Vodicka Studios. Among the leading studio poster designers was Emil Weiss (1896–1964), whose posters for men's fashions, nightspots like the Alhambra and Lucerne Cabaret-Restaurant, and the Walter Junior automobile were strongly influenced by American, German, and French tendencies. There was a marked difference between the advertising agency posters, which adopted the latest techniques from abroad, and those of independent poster designers such as František Kysela and Zdeněk Rykr (1900–1940), who were engaged in other activities like painting, book design, and illustration. Of all the Czech commerical artists in the interwar years, Kysela, whose design repertoire ranged from posters to textile patterns and tapestries, was the most versatile, working in styles that varied from highly illustrative to conceptual and Functionalist.

Following the early interest in typography by Preissig and others involved in the Book Beautiful movement, little progress was made in developing a modern Czech typeface until 1932 when Oldřich Menhart (1897–1962) designed Menhart Antiqua and Menhart Cursive for the Bauer Foundry in Germany. Though influenced by Preissig's Antikva, Menhart eschewed his predecessor's more idiosyncratic artistic approach, concentrating instead on calligraphy and earlier typography as sources.

The 1920s saw an emphasis on creating an inherently Czech typeface in accord with nationalist aspirations. Menhart addressed the problem not by drawing on Czech folkloric or decorative elements but instead by taking into account the peculiarities of the Czech language with its exceptional number of diacritical marks. His typefaces for Bauer, which presented reasonable solutions to the peculiarities of Czech typesetting, were the first Czech faces to achieve international recognition and they prepared the way for the designer's subsequent Menhart Roman (Fig. 25.08) and Italic for the Monotype Corporation in 1936 as well as for his numerous typeface designs after World War II.

Fig. 25.08: Oldřich Menhart, Menhart Roman typeface, 1933. Courtesy The Newberry Library, Chicago, wing_z_40545_4815_p9d+I83.

Avant-garde graphic design: Devětsil to Surrealism

Karel Teige was the principal theorist of Czech avant-garde graphic design in the 1920s and 1930s. For about a decade, beginning in the early 1920s, he published a series of manifestoes that promoted film, photography, and photomontage as alternatives to painting and sculpture. As the ideal medium of expression, he espoused the *obrazové básně* or "picture poem," which was a rigourous composition of photographic fragments that could also include text. Teige considered the picture poem to be a visual storytelling device that could take the place of writing. In 1924, he incorporated it into his theory of Poetism, which had both a social and aesthetic dimension. As a social theory, Poetism called for a new society that would be achieved through revolutionary struggle, but unlike conventional political rhetoric, it incorporated the individual's need for an emotional experience of the world. To this end, Teige juxtaposed the political and intellectual rigor of Constructivism with the freedom and poetry of Poetism. He believed that Constructivism was the basis of life and Poetism was the "crown of life," representing the supremacy of poetry, whose purpose was pleasure rather than politics.

Though he had made picture poems as free art works in the early 1920s, Teige believed their best application and that of Poetism to be the book cover. Along with the cover, he thought the text should feature a typographic design that brought out its expressive elements. His closest collaborators in the production of books that exemplified his theory were the poets Vítěslav Nezval (1900–1958), Jaroslav Seifert (1901–1986), and Konstantin Biebl (1898–1951), all members of Devětsil. Among the earliest picture poems to appear on a book cover was fellow Devětsil member Otakar Mrkvička's (1898–1957) photomontage for Seifert's poetry collection *Samá Láska* (*Pure Love*) in 1923. However, a stronger impact was made the following year by Jindřich Štyrský's cover for Nezval's book of poems and essays, *Pantomima* (*Pantomime*), with typography by Teige. The poetic cover featured a photograph of a dreamy Pierrot juxtaposed on a map and surrounded by a sailboat at sea, planes in flight, palm trees, and an elaborate bouquet of flowers. The numerous images of travel on the cover exemplified the Devětsil members' interest in visiting far-off places (Plate 26).

In 1925, Teige collaborated with Seifert on a book of poems, *Na vjnach TSF* (*On the Airwaves*), for which he created a Dada-inspired typographic cover that featured large 19th-century Egyptian letters along with a drawing of a radio speaker and the proverbial Dada icons—closed hands with pointing fingers aimed in this case at the date of publication. Teige sought to give each poem in the book a distinctive visual format, which became the typographic counterpart of a picture poem. For the poem "Circus" he depicted the phrase "a big balloon" with a round black ball, and he laid out the poem "Abacus [of Love]" in the form of an abacus. For Nezval's 1926 book of poems, *Abeceda* (*Alphabet*), Teige merged typography and dance by showing the dancer Milča Mayerová in photographic poses that depicted the 26 letters of the Roman alphabet (Fig. 25.09). In a public performance, Nezval recited the poems to Mayerová's dance accompaniment and Teige used photographs from the performance for the book. He devoted one page to each letter in which the dancer's pose was framed by heavy black lines that either signified or complemented the typographic forms themselves. Teige called this an example of "typofoto," in which lettering and photography were combined in a single composition.

He introduced another technique—the abstract typographic composition—in two books of poems by Konstantin Biebl, *S lodí jež dováží čaj a kávu* (*On the Ship Bringing Tea and Coffee*) and *Zlom* (*Fissure*), both published in 1928. In these books the layouts were geometric, consisting of rectangular blocks of color combined with line arrangements and punctuated by letters, words, numbers, or other typographic signs such as arrows and question marks in different typefaces. These recall comparable experiments by the

Fig. 25.09: Karel Teige, *Abeceda*, layout, 1926. Collection Merrill C. Berman. Photo: Jim Frank and Joelle Jensen.

Dutch designer Piet Zwart in the same period, but Teige related his designs to Biebl's poems as parallel visualizations to his designs for the book covers as well. (Plate 27).

A number of Czech publishers including Aventinum, Melantrich, Odeon, and František Borový were willing to publish modern books by authors and designers in the Devětsil circle and also by others. The Czech reading public generally accepted these books although professional typographers found much to criticize in Teige's work. The leading publisher of the Devětsil volumes was Odeon, whose director was Jan Fromek. Beginning in 1925, when he founded the press, Fromek employed Teige as an author, typographer, and translator, also using him as an editor. By 1931, when

Devětsil ceased to exist, Odeon had published about 130 books with avant-garde designs.

Besides Teige, other Devětsil designers—Jindřich Štýrský (1899–1942), his partner Toyen (a.k.a. Marie Čermínová) (1902–1980), Josef Šíma (1881–1971), František Muzika (1900–1974), and Vít Obrtel (1901–1988)—did covers and illustrations for avant-garde books. All were engaged in other arts besides book design. Muzika collaborated with Teige and was for a time the artistic editor for Aventinium. Štýrský and Toyen left for Paris in 1925, where they invented a new aesthetic theory, Artificialism. It maintained the poetic component of Poetism but they intended it to liberate their painting by eliminating the Constructivist base that Teige considered essential to Poetism. Šíma had moved to Paris in 1921, where he was influenced by Cubism and Purism. His work for Czech publishers, though influential, was as an illustrator rather than a designer.

By the early 1930s, a number of Czech artists became interested in Surrealism, including Štýrský and Toyen who had by then returned to Prague. Štýrský's dramatic yet mysterious covers for the Czech versions of the French Fantomas detective thrillers foreshadowed what would become a stronger Surrealist tendency in several years. Teige too was attracted to the freedom of the unconscious that Surrealism encouraged even as he became more active in leftist politics.

In 1934, Štýrský, Toyen, and Teige became members of the newly-formed Prague Surrealist group, which held joint exhibitions with its French counterpart and translated writings of French Surrealist authors. Surrealism also began to influence Czech avant-garde book design. For a Czech edition of writing by Paul Eluard, Štýrský made a collage for the cover from old engravings and then created four additional collages to illustrate the texts. Teige began to make erotic collages in which he populated fantastic landscapes with nude women and their body parts. He also designed Surrealist-inspired photomontage covers for a number of Nezval's books in the 1930s to represent the poet's own growing infatuation with Surrealism and eroticism. However, he retained a strict Constructivist approach for the design of the books on architecture and housing that he published in the early 1930s.

Functional graphic design

During the 1930s, Functionalism was as evident in Czech graphic arts as it was in architecture and household goods. It was strongly influenced by the principles of the German graphic designer Jan Tschichold, notably as he stated them in the aforementioned special issue of *Typographische Mitteilungen* in 1925 and then in his book *Die Neue Typographie* of 1928. Tschichold asserted that typography should be purposeful not decorative and he espoused san serif type, asymmetric composition, and the use of photographs rather than drawings. For Tschichold, the new typography could be applied to cultural forms such as books and posters as well as all forms of commercial design like logotypes, stationery, and brochures (see Chapter 21). Teige too had argued for a more modern graphic design and had drawn on avant-garde artistic precedents such as Constructivism and Dada. In his seminal essay of 1927, "Modern Typography," published in the Czech graphic design journal *Typografia*, he noted that Constructivism had taken root in Czech graphic design during the previous few years and he sought to distinguish its true principles from its more superficial decorative applications. In a set of six mandates for modern typography, he advocated clearly legible types, a balance of space and type according to optical laws, and a combination of images and type into "typophotos." He also celebrated Herbert Bayer's Universal typeface although he subsequently proposed several changes to individual letters.

Teige's book covers from the 1920s that were based more on Constructivist principles than poetic impulses were important precedents for the Functionalist graphic design of the 1930s, as were his strong covers for the journal *ReD* (*Revue Devětsil*), which may well have been inspired by the declarative

lettering of Alexander Rodchenko's covers for the Soviet arts journal *Lef*. Published between 1927 and 1931, *ReD* featured on its covers a bold title—composed of separate stencil elements—combined with strong bars of color that framed or complemented additional type and images.

Though Teige created the earliest examples of Functionalist graphic design in Czechoslovakia, Ladislav Sutnar had the greatest impact on its spread within the country. In 1932, he became director of the State School of Graphic Art, where he established a curriculum for modern graphic designers. Founded in Prague in 1920, the school was intended to train students for careers in printing, bookbinding, graphic design, and photography but it only achieved its distinctive character under Sutnar's leadership during the 1930s. Among the reforms he introduced were a course in advertising photography, and instruction in modern art and printing techniques such as airbrush, offset, and rotogravure. He also added courses on cinematography and newspaper design, while shifting the emphasis of the bookbinding course from the creation of expensive leather bindings to the design of cloth books for mass production.

Sutnar also oversaw the design and production of several important books at the school. Together with Augustin Tschinkel (1905–1983), a professor of drawing, Sutnar designed a civics reader for the Ministry of Education that featured Otto Neurath's pictorial statistics. It was an early introduction of Neurath's system to Czechoslovakia. Tschinkel had worked for a time with Neurath in Vienna and was strongly influenced by the graphic style of Gerd Arntz, the German artist who devised Neurath's pictorial iconography.

In 1935, the State School of Graphic Art published *Fotografie vidí povrch* (*Photography Sees the Surface*), a collaboration between Sutnar and the photographer Jaromir Funke. One of the most important books on photography to be published in Czechoslovakia between the wars, it explored questions of visual perception through comments by scholars in various fields related to photographs done by the school's students. The school also brought out Tschinkel's handbook for designers entitled *Symbol, Rébus, Písmeno* (*Symbol, Rebus, Letter*).

By the time Sutnar became head of the State School of Graphic Arts, he was already director of exhibitions for the Czechoslovak Arts and Crafts Association and art director for the publishing house Družstevní práce (Cooperative Work). Two years after he became a member of the Arts and Crafts Association in 1924, the organization changed the name of its journal to *Výtvarné snahy* (*Art Endeavors*) and began to focus more on modern living. The journal published examples of furniture and interiors elsewhere in Europe and reprinted articles by important architects and designers of the European avant-garde. Sutnar was the co-editor from 1926 to 1930 and designed many of the covers, drawing heavily on Dutch, Russian, and German avant-garde examples.

As the designer for all the exhibitions of the Czechoslovak Arts and Crafts Association, Sutnar played an important role in the promotion of Czech products at home and abroad. For the organization's participation in Brno's *Modern Commerce Exhibition*, held in 1929, he created an exhibit on modern advertising, using photographic fragments and the emerging techniques of information graphics to make a dramatic presentation. As an exhibition designer, he was as innovative as El Lissitzky in the Soviet Union and Herbert Bayer in Germany. He understood that an exhibition was more than a display of objects. It was a total experience that incorporated all the senses; hence he integrated bold text panels with abstract surface designs and three-dimensional forms to frame the objects on display. Besides the Brno exhibition, his techniques were evident in his exhibit designs for the International section of the Book Exhibition in Leipzig in 1927, the Modern Czechoslovak Textile Exhibition in 1929, the Czech section of the International Hygiene Exhibition in Poznań, Poland, in 1933, and the Czech Pavilion at the 1937 World's Fair in Paris.

One ambitious project for the Arts and Crafts Association was the Baba Settlement Exhibition, a display of Functionalist houses that the association organized in 1932. Inspired by the Deutscher Werkbund and built outside the center of Prague, the housing estate, which might be compared in some ways to the Weissenhof Siedlung in Stuttgart, was co-organized by Sutnar along with the architect Pavel Janák. Sutnar designed the identity program for the exhibition from the logo, signage, and letterhead to all the promotional materials and particularly the catalog. His involvement with the Baba project thrust him into the center of contemporary Czech debates about modern housing, many inspired by the CIAM congresses, which Czech Functionalist architects attended.

In 1931, he co-authored a book, *Nejmenší Dům* (*The Minimum House*), based on a competition that the Arts and Crafts Association held jointly with the Education Ministry. His cover for the book, which featured a red square poised on an angled grid in and around which Sutnar placed some small photographic figures, was one of the most conceptual covers produced by any Functionalist designer in Czechoslovakia. Sutnar chose a red square, familiar from Lissitzky's graphics, to signify the mimimal house, and a grid to suggest an orderly city or community plan. The square, set against a white ground like a painting by Malevich, became the iconic focus of the cover to which the diagonal title was attached. Sutnar's composition broke every convention of book cover design, locating itself, to paraphrase Lissitzky's term for the Proun, between a book cover and an abstract work of art (Fig. 25.10).

Though Sutnar was actively involved with the Czechoslovak Arts and Crafts Association from the mid-1920s to 1939, his primary source of employment was the Družstevní práce, the cooperative he joined in 1929. There, as previously discussed, he directed its design outlet and gallery, Krásná jizba, and was in charge of design for the publishing division, which produced a steady stream of books as well as two pictorial magazines, *Žijeme* (*For Life*) and *Panoráma*

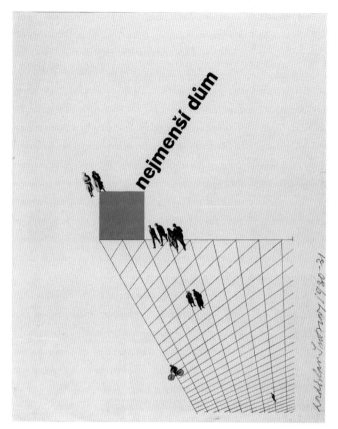

Fig. 25.10: Ladislav Sutnar, *The Minimum House*, cover, 1931. Collection Merrill C. Berman. Photo: Jim Frank and Joelle Jensen.

DP. Družstevní práce started in 1922 as a cooperative of shareholders who wanted to publish quality fiction. With a membership that was distinctly middle class and largely partial to the Social Democratic Party, the staff began to favor literature that was socially critical and left-oriented, although Družstevní práce's politics were broadly socialist rather than doctrinaire leftist.

Committed to photography as his visual medium, Sutnar redesigned the covers of *Žijeme* to include photographs and parts of photographs set against plain backgrounds with frequently distorted spatial perspectives. To strengthen Družstevní práce's image, Sutnar brought together several of its earlier publications to form *Panoráma DP*. He changed the format and began to feature extensive photographic

advertisements by Josef Sudek for Krásná jizba. As previously mentioned, Sudek photographed the glass, ceramic, and metal products from unusual perspectives to accentuate their formal qualities both individually and in patterns (see Fig. 25.05).

For the publishing division, Sutnar created a new DP logotype and forged distinctive looks for the various series of books that Družstevní práce brought out. Unlike Karel Teige's individually distinctive book covers, Sutnar strove to create a set of standard but variable formats, relying frequently on repeatable devices such as full-page or partial-page photographs and titles in san serif type either laid on top of the photographs or reversed out of rectilinear boxes. Rather than poetic images, he sought a factual quality in his photographic covers, some of which, particularly those for books with political themes, resembled John Heartfield's covers for the Malik Verlag in Germany. One series that Sutnar treated more playfully was a collection of plays by the Anglo-Irish dramatist George Bernard Shaw. Each cover featured a different photograph of the dramatist, placed within a composition of geometric red and black elements on a white ground (Fig. 25.11). Besides doing his own covers, Sutnar commissioned photographic covers from other designers including Karel Teige and the artist Antonín Pelc (1895–1967). He also paid careful attention to the bindings, drawing on experimental work from the State School of Graphic Art's bookbinding workshop. Bindings often had the book's title printed on the front or spine, sometimes accompanied by an abstract design.

Between his many projects for the Czechoslovak Arts and Crafts Association and Družstevní práce, Sutnar was highly influential across various fields in the 1930s. He pioneered new techniques of exhibition design that enhanced the presence of Czechoslovak goods and activities abroad, while also applying similar strategies to the display and promotion of household goods in a retail space. As well, he provided a new Functional look for magazines and created a contemporary style for the covers and contents of

Fig. 25.11: Ladislav Sutnar, *Captain Brassbound's Conversion*, cover, 1932. Jerri Zbiral, Alan Teller/The Collected Image.

mass-produced books. The State School for Graphic Art, which he directed, became a primary source for training young designers and photographers for the needs of the modern world.

Besides Sutnar, Zdeněk Rossman was a leading Functionalist graphic designer. Rossman was a member of the Brno chapter of Devětsil. He did the layouts for the chapter's journal, *Pásmo* (*Zone*), published between 1924 and 1926, and then he designed the bold cover for *Fronta*, a cultural anthology that the chapter published in 1927. The Brno chapter of Devětsil dissolved that year after which Rossman and his wife briefly studied at the Bauhaus. As previously stated, Rossman became head of the graphic design program at the School of Applied

Arts in Bratislava when he returned from Germany in 1931 and there he introduced a Functionalist curriculum. In 1938, he published an important book, *Lettering and Photography in Advertising*, which presented examples of Functionalist aesthetics. Its cover consisted of a single eye on a white ground from which radiated lines to the important words of the title, thus signifying their connection to sight.

During the 1930s, photography became widespread in advertising. Sudek's experimental work for Krásná jizba was an important precedent as was the German advertising photography of Albert Renger-Patzsch along with the work of Walter Peterhans, who taught photography at the Bauhaus. Emanuel Hrbek (1897–1975), a Functionalist graphic designer, promoted modern photography for advertising at the School of Applied Arts and Crafts in Brno, where he encouraged students in his graphic design and advertising courses to take up the medium. Among them were a number who pushed photography's boundaries during the 1930s to incorporate techniques associated with Surrealism such as automatism, chance, and dream imagery.

At the State School of Graphic Art in Prague, Karel Novák (1875–1950) and then Jaromir Funke also taught advertising photography. Funke began to teach the subject at the Bratislava School of Applied Arts and subsequently undertook a number of advertising projects with Sutnar. One of the strongest Czech advertising photographers was Jaroslav Rössler (1902–1990), the only member of Devětsil who specialized in photography. Rössler published in the Czech avant-garde journals and then left for France in 1927, remaining there until 1935. Though many of his best advertising photographs were done abroad, the high quality of his work in the genre was surely an influence on other photographers at home. Bohumil Šťastný (1905–1991) was also a versatile advertising photographer, although he worked for many years as an active photojournalist for the illustrated magazine *Pestrý týden* (*Colorful Week*), which also employed Rössler as a freelancer. Other illustrated magazines enjoyed a wide circulation in the 1930s and provided work for a group of magazine photographers including Václav Jírů (1910–1980), who was active as well in advertising campaigns for the Aero car company.

Some Czech photojournalists may have been influenced by the work of the German photomontagist John Heartfield, who escaped from Germany in 1933 when Hitler came to power and lived in Prague for much of the period between 1933 and 1938. He continued to create photomontages for the German workers' magazine *AIZ*, which was produced there and then smuggled into Germany. He also continued to work for his brother's publishing house, Malik-Verlag and did occasional work for Czech publishers of books and magazines.

Poland

After a long tradition of independence from the 10th to the late 18th century, Poland was partitioned between Russia, Austria, and Prussia and did not become a nation again until the inauguration of a new Polish Republic in 1918. A parliament governed the republic until 1926 when Marshal Józef Piłsudski took over the government and instituted a dictatorship that lasted until his death in 1935, when a weak democracy was instituted until the German invasion in 1939.

During the time of partition, a sense of Polish community was maintained through the arts and other intellectual pursuits including the applied arts. In the late 19th and early 20th centuries, Cracow, which was located in the province of Galicia, a part of the Austro-Hungarian Empire, became the leading center of applied arts activity among the Poles, largely because the authorities did not regulate or suppress the cultural activities of minorities, especially as they pertained to the expression of national identity. Following independence, Poland's cultural center shifted to Warsaw although designers and architects from Cracow continued to be influential.

Nationalism and the Arts and Crafts influence before independence

Cracow became a center of Polish arts and crafts as early as 1868 when Adrjan Baraniecki (1828–1891), a Pole who had met John Ruskin in London and been impressed with Henry Cole's South Kensington Museum, decided to establish a Museum of Industry with support from the mayor of Cracow. Baraniecki's aim was to present models of craft excellence that could counter the tide of cheap mass-produced goods that were pouring into the predominantly agricultural region from the industrial centers of the Austro-Hungarian Empire, namely the Czech lands of Bohemia and Moravia. He amassed a huge collection of artifacts from tools to tapestries and promoted educational courses both for Galician craftsmen as well as for the general public.

After the architect Tadeusz Stryjeński (1849–1943) became director of the museum in 1907, he established a group of workshops both before and after the new building he designed was erected in 1913. These included a bookbinding studio, a metal workshop, a carpentry workshop, and studios for printing and photography. Their contribution to improving the quality of Galician goods was enhanced by the proximity of the National Institute for the Promotion of Handicraft and Industry, which shared space in the new museum with them. Through its journal, *Handicraft Review*, and the publication of translated books by foreign design theorists such as Hermann Muthesius, as well as through exhibitions and other activities, the museum played an important role in fostering an indigenous Arts and Crafts movement in Galicia.

Where Baraniecki was concerned with issues of production, labor, and the quality of goods, Stanisław Witkiewicz (1851–1915), an author, artist, and art critic, was more interested in discovering a national Polish style. He believed he had found it in the folk culture of the Górale or highlanders who lived in and around Zakopane in the foothills below the Tatra Mountains. Historian David Crowley has noted that the Górale lived as farmers and shepherds untouched by industry or the bureaucracy of the Austro-Hungarian monarchy. Witkiewicz was fascinated by their wooden furniture and household objects, which he felt were quintessentially Polish, and he was also taken with the vernacular design of their log cabins, especially the half-gabled roofs.

Having moved to Zakopane, Witkiewicz and some architectural colleagues created their own interpretation of the Zakopane style in several houses they built. Witkiewicz's House under the Firs, designed for an economist and historian and completed in 1897, was an attempt to elevate the Górale vernacular to the status of a *Gesamtkunstwerk* or total work of art similar to William Morris's Red House in England, or Henry van de Velde's Bloemenwerf in Uccle, Belgium. In both of those buildings, the architectural design was integrated with a complete interior as it was in Zakopane.

The House under the Firs had a steeply pitched roof with a series of decorated gables, stepped windows, and a stone base on which the wooden frame was erected. Witkiewicz adapted the rich local ornament—stylized suns, thistles, and flowers—for door frames, gable ends, and structural beams. He applied it as well to all the furniture and other interior elements that he and his friends designed. Local craftsmen produced everything including most of the fabric coverings and curtains as well as two large ovens that heated the house. For Witkiewicz, the combination of vernacular forms and local craftsmanship in Zakopane clearly embodied the nationalist Polish style that he sought when he arrived there. In an attempt to export the style, he created designs for a porcelain jug and bowl based on a local ladle for goat's milk. A French ceramics factory in Sèvres produced these and marketed them under the rubric *Le Style Polonaise* (The Polish Style).

Other artists, architects, critics, and designers in Cracow supported the Zakopane style, which was one reason for their founding the Polish Applied Arts Society (Towarzystwo Polska Sztuka Stosowana) in 1901. Another stimulus was their espousal of Arts and Crafts ideals expressed in the Polish translations of writings by John Ruskin and William Morris around the turn of the century. Leading members of the society included artists Karol Tichy (1871–1939) and Stanisław Wyspiański (1869–1907), sculptor Jan Szczepkowski (1878–1963), and architect Józef Czajkowski (1872–1947). The society was intent on preserving traditional Polish culture, which it sought to do through restoration projects, attention to the preservation of vernacular objects, and an adoption of traditional forms for contemporary designs.

The work of the Applied Arts Society members drew from various sources, not just the Polish vernacular. Located in Cracow, within the Austro-Hungarian monarchy, members were also influenced by events in Vienna, notably the Secession exhibitions and the formation of the Wiener Werkstätte. As individual commissions for either commercial or residential interiors increased, the design language became more contemporary and cosmopolitan. Tichy, for example, was strongly influenced by the spare designs for chairs and cabinets of Josef Hoffmann in Vienna. One of Szczepkowski's manufactured table lamps that was produced by the M. Jarry factory had a stylized bronze bird as its base and a two-tiered fringed shade, while Czajkowski's decorative chairs for a Cracow restaurant recalled the form of the Greek klismos with its curved legs and back.

Wyspiański may have been the best known member of the society as he was a prominent painter, stained glass artist, and a playwright who was considered to be the founder of Polish modern drama. One of his major projects was the dramatic interior for the Church of St. Francis in Cracow, where he combined elaborate frescoes with richly colored stained-glass windows. As historian Józef Mrozek points out, Wyspiański created his own idea of a national style through the range of commissions he undertook, including the furniture he designed as part of the scenery for one of his own plays.

In 1913 some members of the society formed the Warsztaty Krakówskie (Cracow Workshops) with a few other colleagues to create a more cohesive and socially focused working environment. Housed in the Museum of Industry, the Cracow Workshops intended to bring together artists and craftsmen to "enoble production through handicraft." Like similar workshops in England, Germany, Austria, and Russia, the Cracow Workshops proposed to raise the level of craft production as an antidote to the welter of mass-produced goods that had flooded the market in Galicia. Likewise, the founders hoped to bring quality goods to everyone, thus echoing the ideal of William Morris and other founders of the Arts and Crafts movement. There was little that the workshops were able to accomplish before war broke out in 1914, but they played a prominent role in the early development of the decorative arts in the new Polish Republic after the war.

A parallel initiative to the various crafts societies and workshops in Cracow was the founding and development of the School of Fine Arts in Warsaw, which was part of the Russian partition. A private school, it opened officially in 1904 with a small faculty of prominent artists among whom was Karol Tichy. The school differed from its predecessor, the Cracow Academy of Art, in two significant ways. From the beginning there was a commitment to the applied arts as well as the fine arts and by 1907 two applied arts studios were producing designs for lamps and lampshades, kilims, ceramics, and advertising graphics. The second difference was that the school began to admit women after 1920 and soon more than half the students were female.

The Cracow School and the continued quest for a national style

Following independence, Warsaw became the center of the new Polish government and also began to assume the role of the nation's cultural capital. As a result, a number of artists, designers, and architects from Cracow moved there. Some obtained positions at the Warsaw School of Fine Arts, which the state took over

in 1922 and which achieved the status of an Academy ten years later. Karol Tichy became the school's director and Józef Czajkowski formulated its new educational program. The Cracow School, as this loose network of like-minded artists and designers was called, shared a dislike for the industrial products that modernists at the Bauhaus and elsewhere in Europe promoted, preferring instead to encourage the production of high-quality craft products, which had been their aim since the turn of the century.

After 1918, the original Cracow Workshops retained its base in the city's Museum of Industry. The remaining members still espoused the revival of handicraft production, although they were not able to create a market for their own products. Their survival, until bankruptcy forced them to close in 1926, came from a government commission in 1922 to produce many of the Polish exhibits for the 1925 Paris Exposition Internationale des Arts Décoratifs. The commission for the Polish Pavilion went to Józef Czajkowski, a founder of the Workshops, whose design combined a modernized classical facade topped by several rows of angular sculptural elements. Behind it was a tower of metal chevrons that was illuminated at night. Although the building was considered at the time to represent a new national style, it nonetheless strongly recalled the earlier Czech Cubist facades of Josef Chochol and Josef Gočár.

The interior by contrast was extremely traditional, featuring heavy wooden rustic benches designed by Karol Stryjeński (1887–1932), who derived their forms from the wooden furniture of the Górale people near Zakopane. Also featured in the pavilion were six large painted frescoes depicting Slavic myths and peasant festivals by Stryjeński's wife Zofia Stryjeńska (1891–1976). As a young woman, Stryjeńska attended the prestigious all-male Art Academy in Munich for a year and a half disguised as a man. After returning to Cracow, she illustrated many books with themes from Polish folklore before undertaking the panels for the Paris exhibition.

The Polish exhibits at the Paris exposition were spread across several venues and featured objects made in a number of Polish workshops as well as in various schools of applied art. The Poles won 172 prizes, more than any other nation, and in that sense, the exhibit was a glorious justification of the Cracow School argument for a new culture of handicrafts. But in the eyes of some critics and officials, it was a failure because it contributed little or nothing to the creation of a modern industrial economy.

Opposing this critique was a group of Cracow School members who were professors at the Warsaw School of Fine Arts, notably Czakowski, Wojciech Jastrzębowski (1884–1963), Stryeński, and Tichy. The year after the Paris exposition, they and others formed a new cooperative workshop, Ład (Harmony), just as its predecessor, the Cracow Workshops, was going bankrupt. Ład's intent was to design furniture, ceramics, silverware, interiors, and textiles as its members had already done for many years. Ład weavers became specialists in the production of one-off kilim rugs, while its ceramists developed simple forms and furniture and its designers created furniture with basic construction. Metalwork, however, continued to draw on the Zakopane style. As the inheritor of the Cracow School ideals, Ład was successful in large part due to the financial support it garnered from the government, particularly the Ministry of Industry and Trade and the National Economic Bank.

After Marshal Józef Piłsudski became the nation's dictator in 1926, the Cracow School aesthetic continued as a national style. Given the absence of an enlightened middle class to support modern design as could be found in Prague, major commissions for the Cracow School therefore came from the government. These included the design of government buildings such as the Ministry of Religion and Public Education of 1928 and the National Economic Bank, which was constructed between 1928 and 1935. The competition for the Ministry of Religion interior was won by Wojciech Jastrzębowski, who introduced a ceremonial

modernism in which he juxtaposed geometric motifs with traditional Polish symbols and native materials.

The Cracow School approach was combined with a modernist vocabulary in an unusual government project of 1929–1931: the design of a summer residence for the state president, Ignacy Mościcki. The architect, Adolf Szyszko-Bohusz (1883–1948), a member of the Cracow School, nonetheless adopted a modernist rhetoric by imposing a series of geometric blocks over an open plan, although he introduced a traditional element by cladding the building in rough sandstone. The interior designers furnished the residence with chromed tubular steel chairs and desks that were custom-made by the firm of Konrad Jarnuszkiewicz, which produced a line of such furniture for the market. The choice of modern exterior and interior elements for a government commission was unusual and remained something of an anomaly in the years to come.

The cultural status of the Cracow School was further enhanced after Jastrzębowski became director of the Department of Art in the Ministry of Religion and Public Education in 1928. This position gave him authority over the art schools as well as the power to dispense various commissions and appointments. Several years later, Władysław Skoczylas (1883–1934), a wood engraver who continued to draw on themes from the Zakopane region, became rector of the Warsaw School of Fine Arts and then president of the Institute for the Promotion of Art. The Institute's director was Karol Stryjeński, also a strong advocate of the Zakopane style.

In 1929, Ład was invited to design ten rooms at the Universal National Exposition in Poznań, one of Poland's major industrial centers. Held under the auspices of the Ministry of Trade, the exhibition celebrated a decade of national independence. In a statement published in the catalog, Ład continued to promote the experimental workshop model, defining the workshop's role as a place to prepare prototypes for industry. Rejecting large factories as sites of production, the Ład designers believed that the purpose of machines was simply to copy the forms that had been originally produced by hand. In this sense their position was somewhat similar to Henry van de Velde's defense of the artist at the 1914 Deutscher Werkbund exhibition in Cologne. Their commitment to what one critic called "modernized folk art," was evident in the room designs in Poznań, where viewers could see examples of furniture and textiles whose designers had sublimated more overt expressions of folkishness to modern forms that nonetheless incorporated folk references.

Given Piłsudski's political aim of relating Poland to the rest of Europe while still retaining a strong national identity, the government's support of Ład made sense. During the 1930s, in fact, the workshop received a number of prestigious state commissions including the design of interiors for major Polish embassies in London, Paris, and other cities. Even though critics in the 1930s found good reason to denigrate Ład's influence, particularly in light of the growing CIAM-inspired debates about modern architecture and minimal dwellings, the cooperative had nonetheless proven its worth as an instrument of national propaganda and thus continued to remain in official favor.

The avant-garde and Functional design

In 1923, the New Art Exhibition, held in Vilnius, Latvia, displayed the work of a group of Polish artists who the next year would form an association in Warsaw and launch a journal, *Blok*, to promote Constructivism in Poland. One of the two co-organizers of the exhibition was Władysław Strzemiński (1893–1952), an artist who had studied engineering and art in Russia, where he was born. He held positions in IZO, the Russian government's Department of Fine Arts, and in addition he was a representative of Kazimir Malevich's UNOVIS group in Smoleńsk. His wife, the sculptor Katarzyna Kobro (1898–1951), born in Russia as well, worked with him in Smoleńsk and also contributed to the Vilnius exhibition. Other artists who exhibited in Vilnius and were to be active in the Polish Constructivist

movement were Mieczysław Szczuka (1898–1927), Henryk Stażewski (1894–1988), and Teresa Żarnower (1895–1950).

Blok, whose editors were Szczuka and Żarnower, first appeared in March 1924 with a design that featured bold black letters for the title and a newspaper format. Heavy black rules divided sections of text, which alternated with photographs (Fig. 25.12). Along with the articles, the journal also published drawings of Constructivist interiors that had no influence on actual projects at the time but at least provided an alternate modernist vision to the traditional designs of the Cracow School.

Within a year, the *Blok* group had split into two factions, one based on Strzemiński's theory of *Unizm* (Unism), which posited art as an autonomous practice that could influence life, and the other derived from Szczuka's utilitarian theory, which claimed that art should be dictated by social needs. For Szczuka, industrial design, stage design, architecture, and film were all activities worthy of the modern artist's engagement. His ideas were embodied in the manifesto "What is Constructivism?," which was published in *Blok* 6–7. There, Constructivism was applied to art as a whole rather than to any particular branch such as painting or poetry. The manifesto also rejected handmade forms such as the Cracow School advocated and instead promoted mechanization as "an absolute objectivism of form." Most important was the assertion that problems of art and society were indivisible. By the end of 1925, Strzemiński and his supporters had left the journal and it ceased publication the following year. In 1930–1931, Strzemiński and Kobro sought to institute a new avant-garde design curriculum at the Girls' High School of Industry and Commerce in Koluszki, a town in central Poland not far from Łódź. In a program where the school was teaching girls to design and produce clothing, they introduced a radical curriculum based on a set of formal exercises, which moved from arranging lines on a plane to designing a dress based on the architectonic lines of the human body. Although the

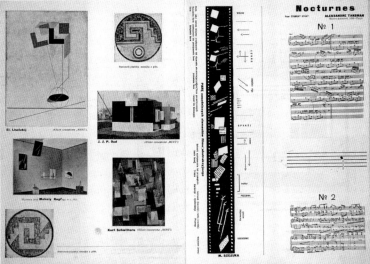

Fig. 25.12: *Blok*, cover and page spread, 1924. Beinecke Rare Book and Manuscript Library, Yale University.

program lasted for only a year, Strzemiński later claimed that its results had surpassed those of the Bauhaus.

Within the Polish discourse of the applied arts in the mid-1920s, Szczuka's critique of bourgeois taste that had been put forward in *Blok* was marginal. The Cracow School was still dominant and its values were not easily challenged, especially by someone whose criticism was based on left-wing internationalist ideology. One of Szczuka's actual projects, however, was acting as an organizer of the First International Exhibition of Modern Architecture in 1926. He collaborated on the exhibition with several professors from the Warsaw Polytechnic, where modernist ideas had already found a more welcome reception than they did at the Warsaw School of Fine Arts.

Almost concurrently with the demise of *Blok*, a new journal, *Praesens*, began publication by a recently-formed association of architects and painters with the same name. Initiated by the architect Szymon Syrkus (1893–1964), *Praesens* had a more pragmatic focus than *Blok*. Syrkus had contacts with modern architects abroad and wanted to connect the issues of Polish housing and town planning to wider European debates. Though Strzemiński was also a member of

Praesens and his book *Unizm* was published by the association, he eventually had a falling-out with Syrkus and left the group. Strzemiński continued to consider Functionalism as an abstract quality of spatial design similar to Malevich's philosophical idea of architecture and thus he disagreed with the more practical concerns of the Praesens architects related to minimum dwellings and general issues of housing design and architecture.

Syrkus and other Praesens members were interested in the design of interiors, but their approach to the domestic interior was rebuffed by the government planners of the Universal National Exhibition in Poznań. Whereas Ład was given its own wing in the Palace of Art, Praesens was largely excluded from the official displays and instead had to make its ideas known through the design of commercial pavilions for industrial firms that manufactured products such as fertilizer and cement.

The ideas of the Praesens architects about modern housing were more evident at Warsaw's Minimum Flat exhibition, held in 1930. The premise of the exhibit was to explore the problem of *Existenzminimum* (minimum dwelling space) that was currently at the heart of the CIAM debates. For the exhibition, the Warsaw Housing Cooperative allocated 20 flats whose interiors modern architects could arrange with inexpensive furniture. For one flat, Szymon and Helena Syrkus created some custom-made pieces of tubular iron furniture, which was manufactured by the firm of Konrad Jarnuszkiewicz, the company that made the chromed steel furniture for the president's summer residence. The significance of the Syrkuses' metal furniture, however, was more in its proposed application to the Polish working-class interior than in any original advance on what Marcel Breuer, Mart Stam, or Mies van der Rohe had already done. The one original contribution of the Syrkuses was a metal bed that could stand upright in a corner when not in use. A curtain could be pulled around it to conceal its function and integrate it with the daytime decor. According to one journalist, the best interior in the Minimum Flat exhibition was by two other Praesens members, the architects Stanisław Brukalski (1894–1967) and his wife Barbara Brukalska (1899–1980), both graduates of the Warsaw Polytechnic. They produced simple prototypes for cupboards and armchairs made of laminated plywood, which were recognized for their efficiency.

The next year Syrkus and his wife created additional metal furniture for the rooms of a small sanitorium they designed in Konstancin. Like the furniture for the Modern Housing Exhibition, it was manufactured by Konrad Jarnuszkiewicz, whose firm, unfortunately, did not introduce it to a wider domestic market. The company did, however, produce various lines of furniture made from steel tubing for residences, hospitals, offices, and gardens. Among its models was a cantilever chair with a plywood seat, back, and armrests for which Marcel Breuer's Bauhaus chair of 1928 was surely a source.

In their design of moderately priced housing estates in the early 1930s, Brukalski and Brukalska introduced a more industrial "kitchen laboratory," along the lines of Greta Schütte-Lihotsky's Frankfurt kitchen of several years earlier, but subsequently they softened their industrial look with free-standing wooden kitchen furniture for their villa entry in the Housing Building Exhibition of 1935. An important source of furniture designs for serial production in the 1930s was the Studio of Interiors and Utensils that the architect Stefan Sienicki (1897–1970) established in the Faculty of Architecture at the Warsaw Polytechnic. Sienicki, a former furniture designer for Thonet Mundus, directed his studio towards the creation of prototypes for the Polish furniture industry which, as David Crowley has noted, consisted primarily of small manufacturers and workshops. Hence, Sienicki fostered projects that used native materials and appealed to a conservative middle class, recognizing as well the limited capability of the nation's factories and workshops to produce high-end industrial furniture for a mass market.

The neglected profession of industrial design

During the 1920s and 1930s, the profession of industrial design was unknown in Poland. Artists, craftsmen, and architects produced furniture and household objects but the design of electrical appliances, cars, trains, ships, and planes was the work of engineers. The Elektrit Company, a manufacturer of radios, produced its first radio in 1927 and by the end of the decade was making around 90 percent of the nation's receivers. The firm employed engineers and technicians to keep the technology current, while the wooden housings with their boxy shapes and rounded edges were most likely done by craftsmen. The Elektrit Automatic Z of 1938–1939 featured 12 push buttons with the names of broadcasting stations on them, although they were complemented by a knob in case the owner wanted to find the stations manually.

Unlike Czechoslovakia, Poland did not have an automobile industry, although the country did manufacture one car, the CWS T-1, which was first produced in 1928 as a four-seat coupe designed especially for Polish road conditions. Production was short lived, however, and it was taken out of production in 1931. More enduring was the stream-lined railroad engine, known as the Pm36, that was designed in 1937 for the Polish national railroad by engineers in the Aerodynamics Institute at the Warsaw Polytechnic. The shell design was done by a team under the direction of Kazimierz Zembrzuski (1905–1981), while another team handled problems of construction. The shell was attached to a skeletal frame and covered all the machinery except for three drive wheels. In appearance, the Pm36, with its swept-back form, was similar to other streamlined locomotives that were designed around the same time in the United States, Britain, the Soviet Union, and elsewhere. Some were done by engineers and others by industrial designers.

One ambitious project of the 1930s was the two Polish ocean liners, the M/S *Piłsudski* and the M/S *Batory*, both of which sailed for the Gdynia America Line. The first was completed in 1934, the second in 1936, though sadly a German mine sank the *Piłsudski* in 1939. The two ships were designed primarily to take Polish emigrants to North America and then to serve as links between them and Poland. They were constructed in an Italian shipyard but Polish architects and designers did the interior design and furniture to emphasize the ships' nationalist character. Unlike earlier government commissions in the 1920s, Cracow School architects and designers did not dominate the project. They shared the interior design of both ships with modernist artists and architects, a collaboration that represented a new accomodation among the different schools of thought about architecture and design in Poland.

Graphic design

Commercial art and typography

The same cultural ferment in Cracow that fostered the applied arts movement at the end of the 19th century generated the first artistic posters in Poland. Many were done for art exhibitions and other cultural events by artists associated with the Młoda Polska (Young Poland) movement as well as with the Polish Applied Arts Society. Initially Art Nouveau was an influence,

as in a poster by Teodor Axentowicz (1859–1938) for the Cracow art society, Sztuka (Art). His image of a beautiful woman in a Polish folk costume recalls the posters of Alphonse Mucha in Paris.

Similar to movements in Brussels, Vienna, or Munich, Młoda Polska artists were interested in dissolving the boundaries between the fine and applied arts. Besides making posters, they also designed books and periodicals such as *Życie* (*Life*), the literary magazine attached to Młoda Polska which promoted a modern style of typography, illustration, and page layout similar to *Jugend* in Munich and *Ver Sacrum* in Vienna.

Some members of the Polish Applied Arts Society also designed posters to promote the society's exhibitions and other cultural events. Among them were Józef Czajkowski, Wojciech Jastrzębowski, Józef Mehoffer (1869–1946), Stanisław Wyspianski, and Karol Frycz (1877–1963), all of whom were active in the applied arts or architecture. Besides Art Nouveau and the folk art of the Zakopane region, poster designers were open to other influences such as the French fashion illustrators as well as artists in Germany and Italy like Julius Klinger and Leonetto Cappiello. In general, the Polish posters did not break any new ground but those by Frycz displayed varied drawing styles of some interest as well as idiosyncratic lettering. Artists in Warsaw also produced posters during this period, many of which had bilingual Polish and Russian texts.

As with the applied arts, after World War I, the center of the graphic arts shifted to Warsaw. The first modern poster artists in Poland whose work could rival that of artists elsewhere in Europe were former students of Zygmunt Kamiński (1888–1969) and Edmund Bartłomiejczyk (1885–1950), who taught drawing courses in the Department of Architecture at the Warsaw Polytechnic. Both had absorbed the ambition of the Polish Applied Arts Society to elevate the artistic level of daily life objects. Kamiński held the chair for freehand drawing and developed an intensive four-year drawing curriculum that began with geometric shapes and then moved on to nature, plaster casts, and live models. Under Kamiński's tutelage, students learned to work in different media including pencil, pen, chalk, and paint. From 1917, Bartłomiejczyk headed the program in perspective drawing, where students were taught to render three-dimensional forms in flat space. He was a skilled woodcut artist with an extensive background as a book illustrator and engraver as well as a designer of postage stamps, banknotes, and advertising leaflets. Both Kamiński and Bartłomiejcyzk also designed posters, but they worked in an illustrative style that broke no new ground in the medium.

Given their extensive training in visual art, it was thus not surprising that some students at the Warsaw Polytechnic decided to become poster artists rather than architects. The most successful of them was Tadeusz Gronowski (1894–1990), who was probably the first artist in Poland to embrace the modern style of advertising poster that was prominent elsewhere in Europe. Gronowski never practiced architecture, but instead built a career in graphic design. He was, however, able to use much that he had learned at the Polytechnic, notably the disciplined representation of objects in space and the simplification of forms that differed greatly from the more painterly poster tradition of the early post-war years. In 1923, he co-founded one of the first Polish advertising studios, Plakat (Poster), with Jerzy Gelbard (1894–1944) and another partner.

Cassandre was a strong influence on Gronowski and he became familiar with Cassandre's work through frequent visits to Paris. Besides mastering modern techniques of reproduction that included the airbrush, Gronowski was instrumental in shifting Polish poster design from an illustrative style to a more conceptual one, whereby an image could convey an idea rather than simply function as an illustration. This was evident in an early poster that helped build his reputation, an advertisement for Radion, a washing compound whose efficacy Gronowski portrayed by showing one black cat jumping into a sudsy pail of the compound and another white cat jumping out (Plate 28). Accompanying the image was the concise slogan, "Radion cleans for you."

Gronowski worked for diverse clients—manufacturers of soaps, chocolates, or cigarettes, as well as government agencies and organizations that supported social causes. He also helped to promote the inauguration of Poland's national airline, LOT, which the Ministry of Civil Air Transportation established in 1928. Gronowski designed the first logo for the airline, an abstract image of a crane in flight—and then helped encourage the airline's passenger business through a number of posters that gave both the planes and the passengers a fashionable look. He did illustrations as well for various popular magazines, thus defining a type of diverse modern graphic design practice that had not existed in Poland before.

Other poster designers who were trained at the Warsaw Polytechnic as architects included Stefan Osiecki (1902–1939), Adam Bowbelski (1903–1968), Maciej Nowicki (1910–1951), Stanisława Sandecka (1912–d.o.d. unconfirmed), Janusz Alchimowicz (1907–1945), Marian Walentynowicz (1896–1967), Jerzy Hryniewiecki (1908–1989), and Jerzy Skolimowski (1907–1985). In general, these men and women, like Gronowski, drew significantly from the French *moderne* poster style as well as from the visual rhetoric of streamlining. Their images were spare, they worked primarily with flat colors, and their lettering was always well formed and integrated with their overall designs. Nowicki and Sandecka, who later married, formed the Studio for Art Graphics, collaborating as well with Bowbelski, while Osiecki and Skolimowski worked together, sometimes with several other partners. With very few exceptions, these designers avoided photography in their poster designs as their training in drawing and painting was extremely strong. They were recognized internationally at the 1937 World Exposition in Paris, where their posters garnered a number of prizes. Besides graphic design, some of them also designed exhibitions and interiors.

More graduates of the Polytecnic might have

continued in architecture at the time except that the Polish economy suffered greatly during the 1930s and there was little work for architects. There was, however, a great need for graphic design since commerce, industry, and government all sought modern visual forms to communicate with the public.

Meanwhile, in 1926 Bartłomiejcyzk moved to the Warsaw School of Fine Arts, where he became head of the newly formed Faculty of Applied Graphic Design, a studio that complemented the Faculty of Artistic Graphics, which taught printmaking and other graphic arts and was headed by the traditional woodcut artist Władysław Skoczylas. Students who studied graphic design with Bartłomiejcyzk at the School of Fine Arts generally adopted a more painterly approach than those at the Warsaw Polytechnic. Among them were Edward Manteuffel (1908–1941), Antoni Wajwód (1905–1944), and Jadwiga Hładki (1904–1044). In 1933, these three formed a studio, Mewa (Seagull), where they worked together until 1936. Some consider this studio to have been the most important in Poland during the interwar years. The three principal designers had diverse talents and worked on a range of commissions from posters and stamp designs to large painted murals.

Although many poster designers and graphic artists came from the Polytechnic or the School of Fine Arts, some who gained prominence either studied at other schools or were self-taught. In 1933, Jan Lewitt and Jerzy Him, who changed his name to George Him when he settled in England, formed Lewitt-Him to produce posters and advertising with a humorous touch, and in 1937 they moved to London where their understated wit was more in tune with the British sensibility. Stefan Norblin (1892–1939), a painter, illustrator, and graphic artist, studied in Germany and Belgium, where he developed a realistic style that state authorities favored for a series of posters to promote Polish tourism in the mid-1920s. Norblin featured heroic portrayals of Polish types—a miner from Silesia, men and women in folk dress from Łowicz, and a mountaineer

in traditional costume from Zakopane (Fig. 25.13). Tadeusz Trepkowski (1914–1954), who studied at the Graphics Industry School and the Municipal School of Decorative Art and Painting in Warsaw, introduced a new dramatic element to poster design in a series of posters on social themes that he did in the late 1930s. His intense visual statements derived their impact from terse copy lines combined with forceful images such as a bandaged hand set against a torn phototograph of clenched fists and hammers on a poster that advocated more care in the workplace to avoid accidents.

The graphic design profession received a boost in 1933 when Gronowski and ten other designers acted on an initiative from Edmund Bartłomiejcyzk to form the Circle of Graphic Advertising Artists (KAGR), an organization that quickly grew in size. The KAGR promoted the work of its members through exhibitions and competitions around Poland. Some KAGR members were also involved with a monthly journal, Reklama (Advertising), that discussed current issues related to design.

With the well developed courses in lettering in Poland's art and architecture schools, poster designers and other commercial artists were able to produce elegant and original texts for their posters and other graphic work by hand. There was little advance in the design of printing types except for Antykwa Półtawskiego (Półtawski Antiqua), a typeface drawn in 1928 by Adam Jerzy Półtawski (1881–1952), who also designed independent Poland's first banknote. Like Oldřich Menhart in Czechoslovakia, Półtawski designed a typeface that he believed was suitable for setting in his own language. This meant creating special forms for certain letters that otherwise seemed distorted when printed. While some felt that Półtawski Antiqua, which a Warsaw foundry originally cast in 1931, contributed to the creation of a modern Polish style in book design, others thought that some of the letters, particularly the italics, were not well developed. However, after World War II, the Polish state type foundry redrew and cast Półtawski Antiqua, which

Fig. 25.13: Stefan Norblin, Poland, Zakopane, poster, 1925. © Lebrecht Music and Arts Photo Library/Alamy.

subsequently became Poland's most popular typeface for a time.

The avant-garde influence: advertising, pubication design, typography

As in other countries where avant-garde poets radically altered conventional typographic formats for book covers and poetry layouts, the same was true for poets associated with Poland's Futurist movement. Among them were Aleksander Wat (1900–1967) and Anatol

Stern (1899–1968), who published *Gga: The First Polish Almanac of Futurist Poetry* in 1920. Its format was square and the title consisted of heavy oversized black letters. The principal influence for other books that Futurist poets published between 1919 and 1922 was not Marinetti's Italian Futurism with its disruption of verbal syntax and its celebration of modern technology but rather Russian Futurism and Dada, both of which depended on subversive plays with verbal meaning. Wat and Stern acknowledged that words had weight, sound, color, and shape, but they resisted the syntactic disruptions of Marinetti's "words in liberty."

In 1921, the poet Bruno Jasieński (1901–1939) published several Futurist manifestoes in a newspaper format with large black letters for the titles and then different typefaces and point sizes for the texts. However, he laid out the texts in a conventional format characterized by flush left and right margins. The last important Futurist publication was *Knife in the Stomach*, a broadside, also in a newspaper format, that appeared later in 1921 after Jasienski's manifestoes. Consisting mostly of Futurist poems, its provocative title was laid out in large black letters while the phrase, "We piss in all colors," taken from the Zurich Dadaists, was placed below it in somewhat smaller but still bold type.

By 1922, the Futurist movement had ended and Wat, Stern, Jasieński, and the other poets moved on to new endeavors. Wat, who became a communist, lost interest in poetry and literature, choosing instead other forms of writing that were more socially directed. In 1924, he joined with the poet Stanisław Brucz (1899–1978) and the artist Henryk Berlewi (1894–1967) to form an advertising agency called Reklama Mechano (Mechno Advertising). Berlewi had a prior interest in Futurism and Dada, but converted to Constructivism after he met the Russian artist El Lissitzky in 1921, when Lissitzky was passing through Warsaw on his way to Berlin. Shortly after that meeting, Berlewi, who had been active in the design of Yiddish publications in Poland as Lissitzky had in Russia, spent several

Fig. 25.14: Henryk Berlewi, exhibition poster, 1925. Collection Merrill C. Berman. Photo: Jim Frank and Joelle Jensen.

art and life by producing modern advertising that possessed the visual qualities of his Constructivist paintings. Wat wrote the copy for the firm's brochure, which promised clients rapidity and low cost as well as ingenuity, simplicity, and beauty. The agency was only active between 1924 and 1926, during which time one of its major projects was a brochure for Plutos Chocolate, which featured Wat's tight copy lines that Berlewi laid out on crossed diagonals. Berlewi chose red and black for the text, which he printed on a bright yellow ground. Although an example of commercial graphic design, the brochure continued the experimentation with layouts that first interested Wat and the other Futurist poets.

Stern and Jasieński turned towards more socially committed poetry and in 1924 they jointly published a volume of poems, *Earth to the Left*, with a photomontage cover by Mieczysław Szczuka, the principal organizer of Blok and the co-editor of its journal (Fig. 25.15). Szczuka was most likely attracted to Stern and Jasienski because of political sympathies. The same year that he designed the cover for their book and also co-founded *Blok*, he became the editor of the Polish Communist Party's journal, *Nowa Kultura* (*New Culture*), which he laid out according to the same Functional tenets that he employed for *Blok*.

Szczuka was the first theorist of photomontage in Poland and used the technique extensively in his work as a designer of book and periodical covers, political dailies, and propaganda posters. He chose photomontage because he believed that it met the needs of an industrialized mass society better than painting did. It was inexpensive to reproduce and could be widely disseminated. Photomontage also substituted a mechanically precise means of reproduction for the individual gesture of the artist.

Szczuka created photomontage illustrations for another poem by Alexander Stern, *Europa*, for which his close collaborator, the artist Teresa Żarnower (1895–1950), designed the cover. The book was published in 1929, two years after Szczuka died in a

years in Berlin, where he mingled with international Constructivists like Theo van Doesburg and László Moholy-Nagy and was active like Lissitzky in the city's community of Jewish artists. In Berlin, Berlewi created a form of non-objective art that he called *Mechno-Faktur*, which consisted of arrangements of flat geometric shapes on a surface. His poster for a 1925 exhibition of his art in Warsaw's Austro Daimler showroom combined geometric shapes with stencil letters in a dense composition that featured all the elements in red and black on white as was the case with his paintings (Fig. 25.14).

Though Berlewi was a member of Blok, he did not play a central role in the movement or its journal. Instead, he tried to break down the barrier between

Fig. 25.15: Mieczysław Szczuka, *Earth to the Left*, cover, 1924. Muzeum Sztuki, Łódź.

mountain-climbing accident. Żarnower's lettering on the cover was bold and declarative as it had been on her 1926 poster, *Amnesty for Political Prisoners*. After Szczuka's death, she continued to design the left-wing social and political magazine *Dźwignia* (*Lever*), which he had begun to publish in 1927 and which ceased publication the following year.

Żarnower was a photographer as well as an artist, designer, and creator of photomontages. She used photography and photomontage extensively in her propaganda posters for the Polish Communist Party's election campaign of 1928, which combined strong photomontage images and Functional typography. She continued her left-wing political commitment in the early 1930s with her graphic work for several publications—*Miesięcznik Literacki* (*Literary Monthly*) and *Czerwony Sztandar* (*Red Banner*)—that were controlled to one degree or another by the party. Another designer who used photomontage extensively for left-wing political purposes was Mieczysław Berman (1903–1975),

a graduate of the Warsaw School of Fine Arts, who drew heavily on the ironic photographic juxtapositions of John Heartfield. In addition to doing political graphics and free photomontage compositions, Berman worked extensively as a commercial artist, designing posters that frequently included photographs or photographic elements.

Besides its adoption by members of the avant-garde, photomontage was used extensively by the popular press. One of its major proponents was Janusz Maria Brzeski (c. 1907–c. 1957), who had worked briefly for the illustrated magazine *Vu* in Paris. In Poland, Brzeski introduced the ideas of *Vu* in photomontage illustrations for commercial weekly magazines published by the Illustrowany Kurier Codzienny (Illustrated Daily Courier) press syndicate. From 1931 to 1934, Brzeski was the graphic designer for the syndicate's sensationalist crime magazine *Tajny Detektyw* (*Private Eye*), where his photomontages combined mug shots of criminals with actual crime scenes and other photographs that suggested the reasons for the crimes and the circumstances surrounding them (Fig. 25.16). After several years of publication, however, *Tajny Detektyw* proved too lurid for the Polish public and it folded. Brzeski moved on to become the art director of another IKC publication, the new weekly women's magazine *As* (*Ace*).

Brzeski also made experimental films, believing in a close relation between film editing and arranging sequences of press photographs. In fact, his strategies for magazine layouts influenced his films and vice versa. In 1932 he founded the Cracow studio SPAF (Polish Avant-Garde Film Studio) together with Kasimierz Podsadecki (1904–1970), who also did photomontage illustrations, many quite grotesque, for the IKC. Podsadecki worked mainly for IKC's weekly magazines *Na Szerokim Świecie* (*Across the Wide World*) and *Światowid* (*Worldseer*). He and Brzeski mounted a strong critique of modern technological society in their collaborative montage film *Beton* (*Concrete*) in 1933.

Podsadecki was as much interested in modern typography as he was in photomontage. In 1926–1927,

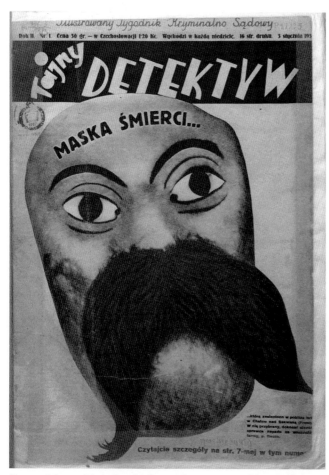

Fig. 25.16: Janusz Maria Brzeski, *Private Eye*, cover, 1932. Mazovian Library.

he designed the second series of the avant-garde journal *Zwrotnica* (*Railway Switch*), whose first series had been published beginning in 1922, preceding *Blok* by two years. Founded by the poet Tadeusz Peiper (1891–1969), *Zwrotnica* was a forum for discussions of contemporary poetry. Podsadecki provided experimental typographic covers whose elements he arranged in complex syntactical designs. He also created innovative layouts for the journal's advertisements, frequently alternating letters of different weights and sizes, arranging words on vertical and horizontal axes, and repeating words for rhythmic effects.

Podsadecki had been inspired by earlier typographic designs of Władislaw Strzemiński in *Blok*

as well as the first series of *Zwrotnica*. As previously discussed, Strzemiński believed that all forms should have a constructive quality, hence his interest in typography as well as painting, sculpture, and architecture. He therefore approached typographic layouts, not from the perspective of the traditional line-by-line page layout but as visual compositions whose parts had to cohere in an organic whole.

This approach was evident in his hand-lettered covers and his typographic designs for a play by the poet Tadeusz Peiper and several books of poems by the poet Julian Przyboś. For Peiper's play of 1926, *Szósta!, Szósta!* (*The Sixth! The Sixth!*), Strzemiński drew expressive letters in different sizes and weights as he did for Przyboś' poetry book *Oburacz* (*With Two Hands*). For the cover of a later book of poems by Przybos, *Z Ponad* (*From Above*), Strzemiński drew extremely distorted letters, which he organized in a multicolored composition that challenged the boundaries between lettering and abstract painting (Fig. 25.17). He continued to push the same boundaries in his typographical layout of the poems, where he broke the lines up into individual words and phrases that he arranged horizontally and vertically in combination with heavy black horizontal and vertical rules.

Z Ponad was published by a.r. (revolutionary artists), an avant-garde group in which Strzemiński played a leading role. Set up in 1929 and lasting until 1936, a.r. was primarily concerned with the visual arts and poetry. Its principal achievement under Strzemiński's leadership was the establishment of a museum of modern art in Łodz, which is still Poland's greatest repository of Constructivist painting and sculpture. Strzemiński also initiated a book series for which he designed all the volumes.

During the 1930s, he actively promoted modern typography. In the a.r. book series, he published a volume on Functional printing by his students at the Public Vocational School in Łódz, where he was the headmaster and taught courses in typography and printing. Strzemiński also introduced a new alphabet constructed with segments of straight lines and curves

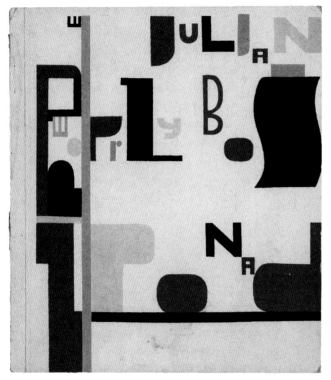

Fig. 25.17: Władislaw Strzemiński, *Z Ponad*, cover, 1930. Collection Merrill C. Berman. Photo: Jim Frank and Joelle Jensen.

in an a.r. newsletter of 1932 (Fig. 25.18). Through a.r., he organized the International Exhibition of Typography, held in Łodz the same year, where some of Europe's best modern graphic designers exhibited. In 1933 he

published a major theoretical article on typography in the deisgn magazine *Grafika Polska* (*Polish Graphics*) and in 1938 he edited a Polish version of Jan Tschichold's 1936 book *Typographische Gestaltung*, which appeared in Polish as *Druk nowoczesny* (*Modern Typography*). Strzemiński's own book on typography, *Zasady Kompozycji Reklamowej* (*The Principles of Advertising Composition*) came out in 1939 as the final volume in the a.r. series, but the entire edition was destroyed by the Nazis when they occupied Poland that year.

It is curious that Strzemiński's important contributions to modern typography occurred on the margins of Polish culture. His own work was most evident in short-lived avant-garde magazines and his teaching was confined to little-known vocational schools outside Warsaw and Cracow. Adam Jerzy Półtawski's traditional Półtawski Antiqua was the principal commercially produced Polish typeface during these years when no Polish san serif equivalent of Futura, Kabel, or Gill Sans appeared. And despite the vigorous avant-garde work of Strzemiński, Podsadecki, Szczuka, Stażewski, and Zarnower, no strong advocates of Functional typography arose to influence mainstream Polish publishing or advertising.

Austria

Although strong forces wanted Austria to rejoin

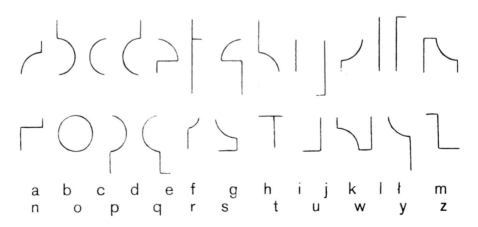

Fig. 25.18: Władislaw Strzemiński, experimental alphabet, 1932. Muzeum Sztuki, Łódź.

Germany, a new independent republic was established in 1919, following the collapse of the Austro-Hungarian Empire. It was, however, a mixed blessing and failed to satisfy all the factions whose interests ranged from reviving the Hapsburg monarchy to uniting with Germany. Neither of these suited the ruling European powers and the formation of an independent democratic government became the Austrians' most realistic opportunity.

Amidst widespread poverty and social chaos, a new government formed and over the next several years managed to stabilize the economy, which made economic reconstruction viable. Though a moderate party ruled the national legislature, socialists controlled the government of Vienna, thus prompting the name "Red Vienna" for Austria's largest city. However, both the socialists and the ruling moderates in the national legislature shared an antipathy to Soviet communism and took strong measures to reduce the power of the Austrian Communist Party. Distinctive election posters for the socialists in 1920 were designed by a Hungarian, Mihály Biro (1886–1948), who, before coming to Vienna, was active as a poster artist in Budapest where he supported the short-lived regime of the communist Béla Kun.

Building a socialist culture in Vienna

The working class, which had been nearly invisible during the years when bourgeois culture—the Vienna Secession, Adolf Loos, and Sigmund Freud—determined Vienna's identity, now became a major force in the creation of a new urban cultural life. Central to the program of the Austrian Socialist Party (SDAP), also known as Austro-Marxists, was an active program of social housing, which resulted in the construction of almost 70,000 new domiciles between 1919 and 1934, of which almost 59,000 were in apartment blocks. Unlike Germany, where an ambitious housing program was allied with new forms of modern architecture, those in charge of the Viennese housing program chose a mélange of outmoded styles that seemed to confirm the

workers' Viennese identity rather than ally them with an international modern movement. One of the largest and most fortress-like of these "people's palaces" was the Karl-Marx-Hof, that the city planner Karl Ehn (1884–1957), a former student of Otto Wagner, designed.

Despite the monumentalism of the building exteriors, however, the interiors tended to be quite small. The municipality established the Vienna Household Furnishings Company to provide furniture for the new dwellings. The company sold pieces that it designed itself as well as mass-produced furniture from other sources. Socialist Party publications praised the modular furniture units that were intended for the new apartments, but they were too expensive for many people, who had to make do with the larger pieces of furniture they brought from their previous tenement dwellings. To complement the new small domiciles, the housing projects included communal facilities such as laundries, bathhouses, medical clinics, libraries, kindergartens, and shops. There were considerable debates in the press about the advantages of collective facilities such as communal kitchens, but the Viennese workers rejected such proposals, preferring instead the conventional layouts of traditional dwellings. They also preferred more traditional kitchens and the mechanized Frankfurt kitchen, designed by an Austrian architect, Greta Schütte-Lihotsky, although she was an Austrian, was absent from the Viennese housing designs as well.

Through the creation of a total working-class culture, the Austrian Socialist Party sought to mold its members into new types of human beings. Important components of this culture were the party's many publications, including daily newspapers, periodicals, and books. Without designers of John Heartfield's caliber, they tended to lack distinction. One of the illustrated magazines, *Der Kuckuck*, followed the model of the German photographic weekly, the *Arbeiter Illustrierter Zeitung*, encouraging an Austrian movement of worker photographers just as the *AIZ* had in Germany.

Otto Neurath's pictorial statistics

The most significant cultural legacy of the Viennese Austro-Marxist program during the 1920s and early 1930s was the system of pictorial statistics devised by Otto Neurath (1892–1945), a philosopher, sociologist, and economist, for his Gesellschafts-und Wirtschaftsmuseum (Museum of Society and Economy). Funded by the municipality of Vienna, the museum's purpose was to publicize information about economic and social phenomena through pictorial charts. Neurath critiqued the Socialist Party's preference for the verbal rather than the visual, as evidenced in its extensive publishing program, and he believed that the workers could be better informed through a rational display of pictorial information.

To achieve this he developed strict rules for the visual display of social data. A major contribution to the tradition of statistical displays was not to represent quantities with figures of different sizes but rather to establish a uniform size and then multiply the number of figures to achieve a representation of the desired quantity. For easy reading he chose flat two-dimensional figures and used color to distinguish different types of figures. For the texts, he selected Paul Renner's Futura type because of its clarity. Neurath's system was first of all a product of his desire as a socialist to provide the working class with a view of the world that could be easily grasped through pictorial means. Second, as a philosopher involved in the Viennese Neo-Positivist movement that identified rationality as the core of philosophic discourse, he strove to describe the world in a clear and orderly way through visual techniques.

To produce the large number of charts that he displayed in the museum and contributed to exhibitions elsewhere, Neurath assembled a team with a distinct set of functions. Marie Reidemeister (1898–1986), a mathematician and physicist, was the museum's "transformer" whose job was to gather statistical data on a given subject and then distill it down to a cluster of facts that could be illustrated with pictorial statistics. Eventually she became Neurath's wife and lifelong collaborator.

In 1929, Neurath hired the German artist Gerd Arntz (1902–1988), who codified the style of the pictorial figures. They became progressively more abstract yet allowed for distinctions of differences in ethnicity, religion, or profession. Arntz also devised figures to represent industrial and agricultural products.

What came to be called the Vienna Method of Pictorial Statistics received wider recognition with the publication of the *Society and Economy Atlas* in 1930 (Fig. 25.19). Consisting of 100 pictorial charts and 30 text tables, the atlas served as a visual encyclopedia of historical and contemporary facts related to population, trade, technology, labor, and other social phenomena.

In 1934, when a contract with the Soviet Union to establish an ISOTYPE Institute there ended, Neurath, with Marie Reidemeister and several others including Gerd Arntz, emigrated to the Netherlands where they established an institute called the Mundaneum to further promote the use of the Vienna Method, which was renamed the International System of Typographic Picture Education or ISOTYPE in 1935.

Design for the middle class

Despite the active development of Vienna's working-class housing program, the central government chose to ignore it when determining its participation in the 1925 Exposition des Arts Décoratifs in Paris. It decided instead to fall back on the Viennese reputation for the production of luxury goods. Josef Hoffmann, a founder of the Vienna Workshops, supervised the extensive complex of buildings and exhibits. He designed the main pavilion, which he fashioned in a spare classical style to which he had reverted following the ground-breaking modernism of his pre-war Purkersdorf Sanitorium and Palais Stoclet. Despite the lavishness of the Austrian exhibits, they did not engage the French public and were criticized at home as a colossal failure. Many of the objects on display were designed by the Vienna Workshops and by Hoffmann's students from the School of Applied Arts. The Workshops had experienced a financial crisis in 1914. Reorganized as a

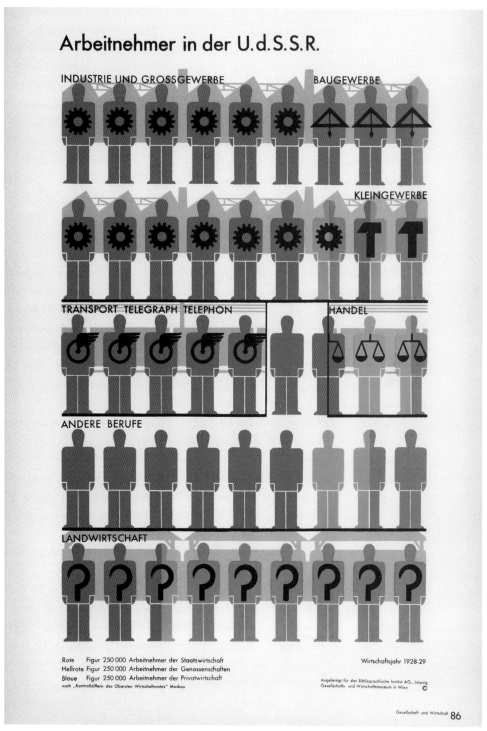

Fig. 25.19: Otto Neurath and Gerd Arntz, *Society and Economy Atlas*, 1930. Collection Merrill C. Berman. Photo: Jim Frank and Joelle Jensen.

new private company, they sought to continue their production of expensive hand-made goods even as the economic and social climate changed after World War I.

The man who shaped the Workshops' new decorative style was Dagobert Peche (1887–1923), a versatile craftsman whom Hoffman hired in 1915. Peche's first major activity was to set up and manage a new cluster of studios, where artists with various skills could experiment. They were provided with materials and working space and the Workshops put their most successful designs into production. Most of the participants were female students of Hoffmann's from the School of Applied Arts. Noting the Workshops' WW (Wiener Workstation) acronym, the poster artist Julius Klinger, who was critical of craft production, sarcastically referred to the products that originated in the Workshops' studios as "Wiener Weiberkunstgewerbe," or "Viennese women's crafts."

Peche admired the ornate decoration of the Baroque and Rococo periods, which strongly influenced his own work. He had little interest in utilitarian objects and preferred to add decorative elements to everything he designed. Working with different materials, he produced a full range of products from silver tea services and lamps to ceramic vases, glassware, furniture, clothing, jewelry, and wallpaper. He stated his ideas on the decorative arts in "The Burning Bush," an unpublished manuscript of 1922, where he celebrated the creative talents of the artist even as he argued that the Vienna Workshops had to be run as a business.

Peche's aesthetic was more delicate than Hoffmann's, although it was rich in color, pattern, and iconography. His premature death in 1923 was a great loss to the Workshops. Other artists such as the fashion and textile designers Maria Likarz (1893–1956) and Mathilde Flögl (1893–1950), both former students of Hoffman's at the School of Applied Arts, produced creditable designs but could not rival Peche's fecund imagination. For a number of reasons, the quality of

the Workshops' production began to decline in the late 1920s and it finally had to close in 1932. From its inception, the Vienna Workshops had furnished the Viennese upper middle class with a domestic and sartorial identity. In its second phase after the war, it had also helped to provide that same segment of society with an escape from the nation's economic crisis and the aggressive spread of working-class culture.

A rival to the Vienna Workshops, though lesser known, was Haus & Garten (House & Garden), a studio run by two architects, Josef Frank (1855–1967) and Oskar Wlach (1881–1963), between 1925 and 1933. Frank became the principal designer, while Wlach managed the business. The studio produced a wide selection of domestic furnishings—sofas, chairs, tables, beds, desks, carpets, and lamps. The pieces were on display in a Vienna showroom but generally had to be custom ordered. Frank also designed textiles, a practice he would develop further when he later began to design for the Swedish furnishings shop Svenskt Tenn in Stockholm.

Unlike the Vienna Workshops, Frank's aesthetic could be characterized as soft modernism, which would later be compatible with the next phase of his career in Scandinavia. His wooden chairs, for example, featured pared down frames that were frequently combined with fabric-covered padded support. Frank would also add a covering of fabric to a geometric cabinet design. He used expensive woods and demanded a high quality of craftsmanship. As a textile designer, he favored dense colorful patterns of small elements, frequently drawn from nature. Though he did not dispute the value of mass-production, he was reluctant to give up craftsmanship completely, believing strongly that it added a quality of comfort to the domestic interior. Hence the furniture was expensive and the firm's clientele was almost exclusively upper middle class.

Frank's designs for Haus & Garten influenced a number of younger Austrian architects and interior designers who were sometimes grouped together as representatives of *Wiener Wohnkultur* (Viennese domestic culture), a name used to describe a kind of comfortable modern interior that served as an alternative to the colder industrialized counterparts with tubular steel furniture in Germany.

It was actually an Austrian furniture company, Thonet, that dominated the European market in tubular steel furniture. From its beginning in the 1830s, Thonet had produced bentwood furniture but then entered into the production of tubular steel pieces in the late 1920s. In 1922, Thonet, which had been privately held since its inception, joined the world's largest furniture conglomerate Kohn-Mundus, then located in Zurich. The firm continued to operate independently and remained one of Austria's largest exporters of finished goods, even though it also had manufacturing facilities abroad, notably in Germany and the United States.

Thonet experienced a bentwood revival during the 1920s, in part because of the chairs' spare designs, which complemented the new modern aesthetic. The bentwood furniture received an additional impetus from Le Corbusier, who used it in his early interiors and considered its design to be classic. Thonet furniture was also widely seen in various interiors at the 1927 Weissenhof housing exhibition in Stuttgart. At home, Thonet continued to produce new models that were created in-house, but also began to commission well-known architects to design chairs for them. Of these, most were done by architects abroad, but Josef Frank also designed one.

In 1929, Thonet sponsored a chair competition in Vienna to elicit new bentwood designs. Of 4,000 entries, however, the distinguished jury found little to admire, recognizing that the company's best bentwood designs may have been its earliest ones. Around the same time, Thonet began to produce other types of furniture in tubular steel along with heavily upholstered club chairs and couches. The mainstay of Thonet's business, however, was the institutional market for which it made many types of furnishings for schools, theaters, and retail spaces. By 1938, after the Nazis had occupied Austria, much of Thonet's production had shifted to Germany or the United States. Due to the ensuing war and the destruction it wrought, Thonet would have to completely rebuild its European operations after the end of hostilities in 1945.

The Austrian Werkbund

The Austrian Werkbund, an offshoot of its parent association in Germany, was founded in 1912 but was far less active than its German counterpart. After an initial flurry of activity, which included hosting the German Werkbund's 1912 congress in Vienna, the Austrian branch became mired in disagreements, which effectively paralyzed it until the late 1920s. One major difference between the Austrians and the Germans was that the Austrians did not share the Germans' interest in uniting art and industry. Austria had never embraced industrialization, and the Werkbund members fell back on what had always been Austria's rationale for this— quality was more important than quantity and quality could best be attained by supporting fine craftsmanship rather than mass production.

Around 1928, Joseph Frank led a move to reinvigorate the association, which resulted in the selection of new leadership. But Frank was unclear about what direction the revived Werkbund should take, although he was certain that it should retain a strong commitment to the handicrafts. In 1930, the Austrian Werkbund decided to create a model housing estate similar to the 1927 Weissenhof exhibition in Stuttgart, which had been organized by its German counterpart.

Under the direction of Frank, the project was completed in 1932. As in Suttgart, both Austrian and international architects were invited to participate. These included Adolf Loos (1870–1933) and Richard Neutra (1892–1970) from Austria, Gerrit Rietveld from the Netherlands, Hugo Häring (1882–1958) from Germany, and André Lurçat (1894–1970) from France.

Frank had contributed to the design of some of the high-density worker housing that was supported by the socialist-dominated municipality in Vienna and he was extremely dissatisfied with it. He conceived the Werkbund estate as an alternative, although the focus on single-family homes was directed to the middle class rather than the workers. The challenge of the program was to extract the maximum comfort from a minimum of space, although the definition of what was minimal would have seemed quite ample to the planners of the working-class housing blocks.

The construction of the estate was the Austrian Werkbund's last positive act. Following its completion, a growing right-wing nationalist group within the association, surely emboldened by Hitler's election as the German chancellor, began to protest against its Jewish members such as Josef Frank. A number of the right-wingers resigned and many reunited in a new group led by Josef Hoffmann. By the end of 1933, the Austrian Werkbund had split into two camps: the "Old Werkbund," consisting almost exclusively of socialists and Jews, and the "New Werkbund," whose conservative and Roman Catholic members followed Hoffmann and several others like him. By early 1934, the "New Werkbund" had become the official New Austrian Werkbund, purged of all Jews and leftists. Its two vice-presidents were the prominent architect-designers Joseph Hoffmann and Peter Behrens.

The division within the Werkbund mirrored the larger split between the socialists and the emerging right wing in Austrian society. In early 1934, all political parties were abolished except the conservative Fatherland Front. Several months later an authoritarian constitution was put in place and Austria became a federal state rather than a republic. In 1938, the Nazis invaded the country, which was incorporated into the rapidly expanding Third Reich.

Commercial art

Austria's strongest activity in the graphic arts before World War I was not in the commercial sector as in Germany but rather in the sphere of culture. Dense intricately-lettered posters by Kolo Moser and Alfred Roller for the Secession exhibitions and artistic posters

for the Cabaret Fledermaus and the Kunstschau by Berthold Löffler (1874–1960) defined the Viennese visual style of the pre-war years (see Chapter 12).

After the war, however, it was the German *sachplakat* or "fact poster" that most strongly influenced the development of commercial art in Austria, particularly in Vienna. The strongest proponent of the *sachplakat* was Julius Klinger (1876–1942), who had worked as a commercial designer in Berlin from 1897 to 1915. He, Lucian Bernhard, and others created the *sachplakat*, particularly through the commissions they undertook for the Berlin lithography firm Hollerbaum & Schmidt.

Following World War I, Klinger opened a commercial art studio in Vienna, where he also taught modern advertising art. However, more students studied graphic art at the School of Applied Arts, where their teachers included some of the major artists of the Vienna Secession. Alfred Roller was head of the school and Berthold Löffler among others taught art classes. Rudolf von Larisch (1856–1934), the specialist in lettering whose writings had strongly influenced the Secession poster artists, taught both at the School of Applied Arts and the Graphische Lehr und Versuchsanstalt (Graphic Education and Research Institute).

Klinger was opposed to the Secession style, espousing instead an aesthetic of simplicity that he believed to be in accord with Adolf Loos's ideas. Like Lucian Bernhard, he favored flat colored forms instead of modeling, and his advertising posters featured strong images and prominent lettering instead of detailed anecdotal scenes. Besides posters, he designed stationery, trademarks, advertisements, and packaging, demonstrating to other commercial artists the variety of commissions they might undertake. Klinger was skilled at lettering as well as drawing and the roman alphabet with spiky serifs that he designed and used for many of his posters was later developed into a typeface. One of his strongest campaigns was for Tabu, a firm that produced cigarette papers. Beginning in 1918, he popularized the company's products with designs that ranged from small newspaper announcements to large billboards and wall paintings. Like many Viennese, Klinger had a sharp wit, which was often evident in his posters such as one for Olleschau, another producer of cigarette papers, where the O becomes a leitmotif in the construction of the humorous trademark figure's body as well as in the smoke rings he is blowing.

Klinger was a great promoter of Viennese commercial art. In 1923, he founded a group of designers called the Vienna Group. Among its members were Willy Willrab, who later moved to Germany, Herman Kosel (1896–1983), and Rolf Frey (dates unconfirmed). For a time Kosel and Frey ran a joint studio until Frey moved to Germany around 1926. The group espoused modernity particularly through their appreciation of Charlie Chaplin, the French fashion illustrations of Charles Martin, and the acerbic wit of their own countryman, Karl Kraus.

The same year that Klinger established the Vienna Group, he found a publisher in Chicago to produce a book of their work. Entitled *Poster Art in Vienna*, the book's beautiful color reproductions helped to spread their reputation although it did not appear to attract American clients in any number nor did it have any significant impact on commercial artists in the United States.

The artists in the Vienna Group worked in a style that was similar to Klinger's although there were also differences. Some of Willrab's posters, for example, featured large three-dimensional letters that became dominant shapes. Kosel-Frey remained closer to Klinger, drawing heavily on the German caricature style of *Simplissimus* and *Die Lustige Blätter*, although in the 1930s, Kosel won a prize for a poster in a more somber style that presented Vienna as a tourist destination. Besides the artists in the Vienna Group, others were also strongly influenced by the German *sachplakat*. Posters of Heinrich Blechner (1895–1983) for Odol mouthwash, and Alexander Exax (1896–1994) for Steyr ball bearings are good examples. Hans Wagula (1894–1964) produced similar work but also

became known for his travel posters, which depicted inviting views of vacation spots in strong flat colors. Austrian commercial artists also had a rich resource for expressive letters in Rudolf von Larisch's multiple volumes of lettering examples, which he gathered from artists throughout Europe. Published between 1900 and 1909, these books remained a strong source of ideas for decorative lettering styles even though many poster artists had begun to favor a plainer san serif letter by the late 1920s.

The most important commercial artist in Austria in the generation after Klinger was Josef Binder (1898–1972), who had served a brief apprenticeship with a printing and publishing house in Vienna and attended classes at the School of Applied Art after the war. He opened his own studio in 1922 and began immediately to work in a modern style. Like Klinger, he designed trademarks and other advertising material besides posters. An excellent draftsman, his roots were in freehand drawing and his work never reflected the style of humorous drawings that was frequently evident in the work of Klinger and Kosel-Frey, for example. Binder was one of the first commercial artists to produce drawings with an airbrush, which until the 1920s had been used primarily for retouching photographs.

One of his memorable creations was a 1924 poster for Meinl coffee that featured a small brown-skinned boy with a fez sipping the brew. Known as the Meinl moor, this image, which conveyed the exotic Ethiopian origin of the product, became the company's logo and has been updated a number of times over the years (Fig. 25.20). In another poster, for Meinl tea, Binder conveyed its Asian origin by depicting a Chinese junk manned by a boatman in a coolie hat. His work for Julius Meinl was complemented by that of Otto Exinger (1897–1957), a poster designer who joined Meinl's in-house design studio in 1926. Exinger later became the studio's director and continued to supervise the company's advertising until his death in 1957.

Britain, was not a colonial power, the employment of stereotypical figures in Binder's work and that of other European graphic designers makes clear a widespread worldview during the 1920s and 1930s that found stereotypical depictions of non-Europeans to be perfectly acceptable. Binder's studio became an important training ground for other Viennese commercial artists such as Lois Gaigg (dates unconfirmed), a talented and prolific poster designer who established her own studio in 1934. She was killed during World War II.

By the time Binder left Vienna for the United States in 1936, other artists had begun to work in a related modern style. Many had joined the Bund Österreichischer Gebrauchsgraphiker (League of Austrian Graphic Designers), which was founded in 1927 and helped to move graphic design from a commercial art that had its roots in painting and drawing to a more mature profession.

Hungary

During the time Hungary was part of the Austro-Hungarian Empire, the nation experienced exceptional economic growth, although industry could not expand quickly enough to prevent many people from emigrating. The living standards of the rural population were extremely low and those of the uneducated working class were not much better. Budapest continued to grow rapidly as did its middle class. At the end of World War I, the monarchy was defeated and in 1918 Count Mihály Károlyi became the Prime Minister. But his administration was brief, due to a coup that installed Béla Kun as the head of a short-lived Communist republic. After three months of unstable governance, the Communists were ousted and a new Kingdom of Hungary was established. King Charles IV was not called back and instead the parliament elected Admiral Miklós Horthy as Regent for an indefinite period. Horthy was an authoritarian ruler who remained in power until World War II. Industry grew very little under his reign. Hungary had to rebuild its economy because of the loss of a great deal

Fig. 25.20: Josef Binder, Meinl Kaffee, poster, 1924. MAK - Austrian Museum of Applied Arts/Contemporary Art. Photograph: © MAK.

Though Binder's posters differed considerably from those of Klinger and his circle, he did share with Klinger the belief that a good poster had to feature a strong image that stood out from a plain background. Like Ludwig Hohlwein in Germany, his images varied from handsome European sportsmen and men about town to an array of exotic figures from Africa, Asia, and the Middle East. These included bare-breasted African women carrying water jars, smiling Chinese coolies with slit eyes advertising Arabian tea, and dark-skinned serving boys promoting coffee. Though Austria, unlike of territory, population, and industry due to the Treaty of Trianon, signed with the Western powers in 1920. Hungary was also isolated from the victors of World War I and consequently did not participate in the 1925 Exposition Internationale des Arts Décoratifs in Paris, an event that intensely focused applied arts activity in Czechoslovakia and Poland. In spite of difficulties, there were positive achievements in particular sectors of Hungarian industry due to the strong vision and management of individual companies.

Art and industry in the Austro-Hungarian Empire (Dual Monarchy)

By 1900, Hungary had long recognized the importance of the applied arts and established some of the institutions that were necessary to foster their growth. As part of the Dual Monarchy, Hungary was also influenced by the applied arts in Vienna, which were highly developed in the years before World War I, as well as the applied arts in Munich, Berlin, and Paris, where a large number of Hungarians studied.

It was actually the Deutscher Werkbund that stimulated the formation of a Hungarian group to improve the quality of Hungarian goods. The Werkbund's activities were first reported in Hungary by the president of the National Society for Industry, who proposed the establishment of an Industrial Arts Center to foster quality industrial production and provide a place where craftsmen could market their products. Although that plan did not come to fruition, the news of the Werkbund did stimulate the founding of a comparable group in Budapest, Magyar Művészi Munka (Hungarian Quality Work Society), which was inaugurated in 1913, the same year as the Austrian Werkbund. The society's charter stated the hope of the founders to raise the quality of industrial products through the cooperation of artists, industrialists, and craftsmen. It also signaled their wish to align their objectives and activites with the German and Austrian Werkbunds and expressed the hope that their association might be known abroad

as the Hungarian Werkbund. Founding members included architects and applied artists such as Ödon Lechner (1845–1945), Hungary's leading Art Nouveau architect; the architect József Vago (1877–1947); and Lajos Kozma (1884–1948), an architect who became one of Hungary's major designers of shop facades, interiors, furniture, and books as well as a prominent design educator. However, with war imminent, there was little opportunity for the new society to launch a program, nor did anything come of it directly after the war.

Though its representation at foreign exhibitions before World War I emphasized Hungary's folk heritage, the monarchy had a number of enterprises such as the aforementioned Ganz & Company that were quite advanced in engineering and the manufacture of industrial products. Around 1908, two factories began to produce small delivery vans for the Hungarian Postal Authority, both using engines designed by the mechanic and inventor János Csonka (1852–1939), who is credited with the design of the first Hungarian automobile in 1902. The box-like vans differed little in design from the touring cars of the day, but the idea of using the rear section for storage was novel and Hungary was one of the first countries in Europe to motorize mail delivery. In 1908, Csonka also began to build small experimental cars that the Postal Authority purchased to collect mail. Though hardly a match for the superior designs of cars from abroad, some were nonetheless adapted as passenger vehicles. Hungarian-made cars produced by MARTA Hungarian Automobile Ltd also replaced the horse-drawn carriages of Hungary's major taxi company. As well, MARTA competed successfully for a contract from the city of Budapest to build double-decker city buses following the London model. A number were completed, but after World War I, Romania annexed the region where the MARTA factory was located and the factory ceased to operate.

Though high-end furniture in Hungary during the Dual Monarchy tended towards heavy ornamentation and a Neo-Baroque style, a furniture company owned by Sándor Buchwald (1837–1919) produced simple folding chairs and tables, along with stationary benches, for gardens and parks. The pieces he designed consisted of metal frames with either wood or metal slats for the seats and backs. The different designs were variations on basic models although Buchwald's ability to use some of the same parts in different models does not appear to have been as well thought out as it was by the Thonet company, whose furniture was primarily for indoor use.

The graphic arts before independence

Given the modest size of the market for mass-produced books, advances in their design were limited. The revival of Hungarian book printing began in the 1880s when the middle classes started to demand higher quality in its printed matter. A major journal that adopted a new design format was the literary magazine *Nyugat* (*West*), which was founded in 1908. It published both poetry and prose in a range of styles from symbolism and naturalism to impressionism. Elek Falus (1884–1950), who combined motifs from Art Nouveau with elements of Hungarian folk art, designed the title page and some covers, as well as the covers of books the journal published.

Art Nouveau was also highly influential in the early development of the Hungarian poster although sources ranged widely from Jules Chéret to Lucian Bernhard and the caricaturists of *Simplicissimus*. Árpád Basch (1873–1944), who studied art in Munich and Paris, brought a naturalistic sensibility to poster design, but he was also extremely attentive to lettering and its relation to an image. The poster designer who best conveyed a picture of the Hungarian middle class under the Dual Monarchy and after Horthy came to power was Géza Faragó (1877–1928), who had studied with Alfonse Mucha in Paris. His posters featured stylishly dressed men and women enjoying the comforts of middle-class life. Faragó was essentially an illustrator who added lettering to his images as in his well-known poster for Törley Champagne, which depicts an effete young man in evening dress smoking a cigarette while his champagne glass, gloves, and a drooping rose rest on a nearby table (Plate 29).

The applied arts in the interwar years

Following the collapse of Béla Kun's short-lived Communist republic, artists and intellectuals left Hungary in large numbers. Many went to Vienna, where the Socialist government offered some compatibility, and others departed for Germany. László Moholy-Nagy joined the avant-garde milieu in Berlin and after several years was called to Weimar to become a member of the Bauhaus faculty. Before Moholy arrived at the school, many Hungarian students had already been drawn to the Bauhaus. Some formed an alliance they called the KURI group, which lobbied for the appointment of Moholy-Nagy to the faculty after Johannes Itten left. Though many of the Hungarian students distinguished themselves at the school, Marcel Breuer is the one who is best known because of his innovative furniture designs and the fact that he became a teacher there following his tenure as a student.

One of the Hungarians who spent time in Weimar without actually enrolling in the Bauhaus was Sándor Bortnyik (1893–1976), a painter active in Hungarian avant-garde circles before he left Hungary after the Communist coup. When Bortnyik returned home in 1925, he was unable to obtain any state commissions because of his prior left-wing activity. He began to work as an independent graphic designer, producing posters, book covers, and other printed materials, and in 1928 he founded a small school, Műhely (Workshop), which he kept going for ten years with a staff of part-time teachers. The program was based on Bauhaus ideas and the most advanced thinking of the avant-garde in other countries. The part of the program that produced the most visible results was graphic design, which is the field that Bortnyik himself was working in at the time. Among the students at the Műhely was Gyorgy Kepes (1906–2001), who later worked in Berlin as an assistant to Moholy-Nagy and then had a distinguished career as a visual arts educator in the United States. Another prominent alumnus was the painter Victor Vasarely, who was associated with the international op art movement.

Under the conservative cultural policies of the Horthy regime, modern design such as Bortnyik espoused at the Műhely received no public support. However, modernism was evident to some degree in the design of occasional commercial interiors and store facades such as Lajos Kozma's Budapest fashion house interior of 1928 and his Apostol Pharmacy of 1929, both done in an Art Deco style. As a furniture designer during the 1920s, Kozma adopted an ornate aesthetic. One critic dubbed his mixture of swirling Baroque elements and refined folk art motifs "Kozma Baroque." Kozma's designs, however, were part of a broader craft ethos that was also evident in selected furniture, ceramics, and textiles by others. In the mid-1930s, this ethos gained wide currency through the designs of Kató Lukáts (1900–1990), notably the candy wrappers and boxes she created for the Frigyes Stühmer Company,

Though Hungary experienced no modern movement equivalent to Functionalism in Czechoslovakia, there was a gradual shift in the late 1920s towards a more Functional approach to furniture. A major participant in this shift was the furniture factory owned by Károly and János Lingel. Known for its office furniture in the American style, the company began to manufacture a line of modular utility home furniture after 1927. Marketed under the name Varia, their line consisted of 14 types of modular units that could generate an enormous number of permutations and combinations.

The shift to more Functional furniture was also stimulated by the founding of the progressive architecture and design magazine *Tér és Forma* (*Space and Form*), which appeared in 1928 and continued publication until 1945. It was supported as well by the debates around minimum living space that had been occurring within CIAM, and which included

Hungarian participants. The Hungarian CIAM group also organized two exhibitions that explored aspects of collective living and public low-cost housing. Both topics challenged the policies of the Horthy government, which responded to the second exhibition by sending the police to shut it down.

At the Budapest Furniture Fair in 1931, Lajos Kozma introduced a spring-backed chair for mass-production that could be made with considerable variations. It was put into production by the Jószef Heisler Furniture Factory and was available in different materials including a choice of wooden or steel-plate frames. Shortly thereafter Kozma created several pieces of tubular steel furniture for another manufacturer, thus solidifying his move from Baroque ornamentalist to modern designer.

In 1932, Kozma helped establish the Magyar Műhely-Szövetség (Hungarian Workshop Alliance), an organization better known by its alternative name, the Hungarian Werkbund. Like its predecessor, the Hungarian Quality Work Society, which was founded in 1913, the aim of the Hungarian Workshop Alliance was to improve the quality of industrial goods. By this time the Deutscher Werkbund—equally the model for its 1913 and 1932 Hungarian counterparts—had also become involved with the improvement of modern living spaces and household furnishings. It did so through its sponsorship of the Weissenhof Siedlung in 1927, a project that would influence the activities of the new Hungarian Alliance. Others besides Kozma who were active in the Alliance's founding included Farkas Molnár (1897–1945), an architect who had been part of the Bauhaus community and then later helped organize the Hungarian CIAM delegation; Sándor Bortnyik; the ceramist Géza Gorka (1894–1971); the artist Anna Lesznai (1885–1956); and the publisher Imre Kner (1890–1945).

As with its predecessor organization, the activity of the Hungarian Workshop Alliance was interrupted by war before it had a chance to fully develop its program. It was, however, able to mount several exhibitions, support the annual Budapest Furniture Fair with work by its members, and participate in additional exhibitions as well. Despite its other activities that included lectures and publications, historian Gyula Ernyey believes that the Alliance did not have a significant influence on Hungarian architecture or design as its counterpart, the Deutscher Werkbund, had on German culture from its founding in 1907 until Hitler came to power in 1933. However, Hungary's participation in the major world's fairs of the 1930s, for example the Milan Triennale in 1933 and the Paris World's Fair in 1937, evoked positive commentaries by historians and critics of the period.

The industrial sector

Even though the Hungarian economy performed poorly during the interwar years, a modest culture of invention had formed during the years of the Dual Monarchy and enabled the development of a few strong companies, particularly in the fields of telecommunications and transportation. The 1920s saw a constantly rising demand for radio sets whose numbers increased from 17,000 in 1925 to 420,000 by 1938. The Orion Electric Company, a leading manufacturer of radios, was established in 1913 as the Wolfram Lamp Factory before it changed its name in 1923. Following the name change, József Bottlik (1897–1984), an artist who had turned to commercial art, designed a logo for Orion consisting of the company name, a jagged line that looked like radio waves, and three heads of speaking figures. Bottlik was conscious of the company's need to have a dignified visual identity and worked on its image throughout his career. The designs for the radio cabinets were conservative, changing little from year to year except for the size of the models and the location of the speakers and dials. Essentially, they were polished wooden boxes with mesh fabric to cover the speakers. The larger ones were free-standing furniture pieces that combined phonographs with the radios. As a local company, Orion faced stiff competition from the Dutch conglomerate Philips, which manufactured many other products besides radios. Philips's chief designer in Hungary was Dezsö Bozzay (1912–1974), whose radio housings of polished wood had a clean simplified appearance, exemplified by the Europa Star of 1936.

In automobile design, Hungary produced no car like the Czech Skoda or Tatra that could reach a significant market. Instead, cars manufactured by the MAG company between 1911 and 1934 tended to be heavy and somewhat behind the latest developments. One of the MAG engineers, Jenő Fejes (1877–1952), left the firm in 1917 to start his own enterprise, the Fejes Plate Engine Manufacturing Company. His intention was to manufacture cars with a new steel plate engine that he invented and to build up the entire car with pressed and welded iron sheets. Costs for production were well below other cars in the domestic market and the design of the car body was decent. But the company was undercapitalized and had to cease operations in 1931.

Hungary was more successful in the design of railroad engines, building on the exemplary achievements of Ganz & Company since the late 19th century. Kálmán Kandó (1869–1931) rejoined the staff of the Ganz factory in 1917 after some years working in Italy. His aim was to construct a second generation of electric railways that would enable the alternating current produced in Hungary to provide the power for the nation's railroads. In 1929, MÁV, the Hungarian National Railway, electrified one of its main lines for which Kandó designed two new electric locomotives, one for fast trains and one for slow. Their plain box shapes, which differed from the more traditional forms of the steam locomotives, were also designed by Kandó, who was equally at home with the engineering and the aesthetic aspects of his machines.

MAV worked as well on a streamlined steam locomotive, MÁV No. 242. In the early 1930s, it was one of many being designed in various countries. Put into service in 1936, it had an attractive somewhat swept-back form, although compared with the bullet-nosed shapes of its American counterparts by Henry Dreyfuss and Raymond Loewy, its design was on the conservative side. However, it was strong on the engineering, achieving a speed of more than 100 miles per hour.

One of MAV's most distinctive designs of the 1930s was the Árpád lightweight engine of 1934. Known as a railcar, it carried about 70 passengers and generally ran alone, although it could haul additional carriages if necessary. It was built by Ganz & Company, which had already produced several similar railcars for other lines. The Árpád had a light steel structure and was designed for about 70 passengers. It was created for maximum comfort and offered a smooth ride even at high speeds. Ferenc Zámor (1877–1960), a mechanical engineer, and his internal team designed the engine with consultation by the artist and interior designer Ferenc Szablya-Frischauf (1867–1962). The Árpád was a perfect combination of technical efficiency and quality design. Its external form was clean and balanced, while its interior was spacious and tasteful. After the international success of the Árpád, Ganz & Company manufactured a series of longer railcars for several countries including Egypt and Argentina.

Graphic design: the avant-garde and commerce

In the years leading up to World War I, leftist intellectuals in Budapest were intently discussing ways to serve the masses with their art. Lajos Kassák (1887–1967), a writer and critic who was associated with the Activists, a group of socially conscious artists, had a radical vision of a new socialist society and in 1916 he founded a journal, *A Tett* (*The Deed*), to publish his own work as well as writing and art by others whose ideas he found sympathetic. The declarative covers were indicative of the journal's provocative contents and the government authorities soon shut it down after less than a year. Within weeks of its demise, Kassák started another journal, *Ma* (*Today*), which soon became the voice of the Hungarian avant-garde.

In the first issue of *Ma*, Kassák published an article entitled "The Poster and the New Painting,"

in which he aligned good posters with "a spirit of radicalism." He saw the poster as breaking through the sluggish masses or hostile currents, noting that "it [the poster] leaps on to the stage as an absolute force on its own." Kassák's fervent description of the poster as an active part of the social process certainly helped to encourage the vigorous lithographic placards that appeared in 1919 to support Béla Kun's Communist coup. So did the powerful political poster of Mihaly Biró (1886–1949), done for the Social Democratic Party in 1913, which showed a muscular nude man wielding a giant sledgehammer. Biró painted the figure in red on the front page of a Budapest newspaper, the *People's Voice*.

To support Kun's Republic of Councils, radical artists, many of them Expressionists, drew powerful images portraying the Communists as a strong and visionary cadre that was ready to smash the old Hungarian culture and build a new one. Béla Uitz's "Red Soldiers, Forward!" depicted several lines of men with shouldered rifles, earnestly marching, metaphorically, into the future (Fig. 25.21). Other posters were equally enthusiastic about a Communist victory in Hungary. Bertalan Pór's "Proletarians of the World, Unite!" was an expressive image of several stylized nude figures waving red flags, while Robert Berény depicted a revolutionary figure calling out "To arms! To arms," with an unfurled red banner in hand. Biró's nude figure with a sledgehammer was also revived with the newspaper background replaced simply by the date, "May 1, 1919," an official Soviet holiday that also commemorated the existence of the Hungarian Communist regime.

The plethora of posters that supported the Kun government was the last hurrah of the Hungarian left, as most went into exile shortly after the Kun regime collapsed. Kassák, with a group of artists and writers in the *Ma* circle, went to Vienna, where Kassák continued to publish the journal, whose covers he mainly designed himself. Though not trained as an artist, he also began to make Constructivist

Fig. 25.21: Béla Uitz, Red Soldiers, Forward!, poster, 1919. Hungarian National Gallery. Photo: Zsuzsa Berényi © DACS 2017.

art consisting of geometric lines and shapes and he brought this new Constructivist look to *Ma*'s covers as well as the covers of several books he designed for *Ma* and for Viennese publishers. One example of a book that *Ma* published was *Total Stage*, written by János Mácza, an experimental playwright and theorist of avant-garde set design (Fig. 25.22). In his shift from Expressionist graphics to Constructivist form, Kassák was surely aware of van Doesburg's redesigned covers for *De Stijl* whose look some issues of *Ma* resembled. In 1921, Kassák published in *Ma* his theory of *Bildarchitektur* (Picture Architecture), in which he enunciated a philosophical basis for the geometric forms he was currently using and would continue to use in his art. *Bildarchitektur* also gave Kassák a theoretical basis for Constructivist graphic design. In 1926, he stopped publishing *Ma* and returned to Budapest, where he started yet another publication, a social and political journal, *Dokumentum*, which was soon suppressed by the Horthy regime. Realizing that

the political climate in Hungary was not hospitable to his idealistic social visions, Kassák turned towards more local topics, which he addressed in a new journal, *Munka* (*Work*). The cover designs for both *Dokumentum* and *Munka* represented Kassák's own version of Functionalism, which seems to have evolved from his Constructivist origins. The typography was san serif, sections of text were separated by colored rules, and Kassák was more inclined, as in his designs for *Munka*'s covers and for a series of his own books, to adopt standardized formats.

In the late 1920s, Kassák did more practical work, designing Functionalist book covers for several Budapest publishers, as well as creating covers for *Magyar Grafika*, a magazine of printing and graphic design, where he also published an important article, "Towards an Elemental Typography," in 1928. He was one of the very few Hungarian designers to incorporate photographs into his book and periodical covers or posters, sometimes using cropped images but also

Fig. 25.22: Lajos Kássak, *Total Stage*, cover, c. 1924. Collection Merrill C. Berman. Photo: Jim Frank and Joelle Jensen.

occasionally using fragments as in his poster for a Budapest movie theater.

Kassák's Constructivist/Functionalist graphic design differed somewhat from the approach of Sándor Bortnyik and Robert Berény (1887–1953), both fellow political activists before they went into exile. When they returned to Hungary from Germany, they began to work as commercial artists, concentrating on posters, although they did other things as well. The two had a close relationship with Modiano, a company based in Italy whose Hungarian branch specialized in cigarette papers. Modiano courted poster artists through a series of competitions, and as a result a number of Hungrian artists including, besides Bortnyik and Berény, Mihály

Biró, István Irsai (1896–1967), who would later work in Palestine under the name Pesach Irsai, and Imre Lányi (dates unconfirmed) created posters for the firm. These particular designers as well as some others worked in the modern poster style of Cassandre in France or the *sachplakat* designers in Germany. Most of the Modiano posters featured a single image on a flat background with only the name of the company as a text. Bortnyik adopted Herbert Bayer's Universal alphabet, the letters of which he most likely drew by hand. Berény experimented with flat shapes, which produced a tension in one poster between an abstract composition and the image of a stylish figure smoking a cigarette. Posters in the modern style tended to advertise consumer products such as cigarettes, champagne, clothing, newspapers, or household goods. By contrast, official posters for the Hungarian tourist office by artists including György Konecsni (1908–1970) depicted men and women in folk costumes, their airbrushed forms appearing similar to the representations of idealized figures in the posters of other authoritarian regimes.

Compared to even the few examples of modern design by Hungarian poster artists or the rare Constructivist book covers by Lajos Kassák, Hungarian publishers remained wedded to traditional book formats. The most interesting of them, however, was Imre Kner (1890–1944), whose Kner Printing House was responsible for the revival of Hungarian printing. Working initially with only limited typefaces since no modern Hungarian typefaces were designed before World War II, Kner joined together with the architect and designer Lajos Kozma, who created an extensive series of borders, vignettes, ornaments, and initials that he derived from historic sources, particularly the Baroque. For Kozma, reflecting in the early 1920s, the Baroque was the last good period for decoration and ornament and it represented for him the first style with a Hungarian character. As in his furniture and some of his architecture of the early 1920s, Kozma returned to Baroque and folk art sources to create the printing devices he drew for

Kner. The two represented their typographic views in several small volumes, which one critic dubbed the "Three Tiny Books." These featured Hungarian folk tales and stories that were printed with ornaments and hand-colored woodcut illustrations by Kozma. The collaboration of Kner and Kozma was strongest in the early 1920s, when Kner published several series of well-known Hungarian texts and classics of world literature, all with woodcut initials, devices, and illustrations based on Kozma's drawings. In the late 1920s, the Bodoni typeface became available in Hungary and Kner changed his design philosophy to accommodate its modern, though still classical, characteristics. Given his influence among book publishers, a number of others followed suit.

Yugoslavia

Following World War I, the Paris Peace Conference that the victorious nations organized in 1919 divided up the Balkans to create a new Kingdom of Serbs, Croats, and Slovenes. It was intended to unite a more heterogeneous group of territories than existed anywhere else in Central Europe. During the interwar years, the diversity of this new nation was sustained only with enormous effort. The initial constitution established a highly centralized state in which an elected assembly and a Serbian king jointly held legislative power. After a decade of struggle, King Alexander I discontinued the parliament and declared a royal dictatorship. At the time he also changed the name of the country to the Kingdom of Yugoslavia. Though he promised to unite the population, he failed to do so, nor did he do much to improve the weak economy. In 1934, a group of Croatian nationalists assassinated him, and Milan Stojadinović, a former finance minister, became the new premier. Stojadinović replaced many of the king's accomplices, loosened the censorship laws, and began to address the country's economic problems. He remained in office until 1939, when the Prince Regent replaced him partly because he was unable to negotiate successfully with the Croatians and partly because he

sought to create his own group of followers, following Mussolini's tactics by calling them Green Shirts instead of the Duce's Black Shirts.

Although Yugoslavia was endowed with natural resources, the territories it contained had little industry when they were first united nor did they develop much more in the interwar years. There were a few textile factories but the country's economic policy was based primarily on trading raw materials for finished goods, first with Italy and then after 1935 with Germany, which became its main trading partner. This relationship was disrupted in 1941 when Germany invaded Yugoslavia.

Commercial and applied arts before 1919

Among the peoples who were joined together as the Kingdom of Serbs, Croats, and Slovenes, the Croats and Slovenes had a particularly strong relation with Western Europe. Both had been subject to the Dual Monarchy of Austria-Hungary, with Slovenia being controlled by the Austrians, and Croatia ruled by the Hungarians. Zagreb was the cultural capital of Croatia, while Ljubljana and Belgrade were the cultural centers in Slovenia and Serbia respectively.

At the beginning of the 20th century, Zagreb was an important center for the decorative arts. A Museum of Arts and Crafts, founded to defend the crafts against the incursion of industrialization, opened in 1879. It was designed by the architect Herman Bollé (1845–1926), who also founded Croatia's first school of applied arts, the Royal County Craft School, in 1882. As an architect, Bollé designed a number of important churches in Zagreb as well as the important Mirogoj Cemetery, but he also believed strongly in the applied arts and fostered Croatia's involvement in many exhibitions leading up to the 1900 Exposition Universelle in Paris. Serbia too fostered participation in international fairs. Following its participation in the same Paris exhibition, its pavilion for the 1911 Turin exhibition was designed in a Byzantine style

Fig. 25.23: Jadviga Matkovska, Penkala-Moster Company, poster, c. 1907. Getty Images.

mechanical pencil tucked behind it, was devised by the inventor himself and drawn by an artist, Penkala's sister-in-law Jadviga Matkovska (dates unconfirmed) (Fig. 25.23). The trademark was subsequently redesigned and used widely in the company's advertising and promotional products.

By the end of the 19th century, printing houses in Zagreb, Belgrade, and Ljubljana were equipped with presses for color lithography. Most posters for industry were anonymous, while those by known artists primarily advertised cultural events. Similar to other parts of Eastern Europe, Art Nouveau and the Vienna Secession were strong influences. Examples are a poster for the Zagreb literary magazine *Mladost* (*Youth*) of 1898 by the artist Bela Čikoš-Sesia (1864–1931) that features an ethereal young woman with a heavy outline around her hair reminiscent of Mucha's or Privat-Livemont's style, and another of 1915 by Tomislav Krizman (1882–1955) for a concert that owes more to the Vienna Secession with its strong lettering and a dominant symbolic figure (Plate 30). Other artists who designed posters during this period included the Croatian painter Menci Klement Crnčić (1865–1930), who was also a book illustrator and a caricaturist; Ljubo Babić (1890–1974), who, besides painting, illustrated books and designed theater sets; and the sculptor Ivan Meštrović (1883–1962).

Tradition and modernism in crafts and design

The forging of the different territories into a new nation did not, however, result in a singular Yugoslav culture. Instead, prior national traditions continued to prevail although the central government in Belgrade did attempt to meld aspects of them together for international purposes. This was evident in the ambitious Yugoslav participation at the 1925 Exposition Internationale des Arts Décoratifs in Paris. The director of the exhibition team was Tomislav Krizman, the Zagreb artist, who was closely associated with the Vienna Secession. Consequently the pavilion, designed

with furniture that recalled the craftwork of Russian peasants.

Though Croatia did not have a strong industrial culture, Zagreb was nonetheless home to Eduard Penkala (1871–1922), who invented the first mechanical pencil in 1906 and the first solid ink fountain pen the following year. He and an associate quickly formed the Penkala-Moster Company and set up a factory to manufacture the "automatic pencils" and then the pens. The company's unusual trademark, a caricature of Penkala with a pointed nose and big ear that had a by Stjepn Hribar (1889–1965), subordinated the inevitable folk ornamentation to a more classical structure. The furniture, designed by Srečko Sabljak (1892–1938), a professor at the Craft School in Zagreb, referenced refined Secessionist models rather than more rustic folk or peasant designs. The range of objects on display was quite broad, extending from books and pottery to glass, furniture, and textiles. Most of the exhibitors were Croatian, due in large part to the long tradition of applied arts at the Zagreb Craft School. There were, however, also urban plans for Belgrade that were formed by several Serbian architects.

Surprisingly, the Slovenian architect Jože Plečnik was barely represented in the Yugoslav exhibit, perhaps because he was heavily involved in the restoration of the Prague Castle at the time. In later years, however, Plečnik worked extensively in Slovenia. Though he designed several substantial buildings in the capitol, Ljubljana, along with their interiors, the university library, completed between 1936 and 1941, was his major achievement. For the reading room, Plečnik created an elaborate metal chandelier, which displayed his encyclopedic knowledge of ancient craft styles and materials. The chandelier complemented the wooden chairs and long desks that rested on marble bases. Plečnik's attention to detail was evident as well in his furniture for a private villa in Ljubljana owned by the Prelovšek family, where he synthesized Egyptian and Greek models for a set of elegant living room chairs that were covered in black lacquer. He also designed more austere models for the dining room and library.

Besides his designs for interiors, Plečnik was interested in all the details of Ljubljana's cityscape and undertook numerous commissions for urban artifacts. His street lamps perched on classical concrete columns are of several varieties as are the kiosks he designed for the city's Three Bridges. Plečnik occupied a unique position among architects and designers of interiors in Central Europe. He was neither a modernist nor a conventional traditionalist. Following the thinking of his mentor, Gottfried Semper, he drew extensively on historical sources and a vast knowledge of materials, while carefully considering the adaptation of both to modern environments.

Plečnik's immersion in history can be contrasted with the emerging modern architectural movement in Yugoslavia, which was comparable to that in other Eastern European countries. By 1928, such a movement had begun in Serbia and one of its members, Dragiša Brašovan (1887–1965), was chosen to design Yugoslavia's pavilion for the 1929 World's Fair in Barcelona. His mildly decorative modernist structure was initially awarded the first prize for a pavilion design, but the prize was subsequently withdrawn and given instead to Mies van der Rohe. In Ljubljana, the architect Ivo Spinčič (1903–1985), after returning in 1925 from Vienna where he had studied with Peter Behrens, became a proponent of Functionalism, which he exemplified in several domestic dwellings as well as in the plain geometric furniture and unornamented table lamps he designed in the early 1930s.

Except for projects of the avant-garde, Functionalism was little evident in Yugoslavia's commercial graphics. Instead, illustrators and poster designers looked to the work of designers abroad, which they would have known through magazines like *Gebrauchsgraphik* and the *Gazette du Bon Ton*. The first publicity agencies appeared in Ljubljana in 1926, Zagreb in 1928, and in Belgrade around the same time.

Otto Antonini (1892–1959) was a commercial artist in Zagreb, best known as the editor and cover designer for *Svijet* (*World*), a lively magazine that he inaugurated in 1926 to chronicle the lifestyles of the city's wealthy class. *Svijet* followed in some ways the direction of the French *Vogue*, although it dealt with far more than fashion. On the covers that Antonini drew weekly for seven years, he depicted images of modernity that were embodied in his elegant drawings of upper-class men and women engaged in leisure activities. Antonini, who had trained as a fresco painter in Siena, was a versatile illustrator whose style could range from caricature to serious portraits. His covers for *Svijet* changed regularly, providing ample evidence of his versatility. Besides the covers, Antonini laid out each issue, choosing the typography and determining the relation of the text to the pictures.

One of the illustrators for *Svijet* in the 1930s was Pavao Gavranić (1905–1973) who, with Sergije Glumac (1903–1964), was a leading poster designer in Zagreb. A former student of Ljubo Babić at the Zagreb Art Academy, Gavranić also contributed illustrations to newspapers and magazines. As a poster designer, his style ranged from romantic realism to caricature. He could choose an unusual angle to make a figure in a product advertisement more interesting or he could fill the landscape on a travel poster with a dramatic burst of light. Other posters of his featured caricature figures that functioned similarly to trademarks. Gavranić worked on posters for many companies in the 1930s as well as for trade shows, cultural festivals, and other public events. Though he continued to paint, he can be considered one of Croatia's first professional graphic designers.

The first graphic design studio was probably Atelier TRI (Atelier Three), which was active between 1929 and 1941. Its members were Vladimir (dates unconfirmed) and Zvonimir Mirosavljević (dates unconfirmed) along with Božidar Kocmut (1899–1977). They differed from Gavranić in their quest for a less painterly and more designerly approach to posters, as was evident in Kocmut's poster for the 14th Zagreb Fair, which depicted two initials extending from twin skyscrapers that were sketchily depicted in a commercial Cubist style.

The study of modern advertising in Croatia received an impetus in the early 1930s when the philosopher and writer Miroslav Feller (1901–1961) founded Imago, an institute for the scientific analysis of advertising. Participants in the institute's activities, which included the brief publication of a magazine called *Reklama* (*Advertising*), included Sergije Glumac, the members of Atelier TRI, and the painter and graphic artist Anka Krizmanić (1896–1987). In Belgrade, the Serbian artist Dušan Janković (dates unconfirmed) did the occasional poster for a Surrealist performance in the early 1920s and later worked for commercial clients, designing posters in the Serbian language with Cyrillic characters in order to address a local audience.

The avant-garde and its publications

The huge success of Otto Antonini's weekly magazine *Svijet* throughout Croatia was a clear indication that the population was more interested in the dream of a glamorous lifestyle than in the radical vision of a new society. Zagreb was thus not fertile ground for the growth of an avant-garde movement, although the poet Ljubomir Micić (1895–1971) sought to establish one there. In 1921, he formed a group called Zenit (Zenith), consisting of artists, poets, and critics. Central to Zenit's activities was the publication of a journal by the same name. It began to appear more or less monthly in early 1921 and ceased publication in 1924 after more than 40 issues, when it was shut down by government authorities in Belgrade.

Like the Hungarian Lajos Kassák, Micić called for a revolution that would be political and social as well as cultural. Though he published writers from avant-garde movements throughout Europe, he was a staunch nationalist. Initially, the look of his journal was influenced by the gestural and emotional layouts of Expressionist publications, but after a trip to Germany in 1922 he adopted a Constructivist approach to design, while also interjecting Dada and Futurist elements. In 1922, El Lissitzky designed the cover for a special issue of *Zenit* on Russian avant-garde art that he edited together with Ilya Ehrenburg.

As a poet, Micić shared with his predecessors Apollinaire, Marinetti, and van Doesburg an understanding that the purpose of altering a text typographically was to create new poetic meaning and not simply to produce modern layouts. In this sense, he espoused Lissitzky's dictum that the new book demanded a new form or reading. Like Karel Teige in Prague or Władysław Strzemiński in Łódź, Micić commissioned and published books in addition to editing his journal. He designed the books and their covers as well. The first one was a polemical *Manifesto of Zenitism*, which was followed by several others with his own texts including *Kola za spasavanje* (*Emergency Vehicle*) of 1922 and *Aeroplan bez motora* (*Airplane without an Engine*) of 1925.

Zenit was the first and most important of Yugoslavia's interwar avant-garde journals. Dragan Aleksić (1901–1958) initially published a number of Dada texts in *Zenit*, but after a falling out with Micić he brought out his own journal, *Dada Tank*, with typography that followed the conventions of Dada elsewhere. Because of Aleksić's strong language, the state censors intervened, which led to a second edition

of his journal, *Dada Jazz*, which had equally strong typography but eliminated the obscene words and phrases. *Dada Jazz* prompted Branko Ve Poljanski, Micić's brother, to attack Aleksić's interpretation of Dada in yet another magazine, *Dada-Jok*, which he laid out similarly to other Dada publications of the time.

Zenit was also the stimulus for an additional journal, *Tank,* which originated in 1927 with a group of Slovenian Constructivist artists who were living in Trieste, an Italian city that borders on Slovenia. The central figure of the group was August Černigoj (1898–1985), who had studied briefly at the Bauhaus. He was interested in education as well as art and attempted unsuccessfully to open a school in Trieste based on Bauhaus ideas. Like *Zenit*, *Tank* solicited work from many foreign contributors and based its design on Constructivist principles (Fig. 25.24). The *Tank* manifesto in the first issue featured words in different type sizes, important words in bold letters, and a typographic arrangement that separated key words in order to emphasize their importance in the text. Černigoj also produced a linocut for the second issue in order to energize words and word fragments by joining them with black and white formal elements in a dynamic composition. *Tank* did not call for a political revolution. Instead, it challenged the prevailing conservative artistic culture in Slovenia with fiery rhetoric and a strong graphic format. Historian Steven Mansbach notes that *Tank* helped to identify Ljubljana as a center of the European avant-garde during a brief period, but its strong language must have made the Slovenian authorities nervous and they suppressed a third issue after two had already been published.

Given the rapid crackdown on *Tank* in Ljubljana, it is worth noting that a more blatantly political magazine, *Nova Literatura* (*New Literature*), was able to begin publication in Belgrade the following year. Twelve issues appeared and it ceased publication in 1930. *Nova Literatura* was published by the Nolit publishing house, which Pavle Bihalji (1898–1941) and his brother Oto had founded. Nolit (a condensation

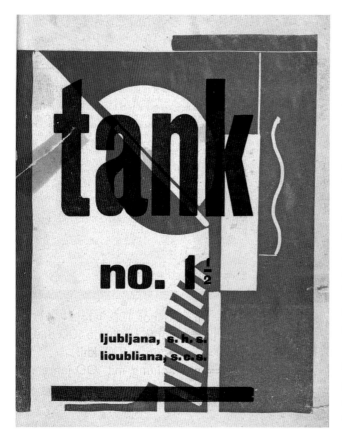

Fig. 25.24: August Černigoj, *Tank,* cover, 1927. Slavic and Baltic Division, The New York Public Library, Astor, Lenox and Tilden Foundations.

of *Nova Literatura*) also published left-wing books by local and foreign authors. Articles in *Nova Literatura* were in the Serbian language though they were written mainly by leftist authors abroad—Bertolt Brecht, Kurt Tucholsky, and Anna Seghers in Germany; Maxim Gorky in the Soviet Union; and Upton Sinclair in the United States. Illustrations were by foreign artists like Pablo Picasso, George Grosz, and Otto Dix and local artists as well.

What distinguished *Nova Literatura* graphically from other socially oriented publications, however, were the photomontages of Pavle Bihalji, which were strongly influenced by the work of John Heartfield. Unlike Czechoslovakia and Poland, photomontage was

Fig. 25.25: *Contimporanul*, cover, 1924. Biblioteca Academiei Romane.

little known in Yugoslavia, and Bihalji's were among the few examples to be seen in the country. Bihalji also created photomontage covers for books published by Nolit, following the example of the covers that Heartfield designed for the Malik Verlag in Berlin. The Minerva publishing house in Zagreb followed suit by commissioning Franjo Bruck (dates unconfirmed) to create photomontage covers for a series of books by the prominent Croatian writer Miroslav Krleža.

Romania
The avant-garde

The situation for avant-garde Romanian poets and artists was similar to that in Yugoslavia. They lived in a conservative culture and tried to change it by publishing new literature and exhibiting new art. A central figure in this movement was Marcel Janco, who was among the first to join the nascent Dada movement in Zurich when it began in 1916 (see Chapter 18). After several years in Western Europe, Janco returned to Romania in 1921. He was instrumental in founding the avant-garde journal *Contimporanul* in 1922 and remained involved with it as a writer and artist for the ten years of its existence. The covers varied in typographic format although they were not as brash or polemical as those of subsequent Romanian journals (Fig. 25.25).

Two years later, *Contimpuranul*'s claim to speak for the Romanian avant-garde was challenged by *75 HP* (a reference to a powerful automobile), a new journal created by a young poet, Ilarie Voronca (1903–1946), and his friend, the artist Victor Brauner (1903–1966). Brauner's polemical cover of the single issue consisted of large letters and numbers combined with abstract forms on the front and texts printed horizontally, vertically, and diagonally on the back (Fig. 25.26). The issue contained two manifestoes. The first by Voronca, which he called an Aviogram, had a layout that reflected many prior sources including the calligrams of Apollinaire and the words-in-liberty of Marinetti. The principle objective of the second, which was entitled "Pictopoetry" and was co-written with Brauner, was to

Fig. 25.26: Victor Brauner, *75 HP*, cover, 1924. Biblioteca Academiei Romane. © ADAGP, Paris and DACS, London 2017.

dissolve the difference between poetry and art through paintings that would integrate words into the compositions, a practice initiated by the Cubists and continued by other avant-garde artists.

Though there was only one issue of *75 HP*, its visual format was the strongest of the Romanian avant-garde journals though it was higher on polemics than on the sustained critical opinion that the other publications provided. Also appearing in 1924, *Punkt* (*Period*) was a weekly review, though it too lasted for only a brief period. After an experimental beginning, the format became more like a newspaper, with the visual polemics embodied in a bold masthead featuring the title and issue number. Around the same time that *Punkt* was founded, yet another journal, *Integral*, was established. Among its editors were Voronca and the painter Max

Herman Maxy (1895–1971), who did the linocut covers for the 15 issues in a strong Constructivist format that recalled the declarative design of Rodchenko's *Lef* covers in Moscow. *Integral* was open to ideas from all avant-garde movements, but that weakened its influence since it never developed a strong enough position of its own. Maxy was additionally involved with an Academy of Decorative Art that was founded in Bucharest in 1924 to further the spirit of the Bauhaus and he designed some furniture and lighting that was exhibited abroad around 1931.

In the end, as historian Steven Mansbach has noted, the Romanian avant-garde made little impact on the wider society since it concentrated much of its energy on internal debates about artistic matters. Although there was a school of applied art in Bucharest, it was not central either to the avant-garde, the government, or representatives of the country's small manufacturing sector. Hence it did not achieve either the national or international notoriety that might otherwise have been possible.

Estonia and Latvia

During the 1920s and 1930s, Estonia and Latvia were preoccupied with establishing their identities as modern nations, having declared their independence from Russia. Neither could boast of a strong industrial base, although there were a few enterprises with deep roots in the Baltic lands. Latvian attempts to produce furniture or household goods were modest. In 1924, three artists—Romans Suta (1896–1944), his wife, Aleksandra Belcova (1892–1981), and Sigismunds Vidbergs (1890–1970)—formed Baltars, a porcelain workshop to manufacture and sell modern ceramic objects for daily use. Inspired partly by the Soviet tea sets and plates with avant-garde Suprematist designs and partly by native folk culture, they and other artists made designs for plates that initially represented folkloric themes in a modernist idiom but became increasingly decorative by 1928 when the factory had to close due to financial difficulties.

One of the Baltic states' strongest enterprises was in Estonia, where the A. M. Luther Company for Mechanical Woodworking was founded in 1877 and first began producing furniture in 1883. The company had its initial success with plywood seats and by the end of the 19th century had developed a diversified line of products that ranged from domestic furniture made of curved plywood to folding armchairs and office furniture that followed American precedents. A separate factory produced plywood hatboxes and suitcases.

In 1897, the Luther company, which marketed its furniture and plywood sheets under the name Luterma, formed a sister firm, the Venesta Plywood Company, to sell its plywood sheets in Great Britain. By the 1930s, Venesta would be involved as a partner in the design and production of Britain's most modern furniture.

Following independence, Luterma collaborated with prominent Estonian architects on important government commissions such as the new parliament building in Tallin, Estonia's capital city. One of the two architects, H. Johanson (dates unconfirmed) designed several different chairs with traditional folk

Fig. 25.28: Peet Aren, Koit, poster, n.d. Art Musem of Estonia.

references for the parliament's assembly hall and Luterma produced them in multiple exemplars.

The company's primary focus, however, was on mass-produced furniture for the domestic home market. A group of designers was hired to supervise the design and development of new products in the Furniture Department. One focus was on furniture that would cater to the needs of the expanding working class who were moving into the newly constructed modest-sized apartments and houses in Tallin, but Luterma also produced for the middle-class market as well (Fig. 25.27). The company embraced the concept of standardized types, as Hermann Muthesius had espoused at the 1914 Werkbund exhibition in Cologne, rather than create idiosyncratic decorative designs. In the mid-1930s, Luterma participated in an initiative of the Ministry of Economics called "Furniture for Everyone" to manufacture flexible modern designs

Fig. 25.27: Luterma, bistro chairs, c. 1900. Kolonn.

with interchangeable standardized units that could be arranged in multiple combination.

One of the leading Estonian graphic artists during this period was Peet Aren (1889–1970), a modern painter and woodcut artist who also created commercial art in many forms from menus to advertising posters. His colorful illustrations recalled work by late 19th-century artists such as Maxfield Parrish. He also specialized in lettering in several different styles that sometimes accompanied his drawings but was also featured in its own right (Fig. 25.28).

Bibliography
Bibliographic essay

There is no general history of design in Central and Eastern Europe during this period, although some information can be found in general histories of art such as Timothy O. Benson, ed., *Central European Avant-Gardes: Exchange and Transformation, 1910–1930*; Dubravka Djurić and Miško Šuvaković, eds., *Impossible Histories: Historical Avant-gardes, Neo-Avant-gardes, and Post-Avant-gardes in Yugoslavia, 1918–1991*; and S. A. Mansbach, *Modern Art in Eastern Europe: From the Baltic to the Balkans, ca. 1890–1939*. Mansbach also edited a special issue of the *Art Journal* on the avant-gardes of Eastern Europe. See *Art Journal* 49, no. 1 (Spring 1990). David Crowley published an essay on "Art Deco in Central Europe," and Reino Liefkes on "Germany, Austria and the Netherlands," in Charlotte Benton, Tim Benton, and Ghislaine Wood, eds., *Art Deco 1910–1939* and there is additional material on the topic in the catalog *L'Art Deco en Europe*. Czech modernism and the Czech avant-garde are covered extensively in a number of books and exhibition catalogs: Jaroslav Anděl, *The New Vision for the New Czech Architecture, 1918–1938*; *El Arte de la Vanguardia en Checoslovaquia, 1918–1938/The Art of the Avant-Garde in Czechoslovakia, 1918–1938*, the catalog of an exhibition at the IVAM in Valencia, Spain; *Czech Functionalism, 1918–1938*; *Czech Modernism 1900–1945*; *Czech Photographic Avant-garde, 1918–1948*;

Prague 1891–1941: Architecture and Design; and *Prague, 1900–1938: Capitale secrète des avant-gardes*.

Books and catalogs on specific Czech movements are Alexander von Vegesack, ed., *Czech Cubism: Architecture, Furniture, and Decorative Arts 1910–1925* and Jiri Svestka and Tomás Vlcek, *1901–1925 Kubismus in Prag: Malerei Skulptur Kunstgewerbe Architektur*; *Devětsil: Ceska Vytvarna Avantgarda*, the catalog of an exhibition in Prague; *Devětsil: Czech Avant-Garde Art, Architecture, and Design of the 1920s and 1930s*, the catalog of another exhibit in Oxford; and *Art Deco Boemia, 1918–1938. Das Bauhaus im Osten; Slowakische und Tschechische Avantgarde 1928–1939*, edited by Susanne Anna, contains a group of essays that discuss the Czech version of the Bauhaus in Bratislava. Iva Mojzisová provides additional material on the school in her article, "Avant-garde Repercussions and the School of Applied Arts in Bratislava, 1928–1939," *Journal of Design History* 5, no. 4 (1992). On Czech book design see *The Czech Avant-Garde and Czech Book Design: The 1920s and 1930s*, the special 1984 supplement to the journal *Afterimage*; *The Czech Avant-Garde and the Book, 1900–1945*; the special issue on Czechoslovakia in *Fine Print: The Review for the Arts of the Book* 13, no. 1 (January 1987); and Esther Levinger's article, "Czech Avant-Garde Art: Poetry for the Five Senses," *Art Bulletin* 81, no. 3 (September 1999). Books and catalogs dedicated to individual architects, designers or photographers include Vladimir Birgus and Jan Mlčoch, eds., *Jaroslav Rössler: Czech Avant-Garde Photographer*; Eric Dluhosch and Rostislav Svácha, *Karel Teige 1900–1951: L'Enfant Terrible of the Czech Modernist Avant-Garde*; *Jan Kotěra, 1871–1923: The Founder of Modern Czech Architecture*; *Ladislav Sutnar: Prague – New York – Design in Action*; and Jiři Mucha, *Alphonse Maria Mucha; His Life and Art*.

David Crowley's *National Style and Nation-State: Design in Poland from the Vernacular Revival to the International Style* is the essential text in English for the story of design in Poland from the turn of the century to the 1930s. Further material on

Polish design can be found in the extensive volume *Rzecy Pospolite, Polskie Wyroby, 1899–1999/Common Wealth, Polish Products, 1899–1999*; Czesława Frejlich, ed., *Out of the Ordinary: Polish Designers of the 20th Century*; and in the comprehensive study of the Cracow Workshops, Maria Dziedzec, ed., *Warsztaty Krakowskie, 1913–1926/The Krakow Workshops, 1913–1926*. Hilary Gresty's and Jeremy Lewison's catalog *Constructivism in Poland, 1923–1936* provides thorough documentation of that wing of the Polish avant-garde. See also Esther Levinger, "Return to Figuration: Władislaw Strzeminski and the Move from Idealism," *Art History* 24, no. 1 (February 2001). The extensive literature on Polish posters includes Szymon Bojko, *Polska Sztuka Plakatu*; *Das Polnische Plakat von 1892 bis Heute aus dem Sammlungen des Plakatmuseums Wilanów*; *Polski Plakat Filmowy: 100-Lecie Kina w Polsce 1896–1996/Polish Film Poster: 100th Anniversary of the Film Poster in Poland 1896–1996*; and *Polski Plakat Teatralny 1899–1999/Polish Theater Poster 1899–1999*.

Design in Austria with the exception of the Wiener Werkstätte is not well documented. Jane Kallir, *Viennese Design and the Wiener Werkstätte* provides good coverage of the Werkstätte after the initial period as does Peter Noever, ed., *Dagobert Peche and the Wiener Werkstätte*. Helmut Gruber's *Red Vienna: Experiment in Working-Class Culture, 1919–1934* by contrast addresses the large-scale construction of low-cost housing, while Christopher Long's excellent monograph *Josef Frank: Life and Work* provides helpful background material on Frank's design milieu besides discussing his own work. Nader Vossoughian's *Otto Neurath: The Language of the Global Polis* is a detailed biography of the Austrian founder of the ISOTYPE movement.

Gyula Ernyey, *Made in Hungary: The Best of 150 Years in Industrial Design* is an authoritative source of information on Hungarian industrial design. Juliet Kinchin discusses Hungarian furniture in "Modernity and Tradition in Hungarian Furniture, 1900–1938; Three Generations," *The Journal of Decorative and Propaganda Arts* 24 (2002). There is considerably more material, however, on the Hungarian avant-garde. See *Lajos Kassák y la Vanguardia Húngara*; S. A. Mansbach, *Standing in the Tempest: Painters of the Hungarian Avant-Garde 1908–1930*; and the Hayward Gallery catalog, *The Hungarian Avant-Garde, The Eight, and The Activists*. Rudolf Tőkés provides background to the avant-garde's early difficulties in Hungary in *Béla Kun and the Hungarian Soviet Republic: The Origins and Role of the Communist Party of Hungary in the Revolutions of 1918–1919*. Éva Bajkay-Rosch writes about "Hungarians at the Bauhaus," in the volume of conference papers, *ICSAC Cahier 6/7*, 1987, while John Halas' "Encounter with Moholy-Nagy," *STA Journal* 1, no. 3 (Summer 1980), describes his own activity at Alexander Bortnyik's design school, the Mühely. On Hungarian posters, see Tibor Szántó, *A Magyar Plakát*, while György Haiman's article "Imre Kner and the Revival of Hungarian Printing," *Design Issues* 7, no. 2 (Spring 1991) provides helpful material in English on this important Hungarian printer and publisher.

On other countries in the region, see Damjan Prelovšek's authoritative biography, *Jože Plečnik: 1872–1957*; Tom Sandqvist's study of Hungarian Dada, *Dada East: The Romanians of Cabaret Voltaire*; the special Yugoslav theme issue of *The Journal of Decorative and Propaganda Arts* 17 (Fall 1990); S. A. Mansbach with Wojciech Jan Siemaszkiewicz, *Graphic Modernism From the Baltic to the Balkans 1910-1935*; and Zelimir Koscevic's earlier article "The Poster in Yugoslavia," *The Journal of Decorative and Propaganda Arts* 10 (Fall 1988). Jüri Kermik, *Lutheri Vabrik: Vineer ja Möbel, 1877–1940/The Luther Factory: Plywood and Furniture, 1877–1940* is a detailed study of the Luther Furniture Factory in Estonian and English, while Leonhard Lapin's *Eesti XX Sajandi Ruum /Space in 20th Century* also deals with furniture design as well as related topics.

Books

General

L'Art Deco en Europe. Bruxelles: Societé des Expositions du Palais des Beaux-Arts, 1989.

Benson, Timothy O., ed. *Central European Avant-Gardes: Exchange and Transformation, 1910–1930.* Cambridge, MA, and London: MIT Press, 2002.

Djurić, Dubravka and Miško Šuvaković, eds. *Impossible Histories: Historical Avant-gardes, Neo-Avant-gardes, and Post-Avant-gardes in Yugoslavia, 1918–1991.* Cambridge, MA, and London: MIT Press, 2003.

Mansbach, S. A. with Wojciech Jan Siemaszkiewicz. *Modern Art in Eastern Europe: From the Baltic to the Balkans, ca. 1890–1939.* New York: Cambridge University Press, 1999.

—*Graphic Modernism From the Baltic to the Balkans 1910–1935.* With an essay by Robert H. Davis Jr. and Edward Kasinec. New York: The New York Public Library, 2007.

Rothschild, Joseph. *A History of East Central Europe.* Seattle and London, University of Washington Press, 1974.

Czechoslovakia

Anděl, Jaroslav. *The New Vision for the New Czech Architecture, 1918–1938.* Zurich: Scalo Verlag, 2006.

Anna, Susanne, ed. *Das Bauhaus im Osten; Slowakische und Tschechische Avantgarde 1928–1939.* Ostfildern-Ruit: Verlag Gerd Hatje, 1997.

Art Deco Boemia, 1918–1938. Milan: Electa, 1996.

El Arte de la Vanguardia en Checoslovaquia, 1918–1938/ The Art of the Avant-Garde in Czechoslovakia, 1918–1938. Valencia: IVAM Centre Julio Gonzalez, 1993.

Birgus, Vladimír and Jan Mlčoch, eds. *Jaroslav Rössler: Czech Avant-Garde Photographer.* Cambridge, MA, and London: MIT Press, 2004.

The Czech Avant-Garde and Czech Book Design: The 1920s and 1930s. Madison, NJ: Florham-Madison Campus Library, Fairleigh Dickinson University, n.d.

Czech Functionalism, 1918–1938. Foreword by Gustav Peichl. Introductory essay by Vladimir Slapeta. London: Architectural Association, 1987.

Czech Modernism 1900–1945. Boston, Toronto, and London: Bullfinch Press, 1989.

Czech Photographic Avant-garde, 1918–1948. Cambridge, MA, and London: MIT Press, 2002.

Devětsil: Česká Výtvarná avantgarda Dvacátých Let. Prague: Galerie hlavního města Prahy, 1986.

Devětsil: Czech Avant-Garde Art, Architecture, and Design of the 1920s and 1930s. Oxford: Museum of Modern Art, London: Design Museum, 1990.

Dluhosch, Eric and Rostislav Svácha. *Karel Teige 1900–1951: L'Enfant Terrible of the Czech Modernist Avant-Garde.* Cambridge, MA, and London: MIT Press, 1999.

Jan Kotěra, 1871–1923: The Founder of Modern Czech Architecture. Prague: Municipal House/Kant, 2001.

Kroutvor, Josef. *Poselství Ulice: z Dějin plakatu a promĕn doby.* Prague: Comet Publishers, 1991.

Ladislav Sutnar: Prague – New York – Design in Action. Prague, Museum of Decorative Arts and Argo Publishers, 2003.

Mamatey, Victor S. and Radomír Luža, eds. *A History of the Czechoslovak Republic, 1918–1948.* Princeton NJ: Princeton University Press, 1973.

Mucha, Jiři. *Alphonse Maria Mucha; His Life and Art.* London: Academy Editions, 1989.

Novák, Arne. *Czech Literature.* Translated from the Czech by Peter Kussi. Ann Arbor: Michigan Slavic Publications, 1976.

Prague 1891–1941: Architecture and Design. Edinburgh: City Art Centre, 1994.

Prague, 1900–1938: Capitale secrète des avant-gardes. Dijon: Musée des Beaux-Arts, 1997.

Sayer, Derek. *The Coasts of Bohemia: A Czech History.* Princeton NJ: Princeton University Press, 1998.

Stoletî Besignu. Praha: Umeleckorprumyslového Muzea v Prazw, 1984.

Svestka, Jiri and Tomás Vlcek. *1901–1925 Kubismus in Prag: Malerei Skulptur Kunstgewerbe Architektur.* Stuttgart: Verlag Gert Hatje, 1991.

von Vegesack, Alexander, ed. *Czech Cubism: Architecture, Furniture and Decorative Arts 1910–1925.* New York: Princeton Architectural Press/Vitra Design Museum, 1992.

Poland

Bojko, Szymon. *Polska Sztuka Plakatu*. Warszawa: Wydawnictwo Artystyczno Graficzne, 1971.

Crowley, David. *National Style and Nation-State: Design in Poland from the Vernacular Revival to the International Style*. Manchester and New York: Manchester University Press, 1992.

Dziedzec, Maria, ed. *Warsztaty Krakowskie, 1913–1926/ The Krakow Workshops, 1913–1926*. Krakow: Jan Matejko Academy of Fine Arts, 2009.

Frejlich, Czesława, ed. *Out of the Ordinary: Polish Designers of the 20th Century*. Warsaw: Adam Mickiewicz Institute, 2011.

Gresty, Hilary and Jeremy Lewison. *Constructivism in Poland, 1923–1936*. Cambridge: Kettle's Yard Gallery in association with Muzeum Sztuki, Lodz, c. 1984.

Das Polnische Plakat von 1892 bis Heute aus dem Sammlungen des Plakatmuseums Wilanów. Berlin: Hochschule der Künste, 1980.

Polski Plakat Filmowy: 100-Lecie Kina w Polsce 1896–1996/Polish Film Poster: 100th Anniversary of the Film Poster in Poland 1896–1996. Cracow: Galeria Plakatu, 1996.

Polski Plakat Teatralny 1899–1999/Polish Theater Poster 1899–1999. Cracow: Dydo Poster Collection, n.d.

Rzeczy Pospolite, Polskie Wyroby, 1899–1999/Common Wealth, Polish Products, 1899–1999. Warsaw: Bosz, n.d.

Austria

Gruber, Helmut. *Red Vienna: Experiment in Working-Class Culture, 1919–1934*. New York and Oxford: Oxford University Press, 1991.

Kallir, Jane. *Viennese Design and the Wiener Werkstätte*. Foreword by Carl E. Schorske. New York: Galerie St. Etienne/George Braziller, 1986.

Long, Christopher. *Josef Frank: Life and Work*. Chicago and London: University of Chicago Press, 2002.

Mendenhall, John. *Swiss and Austrian Trademarks 1920–1950*. San Francisco: Chronicle Books, 1997.

Noever, Peter, ed. *Dagobert Peche and the Wiener Werkstätte*. New Haven and London: Yale University Press, 1998.

Vossoughian, Nader. *Otto Neurath: The Language of the Global Polis*. Rotterdam: NAi Publishers, 2008.

Hungary

Ernyey, Gyula. *Made in Hungary: The Best of 150 Years in Industrial Design*. Budapest: Rubik Innovation Foundation, 1993.

The Hungarian Avant-Garde, The Eight, and The Activists. London: Hayward Gallery, 1980.

Lajos Kassák y la Vanguardia Húngara. Valencia: IVAM Center Julio Gonzalez, 1999.

Mansbach, S. A. *Standing in the Tempest: Painters of the Hungarian Avant-Garde 1908–1930*. Santa Barbara: Santa Barbara Museum of Art, Cambridge, MA, and London: MIT Press, 1990.

Szántó, Tibor. *A Magyar Plakát*. Budapest: Corvina, n.d.

Tökés, Rudolf. *Béla Kun and the Hungarian Soviet Republic: The Origins and Role of the Communist Party of Hungary in the Revolutions of 1918–1919*. New York and Washington: Praeger/London: Pall Mall Press, 1967.

Yugoslavia

Prelovšek, Damjan. *Jože Plečnik: 1872–1957*. Translated from the German by Patricia Crampton and Eileen Martin. New Haven and London: Yale University Press, 1997.

Romania

Sandqvist, Tom, *Dada East: The Romanians of Cabaret Voltaire*. Cambridge, MA, and London: MIT Press, 2006.

Estonia

Kermik, Jüri. *Lutheri Vabrik: Vineer ja Möbel, 1877–1940/The Luther Factory: Plywood and Furniture, 1877–1940*. Tallin: Eesti Arhitektuurimuuseum, 2004.

Lapin, Leonhard. *Eesti XX Sajandi Ruum /Space in 20th Century Estonia*. Tallin, 1999.

Chapters in books

Bennett, Ian, "Germany and Austria," in Phillipe Garner, ed. *Encyclopedia of the Decorative Arts, 1890–1940*. New York: Galahad Books, 1978.

Crowley, David, "Art Deco in Central Europe," in Charlotte Benton, Tim Benton, and Ghislaine Wood, eds. *Art Deco – 1910–1939*. Boston, New York, and London: Bulfinch Press, 2003.

Koller, Gabriele, "L'Esprit de la Tradition. L'Art Déco en Autriche," in Helena Dahlbäck Lutteman, ed. *L'Art Déco en Europe: Tendances Décoratives dans les Arts Appliqués vers 1925*. Bruxelles: Société des Expositions du Palais des Beaux-Arts, 1989.

Liefkes, Reino, "Germany, Austria and the Netherlands," in Charlotte Benton, Tim Benton, and Ghislaine Wood, eds. *Art Deco – 1910–1939*. Boston, New York, and London: Bulfinch Press, 2003.

Articles

Art Journal 49, no. 1 (Spring 1990). Special issue edited by S. A. Mansbach on the avant-gardes of Eastern Europe.

Bajkay-Rosch, Éva, "Hungarians at the Bauhaus," *Bauhaus. ICSAC Cahier* 6/7 (1987).

The Czech Avant-Garde and the Book, 1900–1945. Visual Studies Workshop, 1984. Special supplement to *Afterimage*.

Fine Print: The Review for the Arts of the Book 13, no. 1 (January 1987). Special issue on Czechoslovakia.

Haiman, György, "Imre Kner and the Revival of Hungarian Printing," *Design Issues* 7, no. 2 (Spring 1991).

Halas, John, "Encounter with Moholy-Nagy," *STA Journal* 1, no. 3 (Summer 1980).

The Journal of Decorative and Propaganda Arts 17 (Fall 1990). Yugoslavian theme issue.

Kinchin, Juliet, "Modernity and Tradition in Hungarian Furniture, 1900–1938; Three Generations," *The Journal of Decorative and Propaganda Arts* 24 (2002).

Koscevic, Zelimir, "The Poster in Yugoslavia," *The Journal of Decorative and Propaganda Arts* 10 (Fall 1988).

Levinger, Esther, "Czech Avant-Garde Art: Poetry for the Five Senses," *Art Bulletin* 81, no. 3 (September 1999).

—"Return to Figuration: Władislaw Stryeminski and the Move from Idealism," *Art History* 24, no. 1 (February 2001).

Mojzisová, Iva, "Avant-garde Repercussions and the School of Applied Arts in Bratislava, 1928–1939," *Journal of Design History* 5, no. 4 (1992).

Rypson, Piotor, "Znacki firmowe w dsudziestroleciu"/ "Polish Trade Marks in the Interwar Period," *Piktogram* 15 (2010/11).

Chapter 26: Scandinavia 1917–1945

Introduction

Sweden, Denmark, and Norway declared neutrality when World War I broke out, while Finland, then a part of Russia, gained its independence at the time of the Russian Revolution in 1917. Because of the war, the Scandinavian countries suffered hardships due to a disruption of trade relations. During the 1920s, when trade conditions improved, Sweden prospered. Denmark and Norway had unemployment problems although Norwegian industrial production did increase. To a greater extent than the other Scandinavian countries, Finland's economy was still dominated by agriculture since the new nation had little incentive or opportunity to build an industrial base while annexed to Russia. The Great Depression of the early 1930s affected all the Nordic nations although Sweden had almost completely recovered by the end of the decade.

Though political situations differed somewhat within the Nordic countries, all had relatively liberal governments during the interwar years. Many reforms were instituted ranging from ensuring the vote for women, increasing social services, and regulating the work week. In Sweden, the reform program of the 1930s was characterized by the term *folkhemmet*, which defined Swedish society as a "people's home" that would take care of the population's needs. The term was coined by then Prime Minister Per Albin Hansson.

None of the Scandinavian countries were extensive manufacturers of mass-produced products, although several had industries that were internationally successful. In general, the Nordic countries exported more raw materials and agricultural products than manufactured goods, while all produced some goods in smaller quantities for home consumption. Consequently, the crafts continued to play a considerable role in their economies and numerous debates occurred during the interwar years about the value of the crafts as a means of production.

Sweden

In Sweden, the Deutscher Werkbund influence was evident in the reorientation of Sweden's Svenska Slöjdföreningen (Swedish Society of Crafts and Design). Its secretary was the critic Erik Wettergren (1883–1961), who, along with Gregor Paulsson (1889–1977), an art historian at the Swedish National Museum, sought to bring about a collaboration between Swedish industry and the country's young designers who wanted to create a new modern aesthetic that was suitable to mass production. Paulsson, who spent time in Germany before World War I, was the central figure in the society from the time he joined it in 1916 until the 1930s. He served as the society's director between 1920 and 1933 and edited its periodical, *Svenska Slöjdföreningens Tidskrift* (*Swedish Society of Crafts and Design Magazine*) between 1920 and 1934. In Germany he had been taken with the aims of the Deutscher Werkbund, particularly the ideas of its prime mover, Hermann Muthesius, but he was also strongly influenced by the writings of the early Swedish design reformer Ellen Kay (1849–1926) who argued in her pamphlet *Skönhet åt alla* (*Beauty for All*) of 1899 that ethics and aesthetics were closely related. Enhancing public taste and raising design standards for everyone, Kay claimed, could help bring about social reforms.

Paulsson's important book of 1919, *Vackrare vardagsvara* (*More Beautiful Things for Everyday Use*), was a powerful call to provide attractive objects for everyone. He aligned himself with the wing of the Werkbund that called for an industrial aesthetic and mass-produced goods, thus playing down the rustic country style that Ellen Kay preferred and the belief in the craftsman that William Morris emphasized. For Paulsson, the artist was to create beautiful forms that could then be shared with everyone through industrial production.

In 1917, the Swedish Society of Crafts and Design launched a polemic to bring good design to the working class with its Home Exhibition, held in Stockholm. Prominent Swedish architects and designers such as Gunar Asplund (1885–1940) and Carl Malmsten (1888–1972) designed model rooms with unpretentious furniture as well as glassware, porcelain, and other domestic wares. Among the furniture designs were historic styles along with more simplified pieces that were better suited for standardization and mass production. Two years earlier, the Society of Crafts and Design had established an agency to find work for artists in Swedish industries and by the time of its exhibition several industries, notably the glass manufacturer Orrefors and the Gustavsberg Porcelain Factory, had hired artists to work as in-house designers. Several of the glassware artists designed plain glassware that broke with the more complicated faceting of earlier pieces. A leading manufacturer of such designs was the Kosta Glassworks, which brought out its first examples of inexpensive glassware and ceramic dinner services.

Wilhelm Kåge (1889–1960), a former poster designer, joined the Gustavsbergs Porslinsfabrik (Gustavsberg Porcelain Factory) in 1917 and that year he designed an inexpensive dinner service with three different kinds of ornamentation called Liljeblå (Blue Lily). The service featured Kåge's blue flower and border designs on a plain white ground (Plate 31), recalling earlier designs from the 19th century. Its price was sufficiently low for it to become known as the Workers' Service. Although it remained in production until the 1940s, it was purchased primarily by progressive intellectuals rather than the workers for whom it was originally intended.

Kåge's dinner service exemplified the Society of Crafts and Design's interest in inexpensive well-designed objects. The society had preceded the Home Exhibition with a competition for inexpensive interiors and industrially produced goods of high quality. Thus all the designers and architects who entered had to indicate the costs of their goods and interiors to the consumer. The organizers had sufficient entries to display 23 furnished rooms for small apartments along with a host of other objects for the home, including glass, ceramics, and furniture. As design historian Cilla Robach has noted, most of the objects had their origin in those that filled the 19th-century rural home or else displayed the simplicity of 18th-century design. For the exhibition's purpose, any objects that represented the "democratization of beauty" were preferable to highly original but expensive alternatives.

By contrast to the Gustavsberg Porcelain Factory's emphasis on ceramic design for the working class, the Orrefors Glasbruk (Orrefors Glass Factory) hired Simon Gate (1883–1945) in 1916 and Edward Hald (1883–1980) the following year to emphasize glassware for a more affluent clientele. Both men were painters, Hald having studied with Henri Matisse in Paris, and neither had any previous experience with glass. With the help of Orrefors' craftsmen, Gate

Fig. 26.01: Simon Gate, Orrefors glass, c. 1925. © Les Arts Décoratifs, Paris/Jean Tholance/akg-images. © DACS 2017.

developed a genre known as Graal, which involved cutting figures from layers of colored glass that had been laid on a clear surface, then reheating the glass and covering it with a layer of clear crystal. Hald also worked in this genre and both men additionally created drawings that were then engraved into layers of soft clear glass. Gate preferred Neo-Classical subjects, mostly mannered nudes that were cut in deep relief (Fig. 26.01) while Hald depicted male and female figures with a lighter touch. In the late 1920s, Orrefors brought in a third artist, the sculptor Vicke Lindstrand (1904–1983) who put more emphasis on the forms of the vessels and the reflective qualities of the glass, while also continuing the engraving techniques that Gate and Hald had initiated.

Orrefors glassware by Gate and Hald was extremely well received at the 1925 Exposition Internationale des Arts Décoratifs in Paris, where Orrefors won a gold medal. Though Gregor Paulsson was the superintendent of the Swedish Pavilion, it did not feature the populist designs that were on display at the Home Exhibition. The Swedish government most likely wanted to emphasize furniture and decorative arts for export and thus requested a pavilion more in keeping with the conventions of Swedish tradition. Hence, it was designed in the Neo-Classical style that represented the country's strongest design heritage.

Fig. 26.02: Gunnar Asplund, "Senna" chair, 1925. Wright Auction House.

Among the furnishings were traditional chairs by Carl Malmsten (1888–1972) as well as an expensive furniture suite by the architect Gunnar Asplund (1885–1940). Though Asplund would become the chief architect for the modernist Stockholm Exhibition of 1930, his conception of furniture design at this point, exemplified by his "Senna" chair that was made of mahogany, leather, and ivory (Fig. 26.02), looked back to the style of the National Romantic movement rather than forward to the Deco designs of the French or the steel furniture of the Germans.

Paulsson was a pragmatist who accommodated the Swedish government's intention to project an international image based on tradition, but in fact he was equally taken with Le Corbusier's prefabricated Pavilion de l'Esprit Nouveau as was Uno Åhrén (1897–1977), one of Sweden's first modernist architects who, along with Asplund, played a major role in the Stockholm Exhibition of 1930. He then designed a Swedish factory for the Ford Motor Company in 1930–1931. He also collaborated with the Swedish sociologist and social reformer Gunnar Myrdal on a 1934 publication on social housing that would later become influential in planning the social democratic Swedish society.

In the years just after the Paris Exhibition, the Swedish Society of Crafts and Design increased the pressure on companies to hire artists and architects for design positions. The bus manufacturers Tidaholms Bruk and Hägglund & Söner recruited the Functionalist architects Eskil Sundahl (1890–1974) and Sigurd Lewerentz (1885–1975) as designers, while a more unusual relation developed between the portrait painter Helmer Mas Olle (1884–1969) and the fledgling Swedish automobile manufacturer Volvo, whose intention was to build a car more suited to the Nordic climate than the American imports. Mas Olle styled ten prototype bodies for the ÖV4, which Volvo began to sell in 1927 (Fig. 26.03). For a number of reasons, however, Volvo subsequently turned over the design function to its engineers who took the safer route of using American cars as models.

Fig. 26.03: Helmer Mas Olle, Volvo ÖV4, 1927. © Heritage Image Partnership Ltd/Alamy.

Another artist, the Norwegian painter Jean Heiberg 1884–1976), created a successful design for a new cradle telephone that the Swedish telephone company Ericsson adopted. Earlier, Ericsson's first phone to combine the speaker and receiver in a single handset, the Model 88, had achieved wide success in Europe after its launch in 1908. Two decades later, Heiberg, working with the Norwegian engineer Johan Christian Bjerknes (1889–1983) at the Norsk Elektrisk Bureau, a Norwegian subsidiary of Ericsson's, designed a modern sculptural version of the cradle telephone, which went into production in 1932. Manufactured with a Bakelite casing that replaced the existing metal one, the DHB 1001, as it was called, consisted of a curved base that housed the dialing mechanism and a rounded handset that rested on the base (Fig. 26.04). The Ericsson phone based on Heiberg's and Bjerknes's design became the standard model for the Swedish Telephone Company, and the British Post Office adopted a variant for use in Great Britain.

Besides its campaign to improve the quality of everyday goods by pressuring companies to hire artists, the Swedish Society of Crafts and Design entered into its own collaboration with a large furniture

manufacturer, AB Svenska Möbelfabrikerna, to mass-produce furniture of high quality for a wide public. The company's collaboration with the Swedish Society of Crafts and Design was only a small part of its large output, which comprised about 100 different furniture suites as well as individual pieces such as card tables. The society's collaboration with AB Svenska Möbelfabrikerna represented a firm commitment to creating attractive goods by industrial means rather than encouraging the many small craft-based workshops that comprised the bulk of Sweden's furniture industry and for which there was still strong support. Some of Sweden's leading furniture craftsmen and architects designed furniture for the Nordiska Kompaniet, a large department store that had its own furniture workshops. Gemla, a company that produced toys as well as furniture, began producing its own version of bentwood furniture with the help of specialists from abroad.

Svenskt Tenn (Swedish Pewter), an interior design company that Estrid Ericson (1894–1981) founded in 1924, also produced furniture as well as textiles. In its own Stockholm shop, the company sold both, along with the modern pewter that Ericson favored and from which the company took its name. In 1933, the Austrian designer and architect Josef Frank (1885–1967), who had emigrated to Sweden from Austria that year, began to produce textile and furniture designs for Svenskt

Fig. 26.04: Jean Heiberg and Johan Christian Bjerknes, Ericsson DHB 1001 telephone, 1932. © 2014. Digital image, The Museum of Modern Art, New York/Scala, Florence.

Tenn, becoming the company's chief designer two years later. Frank favored complex textile patterns, many derived from plants or animals (Plate 32), while his taste in furniture reflected a simplified Neo-Classicism that was modern without being strictly Functionalist.

Despite the successful participation of a few artists and architects with industrial companies, engineers designed most industrial products, emphasizing a split within all the Scandinavian countries between the artists, craftsmen, and architects who designed furniture, ceramics, textiles, and other domestic goods, and the engineers who were mainly responsible for industrial products. For example, Gustav Dalén (1869–1937), the chief engineer of Svenska AB Gas Accumulator Company, designed the revolutionary Aga stove in 1922 (Plate 33). It was named after the initials of the company, which replaced the prior gas burners with two large hotplates that could deliver intense heat from an internal storage unit. The stove had dual ovens that maintained different temperatures from the hotplates as they were not the same distance from the heat source. A thermostat controlled the heat, so no knobs or dials were required. The Aga ranges were first imported into Great Britain in 1929 and achieved considerable success there, thus contributing to Sweden's economic recovery in the 1930s.

Several other industrial companies introduced important new appliances and models during the interwar period. Elektrolux, formed in 1919 from a merger between the Lux vacuum company and another Stockholm company, Elekromekanista, introduced its new vacuum cleaner, the Model V, in 1921. Designed by Axel Wenner-Gren (1881–1961), inventor of one of the first vacuum cleaners, the Model V featured a cylinder perched on runners with a sweeper attached to an extended flexible hose. This model became the prototype of other vacuum cleaners for many years to come (Fig. 26.05).

In 1925, the company purchased the rights to a machine designed by two Swedish engineering students that converted heat to cold and produced its first

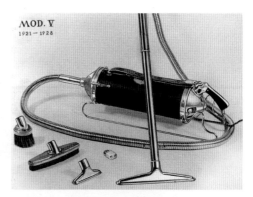

Fig. 26.05: Axel Wenner-Gren, Elektrolux Model V vacuum cleaner, 1921. Electrolux PLC.

refrigerator, the Electrolux L1, between 1931 and 1937. The company continued to manufacture refrigerators in large volume and by the mid-1930s had established factories in Great Britain, France, and the United States to produce its growing range of appliances. In the late 1930s, Electrolux intensified its marketing by commissioning the American industrial designer Raymond Loewy to design several products in the streamline style, notably a cylinder vacuum cleaner, a floor polisher, and the stylized L3000 refrigerator.

Sweden was also an active manufacturer of motorcycles during the interwar years. They were made by Husqvarna (Mill House), one of Sweden's oldest industrial firms, which was founded in 1689. Originally the company made musket barrels, but with the construction of a foundry in 1872, Husqvarna began to manufacture a broad range of household appliances from wood-burning stoves to sewing machines. In 1896, the company produced its first bicycle and from 1903 it began to manufacture motorcycles. Initially Husqvarna bicycle frames were fitted with single-cylinder engines from other manufacturers, but in 1920 the company initiated the manufacture of its own engines. Two years later, Husqvarna began to market a large four-cycle machine that was comparable in size to the Indian, the Harley-Davidson, and the BMW (Fig. 26.06). Around 1929 the engineer and designer Folke Mannerstedt (1901–1987) joined the firm with a mandate to improve

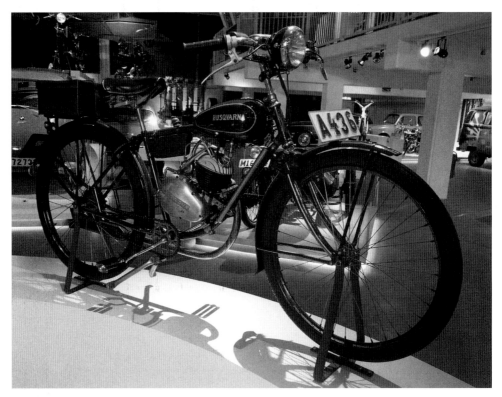

Fig. 26.06: Husqvarna motorcycle, 1938. Wikimedia/Alf van Beem.

the competitive capacity of its motorcycles in European races.

An expert in the use of light alloys for the engines as well as the body designs, Mannerstedt helped Husqvarna become a successful racing competitor. In the mid-1930s, however, the company stopped entering races, ceased production of its large engines, and concentrated on building smaller cycles with two-stroke engines. In part because these machines did not require a driver's license, they proved to be very popular and Husqvarna sold thousands of them.

While companies that made industrial products had no problems encasing them in clean modern forms, the debate between *funkis* (Functionalism) and *tradis* (tradition) intensified in the late 1920s within the Swedish Society of Crafts and Design, as Gregor Paulsson, Uno Åhrén, and others promoted a comparable Functional aesthetic for household goods

and architecture. Led by the furniture designer Carl Malmsten, the "traditionalists" defended the role of the individual craftsman. Nonetheless the Functionalists prevailed and in 1930 the society, led by Paulsson, organized the Stockholm Exhibition, an extensive display of household goods and architecture that firmly grounded Functionalism as a dominant aesthetic in Swedish design.

The architect Gunnar Asplund designed the principal structures—the main restaurant with its glazed walls and Corbusian roof garden and the plain exhibition halls. On display was the full range of household goods—furniture, textiles, glass, ceramics, and metalwork. Visitors could also see inexpensive interiors for the working class, as well as hospital and hotel interiors for an industrialized society. The exhibition gave a new impetus to the society's program of "beautiful things for everyone," and led to further designs for low-cost and mass-produced household goods, many in the new Functional style. Among the leading examples of such goods at the exhibition and in the years that followed were Wihelm Kåge's Praktika earthenware service for Gustavsberg in 1933 and the Eva chair by cabinetmaker Bruno Mathsson (1907–1988), which was made of laminated bentwood and webbed fabric. Unlike Kåge's earlier Blue Lily service whose design derived from a Swedish folk style, the Praktika earthenware dishes had a plain green ring around each bowl and plate, avoiding any reference to a national tradition. They were also designed to nest within each other for economic storage, particularly in smaller flats. However, despite critical praise, they did not appeal to Sweden's mass market, nor did Mathsson's chair, which he designed in 1934. The curves of the bent wood and the resilience of the webbing derived from his research into forms that would provide the most comfort to the sitter, but both broke with the traditions and techniques of Swedish furniture manufacturing, resulting in Mathsson producing the chair in his own workshop since he could not find an existing manufacturer to do it (Fig. 26.07). Mathsson's choice of wood and fabric were exemplary of the Nordic preference for natural materials, and the use of such materials came to characterize Swedish Modern. Though tubular steel furniture was widely shown at the Stockholm Exhibition, it did not receive a very welcome reception in Sweden or anywhere else in Scandinavia.

As a follow-up to the exhibition, in 1931, five architects—Uno Åhrén, Gunnar Asplund, Wolter Gahn (1890–1985), Sven Markelius, and Eskil Sundahl (1890–1974)—along with Gregor Paulsson issued a book-length manifesto in support of Functionalism. Polemically titled *Acceptera!* (*Accept*), it was a plea to the public to recognize Functionalism, standardization, and mass production as valuable components of a new set of cultural values.

For the designers and architects such as Uno Åhrén who espoused Functionalism, the Functionalist philosophy was part of a desire to construct a socially

Fig. 26.07: Bruno Mathsson, Eva chair, 1934. © Les Arts Décoratifs, Paris/Jean Tholance/akg-images.

progressive environment that would meet everyone's needs. This resulted in new architectural typologies such as the service-flat housing block that the architect and planner Sven Markelius (1889–1972) designed in collaboration with the sociologist Alva Myrdal (1902–1986). Similar to some of Moisei Ginzburg's 1930s Constructivist experiments in Russia, the intent of the block that Markelius designed was to relieve professional women with children of responsibilities for childcare, cooking, laundry, and other domestic functions by providing communal facilities for these functions.

Attention to social needs was also evident at the Gustavsberg Porcelain Factory after the Kooperativa Förbundet (Swedish Co-operative Union and Wholesale Society) acquired it in 1937. Better known for its high profile dinnerware, Gustavsberg also began to produce bathroom porcelain such as bidets, sinks, and tubs in 1939. Under the leadership of Hjalmar Olson (1902–1990), a pioneer in the field of design management, Gustavsberg sought to juggle a profitable balance sheet with a strong sense of social responsibility. This challenge paralleled that faced by the architects and designers of the modern movement in Germany during the 1920s, but Sweden was able to move forward with a socially progressive design program in the 1930s because its government was dominated by Social Democrats rather than the repressive Nazi regime that came to power in Germany around the same time.

Denmark
Household goods and furniture

In Denmark, the Landsforeningen Dansk Kunsthaandvaerk (Danish Society of Crafts and Design) was founded in 1907, but it did not promote a new design direction in Denmark as strongly as the Society of Crafts and Design did in Sweden. Instead, several organizations—the Danske Kunstindustrimuseum (Danish Museum of Decorative Arts), the Department of Furniture and Interior Decoration at Det Kongelige Danske Kunstakakademi (The Royal Academy of Fine Arts), and the Københavns Snedkerlaug (Copenhagen Cabinet Makers' Guild)—worked along common lines. As a counterpart to The Royal Academy of Fine Arts, the Museum of Decorative Arts established its own Haandvaerkerskole (School of Crafts), whose first director was Hans Tegner (1853–1952), an artist, illustrator, and designer of stamps and banknotes who was also the design director of the porcelain manufacturer Bing & Grøndahl between 1907 and 1932.

Beginning in 1927, the Cabinet Makers' Guild initiated an annual exhibition, and later a competition, at the Museum of Decorative Arts to promote the design of new furniture. The guild's major figure in the 1920s was Kaare Klint (1888–1954), who was trained as an architect before founding the department of furniture and interior decoration at The Royal Academy of Fine Arts in 1924. Like most Danish architects of his day, Klint was strongly influenced by Neo-Classicism but he also researched earlier styles and materials to discover principles and technique for contemporary design. His own chairs were based on a careful study of prior designs such as the knock-down chair used by the British Army abroad and the folding chair found on the decks of passenger ships.

With his students at the Kunstakademi, Klint collected and correlated data on the human body to enhance the development of furniture that corresponded to the body's characteristics. This was an early example of gathering human data for design purposes, a practice that later developed into the science of ergonomics. Klint also placed great emphasis on craftsmanship, thus characterizing the Danish approach to furniture design as an alternative to the industrially based aesthetic of the German modern movement.

Klint's folding deck chair of 1933 for the furniture manufacturer Rudolph Rasmussen, with its wooden frame and cane surfaces, exemplifies his combination of craft skill and rational proportion (Fig. 26.08). His interests, however, ranged beyond chairs and he worked closely with his students to develop a rational approach to storage furniture such as cupboards and cabinets.

Modern Danish furniture owes a great debt to Klint, not only for his own designs but also for the influence he had on his many assistants and students who also became prominent designers. Mogens Koch (1898–1992) was a former assistant whose MK Safari chair of 1932 retained Klint's interest in rational form but departed radically from Klint's approach with its use of tightly woven fabric for the back and seat. Koch's chair parallels closely the precedent of a similar folding chair that Gerd Hassenpflug designed at the Bauhaus in 1928. Like Bruno Mathsson's Eva chair, created two years later in Sweden, the Safari chair was too radical to attract a manufacturer when it was designed and was not put into production until 1960. Koch's subsequent furniture was less controversial and included various pieces that were inspired by earlier historical types. Like Koch, Ole Wanscher (1903–1985), a student of Klint's, also based his designs on historic precedents, particularly those of the 18th century, although one of his better known pieces, produced in 1960, was derived directly from an early Egyptian folding stool.

The rising quality of Danish modern furniture was due in large part to the enlightened views of a few progressive manufacturers who collaborated

Fig. 26.08: Kaare Klint, deck chair for Rudolph Rasmussen, 1933. Dansk Møbelkunst Gallery.

closely with the Copenhagen Cabinet Makers' Guild. Unlike most Danish furniture companies, these firms were interested in producing high-quality designs at moderate prices for a broad public. The firms included Jacob Kjaer, Rudolph Rasmussen, A. J. Iversen, and Fritz Hansen. Of these, Fritz Hansen was the first to market modular sectional furniture that could be put together in different combinations.

In 1926, Poul Henningsen (1894–1967) and a group of fellow architects initiated a radical call for a new social approach to design. They declared it in the first issue of their magazine *Kritisk Revy* (*Critical Review*), which they published until 1928. The group had little interest in aesthetics and placed their emphasis on social needs. According to Henningsen, the designer should focus on a single useful object and develop its possibilities. His own specialty was lighting and he had begun to design hanging and table lamps for the lighting manufacturer Louis Poulson in 1924. Known as the PH series, these lamps diffused the light through several layers of metal shades whose curvatures Henningsen carefully calibrated to reduce the glare of the electric bulb (Fig. 26.09). Over the years, Henningsen continued to refine his design, adding more and more layers to the lamps. He opposed any

celebration of the crafts and designed his lamps for mass production. Their modern industrial aesthetic made them popular abroad, especially in Germany where the Deutscher Werkbund and the builders of the Neue Frankfurt promoted them. Though known primarily for his lighting, Henningsen was interested in other uses of industrial materials. His tubular steel furniture for the manufacturer V. A. Høfding was formed from curved pieces of steel to which were attached leather and fabric-covered seats and backs. For another manufacturer he designed a piano with curved steel legs and a transparent acrylic cover in a steel frame.

Henningsen thoroughly subverted the conventions of standard object and furniture types with his industrial aesthetic that was based on a radical social agenda. Less radical though also socially conscious was Kaj Bojesen (1886–1958), a silversmith who had trained in the workshop of Georg Jensen. By 1931, Bojesen had established his own workshop and begun to design

Fig. 26.09: Poul Henningsen, PH 4-3 table lamp, 1927. © 2014. Digital image, The Museum of Modern Art, New York/Scala, Florence.

tableware with plain forms that was suitable for mass production. Ultimately his designs were produced for a wider market in stainless steel. Another prominent designer of silver was Kay Fisker (1893–1965), an architect rather than a silversmith. As a writer for the architectural journal *Arkitekten* (*The Architect*) between 1919 and 1927, Fisker promoted modern design through polemics, while as a designer for the manufacturer A. Michelsen, he produced silver tea services, cocktail shakers, and pitchers in pure sculptural forms with subtle historical associations. Fisker was less successful as a designer of furniture. His wingback chair of the 1930s was an attempt to modernize the 18th- and 19th-century models by substituting curved wooden arms for the earlier upholstered ones and plain wooden legs for the more ornate legs of the earlier models.

The success that Georg Jensen had achieved before World War I (see Chapter 17) through his designs and those of Johan Rohde and other designers continued to ensure the firm's success in the interwar years. One of Jensen's leading designers during this period was Harald Nielsen (1892–1977), who created simple unadorned silver teapots and other hollow ware as well as flatware patterns. His Pyramid flatware of 1927, which featured a stepped design at the base of each piece of cutlery, recalled the forms of Art Deco and became one of the firm's best selling designs. When Georg Jensen died in 1935, the company was managed by his son Jørgen and continued its successful course.

A counterpart to Nielsen's plain unadorned forms in silver was the glassware that Jens Bang (1890–1965) designed for the Holmegaards Glasværk (Holmegaard Glass Factory) in the 1920s. Bang joined Holmegaard's design office in 1924 and became its artistic director in 1928. The clear Purist forms that he designed for Holmegaard during the 1920s were in marked contrast to the elaborately decorated glassware that Simon Gate and Edvard Hald were designing for Orrefors in Sweden at the time. Bang's Hogla beer glass of 1928, a beautifully shaped sculptural vessel with a thick transparent stem and base, marked a turning point for

Holmegaard's shift to mass production. His Primula glassware of 1930 played more with curved forms and varied stem shapes but still preserved the pristine sense of form that characterized his work with Holmegaard until he left in 1942.

Industrial products

As in Sweden, Danish entrepreneurs, engineers, and informal designers were primarily responsible for the design of electrical goods and transportation during the interwar years. In 1910, the year Axel Wenner-Gren introduced his cylinder vacuum in Sweden, two Danish entrepreneurs, Peder A. Fisker (1875–1975) and H. M. Nielsen (1870–1954), patented a canister vacuum cleaner after founding a company to produce small electric motors four years earlier. The Nilfisk vacuum, which took its name from the company's founders, was the first portable vacuum cleaner of its type. It was regarded as a technological breakthrough because the designers condensed so much cleaning power into a small object. During the 1930s, it took on a more elegant appearance in order to appeal to the housewives who were its primary users.

Fisker & Nielsen also produced a popular motor-cycle, the Nimbus, which Peder Fisker designed. His first design, the Model A, was manufactured between 1919 and 1923. It was known as "The Stovepipe," because of its large rounded frame, which also functioned as a gas tank. A new Model B was basically the same machine with an improved front fork. The early models of the Nimbus were produced primarily for domestic consumption, though they never became big sellers because they cost almost as much as Henry Ford's Model T automobile. In 1934, Fisker's son Anders designed a more streamlined and longer-lasting version, the Model C, which was called "The Bumblebee" after the sound of its exhaust.

Bang & Olufsen, which in later years became the premier manufacturer of high-end sound equipment, was founded in 1925 by two engineers, Peter Boas Bang (1900–1957) and Andreas Grøn Olufsen (1897–1949).

Fig. 26.10: Bang and Olufsen, Beolit 39 radio cabinet, 1939. Wikimedia/Theredmonkey.

Their products, including an early radio with push-button tuning, were innovative from the start and displayed their strategy of combining sophisticated technology and visual elegance. This was evident in their streamlined Bakelite radio cabinet of 1939, the Beolit 39 (Fig. 26.10).

Shops and showrooms

Besides being a designer of tableware, Kaj Bojesen was also the driving force in the establishment of Den Permanente, a cooperative association with a large showroom in Copenhagen, where artists could display and sell their own designs. As a vehicle for distribution, Den Permanente gave individual designers access to the market, thus bypassing the traditional attitudes and taste of many Danish manufacturers. Progressive merchants could play a similar role. In Copenhagen, Kaj Dessau (1897–1987) created BO (Living), a retail outlet for interior furnishings and household goods that strongly influenced the Danish reception of modern design. The store featured everything for the home: furniture, upholstery fabrics, ceramics, glass, and lighting fixtures. Dessau based his commitment to sell well-designed goods at attractive prices on his knowledge of the Bauhaus, the Deutsche Werkstätten, and Britain's Design and Industry Association. He also looked carefully at Sweden's handicraft organizations and furniture factories.

In the store's first phase, Dessau strongly emphasized Swedish goods including some small exhibits of objects from the Stockholm Exhibition, but he began to promote Danish goods in 1935 when he opened an exhibition that featured furniture, rugs, and upholstery made in his own workshops. The director of his weaving workshop was Marianne Strengell (1909–1988), who left for the United States in 1937 to head the weaving department at the Cranbrook Academy of Art.

Dessau also fostered the establishment of other workshops by committing to selling their wares. Among these was Saxbo, which featured stoneware colored with the rich glazes of Natalie Krebs (1895–1978). The workshop mass-produced high-quality stoneware for sale at low prices, a value that accorded with Dessau's own views. Saxbo also featured the expressive artistic vessels of Axel Salto (1889–1961), who worked as well for the Royal Copenhagen Porcelain Factory, where he developed many stoneware pieces that anticipated the post-war interest in organic forms.

In part due to Dessau's promise to sell her screen-printed fabrics, the fabric designer Marie Gudme Leth (1910–1997) founded her own textile workshop, Dansk Kattuntrykkeri (Danish Calico Print Works). Leth's fabrics featured images drawn in a folkloric style rather than abstract patterns. However, she was not nostalgic. Her fabrics Landsby (Village) I and II of 1935 and 1936 feature rural houses and windmills but include images of factories to acknowledge the presence of industrialization. Dessau also collaborated with the Haderslev Klaedefabrik (Haderslev Cloth Mill), a factory that produced rugs woven on power looms. The "Hadersbo rugs" featured abstract patterns designed collaboratively by Brita Drewsen (1887–1983) and Dessau himself. By 1941, BO had become an important promoter of modern design in Denmark through its network of workshops and its creative exhibitions, but Germany's invasion of Denmark in 1940 led Dessau, a Jew, to close his store the following year. He moved to Sweden in 1943 and there he found a welcome reception for his ideas before he eventually settled in Switzerland.

As in other countries that the Nazis occupied, initiatives to design modern dwellings and household goods dwindled and only experienced a resurgence after Western Europe was liberated in 1945.

Norway

Both Norway and Finland gained their independence considerably later than Sweden and Denmark, a factor that may account for a continuing influence of folk culture and National Romantic ideals in both countries at a time when the two older nations were more readily absorbing influences from abroad. Norway did not have its own design organization until 1918 when the Landsforbundet Norsk Brukskunst (Norwegian Society of Crafts and Design) was formed.

Through exhibitions, publications, and contacts with industry, the Landsforbundet became an important forum for design debates between the wars. Its president for the first several years was the architect Harald Aars (1875–1945) and its vice-chairman Jacob Tostrup Prytz (1886–1962), head of the firm Jacob Tostrup, a leading producer of household goods and jewelry in gold and silver. Prytz remained with the Landsforbundet for almost 30 years. Other members included Hans Aall (1869–1946), founder and director of the Norsk Folkemuseum (Norwegian Folk Museum), and Thor B. Kielland (1894–1963), an art historian who became curator of the Oslo Museum of Decorative Art in 1928, along with textile, furniture, and ceramics artists. As the late design historian Frederik Wildhagen has shown, topics of the initial debates within the Landsforbundet paralleled those occurring in Germany, Sweden, and Britain: notably how to produce attractive products for everyone and how to relate handicrafts to mass production. Initially the Landsforbundet supported a program similar to Gregor Paulsson's in Sweden. In 1920, it organized the exhibition "New Homes," a display of low-cost domestic environments that recalled the similar Swedish exhibition of several years earlier. By the mid-1920s, its social program and its discussions of machine aesthetics had waned.

Neo-Classicism became the preferred form language as it was in Sweden, and the urban middle class the primary consumption community. In 1929, a group of craft-oriented artists broke away from the Landsforbundet to form a new group, the Prydkunstnerlaget (Association of Decorative Artists), that wished to replace the emerging Neo-Classicism with a vernacular Norwegian tradition. The group also criticized the anonymous quality of mass production and sought to relocate design in the crafts. From 1931, this group was known as the Brukskunstnerlaget (Association of Applied Artists) and that year it became a subgroup within the Landsforbundet Norsk Brukskunst.

Despite these turns, some designers and manufacturers chose to design and produce household wares in a modern style. Unlike Denmark, this was less the case in furniture than in ceramics and metalware. One exception among furniture designers was Herman Munthe-Kaas (1890–1977), whose cantilevered tubular steel armchair known as the "F-17" of 1929 followed closely the basic form of Marcel Breuer's Cesca chair of 1928. Munthe-Kaas added a softer seat and back support covered by fabric, though he retained Breuer's wooden arm rests.

In ceramics, Nora Gulbrandsen (1894–1978) was recommended by the Landsforbundet to the Porsgrund Porselaensfabrik (Porsgrund Porcelain Factory), where she served as artistic director between 1928 and 1945. More than any other Nordic ceramist in this period, Gulbrandsen studied the avant-garde design language of the Russian Constructivists and the Bauhaus. A coffee set she designed between 1929 and 1931 featured shaded areas in different colors that recall the mass-produced German ceramics of the period, but she accented the pieces with strong red stripes and round red knobs on the vessel covers (Plate 34). Another coffee service, Model no. 1848, featured a pattern of alternating blue and cream diamonds with small brown patterns on the lighter surfaces. A related effort to introduce modern forms in glass was undertaken by Sverre Petterson (1994–1958), the first artistic director

Fig. 26.11: Jacob Jacobsen, Luxo L-1 lamp, 1937. Photo by Nils Petter Dale, Norway. © Luxo.

at the Hadeland Glasverk (Hadeland Glass Factory). Petterson, however, looked to the Art Deco style as his source rather than to the avant-gardes. The influence of Art Deco was also evident in the silver objects that Thorbjørn Lie-Jørgensen (1900–1961) designed for the firm David-Andersen and it could be seen in some of the metalware that Arne Korsmo (1900–1968) designed for Jacob Tostrup.

Modernism in Norway also took other forms. Industrial expansion was stimulated by efforts to harness the country's immense waterpower as well as by shipping, mining, and fish exports. Because of Norway's rich endowment of natural resources, there was less emphasis on the development of manufacturing, and in this regard, Norway lagged behind Sweden and Finland. As mentioned earlier, the Elektrisk Bureau in Oslo, a subsidiary of the Swedish firm Ericsson, produced a model for a telephone receiver that remained the basic typology of that object for many years.

One exportable industrial product of note was the Luxo lamp, which the engineer and lighting designer Jacob Jacobsen (1901–1996) adapted from George Carwardine's Anglepoise lamp of 1934. That same year

Jacobsen designed a variation on the Anglepoise lamp, which he called the Luxo L-1 (Fig. 26.11). Though it had a similar balancing system, Jacobsen's lamp had a more finely shaped cover and base as well as an overall more attractive form. It went on the market in 1937. Jacobsen also eventually acquired the American production rights for Carwardine's spring tension principle and during the 1940s he monopolized the sale of flexible-task lamps in Europe and the United States.

Finland
Origins of Finnish craft ideology

Finland was the last of the Nordic countries to achieve independence. Separating from Russia in 1917 as a consequence of the Russian Revolution, the new nation created its first constitution in 1919. Design debates during the National Romantic period at the beginning of the century had been strongly weighted towards craft activity, and this direction persisted after Finland's separation from Russia. At the time, Finland was a predominantly agricultural country, a situation that supported the heavy craft orientation.

In 1871, the educator Carl Gustaf Estlander (1834–1910) was instrumental in founding a new school of arts and crafts to provide better training for the young people who worked in Finland's handicraft industries. Four years later Estlander helped establish the Konstflitföreningen i Finland (Finnish Society of Crafts and Design), which took over the management of the school. Fifteen years later it became the National Central School of Industrial Arts. From 1902 to 1912, its director was Armas Lindgren (1874–1929), a partner in the firm of National Romantic architects Gesellius, Lindgren, and Saarinen (see Chapter 12). Lindgren brought to the school ideas from the British Arts and Crafts movement and the Deutscher Werkbund.

Given the predominance of agriculture and lack of industry in Finland at the time, it was the Arts and Crafts values of Ruskin and Morris that predominated. In 1911, a group of students who had received their training under Lindgren formed a designers' association called Ornamo, which sought to raise the social position of those in the applied arts to that of the architect and fine artist. Ornamo also devised rules for competitions and gained from the government the commission to organize Finland's Pavilion at the 1925 Exposition Inernationale des Arts Décoratifs in Paris.

The strongest advocate for craft production in Finland and a collaborator with Ornamo was Arttu Brummer (1891–1951). Trained as a furniture designer at the Central School of Industrial Arts, Brummer began to teach there in 1919 and had a major impact on several generations of students. He was a strong advocate of handicrafts, which he believed were more humane than machine production, and he believed that handicrafts were always preferable when they could compete economically with mechanized industries.

As a designer, Brummer created furniture for several national projects such as the Finnish Pavilion at the 1925 Exposition Internationale des Arts Décoratifs and the new Parliament House that the architect Johan Sigfrid Sirén (1889–1961) designed in the classical style and completed in 1931. Brummer also began to design glassware in the early 1930s, winning first prize in 1932 for an air bubble glass vase in a competition sponsored by the Karhula Glassworks.

With strong links to the Arts and Crafts movement and the National Romantic architects such as Lindgren, Brummer urged his students to look to nature as a source for their designs. In contrast to Gregor Paulsson in Sweden, he considered a hand-made object to be a "living individual being," while he believed mechanical objects to be stiff and cold. Though he taught his students to cultivate their own creativity, he also framed such expression within a national agenda. He conflated the expression of Finnish identity with racial purity, and in an article of 1923 he cited the example of the "negro peoples" who had created something original, though not of a high spiritual level, by avoiding racial intermixing. Inherent in Brummer's aesthetics was a claim to European cultural superiority, a view that is not dissimilar from the widely held views of colonial peoples that one finds elsewhere in Europe at the time. Brummer's main goal as an educator and theorist, however, was to challenge his students to contribute to a worthwhile life by designing objects that could uplift people's spirits. His belief in nature as a source of forms and his espousal of a national identity in design had a strong influence on designers—many his former students—who worked in the Finnish glass, ceramics, metal, textile, and furniture industries.

From craft to mass production

The three major glassworks in Finland were Iittala, the oldest of Finland's glass factories, founded in 1881; the Karhula Glassworks, founded in 1889; and the newest factory, Riihimäki, which was established in 1910. Karhula acquired Iittala in 1917 and the new company marketed its glassware under the name Karhula-Iittala until 1959. Initially Karhula produced bottles and household glass, copying its designs from elsewhere. After acquiring Iittala, Karhula concentrated on bottles and pressed glass while Iittala, the smaller firm, specialized in blown glass. Riihimäki was the largest and perhaps the most diverse of the three companies, manufacturing lighting glass for the company Taito Oy from 1927 as well as glass for containers and household use.

Instead of hiring designers, all three companies began to organize competitions in the late 1920s in order to discover designs for production. In 1932, however, Karhula hired Göran Hongell (1902–1973) as its part-time artistic advisor. Hongell, who trained as a decorative artist at the Central School of Industrial Arts, had previously won several competitions for glassware. After joining Karhula, he continued to design for the company as well as Iittala for many years after that.

The same year that Hongell joined Karhula, the glassworks held another competition, which happened to mark the first impact of Functionalism on the Finnish glass industry. The competition had a category for pressed glass, the only type of glass that could be

Fig. 26.12: Aino Aalto, Bölgeblick glass, 1932. © 2014. Digital image, The Museum of Modern Art, New York/Scala, Florence.

mass-produced at the time. One of the prizes in that category was garnered by the architect Aino Aalto (1894–1949), whose entry consisted of a drinking glass, pitcher, small bowl, sugar bowl, and creamer. Titled Bölgeblick (Wave View), the glassware featured stepped and ribbed rings (Fig. 26.12). It was simple and durable, displaying the characteristics of "good design for all" that had become associated with Nordic Functionalism.

The popularity of Aalto's Bölgeblick series paved the way for other unadorned Functionalist glassware. In 1933, Aino and her husband, the architect Alvar Aalto (1898–1976), won a prize in a competition sponsored by Riihimäki. Known as Riihimäki Flower, the set they designed consisted of different-sized glasses with flared rims as well as bowls and plates, all of which could be stacked. The spare minimal forms were considered too extreme at the time and the set was not put into production until 1953. However, in 1938, Karhula-Iittala launched Göran Hongell's pressed glass Silko series of glasses, pitcher, plates, and bowls, a project surely engendered by the success of Aino Aalto's Bölgeblick glassware, which had gone to market four years earlier.

In 1936, Alvar Aalto won another Karhula-Iittala competition with a design for a vase, whose undulating contours were supposedly inspired by the Finnish shoreline. The asymmetric form was unusual

and therefore complicated to produce. The vase was named Savoy because one was placed on each table in the expensive Helsinki restaurant by that name for which Alvar and Aino Aalto designed the furnishings and fixtures.

The production of Finnish ceramics underwent a transformation from craft to mass production that was similar to the glass industry. Finland's largest ceramics factory was Arabia. Founded in 1873, it was originally a subsidiary of the Rörstrand Porcelain Factory in Sweden, which ran it to serve the Russian market. In 1916, Finnish investors bought Arabia from Rörstrand. Under the directorship of Carl Gustav Herlitz (1882–1961), who succeeded his father, Arabia embarked on an ambitious expansion program that involved bringing electricity to the factory, adding a laboratory, and installing the world's longest tunnel kiln in 1929. Herlitz also introduced a more efficient method for producing sanitary ware such as washbasins and toilet bowls. Adapting the same technique to the production of tableware reduced costs by a third. Though best known for its high-profile tableware, Arabia produced a wide range of ceramic products and during the 1920s and 1930s was Europe's largest porcelain factory. The company established an export department in 1929 and beginning with exports to neighboring Sweden and Estonia, eventually expanded to more than 30 countries including North America and South America, where Argentina became an especially strong trading partner.

Arabia began to hire artists in the 1890s, especially to design its ceramicware. In 1912, Eric O. W. Ehrstrom (1881–1934), who had created the metalwork for some of the buildings by the National Romantic architects Gesellius, Lindgren, and Saarinen, designed a set of ceramic tableware with stylized ornaments that Arabia produced for the American market. During the 1920s, Arabia hired a number of young applied artists such as Greta-Lisa Jäderholm-Snellman (1894–1973), Svea Granlund (1901–1986), Tyra Lundgren (1897–1979), Olga Osol (1905–1994), and Friedl Holzer-Kjellberg (1905–1993). Much of their work was to provide

Fig. 26.13: Greta-Lisa Jäderholm-Snellman, Arabia coffee service, c. 1930s. Photo: P.J.Bögelund/Design Museum.

decoration for the tableware but several including Greta-Lisa Jäderholm-Snellman, designed their own services (Fig. 26.13). Both Jäderholm-Snellman and Lundgren helped to enhance Arabia's reputation abroad by garnering prizes at the Milan Triennale in 1933.

By the 1930s, Arabia was producing as many as 30,000 different products, which fostered a need for greater efficiency. Management introduced time and motion studies, limited automation, and a department of production planning. In 1932, the company hired Kurt Ekholm (1907–1975) as its artistic director. Eckholm, a Finn, had studied at the Royal Institute of Technology in Sweden, where he came into contact with Gregor Paulsson's philosophy of "good design for all" as well as the Functionalist movement, both of which strongly influenced him. At Arabia he set up an art studio, which produced many memorable designs until he left in 1949. With the intention to build a strong international reputation for Arabia, Ekholm gave his artists wide latitude to develop new products. Among the ceramic artists who joined the

studio during the 1930s was Toini Muona (1904–1987), who had studied at the Central School of Industrial Arts, as had most of the other ceramists, and then won gold medals at all the major world's fairs in the 1930s. In 1935, Arabia began to market Eckholm's simplified AH dinner service, his initial response to the Swedish emphasis on quality design for everyone. The service consisted of numerous pieces without decoration—plates of different sizes, trays, and bowls. It came in several colored metallic glazes including a warm orange.

The following year, Arabia produced another of Ekholm's plain services, AR, which also went by the name Sinivalko (Blue White) after the thick blue band that ringed all the pieces. Like Wilhelm Kåge's 1933 Workers' Service for Gustavsberg in Sweden, an obvious model for Ekholm, the AR dishes stacked efficiently to save storage space. The service went beyond the range of dishes Ekholm designed for the AH set, adding a sauceboat, a salad bowl, and a jug. In addition, Olga Osol designed a tureen and lid. The

AR range was manufactured until 1940 when it was replaced by another Functionalist design by Osol.

Metalwork also developed from a craft to a component of industrial production. The leading manufacturer of metal products was Taito Oy, a firm that a group of craftsmen, artists, and a factory owner founded in 1918. The chief designer and principal figure was the artist and metalsmith Paavo Tynell (1890–1973), who also taught metal arts at the Central School of Industrial Arts, where he recruited designers for Taito. The firm produced a wide range of metal objects from ecclesiastical silver vessels for St. Paul's Cathedral in Helsinki to the huge bronze doors of Johan Sirén's Parliament House. Beginning in the 1930s, Taito's main emphasis was on lighting fixtures, and after World War II these became its exclusive products, with Tynell designing many of them. Others were designed by Gunnel Nyman (1909–1948), a former student at the Central School of Industrial Arts who worked for Taito in the early 1930s. She also designed furniture for the Boman company and produced glassware for Riihimäki and Karhula.

Because of its vast forests, furniture production was a major industry in Finland. Before its separation from Russia, historic styles were dominant, but Eliel Saarinen and others in the National Romantic movement had begun to explore folklore and Finnish traditional design as additional sources. During the interwar years, furniture designers came from two backgrounds. Some were architects and others were trained at the Central School of Industrial Arts in a succession of programs whose names changed from "furniture composition" to "furniture drafting," and finally to "furniture art." Besides Arttu Brummer, who designed furniture but did not teach in the furniture design program, an important figure at the Central School was Werner West (1890–1959), who was one of the first furniture designers in Finland to emphasize the importance of designing for industry and mass production. Besides teaching, he was associated for many years with Stockmann's Department Store,

Helsinki's principal shopping emporium. In 1919, Stockmann bought the Kerava Furniture Factory and at the same time established its own design office. West became head of that office in 1924 and in 1929–1930 he supervised the interior design for Stockmann's new building, which the architect Sigurd Frosterus (1876–1956) designed. All the furniture for the interior was produced at the Kerava Factory.

Stockmann's design office was modeled after a similar one at the Nordisk Kompaniet, a department store in Stockholm. Besides producing furniture for sale in the store, the Stockmann office designed interiors for the Café Nissen in Helsinki, the National Museum of Finland, the Finnish Insurance Company, and Helsinki's Hotel Torni. West's own furniture was spare. He was an early modernist though not a strict Functionalist. His style is exemplified by a chair produced at the Kerava Factory that had a plain birch frame with a seat and back of tightly woven wicker. Several of West's students from the Central School of Industrial Arts became successful designers for Stockmann's. Lisa Johansson-Pape (1907–1989) created furniture for the company as early as 1930 before joining the office as a designer in 1937. She remained on the staff until 1949, dividing her time between furniture, textiles, interiors, and lighting. Subsequently she continued to work for Stockmann's as an independent designer. Besides his employment with Stockmann's, Runar Engblom (1908–1965) returned to the Central School of Industrial Arts after World War II and became an influential teacher of furniture design there.

Engblom also worked for Asko Furniture Ltd, as did another of West's students, Maija Heikinheimo (1908–1963). While Engblom worked as a freelance designer, Heikinheimo became the first furniture designer to be permanently employed by the firm. She remained there from 1932 to 1935, when she joined Artek, the company that was founded to produce and sell furniture by Aino and Alvar Aalto.

Asko Furniture Ltd was the first factory in Finland to mass-produce furniture. Its products were traditional furniture suites, although Heikinheimo, and after her Ilmari Tapiovaara (1914–1999), another of Werner West's former students, were instrumental in introducing a modern Functionalist line. After graduating from the Central School of Industrial Arts, Tapiovaara worked in the London office of Artek and then served an apprenticeship in the architectural office of Le Corbusier in Paris. With this background, he returned to Finland and worked as the art director for Asko from 1937 to 1940.

Though middle-class Finns preferred wooden furniture for their homes, tubular steel pieces were produced in a limited range during the 1930s, primarily for public places such as hotels and cafés. The most prominent designer of such furniture was the Functionalist architect Pauli Blomstedt (1900–1935). Working with the Merivaara company, a leading manufacturer of hospital furniture, Blomstedt created several pieces that could be used either in a hotel or a hospital, notably a tubular steel frame bed on wheels, a simple desk and chair, some small nesting tables, and a more plush cantilevered easy chair with back and seat cushions. That an architect designed this furniture signifies the differing receptivity to Functionalism between architects and applied artists. Finnish architects were far more open to the new Functionalist aesthetic and its implications for an international style than the applied arts community, which was more susceptible to Arttu Brummer's call for a nationalist approach to form.

The Aaltos and Artek

In an article of 1940 entitled "Temples or Doghouses," Arttu Brummer referred to Alvar Aalto's furniture designs as "aristocratic creations," claiming they did not meet the needs of ordinary people. Brummer criticized Aalto's form language because of its originality, inferring that it was too distinctive to be part of a nationalist rhetoric. It is true that Functionalism did not find particularly fertile ground in Finland during the 1920s and 1930s, but Brummer was inaccurate

in claiming that Aalto's designs were elitist just as he refused to acknowledge the degree to which Aalto's architecture of the late 1930s had come to embody a robust Nordic identity.

Aalto was an active furniture designer from the end of the 1920s into the 1940s. His wife Aino also worked in the field but her accomplishments are frequently overlooked. Both Alvar and Aino Aalto studied architecture at the Institute of Technology in Helsinki. Aino went to work in Alvar's office in 1924 and they married the same year. In 1927 the Aaltos moved from Jyväskylä to Turku, where both designed furniture for their home. Early on they experimented with bending flat sheets of wood. Aino designed small-scale modern pieces for the children's nursery—a child's bed, nesting tables, and childrens' chairs of curved wood with tubular steel legs. Other pieces of hers included wall-fixed shelves, low bookcases, and a bed for an older child.

In his architectural commissions that preceded the Paimio Sanatorium, a hospital for tuberculosis patients (1929–1933), and the Viipuri Library (1930–1935), Alvar selected modern furniture from catalogs such as Thonet's. He was particularly partial to Marcel Breuer's Wassily chair and tubular steel nesting tables, which he also ordered for his own home. He considered furniture to be an integral part of a building, a conviction he may have adopted from the National Romantic belief of Armas Lindgren, one of his teachers and a partner of Eliel Saarinen, who designed the furniture for Hvittrask, the home and studio Lindgen shared with his two partners, Gesellius and Saarinen, and their families.

By the time Aalto began to create furniture for his public commissions, he decided on wood rather than tubular steel. As a practical matter, wood was plentiful in Finland, but Aalto also believed it had more humane qualities. For the Viipuri Library, he designed a three-legged stacking stool with curved birch L-shaped legs that supported interchangeable round tops (Fig. 26.14). He was assisted in his research on how to curve

Fig. 26.14: Alvar Aalto, three-legged stacking stool, 1932–1933. © V&A Images/Alamy. © DACS 2014.

the legs by Otto Korhonen (1884–1935), co-founder and managing director of the Furniture and Construction Work Factory in Turku, which manufactured the stools and made all of Aalto's other furniture.

The Viipuri stool was a prelude to the full range of furniture and fixtures that Alvar and Aino designed for the Paimio Sanatorium in 1931–1932. The building itself, with its clearly articulated composition of connected volumes, was perhaps the first in Finland to be built in the new international style. As a building type, Josef Hoffman's Purkersdorf Sanatorium outside Vienna is a viable precedent and, like the Aaltos, Hoffman designed the interior furnishings and lighting. For Paimio, Alvar worked with Otto Korhonen to create several chairs of bent birch and molded plywood.

The technique they developed for bending birch or other wood pieces into curved forms was perhaps their most significant contribution to furniture design. Known as the "bent knee," it enabled them to produce organic forms that had flexibility and resilience without being constrained by the conventional stiffness of wood. To make the wood flexible, a workman sawed grooves in a solid piece of birch at the end. He then glued thin wooden slats into the grooves and bent the wood to a preferred angle.

This technique was evident in Aalto's Paimio chairs. The simplest of them, Armchair 51, consists of a seat and back made from a single sheet of curved plywood supported by a frame of bent laminated birch. The more widely known is Armchair 41, which is based on a similar idea but the seat and back are made of a more generously curved plywood sheet with the back dropped lower to allow more comfort for the sitter. Instead of four legs, the frame consists of closed curved beech supports whose organic forms complement the rounded plywood (Fig. 26.15). A third chair was Aalto's and Korhonen's first experiment with a cantilevered armchair where they substituted bent laminated birch for the resilience of tubular steel. The first experimental chairs with curved plywood seats and backs are less known today but the cantilever principle was adapted to a more elegant version that substitutes webbing made of black woven strips for the original plywood. The factory also produced a version of Aino Aalto's child's nursery chair, though it substituted curved wooden legs for the original tubular steel.

Aino's Paimio furnishings are formally less notable than her husband's, but are eminently practical, conforming closely to existing hospital typologies. Her hospital bed of painted tubular steel is cheap and durable as are her three-legged tubular steel stools with flat plywood seats. Similarly, her bedside locker of molded plywood is plain and easily moveable, while her bedside table with its tubular steel frame and plywood top would have easily served as a temporary support for a food tray.

The Paimio commission is also important because of the Aaltos' collaboration with other major Finnish manufacturers, notably Arabia, which produced the porcelain washbasins based on Alvar's designs, and Taito Oy, which manufactured several of Alvar's lamps for the sanatorium—one the architect's wall lamp with

Fig. 26.15: Alvar Aalto, Paimio Armchair 41, 1932. Saint Louis Art Museum, Missouri, USA/Bridgeman Images. © DACS 2014.

a rounded conical shade of lacquered sheet metal that covered the bulb completely to produce a soft glow; and the other a clip-on lamp with a more conventional metal shade. The Paimio commission may have been instrumental in Taito Oy's shift to mass-produced lighting as it gave the company a chance to develop an industrialized production process for a guaranteed number of fixtures.

In 1933, the British critic P. Morton Shand, who coined the enduring term "Swedish grace" after visiting the Stockholm Exhibition of 1930, mounted an exhibition of Alvar's furniture at the London department store Fortnum and Mason. It was immensely successful, leading Shand and several partners to form Finmar, a company that imported and sold the furniture in Britain (see Chapter 23). Siegfried Giedion, the Swiss architecture critic and a founder of wohnbedarf, the chain of modern home furnishing stores in Zurich and Berne, invited Aalto to distribute his furniture in Switzerland, resulting in the design of several pieces that helped to spread the interest in it abroad.

To facilitate this process, the Aaltos joined together with Maire Gullichsen (1907–1990) of the Ahlström family that owned large timber interests

as well as the Karhula-Iittala glassworks, and the art historian Nils-Gustav Hahl (1904–1941) to form Artek, a company whose purpose was to market the furniture, glass, and textiles of the Aaltos. Artek—a contraction of art and technology—also had a gallery that organized exhibitions of modern and applied art, including paintings by Picasso and Léger and sculpture by Calder, with the aim of developing a modern artistic culture in Finland. As well, the company undertook many commissions for public interiors ranging from a military hospital and a prominent hotel to the Savoy Restaurant, designed by Alvar and Aino Aalto, which was Artek's crowning achievement. The various interiors were furnished largely with furniture and decorative arts by the Aaltos, though some other designers also created products for Artek. Nils-Gustav Hahl and Aino Aalto were the first managers, and Aino continued alone after Hahl died in World War II. Maija Heikinheimo, who left Asko Furniture Ltd to join Artek, remained with the firm for almost 30 years. She was active in the design of interiors including many for Alvar Aalto's own buildings and she also made working drawings for furniture from Aalto's sketches. Initially, his furniture was more popular abroad than in Finland, perhaps for the reason that Arttu Brummer cited. It was too novel to fit within the traditional Finnish home, hence its domestic reception had to wait until a broader public embraced modernism as a suitable aesthetic for domestic furnishings.

Though Artek tended to feature Alvar's designs more than Aino's, the two continued to collaborate on interiors and exhibition designs. The Finnish government commissioned Aalto to design its pavilions for the 1937 World's Fair in Paris and then the 1939 World's Fair in New York. Alvar designed the New York pavilion, but he and Aino collaborated on the interior exhibition. Their approach was nationalistic rather than simply artistic. Where the Swedes emphasized decorative arts and home furnishings, the Aaltos represented the entire culture. Though the exhibit was extensive, the dominant image was the undulating

Fig. 26.16: Alvar and Aino Aalto, Finnish Pavilion, New York World's Fair, 1939. © Ezra Stoller/Esto World's Fair 1939, Finnish Pavilion, Location: Queens NY, Architect: Alvar Aalto © Ezra Stoller/Esto. © DACS 2014.

wall of wooden slats in which were embedded gigantic photographic images of Finnish life (Fig. 26.16). If the Aaltos' furniture of the early 1930s was too internationalist for domestic consumption, their 1939 World's Fair exhibit traded on one of the most profound myths of Finnish nationalism, notably the forest as a source of inspiration, identity, and wealth. The latter was conveyed through clusters of wooden objects such as propellers, skis, and axe handles, while large statistical tables and enormous cheeses were also made of wood. The scale of the pavilion and the dense clusters of objects recalled El Lissitzky's Soviet exhibitions of the late 1920s and early 1930s—particularly the Pressa in Cologne with its lengthy photographic mural—and his display for the International Fur Trade Exhibition in Leipzig. Though one might find similarities in the exhibitions of Lissitzky and the Aaltos in terms of style,

the exhibition in New York nevertheless showed how far Finland had come as an independent nation since its separation from Russia little more than 20 years earlier.

Scandinavian Graphic Design: Advertising and the Book Arts

The Scandinavian countries had strong craft traditions on which to build practices of design for mass production during the interwar years, but they were less developed in the printing and graphic arts. All had relatively high levels of literacy but they depended on imported printing equipment and type for the production of books, newspapers, and magazines. Poster design with a strong illustrative component began in the later 19th century, but the styles were imported primarily from France and Germany. The posters of Lucian Bernhard and other *sachplakat* artists were an influence as was the general approach to commercial art that was promoted in the pages of the German magazine *Das Plakat*.

Designers who became prominent in the book and advertising industries were for the most part trained as artists or illustrators, a background they also shared with some artists who worked in the ceramics, glass, and furniture industries. By 1930, the debate between *tradis* and *funkis*, tradition and Functionalism, also raged among printers and book designers. It had less effect on advertising artists, who designed very few posters or other forms of advertising according to the Functionalist tenets of the New Typography.

In Sweden, the "artistic" poster gained some recognition in the period between 1910 and 1920. One of the first artists to become a poster designer was Wilhelm Kåge, the ceramist who initially studied painting in Sweden and then poster design in Munich, where he would have seen the posters of Ludwig Hohlwein and others working in a related style. Kåge abandoned graphic design in 1917 when the Gustavsberg Pottery recruited him to become a ceramic artist.

In addition to the applied arts, the Swedish Society of Crafts and Design was also trying to improve the quality of the graphic arts in accord with Gregor Paulsson's philosophy. Just as the organization supported Orrefors glassworks' hiring the artists Edvard Hald and Simon Gate to design glassware, so did they encourage the publisher P. A. Norstedt & Sons to bring in the artist Akke Kumlien (1884–1949) as a full-time "artistic advisor." From the time Kumlien began there in 1916 and for many years following, he designed myriad books with covers and title pages in an elegant Neo-Classical style. He also created an important and widely used Swedish typeface, Kumlien, which the Stempel Foundry in Germany released in 1943. Kumlien's approach to book design paralleled the strong Neo-Classical influence in Swedish architecture during the teens and 1920s. Though he was considered a traditionalist compared to the new Functional style that was introduced to Sweden with the Stockholm

Exhibition of 1930, his book covers nonetheless have a clean modern look. He drew the letters himself as he did the refined ornaments and rules. Kumlien's successor after World War II was Karl-Erik Forsberg (1914–1995), who had worked previously as artistic director and a book designer for the publisher Almqvist & Wiksell. Earlier, Forsberg had trained as a compositor in Basel and like Kumlien also designed typefaces including Parad in 1938 and Lunda in 1941. Both were released by the Berling Type Foundry in Lund. An early tendency towards a more contemporary style of typography was evident in the journal *flammen*, edited by the painter Georg Pauli (1855–1935) who had been a proponent of Cézanne and Cubism in Sweden. Pauli's sources for a new typography were the free typography in the poems of Mallarmé and Marinetti.

Just as the Stockholm Exhibition was influential in introducing Functionalism to the applied arts, so did it have an influence on advertising and typography. The official poster for the exhibition, whose principal image was the date of the exhibition in large silhouette numbers, was designed by the architect Sigurd Lewerentz (1885–1975), an important early modernist. Lewerentz was also responsible for the illuminated signboards on the tall advertising mast that served as a key icon of the exhibition site.

The exhibition had a particularly strong effect on Anders Billow (1890–1964), who adopted a Functionalist style in the books he designed for the printer Nordisk Rotogravyr (Nordic Rotogravure). Following Moholy-Nagy and others in Germany who claimed that the photograph was the new storytelling device of civilization, Billow came to specialize in books and periodicals that featured photographs in their design. He wrote frequently for the magazine of the Swedish Touring Club, proposing guidelines for amateur photographers, and he was also responsible for the editing and design of the organization's frequent publications. In the battle between *tradis* and *funkis*, the widespread popularity of Billow's publications for the Swedish Touring Club represented a victory for the Functionalists, although many book designers continued to work in a traditional style. San serif type never became as popular in the Nordic countries as it did elsewhere in Europe. Its simple lines conveyed to many Nordic designers the same cold quality that tubular steel did.

During the 1920s, Swedish advertising artists still featured painted or drawn illustrations, frequently influenced by French poster artists or the German *sachplakat*. By the end of the decade, some artists

Fig. 26.17: Anders Beckman, Fly with Aerotransport, poster, 1934. The National Library of Sweden.

began to use photography and photomontage. This was prevalent in posters for Esselte Reklam, one of Sweden's leading advertising agencies. It was also evident in the work of Anders Beckman (1907–1967), who became a leading exponent of a modern poster style during the 1930s. Beckman combined selected photographs with an airbrush technique, hand-painted images, and bold san serif lettering, which sometimes dominated his compositions. A major client was the Swedish airline AB Aerotransport, the predecessor of SAS, for whom Beckman designed a number of posters in a simplified style. A poster of 1934, "Fly with Aerotransport", recalling the travel posters of Herbert Matter in Switzerland, incorporated the photograph of an airplane, whose speed Beckman indicated with airbrushed lines, and photographic images of passengers waiting to board, both subordinated to the large letters for "Fly," which dominate the poster (Fig. 26.17).

Beckman, who ran a small studio in Stockholm, was instrumental in raising the status of the advertising artist in Sweden. In 1936, he joined with other artists to form the Swedish Poster Artists' Association, whose members showed their work at an art gallery, the Galerie Moderne, in 1937. With Göta Trädgårdh (1904–1984), Sweden's leading fashion illustrator and textile designer, he founded a school to provide practical training for future designers in Sweden's creative industries. Unlike the more academic schools elsewhere in Scandinavia, Anders Beckman's School, as it was known, forged a close relation between the students and the professional work of its teachers. Housed in an apartment, it remained small, though over the years it produced many of Sweden's outstanding designers in the advertising and fashion industries.

The new Functionalist ideas in book design and commercial art were less influential in the other Nordic countries. Denmark had a strong tradition of commercial art that could be traced back to the logotype and beer label for the large Danish brewery Carlsberg that architect and artist Thorvald Bindesbøll (1846–1908), better known for his earthenware

Fig. 26.18: Thorvald Bindesbøll, Carlsberg Pilsner label, 1904. Carlsberg archives.

ceramics, designed in 1904 (Fig. 26.18). Knud V. Engelhardt (1882–1931) is sometimes considered to be Denmark's first professional designer. With a background in architecture and the crafts, he interested himself in all forms of design. An early project for the Copenhagen Tramways in 1910, which he undertook with Ib Lunding (1895–1983), combined the production of destination signs and brochures with the "hard" design of the tramway cars and their interiors. The year before, Engelhardt had shown his interest in combining decoration and utility in a new design for the Copenhagen telephone directory, whose expressive gilded letters on the cover recall the highly stylized forms of the Vienna Secession artist Alfred Roller. However, inside the directory he created a clear hierarchy of information using a combination of simple and bold letters, scale, and formal spacing to create

a rational organization of the information. Calling himself an "Architect and Printer," Engelhardt designed many logotypes and emblems as well as catalogs, books, and alphabets. His practical lettering is evident in the street signs he created for the municipality of Gentofte, to the north of Copenhagen, in 1927.

Engelhardt's generalist tendency was also evident in the work of Gunnar Biilman Petersen (1897–1968), who worked for a time in Engelhardt's studio. Petersen designed books, logotypes, advertisements, and alphabets. Though his early alphabet designs featured san serif letters, he became increasingly interested in Latin lettering. Besides graphics, he also designed wine bottles and participated in the design of the world clock atop Copenhagen's Town Hall. Beginning in 1925, Petersen taught graphic arts at the Royal Danish Academy of Fine Arts where he influenced many students, particularly with his emphasis on typography. In 1949, he became the head of a newly established Department of Industrial Art at the Academy, although typography remained his primary interest.

Among book designers, Kai Friis Møller (1888–1960) exemplified the classical approach and preference for fine printing as opposed to mass-produced books. Architects, however, were more inclined to adopt the new *funkis* style of the 1930s. In 1932, the architect Steen Eiler Rasmussen (1898–1990) had arranged a seminal exhibition of British applied arts, "Britisk Brugskunst," for which he designed a catalog that closely followed the tenets of Tschichold's New Typography. It featured photographs and blocks of text that were placed asymmetrically on the pages with ample white space and large page numbers. That same year the architect and silversmith Kaj Fiskers adapted Functionalism to Neo-Classical rhetoric when he redesigned the professional journal *Arkitekten* in a clean symmetrical style with a clear hierarchy and plenty of white space. The following year the co-editors Steen Eiler Rasmussen and Willy Hansen redesigned the journal according to the tenets of the New Typography, with an asymmetrical flush-left layout that included a bold san serif title.

Danish poster artists showed little interest in the New Typography, preferring instead to continue a tradition of drawn images, frequently derived from techniques of caricature but also influenced by French and German poster artists. As in France during the 1890s, Danish posters frequently promoted cabarets, plays, and during the interwar years, films. Valdemar Andersen (1875–1978), who became active as a poster designer around 1900, is considered to be the first major poster designer in Denmark comparable to Jules Chéret in France. Initially he was strongly influenced by Toulouse-Lautrec and developed a related style of narrative, though less painterly and more illustrative.

Besides posters, Andersen employed the same illustrative technique to the design of book covers. Others who followed him were Thor Bøglund (1890–1959), who took a special interest in lettering and whose style was more influenced by Lucian Bernhard and Ludwig Hohlwein, and Sven Brasch (1886–1970), perhaps the most prolific Danish poster designer and illustrator in the interwar years. Brasch had a keen ability to depict the activities of daily life, particularly those of the Danish middle class. His covers for popular magazines such as *Tik Tak*, *Pressens*, and *Vore Damer* (*Our Women*) showed elegant men and women in fancy dress or even bathing attire while some of these figures also appeared, along with other images, in the many drawings he did for book covers and magazines. Brasch was well known for his movie posters, which he mainly produced as lithographs or linocuts. He did about 500 in the years between World War I and the 1930s. They frequently featured images of the films' stars created in various styles, such as his portrait of Greta Garbo whom he portrayed with a gestural line and lightly textured hair and ruffles (Fig. 26.19). The prolific Brasch also did many posters and advertisements to promote commercial products. An outstanding draftsman, he ranged from the derivative to the personally expressive. This flexible approach to commercial art may have mitigated against developing a distinct personal style that would have made his work better known internationally.

In Norway, Sverre Pettersen (1884–1959) was a decorative artist who was also an influential book designer. Though Norwegian designers produced ambitious luxury books, little progress was made in improving the design of more popular machine-printed editions. There were, however, some experiments in the early 1930s that made a positive impression when they were displayed in Sweden. The advertising and book artists tended to follow foreign examples, though the painter Per Lasson Krogh (1889–1965), who had a distinctive illustrative style, was known internationally as a poster designer during the 1920s. Among his

Fig. 26.19: Sven Brasch, *The Mysterious Woman*, poster, 1929. Design Museum, Denmark. © DACS 2017.

Fig. 26.20: Topi Vikstedt, *God Passes*, cover, 1929. Courtesy National Library of Finland.

continued to work as an illustrator and book designer for various publishers. Subsequently he formed another office for illustration and commercial art with his wife Karin. As an independent artist, Vikstedt designed many book covers for Otava Publishers, a firm he joined in 1923 as the resident book designer (Fig. 26.20). Although he never gave up classicism completely, he did begin to draw more modern covers for Otava, particularly in a Cubist style. In 1926, Vikstedt was a founder of the graphic design department in the Central School of Arts and Crafts, thus contributing to the beginning of formal graphic design education in Finland.

During the 1930s, modern designs appeared selectively in Finnish advertising. The airbrush posters of Eric Gardberg (1905–1969) for Stockmann's Department Store recalled French fashion illustration of the period. Other artists such as Einari Wehmas (1898–1955), Jorma Suhonen (1911–1987), and the team of Göran Hongell, primarily a designer of glassware, and Gunnar Forsström (1894–1958) designed posters in styles that ranged from the Cubist-inspired work of Wehmas to the posters of Suhonen and Hongell and Forsström that featured flat colors and san serif lettering. Suhonen's poster, *Visit Finland*, was done in anticipation of the 1940 Olympics that Finland had hoped to host before that hope was dashed by the onset of World War II (Plate 35).

Bibliography
Bibliographic essay

One of the early surveys of Scandinavian design that included this period is David McFadden, ed., *Scandinavian Modern Design 1880–1980*, the catalog of an exhibition at the Cooper-Hewitt Museum in New York. Charlotte and Peter Fiell's *Scandinavian Design* is predominantly a visual record, while Kjetil Fallan's *Scandinavian Design: Alternative Histories* exemplifies the most recent scholarship on the subject. Erik Dal, *Scandinavian Bookmaking in the Twentieth Century* is an indispensable guide to this little-known topic of book

clients were a brewery and the newspaper *Dag Bladet*. Olaf Krohn (1863–1933) and other artists associated with the Fabritius advertising agency also produced posters.

One of the early local design offices that created advertisements and advertising posters in Finland was De Tre (The Three), founded around 1913 by Toivo (Topi) Vikstedt (1891–1930), Bruno Tuukkanen (1891–1979), and Harry Röneholm (1892–1951). After two years, the principals went their separate ways. Vikstedt design. Essays on modern Scandinavian design include Jennifer Hawking Opie, "Lovely Neoclassical Byways: Art Deco in Scandinavia," in Charlotte Benton, Tim Benton, and Ghislaine Woods, eds., *Art Deco 1910–1939*; and the late Frederick Wildhagen, "The Scandinavian Countries: Design for the Welfare Society," in *History of Industrial Design 1919–1990: The Domain of Design.*

Utopia & Reality: Modernity in Sweden, 1900–1960 is the catalog of an exhibition at the Bard Graduate Center in New York, which includes a number of important essays. Other useful essays are Gillian Naylor, "Swedish Grace … or the Acceptable Face of Modernism?" in Paul Greenhalgh, ed., *Modernism in Design*; and Gunilla Frick, "Radical Change or Stagnation? Swedish Post-war Decorative Art," *Scandinavian Journal of Design History* 6 (1996) and "Furniture Art or a Machine to Sit On? Swedish Furniture Design and Radical Reforms," *Scandinavian Journal of Design History* 1 (1991).

Modern Danish design is covered in the exhibition catalog *Dansk Design 1910–1945: Art deco & funktionalisme*, while Svend Erik Moller, ed., *Danish Design* is an older survey of the subject. More current scholarship is evident in a number of articles: Kevin Davies, "Twentieth Century Danish Furniture Design and the English Vernacular Tradition," *Scandinavian Journal of Design History* 7 (1997); Steen Ejlers, "Architects in Danish Graphic Design," *Scandinavian Journal of Design History* 7 (1997); Lise Osvald, "The Story of Kaj Dessau's BO, 1928–1941," *Scandinavian Journal of Design History* 3 (1993); Charlotte Paludan, "Marie Gudme Leth: A Pioneer in Danish Textile Design," *Scandinavian Journal of Design History* 5 (1995); and Claire Selkurt, "New Classicism: Design of the 1920s in Denmark," *The Journal of Decorative and Propaganda Arts* 4 (Spring 1987).

Recent scholarship on Norwegian industrial design is exemplified by Kjetil Fallan's 2007 doctoral dissertation, *Modern Transformed: The Domestication of Industrial Design Culture in Norway, ca. 1940–1970.* It complements an earlier, more extensive, survey, by the late Frederik Wildhagen, *Norge i Form: Kunsthåndverk*

og Design under Industrikulturen. Studies of Finnish design history are more numerous. Most recently, Pekka Korvenmaa has published a brief survey, *Finnish Design: A Concise History.* Marianne Aav and Nina Stritzler-Levine, eds., *Finnish Modern Design: Utopian Ideals and Everyday Realities, 1930–1997* is the catalog of an exhibition at the Bard Graduate Center, while Ulf Hård af Segerstad, *Modern Finnish Design* is a much earlier survey. More specialized books, notably about Aino and Alvar Aalto and Artek are the exhibition catalog *Artek 1935 – Artek 1985*; and Thomas Kellein, *Alvar & Aino Aalto. Design: Collection Bischofberger.* Ilkka Huovio's doctoral dissertation, *Invitation from the Future: Treatise of the Roots of the School of Arts and Crafts and its Development into a University Level School 1871–1973,* is a detailed account of how Finland's most important design school developed. Päivi Hovi-Wasastjerna's *Mainoskuva Suomessa: Kehitys ja Vaikutteet 1890-Luvulta 1030 – Luvun Alkuun,* a history of Finnish advertising art, is based on her doctoral dissertation, the first completed at the University of Art and Design in Helsinki. Two articles that focus on the Aaltos and Artek are William C. Miller, "Furniture, Painting, and Applied Designs: Alvar Aalto's Search for Architectural Form," *The Journal of Decorative and Propaganda Arts* 6 (Fall 1987); and Renja Souminen-Kokkonen, "Designing a Room of One's Own: The Architect Aino Marsio-Aalto and Artek," *Scandinavian Journal of Design History* 7 (1997).

Books

General

Dal, Erik. *Scandinavian Bookmaking in the Twentieth Century.* Urbana, Chicago, and London: University of Illinois Press, 1968.

Fallon, Kjetil. *Scandinavian Design: Alternative Histories.* London and New York: Berg, 2012.

Fiell, Charlotte and Peter, *Scandinavian Design.* Cologne: Taschen, 2002.

McFadden, David, ed. *Scandinavian Modern Design 1880–1980.* New York: Abrams, 1982.

Sweden

Creagh, Lucy, Helena Kåberg, and Barbara Miller Lane, eds. *Modern Swedish Design. Three Founding Texts.* New York: Museum of Modern Art, c. 2008.

Design in Sweden. Stockholm: The Swedish Institute, 1972.

Plath, Iona. *The Decorative Arts of Sweden.* New York: Dover Publications, 1948.

Utopia & Reality: Modernity in Sweden, 1900–1960. New Haven and London: Yale University Press, 2002.

Denmark

Dansk Design 1910–1945: Art deco & funktionalisme. Copenhagen: Det Danske Kunstindustrimuseum, 1997.

Moller, Svend Erik, ed. *Danish Design.* Copenhagen: Det Danske Selskab, 1974.

Norway

Wildhagen, Frederik. *Norge i Form: Kunsthåndverk og Design under Industrikulturen.* Oslo: J. M. Stenersens Forlag, 1988.

Finland

Aav, Marianne and Nina Stritzler-Levine, eds. *Finnish Modern Design: Utopian Ideals and Everyday Realities, 1930–1997.* New Haven and London: Yale University Press, 1998.

Artek 1935 – Artek 1985. Helsinki: Taideteollisuusmuseo, 1985.

Hård af Segerstad, Ulf. *Modern Finnish Design.* New York and Washington: Praeger, 1969.

Hovi-Wasastjerna, Päivi, *Mainoskuva Suomessa: Kehitys ja Vaikutteet 1890–Luvulta 1030 – Luvun Alkuun.* Helsinki: Taideteollisen Korkeakoulun Juikaisusarja, 1990.

Kellein, Thomas. *Alvar & Aino Aalto. Design: Collection Bischofberger.* Ostfildern: Hatje Cantz Verlag, 2005.

Korvenmaa, Pekka. *Finnish Design: A Concise History.* Helsinki: University of Art and Design, 2009.

Chapters in books

Naylor, Gillian, "Swedish Grace … or the Acceptable Face of Modernism?" in Paul Greenhalgh, ed. *Modernism in Design.* London: Reaktion Books, 1990.

Opie, Jennifer Hawkins, "Lovely Neoclassical Byways: Art Deco in Scandinavia," in Charlotte Benton, Tim Benton, and Ghislaine Woods, eds. *Art Deco 1910–1939.* Boston, New York, and London: Bullfinch Press, 2003.

Wildhagen, Frederik, "The Scandinavian Countries: Design for the Welfare Society," in *History of Industrial Design 1919–1990: The Domain of Design.* Milan: Electa, 1991.

Articles

Davies, Kevin, "Twentieth Century Danish Furniture Design and the English Vernacular Tradition," *Scandinavian Journal of Design History* 7 (1997).

Ejlers, Steen, "Architects in Danish Graphic Design," *Scandinavian Journal of Design History* 7 (1997).

Frick, Gunilla, "Furniture Art or a Machine to Sit On? Swedish Furniture Design and Radical Reforms," *Scandinavian Journal of Design History* 1 (1991).

—"Radical Change or Stagnation? Swedish Post-war Decorative Art," *Scandinavian Journal of Design History* 6 (1996).

Gram, Magdalena, "National Typography as Exemplified by Akke Kumlien," *Scandinavian Journal of Design History* 5 (1995).

Miller, William C. "Furniture, Painting, and Applied Designs: Alvar Aalto's Search for Architectural Form," *The Journal of Decorative and Propaganda Arts* 6 (Fall 1987).

Osvald, Lise, "The Story of Kaj Dessau's BO, 1928–1941," *Scandinavian Journal of Design History* 3 (1993).

Paludan, Charlotte, "Marie Gudme Leth: A Pioneer in Danish Textile Design," *Scandinavian Journal of Design History* 5 (1995).

Selkurt, Claire, "New Classicism: Design of the 1920s in Denmark," *The Journal of Decorative and Propaganda Arts* 4 (Spring 1987).

Souminen-Kokkonen, Renja, "Designing a Room of One's Own: The Architect Aino Marsio-Aalto and Artek," *Scandinavian Journal of Design History* 7 (1997).

Dissertations and theses

Fallan, Kjetil. *Modern Transformed: The Domestication of Industrial Design Culture in Norway, ca. 1940–1970.* PhD Dissertation, Norwegian University of Science and Technology, 2007.

Huovio, Ilkka. *Invitation from the Future: Treatise of the Roots of the School of Arts and Crafts and its Development into a University Level School 1871–1973.* PhD Dissertation, University of Tampere, 1998.

Chapter 27: Italy, Germany, the Soviet Union, and Portugal 1922–1940

Introduction

No single model characterizes the way design was managed in the European dictatorial regimes from the 1920s to World War II. Benito Mussolini became Italy's Prime Minister in 1922 and remained in office until his ouster in 1943. Though he fostered an architectural and visual rhetoric that was grandiose and bombastic, modernist architecture, furniture design, and graphics also flourished during his reign. In essence, Mussolini had no overarching vision of how design could serve the state, although much public architecture and most propaganda employed an imposing style that easily became associated with the Fascist Party.

In Germany, the architects and designers who forged a new modern style in the Weimar Republic before Hitler came to power were harassed by the Nazis after Hitler became Chancellor and most left Germany. The Nazi Party sought to instate a traditional *Heimat* or homeland style that was associated with conservative nationalist traditions. The party's heavy hand was most evident in its visual propaganda, which ranged from posters to exhibitions, but it could also be seen in architecture, where classicism determined the rhetoric of public buildings and folk forms the appearance of numerous smaller structures and private dwellings. Nonetheless, many design values from the Weimar years continued, though in a different form, particularly the aim to provide decent housing for the working class and basic functional furniture forms for the home and workplace. As well, Henry Ford's example of a low-cost mass-produced automobile that was accessible to large numbers of people became an ideal of Hitler's even though the decision to produce armaments in the late 1930s prevented him from realizing it. In essence, the Nazis pursued a design policy of what the late historian John Heskett called "modernism and archaism," shifting from modernity to tradition as it suited the needs of a particular policy or strategy.

In the Soviet Union, Joseph Stalin had no use for the modern ideas of the avant-garde and from the time he became the undisputed leader of the nation in the late 1920s, he cracked down on avant-garde proposals to create new architecture, graphics, and all other forms of design. He closed the national design school, Vkhutemas, and instituted a monumental style of Socialist Realism that was adopted for all art forms from literature and painting to photography, exhibitions, and architecture. The style was particularly evident in the Soviet arts and in propaganda but could be seen as well in the heavy-handed buildings that were constructed during Stalin's reign.

When António de Oliveira Salazar became Prime Minister of Portugal in 1926, he instituted what came to be called the Estado Novo or New State. He established a Secretariat of Propaganda but did not espouse a ponderous visual style. In fact, many of the artists who worked for the Estado Novo came from the modernist milieu that preceded it. However, like Mussolini, Hitler, and Stalin, Salazar promoted large propagandistic exhibitions that became highly visible examples of state power.

Italy

Fascism

The political chaos in Italy following World War I was fertile ground for the emergence of new social movements. The Fascist Party, led by Benito Mussolini, a former journalist, was the one that quickly triumphed. To oppose the Socialists and Catholics, Mussolini formed a group of paramilitary squads that engaged in street brawls and other forms of violence to intimidate the opposition parties and the public. The black shirts they wore, and which gave them their name, derived from the red shirts worn by the followers of Giuseppe Garibaldi, who led the struggle for a united Italy in the 1860s.

In October 1922, Mussolini marshaled 25,000 of his supporters for a March on Rome. To stave off a civil war, King Victor Emmanuel III named Mussolini Prime Minister and asked him to form a new Fascist government. By 1926, the Fascists had abolished elections, censored the press and other public media, and dissolved all opposition parties. Mussolini adopted the title "Il Duce," (The Leader) and introduced the slogan, "Mussolini is always right."

As a former journalist, Mussolini was aware of propaganda's importance. He recognized the need to create an aura of pomp and ceremony to reinforce his own power and that of the Fascist Party. In fact, he founded his own newspaper, *Il Popolo d'Italia* (*People of Italy*), in 1914, and after the Fascists came to power, this paper continued to be a principal propaganda organ of the Fascist regime. The paper also published an annual Fascist almanac and a weekly magazine, *La Rivista Illustrata del Popolo d'Italia* (*The Illustrated Review of People of Italy*), whose covers were created by Italy's best modern illustrators and designers—Xanti Schawinsky, Fortunato Depero, Enrico Prampolini, Mario Sironi, and Bruno Munari among them.

Most of the propaganda iconography that Mussolini adopted came from Roman history. In 1926, he appropriated as the official emblem of the party the fasces, a bundle of elm or birch rods bound together with an axe. Roman guards called *lictors* originally carried them as symbols of unity and power. Historian Dennis Doordan notes that the fasces were omnipresent during the Fascist years. They appeared on building facades as the swastika did in Germany and designers adopted them for a wide range of goods from jewelry and desk accessories to furniture and wall lamps.

The ubiquity of the fasces was part of the Fascist identification with Rome and the revival of its glory. As Il Duce, Mussolini likened himself to Caesar. He

supported a cult of *Romanità* or Roman-ness through which he sought to identify the Fascists as the party that would revive Rome's past glory. They promoted the Roman salute instead of the handshake and adopted Roman numerals for counting the years after 1922. These were combined with E.F. (Era Fascista) instead of the conventional A.D. (Anno Domini).

Gradually Rome became the center of Fascist activity and architects sought to revive its earlier splendor with grandiose projects such as the Foro Mussolini (Mussolini Forum). Historian Simonetta Falasca-Zamponi makes the point that by linking Fascism to Rome, Mussolini wanted to persuade people that the movement was a natural consequence of Italian history. Thus, references to Rome were not nostalgic but instead reinforced the idea that Roman history was the foundation on which to build a strong future.

Whereas Hitler established a Ministry of Propaganda and Enlightenment under Joseph Goebbels shortly after he became Chancellor, Mussolini did not create an Undersecretariat for Press and Propaganda until 1933, ten years after the Fascists came to power. Prior to that, the press, film, radio, and other forms of propaganda were managed from his press office. It was only in 1937 that the regime established a full-scale propaganda ministry, which was called the Ministry of Popular Culture (Minculpop). It combined all the previous propaganda offices and for the first time countered the regime's former emphasis on negative censorship with a positive approach intended to promote Fascist principles more actively in all fields of social life.

Unlike Hitler, Mussolini was surprisingly open to diverse forms of art and architecture. Although the work most closely associated with the Fascist regime tended towards the monumental, abstract artists were allowed to show their work as were modern designers and architects whose furniture, interiors, and buildings were far more prevalent in the various exhibitions of applied art and design during the Fascist years than in

Fig. 27.01: *Gioventù Fascista*, cover, 1931. The Wolfsonian–Florida International University, Miami Beach, Florida, Gift of Steven Heller, XC2008.07.17.210. Photo: David Almeida.

and even school notebooks called Quaderni, whose covers featured a variety of propaganda illustrations, the regime published *Gioventù Fascista* (*Fascist Youth*), with covers in a contemporary style by many well-known designers (Fig. 27.01).

Mussolini's chauvinistic attitude towards women resulted in their near absence from official propaganda imagery, while his macho view of men was evident in the presentations of male cadres who bonded as they demonstrated their devotion to Fascist ideals. A 1933 poster by C. V. Testi (dates unconfirmed) that promoted the Exhibition of the Fascist Revolution in Rome exemplifies this view. Three square-jawed militaristic figures, who recall the soldiers of a Roman legion, signify a strong devotion to the party's ideals as they march forward (Plate 36). The strong diagonal— a compositional device evident in many Fascist posters and publications—conveys a sense of dynamic movement. The concentration of male imagery was confined to Fascist Party propaganda, however, and was not paralleled by the general iconography of Italian advertising.

The regime also used design to promote its accomplishments, and different ministries hired designers to undertake various projects. Among these, the Ministry of Public Works stands out for the ambitious publications and exhibitions it commissioned during the 1930s. Much of the work was done by Attilio Calzavera (1901–1952), who began his association with the ministry in 1932. For more than a decade, he designed publications and exhibitions that mingled avant-garde elements with the obligatory Fascist rhetoric. His major achievement among the publication designs was the voluminous report, *Opere Pubbliche 1922–1932* (*Public Works 1922–1932*), which documented ten years of construction projects undertaken by the Fascist regime (Fig. 27.02). On the cover, Calzavera represented the Roman numeral X or ten as a building that supported the numbers for the years bracketing the decade. The power of the forms was enhanced by the three-dimensional numbers,

built projects or mass-produced objects either for the regime or the market.

The principal icon of the Fascist regime was Mussolini himself. His strapping form and shaven head could be seen everywhere, even in school textbooks. Besides depicting Mussolini, Fascist Party magazines and posters portrayed marching cadres of young male Blackshirts or squadristi, while the children, mainly boys, who were members of the Opera Nazionale Balilla, the party organization charged with their indoctrination, were shown in their specially designed uniforms—short pants, black shirts, and black hats with tassels. The regime produced many publications for the Balilla organization. Besides posters, handbooks,

Fig. 27.02: Attilo Calzavera, *Opere Pubbliche 1922–1932*, cover, 1933. The Wolfsonian–Florida International University, Miami Beach, Florida, The Mitchell Wolfson, Jr. Collection, 83.2.979. Photo: David Almeida.

dramatic perspective, and stark contrast of light and dark. Calzavera's title page and ten chapter headings were equally dramatic, combining images depicted from unusual angles with bold black letters that recalled those of Futurist publications. Calzavera also designed a series of impressive exhibitions for the Ministry of Public Works and several other government bodies that set high standards in this field.

While Mussolini did not fully exploit the propaganda potential of radio and film, he placed great emphasis on large public exhibitions to reinforce Fascist

ideals. These in fact were the most highly developed forms of Fascist propaganda and also the most original. The first of them and the one that defined the scale and rhetoric of those that followed was the Mostra della Rivoluzione Fascista (Exhibition of the Fascist Revolution), which was held in Rome in 1932. Its purpose was to commemorate the first ten years of Fascist rule by celebrating the March on Rome and the years that preceded it. The director and lead designer was Dino Alfieri (1886–1966), a Fascist politician who subsequently became deputy director for Press and Propaganda and later Minister of People's Culture.

More important than formal techniques was the overall capacity of the exhibition to evoke in the spectators an emotional loyalty to Fascism. It did not feature a single design style but instead provided a vehicle for modernist architects to work side by side with more traditional artists and designers. The layout consisted of multiple rooms that traced the rise of the Fascist Party in a chronological manner before leading the public into a series of spaces that glorified Fascism and the actions that brought the Fascists to power. Among the project's architects was Giuseppe Terragni (1904–1943), who was allied with the nascent Rationalist movement. In his design for the Room of 1922, which dramatized the events prior to the Fascist takeover that year, Terragni used a variety of bombastic techniques, some likely inspired by Expressionist stage design and others by El Lissitzky's display of the Soviet press, held at Cologne's Pressa Exhibition in 1928.

Terragni combined models, dramatic lighting, photomontage, and huge cut-out figures to celebrate the heroic actions of the party cadres. The apotheosis of his design was a three-dimensional wall construction entitled "Adunate" (Mass Meeting). It featured several large airplane propellers whose blades, covered with photographs of mass rallies, were set against a backdrop of hundreds of plaster hands in a Fascist salute. Pointed towards the sky, the hands represented "the rising tide of Fascism," as one critic wrote.

Terragni's powerful display was complemented by the quietly dramatic Gallery of Fasci created by the painter Mario Sironi (1885–1961), a leader of the conservative Novecento art movement, and the serene Chapel of Martyrs, designed by the Rationalist architect Adalberto Libera (1903–1963) and Antonio Valente (dates unconfirmed), an architect and designer of theater and film sets. Libera, along with Mario del Renzi (1897–1967), also designed the modernistic facade of the exhibition hall, which featured four huge stylized fasces, aligned as classical columns and combined with large three-dimensional letters that spelled out the exhibition's name.

The exhibit was an enormous success and prompted numerous others that focused on issues of politics and economics. Among these were the Mostra Aeronautica (Aeronautical Exhibition) of 1934, the Mostra Augustea della Romanità (The Augustan Exhibition of Romanness) in 1937, and the Mostra della Razza (Exhibition of the Race) in 1942. Although modern architecture and design were less evident after 1935 in the official Fascist displays and the buildings that housed them, the design of exhibitions, as in the Soviet Union, nonetheless remained an activity where avant-garde techniques could serve the purposes of political propaganda.

Futurism

Before World War I, Mussolini and Filippo Tommaso Marinetti, the founder of the Futurist movement, had much in common. For a time, both were interested in anarchism, supported violence and war, and opposed those who governed Italy—the king, the Church, and the bureaucracy. After the war, Marinetti became a member of the Fascist movement's central committee and ran for parliament in 1919 as one of the new Fascist Party's first candidates. But he was more a poet than a politician and his extreme demands for change were soon at odds with Mussolini's pragmatic and tactical approach. Nonetheless, Mussolini supported the first post-war Futurist exhibition in 1919 and continued

to tolerate Marinetti and the Futurists, while keeping them from positions of political or cultural power.

Marinetti kept on recruiting new members of the Futurist movement after the war. They belonged to what has been called the Second Futurism to distinguish it from the polemical avant-garde activity that occurred earlier. The various artists, designers, and architects who called themselves Futurists in this period produced new projects, although few were as radical as the pre-war paintings of Boccioni, Carrà, and Balla, the architectural drawings of Sant'Elia, or the first typographic compositions of Marinetti and Ardengo Soffici. Marinetti published his book *Les Mots en Liberté Futuriste* in 1919, thus keeping alive his dramatic typography, but he had created most of the contents before and during World War I. The various Futurist exhibitions in the 1920s were oriented more to the past and the present than to the future, although Marinetti did launch one new Futurist initiative in 1929, *Aeropittura*, which consisted of painting and sculpture dedicated to aviation. The Futurists' interest in airplanes and flying paralleled the Fascists' interest in flight. Not only did Italy set up a Ministry of Aeronautics in 1923 to unite military and civil aviation—the second country to do so after Great Britain—but Italo Balbo, who became the Air Minister in 1926, accomplished an amazing feat in 1933, when he led a fleet of 24 Italian S-55 flying boats on a round-trip flight from Rome to the Century of Progress exhibition in Chicago, Illinois.

Ultimately the Futurists' fascination with machines was rhetorical rather than practical. Paradoxically, most of the furniture pieces and decorative objects they made were crafted by hand. In 1915, Giacomo Balla (1871–1958) and Fortunato Depero (1892–1960) wrote an important manifesto, *Ricostruzione Futurista dell'Universo* (*Futurist Reconstruction of the Universe*), in which they called for new kinds of objects that could populate a dynamic universe. For Balla and Depero, there was no limit to what could be done. It was all a matter of imagination and will. Watching an airplane ascending while a band played in a town square might lead to concerts in the sky; the need to vary one's environment led to the idea of transformable clothes; and the combination of speed and noise generated the idea for a rotoplastic noise fountain. While none of these projects was practical, they signified a vision that was attuned to the possibilities of a new modern environment.

Between 1915 and 1920, Balla produced many maquettes for patterned lamps and lampshades, carpets, cushions, fans, and tiles. He made wooden screens, chairs, and dressers that he covered with brightly colored curved and angular shapes and he created dramatic designs for interiors and Futurist clothing. He also assembled large flowers and plants from wooden planes to emphasize his and Depero's concept of an "artificial landscape." Central to their aesthetic was an interest in movement, speed, and lines of force, which enabled them to generate a large variety of novel objects.

Though Balla had done much of his decorative work by 1920, he did create a few objects after that time including a colorful coffee service in 1928 (Plate 37). Depero was the more active of the two men during the

Fig. 27.03: Fortunato Depero and Fedele Azari, *Depero Futurista*, cover, 1927. The Wolfsonian–Florida International University, Miami Beach, Florida, The Mitchell Wolfson, Jr. Collection 83.2.459. © DACS 2017.

Fascist years. In 1919 in his hometown of Rovereto, he opened his Casa d'Arte Depero (Depero House of Art), which was modeled on a similar Casa d'Arte of Balla's. Depero designed furniture, toys, tapestries, pillows, and clothing that were produced in one-off versions or limited runs. A small team of women, headed by his wife Rosetta, wove the tapestries and fabrics. They also sewed the garments and pillows and embroidered them with Depero's designs. A team of men made the furniture and most likely the wooden toys. In the logo that Depero designed to promote the Casa d'Arte he placed a woman, probably his wife, at a work table or loom within a house, while a larger figure composed of dynamic curves, presumably himself, looks in from outside.

Besides designing objects, Depero created occasional interiors, notably a wildly decorated one for the Cabaret del Diavolo in Rome, where he designated a sequence of three rooms as Inferno, Purgatory, and Paradise after Dante's epic poem, *The Divine Comedy*. He was active as an advertising artist and illustrator, collaborating with major clients, particularly Campari, the company that made cordials and other drinks, for whom he did many whimsical advertisements with abstract figures and ornaments. He also provided covers and drawings for journals and mass-circulation magazines. In 1927, Depero teamed up with Fedele Azari (1895–1930), an aviator and fellow Futurist, to publish a book of his advertising graphics, *Depero Futurista*. Instead of a binding, however, the pages and cover were held together with two nuts and bolts, exemplifying the Futurist idea of the book as an object (Fig. 27.03). He continued his polemics and self-promotion in a 1932 publication, *Manifesto dell'arte pubblicitaria futurista* (*Manifesto of Futurist Publicity Art*), which affirmed a strong relation between Futurism and advertising and characterized advertising as the art of the future.

Depero's most ambitious advertising project was a kiosk he designed for the publishing house Bestetti, Tuminelli & Treves in 1927. Created for the

Fig. 27.04: Fortunato Depero, kiosk for Bestetti, Tuminelli & Treves, 1927. The Museum of Modern and Contemporary Art of Trento and Roverto. © DACS 2017.

third Monza Biennale, it was an example of what he called "typographic architecture." Attached to the small building were huge three-dimensional letters that spelled out the publisher's name. On either side of the structure were columns of letters that repeated words from the facade (Fig. 27.04). Inside, Depero continued his architectural approach to typography with designs for display stands that were shaped like huge letters. His combination of a building and a billboard relates to the dynamic objects that he and Balla called for their leaflet of 1915 in *Futurist Reconstruction of the Universe*. While Depero proposed a similar stand for Campari, which was never built, the Monza kiosk more than likely influenced the subsequent use of large three-dimensional letters on the facades of buildings designed for the Fascist regime. A good example is the facade for the Exhibition of the Fascist Revolution that Adalberto Libera and Mario del Renzi designed in 1932. Depero

also exploded letters into three-dimensional forms in some of his paintings and advertising graphics as a way of making them more dynamic. This technique could also be seen on many Fascist posters and magazine covers.

Following the lead of Balla and Depero, other Futurists established studios to produce hand-crafted goods as well as advertising. Among them was Pippo Rizzo (1897–1934), who brought Futurist ideas south to Palermo in Sicily. In his own Casa d'Arte, Rizzo formed a group to make furniture and decorative objects, while also producing fashion designs and advertising. The work of the studio was shown locally as well as at several of the larger exhibitions of decorative art and design in Monza and Milan between 1923 and 1930.

In the town of Albisola, Tullio D'Albisola (née Mazzotti) (1899–1971) designed and produced

Fig. 27.05: Tullio D'Albisola, Futurist ceramic jug, date unconfirmed. Private Collection.

Futurist ceramics in the Casa Mazzotti, a ceramics factory that his father founded. D'Albisola introduced Futurist elements into his own ceramics as early as 1925 and by 1929 he was exhibiting pieces with unusual shapes and strange combinations of forms to which he gave special names such as arc vases, Futurist plates, flower antipasto services, projectile vases, and electric bonbonnières (Fig. 27.05). Beginning in the 1930s, when the Mazzotti factory moved to new premises, D'Albisola invited other Futurists to design ceramic objects that the factory could produce. Among those who responded were the sculptor Mino Rosso (1904–1963), Bruno Munari (1907–1998), Farfa (a.k.a. Vittorio Osvaldo Tommasini) (1881–1964), and Marinetti's wife Benedetta (1897–1977), who designed *piatti murali* or mural plates. Some of the Futurist ceramics produced at the Mazzotti factory were decorated with pictures of airplanes, thus aligning them with the *Aeropittura* Futurists. D'Albisola, who was a poet and polemicist as well as an artist, in fact coined the term "aeroceramics" and also published a "Manifesto of Futurist Ceramics" with Marinetti in 1938. He intended his own work to challenge the more conventional ceramic production of Sevrès and the Vienna Workshops and, closer to home, the Italian ceramics based on classical

ideals that Gio Ponti designed for the ceramics factory Richard-Ginori.

Futurist decorative objects were of considerable aesthetic interest, but they had little influence on the design of commercial goods. The case was different for Futurist graphic arts. Since the founding of Futurism in 1909, Marinetti and other Futurists had designed books as well as posters and other forms of publicity to promote their exhibitions and performances. Depero was the first of the Futurists to work extensively as an advertising artist, but others became active as well. Futurism had a major impact on Italian advertising and graphic design during the interwar years as was evident in the special issues devoted to it by several leading magazines in the field.

Nicolai Diulgheroff (1901–1982), a Bulgarian who trained as an architect and was a former Bauhaus student, designed many advertising posters, publication covers, and exhibitions as well as ceramics for D'Albisola's Casa Mazzotti. A member of the Turin Futurists, he invented a form of dynamic composition for what he called *cartelli lanciatore* or hurled posters. These featured abstract depictions of objects, forms, and letters that moved in multiple directions along diagonal axes or otherwise created the impression of motion. Some of Diulgheroff's designs, such as those for the covers of the *Almanacco dell'Italia* (*Almanach of Italy*), were less dynamic but nonetheless featured energetic arrangements of bold letters and forms.

Both Vinicio Paladini (1902–1971) and Ivo Pannaggi (1901–1981) were members of the political left who were active in the Futurist movement in the early 1920s. They brought to their work influences from Russian Constructivism, Dada, and the Bauhaus and these were particularly evident in the book covers they designed for several progressive Italian publishers. The Soviet book covers of Alexander Rodchenko were a strong reference for both men, who were among the first to use photomontage in Italy.

The rhetoric of Futurist graphics with its emphasis on modernity, speed, and technology had a strong influence on the look of Fascist propaganda, particularly posters, whose lettering tended to be blocky and sculptural like that adopted by many Futurists. However, two designers active in the *Aeropittura* movement, Bruno Munari (1907–1998) and Riccardo Castagnedi (1912–1999), who adopted the professional name Ricas, forsook the conventions of Futurist graphics for an approach that drew more heavily on other avant-garde movements—Dada, Surrealism, and the New Typography. In 1929, Munari began to work in advertising, freelancing in different studios including Cossio, which pioneered the use of

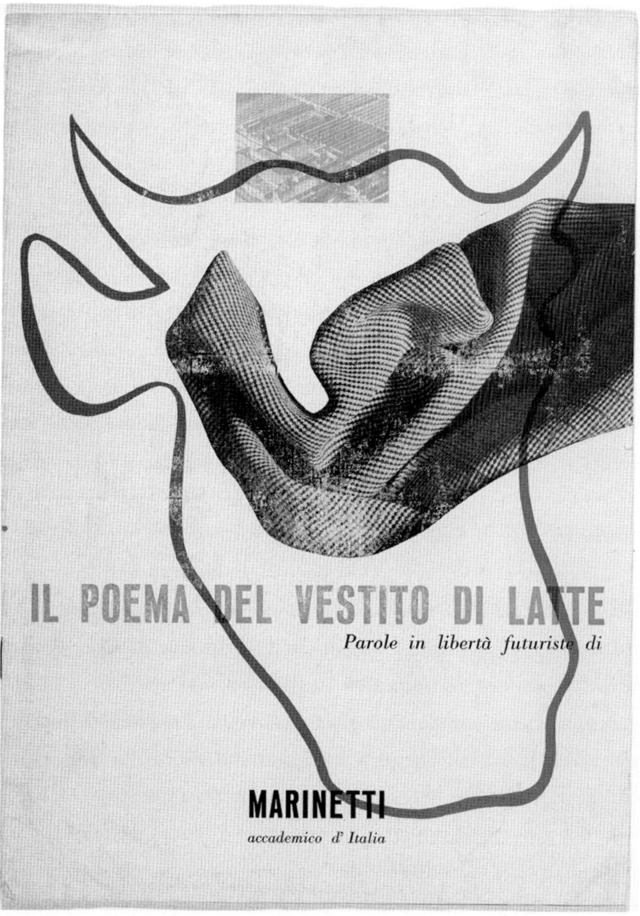

Fig. 27.06: Bruno Munari, *Il Poema del Vestito di Latte*, cover, 1937. The Wolfsonian–Florida International University, Miami Beach, Florida, The Mitchell Wolfson, Jr. Collection, 84.2.419, Photo: David Almeida.

animated advertising cartoons in Italy. The following year, Munari and Ricas opened their own graphic design studio, one of the first in Italy. Studio Ricas + Munari was extremely active until it closed in the late 1930s. Both artists designed numerous covers for *L'Ala d'Italia*, the Fascist aviation magazine, where they introduced new techniques of collage, photomontage, and more conceptual graphics. In 1937, Munari designed the cover and layout for a long poem of Marinetti's entitled *Il Poema del Vestito di Latte* (*The Poem of the Milk Vest*) (Fig. 27.06). For his design, Munari made no reference to Marinetti's earlier cacophonous typographic compositions, adopting instead the approach of the New Typography. Like El Lissitzky, Munari gave the book a cinematic feel by distributing photographs and photographic fragments throughout the text, which was set in a modern face and laid out with extremely wide leading to create a feeling of space on the pages. Though Munari's work was heavily influenced by Dada and Surrealism, he and Ricas were among the first Italian graphic designers to introduce the influence of the New Typography in Italy.

In exhibition design, Enrico Prampolini (1894–1956) was the most prominent of the Futurists. An early member of the Futurist movement who was widely known in Europe for his abstract paintings and theater sets, Prampolini designed numerous exhibitions for the Fascist regime. An early project was a room, created jointly with another Futurist, Gerardo Dottori (1884–1977), for the Mostra della Rivoluzione Fascista in 1932. This was followed by numerous designs for other exhibitions in the 1930s: the II Mostra Nazionale di Plastica Murale per l'Edilizia Fascista (2nd National Exhibition of Plastic Murals for Fascist Buildings) in 1936, where Prampolini experimented with three-dimensional wall murals or *murale plastici* that combined painting and sculpture; the Mostra Nazionale del Dopolavoro (National Exhibition of the After Work Organization) in 1938; the Mostra Autarchica del Minerale Italian (Autarchic Exhibition of Italian Minerals) in 1938–1939; and the Mostra d'Oltremare (Exhibition of Overseas Territories) in 1940. For the latter, Prampolini designed the Pavilion of Electronics, where he created large curved metal structures to organize the space and introduced an upside down spiral in the shape of a cone to symbolize the connection of electrical energy between the sky, the ceiling, and the floor. For the same exhibition, Prampolini reinforced Italy's colonial aspirations with a large mural attached to the exhibition's restaurant that benignly depicted African women in native dress along with primitive hunters whose portrayal recalled the early cave paintings of Lascaux or Altamira.

On the whole, Futurism's relation to Fascism was a complicated affair. The range of participants in the Second Futurism was far more diverse than the handful of artists who inaugurated the movement, and the interests of the later Futurists were more varied. Hence, it is not possible to speak of a unified position of Futurism towards Fascism. Some, like Prampolini, furthered their own artistic ideas through projects for the state, and Futurist visual and verbal rhetoric found its way by multiple routes into the cultural practices and products of the regime. Though Marinetti remained in contact with Mussolini throughout the 1930s, other Futurists had no contact with the Fascist Party nor did their work reference its aims and purposes.

The Novecento and the crafts debate

When Mussolini came to power, Italy was a nation of many small craft enterprises and a few large industrial concerns. Historic styles dominated the decorative arts, although at the turn of the century the nation had its own variants of Art Nouveau, Stile Liberty (Liberty Style) and Stile Floreale (Floral Style). Both were highly ornate but nonetheless served as counters to the prevalent historicism. By the end of World War I, their influence had declined and historic styles reigned once more. These were all too evident at the Esposizione Regionale Lombarda d'Arte Decorativa (Lombardy Regional Exposition of Decorative Art), the nation's first survey of decorative arts after the war. Held in 1919

in Milan, the center of fashionable taste in northern Italy, the exhibit demonstrated that the country was still undeveloped in the applied arts.

Among the organizers was the art critic and publisher Guido Marangoni (dates unconfirmed). He was an active member of the Società Umanitaria (Humanitarian Society), a socialist organization in whose building the exhibition was held. The Humanitarian Society was founded in Milan in 1893 to improve the conditions of the working class. Its projects included experimental schools for children under the direction of Maria Montessori, employment offices, and a theater. In 1903 it opened a workshop-school of applied industrial art, which provided classes and instruction for aspiring artists and craftsmen. Basing its philosophy on the Arts and Crafts ideals of William Morris, the school attracted as its teachers some of Milan's leading designers of furniture and decorative arts including Duilio Cambellotti (1876–1960) and Alessandro Mazzucotelli (1865–1938).

The year before the Lombardy exhibition, Marangoni began to campaign for a university of applied arts to train craftsmen at a higher level. At the same time, he urged the inauguration of an international decorative arts exhibition. Within several years, both were realized in the town of Monza—the school in 1921 and the exhibition in 1923. Called ISIA (Istituto Statale Industrie Artistiche/State Institute of Artistic Industry), the school, which historian Anty Pansera has referred to as the Italian Bauhaus, quickly developed a program that moved from training in regional crafts to instruction in the modern applied arts. Though some of the professors continued to promote an earlier decorative style, others who joined the faculty such as the critic Edoardo Persico (1900–1936) and the architect Giuseppe Pagano (1896–1945) sought to modernize the curriculum to prepare students for work in industry. The school was particularly strong in advertising and poster design due to faculty members Fortunato Depero, Marcello Nizzoli (1887–1969), and Mario Sironi (1885–1961). Although there were other schools of applied art in Italy, ISIA became the one that most actively emphasized training in design for the contemporary world.

Fascist economic policies in the 1920s favored small craft enterprises and the regime established two organization that offered classes for craftsmen—ENAPI (Ente Nazionale per l'Artigianato e le Piccole Industria/National Organization for Craftsmanship and Small Industries) and the OND (Opera Nazionale Dopolavoro/National Afterwork Organization). ENAPI also promoted competitions for designs produced by artists that were executed by artisans and it subsequently sold the objects that resulted at decorative arts exhibitions and trade fairs. From 1928, the organization was headed by the artist and architect Giovanni Guerrini (1887–1972), who had designed the poster for the 1925 decorative arts exhibition in Monza and whose own taste was decidedly Neo-Classical.

The international decorative arts exhibition that Marangoni initiated in Monza's Villa Reale began as a Biennale and was then transformed into a Triennale in 1930. As a Biennale it initially emphasized regional crafts but gradually moved to more sophisticated displays of applied arts and architecture. At the third Biennale of 1927, the dominant Italian exhibitors were the applied artists, led by the architect Gio Ponti (1891–1979), who were associated with the Novecento group. Though a number of architects and applied artists espoused the values of the group, it began in 1922 as a movement of painters, sculptors, and writers that was promoted by Mussolini's mistress, the art critic Margharita Sarfatti (1880–1961). The Novecento artists sought a modern style that retained strong elements of Italian tradition, particularly Neo-Classicism.

Ponti, who trained as an architect at the Milan Politecnico, adopted aspects of Neo-Classicism when he joined the Tuscan ceramics manufacturer Richard-Ginori in 1923 as its artistic director. With more than 1,000 employees, Richard-Ginori was a leader in Italy's ceramics sector. During the time Ponti was with the firm between 1923 and 1930, he created almost 1,000 designs

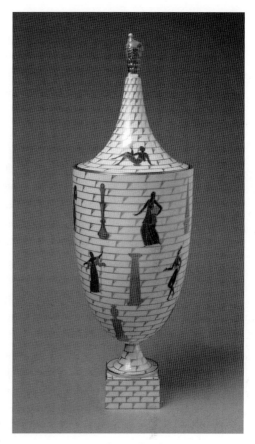

Fig. 27.07: Gio Ponti, "An Archaeological Stroll," ceramic urn with cover, 1925. © 2014. Image copyright The Metropolitan Museum of Art/Art Resource/Scala, Florence.

for hand-painted vases, plates, urns, ashtrays, candy dishes, and other objects in porcelain and majolica. His designs for molds referenced classical forms similar to those that Josiah Wedgwood produced in the 18th century, but his decorative drawings, which were hand painted on the forms by artisans, were graceful and frequently witty depictions of classical figures in a more contemporary style reminiscent of French fashion illustration (Fig. 27.07). Besides the classical figures, Ponti produced numerous images of modern life, adding jockeys, skiers, and circus performers to his classical repertoire. Although he and other Novecento designers emphasized *Italianità* or Italian-ness in their designs,

Ponti was heavily influenced by the Wiener Werkstätte, modeling his practice to some degree on that of Josef Hoffmann, like him an architect who worked in the applied arts. Émile-Jacques Ruhlmann, the French decorator and furniture designer, was another likely model.

Ponti introduced the decorative styles of Austria and France to the comfortable Milanese middle class, who were the principal customers for Richard-Ginori's ceramics. In the Italian context, his work with Richard-Ginori might be considered the first serious collaboration between a designer and a major factory in Italy, although it would remain a rare example until after World War II.

Richard-Ginori was a principal exhibitor in the Italian Pavilion at the 1925 Exposition Internationale des Arts Décoratifs, where Ponti won the grand prize for his ceramics. Also on display there were the incised glass pieces of Guido Balsamo Stella (1882–1941), who was strongly influenced by the Orrefors glassware of Sweden. The pavilion itself was a massive classical edifice by the Roman architect Armando Brassini (1875–1965), who defined the monumental style of Fascist architecture with Marcello Piacentini (1881–1960) in the 1930s. Novecento designs dominated the Italian pavilion except for an anomalous display by three Futurists—Balla, Depero, and Prampolini—that may have resulted from Marinetti's friendship with Mussolini.

While at Richard-Ginori, Ponti opened a studio with the architect Emilio Lancia (1890–1973) in 1926 and the two launched Domus Nova, a line of refined but moderately priced furniture that included pieces for the living room, dining room, and bedroom. It was commissioned by La Rinascente (The Renaissance) department store in Milan, which traditionally sold more expensive furniture. With their absence of surface ornament, the Domus Nova pieces were decidedly modern although some contained muted references to earlier styles, particularly Neo-Classicism. Like Richard-Ginori's attempts to introduce aspects of mass production to its manufacturing process, the furniture in the Domus Nova line was also mass-produced on a limited scale. La Rinascente, which was established in 1917, was named by the Italian poet Gabriel d'Annunzio who also coined its signature slogan, "New Italy impressed in every style." A further cultural reference was its original logo created by Adolfo De Carolis (1874–1928), the artist who illustrated many of d'Annunzio's books.

Additional furniture and decorative objects in the Novecento style were produced by Il Labirinto (The Labyrinth), a society of architects and designers that was founded in 1927. Modeled on the Wiener Werkstätte, Il Labirinto was created to produce furniture and decorative objects for a discerning middle-class public, following not only the same production model as the Viennese but their marketing approach as well. As in other Novecento design groups, Ponti was a central figure. Besides him and Lancia, other members were the architect Tomaso Buzzi (1900–1981), a designer of furniture and glass; Paolo Venini (1895–1959), founder of a leading glass factory in Murano; Pietro Chiesa (1892–1948), who also specialized in glass objects; the Contessa Carla Visconti di Modrone Erba (dates unconfirmed); and the architect Michele Marelli (dates unconfirmed).

Il Labirinto was short-lived and may have made its greatest impact at the 1927 Monza Biennale, which was the moment when Novecento designers gained wide public recognition and helped to redirect the Biennale away from the rustic regional furniture that had dominated the two earlier editions. The group was also a spawning ground for additional collaborations among its members as well as for several other decorative arts enterprises. In 1928, Carla Visconti di Modrone Erba, with two partners, Bice Pittoni and the fashion designer Maria Monaci Gallenga (1880–1944), opened the Boutique Italienne in Paris, which served until 1934 as a source of Italian fashion. In the early 1930s, Ponti helped to establish Fontana Arte, a firm that would come to specialize in lighting, although it initially produced furniture and glass objects. Fontana Arte resulted from the 1933 merger of a studio founded by Luigi Fontana (1827–1908) and the Bottega Pietro Chiesa, which created modern decorative objects such as Chiesa's table of 1932, made from a single strip of bent glass. Chiesa became the artistic director of Fontana Arte and was responsible for much of its lighting design. His floor lamp of 1933, known at the Luminator, was one of the first truly modern objects to be mass-produced in Italy. Designed to cast indirect light on the ceiling, it consisted of a polished metal tube on a base that gracefully expanded into a funnel shape where the lighting source was housed.

In ceramics, besides the many products of Richard-Ginori, the Novecento style was evident in the tea and coffee services, tureens, and dinnerware made by the Società Ceramica Italiana in Laveno. The firm's artistic director was Guido Andlovitz (1900–1965), who, like Ponti, had studied architecture at the Milan Politecnico. He joined the Società in 1923, the same year that Ponti began to work for Richard-Ginori, and he remained with the company until 1942. Besides improving the technical quality of its products, Andlovitz invented many new forms and specialized in decorations for the ceramics that had the lightness and grace of rococo paintings.

Though many designers exemplified Novecento values, Ponti had a larger vision of how the style might influence the taste of the Italian middle class in Milan and the industrial north. Following the success of the Novecento exhibits at the 1927 Monza Biennale, he founded a magazine, *Domus*, the following year to promote a broad version of the Novecento style as the quintessence of Italian middle-class modernism. *Domus* provided wide coverage of new tendencies in architecture and home furnishings, while continuing to propound the virtues of *Italianità* as they were exemplified in the Neo-Classical architecture, furniture, and decorative arts that he and others were creating. Though Ponti rejected the machine aesthetic, he embraced mass production and was instrumental

in instigating the gradual shift away from small craft workshops towards more modern means of production.

Rationalism and the Triennales

Although the 3rd Monza Biennale in 1927 was hailed as a triumph for the Novecento designers, it was also significant for another reason. It introduced a display of speculative drawings of modern buildings by Gruppo 7, a coterie of young architects, who were all recent graduates of the Milan Politecnico. They came to be known as Rationalists because they identified with the rigorously designed architecture of the European modern movement. At the end of 1926, they published several articles in which they declared themselves the bearers of a new spirit in opposition to both the Novecento and the Futurists. Gruppo 7 consisted of Luigi Figini (1903–1984), Gino Pollini (1903–1991), Giuseppe Terragni (1904–1943), Adalberto Libera (1903–1963), Guido Frette (1901–1984), Sebastiano Larco (dates unconfirmed), and Carlo Enrico Rava (1903–1986). Among the foreign architects and movements they admired were Le Corbusier, *De Stijl*, and the Russian avant-garde.

Along with an exhibit of German applied arts organized by Bruno Paul, the presence of Gruppo 7 marked a shift in the Biennale's agenda from promoting regional crafts to exhibiting modern architecture and design. Not surprisingly, the 3rd Biennale was the last for Guido Marangoni as director general. Marangoni, who founded the event in 1923, did much for the applied arts by initially proposing the Biennale and managing it through three editions, but his interests in Italy's regional and rustic decorative arts were being outstripped not only by the Rationalists but also by the cosmopolitan Neo-Classicism of the Novecento designers.

In 1928, the same year that *Domus* began publication, Marangoni founded *La Casa Bella*, a magazine whose focus was the household interior as well as the decorative and industrial arts. *La Casa Bella* adopted a more eclectic editorial policy than *Domus*. After

Marangoni opened it to a plurality of voices, a group of architects including Alberto Sartoris (1901–1998) and Giuseppe Pagano began to push for an "engagement with modernity." Marangoni, recognizing that the editorial direction was moving away from his own convictions, relinquished his position as editor in 1929. Several years later, the magazine changed its name to *Casabella*, and under the guidance of Pagano and the critic Edoardo Persico it served as a vociferous advocate for modernism in Italy

By 1930, the Biennale had become a Triennale and its name was changed to the Espozizione triennale internazionale delle arti decorative e industriali moderne (International Triennale Exhibition of Decorative and Modern Industrial Arts). The new directors' injection of the adjective "industrial" confirmed the end of the exhibition's interest in regional folkloric craft and its new emphasis on modern industrial arts. As a Triennale, it was the principal site for the exhibition of modern Italian architecture and design. The shift from traditional regionalism to international modernism was due in part to the influence of foreign exhibitors whose more developed ideas of design highlighted the somewhat backwards situation of Italy's applied arts.

At the 1930 Triennale, which remained in Monza until it moved permanently to Milan in 1933, Gruppo 7 made a strong showing with its design for an electric house—the Casa Elettrica. The building was funded by the Società Edison to demonstrate a modern way of life. It was filled with electric appliances, few of which could be found in the typical Italian home. Figini and Pollini received the commission and invited several other architects to join them in executing it. The small villa, comprised of rectilinear surfaces including a partial glass facade and a flat roof, was a polemical call for a new architecture that was appropriate for the industrial era (Fig. 27.08). The project's modernity was reinforced by the roof terrace, the two levels of the

Fig. 27.08: Luigi Figini, Gino Pollini et. al., Casa Elettrica, 1930. Archivio Fotografico © La Triennale di Milano.

living room, and by Piero Bottoni's kitchen design, which was based on the efficiency methods of Frederick Winslow Taylor. These had already been incorporated into the Frankfurt kitchen in Germany and came to represent throughout Europe a striving for a modern lifestyle. Historian Dennis Doordan points out that neither the Futurists, who continued to celebrate craft production as the source of their inventive objects, nor the *Novecentrists*, with their advocacy of a comfortable lifestyle and their reluctance to explore the potential of technology, were as suitable as the Rationalists to design the Casa Elettrica. Given how rare electrical appliances were in the Italian home and how few advocates for them there were within the architecture and design communities that had coalesced around the Biennales, the Casa Elettrica stood out with its clarion call for a new way of living.

Compared to the modern homes on display at the Weissenhof Siedlung in Stuttgart three years earlier, the Casa Elettrica was not particularly distinguished, but within the Italian context, it marked a new direction for Italian architects and designers even though the Rationalist philosophy had great difficulty moving forward. On the one hand, the public was not yet ready to absorb all the new household technology nor was Italian industry geared up to produce it. On the other hand, by the mid-1930s the architects closest to Mussolini, those around Marcello Piacentini and Armando Brassini, had closed ranks behind a monumental classicism, thus precluding the Rationalists from any major government commissions. Hence their polemics were played out primarily as projects for the Triennales, where they could at least present their ideas for architecture and furniture in built form rather than in the sketches and drawings to which their Futurist predecessors had been limited.

Although the Casa Elettrica received considerable publicity, it was a rare example of modernity at the 4th Triennale, which was still heavily populated with displays of crafts, traditional arts, and modern applied art rather than industrial products. Its directors,

in fact, were Gio Ponti, the painter Mario Sironi, and the architect Alberto Alpago-Novello (1889–1985), all leading figures of the Novecento. Ponti and Emilio Lancia, in fact, designed a Neo-Classical vacation house, which included furniture in the Novecento style from La Rinascente. Ponti also invited Joseph Hoffmann to curate an Austrian exhibit that featured examples of Viennese decorative art, which he very much admired. The Deutscher Werkbund organized the German display, which presented the results of 20 years' collaboration between artists and industry. Though it gained less attention than either the Casa Elettrica or the Novecento projects, the significance of the German exhibit was not lost on Edoardo Persico, soon to become a leading apostle of Rationalist design. Persico contrasted the Werkbund display with "the minor subjectivism of the neo-classicists." The Germans, he said, "teach us that rationalism is not just an architectural formula or a method, but a moral system, a social order."

Although the Rationalists built little for the Fascist Party, one significant project was the Casa del Fascio (House of Fascism) that was designed by Giuseppe Terragni of Gruppo 7 in 1932 in the town of Como and was completed in 1936. Terragni, who received the commission with the help of his older brother, the town's mayor, proposed an architecturally advanced structure with a gridded facade of positive and negative spaces based on geometric proportions. The rational organization of the design was continued in the interior, notably the main meeting room for which Terragni designed chairs of bent tubular steel that seemed a compromise between the direct linear forms of the Germans and a muted version of the *Stile Floreale*. Covering one wall of the room was a mural comprised mainly of geometric forms. It was done by Mario Radice (1898–1987), a Como artist who was strongly influenced by Léger, van Doesburg, and Mondrian. As the single iconic element in an otherwise abstract composition, Radice included a stylized portrait of Mussolini (Fig. 27.09). Working at about the same time on his bombastic exhibit for the Mostra della Rivoluzione Fascista in Rome, Terragni may have had some sense that the future of Fascist architecture lay with the monumental forms and emotionally excessive gestures of Fascist propaganda rather than the cool rationalism of his Casa del Fascio.

Another counterpoint to the overblown theatrics of the Rome exhibition was the Sala delle Medaglie d'Oro (Hall of Gold Medals) at the Exhibition of Italian Aviation in 1934. It was designed by the modernist critic Edoardo Persico and Marcello Nizzoli (1887–1969), a painter and poster artist who would later become the principal product designer for Olivetti. The two created an exhibit of gridded linear frames on which they hung flat panels of photographs and text that described the exploits of 26 Italian aviators who fought valiantly in World War I and received medals for their heroism. Persico was a committed anti-Fascist and may have seen

the rational structure and information-based graphics of this project as a way to undermine the emotional propaganda of the earlier Mostra della Rivoluzione Fascista, which set the tone for almost all subsequent Fascist exhibitions. He and Nizzoli designed a similar grid of metal tubes for Milan's Galleria, where it was temporarily installed as a space for exhibiting photographs.

In the same year, Persico and Nizzoli collaborated on the design of two commercial interiors for the Parker Pen Company in Milan, both of which stood as modest testaments to modern design against the traditionalism of the city's Novecento architects such as Giovanni Muzio (1893–1982). Glass was the principal material for the Parker Pen interior designs, whether it served as the backdrop for the large san serif letters the designers devised to spell out the company's name in the shop window or whether it comprised the transparent rectangular cases full of pens and small

Fig. 27.09: Giuseppe Terragni, Casa del Fascio, meeting room with mural by Mario Radice, 1936. Archives de la construction moderne–EPFL, fonds Alberto Sartoris.

objects that were hung orthogonally and elegantly framed with thin black metal strips. To architects who opposed the politics of Fascism, the strict geometrical order and spare design of the Parker Pen shops might have signified, as Stephen Leet suggests, the possibility of designing outside the dictates of the state. It is also important to note that the Parker Pen Company was American, even though the shops were commissioned for its Italian branch. This may have made it more likely for the company to select a Rationalist design rather than a Novecento proposal.

Unlike Terragni, Figini and Pollini received no commissions from the Fascist Party. In 1932, they exhibited furniture designs at the Galleria Il Milione in Milan, where Edoardo Persico was the director. Under Persico's guidance, Galleria Il Milione had become an important exhibition space for modern art and design. In the statement for their exhibition, Figini and Pollini declared that furniture had to re-enter architecture and be subjected to the same laws and sense of measure as a building. The next year they won a competition for the design of a radio-phonograph sponsored by the National Gramophone Company. Their prototype—an unadorned rectangular box on four metal legs—presented the apparatus as a piece of modern furniture that challenged the traditional phonographs, which had elaborate housings replete with decorative ornament. They won another furniture competition at the 6th Triennale for a minimal desk that consisted simply of a flat writing surface, supported by a rectangular storage section and two metal legs. For that same exhibition, they designed a small Villa for an Artist, in which they placed modern furniture as Terragni had done in the Casa del Fascio.

Held in 1933, the 5th Triennale was the first to take place in Milan, where it was housed in the new Palace of Art designed by the Milanese Novecento architect Giovani Muzio (1893–1982). Beginning with the 1930 Triennale, sponsorship and control of the exhibition shifted to the national government, which continued to support it through the duration of the Fascist regime. Prominent officials were always part of the administration as were Gio Ponti along with Marcello Piacentini, the leading Fascist architect. Nonetheless, the Triennale was always open to new proposals and remained a principal site for the Rationalists to present new architectural projects and designs for furniture and household objects.

There are several possible reasons for the Fascist regime's liberal attitude towards the Triennale. First, the Fascists were interested in mass production even though there was little of it in the Italian consumer goods sector. The Triennale was thus a laboratory, where new ideas for mass-produced products might arise and gain public attention. This was the case for the exhibition of radios at the 7th Triennale in 1940. Second, the Triennale provided excellent publicity that enabled Italy to compete in the more cosmopolitan European world of architecture and applied arts, where France maintained a strong lead during the 1930s. It was also a place to showcase examples of current work being done elsewhere. This occurred through exhibits from other countries such as the one designed by Max Bill that the Swiss government sent to the 6th Triennale in 1936. At that same exhibition, Alvar Aalto's birch furniture from Finland was on display and he received a gold medal.

As a member of the Triennale administration, Piacentini appeared to tolerate the projects of the Rationalists within the confines of the exhibition itself, but he maintained a strict adherence to monumental classicism when it came to government commissions; thus little of the experimental work that was shown at the Triennale found its way into the official canon of Fascist architecture or design. Though furniture and appliances were less polemical than buildings, the Rationalists were still not high on the list of those selected to design the furnishings for official structures such as ministries and embassies. Among the designers who did get such commissions was the Stile Liberty furniture maker Eugenio Quarti (1867–1929) and his son Mario (1901–1974), who specialized in handcrafted luxury pieces. After adopting a more classical Novecento look, Quarti and his son designed the furniture for two of Piacentini's buildings—the Ministry of Justice and the National Fascist Institute for Social Security. The Novecento influence was also evident in the furniture Gio Ponti designed at Piacentini's invitation for the antechamber of the Ministry of Corporations in 1933–1934.

The 6th Triennale in 1936, organized by Giuseppe Pagano and Edoardo Persico, was dedicated to Rationalist architecture and design. It brought to public attention the potential of rational planning through displays dedicated to housing, furnishings, and urbanism. What differentiated this Triennale from those that had preceded it was that Rationalist design was evident in the plan of the entire exhibition from the decision to substitute three major sectors for the myriad small pavilions to the gridded display stands that were prevalent in many of the individual exhibits. The 6th Triennale embodied in built form the strong arguments for modernism that Pagano and Persico had been making for several years in *Casabella* and it represented a moment of triumph for the Rationalist position even though a period of resistance to modernism was soon to follow.

The display system that Persico and Nizzoli had introduced at the Exhibition of Italian Aviation two years earlier was widely adopted throughout the Triennale. Pagano and Guarniero Daniel (dates unconfirmed) used it for their Exhibition of Vernacular Architecture that featured Pagano's photographs and it was evident in Pagano's Exhibition of Construction Technology and Building Materials. Even a small exhibition of antique gold work designed by Franco Albini (1905–1977) and Giovanni Romano (dates unconfirmed) was presented in horizontal glass cases supported by vertical poles, recalling Persico's and Nizzoli's earlier designs for the Parker Pen shops.

After graduating from the architecture program at the Milan Politecnico, Albini worked for several years in Gio Ponti's studio before he adopted a more

Functionalist approach to design. He joined the team led by Pagano that designed a Corbusian steel frame house for the 5th Triennale, and for the 6th Triennale he presented a Room for a Man, in which he efficiently organized a minimal space replete with horizontal and vertical planes and volumes that fulfilled the functions of storage, writing, and sleeping. It was in fact the domestic equivalent of Persico's and Nizzoli's Parker Pen shops, demonstrating that rational design could be both efficient and elegant. Albini also included in the room several tubular steel cantilever chairs with padded seats and backs that he had designed.

During the 1930s, Albini created shop interiors and exhibitions, while also producing some furniture including several radical prototypes. In addition he worked with a team of architects on low-cost housing, which was built according to Rationalist principles. "Veliero," his prototype for a tensile bookshelf of 1938–1940 was a novel experiment in furniture construction (Fig. 27.10). Intended to serve both for the storage of books and as a room divider, it consisted of shelves made from strong Securit glass suspended within a frame of V-shaped wooden compression members that were held in place with steel cables.

One concession to the rhetoric of Fascist propaganda at the 6th Triennale was the Salone d'Onore (Hall of Honor) designed by Persico, Nizzoli, and Giancarlo Palanti (1906–1977). Here classicism and modernism tempered each other in the subtle organization of space, but the column of photographs depicting Roman leaders from the past was clearly intended to reinforce the imperial ambitions of the Fascists even as Persico anticipated that the team's design might be read as an expression of hope for a peaceful Europe.

Sadly Persico died just as the exhibition opened. His belief that rational design could survive and spread under the Fascists animated his multifarious activities as a writer, editor, designer, and organizer. Unlike him, his fellow *Casabella* editor, Giuseppe Pagano was a member of the Fascist Party and actively promoted the compatibility of Fascism and modernism until he

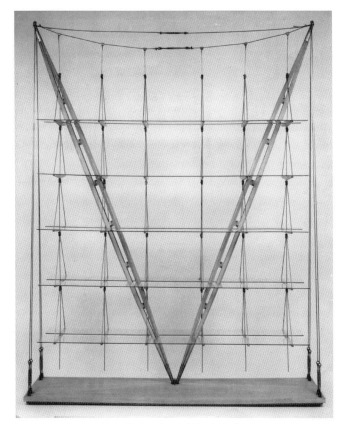

Fig. 27.10: Franco Albini, "Veliero" tensile bookshelf, 1938. © Fondazione Franco Albini – www.fondazionefrancoalbini.com

for more than 25 years earlier at the 1914 Werkbund exhibition in Cologne, thus indicating how slowly Italy had progressed in industrializing its manufacturing sector compared to the Germans.

Besides the various companies that produced electrical appliances, office equipment, bicycles, cars, and motorcycles, several firms did market machine-made furniture successfully. Gabriele Mucchi (1899–2002), who was both a civil engineer and a painter, worked with Emilio Pina, the owner of a small factory, to produce tubular steel furniture in the mid-1930s. Perhaps their most successful chair was the S5 of 1934, a stacking chair with a chrome frame and a woven wicker seat and back. In addition, Mucchi designed a chaise longue that Pina manufactured. A. L. Colombo also produced a line of tubular steel furniture, although its pieces were mainly derivative of other designs. One of the most original tubular steel chairs was designed by the architect Piero Bottoni (1903–1973), who collaborated with Figini and Pollini on the Casa Elettrica at the 4th Triennale. When Bottoni designed it in 1929, many Italian companies rejected the chair before it was picked up by the international firm Thonet-Mundus the following year.

During the 1930s, the Rationalists made their greatest mark as producers of prototypes and models. Their sphere of influence was primarily the Triennale exhibitions, although one or another architect or designer did secure an occasional commission from a private or corporate client. Historian Anty Pansera calls this period a time of "proto-design," viewing not only the Rationalists but also Novecento designers like Ponti as preparing the way for a more intense engagement of design with industry after the war.

Industry under the Fascist regime

Among the first acts of the Fascist regime when it came to power in 1922 was to reduce its control over industry. The Fascists supported the large companies by curtailing the power of the working class and interfering minimally in the way companies conducted

became disillusioned with Fascism and resigned from the party in 1942.

Despite the many propositions at the 6th Triennale for mass-produced housing and furniture, there was still little of it in Italy. For the 7th Triennale, held in 1940, a year after Mussolini had formed a military alliance with Hitler (the Pact of Steel), Pagano organized a Mostra internazionale della produzione in serie (International Exhibition of Serial Production) in which he presented various types of mass-produced objects in different sectors from furniture and ceramics to housing. His intent was to move beyond one-off objects by claiming that "a beautiful model is of no use if it can't be correctly and excellently produced." Pagano was arguing for the same kind of "standard" or "uniform" types that Hermann Muthesius had called their affairs. They also supported small craft enterprises through ENAPI (Ente Nazionale per l'Artigianato e le Piccole Industrie/National Corporation for Handicrafts and Small Industry), which organized classes and workshops to promote small-scale production. During the late 1920s and early 1930s the Confindustria (Confederazione Generale del Industria Italiana/ General Confederation of Italian Industry) was the major force in the private sector, including among its members not only large firms but also small enterprises with as few as five employees. During this time the government attempted to establish a third economic way between communism and capitalism—corporativism—that would have integrated companies and workers into large units or corporations whose activities would be controlled by the state. However, it was evident by the early 1930s that the system was not developing as anticipated.

To combat the harmful effects of the Great Depression, the regime adopted a policy of large-scale economic intervention. In 1933, the government established the IRI (Istituto per la Ricostruzione Industriale/ Institute for Industrial Reconstruction) to take over much industrial financing from the banks and to integrate industry into a political system that would severely curtail its autonomy. As a result, the IRI controlled significant shares of Italy's largest industries. Despite its funding for ENAPI, the regime had always favored the development of heavy industry over medium-scale consumer-oriented firms, which were hampered by an inadequate allocation of raw materials as well as a lack of government support for creating new markets overseas. This policy helps to explain why most design innovations that were introduced at the Triennales, which would have been produced by such firms, did not go beyond the prototype stage. Among the few industries that had successful systems of mass production were Fiat, which produced cars and other vehicles, and Olivetti, the manufacturer of office machines.

After the Fascists attacked Ethiopia in 1935, the League of Nations imposed sanctions on Italy that curtailed the import of raw materials from abroad and the sale of Italian goods in foreign markets. In March 1936, Mussolini introduced the term *autarky* to characterize the government's control over the economy and its drive for economic self-sufficiency. As a result, Italian companies concentrated on the home market and certain domestic materials such as aluminum became widely used for furniture and industrial products. An early demonstration of aluminum's potential was Gio Ponti's design for the headquarters of Montecatini, Italy's largest mineral and chemical company as well as a major producer of the metal. Ponti chose aluminum for the roof and gates of Montecatini's office building and employed it for all the office furniture. He designed various models for desks, typists' tables and chairs, a number of which were put into production. His aluminum typist's chair adapted design elements from the tubular steel furniture of the prior decade but featured a heavier base and knobs to adjust the seat height and back. To advocate the use of aluminum more widely, the government sponsored the Exhibition of Italian Autarkic Metal in 1939. Held in Rome, its intent was to promote materials like aluminum and discourage the use of iron, which was needed for military purposes.

Consumer products

Even though the Edison Company was able to fill every room of the Casa Elettrica with electrical appliances, few Italian homes had electricity and few companies introduced new appliances to the domestic market during the Fascist years. Firms from abroad such as Frigidaire did achieve modest sales in Italy and remained in part because they were successful against local competitors like Fiat. In 1928, SCAEM, a company that manufactured domestic appliances, introduced a vacuum cleaner with a Marelli motor that was based on models developed elsewhere, notably by Electrolux in Sweden. The vacuum cleaner was horizontal and had runners like its Swedish predecessor. However, it came with a group of brushes whose wooden handles may well have been produced by artisans. SCAEM produced other electric appliances as did another company, the Società Anonima Zerowatt, which manufactured a range of electric fans, irons, coffee makers, and related products that for the most part derived from those produced by foreign companies like the AEG in Berlin. One appliance that was widely used in Italy was the Necchi sewing machine. Originally a copy of the American Singer machine, by 1934 Necchi had produced a more original model, the BDA, which became a successful mass-produced product.

While sales of Italian electrical appliances were acceptable, they were less than they might have been because adequate methods of promoting them were lacking. Italy had no equivalent of the annual French Salon des Arts Ménagers, where new domestic appliances were introduced to the public. Meanwhile, the leading design magazines such as *Domus* and *Casabella* similarly promoted a culture that centered on architecture, interiors, and household furnishings rather than industrial products.

Perhaps the most original of Italy's consumer products were its coffee makers. Various companies manufactured the large machines that forced water heated by steam through fine-grained coffee to produce

Fig. 27.11: Alfonso Bialetti, Moka Expess coffee maker, 1933. © MARKA/Alamy.

espresso. The first Italian espresso machine was most likely made by La Pavoni, which initially introduced it in 1905 and then manufactured it in larger versions for bars and restaurants in the 1920s and 1930s. In 1933, Alfonso Bialetti (1888–1970) began to market the Moka Express, a small aluminum stovetop espresso maker for the home (Fig. 27.11). Its faceted form suggests a relation to Art Deco, and Bialetti, a metalworker and inventor rather than a decorative artist, may well have adopted the design from the higher-priced silver Novecento tea and coffee services that were then on the market. Although the Moka Express became Italy's leading coffee maker during the 1930s, it was produced by artisanal methods until after World War II when Bialetti's son Renato expanded the market through mass production.

Considerable design attention was devoted to the radio, whose manufacture received an additional impetus due to its use as a propaganda medium. The first Italian radios were furniture pieces and artisans made their wooden housings. They had traditional ornamentation and were expensive to produce. In 1930, Radiomarelli, a company associated with the Magneti Marelli factory, which was making car batteries, began to mass-produce radios to meet a growing demand.

By the 1930s, radio had become a mass medium, In 1938, the number of sets had risen to more than 1,000,000, although this was an insignificant number considering a population of 43 million people. To boost radio ownership for propaganda purposes, the Fascists introduced a subsidized inexpensive model called the Radio Balilla in 1937 (Fig. 27.12). They named it after a young man in 18th-century Genoa who is said to have led a revolt against the Hapsburg army. Balilla was also the name of the official Fascist youth organization as well as a car produced by Fiat.

Experimental radio designs were produced for several Triennale competitions, which culminated in a special exhibition devoted to the radio at the 7th Triennale of 1940. The boldest design in that exhibition was Franco Albini's receiver, which embedded the tuner

Fig. 27.12: Radio Balilla 650, 1937. © dario Fusaro/Marka/SuperStock.

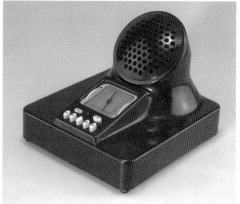

Fig. 27.13: Luigi Caccia Dominioni, Livio and Pier Giacomo Castiglioni, Phonola radio, 1939. Quittenbaum Kunstauktionen GmbH.

parts, and their design of the casing form made the Phonola one of the first real industrial design objects in Italy, one that pointed the way to the many inventive products that Italian designers would create in the post-war years.

The Olivetti design program

Of all the Italian companies in the interwar period, Olivetti, founded in 1908 (see Chapter 17), was the one that most actively integrated architecture, product design, and advertising into a cohesive design program. There was a precedent for such a project in the AEG, when Peter Behrens was its director of design from 1908 to 1914, but Behrens' program did not have much influence on other large companies. In the case of Olivetti, it was Adriano Olivetti (1901–1960), son of the company's founder and its director from 1929, who instigated the design changes. On a trip to the United States, he observed new rationalized methods of organization and production, which he began to apply to his own company as a response to the economic crisis of 1929. Shifting from piecework to more efficient production methods, he reduced the manufacturing time of a typewriter from twelve hours to four and increased the volume of production by 30 percent.

and the speaker in a sheet of the transparent material, Securit, that was supported by an additional sheet behind it. However, the design that changed the Italian idea of a radio from a piece of furniture to an electrical appliance was the Phonola, designed by the architects Luigi Caccia Dominioni (1913–d.o.d. unconfirmed), Livio (1911–1979) and Pier Giacomo Castiglioni (1913–1968) and for the Phonola Company, which launched it in 1939. Drawing on American product styling of the period, the Phonola, whose name may well have derived from the earlier American phonograph called a Victrola, was the first Italian radio with a casing made of Bakelite, a synthetic resin, instead of wood. The Phonola was available in different colors and its angled control panel and raised speaker resembled a telephone, which was an object the Italian public could already recognize as a machine (Fig. 27.13). According to several scholars, the designers' engagement with a new material, their arrangement of the mechanical

In 1931 he established the Ufficio Sviluppo e Pubblicità (Office of Development and Publicity) to bring together artists, designers, and poets with a modern outlook. As head of the office he appointed Renato Zveteremich (dates unconfirmed), who had extensive contacts with members of the Milanese art and design community. Two years later he commissioned Figini and Pollini, the Gruppo 7 architects, to modernize and extend the Olivetti factory buildings in Ivrea and he subsequently commissioned them to design a new administrative center and then worker housing and community facilities. Like his father, Adriano was committed to the well-being of his workers and he envisioned Ivrea as an ideal factory town with suitable living and recreational facilities for them.

The first new product under Adriano's management was the MP1, Olivetti's earliest portable typewriter. Manufactured in 1932, it was designed by the engineer Aldo Magnelli (dates unconfirmed), probably assisted by his brother, the abstract painter Alberto Magnelli (1888–1971). Most important for future Olivetti designs was the casing, which for the first time was divorced from the mechanical parts. Due to a reduction in parts, the MP1 was considerably flatter than its predecessors, thus setting a precedent for the design of future portable typewriters. A 1935 poster by the artist Xanti Schawinsky presented the MP1 as a typewriter for the new female workforce in the office. Its association with an attractive stylishly-dressed woman, and its appealing color positioned it as an object of style as well as function. Schawinsky's poster—a tinted photomontage—which represented the emerging modern graphic approach of the Studio Boggeri with whom Schawinsky collaborated at the time, enhanced Olivetti's sense of style (Plate 38). Schawinsky also created a new logo for the company, which consisted of the company's name in large lower-case letters that suggested those on the typewriter keys.

The second typewriter designed under Adriano's leadership was the Studio 42, which the company began to market in 1935. A result of Adriano's interest in bringing together artists and architects to handle his design work, Xanti Schawinsky and the two architects Figini and Pollini in collaboration created it with the engineer Ottavio Luzzati (dates unconfirmed). Designed for both home and office, the Studio 42 had a larger housing than the MP1, although it broke with the earlier boxy vertical typewriter forms and was also produced in colors other than black to fit in easily with other home furnishings.

In 1935, Marcello Nizzoli began to do advertising work for Olivetti. Some time thereafter he met Adriano who invited him to work on the company's products. His first design for the company was the Summa calculator of 1940, a machine that had the rounded form that would characterize Nizzoli's designs for Olivetti typewriters after the war.

Adriano also wanted to create a new type of publicity and he originally hired Schawinsky to head his advertising office perhaps because of Schawinsky's prior Bauhaus experience. Schawinsky left for the United States in 1936 and subsequently the poet, mathematician, and artist Leonardo Sinisgalli (1908–1981) and Giovanni Pintori became heads of the advertising section. Pintori had studied art at ISIA in Monza, where Persico, Pagano, and Nizzoli taught. Both Sinisgalli and Pintori played an important role in making Olivetti advertising world-famous in the post-war years. Other artists who contributed to the advertising program were Constantino Nivola (1911–1988), who had studied with Pintori at ISIA in Monza; the abstract painter and photographer Luigi Veronesi (1908–1998); and the designers Bruno Munari and Erberto Carboni (1899–1984).

During the interwar years, Olivetti was the rare company in Italy or elsewhere that was guided by the exceptional artistic and social vision of its top management, and its design office functioned as an experimental studio or laboratory for the development of a modern corporate design strategy. Adriano Olivetti was the one who recognized the value that artists and architects of quality could contribute to the entire design process of his company. An adherent of Rationalism, he hired creative people who brought a modern vision to the design of Olivetti's architecture, products, and advertising. He also helped to establish the profession of industrial design in Italy by hiring artists and architects to collaborate with engineers in the design of products that were innovative both mechanically and formally.

Transportation

At the beginning of the 1920s, Fiat opened its Lingotto automobile factory, a huge building of reinforced concrete with a test track on the roof. Designed by the architect and naval engineer Giacomo Matte-Trucco (1869–1934), the factory signified Fiat's intention to become a modern industrial company that could mass-produce automobiles just as Henry Ford did in the United States. The company had begun the process as early as 1912 with the Fiat Zero, following the example of Henry Ford's Model T.

During World War I, Fiat supplied the Italian military with armaments and entered the 1920s with 30,000 workers. The company also diversified its production to include numerous forms of transport—streetcars, buses, airplanes, and railroad cars among them. As mentioned earlier, it even made refrigerators. Fiat's founder, Giovanni Agnelli, was a supporter of Mussolini and during the Fascist period the company received considerable aid from the Italian government.

Applying American methods of mass production, Fiat changed the Italian system of automobile manufacturing from one where a factory would give a coachbuilder a chassis and the coachbuilder would install a custom-designed body on it. Instead, Agnelli established separate departments for the design and production of engines and auto bodies. Although Fiat had its own designers, it continued to collaborate with the coachbuilding firms that had traditionally specialized in the design of auto bodies. In 1932, Fiat introduced its model 508 under the patriotic name Balilla. It was also Italy's first low-priced car and by 1937 more than 113,000 had been sold. Marcello Dudovich promoted the elegance of the car in his 1932 poster that compared it to a stylishly dressed female and described its form as having "the elegance of a woman" (Fig. 27.14).

Fiat was also the first company to challenge the formal tradition of European coachbuilding when it introduced the Fiat 1500, a response to the streamlined design of the Chrysler Airflow, in 1934. Mario Revelli de Beaumont (1907–1985), a designer who collaborated with numerous Italian automobile manufacturers,

Fig. 27.14: Marcello Dudovich, The New Balilla for Everyone, poster, 1932. © Universal Images Group/DeAgostini/Alamy. © DACS 2017.

LA VETTURA PICCOLA PIÙ BELLA E COMODA DEL MONDO

La FIAT 500 ha, nel suo piccolo
le stesse doti della FIAT 1500 :

sicurezza
stabilità
meraviglioso molleggio
grande visibilità e silenziosità
comodo viaggiare
guida facile entusiasmante

Tutti i cristalli sono Securit

— 2 posti amplissimi e posto per abbondante bagaglio.
— 4 cilindri; motore di grande elasticità e rendimento.
— 4 velocità e retromarcia, con 3ᵃ silenziosa e sincronizzatore.
— Sospensione anteriore speciale a ruote indipendenti.
— Guida con comando indipendente alle due ruote.
— Freni idraulici sulle 4 ruote.
— Ammortizzatori idraulici.

Carrozzeria interamente metallica, tetto compreso.

Fig. 27.15: Dante Giacosa, Fiat 500 "Topolino," brochure, 1936. The Wolfsonian–Florida International University, Miami Beach, Florida, The Mitchell Wolfson, Jr. Collection, XB1993.3 Photo: David Almeida.

was responsible for the design. Fiat's introduction of a streamlined car in Europe was yet another example of how American design and production influenced the company's policies and practices. Fiat continued to follow the American model with an inexpensive mass-produced car for two people, the Fiat 500. Affectionately known because of its size as the "Topolino," the Italian nickname for Mickey Mouse (Fig. 27.15), its form and engine were both designed by Dante Giacosa (1905–1996), a mechanical engineer who joined Fiat in 1927 and spent his entire career with the company. At the time of its initial production in 1936, the Topolino was one of the smallest cars in the world and its low price made it even more affordable than the Balilla. The curved front grill and slightly swept-back front windows were also influenced by American streamlining but less so than the larger Fiat 1500 that preceded it.

Fiat led the Italian automobile industry in adopting mass-production techniques, but other manufacturers also sought to modernize their designs. In 1937, Lancia, a company founded in 1907 by Vincenzo Lancia, who had formerly worked for Fiat, introduced the Aprilia coupe, which was styled by the coachbuilding firm that Battista "Pinin" Farina (1893–1966) founded in 1930. Farina, who later adopted Pininfarina as his surname, had worked for a traditional coachbuilder or *carrozeria* as well as for Fiat and understood the need to modernize the coachbuilding business to collaborate with automobile companies interested in mass production. Farina became known for his sensually modeled body designs as exemplified by the rounded shape of the Aprilia, which was as much a piece of sculpture as an aerodynamically-styled vehicle.

A prominent designer for anohter leading car manufacturer, Alfa Romeo, was Vittorio Jano

(1891–1965), who began his career at Fiat in 1911 and moved to Alfa Romeo in 1923, where he designed the Alfa Romeo P2, a successful racing car that helped to identify the company as pre-eminent in world auto racing after it was placed first in numerous Grand Prix competitions. In 1930, Jano also designed the 6C 1750, which established Alfa Romeo in the sports car market, as well as the larger more expensive touring car, the 6C 2300, first produced in 1933. Isotta-Fraschini, founded in 1905, began by importing, repairing, and selling cars. Though it originally made racing cars, the company came to specialize in deluxe limousines for the American upper class. Due to the economic crisis of the 1930s and the disruptions of World War II, Isotta-Fraschini ceased making cars after the war.

On a smaller scale, Moto Guzzi, established near Genoa in 1921, became Italy's leading producer of motorcycles. The original machine was designed by Carlo Guzzi (1889–1964), a former airplane mechanic, who, according to the architect Vittorio Gregotti, did not create a motorcycle with any radical innovations but instead produced a machine that was extremely rational in its assembly of existing technology and in its formal design. In fact, subsequent models changed little until the 1950s.

Mussolini devoted considerable resources to Italy's railroad system, investing heavily in new rolling stock and the completion of new lines. It was in the late 1920s that the motto "during Fascism, the trains ran on time" became widespread. Punctuality was, in fact, crucial, and engineers had to pay personally if their trains were late. Fiat introduced a series of streamlined trains between 1934 and 1939, with later models adopting the rounded grill and swept-back windows that had originated with the company's automobiles. The Breda company of Milan (Società Italiana Ernesto Breda) also introduced several stream-lined designs in the late 1930s. Its ETR 200, Italy's first electric locomotive, entered service in 1936. Originally, it was to be a simple light train until the Fascist Party decided to transform it into a symbol of the regime.

Its aerodynamic form, which was tested in a wind tunnel at the Turin Polytechnic, allowed it to reach a speed of 125 miles per hour. For the coach interiors, Breda commissioned the architects Giuseppe Pagano and Gio Ponti, who introduced a rational style and new materials to enhance passenger comfort, while consulting on the shape of the engine as well.

As discussed in the section on Futurism, flight was an important symbol for the Fascists, and Mussolini enthusiastically promoted advances in aviation. By the 1930s, Italy had a thriving aviation industry with approximately 18 airplane manufacturers as well as other firms that built engines. The leading firms included Fiat, Società Italiana Caproni, and Savoia-Marchetti. They all produced planes for the Italian Air Force, but Caproni and Savoia-Marchetti also took a special interest in the development of civil aviation.

The Società Italiana Caproni was founded in 1908 under another name by an engineer, Gianni Caproni (1886–1957). Until 1950, when the company ceased to operate, it introduced around 180 different aircraft. During World War I, Caproni mass-produced heavy bombers both in Italy and abroad. After the war the company turned its attention to the design of prototypes for passenger and cargo aircraft, while continuing to make bombers as well.

An early attempt by Caproni to create a trans-atlantic passenger carrier was the CA 60 Transaereo, a flying boat with three sets of triple wings, eight engines, and pontoons mounted on either side to provide stability. Designed to carry 100 passengers, only one was built and on its first flight in March 1921 it crashed over Lago Maggiore, breaking up when it hit the water and then sinking to the bottom of the lake. The company was more successful with the CA 73, a light bomber, designed between 1922 and 1924. Conceived as a civil aircraft for ten passengers, it was also the first Italian plane to be constructed entirely of metal. In 1930, the CA 90 set a world's record for altitude and duration. A bomber, it was a plane of considerable size that is thought by some to have been the world's

Fig. 27.16: Alessandro Marchetti, Savoia-Marchetti S-55 flying boat, 1925. © Museum of Flight/CORBIS/Getty Images.

largest aircraft until superseded by the Russian Tupolev ANT-20 in 1934.

The Società Idrovolanti Alta Italia was founded in 1915 but took its post-war name, Savoia-Marchetti, when engineer Alessandro Marchetti (1884–1966) joined the firm in 1922. The company became known for its flying boats and seaplanes, which set a number of speed and endurance records. In 1924, Savoia-Marchetti began to produce the S-55, a flying boat that was perhaps its most famous aircraft. Designed by Marchetti in response to a request from the newly formed Ministry of Aeronautics, it carried passengers and baggage in two pontoon hulls while the pilot and co-pilot occupied a cockpit in the center of the high wing (Fig. 27.16). The two engines were mounted one behind the other on a frame that rested on top of the wing. As previously mentioned, the Minister of Aeronautics, Italo Balbo, commanded a squadron of 24 S-55s that flew in a V formation across the Atlantic to Chicago in 1933. Historian Dennis Doordan has noted that the S-55 became one of the iconic images of the Fascist regime through its multiple reproductions on posters, postcards, paintings, and other visual propaganda. However, despite the

Fascist regime's promotion of the S-55 as a symbol of modernity, Italy's own national airline, Ala Littoria, formed in 1934 through the union of several smaller lines, used mainly German and Dutch planes until it was able to adapt some of Italy's own military aircraft, particularly the three-engine monoplanes that Savoia-Marchetti built for civilian use.

Italy lagged behind other European countries in commercial shipbuilding and did not begin to compete seriously in this endeavor until the early 1930s, when two transatlantic ocean liners were launched, the *Rex* in 1932 by the Compagnia Italia in Genoa, and the *Conte de Savoia*, inaugurated the following year by Lloyd Adriatico in Trieste. Both were a tribute to Italian naval engineering and shipbuilding capabilities, the *Rex* having been built by the well-established Ansaldo & C., which owned shipyards in Genoa and Naples. The year the *Conte de Savoia* was launched, it won an award for crossing the Atlantic in four days, a feat of technological prowess comparable to the transatlantic flight of Italo Balbo's S-55 squadron the same year. Such accomplishments were celebrated by the Fascist regime as evidence of its modernity and its capacity to organize human and technological resources for impressive practical ends.

At the beginning of the 1930s, the interiors of Italian passenger ships were decorated in historic styles, following the British example. However, some of the French and German ships had broken with this tradition by the late 1920s and introduced deluxe modern interiors with expensive furnishings and rich materials. Lloyd Adriatico was the first Italian company to follow this trend. For the interiors of the *Conte de Savoia*, it hired the engineer Gustavo Pulitzer Finali (1887–1967), whose chosen style, which was evident in his grand Salone Colonna, was somewhere between the Novecento and the Viennese Secession. In fact, ship interiors had become a theme for the Triennales and Gio Ponti wrote favorably of Pulitzer Finali's work in *Domus*.

Commercial graphics, typography, and book design

Advertising

During the interwar years, Italian advertising graphics flourished even as they competed with the heavy-handed propaganda of the Fascist regime. While Fascist posters, publications, and even postage stamps had a distinctive though not rigid visual style, advertising posters and popular magazine covers remained extremely diverse, and some poster artists and illustrators moved back and forth between propaganda and commercial design. By the early 1930s, modern graphic techniques that had been derived from the Bauhaus, the New Typography, and new graphic practices in Switzerland competed with the more traditional techniques of advertising.

The poster continued to play a major role in Italian commercial graphics with Milan remaining the center of the advertising industry. Following World War I, the leading poster artists were Leonetto Cappiello (1875–1942), Marcello Dudovich (1878–1962), and Achille Mauzan (1883–1952), all of whom had been previously prominent. Cappiello was an Italian who moved to Paris in 1897; Mauzan was born in France but migrated to Italy in 1905; and Dudovich had been one of the prominent poster designers who worked for Riccordi, the large Milanese lithography firm before the war.

Cappiello began his career in France as a caricaturist, working for many magazines and satirical journals. He produced his first posters within the Parisian milieu that was dominated by Jules Chéret, but Cappiello departed from Chéret's more narrative scenes by featuring single figures against solid colored backgrounds. He did not go as far as poster artists like Lucian Bernhard, who reduced their designs to a drawing of the product accompanied by large letters with the manufacturer's name, but his emphasis on one figure or occasionally two associated the figures directly with the product that was advertised. Cappiello's posters were often filled with fantasy and whimsy: a woman in diaphanous clothing holding a gigantic glass of champagne; another with butterfly wings prancing through the air clutching a bottle of Gancia extra dry spumante in one hand and a foaming glass of spirits in the other; a female figure in an extravagant costume astride a bucking unicorn with an open box of Wamar biscotti in one hand; or a poster from the early 1920s for Campari, the manufacturer of cordials and bitters, depicting a clown holding a bottle of bitters while dancing inside an orange peel that swirled around him (Fig. 27.17). Cappiello worked for many Italian clients, continuing to associate products with fantasy imagery in a style that became increasingly nostalgic. Mauzan, who had created one of the most powerful Italian recruiting posters during World War I, reverted to a more superficial illustrative style after the war, playing heavily on French fashion illustration and comic drawings to promote toothpaste, perfume, and hair lotion.

Both Cappiello and Mauzan were represented in Italy by Studio Maga, an agency that Giuseppe Magagnoli (1879–1933) founded in Bologna around 1916. Magagnoli, who was more an entrepreneur than an artist, had contracts to represent both Cappiello and Mauzan in Italy and in addition gathered around him a stable of poster artists who were among the best in Italy.

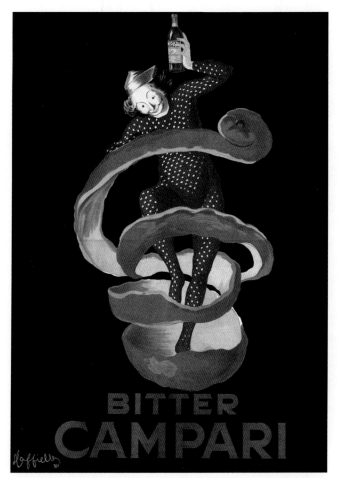

Fig. 27.17: Leonetto Cappiello, Bitter Campari, poster, 1921. © 2014. White Images/Scala, Florence.

They included Aleardo Terzi (1870–1943), Mario Pozzati (1888–1947), Severo Pozzati (1895–1983), and Marcello Nizzoli, Their posters were sometimes signed with the studio name even though the artists had considerable leeway to develop their own styles.

Dudovich continued to work as he had before the war, depicting the wealthy Milanese. He worked for numerous clients during the Fascist years but also did an extended series of large lithographic posters for the Milanese department store La Rinascente. As much as anyone, Dudovich created a visual portrait of the affluent Milanese middle class, the consumers who went to elegant restaurants and cafés and who bought the expensive furniture and decorative objects that Gio Ponti and other Novecento designers created (Fig. 27.18).

Markets for national brands developed slowly in Italy but companies that did establish brand names for their products—whether liquors, clothing, beauty aids, appliances, or automobiles—often hired poster artists to advertise them. Some of these companies—Buitoni, Martini, Fiat, Pirelli, La Rinascente, and later Olivetti and Motta—set up their own internal advertising offices, while others like Campari worked in a more individual way with graphic artists. Though Fiat embraced the efficiency of American manufacturing, its advertising program failed to achieve any unity even though many well-established artists worked for the company. While the advertising office did produce some excellent posters, the overall production was uneven and lacked visual coherence. Campari, which also collaborated with many different artists, employed them more creatively and produced some exceptional publicity such as the black and white newspaper advertisements that Fortunato Depero did. Olivetti was perhaps the only company or one of the very few that understood the concept of a house style, which it achieved through the guidance of its Office of Development and Publicity.

As early as 1917, however, the poster artist Luciano Ramo (1886–1959) argued that modern advertising required that the creativity of the artist be subordinated to scientific strategies of persuasion. Besides the art directors and poster impresarios like Giuseppe Magagnoli, a new type of professional, who preferred to be known as an advertising technician or *tecnico pubblicitario*, emerged. In general these experts did not have artistic backgrounds and considered advertising to be a problem of sales rather than art. Magagnoli was skeptical of them, and Studio Maga's house organ *Il pugno nell'occhio* (*A Punch in the Eye*) attacked their "cabalistic formulae" and claimed that they were only able to address an "audience of imbeciles." Magagnoli,

Fig. 27.18: Marcello Dudovich, Sea and Mountains at La Rinascente, poster, 1920s. Mondadori via Getty Images. © DACS 2017.

of the Cubists on the one hand and the reductive formal compositional techniques of the Purists on the other. Initially Sepo worked in Italy through the Studio Maga but later joined the Dorland advertising agency in Paris and in 1932 he founded his own Parisian studio, IDEA, which continued until the 1950s. Sepo's work was closest to Cassandre's in its embrace of modern formal techniques, its emphasis on lettering as an integral part of the composition, and its ability to introduce the product with extreme visual economy. In 1928, he began to collaborate with a shirt manufacturer, Noveltex, an account obtained through Studio Dorland, and he created for them a series of posters depicting either a shirt or just a shirt collar on a flat ground of geometric shapes and limited colors. Although these posters did not result from the scientific strategies of persuasion that the advertising technicians espoused, they nonetheless advanced beyond the more eclectic imagery of Cappiello or Mauzan by maintaining a consistent formal structure for the entire series as well as the same scale and placement of the company name within each composition.

Federico Seneca (1891–1976) was initially influenced by Marcello Dudovich, but he developed his own poster style through his association of many years with Buitoni-Perugina, a large food company that sold pasta under the Buitoni name and chocolates under the name Perugina. Working with a range of clients, Seneca featured single figures against colored backgrounds, but the figures were more abstract than Cappiello's. Seneca drew them like trademarks, without facial features and with an emphasis on the rounded formal shapes of their bodies, whether bare-breasted African women with baskets of cocoa beans for Perugina, a man in formal attire sipping a cordial for Ramazzotti, a seated man in a turban for Modiano cigarette papers, or his well-known green nun and chef with a bowl of pasta for Buitoni (Fig. 27.19).

By the beginning of the 1930s, the influence of Cappiello had waned and poster artists were drawing more inspiration from French fashion illustrators

who frequently discussed poster concepts with his clients before he gave an assignment to an artist, believed instead that it was more effective to create a visual trick that would surprise the audience and enable them to remember a product.

In fact, following Cappiello's emphasis on the single figure, other poster artists created distinctive images that became closely associated with particular goods. Severo Pozzati (1895–1983), who adopted the professional name Sepo, was adept at isolating an object or human figure for this purpose. He had moved to Paris in 1920, where he absorbed the formal strategies

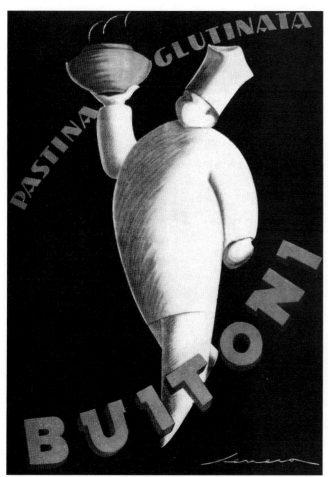

Fig. 27.19: Federico Seneca, Buitoni, poster, c. 1928. © Lordprice Collection/Alamy.

like Georges Lepape, the modern French style of Cassandre, Carlu, or Leupot, the Austrian airbrush posters of Joseph Binder, the German posters of Ludwig Hohlwein, or those of Swiss designers like Herbert Matter. The work of all these designers was published in the illustrated commercial art magazines like *Gebrauchsgraphik* that circulated widely in Europe. Among the Italian artists who created advertising posters in this genre were Mario Gros (1888–1977), Giovanni Mingozzi (1891–d.o.d unconfirmed), Paolo Garretto (1903–1989), Mario Puppo (1905–1977), Araca (1898– d.o.d unconfirmed), Giorgio Federico Dabovich (1902–1956), the Austrian Franz Lenhart (1898–1992),

whose travel posters promoted the Tyrol in Austria as well as Italian sites, and Filippo Romoli, 1928–1968), who worked in Genoa rather than Milan where most of the other artists were situated. Plinio Codognato (1878–1940) kept the Futurist tradition alive with his dynamic posters that advertised automobiles and automobile races. The Novecento painter Mario Sironi was also an active poster designer for commercial clients as well as the Fascist regime, although his designs remained painterly and were not entirely successful as either propaganda or advertising.

Though Marcello Nizzoli produced advertising posters within the above-mentioned genre during the first part of his career, he was something of a special case. Trained as a painter in Parma, he had developed a modern poster style but not one that could easily be traced. Besides an interest in the painters of the Novecento, he employed the dynamic perspective of the Futurists, while in several posters of 1926 for Campari, he created stilllifes with a Campari bottle that revealed a strong debt to Cézanne. Posters he did for the various Triennales or events promoted by the Fascist Party employed heavy geometric lettering and strong iconic forms. By 1934, when he began to collaborate with Edoardo Persico on the design of exhibitions and retail spaces, Nizzoli was committed to Rationalism, an approach that he brought with him to Olivetti when he first worked for the company in 1935. Nizzoli helped to transmit a modern graphic style to younger graphic designers such as Giovanni Pintori through the courses in advertising techniques that he taught at ISIA in Monza during the 1930s.

An important poster artist in the interwar years working completely outside the prevailing influences on other designers was Gino Boccasile (1901–1952), who began his career as a caricaturist for satirical journals and an illustrator for fashion magazines. Though his many advertising posters depicted men and women, he came to specialize in female pinups, shapely women with large breasts whom he sometimes depicted with their eyes closed in a supposed state of ecstasy. Boccasile was also the principal poster propagandist for the Fascists during World War II, depicting the Fascist male as a muscular hero just as Mussolini wished him to be seen and often creating racist imagery that demeaned Jews and African-Americans, the latter recalling derogatory depictions of Africans while Italy was a colonial power. After the war, Boccasile returned to creating advertising posters that depicted the same buxom women whose seductive shapes were associated with a variety of products.

Boccasile and other poster artists who had many clients frequently worked in Milanese studios which were numerous. Boccasile originally worked in the studio of Alphonse Mauzan and then moved to the ACTA studio. The Officine Grafiche Ricordi, one of the oldest of these studios, was established early in the century and specialized in the design and lithographic printing of posters and sheet music. After World War I, Studio Maga was certainly one of the largest producers of advertising posters. Other studios included UPI; Agencia Gros-Monti, co-founded by the poster artist Mario Gros; Arti Grafiche Pirovano; and IMA (Idea Method Art). These studios specialized in the design and sometimes printing of advertising posters and other commercial art, but others were established with the aim of introducing the more scientific American style of advertising to Italy. Known as advertising agencies instead of graphic art studios because they produced entire campaigns rather than graphic design alone, they included the ACME-Dalmonte agency, the first and perhaps most important of these, founded in 1922 by Luigi Dalmonte Casoni (1881–1966), a former illustrator and graphic artist who had worked briefly for an advertising agency in New York; and Balza-Ricc, established in 1931 by Giulio Ricciardi (dates unconfirmed) and Pier Luigi Balzaretti (dates unconfirmed), former head of La Rinascente's advertising office in Milan. *L'Ufficio Moderno* (*The Modern Office*) was the principal publication where the theories and methods of the advertising agencies were discussed.

Typography and book design

From the turn of the century until World War II, the major figure in the world of Italian book arts and typography was Raffaello Bertieri (1875–1945), a publisher with a background in printing. His principal forum was *Il Risorgimento Grafico* (*The Graphic Renaissance*), the printing journal he founded in 1902 (see Chapter 17), while the publishing house in which he was a partner, Bertieri & Vansetti, set high standards for book printing.

Bertieri was a nationalist who argued for the establishment of an Italian printing office along with Italian foundries, typefaces, and schools of graphic art. These goals were not lost on the Fascists who adopted them as part of their program though subsequently paid minimal attention to them. Bertieri espoused the typefaces of the Italian Renaissance as models for modern fonts. In the pages of his journal, he wrote extensively about the printing arts, arguing strongly for the legibility of typefaces and for the appropriate use of varied faces in different kinds of publications. He also accommodated the journal to modern trends and changed its design accordingly over time.

In 1918, Bertieri became the director of the Scuola del Libro (School of the Book), which the Società Umanitaria had established in 1902 in Milan. The school's aim, which was similar to the society's aforementioned school for the applied arts that was founded a year later, was to foster a revival of the book arts, presumably following the Arts and Crafts movement and subsequent reforms in Germany. Bertieri headed the Scuola del Libro until 1925, during which time he made it more responsive to the technical needs of the graphic arts community. Among the prominent students in the 1920s were Attilio Rossi (1909–1994) and Carlo Dradi (1908–1982), both founders in 1933 of *Campo Grafico*, the magazine that promoted a modern graphic style in Italy.

Bertieri also had a close association with the Nebiolo foundry in Turin and collaborated with them on the production of various typefaces. The

A
BCDEFGHI
JKLMNO
PQRS
TU
V
XYZ

Fig. 27.20: Alessandro Butti and Raffaello Bertieri, Paganini typeface, 1928. Museum of printing and graphic communication, Lyon.

first was Inkunabula, which the foundry copied from a Venetian alphabet of 1476 by Erhard Ratdolt and released in 1911 (Fig. 27.20). But Inkunabula, previously mentioned, was an undistinguished face that had limited use, although it was adopted for *Il Risorgimento Grafico* (see Chapter 17). More successful was the design of Paganini, another Nebiolo face on which Bertieri collaborated with Alessandro Butti (1893–1959), art director of the Nebiolo foundry. Introduced in 1928, Paganini—a roman type somewhat similar to the French Cochin—remained in circulation for a considerable time although it was eventually eclipsed in popularity by various revivals of Bodoni that Bertieri, in fact, helped to promote. Other fonts cast by the Nebiolo foundry for which Bertieri was responsible include Sinibaldi in 1926, Iliade in 1930, and Ruano in 1933. Despite his espousal of typographic legibility and clarity, none of the typefaces for which Bertieri was responsible, with the exception of Paganini, were widely used and they quickly went out of circulation, largely because Bertieri was more interested in producing a national typeface with roots in Italian tradition than in creating one that was above all legible and functional.

Besides Bertieri's faces, which were rooted in the Italian Renaissance, Nebiolo also produced contemporary types. In 1930, the foundry published its own version of Futura, which it called Semplicità (Simplicity). A more original modern font was Neon (also listed as Neondi), designed by the painter Giulio da Milano (1895–1990) in 1935. At the time, da Milano was the director of type design for Nebiolo, a position that Alessandro Butti took over the following year. Another modern face, Triennale, was introduced two years earlier by the Fonderia Reggiani in Milan, coinciding with the first Triennale to be held in Giovanni Muzio's new Palazzo dell' Arte.

In 1927, the German printer, typographer, and printing scholar Hans Mardersteig (1892–1977) moved his press, the Officina Bodoni, from Switzerland to Verona, Italy, where he had won a competition to print the complete works of the Italian poet Gabriele d'Annunzio. Settling in Verona, Mardersteig, who changed his name to Giovanni, spent ten years producing 49 volumes of d'Annunzio's writings. Hand-set in the Bodoni typeface, the books achieved the highest level of design and printing excellence. Mardersteig also designed several typefaces of his own during this period, notably Zeno, which was realized by the French punchcutter Charles Malin in 1935–1936. Mardersteig became more active in Italian publishing circles after World War II when he set up a commercial press, the Stamperia Valdonega, in Verona.

Modern graphic design

Italy's long tradition of avant-garde typography began with the publication of F. T. Marinetti's sound poem *Zang Tumb Tumb* in 1914. While the poem helped to foster a spate of experimental Futurist books, magazines, and advertising in the interwar period, neither it nor the work that followed from it was central to the modern graphic design movement that emerged at the beginning of the 1930s. Instead, the architecture of Gruppo 7 aroused interest in the wider European Rationalist movement and contributed to the development of such magazines as *Casabella*, which promoted a culture of modernity in Italy.

Shortly after Edoardo Persico became associated with *Casabella* in 1930, he initiated a gradual process of visual transformation that resulted several years later in the magazine becoming Italy's first publication designed according to the principles of the New Typography and Bauhaus Rationalism. Persico selected the Nebiolo foundry's san serif typeface Serenità for the text, which he combined with wide margins, ample white space, and photographs. His most significant

Fig. 27.21: Carlo Dradi, Attilio Rossi, and Battista Pallavera, *Campo Grafico*, cover, 1933. © Archive Tipoteca Italiana, Italy.

innovation, however, was the two-page spread, which he conceived as a single layout or "two pages in one." He continued to experiment with the design of the publication until he stabilized it in 1934 with a more or less square format and a cover that featured the title, issue number, and an image arranged in a formal composition on a white ground.

Persico's experimental *Casabella* covers and layouts marked the beginning of a modern movement in Italian graphic design that grew throughout the 1930s as a counterforce to the ponderous rhetoric of Fascist propaganda. It opposed as well the more traditional approaches to typography and layout that Raffaello Bertieri and other authors emphasized in the pages of *Il Risorgimento Grafico*.

Modern graphics received an impetus in 1933 from three important events: the exhibition of contemporary German graphic design that Paul Renner curated for the Deutscher Werkbund at the 5th Triennale; the founding of *Campo Grafico*, Italy's first magazine devoted to modern graphic design; and the establishment of the Studio Boggieri, the first independent design office in Italy dedicated to the Rationalist graphics that were already well developed in Germany and Switzerland. Besides these events, the continued growth of Olivetti's advertising program added yet another site of activity to the new movement.

Campo Grafico was founded by Attilio Rossi and Carlo Dradi. At the Scuola del Libro, the two studied with the artist and illustrator Guido Marussig (1885–1971), who shifted his course from the traditional decoration of books to a structural method of book design. Neither the editorial policy nor the design approach of *Campo Grafico* were rigid and the editors changed the covers, layouts, and typography with each issue to maintain a spirit of experimentation (Fig. 27.21). They designed some covers themselves, collaborated with designers such as Battista Pallavera (dates unknown) and commissioned covers from numerous artists and designers including Enrico Kaneclin (dates unconfirmed), Giovanni Fraschini (dates unconfirmed),

Atantasio Soldati (1896–1953), and Luigi Veronesi (1908–1998). They also expanded their definition of graphic design to include ordinary objects of daily life such as train tickets, coupons, and business cards. This provoked the adverse response from some that they were simply presenting "a review of the ugly." The leading collaborators included the printer, editor, and typographer Guido Modiano (1899–1943), and the designer Bruno Munari.

Campo Grafico became an important rallying point for designers, artists, and critics who were interested in the connection between graphic design and modern art. The editors forged relations with Italy's first abstract painters such as Lucio Fontana, Atanasio Soldati, and Luigi Veronesi and published articles that featured photomontages and abstract paintings, along with examples of the best modern graphic design from Italy and abroad. According to Rossi, they traced their roots to the Bauhaus, the *Esprit Nouveau* of Le Corbusier and Ozenfant, and Adolf Loos's *Ornament and Crime*. The editors and contributors campaigned actively for a typographic renewal, which was expressed as much through the journal's experimental layouts as through the written texts. *Campo Grafico* appeared regularly until 1939, when financial exigencies forced its closure. The final issue was a paean to Futurism, thus returning Italian graphic modernism to one of its earliest sources.

Antonio Boggeri (1900–1989) trained as a violinist and subsequently developed a passion for abstract photography after he encountered Moholy-Nagy's seminal book, *Painting, Photography, Film*. His belief that photography could also be an important component of modern advertising influenced his decision to found the Studio Boggeri in 1933. Stimulated by Paul Renner's exhibition of modern graphics at the 5th Triennale, Boggeri decided to seek out designers who had some relation to the Bauhaus or who worked outside of Italy.

He was fortunate in attracting the Swiss artist Xanti Schawinsky, who was a student at the Bauhaus between 1924 and 1929. Schawinsky left Germany in 1933 because of the Nazis and emigrated to Italy, where Boggeri recruited him. At the beginning, Schawinsky and the Hungarian designer Imre Reiner, who lived across the border in Switzerland, were the mainstays of the studio. Much of Schawinsky's work consisted of painted posters, although he began to use photography extensively in his projects for Olivetti. Reiner contributed a refined Constructivist approach that was already prevalent among progressive Swiss graphic designers.

Schawinsky, who strongly influenced a number of younger Italian designers, remained with Studio Boggeri until 1936 when he left for the United States. By that time, however, Boggeri had begun to work with a number of other designers including Marcello Nizzoli, Erberto Carboni, Remo Muratore (1912–1983), Bruno Munari, and Riccardo Castagnedi (Ricas).

Overall, the studio's work had much in common with the Swiss version of the New Typography that one could see in the designs of Max Bill, Richard Lohse, Anton Stankowski, or Hans Neuburg. This quality was enhanced by the Swiss designer Max Huber (1919–1992), who joined Studio Boggeri in 1940. While the graphic pieces produced by Boggeri's designers shared an underlying structure, they were not rigid examples of a singular visual style. What they shared was a commitment to photography—a medium appropriate for many of the studio's industrial clients—a preference for san serif typography, and a limited color palette, frequently confined to black or gray, white and red. The studio also adopted some strategies of the advertising agencies by designing coordinated graphics programs that included logotypes, exhibits, letterheads, and product catalogs as well as the standard promotional materials.

Many examples of the new Italian design were displayed at the 7th Triennale of 1940 in a special graphics exhibition curated by Guido Modiano, who had collaborated with *Campo Grafico*. Among those selected to show their work were Carboni, Dradi, Rossi,

Munari, Muratore, Nizzoli, Veronesi, and Ricas. This recognition was important as it signaled a perceived compatibility with the Fascist regime, even though the measured forms of the work itself were as far from the visual bombast of the government's propaganda as one could imagine.

Germany
The importance of propaganda

In 1919, Adolf Hitler, an Austrian who served in the German Army during World War I, joined an obscure political organization, the German Workers' Party (DAP), which in 1920 changed its name to the National Socialist German Workers' Party (NSDAP). Hitler became the party's chief propagandist, and soon its leader, propounding a mix of German nationalism, anti-Semitism, and antagonism to big business. The party set out to court the small shopkeepers, tradesmen, and craftsmen who were threatened by the rise of the large German corporations and angered by the harsh reparations that the Allied victors demanded after Germany's defeat in World War I.

Believing that the masses had to be bullied by a strong-willed leader, Hitler adopted the tactics of a street fighter, organizing his own paramilitary squads, the SA, who staged demonstrations and engaged in street fights. In 1923, he was jailed for his role in a rowdy Munich beer-hall brawl in which he urged the crowd to overthrow the Berlin government. Tried for treason, he was sent to prison where he wrote *Mein Kampf* (*My Struggle*), a book in which he exposed his virulent racism and his belief in the right of the strong to dominate the weak (Fig. 27.22). In a salient chapter on war propaganda, he recognized the superior efforts of the Allied forces during World War I and enunciated a propaganda strategy for the future. Regarding the masses, he wrote that "they always require a certain time before they are ready even to notice a thing, and only after the simplest ideas are repeated thousands of times will the masses finally remember them."

In the following years, after his release from prison, Hitler built the NSDAP into a mass party, replete with uniforms, rituals, and a powerful symbol, the swastika, which served as a visual rallying point for the party's members. The swastika was an ancient symbol that has its probable origin about 3,000 years ago among the Aryans in India. In the years before Hitler adopted it, the swastika was associated with several anti-Semitic groups that promoted the superiority of the Aryan race. Hitler also devised a special party flag that had a red ground on which was a white circle with a black swastika in the center. During the years between 1933 and 1945 when the Nazis ruled

Fig. 27.22: *Mein Kampf*, cover, 1939. © Stephen French/Alamy.

Germany, this flag replaced the red, white, and black striped one of the Weimar Republic.

Among Hitler's first acts after becoming Chancellor of Germany in January 1933 was to establish a Ministry for Popular Enlightenment and Propaganda. As its head, he appointed Joseph Goebbels (1897–1945), a doctor of philosophy who joined the Nazi Party, as the NSDAP came to be called, in 1924 and became its propaganda chief by the end of the decade. Goebbels shared Hitler's belief that the masses could be conquered by pervasive propaganda and simplistic slogans. One of his first tasks was to reorganize all the artists, filmmakers, designers, architects, writers, and other creative people into new organizations that ensured the members' loyalty to the party.

Goebbels was also involved in the creation of an organizational manual that dictated where and how the official Nazi symbols, notably the swastika and the eagle, were to be used. The applications ranged from banners, uniforms, and emblems to stationery, plaques, and postage stamps (Plate 39). As with the use of corporate logotypes in later years, the swastika could be miniaturized for a commemorative medal or enlarged as a symbol on a public building.

Graphic design, typography, and exhibitions

Taking a cue from the bourgeois press, the Nazi party launched its own series of newspapers and illustrated magazines during the 1920s. The first of these party papers was the *Völkischer Beobachter* (*People's Observer*), which Hitler began to publish in 1925. Instead of the lengthy articles and academic discussions of the liberal and left press, the *Beobachter* featured short vicious propaganda pieces with shocking photographs of atrocities against unsuspecting women that were alleged to have been committed by Jews or Communists. The *Beobachter* and other Nazi publications demonized these two groups as enemies of Germany and portrayed them in derogatory ways throughout the years that the Nazis were in power. Even more strident than the *Völkischer Beobachter* were *Die Angriff* (*The Attack*), founded by Goebbels in 1927, and *Der Stürmer* (*The Striker/Attacker*), a virulent anti-Semitic paper inaugurated in 1923 by Julius Streicher in Nuremberg. The design of both papers was heavy-handed, featuring aggressive mastheads and bold headlines in Fraktur type. The party also established its own illustrated weekly, the *Illustrierter Beobachter* (*Illustrated Observer*), in direct imitation of the bourgeois weeklies published in Berlin, Munich, and elsewhere. Like the left-wing *Arbeiter Illustrierte Zeitung*, it was a propaganda magazine and its photographs of party meetings, demonstrations, and processions were intended to glorify the Nazi

Fig. 27.23: *Illustrierte Beobachter*, cover, 1932. © Lebrecht Music and Arts Photo Library/Alamy.

movement (Fig. 27.23). Between 1931 and 1938, the Nazis also published an unsuccessful humor magazine, *Die Brennessel* (*The Nettle*), whose chief cartoonist was Josef Plank (dates unconfirmed), known as Seppla. He specialized in cartoons that caricatured and ridiculed Nazi enemies, notably the Jews and Communists, and later the British and Americans. One cartoon depicted Winston Churchill as an octopus seeking to embrace the entire globe in its grip.

The Nazis relied heavily on posters to promote specific events and to reinforce positive stereotypes of ideal Germans. These were of several types. During the election of 1932, the party published several posters that featured tough lantern-jawed street fighters looking straight ahead with determined gazes. The artist who specialized in drawing these types was Hans Schweitzer (1901–1980), whose artistic name was Mjölnir, a Nordic term meaning "that which smashes." Mjölnir had been doing illustrations for the Nazi press since the early 1920s. Whether he was producing his images as drawings or woodcuts, his style was crude and highly gestural. A woodcut poster of the late 1920s features a row of determined brown shirts, one with a head bandage from a street fight. Behind them is a Nazi flag and below, cut in rough letters, is the description, "The organized will of a nation" (Fig. 27.24).

The artist who specialized in images of handsome Nazis was Ludwig Hohlwein, who, as described earlier, was the foremost advertising artist of the Weimar Republic. It is not surprising that Hohlwein would have embraced the Nazi cause. During the 1920s, he specialized in depictions of wealthy men and women who would appear to have had little interest in the progressive politics or innovative art forms of the German left. Hohlwein's Nazi figures possessed the same self-confidence as did his Weimar types only now they were dressed in uniforms or nationalistic Bavarian folk costumes (Plate 40). Other prominent commercial artists during the Weimar years who later did posters for the Nazis include Otto Ottler, Jupp Wiertz, Willi Petzold (dates unconfirmed), and Valentin Zietara.

Although the Nazis promoted a return to German tradition in cultural expression, their adoption of traditional forms was selective. In architecture, the traditional folk form of the half-timbered house was chosen for youth hostels, while civic buildings, mostly designed by Hitler's principal architect Albert Speer, used a classical language. In typography, the Nazis called for a return to traditional Fraktur type, although san serif and roman alphabets were widely available. Nonetheless, following Hitler's assumption of power the German type foundries rushed out a series of modernized Fraktur black letter typefaces, all of which,

Fig. 27.24: Mjölnir, The Organized Will of the Nation, poster, late 1920s. © war posters/Alamy.

they claimed, possessed a German character. Despite that claim, however, these typefaces combined calligraphic elements of the traditional black letter with a modern geometric quality such that they had an angular rather than a flowing appearance.

The Berthold Foundry released Deutschland and Deutsch, the latter designed by Georg Trump (1896–1985); Ludwig & Meyer produced National; and the Stempel Foundry created Tannenberg (Fig. 27.25). The Bauer Foundry, which several years earlier had released

Fig. 27.25: Tannenberg typeface, advertisement, 1933. The Wolfsonian–Florida International University, Miami Beach, Florida, The Mitchell Wolfson, Jr. Collection, XC1994.4360. Photo: David Almeida .

Paul Renner's modernist san serif Futura to great fanfare, produced a black letter type, Element, that the graphic designer Max Bittrof created. In its advertising, Bauer even co-opted the language of the Weimar avant-garde, calling Element "the clear German script of the new typography."

The adoption of traditional graphic forms was selective and, following the crudely designed Nazi publications of the 1920s, rarely applied to advertising or mass circulation publications during the 1930s. The international advertising agency Studio Dorland, whose principal designer in Berlin was Herbert Bayer, continued to produce modern advertising and publication designs. After leaving the Bauhaus in 1928, Bayer joined the agency following a brief stint as art director of *Vogue*'s German edition. He remained at Dorland until 1938 when he left Germany for the United States. While at the agency he moved away from a strict interpretation of the New Typography to incorporate photomontage and Surrealist images in some of his advertisements and cover designs.

Among Dorland's major clients was *Die Neue Linie* (*The New Line*), a fashion magazine. As art director, Bayer conceived the covers and supervised the interior layout (Fig. 27.26). He also worked on a number of major exhibitions between 1933 and 1938. Although the stated aim of these was to promote German trade and industry, they served to present a new image of Germany that conformed to the political and cultural values of the Nazi Party. Several organizations were involved with the promotion of exhibitions. One was the Institut für Deutsche Kultur und Wirtschaftspropaganda (Institute for German Culture and Economic Propaganda) and another was the Amt für Ausstellungs- und Messewesen (Office for Exhibitions and Trade Show Affairs). The participation of these organizations in exhibition planning was a clear indication that all exhibitions were intended to convey a propaganda message.

The modernist rhetoric of a number of these exhibitions makes clear that the Nazis moved

Fig. 27.26: Herbert Bayer, *Die Neue Linie*, cover, 1930. The Wolfsonian–Florida International University, Miami Beach, Florida, The Mitchell Wolfson, Jr. Collection, XB1999.210.3. Photo: David Almeida. © DACS 2017.

strategically between modern and traditional design, depending on the purpose of the project. Aimed at a foreign as well as a domestic audience, the exhibits that Bayer designed could be presented in a modern style while also demonstrating in their content the traditional nationalist values espoused by the Nazis. Bayer designed a trilogy of exhibitions—Deutsches Volk – Deutsche Arbeit (German People – German Work) of 1934, Das Wunder des Lebens (The Wonder of Life) of 1935, and Deutschland Ausstellung (Germany Exhibition) of 1936. For the first of the exhibitions,

Deutsches Volk—Deutsche Arbeit, Bayer was assisted by other designers including former Bauhaus faculty Walter Gropius, Joost Schmidt, Lilly Reich, and Mies van der Rohe. The exhibit presented modern German industrial objects against a backdrop of photomontage cultural narratives. The catalog cover for the third exhibit Deutschland Ausstellung suggests Germany's imperial aims by showing a map of the country at the top of a globe with all the lines marking time zone divisions converging at one point inside its borders. The catalog text, which combined blue and brown tinted photographs that portrayed a cross-section of German life under the Nazis, reinforced the cover image by addressing Germany's need for *Lebensraum* or living space, while promoting the endurance of German folk culture despite the continuing process of industrialization. Within the exhibition, a large triangular panel showed Hitler with a raised clenched fist followed by workers, soldiers, and youth group members who gradually disappear into an anonymous mass that stretches backwards to a seemingly infinite vanishing point.

Other exhibitions the Nazis promoted include Die Küche—das Reich der Frau (The Kitchen—the Woman's Domain), and Schaffendes Volk (A Nation at Work), a large exhibition that promoted the Nazi's Four-Year Plan for economic self-sufficiency and urged the public to buy German goods. Several other exhibitions demonized Germany's enemies: Das Ewige Jude (The Eternal Jew) and Der Bolschevismus (Bolshevism), both held in 1937. The poster for *Das Ewige Jude* featured a stereotypical Jewish money-lender, while the Bolsheviks were personified on the Bolshevism exhibition poster as a bloodthirsty spider attempting to encircle the globe with its hairy legs (Plate 41). As propaganda media, exhibitions proved to be extremely effective. Designers created atmospheres of total immersion where the public was surrounded by dramatic lighting, enormous photographs, and objects whose powerful presentation highlighted their polemical value.

The industrial machine

In his rise to power during the 1920s, Hitler had consistently courted the German craft classes, promising them a greater role in a Nazi economic program. Following his election, however, he announced that the nation's highest industrial priority would be rearmament. After Germany's defeat in World War I, the victorious Allies had forbidden Germany to rearm but Krupp, the nation's largest armaments firm, illegally circumvented this restriction first by designing artillery in a German factory under the guise of making machine tools and then by developing several tank prototypes and other weapons. Gustav Krupp was an early supporter of the Nazis and his firm became the party's leading weapons manufacturer.

The design of automobiles and road transport vehicles was revitalized by the push to create a national highway system or *Reichsautobahn*. Widely publicized as one of the Nazis' greatest domestic achievements, the *autobahn* was intended to serve several principal purposes. First, it facilitated movement between cities within Germany and encouraged attendance at mass rallies and other meetings, and second, it encouraged tourists from other countries to tour Germany by car. Robert Zinner's poster, done in an academic painterly style, depicts the *autobahn* for foreign tourists as a seamless route for cars to move through a vast wooded and mountainous landscape into an infinite distance (Fig. 27.27). Another by-product of the *autobahn* system was a network of roads along which to move military equipment to the east. However, scholars have noted that the routes chosen do not correspond to the highest priorities of military strategy and thus military needs are not seen in retrospect as a principal intent of the *autobahn's* construction.

Fig. 27.27: Robert Zinner, Reich Highways in Germany, poster, 1936. The Wolfsonian–Florida International University, Miami Beach, Florida, The Mitchell Wolfson, Jr. Collection, XX1990.3104. Photo: Lynton Gardiner.

Shortly after his election as Chancellor, Hitler announced at the Berlin automobile show that he intended to support the production of a Deutsche Volkswagen or German people's car. Later that year, he met the Austrian automotive engineer Ferdinand Porsche (1875–1951), who had long been interested in building a small car. Hitler gave Porsche a contract to build three prototypes based on an earlier design of his own. In 1936, the prototypes known as the VW3 were put through a rigorous testing process. Two years later, construction began on a factory to produce the cars as well as a town where it was to be located. Called Wolfsburg, the town was a Nazi variation of the socialist German town plans of the 1920s mixed with the British garden city model of Ebenezer Howard.

Fig. 27.28: Ferdinand Porsche, Kdf Wagen, prototype, 1938. © Volkswagen AG.

One stark difference between the Nazi new towns of the 1930s and their predecessors was the pitched roofs of all the dwellings rather than the flat roofs of the earlier socialist housing.

In 1939, after further testing and changes, several prototypes of the volkswagen were produced to test the capacity of the factory and to demonstrate what the final version would look like (Fig. 27.28). Once these prototypes rolled off the line, Hitler abruptly changed the name of the car to the KdF Wagen, to link it with Robert Ley's *Kraft durch Freude* or Strength through Joy movement, whose purpose was to organize leisure time activities for German workers. An elaborate campaign was orchestrated in which the German public was invited to invest 5 marks a week towards the purchase of a car that would eventually cost around 1,000 marks, then equivalent to about $250. However, once Hitler began his *Drang nach Osten,* his expansion towards the East, which started with the annexation of Austria and acquisition of the Sudetenland in 1938, followed by the invasion of Poland the following year, the demand for military equipment superseded the production of an inexpensive people's car and instead of producing the KdF Wagen, the Wolfsburg factory began to make military vehicles. The factory was bombed during World War II and did not begin producing civilian cars until the Volkswagen company was completely restructured after Germany surrendered.

Working at the other end of the transportation spectrum, the Nazis began to promote commercial air travel in giant dirigibles, first the *Graf Zeppelin*, which made regular trips to South America, and then the much larger LZ 129 *Hindenburg*. Completed in 1936 and designed especially for the North Atlantic route, the *Hindenburg* was almost as long as the *Queen Mary*, the largest ocean-going liner at the time. The interior design was planned and supervised by the architect Fritz August Breuhaus de Groot (1883–1960), already famous as a designer of luxury villas and interiors for passenger ships, trains, and airplanes. Distributed along the two decks of the passenger area that was located in the belly of the enormous airship were an elegant dining room, public rooms for writing and smoking, 25 double cabins, a kitchen, and rooms for the crew (Fig. 27.29). Because of a need for the dirigible's light weight, the furniture was mainly aluminum, including the piano, whose metal structure was covered with yellow leather. Some pieces, however, were made of tubular steel. Breuhaus de Groot, who had also designed tubular steel furniture for Thonet, modeled the chairs on existing types, adopting padded seats and backs for added comfort. During 1936 more than 1,000 passengers crossed the Atlantic in the *Hindenburg*, but on the first trip of 1937, the airship burst into flames shortly before landing in Lakehurst, New Jersey, severely challenging the credibility of airship transport and effectively shifting the focus of transatlantic air travel to new airplane designs.

Just as Ferdinand Porsche had begun developing designs for a small vehicle before being invited by Hitler to produce an official people's car, so did Walter Maria Kersting (1889–1970), an active Werkbund member, design a prototype for an inexpensive people's radio in 1928. Shortly after Hitler became Chancellor in 1933, the Nazis adopted it as the Volksempfänger (People's Receiver) VE 301. The radio was manufactured to standard specifications by several companies and sold cheaply to the public as a way to ensure that everyone would be able to listen to the Fuehrer's speeches. The housing was a simple modernist form made of Bakelite, but to give it a Nazi brand identity a subtle swastika pattern was woven into the grille cloth that covered the speaker. During World War II, German citizens found that they could only receive those stations that were controlled by the German propaganda ministry and were thus unable to listen to news from the BBC and other Allied broadcasters. The importance of the Volksempfänger for the dissemination of domestic propaganda was emphasized in a poster that depicts the

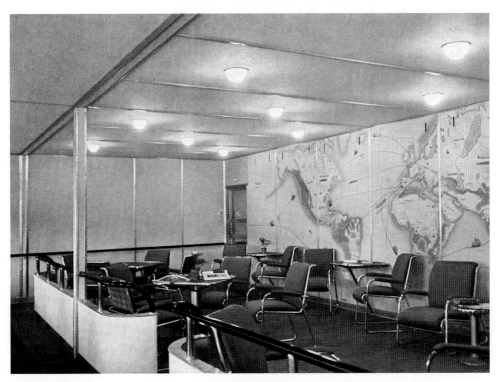

Fig. 27.29: Fritz August Breuhaus de Groot, *Hindenburg* airship lounge, 1936. The Wolfsonian–Florida International University, Miami Beach, Florida, The Mitchell Wolfson, Jr. Collection, XC1992.441.1.

Fig. 27.30: All Germany listens to the Führer with the Volksempfänger, poster, 1936. © war posters/Alamy.

German masses gathered around the radio as if it were the Führer himself (Fig. 27.30).

In general, the Nazi regime had no formal policy on whether modern or traditional forms of furniture or other domestic products best represented the regime. An advocate of traditional craftsmanship like Fritz Spannagel argued in his book *Unsere Wohnmöbel* (*Our Domestic Furniture*) of 1937 that machine production was acceptable only if it resulted in well-made objects that had a comfortable family-oriented form, while others continued to espouse furniture made of steel tubing such as Mies van der Rohe's cantilever chairs for Thonet.

However, the use of steel was restricted for domestic goods because it was needed for military purposes.

Furniture produced for Nazi organizations such as the Deutsche Arbeitsfront (German Labor Front) tended to be simple in form though usually made of wood. Unlike architecture, where the flat roof was identified with the dwellings of an inferior Mediterranean race, furniture forms were hardly controversial. What the modern movement had contributed to German furniture design, however, was to obviate the need for decorative ornament, which had seemed obligatory before the Jugendstil. This was evident in the furniture designed by the Schönheit der Arbeit (Beauty of Work) office of the German Labor Front. Under the direction of its chief designer, Karl Nothelfer (dates unconfirmed), the office designed and commissioned furniture and other standard products for work environments and housing projects. For architect Herman Giesler's party education center, the staff designers created wooden chairs with slightly curved backs like Windsor chairs, along with long plain wooden tables, while office furniture produced by the same organization featured basic chairs and practical wooden desks with clean flat surfaces and adequate storage space.

Furniture for Hitler's residencies and the Chancellery were produced in the Vereinigte Werkstätten of Munich (Munich United Workshops), much of it under the guidance of the architect Gerdy Troost (1904–2003), wife of the architect Paul Ludwig Troost who designed buildings for the Nazi Party. As Frederic Spotts notes, Hitler favored a plain style, but a complementary tendency towards the ornate and decorative is evident in his surviving sketches for fireplaces, sideboards, mantels, a sofa, and large wooden tables.

A principal supplier of Nazi uniforms was Hugo Boss (1885–1948), who founded a clothing company in 1924, went into bankruptcy due to the harsh economic climate, and then began to rebuild his business in 1931, the year he joined the Nazi Party. He became an official supplier of uniforms to various party organizations including the Sturmabteilung, Schutstaffel, Hitler Jugend, and the National Socialist Motor Corps. To meet the demand for more uniforms in the later years of the war, Boss took both prisoners of war and forced laborers into his workforce.

The Soviet Union
The Five-Year Plans 1928–1941

With the death of Vladimir Ilyich Lenin in 1924, leadership of the Communist Party shifted to a ruling triumvirate that included Joseph Stalin, then the party's general secretary. By 1928, Stalin had made himself the most powerful figure in the party hierarchy and a year later his position as the party's next leader was secured.

Unlike his rival Leon Trotsky, who believed that communism had to spread beyond the Soviet borders in order to succeed, Stalin espoused a doctrine of "socialism in one country." He called on the Russian people to make immense sacrifices in order to achieve heroic goals that would turn the Soviet Union into a leading economic and political power. These goals were codified in a succession of Five-Year Plans, which ended the more open economic climate of the NEP years.

The First Five-Year Plan began in 1928. Its principal features were the replacement of private farms with large state agricultural collectives and the launching of enormous industrial projects. Whereas peasants under the NEP were allowed to till their own lands and sell their produce in the market-place, Stalin consolidated their private lands into large state-run collective farms, thus forcing all the peasants to work primarily for the state. This collectivization of agriculture was a brutal process that occurred at great personal expense to the peasants, and millions died in a devastating famine of 1933.

Stalin's increasingly centralized rule also affected the arts. In 1932 a government decree mandated the end of all independent artists' groups, which were replaced by associations organized according to specialties such as the visual arts, architecture, music, or literature. At the Writers' Congress of 1934,

Socialist Realism was pronounced the official aesthetic in literature and the other arts. Its aim was to glorify the state and its leaders by producing mythic narratives of heroic acts and achievements. Stalin also introduced a personality cult, which required artists and writers to depict him as the nation's benefactor in all realms from education and industrialization to culture and agriculture.

But he was an insecure leader and exercised his power by ordering the deaths of millions of innocent people whom he suspected of being disloyal or saboteurs. By the late 1930s, the Great Purge, as the annihilation of many Soviet citizens was called, had eliminated a large cadre of the nation's talented engineers, artists, managers, and even high-ranking military officers. This had a devastating effect on Soviet life and induced a climate of fear that reigned until Stalin called the nation together to resist the German invasion in 1941.

Propaganda

Exhibitions

The inauguration of the First Five-Year Plan brought with it a move to present a new image of the Soviet Union abroad, one that could begin to compete with the Western powers, not just on ideological grounds but in terms of social and economic accomplishments. A principal vehicle for this was the large-scale exhibitions that the Soviet government sent overseas between 1928 and 1930. El Lissitzky became the leading expert in the design of such displays. Following his design for the All-Union Polygraphic Exhibition in 1927, Lissitzky was asked to head a team that would create a massive display for a Soviet Pavilion at the Pressa, an international exhibition on the press, advertising, and publishing that the German government organized in Cologne in 1928.

The scale of the exhibit, which included 20 different sections and more than 220 separate stands, was greater than anything Lissitzky had worked on before and set a new standard for large state displays.

Fig. 27.31: El Lissitzky, *Pressa*, catalog, 1928. © Heritage Image Partnership Ltd/Alamy.

The aesthetic, which could only be characterized as bombastic, was a far cry from the complex formal arrangements of Lissitzky's earlier Proun paintings or the subtle typographic arrangements of his avant-garde publications. However, it was at this point that Lissitzky actually became a state designer, seeking some compromise between his own aesthetic convictions and the government's brief.

The centerpiece of the exhibition was a large red star with political texts wrapped around it and a dramatic circular form with a series of floating spheres suspended above it. Information was presented on moving vertical conveyor belts and huge graphics spelled out "U.S.S.R," while stands in the shape of human figures provided statistics on Soviet achievements in all forms of publishing. A set piece of the exhibition was the extended photomontage wall mural that Lissitzky created with Sergei Senkin. They combined large numbers of photographs to tell the story of how the Soviet press was contributing to the education of the masses. The photomontage mural was

also the source for Lissitzky's innovative catalog, whose pages folded out in accordion style (Fig. 27.31).

The Soviet Pressa display garnered wide acclaim in the foreign press and led to Lissitzky's selection to coordinate the design of other Soviet exhibitions in Germany, notably the section on Soviet photography and film for the Werkbund's Film und Foto exhibition in 1929, the International Hygiene Exhibition in Dresden, and the International Fur Trade Exhibition in Leipzig. For the latter two exhibitions, which were held in 1930, Lissitzky introduced a grand narrative consisting of photographs, films, and texts, all presented in novel displays. The designs involved many different components that he and his team shaped into three-dimensional stories about the Soviet Union's achievements.

Posters

During the NEP, when the nation's focus was on rebuilding the economy, the depiction of workers, peasants, and soldiers fighting against the White Army and the paunchy titans of capitalism subsided.

Fig. 27.32: Gustav Klucis, We Will Repay the Coal Debt to the Country, poster, 1930. © Fine Art Images/SuperStock.

Propaganda posters were revived, however, with the beginning of the First Five-Year Plan, but this time the principal figures were male and female workers whose labor was extolled as the backbone of the plan. Along with the consolidation of artists' organizations came the centralization of poster production as well. The coordinating agency for posters was ISOGIZ, the State Publishing House for Art, which commissioned posters on diverse themes. These initially featured dedicated Soviet workers, but later in the 1930s Stalin's image began to appear more frequently as part of the cult of personality.

Gustav Klucis produced a series of photomontage posters at the beginning of the 1930s that integrated Soviet workers and farmers into collective instruments of labor. His poster of three miners, who ranged from youthful to aging, depicted them moving forward in a phalanx, shouldering their drills and sledge hammers as if they were marching off to war (Fig. 27.32). Klucis adopted a similar military rhetoric to portray an army of collective farmers driving their tractors in a convoy, with each tractor bearing a red banner. His wife, Valentina Kulagina (1902–1987), was one of several female poster artists who depicted women workers. As opposed to the Civil War period, when the portrayal of a woman worker was rare, women were frequent

Fig. 27.33: Natalia Pinus, Women in the Collective Farms are a Great Force, poster, 1933. © Fine Art Images/ SuperStock.

subjects in Five-Year Plan posters, particularly as farm workers. A triptych poster from 1933 entitled *Women in the Collective Farms are a Great Force*, by Natalia Pinus (1901–1980), a student of Klucis', shows Stalin flanked by two women, one driving a tractor and the other threshing wheat (Fig. 27.33). By this time, critics were calling for more individualized portrayals of workers. Evidence of such portrayals could be seen increasingly in Socialist Realist paintings as well as in posters such as Pinus's. The insertion of Stalin in the triptych links him to positive images of collective farm workers, a representation that belies the ruthless politics of agricultural

collectivization. The discrepancy between appearance and reality distinguishes much Soviet propaganda of the 1930s from that of the Civil War period, when images of workers, peasants, and soldiers built solidarity for a struggle against a common enemy.

Publications

Although bold Constructivist graphics were no longer evident on book and journal covers by the end of the 1920s, the rigorous structure of Constructivism had become the core foundation of book design and persisted throughout the 1930s. While decorative elements returned to architecture and floral patterns began to appear once again on Soviet textiles, book design maintained its Constructivist rigor without revealing its source. San serif types and lettering were still in use and opponents of the avant-garde failed to recognize that the aesthetic of the enemy had become the subversive norm. Nonetheless, few books from the 1930s stand out as distinctive with the exception of the lavish commemorative volumes that Lissitzky, Rodchenko, and Stepanova were invited to design to promote the military and economic achievements of the Soviet state.

The most ambitious publishing venture of the 1930s was *USSR in Construction*, an illustrated monthly magazine whose aim, according to the editors, was to "reflect in photography the whole scope and variety of the construction work now going on in the USSR." The publication was intended for both domestic and foreign audiences. It provided readers at home with a photographic narrative of contemporary Soviet life, featuring controlled depictions of how people lived in the different regions of the country, along with inspirational images of shock workers at building sites, happy farm laborers, and an array of new consumer goods from decorative clocks to automobiles. For foreign audiences, *USSR in Construction* was a propaganda vehicle that presented the Soviet Union as an emerging industrial power and a paradise of social equality.

"TODAY, WHEN THE TURBID WAVE OF FASCISM IS BESPATTERING THE SOCIALIST MOVEMENT OF THE WORKING CLASS AND BESMIRCHING THE DEMOCRATIC STRIVINGS OF THE BEST PEOPLE IN THE CIVILIZED WORLD, THE NEW CONSTITUTION OF THE USSR WILL BE AN INDICTMENT AGAINST FASCISM, DECLARING THAT SOCIALISM AND DEMOCRACY ARE INVINCIBLE. THE NEW CONSTITUTION OF THE USSR WILL SERVE AS MORAL ASSISTANCE AND REAL SUPPORT TO ALL THOSE WHO ARE TODAY FIGHTING FASCIST BARBARISM."

– J. STALIN
"ON THE DRAFT CONSTITUTION OF THE USSR"

Fig. 27.34: El Lissitzky, *USSR in Construction*, Stalinist constitution, happy Soviet people, page from the "Constitution" issue, 1937. Howard Garfinkel and Larry Zeman, Productive Arts, USA.

Fig. 27.35: Alexander Rodchenko, *USSR in Construction*, "White Sea Canal" issue, cover, 1933. Howard Garfinkel and Larry Zeman, Productive Arts USA. © Rodchenko & Stepanova Archive, DACS, RAO, 2017.

The magazine was initially published in four languages—Russian, English, German, and French. Later a Spanish edition was added. It had a lavish budget and was beautifully printed by rotogravure. Expensive special effects were created with die-cuts, gatefolds, and other experimental graphic techniques. There was no permanent art director and issues were assigned to different freelance designers. Nikolai Troshin (1897–1990), a former Vkhutemas student and creator of children's books with his wife Olga Deinika (1897–1970), designed many of the issues over the 11 years that *USSR in Construction* was published,

while Deinika created the original title lettering, which remained on the magazine's covers throughout the length of its publication. Initially, the editors covered a variety of themes each month, but after several years they decided to devote each issue to a special topic.

Troshin had suggested inviting Lissitzky, Rodchenko, and Stepanova to design some of the issues. Lissitzky's first assignment in 1932 was an issue devoted to the completion of the Dnieper Dam and Power Station. As with his exhibition designs, he created a dramatic narrative that began with the taming of a mighty river and ended with Stalin turning on the power. Of the many issues he designed, sometimes alone and sometimes with his wife Sophie, the most elaborate was a special one devoted to the Soviet Constitution of 1937 (Plate 42). For this project, Lissitzky created an "epic narrative" style in which he adopted a multitude of visual devices to describe how the Constitution represented the rights of the diverse ethnic groups that populated the Soviet Union's 15 republics (Fig. 27.34).

The subject of Rodchenko's first issue in 1933 was the White Sea Canal, a waterway that was built largely by prisoners (Fig. 27.35). Rodchenko combined his own commanding photographs of the canal and its locks with manipulated photomontages of the workers. The issue presented the completion of the canal as a heroic effort that brought new life to the laborers, while in fact they worked under inhumane conditions. As an avant-garde photographer and designer, Rodchenko had to grapple with the contradiction between the formal aesthetic of his photographs and the editors' demand to insert them in a narrative that made an uplifting story out of a harsh reality. For other issues, he and his wife Stepanova worked as a team and many of the magazines they designed featured subjects that were far less politically charged than the White Sea Canal. These included issues on Soviet gold and timber as well as one on Soviet parachutists that included several unusual foldout sections as well as a number of striking layouts.

Although Socialist Realism was the official style of

Soviet artists, its equivalent in graphic design was never clearly codified. Hence the Lissitzkys, Rodchenko, and Stepanova could employ various avant-garde strategies in their layouts for books and magazines in the 1930s. Lissitzky created an "epic narrative" style that incorporated visual elements as varied as cartoons, pictorial statistics, and photomontage, while Rodchenko and Stepanova produced spreads with tight structures that recalled their designs of the 1920s.

A special feature of the magazine was its use of maps and pictorial statistics. The latter were based on the ISOTYPE technique or representing statistics graphically that Otto Neurath had developed in Vienna in the 1920s (see Chapter 25). In the early 1930s, Neurath and the German designer Gerd Arntz, who actually created many of the ISOTYPE figures that Neurath employed, were invited to Moscow to found an institute where Soviet designers would be trained in the ISOTYPE method. Known as ISOSTAT, the institute reported to the Central Committee of the Communist Party and prepared people to work in local offices around the country.

Consumer goods, heavy industry, and transport

The emphasis of the initial Five-Year Plans on collectivized agriculture and heavy industry meant that less attention was given to the manufacture of consumer goods. With the closing of the Vkhutemas-Vkhutein in 1930, there was no comparable school for the training of industrial designers. Factories either relied on designs from the past, adapted craft techniques to industrial production, or copied their designs from Western models. There were nonetheless a few trained industrial designers such as Abram Damski (dates unconfirmed), who studied with Rodchenko at the Vkhutemas, and subsequently became a specialist in lighting design. For the *Pravda* newspaper building he created a ceiling lamp consisting of extended curved glass sections that wrapped around the bulb, while also producing designs for several hanging fixtures as well as a metal table lamp. Although these objects embodied a modernist aesthetic at a time when few other Soviet products did, they nonetheless recalled Western models, particularly the lamps the AEG produced in Berlin and the Kandem table lamps that Marianne Brandt designed at the Bauhaus.

In 1935, the first line of the Moscow Metro opened to be followed several years later by two others. The design and construction of the Metro was a major achievement of the Five-Year Plans. The project involved various teams of engineers, architects, artists, and designers who created everything from the lavish station decors to the modern cars, myriad platform kiosks, ticket counters, and uniforms for the Metro personnel. Each station was designed by a different group of architects, and had a distinctive look. The dominant style was monumental classicism, and the expansive station interiors with their marble floors, decorated surfaces, and other artistic accoutrements recalled the grandeur of the czar's Winter Palace. This decor contrasted sharply with some of the train interiors by Vladimir Stenberg, the Constructivist stage designer and poster artist, who did them in a modern style with chromed steel armrests.

Despite its conservative architecture, the Metro was one of the most impressive Soviet design projects of the 1930s. It drew on the expertise of many different design professionals in a way that no other projects in the Soviet Union had previously done. The Metro was part of an even larger project to turn Moscow into a modern metropolis. An ambitious construction program produced a series of gigantic apartment buildings adorned in a decorative classicism that ringed the inner city. Boulevards were made extremely wide to accommodate the new automobiles that the Soviets began to produce in the 1930s.

The automobiles came from several factories, notably the Zavod Imeni Stalina (Stalin Factory), whose cars featured the acronym ZIS, and the Gorky Automobile Factory, which produced the GAZ line of automobiles and light trucks. The ZIS factory

Fig. 27.36: ZIS 101 automobile, 1936. © RIA Novosti/Alamy.

originally belonged to AMO (Moscow Automobile Enterprise), which had begun to manufacture cars before the Revolution in 1916. The Bolsheviks took it over but it produced few cars until the beginning of the First Five-Year Plan at which time an American company, A. J. Brandt, rebuilt it.

The plant manufactured a series of small cars with a Buick straight eight engine in 1933, but its first distinctive design was the ZIS 101, a limousine inspired by Packard designs of the time, that rolled off the assembly line in 1936. This car, which had an aerodynamic body that followed the streamlining trend in the United States (Fig. 27.36), remained in production until 1940, when a new version was manufactured with a modified front end. In 1939, Valentin Rostkov (dates unconfirmed), who went on to have a successful career as a car designer, created a two-seat sport model of which only one of several prototypes was manufactured. The company was later renamed Zavod Imeni Likhachova (Likachova Factory) or ZIL after the name of one of its plant directors, Ivan Alekseevich Likhachev.

The Ford Motor Company signed an agreement with the Soviet government in May 1929 to build a new automobile manufacturing plant at Nizhni-Novgorod and sent some of its engineers to provide technical assistance. Named the Gorky Automobile Factory after the famed Soviet writer, it was designed to produce a Soviet version of the Ford Model-A passenger car and a light truck. The first car rolled off the assembly line in 1930. It was a Model A, known in the Soviet Union as the GAZ-A, after the name of the factory. By the late 1930s, the factory was producing between 80,000 and 90,000 automobiles a year. Its light truck, called the GAZ-AA, remained the leading Soviet vehicle of its type until the 1950s.

Besides automobiles and trucks, Soviet planners gave a high priority to the design of more powerful tractors, which were badly needed for the large collective farms. Following the 1917 Revolution, the Soviet Union began to import American Fordson tractors, made by the Ford Motor Company. These transformed Soviet agriculture, which hitherto was based on primitive methods of cultivation. By 1926, more than 25,000 Fordsons were in use. With the inauguration of the First Five-Year Plan, however, the government wanted to reduce its dependency on foreign suppliers and by the early 1930s the Kharkov Tractor Works had become the leading factory for the production of well-designed Soviet tractors.

Though the czars originally had to import railway equipment for the first phase of their extensive railroad construction in the 19th century, Russia was producing its own locomotives by 1902. The Kolomna Locomotive Works was a leading manufacturer and supplied engines to most of Russia's railway lines including the Moscow–Kazan Railway whose chief engineer, E. Noltein (dates unconfirmed), was responsible for a number of innovations in locomotive design. After the revolution, the Kolomna Works continued to be a major producer of locomotives, as did the Bryansk Engineering Works. A leading Soviet locomotive designer was L. Lebedyansky (dates unconfirmed), who was responsible for several important freight and passenger locomotives during the 1920s and 1930s. His sleek dynamic FD locomotive was a symbol of the industrial push of the 1930s, while his IS design showed

early evidence of American streamlining. Lebedyansky developed the streamline design further in his *Krasnaya Strela* (*Red Arrow*) locomotive, whose first exemplar the Kolomna Works completed in 1937. Its swept-back appearance and aerodynamic shell made the locomotive a powerful sign of Soviet modernism, as it hauled passengers along the prestigious Moscow–Leningrad route in the late 1930s. Streamlining was also evident in other locomotives such as the bullet-nosed engine of 1938, the 2-3-2V, built at the Voroshilovgrad Works, which recalls Raymond Loewy's earlier design for a Pennsylvania Railroad locomotive in 1936 (Fig. 27.37).

With a growing confidence that came from the completion of major public works like the Dnieper Dam and Power Station during the First Five-Year Plan, Stalin launched a cult of gigantism, mandating that everything—whether a building, a factory, a farm, or an airplane—be larger than anything that the West had produced. In aviation, this led to Andrei Tupolev's design

Fig. 27.37: 2-3-2V locomotive, 1938. Wikimedia.

Fig. 27.38: *Maxim Gorky* propaganda airplane, 1934. akg-images/RIA Nowosti.

of the *Maxim Gorky*, an eight-engine airplane dedicated to the dissemination of propaganda. To commemorate the 40th anniversary of Gorky's writing career, magazine editor Mikhail Koltsov proposed that an airplane be built in his honor and funds were raised, largely from public subscriptions. The plane was intended to be a flying equivalent of the propaganda trains and ships that were widely used during the Civil War (Fig. 27.38). Besides a salon for press conferences, it had cabins for 70 people, a press, a radio center for broadcasting to the ground, photographic and film laboratories, film projectors, and a separate power and telephone center, along with a kitchen, restaurant, and sleeping berths. Not only was the design of such a gargantuan agit airplane unprecedented, but the plan also called for equipment that did not yet exist, such as a light printing press. Tupolev came up with the idea to make one out of a light metal, duralumin, rather than cast iron. Thus, many different factories besides Tupolev's Experimental Design Bureau were involved in the *Maxim Gorky*'s total design. After a number of successful demonstration flights, the plane crashed when a pilot performing an aerial stunt collided with another plane. Although it was not rebuilt, many of the *Maxim Gorky*'s pioneering features were used successfully in later aircraft designs.

Portugal
The First Republic

In May 1926, Portugal's First Republic ended in a military coup, having lasted only 14 years following the collapse of the monarchy in 1910. Shortly thereafter, a newly elected constituent assembly quickly wrote and passed a constitution, but the young republic was plagued with political and economic problems that disrupted its stability. The Portuguese economy was largely agricultural and the wealthy traded in raw materials that they extracted from Portugal's colonies. Both impeded the development of an industrial culture as was occurring elsewhere in Europe.

There was a sufficiently large consumer class to support an advertising industry, which mostly promoted goods from abroad and services although domestic foodstuffs and wines were also advertised widely. Raul de Caldevilla (1877–1951), who had studied advertising at the School of Advanced Commercial Studies in Paris, held consular positions in Spain, and worked as a commercial agent in Argentina, founded Portugal's first advertising agency in 1914. He had a good understanding of marketing and believed the poster to be at the center of any successful advertising campaign, although he was also the first in Portugal to make an advertising film. The agency he headed, ETP (Escritório Técnico de Publicidade/Technical Advertising Agency), was in Porto, the center of the nation's wine industry, and a number of Caldevilla's

Fig. 27.39: George Massiot-Brown, Sandeman's Port, poster, 1928. "The Sandeman Don" courtesy of Sogrape Vinhos.

clients were makers of wines and liqueurs. In 1916 the agency name was changed to ETP-Raul de Caldevilla e Companhia Limitada (ETP-Raul de Caldevilla and Company Ltd) and in 1919 it became ETP-Empreza Técnica Publicitária Film Gráfica Caldevilla (ETP-Technical Advertising Enterprise Graphic Film Caldevilla). One of Caldevilla's leading poster designers was Diogo de Macedo (1889–1959), a sculptor who had lived and studied in Paris, and some of his posters were strongly influenced by French fashion illustration, particularly the drawings of Erté. This is evident in a poster for Bi-Cacao-Chauve, a cacao liqueur, which depicts a heavily made-up woman in 18th-century dress delicately holding a small glass of liqueur in one hand and a bottle in the other.

Actually, the most memorable of the Porto wine posters was not by a Portuguese artist. It featured a silhouette figure, known as the Sandeman Don, in a black traditional student's cape from Coimbra and a wide-brimmed Spanish hat (Fig. 27.39). The figure, which became a widely recognized trademark, was drawn in 1928 by George Massiot-Brown (dates unconfirmed) for the House of Sandeman, an English wine company that was founded in 1790 in England and then established in Porto in 1810.

Other advertising imagery was produced in Porto by Empreza do Bolhão Limitada, which had facilities for printing lithographic posters and wine labels that it took over from ETP. Poster and wine label designers were primarily artists without training in commercial design. While the posters were largely based on examples from Paris, where the work of Cappiello continued to be an influence, wine label design was more original, having a tradition that extended as far back as the late 18th century.

In Lisbon, many artists contributed satirical illustrations to the new cultural journals and magazines that were started after the fall of the monarchy. Much of this work was recognized in 1912 at the First Salon of Humorists and at subsequent salons. It was from this culture of caricature and humorous drawings that some of Portugal's leading modern painters, illustrators, and graphic artists emerged. These included Emmerico Hartwich Nunes (1888–1968), José Sobral de Almada Negreiros (1893–1970), António Soares (1894–1978), Jorge Nicholson Moore Barradas (1894–1971), and José Stuart Carvalhais (1887–1961). Stuart Carvalhais was the founder in Portugal of the *banda desenhada* or full-page comic format that is the forerunner of today's graphic novel, while Emmérico Nunes also contributed to this medium. Stuart Carvalhais was also a well-known illustrator of magazine, book, and sheet music covers.

Almada Negreiros (1893–1970) was a magazine art director and one of the founders of Portugal's first modern literary magazine, *Orpheu*, in 1915. Another

Fig. 27.40: Emmerico H. Nunes, *ABC*, cover, 1923. Private Collection.

early magazine art director was Fernando Correia Dias (1892–1935), who worked for numerous magazines including *A Rajada* (*A Gust*) and *Arte e Letras* (*Art and Letters*), for which he also did satirical drawings. António Soares and Jorge Barradas established one of Lisbon's first commercial art studios in 1915, but they had to close it after a relatively short period for lack of commissions and clients.

The publications to which these artists contributed drawings were varied. Some were launched shortly after the republic was established while others did not appear until the early 1920s or even around the time of the military coup. Among those published in this period were *ABC*, a general magazine (Fig. 27.40), and *ABC-Zinho*, a magazine for children that was directed by two architects, Cottinelli Telmo (1897–1948) and Manuel Oliveira Ramos (dates unconfirmed); *Ilustração* (*Illustration*); *Sempre Fixe*, a satirical weekly that featured the comic strips of Eduardo Teixera Coelho (1919–2005); and *Contemporânea* (*Contemporaneous*), a magazine under the literary and artistic direction of the architect José Pacheco (1885–1934), who had done the first cover for *Orpheu* and founded *Contemporânea* as a successor. Besides the aforementioned illustrators and art directors, these new magazines attracted a group of slightly younger artists like Bernardo Loureiro Marques (1898–1962), Carlos Botelho (1899–1982), and Jaime Martins Barata (1899–1970), along with Tomás José de Mello (a.k.a. Thomaz de Mello) (1906–1990), who published caricatures under the name Tom. In addition to drawing for the weekly and monthly magazines, these artists were also active as designers of book covers and posters for commercial enterprises. A number of them were part of Portugal's first generation of modernist painters and some also worked for the new regime after the military coup.

The Estado Novo

In 1932, António de Oliveira Salazar became Prime Minister of Portugal and ruled the country with an iron hand until 1968. Salazar was an economist who brought order to Portugal's chaotic economy after the military government appointed him finance minister in 1928. In 1930, he assimilated Portugal's colonies into his comprehensive economic system and continued to include them in his vision of a larger Portuguese Empire after the ratification of the new constitution in 1933 and the establishment of the Estado Novo (New State).

Salazar was not a dictator who wantonly destroyed those who opposed him but he was concerned with civic order and stability at all costs and thus instituted a program of censorship and repression to ensure that no opposition voices were heard. He also fostered youth groups, educational reform, and a plethora of celebratory events to spread the benign image of a

Fig. 27.41: Fred Kradolfer, Portuguese Colonial Exhibition in Paris, poster, 1937. Biblioteca Nacional de Portugal.

stable and productive empire among the Portuguese people.

To further this aim, he established the SPN (National Secretariat of Propaganda) in 1933 and named António Ferro (1895–1956), a cultural critic, to head it. For almost 20 years, Ferro had collaborated with the authors and artists who were promoting a modern culture in Portugal and it was to this group that he turned after he became head of the propaganda secretariat, which was renamed the SNI (Secretariat of Information, Popular Culture and Tourism) in 1944.

Though Ferro began as a cultural modernist, he was also a strong nationalist. He espoused Salazar's vision of a Portuguese Empire and fostered the image of Portugal itself as a country consisting of different regions, each with its own customs and traditions. Ferro admired Mussolini and took from the Italian Fascists the idea of the large exhibition as an instrument to impress the tenets of state ideology on the public. He also believed strongly in the poster as an effective means to promote tourism, exhibitions, and other special events.

Ferro became Portugal's principal patron of modern design. As an art critic, author, and editor of cultural publications, he was no stranger to modernism and he did not see a conflict between it and the statist values of the Salazar regime. One reason that Salazar appointed him was that he believed Ferro could establish good relations with the art community. To assist him, Ferro brought together a team of artists and designers whom he drew from the modernist milieu of the First Republic. Among them, however, was a recent immigrant to Portugal, the Swiss poster artist Fred Kradolfer (1903–1968). Having studied and worked in Zurich, Munich, Paris, and elsewhere in Europe, Kradolfer came to Lisbon in 1924. He brought a sophisticated European approach to poster design that was lacking in Portugal, whose tradition derived primarily from illustration and fine art. Kradolfer's own work can be referenced most accurately to the French modernism of Cassandre, Colin, and Carlu.

Like them, he was as adept at lettering as he was at creating images. These skills are evident in his poster to promote the Portuguese Pavilion at the Paris International Exhibition of 1937. To signify Portugal's imperial status, Kradolfer chose the head of an African woman, whom he clearly branded with large lips, huge ringed earrings, and close-cropped hair. He connected her image to the lettering below with a rectangular shape that also suggested her neck (Fig. 27.41).

Kradolfer joined Atelier ARTA and subsequently collaborated with the poster artist and exhibition designer José Rocha (1907–1982), who founded one of Lisbon's first advertising agencies in 1936. Surprisingly Rocha called the agency ETP (Estúdio Técnico de

Publicidade/Technical Advertising Studio), which was the same acronym as Caldevilla's earlier advertising studio in Porto. Working for ETP, Kradolfer produced a plethora of advertising materials from posters to packaging.

Besides Kradolfer, Ferro's propaganda team included José Rocha and the artists Bernardo Marques, Tomás de Mello, Emmérico Nunes, and Paulo Ferreira (1911–1999). Other designers who were involved with the propaganda secretariat were Almada Negreiros and Roberto Araújo (1908–1969), as well as Maria Keil (1914–2012), who was also associated with José Rocha's studio, ETP. Ferro's group worked on many projects including the design of exhibition pavilions, publications, and poster campaigns. To encourage modern poster design, Ferro held up the work of the French designer Paul Colin as a model. Tourism was a principal concern of Ferro's and he encouraged poster design as a way to attract visitors to the country's different regions. He also shifted his earlier advocacy of pictorial modernism to the promotion of Portugal's folkloric traditions and historical icons. In 1937, the propaganda secretariat published *Several Images of Portuguese Popular Art* for distribution in France. In his introduction, Ferro referred to the "vast living museum of Portuguese folklore" which was illustrated in the book by Paulo Ferreira, who also did the layout. The folk art theme was used for another book, *Portugal*, whose cover was designed by Bernardo Marques (Fig. 27.42).

Ferro's principal contribution to the propaganda efforts of the Salazar regime, however, was his promotion of large exhibitions, which occurred with considerable frequency. They began with the Portuguese Colonial Exhibition in Porto in 1934 and continued with the Celebration of the National Revolution in 1936, and the Congress of Portuguese World Expansion in 1937. The series culminated with the mammoth Portuguese World Exhibition of 1940. For these as well as the Portuguese pavilions for exhibitions abroad—Paris in 1937 and New York and San Francisco in 1939—Ferro relied on his team of artists

Fig. 27.42: Bernardo Marques, *Portugal*, cover, 1944. Private Collection.

Fig. 27.43: Portuguese World Exhibition entrance, 1940. Private Collection.

and designers who collaborated with architects to create interiors that united all the arts within comprehensive symbolic narratives that reinforced Salazar's emphasis on God, nation, and family.

The most ambitious project of the propaganda secretariat was the Portuguese World Exhibition of 1940, which jointly commemorated the founding of the Portuguese nation in 1140 and the restoration of its independence from Spain 500 years later. Unlike the World's Fair that opened in New York the previous year and to which Portugal contributed a pavilion, the Lisbon exhibition looked to history rather than the future. Its aim was to create a seamless continuity between the nation's prior achievements, which included the building of a colonial empire, and its present, which was seen as the outcome of a heroic and virtuous past. Though inspired by the 1932 Exhibition

of the Fascist Revolution in Rome, which sought to construct a historical narrative of the Fascist Party, the Portuguese World Exhibition commemorated the history of the Portuguese nation rather than simply the achievements of the Estado Novo.

Coordinated by the architect Cotinelli Telmo, who also directed Portugal's first sound film, *Song of Lisbon*, in 1933, the exhibition consisted entirely of Portuguese pavilions with the exception of one from Brazil, Portugal's former colony. The architecture was monumental and replete with images of heroic figures such as the knights carved in relief on the four massive columns of the exhibition entrance (Fig. 27.43). For the pavilions, artists executed murals and wall reliefs that embodied historical narratives and allegories, while also depicting Portugal's colonies as beneficiaries of the nation's civilizing mission. Designers created numerous charts, diagrams, and displays for the different pavilions and coordinated all the graphics for the guidebook, posters, and other publicity materials.

The monumentality of the exhibition and the grandeur of its design was a result that no one could foresee in the days of the First Republic, when many of the artists and designers who later worked actively for António Ferro's National Secretariat of Propaganda were showing their drawings and caricatures at the humor salons and publishing them in the flourishing satirical and literary press. What may have seduced them into collaborating with the Salazar regime was the deceptive freedom Ferro gave them to create a modern visual culture within the framework of a discretely repressive state.

Bibliography
Bibliographic essay

Although there is considerable literature about the art and politics of the various dictatorial regimes in the 1920s and 1930s, there is less about design, except for an abundance of books and articles on propaganda. Wendy Kaplan's catalog *Designing Modernity: The Arts of Reform and Persuasion, 1885–1945* contains a number of valuable essays about design in Italy and Germany, while Anthony Rhodes, *Propaganda: The Art of Persuasion, WWII*, edited by Victor Margolin, includes ample material about propaganda during dictatorships in the years before and during the war. The Rhodes volume is supplemented and amplified by Steven Heller, *Iron Fists: Branding the 20th Century Totalitarian State*, which describes the propaganda apparatuses in Italy, Germany, and the Soviet Union during the dictatorial regimes and through World War II. The exhibition catalog *Annitrenta: Arte e Cultura in Italia* provides material on various cultural aspects of Italy under the Fascists as do Marla Susan Stone, *The Patron State: Culture & Politics in Fascist Italy*; Edward R. Tannenbaum, *The Fascist Experience: Italian Society and Culture, 1922–1945*; Doug Thompson, *State Control in Fascist Italy: Culture and Conformity, 1925–43*; and

Adam Arvidson, "Between Fascism and the American Dream," *Social Science History* 25, no. 2 (Summer 2001). General literature on design, crafts, and exhibitions in Italy includes Emilio Ambasz, ed., *Italy: The New Domestic Landscape: Achievements and Problems of Italian Design*; Silvia Barisone, Matteo Fochessati, and Gianni Franzone, eds., *The Wolfsonian Collection of Genoa*; Irene de Guttry, Maria Paola Maino, and Mario Quesada, *Le Arti Minori d'Autore in Italia dal 1900 al 1930*; Simonetta Falasca-Zamponi, *Fascist Spectacle: The Aesthetics of Power in Mussolini's Italy*; David Forgacs, *Italian Culture in the Industrial Era, 1880–1980*; Alfonso Grassi and Anty Pansera, *L'Italia del Design: Trent'Anni di Dibattito*; Vittorio Gregotti, *Il Disegno del Prodotto Industriale: Italia, 1860–1980*; Penny Sparke, *Italian Design: 1870 to the Present*; M. Michail and Cristina Tonelli, *Il Design in Italia 1925/43*; Anty Pansera, *Storia del Disegno Industriale Italiano*; Tony del Renzio, "Italy – The Italian Experience," in Barbie Campbell-Cole and Tim Benton, eds., *Tubular Steel Furniture*; Andrea Nulli and Giampiero Bosoni, 'Italy: The Parallel History of Design and Consumption," in *History of Industrial Design, 1919–1990: The Dominion of Design*; and Jeffrey T. Schnapp, "Epic Demonstrations: Fascist Modernity and the 1932 Exhibition of the Fascist Revolution," in Richard J. Golsan, ed., *Fascism, Esthetics, and Culture*. On specific topics of Italian design see the following on automobiles: Angelo Tito Anselmi, ed., *Carrozzeria Italiana: Advancing the Art and Science of Automobile*; and the monograph by Antoine Prunet, *Pininfarina: Art and Industry 1930–2000*. Books on Olivetti include the classic catalog *Design Process Olivetti, 1908–1978* and Sibylle Kicherer, *Olivetti: A Study of the Corporate Management of Design*. Anty Pansera's *Storia e Cronaca della Triennale* is the definitive book on that subject, while her article "The Triennale of Milan: Past, Present, Future," *Design Issues* 2, no. 1 (Spring 1985) is a good introduction to the Triennale. The literature on Futurism is extensive. Perhaps the most comprehensive volume is the large exhibition catalog, edited by Pontus Hulten, *Futurismo*

& *Futurismi* but see also *Balla, Depero: Ricostruzione Futurista dell'Universo*; Enrico Crispolti, ed., *Futurismo e Meridione*; *Fortunato Depero, My Own Futurism*; Giovanni Lista, *Le Livre Futuriste de la Libération du Mot au Poème Tactile*; Claudia Salaris, *Il Futurismo e la Publiccità*; and the short survey by Caroline Tisdall and Angelo Bozzolla, *Futurism*. Art Deco in Italy is covered in Fabio Benzi, *Il Deco in Italia*; Tim Benton, "Italian Architecture and Design," in Charlotte Benton, Tim Benton, and Ghislaine Wood, eds., *Art Deco 1919–1939*; and Rosanna Bossaglia, "L'Art Déco Italien," in *L'Art Deco en Europe: Tendances Décoratives dans les Arts Appliqués vers 1925*. Monographs on Italian product designers and architect-designers include Albrerto Bassi and Laura Castagno, *Giuseppe Pagano*; *Franco Albini: Architecture and Design 1934–1977* with essays by Franca Helg, Stephen Leet, and Alberto Sartoris; Ugo La Pietra, ed., *Gio Ponti*; and Marco Romanelli, *Gio Ponti: A World*.

The literature on Italian graphic design during this period is equally extensive. Good overall studies are Giorgio Fioravanti, Leonardo Passarelli, and Silvia Sfligiotti, *La Grafica in Italia*; Giancarlo Iliprandi, Alberto Marangoni, Franco Origoni, and Anty Pansera, *Visual Design: 50 Anni di Produzione in Italia*; Karen Pincus, *Bodily Regimes: Italian Advertising under Fascism*; and Giuseppe Priarone, *Grafica Pubblicitaria in Italia negli Anni Trenta,* while more specialized books and articles include Sergio Coradeschi, "The Novecento Style in Italy: Commercial and Graphic Design," *The Journal of Decorative and Propaganda Arts* 3 (Winter 1987); Steven Heller and Louise Fili, *Italian Art Deco: Graphic Design Between the Wars*; Luigi Menegazzi, *Il Manifesto Italiano* and *Settant'Anni di Manifesti Italiani della Raccolta delle Stampe A. Bertarelli*; and Pepa Sparti, ed., *L'Italia che Cambia Attraverso i Manifesti della Raccolta Salce*. Books and articles on individual graphic designers and design offices include Germano Celant, *Marcello Nizzoli*; Enrica Torelli Landini, *Attilio Calzavara: Works and Commissions of an Anti-Fascist Designer* and the short article by the same author,

"Attilio Calavera: Stories from an Archive," *The Journal of Decorative and Propaganda Arts* 16 (Summer 1990); Dennis Doordan, "The Advertising Architecture of Fortunato Depero," *Thr Journal of Decorative and Propaganda Arts* 12 (Spring 1989); Leo Lecci, ed., *Filippo Romoli: Manifesti d'Artista, 1928–1968*; *Lo Studio Boggeri, 1933–1981*; *Xanti Schawinsky: Malerei, Bühne, Graphikdesign, Fotografie*; and Aldo Tanchis, *Bruno Munari: Design as Art*.

Writing on design in the Third Reich is scattered among a number of sources. There is abundant literature on Nazi propaganda and architecture but little on product design. A seminal article is John Heskett, "Modernism and Archaism in the Third Reich," *Block 3* (1980). Winifred Nerdinger, ed., *Bauhaus-Moderne im Nationalsozialismus: Zwischen Anbiederung und Verfolgung* also deals with design during this period, while Gert Selle, *Design – Geschichte in Deutschland: Produktkultur als Entwurf und Erfahrung* includes the interwar period in a broad overview of German design. Nazi graphic design is covered in Jeremy Aynsley, *Graphic Design in Germany, 1890–1945*, while other books touch on the relation of particular graphic designers and typographers to the broader design environment under the Nazis. These include Christopher Burke, *Paul Renner: The Art of Typography*; Leslie Cabarga, *Progressive German Graphics 1900–1937*; Gerald Cinamon, *Rudolf Koch: Letterer, Type Designer, Teacher*; and H. K. Frenzel, *Ludwig Hohlwein* and Christian Schneegass, ed., *Ludwig Hohlwein: Plakate der Jahre 1906–1940*. Graphic design that opposed the Nazis is discussed in James Fraser, ed., *Malik-Verlag, 1916–1947: Berlin, Prague, New York* and Peter Pachnicke and Klaus Honef, eds., *John Heartfield*.

While much of the literature on Soviet design emphasizes the period before the Five-Year Plans, there are several publications that discuss the later period—Alexander Lavrentiev and Yuri V. Nasarov, *Russian Design: Traditions and Experiment, 1920–1960* and Raymond Hutchings, *Soviet Science, Technology, Design: Interaction and Convergence* are among them.

William L. Blackwell, *The Industrialization of Russia: An Historical Perspective* looks at industrialization, which had a bearing on how design developed during the initial Five-Year Plans. L. L. Kerber, *Stalin's Aviation Gulag: A Memoir of Andrei Tupolev and the Purge Era* focuses on the aircraft designer Tupolev, while books related to Russian shipbuilding and naval architecture include Mairin Mitchell, *The Maritime History of Russia, 1848–1948* and David Woodward, *The Russians at Sea: A History of the Russian Navy.* In general, the books on avant-garde figures also address their activities during the Stalin period, albeit not extensively. These include Alexander Lavrentiev, *Varvara Stepanova: The Complete Work*; Sophie Lissitzky-Küppers, *El Lissitzky: Life, Letters, Texts*; Selim O. Khan-Magomedov, *Rodchenko: The Complete Work*; and John Milner, *Vladimir Tatlin and the Russian Avant-Garde.* There is actually a considerable amount of material on graphic design during the Stalin years before World War II. I devote a chapter of my book *The Struggle for Utopia: Rodchenko, Lissitzky, Moholy-Nagy, 1917–1946* to the projects of Lissitzky and his wife Sophie Küppers and Alexander and Varvara Stepanova for *USSR in Construction.* Russian book design during the Plan years is described in Susan Compton, *Russian Avant-Garde Books, 1917–1934* and Margit Rowell and Deborah Wye, *The Russian Avant-Garde Book, 1910–1934.* With essays by Jared Ash, Nina Gurianova, Gerald Janecek, Margit Rowell, and Deborah Wye, Leah Dickerman, ed., *Building the Collective: Soviet Graphic Design, 1917–1937: Selections from the Merrill C. Berman Collection* considers Soviet design more broadly during a similar period as does Alla Rosenfeld, ed., *Defining Russian Graphic Arts, 1898–1934: From Diaghilev to Stalin.* Two books that look specifically at posters are Victoria E. Bonnell, *Iconography of Power: Soviet Political Posters under Lenin and Stalin* and Klaus Waschik and Nina Baburina, *Werbe für die Utopie: Russische Plakatkunst des 20. Jahrhundert.*

The literature on design in Portugal during the interwar years is not extensive but useful material can be found in Margarida Acciaiuoli's study of the large state exhibitions, *Exposições do Estado Novo, 1934–1940*; Theresa Lobo's *Cartazes Publicitários: Colecção de Empreza do Bolhão*; and the article by Helena Barbosa, Anna Calvera, and Vasco Branco, "Portugal's First Advertising Agency: Raul de Caldevilla and the ETP, 1914–1923," *Design Issues* 25, no. 1 (Winter 2009).

Books

General

Deparo, Fortunato, *My Own Futurism*. Evanston: Mary and Leigh Block Gallery, 1992.

Frampton, Kenneth. *Modern Architecture: A Critical History*, 3rd ed. New York and London: Thames and Hudson, 1992 (c. 1980).

Heller, Steven. *Iron Fists: Branding the 20th Century Totalitarian State*. New York and London; Phaidon, 2008.

Kaplan, Wendy, ed. *Designing Modernity: The Arts of Reform and Persuasion, 1885–1945*. London and New York: Thames and Hudson, 1995.

Rhodes, Anthony, *Propaganda: The Art of Persuasion, WW II*. Edited by Victor Margolin. New York: Chelsea House, 1976.

Sembach, Klaus-Jürgen, Gabriele Leuthäuser, and Peter Gössel. *Twentieth-Century Furniture Design*. Köln: Taschen, 2002.

Weill, Alain, *The Poster*. Boston: G. J. K. Hall, 1985.

Italy

Ambasz, Emilio, ed. *Italy: The New Domestic Landscape: Achievements and Problems of Italian Design*. New York: The Museum of Modern Art, 1972.

Annitrenta: Arte e Cultura in Italia. Milan: Mazzotta, 1982.

Anselmi, Angelo Tito, ed. *Carrozzeria Italiana: Advancing the Art and Science of Automobile Design*. Milan: Automobilia, 1980.

Balla, Depero: Ricostruzione Futurista dell'Universo. Modena and Milan: Fonte d'Abisso Editore, 1989.

Barisone, Silvia, Matteo Fochessati, and Gianni

Franzone, eds. *The Wolfsonian Collection of Genoa.* n.p.: Skira, 2005.

Bassi, Albrerto and Laura Castagno. *Giuseppe Pagano.* Bari: Editori Laterza, 1994.

Benzi, Fabio. *Il Deco in Italia.* Milan: Electa, 2004.

Celant, Germano. *Marcello Nizzoli.* Milan: Edizioni di Comunità, 1968.

Crispolti, Enrico, ed. *Futurismo e Meridione.* Napoli: Electa Napoli, 1996.

De Grand, Alexander. *Italian Fascism: Its Origins & Development,* 2nd ed. Lincoln: University of Nebraska Press, 1989 (c. 1982).

de Guttry, Irene, Maria Paola Maino, and Mario Quesada. *Le Arti Minori d'Autore in Italia dal 1900 al 1930.* Bari: Editori Laterza, 1985.

Design Process Olivetti, 1908–1978. Pittsburgh: Carnegie-Mellon University, 1979.

di Grazia, Victoria and Sergio Luzzatto. *Dizionario del Fascismo,* 2 vols. Turin: Einaudi, 2003.

Doordan, Dennis. *Building Modern Italy: Italian Architecture 1914–1936.* New York: Princeton Architectural Press, 1988.

Falasca-Zamponi, Simonetta. *Fascist Spectacle: The Aesthetics of Power in Mussolini's Italy.* Berkeley, Los Angeles, and London: University of California Press, 1997.

Fioravanti, Giorgio, Leonardo Passarelli, and Silvia Sfligiotti. *La Grafica in Italia.* Milan: Leonardo Arte, 1997.

Forgacs, David. *Italian Culture in the Industrial Era, 1880–1980.* Manchester and New York: Manchester University Press, 1990.

Fortunato Depero, *My Own Futurism.* Evanston; Mary and Leigh Block Gallery, 1992.

Franco Albini: Architecture and Design 1934–1977. Essays by Franca Helg, Stephen Leet, and Alberto Sartoris. New York: Princeton Architectural Press, 1990.

Grassi, Alfonso and Anty Pansera. *L'Italia del Design: Trent'Anni di Dibattito.* Casale Monferrato: Marietti Editore, 1986.

Gregotti, Vittorio. *Il Disegno del Prodotto Industriale: Italia, 1860–1980.* Milan: Electa, 1982.

Heller, Steven and Louise Fili. *Italian Art Deco: Graphic Design Between the Wars.* San Francisco: Chronicle Books, 1993.

Hulten, Pontus, ed. *Futurismo & Futurismi.* Milan: Bompiani, 1986.

Iliprandi, Giancarlo, Alberto Marangoni, Franco Origoni, and Anty Pansera. *Visual Design: 50 Anni di Produzione in Italia.* Introduzione di Gillo Dorfles. Con i Contributi de Cesare Colombo e Maurizio Vitta. Milan: Idealibri, 1984.

Kicherer, Sibylle. *Olivetti: A Study of the Corporate Management of Design.* New York: Rizzoli, 1990.

Landini, Enrica Torelli. *Attilio Calzavara: Works and Commissions of an Anti-Fascist Designer.* Miami Beach: The Wolfsonian Foundation, and Florence: Amalthea, 1994.

La Pietra, Ugo, ed. *Gio Ponti.* Essays by Enzo Frateili, Agnoldomenico Pica, and Vittoriano Viganò. New York: Rizzoli, 1988.

Lecci, Leo, ed. *Filippo Romoli: Manifesti d'Artista, 1928–1968.* Genoa: Fondazione Carige, 2006.

Lista, Giovanni. *Le Livre Futuriste de la Libération du Mot au Poème Tactile.* Modena: Edizioni Panini, 1984.

Menegazzi, Luigi. *Il Manifesto Italiano, 1882–1925.* Milan: Electa Editrice, 1975.

—*Il Manifesto Italiano.* Milan: Arnoldo Mondadori Arte, 1989.

Michail, M. and Cristina Tonelli. *Il Design in Italia 1925/43.* Bari: Editori Laterza, 1987.

Pansera, Anty. *Storia e Cronaca della Triennale.* Milan: Longanesi, 1978.

—*Storia del Disegno Industriale Italiano.* Bari: Editori Laterza, 1993.

Pincus, Karen. *Bodily Regimes: Italian Advertising under Fascism.* London and Minneapolis: University of Minnesota Press, 1995.

Priarone, Giuseppe. *Grafica Pubblicitaria in Italia negli Anni Trenta*. Firenze: Cantini Editore, 1989.

Prunet, Antoine. *Pininfarina: Art and Industry 1930–2000*. New York: Rizzoli, 2000.

Romanelli, Marco. *Gio Ponti: A World*. Milan: Editrice Abitare Segesta, 2002.

Salaris, Claudia. *Il Futurismo e la Publiccitá*. Milan; Lupetti & Co. Editore, 1986.

Settant'Anni di Manifesti Italiani della Raccolta delle Stampe A. Bertarelli. Milan: Civica Raccolta delle Stampe A. Bertarelli, 1972.

Sparke, Penny. *Italian Design: 1870 to the Present*. London: Thames and Hudson, 1988.

—*A Century of Car Design*. Hauppauge, NY: Barron's, 2002.

Sparti, Pepa, ed. *L'Italia che Cambia Attaverso i Manifesti della Raccolta Salce*. Rome: Artificio, 1990.

Stone, Marla Susan. *The Patron State: Culture & Politics in Fascist Italy*. Princeton NJ: Princeton University Press, 1998.

Lo Studio Boggeri, 1933–1981. Milan: Electa Editrice, 1981.

Tanchis, Aldo. *Bruno Munari: Design as Art*. Cambridge, MA: MIT Press, 1987 (c. 1986)

Tannenbaum, Edward. R. *The Fascist Experience: Italian Society and Culture, 1922–1945*. New York and London: Basic Books, 1972.

Thompson, Doug. *State Control in Fascist Italy: Culture and Conformity, 1925–43*. Manchester and New York: Manchester University Press, 1991.

Tisdall, Caroline and Angelo Bozzolla. *Futurism*. New York and Toronto: Oxford University Press, 1978.

Xanti Schawinsky: Malerei, Bühne, Graphikdesign, Fotografie. Berlin: Bauhaus-Archiv, 1986.

Germany

Aynsley, Jeremy. *Graphic Design in Germany, 1890–1945*. London and New York: Thames and Hudson, 2000.

Burke, Christopher. *Paul Renner: The Art of Typography*. New York: Princeton Architectural Press, 1998.

Cabarga, Leslie. *Progressive German Graphics 1900–1937*. San Francisco: Chronicle Books, 1994.

Cinamon, Gerald. *Rudolf Koch: Letterer, Type Designer, Teacher*. New Castle: Oak Knoll Press, and London: The British Library, 2000.

Fraser, James, ed. *Malik-Verlag, 1916–1947: Berlin, Prague, New York*. New York: Goethe House, 1984.

Frenzel, H. K. *Ludwig Hohlwein*. Berlin: Phönix Illustrationsdruck und Verlag, 1926.

Nerdinger, Winifred, ed. *Bauhaus-Moderne im Nationalsozialismus: Zwischen Anbiederung und Verfolgung*. Munich: Prestel, 1993.

Pachnicke, Peter and Klaus Honef, eds. *John Heartfield*. New York: Harry N. Abrams, 1992

Rhodes, Anthony, *Propaganda: The Art of Persuasion, WW II*. Edited by Victor Margolin. New York: Chelsea House, 1976.

Selle, Gert. *Design – Geschichte in Deutschland: Produktkultur als Entwurf und Erfahrung*. Cologne: DuMont Buchverlag, 1987.

Schneegass, Christian, ed. *Ludwig Hohlwein: Plakate der Jahre 1906–1940*. Stuttgart: Staatsgalerie, 1985.

Spotts, Frederic. *Hitler and the Power of Aesthetics*. London: Hutchinson, 2002.

Soviet Union

Blackwell, William L. *The Industrialization of Russia: An Historical Perspective*. New York: Thomas Y. Crowell, 1970.

Bonnell, Victoria E. *Iconography of Power: Soviet Political Posters under Lenin and Stalin*. Berkeley, Los Angeles, and London: University of California Press, 1997.

Compton, Susan. *Russian Avant-Garde Books, 1917–1934*. Cambridge, MA: MIT Press, 1993.

Dickerman, Leah, ed. *Building the Collective: Soviet Graphic Design, 1917–1937: Selections from the Merrill C. Berman Collection*. New York: Princeton Architectural Press, 1996.

Hutchings, Raymond. *Soviet Science, Technology,*

Design: Interaction and Convergence. London, New York, and Toronto: Oxford University Press, 1976.

Kenez, Peter. *A History of the Soviet Union from the Beginning to the End*. Cambridge: Cambridge University Press, 1999.

Kerber, L. L. *Stalin's Aviation Gulag: A Memoir of Andrei Tupolev and the Purge Era*. Edited by Von Hardesty. Washington and London: Smithsonian Institution Press, 1996.

Khan-Magomedov, Selim. *Rodchenko: The Complete Work*. Introduced and edited by Vieri Quilici. Cambridge, MA: MIT Press, 1987.

Lavrentiev, Alexander. *Varvara Stepanova: The Complete Work*. Edited by John Bowlt. Cambridge, MA: MIT Press, 1988.

Lavrentiev, Alexander and Yuri V. Nasarov. *Russian Design: Traditions and Experiment, 1920–1960*. London: Academy Editions, 1995.

Lissitzky-Küppers, Sophie. *El Lissitzky: Life, Letters, Texts*. London: Thames and Hudson, 1968.

Margolin, Victor. *The Struggle for Utopia: Rodchenko, Lissitzky, Moholy-Nagy, 1917–1946*. Chicago and London: University of Chicago Press, 1997.

Milner, John. *Vladimir Tatlin and the Russian Avant-Garde*. New Haven and London: Yale University Press, 1983.

—*A Dictionary of Russian and Soviet Artists, 1420–1970*. Woodbridge: Antique Collectors' Club, 1993.

Mitchell, Mairin. *The Maritime History of Russia, 848–1948*. London: Sidgwick and Jackson, 1949.

Nove, Alec. *An Economic History of the USSR, 1917–1991*. London: Penguin Books, 1992.

Rosenfeld, Alla, ed. *Defining Russian Graphic Arts, 1898–1934: From Diaghilev to Stalin*. New Brunswick: Rutgers University Press and the Jane Voorhees Zimmerli Art Museum, 1999.

Rowell, Margit and Deborah Wye. *The Russian Avant-Garde Book, 1910–1934*. With essays by Jared Ash, Nina Gurianova, Gerald Janecek, Margit Rowell, and Deborah Wye. New York: The Museum of Modern Art, 2002.

Treadgold, Donald W. and Herbert J. Ellison. *Twentieth Century Russia*. Boulder: Westview Press, 2000.

Waschik, Klaus and Nina Baburina. *Werbe für die Utopie: Russische Plakatkunst des 20. Jahrhundert*. Bietigheim-Bissingen: Editions Tertium, 2003.

Woodward, David. *The Russians at Sea: A History of the Russian Navy*. New York and Washington: Praeger, 1965.

Portugal

Acciaiuoli, Margarida. *Exposições do Estado Novo, 1934–1940*. Lisbon: Livros Horizonte, 1998.

Lobo, Theresa. *Cartazes Publicitários: Colecção de Empreza do Bolhão*. Lisbon: Edições Inapa, n.d.

Chapters in books

Benton, Tim, "Italian Architecture and Design," in Charlotte Benton, Tim Benton, and Ghislaine Wood, eds. *Art Deco 1919–1939*. Boston, New York, and London: Bulfinch Group, 2003.

Bossaglia, Rosanna, "L'Art Déco Italien," in Helena Dahlbäck Lutteman, ed. *L'Art Déco en Europe: Tendances Décoratives dans les Arts Appliqués vers 1925*. Bruxelles: Société des Expositions du Palais des Beaux-Arts, 1989.

De Guttry, Irene and Maria Paola Maino, "Forging Modern Italy; From Wrought Iron to Aluminum," in Wendy Kaplan, ed. *Designing Modernity: The Arts of Reform and Persuasion, 1885–1945*. London and New York: Thames and Hudson, 1995.

del Renzio, Tony, "Italy – The Italian Experience," in Barbie Campbell-Cole and Tim Benton, eds. *Tubular Steel Furniture*. London: The Art Book Company, 1979.

Doordan, Dennis, "Political Things: Design in Fascist Italy," in Wendy Kaplan, ed. *Designing Modernity: The Arts of Reform and Persuasion, 1885–1945*. London and New York: Thames and Hudson, 1995.

Heskett, John, "Design in Inter-War Germany," in Wendy Kaplan, ed. *Designing Modernity: The Arts of*

Reform and Persuasion, 1885–1945. London and New York: Thames and Hudson, 1995.

Lamonica, Marianne, "A 'Return to Order': Issues of the Vernacular and the Classical in Italian Inter-War Design," in Wendy Kaplan, ed. *Designing Modernity: The Arts of Reform and Persuasion, 1885–1945*. London and New York: Thames and Hudson, 1995.

Nulli, Andrea and Giampiero Bosoni, "Italy: The Parallel History of Design and Consumption," in *History of Industrial Design, 1919–1990: The Dominion of Design*. Milan: Electa, 1991.

Schnapp, Jeffrey T., "Epic Demonstrations: Fascist Modernity and the 1932 Exhibition of the Fascist Revolution," in Richard J. Golsan, ed. *Fascism, Esthetics, and Culture*. Hanover and London: University Press of New England, 1992.

Articles

Anysley, Jeremy, "Pressa Cologne, 1928: Exhibitions and Publication Design in the Weimar Period," *Design Issues* 10, no. 3 (Autumn 1994).

Arvidson, Adam, "Between Fascism and the American Dream," *Social Science History* 25, no. 2 (Summer 2001).

Barbosa, Helena, Anna Calvera, and Vasco Branco, "Portugal's First Advertising Agency: Raul de Caldevilla and the ETP, 1914–1923," *Design Issues* 25, no. 1 (Winter 2009).

Coradeschi, Sergio, "The Novecento Style in Italy: Commercial and Graphic Design," *The Journal of Decorative and Propaganda Arts* 3 (Winter 1987).

Doordan, Dennis, "The Advertising Architecture of Fortunato Depero," *The Journal of Decorative and Propaganda Arts* 12 (Spring 1989).

Heskett, John, "Modernism and Archaism in the Third Reich," *Block* 3 (1980).

Landini, Enrica Torelli, "Attilio Calavera: Stories from an Archive," *The Journal of Decorative and Propaganda Arts* 16 (Summer 1990).

Pansera, Anty, "The Triennale of Milan: Past, Present, Future," *Design Issues* 2, no. 1 (Spring 1985).

Chapter 28: The United States 1917–1941

Introduction

World War I began in 1914 but the United States did not enter the conflict until early 1917. Supporting the Allies who were fighting against Germany, the Americans initially provided naval support to the British and only sent ground troops abroad in the spring of 1918, just eight months before the Germans surrendered and the war ended. Consequently the United States government suffered far fewer losses than other countries involved in the war, all of which were economic rivals.

As a result, America was the preeminent industrial nation after World War I and its economy expanded rapidly during the 1920s, due to a combination of technological advances, managerial innovation, and aggressive marketing. These tendencies were all in place by the late 19th century but they were both accelerated and refined after the war. What also contributed to American economic growth in the 1920s was an increasing involvement with foreign markets for selling finished goods as well as obtaining raw materials.

Many large companies developed their research activities following the earlier models of Kodak, General Electric, and Westinghouse. By 1929 there were more than 1,000 industrial laboratories in the United States, up considerably from only 100 before World War I. During the 1920s, for example, Du Pont had a staff of 1,000 scientists, engineers, and technicians who worked in several labs. The company's aim was to shift from the manufacture of armaments to chemical products including rayon fibers and cellophane films.

A major breakthrough was the invention of nylon, often considered to be the first synthetic fiber, and in 1938 Du Pont successfully introduced nylon stockings as an affordable alternative to silk. Other synthetic materials that were invented in Du Pont's labs included neoprene, a rubber substitute, and various enamels such as the quick-drying Duco and Dulux, which enabled Du Pont to dominate the automobile paint market in the 1930s.

The new materials that came out of the Du Pont labs were part of a much larger stream of synthetics that were widely adopted during the 1920s and 1930s for new products. Many were variants of celluloid, a thermoplastic that was invented in the mid-19th century, but others came later: Monel—a stainless metal alloy created in 1901 and composed primarily of nickel and copper; Bakelite—a synthetic plastic that was developed around 1909; and Formica—a composite that was invented by two researchers at Westinghouse in 1912. Originally used for electrical insulation, Formica was employed extensively in the 1920s and 1930s as a surface laminate for kitchen furniture and counter tops.

Two of the most significant materials created during the interwar period were Plexiglas, an acrylic plastic developed in 1933, and fiberglass, a durable material made from bundles of glass fibers that was invented in 1938 by Russell Slayter (1896–1964), a researcher at Owens-Corning. Originally used for insulation purposes, fiberglass was later adopted for the manufacture of furniture, automobiles, and even surfboards. In general, manufacturers were quick to make use of all the new materials for many different products from combs and bathroom accessories to clocks and radios.

Historian Thomas Hughes has noted that the rise of large corporate research laboratories came to replace independent inventors like Thomas Edison as the primary source of American innovation, yet he also states that these laboratories were more conservative in their methods; consequently, radical breakthroughs such as the invention of the jet engine, the helicopter, magnetic recording, and air conditioning were still made by independent inventors, who were now peripheral to the national research effort rather than central to it as Thomas Edison had once been.

The intensification of research activity resulted in exceptional productivity and created a surplus of goods that American manufacturers actively marketed both at home and abroad. The European economies had been weakened by the war, and a strong demand for American products existed. Large American retailers like Woolworth's, Montgomery Ward, and A & P opened stores abroad and introduced American retail techniques to their new environments including mail order catalogs, appealing packaging, money-back guarantees, and high-pressure sales tactics.

Other American companies became international conglomerates during this period through investing in or purchasing foreign competitors. By 1930, for example, General Electric either controlled or influenced most of the major electrical companies worldwide. American automobile manufacturers also came to dominate world markets by opening assembly plants in Europe, Latin America, and more distant countries such as Japan, Turkey, Australia, and the Soviet Union.

World War I had shown American industrialists how important foreign resources were and prompted a shift from consuming domestic raw materials to strategies for obtaining needed materials abroad. The industrialists successfully enlisted the government's help in gaining access to oil in the Middle East and Latin America, extracting rubber from Liberia, and purchasing failing sugar mills in Cuba and banana plantations in Central America. By 1929, the United States, with British partners in numerous cases, also controlled production of many of the world's resources including nickel, aluminum, asbestos, copper, iron, tin, and manganese.

The corporate shift from a national economy to an international one occurred for a number of reasons.

First, the American government provided political and diplomatic resources to support it. Second, it was facilitated by the managerial efficiency of large companies such as General Electric, Ford, and Standard Oil. Third, these companies viewed the world and its resources from an entrepreneurial rather than a colonial perspective which stimulated more aggressive and inventive methods of economic accumulation. Fourth and finally, the government introduced harsh trade and monetary policies that maintained high tariffs at home, while exerting stringent terms on foreign nations for the repayment of loans.

Herbert Hoover, an engineer who served as Secretary of Commerce from 1921 to 1929, strongly supported the expansion of American enterprise abroad without government regulation. At home, he was a strong advocate of industrial efficiency and played a major role in producing the *Waste in Industry Report* of 1921, which advocated the standardization and simplification of manufacturing practices to reduce industrial waste. As Secretary of Commerce, Hoover inaugurated a new Division of Simplified Practices to foster agreement among producers and consumers on how to cut down the number of sizes and models of consumer products. He continued to advocate such policies after he became President in 1929.

Others outside the government joined the movement to eliminate waste. Among them was Stuart Chase, a statistician who wrote a series of books during the 1920s—*The Tragedy of Waste* (1925), *Your Money's Worth* (1927), which he co-authored with F. J. Shlink, and *Men and Machines* (1929)—in which he claimed that American industry was manufacturing far more than people needed and that many products were of dubious quality. Chase was particularly critical of the squandered resources that had gone to produce "junk and litter and waste." In a prescient statement of 1932, he wrote, "Our children and our grandchildren will have a bitter bill to pay. We are living on our economic capital where other ages have lived on their economic income."

Chase also called attention to the lack of facilities to evaluate new products. In *Your Money's Worth*, he and his co-author cited the Bureau of Standards, a federal laboratory that was housed within the Department of Commerce over which Herbert Hoover presided for eight years, as a good example of a regulatory agency that could evaluate products and identify those that were poorly made. Chase was active in the nascent consumer movement of the early 1930s that led to the founding of the Consumers Union, an independent product-testing and information organization, in 1936.

Chase's arguments for the economic use of resources and the reduction of waste were countered by spokesmen from the advertising industry, notably Roy Sheldon and Egmont Arens, who argued in their book *Consumer Engineering* (1932) that the real problem of the American economy was underconsumption. The function of the advertising agency, they stated, was to convince American consumers that new products ought to be replaced frequently even if they were still serviceable. For these advertising men, design was simply a technique to make products look attractive in order to increase their sales appeal.

The term "consumer engineering" was introduced by advertising executive Ernest Elmo Calkins (1868–1964) in an address to a convention of advertising professionals some time before 1932. Sheldon and Arens developed the concept in their book, calling "consumer engineering" the new business science. They justified the approach by claiming that resources were available in abundance and that consumers preferred a steady stream of new products. What was positive about their approach to design was their emphasis on improving the quality of products to make them more appealing, but in making that argument they paid no heed to the warnings of Chase and others that the prodigious waste of what they called "progressive obsolescence" would leave a debt for future generations to pay.

Like most advertisers, manufacturers, and designers in the interwar years, Sheldon and Arens identified women as the nation's primary consumers.

In 1920, women won the right to vote. This new opportunity was coupled with their growing presence in the workforce, primarily in secretarial jobs and other "pink collar" occupations. However, large numbers of married women stayed at home and most advertising was targeted to them.

Electrification in American homes increased from 24 percent in 1917 to almost 90 percent by 1940. This created a huge market for electrical appliances of all kinds. The fastest-selling new products of the 1920s were telephones, radios, and automobiles. The number of telephones jumped from about 1 million in 1900 to over 20 million in 1930. The rapid spread of radio, which surpassed automobiles in sales per capita, resulted in national broadcast networks that enabled people to share in the live transmission of cultural and news events, while making it possible for advertisers to address the listening public as a national market.

However, the growth in automobile sales far surpassed any other industry. From fewer than 500,000 cars and other vehicles in 1900, the number jumped to nearly 10 million in 1920, more than 26 million in 1930, and began to level off at 32 million in 1940. The sale of automobiles, led by the inexpensive models of Henry Ford but fueled as well by the styling of General Motors, transformed the American landscape and generated enormous industries of road building, gasoline distribution, and the construction of suburban homes.

The Depression and the New Deal

The economic boom of the 1920s was shattered by the Stock Market Crash of October 1929, which led to the Great Depression of the 1930s. When Franklin D. Roosevelt was elected President in 1932, around 25 percent of the workforce was unemployed and family income had dropped almost 40 percent since the market crashed. During his first 100 days in office, Roosevelt introduced a series of bills that stabilized the banking system, provided new regulatory powers for the government, and established the Tennessee Valley

Authority, a vast project to build dams and power plants in an impoverished region of the country. Congress also created the National Recovery Administration to help business leaders regulate prices, wages, and other matters, although the program ended when the Supreme Court invalidated it in 1935 because of administrative problems.

The aggregate of Roosevelt's proposals were known as the New Deal. One of its aims was to stimulate the economy by creating thousands of jobs. Among the agencies the Roosevelt administration founded for this purpose were the Civilian Conservation Corps, which employed 2,500,000 young men to improve huge areas of forestland by planting trees and by other means; and the Works Progress Administration, which employed more than 2,000,000 workers annually, including many artists, writers, musicians, actors, and also designers, to paint murals, write plays, create posters, and generally improve thousands of schools, hospitals, airports, and other facilities. Besides the work programs, the federal government also established a new agency, the Social Security Administration, to ensure an income for retired workers. Between 1932 and 1937, President Roosevelt reduced employment to 9 percent, although the latter figure remained stable until American industry geared up with full force in 1942 to manufacture arms, uniforms, and equipment for World War II.

Design Promotion

When Herbert Hoover became Secretary of Commerce in 1921 and began to develop programs and policies to advance American industry and its impact on the economy at home and abroad, he could not have imagined that before the end of the decade, product styling would be recognized as an important stimulus to the sale of everything manufactured in America from kitchen stoves to automobiles. With a background as a mining engineer, Hoover understood industry in terms of efficiency and devoted considerable energy to reducing the waste in the manufacturing system.

But when an invitation came to the United States government from the organizers of the Exposition Internationale des Arts Décoratifs in Paris to design and build an American Pavilion for the exposition, Hoover did not immediately recognize the strategic value of participating. Instead, he sought the opinion of selected manufacturers and abided by their assessment that the United States had nothing of value to display. Given that advice, he was unable to recommend the construction of a pavilion although he did later send a delegation to Paris to assess the exhibits and prepare a lengthy report on their significance for American industry.

In a telephone address to the 4th Annual Exhibition of Women's Arts and Industries in 1925, Hoover revealed his belief that industrial art was women's work and that its primary purpose was to uphold the "canons of art and taste." His response suggests that as an engineer, he thought the hard design of fashioning an object and developing its mechanical function to be a man's job, while its decoration could be left to the refined sensibilities of a woman. Given such ideas, it was not unexpected that he did not recognize the value of the Paris exhibition for America's economy.

The delegation that Hoover sent to Paris included members of many trade associations as well as a number of delegates at large. One of the leaders was Charles R. Richards (1865–1936), who had prompted Hoover to organize the delegation. He was moved in part by the extensive survey of American applied arts that he undertook in 1920. Entitled *Art in Industry*, it covered a large number of manufacturing sectors from furniture and lighting design to printing, fashion, textiles, wallpaper and ceramics. It also included an extensive discussion of applied arts education in Europe and an account of schools of applied art in the United States. Though well documented, the survey unfortunately did not persuade the federal government—one of its funders—to invest in industrial arts education, thus leaving this important activity to the states or to private initiatives.

Nonetheless, Richards remained a leading advocate for the applied arts. At the time the Paris exhibition closed, he was director of the American Association of Museums and he organized a show of more than 400 objects from the exhibition that traveled to a number of museums on the east coast and in the Midwest, thereby bringing some examples of European modern design to a public that more than likely knew little of it.

Another commission member who actively enhanced the museum's role in improving the applied arts was Richard Bach (1887–1968). In 1918 he was appointed head of a new Department of Industrial Relations at the Metropolitan Museum of Art, where his responsibility was to encourage industry to use the museum's collections as a stimulus for the design of new products. This was one way to extend the museum's influence in enhancing the aesthetic quality of daily life. Throughout the 1920s and the 1930s, Bach played an important role in promoting the applied arts through a series of annual exhibitions that he organized, although his conception of design for many years was based on the application of historic precedents to the fashioning of contemporary goods.

The Metropolitan's commitment to display applied art had its precedent in John Cotton Dana's previously mentioned ground-breaking exhibitions at the Newark Museum some years earlier (see Chapter 17). During the 1920s, Dana continued to mount applied arts exhibitions, which included the display of inexpensive everyday objects, in order to improve the public's taste. Bach's counterpart in Chicago was Herman Rosse (1887–1965), who headed the Department of Decorative Design at the Art Institute in the early 1920s. Rosse, whose background was in architecture and interior design, later went on to work in the film industry as an art director and a designer of sets and costumes.

Before 1924, the exhibitions that Bach organized at the Metropolitan Museum of Art were promoted as displays of products based on objects in the museum, but after that the annual shows were advertised more broadly as exhibits of American industrial art. Historian Wendy Kaplan has pointed out, however, that the department stores played a far greater role than the museums in stimulating public taste. With no commitment to objects from the past, they could espouse a new modern style and did so, originally by presenting many objects from Europe. The Paris exhibition was a primary stimulus, but eventually the stores sought to introduce modern furniture and decorative objects by designers in America.

The first of these department store exhibitions was Macy's Art-in- Trade show of 1927. It was designed by Lee Simonson (1888–1967), who brought to the department store the same sense of visual drama that had made him one of New York's leading theater set designers. Macy's followed that show a year later with another, more ambitious, exhibition, Art-in-Industry. Organized by the head of Macy's new department of design, the painter Austin Purvis (dates unconfirmed), and designed by Simonson, it also featured work by leading European designers—Joseph Hoffmann, Maurice Dufresne, Bruno Paul, and Gio Ponti. Given the talent involved, it is not surprising that the exhibition drew 100,000 visitors in one week, a figure surpassed only by Macy's rival, Lord & Taylor, whose exhibit of modern French decorative art the same year was seen by over 200,000 visitors. Spurred by the large attendance at these New York events, other department stores across the country began to mount their own shows of modern furniture and decorative arts.

Modern Design: The First Wave

The report of the commission that Herbert Hoover appointed to visit the Exposition Inernationale des Arts Décoratifs was extremely positive in its assessment of modern design. As the authors noted, "the modern movement in applied art is destined to play a large part in the near future in many important fields of production throughout the western world." Speaking in the language of marketing and trade, they wrote that the nation that could best adapt the principles and aesthetic practices of the modern movement to conditions of mass production and consumption would gain a distinct trade advantage. The report strongly critiqued the American tendency to "copy, modify, and adapt the older styles with few suggestions of a new idea," and urged American industrial leaders to reduce their dependence on foreign and antiquarian models by creating a modern American style. The authors also urged improvements in American design education and the extension of current copyright legislation to protect design, a project picked up by others and passed into law in 1930.

A number of these points had already been made by Richards in his 1920 report, *Art in Industry*, and the recommendations in the new document garnered hardly any more response from the Department of Commerce than Richards had received from the government following the completion of his earlier document.

The lack of government comprehension of design as a strategic activity to improve domestic sales and foreign trade was in stark contrast to America's leading competitors in Germany, France, and Britain where government support for the applied arts had begun as early as the mid-19th century and continued with the establishment of museums, design schools, and government-funded councils to strengthen the public understanding of design.

Nonetheless, a number of designers in the United States, most of them immigrants from Europe, had begun to foster a loosely-knit movement to counter the historic styles with a new modern vocabulary. Independent of the consultant designers who are generally considered to have created a distinctly American industrial design practice, the European émigrés brought a craft tradition to the production of furniture and household objects with modern forms. Though much of their work was for individual clients or was produced in small runs, they nonetheless established precedents that were frequently adopted by the large manufacturers of furniture, ceramics, and metalware, and some of them worked for these companies as well. Most of the émigrés were located in New York, although by the 1930s a few had moved to other cities like Chicago or Pittsburgh.

One of first designers to arrive from Europe was Ilonka Karasz (1896–1981), who came to New York from Budapest, Hungary, in 1913. She was an early promoter of modern decorative arts and distinguished herself as an artist and teacher as well as a designer of textiles, carpets, silver, ceramics, furniture, and wallpaper. As a designer of textiles, Karasz experimented with one-off batiks, while also working as a freelance designer for the silk-printing firm, H. R. Mallinson. Her tea and coffee set of ribbed electroplated nickel silver for Paye and Baker had a starkness that recalled Marianne Brandt's Metal Workshop projects at the Bauhaus, while her furniture designs, though not mass-produced, were influential for their early commitment to basic linear and planar forms. This was evident in a desk she designed around 1928, which was composed entirely of horizontal and vertical planes similar to Gerrit Rietveld's Red and Blue chair and the earlier Prairie School furniture of Frank Lloyd Wright. In addition to her active and varied career as a designer of furniture and utilitarian objects, Karasz was also a successful advertising and magazine illustrator, known especially in the interwar years for her gently humorous *New Yorker* covers. Her sister, Mariska Karasz (1898–1960), pursued several careers in fashion and textiles, initially gaining recognition as a designer of women's clothing and then custom clothing for children. After World War II she concentrated mainly on embroidered wall hangings.

Other designers came from Vienna, where they had been exposed to the aesthetics and practices of the Wiener Werkstätte. A major figure within this group was Paul Frankl (1886–1958), who arrived in the United States in 1914 after studying architecture in Berlin. In Europe, Frankl critiqued the Deutscher Werkbund for not fostering enough mass-produced goods, but in

Fig. 28.01: Paul Frankl, Skyscraper bookcase, c. 1927.
Gift of the Antiquarian Society through Mr. and Mrs.
Thomas B. Hunter III and Mr. and Mrs. Morris S.
Weeden, 1998.567, The Art Institute of Chicago.

America he mainly designed furniture and interiors for
individual clients. Embracing the fast-moving modern
culture of New York, Frankl created the first of his
signature Skyscraper bookcases around 1925 and for
several years he continued to produce variants in a small
workshop (Fig. 28.01). These included both separate
pieces and some that combined multiple functions.
Initially, the Skyscraper pieces proved popular and
others quickly copied them. The Johnson Furniture
Company, a large Grand Rapids manufacturer, introduced mass-produced versions of the stepped furniture
in their "Dynamique Creations" line, which they billed
as "authentic modernist" design.

Besides designing, Frankl was an active promoter
of modern design and complemented his furniture and
interior design activities with importing French textiles
that had patterns by well-known designers including

Raoul Dufy, François Jourdain, and Paul Poiret. When
Poiret toured the United States in 1923 to promote his
new fashions, however, he was dismayed to discover
that American manufacturers had copied many of his
designs.

More than any other European émigré modernist,
Frankl publicized modern design beyond the elite
circles of wealthy New York and East Coast clients. In
1928 he prepared a home study course on contemporary
decorative art and undertook several national speaking
tours to stimulate interest in the subject, especially
among employees in department stores. The same year
he published a book, *New Dimensions: The Decorative
Arts of Today in Words & Pictures*, in which he explained
and promoted modern design across all the decorative
arts from furniture to ceramics, including as well theater
sets, shop windows, and posters. Amply illustrated, the
book featured numerous photographs of Frankl's own
furniture, thus presenting his pieces within a larger
context of modern European design.

Frankl was an admirer of Frank Lloyd Wright,
whom he persuaded to write a gracious foreword
to the book. In his brief text, Wright referred to a
crusade "in the cause of Style as against 'styles'." Why
Wright himself did not play a larger role in promoting
modern design after the Paris exposition is a worthwhile question. His lack of prominence in New York
can be partially attributed to his personal arrogance. He
visited the Paris exposition and expressed his distaste
for what he saw, just as he disdained the skyscraper as
a building type and reacted against the 1938 Bauhaus
exhibition at the Museum of Modern Art. When
Macy's organized its Art-in-Industry exhibition in
1928, Wright, America's leading modernist architect
whose buildings and furniture designs had influenced
Europeans as early as 1911, was not invited to participate. At the same time, he refused invitations to join
exhibitions of modern design such as the Metropolitan
Museum's 1929 exhibit on architects and the industrial
arts, and the 1933 Century of Progress exhibition in
Chicago.

Consequently it was predominantly European émigrés who constituted the first wave of modernists. Besides Frankl, the architect Joseph Urban (1872–1933) also came from Vienna. Active as a designer of productions for the Metropolitan Opera and the Ziegfeld Follies several years after coming to the New York in 1912, he also managed the short-lived gallery that sold decorative objects manufactured by the Wiener Werkstätte. Besides achieving fame as a production designer and recognition as an architect, Urban coordinated the color scheme for the Century of Progress exhibition, which opened in Chicago in 1933. He was assisted there by another Viennese, Wolfgang Hoffmann (1900–1969), who emigrated with his wife Pola to New York in 1925. Son of Wiener Werkstätte founder Joseph Hoffmann, Wolfgang worked with Joseph Urban before he and Pola (1902–d.o.d unconfirmed), also a designer, opened their own studio, where they created custom furniture for private clients. Following the Chicago fair, Hoffmann became the resident designer for the Howell Co., a large Chicago manufacturer of mass-produced tubular steel furniture.

Vally Wieselthier (1895–1945), who headed the ceramics workshop at the Wiener Werkstätte in its later years, came to New York in 1929. She established a career as a designer of varied household goods from ceramics to glassware, textiles, and furniture. She also designed jewelry as well as the metal elevator doors for Ely Jacques Kahn's Squibb Building.

Several émigré designers from Germany were former students of Bruno Paul, one of the few applied artists who were founding members of the Deutscher Werkbund in 1907. Paul was initially active in the Munich *Jugendstil* and was subsequently appointed director of the Berlin applied arts museum in 1903. Kem Weber (1889–1963) was recommended by Paul to help design the German section of the Panama–Pacific International Exposition in San Francisco. Weber arrived there in 1914 to supervise the construction and was unable to return to Europe when war broke out. After teaching art and running a small design studio in Santa Barbara, he moved to Los Angeles in 1921 and joined the furniture company Barker Bros., where he became art director that same year, exercising responsibility for store interiors and packaging.

In 1927, Weber opened his own studio, calling himself an industrial designer. Though he remained a consultant to Barker Bros., he followed the lead of Bruno Paul, becoming active in other fields of design as well. Weber designed furniture for various manufacturers, created commercial, residential, and office interiors, and designed pewter and silver for the Porter Blanchard Silver Company. He was one of the few modernists in southern California in the 1920s and helped to build a modest culture of modern design there, along with the architects Richard Neutra and Rudolf Schindler.

One of Weber's best-known designs is his "Airline" chair of 1934–1935, which had a swept-back look, perhaps to follow the "streamline" aesthetic. But the shape of the side supports was less significant than the structure, which featured a cantilevered seat and a knockdown design that made shipping inexpensive. Although the Disney Studios purchased 300 for their projection theaters, Weber was not able to find a company that would manufacture them for a mass market.

Walter Von Nessen (1889–1943), also a student of Paul's, came to New York in 1925 and two years later he established Nessen Studios, where he designed and fabricated architectural lighting and metal furniture. Among the customers he served were a number of leading architects who commissioned him to create lighting as well as other household objects for their clients. In the late 1920s and early 1930s, Von Nessen, who also adopted new materials such as chrome, spun aluminum, Bakelite, and fiberglass, had scant competition as a designer of modern lighting. One of his best-known designs, a copper lamp from the early 1930s with a swing arm, set a new standard for modern lighting within the industry even though it was not manufactured in large numbers. Von Nessen collaborated closely with his wife Greta (1900–1978), whom he met while working as a designer in Sweden before he came to the United States.

Other students of Paul's were Frederic Buehner-Warner (1908–1971), who came to the United States in 1929 and specialized in the design of aluminum housewares, which he branded with his trademark name Buenilum; and Peter Müller-Munk (1904–1967), a silversmith who arrived in New York in 1926. After a year as a designer for Tiffany's, Müller-Munk opened his own studio, where he researched traditional techniques of silver production. As a designer, he was best known for his angular chromium-plated brass pitcher, which was shaped like a silhouette of the French ocean liner *Normandie* (Fig. 28.02). It was made by the Revere Copper and Brass Co. in 1935. Müller-Munk turned from craft-based production to industrial design and worked on home appliances, cameras, and commercial machinery. He also taught in one of the first American industrial design programs at the Carnegie Institute of Technology in Pittsburgh.

For a brief period, Erik Magnussen (1884–1960), a self-taught silversmith from Denmark who came to New York in 1925, served as the artistic director of the Gorham Silver Company, which was previously known for its conservative designs in the traditional American Colonial Style. Working independently from other Gorham designers, Magnussen created pieces in the *moderne* style and was particularly noted for his faceted cubistic coffee service of burnished silver, which he called the "Lights and Shadows of Manhattan." It was designs like Magnussen's, which were strongly influenced by Cubism, that prompted some American critics to refer to them as "Zig Zag Moderne." Within the Gorham company culture, however, some of the other designers resented Magnussen's modernist sensibility and he left in 1929 to start his own business. Magnussen returned to Denmark in 1939 and became known after World War II as a jewelry designer.

The iconic skyscraper designs for furniture and decorative objects were one manifestation of the European-inspired American *moderne*, which critics referred to as "modernistic design." The motif was also evident in Louis Rice's "Skyscraper" tea service of 1928; Abel Faidy's 1927 settee with a back consisting of a skyscraper form; Joseph Sinel's scale for the International Ticket Scale Company of 1929; and the "Skyscraper" cocktail set designed by Norman Bel Geddes in 1937.

Besides the émigrés, some American designers were committed to modern design, but unlike the Europeans, they were not trained in craft techniques. Donald Deskey (1894–1989) became interested in design after visiting the Paris exhibition and most likely the Dessau Bauhaus. His initial commissions after opening a New York office in 1926 were the design of the first modern department store display windows for Franklin Simon and Saks Fifth Ave. This led to meetings with several manufacturers that resulted in commissions for textiles, fabrics, carpets,

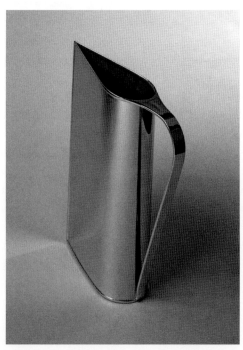

Fig. 28.02: Peter Müller-Munk, *Normandie* pitcher, 1935. Brooklyn Museum of Art, New York, USA/H. Randolph Lever Fund/Bridgeman Images.

and wallpaper, which were carried out through the Deskey-Vollmer studio that Deskey set up with Phillip Vollmer (dates unconfirmed) in 1927.

Gilbert Rohde (1894–1944), the son of a cabinetmaker, was influenced, like Deskey, by the Paris Exposition des Arts Décoratifs. After a visit to the exhibition, Rohde began designing furniture and sold some of his early work through the New York department store Abraham and Strauss. A modernist who was intrigued with German furniture, Rohde worked in chrome and Bakelite as well as other contemporary materials. By 1930 he had created furniture for private clients and retail interiors, while the Heywood-Wakefield Company, a manufacturer of modern furniture in wood, hired him to design a line of indoor and outdoor pieces. One of the first examples of mass-produced modern furniture in America was a bentwood side chair Rohde designed for the company. It sold more than 250,000 exemplars in less than a decade. Rohde is best known, however, as the man who introduced the Herman Miller Company to modern design after he was hired as design director in 1933.

Eugene Schoen (1880–1957), by contrast to Rohde, was dedicated to high-style furniture that was influenced by Austrian, German, and French examples. Trained as an architect, Schoen specialized in interiors for private residences as well as banks, theaters, and department stores. He also designed a nightclub for the ocean liner *Leviathan*, and consulted on the New York State Pavilion for Chicago's Century of Progress exhibition. Of all the designers in New York, Schoen's sensibility was most like that of the French decorators, given his interest in Neo-Classical forms and his taste for luxurious materials.

With the exception of Kem Weber in Los Angeles, the émigré designers worked mainly in New York and organized various exhibitions and a designer's association to promote their work. The American Designer's Gallery, which held the first of several exhibitions in 1928, adopted a similar strategy to Macy's Art-in-Industry display of the same year by dedicating separate rooms to individual designers. This strategy also had its precedents in European exhibitions going back at least as far as the Paris Exposition Universelle of 1900, when Samuel Bing devoted suites of rooms to Eugene Gaillard, Georges de Feure, and other applied artists whose work he was selling. It was as well a strategy of the French artist-decorators who, in their exhibitions of the interwar years, designated rooms and even pavilions for department stores and particular designers.

The first exhibition in the American Designer's Gallery featured ten rooms by individual designers as well as cases with other objects. Its intent was to promote a new vision of what American design could be. Among the participants were Paul Frankl, Wolfgang and Pola Hoffmann, Donald Deskey, Ilonka Karasz, Peter Müller-Munk, Herman Rosse, the German designer Winold Reiss (1886–1953), Joseph Urban, and the architects Raymond Hood (1881–1934), Ely Jacques Kahn (1884–1972), and the Swiss émigré William Lescaze (1896–1969).

The exhibit was even more provocative than its department-store counterparts. Herman Rosse created a dining room whose ceiling, walls, furniture, and even dishes were made of metal, while a highlight of the exhibit was Donald Deskey's "Man's Smoking Room," with its aluminum ceiling, tan and brown cork walls, tube lighting, linoleum floor, and tan pigskin chairs. Although the exhibit rooms represented the real or hypothetical living situations of America's social and economic elite, the publicity created an atmosphere that helped induce some mass manufacturers to market modern furniture and household objects.

Almost all the designers who showed at the American Designer's Gallery also joined the American Union of Decorative Artists and Craftsmen (AUDAC), which was established the same year. The membership of this organization was broadened to include industrial designers, architects, photographers, and craftsmen as well as designers of applied arts and interiors. This was, in part, a response to the Metropolitan Museum's

1929 exhibition The Architect and the Industrial Arts, for which Richard Bach invited a group of leading architects to design rooms of furniture and decorative objects. In 1930, AUDAC, under the leadership of the Austrian Frederick Kiesler (1890–1965), mounted its own exhibition to counter the leading role that Bach had suggested for architects in the applied arts. Though impressive in its scope, the first AUDAC exhibit did not make as great an impact as the second one that Wolfgang Hoffmann and Kem Weber organized at the Brooklyn Museum in 1931. It brought together a broad spectrum of objects including fabrics, furniture, radio cabinets, industrial design, typography, architecture, and the applied arts. According to one critic, the exhibit gave evidence that designers were developing "an original school of American design which is worthy to stand beside the best efforts of other lands."

Following the exhibition, the organizers published a book entitled *Modern American Design*, with a cover in the Deco style by Ilonka Karasz. The book celebrated machine production and promoted a comfortable middle-class life as a primary aim of design. Separate sections were devoted to shop interiors, architecture, the home, and the use of new materials as well as graphic design and commercial photography. While the ample photographs depicted objects and interiors that would have suited a moderately well off clientele, the aspirations of the essayists were towards more democratic design that would be widely available. The critic Lewis Mumford was the most extreme with his polemical attack on conspicuous consumption, his expression of dissatisfaction with the European class system, and his call for a new design ethic that did not play into "snobbery and caste-assertion." For Mumford as well as the other essayists, machine production was an effective means to enhance life and make quality design more widespread.

Despite its two widely visited exhibitions and the publication of its excellent book, AUDAC ceased to function shortly after the Brooklyn exhibition. Had the Depression not made it difficult to continue funding its activities, AUDAC might easily have become the American version of the Deutscher Werkbund or the French Societé des Artistes Décorateurs (SAD), since it had attracted a wide array of prominent industrial designers, applied artists, photographers, graphic designers, and architects. In Germany, the Werkbund continued to promote modern design, architecture, and photography through its important exhibitions and its journal *Die Form*. However, unlike the Werkbund, which had active local chapters throughout Germany, the AUDAC membership was concentrated in New York and lacked support from manufacturers and the government to sustain its activities.

Nonetheless, AUDAC's advocacy of modern design began to bear fruit in commercial enterprises. The most impressive of these was New York's Radio City Music Hall, whose interior design was planned by Donald Deskey. With Edward Durrell Stone as the principal architect, the project was launched by John D. Rockefeller Jr., who joined with the Radio Corporation of America and the impresario S. L. "Roxy" Rothafel to build a spectacular theater that opened in December 1932. Originally planned to bring high-class variety shows to a broad public, Radio City was not successful in that attempt and the management soon switched to showing films, which it combined with a stage show featuring a line of female dancers, the Rockettes.

Though Rothafel originally wanted to design the interior in an elaborate "Portuguese Rococo" style, Deskey persuaded him to adopt a modern style, which he dubbed "Modern Rococo" in order to sell the project. The interior space included 30 lobby areas, as well as foyers and lounges along with rooms for smoking and relaxing. Deskey also designed an office for Rothafel in a modern Deco style. He hired craftsmen to make ceramics, wood panels, and chandeliers, and modern artists such as Stuart Davis, Yasuo Kuniyoshi, Witold Gordon, and Henry Billings to design murals for the different lounges. Ruth Reeves (1892–1966), a designer of textiles, rugs, and wallpaper who was a founder of the American Designer's Gallery and was active in AUDAC, was asked to create wall coverings and a carpet for the Grand Foyer. The theme of her wall coverings was "The History of the Theater," while the carpet consisted of a colorful Cubist-inspired arrangement of musical instruments, all depicted in an abstract manner. Deskey also designed carpets and wallpaper for Radio City, while creating furniture for the public rooms, lounges, and the Rothafel apartment. Most of the furniture was in a Deco style, featuring wood or chrome frames with plush leather for the seats and back. Continuing the new ways of using materials that he first displayed in his "Man's Smoking Room" at the American Designer's Gallery, Deskey combined Bakelite, aluminum, and cork in the overall design with more elegant materials such as marble and gold foil.

The Radio City Music Hall provided wide publicity for the new modern style of interior design, asserting that it was more appropriate for contemporary life than the elaborate historical styles that had previously graced theaters and movie palaces. The scope of the project was at least as grand as the design of the French ocean liner *Normandie*, which showcased the diverse talents of French *moderne* designers, and in historic terms, Radio City's lavish interior design can also be compared to the great royal palaces of Europe. Its particularly American character was the entrepreneurial spirit that brought it into being as well as its appeal to the masses rather than a cultivated elite. Radio City also influenced the subsequent adoption of modern design for the decors of other public spaces such as restaurants, casinos, clubs, and hotels. It was not until after World War II, however, that Deskey had a chance to apply what he had learned in creating the Radio City interiors to the interior design of a luxury ocean liner, the S.S. *Argentina*, for which he hired such well-known modern artists as Loren McIver, José de Rivera, and Isamu Noguchi to contribute work.

The Museum of Modern Art's Critique of "Modernistic" Design

As rich and variegated as the interior decor of Radio City was, to the curators of the Museum of Modern Art (MoMA), located just a few blocks away, it could have been characterized as "modernistic," a term they applied disparagingly to any objects or buildings that did not exemplify the purity of the International Style, their term for the new movement in architecture and design that had emerged in Europe during the preceding decade. Their attitude would have also applied to much of what had been presented at the AUDAC exhibitions as well as in the design shows at the Metropolitan Museum of Art.

MoMA was founded in 1929 to exhibit modern art and sculpture, but its director, Alfred H. Barr Jr., a former professor of art history, soon expanded its mission to include architecture and design as well. The museum's International Style exhibition of 1932, curated by historian Henry Russell Hitchcock and architect Philip Johnson, featured a number of European and American buildings of recent design that exemplified a set of unifying principles based on such elements as a clear articulation of volume and a lack of ornament. The unadorned forms of these buildings were to be sought in everyday objects as well, an argument that Johnson and Barr made in an exhibition of 1934, Machine Art. On the catalog cover was a close-up photograph of a ball bearing, an image intended to exemplify the machine aesthetic that the curators espoused.

In his foreword to the catalog, Barr stated clearly that the role of the artist-designer was not to embellish or elaborate but to refine, simplify, and perfect. Geometry, he wrote, was the basis of beauty and it could be found in the pristine design of a saucepan or the functional form of a machine. This idea was reinforced in the exhibition by combining industrial objects such as springs, laboratory beakers, and propellers with examples of everyday objects for home or office that exemplified a comparable aesthetic (Fig. 28.03). Though Barr did not demand that form follow strictly from an object's function, he did, however, claim that an object's form should at least make its function evident in some way. Adding to Barr's argument, Philip Johnson, in his catalog remarks, positioned the Purist

Fig. 28.03: MoMA, Machine Art exhibition, 1934. © 2014. Digital image, The Museum of Modern Art, New York/Scala, Florence.

design that MoMA advocated between the "French Decorative movement" on one side and streamlining on the other. The principles of streamlining, he argued, and here he may well have been referring to Norman Bel Geddes' 1932 book *Horizons*, "often receive homage out of all proportion to their applicability."

When Barr and Johnson visited the Bauhaus in Dessau on a trip to Europe in 1927, they were impressed by what they saw. After Walter Gropius, director of the school from 1919 to 1928, moved to the United States in 1937 to head the architecture program at Harvard, the museum decided to do a Bauhaus exhibition. This was to be curated by Gropius and his wife Ise, but would stop at 1928, when Gropius left the school, rather than include the period up to 1933 when the Bauhaus was headed first by the leftist architect Hannes Meyer and then by the architect Mies van der Rohe.

The exhibition was designed by Herbert Bayer, a Bauhaus teacher who had moved to the United States a year after Gropius. When the exhibition opened in 1938, it was not very popular with the critics or the public. Perhaps it was the odd-looking student exercises and experimental art and photography by the faculty that put people off, although they may have been equally estranged by some of the applied design as well. From the point of view of a practicing industrial designer, Harold Van Doren, writing in his seminal textbook of 1940, *Industrial Design: A Practical Guide*, stated "[t]he Bauhaus approach lacks, however, the realistic qualities that we Americans, rightly or wrongly, demand," and he further noted that "it will be difficult, I believe, to acclimatize the esoteric ideas of the Bauhaus in the factual atmosphere of American industry."

Around the time of the Bauhaus exhibition, MoMA tried a different strategy to influence popular taste by presenting "Useful Household Objects Under $5.00," the first of an annual show that continued for several years with the cost of the objects rising each year. Given the museum's stringent aesthetic and the curators' antipathy to streamlining, it is hard to imagine that these shows had an impact that was in any way comparable to the more inclusive design exhibitions that Richard Bach was presenting regularly at the Metropolitan Museum of Art. In 1940, Bach mounted his largest show to date. With an attendance of over 139,000, it featured more than 1,000 designed objects with contributions coming from 238 designers, including Russel Wright, Donald Deskey, and other leaders in the field.

The same year as the big Metropolitan show, MoMA established its own Department of Industrial Design. It was headed by an architect, Eliot Noyes (1910–1977), whom Walter Gropius, his former teacher at Harvard, had recommended to the museum. Noyes' first major exhibition was Organic Design in Home Furnishings, which opened in 1941 (Fig. 28.04). It featured the winners in a furniture competition that continued the museum's espousal of Purist modern design. Organic design was defined as a harmonious organization of the parts within the whole and entailed an absence of "vain ornamentation or superfluity." The winners were Charles Eames (1907–1978) and Eero Saarinen (1910–1961), both students at the Cranbrook Academy of Art in Michigan. The chairs they designed in several versions had light plywood shells rather

Fig. 28.04: MoMA, Organic Design in Home Furnishings exhibition, 1941. © 2014. Digital image, The Museum of Modern Art, New York/Scala, Florence.

than elaborate upholstery and were then covered with fabric on top of a rubber base. The two also submitted a number of standardized wooden storage units of different sizes.

The furniture in the exhibition was decidedly middle class. Its precedents were the emerging Scandinavian Modern style as well as the chairs of Thonet, the furniture of the Munich Workshops, and of course the birch chairs and stools of Alvar Aalto. In that sense, Noyes and the competition judges drew heavily on the tradition of European modern design although they also recognized distinctly American contributions such as the rattan armchairs of designers Carl Anderson (dates unconfirmed) and Ross Bellah (1907–2004).

As a result of the exhibition, MoMA was contacted by the newly formed Castleton China Company to recommend a designer for a new dinner service. The company was seeking to distinguish itself and believed that a service by a well-known designer would help. Noyes recommended the Hungarian ceramist Eva Zeisel who had emigrated to New York in 1938 after establishing a reputation in Europe and having worked in the Soviet Union (see Chapter 20).

Seeking to exert its own influence on public taste, the museum worked out an unusual arrangement with Castleton. In exchange for the use of its name, the museum reserved the right to review every piece that Zeisel designed before it went into production.

Although the service was ready around 1943, it could not be put into production until after the war, at which time MoMA introduced it to the public with great fanfare at a special exhibition. The design differed from the existing popular American Modern and Fiesta services in several ways. Both of those were of earthenware and aimed squarely at a popular market. The Castleton service was made of porcelain, recalling the modern European dinner services of European designers like Marguerite Friedländer-Wildenhain and Trude Petri. In line with MoMA's Bauhaus aesthetic, Zeisel's forms were austere (Fig. 28.05). MoMA insisted on a clear glaze over the cream colored forms, allowing colored glazes for several smaller plates to serve as accents although these were later abandoned for a uniform white service. The forms were also thinner than those of other services and had elegant organic curves. What all conveyed—whether plates, cups, or bowls or coffee pots—was a stark geometry that expressed the MoMA aesthetic.

Modern Design in Mass-Produced Products

In the years following World War I, the favored furniture style of many Americans was the Colonial Revival which, as historian Kristina Wilson has noted, became a way to embrace a mythic vision of America's past in the face of the Depression's harsh realities. Despite this, however, one outcome of all the exhibitions that promoted modern design, whether in museums, galleries, department stores, or elsewhere, was a gradual openness of American manufacturers to produce modern furniture or household objects. Some eased into the modern style gradually while others introduced extensive product lines. In Indiana, the Dunbar Company hired Edward Wormley (1907–1995),

Fig. 28.05: Eva Zeisel, Castleton china service, c. 1945. © 2014. Digital image, The Museum of Modern Art, New York/Scala, Florence.

a former designer of period furniture for Marshall Field's department store in Chicago, to create dual lines of traditional and modern pieces beginning in 1931. Though Wormley began with antique designs, he soon augmented them with new furniture for every room in the house. By 1944, Dunbar's modern furniture became so popular that the company dropped its traditional line.

Donald Deskey may have been the first designer in America to create a line of tubular steel furniture for mass production. He initially designed tubular steel tables and chairs for his own company, Deskey-Vollmer, and produced them in limited runs, but around 1928 he created a living room suite of tubular steel couches, easy chairs, and tables for the Ypsilanti Reed Furniture Company, a firm in the Grand Rapids nexus that specialized in mass-produced furniture. Similar to much of the tubular steel furniture produced in the United States in the 1930s, Deskey's pieces were adapted from European models, the difference being that—in the case of the chairs—they combined the comfort of plush cushions and arm rests with spare metal frames. For the same company, Deskey also designed a line of rattan couches, easy chairs, and small tables as well as several sets of tubular steel bridge tables and chairs.

His wooden furniture for the Estey Manufacturing Company was more original and characteristic of the geometric *moderne* aesthetic. For a group of bed frames, chests, vanities, night tables, and other pieces of bedroom furniture, Deskey combined light and dark white holly and burl walnut veneers and handles to create abstract rectilinear compositions that contrasted sharply with traditional ornate bedroom sets.

Heywood-Wakefield, a company that had been manufacturing furniture for 100 years, introduced its Heywood-Wakefield Modern Line along with other modern styles during the 1930s. With designs by Gilbert Rohde, Russel Wright, and others, the company developed a consistent look with its light-colored pieces made of birch and softened with rounded corners. The modern furniture complemented Heywood-Wakefield's more traditional lines, a number of which were created by a prolific staff designer, W. Joseph Carr (dates unconfirmed).

Following Deskey's tubular steel designs for Ypsilanti Reed, other companies also began to produce metal furniture. The largest of them was the Howell Company in Chicago, where Wolfgang Hoffmann became the principal designer in 1934. The company had previously made furniture of wrought iron, but its line underwent a drastic change after the owners saw the tubular steel cantilever chairs designed by Mies van der Rohe and Marcel Breuer. Initially the company imported European examples and adapted them for American use. By the time of the Century of Progress exhibition in 1933, Howell had developed various lines of tubular steel furniture for office, showroom, and home use. More than 80 percent of the pavilions at the fair were furnished with tubular steel pieces and this helped enormously to gain acceptance for them. Where other companies commissioned tubular steel primarily for the living room, Howell developed a line of kitchen furniture including cantilever chairs with backs and seats upholstered in vinyl. These became standard items in kitchens across America (Fig. 28.06). The range of Howell Chromsteel Furniture expanded after Wolfgang Hoffmann joined the company in 1934.

A smaller company that produced metal furniture was started by Warren McArthur (1885–1961) in Los Angles in 1929. McArthur, who was trained as a mechanical engineer, began by making custom furniture but soon developed new methods of joining metal pieces together that made it feasible to produce modest runs for the commercial market. His extensive line of aluminum lounges, sofas, and end tables featured curved tubing and rounded edges and he chose strong contrasting colors for the upholstery. What further distinguished his furniture was a process he used to allow his dyes to become part of the metal rather than remain as outer coats. Thus he was able to

Fig. 28.06: Howell Company, *Modern Chromsteel Furniture*, catalog cover, 1936. Courtesy of the Smithsonian Institution Libraries, Washington, D.C.

market his furniture in colored metal tones with names like Golf Green and Alice Blue. One of the company's signature pieces was McArthur's outdoor lounge chair, which he named "Sun Fast," because it could withstand both sun and rain. The company might have made a greater contribution to modern design in California if McArthur had not needed to relocate his company to upstate New York in 1933 for financial reasons.

When Frank Lloyd Wright was planning the office furniture for the Johnson Wax Building, Warren McArthur was one of two companies that bid on the fabrication. For the large open workspace, Wright had devised three-legged chairs along with desks that had rounded surfaces and metal supports. He finally decided to award the project to Steelcase, based on drawings produced by their engineering department. Wright's Johnson Wax building, with its concomitant

furnishings, was innovative in many ways, most notably for the huge open workspace, a forerunner of the open offices of the post-war years (Fig. 28.07). Wright also designed the furniture according to a system. Not only were the fabrics color coded to specify the employee's department, but the desks came in different shapes and with different attachments and openings for storing files. Originally the chairs had three legs but when they proved unstable Wright redesigned them with four.

In 1930, seeking new business, Gilbert Rohde visited Grand Rapids, the bastion of traditional furniture design, to interest potential clients in manufacturing modern designs. He was successful with the Herman Miller Company, which he persuaded to inaugurate a modern line, while maintaining as well the period styles for which it was known. In 1932, Rohde became Herman Miller's design director, a position he

Fig. 28.07: Frank Lloyd Wright, Johnson Wax headquarters, interior, 1936. Library of Congress, LC-HS503- 2979.

held until his death in 1941. Among his innovations was the Living-Sleeping-Dining group whose pieces were not confined to specific rooms as the conventional large suites of ornate matching furniture were. He thus brought a new flexibility into an ossified system that pervaded most American furniture manufacturing. Rohde also introduced his Executive Office Group (EOG), a system consisting of 15 modular elements that could be joined together in 400 different combinations. The system introduced Herman Miller to the office furniture market, where it was to excel after the war.

Besides designing modern furniture for Herman Miller, Rohde also modernized the company's showrooms. In Chicago he introduced a biomorphic-shaped dropped ceiling, curved Flexwood walls, indirect lighting, a sectional sofa, and a Lucite coffee

table. Rohde's concepts of furniture systems were not widely employed by other manufacturers in the 1930s. However, modular furniture produced by Herman Miller was to become popular after World War II, when George Nelson, Charles Eames, and Robert Probst developed it further. The company also continued its traditional furniture line, which was taken over by Freda Diamond (1905–1998), a furnishings consultant, who designed period pieces for Herman Miller from the late 1930s to the early 1940s.

In 1934, Heywood-Wakefield introduced a line of 60 furniture pieces designed by Russel Wright (1904–1976), whose name became synonymous with modern furniture and housewares by the end of the decade. The pieces, which combined function and comfort, did not do well in the marketplace, but Wright gained the experience that would make his next furniture line, American Modern, a success. Introduced by Conant Bell in 1935, the American Modern line was not influenced by European *moderne* or Bauhaus examples but instead reinterpreted in a contemporary way the honesty and simplicity of American Colonial designs. The line was offered in both dark and light finishes, the latter called "blonde" by Wright's wife Mary (1905–1952), who did all the publicity for his designs.

The American Modern line appealed broadly to middle-class taste. It was intended to fit into a typical suburban home and was offered at a modest price. Like much other modern furniture, it challenged the traditional idea of ensembles that were consigned to particular rooms and placements. Instead, the pieces, which numbered more than 50, could be placed throughout the house. Rather than rectilinear angles, they featured rounded corners, which Wright called "cushion edges." American Modern represented a true democratization of modern furniture, both in style and in price. In addition, Wright and his wife positioned it as an American alternative to European styles, perhaps playing on the promotional phrase Swedish Modern, which had become popular after the Stockholm Exhibition of 1930. American Modern suited Wright, who maintained a strong patriotic attitude throughout his career as a designer, continually emphasizing ways that his designs expressed American values.

Other Applied Arts: Housewares and Textiles

Following the furniture launch by Heywood-Wakefield, Wright and his wife continued the American Modern theme in a line of dinnerware that would become the first American products to be identified by a designer's name. Although the service, like the furniture, was designated as American Modern, it came to be known as Russel Wright dinnerware (Plate 43). First introduced in 1939, it included a large number of pieces that could be mixed and matched, both in terms of function and color. Glazes were added over time and the colors ranged

from yellow and green to coral, grey, blue, and brown. Most distinctive were the shapes. Wright designed soft rounded forms with curved edges that gave the pieces an organic quality. Some serving plates also had a ridge in the middle to separate different kinds of food.

Manufactured by the Steubenville Pottery in Ohio, the dinnerware completely turned the fortunes of an almost-bankrupt company around. Some believe that it was the best-selling dinnerware in American history before production ceased in 1959. One aspect of the service was its functional rather than ceremonial design. Like Wright's American Modern furniture, it was intended to foster a more casual approach to living, particularly as the new suburbanites experienced it. It was also part of a larger vision of modern living that was both relaxed and comfortable.

Besides furniture and dinnerware, Wright also introduced a broader line of housewares that ranged from table linen and bedspreads to fabrics and glass. He designed as well a number of practical serving accessories and other objects in spun aluminum. Of all the American designers in the interwar years, Wright was most identified with an American style that would convey a sense of good taste and comfortable living for middle-class consumers. He was adamant about rejecting the influence of European design, urging members of the New York Fashion Group in a speech of 1938 to "[r]id yourselves of the American inferiority complex, forget European standards, look at the American scene, and have more respect for it."

Around 1940, Russel and Mary Wright launched a huge project called "American Way" to market household goods from more than 70 designers, craftspeople, and manufacturers. It was intended to draw on the best craft and design traditions of the American past to produce a line of contemporary housewares, but managing more than 140 contracts and agreements became too cumbersome and the project ultimately failed.

It is not clear whether Wright's American Modern dinner service was influenced by a slightly earlier design, Fiesta Ware, introduced to the market in 1936 by the Homer Laughlin China Company. Designed by British ceramist Frederick Hurten Rhead (1880–1942), who was on the Laughlin staff, Fiesta Ware was a bold populist service that originally consisted of 34 different pieces in five colors that could be mixed and matched. The flexibility of both the Fiesta Ware and American Modern services was in accord with a similar tendency in furniture design that has been described above. The shift was from standard ensembles in furniture design and fixed patterns in dinnerware to larger numbers of pieces, whether differentiated by type of color that could be interchanged according to the consumer's interest. The design of Fiesta Ware was simple: plain forms for each item with a set of concentric rings near the outer edge (Fig. 28.08). Among the more distinctive forms was the water pitcher, which had a slightly streamlined shape, with the elongated line of the spout continuing with the curved handle. The initial colors were blue, red, yellow, green, and ivory, with other colors and forms being added and then some subtracted while Fiesta Ware was being produced until the 1960s.

The European ceramics tradition was promoted in the United States by Julius Mihalik (1874–d.o.d.

Fig. 28.08: Frederick Hurten Rhead, Fiesta Ware, 1930s. © ZUMA Press, Inc./Alamy.

unconfirmed), a Viennese designer who headed the design department at the Cleveland School of Art. He encouraged his students to go to Vienna to study the work of Michael Powolny, Vally Wiselthier, and others in the Wiener Werkstätte. Among the students who visited Vienna was Viktor Schrekengost (1906–2008), who created a number of distinctive vases and bowls, some with Jazz Age imagery, for the Cowan Pottery in Ohio, a firm that was in the forefront of American ceramic design until it went into receivership in 1930. The firm's founder, Reginald Guy Cowan (1884–1957), was also a potter and one of the first American ceramists to work in a modern style. Cowan hired quite a few young designers during the 1920s and gave them considerable leeway in designing the many vases, bowls, jars, figurines, and even bookends that the firm produced at a relatively low cost. The figures on Schrekengost's ceramic pieces had some similarity to the work Gio Ponti was doing at the time for Richard Ginori in Italy, which is not surprising since both were influenced by the Vienna style. When the Cowan Pottery closed, Schrekengost designed mass-production ceramicware for other companies.

There was no equivalent in glassware design to the enormous popular success of Fiesta Ware and American Modern in ceramic services. One firm that sought to produce glassware in a modern style was the Steuben Glass Works, founded by Thomas Hawkes (dates unconfirmed) and Frederick Carder (1863–1963) in 1903. Carder had a deep knowledge of glassmaking techniques and colors, enabling Steuben to compete successfully with the better-known firm headed by Louis Comfort Tiffany. In 1918, Steuben was purchased by the larger Corning Glass Works and became one of its divisions. During the 1920s, Carder, who had a free hand, continued to work in traditional modes, although one of his innovations was a set of forks, knives, and spoons with glass handles that were sold to British producers of flatware. He left the company in 1933 to become design director of the entire Corning Glass Works.

Around 1932, while Carder still worked for Steuben, the division hired industrial designer Walter Dorwin Teague (1883–1960) to create a range of modern glass objects ranging from bowls, vases, and centerpieces to a variety of crystal stemware. Teague worked with Steuben for about a year, contributing to the company's advertising and public relations plans as well as its design repertoire. After analyzing Steuben's sales and production problems, he recommended a new image that would establish the ownership of Steuben glass products as signs of status. Consequently, his stemware designs had names that suggested elite identity—St. Tropez, Riviera, Blue Empire, and Winston. What Teague contributed to Steuben was more than what a traditional glass designer would have done. He was an industrial designer, already accustomed to working with large companies and analyzing their product lines within a larger framework of promotion and sales.

In 1936, Corning hired the sculptor Sidney Behler Waugh (1904–1963) to reorganize the Steuben Division, and Waugh remained Steuben's chief designer until his death in 1963. Featuring products that highlighted Corning's colorless crystal, Waugh designed a number of crystal bowls with engraved images, frequently mythological figures or animals. These were similar both in style and technique to the Swedish engraved glass of Simon Gate and Edvard Hald for Orrefors, and in their own way fulfilled Teague's recommendation that Steuben position itself as a producer of glass for an elite rather than a mass consumer class.

Besides Corning, the Libbey Glass Company also sought to develop mass-produced modern glassware in the interwar years. The Libbey Glass Company, which achieved an international reputation for cut glass in the 1890s, subsequently pioneered the adoption of new machines for automating the glass-production process. The automated tumbler machine helped Libbey become successful as a manufacturer of glasses for the restaurant industry during the 1920s and 1930s. In the mid-1920s, the company's engineering department had developed a method of producing glassware with a beaded lip around the edge of the glass that made it highly resistant to chipping, and the glasses were sold under the patented trade name No-Nik Safedge. In the late 1920s, Libbey marketed a soda fountain glass, which eventually became an American icon. Produced in several variants, it had a beaded lip, wide top, and a somewhat narrower base.

In the early 1930s, Libbey sought to establish a stronger presence in the domestic housewares market by paying more attention to design. After enrolling some of its engineers in classes in the School of Design at the Toledo Museum of Art, the company turned to professionals for assistance. Following several unsuccessful attempts to work with independent glass designers, Libbey's advertising agency recommended that the company bring in an industrial designer as Corning had done. Libbey hired Donald Deskey, who, like Teague, analyzed the company's product line and marketing strategies in addition to producing a design for a tumbler.

In 1935, Libbey merged with the Owens-Illinois Glass Company, whose president and vice-president strongly believed in design. Walter Dorwin Teague was commissioned to design patterns for pressed glass bricks that were used as architectural elements in buildings, but the company relied on local talent to enhance its flagging sales in the housewares market. Edwin W. Fuerst (1903–1988), a former student and teacher at the Toledo Museum of Art's Design School, became head of design development in 1938. His cordial decanter, glasses, and other pieces made of clear glass and mounted on solid rectangular bases recalled the Scandinavian designs of the period. They were marketed as part of Libbey's Modern American line, which the company established in 1940 to replace the contemporary European art glass that had become difficult to import because of the war. Fuerst also collaborated with Teague on a set of fluted stemware and finger bowls for the State Dining Room in the Federal Building at the 1939 New York World's Fair. However, Teague did not produce a design that could be manufactured within the required time constraints and was consequently dissatisfied with the changes that Fuerst made as well as with the company's decision to market the set to a broader public after the fair. One of Teague's legacies to Libbey, however, was his recommendation that the company hire a woman designer who might have a greater insight into a market that was dominated by female consumers. Advised by its advertising agency, Libbey hired Freda Diamond, who had also designed furniture for Herman Miller, in 1941. Diamond remained as a consultant to Libbey for many years.

Other companies also hired outside designers to create glassware. George Sakier (1897–1988), a former magazine art director and one of the first American industrial designers, designed vases, both fluted and ribbed, for the Fostoria Glass Company, while Reuben Haley (1872–1933), a designer of glass, metal, and ceramicware, created the "Ruba Rombic" series in 1928 for the Consolidated Glass Company, a small firm in the Pittsburgh area that had begun producing art glass two years earlier. Unlike the glassware of the larger firms such as Corning and Libbey that was made for a wide audience, Haley's "Ruba Rombic," which was inspired by the glassware that Art Nouveau designer René Lalique introduced at the 1925 Paris exhibition, was a novelty line whose 30 pieces were made of irregular faceted planes of smoked glass. Though praised by some critics for its Cubist look, the line was too eccentric for a mass market, both visually and functionally, and it went out of production after three years.

At the time of the Paris exhibition in 1925, French textile designers continued to inspire their American counterparts, but by 1930 some American designers, mostly women, had begun to introduce their own original designs, which were adopted for fabrics as well as carpets and wallpapers. Few women who worked as textile or carpet designers in the 1920s or 1930s were trained in those fields. Most were skilled artists who found ways to adapt their artistic skills to commercial purposes. Ruth Reeves spent much of the 1920s in Paris,

where she studied with the modernist painter Fernand Léger. In 1930, she became a consultant to the W & J. Sloane furniture store, which produced several block-printed cotton fabrics with her designs. Among them was "Manhattan," a fabric featuring a montage of images—skyscrapers, bridges, offices, speeding cars, laborers, the Statue of Liberty, and even telephone operators—that conveyed a sense of life in a large metropolis. Another block-printed fabric that Reeves produced for W & J. Sloane, entitled "The American Scene," was similar in design to "Manhattan," although the images were all of small-town or rural life. Dense combinations of images characterized many of her designs, which were used to upholster furniture as well as for other purposes, but Reeves also produced fabrics with geometric patterns for similar uses. She worked for a number of textile and carpet manufacturers, but her most ambitious commission was the wall hangings and carpet that she designed for the Grand Foyer at Radio City Music Hall.

Other women who were active as designers of modern textiles or carpets were Ilonka Karasz; Henrietta Reiss (1889–d.o.d. unconfirmed), an English designer whose abstract patterns were printed on silk and also served as designs for rugs; Marguerite Zorach (1887–1968), who had studied painting in Paris; Hazel Burnham Slaughter (1888–1979); and Helen Dryden (1887–1981), who also designed housewares and automobile interiors. The Dupont-Rayon Company, which manufactured different types of rayon, the first artificial fiber, hired well-known designers of textiles including Ilonka Karasz, Ruth Reeves, and Donald Deskey to produce designs for experimental rayon weaves with different weights and textures. Deskey, one of the few men in the field of textile design, created geometric patterns, many derivative of Cubist paintings, for rugs and fabrics, while producing as well some rather ordinary designs that featured images of flowers, vases, and boats.

Among the most novel fabric designs of the period were those that the Stehli Silk Corporation commissioned from the photographer Edward Steichen

(1879–1973) in 1926 and 1927. The company's designs for silk dress fabrics were based on photographs that Steichen made of common objects such as matches and matchboxes, sugar lumps, mothballs, carpet tacks, and eyeglasses. He presented the objects in abstract patterns by photographing them from above, a technique that also produced heavy shadows, which became part of the pattern.

The Origins of American Industrial Design

Following World War I, the United States experienced a severe recession in which 100,000 businesses went bankrupt. Many companies had invested heavily to increase their production capacity and were faced with large inventories that they couldn't move. Besides the collapse of businesses, more than 450,000 farmers lost their land and 5 million people were unemployed. As the new decade progressed, however, the economy revived and the national manufacturing output expanded throughout the 1920s. Despite growing wealth, income was unevenly distributed, with large numbers of people continuing to live below the poverty level. Consumption increased, though primarily among the middle and upper classes. This was due, in part, to advertising strategies intended to persuade the public that the problem facing the country was not overproduction but underconsumption.

Earnest Elmo Calkins (1868–1964), who co-founded the Calkins & Holden advertising agency in 1902, was a leader in promoting the idea of underconsumption. The aim of advertising as he saw it was to persuade the public to spend more money. Calkins was among the first to recognize that design could contribute to this process by making products more attractive and appealing to the customer. He came to this conclusion through his initial belief that modern artists could help to accomplish this by producing more attractive ads.

In a textbook of 1905, *Modern Advertising*, Calkins stated that advertising should do more than simply announce and describe a product. It should also help to arouse a demand for it. He pursued this end by hiring skilled artists, illustrators, and engravers to create modern advertisements for his clients. He then concluded that improvements in package design and finally the design of products themselves were a natural extension of his initial realization that beauty was a quality that could help to sell more goods. In 1929, Calkins & Holden was, in fact, the first advertising agency to establish an Industrial Styling Division, which was headed by a former journalist and editor, Egmont Arens (1888–1966).

In an article of 1927, "Beauty the New Business Tool," which was published in the widely circulated *Atlantic Monthly*, Calkins described how "good taste passed from the advertisement to the package, and from the package to the product, keeping pace with the growing appreciation of taste on the part of the public due to increased culture and sophistication." Though increased sales based on "eye appeal" were the bottom line for Calkins, he advocated a conception of modern product form that countered the prevailing convention of adopting historic styles. "Beauty is original," he wrote. "It is found in the thing itself." He argued against turning a library into a Greek temple or a railway station into a Renaissance palace. In this sense, he continued a line of thought about appropriate design that began with John Ruskin and William Morris, although, unlike them, he believed firmly that a good design should represent "the aesthetic spirit of the age." Guided by Calkins & Holden and other advertising agencies, manufacturers began to understand the value of design and they looked to the advertising agencies to provide them with experts, a practice that continued throughout the 1930s.

Joseph Sinel (1889–1975), an illustrator who emigrated to the United States from New Zealand in 1918, may have been the first to characterize his services as "industrial design," by which he meant drawings of industrial objects used in advertisements. However, Sinel did go on to design products for various manufacturers, thus helping to reinforce the roots of American industrial design in art and illustration. Like him, the leading industrial designers of the late 1920s and 1930s—Norman Bel Geddes, Henry Dreyfuss, Raymond Loewy, and Walter Dorwin Teague—also began as illustrators or else designers for the theater. Bel Geddes (1893–1958) started as a visionary stage designer. Having collaborated with the German theater director Max Reinhardt, who was known for his Berlin spectacles that included crowds of actors, dramatic lighting, and imposing sets, he was equally ambitious in pushing the boundaries of American stagecraft. Before going into design, he was involved with more than 100 plays, films, and other performances that ranged from opera to circuses. Throughout his career as an industrial designer, his flair for drama would serve as both an asset, based on his capacity to conceive and give form to grand visions, and a liability as he gained a reputation for being impractical and unable to deliver viable solutions to a manufacturer's problems.

Though Henry Dreyfuss (1904–1972) worked under Bel Geddes as a stage designer, he adapted more readily to the needs of his manufacturing clients, resisting simple styling solutions and addressing the function of the product as well. Both Raymond Loewy (1893–1986), an émigré from France, and Walter Dorwin Teague started as illustrators. Loewy, who was also trained as an electrical engineer, brought a French Deco style to his work as a fashion illustrator for *Vogue*, *Harper's Bazaar*, and Saks Fifth Avenue, while Teague had a long career as an advertising artist with Calkins & Holden before he became an industrial designer. As an illustrator, Teague was known for his decorative borders, which were based on his studies of dynamic symmetry and French classical ornament.

The Practice of Industrial Design

Industrial design originated in New York, where most of the large advertising agencies were to be found. All the major industrial designers established offices in the city, as did the majority of designers involved

with furniture, textiles, and other modern applied arts. While there was little overlap between the industrial designers and those working in the applied arts, several of the industrial designers were active with AUDAC and showed their work in the exhibitions of industrial design and applied arts at the Metropolitan Museum of Art and elsewhere.

An additional advantage to being in New York was the presence of the many advertising agencies that were in a position to recommend industrial designers to their clients. It was, in fact, through Stanley Resor, president of the J. Walter Thompson Advertising Agency, that Bel Geddes began to work for manufacturers in the late 1920s. The first of the major American industrial designers to establish his own office, which he did in 1927, Bel Geddes undertook various conceptual projects for clients of J. Walter Thompson, ranging from modern furniture for the Simmons Company to redesigning the scales and sketching images of new factory buildings for the Toledo Scale Company. Perhaps the most successful project of his early career, which did go into production, was his design of a sheet metal stove for the Standard Gas Equipment Corporation in 1933. The project introduced an approach to design that went beyond Calkins' advocacy of beauty as the principal quality that a designer could offer a manufacturer. Bel Geddes undertook a survey that revealed ease of cleaning to be the principal concern of female consumers. Based on the survey results, he introduced a sheet-metal skirt that extended to the floor and he provided covers for the burners. His office also overcame the problem of cracking enamel, which had made stove manufacturers reluctant to use painted sheet metal. As a psychological element, Bel Geddes proposed white as the color of the enamel because of its reference to cleanliness, a decision that sharply contrasted with the traditional black of cast iron stoves. Perhaps due to Bel Geddes' design, other manufacturers such as General Electric and Westinghouse began to favor white for kitchen appliances and for many years it was the dominant color for such goods.

Besides the manufacturing and color innovations, Bel Geddes gave the stove a more graceful form, with rounded corners at the edges of each surface and an orderly display of knobs and compartments for broiling and baking as well as storage. He enhanced sales by devising a system of standardized components that could be mixed and matched to create different stove designs. Another innovation associated with the stove was the promotional campaign Bel Geddes devised to sell it as an object of beauty. Each stove bore his monogram and was marketed as an art object as well as an efficient machine. To emphasize the artistic aspect, Standard Gas Equipment featured Bel Geddes as the one responsible for the design.

Though he devised a clean efficient look for the Standard Gas stove and the manufacturer promoted it successfully as a beautiful object, it was Bel Geddes' advocacy of streamlining that more dramatically captured the imagination of the public as well as other designers. He first introduced the concept in his book *Horizons* of 1932. "An object is *streamlined*," he wrote, "when its exterior surface is so designed that upon passing through a fluid such as water or air the object creates the least disturbance in the fluid in the form of eddies or partial vacua tending to produce resistance." Bel Geddes claimed that streamlining would enhance the efficiency of a vehicle's movement because it reduced air resistance, but in fact it became a styling device as it was applied to the design of everything from trains and toasters to brassieres and typefaces. Historian Jeffrey Meikle has written that the term "streamlining" also became detached from its aerodynamic origins and came to signify for some the efficiency of an industrial system that could merge production, distribution, and consumption into a seamless whole. Streamlining represented for others the capacity of American industry to overcome the economic problems that inhibited an effortless flow of goods from factory to consumer. In its most crass sense, as Meikle points out, when applied to product styling, streamlining could render a product contemporary and

suggest the obsolescence of goods by competitors that lacked it.

In *Horizons*, Bel Geddes featured photographs of model trains, planes, automobiles, boats, and also buildings with streamlined forms that he and his staff had created. Of these, his train model was influential in persuading railroads to exchange streamlined designs for the traditional steam locomotives and boxy passenger cars they had previously been using (Fig. 28.09). Bel Geddes intended to shift the public's attention away from the past. The streamlined models in *Horizons* all pointed towards a future of advanced technology that was embodied in forms without reference to history.

There was a precedent for such forms in the literature of science fiction, whose popularity began to spread during the 1920s. The term "science fiction" was invented by writer and publisher Hugo Gernsback (1884–1967), whose first magazine devoted to the genre, *Amazing Stories*, initially appeared in 1926. Subsequently Gernsback published two other magazines, *Science Wonder Stories* and *Air Wonder Stories*, which were combined into a single publication around 1932. Covers and interior illustrations for all these publications by the illustrator Frank R. Paul (1884–1963) included futuristic vehicles, machines, and even entire cities (Plate 44).

Another vision of the future that preceded *Horizons*, though it was formally different from the models in Bel Geddes' book, was German director Fritz Lang's 1925 Expressionist film *Metropolis*, which was set in a city that featured highways stretching between buildings far above the ground. Though its imagery was not comparable to the models of Bel Geddes, *Metropolis* directly influenced the dramatic drawings of skyscrapers that Hugh Ferris (1889–1962), a New York architect and architectural renderer, published in his 1929 book, *The Metropolis of Tomorrow*. Unlike the Bel Geddes models, the forms of Ferris's buildings were not very dissimilar from buildings that one could observe along the New York skyline. However, like Lang's set, their scale exceeded anything that had previously been

Fig. 28.09: Norman Bel Geddes, model of a streamlined train, *Horizons*, 1932. Harry Ransom Center, The University of Texas at Austin, Image Courtesy of the Edith Lutyens and Norman Bel Geddes Foundation.

built, and in some drawings, Ferris included elevated highways as Lang had done in his film.

It is not clear that Bel Geddes drew directly on any of the aforementioned precedents, but they provided a context for turning the public's attention towards the future, where people might expect to find a new world of streamlined designs. Bel Geddes' vision was also disseminated by other, more widely distributed, publications such as *Popular Mechanics*, which periodically featured illustrations of the stream-lined vehicles that he and other consultant designers envisioned and sometimes designed.

Though Henry Dreyfuss, who established a design office in 1928—a year after Bel Geddes—adopted streamlining for the railroad rolling stock he designed in the late 1930s, he barely applied it to his earlier designs for products, preferring instead to allow the design to emerge from his analysis of what was needed for the overall improvement of a product. It

should be noted that the leading consultant designers were known primarily for their redesigns of existing products rather than their inventions of new ones. Among Dreyfuss's early commissions was his redesign of the General Electric refrigerator. Designers of prior models had preserved the condenser on top as an indispensable icon and even Bel Geddes, whom GE hired around 1930, could not persuade the company to dispense with it. By the time Dreyfuss became a consultant to GE in 1933, the company was ready to change and the Dreyfuss office created a clean white box that concealed the condenser and eliminated the cabriolet legs that had been adopted from historic chair designs.

Both Bel Geddes' Standard Gas stove and Dreyfuss's GE refrigerator adopted a simplified modern visual language for domestic appliances and other industrial products, which Dreyfuss later characterized as "cleanlining." Although the break with historic styles had been made a few years earlier in Europe, modernism was applied there mainly to furniture and lighting rather than appliances such as stoves and refrigerators. Following the lead of Bel Geddes and Dreyfuss, other American manufacturers of radios, cameras, vacuum cleaners, and kitchen appliances would readily adopt the style.

In 1933, a year before the GE refrigerator went to market, Sears Roebuck hired the Dreyfuss office to design a new high-end washing machine that would simultaneously help the company overcome its reputation as a mail-order supplier of goods for farmers, while also introducing a more expensive product that could evade the price wars with other manufacturers

Fig. 28.10: Henry Dreyfuss, Toperator washing machine, 1933. © 2014. Cooper-Hewitt, National Design Museum, Smithsonian Institution/Art Resource, NY/Scala, Florence.

of inexpensive washing machines. Dreyfuss designed a new cleanlined machine that he called the Toperator because the controls were located on the wringer arm above the tub (Fig. 28.10). As he would subsequently do with the GE refrigerator, Dreyfuss concealed the machine's motor in a single shell, with the tub thus giving the machine a smooth attractive appearance that was enhanced by a blue-green enamel shell with chrome rings around it. Just as Standard Gas had capitalized on Bel Geddes' name, so did Sears seek to enhance the prestige of the Toperator by publicly attributing it to Dreyfuss.

Both the Toperator and the GE refrigerator combined styling with mechanical redesign, although styling was the stronger component of each project, However, Dreyfuss' work for Bell Telephone Laboratories demonstrated more clearly how an industrial designer could also work closely with a company's engineers. In 1930, Dreyfuss began his collaboration with Bell Labs by analyzing consumer reactions to its current designs and making recommendations for improving their appearance. This eventually developed into a commission to design what became Bell's Model 302 desk phone, which went into production in 1937 (Fig. 28.11). Dreyfus built on Jean Heiberg's 1930 design for Sweden's Ericsson company, itself a significant advance compared to the awkward proportions of Bell's "French Phone" of 1927, which was the first desk phone to combine the speaker and microphone in a single hand piece. Collaborating with Bell's engineers, Dreyfuss refined both the base and the handset of the Heiberg model, which improved its appearance and function at the same time. Consequently the Model 302 remained Bell's standard desk telephone until around 1950, when it was replaced with a newer model that the Dreyfuss office also designed.

The idea of enclosing the mechanical parts of a machine in a sculpted casing, which became a standard technique of American industrial designers, may well have been introduced by Raymond Loewy in his redesign of the Gestetner duplicator in 1929.

Fig. 28.11: Henry Dreyfuss, Bell desk telephone, Model 302, 1937. Yale University Art Gallery.

Sigmund Gestetner, who met Loewy at a London dinner party, commissioned him to redesign his mimeograph machine within five days. Loewy, who had some training in engineering before he started as an illustrator, analyzed the machine with its many exposed parts and subsequently encased them in a single shell. When the machine was manufactured in 1933, the shell consisted of Bakelite, which was considered to be the first plastic material made of synthetic resins. Like the designs of other consultants, Loewy's redesign of the mimeograph machine improved both its physical appearance and its mechanical functioning.

Based on his success with Gestetner, Loewy began to seek other clients. For two years he supervised radio cabinet design for Westinghouse. He also created fabric designs for Shelton Looms and entered the difficult field of automobile manufacturing by contributing to the design of the 1934 Hupmobile. Around this time, Loewy produced a widely published series of drawings that showed how different objects from telephones and ships to automobiles and dresses would morph over time from traditional versions to streamlined ones.

Like Bel Geddes, Dreyfuss, and Teague, Loewy was adept at self-promotion and presented a carefully crafted image of a designer in the mock-up of a design office that he created with the stage designer Lee Simonson for the Metropolitan Museum of Art's Contemporary American Industrial Art exhibition of 1934. A photograph of the office depicts Loewy as a businessman dapperly dressed in a dark suit. He is seated on a chrome-framed ledge and is surrounded by metal furniture. On a pedestal is a model of the Hupmobile and on the wall are drawings for a stream-lined ship. While this was an effective representation for clients who were less concerned with how new designs came to be than with the assurance that they were acquiring something of value, in fact it concealed one of the consultant designers' greatest accomplishments—their organization of multidisciplinary offices where engineers, architects, draftsmen, and model makers produced the drawings and models for products that in Loewy's words ranged "from a lipstick to a steamship."

In 1935, Sears Roebuck introduced its new Coldspot refrigerator (Fig. 28.12), which Loewy created after securing a commission from the company in 1932 to redesign an outmoded boxy model. Loewy brought his nascent experience in the automobile industry to bear on the project and produced a new version whose shape was slightly rounded but decorated with vertical ribbing on the front and a chrome strip on the side of the door. The lead designer on the project was actually Clare Hodgman (1911–1992), who had worked previously for Harley Earl at General Motors and adapted what he learned in GM's automobile styling section to the design of consumer products. Inside, the storage boxes were neatly arranged and decorated as well with chrome strips. Buoyed by the success of the Coldspot, Sears executives adopted the auto industry's model of "planned obsolescence," following the annual automobile model changes that Alfred Sloan, President of General Motors, pioneered. For the following three years, Loewy introduced changes in the Coldspot every year, a strategy that, as Jeffrey Meikle points out, reduced the drama of industrial design from producing

Fig. 28.12: Raymond Loewy and Clare Hodgman, Coldspot refrigerator, 1935. akg-images.

sweeping changes in an outmoded product to making modest annual adjustments in those that had already achieved success.

Loewy's involvement in other industries did not replicate his succession of annual changes for Sears. In 1937, he picked up International Harvester, a well-known manufacturer of farm equipment, as a new client. Neither International Harvester nor John Deere, a rival farm equipment producer for whom Henry Dreyfuss consulted, was known for bold designs, nor were, in fact, any of their rivals in a market where efficient function and price overrode aesthetic concerns. Loewy's redesign of International Harvester's cream separator provided an attractive casing on a pedestal base for a machine that had previously consisted of exposed parts that were both dangerous and unsanitary. He also helped the company compete against the Fordson, the first mass-produced tractor produced by Henry Ford. Loewy redesigned International Harvester's Farmall tractor by encasing the fuel tank, engine, and radiator

in a streamlined housing, a design that also competed with Dreyfuss' proposed tractor design for John Deere.

One quality that distinguished the leading industrial designers was their ability to think comprehensively about a client's needs. Besides the equipment the Loewy office redesigned for International Harvester, the designers also updated the company's logotype, redesigned the packaging for the myriad replacement parts it distributed, and created clean modern designs for a range of modular International Harvester Servicenters, where new products were sold.

Loewy first recognized retail space design as a distinct activity in 1936 when he established a new division for store planning and design in his office. Headed by William T. Snaith (1907–1978), an architect, stage designer, and designer of interiors, the division employed a number of draftsmen such as Gordon Bunschaft (1909–1990) and Minoru Yamasaki (1912–1986), who later went on to distinguished careers as architects. An early accomplishment of the division was the design of a suburban department store on Long Island for Lord & Taylor, which was considered to be the first in the United States. Subsequent clients included many major department stores on both sides of the Atlantic.

The fourth of the major industrial designers was Walter Dorwin Teague. In their 1936 book, *Art and the Machine*, Sheldon and Martha Cheney characterized Teague as "a typical present-day businessman," contrasting his matter-of-fact approach to design with Geddes' vast plans "involving many and complex factors." The business model Teague offered his clients featured improved product appearance and serviceability as well as increased economy of manufacture. He clearly described his methods, which included studies of production and marketing, and he outlined the steps in "design creation" from preliminary sketches to completed models.

Teague, a former advertising illustrator, began to work for his first manufacturing client, Eastman Kodak, in 1927. The company had obtained his name from Richard Bach at the Metropolitan Museum of Art, and Teague helped Kodak convert their range of cameras from plain black boxes to stylish objects. In addition, Kodak retained Teague to redesign its logo, packaging, showrooms, and exhibitions. He went on to work for many manufacturers of heaters, radiators, office equipment, and other machines, which his staff endowed with clean modern forms.

From Le Corbusier, Teague took the idea that there could be one ideal form for a product, which, if discovered, would not need to change. Therefore, once he had introduced an attractive design he was reluctant to make further changes, although he was obliged to do so when clients believed that a continual stream of new models would enhance sales.

In a speech to professional colleagues in 1925, while he was still an illustrator, Teague had urged them to consider the close relation between all the arts—buildings, furniture, fashion, and the mundane objects of daily life—which he believed ought to display a unity of style that was characteristic of their historic moment. Perhaps it was this belief that motivated his own involvement with many forms of design from retail spaces and facades to exhibitions. In fact, Teague was the first of the major designers to establish a reputation in the exhibit field. He did so initially through the exhibits he designed for the Ford Motor Company, beginning with Ford's pavilion at the 1933 Century of Progress Exhibition in Chicago. Teague's firm described their exhibit work to clients as "visual dramatization" or "industrial showmanship" and, on the basis of the Ford exhibits, attracted other clients including Texaco, United States Steel, Eastman Kodak, and the National Cash Register Company. Though not considered to be the visionary that Bel Geddes was, Teague, as a member of the Board of Design for the 1939 World's Fair in New York, nonetheless helped shift the theme of the fair from a celebration of America's past to the "World of Tomorrow."

William Lescaze (1896–1969), who came to the United States from Switzerland in 1920, was the rare architect to undertake the kind of broad commission on which the consultant designers thrived. He mainly designed schools, homes, and housing developments, but he contributed to the design of at least one large office building, for which he also designed interior furnishings, clocks, and even a desk set. Lescaze worked mainly in the style of the European modernists and it was this approach that appealed to William Paley, president of the Columbia Broadcasting System, who wanted a modern "look" for his budding radio network. Lescaze began a long collaboration with CBS in 1934, when he was hired to convert an existing New York theater into a radio broadcasting facility. Besides the studio, this also involved the design of a microphone housing and a complete visual identity program. Following Lescaze's design of the initial broadcast facility, Paley asked him to design a new building for CBS, which was not constructed although the architect was subsequently able to design a new broadcast facility for CBS in Hollywood. Unlike the consultant designers, Lescaze worked primarily as an architect, but the CBS commission enabled him to engage with other aspects of design, thus providing a contrast to the major consultant designers who moved from smaller objects to architecture rather than the other way around.

Others among the first industrial designers in New York besides the aforementioned Joseph Sinel included Lurelle Guild (1898–1985), who studied fine art and began his career as an illustrator of interiors for fashion magazines. Once he began to work as an industrial designer, Guild provided product sketches for many clients, claiming at one point that he redesigned 1,000 products a year. He was also a skilled metalworker and designed numerous accessories for the Chase Brass and Copper Company as well as a group of aluminum pots, kettles, bowls, pitchers, and vases for Alcoa that sold widely. In the New York showroom that Guild designed for Alcoa in 1936, he broadened the company's promotion of aluminum by incorporating the material into the showroom itself, notably its lighting fixtures, furniture, and display stands.

Others like George Switzer (dates unconfirmed) and Egmont Arens were specialists in packaging. John Vassos (1898–1985) moved between illustration, packaging, and the design of products and interiors. He is probably best known for the books such as *Contempo* and *Ultimo: An Imaginative Narration of Life Under the Earth* that he wrote and illustrated in a Deco style, but in 1932 he designed a turnstile for the Perey Company of New York that was first used at the Brooklyn Museum and then at the 1933 Century of Progress exhibition in Chicago. It became a standard for the turnstile industry, while also lowering Perey's manufacturing costs and significantly increasing sales.

Industrial Design outside New York

Fueled in part by the publicity that New York designers like Bel Geddes and Dreyfuss were attracting for their products, the practice of industrial design began to spread, particularly in the Midwest. In Chicago, the two large mail-order suppliers, Sears Roebuck and Montgomery Ward, had become conscious of design by the early 1930s. At Sears, the ability to produce merchandise of good quality at a low price became a problem after World War I. Managers continued to discover poor-quality goods in various departments and the company instituted a process of quality control. This was difficult to maintain as most of Sears' products came from outside suppliers, although the company did begin to do more in-house design.

As Sears began to diversify its distribution from mail order to retail outlets, it developed protocols for space planning in its stores that included directional signs, interior display equipment, and fixtures such as lighting. In 1932, Sears created its own Store Planning and Display Department, which was headed for years by a company employee, Les Janes (dates unconfirmed). Sears also created a design department, more than likely prompted by the success of rival Montgomery Ward's Bureau of Design, which was established in 1931. In 1934, Sears hired Jack Morgan (1903–1986) as its chief product designer. Morgan had

come from General Motors where he conceived the first automobile bumper that was integrated into a total car design. At Sears he mainly designed appliances but was also responsible for a pair of streamlined roller skates.

The long-time director of Montgomery Ward's Bureau of Design was Ann Swainson (1900–1955), the first female executive at the company. Swainson, who was born in Sweden, studied fine and applied arts at Columbia University and was the director of design at the Chase Brass and Copper Company in Connecticut before Montgomery Ward hired her away. In Chicago she assembled a sizeable staff of architects and designers of products and packaging. Initially they were charged with evaluating the quality and appearance of the myriad items that Montgomery Ward purchased from thousands of outside suppliers, but they began to redesign the company's own products as well.

Swainson's first big challenge at Montgomery Ward was the redesign of the company's mail order catalog, a project that took five years to complete. A major change was the replacement of the antiquated stock woodcuts—initially with metal plates but eventually with modern photographs that included live models. With the introduction of the new catalog, profits increased exponentially.

By 1935, the Bureau of Design had a staff of 18 designers who worked on products, and 14 more who did packaging. The Bureau staff redesigned everything from radios and furniture to refrigerators, clothing, and tableware. Much of Swainson's job was supervising the work of her staff, a task not dissimilar to a consultant designer like Walter Dorwin Teague, who devoted his main energy to soliciting new business while his staff designers produced the initial sketches and prototypes for his clients. Among the designers who worked for Swainson and then went on to establish their own industrial design offices or head those of other companies were Dave Chapman (1909–1978), who was the first Head of Product Design at Montgomery Ward before he left to start his own practice; Richard Latham (1920–1991), who left Ward to join Raymond

Loewy's Chicago office after World War II; Joseph Palma (1909–2007), who became the Bureau's Head Designer after Dave Chapman departed in 1934; and Ellen Manderfield (1916–1999), a former Supervisor of Styling at the Colonial Radio Company (later known as Sylvania), who designed hundreds of products for Montgomery Ward between 1947 and 1951.

Prior to Montgomery Ward's inauguration of its Bureau of Design, other large companies established their own in-house design departments. Beginning in 1927, George Sakier (1897–1988) began designing bathroom fixtures for the American Radiator and Standard Sanitary Corporation, where he became director of the company's own Bureau of Design. Trained as both an artist and an engineer, Sakier not only created modern bathroom fixtures but by 1933 he also designed complete prefabricated bathroom units of which thousands were sold.

In the early 1920s, General Electric established a committee on "product styling" and in 1928 Ray Patten (1897–1948) joined the company to supervise the design of domestic appliances. Initially the work of his staff was called "Appearance Design," a name that was not changed to "Industrial Design" until 1948. Among the innovative products to come from the General Electric design group in the 1930s was the "Unit Kitchen," which the company began to market in 1937. Though such cooking laboratories had their precedents in Georg Muche's Haus am Horn at the Bauhaus exhibition of 1923 and most noticeably in Grete Schütte-Lihotzky's Frankfurt kitchen of 1926, the GE kitchen upgraded those precedents with a host of new appliances including, besides the refrigerator, a garbage disposal unit and a dishwasher. All were produced as modules so they could be arranged in a variety of spaces.

Donald Dohner (1897–1943), who had previously been a consultant to the Westinghouse Electric Company in Pittsburgh while teaching at the Carnegie Institute of Technology, became director of design in the Westinghouse engineering department around 1930. Unlike Ann Swainson at Montgomery Ward, Dohner was directly engaged with the company's engineering staff and helped to develop a number of engineering solutions for electrical appliances. This was in sharp contrast to the way engineers at many other companies dismissed the industrial designers as "style and color boys."

Among the designers who established their own offices outside New York in the early 1930s were Harold Van Doren (1895–1957) and John Gordon Rideout (1898–1951), who opened an office in Toledo, Ohio, in 1933. Possibly the first consultant design office in the Midwest, Van Doren and Rideout attracted a large number of local and regional clients including the Toledo Scale Company, which had earlier rejected Norman Bel Geddes' bold proposals for product and factory designs. For another Toledo firm, the American National Company, they designed a series of children's scooters, wagons, and tricycles with streamlined forms, which went on the market in the early 1930s at about the time streamlining was first applied to various forms of transportation.

According to Sheldon and Martha Cheney, Harold Van Doren was the first designer to experiment with colored plastic materials as exemplified in Van Doren and Rideout's Air-King Midget Radio of 1933. Made of a synthetic called Plaskon with additional metal and glass parts, the radio possessed a Deco skyscraper form, which demonstrated the possibility of molding plastic into myriad fluid shapes. Van Doren and Rideout had previously adopted the skyscraper icon for several scales they designed for the Toledo Scale Company in 1931. The same icon applied to a radio was a radical departure from the wooden cathedral shape of competitors such as Atwater Kent, Crosley, Philco, RCA, and General Electric. The single-piece housing of the Air-King reduced manufacturing costs and its pea green color helped to boost sales by more than 300 percent.

In Milwaukee, Wisconsin, Brooks Stevens (1911–1995) opened an industrial design office in 1933, readily adopting the emphasis on product styling which he believed would appeal to "Mrs. Consumer," a term he used with clients to acknowledge the housewife's purchasing authority. Stevens did not originate the strategy of producing new product models on a continuing basis, but he is credited with coining the term "planned obsolescence," which he defined as instilling in the customer the desire to buy something new a little sooner than would otherwise be necessary.

Though Stevens gained wider recognition after World War II, he designed a number of commercially successful products before the war such as the Steam-O-Matic—the first domestic steam iron—and the Hamilton Clothes Dryer, a recent invention for which Stevens created a white box with rounded corners, similar to Bel Geddes' stove for American Standard. But he was not a formal purist and he added fluted vertical panels to the dryer. These functioned like curtains on either side of a window that enabled the housewife—Stevens' envisioned user—to see the laundry tossing in the machine. One interpretation of this design element was that it reinforced a housewife's feelings of service to her family by revealing the drying process in action.

R. Buckminster Fuller: A Maverick Designer

R. Buckminster Fuller's career as an inventor and designer ran counter to that of the consultant designers. He opposed the belief in planned obsolescence with a philosophy of design that was based on an economical use of the world's resources. In the 1920s and 1930s, few in the design field were concerned with the issues of responsible environmental stewardship that Fuller expressed in his writings and put into practice in his designs.

In 1927, as a response to several family tragedies, Fuller vowed to develop "an art and science of generalized and anticipatory design competence" that would be dedicated to design for social needs. To this end, he established several of his own companies, although he

also collaborated with various manufacturers. Some of these collaborations were experimental but a few of Fuller's designs did reach the market, notably his geodesic dome, which became extremely successful in the post-war years.

In his 4–D Timelock essays of 1927, Fuller first revealed his penchant for global design solutions by introducing his World Town Plan, which advocated advanced scientific and technical means for resolving the world's housing problems. The same year, he designed his first Dymaxion House, which expressed his belief in a "maximum gain of advantage from minimal energy input." It consisted of modular elements with floors that were suspended from a central core (Fig. 28.13). The house could be air delivered by a dirigible and erected in a single day on a prepared foundation. It featured many labor-saving innovations that later became part of mainstream housing construction. Basing his ideas for water usage on ships and airplanes, Fuller devised an efficient system of water filtering and circulation as well as one for waste disposal. In 1931, he developed for the American Radiator Company his first mass-produced bathroom and toilet unit, which he reworked in 1936 with support from the Phelps-Dodge Corporation.

As part of his Dymaxion House design, Fuller was also concerned with a means of transport that could deliver such a structure to a desired building site. While in the U.S. Navy during World War I, he devised a plan for a vertical take-off aircraft, which he continued to develop in the early 1930s. As a first stage in creating such a vehicle, he designed the Dymaxion Car, which had a teardrop shape and three wheels, two in the front and one in the back for steering (Fig. 28.14). Although the car could achieve a speed of more than 100 miles an hour and could carry 11 passengers, it did not get beyond the prototype stage.

Fuller also continued his interest in housing with the development of his Wichita House, a circular dwelling whose floors were suspended from a central mast like the earlier Dymaxion House. He incorporated

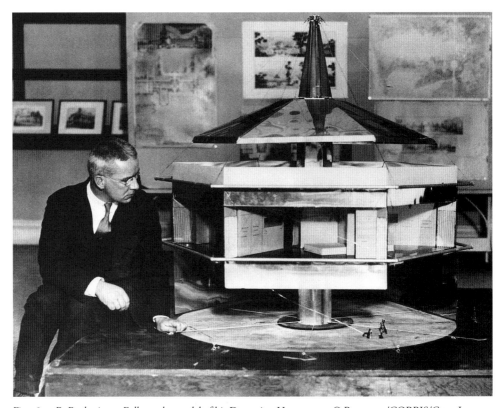

Fig. 28.13: R. Buckminster Fuller and a model of his Dymaxion House, 1930. © Bettmann/CORBIS/Getty Images.

Fig. 28.14: R. Buckminster Fuller, Dymaxion Car, 1933. © Bettmann/ CORBIS/Getty Images.

some of his principles for industrial housing in his Dymaxion Deployment Unit of 1940–1941, which he created in association with the Butler Manufacturing Company. Its purpose was to convert Butler's corrugated grain storage bins into dwelling units. Designed for temporary wartime use as radar stations, hospitals, and dormitories, more than 1,000 were produced before production was curtailed due to a reallocation of steel for higher priority projects.

In essays that Fuller published in his 1938 book *Nine Chains to the Moon* and in surveys he carried out for *Fortune* magazine, he put forth numerous plans for reusing industrial materials while also devising a World Energy Map which was based on a new cartographic projection that facilitated the correlation of population distribution with available energy. Among designers in the 1930s, Fuller was almost alone in his concern for efficient energy use and industrial recycling, issues that would not become central to the design community for years to come.

Women and People of Color as Designers

The chauvinism evident in the way Stevens and other male designers gendered the female consumer worked in two ways for women who aspired to enter the industrial design profession. In some instances it led manufacturers to believe that women designers would have a better sense than men of what their customers wanted and in fact this attitude did result in a few women such as Ann Swainson, Ellen Manderfield, and Irene Pasinski (1923–2002), a graduate of the Carnegie Institute of Technology's industrial design program, developing successful careers in the field. While also successful, Belle Kogan (1902–2000), who opened her own New York office in 1932, described the difficulties she faced as a female designer from some antagonistic manufacturers and skeptical engineers who did not believe a woman had the mechanical ability to design a successful product. Few women had Kogan's determination and many went instead into related fields such as interior, textile, or fabric design, where a woman's sensibility was considered an advantage. Kogan hired other women to work in her studio and is thought to be the first to hire an African-American designer.

If there were few women industrial designers during the interwar years, there were almost no people of color. This had nothing to do with design ability but rather with access to a world of social relations on which design practice depended. Blacks, for example, had long worked in the decorative and mechanical arts (see Chapter 13) but, with rare exceptions, did not have access to manufacturing and sales facilities that would have enabled their work to reach a wide audience. Writing in the February 1940 issue of *Opportunity*, the monthly magazine of the National Urban League, Vernon Winslow (d.o.b. unconfirmed–1993) praised the black artists who had created the "Negro Renaissance," but noted that "where the messages of the white artist were recaptured by white industry, ours fell upon an impoverished helpless group without industrial ownership or participation." What was lacking, according to Winslow, was the means of "industrial translation." In the white world, he wrote, painters could contribute to commercial photography or advertising design while sculptors could assist in designing automobiles or myriad products such as electric irons, radios, or telephones. By contrast, Negro artists were confined to painting, and sculptors to making allegorical figures. Winslow saw a potential breakthrough in the Community Art Centers that had been founded as part of Franklin D. Roosevelt's Works Project Administration (WPA). In these centers, as well as in WPA workshops for the production of posters and furniture, blacks and whites could work side by side, a phenomenon that was not realized at the time in the commercial worlds of industrial and graphic design.

Blacks were, however, active during the 1920s and 1930s as independent inventors because there were no social barriers to obstruct their initiatives. They could obtain patents by submitting the appropriate drawings and consequently sell their patents or find means to market their products themselves. The same was true for women, who had an extensive history of inventing, beginning in the early years of the American republic.

Among African-Americans, Garrett Morgan (1877–1963), an all-around inventor, initially became wealthy as the publisher of an African-American newspaper. One of his first patented inventions was a gas mask that prevented a rescuer from breathing smoke or noxious fumes when entering a room filled with either. He also invented a traffic signal, which was a pole unit in a T-shape that featured three positions, Stop, Go, and a third position that halted traffic in all directions so that pedestrians could safely cross the street. This was a variation on the familiar traffic light, which was first introduced in Detroit by William Potts in 1920. What Morgan added was the possibility of controlling the light from a distance with a mechanical link. He eventually sold his invention to General Electric for $40,000, thus participating in a familiar practice whereby large companies purchased patents from independent inventors for modest sums and then profited from them many times over.

Women of all ethnic backgrounds were also active as inventors. African-American inventors in the 1920s included Mary Jane Reynolds (dates unconfirmed), who patented a gear mechanism for hoisting and loading heavy articles. In 1928, Marjorie Stuart Joyner (1896–1994) received a patent for a permanent wave machine, consisting of a set of thin rods hooked to a hair dryer hood. Joyner ceded the patent rights to the Madame C. J. Walker Manufacturing Company, which used the device extensively in its chain of hair salons, thus ensuring sizeable revenue for the inventor.

One difference between white and black women inventors is that white women had access to positions in major corporations that women of color did not. Beulah Louise Henry (1887–1973), a white woman who lived in New York, was often referred to as the "Lady Edison." Though she was hired by a number of companies in the 1950s and 1960s to develop products for them, she did so after having patented many inventions herself and having run several of her own companies. Henry has been credited with as many as 110 inventions during her lifetime. The first in 1912 was a vacuum ice cream freezer, while the second and third were a handbag and a parasol with detachable cloth covers in different colors. Henry founded the Henry Umbrella and Parasol Company to sell her parasols, and established a second company, B. L. Henry Company, to market other inventions, which included a spring-limbed doll, sponges that held soap in the middle, and the machine that made the sponges. In 1930 she patented a device she called a "protograph," that produced an original typed document and four copies without carbon paper.

At General Electric, Maude Adams (1872–1953) developed an incandescent bulb that was used widely in color film projectors and made other improvements

to projector lamps for showing color films. Edith Clarke (1883–1959), also working at General Electric, secured a patent in 1925 for a calculator that monitored and predicted the performance of electrical transmission lines and for other devices as well. Women produced additional inventions during this period in fields as diverse as home maintenance, agriculture, and medicine. It was thus not for lack of talent that women and people of color were not more active as industrial designers but rather lack of opportunity arising from different kinds of prejudice.

The Growth of the Design Profession

Despite restrictions on who could become a designer, the industrial design profession grew dramatically from the late 1920s to World War II, when many designers were enlisted in the war effort. In one case after another, design had been shown to not only improve the appearance of products and frequently their function as well but also to enable them to be manufactured more efficiently and less expensively and above all to increase sales, often by considerable amounts.

Bel Geddes' *Horizons* was perhaps the first publication that sought to explain to the public what a designer did. Following Earnest Elmo Calkins, who characterized industrial design as an act of styling or making products visually attractive, Bel Geddes described the industrial designer as an artist who could create beauty in the commercial world. "Just as surely as the artists of the fourteenth century are remembered by their cathedrals," he wrote, "so will those of the twentieth be remembered for their factories and the products of those factories."

Eight years later, when Harold Van Doren published *Industrial Design: A Practical Guide*, the profession had already moved through a romantic phase and was becoming more integrated into the manufacturing process. Van Doren, who had been an assistant museum director and an art editor before becoming a designer, was no stranger to the fine arts but he was careful to adopt a business-like tone by identifying mass production and sales competition as the two strongest reasons for hiring a designer.

While product appearance remained paramount for Van Doren, he took great pains to demystify the designer's job by elaborating in detail the techniques involved in producing renderings, clay models, and mechanical drawings. He also equated streamlining with a broad definition of modern form instead of presenting it as a visionary metaphor. "The streamlined tub today," he wrote, "means the modern laundry tub." Discounting the possible efficiency that streamlining might bring to the design of moving vehicles or airplanes, "nonfunctional streamlining" now characterized standard techniques of designing—covering exposed mechanical parts, substituting buttons for levers, and visually relating control panels and dials more effectively to the mechanical functions they enabled. However, curves and rounded corners could also contribute to an appealing product form. Given Van Doren's integration of streamlining into a general vocabulary of visual techniques for the industrial designer, it is not surprising that after World War II, streamlining as Bel Geddes had dramatically propounded it in the early 1930s lost its luster although it remained useful in a functional sense for some forms of transport, notably airplanes and trains.

Transportation Design
Automobiles

During the interwar period, the production and purchase of automobiles grew rapidly. The United States became a society in which large numbers of people owned cars and, in fact, their growing use had a great impact on the economy from the building of roads to the spread of gasoline stations and the construction of suburban homes. By 1929, American manufacturers controlled 85 percent of the world's automobile production, while three large companies—Ford, General Motors, and Chrysler—dominated the domestic market.

In 1921, Henry Ford, who had pioneered the mass production of automobiles, retained the lion's

share of American sales, garnering 55 percent, which far exceeded the 12 percent of Ford's nearest rival, General Motors. By 1924, however, Ford's sales began to decline, largely because Henry Ford refused to change the design of the Model T, while other companies, notably GM, began to introduce annual model changes that proved more attractive to the public. Ford's sales of more than two million cars in 1923 started to decline after that as rivals manufactured models that were more in tune with what the public wanted. Notable among the changes the public preferred was a car with a closed body and a more sculptural design.

Henry Ford was slow to introduce a successor to the Model T. He was also reluctant to hire outside designers, preferring to maintain control over design changes himself. Nonetheless, he was a far-sighted entrepreneur who had diversified into multiple businesses by the end of World War I. He was a master of vertical integration—the coordination of all elements required for the production and distribution of a product—and made this manifest in the construction of his gigantic River Rouge plant, which he began in 1917 and completed in 1928. River Rouge was a vast enterprise, which consisted of 93 buildings and occupied a space one mile long and one and a half miles wide. To transport materials within the huge complex, Ford installed more than 120 miles of conveyor belts, 100 miles of railroad track, and 15 miles of paved roads. Albert Kahn (1869–1942), an architect whose firm specialized in industrial architecture, designed a number of the buildings using a technique of reinforced concrete construction that replaced wood in many factory structures.

Ford's purpose in creating River Rouge, an enterprise that required more than 100,000 employees, was to control all the resources that were required to produce an automobile from the processing of raw materials to the finished product. Ford built a coke oven to manufacture iron, which was then poured into molds to make engine blocks, cylinder heads, and other automotive parts. Steelmaking furnaces and rolling mills were constructed in 1926. With the completion of tool and die plants and facilities for making tires, casting engines, producing transmissions and radiators, and manufacturing other necessary parts for his cars, Ford was able to eliminate external suppliers, thus reducing the cost of parts and maintaining control of their quality. Innovations also resulted from this strategy. His glass plant, for example, produced the first laminated safety glass to be used in a low-priced car.

More than 15 million Model Ts had been manufactured by the time Ford stopped production in 1927. That year the company began to draw up plans for the Model A, which was so named to signify a new beginning. Henry Ford spearheaded the mechanical design himself, communicating with an army of engineers. He left the body styling to his son Edsel (1893–1943), then president of the Ford Motor Company, who created the car as a smaller version of the Lincoln, a luxury vehicle that Ford had been manufacturing since it bought the Lincoln Motor Company in 1922 (Fig. 28.15).

Edsel was assisted in the design of the Model A by Józef Galamb (1881–1955), an engineer who had emigrated to the United States from Hungary in 1905. Galamb joined Ford that year and subsequently became

the company's chief engineer. He played a role in the planning of company's production line in 1913 and designed many of the parts for the Model T. He worked as well on the design of the Fordson tractor before assisting Edsel with the Model A. Subsequently he had a hand in the design of the Ford V-8, a further development of the Model A, which was produced in 1932.

The Model A was successful as a mass-market car, although it was more noteworthy for its price and mechanical features than its styling. Nonetheless by the 1930s Ford had dropped to third place in sales behind General Motors and Chrysler. Lower sales in the United States were compensated, however, by a strong market abroad. In the interwar years, Ford built an international empire that expanded previous factories in England and Germany to include assembly plants in such widespread nations as Turkey, Romania, Australia, and New Zealand. The Ford Motor Company also had strong sales in Latin America, where it remained significantly ahead of General Motors and Chrysler.

Edsel Ford had a better opportunity to exercise his flair for styling through the production of the Lincoln, which he developed into a premier luxury car that competed successfully with its closest rivals, Cadillac and Packard. In 1939 he introduced the Mercury, a lower-end luxury car that was produced to compete with GM's Buick rather than the Cadillac. Following the lead of Alfred Sloan at General Motors, Edsel established a styling department, which was headed by E. T. (Bob) Gregorie (1908–2002), who joined the company in 1932. However, the studio functioned much more informally than did the considerably larger one at General Motors. Gregorie was in charge of all Ford's design, which ranged from automobiles to buses, trucks, and tractors. He remained with Ford until 1946 when he left because top management chose to model a revamped styling department after Harley Earl's at General Motors.

With a previous background in yacht design and a brief tenure under Harley Earl at General Motors, Gregorie worked on the Lincoln Zephyr, Ford's version

Fig. 28.15: Ford Motor Company, Model A, 1927. © Will Daniel/Alamy.

of a streamlined car, which was introduced to the market in 1936, two years after the more highly touted but less successful Chrysler Airflow (Fig. 28.16). The Zephyr was based on a design known as the Dream Car that the Dutch designer John Tjaarda (1897–1962) had created for the Briggs Manufacturing Company, a Detroit firm that supplied Ford and Lincoln with auto bodies. Trained as an aeronautical engineer, Tjaarda had previously designed custom car bodies in California and came to specialize in elegant stylized designs for luxury cars. Briggs hired him to run its recently established design center after he worked briefly, like Gregorie, for Harley Earl at General Motors.

The Briggs Dream Car bore some resemblance to Ferdinand Porsche's Kleinauto or Type 32, which became a prototype for the Volkswagen. Its engine was in the rear and it had a gently curved body with low-slung windows and rounded fenders that hid the back wheels. Although Tjaarda's background in aeronautical design may have contributed to the car's curved form, the Dream Car was not strictly aerodynamic in the sense that Bel Geddes projected in the car models he published in *Horizons*.

Gregorie incorporated many features of Tjaarda's prototype into the design of the Zephyr, which was named after the Chicago, Burlington, and Quincy Railroad's streamlined train of 1934. Among the Zephyr's mechanical changes were a shift of the engine from the rear to the front and the capacity for higher speed and lower fuel consumption. Gregorie's strongest design innovation was raising the hood and supporting it with a swept-back metal grille. The Zephyr was a success and remained in production until 1942 when Ford shifted to wartime work.

Just as the Briggs Dream Car had been the prototype for the Lincoln Zephyr, the latter played a similar role in the development of the Lincoln Continental, whose design Gregorie also supervised. Manufactured originally at the request of Edsel Ford as a custom car for his own use, it attracted sufficient attention to go into limited production in 1939. Edsel was a great admirer of European luxury cars, hence the name "Continental," and he provided sketches from a European trip on which the styling department based its initial clay model of the car. Longer and lower than any of its rivals, the Continental was also distinguished from them by its extended hood, curved sculptural body, and rear tire mount, which became a mark of style that other manufacturers emulated. Unlike the mass-produced Ford, the Continental was a custom car

Fig. 28.16: Bob Gregorie, Lincoln Zephyr, 1936. Hulton Archive/Getty Images.

that was made almost entirely by hand even though its body rested on an adapted Zephyr chassis.

Ford's strongest rival, William Durant (1861–1947) began in 1908 with the ownership of Buick and built up General Motors (GM) initially. He subsequently acquired or helped to establish in fairly rapid succession a string of other automobile manufacturers—Oldsmobile, Cadillac, Elmore, Oakland (later known as Pontiac), and Chevrolet. In 1920, Durant lost control of GM due to a combination of accumulated debts and a difficult market for new cars, and in 1923 Alfred Sloan (1875–1966), who had been a vice-president of GM, became its president. Under his direction, General Motors became a worldwide corporation with interests ranging from automobiles to buses, locomotives, and refrigerators. Sloan developed a strategy of annual model changes for GM cars and organized the production of GM's various models according to a pricing structure that ranged from the Chevrolet on the low end to the Cadillac on the upper. He offered consumers a choice of GM vehicles in different price ranges, enabling them to move up to more expensive cars as their incomes increased. General Motors was not the first automobile company to institute annual model changes. Several makers of luxury cars had begun to do this as early as 1921 in order to justify the cars' high prices. Sloan, however, extended the practice to the mass market.

Sloan was the first automobile executive to recognize the importance of styling and in 1927 he hired Harley Earl (1893–1969) to head a new Art and Color Section at GM. Earl was a California coachbuilder whose father had been in the business since 1889. Before he came to GM, Earl was based in Los Angeles, where he managed Earl Automobile Works, a company founded by his father in 1908 which was subsequently sold to a local Cadillac dealer.

Before General Motors established its new styling division, automobiles were either designed primarily by engineers, or else a luxury car manufacturer would ship a chassis to a coachbuilder of the customer's choice. Earl introduced the customized coachbuilding approach to the design of cars for the mass market. He was a man of high style with a large ego who was capable of defending his team of designers from the engineers who at one point called the Art and Color Section a "beauty parlor."

Earl did not draw well and while in California he developed a technique of sculpting clay models to present his styling ideas to clients. At GM, Earl's model makers would create full-scale exemplars consisting of clay that was applied to wooden armatures. Although other manufacturers had used both clay and wooden models as early as 1916, the full-scale mock-ups produced in GM's Art and Color Section conveyed a sense of drama and showmanship that differed from earlier examples.

Earl built up a staff that included design engineers, clay modelers, body layout men, and others. He also sought commercial and advertising artists, interior decorators, architects, yacht designers, and even designers of jewelry who could be trained to style automobiles. Hired on a trial basis and asked to design details such as grilles, lamps, or fender shapes, many did not qualify for permanent jobs, but quite a number did. In fact, the Art and Color Section served as the training ground for designers who fanned out through the entire auto industry, carrying with them techniques they had learned from Harley Earl. Among those who passed through the section were John Tjaarda, E. T. Gregorie, and Gordon Buehrig (1904–1990), who went on to an outstanding career, first as a designer for Duesenbrg and Auburn and then after World War II for Ford.

Earl divided the designers and modelers into groups and staged competitions for new models. He and other executives judged the entries and selected the best ones for further development. Earl liked drama in his designs and sought to attain it through bold forms, which might include long hoods, bulbous fenders, rounded horizontal grilles, sculpted bumpers, and chrome strips applied to the front and sides of the automobiles.

To enhance efficiency in the production of so many different annual models, he adapted an idea from one of his staff and recommended to management that all GM cars share four basic body shells, which he designated A, B, C, and D. With these in place, the Art and Color Section, whose name was changed to General Motors Styling in 1937, would give the standard bodies distinct identities by adding different grilles, fender lines, hoods, lamps, wheels, hubcaps, instrument panels, upholstery, and other elements.

To maintain the variety that was required for so many model changes, Earl had some of his designers work on single elements rather than overall designs. The results provided a backlog of design components that could be applied to new models. The system of body shells, which was one of the Art and Color Section's major contributions to GM's financial success, became a basic component of General Motors' production strategy. Phil Patton has referred to it as "flexible manufacturing." One consequence of the system was that Earl was able to create a unified look for the entire range of GM cars even though they were marketed in different price ranges. Occasionally, he would make one of GM's lower priced cars look like a scaled-down version of a higher priced one. This was the case with the 1932 Chevrolet, which had all the attributes of the Cadillac of that year.

Within the studio, designers began to distinguish themselves. Frank Hershey (1907–1997), who had a background in custom coachbuilding in California, transformed the 1933 Pontiac by adding a silver chrome streak, which remained a hallmark of the car for years to come. After World War II, Hershey would go on to design the Thunderbird for Ford. He was succeeded as head of the Pontiac studio by Virgil Exner (1909–1973), who later went on to work for Studebaker and Chrysler.

Bill Mitchell (1912–1988) was an advertising illustrator before GM hired him at the end of 1935. Just over a year later, Earl made him the head of the Cadillac studio where he was initially responsible for the Cadillac Sixty Special, a car that influenced the entire auto industry with its elegant form, gracefully curved fenders, flat roof, lack of running boards, and thin chrome outlines around the windows. Mitchell remained with GM for his entire career and replaced Earl as Head of Design when Earl retired at the end of 1959.

One of Earl's major innovations was the creation of the concept car, a vehicle intended to present new design ideas to the public to see which ones might be incorporated into mass-produced models. Such cars were introduced at annual auto shows to create excitement and produce information about what features appealed to the public. In 1938, Earl designed the Buick Y-Job, considered to be the first concept car, which was built on a Buick chassis but possessed many novel features. A two-seater, its elongated hood had a modified bullet shape that was complemented by torpedo-like fenders, which had built in hidden headlamps and curved back into the doors. The small oblong grille was located below the fender nose, and multiple chrome streaks lined each of the four fenders. It also had an electric top that was hidden behind a metal panel in the back of the seats. Although it did not go into production, the Buick Y-Job nonetheless helped to build a reputation for General Motors as the most far-sighted of the major auto manufacturers.

By the end of the 1930s, General Motors had become the most successful of the American car companies. Due to the administrative leadership of Alfred Sloan and the robust design studio headed by Harley Earl, GM managed to produce more cars than its competitors and to stay ahead of them in terms of new styles. But the company was also active in other fields of design. In 1919, GM acquired Frigidaire, a company that manufactured refrigerators. Alfred Sloan invested heavily in improving the refrigerator's cooling system, and the company held its own in the kitchen appliance market although it did not have a comparable impact that GM cars had on automobile sales.

In 1925, General Motors assumed majority ownership of the Yellow Coach Manufacturing Company, a subsidiary of the Yellow Cab Company, which produced buses. A few years later in 1936, GM joined with Firestone Tire, Standard Oil of California, and Phillips Petroleum to form a holding company, National City Lines, to buy up local transit systems around the country. NCL purchased more than 100 streetcar systems in 45 cities. These were ultimately dismantled and replaced with GM buses. Although a Federal Court convicted NCL in 1949 of conspiring to substitute gasoline- or diesel-powered buses for electric transportation, opponents of the decision still question whether any of the streetcar companies would have converted to buses without NCL's intervention.

In 1930, General Motors purchased Electro-Motive Corporation, a railcar builder, and its engine supplier, Winton Engine. Both were renamed as the General Motors Electro-Motive Division. Beginning in 1937, GM designed paint schemes for railroad trains in the Styling Section of this division, which worked for a large number of railroads and was extremely influential in creating a colorful modern Deco look that characterized the railroads' streamline era. GM also built diesel-powered passenger and freight locomotives for a number of railroad lines.

The third major competitor among mass-market automobile manufacturers was the Chrysler Corporation that Walter Chrysler (1875–1950) founded in 1925. He first developed his skills as a mechanical engineer in the railroad industry before moving to automobile manufacturing in 1911, when he joined the Buick Motor Company. There he solved many production problems and eventually boosted Buick's production from 40 cars a day to 500. He became president of Buick and was also named vice-president in charge of production for Buick's parent company, General Motors.

Chrysler left GM in 1920, but soon returned to the industry as chief executive of several failing companies, first Willys-Overland and then Maxwell-Chalmers. In the course of his efforts to revamp Willys-Overland, Chrysler engaged Fred M. Zeder (1886–1951), Owen M. Skelton (dates unconfirmed) and Carl Breer (1883–1970), known as the "Three Musketeers," who had left Studebaker in 1920 to form the Zeder-Skelton-Breer Engineering Corporation (ZSB). After Walter Chrysler moved to Maxwell, he purchased ZSB and the rights to the cars they had been developing. Their first prototype, which bore the Chrysler name, was the Chrysler Six. It had a number of engineering innovations such as a high compression engine and four-wheel hydraulic brakes, which no other manufacturer offered at the time. Maxwell sold 32,000 of this model when it was put on the market in 1924.

The following year, Walter Chrysler purchased Maxwell, and the Chrysler Six became the first car to be sold by his new Chrysler Corporation. It could achieve a top speed of 70 miles per hour, just under that of the Packard, which cost twice as much, and its efficiency rivaled the Duesenberg, a car that was five times more expensive. The Chrysler Six also possessed more equipment than its chief competitor in the mid-sized range, GM's Buick. At least one writer sees the Chrysler Six as having set new technological standards for mass-produced cars.

Shortly after its founding, the Chrysler Corporation began a process of expansion, aimed particularly at competing with General Motors. In 1926, it introduced the Chrysler Imperial, a luxury car intended to challenge GM's Cadillac. Two years later, Chrysler introduced the Plymouth—a car designed to rival another GM car, the inexpensive Chevrolet. At that time Chrysler purchased the Dodge Motor Company and inaugurated yet another new automobile, the De Soto. Now Chrysler had a range of cars that could match General Motors in every price range.

To complement his company's growing influence in the automobile market, Walter Chrysler broke ground in New York for a company office building. For a brief period it would be the tallest building in the world until the Empire State Building eclipsed it. The architect was William Van Alen (1883–1954), who trained in the Beaux-Arts tradition but made his statement as a modernist with his design for the Chrysler Building. The Art Deco style incorporated features then in use on Chrysler automobiles such as the chrome eagles on the corners that replicated hood ornaments on the 1929 Chrysler, and the corner decorations on a higher floor that were based on the hubcap designs from the same car. The signature element was the terraced crown that contributed to the building's Deco look. It consisted of seven concentric circles made of steel cladding and covered with triangular forms.

Walter Chrysler recognized the value of GM's Art and Color Section, and in 1928 he started his own office for stylists to which he gave a similar name, Chrysler Art and Color. The difference between Chrysler and GM, however, was that the Chrysler stylists remained firmly under the control of the engineers and focused initially on ornamental details, interiors, and trim. Working under Oliver H. Clark (dates unconfirmed), the company's body engineers designed most of the exterior bodies. Initially the Art and Color section was headed by Herbert V. Henderson (dates unconfirmed), an interior decorator who had done the homes of various Chrysler executives. He reported directly to Clark. In 1932, Walter Chrysler brought in Raymond Dietrich (1894–1980), who, unlike Henderson, had a strong background in coachbuilding, having been a partner in Le Baron Carrossiers and a designer for the successful Reo Royale 8.

Initially Dietrich worked independently of Art and Color, creating facelifts for several Chrysler and De Soto models. In 1935 he took over Art and Color when Henderson departed, but despite his extensive experience as a coachbuilder, he could not overcome the strong influence of Oliver Clark and the body engineers, so he left the company in 1940.

In 1934, Chrysler introduced one of its most highly publicized cars, the Chrysler Airflow, although it was not to be one of its most successful. The Airflow was promoted as a streamlined car and its design was actually based on a series of wind tunnel tests. Carl Breer, one of the "Three Musketeers" whose engineering firm, ZSB, Walter Chrysler had purchased, initiated the idea for it. Tests quickly confirmed that the traditional box-like automobile body was aerodynamically inefficient and the Chrysler engineers produced instead an aerodynamic body with a curved front end, rounded grill and sunken headlights (Plate 45). Aside from the low-slung body shape, Breer and his team of engineers introduced many technical innovations including a steel body frame, which departed radically from the normal practice of bolting a wooden body structure to a metal chassis. As a result, the Airflow was stronger and lighter than its rivals, due as well to an innovative suspension system that shifted the rear seats to a position ahead of the rear axle so as to produce a smoother ride.

The Chrysler Airflow was a bold move on Walter Chrysler's part. It incorporated numerous technical innovations but was, however, a commercial failure. Its streamlined design was too far ahead of public taste and the car did not sell well, although initial manufacturing defects also contributed to the low public acceptance. Chrysler introduced elements from the Airflow in other models, notably the De Soto, and did no better with them. With some modifications in the body design, the company continued to market versions of the Airflow until 1937, after which it was discontinued. Due in part to the Airflow's lack of success, Chrysler styling in the late 1930s was conservative, and executives were reluctant to adopt any designs that had not already been proven elsewhere. Chrysler Art and Color remained small and continued to be ancillary to the engineering department, which successfully opposed any proposals it did not like.

Most smaller automobile manufacturers concentrated on the luxury market instead of mid-sized or inexpensive models. Rather than hire their own designers, they tended with few exceptions to rely on coachbuilding firms to supply bodies for them. Gordon Buehrig (1904–1990) worked for a number of such manufacturers and created some of the most distinctive designs for this market. He learned to design cars while employed by several firms that built auto bodies and in the late 1920s he worked briefly for Harley Earl at GM. There he developed his own aesthetic of modern car design, which he then applied while subsequently working for several luxury car manufacturers, notably Stutz and then Duesenberg. After moving to the Auburn Automobile Company, another luxury automobile manufacturer, Buehrig designed the Cord 810, a dramatic car with bulging free-standing front fenders and a "coffin-nosed" louvered hood whose grille consisted of horizontal metal strips that extended from the front and wrapped around the sides. Although Buehrig's design was striking, technical glitches contributed to the car's lack of continued success after strong initial interest. Packard, Marmon—which commissioned Walter Dorwin Teague to design the Marmon 16—Peerless, and Pierce-Arrow were other models that competed in the luxury market and Packard was the most successful of these. To survive during the Depression, the company introduced a mid-priced car, the Packard 120, which was manufactured with mass-production techniques while its luxury model still required considerable hand labor and craft knowledge.

Other companies that entered the mid-range market were Studebaker, Hudson, and Nash. Though Nash Motors' styling was less remarkable than that of its competitors from GM or Chrysler, the company invested heavily in research, drawing in part from Kelvinator, a kitchen appliance company that merged with it in 1937. The following year, Nash pioneered an optional air heating and ventilating system that resulted from expertise shared with Kelvinator's engineers and in 1939 added a thermostat to its "Conditioned Air System." In 1936, the year before the Kelvinator merger, Nash introduced another significant feature, "Bed-In-A-Car," which made it possible to convert the back seat into a sleeping compartment by changing the rear seat's position so that two people could sleep with their heads and shoulders on the seat cushion and their feet in the trunk. Nash was also one of the few automobile manufacturers in the late 1930s to hire a woman designer, commissioning Helen Dryden (1887–1981) to design some of its interiors. Dryden, who began as a fashion illustrator, subsequently worked for the Dura Corporation, a manufacturer of auto parts, before establishing her own industrial design firm around 1935. Studebaker commissioned her to design interiors for its 1936 line and she worked for the company again at the end of the decade when Raymond Loewy hired her. Dryden functioned primarily as a consultant, but Hudson was possibly the first automobile manufacturer to hire a woman full-time. In 1939, Betty Thatcher (dates unconfirmed) joined the company where, among other projects, she worked on the instrument panel of the 1941 Hudson.

Besides the conventional cars, there were experimental models that some journalists called Zepps, perhaps named after the German 1932 *Maybach Zeppelin*, which was known for its envelope body shape. By Zepp, the journalists meant a car whose design was too extreme to be taken seriously. One of these was the Scarab, whose first prototype was made in 1932, while a subsequent improved version was completed in 1935, a year after the Chrysler Airflow was introduced. Designed by engineer William Busnhell Stout (1880–1956), who went into automobile design after a pioneering career in aviation, and built by his manufacturing company, its streamlined shape, which was developed from a prototype by John Tjaarda, departed from automobile production norms in a number of ways. It is considered by some to have been the first mini-van. Stout put the engine in the back in order to eliminate the long front hood where engines were normally housed. The frame followed the construction of an aircraft fuselage. It featured a short nose and tapered rear body, bringing the design of an automobile closer to an aircraft form than any other car of the period. Stout eliminated the running boards to provide more interior space and did not bolt down any seats, except for the driver's, to accommodate flexible seating arrangements. While the Scarab received positive reviews as well as skeptical ones, its high price, more than four times that of the Imperial, Chrysler's luxury car, precluded mass production and only nine were built, all by hand. Thus the Scarab was a strange mixture of advanced technology and craft production, which precluded successful sales but not the possibility that mainstream manufacturers would adopt some of its design features for their own purposes.

The proliferation of automobiles developed concurrently with the rise of the American oil industry. Following Ford's mass production of the Model T and then the competition from other manufacturers that began in the early 1920s, a need arose for service stations to dispense gasoline. Early station types varied from prefabricated metal sheds to Colonial-style architecture. By the 1930s, as Phil Patton notes, the oil companies realized that the gasoline station could serve as a package for additional products besides gasoline—oil, tires, and batteries for example. Several large oil companies turned to industrial designers to create stations that could function as brand images. This meant designs that were both distinctive and modern. Norman Bel Geddes designed a prototype station for Socony-Vacuum, while Walter Dorwin Teague's office, which worked for Texaco between 1934 and 1937, created several variations on a basic design that the company adopted for its stations across the country. The most popular variation was the Type C, a box-like structure with a flat canopy over the pumps and two bays for washing and lubricating cars. On each side of the canopy was a large sign with "Texaco" spelled out in three-dimensional letters. The design was both efficient and visually appealing, thus transforming the image of the service station from a vernacular building to an icon that characterized an oil company's identity.

The proliferation of service stations and the construction of roads encouraged many Americans to travel, which stimulated a market for trailers that

Fig. 28.17: Wally Byam, Airstream Trailer, date unconfirmed © Spaces Images/Alamy.

could function not only for portage but for eating and sleeping as well. Between 300 and 400 companies manufactured trailers during the interwar period, but only one, the Airstream Trailer Company, survived the Depression. It was founded by Wally Byam (1896–1962), a lawyer and publisher who designed a trailer in the 1920s with a dropped floor and raised ceiling that enabled campers to stand up inside it. He built these in his backyard but also sold inexpensive plans that enabled purchasers to construct the trailer themselves.

During the 1930s, Byam became associated with William Hawley Bowlus (1896–1967), supervisor of construction for Charles Lindbergh's *Spirit of St. Louis* airplane and a recognized designer of glider aircraft, who was building a trailer of stressed aluminum. He declared bankruptcy in 1936. Byam bought some of his equipment and employed several of his workers. Adopting Bowlus's aircraft construction methods, in early 1936, Byam introduced the Airstream Clipper, named after the famous Pan Am airplane (Fig. 28.17). Made of riveted aluminum sheets, it had a body designed on aerodynamic principles to reduce wind resistance. Byam's reference to the Pan Am Clipper was no coincidence since his trailer was equally revolutionary in terms of comfort. It could sleep four people, carried its own water supply, had a separate galley, and was fitted with electric lights. The Airstream was immensely successful even at a high price, but Byam ceased production during World War II, beginning again after the war ended.

Trains

Although Norman Bel Geddes, Henry Dreyfuss and Raymond Loewy received considerable attention for their proposals and actual designs for streamlining America's railroad trains, Otto Kuhler (1894–1977), a lesser-known German designer of auto bodies who emigrated to the United States in 1923, was equally influential if not more so in transforming the look of America's rolling stock in the 1920s and 1930s.

As the historian Donald J. Bush points out, Reverend Samuel R. Calthrop (dates unconfirmed) patented a design for a tapered "air-resisting train" in 1865, but the idea was not developed at the time. It was renewed when Kuhler, working in New York as a freelance artist, began to publish drawings of streamlined trains around 1928. In 1931, Egmont Arens published an article, "The Train of Tomorrow," which he sent to executives of all the major railroads and that year Norman Bel Geddes also made drawings and models of a tubular streamlined train which he photographed and published the following year in his book *Horizons*.

The same year that *Horizons* appeared, Kuhler received a commission from J. G. Brill and Company, a large manufacturer of streetcars and buses, to participate in the Union Pacific Railroad's competition for an "egg-shaped train." Brill, which at its zenith was the largest manufacturer of streetcars and interurban trains in the United States, had been acquired by the American Car and Foundry Company (ACF), a major manufacturer of railroad rolling stock, in 1926, and Kuhler worked closely with the ACF engineers on the competition, which was ultimately won by Pullman Car and Manufacturing, one of America's largest manufacturers of railroad coaches.

Entering service in 1934, Union Pacific's M-10000 derived its bullet-nosed form and tubular body from extensive wind-tunnel tests. The aluminum body reduced the weight of the train significantly, while its height was considerably lower than other trains, and the doors and windows were set flush with the body to eliminate drag. Besides its innovative exterior design, the M-10000 also had an attractive interior with an appealing color scheme and comfortable seats as well as a buffet kitchen where passengers could buy meals.

Following its commission of the M-10000, Union Pacific ordered another streamlined design for a longer train, which went into service as the *City of Portland* in 1935. While the new train, named the M-10001, retained most exterior features of its predecessor, it was the first streamlined train to incorporate a full dining-lounge car and three sleeping cars divided into compartments and bedrooms, along with a buffet-coach and a post office-baggage car. During the 1930s, Union Pacific also commissioned streamlined trains for its other routes. For trains that would pull more cars, the diesel locomotives were redesigned with longer hoods and vertical grilles to follow automobile styling. The *City of Los Angeles* featured a lounge-observation car with rounded porthole windows covered with Polaroid glass that could be rotated to reduce the glare from outside, while the *City of Denver*'s sleeper-lounge observation car had a glass-enclosed solarium at its far end. Though the design of its rolling stock has received less attention than some of the higher-profile individual trains, Union Pacific adopted a corporate approach to modernizing its entire fleet of trains, providing not only a unified public relations plan, as evidenced by the naming of its trains, and advanced streamlined designs for its engines, but also varied design and comfort innovations on individual trains.

Though Union Pacific's M-10000 may be considered the first streamlined train to be put into service, it was not far ahead of the Burlington Zephyr, which was also introduced in 1934, less than two months after its predecessor (Fig. 28.18). Unlike the M-10000, the Zephyr had a diesel engine and was constructed of stainless steel. Built by the Edward Budd Manufacturing Company for the Chicago, Burlington, and Quincy Railroad, it featured an important design innovation: the Budd Company's patent of a technique called "shot welding," which held the car body together. Whereas traditional welding techniques would weaken the metal pieces at the joints, shot welding entailed pressing two metal surfaces against each other and passing an electric current through the joint to fuse them into a single piece.

The principal designer of the exterior was an aeronautical engineer, Albert Gardner Dean (dates unconfirmed), who created the sloping nose form. He was assisted by the architects Paul Phillipe Cret (1876–1945) and John Harbeson (1888–1986), who

Fig. 28.18: Burlington Zephyr, postcard, 1930s. Getty Images.

devised the horizontal steel fluting along the sides of the trains. Cret, who was born in France and studied Beaux-Arts architecture, designed the Zephyr's passenger compartments in a contemporary style that complemented the streamlined look of the exterior. He featured comfortable upholstered seats in the coach area, indirect lighting, soft colors, and clean, modern seating in the rear lounge car. Cret and Harbeson's architectural firm was based in Philadelphia, where the Budd Manufacturing Company was located, and sustained a long relationship with Budd, designing interiors for most of the streamlined trains it built, including the Santa Fe Railroad's Super Chief of 1937 and a number of other Zephyrs for the Chicago, Burlington, and Quincy Railroad. Although the initial Zephyr carried relatively few passengers, it was most valuable as a public relations vehicle that heralded the revival of railway travel as it crisscrossed the country along with the M-10000 and appeared at the Century of Progress exhibition in Chicago.

Beginning in 1932, Otto Kuhler cemented his reputation as a designer of streamlined locomotives through his work as a consultant to the American Locomotive Company (ALCO). Founded in 1901, ALCO had become the nation's second largest manufacturer of steam locomotives before creating its first successful diesel-electric locomotive in 1924. Kuhler's initial success for ALCO was the Hiawatha locomotive he designed for the Milwaukee Road around 1934. As he had done in his drawings several years earlier, he designed a smooth sheath for the engine whose slightly protruding front recalled the Burlington Zephyr, the difference being that in the Zephyr locomotive the engineer sat at the front while in the Hiawatha design the engineer's seat was at the back. By 1935, when the Hiawatha engines were put into service, they enabled the fastest passenger service of any line in the world. Kuhler also joined with Karl F. Nystrom (dates unconfirmed), Milwaukee Road's chief mechanical officer, to design a striking observation car for the Hiawatha with wide windows dramatically divided by an arched vertical strip.

Among the other rolling stock designs with which Kohler was involved was the Capitol Limited, the Baltimore and Ohio's train that handled the premier run from Washington to New York. For the engine, Kuhler and his two assistants adopted a version of his "bullet nose" form, which became known in the industry as the "Kuhler type." As the railroad wished to revitalize its existing stock, Kuhler replaced the clerestory roofs of the passenger cars with rounded roofs, which helped to produce a streamlined effect. The addition of full skirting to cover the wheels and coverings between the cars to create the appearance of a single continuous form also contributed to the streamline image. In addition, Kuhler devised a system of exterior color for the car bodies. It featured a white lozenge that surrounded the windows on a blue ground. The engine had a white top with gray strips offset with gold stripes and lettering emanating from an emblem on its front along its width on both sides.

Kuhler's work for the Baltimore and Ohio had a strong element of redesigning, since much of the existing equipment was adapted to represent a new streamlined style. This was also the case with his project for the Lehigh Valley Railroad for which he designed a train called the Asa Packer in 1938. It was drawn by a steam locomotive for which Kuhler created a simple forward sloping panel and modest skirting that was painted to suggest speed. Encouraged by the positive response of its patrons, the railroad then commissioned Kuhler to convert two aging steam locomotives into bullet-nosed streamlined vehicles. The following year Lehigh Valley introduced the *John Wilkes*, a converted steam locomotive that was also endowed with Kuhler's signature "bullet nose." Kuhler added a sloping grill that bore a vertical red panel and three chrome strips that wrapped completely around the engine. The train's color scheme was black with horizontal red bands that ran the length of the train.

For the interior, Kuhler introduced a lounge car and refitted the dining car with new furniture and indirect lighting. Trained as an artist, he also created the dynamic cover artwork for the advertising brochure. As his final project for Lehigh Valley in 1940, Kuhler redesigned the railroad's flagship train, the *Black Diamond*, which traveled between New York and Buffalo. As with the *John Wilkes*, Kuhler chose his bullet nose for the redesign and introduced similar changes in the train's interior. As an additional element, he designed new uniforms with red, black, and white trim for the train's attendants.

Henry Dreyfuss' first railroad commission came from the New York Central, which hired his office in 1936 to redesign the Mercury, a 25-year-old train that ran on the Cleveland–Detroit route. Initial discussions about designing a new train almost sank the project, but Dreyfuss revived it with a proposal to drastically cut costs by redesigning existing stock. The design of the M-10000 and the Burlington Zephyr included separate exteriors and interiors, but Dreyfuss' design for the Mercury was the first in which the same designer closely coordinated the exterior and interior designs.

Dreyfuss covered the engine with a swept-back sheath that was very different from Norman Zapf's redesign of the same railroad's *Commodore Vanderbilt* locomotive two years earlier. Adding a striking element to his locomotive design. he cut out a portion of the metal skirt to expose the solid disk wheels, which were illuminated at night to create a dramatic effect. Unlike Otto Kuhler, however, Dreyfuss eschewed an elaborate color scheme for the Mercury, preferring instead a solid gray adorned only with several strips of thin contrasting trim.

Dreyfuss' sober interiors for the observation car, the parlor cars, and the coaches complemented the exterior design perfectly. His redesign of the commuter cars included large windows, which fitted well with the comfortable easy chairs turned at angles towards the windows so passengers could enjoy the views. The parlor cars had movable chairs, tables, and reading lamps, and the complete interior design with its warm colors set a new standard for furnishings that were tasteful and comfortable.

The redesign of the Mercury was extremely successful in attracting new passengers and prepared the way for a second New York Central commission, the design of the railroad's most prestigious train, the 20th Century Limited, which had been providing elegant service for well-to-do passengers on the New York–Chicago run since 1902. This time the railroad executives agreed to purchase completely new locomotives and passenger cars designed to Dreyfuss' specifications.

His design for the locomotive featured a protruding bullet-shaped boiler atop a metal skirt (Fig. 28.19). As with the Mercury locomotive, the wheels were exposed and incorporated as dramatic visual elements of the design. Centered in the rounded bullet shape was a headlight that interrupted the flow of a raised vertical strip that bisected the boiler. Frequently photographed from an angle that emphasized the sculptural contrast of its different parts, the 20th Century Limited locomotive became the seminal icon of the 1930s.

Dreyfuss treated the interior as a total design and attended to every detail. He gave the train a visual brand as if it were a hotel by repeating the logotype, striping, and color scheme on dinnerware, stationery, and even matchbooks. The layout of the buffet-lounge car, sleeping cars, dining cars, and observation car resembled that of a luxury hotel, an impression that was reinforced by the names of the cars, such as Century Club and Century Inn. The lounge cars featured photographic murals on curved walls, while the decor and food in the dining car equaled that of the best Manhattan restaurants. Walls in the lounges were covered in gray leather to complement the blue chairs and settees. After the dinner hour, the table linen was changed and the dining cars were transformed into nightclubs with soft lighting and piped in music. Dreyfuss' interior design created an air of understated luxury that was expressed through a modernist's good taste rather than a decor of excess.

The 20th Century Limited was inaugurated on June 6, 1938, the same day as its rival, the Broadway

Fig. 28.19: Henry Dreyfuss, *20th Century Limited*, c. 1938. © Bygone Collection/Alamy.

Limited, which Raymond Loewy designed for the Pennsylvania Railroad. The two trains ran along the New York–Chicago route and both catered to a wealthy clientele. Loewy's first major project for the Pennsylvania Railroad was carried out in the early 1930s. It was a redesign of the GG-I series electric locomotive prototype, which Loewy transformed from an awkward shape into a "streamstyled" form, with rounded contours and curved gold pin-striping along the sides. Instead of welded steel plates, Loewy proposed a single shell that could be lowered onto the mechanical structure, an idea that was successfully implemented.

Following the GG-I project, Loewy signed a retainer contract with the railroad and offered his views on everything from observation cars and railway stations to menu covers and tea bag tags. He had the opportunity to bring all his interests together in his design for the Broadway Limited, just as Dreyfuss did for the Pennsylvania Railroad's rival. In 1935, Loewy made some sketches that formed the basis of his design

for a bullet-nosed steam locomotive, the S-1. Although it was among the world's largest and fastest locomotives, the railroad built only one. It went into service in 1938 before it became part of the Pennsylvania Railroad's exhibit at the 1939–1940 New York World's Fair.

Loewy designed other locomotives after the S-1, but his work with the railroad culminated in his interior design for the Broadway Limited, a project he carried out with the architect Paul Cret. Powering the Broadway Limited was an electric locomotive from the GG-I series, which pulled the train for part of the trip, sharing the remaining part with a steam locomotive that was rebuilt with a streamlined shrouding or shell. Loewy's and Cret's designs for the train's interior contrasted with those of Dreyfuss. Where Dreyfuss introduced large windows to bring the outside into the train, Loewy and Cret incorporated long sections of wall that cut the passengers off from the outside with cork panels or murals. Views were featured, however, in the lounge cars, which had love seats arranged for looking outward. Like the 20th Century Limited,

Fig. 28.20: Raymond Loewy and Paul Cret, *Broadway Limited*, interior, 1946. © Bettmann/CORBIS/Getty Images.

the interior by Loewy and Cret had all the accoutrements of a high-class hotel and certainly enabled the Broadway Limited to compete favorably with its rival for a class of wealthy customers (Fig. 28.20).

Airplanes

Airplane design after World War I was dominated by European companies, especially Junkers in Germany and Fokker in the Netherlands. In 1923, Anthony Fokker founded a branch of his firm in the United States, where he introduced an early version of the tri-motor plane by adding two engines to one of his wooden aircraft. Both Henry Ford and the engineer William Stout were impressed with Fokker's success. Stout, who had worked in the aviation division of

the Packard Motor Company, competed with Fokker by designing the Air Pullman, the first passenger plane that had a body made entirely of metal—an aluminum alloy called Duralumin. In 1924, Stout sold his company to Henry Ford, and three years later the Ford Motor Company introduced its own tri-motor with a metal body. Dubbed the "Tin Goose," it had a seating capacity of 12 and was the first American plane to carry passengers rather than mail. However, due to a number of factors, Ford began to lose interest in aviation and by 1933 he had left the airplane business.

However, other airplane manufacturers were designing planes for the emerging civil aviation industry, which began to burgeon after Charles Lindbergh's solo flight across the Atlantic in 1927. The Curtiss Airplane and Motor Company, headed by aviation pioneer and aircraft designer Glenn Curtiss (1878–1930), specialized in seaplanes, a strategy that Curtiss adopted to circumvent the worldwide shortage of landing strips. The principal consumer for such planes was Pan American Airways, founded in 1927, which became America's first international carrier. The company's aggressive president Juan Trippe purchased a number of ailing airlines in Central and South America, which gave Pan Am a virtual monopoly of this territory. The company also developed transatlantic flights to Europe and later a Pacific route as well.

Pan Am established a relation with the Russian aircraft designer Igor Sikorsky (1889–1972), who had emigrated to the United States in 1919. The Sikorsky Manufacturing Corporation specialized in seaplanes or flying boats and sold its first practical amphibian, the eight-seat S-36, to Pan Am in 1928, while a larger plane, the S-38, which had nine seats, attracted orders from ten airlines and the U.S. Navy the same year. The S-42, a large efficient flying boat, was purchased by Pan Am in 1934 to open routes across the Atlantic and the Pacific, although the significantly larger M-130, manufactured by the Glenn L. Martin Company and known as the China Clipper, made the first flight across the Pacific in 1935, leaving from Alameda, California, and arriving in Manila after stops in Honolulu and on various Pacific islands. The flight to Manila aroused much public interest and the following year First National Pictures released a film, *China Clipper*, which featured Humphrey Bogart in an early role as the plane's captain.

Pan Am hired Norman Bel Geddes to design the interior of the China Clipper, and he assigned the design aspect to his wife, Frances Waite Geddes (dates unconfirmed). Since comfort was a premium on the Pacific flight—probably the most costly in the airline industry at the time—Pan Am allowed Geddes to reduce the passenger capacity by a third. This enabled her to divide the cabin into compartments with sofas and chairs that converted into beds at night. An additional lounge could also be transformed into dressing rooms before bedtime. Besides providing sleeping facilities, Geddes added other innovations. Historian Jeffrey Miekle has noted that these included a galley kitchen with a cooking range and refrigerator, separate rest rooms for men and women, hot and cold water, and cone-shaped lights. In addition, the blue seat covers and cream-colored wall coverings had zippers so they could be removed for cleaning. Pan Am promoted its transoceanic flights with a series of posters that featured vivid illustrations by the artist Paul George Lawler (dates unconfirmed). He portrayed Pan Am destinations like the Andes and Rio de Janeiro in South America and Hawaii and Pago Pago in the Pacific as exotic places where tourists would discover colorful local cultures.

In the late 1930s, Pan Am contracted with the Boeing Company to build an even larger flying boat to transport passengers on transoceanic routes. In 1938, the airline introduced the Boeing 314, which was the biggest civil aircraft at the time. Also known as the Yankee Clipper, it had a capacity of 90 passengers on day flights and 40 on flights at night. Within a short period the 314 Clipper was flying to destinations in all parts of the world.

The same year that the Yankee Clipper was introduced, Boeing completed work on the Model 307 Stratoliner, which was subsequently employed for several years by Pan Am for long transoceanic flights. The world's first aircraft with a pressurized cabin, it was also the first high-altitude commercial transport and the first four-engine airplane to fly domestic routes as well. Like the streamlined trains of the day, the Stratoliners had individual names like Rainbow, Comet, and Apache and set new standards for speed and comfort. Their exceptionally wide cabins also allowed extra space for overnight berths. For the first time, the crew included a flight engineer to adjust the many settings and systems, thus allowing the captain to concentrate on navigation.

Pan Am was alone in staking out international routes from the United States, while a number of other airlines competed for the domestic business. Transcontinental Air Transport (TAT), a consortium that included the Pennsylvania Railroad, organized the first American coast-to-coast route. In 1929, TAT introduced a mixed air and rail link that required passengers to change several times from trains to planes, but this proved unsuccessful and the consortium collapsed after little more than a year.

TAT merged with Western Air Express to form Transcontinental and Western Air (T&WA), which became known as TWA. The new airline approached Boeing, the leading airplane manufacturer of the early 1930s, for new planes, but Boeing was committed to a contract with United Airlines and could not deliver planes to another customer at the time. TWA then sought out other manufacturers including the Douglas Aircraft Company, which had previously only designed planes for the military. In late 1933, Douglas delivered the DC-1, the first of its DC (Douglas Commercial) planes to TWA. That year Boeing introduced the 247, a more advanced plane which was considered to be the first modern passenger airliner. Its aerodynamic bullet nose and low cockpit preceded the DC-3 by several years, although the body retained a slightly boxy form. The plane had many innovative technical features including a fully cantilevered wing, retractable landing gear, autopilot, and de-icing boots for the wings and tail. It was also capable of crossing the United States at least eight hours faster than its predecessors, the Ford Tri-motor and the Curtiss Condor.

In 1934, TWA took delivery of the DC-2, which was purchased by other airlines as well. American Airlines tried unsuccessfully to convert the DC-2 into a sleeper but found the body too narrow. The company petitioned Douglas to produce a larger plane, which resulted in the DC-3 (Fig. 28.21). To design the new plane, which revolutionized the airline industry, Douglas enlisted more than 400 engineers and draftsmen led by aeronautical engineer Arthur Raymond (1899–1999). According to one industry executive, it was the first plane that enabled an airline to become profitable simply by hauling passengers.

The DC-3 was not only bigger than the DC-2 but it also flew higher and faster than its predecessor, while providing more passenger comfort and safety features. It was distinguished as well by its Duralumin surface and overall aerodynamic form, which rounded out the more angular body shape of the Boeing 247. The DC-3 was initially produced in three models: a day plane that could seat 21, a comfortable overnight Skysleeper for 14 people, and a luxurious Skylounge for a similar number of flyers. By the end of 1936, most American airlines including American, United, and Eastern were flying DC-3s or were planning to convert to them. Besides promoting their technical innovations, the airlines also improved their interior designs, meals, and services that the stewardesses provided.

To compete with the DC-3, Boeing introduced its four-engine 307 Stratoliner in 1938, although, despite its innovations, only ten were produced. Pan Am and TWA were the only airlines to adopt the Stratoliner for passenger service, while one was customized for the American billionaire Howard Hughes after his purchase of TWA. The exterior body featured the rounded streamlined form of the DC-3, while the

Fig. 28.21: Douglas DC-3, 1936. © Aviation History Collection/Alamy.

interior design incorporated the comfortable seating and separate compartments that Frances Waite Geddes had pioneered in the China Clipper.

Besides its role in persuading Douglas Aircraft to build the DC-3, American Airlines pioneered in several areas that were not directly related to aircraft design but were central to the development of a flight system that included traffic control, ticketing, and airports. With its fleet of DC-3s, American embarked on an ambitious service program that led to its Admiral's Club lounges for frequent flyers—the first being established at newly opened La Guardia airport in 1939. It also introduced a centralized process for making reservations, as well as the nation's first air traffic control system.

In 1926, the passage of the Air Commerce Act created a national air transportation network that delegated the construction of airports to local authorities while retaining for the federal government the designation of navigation aids and air routes, as was the case with its control of the nation's waterways. Two models were adopted for the first terminal designs: the depot hangar, which combined a waiting room and offices with an aircraft hangar; and the "simple terminal," which was modeled after a railroad station. These terminals changed significantly both in scale and design as air transport expanded rapidly during the 1930s.

Other modes of transport

Changes in the design of automobiles, trains, and airplanes were far greater than those in other modes of transport. Around 1933, the recently formed Greyhound Corporation hired Raymond Loewy to modernize the look of its bus fleet. By 1936, the company had fielded its Super Coach, which drew some inspiration from the Burlington Zephyr. The conventional engine hood had been dropped and the front was flat. Loewy contributed a visual scheme to enhance the streamlined look. He modernized the Greyhound logo and devised a blue and white color combination, while creating a sense of speed with a two-dimensional depiction of streamlined fenders. Later versions of the Super Coach replaced Loewy's faux fenders with ribbed metal sides like the Burlington Zephyr.

The Indian Motorcycle Manufacturing Company also drew on streamlined forms for its Indian Chief models in the 1920s and 1930s, while Schwinn introduced its streamlined bicycle, the Aerocycle, in 1934. The Aerocycle had flared fenders and a teardrop-shaped tank that contained a built-in headlight like the Chrysler Airflow. It was the first bicycle to have balloon tires, which were wide pneumatic tires that could be fully inflated with relatively low pressure. Even more so than the Indian Chief motorcycle, the streamlined styling of the Aerocycle was primarily for show and was intended mainly to boost bicycle sales. It did not last, as the streamlined elements made the bicycle heavier and more difficult to pedal.

The White Motor Company, which began to produce large semi-trucks and trailers in the 1920s, adopted streamlining in the 1930s for several of its models. Around 1937, the company hired Count Alexis de Sakhnoffsky (1901–1964), an experienced custom car designer, to create concept drawings for streamlined trucks. Several of these led to production vehicles that de Sakhnoffsky designed. One was a truck cab that had a curved front with a shaped grille that resembled those on the more advanced automobiles, and another was a tractor-trailer rig designed for the Canadian brewery, Labatt's, whose cab had a curved grille and pulled a van with a rounded front that fitted snugly against the sloping back of the cab. Metal stripes on the sides of the cab and the van suggested speed, just as they did on numerous trains and automobiles.

Unlike many European countries, transoceanic passenger transport was not a major industry in the United States during the 1920s and the 1930s. Hence, there were no American equivalents to the grand European ocean liners of the period such as the *Normandie* in France, the *Bremen* in Germany, or the *Queen Elizabeth* in Britain. One could argue that the same revolution in taste that occurred in the design of European ship interiors was instead evident in the United States in the design and redesign of railroad coach interiors. Nonetheless, there is at least one example of ocean liner design, Raymond Loewy's interiors for three Panama Line ships—the *Panama*, the *Cristobal*, and the *Ancon*. The Panama Line sailed between New York, Port-au-Prince, Haiti, and the Canal Zone, where the Panama Canal was located. In 1904 the Panama Railroad Company, which also operated a steamship service between New York and the canal, passed from French to U.S. government hands with the transfer of the canal's ownership. To mark the 25th anniversary of the canal's opening, the Panama Line, which belonged to the railroad, inaugurated the three new ships, which were designed by naval engineer George Sharp (dates unconfirmed). Working closely with him, Raymond Loewy's office did the interiors. Loewy started the project in 1936 and the ships were launched in 1938–1939.

To counteract the historical styles that were also being rejected by designers in other countries, Loewy introduced modern furnishings similar to those one might have found in a contemporary New York restaurant or bar. Walls were painted in soft pastel shades to make the passengers feel comfortable, while the dining rooms, bars, and staterooms featured built-in furniture with drawers that opened and closed easily. Stainless steel, aluminum, Formica, and other industrial materials were used extensively for the furnishings. Clearly, Loewy's parallel project to design a new train for the Pennsylvania Railroad would have had some relevance to his design for the three ships, given that all were means of transport intended to provide an experience of luxury and comfort for their well-to-do passengers.

Design Education
Design schools

Although preceded by programs in the decorative arts at various art schools, the first program in the United States to train industrial designers was initiated in 1934 at the Carnegie Institute of Technology in Pittsburgh.

The principal faculty member was Donald Dohner (1897–1943), who had been working as a designer for the Westinghouse Electric Company. Dohner, joined by Alexander Kostellow (1900–1954), a professor of painting, taught an introductory course that showed students how to integrate qualities of art and utility in the design of industrial products. Students also learned about materials, model making, and industrial processes, and were introduced to manufacturing through factory visits. In 1935, Dohner went to Pratt Institute, a New York art school, to start a comparable program, and a year later he hired Kostellow and his wife Rowena Reed (1900–1988), who had taught sculpture at Carnegie, to join the faculty. The Kostellows and Dohner subsequently developed the industrial design program at Pratt, which drew on the Carnegie model, and after Dohner's death in 1944, Alexander Kostellow and Rowena Reed continued to teach in the program for a number of years. Perhaps impressed by the professional program at Pratt, New York University brought in Donald Deskey to help create a department of industrial design in 1940.

From 1927 to 1943, Frederick Keisler (1890–1965), who had collaborated briefly with Adolf Loos and was a former member of the *De Stijl* group, directed the Laboratory for Design Correlation within the Department of Architecture at Columbia University. The program was more commercially oriented than Keisler's avant-garde background might have suggested. Keisler had come to New York in 1926 following extensive activity in European avant-garde circles. In New York he applied himself to commercial projects such as store window design and published a book on the subject, *Contemporary Art Applied to the Store and Its Display*, in 1930. He was also a founding member of AUDAC the same year. Keisler's theoretical interests centered on how humans use space, and he explored these in his design for the Film Guild Cinema in 1929, his biomorphic furniture of the early 1940s, and his "Endless House" project of 1958–1959.

On the West Coast, Walter Baermann (1903–1972), who had attained degrees in architecture and engineering in Germany as well as a doctorate from the University of Munich and who came to the United States in 1929 at the invitation of Joseph Urban, helped to found a privately-funded Graduate School of Design in Pasadena in 1937 and subsequently became its director. During the first year, students were engaged in design projects and workshops that involved industrial materials and processes, while also following lectures and seminars on economics, sociology, and technology. In the second year, problems were on a larger scale and students were required to complete an independent thesis. With the school's inclusion of social science courses, Baermann brought a more rigorous intellectual approach to design training than was typical in other curricula. Perhaps because of the curricular rigor, the school became part of the California Institute of Technology in 1941.

The programs at Carnegie, Pratt, and other schools that followed their lead were pragmatic and professional. They trained students for industry as it was and did not seek to instill in them the motivation to change either the design profession or the conditions in which designers worked. Other programs, however, conceived design education more idealistically, linking it on the one hand to the craft communities of the past in England and Scandinavia, and on the other hand to the European avant-garde movements, particularly as they were evident in the Weimar and Dessau Bauhaus.

The Cranbrook Academy, which opened in 1932 in Bloomfield Hills, Michigan, had its roots in the Arts and Crafts movement and the ideals of Scandinavian National Romanticism. Cranbrook's first director, the Finnish architect Eliel Saarinen (1873–1950), who came to the United States to teach architecture at the University of Michigan in 1923, had long wanted to establish a school for architectural training that would also incorporate the related arts of painting, sculpture, and the handicrafts. Saarinen found a partner in George Booth, a Detroit newspaper publisher and devotee of the Arts and Crafts, who provided both the land and the funding for Cranbrook.

As Saarinen enunciated Cranbrook's purpose, it was not to be a school in the traditional sense but rather a working community, where experienced teachers would guide the students. Like Walter Gropius, who designed the Dessau Bauhaus building and then filled it with furniture and lighting from the Bauhaus workshops, Saarinen also designed a number of buildings for the Cranbrook Educational Community, which included, besides the Cranbrook Academy of Art, the Kingswood School for Girls and the Cranbrook School for Boys along with the Cranbrook Museum and Library. For the director's residence, Saarinen created custom furniture that rivaled the exquisite craftsmanship and restrained elegance of furnishings from the workshops of Vienna and Paris. As heads of the Cranbrook workshops, Saarinen brought some of the teachers from Scandinavia. His wife Loja (1879–1968) was a weaver who established her own studio. Besides heading the Weaving Workshop, she also designed and wove rugs and tapestries with patterns inspired by Scandinavian folk motifs for many of the Cranbrook buildings including the director's residence. Marianne Strengell (1909–1998), another Finnish weaver, came to Cranbrook from Helsinki in 1937 as a weaving instructor. During her years at the school, Strengell designed many commercially successful fabrics that were adopted by such clients as Knoll Furniture, United Airlines, Russel Wright, and General Motors. Another Finnish craftsperson, Maija Grotell (1899–1973), taught ceramics, while the Swedish sculptor Carl Milles (1875–1955) headed the sculpture workshop and undertook numerous commissions for single figures and monumental groups for the Cranbrook campus as well as other locales. In 1941, Saarinen invited Walter Baermann from Pasadena to head the recently created Department of Industrial Design. Asked to prepare a report on the present and future of Cranbrook, Baermann noted that the school's greatest success derived from the relationship between its accomplished faculty and their apprentice students. He found the atmosphere to be "romanticized," and recommended the introduction of a rigorous curriculum for undergraduates and graduates as well as a junior college program. There was considerable resistance to his suggestions and after only a brief tenure at Cranbrook, Baermann left for a job in Washington, DC, in the Office of Civil Defense. Likewise, conversations with car designer Gordon Buehrig about founding a Department of Automobile Design, given Cranbrook's proximity to the auto manufacturers in Detroit, also came to naught.

Those who studied at Cranbrook and some of those who taught there in the 1930s included the Saarinens' son Eero (1910–1961), and their daughter Pipsan Swanson (1905–1979), Charles Eames (1907–1978) and Ray Kaiser Eames (1912–1988), Harry Weese (1915–1998), Benjamin Baldwin (1913–1993), and Harry Bertoia (1915–1978). While still a student, Bertoia supervised the silver and metal workshop whose projects were as good as those done anywhere. Eames, who with Eero Saarinen won first prize in MoMA's Organic Design in Home Furnishings competition, also taught industrial design at Cranbrook. Pipsan Swanson, who trained students in furniture design, and her husband Robert Swanson (1900–1981) introduced a line of functional and flexible furniture, known as Flexible Home Arrangement or F. H. A., in 1939. Florence Schust Knoll (b. 1917), became a leading furniture and interior space planner after World War II. She was a student at the Kingswood School for Girls and the Cranbrook Academy of Art before she went on to study architecture with Mies van der Rohe at the Illinois Institute of Technology.

Whereas many of the émigré modernist designers in New York came from Germany, Austria, or Hungary and drew ideas from the modern craft movements in those countries, the Cranbrook community was built on a strong commitment to the Arts and Crafts tradition as filtered through a modern Scandinavian

sensibility. Although the school's contacts with American industry were minimal before the war, the cohort of students who studied there in the 1930s later introduced a major new approach to American design. Imbued with a craft sensibility and a respect for technology, they engaged experimentally with materials and produced major breakthroughs, especially in the design of furniture. The strength of the Cranbrook approach was initially evident in the impressive amount of work by Cranbrook students, former students, and faculty that was accepted for the Museum of Modern Art's exhibition, Organic Design in Home Furnishings, in 1941. This included the prize-winning furniture of Charles Eames and Eero Saarinen as well as that of Harry Weese and Benjamin Baldwin along with fabrics by Marianne Strengell.

The first-prize winner in the textile division of the Organic Design exhibition was Marli Ehrmann (1904–1982), who had studied textile design at the Bauhaus and at the time headed a program in textile design at the School of Design in Chicago. The school's director was former Bauhaus teacher László Moholy-Nagy. He had come to Chicago in 1937 at the invitation of a civic group, the Association of Arts and Industries, to head up a design school that was originally called the New Bauhaus. During the decade that Moholy was director of the school, it went through several changes, beginning as the New Bauhaus in 1937, then reinventing itself as the School of Design in 1942, and finally becoming the Institute of Design in 1944.

Although some Americans taught at the school, a number of the teachers were European. Marli Ehrmann and Hin Bredendieck were former Bauhaus students; Gyorgy Kepes had worked with Moholy in Berlin and London; Alexander Archipenko (1887–1964) was a Russian sculptor who had been associated with the Cubist movement in Paris; and Marianne Willisch (d.o.b. unconfirmed–1984) was an artist who managed the Austrian Werkbund's shop in Vienna. In 1930, she moved to Chicago, where she joined a group of artists and architects to organize the Chicago Workshops, a cooperative that produced furniture and crafts and sold them in their own shop. George Fred Keck, one of the American teachers at the school, was an architect with an active Chicago practice. He designed several innovative houses for the Century of Progress Exhibition in 1933 including the House of Tomorrow and the Crystal House. Keck headed the architecture department for about five years.

Moholy was a painter and sculptor as well as a photographer, industrial designer, and a graphic artist. Unlike Eliel Saarinen at Cranbrook, he did not emphasize traditional craft techniques in the curriculum. As a former avant-garde activist, he was more interested in experimental work and sought to break down the barriers between the different art and design practices. Though Moholy received most of his financial support from local businesses, particularly the Container Corporation of America, the school did not train students for conventional design jobs in industry. Moholy was an idealist who believed that industry should be guided by more innovative visions and consequently the emphasis of the school was on encouraging students to think about their work in new ways. Due to private funding, financial support was always a problem and the school was never on a secure footing until it was absorbed by the Illinois Institute of Technology in 1949.

Central to the curriculum was the Foundation Course. It was based to some degree on the one at the Bauhaus, which Moholy taught after he replaced Johannes Itten in 1923. In the 1930s, no other design school in America had such a course, whose intent was to open the students' minds to the possibilities of working with different materials. Moholy also believed that artists and designers needed a strong human-istic education so he invited the philosopher Charles Morris and two other professors from the University of Chicago to give courses at the school, which they did for a brief period.

Similar to the Bauhaus in Germany, students completed the Foundation Course and then entered one of the specialized areas. These included photography, product design, textiles, interiors, and architecture as well as a special Light Workshop, headed by Gyorgy Kepes, that incorporated photography, film, typog-raphy, and layout. Kepes based his curriculum on the manipulation of abstract elements—light, space, line, and color—and techniques like photomontage. He described his pedagogy in *The Language of Vision*, an influential book that was published in 1944 by the émigré publisher Paul Theobald in Chicago.

Unlike Cranbrook, whose students and faculty made a major impact on the design of American furniture and interiors after World War II, the influence of Moholy's curriculum was particularly strong in photography whose practice in America his students and faculty helped to transform. In graphic design, Kepes introduced a pedagogical approach that was unknown anywhere else in the United States and after the war a number of the school's students achieved prominence in this field. Many of Moholy's students became design teachers themselves and continued to transmit to their own students the spirit of experimen-tation and wonder that he introduced in the Chicago curriculum.

Another former Bauhaus teacher, Josef Albers (1888–1976) also kept the Bauhaus spirit alive at Black Mountain College, an experimental school that combined the visual, literary, dramatic, and musical arts. Albers and his wife Anni (1899–1994), who had studied weaving at the Bauhaus under Gunta Stözl, came to the United States in 1933, the year Black Mountain was founded. Albers, who was primarily a painter and print maker, taught a design course where students learned to see their environment in a new way. Around 1940, the school introduced some courses in architecture and furniture design, although Black Mountain never had a formal program in either of these areas. Anni Albers directed a workshop for weaving and textile design that prepared students to design for industrial production. The textiles that Albers and her students produced at Black Mountain had a distinctive quality. The patterns were geometric and they featured the thread as a material, while the range of colors was limited primarily to black, white, and natural fibers.

Though Frank Lloyd Wright opposed the pedagogy of the Bauhaus because it did not originate in America, he was not against the apprenticeship system, which Walter Gropius had originally built into the pedagogical design of the Weimar Bauhaus and which Eliel Saarinen introduced at Cranbrook, where Wright lectured occasionally. In a series of six lectures he gave at Princeton University in 1930, Wright called for a new relationship between design and industrial production. To achieve this, he proposed the establishment of corporate-funded decentralized "industrial style centers" in rural areas around the country. According to Wright's idea, master craftsmen at each center would guide small numbers of students in the study of glass-making, pottery, textiles, sheet metal, landscaping, and the arts. Having lauded the use of the machine in his seminal Hull House lecture of 1901, Wright imagined that students at his centers would learn with the latest techniques and be trained on the most modern machines. The other aspect of Wright's proposal was that the students would spend several hours a day working the land and would possibly bring some revenue to the centers by marketing the products they designed. Although Wright found no sponsorship for his idea, he did open his own apprenticeship academy two years later. Known as the Taliesin Fellowship because of its proximity to Taliesin, Wright's home and studio in Wisconsin, its focus, however, was on architecture rather than design, and instead of creating their own designs, students were devoted primarily to supporting Wright's practice.

Two years before the New Bauhaus opened its doors in 1937, the Bauhaus in Germany became the model for another American school, the Design Laboratory, which operated in New York City between 1935 and 1940. Initially the Works Project Administration's Federal Art Project, which was established as part of Franklin Delano Roosevelt's New Deal,

funded it and free tuition was offered to students. The school's director, Gilbert Rohde, already a well-known industrial designer, envisioned the Design Laboratory as a training ground for professional designers. Its mission, he said, was to coordinate training in aesthetics, product design, machine fabrication, and merchandising. When it opened, it included a design school with courses in industrial design, textiles, and ceramics, a graphic arts school, and a school of fine arts. Several of the faculty members, Hilda Reiss and Leila Ulrich (dates unconfirmed), had studied at the Bauhaus for several years in Dessau and Berlin under Mies van der Rohe, and a third teacher, William Priestley (dates unconfirmed), had been at the school briefly before it closed. During the severe WPA budget cuts in June 1937, the Design Laboratory lost all government support, leading members of the faculty and student body to continue it as a private enterprise, which they did until 1940.

The Federal Arts Project also funded Community Arts Centers, which were intended to bring arts and crafts training and exhibitions to rural areas or urban neighborhoods that had little access to art schools, galleries, or museums. A number of centers were established in African-American neighborhoods and of these the Harlem Community Art Center was the most prominent. Between 1937 and 1942, the Harlem Center offered classes in art, craft, and design to large numbers of black students. Until 1938, the center's director was the sculptress Augusta Savage (1892–1962), who was also a prominent arts educator. Then Gwen Bennett (1902–1981), a poet, artist and illustrator, took over the job. Although the faculty of men and women was integrated, African-American women played a prominent role as teachers. They included Louise E. Jefferson (1908–2002), a commercial artist who taught textile design; Octavia Clark (dates unconfirmed), whose specialty was costume design; and Sarah West (dates unconfirmed), who taught metal craft. In Chicago, the South Side Community Arts Center, which opened in 1940, also served as a place where

African-Americans took art classes and where possibilities of working in design were discussed. Its principal founder was the artist Margaret Burroughs (1915–2010) and prominent among those interested in design was William McBride (d.o.b. unconfirmed–2000)

World's Fairs
The Century of Progress 1933–1934

The problems of unemployment, race, and cultural deprivation that the Federal Arts Project addressed were far from the minds of those who planned two major world's fairs during the 1930s—the Century of Progress International Exhibition that was held in Chicago during 1933–1934, and the New York World's Fair, also known as the World of Tomorrow, which took place in Queens, just outside New York, in 1939–1940. What the two exhibitions shared as themes was the role of science and industry in helping to create a better life for everyone. This was demonstrated more explicitly in Chicago, where the organizers aimed to subordinate the display of finished products to "a dynamic presentation of actual processes." By this approach, they wished to show how discoveries in the basic sciences were turned into productive enterprises for the improvement of human life. This goal was reinforced by the inauguration of the city's new Museum of Science and Industry to coincide with the opening of the fair.

The organizers of the New York World's Fair were equally idealistic in stating their aim to foster human betterment, but they were more blatant in presenting American corporate capitalism as the instrument to bring this about. Far more corporations were enlisted as exhibitors at the New York fair than in Chicago, thus adding a strong rhetoric of merchandising to the loftier rhetoric that described a wondrous future for Americans.

The design of the Century of Progress, conceived to celebrate the 100th anniversary of Chicago's founding, was shaped by architects rather than industrial designers. The Architectural Commission in charge of the overall design strategy included some

of America's most distinguished practitioners: Harvey Wiley Corbett and Raymond Hood from New York; Paul Phillipe Cret from Philadelphia; and John Holabird and Louis Skidmore from Chicago. Both Hood and Corbett had put forth visionary plans for transforming Manhattan, although Hood's winning entry for the Chicago Tribune Tower competition in 1922 was the epitome of traditional Neo-Gothic design. Norman Bel Geddes served as a consultant to the commission on lighting and subsequently developed several bold architectural proposals for the fair including a revolving "Aerial Restaurant" that was to be constructed on a high tower, and an "Aquarium Restaurant" that was to be built underwater inside the wall of a dam.

After some deliberation, the commission agreed to adopt a modern style for the exhibition architecture that was constructed along the city's lakefront, although they did not accept any of Bel Geddes' proposals. They decided to counter the White City of the 1893 Chicago Exposition with a scheme of multicolored buildings. Joseph Urban, who had garnered a strong reputation as a designer of stage sets, was appointed Director of Color Coordination and devised a selection of 23 colors to unify the site. Three or four were applied to most buildings, creating a kaleidoscope of hues that gave the exhibition a festive air.

Dominating the commercial sector were the Ford and General Motors pavilions, both of which were enhanced by dramatic night-time lighting. Where General Motors displayed an operating assembly line in accord with the exhibition's intention to show industrial processes, Ford presented a far more dramatic display. It was designed by Walter Dorwin Teague, who pioneered the creation of dramatic exhibits as a field of expertise for industrial designers, arguing that these should be considered works of art just as buildings were.

Historically, architecture had dominated exhibition pavilions at world's fairs, and Teague had to work with a design for the Ford Pavilion by Albert Kahn, the architect of Henry Ford's River Rouge complex who created an impressive round building in the shape of a giant gear. Inside, Teague used multiple visual strategies and devices to convey Ford's history and promote its future. Among the components of his exhibit was a gigantic circular photomural of the River Rouge plant that surrounded a display of automobiles. It was only one of five features that also included exhibits of manufacturing processes, a soybean processing display, and a section where visitors could be driven along 100-foot strips that replicated 19 famous highways of the world. What distinguished Teague's concept of an industrial exhibit from that which prevailed at the time was his emphasis on a total emotional experience that was entertaining as well as informative. As a result of his success in Chicago, the Ford Pavilion set a new standard for corporate exhibits and served as an antecedent to the plethora of dramatic displays that visitors would encounter at the New York World's Fair in 1939.

Modern design was evident in buildings of different scales throughout the Century of Progress. In a section of the exhibition called "Home and Industrial Arts," the Chicago architect George Fred Keck built his "House of Tomorrow," which became one of the fair's most popular attractions (Fig. 28.22). The project was Keck's response to Le Corbusier's idea of the house as a "machine for living." Though its industrial look derived from the central utility core, steel frame,

Fig. 28.22: George Fred Keck, House of Tomorrow, Century of Progress Exhibition, 1933. UIG via Getty Images.

and large glass panels that covered its 12 sides, Keck employed a conventional method of construction that contrasted sharply with the more radical proposal for industrialized building that R. Buckminster Fuller had proposed several years earlier for a related project, his Dymaxion House. The House of Tomorrow, which had its own helicopter hangar on the first floor, was filled with modern furniture pieces, a number of which were made of chromed tubular steel. In fact, as previously mentioned, tubular steel furniture was used extensively elsewhere in the exhibition, a phenomenon that contributed to its growing acceptance in the wider culture.

Besides new houses, the Century of Progress also showcased the latest developments in transportation. Ford displayed John Tjaarda's Briggs Dream Car, while Pierce Arrow showed its new streamlined Silver Arrow, of which only five were built. In the second year of the fair, Chrysler introduced the Airflow. The most experimental vehicle on display, however, was Buckminster Fuller's aerodynamic Dymaxion Car, which had the misfortune to be involved in a fatal accident just outside the fair grounds, a fact that contributed to the reluctance of any major automobile company to put it or a variant of it into production. Streamlining was most dramatically introduced in 1934 by the Union Pacific's M-10000 and Burlington Zephyr railroad trains. The Zephyr made a particularly dramatic entry in May of that year after completing a record-breaking trip of more than 1,000 miles from Denver to Chicago in almost half the time that it took its closest rival.

Although the spectacular display of new architecture, transportation, and technology was planned to encourage a sense of public optimism in the midst of the Depression when millions were out of work and could see little hope for the future, its message was directed at only one part of the population, the country's white majority. Despite the sizeable black population in Chicago, many of whom had come up from the South during the Great Migration that began around 1916, few exhibits recognized their presence in the city and only the rare black employee, with the exception of some entertainers who appeared in stereotyped roles, did more than clean the washrooms. A replica of the log cabin originally built in 1779 by Jean Baptiste Point du Sable, a black Haitian recognized as the founder of Chicago, was one of the few exhibits that acknowledged African-American achievements. Another was the display presented by the National Urban League in the Hall of Social Science. Designed by black artist Charles C. Dawson (1889–c. 1980), it consisted of a large painting of his, depicting the black migration to the North, which was flanked by charts and graphs that revealed through statistics the economic and social advantages that blacks had attained as well as their achievements.

As a parallel to the lakefront exhibition, historian Christopher Reed has described a much fuller depiction of black achievement that was presented at a separate African and American Negro Exhibit, which opened on Chicago's South Side in May 1933, at the same time as the Century of Progress. Here, one could see displays related to ancient African art and architecture along with contemporary art, commercial products, and chronicles of black accomplishments in science, the military, the professions, and culture.

The New York World's Fair 1939–1940

Originally the organizers of the New York World's Fair wanted to honor the 150th anniversary of George Washington's inauguration as the first American president, but the Board of Design, which replaced the Architectural Commission that had planned the Century of Progress exhibition, shifted the emphasis of the exhibition to the future, adopting as its theme, "Building the World of Tomorrow." Central to the decision was the industrial designer Walter Dorwin Teague, a member of the Board of Design, who strongly influenced the layout of the fairgrounds and whose office designed a large number of the corporate pavilions. If architects played a strong role

in determining the look and content of the Century of Progress, industrial designers assumed that role in New York. Not only did they create a considerable number of corporate displays, but they also designed the exhibits that were central to most of the thematic zones. These included production and distribution, transportation, communication, and food.

The central symbol of the exhibition, the Trylon and Perisphere, was designed by the architectural office of Wallace K. Harrison (1895–1981) and André Fouilhoux (1879–1945). The Trylon, a huge three-sided needle that tapered to a point 700 feet above the ground, complemented a large sphere which housed the exhibition's principal thematic exhibit, Democracity, designed by Henry Dreyfuss. To view the exhibit, visitors entered the Perisphere from an escalator and exited across a bridge that connected them back to the Trylon from which they descended along a huge curving ramp called a Helicline (Fig. 28.23).

Democracity was an enormous city diorama that represented urban life 100 years into the future. Drawing on his knowledge of stage design, Dreyfuss devised a combination of revolving platforms and bold lighting, adding dramatic music and narration to convey an emotional experience through total sensorial immersion. For the design, he adopted concepts from present and past urban theorists such as the late 19th-century British town planner, Ebenezer Howard, who introduced the idea of radial Garden Cities with circular green belts between denser living areas. As historian Jeffrey Meikle points out, Democracity was based on a static design that embodied a vision of controlled order. To his credit, Dreyfuss did not propose a high-technology Buck Rogers city that might well have made fair visitors uncomfortable. Instead, he provided a continuity between the present and the future, thus making it all the easier for the fair's corporate exhibitors to persuade the public that they were ready to bring the world of tomorrow into being immediately.

For the focal exhibit in the Transportation Zone,

Fig. 28.23: Walter K. Harrison and André Fouilhoux, Trylon and Perisphere, New York World's Fair, postcard, 1939. Beinecke Rare Book and Manuscript Library, Yale University.

Raymond Loewy took another tack. Instead of considering how cars, buses, and trains might be joined into an efficient national transportation system, he created a Rocketport, which dramatically visualized how rockets would rapidly whisk passengers from one continent to another in the world of the future. In the Food Zone, Russel Wright created an exhibit that used entertaining theatrical techniques to explain the progress in cultivating, processing, and distributing food since

1879. Its apotheosis was a huge ovoid form with a window through which visitors could view a surrealistic display of bejeweled avocados, flying lobsters, and other wondrous scenes.

Though Teague did not design any of the focal exhibits in the theme zones, he created more corporate pavilions than any other designer. The fair, in fact, was a powerful demonstration of Teague's claim that emotionally immersive exhibits were valuable selling tools and worth the expense. For the National Cash Register Company, he devised a gigantic cash register that became one of the fair's principal icons by ringing up the attendance numbers and displaying them prominently. He also created pavilions for other clients: Du Pont, Ford, Consolidated Edison, Kodak, A. B. Dick, and United States Steel. For Consolidated Edison, Teague produced "The City of Light," which included a diorama of New York that was more than a city block in length and higher than a building of three stories. With lighting, sound effects, and a spoken narrative, the display dramatized the role of electricity, gas, and steam in the life of the city. Teague also created another lavish display for Ford, which outdid his exhibit for the company at the Century of Progress. The "Ford Cycle of Production" featured a huge revolving turntable with more than 80 exhibits that demonstrated a progression from raw dirt to finished cars just as Henry Ford had conceived the process at River Rouge. Teague added the "Road of Tomorrow," along which visitors were conducted in cars that took them around the pavilion past murals that depicted superhighways of the future.

As extravagant as the exhibits by Dreyfuss, Loewy, and Teague were, none could equal the elaborate "Futurama" that Norman Bel Geddes designed for General Motors (Fig. 28.24). GM departed from Chrysler and Ford by choosing as its theme not its latest cars or even its efficient production process but rather the physical infrastructure, namely the additional highways, that would be required in the future to support a society that was increasingly dependent on the automobile.

The Futurama was pure theater and drew on all the techniques of staging and lighting that had made Bel Geddes one of America's most prominent theater set designers in the 1920s and early 1930s. Central to the exhibit was a diorama that depicted a future city of 1960. Like Dreyfuss in Democracity, Bel Geddes adopted the ideas of prominent planners and architects. In this case, he relied heavily on Le Corbusier's Ville Contemporaine of 1922, which consisted of residential tower blocks separated by large swathes of parkland and divided by highways. Viewers experienced the diorama from moving seats that carried them across a vast American landscape in miniature that combined farmlands and mountains with a 14-lane highway. With its 500,000 scale model buildings and 50,000 automobiles, the Futurama may well have been the largest diorama ever made. For General Motors, its accuracy was less important than its identity as a generic future landscape, where clean, modern, well-lit highways built at government expense might be eagerly welcomed as a core element of the nation's infrastructure.

The fair also featured an extensive array of pavilions from other countries, all of whom chose to foreground present economic, social, or cultural accomplishments. Besides the pavilion of the Pan American Union, which housed exhibits from various Latin American nations, Brazil constructed a contemporary building by Lucio Costa and Oscar Niemeyer, who would design their country's new capital Brasilia in the early 1950s. Alvar and Aino Aalto showed off Finland's natural resources and their potential as a resource for design in the pavilion they designed for their government (see Chapter 26). Italy's Fascist regime was represented by a monumental building that featured a large statue of Mussolini, while Japan, which by that time had invaded China and established the puppet government of Manchukuo, avoided any evidence of imperial ambitions by basing its pavilion on an ancient Shinto shrine. The Russians constructed a pavilion that followed closely the one they had built at the 1937 World's Fair in Paris, but it was torn down during the second year of the fair after Stalin and Hitler signed the German–Soviet Non-Aggression Pact.

Compared to the exhibits in these national pavilions, those of the American industrial designers were far more deeply embedded in sales and marketing strategies, although this fact was cloaked in lofty rhetoric about the bright future that their corporate

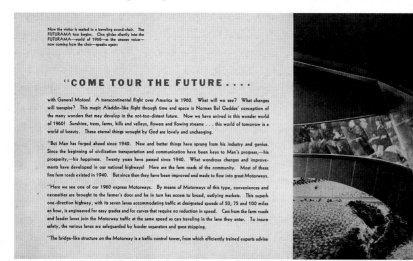

Fig. 28.24: Futurama brochure, page spread, 1940. The Wolfsonian–Florida International University, Miami Beach, Florida, The Mitchell Wolfson, Jr. Collection, 83.20.7. Photo: David Almeida.

clients would help to bring about. Like the Century of Progress, the aim of the New York World's Fair was to lift the nation's spirits and convey an optimistic vision of the future. This ambition was undermined, however, by the fair's financial difficulties in its second year and the rumbles of war in Europe and Asia. Not long after the fair closed, the United States was to be drawn into the conflict, forcing the Roosevelt administration to focus on the production of war materiel rather than consumer goods. After the war, advertising agencies worked hard to reactivate the American consumption impulse, building on the high volume of post-war manufacturing to persuade the American public once again that a better tomorrow was theirs for the buying.

Advertising, Magazines and Books
Advertising

At the end of World War I, theories to enhance the effectiveness of advertising were more highly developed in the United States than anywhere else. Many in the business world were eager to establish advertising as a science of selling and looked for assistance to psychologists like John B. Watson, the founder of behaviorism, who was hired by the J. Walter Thompson agency. Watson sought to make psychology more scientific by grounding it in experimental methods which, when applied to advertising, would motivate consumers to buy products the agency advertised.

The reliance on psychology as a tool for designing advertising campaigns reduced the autonomy of the art director, illustrator, and copywriter who had to work within a motivational framework that guided an ad's production. This approach sharply differentiated the work of American agencies from most European advertising for which the artist had considerable leeway to produce visually stimulating posters or other graphic media. Among agency executives, Earnest Elmo Calkins and his agency, Calkins & Holden, led the field in producing ads of outstanding visual quality.

Calkins & Holden hired leading artists and illustrators such as J. C. Leyendecker (1874–1951), who was widely known for his *Saturday Evening Post* covers as well as his advertising illustrations. For the Arrow Collar campaign, Calkins & Holden art director Tom Hall (dates unconfirmed) decided to depict a handsome male wearing an Arrow Collar as part of a sartorial ensemble instead of simply showing the collar by itself. Just as Charles Dana Gibson had earlier created the Gibson Girl as the turn-of-the-century feminine ideal, Leyendecker's Arrow Collar Man, modeled on his lover Charles Beach, was a suave, impeccably attired masculine persona who charmed the smartly outfitted women of America's leisure class (Plate 46). Leyendecker was also in demand by other manufacturers of men's apparel such as B. Kuppenheimer and Company, Hart, Schaffner and Marx, and Interwoven Sox. For all these clients he created well-dressed male figures, who could easily have stepped out of an F. Scott Fitzgerald novel.

Besides hiring freelance illustrators with high profiles, Calkins & Holden had its own art department, which became a model for other agencies. Walter Dorwin Teague worked in the department for a few years before he became an industrial designer. His ads were known in the industry for their decorative "Teague borders," a consequence of his interest in Rococo ornament. René Clarke (1886–1969) started with Calkins & Holden as an illustrator and eventually became a principal art director. His ads for Wesson Oil were aimed at persuading housewives to replace shortening with liquid cooking oil by depicting oil pouring from a metal Wesson container into a frying pan. This image was sometimes coupled with drawings of a leafy salad or a rich cake, a technique known as selling by association, which the agency employed for other campaigns as well. In a 1927 article, Calkins praised Clarke as an artist who found the "meeting point halfway between the utilitarian demands of business and the unlimited and undreamed-of possibilities of an art that is even now creating its own technique." Though Clarke's depictions of Wesson Oil cans were hardly vanguard art, to Calkins they pointed towards the commercial adoption of artistic modernism as a way to bring the pleasure of modern art to a broad public through promoting products. Despite Calkins' espousal of modernism, however, and its evidence in occasional ads, most campaigns continued to rely on conventional realistic illustration.

Illustrators developed their own styles and were frequently known for a particular kind of drawing or painting. Coles Phillips (1880–1927) specialized in scantily clad flappers with bobbed hair who promoted hosiery as well as more mundane products. The demure models of Clarence Underwood (1871–1929) were less daring though still appealing enough to sell Woodbury and Palmolive Soap. Albert Staehle (1899–1974) was a versatile artist although he specialized in painting animals. His image of a cow feeding her calf with a bottle of Borden's milk led to Borden's Elsie the Cow campaign. Staehle also created the original Smokey the Bear poster in 1944.

Leading women illustrators in the advertising industry included Lucille Patterson Marsh (1890–d.o.d. unconfirmed), Rose O'Neill (1875–1944), and Neysa McMein (1888–1949). Marsh worked extensively for manufacturers of home appliances, attempting to appeal to women's domestic impulse and their capacity to nurture, while Rose O'Neill specialized in coy children who were adopted by Jell-O, Kellogg's, and Oxydol. The Kewpie dolls that O'Neill introduced in some of her ads, were perhaps the first advertising figures to be turned into a separate line of merchandise. The painterly depictions that Neysa McMein did of women had more depth than typical illustrations, and she portrayed them as Egyptian princesses, nurses, or socialites in ads for Palmolive Soap and other major clients. In 1936 she created the image of Betty Crocker for General Mills and continued to update the trademark for a number of years.

Whether illustrators portrayed homey stereotypes of small-town denizens or dapper urbanites, they moved easily during the interwar years between the worlds of advertising and magazine publishing.

The two worlds, in fact, were closely related since most ads were destined for mass-circulation magazines and advertising virtually supported magazine publishing. Covers by Norman Rockwell (1894–1978), J. C. Leyendecker, or Neysa McMein for the *Saturday Evening Post* therefore widened the artists' public recognition and actually enhanced their status within the advertising industry.

The Society of Illustrators was founded in 1901 to promote illustration and soon attracted the leading figures in the field. Aside from organizing social events and gallery exhibitions, society members worked closely with the federal government during World War I to produce propaganda posters. In 1920, the society was incorporated and began to accept women as full-time members. That same year a small group of art directors became charter members of the Art Directors Club, whose founding was strongly promoted by Earnest Elmo Calkins. The club inaugurated a series of annual exhibitions that were intended to explain just what an art director did. By treating the exhibitions as cultural events, the club members could make a better case for their work as a form of art even though it was done for commercial purposes. The exhibitions presented the art director as a middleman between the client and the creative types who produced the art and copy. If an agency or artist wanted to introduce modern art to a campaign, it was up to the art director to convince the client that it made business sense.

Only a few agencies were actively committed to using modern art, notably Calkins & Holden and J. Walter Thompson in New York; Erwin, Wasey & Company in Chicago; and N. W. Ayer and Son in Philadelphia. Perhaps the most successful of these was N. W. Ayer, the nation's oldest advertising agency and the first to hire an art director. For many years the dominant figure in Ayer's art department was Charles T. Coiner (1898–1989), whose career at the agency spanned more than 40 years. Coiner joined N. W. Ayer as a layout artist in 1924. He moved up to art director in 1929 and to vice-president in 1936.

Ayer was fortunate in its selection of clients. Some such as De Beers Consolidated Mines, Climax Molybdenum, and the French Line made luxury products or provided costly services for which modern art became a sign of quality and exclusivity. By contrast, the Container Corporation of America (CCA), another N. W. Ayer client, produced paperboard boxes, but the company's founder and chief executive, Walter Paepcke, understood how modern art could add luster to a mundane product. He was also highly conscious of good design as a company value. In 1936, Paepcke hired Egbert Jacobson as the CCA director of design, perhaps the first time that a designer occupied such a position in an American corporation. Jacobson worked closely with N. W. Ayer on the company's advertising while also implementing a corporate identity program and designing the interiors of CCA's mills and factories.

Where art directors tended to hire commercial illustrators to imitate the styles of European modern artists, Coiner commissioned paintings and drawings directly from European, as well as American, artists who ran the gamut from establishment to avant-garde. These included Pablo Picasso, Raoul Dufy, Marie Laurencin, Salvador Dali, Man Ray, László Moholy-Nagy, and Georgia O'Keefe. Coiner also hired Alexey Brodovitch, Herbert Matter, Gyorgy Kepes, A. M. Cassandre, and Herbert Bayer, all European modernist designers who had either settled in the United States or came for a brief period.

While many of the ads that N. W. Ayer produced followed the conventional separation between a painting or photograph and a block of copy, some were designed in the European style, which featured a closer integration of images and text. This was evident in 12 black-and-white newspaper ads that Coiner commissioned from the French poster artist A. M. Cassandre for the Container Corporation of America in 1937. Besides Cassandre's adoption of ambiguous Surrealistic imagery, the ads were equally radical in their rejection of narrative copy in favor of single words and phrases. One ad promoted CCA's research in paperboard packaging by featuring the heads of three figures, enclosed in a circular form, gazing intensely at a cardboard box. The circle was framed by the word "Concentration," a quality meant to characterize CCA's research efforts. N. W. Ayer also produced a series of wartime ads for CCA that emphasized the company's participation in the war effort. These were done primarily by designers from Europe who made use of the most highly developed visual techniques—collage, photomontage, and angular lines of type. Mo Leibowitz (1918–1974), an American designer working in Philadelphia who embraced European modernism, also contributed to the series.

Until the 1930s, agencies used photographs relatively infrequently in advertisements. Clarence H. White (1871–1925), a founding member of the Photo-Secession, which helped to improve the quality of art photography, was perhaps the first important photographer to take advertising seriously. In 1914, he opened the Clarence White School of Photography in New York, where he developed what Michele Bogart has called "a pedagogy of experimentation." The curriculum emphasized formal design principles as essential components of a photograph and students worked on problems whose solutions depended on composition, lighting, and printing.

Many projects centered on everyday objects, and White encouraged students to dedicate their talents to commercial photography along with fine art. Consequently, a number became leading advertising photographers as well as photojournalists and filmmakers. These included Paul Outerbridge (1896–1958), Anton Bruehl (1900–1983), Margaret Bourke-White (1904–1971), Dorothea Lange (1895–1965) and Ralph Steiner (1899–1986).

Both Outerbridge and Bruehl were in high demand for advertising photography, as was Edward Steichen (1879–1973), who had gained a wide reputation as a photographer of famous people. Steichen received annual contracts from the J. Walter Thompson agency between 1924 and 1931, where he, like the former students of Clarence White, introduced the strong compositional and tonal values of art photography to the commercial sphere. Beginning in 1923, he also worked regularly for Condé Nast publications as a fashion photographer for *Vanity Fair* and *Vogue*.

Advertising photographs were of different types. Like Outerbridge's Ide Collar ad for *Vanity Fair* in 1922, they could feature a single object or group of objects that were dramatically lit (Fig. 28.25). Photographers would also set up narrative scenes that were similar to those of the illustrators or they might feature a model or several models shot from an unusual angle. During the 1920s, photographs were in black and white, but by the mid-1930s, color began to dominate the field.

Throughout the 1920s, champions of

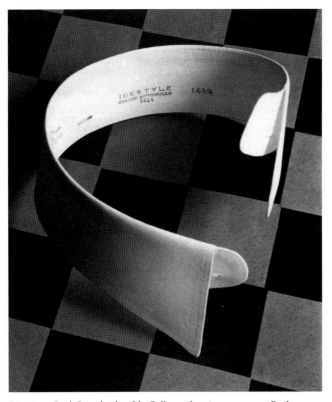

Fig. 28.25: Paul Outerbridge, Ide Collars, advertisement, 1922. Paul Outerbridge, Jr. © 2014 G. Ray Hawkins Gallery, Beverly Hills, CA. New York, Museum of Modern Art (MoMA). Platinum print, 4 ½ x 3 ⅝ inches (11.9 x 9.2 cm). Gift of the photographer. Acc. no.: 393.1972.© 2014. Digital image, The Museum of Modern Art, New York/Scala, Florence.

photography campaigned hard to assert its superiority to illustration. By the early 1930s, they began to succeed. Only 5 percent of magazine advertising featured photographs in July 1927. By 1935, this figure had jumped to 90 percent, thus contributing to the demise of the advertising illustrator.

Though advertisements were mainly produced for mass-circulation magazines, they also appeared on huge billboards that lined highways across the United States. These were owned by companies who sold advertising space just as magazines did. In 1925, the billboard owners formed a trade group, the Outdoor Advertising Association of America, which did much to establish regulations and standards for the industry. Many of the same illustrators who worked on print advertisements created large posters for billboard display. These included J. C. Leyendecker, Norman Rockwell, Clarence Underwood, and McClelland Barclay (1891–1943). What differentiated the billboards from the print advertisements were the prominence of the image and the reduction of copy. Unlike print ads, the image had the primary responsibility to convey the message, while the text had to identify the product and perhaps function as a simple copy line.

Though most billboard images were in a traditional realistic style, there were some initiatives to introduce modern designs. Within the outdoor advertising industry, the West Coast was considered most advanced in applying modern art to billboard advertising, with Foster and Kleiser, the largest agency in that part of the country, leading the way. The company established its own art department in 1917 and offered complete services to clients and advertising agencies. Artists who worked for Foster and Kleiser included Maurice del Mué (1875–1955), Jacob Ansanger (1887–1941), Fred Ludekens (1900–1982), Maynard Dixon (1875–1946), and Otis Shepard (1893–1969). Most were figurative painters who adopted a modernistic style when they joined the company. Shepard, who began to work for Foster and Kleiser in 1917, had a background in commercial art and was the company's art director from 1923 until he left in 1929. He went to Chicago to join the Wrigley Company, which made chewing gum, and he became the company's art director in 1932.

During a long career with Wrigley, Shepard created a distinctive billboard style, perhaps the most modern in outdoor advertising during the 1930s (Plate 47). The flat figures, strong colors, and unusual perspectives that became his hallmark owed a considerable amount to Joseph Binder, the Austrian poster artist who had given a workshop in Chicago in 1934 and moved to New York shortly thereafter. Binder was among a group of European graphic artists who emigrated to the United States in the 1920s and 1930s. Like A. M. Cassandre, he introduced a modern European poster style that featured strong simplified images rather than more detailed illustration. Although he mainly designed posters, Binder also did several billboards for Ballantine's Ale and Beer.

Lucian Bernhard, the most important poster artist in the pre-war German *sachplakat* movement, came to New York in the early 1920s, although he had difficulty getting work as a graphic designer because American advertising agencies found his work too progressive for their clients. Bernhard did pick up several corporate accounts and for almost 20 years he created monthly billboards for the manufacturer of REM cough syrup and for Amoco Gas. Other European designers who occasionally designed billboards in a modern style were Alexey Brodovitch, Xanti Schawinsky, A. M. Cassandre, and Eric Nitsche (1908–1998).

Besides producing advertising campaigns, ad agencies frequently designed packaging for their clients, although independent designers did this as well. In his discussions of beauty as a new advertising tool, Earnest Elmo Calkins recognized that attractive packages could enhance product sales. A book of packaging case studies compiled in 1939 noted that improved packaging had increased sales between 20 percent and 200 percent for a number of the companies studied.

The design of packages had several aspects. One was the physical form of the container and the method of packing the product. Another was the redesign of the package label or container shape in order to attract customers. It was the latter with which advertising agencies and design firms were primarily concerned. After joining Calkins & Holden in 1929, Egmont Arens started an Industrial Styling Division for the agency, where he designed or redesigned packages for many clients. Joseph Sinel combined product design with the design of packages, as did George Switzer, who began as an advertising agency art director before he opened an industrial design office, where he mainly did packaging.

Advertising agencies also recognized the value of trademarks, particularly folksy character marks, in creating brand identity. The invention of such marks began in the late 19th century and continued during the interwar years. While a number were designed within the agencies or in company art departments, many were created by independent artists or designers. Character trademarks were especially popular for consumer products such as food and cigarettes, but gasoline companies like Standard Oil, which adopted the mythical flying horse Pegasus in 1911, occasionally commissioned such marks to provide a visual identity for their otherwise invisible products.

In 1913, R. J. Reynolds Tobacco chose a camel to represent a blended cigarette made of American and Turkish tobacco. The package designer drew the camel in a desert landscape standing between two pyramids (Fig. 28.26). That the pyramids are in Egypt rather than Turkey and neither palm trees nor deserts typify the Turkish landscape did not seem to matter to R. J. Reynolds, which adopted generic Middle Eastern imagery for its brand identity. Nor did the inaccuracy matter to consumers. By 1921, sales of Camel cigarettes accounted for half the American cigarette market. The Phillip Morris bellhop, the icon of another major cigarette company that originated in 1919, was no competition for Camel cigarettes visually but the sound of a live bellhop shouting, "Call for Phillip Morris," could be heard on many radio shows throughout the 1930s and 1940s. One of the most ubiquitous animal

Fig. 28.27: Lucian Bernhard, Cat's Paw logo, 1941. © Jeff Morgan 03/Alamy. © DACS 2017.

Fig. 28.26: R. J. Reynolds, Camel cigarette package, c. 1920s. © jbcn/Alamy.

logos was the black cat that Lucian Bernhard created in 1941 to promote the sale of Cat's Paw Rubber heels (Fig. 28.27). Similar to barber poles in front of barbershops, they were near ubiquitous in shoe repair shops around the country for many years.

Among food trademarks, Mr. Peanut, the trademark of the Planters Nut and Chocolate Company that was introduced in 1918, was actually the idea of a schoolboy who submitted it for a contest run by the company. In 1925, the Minnesota Valley Canning Company introduced an equally whimsical figure, the Green Giant, to brand a new variety of pea. Children were also favorite choices for character trademarks. The makers of Mary Jane candy bars adopted a little cartoon girl as their mark around 1920, while a young boy in a sailor suit, Sailor Jack, and his dog became the brand identity for the caramel-coated popcorn, Cracker Jack, around 1924.

Trademark characters were white unless an ethnic figure could contribute some special quality to

the product (see Chapter 17). The R. T. Davis Mill & Manufacturing Company adopted a black cook whom they called Aunt Jemima as the trademark for their pancake flour. The figure went through several iterations beginning around 1890 but when redrawn around 1917, Aunt Jemima was still an unflattering stereotype characterized by her flashing white teeth. Variations of this figure remained for years even after Quaker Oats took over the brand in 1924.

Indians were also rampant as trademarks for everything from coal and tires to Land O'Lakes butter. In advertisements, Indians were too exotic to take part in the narratives that were directed at the white middle class, but black maids and railroad porters figured prominently in ads for a wide range of goods and services. Character trademarks were associated with consumer products but more abstract marks were devised for other entities such as railroads, airlines, publishers, civic organizations, and small manufacturers. Joseph Sinel, who created many of these in addition to product packaging and advertising illustrations, did a survey of them in *A Book of American Trade-Marks & Devices*, which he compiled in 1924. Advertising agencies or industrial design firms created most company trademarks in the interwar years as part of the comprehensive service they offered their clients.

Magazines and newspapers

Some of the illustrators who were active in the advertising industry were also prominent magazine artists
and were recognized nationally for their covers as
well as paintings and drawings that illustrated the
magazines' contents. Though magazines were largely
published for specific audiences, a few like the *Saturday
Evening Post* cut across a wide swath of middle-class
readers, gaining a circulation of three million by 1937.
The *Post* maintained a staid editorial policy, avoiding
articles and stories that might be controversial or
overly critical. J. C. Leyendecker was the first of their
prominent cover artists, beginning his association with
the magazine around 1906 and continuing until 1943.
Norman Rockwell (1894–1978), who learned much from
Leyendecker, did his first cover for the *Post* in 1916 and
over the course of 50 years completed more than 300
others. Depicting the daily lives of ordinary small-town
white folks, Rockwell's covers conveyed a sense of social
stability to a large number of Americans, countering
the economic uncertainties of the Depression and the
country's widespread racial injustices.

The conservative masthead, typography, and
layout of the *Saturday Evening Post* were consistent
with the contents of the magazine. Few mass-circulation publications of the interwar years, outside the
fashion periodicals, paid attention to design as a factor
that might increase circulation. One exception was
McCall's, a women's magazine, which was redesigned
by its editor Otis Wiese (dates unconfirmed) in 1932.
The makeover was both editorial and graphic. Wiese
hired Henry Dreyfuss to do the visual redesign and
McCall's remained a Dreyfuss client until 1944. The
experience Dreyfuss gained with the magazine probably
emboldened him to propose changes in *Time* magazine's
design to Henry Luce. Dreyfuss counseled Luce to
get rid of the ornamental columns, which he called
"spinach." They had flanked the cover images since the
magazine's inception and a change occurred during
1938. In 1943, Dreyfuss suggested a major revamping of
Time's covers by urging Luce to depict the figures that

graced them weekly against backgrounds that explained
to the readers something about their profession or
pursuits, an idea that Luce accepted.

Time, which Henry Luce founded with Britton
Hadden in 1923, was a new kind of magazine. Instead
of the lengthy essays that had previously characterized
the mass-circulation publications, *Time* published short
anonymously written articles on news around the
world. Luce's and Hadden's rationale was that busy
people did not have time to read long articles. The
single word title was also innovative. It did not identify
a personality, as did *McClure's* or *McCall's*, but rather
a quality. This was equally true for the subsequent
magazines, *Fortune* and *Life*, that Luce inaugurated in
1930 and 1936 respectively.

Time's design was not distinctive, but Luce paid
more attention to design when he started *Fortune,*
a magazine dedicated to describing and explaining
American business. He vowed to make it "as beautiful a
magazine as exists in the United States." To create a look
for it he hired T. M. Cleland (1880–1964), then one of
New York's most successful graphic artists, who had
previously designed typefaces and decorative borders,
books, magazines, and advertisements. Between
1906 and 1908, Cleland was art editor for *McClure's*
magazine, and he later created ads with heavy doses of
historic decoration for the Locomobile, Marmon, and
Cadillac, all cars designed for the luxury market.

Cleland upheld traditional tenets of typography and ornament, preferring the decorative taste
of the French Renaissance to more modern styles. He
designed *Fortune* as he might have a book, choosing
conservative lettering for the magazine's masthead, and
Baskerville, an 18th-century English type, for the body
copy. In fact, Cleland's concept for *Fortune* seemed
out of step with Luce's ambition and he left *Fortune*
after designing only three issues. Eleanor Treacy (dates
unconfirmed) took over as art editor and served in that
position until 1938. She sought to modernize *Fortune*'s
design, although Cleland's format remained in place
until the end of the 1930s.

Cleland's reserved design seemed to contradict Luce's idea that photography would play a central role in *Fortune*'s editorial policy. In 1929, before the first issue of the magazine appeared, Luce hired Margaret Bourke-White, a former student of Clarence White, as a staff photographer. Within several years, she had photographed industrial settings in the United States, Germany, and the Soviet Union for *Fortune*, thus adding a more modern look to the magazine.

When Luce began to publish *Life* in 1936, Bourke-White joined the staff and her picture of the Fort Peck Dam construction was featured on the cover of the first issue (Fig. 28.28). Just as *Time*'s editors changed the way copy was written by publishing shortened texts and introducing a contemporary vocabulary, so did *Life* redefine the role of the picture by building feature stories around photographs as well as using them to convey breaking news. It was the first American picture magazine, following such European precedents as the *Münchner Illustrierte Zeitung* in Germany and *Vu* in France. Luce foresaw an additional didactic function for *Life*, which the editors fulfilled by making use of pictures, diagrams, and charts to explain concepts of science, medicine and aspects of world affairs.

Several months after *Life* appeared, another picture magazine, *Look*, hit the newsstands. Unlike *Life*, however, it did not report the news but relied instead on feature articles that were not directly related to current events.

Luce's ambition to make *Fortune* America's most beautiful publication faced stiff competition from Condé Nast and William Randolph Hearst, both publishers of fashion magazines whose visual formats were shaped by European art directors familiar with the latest trends in modern art and design. Nast had joined *Collier's Weekly* in 1897, where he helped to augment sales by featuring the covers and drawings of Charles Dana Gibson. Around 1909, he began to build his own publishing empire starting with *Vogue*, and then expanding to include *House & Garden* and *Vanity Fair*. To edit *Vanity Fair* he approached

Frank Crowninshield (1872–1947), a former magazine publisher and editor, and a wealthy New York bon vivant. As editor, beginning in 1914, Crowninshield gave *Vanity Fair* an elegant look. Similar to Charles Coiner in advertising, he solicited artwork directly from leading artists and illustrators including Pablo Picasso, Marie Laurencin, Jacob Epstein, Eduardo Benito, Rockwell Kent, Miguel Covarrubias, and Kees van Dongen. Beginning around 1922, *Vanity Fair* also featured photographs by Edward Steichen, Paul Outerbridge, Charles Sheeler, Anton Bruehl, and George Hoyningen-Huene. Crowninshield's taste in modern art and photography was matched by his instinct for good literature and he published some of America's best modern writers.

Although he had impeccable taste in the visual arts, Crowninshield was an art editor rather than a designer and *Vanity Fair*'s visual format as well as that of *Vogue*, whose art director was Heyworth Campbell (d.o.b. unconfirmed–1953), relied too heavily on conventional typography and layout techniques. Nast asked one of his illustrators, Eduardo Benito (1891–1981), who was familiar with the French *moderne* graphic style, to redesign *Vogue*, which Benito did, although he declined to become the magazine's art director when Nast offered him the job. Instead, Nast hired Dr. Mehemed Fehmy Agha, a Turkish cosmopolitan who was working for the German edition of *Vogue* in Berlin (see Chapter 22).

Between 1929 and 1943, Agha completely transformed the look of *Vanity Fair*, *Vogue*, and *House & Garden*. Crowninshield had created a strong foundation at *Vanity Fair* by developing relationships with many modern artists, illustrators, and photographers, while artistic photography had become a staple of *Vogue* after Edward Steichen began working for Nast in 1923. Strongly guided by Benito's redesign of *Vogue*, Agha introduced san serif type to both *Vogue* and *Vanity Fair*, made extensive use of white space, changed the headline shapes, employed asymmetric layouts, and added color photography and two-page photographic spreads. He

Fig. 28.28: Margaret Bourke-White, *Life* magazine, cover, 1936. Time & Life Pictures/Getty Images.

careers in graphic design. Pineles began as Agha's assistant in 1932 and was promoted to art director of a new Nast publication, *Glamour*, in 1939, while Golden worked on *House & Garden* before he moved to CBS in 1937. Dr. Agha left Condé Nast in 1943 to establish his own consulting business and was replaced as art director by Alexander Liberman (1912–1999), who had been working for *Vu* in Paris.

More than any other American magazines in the interwar years, *Vanity Fair*, until it was absorbed by *Vogue* in 1936, *Vogue*, and *Harper's Bazaar*, which was published by William Randolph Hearst, were conduits for European and American modernism in art, photography, and graphic design. This was due largely to the inherent cosmopolitanism of the fashion industry, which indirectly supported both *Vogue* and *Harper's Bazaar*. Dr. Agha's counterpart at *Harper's Bazaar* was Alexey Brodovitch, who had been a successful art director in Paris (see Chapter 22). Brodovitch came to the United States in 1930 to direct a new department of advertising design at the Philadelphia Museum School of Industrial Arts, a position he held until 1938, while also carrying out regular assignments for Charles Coiner at N. W. Ayer.

In Philadelphia, one of Brodovitch's outstanding students was Irving Penn (1917–2009), who subsequently had a long career as a photographer for *Vogue* and other publications. Brodovitch also developed a Design Laboratory for artistic professionals. His first workshops began in Philadelphia in 1933, but later ones held in New York were attended by some of the greatest photographers, graphic designers, and art directors of the post-war years such as Richard Avedon and George Lois.

In 1934, Brodovitch came to the attention of Carmel Snow, the editor of *Harper's Bazaar*, who offered him the position of art director at the magazine. Snow had worked for *Vogue* since 1921 and was named editor of *Bazaar* about the same time that Dr. Agha joined Condé Nast. She was thus familiar with what an art director could contribute to a magazine and, having

also paid attention to the sequence of the page spreads, designing them to attain maximum visual continuity.

Dr. Agha continued to commission covers and illustrations from Benito and Covarrubias, who were already part of the Nast stable, and he drew in other artists who were steeped in modern or avant-garde art such as the Italians Paulo Garretto (1903–1989) and also Fortunato Depero (see Chapter 27), who maintained a studio in New York from 1928 to 1930. Agha invited advertisers to take more risks, and the receptivity of *Vanity Fair* and *Vogue* to modern advertising gave a strong boost to commercial photographers who favored experimentation.

As well, Agha trained a few young designers including Cipe Pineles (1908–1991) and William Golden (1911–1959), who went on to distinguished seen an exhibit installation of Brodovitch's at the New York Art Directors Club, must have recognized in him a potentially strong rival to Dr. Agha.

Like Agha, Brodovitch introduced many new visual ideas to magazine design during his long tenure with *Bazaar*. His influences ranged from Diaghilev's Ballets Russes to the films of Sergei Eisenstein and the architecture of Le Corbusier, and his taste transcended conventional labels of modern or traditional. For example, he selected the eighteenth-century Didot typeface for *Bazaar*'s new logo, highlighting the elegance of its thick and thin strokes. Brodovitch used white space extensively just as Dr. Agha did, but he incorporated photography more dramatically. He was known for his extensive cropping and his cinematic page sequences. His type sensibility was highly refined and he worked with a limited number of typefaces, which he used for dramatic effect. As well, Brodovitch encouraged young talent and was instrumental in launching the career of photographer Richard Avedon (1923–2004).

While there were many magazines for women in the 1920s and 1930s, ranging from the *Ladies' Home Journal*, which was aimed at middle-class homemakers, to *Vogue* and *Harper's Bazaar*, both directed to women of the wealthy fashion set, the market for men's magazines was dominated by special interest publications devoted to sports or other subjects of predominantly male interest or else to pinup pictures, the latter becoming known as "girlie magazines."

When David Smart and Arnold Gingrich founded *Esquire* in 1937, they still relied on pinups by George Petty (1894–1975) and later Alberto Vargas (1896–1982), but elevated the content with fiction by F. Scott Fitzgerald, Ernest Hemingway, and other writers of quality. The magazine's character trademark, Esky, a sprightly womanizer of a certain age with bulging eyeballs and a bushy white moustache, was designed by a black illustrator, E. Simms Campbell (1906–1971), who was a major contributor of cartoons and illustrations to *Esquire* for many years. Though

Campbell specialized in drawing voluptuous white women as well as his signature cartoon character, a little bearded sultan with an amorous appetite, the magazine on occasion published illustrations of his that featured blacks. But *Esquire* was marketed to a white male population and would only print images of blacks to the point that it did not threaten their readership. Based on his success as an *Esquire* illustrator, however, Campbell also did drawings of sexy white females to help sell Barbasol shaving cream, Springmaid Sheets, and other mainstream products.

Campbell was the rare black artist who worked for mainstream publications during the 1920s or 1930s. Instead, the principal outlet for these artists was the black press, also known by the derogatory term "race press," for which a number of artists did layouts or drew cartoons. The oldest of the black newspapers, the *Chicago Defender*, was founded in 1905 and had become America's largest black weekly by World War I. Jay Jackson (1904–c. 1953) joined the *Defender* in 1933 and worked as a hard-hitting editorial cartoonist while also drawing his own comic strip superhero, *Speed Jaxon*, and taking over another strip, *Bungleton Green*, which Leslie Rogers (dates unconfirmed), an early black woman cartoonist, first began to draw for the *Defender* in 1920. Other cartoonists who worked for the *Defender* included Chester Commodore (1914–2004), who joined the staff following World War II, and Jackie Ormes (1911–1985), who began her cartooning career with the *Pittsburgh Courier* and whose panel cartoon *Patty-Jo 'n' Ginger* for the *Defender* took off after the war. Beginning in 1935, Ollie Harrington (1912–1995) drew a regular single-panel cartoon, *Dark Laughter*, for the *Amsterdam News* in New York. Humor was a way for Harrington to express his hatred of racism, which he embodied in his well-known character Bootsie.

Besides newspapers, cultural journals and magazines for an African-American readership provided an outlet for black artists. The major ones were *The Crisis*, edited by activist W. E. B. Du Bois for the National Association for the Advancement of Colored People; *Opportunity*, published by the National Urban League; and *The Messenger*, a socialist journal started by A. Philip Randolph and Chandler Owen that became the official organ of the Brotherhood of Sleeping Car Porters for a brief period. Black artists such as Gwendolyn Bennett (1902–1981), Laura Wheeler Waring (1887–1948), and Alfred Smith (1896–1940) were among those whose drawings served as covers or illustrations for articles.

Aaron Douglas (1898–1979), another black artist, was also a contributor of cover drawings and content illustrations to *The Crisis* and *Opportunity*. Douglas was active in the Harlem Renaissance, a movement promoted by the writer and philosopher Alain Locke during the 1920s to encourage black artists to find the source of their inspiration in African imagery and styles. The silhouette figures with African features that Douglas drew for *The Crisis* and *Opportunity* epitomized Locke's call for black artists to return to their African roots. Though expressions of black identity, they were not militant as was the cover Douglas created for the single issue of *Fire!*, a literary magazine whose zeal for a new black culture he shared.

Books

Many new publishing houses were founded in the 1920s, including Horace Liveright, Covici-Friede, Viking Press, Simon & Schuster, and Random House. Alfred A. Knopf was also among these new publishers. The firm was established in 1917 but did not begin to build a strong reputation until after World War I. These publishers, along with others, were responsible for books by important new writers, both white and black—Sinclair Lewis, Jean Toomer, F. Scott Fitzgerald, Wallace Thurman, Ernest Hemingway, Eugene O'Neill, Langston Hughes, and John Dos Passos among them. The trade publishers' efforts to reach a broad market were complemented by other types of publishers such as George Macy, whose Limited Editions Club and Heritage Club produced handsomely designed editions of literary classics that were available to a select number

of subscribers. There were also small publishers who concentrated on fine letterpress printing such as Joseph Blumenthal's Spiral Press, the Grabhorn Press in San Francisco, and the Ward Ritchie Press in Los Angeles.

In addition to these were the presses at Harvard, Yale, and other universities. At Yale, Carl Purington Rollins (1880–1960), a devotee of the Arts and Crafts movement, headed the Printing Office. He not only maintained high standards of fine letterpress printing for the Yale University Press, where he was responsible for more than 2,000 books, but he enforced these standards as well for a broad range of catalogs, broadsides, diplomas, and other university ephemera.

Among the trade publishers, Alfred A. Knopf was recognized for the exceptional design of its books, due largely to William Addison Dwiggins (1880–1956), who designed his first book for Knopf in 1926. Though Dwiggins, like Rollins, admired Arts and Crafts books, he sought to bring the private press aesthetic to the design of trade books for a mass market (Fig. 28.29). Just as William Morris did at the Kelmscott Press, Dwiggins was a designer who strove to unify all the elements of a book. He emphasized the importance of typography and recognized the need for paper of good quality. Skilled in lettering and a designer of type, Dwiggins also produced an abundance of ornaments and illustrations for his books and their jackets. He developed his own lexicon of ornaments that were neither overly decorative, as Arts and Crafts designs were, nor purely geometric, as were those espoused by some European modernists. Though Dwiggins also worked for other publishers, he designed about 280 books for Knopf during his long association with the press.

Pynson Printers, which Elmer Adler (1884–1961) founded in 1922, did much of Knopf's printing. Besides his association with Knopf, Adler worked with Random House, where he designed a limited edition of Voltaire's *Candide*, which had illustrations by Rockwell Kent (1882–1971), one of the pre-eminent book illustrators of the interwar years. Additionally, Kent's illustrations

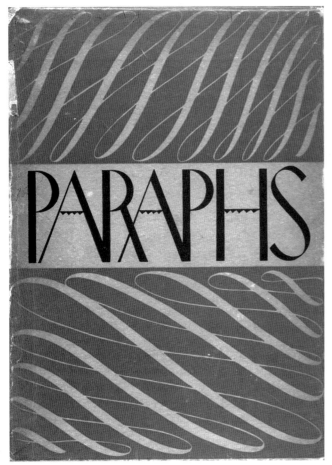

Fig. 28.29: William Addison Dwiggins. *Paraphs*, cover, 1927. Private Collection.

for Random House's *Moby Dick* helped the public to rediscover Melville's novel. Random House published further limited editions in the 1920s with typography by Bruce Rogers, then one of America's best-known typographers, and other adherents of fine printing. During the 1930s, the market for high quality limited editions collapsed and Random House began to concentrate on less expensive trade books, consequently gaining notoriety and recognition for publishing the first American edition of James Joyce's *Ulysses*.

Working for Knopf, Dwiggins defined a new role for the trade book designer by addressing all aspects of a book's design, and he helped to spawn a new profession of freelance book designers. Robert Josephy (1903–1993) was one of the first. During the 1920 and 1930s, he worked for numerous publishers, designing up to 200 books annually. Ernst Reichl (1900–1980), who had been a book designer in Munich before coming to the United States in 1926, designed a large number of books each year for many major trade publishers. Like Dwiggins, Reichl believed that a book design should be subservient to the text and he featured simplicity as a hallmark of his style. Sidney A. Jacobs (dates unconfirmed), the production manager at Knopf who also did freelance designs of his own, was more experimental than either Dwiggins or Reichl, though he was not a doctrinaire modernist. For Carl Heinrich's *Orphan of Eternity*, Jacobs adopted san serif type, which he laid out horizontally and vertically, and he created playful layouts for several volumes of poems by e.e. cummings.

Merle Armitage (1893–1975) was active in Los Angeles during the 1930s and worked independently of the trade book industry in New York. Most of the books he wrote or edited were about creative artists and he designed them to reflect some quality of the individual, whether a photographer like Edward Weston or a musician such as George Gershwin. The title spread for his book on Gershwin displayed a bold gesture. Set in Futura, it ran across two pages and featured Gershwin's name in outsized letters that dwarfed the block of copy and the illustration below it. Though his books were sometimes criticized, Armitage derived his ideas from the work of artists he admired rather than from the traditional tenets of book typography or layout.

George Salter (1897–1967) specialized in book jacket design for trade publishers. He came to New York in 1934, following a successful career in Germany. An expert calligrapher as well as an artist, Salter varied his designs from hand-lettered typographic compositions to illustrative paintings that conveyed a book's mood or atmosphere. His talent for lettering and illustration elevated the quality of jacket design and set high standards for the field. As an example, Salter's jacket for Franz Kafka's *The Trial*, published by Alfred Knopf in 1937, combined his abilities as a calligrapher and artist. The large black letters of the title expressed the ominous aspect of the trial, and Salter's painting depicted the characters involved as ghost-like figures that contrasted with the strong image of the prosecutor in a dark suit. Such covers influenced the design of jackets for all kinds of trade books from crime novels to European classics.

It was rare to find African-American artists working for trade publishers, but the publication of books by black authors offered occasional opportunities for a black artist to create jackets or illustrations. When Alfred Knopf reprinted James Weldon Johnson's *Autobiography of an Ex-Coloured Man* in 1927, Aaron Douglas did the jacket, which he followed at Johnson's request with a series of striking illustrations for the author's *God's Trombones: Seven Negro Sermons in Verse*, produced for another publisher. Douglas also adapted his style to jackets for several other novels including two by French authors that had Africa-related themes. Though he received these commissions during a period of de facto segregation in the publishing industry, Douglas was nonetheless hired as a black artist for books whose contents were explicitly related to African-American or African themes.

One of the more experimental trade publishers who began in the interwar years was New Directions, established by James Laughlin in 1936. Laughlin originally intended to publish books by influential avant-garde writers who had been ignored, but he also republished novels by major Anglo-American authors and eventually brought out English translations of many foreign writers as well. In 1939, Alvin Lustig (1915–1955), a California designer who had been designing books for the Ward Ritchie Press, did his first cover for New Directions, thus beginning an association with the press that reached its apogee after World War II. Lustig considered himself an interdisciplinary designer and his early covers for New Directions showed the influence of modern abstract art rather than

more traditional painting or illustration. His taste in typography ran to modern types like Futura, but he was also adept at inventive hand lettering that resulted in playful linear designs more reminiscent of Alexander Calder's wire sculptures than conventional calligraphy. Lustig used elements from the type case for some of has early New Directions covers as he had for the books of Ward Ritchie, but as his work developed he began to create expressive Surrealistic drawings as well as abstract forms, both of which he combined with typography. Later covers would also feature photographs.

Typography and Gaphic Design
Typography

By the time of World War I, American Type Founders (ATF) in New York had purchased most other American foundries and maintained a near monopoly on type design in the United States. In 1923, ATF produced an extraordinary specimen book and catalog with more than 1,100 pages, many of which contained typographic compositions in two or three colors. Barnhart Brothers and Spindler (BB & S), a large Chicago foundry, had resisted ATF's "type trust" but finally sold out to the company in 1911 with the proviso that it would keep its own name for 20 years. They and ATF had no rivals in the design of type for letterpress printing, but they did face competition from the linotype companies, which saw an advantage to designing their own faces.

American foundries and linotype companies viewed the typographic developments in Europe with cautious interest, a stance that was echoed by leading authors of books and articles on typography such as Edmund G. Gress (1872–1934) and Douglas McMurtrie (1888–1944). Gress, editor of *American Printer*, was perhaps the first to recognize the potential value of modern typography. In the introduction to McMurtrie's *Modern Typography and Layout*, published in 1929, Gress stated that typographic innovations were inevitable and espoused the necessity to guide them along "sane paths." McMurtrie had corresponded with the leading practitioners of the New Typography in

Europe and collected samples from Walter Dexel, El Lissitzky, Theo van Doeburg, Karel Teige, and others. He interspersed these in his book with examples of American advertising layouts, most of which derived from the French Deco style. McMurtrie cautioned against the slavish adoption of European innovations, urging American typographers and designers to concentrate on the basic essentials of dynamic symmetry, function, simplicity, and clear expression. In *Fashions of American Typography 1780 to 1930,* published a year after McMurtrie's book, Gress claimed that simplicity and sanity were hallmarks of modern typography, but he cautioned that those who abandoned typographic tradition and rules ran the risk of creating "typographic chaos and anarchy."

The American foundries and linotype companies emphasized several areas of development. They sought a balance between redesigning traditional fonts and creating new ones in a traditional style. They also devised novel display faces for advertising, and issued their own variations of the best European modern faces. During the 1920s and 1930s, Morris Fuller Benton (1872–1948), one of ATF's principal designers, worked on both traditional and modern types. The modern ones included Chic (1927) and Parisian (1928), which were inspired by the spare elegance of lettering in French fashion advertising, and Broadway (1927), whose combination of black slabs and thin strokes came to characterize American typographic modernism through its adoption for urban signage and its dissemination in various other forms (Fig. 28.30). Benton also designed Stymie Medium and a range of other weights in the Stymie family (c. 1931), along with Tower (1934), and Phenix (1935), which followed his earlier News Gothic Condensed, although with the forms of several letters rounded to make them more stylish.

Other type designers at ATF included Robert Smith (1910–d.o.d. unconfirmed), a lettering designer who was responsible for several modern script faces— Park Avenue (1933) and Brush (1942); and Wadsworth A. Parker (1864–1938), who played a large part, along with Henry Lewis Bullen (1857–1938), in bringing out the 1923 ATF catalog, while also designing two decorative display faces, Gallia (1927) and Modernistic (1928). Both relied heavily on French Deco precedents, although Modernistic was an ornamental version of Benton's Broadway. Gerry Powell (1899–d.o.d. unconfirmed), ATF's Director of Typography for a time, was responsible for several modern faces, Onyx (1937) and Stencil (1937), the latter a heavy slab letter that is still widely used.

In 1929, ATF began to collaborate with the German émigré designer Lucian Bernhard, who created a number of typefaces for the company. The most durable was Bernhard Gothic (1929), one of the first American san serifs to compete with Futura, Kabel, and Gill Sans. It was similar to Futura except for the low crossbars on several letters, which, as type historian Mac McGrew speculates, may have reduced its popularity. Other Bernhard faces for ATF such as Lilith (1930), Bernhard Tango (1934), and Bernhard Tango Swash (1934) were more ornate, while Bernhard Fashion consisted of thin stylized letters that recalled, as did other American display types, the elegant letters of French fashion ads.

In Chicago, Barnhart Brothers and Spindler sought to compete with ATF in the design of new display types for advertising. One of their most prominent faces in this category was Boul Mich (1927), a face that may well have inspired Benton's Broadway of the following year. Cubist Bold (c. 1929), designed by John Zimmerman (dates unconfirmed), was a less successful attempt to create a modern advertising type. It was a heavy black face with awkward triangular shapes jutting out from some of the letters and had nothing to do with the art movement for which it was named.

Barnhart Brothers and Spindler's best-selling type was Cooper Black (1922), designed by Oswald Cooper, a Chicago lettering man. Cooper was a partner in Bertsch & Cooper, a company that offered typesetting, book and magazine layouts, and advertising design to

Fig. 28.30: Morris Fuller Benton, Broadway typeface, 1927. Courtesy The Newberry Library, Chicago, wing_z_40583_039_p158.

Cooper Black

120 Point 3A 3a

OIL sold

96 Point 3A 3a

half 8

24 Point 5A 9a

PINK drapery

18 Point 6A 13a

delighted FRIEND

72 Point 3A 3a

BE paid

14 Point 10A 20a

MAYOR greatly pleased

12 Point 13A 26a

BEAUTIFUL SPRING COATS
finely tailored sport costume

60 Point 3A 4a

3 days IN

10 Point 14A 28a

ENTRANCING MUSICAL DRAMA
collegiate glee club has rehearsal

8 Point 16A 32a

METROPOLITAN BUSINESS INCREASED
builder receives many encouraging reports

48 Point 3A 4a

BOLD style

6 Point 18A 36a

NOTED JURIST GIVES IMPORTANT DECISION
this long disputed question satisfactorily settled

42 Point 3A 4a

4 stage HITS

Characters in Complete Font

A B C D E F G H I J
K L M N O P Q R S
T U V W X Y Z & $
1 2 3 4 5 6 7 8 9 0
a b c d e f g h i
j k l m n o p q r
s t u v w x y z
. , ' : ; ! ? q · — }

36 Point 3A 4a

REAL position

30 Point 4A 7a

inspected HOMES

:[116]:

Fig. 28.31: Oswald Cooper, Cooper Black typeface, 1922. Courtesy The Newberry Library, Chicago, case_wing_z250_a5_bx4_01.

its clients. In 1918, Cooper designed the Cooper Old Style alphabet with rounded serifs for BB & S, whose advertising manager urged him to complete the Old Style family. As a response, he created Cooper Black, which achieved immediate success and influenced a new style of advertising layout with copy composed of dark heavy letters (Fig. 28.31). Cooper followed this typeface with other versions such as Cooper Black

Italic, Cooper Black Condensed, and Cooper Hilite, which was created by cutting thin white lines in Cooper Black to give the letters volume.

Although the linotype technology was introduced in the 1880s, by the 1920s there were still very few typefaces available for mechanical typesetting. However, large American firms, notably Lanston Monotype in Philadelphia, the Mergenthaler Linotype Company in New York, and the Ludlow Typograph Company in Chicago, took steps to remedy the situation. In 1920, Lanston consulted Frederic Goudy, America's most prolific type designer, about developing a program of type design for mechanical printing and soon hired him as their art director, a position he held until around 1939. At the time he joined Lanston, Goudy was a typographic scholar as well as a type designer. He also managed the Village Press, which he had set up with his wife Bertha in 1903 (see Chapter 13). During his affiliation with Lanston Monotype, Goudy began to adapt some of his earlier faces for mechanical typesetting. He also designed numerous new faces, many of which have not worn well. His display faces such as Goudy Heavyface (1925) or Goudy Ornate (1931) had weak designs or were copies of more successful faces by others. Goudy Heavyface was based on Cooper Black, while Goudy San Serif (1930) was an awkward competitor with Paul Renner's Futura. Goudy's most successful typefaces, however, were based on a profound knowledge of typographic history. These included Deepdene (1927), a refined Old Style with some modest Egyptian features, and Goudy Old Style, which he designed in 1915 but later adapted for mechanical setting. Goudy was succeeded as Lanston's art director by Sol Hess (1886–1953), who had joined the company in 1902. Among Hess's jobs was adapting faces from the letterpress foundries for linotype printing as well as designing new ones. Like Morris Fuller Benton at ATF, Hess could work in different styles from traditional to modern. In 1939, he restyled the typography of the *Saturday Evening Post*, adding two new

typefaces to the existing Post type family, Post Stout Italic and Post Black Italic.

The Mergenthaler Linotype Company was originally founded in 1886 to market Ottmar Mergenthaler's line caster typesetting machine. As the leading manufacturer of typesetting equipment for book and newspaper publishers, Mergenthaler had a strong interest in legibility. In 1922, Chauncey H. Griffith (1879–1956), who joined the company in 1906, became vice-president of typographic development with a major responsibility for text types that were marketed to newspaper printers. An early success was Ionic No. 5 (1925), which Griffith and his Legibility Group based on an earlier Victorian model that was noted for the evenness of its strokes. Within 18 months of the typeface's introduction, more than 3,000 newspapers all over the world were using it. Following the success of Ionic No. 5, Griffith and his staff designed additional faces for magazine and newspaper printing, notably Excelsior (1931) and Excelsior No. 2, both of which influenced newspaper typography worldwide. Griffith extended his concern for legibility to the printing of telephone directories by designing Bell Gothic (1937), a condensed san serif in two weights that became the standard for such directories across the United States.

In 1929, Mergenthaler Linotype invited W. A. Dwiggins to design a san serif typeface that could compete with Futura and the other European san serifs. The result was the Metro series beginning with Metroblack (1929–1930) and followed by several lighter variants over the next several years. Metroblack's proportions, according to Paul Shaw, were closer to Gill Sans and its predecessor, Edward Johnston's Underground type, than to the more geometric Futura. Unfortunately, the German Bauer foundry had already established a strong American market for Futura, and the Metro types were not widely adopted. Nonetheless, they proved Dwiggins' ability to make the transition from calligraphy to type design and led to a relationship of more than 25 years that he had as a typographic consultant with Mergenthaler. Although Dwiggins designed the

Metro types primarily for advertising, he preferred text faces, and his subsequent designs such as Electra (1935) and Caledonia (1938) were both refined romans that were well suited for book printing.

In Chicago, Robert Hunter Middleton (1898–1985) joined the Ludlow Typograph Company as a type designer around 1924. Middleton had been a student in the Department of Printing Arts which was established in 1921 at the School of the Art Institute of Chicago. There his teacher and mentor was Ernst Frederick Detterer (1888–1947), who was inspired by William Morris and Edward Johnston. Detterer introduced Middleton to the world of letterpress printing, and during his years at Ludlow, Middleton's commercial work was informed by his deep knowledge of printing history as well as his openness to new tendencies.

Ludlow was a relatively new company when Middleton started there. Its focus was on display advertising and newspaper headlines for which it had to build up a diverse array of typefaces. Like others who made a living designing type for commercial purposes, Middleton created typefaces for Ludlow that covered the spectrum from historic to modern styles. It was inevitable that the company would want its own competitor with Futura, and this resulted in Tempo (1930), which Middleton designed in varying weights. More original were his Delphian Open Title (1928), a delicate yet full-bodied face with white lines cut into the letters, and Stellar (1929), a more expressive san serif counterpart to its European competitors. During his long career with Ludlow, Middleton designed almost 100 typefaces, which ranked him in sheer volume with Frederic Goudy and Morris Fuller Benton. Within the company, a strong supporter of modern typefaces was Douglas McMurtrie, the company's publicist and author of many books on typography including the previously mentioned *Modern Typography and Layout.*

Graphic Design

The term "graphic design" is generally attributed to W. A. Dwiggins, who first used it in a short newspaper article of 1922, "New Kind of Printing Calls for New Design." There he claimed that traditional methods of design were inadequate to assure the high visual quality of printed material produced by new mechanical techniques such as halftone engraving, machine composition, and photogravure. Dwiggins identified three domains of design: the vast amount of workaday printing which, he stated, did not need designers; the domain of printing as a fine art, which was already populated with "printer-artists," by whom he surely meant designers of books and typography like Daniel Berkeley Updike and Bruce Rogers; and lastly the domain of printed matter made for advertising—ads, brochures, letterheads, booklets, and the like. This domain, Dwiggins argued, was badly in need of good design.

In 1928, Dwiggins sought to improve the situation with his book *Layout in Advertising,* which was published the same year as Jan Tschichold's *Die Neue Typographie* (*The New Typography*). Taking on the full range of designed materials from newspaper and magazine advertising to trademarks, letterheads, and packaging, Dwiggins advocated a broad modern approach but did not espouse a specific program as Tschichold did.

At the time Dwiggins published his book, there were relatively few freelance graphic designers in the United States. Most were layout men, who designed print advertising and the occasional trademark or letterhead. In New York, Lucian Bernhard established a practice as an advertising and typeface designer, drawing on his experience in Germany, where he created posters, alphabets, trademarks, and other print materials (see Chapter 17). Dwiggins himself was active in advertising and book design to which he added typography in 1929.

In Chicago, the development of an independent graphic design profession was abetted by the Society of Typographic Arts, which was established in 1927. Despite its title, the organization's founders wanted to represent the interests of "the designer and illustrator as well as those of the type designer and typographer." Around 1934, graphic design in the city received an additional impetus from the establishment of 27 Chicago Designers, a group that was formed to promote the work of its members through an annual book intended for wide distribution in Chicago and elsewhere. Among the designers who were featured in the early volumes were John Averill (dates unconfirmed), Rodney Chirpe (dates unconfirmed), Egbert Jacobson (1890–1966), Robert Hunter Middleton, Ray DaBoll (1892–1982), Bert Ray (dates unconfirmed), Oswald Cooper, and Sid Dickens (dates unconfirmed).

These men had a wide variety of talents and did not provide a unified profile of what practitioners in the graphic arts did. Averill made woodcut illustrations for advertising layouts, DaBoll was a calligrapher, Ray designed publications and advertising flyers, Chirpe created package and product designs, Dickens specialized in industrial styling, packaging, and layouts, Cooper did layouts and type design, Middleton designed type, and Jacobson was the design director of the Container Corporation of America. As tenuous as their professional relationships might have seemed, these were nonetheless sufficient to bring the designers together to solicit new business. As a result, the group made a strong impression with their annual promotional book, which helped to build a national reputation for Chicago graphic art. Chicago talent was also showcased in the Society of Typopgraphic Arts' annual Chicago Printing Exhibition, which helped to promote a distinct graphic identity for the city.

Despite this attention to Chicago graphic design, Charles Dawson (1889–1940), a black artist who established a design studio on Chicago's South Side around 1924, was not included. Dawson's clients were the black businesses that had not previously considered using a designer and he worked for a number of them including Annie Malone's PORO Beauty Schools for which Dawson designed a series of ads that depicted black beauties throughout history, Madagasco hair products, and several enterprises of the Overton Hygienic Company, which was owned by entrepreneur Anthony Overton. At the time Dawson began to work as a commercial artist, there were scarcely any black designers, a condition that remained until many years later.

In New York, the American Institute of Graphic Arts (see Chapter 17) played a similar role to the STA. As in Chicago, the AIGA embraced a cross-section of graphic arts professionals from book designers and art directors to publishers and printing executives. The organization held the first of its annual Fifty Books of the Year exhibitions in 1922 and additionally showcased the national Printing for Commerce exhibitions, beginning around 1936. At the Fifty Books of the Year show in 1940, T. M. Cleland delivered an address, "Harsh Words," in which he castigated the tenets of modernism, whether evident in architecture, furniture, or typography. Although there were graphic designers in the AIGA and elsewhere who agreed with Cleland, many others were open to the new ideas that had originated in Europe and were making their way to the United States.

Modern graphic design was fostered in New York by the Composing Room, a typesetting shop that Sol Cantor (1892–1965) and Dr. Robert Leslie (1885–1987) set up. The Composing Room sponsored the A–D Gallery, which exhibited the work of émigré and young American graphic designers, and PM (Production Manager), a printing magazine edited by Percy Seitlin (dates unconfirmed). PM was one of the few magazines along with Advertising Arts that showcased new American talent as well as the work of designers who were moving to the United States from Europe. Both PM and the A–D Gallery were strong promoters of European modernism and helped to introduce it to the New York design community by exhibiting the work of émigré designers such as George Salter and Herbert Bayer and publishing it as well. In 1940, Leslie dropped the name of PM for his journal and reintroduced it as A/D (Art Direction).

In Brooklyn, Leon Friend, chairman of the Art Department at Abraham Lincoln High School, introduced his students to modern graphic design through a special curriculum that was supplemented by a design club called the Art Squad, whose members completed practical projects for school events and publications. A number of Friend's students went on to become prominent designers, initially including Alex Steinweiss and Gene Federico and later Seymour Chwast and Sheila Levrant de Bretteville. Both Steinweiss and Federico, who began their careers in the late 1930s, belonged to a small group of young American designers who were strongly influenced by modern design in Europe.

Some designers, like Lester Beall (1903–1969) and Paul Rand (1914–1996), first learned about new European tendencies through books and magazines. Beall worked as a freelance illustrator and graphic designer in Chicago before moving to New York in 1935. In Chicago, he showed his interest in the European avant-garde through a series of advertisements for the *Chicago Tribune* in which he brought together photography, collage, and asymmetric layouts. In New York, he began to use photography and photomontage extensively and he combined these with bold arrangements of type, although he did not use san serif types exclusively. Among his New York projects, his covers and spreads for the magazine *Photoengraving* stand out for their high degree of experimentation, which he continued in his cover designs for Abbott Laboratories' house organ *What's New,* where he pioneered the use of modern design in pharmaceutical advertising.

Paul Rand started as a freelance designer in New York around 1934. For a time, he worked in the office of industrial designer George Switzer, creating packaging and advertising, and this led to an opportunity in 1936 to design layouts for *Apparel Arts*, a men's fashion magazine. On the basis of his initial work for this publication, Esquire-Coronet, which owned *Apparel Arts*, offered him a full-time position. Rand distinguished himself for inventive editorial spreads and covers and was soon promoted to art director of Esquire-Coronet's

New York office, where he designed fashion spreads for *Esquire* as well. Besides his work for *Apparel Arts* and *Esquire*, Rand did a series of covers for *Direction*, a left-oriented cultural magazine, beginning in 1938 and continuing until 1945. Similar to Beall's covers for *Photoengraving*, *Direction* offered Rand a chance to explore new ideas without commercial constraints. He was less formally experimental than Beall, but he displayed a witty approach to design that resulted in unusual juxtapositions of drawn and collaged images. Neither he nor Beall copied the Europeans. Instead, they adopted techniques that were new to them and added their own sensibilities, which were more eclectic than the Europeans'. Rand had a strong sense of metaphor and played with the multiple meanings of an image. This was evident in the 1940 Christmas cover for *Direction*, where he made reference to the German occupation of Czechoslovakia and Poland by featuring crossed strips of barbed wire that functioned as ribbon-like wrapping for a gift package as well as an enclosure for war prisoners. In 1941, Rand became the art director of a newly formed advertising agency, William H. Weintraub & Co., where he worked on campaigns for Disney Hats, Coronet Brandy, Dubonnet, and El Producto Cigars, among others. His ads were filled with visual wit and added a humorous sensibility to American advertising that would be further exploited by others in the post-war years.

During the 1920s and 1930s, a number of graphic designers who worked in a modern style arrived in the United States from Europe. Some sought new work opportunities, while others came because of the deepening political crisis. Most settled in New York. The contributions of some like Lucian Bernhard, Mehemed Fehmy Agha, Alexey Brodovitch, Joseph Binder, A. M. Cassandre, Gyorgy Kepes, and George Salter have been discussed already. Others included Herbert Matter and Erik Nitsche from Switzerland; Will Burtin (1909–1972), Hans Barschel (1912–1998), and Herbert Bayer from Germany (see Chapters 21 and 27); the Hungarian Albert Kner (1899–1976);

Xanti Schawinsky from Milan (see Chapter 27); the Czech Ladislav Sutnar, who had been his country's leading modernist designer before he came to New York to install the Czech government's pavilion for the 1939 World's Fair and was stranded after the German invasion of Czechoslovakia (see Chapter 25); and the Frenchman Jean Carlu a prominent poster designer who, like Sutnar, had come to New York to organize an exhibition at the 1939 World's Fair for the French Information Service and chose to remain after the Germans occupied France (see Chapter 22). All stayed in the United States after World War II except for Carlu, who returned to France in 1953. Through their work, teaching, and in some cases exhibitions, these European modernists gained recognition, and even before World War II they began to have a significant impact on American graphic design. Kepes' teaching in Chicago was discussed earlier. In New York, Will Burtin began to teach at Pratt in 1939, and Bayer conducted a successful design course at the American Advertising Guild in New York. The influence of the Europeans was to be felt more strongly after World War II when they and a number of their students attained prominence as art directors, teachers, or freelance designers.

U.S. Government Programs

In addition to funding the Design Laboratory in New York and the Community Art Centers, the Federal Art Project (FAP) supported artists through its Poster Division, which produced about 35,000 poster designs between 1935 and 1943. The main studio was in New York, but by 1938, others had been set up in 18 states. Richard Floethe (1901–1988), a German printmaker and illustrator who had studied at the Weimar Bauhaus, headed the New York studio, which produced more posters than any other.

European modernism was a strong model for many FAP designers, far more than it was for designers who worked for commercial clients. Among the poster artists whose influence could be seen in the FAP posters were E. McKnight Kauffer, A. M. Cassandre, and Joseph Binder. The Poster Division broke the race barrier by employing a number of African-American artists, as did the Federal Art Project in general. Many women also designed posters for the division.

Posters announced cultural events, promoted health and safety, and encouraged tourism. Most were produced by the silk-screen method, which allowed for multiple colors while costing considerably less than lithography. Among the many artists besides Richard Floethe who worked in the program were Vera Bock (1905–d.o.d. unconfirmed), Anthony Velonis (1911–1997), Cleo Sara (dates unconfirmed), Jerome Roth (dates unconfirmed), and Katherine Milhous (1894–1977). Though many of the FAP poster designers were artists and returned to painting or printmaking when they left the WPA, others continued their careers as illustrators or graphic designers.

The government also hired professional designers for special projects. In 1933, Charles Coiner, the art director for N. W. Ayer in Philadelphia, was commissioned to design a symbol for the National Recovery Administration (NRA). It was intended for a sticker or window card that businesses could display to show their support for the NRA. Coiner chose a blue American eagle with a gear wheel in one claw to signify industry and three lightning bolts in the other to represent energy and determination. In 1937 the Rural Electrification Administration (REA), that did not yet have electricity, commissioned Lester Beall to design a set of posters to promote the REA in rural areas. Beall created several simple images to illustrate the benefits of electricity—a light bulb, a water faucet, a washing machine, and radio among them (Plate 48). He designed two additional series with photographic images, mainly of rural dwellers, to suggest satisfaction with the program and to indicate its positive benefits. The government also made use of "pictorial statistics," the technique for representing social data that was invented in Vienna by Otto Neurath (see Chapter 25) and promoted in the United States by a student of Neurath's, Rudolph Modley (dates unconfirmed), author of several books on the subject.

Bibliography
Bibliographic essay

There is a considerable body of literature on the 1920s and 1930s in the United States. For general background I relied on Alan Brinkley, *The Unfinished Nation: A Concise History of the American People*; William E. Leuchtenberg, *The Perils of Prosperity, 1914–1932,* 2nd ed.; Alice G. Marquis, *Hopes and Ashes: The Birth of Modern Times, 1929–1939*; Cabell Phillips, *From the Crash to the Blitz*; Emily S. Rosenberg, *Spreading the American Dream: American Economic and Cultural Expansion, 1890–1945*; and William H. Young with Nancy K. Young, *The 1930s. American Business Abroad: Ford on Six Continents* by Mira Wilkins and Frank Ernest Hill chronicles the international operations of the Ford Motor Company.

Books and articles that emphasize technology and invention include William E. Akin, *Technocracy and the American Dream: The Technocrat Movement, 1900–1941*; Ruth Schwartz Cowan, *A Social History of American Technology*; Brian Horrigan's essay, "The Home of Tomorrow, 1927–1945," in Joseph Corn, ed, *Imagining Tomorrow: History, Technology, and the American Future*; Thomas Hughes, *American Genesis: A Century of Invention and Technological Enthusiasm, 1870–1970*; David F. Noble, *America by Design: Science, Technology, and the Rise of Corporate Capitalism*; Phil Patton, *Made in USA: The Secret Histories of the Things that Made America*; and Ronald C. Tobey, *Technology as Freedom: The New Deal and the Electrical Modernization of the American Home.* Several books and studies focus on particular cities. James Sloan Allen writes extensively about the Container Corporation of America in *The Romance of Commerce and Culture: Capitalism, Modernism, and the Chicago–Aspen Crusade for Cultural Reform*, and John Zukowsky included Chicago design in a major exhibition, the second of two, on Chicago architecture and design at the Art Institute of Chicago.

The catalog, edited by Zukowsky, is *Chicago Architecture and Design, 1923–1993: Reconfiguration of an American Metropolis.* Lloyd Engelbrecht's PhD dissertation *The Association of Arts and Industries: Background and Origins of the Bauhaus Movement in Chicago* discusses the formation of the association and its role in establishing the New Bauhaus in Chicago. The Toledo Museum of Art also mounted an exhibition of local design and published a catalog entitled *The Alliance of Art and Industry: Toledo Designs for a Modern America.*

Books that focus on the decorative arts are Richard Guy Wilson, Dianne H. Pilgrim, and Dickran Tashjian, *The Machine Age in America, 1918–1941*, the catalog of an exhibition at the Brooklyn Museum; Karen Davies, *At Home in Manhattan: Modern Decorative Arts, 1925 to the Depression*; Alastair Duncan, *American Art Deco*; Charlotte and Peter Fiell, eds., *30s/40s Decorative Art: A Source Book*; Paul T. Frankl, *New Dimensions: The Decorative Arts of Today in Words & Pictures*; Martin Greif, *Depression Modern: The Thirties Style in America*; J. Stewart Johnson, *American Modern, 1925–1940: Design for a New Age*; R. L. Leonard and C. A. Glasgold, *Modern American Design by the American Union of Decorative Artists and Craftsmen*; Rudolph Rosenthal and Helena L. Ratzka, *The Story of Modern Applied Art*; Kristina Wilson, *Livable Modernism: Interior Decorating and Design during the Great Depression*; Frederick P. Keppel and R. L. Duffus, *The Arts in American Life*; and Marta Sironen, *A History of American Furniture.* Charles R. Richards' report of 1929, *Art in Industry*, is essential reading.

Monographs on designers include David Gebhard and Harriette Von Breton, *Kem Weber: The Moderne in Southern California, 1920–1941*; David Hanks, *The Decorative Designs of Frank Lloyd Wright*; Jonathan Lipman, *Frank Lloyd Wright and the Johnson Wax Buildings*; Robert McCarter, *Frank Lloyd Wright*; Christopher Long, *Paul T. Frankl and Modern American Design;* and *Eva Zeisel: Designer for Industry,* the catalog of an exhibition at the Musée des Arts Décoratifs de Montréal with an essay by Martin Eidelberg.

There is an equally extensive body of literature

on American industrial design during this period, including books on invention. The most thorough survey of the subject remains Jeffrey Meikle's *Twentieth Century Limited: Industrial Design in America, 1925–1939*. A specific aspect of American industrial design was the subject of a book by Meikle's doctoral student, Christine Cogdell, *Eugenic Design: Streamlining America in the 1930s,* while Meikle's book followed Donald Bush's *The Streamlined Decade*, adding considerably more archival research. Meikle also published *The City of Tomorrow; Model 1937* as one of the pamphlets in a series released by Pentagram and also *American Plastic: A Cultural History*, which looked at plastic from a cultural rather than a technological perspective. Other surveys of industrial design or streamlining during the interwar years include Sheldon and Martha Cheney, *Art and the Machine: An Account of Industrial Design in 20th-Century America*; Martin Eidelberg, ed., *Design 1935–1965: What Modern Was. Selections from the Liliane and David M. Stewart Collection*, the catalog of an exhibition at the Musée des Arts Décoratifs de Montréal; Claude Lichtenstein and Franz Engler, *Streamlined, a Metaphor for Progress: The Aesthetics of Minimized Drag*; David A. Hanks and Anne Hoy, *American Streamlined Design: The World of Tomorrow*; John Perrault, *Streamline Design: How the Future Was*, the catalog of a small exhibition at the Queens Museum in New York, while more general books are Arthur Pulos' *American Design Ethic: A History of Industrial Design to 1940*, the first in a two-volume survey of American design history by a pioneer researcher in the field; Jeffrey Meikle's short volume, *Design in the USA*; and Gregory Votolato's *American Design in the Twentieth Century*. Pulos also wrote an essay on the subject "United States: The Wizards of Standardized Aesthetics" for the more comprehensive volume *History of Industrial Design 1919–1990: The Domain of Design*. Terry Smith includes some material on industrial design in *Making the Modern: Industry, Art, and Design in America*. On the design of automobiles, see Stephen Bayley, *Harley Earl* and David Gartman's

sociological study, *Auto Opium: A Social History of American Automobile Design*; on trains, the reader can consult Bob Johnston and Joe Welsh with Mike Schafer, *The Art of the Streamliner* and on airplanes see Carroll Glines and Wendell F. Moseley. *The DC-3: The Story of a Fabulous Airplane*. Several books that focus on particular companies and make reference to their involvement with design are Ralph Caplan, *The Designs of Herman Miller Pioneered by Eames, Girard, Nelson, Propst, Rohde*; Boris Emmet and John E. Jeuck, *Catalogues and Counters: A History of Sears, Roebuck and Company*; Roland Marchand, *Creating the Corporate Soul: The Rise of Public Relations and Corporate Imagery in American Big Business*; and Alfred P. Sloan Jr., *My Years with General Motors*.

Design and issues related to it at the Century of Progress and the 1939 New York' World's Fair are discussed in Robert W. Rydell's general study, *World of Fairs: The Century-of-Progress Expositions* and in more specific books and articles: Barbara Cohen, Steven Heller, and Seymour Chwast, *Trylon and Perisphere: The 1939 New York World's Fair*; *Official Guide Book, New York World's Fair 1939*, and two articles on African-American participation in the Century of Progress, August Meier and Elliott M. Ridwich, "Negro Protest at the Chicago World's Fair, 1933–1934," *Journal of the Illinois State Historical Society* 59 (1966) and Christopher Robert Reed, "A Reinterpretation of Black Strategies for Change at the Chicago World's Fair, 1933–1934," *Illinois Historical Journal* 81 (Spring 1988).

There are numerous monographs on American industrial designers who rose to prominence during this period and a few on companies that promoted good design. These include Glen Adamson, *Industrial Strength Design: How Brooks Stevens Shaped Your World*; *The Designs of Raymond Loewy*; Russell Flinchum, *Henry Dreyfuss, Industrial Designer: The Man in the Brown Suit*; David A. Hanks with Jennifer Toher, *Donald Deskey: Decorative Designs and Interiors*; Paul Jodard, *Raymond Loewy*; Angela Schönberger, *Raymond Loewy: Pioneer of American Industrial Design*;

William Lescaze: The Rise of Modern Design in America; the IAUS catalog, *William Lescaze*; Martin Pawley, *Buckminster Fuller;* and John McHale, *R. Buckminster Fuller.*

Classic texts by industrial designers are Norman Bel Geddes, *Horizons*; Roy Sheldon and Egmont Arens, *Consumer Engineering: A New Technique for Prosperity*; and Harold Van Doren, *Industrial Design: A Practical Guide.* Raymond Loewy published several books including *The Locomotive*, a large picture book called *Industrial Design*, and his memoir, *Never Leave Well Enough Alone.* Walter Dorwin Teague's memoir, *Design This Day: The Technique of Order in the Machine Age*, like Loewy's, has useful material about the author's design activities in the 1930s. Some of Buckminster Fuller's writings from this period can be found in his collection, *Nine Chains to the Moon.* Hugh Ferris's *The Metropolis of Tomorrow* is an album of his futuristic architectural drawings. The critical writing of Stuart Chase during this period provides a helpful counter-argument to the generally optimistic writing about industrial design. See his books *Men and Machines, The Tragedy of Waste,* a book written with F. J. Schlink, and *Your Money's Worth: A Study in the Waste of the Consumer's Dollar.* Richard Vangermeersch, *The Life and Writings of Stuart Chase (1888–1985)* provides analyses of Chase's work. On invention, Patricia Carter Sluby, *The Inventive Spirit of African Americans: Patented Ingenuity* describes numerous inventions by African-Americans, while Autumn Stanley chronicles those by women in *Mothers and Daughters of Invention: Notes for a Revised History of Technology.*

The role of the Museum of Modern Art in promoting modern design in America as well as background on its department of architecture and design is chronicled in Russell Lynes, *Good Old Modern: An Intimate Portrait of The Museum of Modern Art.* See also Eliot Noyes, *Organic Design in Home Furnishings,* the catalog of the exhibition by the same name. Among design programs and schools during these years, the New Bauhaus, which became the School of Design and

then the Institute of Design, is the most widely covered. See *50 Jahre New Bauhaus: Bauhausnachfolge in Chicago*; Achim Borchardt-Hume, *Albers and Moholy: From the Bauhaus to the New World*; Margret Kentgens-Craig, *The Bauhaus in America: First Contacts, 1919–1936*; and *Moholy-Nagy: A New Vision for Chicago,* the catalog of an exhibition at the Illinois State Museum. Moholy's major writings from this period are published in English as *The New Vision and Abstract of an Artist.* Mary Emma Harris, *The Arts at Black Mountain College* tells the story of that institution where Josef Albers, another Bauhaus faculty member, taught, while thus far *Design in America: The Cranbrook Vision, 1925–1950* is the definitive work on the Michigan school. Jim Lesko's article "Industrial Design at Carnegie Institute of Technology, 1934–1967," *Journal of Design History* 10, no. 3 (1997) describes the beginning of the industrial design program at that institution, while Paul Makovsky's MA thesis, *The Forgotten Bauhaus: The Design Laboratory, New York City, 1935–1940,* provides important information on the short-lived school where Gilbert Rohde taught.

Some general surveys of graphic design that include material on this period are R. Roger Remington with Lisa Bodenstedt, *American Modernism: Graphic Design 1920 to 1960*; R. Roger Remington and Barbara Hodik, *Nine Pioneers in American Graphic Design*; Philip Meggs, *A History of Graphic Design*, 3rd ed.; and Leon Friend and Joseph Hefter, *Graphic Design: A Library of Old and New Masters in the Graphic Arts.* A more specialized publication is Christopher de Noon, *Posters of the WPA, 1935–1943.*

The history of American advertising is generally not included in histories of graphic design yet the literature as advertising relates to design is extensive. Some books include Michele H. Bogart, *Artists, Advertising, and the Borders of Art*; Stephen Fox, *The Mirror Makers: A History of American Advertising & Its Creators*; Otis Pease, *The Responsibilities of American Advertising: Private Control and Public Influence, 1920–1940*; and Jackson Lears, *Fables of Abundance: A Cultural History* of Advertising in America. Earnest Elmo Calkins, "And Hearing Not_": Annals of an Adman and Business the Civilizer provide insight into Calkins' thoughts about the relation of art and advertising. Ancillary to the literature on advertising would be Alfred Q. Maisel, comp, 100 Packaging Case Histories; and Joseph Sinel, comp, A Book of American Trade-Marks and Devices. Catherine Gudis, Buyways: Billboards, Automobiles, and the American Landscape is dedicated specifically to billboards.

The literature on American magazines includes: James L. Baughman, Henry R. Luce and the Rise of the American News Media; Edna Woolman Chase and Ilka Chase, Always in Vogue; and Caroline Seebohm, The Man Who Was Vogue: The Life and Times of Condé Nast. Virginia Hagelstein Marquardt's essay, "Art on the Left in the United States, 1918–1937," in her own edited book, Art and Journals on the Political Front, 1910–1940, discusses the design of a special genre of little magazines.

Histories of American book publishing include Joseph Blumenthal, The Printed Book in America; and John Tebbel, A History of Book Publishing in the United States, Volume 3: The Golden Age between Two Wars, 1920–1940. There is a rich literature on American typography. David Consuegra's American Type Design & Designers provides an excellent overview. More specialized volumes are The Book of Oz Cooper; Edmund Gress, Fashions in American Typography, 1780–1930; Steven Heller, Deco Type: Stylish Alphabets of the '20s and '30s; Douglas McMurtrie, Modern Typography and Layout and Type Design: An Essay on American Type Design with Specimens of the Outstanding Types; and RHM Robert Hunter Middleton, The Man and His Letters: Eight Essays on His Life and Career. There are numerous monographs on modern illustrators and designers including: Gwen Finkel Chanzit, Herbert Bayer and Modernist Design in America; Arthur Cohen, Herbert Bayer: The Complete Work; Herbert Bayer: Kunst und Design in Amerika, 1938–1985. Essays by Eckhard Neumann and Magdalena Droste; Herbert Bayer:

Painter, Designer, Architect; R. Roger. Remington, Lester Beall: Trailblazer of American Graphic Design; Roger Remington and Robert S. P. Fripp, Design and Science: The Life and Work of Will Burtin; Andy Grundberg, Brodovitch; Steven Heller, Paul Rand; Manfred Heiting, Paul Outerbridge 1896–1958; Michael Schau, J.C. Leyendecker; Martha Scottford, Cipe Pineles: A Life of Design; and Thomas S. Hansen, Classic Book Jackets: The Design Legacy of George Salter. The brief article by Sarah Bodine and Michael Dunas, "Dr. Robert Leslie, 100 Years Old," AIGA Journal of Graphic Design 3, no. 4 (1985), provides information about an important figure in the introduction of modern graphic design to the United States.

A number of books discuss magazines and journals that were connected specifically with African-Americans or women: Walter C. Daniel, Black Journals of the United States; Abby Arthur Johnson and Ronald Maberry Johnson, Propaganda and Aesthetics: The Literary Politics of African-American Magazines in the Twentieth Century; and Kathleen L. Endres and Therese L. Lueck, eds., Women's Periodicals in the United States. Amy Helene Kirschke's Aaron Douglas: Art, Race, and the Harlem Renaissance is a biography of an African-American artist who also designed covers for books and journals.

Books

50 Jahre New Bauhaus: Bauhausnachfolge in Chicago. Berlin: Bauhaus-Archiv and Argon Verlag, 1988.

Adamson, Glenn. Industrial Strength Design: How Brooks Stevens Shaped Your World. Milwaukee: Milwaukee Art Museum, and Cambridge, MA, and London: MIT Press, 2003.

Akin, William E. Technocracy and the American Dream: The Technocrat Movement, 1900–1941. Berkeley, Los Angeles, and London: University of California Press, 1977.

Albrecht, Donald, Robert Schonfeld, and Lindsay Stamm Shapiro. Russel Wright: Creating American Lifestyle. New York: Cooper-Hewitt, National Design Museum and Harry N. Abrams, 2001.

Allen, James Sloan. *The Romance of Commerce and Culture: Capitalism, Modernism, and the Chicago–Aspen Crusade for Cultural Reform.* Chicago and London: University of Chicago Press, 1983.

The Alliance of Art and Industry: Toledo Designs for a Modern America. Toledo: Toledo Museum of Art. Distributed by Hudson Hills Press, New York, 2002.

Baughman, James L. *Henry R. Luce and the Rise of the American News Media.* Boston: Twayne Publishers, 1987.

Bayley, Stephen. *Harley Earl.* London: Grafton, 1990.

Bel Geddes, Norman. *Horizons.* New York: Dover, 1977 (c. 1932).

Bienenstock, N. I. *A History of American Furniture.* n.p.: Furniture World – Furniture World South, 1970.

Blumenthal, Joseph. *The Printed Book in America.* Hanover and London: University Press of New England, 1989 (c. 1977).

Bogart, Michele H. *Artists, Advertising, and the Borders of Art.* Chicago and London: University of Chicago Press, 1995.

The Book of Oz Cooper. Chicago: The Society of Typographic Arts, 1949.

Borchardt-Hume, Achim. *Albers and Moholy: From the Bauhaus to the New World.* London: Tate Publishing, 2006.

Brinkley, Alan. *The Unfinished Nation: A Concise History of the American People.* New York: Alfred A. Knopf, 1997.

Bush, Donald J. *The Streamlined Decade.* New York: George Braziller, 1975.

Calkins, Earnest Elmo. *Business the Civilizer.* With an introduction by John Cotton Dana. Boston: Little, Brown and Co., 1928.

—*"And Hearing Not_": Annals of an Adman.* New York: Charles Scribner's Sons, 1946.

Caplan, Ralph. *The Designs of Herman Miller Pioneered by Eames, Girard, Nelson, Propst, Rohde.* New York: Whitney Library of Design, 1976.

Chanzit, Gwen Finkel. *Herbert Bayer and Modernist Design in America.* Ann Arbor and London: UMI Research Press, 1987.

Chase, Edna Woolman and Ilka Chase. *Always in Vogue.* Garden City: Doubleday & Co., 1954.

Chase, Stuart. *The Tragedy of Waste.* New York: Macmillan, 1928 (c. 1925).

—*Men and Machines.* New York: Macmillan, 1929.

Chase, Stuart and F. J. Schlink. *Your Money's Worth: A Study in the Waste of the Consumer's Dollar.* New York: Macmillan, 1931.

Cheney, Sheldon and Martha Cheney. *Art and the Machine: An Account of Industrial Design in 20th-Century America.* New York and London: Whittlesey House, 1936.

Cogdell, Christina. *Eugenic Design: Streamlining America in the 1930s.* Philadelphia: University of Pennsylvania Press, 2004.

Cohen, Arthur. *Herbert Bayer: The Complete Work.* Cambridge, MA, and London: MIT Press, 1984.

Cohen, Barbara, Steven Heller, and Seymour Chwast. *Trylon and Perisphere: The 1939 New York World's Fair.* New York: Harry Abrams, 1989.

Consuegra, David. *American Type Design & Designers.* New York: Allworth Press, 2004.

Cowan, Ruth Schwartz. *A Social History of American Technology.* New York and Oxford: Oxford University Press, 1997.

Daniel, Walter C. *Black Journals of the United States.* Westport, CT, and London: Greenwood Press, 1982.

Davies, Karen. *At Home in Manhattan: Modern Decorative Arts, 1925 to the Depression.* New Haven: Yale University Art Gallery, 1983.

de Noon, Christopher. *Posters of the WPA, 1935–1943.* Los Angeles: The Wheatley Press in association with the University of Washington Press, 1987.

Design in America: The Cranbrook Vision, 1925–1950. New York: Harry N. Abrams in association with the Detroit Institute of Arts and the Metropolitan Museum of Art, 1984.

The Designs of Raymond Loewy. Washington, DC: Smithsonian Institution Press, 1975.

Dreyfuss, Henry. *Designing for People*. Foreword by R. Buckminster Fuller. New York: Grossman Publishers, 1967 (c. 1955).

Duncan, Alastair. *American Art Deco*. New York: Harry N. Abrams, 1987.

Dwiggins, W. A. *Layout in Advertising*, rev. ed. New York: Harper & Bros., 1948 (c. 1928).

Eidelberg, Martin, ed. *Design 1935–1965: What Modern Was. Selections from the Liliane and David M. Stewart Collection*. Montréal: Musée des Arts Décoratifs de Montréal, 1991. Distributed by Harry N. Abrams, New York.

Emmet, Boris and John E. Jeuck. *Catalogues and Counters: A History of Sears, Roebuck and Company*. Chicago: University of Chicago Press, 1950.

Endres, Kathleen L. and Therese L. Lueck, eds. *Women's Periodicals in the United States*. Westport, CT, and London: Greenwood Press, 1995.

Eva Zeisel: Designer for Industry. Catalog essay by Martin Eidelberg. Montréal: Musée des Arts Décoratifs de Montréal, 1984. Distributed by the University of Chicago Press and Macmillan of Canada.

Ferris, Hugh. *The Metropolis of Tomorrow*. New York: Ives Washburn, 1929.

Fiell, Charlotte and Peter Fiell, eds. *30s/40s Decorative Art: A Source Book*. Cologne: Taschen, 2000.

Flinchum, Russell. *Henry Dreyfuss, Industrial Designer: The Man in the Brown Suit*. New York: Cooper-Hewitt National Design Museum and Rizzoli, 1997.

Fox, Stephen. *The Mirror Makers: A History of American Advertising & Its Creators*. Urbana and Chicago: University of Illinois Press, 1997 (c. 1984).

Frankl, Paul T. *New Dimensions: The Decorative Arts of Today in Words & Pictures*. New York: Brewer & Warren, 1928.

Friend, Leon and Joseph Hefter. *Graphic Design: A Library of Old and New Masters in the Graphic Arts*. New York and London: Whittlesey House, 1936.

Fuller, R. Buckminster. *Nine Chains to the Moon*. New York: Anchor Books, 1971 (c. 1938).

Gartman, David. *Auto Opium: A Social History of American Automobile Design*. London and New York: Routledge, 1994.

Gebhard, David and Harriette Von Breton. *Kem Weber: The Moderne in Southern California, 1920–1941*. Santa Barbara: The Art Galleries University of California, 1969.

Glines, Carroll and Wendell F. Moseley. *The DC-3: The Story of a Fabulous Airplane*. Philadelphia and New York: J.B. Lippincott, 1966.

Greif, Martin. *Depression Modern: The Thirties Style in America*. New York: Universe Books, 1981.

Gress, Edmund. *Fashions in American Typography, 1780–1930*. New York: Harper & Bros., 1931.

Grundberg, Andy. *Brodovitch*. New York: Harry N. Abrams, 1989 (Documents of American Design).

Gudis, Catherine. *Buyways: Billboards, Automobiles, and the American Landscape*. New York and London: Routledge, 2004.

Hanks, David. *The Decorative Designs of Frank Lloyd Wright*. New York: E. P. Dutton, 1979.

Hanks, David A. and Anne Hoy. *American Streamlined Design: The World of Tomorrow*. Paris: Éditions Flammarion, 2005.

Hanks, David A. with Jennifer Toher. *Donald Deskey: Decorative Designs and Interiors*. With a special essay by Jeffrey L. Meikle. New York: E.P. Dutton, 1987.

Hansen, Thomas S. *Classic Book Jackets: The Design Legacy of George Salter*. Foreword by Milton Glaser. New York: Princeton Architectural Press, 2005.

Harris, Mary Emma. *The Arts at Black Mountain College*. Cambridge, MA, and London: MIT Press, 1987.

Heiting, Manfred. *Paul Outerbridge 1896–1958*. Cologne, London et al.: Taschen Verlag, 1999.

Heller, Steven. *Deco Type: Stylish Alphabets of the '20s and '30s*. San Francisco: Chronicle Books, 1997.

—*Paul Rand*. Foreword by Armin Hofmann. London: Phaidon Press, 1999.

Herbert Bayer: Kunst und Design in Amerika, 1938–1985. Essays by Eckhard Neumann and Magdalena Droste. Berlin: Bauhaus-Archiv, Museum für Gestaltung, 1986.

Herbert Bayer: Painter, Designer, Architect. New York: Reinhold and London: Studio Vista, 1967.

Hughes, Thomas. *American Genesis: A Century of Invention and Technological Enthusiasm, 1870–1970*. New York: Viking, 1989.

Jacob, Mary Jane and Jacquelynn Bass, eds. *Chicago Makes Modern: How Creative Minds Changed Society*. Chicago and London: University of Chicago Press, 2012.

Jodard, Paul. *Raymond Loewy*. New York: Taplinger, 1992 (Design Heroes).

Johnson, Abby Arthur and Ronald Maberry Johnson. *Propaganda and Aesthetics: The Literary Politics of African-American Magazines in the Twentieth Century*. With a new introduction. Amherst: University of Massachusetts Press, 1991 (c. 1979).

Johnson, J. Stewart. *American Modern, 1925–1940: Design for a New Age*. New York: Harry N. Abrams in association with the American Federation of Arts, 2000.

Johnston, Bob and Joe Welsh with Mike Schafer. *The Art of the Streamliner*. New York: Metro Books, 2001.

Kentgens-Craig, Margret. *The Bauhaus in America: First Contacts, 1919–1936*. Cambridge, MA, and London: MIT Press, 1999.

Kepes, Gyorgy. *The Language of Vision*. Chicago: Paul Theobald, 1944.

Keppel, Frederick P. and R. L. Duffus. *The Arts in American Life*. New York and London: McGraw-Hill Book Co., 1933.

Kiesler, Frederick. *Contemporary Art Applied to the Store and Its Display*. New York: Brentano's, 1930.

Kirschke, Amy Helene. *Aaron Douglas: Art, Race, and the Harlem Renaissance*. Jackson: University Press of Mississippi, 1995.

Kyle, David. *A Pictorial History of Science Fiction*. London et al.: Paul Hamlyn, 1977.

Lears, Jackson. *Fables of Abundance: A Cultural History of Advertising in America*. New York: Basic Books, 1994.

Leonard, R. L. and C. A. Glasgold. *Modern American Design by the American Union of Decorative Artists and Craftsmen*. New York: Ives Washburn, 1930.

Leuchtenberg, William E. *The Perils of Prosperity, 1914–1932*, 2nd ed. Chicago and London: University of Chicago Press, 1993 (c. 1958).

Lichtenstein, Claude and Franz Engler. *Streamlined, a Metaphor for Progress: The Aesthetics of Minimized Drag*. Baden: Lars Müller, n.d.

Lipman, Jonathan. *Frank Lloyd Wright and the Johnson Wax Buildings*. Introduction by Kenneth Frampton. New York: Rizzoli, 1986.

Loewy, Raymond. *Never Leave Well Enough Alone*. New York: Simon and Schuster, 1951.

—*Industrial Design*. Woodstock, NY: The Overlook Press, 1979.

—*The Locomotive*. New York: Universe, 1987 (c. 1937).

Long, Christopher. *Paul T. Frankl and Modern American Design*. New Haven and London: Yale University Press, 2007.

Lynes, Russell. *Good Old Modern: An Intimate Portrait of The Museum of Modern Art*. New York: Atheneum, 1973.

Maisel, Albert Q., comp. *100 Packaging Case Histories*. New York: Breskin Publishing Corp., 1939.

Marchand, Roland. *Advertising the American Dream: Making Way for Modernity, 1920–1940*. Berkeley, Los Angeles, and London: University of California Press, 1985.

—*Creating the Corporate Soul: The Rise of Public Relations and Corporate Imagery in American Big Business*. Berkeley, Los Angeles, and London: University of California Press, 1998.

Marquis, Alice G. *Hopes and Ashes: The Birth of Modern Times, 1929–1939*. New York: The Free Press, 1986.

McCarter, Robert. *Frank Lloyd Wright*. London; Reaktion Books, 2006 (Critical Lives).

McHale, John. *R. Buckminster Fuller*. New York: George Braziller, 1962.

McMurtrie, Douglas. *Type Design: An Essay on American Type Design with Specimens of the Outstanding Types*. With an introduction by Frederic W. Goudy. Pelham, NY: Bridgeman Publishers, 1927.

—*Modern Typography and Layout*. Chicago: Eyncourt Press, 1929.

Meggs, Philip. *A History of Graphic Design*, 3rd ed. New York: John Wiley & Sons, 1998 (c. 1983).

Meikle, Jeffrey L. *American Plastic: A Cultural History*. New Brunswick, NJ: Rutgers University Press, 1995.

—*Twentieth Century Limited; Industrial Design in America, 1925–1939*. 2nd ed. with a new preface and enhanced photographs. Philadelphia: Temple University Press, 2001.

—*Design in the USA*. Oxford, New York et al.: Oxford University Press, 2005 (Oxford History of Art).

—*The City of Tomorrow; Model 1937*. London: Pentagram Design, n.d. (Pentagram Papers 11).

Moholy-Nagy, László. *The New Vision and Abstract of an Artist*. New York: George Wittenborn, 1947 (The Documents of Modern Art).

Moholy-Nagy: A New Vision for Chicago. Chicago: Illinois State Museum and the University of Illinois Press, 1990.

Noble, David F. *America by Design: Science, Technology, and the Rise of Corporate Capitalism*. New York: Alfred A. Knopf, 1977.

Noyes, Eliot F. *Organic Design in Home Furnishings*. New York: Arno Press, 1969 (c. 1941).

Official Guide Book, New York World's Fair 1939. New York: Exposition Publications, 1939.

Patton, Phil. *Made in USA: The Secret Histories of the Things that Made America*. New York: Penguin Books, 1993.

Pawley, Martin. *Buckminster Fuller*. London: Taplinger, 1990 (Design Heroes).

Pease, Otis. *The Responsibilities of American Advertising: Private Control and Public Influence, 1920–1940*. New Haven: Yale University Press, 1958 (Yale Publications in American Studies 2).

Perrault, John. *Streamline Design: How the Future Was*. New York: The Queens Museum, 1984.

Phillips, Cabell. *From the Crash to the Blitz*. New York: Macmillan, and London: Collier-Macmillan, 1969 (The New York Times Chronicle of American Life).

Pulos, Arthur J. *American Design Ethic: A History of Industrial Design to 1940*. Cambridge, MA, and London: MIT Press, 1983.

Remington, R. Roger. *Lester Beall: Trailblazer of American Graphic Design*. New York and London: W.W. Norton, 1996.

Remington, R. Roger and Robert S. P. Fripp, *Design and Science: The Life and Work of Will Burtin*. Aldershot: Lund Humphries, 2007.

Remington, R. Roger and Barbard Hodik. *Nine Pioneers in American Graphic Design*. Cambridge, MA, and London: MIT Press, 1989.

Remington, R. Roger with Lisa Bodenstedt. *American Modernism: Graphic Design 1920 to 1960*. London: Laurence King Publishing, 2003.

RHM Robert Hunter Middleton, The Man and His Letters: Eight Essays on His Life and Career. Chicago: The Caxton Club, 1985.

Richards, Charles R. *Art in Industry*. New York: Macmillan, 1929.

Rosenberg, Emily S. *Spreading the American Dream: American Economic and Cultural Expansion, 1890–1945*. New York: Hill and Wang, 1982.

Rosenthal, Rudolph and Helena L. Ratzka. *The Story of Modern Applied Art*. New York: Harper & Bros., 1948.

Rydell, Robert W. *World of Fairs: The Century-of-Progress Expositions*. Chicago and London: University of Chicago Press, 1993.

Schau, Michael. *J.C. Leyendecker*. New York: Watson-Guptill, 1974.

Schönberger, Angela, ed. *Raymond Loewy: Pioneer of American Industrial Design*. Munich: Prestel, 1990.

Scottford, Martha. *Cipe Pineles: A Life of Design*. New York and London: W.W. Norton, 1999.

Seebohm, Caroline. *The Man Who Was Vogue: The Life and Times of Condé Nast*. New York: Viking Press, 1982.

Sheldon, Roy and Egmont Arens. *Consumer Engineering: A New Technique for Prosperity*. New York: Arno Press, 1976 (c. 1932).

Sinel, Joseph, comp. *A Book of American Trade-Marks and Devices*. New York: Knopf, 1924.

Sironen, Marta K. *A History of American Furniture*. Edited by N. I. Bienstock. East Stroudsburg, PA, and New York: The Towse Publishing Co., 1936.

Sloan, Alfred P. Jr. *My Years with General Motors*. Edited by John McDonald and Catharine Stevens. Garden City, NY: Doubleday & Co., 1964.

Sluby, Patricia Carter. *The Inventive Spirit of African Americans: Patented Ingenuity*. Westport, CT, and London: Praeger, 2004.

Smith, Terry. *Making the Modern: Industry, Art, and Design in America*. Chicago and London: University of Chicago Press, 1993.

Sparke, Penny. *A Century of Car Design*. Hauppauge, NY: Barron's, 2002.

Stanley, Autumn. *Mothers and Daughters of Invention: Notes for a Revised History of Technology*. Metuchen, NJ: Scarecrow Press, 1993.

Teague, Walter Dorwin. *Design This Day: The Technique of Order in the Machine Age*. New York: Harcourt Brace and Company, 1940.

Tebbel, John. *A History of Book Publishing in the United States, Volume 3: The Golden Age between Two Wars, 1920–1940*. New York and London: R.R. Bowker, 1978.

Tobey, Ronald C. *Technology as Freedom: The New Deal and the Electrical Modernization of the American Home*. Berkeley, Los Angeles, and London: University of California Press, 1996.

Van Doren, Harold. *Industrial Design: A Practical Guide*. New York and London: McGraw Hill, 1940.

Vangermeersch, Richard. *The Life and Writings of Stuart Chase (1888–1985)*. Amsterdam et al.: Elsevier, 2005 (Studies in the Development of Accounting Thought vol. 8).

Votolato, Gregory. *American Design in the Twentieth Century*. Manchester and New York: Manchester University Press, 1998 (Studies in Design and Material Culture).

Wilkins, Mira and Frank Ernest Hill: *American Business Abroad: Ford on Six Continents*. With an introduction by Allan Nevins. Detroit: Wayne State University Press, 1964.

William Lescaze. New York: Rizzoli, n.d. IAUS Catalog 16.

William Lescaze: The Rise of Modern Design in America. *Syracuse University Library Associates Courier* 19, no. 1 (Spring 1984).

Wilson, Kristina. *Livable Modernism: Interior Decorating and Design during the Great Depression*. New Haven and London: Yale University Press in association with Yale University Art Gallery, 2004.

Wilson, Richard Guy, Dianne H. Pilgrim, T, Dickran Tashjian. *The Machine Age in America, 1918–1941*. New York: The Brooklyn Museum in association with Harry N. Abrams, 1986.

Young, William H. with Nancy K. Young. *The 1930s*. Westport, CT, and London: Greenwood Press, 2002 (American Popular Culture Throughout History).

Zukowsky, John, ed. *Chicago Architecture and Design, 1923–1993: Reconfiguration of an American Metropolis*. Munich: Prestel Verlag, 1993.

Chapters in books

Horrigan, Brian, "The Home of Tomorrow, 1927–1945," in Joseph Corn, ed. *Imagining Tomorrow*. Cambridge, MA: MIT Press, 1986.

Marquardt, Virginia Hagelstein, "Art on the Left in the United States, 1918–1937," in Virginia Hagelstein Marquardt, ed. *Art and Journals on the Political*

Front, 1910–1940. Gainesville et al.: University Press of Florida, 1997.

Pulos, Arthur, "United States: The Wizards of Standardized Aesthetics," in *History of Industrial Design 1919–1990: The Domain of Design*. Milan: Electa, 1991.

Articles

Bodine, Sarah and Michael Dunas, "Dr. Robert Leslie, 100 Years Old," *AIGA Journal of Graphic Design* 3, no. 4 (1985).

Lesko, Jim, "Industrial Design at Carnegie Institute of Technology, 1934–1967," *Journal of Design History* 10, no. 3 (1997).

Meier, August and Elliott M. Ridwich, "Negro Protest at the Chicago World's Fair, 1933–1934," *Journal of the Illinois State Historical Society* 59 (1966).

Reed, Christopher Robert, "A Reinterpretation of Black Strategies for Change at the Chicago World's Fair, 1933–1934," *Illinois Historical Journal* 81 (Spring 1988).

Dissertations and theses

Engelbrecht, Lloyd C. *The Association of Arts and Industries: Background and Origins of the Bauhaus Movement in Chicago*. PhD dissertation, University of Chicago, 1973.

Makovsky, Paul. *The Forgotten Bauhaus: The Design Laboratory, New York City, 1935–1940*. MA thesis, University of Toronto, n.d.

Plate 01: Alexander Apsit, Year of the Proletarian Dictatorship, poster, 1918. © Image Asset Management Ltd/Alamy.

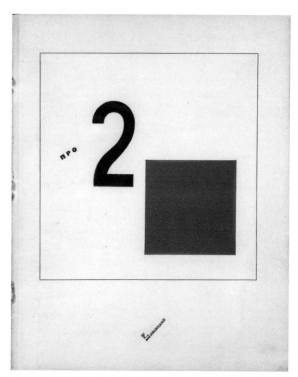

Plate 02: El Lissitzky, *About Two Squares*, cover, 1922. © Heritage Image Partnership Ltd/Alamy.

Plate 03: Varvara Stepanova, design for *sportodezhda*, 1923. © Heritage Image Partnership Ltd/Alamy. © Rodchenko & Stepanova Archive, DACS, RAO, 2017.

Plate 04: M. Bulanov, Mosselprom Tobacco, 1927. © PARIS PIERCE/Alamy.

Plate 05: Bruno Taut, *Alpine Architecture*, text and illustrations, 1919. Beinecke Rare Book and Manuscript Library, Yale University.

Plate 06: Hannah Hoch, *Cut with the Kitchen Knife Dada through the Last Weimar Beer-Belly Cultural Epoch of Germany*, photomontage, 1919–1920. akg-images/Erich Lessing. © DACS 2017.

Plate 07: Joost Schmidt, Bauhaus exhibition poster, 1923. Getty Images.

Plate 08: Herbert Bayer, Bauhaus exhibition catalog, 1923. Collection Merrill C. Berman. Photo: Jim Frank & Joelle Jensen. © DACS 2017.

Plate 09: Jan Tschichold, *Die Frau ohne Namen*, poster, 1927. Collection Merrill C. Berman. Photo: Jim Frank and Joelle Jensen.

Plate 10: Compagnie des Arts Français, hand-painted screen, 1920s. © Les Arts Décoratifs, Paris/Jean Tholance/akg-images.

Plate 11: Theo van Doesburg, Café Aubette, design for Grand Salle, 1928. © 2014. Digital image, The Museum of Modern Art, New York/Scala, Florence.

Plate 12: Anon., Marseille, Exposition Coloniale, poster, 1906. akg-images.

Plate 13: Charles Martin, *Sports et Divertissements*, illustration, 1923. The Bridgeman Art Library/Getty Images.

Plate 14: Paul Colin, *Revue Négre*, poster, 1925. © The Art Archive/Alamy. © ADAGP, Paris and DACS, London 2017.

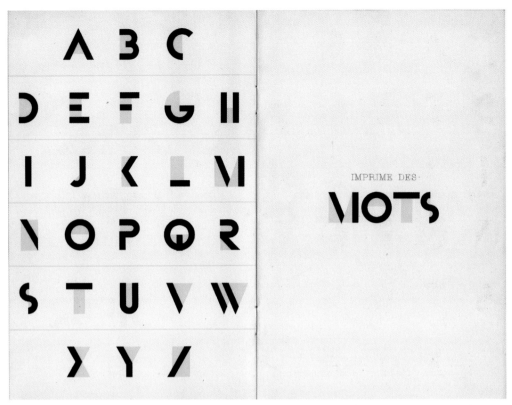

Plate 15: A. M. Cassandre, Bifur, type specimen book, 1929. Museum of printing and graphic communication, Lyon. © MOURON. CASSANDRE. Lic 2016-23-11-04 www.cassandre.fr.

Plate 16: Gerald Spencer Pryse, British Empire Exhibition, poster, 1924. Yale Center for British Art, New Haven, CT, USA/Gift of Henry S. Hacker, 1965/Bridgeman Images.

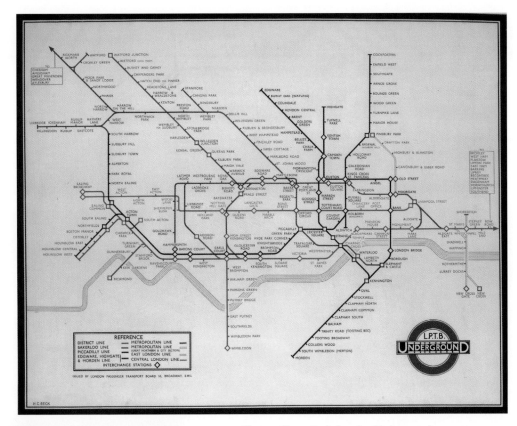

Plate 17: Henry Beck, London Underground map, 1933.
© TfL from the London Transport Museum collection.

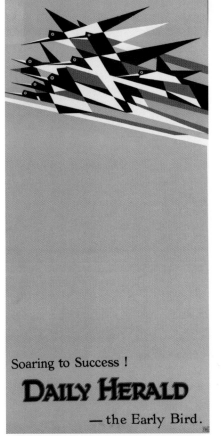

Plate 18: E. McKnight Kauffer, *Daily Herald*, poster, 1917. Library of Congress.

Plate 19: Pat Keely, Night Mail, poster, 1939. © Royal Mail Group, Courtesy of The Postal Museum, 2017.

Plate 20: Gerrit Rietveld, Red and Blue chair, c. 1923. © Picture Partners/Alamy. © DACS 2017.

Plate 21: Vilmos Huszár, Miss Blanche Virginia Cigarettes, poster, 1926. Collection Merrill C. Berman. Photo: Jim Frank & Joelle Jensen. © DACS 2017.

Plate 22: Hendrik Nicolaas Werkman, *The Next Call* 6, 1924. Collection Merrill C. Berman. Photo: Jim Frank and Joelle Jensen.

Plate 23: Pierre Gauchat, Exposition Nationale Suisse, poster, 1929. Photograph courtesy of the Musem für Gestaltung Zürich, Poster Collection.

Plate 24: Josep Renau, The fruit of the farmer's work is as sacred as the worker's salary, poster, 1937. © Iberfoto/SuperStock.

Plate 25: Celest Polychroniadi, Greece, poster, 1938. E.L.I.A. Archive/M.I.E.T. (Literary and Historical Archive/National Bank of Greece Cultural Foundation).

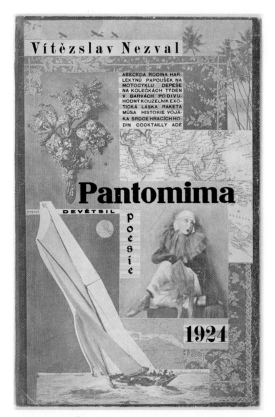

Plate 26: Jindřich Štyrský and Karel Teige, *Pantomima*, cover, 1924. The Wolfsonian–Florida International University, Miami Beach, Florida, The Mitchell Wolfson, Jr. Collection, XC1993.169. Photo: David Almeida.

Plate 27: Karel Teige, *On the Ship Bringing Tea and Coffee*, cover, 1928. The Wolfsonian–Florida International University, Miami Beach, Florida, The Mitchell Wolfson, Jr. Collection, 83.2.622. Photo: David Almeida.

Plate 28: Tadeusz Gronowski, Radion, poster, 1926. Poster Museum, Wilanów.

Plate 29: Géza Faragó, Törley Champagne, poster. Courtesy Törley Archive.

Plate 30: Tomislav Krizman, Marya Delvard, concert poster, 1907. Department of Prints and Drawings of Croatian Academy of Sciences and Arts.

Plate 31: Wilhelm Kåge, Liljeblå (Blue Lily) dinner service, 1917. Photo Bukowski auctions. © DACS 2017.

Plate 32: Josef Frank, Svenskt Tenn, textile design, 1943–1944. Svenskt Tenn.

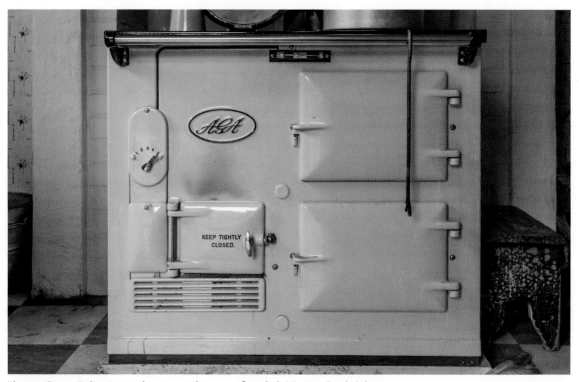

Plate 33: Gustav Dalén, Aga cooking range, date unconfirmed. © Maurice Crooks/Alamy.

Plate 34: Nora Gulbrandsen, coffee set, Porsgrund Porselaensfabrik, 1929–1931. Østfoldmuseene, Moss by- og industrimuseum. Photo: Trine Gjøsund. © DACS 2017.

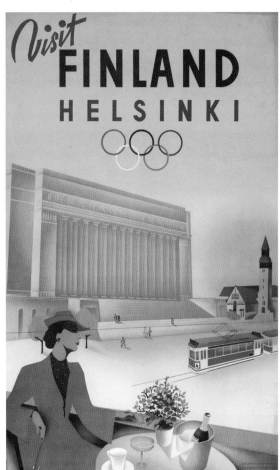

Plate 35: Jorma Suhonen, Visit Finland, Helsinki, poster, 1935. Library of Congress.

Plate 36: C. V. Testi, Exhibition of the Fascist Revolution, poster, 1932. © Leemage/Corbis/Getty Images.

Plate 37: Giacomo Balla, coffee service, 1928. © 2014. DeAgostini
Picture Library/Scala, Florence. © DACS 2017.

Plate 38: Xanti Schawinsky, Olivetti MP1 typewriter, poster, 1935.
Archivio Storico Olivetti, Ivrea, Italy.

Plate 39: *National Socialist Party Organization Manual*, page spread, 1937. Courtesy Jeff Clark.

Plate 40: Ludwig Hohlwein, The German Student Fights for the Führer and the People, poster, 1930s. © Prisma Bildagentur AG/ Alamy. © DACS 2017.

Plate 41: Bolshevism, poster, 1937. Library of Congress.

Plate 42: El Lissitzky, *USSR in Construction*, "Constitution issue," cover, 1937. Howard Garfinkel and Larry Zeman, Productive Arts, USA.

Plate 43: Russel Wright, dinnerware, 1939. Image © Metropolitan Museum of Art, John C. Waddell Collection, Gift of John C. Waddell, 2002 (2002.585.17a-j).

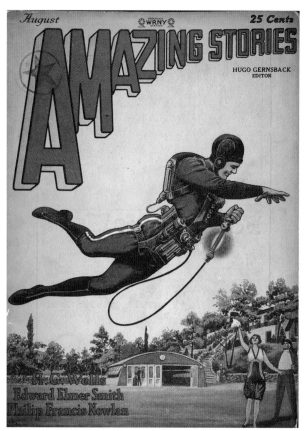

Plate 44: Frank R. Paul, *Amazing Stories*, cover, 1928. Used with the acknowledgement of the Frank R. Paul Estate.

Plate 45: Chrysler Airflow Eight, 1934. The Wolfsonian–Florida International University, Miami Beach, Florida, The Mitchell Wolfson, Jr. Collection of Decorative and Propaganda Arts, Promised Gift, WC2005.1.3.102.001. Photo: David Almeida.

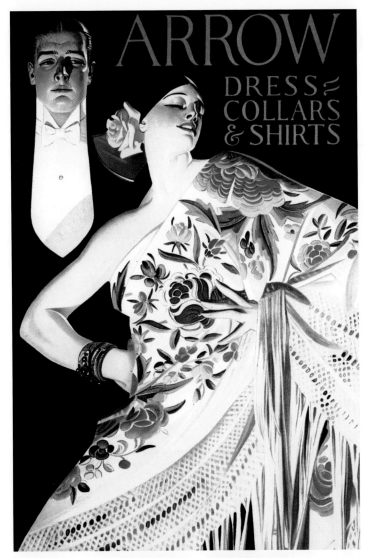

Plate 46: J. C. Leyendecker, Arrow Dress Collars and Shirts, advertisement, early 1920s. akg-images.

Plate 47: Otis Shepard, Wrigley Company billboard, 1930s. Image Courtesy of The Advertising Archives.

Plate 48: Lester Beall, REA Radio, poster 1937. The Wolfsonian-Florida International University, Miami Beach, Florida, The Mitchell Wolfson, Jr. Collection, TD1991.174.3. Photo: Bruce White. © Dumbarton Arts, LLC/VAGA, NY/DACS, London 2017.

Plate 49: *Bohemia*, cover, 1929. The Wolfsonian–Florida International University, Miami Beach, Florida, The Vicki Gold Levi Collection, XC2002.11.4.316.25. Photo: Silvia Ros.

Plate 50: Andrés García Benítez, *Carteles*, cover, 1936. Vicki Gold Levi Collection. Photo: Montreal Museum of Fine Arts, Brian Merrett.

Plate 51: Ernesto Garcia Cabral, *Revista de Revistas*, cover. CONADICOV archives.

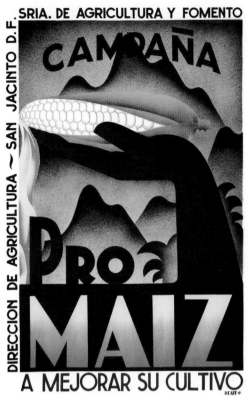

Plate 52: Gabriel Fernández Ledesma and Francisco Díaz de León, Campaign for Corn, poster, 1938. CONADICOV archives

Plate 53: Tarsila do Amaral, *Pau-Brasil*, cover, 1925. Biblioteca Brasiliana Guita e José Mindlin Universidade de São Paulo.

Plate 54: Tomás Santa Rosa, *Cacáu*, cover, 1932. Biblioteca Brasiliana Guita e José Mindlin Universidade de São Paulo.

Plate 55: Paul Dufresne, *Zig-Zag*, cover, 1905. Private Collection.

Plate 56: Luis Fernando Rojas, Ratanpuro is the better tea, poster, 1903. Private Collection.

Plate 57: Achille Mauzan, Crosley Radio, poster, 1930. Private Collection.

Plate 58: Melchior Méndez Magariños, *The Man Who Ate a Bus*, cover, 1927. Collection Miguel Oks.

Plate 59: Peter Ewart, Canadian Rockies, poster, 1941. Canadian Pacific Archives, A.6147.

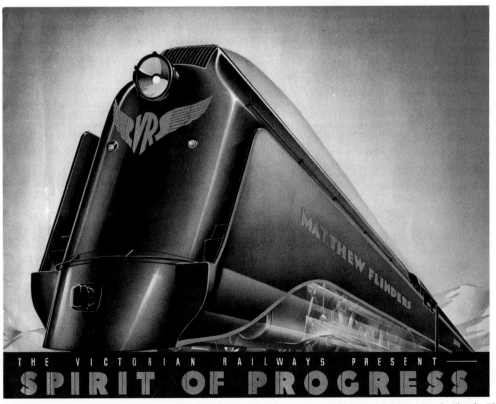

Plate 60: Victoria Railways, *Spirit of Progress*, 1937. The Wolfsonian–Florida International University, Miami Beach, Florida, The Mitchell Wolfson, Jr. Collection, TD1989.22.43. Photo: David Almeida.

Plate 61: Leonard Mitchell, New Zealand, poster, 1930s.
Alexander Turnbull Library, Wellington, New Zealand.

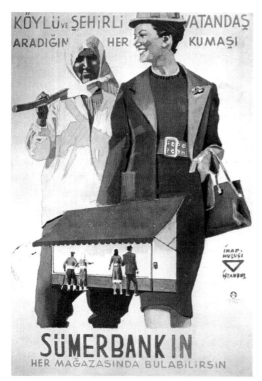

Plate 62: İhap Hulusi Gorey, Sumerbank, poster, c. 1930s.
Courtesy Sadik Karamustafa.

Plate 63: *Bullet in the Heart*, poster, 1944. Courtesy A. Bou
Jawdeh.

Plate 64: Arieh El-Hanani, Flying Camel emblem, Levant Fair, poster, 1934. Courtesy David Tartakover.

Plate 65: Franz Krausz, Visit Palestine, poster, 1936. Boston Public Library.

Plate 66: Geoffroy d'Aboville, Syria and Lebanon, poster, c. 1920s. CPA Media Co. Ltd./Pictures From History.

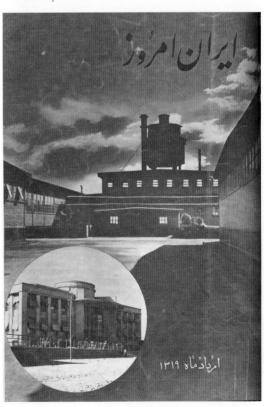

Plate 67: *Iran-e Emruz*, cover, 1930s. Middle East Department, The University of Chicago Library.

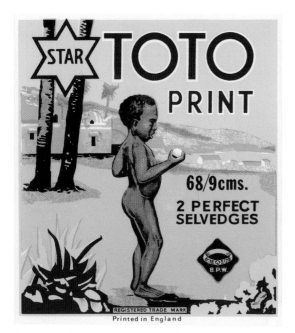

Plate 68: Star Toto Print, cotton bale label, c. 1920s. © Mary Evans Picture Library/Alamy.

Plate 69: Jeanne Thil, Transatlantique, poster, c. 1930. Private Collection/Photo © Christie's Images/Bridgeman Images.

Plate 70: Charles-Jean Hallo, Air Afrique, poster. Private Collection.

Plate 71: Alexander De Andreis, Banania, poster, c. 1915. Getty Images.

Plate 72: Sunlight Soap, poster, 1930. CPA Media Co. Ltd./ Pictures From History.

Plate 73: Austin Cooper, See India, poster 1930s. SSPL via Getty Images.

Plate 74: Zhou Muqiao, Xiehe Trading Company, poster, 1914. Collection: Museum of Applied Arts & Sciences, Sydney. Photographer unknown.

Plate 75: Zhiying Studio, The Great Eastern Dispensary Ltd., poster, 1930s. Print Collector/Getty Images.

Plate 76: *The Ark*, cover, 1937. Photographer: Zhou Bo.

Plate 77: Qian Juntao, *Literature Monthly* 1, cover, 1935. Photographer: Zhou Bo.

Plate 78: Tsunetomi Kitano, Exhibition of Export Articles, 1911. CPA Media Co. Ltd./Pictures From History.

Plate 79: Hashiguchi Goyo, Mitsukoshi Department Store, poster, 1911. CPA Media Co. Ltd./Pictures From History.

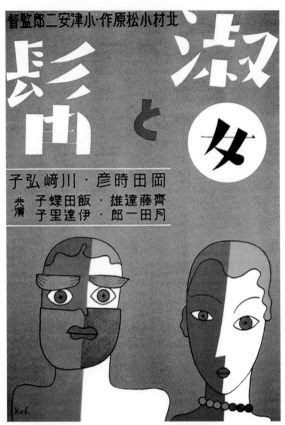

Plate 80: Kono Takashi, *The Lady and the Beard*, poster, 1931. CPA Media Co. Ltd./Pictures From History.

Plate 81: Yamana Ayao, *Nippon*, cover of first issue, 1934. CPA Media Co. Ltd./Pictures From History.

Plate 82: Modern Beauties in Manchurian, postcard. The Wolfsonian–Florida International University, Miami Beach, Florida, The Mitchell Wolfson, Jr. Collection, XC1996.335.1. Photo: David Almeida.

Plate 83: Utility furniture booklet, cover, c. 1943. © Amoret Tanner/Alamy.

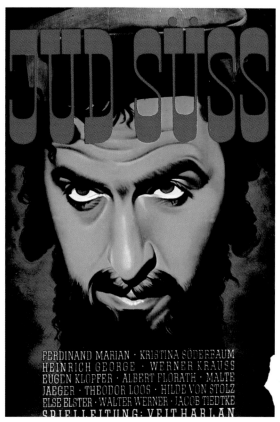

Plate 84: *Jud Süss*, poster, 1940. Getty Images.

Plate 85: Bernard Villemot, Patrie, poster, 1942. Private Collection/Giraudon/Bridgeman Images. © ADAGP, Paris and DACS, London 2017.

Plate 86: Gino Boccasile, poster, c. 1942. akg-images.

Plate 87: Fougasse, Careless Talk Costs Lives, poster, 1940.
Victoria and Albert Museum, London.

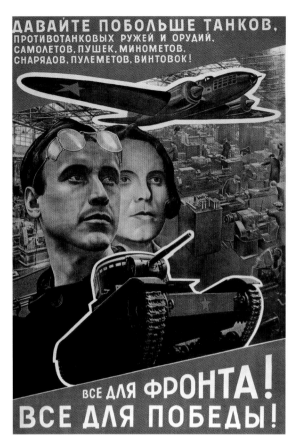

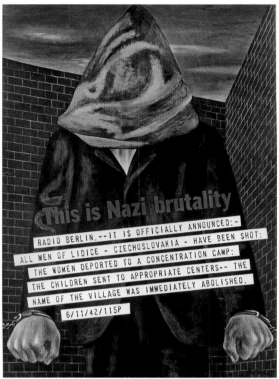

Plate 88: El Lissitzky and Nikolai Troshin, Everything for the Front. Everything for Victory, poster, 1942. © Image Asset Management Ltd/Alamy.

Plate 89: Ben Shahn, This is Nazi Brutality, poster, 1942. The Wolfsonian–Florida International University, Miami Beach, Florida, The Mitchell Wolfson, Jr. Collection, TD1989.121.3. Photo: Bruce White. © Estate of Ben Shahn/DACS, London/ VAGA, New York 2017.

Chapter 29: Latin America: Cuba, Mexico, and Brazil 1900–1939

Introduction

In 1902, Cuba gained its independence from Spain, the last country in Latin America to do so. Political independence, however, did not translate easily into democratic governance in the region and much of Latin America continued to be ruled by wealthy elites or dictators in the period prior to World War II. By the end of the 1930s and the beginning of the 1940s, fascist governments in Italy, Germany, Spain, Portugal, and the Soviet Union became powerful precedents for the rise of dictators and authoritarian leaders in some Latin American countries such as Getulio Vargas in Brazil, Lázaro Cárdenas in Mexico, and in General Agustín Pedro Justo in Argentina.

Until World War I, the ruling classes, which controlled their respective nations' land and resources, preferred to export raw materials and agricultural produce rather than create industrial economies. In Brazil, plantation owners exported coffee, which was also central to the economies of Colombia and Central America. In addition, the latter relied heavily on marketing bananas. Beef and grains were leading exports in Argentina as was sugar in Cuba, while tin mining in Bolivia, copper mining in Chile, and silver mining in Peru enabled those countries to participate respectively in the international economy. In the late 1920s, the discovery of oil deposits in Mexico and Venezuela provided substantial income from abroad. In all these enterprises, local peasants performed the unskilled hard labor, while skilled workers were brought in from overseas to fill positions that required prior training or education.

Within the local Latin American social hierarchies, entrepreneurs were not held in high regard, consequently immigrants became the leading businessmen. Spaniards, Italians, and Germans were prominent in Argentina, Germans and Italians in Uruguay, while Portuguese, Italians, and Germans constituted the main immigrant populations in Brazil. Local elites encouraged immigration to offset the lack of skilled laborers, and immigrants found ample opportunities to establish enterprises that ranged from printing plants to the manufacture of durable goods.

Despite the emphasis on exporting agricultural products and raw materials, industrialization developed gradually in a few Latin American countries before World War I. The war, which cut off Latin America from its European suppliers, accelerated the process of import substitution, or replacing imported products with locally made goods. By the end of the 1920s, active industrial sectors had begun to burgeon in Argentina, Brazil, Chile, Mexico, and Uruguay.

Unlike Europe or the United States, where the invention of new machines and devices helped to transform small craft workshops into large mechanized factories, industrialization in Latin America happened in a more piecemeal fashion. Some enterprises such as large breweries, flourmills, and cigarette factories imported advanced machinery, but many products such as foodstuffs, leather goods, metalware, furniture, and clothing were largely produced in workshops with limited numbers of workers. Frequently these were family businesses. As the economic historian Colin Lewis points out, the small workshops continued to operate alongside the more advanced factories, thus making it impossible to transform entire industries. Importing machinery was difficult but a number of repair shops that had been established to maintain foreign machines, including railway locomotives, were able to develop into shops that could build their own machinery, which they then marketed within the country.

A further obstacle to the transformation of small labor-intensive enterprises into larger factories was the reluctance of banks to finance their expansion. These small businesses persisted as well because governments were slow to establish departments or ministries of industry that could develop national policies to support industrial development. One exception to limited local production was the manufacture of weapons, which was carried out in national armories. Weapons production was expanded in Brazil during the Vargas dictatorship in the late 1930s to include the development of Latin America's only indigenous aircraft industry.

The isolation of Europe from Latin America because of World War I cleared the way for the United States to develop an aggressive policy of marketing its goods in the southern hemisphere. Conversely, the United States became the largest market for Latin American exports.

The aim to increase American trade with Latin America was initiated in 1889 at the First International Conference of American States, held in Washington, DC. At subsequent conferences convened at periodic intervals, this interest was advanced through various inter-American organizations and committees that led to the formation of the Pan American Union, which established its headquarters in Washington. Shortly after Franklin D. Roosevelt became President in 1933, he launched the Good Neighbor Policy through which he sought to develop relations between the United States and the Latin American nations that were based on mutual cooperation and trust. The policy was motivated in part to protect and further American economic interests in Latin America, which by this time were extensive.

Writing in 1936, business historian Dudley Phelps mentioned six variants of product manufacturing and marketing that American companies employed in Latin America. These ranged from complete production in a local plant to designing the packaging for already finished imported goods. In between, Phelps included the local assembly of products based on parts designed to American specifications. As an example, he cited the Otis elevator whose production in Argentina featured a combination of manufacturing and assembly, whereby the core apparatus was imported and other parts were made locally.

When Ford and General Motors began to sell automobiles in Latin America in the mid-1920s, they established assembly plants that required few locally manufactured parts. Firms such as National Cash Register, Singer Sewing Machines, International Harvester, and the United Shoe Manufacturing Corporation employed large numbers of local people, who were hired primarily for marketing operations, although some assembly was often involved. The prevalence of these American companies with their widespread distribution and advertising networks and their highly-developed manufacturing methods made it difficult for local enterprises to compete. Consequently there was considerably less local production of durable goods than there was in the non-durable sectors that included cosmetics, soap, liquor, tobacco, and foodstuffs. Local enterprises also made clothing and shoes, profiting from textile manufacturing, which was far more advanced in Latin America than was the production of machines, appliances, or transport vehicles.

Because so many durable goods came from abroad, even if some were assembled locally, there was little opportunity to develop a profession of industrial design compared to Europe or the United States, where manufacturers with advanced production capabilities relied on designers to create new products for the market. Consequently, product design in Latin America before World War II was practiced primarily as a decorative art with a concentration on furniture for one-off and serial production. Also included were other objects for domestic use such as lamps, glassware, ceramics, and ironwork. As a counterpart to the trained decorative artists, some of whom came from abroad and others who were trained in local art schools, craftsmen in small workshops continued to make objects for daily use such as furniture and pots and pans, while some factories produced locally-designed stoves, refrigerators, and even vehicles such as trucks or buses.

When the Museum of Modern Art in New York held a Latin American industrial design competition in 1940 to coincide with the competition for its exhibition, Organic Design in Home Furnishings, entries were received from 17 countries. Several of the winning designs came from European architects or designers who had emigrated to Latin America: Bernard Rudofsky (1905–1988) in Brazil and two former Bauhaus students in Mexico, Michael van Beuren (1911–2004) and Klaus Grabe (dates unconfirmed). Also from Mexico, the Cuban émigré designer Clara Porset (1932–1981) and her husband Xavier Guerrero (1896–1974) submitted an exemplary prize-winning suite of furniture conceived for rural use featuring cabinets, tables, and a cot and chair that used a traditional webbing material called *ixtle*.

Compared to the near absence of industrial designers, commercial artists were active throughout Latin America. Producing illustrated advertisements for newspapers and magazines was a primary task. Advertising posters were displayed less widely than in Europe but were nonetheless commissioned to promote products as well as films in the emerging domestic and imported film industries in Argentina, Mexico, Brazil, and Cuba. Commercial artists also found ample work designing packaging and labels as well as the occasional logotype for domestic and foreign companies.

The middle classes in all Latin American countries grew rapidly between 1900 and 1939, partly due to immigration but also to the expansion of public and higher education and the growing number of jobs in industry and the public sector. One consequence was a rise in literacy that led to a proliferation of newspapers, journals, books, and magazines. Publishers employed large numbers of artists, art directors, and caricaturists to illustrate and design their publications, which formed the basis for public discourse about politics and culture in the various countries. Argentina had the largest middle class and consequently became a center of book publishing for all Latin America, but almost every country published some books and had one or more illustrated magazines that featured articles on topics ranging from film and furniture to art, politics, music, and literature.

Latin Americans were well informed about cultural tendencies in Europe and the United States to which they were exposed through reading, travel, and visits from prominent foreign visitors such as F. T. Marinetti, Blaise Cendrars, and Le Corbusier. Many Latin American artists and intellectuals strove to be modern, but they wished to be so on their own terms, hence modern tendencies from abroad were filtered through strong impulses to forge national identities, which frequently incorporated indigenous themes. French culture had been the dominant influence on Latin American intellectuals in the 19th century and continued to be so in the 20th. In architecture, the Art Deco style, first introduced at the 1925 Exposition Internationale des Arts Décoratifs in Paris, captured the imagination of numerous Latin American architects though many continued to rely on classical styles and in some cases indigenous forms. There was less interest in the more austere and politically engaged modern movement in architecture of Germany and the Netherlands or the radical architectural propositions of the Soviet Constructivists, but Le Corbusier's visits to several Latin American countries introduced architects to his version of the modern movement, which took root particularly in Argentina, Brazil, and Mexico. The Bauhaus had little influence on design or design pedagogy in Latin America, with the exception of Mexico, where the architect and former Bauhaus director Hannes Meyer lived for some years, beginning in 1939, and Josef and Anni Albers visited in the 1930s.

Latin American artists and writers were cognizant of the European avant-garde movements—Expressionism, Cubism, Futurism, and Dada—and these exercised a considerable influence on them. Latin America, however, had its own avant-gardes, which produced modern paintings, sculptures, novels, and poetry. They also spawned literary journals with layouts that were sometimes playful and covers that were always visually striking.

Hollywood had the strongest influence on the Latin American cinema, which developed primarily as an art form for the masses rather than the elite. Latin American film industries had their own directors, actors, and technicians, but they faced heavy competition from American film companies, which frequently made movies in Spanish for Latin American audiences.

Despite the strong influences from Europe and the United States, Latin American artists and intellectuals were deeply concerned with issues of cultural independence and national identity. Consequently, they looked abroad for the latest developments but adapted them to their own conditions and concerns. Advances were made as well through the many accomplished immigrants who contributed to the development of the decorative and commercial arts in most Latin American countries.

Cuba

Cuba was the last colony in Latin America to gain independence from Spain. The Treaty of Paris that Spain and the United States signed in December 1898 recognized Cuba's liberty, but the United States continued to occupy the country until 1902, departing only when the Cubans agreed to append the Platt Amendment to their Constitution. This amendment, which remained in place until 1934, gave the United States the right to intervene militarily in Cuba whenever it perceived the property and rights of American citizens to be endangered.

By the time of independence, the United States was heavily involved in the Cuban economy. It had, in fact, tried to purchase Cuba from Spain several times during the 19th century. Despite Spain's refusal to sell the colony, by 1902 the United States nonetheless controlled a sizeable percentage of mineral exports and owned most of Cuba's sugar and cigarette factories.

As a colonial power, Spain had little interest in fostering industrial innovation in Cuba, preferring instead the traditional agricultural and mining enterprises. The Spaniards could count on the cheap labor of thousands of Africans who had been brought to Cuba in the 18th and 19th centuries to work on the sugar and tobacco plantations as slaves and were only emancipated in 1886.

Cuba was particularly attractive as a market to American companies because they could operate there without political resistance or trade barriers. Those living in Cuba had access to the latest American furniture styles, home appliances, and new mechanical devices. Literally hundreds of American companies opened sales offices in Cuba and sold everything from sawmill equipment and modern bathroom and toilet fixtures to gas kitchen ranges and soda fountain machinery. The American Talking Picture Company distributed a complete line of phonographs and gramophones, while another company was the dealer for Victor Talking Machines, and an office supply store had the exclusive right to sell Underwood Typewriters. American products were also on sale at El Encanto, Cuba's leading department store, which two Cuban partners founded in 1888. In Havana, its competitors were Floglar; Fin de Siglo, whose art director was Enrique Garcia Cabrera (1893–1949); and Woolworths, but in many other Cuban cities where El Encanto established subsidiaries it had a more exclusive market.

American automobiles were popular in Cuba as early as 1900 and many of the early manufacturers had dealerships there. As in the United States, it was the lower price of the Ford, known in Cuba as *el fotingo* (the jalopy), that made automobile ownership possible for many Cubans. By the end of the 1930s, Ford had dealerships across the island.

Tourism began slowly around 1915, but by the mid-1920s it had begun to rival sugar and tobacco as a major source of national income. Gambling and sensuality were major attractions and tour operators worked hard to create an image of Cuba as a tropical paradise. It was referred to, in fact, by many as the "Paris of the Caribbean." The tourist experience was shaped by North American tastes, and travel agents promoted the island as a place to unwind and have fun. This image was evident in all the tourist advertising, promotional materials, and souvenirs and was the basis for a series of light-hearted musical films such as *Weekend in Havana* and others that followed it after World War II.

The tropical paradise that was promoted to the tourists was at odds with the reality of life on the island. Although there was a well-established middle class that complemented the much smaller cadre of wealthy families, major social inequities existed, especially outside Havana within the rural population. From the time of independence, Cuba had a series of corrupt leaders who caused great anger and frustration among the politically active populace. In 1923, during the presidency of Alfredo Zayas, a group of students protested against the government's dishonest practices and this led to the formation of a new political organization, the Falange de Acción Cubana. Two years later the Cuban Communist Party was formed. These organizations were the first to mobilize a new generation of political activists who protested against the corruption of their leaders.

In 1925, Gerardo Machado was elected president. When his first term ended, he refused to step down and continued illegally into a second term. One of the numerous sources of opposition to Machado was the Grupo Minorista (Minority Group), a loose affiliation of writers and artists who came together to promote a new literary and artistic culture, and also continue the resistance to political corruption that had started with the protests of 1923. Machado remained in power until 1933, when the army forced him out. He was replaced by an army sergeant, Fulgencio Batista, who ruled Cuba until 1944 with American support as an unelected strongman behind a facade of puppet presidents. After winning the election of 1952, Batista came to power again and remained in control of the government until an army led by Fidel Castro toppled it in 1959. Batista was known for his friendship with the American gangster Meyer Lansky, who solidified Mafia control of widespread gambling operations in Cuba.

The decorative arts

When Fernando Aguado y Rico (1859–1941) founded the Escuela Preparatoria de Artes y Oficios (Preparatory School for Arts and Trades) in 1882, his aim was to provide training for young men in carpentry, mechanical pursuits, and industrial chemistry. He envisioned the Escuela as a mechanical training school rather than a school of applied arts, and his curriculum was based on those he observed in Europe and the United States. Free instruction was offered in day and evening classes to students as young as 12 years old. The intent of the program was to produce graduates whose knowledge was less than that of professional engineers and scientists but adequate to work in existing industrial enterprises such as mechanized sugar mills and construction firms. The school was the first in Cuba to prepare students for different trades and was also one of the first trade schools in Latin America. After several years, its name was changed to Escuela Superior de Artes y Oficios de La Habana (Higher Arts and Trades School of Havana) and then in 1938 the name of its founder, Fernando Aguado y Rico, was added.

By 1921, when the commercial and decorative artist Enrique Garcia Cabrera was appointed professor of decorative painting, the school had begun to devote more attention to the decorative arts. While the Escuela Superior started as a school for poor students including many who were children of former slaves, this was not the case for the Academia Nacional de Bella Artes San Alejandro (National San Alejandro Fine Arts Academy), which was founded in 1918. The academy initially offered courses in the fine arts but then added decorative arts classes. Garcia Cabrera taught there after moving from the Escuela Superior de Artes y Oficios.

Initially, American styles in furniture and interiors had great influence on the development of interior decoration in Cuba. The New York firm of

H. F. Huber opened an office in Havana and received a number of commissions to decorate the homes of wealthy Cubans. Others companies followed. Tiffany and Company also opened a branch in Havana, specializing in designs for shop windows and lamps for private residences. Teodoro Bailey (dates unconfirmed) opened a studio that was dedicated to the design of artistic furniture and the decoration of interiors. Bailey had a special interest in Spanish Renaissance styles and advocated heavy wood paneling or molding for dining rooms as an example.

Spanish historicist furniture was popular in Havana, and Cuban craftsmen capably reproduced replicas of original pieces using local woods. For a time, Bailey wrote a regular column on "Architectural Art" for the popular journal *Social*, where he espoused historic styles. Following the 1925 Exposition Internationale des Arts Décoratifs, however, *Social* began to promote the French *style moderne*, later known as Art Deco. It was publicized in other magazines as well including *El Arquitecto* (*The Architect*) and the illustrated monthly *Arte y Decoración* (*Art and Decoration*), which was first published in 1931.

During the 1930s, Cuban architects designed important public buildings and private residences in the Deco style. Prominent among these was the Edificio Bacardi, a corporate office building financed by the Bacardi rum distillery, and the Edificio López Serrano, which housed a number of luxury apartments. Both buildings integrated decorative components such as ornamental stone sculptures, ironwork, carved doorways, tile flooring, and figurative metal panels. Other buildings in the Deco style such as cinemas, hospitals, and various private suburban villas also incorporated such elements.

Carpenters, plasterers, and ironworkers worked independently in cooperative workshops or as employees of large companies. Leading firms included Pi y Brioso S.A. for woodwork; Duque y Compañía for plasterwork; and La Insular, a national factory that specialized in lamps of bronze and wrought iron. The Cerrajería Artística Basora (Basora Artistic Metalworks) specialized in wrought iron fences that were designed in a modern style. Enrique García Cabrera was well known for his design of figurative panels in nickel silver and other metals. His Deco-inspired panel for the vestibule of the Edificio López Serrano depicts a nude figure in motion framed by geometric linear elements that include three airplanes as decorative motifs.

Furniture in both historic and modern styles was frequently custom-made or else produced as multiples in small workshops. Designs were generally derived from existing pieces, although adaptation to the hot climate was essential. Designers featured Cuban woods, but they often substituted wicker for upholstery. Among modern styles, the French *style moderne* was the most admired, while there was little interest in the European Functionalist furniture that Thonet and several other companies distributed. Metal furniture was generally considered to be most appropriate for offices or hospitals. Those companies that did manufacture furniture in metal eschewed Functionalist forms and instead produced custom-made ornate consoles of wrought iron or steel that were often combined with marble tops. Metal furniture was also promoted for outdoor patios.

The one designer who espoused modernism in furniture and interior design was Clara Porset (1895–1981), who had an atypical education for a Cuban woman. She attended a private secondary school in New York, went on to Columbia University, and then to Paris, where she collaborated on projects with the furniture designer and decorator Henri Rapin (1873–1939) while also taking art history and theory courses at the École de Beaux Arts and the Sorbonne. After her return to Cuba, she began to design custom furniture for clubs, schools, and private residences. She opposed the historic styles that Teodoro Bailey promoted so vigorously, and began to give public lectures about interiors, substituting the term "interior design" for the more widely used "interior decoration". In 1931 she presented a seminal lecture in Havana on contemporary interior design and its adaptation in Cuba, in which she distinguished between decoration as adornment and the new German Functionalist concept of interior design as the organization of a closed space.

Despite her commercial success in Cuba, Porset retained her interest in Bauhaus-inspired Functionalism and in 1933 she left for the United States to study with Joseph Albers, the émigré Bauhaus teacher, at Black Mountain College in North Carolina. Returning to Cuba after a summer at Black Mountain, Porset continued her design practice but also took an interest in design education for young women, becoming the Artistic Director of the Escuela Técnica para Mujeres (Technical School for Women). Opposed to the Batista regime, she was active in public protests, lost her teaching position and some professional opportunities, and in 1936 after a short stay in New York she emigrated to Mexico, where she had an illustrious career as a professional designer, teacher, and cultural activist.

Graphic design

Advertising and magazines

Compared to other countries in Latin America where American products were less pervasive, Cuba was saturated with American goods, hence advertising agencies from the United States were operating in Cuba as early as the late 19th century. After the country achieved independence, a flood of American agencies opened offices in Havana, N. W. Ayer, McCann-Erikson, and J. Walter Thompson among them. Less familiar firms included the West Indies Advertising Company, the Havana Advertising Company, and the W. B. Elliott Company, which specialized in billboard ads.

For print advertising, the graphics would often be designed in New York and the original copy would be adapted for Cuban consumers and translated into Spanish. Lithographic posters were widely used and one enterprising advertising agent announced the opportunity to advertise with modern electric signs. The plethora of American agencies ensured that the most

up-to-date advertising techniques were introduced in Cuba, often many years before they were adopted elsewhere in Latin America. Thus, Cuba developed a highly sophisticated class of consumers who took many of their lifestyle cues from the latest American trends.

Although numerous American advertising agencies relied on art directors and artists in New York, Cuba had a cadre of extremely talented artists, art directors, and caricaturists who produced a rich visual culture consisting of advertisements, posters, magazine covers and layouts, illustration, and caricatures. Central to this culture were three magazines—*Bohemia*, *Social*, and *Carteles*—all founded by Cubans. Miguel Ángel Quevedo Pérez (dates unconfirmed) published the first issue of the weekly illustrated magazine *Bohemia* in 1908. Modeled on European publications such as *The Illustrated London News,* it featured extensive news coverage as did illustrated magazines elsewhere, but Quevedo Pérez also published poems and stories as well as articles on all the arts. *Bohemia*, which was widely read throughout Latin America, became a principal voice of opposition to the regime of Fulgencio Batista.

The first covers were conservative, with lettering and imagery reminiscent of Art Nouveau. Visual material in the early issues included reproductions of art by Leopoldo Romañach (1862–1951), Antonio Rodríguez Morey (1874–1967), and Armando G. Menocal (1863–1942), all traditional figurative or landscape painters who had studied at the National Academy of Fine Arts. Covers also featured academic paintings. By the late 1920s, *Bohemia* had modernized its masthead and was publishing some covers in the Art Deco style, although the visual range of its artists was still quite diverse (Plate 49).

Social was launched by Conrado Massaguer (1889–1965), an artist of many talents who was known for his biting political caricatures as well as his magazine cover illustrations, and advertisements. In 1910 he founded an advertising agency, Mercurio, with Laureano Rodríguez Castells (dates unconfirmed). The following year he had his first one-man exhibition of caricatures and in 1913, along with his brother Oscar, he founded his first magazine, *Gráfico*, with which he remained involved until 1918. He left Mercurio in 1915 due to differences with his partner and the next year he established a new advertising agency, Anuncios Kesevén, where he did the drawings for many ads that were published in Havana's thriving weekly and monthly magazines.

In 1916, Massaguer published the first issue of *Social*, a monthly magazine that lasted until 1938. Its intended audience was wealthy Cubans in the middle and upper class. It was beautifully printed and its features ranged from art and architecture, to sports, hygiene, fashion, and politics (Fig. 29.01).

Fig. 29.01: Conrado Massaguer, *Social*, cover, 1926. The Wolfsonian–Florida International University, Miami Beach, Florida, The Vicki Gold Levi Collection, XC2002.11.4.313.2. Photo: David Almeida.

Besides drawing most of the covers himself, Massaguer created the logotype, and some of the section titles, illustrations, and caricatures. A special feature was the Massa-Girl, a youthful vibrant young woman who was Massaguer's version of the American Petty girl.

In 1921, Massaguer hired the painter and illustrator Rafael Ángel Surís (dates unconfirmed) as the assistant art director of *Social* in charge of the page layouts. Among Suris's innovations was the use of various themes for the table of contents. In a series on the zodiac, he added small pen and ink drawings of female nudes with flowing hair to the margins, suggesting a lingering relation to Art Nouveau. Several years after he joined *Social*, Surís moved to New York, where he worked for *Harper's Bazaar* and other publications.

Massaguer commissioned Havana's most talented artists, illustrators, and caricaturists to do covers and illustrations. They included José Manuel Acosta (1895–d.o.d unconfirmed)**,** a modernist painter and photographer; Enrique García Cabrera, one of Cuba's first commercial artists who also designed metal decorative panels for public buildings and private residences; Rafael Blanco (1885–1955), a caricaturist and illustrator; Enrique Riverón (1902–1998), one of Cuba's first abstract painters and collagists who also published cartoons in *The New Yorker*, contributed to Chilean magazines, and worked briefly as an animator for Walt Disney; Rafael Lillo Botet (dates unconfirmed), a Spanish émigré artist known for his caricatures and advertising posters as well as for co-founding the illustrated magazine *Pay-Pay* in 1913; and Jaime Valls (1883–1955), a leading commercial artist, illustrator, caricaturist, and painter. Valls was born in Catalonia, Spain, and came to Havana in 1901 at the age of 18. He studied sculpture in Barcelona, where he absorbed the culture of Modernisme or Spanish Art Nouveau. In Havana, he soon established himself as an accomplished caricaturist, illustrator, and poster designer and quickly developed into Cuba's most prominent advertising artist, creating posters as well as magazine advertisements. At the same time, Valls became the political caricaturist for the magazine *La Discusión* (*The Discussion*), a position he held for many years. As a poster artist, he was familiar with the directness of the Germans as well as the refined drawing techniques of the French designers. Among Cuban artists, he had the greatest understanding of the recent European poster movements and consequently won first prize in every poster competition that was held in Havana.

Massaguer collaborated as well with the Cuban fashion illustrator Rogelio Dalmau (1900–1954), who lived in Paris but nonetheless contributed fashion

Fig. 29.02: Conrado Massaguer, Orange Crush, poster, date unconfirmed. The Wolfsonian–Florida International University, Miami Beach, Florida, The Vicki Gold Levi Collection, XC2002.11.4.263. Photo: David Almeida.

and furniture illustrations to *Social*. These artists also worked regularly for other magazines including *Bohemia* and *Carteles* and some of them were active advertising designers and illustrators as well.

Social folded in 1937, due to the difficult political situation created by the Batista regime, which Massaguer opposed. With his brother, Massaguer also co-founded *Carteles* (*Posters*), which the two launched in 1919. The same year Massaguer brought out a children's magazine, *Pulgarcito* (*Tom Thumb*). *Carteles* became a popular weekly and like *Social* covered all aspects of contemporary life. Its most regular cover artist was Andrés García Benítez (1916–1981), also known for his fashion design and theater productions. The graphic virtuosity of Andrés, as he usually signed his work, ranged from a refined Deco line to a light-hearted comic style and a more somber dramatic rendering technique.

By the mid-1930s a few of Cuba's modern artists had embraced Afro-Cuban themes such as the depiction of dark-skinned dancers and scenes of rural life. Andrés and other commercial artists appropriated this imagery for magazine covers, thus providing a contrast to the prior depictions of stylish urban women sporting the latest American or European fashions (Plate 50).

Besides his artistic and editorial projects, Massaguer was active in many organizations, a number of which he initiated himself. In 1919 he was President of the Havana Advertising Club. He was also a founder of the Asociación de Pintores y Escultores (Association of Painters and Sculptors), which sponsored the Primer Salon de Humoristas (First Humor Exhibition) in 1921 and he was as well a founding member of the Grupo Minorista, whose members published a number of articles on literary and political themes in *Social*. In 1927, they established their own avant-garde journal, the *Revista De Avance*, which they published until 1930. That same year they published in *Carteles* a manifesto that expressed their opposition to the dictatorial regime of Gerardo Machado and called for artistic, scientific, and educational reforms. Other members of the Grupo Minorista—Eduardo Abela (1889–1965), Jaime Valls, and José Manuel Acosta—were also active commercial artists.

In 1924, Massaguer moved for about a year to New York, where he continued to run *Social* while also contributing drawings and caricatures to many major American magazines, *The New Yorker*, *Collier's*, *Vanity Fair*, *Red Book*, *Cosmopolitan*, *Literary Digest*, and *Town and Country* among them. During the period up to the end of World War II, he spent time in Havana, Paris, Geneva, and New York, involved with *Social* and *Carteles*, while also doing advertising illustrations and continuing to contribute drawings and caricatures to many publications in Havana and

Fig. 29.03: Conrado Messaguer, *Life*, *Havana Number*, cover, 1928. The Wolfsonian–Florida International University, Miami Beach, Florida, The Vicki Gold Levi Collection, XC2002.11.4.384. Photo: David Almeida.

abroad. He designed advertising for the American soft drink Orange Crush (Fig. 29.02) and in 1928 he designed the cover for the Havana number of *Life Magazine* (Fig. 29.03).

Scholars and critics who write about the early decades in Cuba following independence consider Massaguer to be one of the leading creators of magazine covers, illustrations, and advertising art. They also identify Enrique García Cabrera and Jaime Valls as the other pioneer commercial artists. Cabrera, previously mentioned, published comic drawings in *Bohemia*, *Carteles*, and other magazines and newspapers. He also designed posters for commercial clients such as Tivoli Beer (Fig. 29.04).

Initially Valls was associated with various Havana advertising agencies, but eventually he established his own studio, La Casa Valls. He referred to his advertisements as "graphic propaganda" and was guided by the American model in setting up his own "publicity bureau." Unlike Massaguer who sketched quickly, Valls's advertising drawings were extremely detailed, and included refined lettering, frequently adopted from American or European Deco examples.

As a member of the Grupo Modernista, Valls participated in its call for a new modern art. In 1927, he traveled to Paris with Eduardo Abela, another Minorista member. There they encountered a Cuban creative milieu, which included the novelist and musicologist Alejo Carpentier, who encouraged them to take up Afro-Cuban themes. After his return to Havana, Valls began a series of drawings and paintings that portrayed the daily life of Cuban blacks and mestizos. His depictions of these themes formed part of the Cuban "new art" and also appeared occasionally as magazine covers for *Bohemia* or *Carteles*, both of which were receptive to such themes in the 1930s.

Eduardo Abela began to depict Afro-Cuban as well as rural themes in his paintings and drawings while he was in Paris, but he became a cartoonist when he returned to Havana, inventing a character whom he called "El Bobo" (The Fool). This character appeared in

Fig. 29.04: Enrique García Cabrera, Tivoli Beer, poster, 1920s. Private Collection.

cartoons on the pages of the newspaper *El Diario de la Marina* from 1930 to 1934, during which time he was widely recognized as a critical voice of opposition to the political regime of Machado.

Film posters

Cubans were avid filmgoers during the 1920s and 1930s. Though films from Europe and elsewhere in Latin America were distributed in Cuba, many came from American distributors who considered the island to be part of an extended market just as manufacturers of other products did. A few Cuban films were also made during this period. Among the lavish theaters built in the Art Deco style during the 1930s were the Cine Moderno, the Teatro Fausto, and the Teatro

Lutgardita, whose fantasy decor was inspired by Mayan motifs.

The first film posters were created abroad and arrived in Cuba along with the imported films. Advertisements were then produced locally and published in newspapers and magazines. Lobby cards with photographs from the films were also done abroad and distributed to the local theaters. The few posters designed in Cuba before 1940 were printed by offset lithography in New York or by the Lithographic Company of Havana. However, unlike Mexico, none of the Cuban film poster designers were closely connected to the film industry, although a few Cuban companies—Studio Chromos, Reguera, Barrios, Rivadulla-Alonso, and Vargas—were commissioned to create large paintings that depicted scenes from the films.

At the beginning of the 1940s a breakthrough in film poster design occurred when Eladio Rivadulla (1923–1998), who studied painting, drawing, and sculpture at the National School of Fine Arts, began designing and printing posters using the low-budget silkscreen process. Rivadulla received his commissions from the film distributors with whom he negotiated the design concept, budget, and other matters. Following his designs, the posters were produced by a skilled technician and then delivered to the distributor.

Rivadulla created his first posters for American and Mexican films. His 1942 poster for *Tarzan y el Tesoro Oculto* (*Tarzan and the Secret Treasure*) was guaranteed to excite an audience. With bold colors, it featured a muscle-flexing Tarzan, drawn in comic-book style, charging through the jungle—an image combined with leaping tigers and a herd of rampaging elephants. In several other posters produced around the same time, Rivadulla gave even more visual prominence to the lead actors, as he did by depicting the head of actor Jorge Negrete in a poster for the Mexican film *Caminos de Ayer* (*Yesterday's Roads*) or that of Gary Cooper in William Wellman's *Beau Geste*. Rivadulla continued to produce film posters after World War

II and his pioneering silkscreen technique became an important precedent for Cuban poster artists once the Cuban film industry became active after the revolution.

Tourist graphics

The massive influx of tourists during the 1920s and 1930s prompted the need for extensive publicity materials. Since most of the tourists were Americans, these materials had to be printed in English. While artists were sometimes identified, often they were not. Some worked in the United States, where travel promoters created materials for domestic distribution, and in Cuba, others most likely worked for advertising agencies in Havana.

In 1934, the Corporación Nacional de Turismo (National Tourist Corporation) was set up to coordinate the various industries involved with tourism. It replaced an earlier organization, the Comisión Nacional para el Fomento del Turismo, which had been established in 1919. While the official tourist organization published materials for visitors, individual enterprises such as hotels like the Plaza and the Lincoln, restaurants such as La Florida, and bars such as La Bodeguita del Medio created their own brochures, menus, and souvenir labels. As early as 1912, the Cuba Railroad Timetable in English was illustrated with reproductions of romantic paintings of rural landscapes and picturesque small towns. Brochures that advertised hotels, cruises, tours, restaurants, and bars featured several types of illustrations. One type portrayed suave tourist couples sitting in a nightclub or dining on a hotel patio while local performers entertained them. Another featured seductive images of the performers themselves, and a third depicted clichés of traditional Cuban life such as a *guajiro* or rural dweller from Camaguey in central Cuba doing a folk dance with a woman in a long Spanish-style dress with her hair pulled back in a bun. Almost all the Cubans portrayed in such publicity were white or at least very light skinned. This unspoken convention of Cuban tourist graphics was in sharp contrast to the representation of blacks and mulattos by some of

Cuba's modern painters and commercial artists who were exploring the Afro-Cuban experience.

Mexico

Porfirio Díaz, a former general, became president of Mexico in 1876 when he overthrew his rival, Sebastián Lerdo. Díaz ruled Mexico until 1910, during a period known as the *Porfiriato*. Under him, the country experienced a period of strong economic growth. However, despite the existence of a modest middle class, the divide between the small wealthy elite and the large mass of poor uneducated peasants was extreme.

Díaz governed with a council of *científicos* or intellectuals who advised him on economic and social planning and policy. He built up Mexico's infrastructure by modernizing the ports, introducing telegraphic communication, and in 1909, uniting the country's different railroad lines in a single government corporation, Ferrocarriles Nacionales de México (Mexican National Railroads) (FNM).

Díaz courted foreign investors aggressively and they soon dominated the Mexican economy. The Americans and British owned the mines and oilfields, the French were in textiles, the Germans in the production of hardware and pharmaceuticals, and the Spanish were active in food businesses. The economy was transformed during the Díaz regime when large vertically integrated companies that were mainly foreign-owned replaced a production system of small artisan workshops. Factories, whether they produced steel, cement, or beer, had the latest foreign equipment, which was operated and maintained by foreign technicians.

Few Mexican entrepreneurs emerged during the *Porfiriato*. Most of the wealthy elite owned natural resources or haciendas, which were large land holdings, where they produced agricultural goods. Hacienda owners had little interest in modern agricultural machinery since cheap peasant labor was readily available.

Like presidents before him, Díaz promoted a positive image of Mexico in the world. Consequently the country participated regularly in world's fairs, beginning with London in 1867 and Vienna in 1873. In 1876, the year Díaz became president, Mexico was one of the few Latin American countries to take part in the Centennial Exhibition in Philadelphia. At the 1889 World's Fair in Paris, where technological modernization was featured in the Galerie des Machines, the Mexican pavilion was an Aztec Palace, which conveyed the promise of Mexico's future by displaying the glories of its past.

To commemorate the centenary of Mexican independence, which was to be held in 1910, Díaz planned a huge celebration that would display the nation's progress and, as Mauricio Tenorio Trillo has noted, present Mexico to the world as a modern nation. Early in the planning process a proposal for a world's fair was made but this never materialized. Instead, the center of festivities for the centenary was Mexico City. Besides the inauguration of parks and monuments, Díaz introduced industrial projects, founded a National University, and initiated construction of the new imposing Legislative Palace. Unlike the centenary celebrations in some other Latin American countries, no display of domestic industrial products was planned. Most consumer products were still imported and there was not sufficient incentive to manufacture more at home since Mexico did not have a large enough middle class to constitute a viable national market.

The impoverished conditions of the landless masses were a major cause of the Mexican Revolution, which began in 1910, the same year as the Centennial. Díaz was single-minded in his goal of economic development and repressive in his rule. Critics of his regime included Francisco Madero, a leader of the anti-re-election movement, and several rebel leaders including Emiliano Zapata and Pancho Villa, who both commanded bands of guerilla fighters.

Madero challenged Díaz in the election of 1910 and was elected president but had to step down after a short period following attacks from both the right and the left. General Victoriano Huerta seized power

but, like Madero, was unable to govern due to fierce opposition from the rebel leaders, who were joined by the politician Venustiano Carranza.

In early 1914, Heurta resigned and continuous fighting followed. Villa's forces were defeated by troops loyal to Carranza, and Zapata's rebel band temporarily withdrew from the conflict. In May 1915, Carranza assumed the presidency and shortly thereafter headed a convention where a new Mexican Constitution was written. Adopted in 1917, it included provisions that gave the government power to redistribute land, restricted the power of the Catholic Church, and introduced new rights for workers.

In 1919, Carranza's troops murdered Zapata, but the following year Carranza made the mistake of attempting to choose his own successor, an act that met with strong opposition and led to his replacement by Álvaro Obregón, a general who launched an ambitious program of social reform that did much to stabilize the political situation. In 1923, an unknown assassin murdered Pancho Villa, thus eliminating the last rebel leader and enabling a peaceful succession of power when Obregón stepped down in 1924 and Plutarco Elías Calles became the new president.

The Obregón government did not adequately address the demands for land redistribution but it made a serious commitment to education. Obregón appointed José Vasconcelos, a writer, philosopher, and political figure, as Secretary of Public Education and appropriated large sums of money for an ambitious program of school construction, recruitment and training of teachers, and special projects such as the Open Air Schools, where thousands of children, especially in rural areas, received artistic training in informal outdoor settings. Vasconcelos created a new type of rural school, La Casa del Pueblo (House of the People), which offered multiple activities in the arts and sports as well as training in sanitation and agriculture. During his four-year tenure as Secretary of Education, Vasconcelos created more than a thousand of these schools.

Vasconcelos also initiated the Mexican mural movement. Diego Rivera, José Orozco, and David Alfaro Siquieros among other artists were hired to create murals in schools and in the new Secretariat of Public Education in Mexico City. Vasconcelos encouraged the muralists to draw on indigenous themes as a means to assert an identity that was true to the spirit of the Latin people. In his 1925 book *La Raza Cósmica* (*The Cosmic Race*), written when he was no longer Secretary of Education, Vasconcelos argued that the people of the Americas formed an Ibero-American melting pot. Their racial mingling, he argued, could become the source of a vibrant new civilization.

Land reform had to await the presidency of Lázaro Cárdenas, who governed Mexico from 1934 to 1940. Though Obregón and the presidents who followed him had to distance themselves from the elitist values of the *Porfiriato* and respond to some demands of the revolution, none took its concerns as seriously as Cárdenas. He appropriated 44 million acres of hacienda land and distributed it to the peasants, largely through collective organizations called *ejidos*, in which land given to people in individual villages was collectively owned and most often cultivated in common.

Cárdenas also extended additional benefits to urban industrial workers, who gained unprecedented unionization rights and wage increases. However, he was more committed to the development of rural Mexico than to the growth of urban centers or the construction of large industrial plants. In a speech delivered at the University of Virginia in 1935, Ramón Beteta, a prominent official in the Cárdenas government, explained Cárdenas's development policy in terms that were reminiscent of William Morris. Like Morris, he associated capitalism with the evils of industrialization that included urbanism, exploitation, waste, and shoddy goods. Also in the Arts and Crafts spirit, he espoused small industrial communities where goods that satisfied people's needs would be produced. He did not oppose machines but did reject the mechanization of workers. He extolled the craftsman as a

producer of beautiful products and observed that their artistic sense would still be expressed if they used machines properly.

Cárdenas may have based his idea for the *ejido* on the Soviet *kolkhoz* or collective farm movement that Joseph Stalin initiated at the end of the 1920s, the difference being that the Mexican president did not advocate state ownership of the land or accrual of the profits that derived from it. He made a point to distance himself from Stalin by inviting Leon Trotsky, a rival of Stalin's, to come to Mexico where Trotsky was subsequently brutally murdered by a Soviet agent. Cárdenas also opened Mexico to thousands of Republican refugees from the Spanish Civil War, among whom were a number of distinguished artists, designers, and intellectuals. As well, he invited the former Bauhaus director Hannes Meyer, who first visited Mexico in 1938, to found an Institute for Planning and Urbanism at the National Polytechnic Institute in Mexico City, which Meyer did the following year. In 1944–1945, Meyer headed the Hospital Planning Commission, which established the construction requirements for all Mexican hospitals.

In March 1938, Cárdenas expropriated all of Mexico's oil resources and then nationalized the American and Anglo-Dutch oil companies. Several months later he created Petróleos Mexicanos (PEMEX), a government company that had exclusive rights to extract, refine, and sell Mexican oil. His successor was Manuel Ávila Camacho, who slowed down the pace of land reform and introduced a massive literacy campaign but spent much of his presidency engaged with issues related to World War II.

Manufacturing, decorative arts, and design

Mexico's production of consumer goods before World War II was limited. The urban middle class expanded during the 1920s and 1930s, but the largest segment of the population was rural and poor. William Beezley describes rural dwellers as living for the most part without chairs, tables, or beds, sleeping on mats called *petates* and cooking with earthen pottery.

The middle class shopped in the grand urban department stores—El Puerto de Liverpool (Port of Liverpool), El Palacio de Hierro (The Iron Palace), and El Centro Mercantil (The Mercantile Center). These stores carried a wide range of goods from Europe and the United States. They also manufactured goods in their own workshops. The Palacio de Hierro, for example, announced in its catalog of 1904 that it had the capability to produce furniture in various styles with advanced machinery and local materials at prices lower than competition from abroad.

Some Mexican craftsmen and decorative artists were aware of the Art Deco style but it was not widely used in the design of furniture or other consumer products. In France, decorative artists frequently appropriated motifs from non-European cultures, which they combined with exotic materials and modern forms. Deco designers in Mexico tended to adopt local folkloric or pre-Hispanic motifs, attempting as in other Latin American countries to ally modernism and nationalism. Ceramists incorporated motifs from Mayan or Aztec pottery with reasonable success since the motifs were subordinated to the forms of simple containers, but the design of custom furniture with such motifs was less successful. A living room suite with stepped Aztec designs appended to the chair and bench forms, for example, displayed the same inappropriate adaptations of historic ornament that were rampant during the Victorian era in Europe. Pre-Hispanic ornament was also adopted for the Mexican government's neo-Mayan pavilion at the 1929 Iberoamerican Exhibition in Seville, Spain. Designed by Manuel Amáblis (1883–d.o.d unconfirmed), the pavilion had a plan that was based on a Nahuatl symbol, while its extensive ornament was superficially grafted onto a modern building that had little relation to a Mayan temple.

Art Deco did, however, have a strong influence on modern Mexican architecture and was evident in the design of some public buildings and private residences in Mexico City. Among the public buildings, the Edificio de la Alianza de Ferrocarrileros Mexicanos, the Estación de Policia y Bomberos, the Central de Teléfonos Antonio Caso, and the Banco de Mexico are prominent examples. Private residences with Deco elements were built in several developments or *colonias* in Mexico City. Many of these buildings included work by skilled craftsmen. Ironworkers created intricately designed gates and railings, modern lighting fixtures were custom-made, woodworkers installed decorative paneling, and ceramists created external ornament that might include pre-Hispanic iconography or, in the case of the Oficinas de Teléfonos, reliefs of telephones set against maps of Mexico. Large concrete Deco letters in relief were also incorporated into the facades of some buildings.

Agricultural equipment

The design of agricultural equipment changed slowly. In the 1890s the predominant implement was a single-handled plow that farmers hooked to the horns of an ox that pushed rather than pulled it. When two-handled plows were imported, peasants often chopped off one of the handles so that the plow resembled the ones they were already accustomed to. An American farm implement company began to manufacture one-handled plows for export and these survived well into the 20th century. Local factories also started to make farm equipment and by the end of the 1930s, about 15 were doing so. They were small establishments and dedicated their production primarily to the traditional plows, although they produced other agricultural tools in limited quantities. No Mexican factories made tractors. To implement his agricultural reforms, Lázaro Cárdenas had to import large numbers of these, which he leased to the *ejidos*.

Cars and airplanes

As elsewhere in Latin America, Mexico did not manufacture its own automobiles in the period before World War II, although the major American automobile companies opened assembly plants there. Buick was the first in 1922, followed in 1925 by the Ford Motor Company, and Chrysler around 1937. At the beginning of the 1920s a Mexican firm attempted to market an automobile designed specifically for domestic consumption. Named the Anáhuac after a center of Aztec civilization, it was to have been made by an American company but only four were ever built.

Earlier, in 1915, President Carranza authorized the establishment of the Talleres Nacionales de Construcciones Aeronáuticas (TNCA) (National Workshop for Aeronautic Construction), which launched the military aviation industry in Mexico. The TNCA was overseen by Gustavo Salinas, head of the government's new Department of Aeronautics, and was directed by two engineers, a Mexican, Juan Guillermo Villasana (dates unconfirmed) and an Italian, Francisco Santarini (1883–1954). Villasana was a pioneer of Mexican aviation who had been recognized around 1912 for an original propeller design that was made of several different woods and enabled a plane to rise and descend more easily. Dubbed the Anáhuac propeller, it became widely known in the aviation field.

The TNCA began as a repair and maintenance shop for the few foreign planes that the government owned, but it soon began to produce planes of its own design. The workshop is noteworthy for its rational division of technical, mechanical, and design tasks, which facilitated the recruitment of personnel with specialized skills. In 1916, the TNCA completed its first two planes, one a biplane that initiated its Series A. The planes were fitted with foreign engines but the workshop made a breakthrough the following year when it produced a Series A plane made entirely with parts that had been designed in Mexico, specifically the Anáhuac propeller and a rotary engine that also bore a patriotic name—*Azatl* ("white heron" in the Náhuatl language).

For the next several years, the workshop continued to design and manufacture more airplanes— additional Series A biplanes, "parasol" planes in the H Series, and several smaller aircraft known as Series C. The workshop had received unqualified support from President Carranza but attitudes began to change after he left office and was assassinated in 1920. The TNCA designed and produced new planes including the Series B and Series E, but it also began to copy foreign aircraft and use engines from abroad for some of its own models. By the time the workshop closed in 1940, the government had ceased to produce its own planes and reverted to its earlier policy of purchasing aircraft abroad.

Graphic design

Magazines, journals, and newspapers

With the end of the Díaz regime in 1910 and the beginning of the Mexican Revolution, various magazines and newspapers that had flourished under Díaz either ceased publication or did so within several years. A number of illustrated magazines were published during the Díaz years. Among them, the most popular was *El Mundo Ilustrado* (*The World Illustrated*), a weekly that began as *El Mundo Semanario Ilustrado* in 1894 and changed its name in 1900. Despite its extensive attention to fashion and social events, *El Mundo Ilustrado* was a serious publication that also covered the economy, science, literature, and the arts (Fig. 29.05). Its aim was to represent the progress and modernity of the Díaz regime rather than offer a critical counterpoint to it.

The magazine was printed with the latest imported equipment, including rotary presses and linotype machines. There were three departments for visual production: one that produced original artwork, another that made engravings, and a third for photography. These departments sometimes borrowed photographs from readers to use as the basis for engravings. Original drawings and engravings were also commissioned from established artists, many of whom had studied at the Academia San Carlos in Mexico City and did commercial art to make a living. Among them were Julio Ruelas (1870–1907), Antonio Gedovius (dates unconfirmed), and Antonio Bribiesca (dates

EL MUNDO ILUSTRADO

Año XL.—Tomo II.—Número 22.   MEXICO, NOVIEMBRE 27 de 1904.

Director: LIC. RAFAEL REYES SPÍNDOLA,
Secretario de Redacción: José Gabriel Eguía.

Sra. Doña Carmen Romero Rubio de Díaz
En cuyo honor se celebró la brillante soirée del 19 del actual

Fig. 29.05: *El Mundo Illustrado*, cover, 1904. CONADICOV archives.

unconfirmed). They created covers, illustrated literary works, and sometimes designed decorative vignettes.

A special supplement to El *Mundo Ilustrado*—*De las Damas* (*Of the Ladies*)—was profusely illustrated with fashion drawings, vignettes, and Art Nouveau headings by Alfredo Flores (dates unconfirmed). He had developed an illustrative style that was based heavily on the European Art Nouveau posters of the 1890s and he adapted it for other purposes. Besides illustration and advertising, he specialized in headings, vignettes, and typographic ornaments for editorial layouts. Although numerous publications solicited his services, Flores worked extensively for *El Mundo Ilustrado*.

Other illustrated publications of the Porfirean years included *Seminario Ilustrado* (*Weekly Illustrated*) (1894–1900) and *El Tiempo Ilustrado* (*The Illustrated Times*) (1887–1912). The leading daily papers were *El Universal*, which first appeared in 1888, and *El Imparcial*, which began publication in 1896. Both were founded by Rafael Reyes Spíndola, one of Diaz's intellectual advisors or *cientificos*, and consequently they tended to support the regime. A rare publication that criticized the Díaz government was *El Hijo de El Ahuizote* (*The Son of the Ahuizote* [a mythical animal]), a magazine founded in 1885 that featured caricatures, including drawings by José Guadalupe Posada, who can be considered the founder of Mexican caricature and political cartoons (see Chapter 15).

The leading cultural magazine of the *Porfiriato* was the *Revista Moderna* (*Modern Review*), which was published between 1898 and 1911. Its managing editor was the lawyer, journalist, and scholar Jesús Urueta, and its principal artist was Julio Ruelas (1870–1907), who left an indelible visual stamp on the publication. Before Ruelas began contributing to the *Revista Moderna*, he studied in Germany where he was attracted to the Romantic painters and Dürer's engravings. French Symbolism also made a strong impression on him and many of his drawings evinced a macabre element.

Ruelas's masthead for the *Revista Moderna* depicted a supine nude woman entwined with a serpent who has bound her to the letters of the title by wrapping his body around her (Fig. 29.06). Ruelas also employed a sinuous Art Nouveau line in some of his drawings. For the *Revista Moderna,* he produced illustrations, vignettes, ornaments, and advertisements, as well as the masthead design. All contributed to the journal's fin-de-siècle appearance.

The *Revista Moderna* sought a strong intellectual presence, publishing Spanish translations of Novalis, Poe, and Baudelaire, the poems of Ruben Darío, one of Latin America's first modernist poets, and articles on art and architecture. During its existence, it was considered by some to be the principal voice of literary modernism

MASCARAS.

J·R·
-03-

LUIS G. URBINA.

———

 L mirar á Urbina recuerdo, casi sin querer, una frase de mi pobre artista Jesús Contreras: "Urbina alcanzó ya los honores del Museo del Louvre; está allí sonriente, desnudo alegre y fuerte, con el nombre de *Sileno jóven.*"

Y en efecto, esa es la idea que traen á la memoria aquella cabeza amplia y cubierta con típica cabellera rizada, aquel *embonpoint* incipiente, aquellos ojillos que suelen reir, cantar, decir gracias y enterneceros y aquella nariz subversiva que recuerda también la de Alejandro el Grande, Alejandro Dumas, el mulato divino que durante tantos años ejercitó el más noble, trascendental y hermoso de todos los ministerios: el de divertir y agradar.

Mas este hombrecillo parecido al "ayo y maestro del dios de la risa," este muchacho locuaz y gracioso, qué músicas tan hermosas oye, qué canciones tan delicadas sabe cantar.

Creo que fué Saint Victor quien asimiló la poesía moderna á los potingues de las hechiceras, compuestos al mismo tiempo de leche, miel, hojas de rosa, sangre de niños, cascabeles de serpiente y corazones de mujer. Esa es la poesía de Urbina: lo más grato, lo más risueño, lo más delicado; y al mismo

Fig. 29.06: Julio Ruelas, *Revista Moderna*, cover, 1903. CONADICOV archives.

in Latin America. In several ways, the *Revista Moderna* can be compared to *The Yellow Book* in England and Ruelas to Aubrey Beardsley, *The Yellow Book's* leading artist. However, Beardsley remained a draftsman and

illustrator, while Ruelas was also a highly accomplished painter and printmaker.

With Diaz's electoral defeat and the political chaos that followed, opposition to critical journalists subsided, which opened the way for a new wave of publications whose contributors were more outspoken about political events than those of the *Porfiriato*. These publications, both weekly illustrated magazines and daily papers, provided opportunities for an emerging generation of caricaturists, cartoonists, and illustrators. Among the new weeklies were *Multicolor*, *La Ilustración Semanal* (*Weekly Illustration)*, *La Ilustracíon Mexicana* (*Mexican Illustration*), and *Revista de Arte* (*Art Review*), all founded between 1911 and 1916. *Multicolor* was a transitional publication that featured caricatures attacking Francisco Madero. During its brief life until 1914, it published drawings by a number of young artists who achieved prominence in later years including Ernesto "El Chango" García Cabral (1890–1968), who became one of Mexico's leading illustrators with work ranging from magazine covers to film posters; Santiago De la Vega (1885–1950); Atenedoro Pérez y Soto (1883–1960); Clemente Islas Allende (1892–1958); and Alfredo Zalce (1908–2003), later to become one of Mexico's most important modern artists and an active collaborator in the revolutionary Taller de Gráfica Popular.

Another important illustrated weekly of this interim period was *Revista de Revistas*, which was initially founded in 1910. It experienced numerous editorial changes until it emerged in the 1920s as an important chronicle of contemporary Mexican life. Compared to the expensive illustrated magazines in the Díaz years, *Revista de Revistas* was relatively inexpensive and was oriented to a mass audience. It had a dynamic graphic layout and an editorial policy that featured articles of general interest rather than political commentary. Magazines like *Revista de Revistas* and *El Universal Ilustrado* had their own art departments, which produced illustrations and photoengravings, but they also hired outside artists for covers and other assignments. Many of the *Revista de Revistas* covers were done by Ernesto García Cabral and featured wry cartoons and scenes of daily life among the middle and upper class, the magazine's principal readers (Plate 51). García Cabral had previously studied in Paris, where

he went in 1912 with a scholarship from the short-lived Madero government and where he collaborated with French humor magazines such as *Le Rire* and *La Vie Parisien*. He worked for *Revista de Revistas* after his return in 1919 and produced drawings for many other Mexican magazines including *Frivolidades* (*Frivolities*), *Zig-Zag*, and *Fufurúfu*. In 1929, García Cabral founded *Fantoche*, a comic weekly whose humor was decidedly not political.

The emergence of cartoons and comic strips that depicted the humor of daily life as opposed to political caricature was a characteristic of the 1920s and 1930s, when various humor magazines were popular. García Cabral, Andrés Audiffred (1895–1958), and Juan Arthenack (1891–1940) were among the artists who popularized these forms of graphic art. Both Garcia Cabral and Audiffred later carried their cartooning talents over to film publicity, becoming leading film poster artists in the post-war years.

Arthenack, who studied fine art at the Academia de San Carlos, initially published humorous drawings in the daily newspapers. In 1928, he created the comic strip, *Adelaido el Conquistador* (*Adelaido the Conqueror*), about a young man who dressed in stylish clothes in order to pursue his romantic conquests. In 1932, Arthenack began to edit a children's magazine with the same name as his comic strip and that year *Adelaido the Conqueror* appeared as a comic book, the first in Mexico with strips by a single author. Arthenack was also the founder of a short-lived political humor magazine, *El Turco* (*The Turk*), which was shut down by the regime of Plutarco Elías Calles as soon as it was published.

An exceptional caricaturist and illustrator was Miguel Covarrubias (1904–1957), who paradoxically established his reputation in New York rather than Mexico. Before moving to New York in 1924, he contributed drawings and caricatures to various small publications in Mexico including *La Falange*, *Policromías*, and *Zig-Zag*. In New York he became a successful caricaturist and illustrator for *Vanity Fair* and *The New Yorker*, and in the early 1930s his travels in Asia resulted in the book he wrote and illustrated, *Island of Bali*. After returning to Mexico in the early 1940s, Covarrubias taught anthropology and headed the dance department at the National Institute of Fine Arts.

The leading dailies that emerged in the period after the Díaz regime were *El Universal*, launched in 1916, and *Excélsior* the following year. These papers became models for the modern Mexican press, creating a division of labor between the editors, reporters, columnists, and art staff. *El Universal* published caricatures and humorous illustrations, and among the young artists it hired were Carlos Dionisio Neve (1890–1962) and Andrés Audiffred. Both became pioneers of the Mexican comic strip. Neve worked extensively for *El Universal*, while collaborating occasionally with other publications including *Revista de Revistas, Tricolor,* and *Revista Ilustrada.* He was also a serious book and magazine illustrator as well as an advertising artist. Audiffred drew a number of comic strips for *El Universal* along with *Zig-Zag, Nueva Era*, and other publications. As a cartoonist and comic strip artist he was known for his ability to depict stereotypical figures of daily life.

In 1917, *El Universal* launched a weekly illustrated magazine, *El Universal Ilustrado*. Published until 1940, it was similar in format to the earlier *Porfirian* publication *El Mundo Ilustrado*, but more open to a range of literary and political voices. In the 1930s, it was home to the work of many emerging photographers. *El Universal Ilustrado*, which became *El Ilustrado* in 1928, conveyed a new sense of modernity during the 1920s and 1930s, one centered on a growing cultural confidence and an engagement with the problems and issues in Mexico as it developed after the revolution. Among the illustrators who worked for the publication were Gabriel Fernández Ledesma (1900–1983), who emerged as one of Mexico's few modern graphic designers in the 1930s; Jorge Duhart (dates unconfirmed); Andrés Audiffred; and Fernando Bolaños Cacho (dates

unconfirmed). Photography was also an important part of *El Mundo Ilustrado,* and photographs were presented in essays according to diverse layout strategies. They appeared in montages, in editorial sequences, or with decorative borders around them. Sometimes they were accompanied by hand-lettered article titles as well. Creating these layouts was the work of art directors, who developed inventive ways of using photographs that paralleled similar layout strategies in European illustrated magazines of the same period.

Photographic layouts—some quite experimental—were used extensively in other magazines including *El Mapa: Revista de Turismo (The Map: Tourism Review)*, *Rotográfico (Rotographic)*, and *Rotofoto,* a magazine for which photography was central to its editorial policy. *Rotofoto* was founded in 1937 by the journalist José Pagés Llergo (1910–1989), who was also a founder and co-editor of the illustrated magazine *Hoy (Today)*. The most likely model for *Rotofoto* was *Life* magazine, which began publication the year before in New York, but, given *Rotofoto*'s strong commitment to the goals of the revolution, Llergo may also have had in mind the Soviet photo magazine *USSR in Construction*.

Rotofoto published the work of numerous Mexican photographers, whose names figured prominently in the credits, and it did much to foster a culture of photojournalism in Mexico. Advertising itself as a "revista supergráfica" (supergraphic magazine), it published high-contrast black and white images, and the photographers were not averse to catching prominent officials off-guard, as Eric Salomon did with his small Ermanox camera in Germany (see Chapter 21). Besides its innovative layout, the magazine's ads were also photographic and represented the most advanced Mexican advertising concepts of the period. Due to its provocative political reporting, the magazine only lasted for 11 issues, its closing caused by the coverage of a rebellion in the region of Huasteca that led to the leader of Mexico's most powerful labor union instigating a strike at the magazine and supporting an attack on its facilities.

Advertising

During the Díaz regime, the audience for advertising was predominantly the urban middle class, which was relatively modest in size compared to the large number of rural peasants. Unlike Paris and other cosmopolitan cities, however, where posters announcing new products were displayed regularly on kiosks and billboards, advertising in Mexico appeared primarily in the weekly magazines and the daily newspapers. During the *Porfiriato*, when most goods were imported, many ads were created abroad, primarily in France and the United States, and then adapted with Spanish-language copy for publication in Mexico. Among the indigenous companies producing their own advertising were El Buen Tono, Mexico's largest cigarette company, and various breweries like Compañía Cervecera Toluca and Cervecería Cuauhtémoc Moctezuma. The large department stores also had publicity departments, where they created their own advertisements and catalogs.

Initially, independent advertising agencies would solicit and acquire advertisements for individual publications or groups of publications. These agencies included Tip Artística de México, the Compañía Anunciadora Mexicana, the Mexican General Advertising Company, and B. & G. Goetschel. Given the lack of commercial art studios, ads were frequently produced in lithography and photoengraving shops and other printing establishments, which would hire artists to create the designs. The artist Alfredo Flores, a specialist in Art Nouveau designs, was affiliated, for example, with the printer Armando Salcedo. Various weekly magazines at the turn of the century, notably the *Revista Moderna*, published advertisements that were heavily influenced by French Symbolism and Art Nouveau. Their leading advertising designers were the same artists who created their illustrations and vignettes: Julio Ruelas, Roberto Montenegro (1885–1968), Germán Gedovius (1867–1937), Alberto Garduño (1885–1948), Rafael de Zayas (1880–1961), and also Alberto Flores.

As Julieta Ortiz Gaitán has shown, the artists produced complete compositions with images and lettering, although the quality of the latter varied greatly. The iconography was often drawn from the tradition of painting and frequently had little to do with the product advertised. Julio Ruelas, for example, created several ads for the Banco Minero de Chihuahua (Miner's Bank of Chihuahua) that depicted a semi-nude man with a hammer and chisel, who represented the bank's funding of successful mining operations. Another ad by Ruelas for a soap company showed a winged fairy proffering an array of soaps to a seated woman in a flowing classical garment with one breast exposed. More successful was Roberto Montenegro's Symbolist-inspired advertisement for La Droguería de la Profesa that showed a woman with her eyes closed holding a bouquet of flowers from which arises a will-o'-the-wisp with a bottle of perfume.

With the ending of the *Porfiriato* and the ensuing transitional period during the revolution, advertising was in a fluid state. During the 1920s and 1930s, however, new styles emerged with strong influences from the current advertising tendencies in the United States and Europe. This resulted in new ways of depicting products and their relations to consumers as well as in new drawing styles; realism, on the one hand, coming from American advertising, and Art Deco, on the other, coming from France. Photography was also used extensively.

One of the leading advertising agencies was Maxim's, which was founded in 1909 by the Spanish artist Máximo Ramos (dates unconfirmed). Other agencies included Excélsior Publicidad, LBA Publicistas, and Mike Studio. Maxim's was among the first agencies in Mexico to produce its own artwork. The most prominent artist in the studio was Manuel Agustín López (dates unconfirmed), known as Cav. He pioneered Maxim's geometric style, which was most evident in its ads for the men's clothing company Bücher Brothers. These ads featured an elegantly dressed gentleman, reminiscent of Ludwig Hohlwein's male figures, beside a geometric form—whether a circle, square, or diamond—which was set against a solid background. The style was also evident in work by other artists in the agency such as Carlos Neve (dates unconfirmed), whose ads for the men's hat retailer Casa Tardan featured a male silhouette in black as a trademark. While the ads produced by Maxim's employed sophisticated contemporary imagery, the typography was extremely weak when compared to some other ads that adopted Art Deco lettering and used it in a way that was more compatible with the imagery. French fashion illustration and poster art—especially drawings by Erté and posters by Charles Gesmar—remained a strong influence on the depiction of women. Ludwig Hohlwein was a comparable influence on the portrayal of men, not only in the ads by Cav. López but also in those for Stetson hats drawn by Gómes Linares (dates unconfirmed). James Leyendecker's Arrow Collar man was also popular in Spanish versions of the American ads.

One consequence of the Mexican Revolution was a new pride in the depiction of national identity. Thus various advertisements, particularly for products made in Mexico, featured Mexican cowboys or *charros*, and women in traditional dress who were known as *chinas poblanas*. We can contrast these nationalistic ads with another group that promoted American products, where human figures were generic modern types without a specific nationality. As in other Latin American countries in the period after World War I, the presence of goods from the United States increased. Consequently many ads for American products, such as Palmolive Soap, Westinghouse and Philco radios, Victor Phonographs, Stetson Hats, and Arrow Collars, appeared. Mexican illustrators drew some and others were based on American ads in which Spanish text was substituted.

Calendar art

Another popular means of advertising was the calendar. Its precedent was the late 19th-century almanac, which contained information about the weather, religious festivals, preferred times for planting, and other advice in addition to advertising. What followed the almanac was the illustrated calendar or "chromo" which began to achieve popularity in the 1930s. The attraction to the "chromos" was part of a growing sense of identity or "Mexicanidad," which led to the rejection of American calendars with recycled images that had previously dominated the market.

Calendars were of two types. One featured a custom illustration that a particular company commissioned. The second type was generic and could be ordered by a customer whose company name would be printed on the calendar. The first company to print calendars in Mexico City was Enseñanza Objectiva, a print shop that was founded in 1922 and began to produce calendars in 1935. The other leading calendar printers were Litografía Latina (Latin Lithography), a small company that had earlier built a reputation printing bottle labels and packaging, and Galas de México, founded in 1913 and soon thereafter expanded to other countries in Latin America.

Principal advertisers were cigarette and beer companies, who embedded their products in nationalistic imagery. The iconography of the "chromos" embodied different myths that ranged from pre-Hispanic legends to scenes of smiling rural workers and Mexican *charros*. Though not commissioned by the government, the popular images reinforced official efforts to promote a national identity. One of the most popular images was done for El Aguila (The Eagle) Cigarettes in 1941. Entitled *La leyenda de los volcanes* (*Legend of the Volcanoes*), it depicts a scene from the legend of Iztacíhuatl, which recounts the story of an Aztec princesss who married a prince from another tribe. When she died, he brought her body to the peak of a volcano, placed it on a bed of flowers, and then lay down next to her to die. The painting by Jesús de la Helguera (1910–1971) exploited the erotic elements of the story through the artist's depiction of the princess's voluptuous pose and the prince's muscular physique.

Helguera, the most popular of the calendar painters, was born in Mexico but raised in Spain. He returned home in 1936 at the start of the Spanish Civil War and pursued an illustrious career as a calendar artist until the production of calendars began to decline in the 1960s. The other leading artists in the initial period of calendar art were Antonio Gómez R. (dates unconfirmed), who had worked as an illustrator for various cultural magazines; Eduardo Cataño (1910–d.o.d. unconfirmed), a graduate of the San Carlos Academy; Jaime Sadurní (1915–1988); and Armando Drechsler (dates unconfirmed), a German who emigrated to Mexico in the 1920s. Drechsler came to calendar art from portrait painting and also popularized an Art Deco illustrative style in his murals for commercial clients.

Film posters

The cinema was popular in Mexico from the beginning of the 20th century, following the earliest films projected with Edison's kinetoscope and Lumière's cinematographe. Mexican directors made a number of silent films, but the American studios dominated the Mexican industry. Following the introduction of sound in 1931, these studios were at a disadvantage because they had difficulty finding actors with credible Spanish accents. After a decade of inactivity during the 1920s, the Mexican film industry revived and entered what has been called a "Golden Age." Stars like Cantinflas, Jorge Negrete, and Dolores del Rio dominated screens in Mexico and in many other Latin American countries where Mexican films were shown (Fig. 29.07).

Silent films were promoted with unimaginative newspaper ads, flyers, and program books, while strong visual film posters appeared during the early years of sound films and flourished thereafter. Producers contracted with agencies or individual artists for their posters and newspaper ads. The largest publicity agency in the 1930s was Vargas Publicidad, headed by Juan Antonio Vargas Ocampo (1901–1955), who had previously founded the popular magazines *Zig-Zag* and *Revista de Revistas* and had been involved with film publicity since 1931. Working under Vargas in the early years were a number of young artists including Leopoldo Mendoza (1921–1994), who began as an apprentice at the Vargas studio; Heriberto Andrade (1931–d.o.d. unconfirmed); and Juan Antonio Vargas Briones (1919–1970), the founder's son.

As part of the labor union movement that had been strengthened during the administration of Lázaro Cárdenas, Vargas Ocampo and two partners founded the publicity branch of the filmmakers' union in 1940. It included separate sections for journalists, publicists, and artists. By 1944, the union had gained enough strength to require all artists who designed movie

Fig. 29.07: *Ahi Esta el Detalle*, poster, 1940. CONADICOV archives.

posters, with rare exceptions, to be members. After that time, most posters were produced by a single agency, Ars-Una.

Though film posters became widespread after World War II, a number of artists besides those working for Vargas Publicidad established themselves before that time. Cartoonists and caricaturists like Antonio Arias Bernal (1913–1961) and Andrés Audiffred, who were well known for their drawings in the newspapers and illustrated magazines, designed posters for comedies, while a distinct style emerged for dramas and historical films. Strongly shaped by Josep Renau (1907–1982), who emigrated to Mexico as a refugee from the Spanish Civil War, this style was also influenced by other Spanish artists as well. Arriving between 1939 and the early 1940s, they included, besides Renau, who had been an active poster designer for the Spanish Republican cause, his brother Juanino (1900–1989), Francisco Rivero Gil (1899–1972), Ernesto Guasp (1910–1983), and José (Josep) Spert (1906–1950). Renau had been influenced by John Heartfield's photomontage technique, the angular drawing styles of various avant-garde artists, and the graphics of the Russian avant-garde. While these influences were not blatantly evident in his film posters, they did contribute to his approach to the poster as an integrated design rather than an illustration with lettering added.

Book publishing
Relatively few books were published in Mexico during the *Porfiriato* and serious book publishing in Mexico did not begin until the Díaz regime ended. Books published by Hermanos Porrúa and Andrés Botas were among the first to appear. Porrúa specialized in reference books rather than literature, although the firm reprinted a series of classical texts in inexpensive editions. Editorial Botas published books primarily by Mexican authors including the novelists and essayists Alfonso Reyes and José Vasconcelos, as well as Martín Luis Guzmán, who wrote several novels about the Mexican Revolution. Among the firm's foreign authors

were Anatole France, Paul Verlaine, and the Portuguese realist writer José Maria de Eça de Queiroz. Editorial Botas also published many books by new authors. The press was recognized for its illustrative jacket designs, though little is known about the artists who did them. The illustrations were complemented by strong title lettering in different styles.

In 1916, Julio Torri, Rafael Loera y Chávez, Agustín Loera y Chávez, and the historian Manuel Toussaint, all leading cultural figures of the period, founded Editorial Cultura. In the spirit of the revolution, they had a strong interest in books about Mexican culture as well as in the broad dissemination of classic literary texts. They published books by Dr. Atl, the pseudonym for Gerardo Murillo, a strong proponent of the new revolutionary Mexican art, and other volumes about art, architecture, and literature. Some of their early books were designed by Francisco Díaz de León (1897–1975), who later founded the Escuela de Artes del Libro (School of Book Arts). Diaz de León became interested in woodcuts through the French artist Jean Charlot, who rediscovered Jose Guadalupe Posada and while in Mexico consequently promoted the woodcut as an artistic medium. In the 1925 book of poems that Díaz de León designed for Editorial Cultura, *Campanitas de plata: libro de niños* (*Little Silver Bells: A Children's Book*) by Mariano Silva y Aceves, he produced 54 original woodcut illustrations as well as a woodcut cover and paragraph initials. The next year he designed Manuel Toussaint's *Oaxaca*, creating a strong woodcut cover and illustrations, as well as a classical typographic layout that helped launch his lifelong devotion to book design. Díaz de Léon refined his talent in this area through the design of other books for Editorial Cultura as well as for another press that was established in the post-revolutionary period, the Imprenta Mundial. In 1934, the Fondo de Cultura Económica was founded with the aim of publishing books on economics, although the editors soon diversified into other areas of the humanities and social sciences. The Fondo's book covers were mainly typographic, but vignettes were sometimes used.

The most experimental books were published by the Estridentistas, an avant-garde group that the poet Manuel Maples Arces (1898–1981) led between 1922 and 1927. Maples Arces published the first Estridentista manifesto at the end of 1921 in *El Universal Ilustrado*. Similar to Marinetti's "Futurist Manifesto" of 1909, Arces praised modern machines. He also attacked Mexican culture of the past, and proposed a new avant-garde aesthetic. Cubism, Dada, Futurism, Russian Constructivism, and German Expressionism were all influences to which the Estridentista poets and artists

Fig. 29.08: *Crisol: Revista de Critica*, cover, 1932. The Wolfsonian–Florida International University, Miami Beach, Florida, Purchase, FIU Faculty Development Funds, XC2011.01.2.1, Photo: David Almeida.

responded and these were manifest in the covers of their publications as well as the dynamic typography of their texts. Several of their books were published by Editorial Cultura. *Avion*, a book of poems by Kyn Taniya (nom de plume for Luis Quintanilla) was the first. It was followed by Arces's long poem *Urbe: super-poema bolchevique en 5 cantos* (*Urbe: Bolshevik Super-Poem in 5 Cantos*), with a woodcut cover by Jean Charlot. The cover displayed large title letters, combined with stencil letters and an image of two large apartment blocks that represent the poem's urban theme. The choice of red and black on a neutral ground recalls the colors favored by the Russian Constructivists. Less dramatic but equally experimental was Roberto Montenegro's cover for another Estridentista book published by Editorial Cultura—Kyn Taniya's collection of poems, *Radio*. The cover featured an array of black shapes on which were distributed the letters of the title and which revealed beneath them diverse intricate linear patterns.

Between 1921 and 1928, the Estridentistas maintained their own publishing house, Ediciones Estridentistas, which published two journals: *Irradiador: Revista Internacional de Vanguardia* (*Illuminator: International Avant-Garde Review*) and *Horizonte*. Published in 1923, *Irradiador* survived for only three issues while *Horizonte*, which began publication in 1926, lasted for ten. Maples Arces was also involved with another literary publication, *Crisol: Revista de Critica* (*Crucible: Critical Review*), whose other collaborators included Diego Rivera (1896–1957) (Fig. 29.08). The journal's political orientation was leftist and the illustrations by Leopoldo Méndez and Fermin Revueltas among others often featured images of workers and revolutionaries.

The block title letters and large numbers on the *Irradiador* covers reflected the group's interest in Russian Constructivism, and evince a similarity to Alexander Rodchenko's designs for the Soviet literary journal *Lef*, which he initiated the year before. Covers for *Horizonte*, created by its editors—two artists associated with the Estridentistas, Leopoldo Méndez (1902–1969) and Ramón Alva de la Canal (1892–1985)—were directed more to local sensibilities, recognizing the fact that the magazine, along with the other publications of Ediciones Estridentista, was supported by the Governor of the State of Veracruz and was intended for a wide audience.

Ediciones Estridentista also published books of poetry, novels, and essays, some of which had covers that incorporated avant-garde tendencies. These included Ramón Alva de la Canal's cover design for German List Arzubide's 1926 essay *El Movimiento Estridentista* (*The Estridentista Movement*), which featured a dynamic depiction of the title letters integrated into a Futurist-like pattern of two- and three-dimensional forms. In retrospect, the Estridentista publications were influential in two ways. First, their incorporation of avant-garde visual ideas influenced work by other Mexican designers in the 1930s, notably Gabriel Fernández Ledesma and Francisco Díaz de León, who adopted related approaches for the catalogs and exhibition announcements they designed for the Ministry of Public Education; and second, the political woodcut covers and illustrations that Méndez and Alva de la Canal created for *Horizonte* and for several books published by the press presaged the powerful woodcut graphics that artists produced at the Taller de Gráfica Popular, beginning in the late 1930s.

Graphic design for the government

When José Vasconcelos became Mexico's first Secretary of Public Education in 1920, he inaugurated an educational and cultural program that involved the extensive publication of books, as well as pamphlets, flyers, and other publicity materials. When he hired artists and designers to assist with his publishing and promotional activities, he established a precedent that was followed by his successors as well as by administrators in other government departments. The sheer volume of printed material over which Vasconcelos had control necessitated careful attention to its design, and

during the course of his tenure until 1924 the development of government publishing showed significant improvement.

Under the direction of the essayist and short-story writer Julio Torri (1889–1970), a founder of Editorial Cultura, the Editorial Department of the Secretaría de Educación Pública (SEP) (Ministry of Public Education) published inexpensive editions of many classic literary works. It was most likely the painter Valerio Prieto (1882–1932), an artist with some prior experience designing bookplates, who designed a number of these books. The design approach was to adopt the best examples from the history of printing. The page layout of Homer's *Iliad*, for example, employs the wide margins, delicate initials, and illustrations with fine lines that one might have seen in a book by Aldus Manutius. The Kelmscott Press books of William Morris may also have been an influence, particularly as they exemplified the care that Morris gave to all parts of the book: typography, illustration, layout, and binding.

The Editorial Department published other books besides the classics. An important one was *Lecturas para Mujeres* (*Readings for Women*) by the Chilean poet and educator Gabriela Mistral, whom Vasconcelos had invited to Mexico. This book in particular suggests some influence from the Kelmscott Press though without the consistency of Morris's typographic taste. The ornament and title are embossed on the cover, while the eclectic title page features the name of the book framed by an ornamental border. The letters, however, are drawn with curious decorative filigrees that are closer to 19th-century display typography than to the classic types of earlier books.

Eclecticism was also evident in the ministry's journal *El Maestro: Revista de Cultura Nacional* (*The Teacher: Review of National Culture*), which was first published in 1921. The cover of the initial issue featured a female figure holding an open book in one hand—an allegorical image drawn directly from 19th-century European sources (Fig. 29.09). This conservative design tendency continued during the journal's first year, along

Fig. 29.09: *El Maestro*, cover, 1921. CONADICOV archives.

by Vasconcelos, they were designed and illustrated by the artists Roberto Montenegro and Gabriel Fernández Ledesma (1900–1983). Both had studied painting at the Escuela Nacional de Bellas Artes (National School of Fine Arts), and Montenegro, the older of the two, had spent some years in Europe where he came into contact with Cubism and developed an illustrative style that was reminiscent of Aubrey Beardsley. When he returned to Mexico after the revolutionary fighting ceased, Vasconcelos named him head of SEP's Departamento de Artes Plásticas (Department of Plastic Arts) and gave him a number of mural commissions. In 1921, the year he joined SEP, Montenegro organized the country's first exhibition of Mexican arts and crafts, which challenged the hegemony of the European fine arts and affirmed the value of Mexico's own folk culture.

Fernández Ledesma had become involved in Vasconcelos's populist program of art education, where he developed an interest in the technique of wood

Fig. 29.10: Roberto Montenegro and Gabriel Fernández Ledesma, *Lecturas clásicas para niños*, cover, 1925. CONADICOV archives.

with various visual references to Art Nouveau. The covers for the following two years, however, rejected the European influence and instead featured iconography associated with Mexican history and culture. Notable among these covers was one by Diego Rivera that presented the journal's title letters as if they were Mayan glyphs.

The design of books within the Ministry of Public Education reached a new level with *Lecturas clásicas para niños* (*Classic Readings for Children*), whose two volumes were published in 1924 and 1925 (Fig. 29.10). Initiated engraving that had been introduced to the open air schools by the French artist Jean Charlot. It is not clear how Fernández Ledesma and Montenegro divided the work of illustrating and designing the *Lecturas clásicas para niños*, but both seem to have been inspired by William Morris's Kelmscott Press books. Though consigned to available types, they introduced each story with small woodcut vignettes and large initials and maintained a consistent layout throughout. At the end of each story was a small ornament that either suggested a pre-Hispanic design or was an animal form.

The books that SEP brought out while Vasconcelos was Secretary of Public Education raised the standards of book design in Mexico and stimulated various independent publishers such as Editorial Cultura to strive for quality in the design of their own publications. After Vasconcelos left SEP in 1924, subsequent administrators continued to recognize the value of design. In 1926, the ministry funded a cultural magazine, *Forma*, that Fernández Ledesma founded and edited until it ceased publication in 1928. The magazine was important in two senses. First, it strongly supported modern art in all its contemporary forms—film, photography, painting, and the relatively new techniques of wood and metal engraving—and it also sustained Roberto Montenegro's attention to the popular arts. Second, editing and designing the publication gave Fernández Ledesma the opportunity to experiment with the typography and photographic layouts. In addition to metal type, he cut large wooden initials by hand and combined photographs and woodcuts in the same layouts. He also used ample white space, which was unusual for a graphic designer at this time. The magazine's illustrations included woodcuts by the leading artists of the period.

While editing *Forma*, Fernández Ledesma remained involved with the open air schools, as did his compatriot and childhood friend Francisco Díaz de León, who shared his interest in wood engraving and typography. After designing some books for the Editorial Cultura, Díaz de León started to work with the editorial department of the SEP in 1928. That year he and Fernández Ledesma, along with 28 other artists, founded the i30–30i Group, whose aim was to challenge the traditional art education of the School of Fine Arts, seeking to merge it with the trade schools and transform it into a public art school that would serve the masses instead of a small elite. The group published several issues of a small journal and a few manifestos that recalled the political broadsides of the 19th century. One consequence of the group's agitation was that in 1929 the director of the School of Fine Arts put Díaz de León in charge of a print workshop, which he named Artes del Libro (Arts of the Book) and where he started to train book illustrators in the techniques of the woodcut as well as etching and engraving.

At the beginning of the 1930s, Fernández Ledesma and Díaz de León directed a small art gallery within the Fine Arts Department of the Ministry of Public Education and for this gallery they designed posters, exhibition announcements, and catalogs that transformed graphic design in Mexico. The colors of their posters were limited for the most part to red, black, and white, although they occasionally chose festive folkloric colors when appropriate for particular exhibitions. The two designers adopted graphic elements from the various European avant-garde movements—the playful lettering of the Dadaists, the strong polemical compositions of the Russian avant-garde, and the geometric formalism of the New Typography. References ranged from Lissitzky and Rodchenko to Tschichold and Moholy-Nagy, but these were combined with a typographic approach that was not restricted to san serif letters. The typographic mix is evident in a poster that Fernández Ledesma designed for an exhibition in the ministry gallery, where he combined large Egyptian letters with san serif ones, all arranged in a composition of horizontal and vertical type lines (Fig. 29.11).

Fernández Ledesma and Díaz de León also differed from their European predecessors in their use of woodcut illustrations instead of photographs. This resulted from their desire to build a national

EXPOSICION DE LA
ESCUELA SUPERIOR DE CONSTRUCCION DE ARTE
EN LA
SALA DE
DEL 22 DE FEBRERO
AL 6 DE MARZO · 1933

Fig. 29.11: Gabriel Fernández Ledesma, Exposición de la Escuela Superior de Construcción, poster, 1933. CONADICOV archives.

and Writers (LEAR), while continuing to design posters for social groups and political causes.

In 1937, the Ministry of Public Education agreed to fund the Escuela Mexicana de las Artes del Libro (Mexican School of Book Arts) that Díaz de León had proposed. Housed initially in the Department of Workers' Education, the school opened its doors at the end of the following year. Díaz de León's intent was to train workers in printmaking, drawing, and photography as well as the traditional arts of bookbinding and typography. He assembled a distinguished group of professors and educated a considerable number of students, some of whom like Isidoro Ocampo (1910–1983) went on to distinguished careers in book illustration, art direction, and design. Díaz de León continued to direct the school until 1956.

During the Cárdenas regime, Díaz de León was also involved with several official publications including *El Maestro Rural* (*The Rural Teacher*), which was published by the Ministry of Public Education, and *Mexican Art and Life*, for which he was the art director. The latter was a propaganda magazine directed to a North American audience. Both magazines had large formats and featured photographs and photomontages of contemporary Mexican life, which suggested some influence from the Soviet magazine *USSR in Construction*.

Mexican Art and Life was published by the Departamento Autónomo de Prensa y Publicidad (Autonomous Department for Press and Publicity) (DAPP), which Cárdenas had organized in late 1936 to consolidate his control over the government's publicity and propaganda efforts for domestic as well as foreign audiences. Among DAPP's other activities was the distribution of posters for various social campaigns. These were designed by capable artists with an awareness of contemporary styles and a developed sense of lettering. Gabriel Fernández Ledesma and Francisco Díaz de Leon, for example, designed a poster for a campaign to grow corn that featured a single icon—a hand with an ear of corn—coupled with large san serif letters (Plate 52).

culture instead of adopting an aesthetic that was driven solely by a machine metaphor. From 1935 to 1938, Fernández Ledesma directed the exhibition gallery in the Palace of Fine Arts, where the exhibits ranged from Japanese prints to Soviet posters. He and Díaz de León created posters and other materials for these exhibitions, continuing to refine the strong graphic language they had begun to use earlier.

During the 1930s, both designers belonged to the milieu of politically progressive artists and writers that supported the socialist program of the Cárdenas regime. In 1933, Fernández Ledesma was a founding member of the militant League of Revolutionary Artists

Fig. 29.12: Francisco Eppens, postage stamps, late 1930s. CONADICOV archives.

Another source of modern design in the Cárdenas administration was the Talleres de Impresíon de Estampillas y Valores de México (TIEV), where the artist Francisco Eppens (1913–1990) employed an Art Deco style of drawing and lettering between 1935 and 1953 to create several hundred innovative stamp designs on diverse subjects. Prior to Eppens, Mexico, like most countries, adopted the conservative convention of printing engraved portraits of famous citizens on its stamps. Eppens' designs not only replaced engraving with rotogravure printing, but they also consisted of

sophisticated airbrush drawings. During the Cárdenas years the stamps heroically depicted rural and factory workers, while also illustrating government anti-malaria, literacy, and reforestation campaigns (Fig. 29.12). Airmail stamps portrayed muscular allegorical figures who symbolized the glory of flight.

Leftist political graphics

In the wake of the Mexican and Russian Revolutions, various leftist organizations formed in Mexico. The Communist Party of Mexico was founded in 1919, the Confederación General de Trabajadores in 1921, and the Sindicato de Obreros Técnicos, Pintores y Sculptores (Union of Technical Workers, Painters, and Sculptors) (SOTPE) in 1923. Among the leaders of the latter group—the first organized by artists—were Xavier Guerrero (1896–1974), Diego Rivera, David Siqueiros (1896–1974), and José Clemente Orozco (1883–1949), all of whom were active in the Mexican mural movement. In 1924, SOTPE members adopted the woodcut as a visual means to reach urban workers whom they thought might not see their murals. They started a newspaper, *El Machete* (*The Machete*), which revived the political broadside of the 19th century that had been a vehicle for the woodcuts of Manuel Manilla and José Guadalupe Posada (see Chapter 15). *El Machete*'s polemical intent was evident in Xavier Guerrero's drawing for its masthead, a hand clenching the handle of a machete with the title written on the blade (Fig. 29.13). Besides reviving the broadside tradition, *El Machete* continued the political criticism begun by the caricature magazines of a few years earlier—*El Hijo de El Ahuizote* and *Multicolor*—only the newspaper's medium was the woodcut rather than the line drawing and its criticism focused on the entire ruling class and not just individual politicians. Guerrero, Siqueros, and Orozco created trenchant woodcut images, some of which illustrated satirical *corridos* or ballads. The ballad sheets could be separated from the newspaper and posted in the streets, making their political messages accessible to a wide audience. Within a year, *El Machete*

Fig. 29.13: *El Machete* with a masthead by Xavier Guerrero, front page, 1935. CONADICOV archives.

had become the official organ of the Communist Party, and the hammer and sickle were added to the masthead. The paper ceased publication in 1929, the year before the party was banned by President Plutarco Calles.

Another radical artists' group, the Liga de Escritores y Artistas Revolucionarios (League of Revolutionary Artists and Writers) (LEAR), formed in 1933. It drew in some members of SOTPE but included other new members as well, many of whom were also members of the Communist Party of Mexico. LEAR supported the Soviet Union and criticized the Mexican government. Although President Cárdenas instituted broad social reforms, LEAR members opposed him for his first two years in office. Initially LEAR promoted the working class and affirmed its solidarity with the Soviet Union, but by 1936 it had become a broad Popular Front organization that united with other groups to oppose fascism in Mexico and abroad.

Beginning in 1934, LEAR published a magazine, *Frente a Frente* (*Front to Front*), which took its title from the idea of class warfare. In the magazine's first three issues, considered as its initial phase, the editors employed woodcuts almost exclusively as illustrations. The cover of the first issue by Leopoldo Méndez (1902–1969), revived the 19th-century print style known as the *calavera*, which featured skeletons in the roles of people. Méndez's cover, which depicted a crowd of skeleton-people inaugurating the Palace of Fine Arts in Mexico City, portrayed Diego Rivera and Carlos Riva Palacio, president of the new National Revolutionary Party, as observers yet collaborators in the celebration. LEAR also began to publish a series of large broadsides, which publicized political issues. Directed to the working class, they combined woodcut illustrations with political texts. The woodcuts that Méndez created for these broadsides inaugurated a new type of political print that illustrated dramatic political conflicts in stark and violent terms.

After the first three issues of *Frente a Frente*, there was a change of editors and a new series with a different format began. Photographs, many from European sources, were now used almost exclusively to correspond with a shift to more news stories. Covers, which featured photographs and photomontages, more often depicted world events rather than domestic conflicts. The work of John Heartfield and the Russian Constructivists were known in Mexico and one cover of *Frente a Frente* incorporated work by both. Twelve issues of the journal appeared and its demise coincided loosely with the dissolution of LEAR, sometime in 1937 or 1938.

From the ashes of LEAR, the Taller de Gráfica Popular (Popular Graphics Studio) (TGP) was born. The idea came from Leopoldo Méndez, who joined with Luis Arenal (1908/1909–1985) and Pablo O'Higgins (1904–1983) to set up a workshop where artists could produce their own prints as well as graphics to publicize political events and promote social causes. In their founding statement, the members of the TGP declared their commitment to working collectively in order to serve the Mexican people. Besides individual prints and suites of prints and occasional book illustrations, members produced brochures, leaflets, flyers, posters, banners, and backdrops for political demonstrations, labor rallies, and other public events. A favorite medium was the flyer or *volante*, which could be produced cheaply in different media. Many were illustrated with linoleum cuts, which, along with lithography and handset type, was a favored means of production. Artists active in the early years included Alberto Beltrán (1923–2002), Angel Bracho (1911–2005), Francisco Dosamentes (1911–1986), Francisco Mora (1922–2002), Isidoro Ocampo, José Chavez Morado (1909–2002), and Alfredo Zalce.

Among the initial projects, besides prints, were *volantes* to promote the TGP and solicit work. An early *volante* by Xavier Guerrero seeking subscriptions for monthly broadsides includes a linocut logo for the workshop, which he probably designed. Another *volante* by José Chavez Morado promoted graphic propaganda as a means to unite communities against oppression. The linocut image depicted a man, accompanied by a cowboy with a lasso, giving the boot to an old gunslinger. The TGP continued the strong anti-fascist commitment of the LEAR, which was reflected in the imagery of many of the early prints. Alfredo Zalce, for example, who had previously published caricatures in *Multicolor* and other popular magazines, produced a broadside with comic drawings entitled *Calaveras Vaciladoras de la Guerra* (*Vacillating Calaveras Against the War*).

Brazil

After a coup overthrew the Brazilian monarchy in 1889 and the country became a republic, modernization accelerated. At the beginning of the 20th century, coffee was the country's leading export and the success of the coffee industry contributed to expanded urbanization in Rio de Janeiro, which became the country's capital, and Sao Paulo, both located in coffee-producing states. Emigrants came to Brazil in increasing numbers, largely from Italy, Portugal, Spain, and Germany, and as in Argentina and Uruguay, many established their own enterprises. The printing industry in Rio de Janeiro and Sao Paulo, for example, was largely founded by immigrants, especially Italians.

With urban growth, the division between the living standards of city and country dwellers increased. Modernization continued in the cities, particularly in the arts, business, and the development of progressive social mores and political values. Meanwhile, society in rural areas remained undeveloped. Large numbers of country dwellers worked under difficult conditions for wealthy owners of cattle farms, coffee plantations, and other agricultural enterprises. Despite the predominance of agricultural exports in the Brazilian economy, a growing interest in industry also existed, although there was little incentive to emphasize it until after World War I, when foreign imports dropped off and the need for domestic products became stronger.

Throughout the 1920s, various groups including some military officers challenged the prevailing politicians with demands for a stronger central government, agrarian reform, better working conditions, and a greater commitment to industrialization. In 1930, the ruling elite was ousted and Getúlio Vargas, former governor of Brazil's southernmost state, Rio Grande do Sul, became the new president. In 1937, Vargas assumed dictatorial powers and established the Estado Novo (New State), which he ruled until a military coup forced him to resign in 1945. Vargas had a strong commitment to industrialization and he fostered centralized efforts to increase Brazil's industrial independence, particularly in the production of military equipment. During his regime, he fostered a national steel industry, established the Fábrica Nacional de Motores (National Motor Factory), and supported the most advanced aircraft industry in Latin America.

Decorative arts and furniture

The first Brazilian training school for skilled workers in the decorative arts was the Liceu de Artes e Ofícios de Sao Paulo (Sao Paulo School of Arts and Trades), which began as the Society for the Propagation of Popular Instruction in 1873 and then changed its name in 1882, when the curriculum was reformed. Modeled on the ideals of William Morris and the British Arts and Crafts movement, the school aimed to train artisans and workers for local industries. It introduced a curriculum that included some mechanical design as well as numerous courses in fields such as cabinet-making, wood and metalworking, and locksmithing. In 1895, the school underwent a broader reform under the direction of an architect-engineer, Francisco de Paula Ramos de Azevedo (1851–1928), who wanted to create a School of Fine Arts. He introduced courses in drawing, clay and plaster modeling, and painting, which he combined with professional training in carpentry, cabinetmaking, metal and woodworking, and the graphic arts among other courses. After 1905, the Liceu began to license and sell the furniture and other products from its workshops just as the Bauhaus would do some years later.

The school had its own building, which Ramos de Azevedo and a collaborator, Domiziano Rossi

(1865–1920), designed in an eclectic Italian style. By 1905, students and graduates were involved in the design of decorative elements for numerous public buildings in Sao Paulo. These projects included facade ornaments, ironwork, and furniture, which were also commissioned for various private residences, along with ceramic tiles and vases and cast bronze ornaments. The enormous chandelier and the furniture of the Sao Paulo Municipal Theater were produced at the school as were the decorative friezes of the building that the Banco de Sao Paulo occupied. Art Nouveau influences could be seen in some of the villas that Sao Paulo coffee magnates and other entrepreneurs commissioned around the turn of the century, and the style was found as well in other parts of Brazil.

Similar to architecture, where its influence was modest, Art Nouveau did not have a great impact on the decorative arts. In ceramics, the leading Brazilian figures were Teodoro Braga (1872–1935), his student Manoel Pastana (1888–d.o.d. unconfirmed), and Fernando Correia Dias (1893–1935), all of whom trained as painters. Working in other media as well, they were more interested in the indigenous examples from Brazil's nativist cultures than they were in European models. Braga and Pastana were from Belém in the Amazon region and made strong references to the region's pre-Columbian Marajoara culture in their work. Ceramic vases from the early 1920s that are attributed to Braga display raised figures of Amazonian fauna—notably beetles and alligators—although as scholar Paulo Herkenhoff points out, Braga did not develop the symbolic meanings of these figures as was the case in the original Marajoara pottery. In 1927, when he participated in the applied arts section of the National Salon of Fine Arts in Rio de Janeiro, Braga showed a group of vases in wrought metal for which he transformed the symbolic language of Marajoara ornamentation into modern motifs that suggested Art Deco. Braga later taught at the Escola Paulista de Belas Artes (Sao Paulo School of Fine Arts), which had been founded in 1925 and where the modern architect and

city planner Lucio Costa (1902–1998) was briefly the director in 1930.

Manoel Pastana, like Braga, produced vases and other objects in metal that had applied animal forms. A number of these objects recreate symbols and legends from Amazonian tribes. Besides his completed work, Pastana made many renderings of objects that were decorated with figures of Amazonian flora and fauna. These ranged from furniture and lamps to coffee and tea sets, trays, and also parasols. Pastana's designs were eccentric. Had they been produced, they would have been regarded as novelties rather than modern decorative objects. His drawing for a coffee and tea set with toucan and palm tree motifs, for example, recalls the Wedgwood teapots whose forms were derived from fruits and vegetables.

The artist Fernando Correia Dias (1893–1935), who emigrated to Rio de Janeiro from Portugal in 1914, was also known for ceramic pots, plates, and urns that were painted with native motifs. Though Portuguese, Correia Dias adapted his designs from the same sources as did Braga and Pastana. Primarily a graphic designer, he also drew numerous vignettes based on Marajoara patterns or Amazonian flora or fauna. Dias characterized his vignettes and ceramic designs as "nationalist," and considered them a contribution to a new Brazilian cultural identity.

By contrast, the furniture industry adopted a wide range of European styles from conventional historic periods to Art Deco and German modernism. One of the large firms that specialized in furniture and interiors in historic styles was Laubisch, Hirth and Company, which employed more than 350 people including cabinetmakers, carpenters, upholsterers, and others who reproduced existing historic models as custom pieces for the firm's clients.

European modern design made its first impact in Brazil through the work of John Graz (1891–1980), a Swiss artist who came to Sao Paulo in 1920. He had studied decorative arts at the École de Beaux Arts in Geneva and was then a student of decorative art, poster design, and advertising at the School of Fine Arts in Munich, where he became familiar with the modern poster work of Ludwig Hohlwein and others.

Subsequently, Graz learned about the Cubists and Fauves in Paris before he began a successful career as a commercial and decorative artist and illustrator in Geneva. After he came to Sao Paulo, he married the Brazilian craftswoman and decorative artist Regina Gomide (1897–1973), whom he had met several years earlier in Europe and with whom he would collaborate on numerous projects for interiors.

Initially Graz showed his paintings and worked as an illustrator, but by the late 1920s he began to focus on interior design. He adopted visual motifs from the Cubists and the French Art Deco designers, while also applying geometric forms where appropriate. His clients tended to be wealthy Paulistas for whom he designed homes with everything from metal gates, painted murals, and stained-glass windows to modern furniture, bathroom fixtures, and gardens. Graz is sometimes considered to be Brazil's first comprehensive designer as well as the first in Brazil to use metal in interior design. He incorporated metal tubing into some of his furniture and also adopted copper and steel sheeting for other decorative purposes. Regina Gomide worked in various decorative arts. She made pillows and tapestries that featured modern motifs and also designed rugs with geometric forms.

Along with Graz and Gomide, various other architects, artists, and designers were interested in the modern interior. During the 1930s, the painter and sculptor Cássio M'Boi (1903–d.o.d unconfirmed) created a series of carpets with strong geometric designs, along with occasional furniture pieces. A number of artists and architects designed modern furniture for their own homes and for occasional clients. Among them was the Russian émigré architect Gregori Warchavchik (1896–1972), who introduced modern architecture to Brazil. He came to Sao Paulo in 1923 and by 1928 he had built a house for himself, which was considered to be the first modern residence in the country. Two years

later he built a second house, the Casa Modernista, which he opened to the public as an exhibition home. He designed most of the modern furniture that was displayed in its various rooms, thus giving the public a chance to see what a modern interior might look like.

As Maria Cecilia Loschiavo dos Santos has noted, Warchavchik developed a complete range of furniture between 1928 and 1933, with all pieces executed according to modernist principles. He worked in wood, using geometric planes and volumes to create tables, chairs, desks, and shelves. He also designed chairs with curved chrome tubing and upholstered seats. For the reading room of the Paulista Association of Medicine, Warchavchik created a long table and chairs consisting mainly of wooden planes in varied shapes. But the chairs had planar siding that was wider than necessary, giving them a ponderous appearance despite the designer's rationalist intentions.

Another designer of modern furniture was the Lithuanian artist Lasar Segall (1891–1957), who first visited Brazil in 1912 and returned to stay in 1923. Though primarily a painter—Segal was a founder of the Dresden Secession—he was also interested in furniture design, particularly for his own residence, and relied on geometry, although he was not as reductive as Warchavchik. The architect Henrique Mindlin (1911–1971), who taught at the Mackenzie Engineering School, also experimented with modern furniture, producing pieces for several clients whose houses he designed. Similar to other modernist furniture designers, Mindlin featured planar surfaces, but his background in engineering as well as architecture enabled him to consider some subtle structural elements that made his work distinctive. By contrast, the furniture designs of the Brazilian architect Flávio de Carvalho (1899–1973) were more eccentric than those of the other modernists due to his strong interest in individual expression.

The pieces by these architects and artists were important for the future of Brazilian furniture design even though they were not mass-produced. Their effect on the furniture industry was to disencumber other designers of the historicist styles that had dominated furniture design for the homes of middle-class and wealthy patrons. However, the mass furniture market was quite conservative and consequently Brazil lacked furniture companies like Thonet in Europe or Heywood-Wakefield in the United States that were ready to invest in modern design.

Nonetheless, as Maria Cecilia Loschiavo dos Santos has shown, there were various companies that sought to produce furniture that was distinct from the replication of historic styles. In 1890, the Companhia de Móveis Curvados (Curved Furniture Company) found a way to mass-produce curved wooden furniture using Thonet's bending process, only with Brazilian woods. Several decades later another furniture company, Indústria Cama Patente, began to manufacture beds and cribs with bent wood. Based on a design of 1915 by Celso Martinez Carrera (1884–1955), a Spanish immigrant who worked for the company, Indústria Cama Patente was able to replicate the iron beds that had been produced in Britain since the 1830s. Following World War I, Cama Patente's wooden bed became a prime example of import substitution, since it had become impossible to import iron. Consequently the bentwood model was available to medical clinics, which had previously purchased iron beds. The wooden bed was also immensely successful throughout the country for domestic use as it was sold at a comparatively low price and was thus widely purchased by working-class and middle-class customers.

Industrial products

Brazil had participated in major international exhibitions abroad since the 1860s, although its pavilions offered little to convincingly document the rise of a modern nation. In 1908, however, when the country mounted its own national exhibition to commemorate the 100th anniversary of trade with the Atlantic nations, a large number of domestic industries displayed their wares. At the time, official estimates counted approximately 3,000 industrial establishments, though most of them were small. Textiles were the most important products and the leading industrial centers were Rio de Janeiro, Sao Paulo, and Rio Grande do Sul. Despite the emergence of industrial enterprises in these centers, the pavilion designs featured pastiches of European historic styles as exemplified by the pavilion for the state of Sao Paulo with its myriad cupolas and heavy Baroque ornamentation.

Industrial production continued to expand, although without any dramatic leaps or startling innovations until the Estado Novo. Small manufacturers made carts, wagons, and sailboats, drawing on traditional craft skills. The production of refrigerators had begun before World War I and continued thereafter. One of the oldest industries was the fabrication of agricultural equipment, which began in the 19th century. The manufacture of simple tools developed into the design of agricultural machines for coffee and rice production.

This level of manufacturing, which consisted primarily of small craft workshops and machine shops, was typical for other countries besides Brazil that were trying to industrialize during this period. In some instances, the machine shops developed into factories and adopted more advanced methods of production. However, Brazil provided relatively few opportunities for learning technical skills. Industrialists found it cheaper to hire skilled workers and engineers in Europe and the United States and thus made few demands on the government for local training institutions.

It was not until the 1920s and 1930s that factories in Brazil began to produce heavy machinery, transportation equipment, and electrical appliances in any significant volume. A number of these factories were subsidiaries of foreign companies whose products were designed abroad and manufactured in Brazil. After World War I, such factories were mainly owned by American companies. Lamps were produced at a factory General Electric ran in Rio de Janeiro, while a subsidiary of International Harvester made agricultural

Fig. 29.14: Companhia Mogiana de Estradas de Ferro, *automotriz*, 1937. Arquivo Público do Estado de São Paulo.

machinery, and office equipment was manufactured at a factory that Addressograph-Multigraph owned. During the 1930s, the Dutch electronics conglomerate Philips manufactured radios with streamlined Bakelite housings and sold them widely at a moment when radio broadcasting was just becoming popular.

Automobiles were assembled in Brazil in factories owned by General Motors, Ford, and Chrysler. A local coachbuilding firm, Companhia Grassi in Sao Paulo, designed and built intercity buses and other vehicles on imported chassis. In 1933, Grassi designed a bus for the General Transport Company, a subsidiary of the Sao Paulo Railway Company. Known as "King Kong" because of its imposing appearance, it was intended to transport passengers between Sao Paulo and Santos. The Grassi designers also introduced streamlined buses, adopting the techniques of American auto styling. Unlike their counterparts designed by rival companies, the Grassi vehicles no longer had the extended engine frames but instead featured frontal sections with slightly rounded forms and stylized grills reminiscent of American luxury cars. Compared to other companies

in Brazil that produced buses during this period, Grassi was by far the most sophisticated and perhaps the only one that adopted advanced American styling.

As early as the 1920s, the railroad industry had developed sufficiently to produce, albeit on a small scale, locomotives and railroad cars that were designed by engineers or were based on foreign models. One of the first railroad companies in Brazil was the Companhia Mogiana de Estradas de Ferro, which was founded in 1872 to serve the states of Sao Paulo and Minas Gerais. In 1921, the company manufactured a steam locomotive known as the Mikado, which won a grand prize at the 1922 exhibition in Rio that commemorated a century of independence from Portugal, and in 1937 the firm introduced its first *automotriz*, a railroad car that did not need to be pulled by a locomotive because it had its own motor (Fig. 29.14). The styling was adopted from American streamlined trains of the same period. The major production of ships was in the Brazilian government's naval shipyard in Rio de Janeiro, which had more than 500 employees, but there were also government shipyards in other parts of the country. In addition, large vessels were produced in private shipyards such as that of M. Buarque and Company.

Manufacturing and the Estado Novo

Shortly after Getúlio Vargas assumed dictatorial powers in 1937, the new constitution gave the state the right to intervene in the economy when it saw fit. The government's authoritarian and technocratic role was intended to make Brazil self-sufficient in consumer goods, but it also appealed to the military, which was able to command basic industries to produce its own materiel. The term "nationalization" was adopted, not to mean complete government control of industry but instead to signify the adoption whenever possible of local raw materials and semi-finished components.

The Vargas administration was particularly interested in large enterprises. Among its projects were the nation's first integrated steel mill in Volta Redonda and the National Motor Factory, which was established in 1943. The design demands of the regime were essentially for engineers, who were required for shipbuilding, railroad expansion, weapons manufacture, and the new aircraft industry. In 1930, the army had established the Escola Técnica do Exército (Military Technical School), where it trained staff for factories and industrial laboratories. Following the design of Brazil's first aircraft by Antonio Guedez Muniz (1900–1985), the technical school created a program in aeronautical engineering.

Guedez Muniz was the pioneer of the Brazilian aircraft industry. He designed his first airplanes while attending the School of Aeronautics in France. In 1935, back in Brazil, he supervised the production of two prototypes of his first Brazilian plane, the M-7. For the design, he had to coordinate the efforts of several different enterprises, which produced both the technical components and the fabric for the wing skin. Guedez Muniz also advocated the use of Brazilian woods for the frames. In 1936, with the support of Getúlio Vargas, the Companhia Nacional de Navegação Aérea (National Company for Aerial Navigation) (CNNA)

manufactured the first two of Guedez Muniz's M-7 aircraft and later constructed others. The CNNA also produced several of his subsequent designs—the M-9, and then the M-10 and M-11. The latter was a small monoplane similar to the Piper Cub, which was made entirely of Brazilian woods. The Empresa Aeronáutica Ypiranga was a company that initially made two gliders, known as Primary and Secondary, which were both copied from German examples. The firm also produced the prototype of a single-engine biplane but only five were built.

Exhibitions during the 1930s

When Vargas came to power in 1930, he had no strong interest in national or international exhibitions. Brazil did not participate in either the Century of Progress Exhibition in Chicago (1933–1934) or the Brussels World's Fair in 1935, but in 1936, Vargas supported a proposal for a national event, the Exposição do Estado Novo (Exhibition of the New State). The proposal was approved, planning initiated, and the exhibition opened in December 1938 in Rio de Janeiro. Its purpose was to counter the divided political culture of the previous period and project the image of a unified political state that had eliminated regional differences. The new unity was symbolized by a monumental rectilinear tower that rose above the exhibition entrance, bearing in large relief letters the words "O Novo Brasil 1930–1938" ("The New Brazil 1930–1938"). The various pavilions featured extensive displays of information graphics—graphs, maps, photographs, and models—that publicized the achievements of the Vargas regime.

Historian Daryle Williams has noted that the Exposição do Estado Novo was a prelude to the positive national image that the Vargas regime would present at three very different events—the Golden Gate International Exhibition in San Francisco and the New York World's Fair, known as the "World of Tomorrow," both in 1939, and the Exposição do Mundo Português (Exhibition of the Portuguese World) in Lisbon the following year. For the two American fairs, the regime presented the image of a modern Latin American nation that could hold its own with its North American counterpart, while for the Lisbon exhibition, which served its own propaganda purposes for Portugal's dictator António de Oliveira Salazar (see Chapter 27), Brazil had the opportunity to assert its role as a powerful presence in the Portuguese-speaking world.

The New York pavilion was designed by architects Lucio Costa (1902–1998) and Oscar Niemeyer (1907–2012), both strong disciples of Le Corbusier. Costa had led the team that developed the new Ministry of Education and Health, a Corbusian structure that was among the first modern buildings in Latin America. In order to create a modern pavilion for the New York fair, the government had to overturn a decree that mandated the design of all buildings representing Brazil abroad to be in the Neo-Colonial style. Wishing to draw attention away from the fact that the Vargas regime was a dictatorship, the government adopted modernism as the prevailing trope of it exhibit. This was evident first of all in the building, whose basic modernist rhetoric eschewed any association with Spanish-American, colonial, or nativist styles. The exhibit inside featured a display of Brazilian commodities that included tropical hardwoods, fibers, and mineral ore. At this stage of industrial development, Brazil had little to show in the way of manufactured goods that were worthy of export. Instead, the exhibit featured raw materials and their potential industrial applications. The exhibition strategy was to present these materials in a simple manner and to avoid the cluttered rhetoric of a typical museum display. Central to the exhibit besides raw materials was coffee, still Brazil's principal consumer product. The pavilion featured a display that explained the coffee-growing cycle and had a coffee bar that was decorated with tropical motifs.

The image of Latin American modernism that the pavilion projected was influential in developing numerous cultural ties between Brazil and the United States. Of particular significance was the Brazil Builds exhibition that the Museum of Modern Art presented in 1943. It contrasted a broad panorama of new buildings that had been constructed during the Vargas years with the richness of Brazil's architectural past. The exhibit was part of President Franklin Roosevelt's Good Neighbor Policy, which also included a visit by Walt Disney to Latin America to explore possible cooperative projects. One result was Disney's creation of the animated Brazilian parrot Zé Carioca, who was inspired by a drawing sent to him by the Brazilian caricaturist J. Carlos. Zé Carioca first appeared in the Disney cartoon *Saludos Amigos* in 1942 with singer Carmen Miranda, the "Brazilian Bombshell."

The Brazilian pavilion for Lisbon showed no traces of the modernism that characterized Costa's and Niemeyer's New York building. Its entrance, in fact, signified that Brazil's cultural roots preceded the arrival of the Portuguese by depicting sculptural figures that were drawn from the pre-Columbian Marajoara civilization. These were designed by architect Roberto Lacombe (dates unconfirmed) who was also in charge of creating the interior exhibit, which featured separate displays that were dedicated to health reform, transportation, the press, and related topics. Whereas, the interior design of the New York pavilion played down the dictatorial presence of Vargas, the Lisbon pavilion featured a large photomontage mural that chronicled the achievements of the Vargas regime. The differences in design between the New York and Lisbon pavilions showed how the Vargas regime was navigating between the image of a Latin American nation that could serve as a useful ally to American interests—which it did during World War II—and a country that presented itself to its former colonial occupier as a strong unified nation whose coherence was enforced by the authoritarian power of Getúlio Vargas.

Graphic design

The influence of the Semana de Arte Moderna

Modern art was introduced to Brazil through the Semana de Arte Moderna (Modern Art Week), held in Sao Paulo in 1922 in conjunction with the

International Exhibition of the Centennial of Brazilian Independence, which was intended to commemorate Brazil's accomplishments since gaining independence from Portugal. In its own way, the Modern Art Week participated in this declaration of independence. The concern of the organizers was to distinguish modernism in Brazil from its origins in Europe. Most of the artists involved had studied or traveled in Europe and their intent in embracing Brazilian culture was not to create a nostalgic nativist art. Rather, they sought to define modernism with a Brazilian character, not only in painting and sculpture but in architecture, literature, and music as well.

This intent was evident even in the design of the catalog cover by Emiliano Di Cavalcanti (1897–1967), one of the Modern Art Week organizers, which featured a loosely rendered ink drawing of a nude woman on a pedestal surrounded by foliage and decorative forms. By the time of the Modern Art Week, Di Cavalcanti had already established himself as a caricaturist and illustrator as well as a painter. His drawings graced the covers of the leading Sao Paulo publications, while he assumed a more serious style of illustration for books and magazines that was influenced by the stark black and white contrasts of Aubrey Beardsley as well as other European artists. His book covers drew on abstract design elements and lettering associated with avant-garde art.

Leading artists and theorists besides Di Cavalcanti who participated in the Modern Art Week include the poet and polemicist Oswald de Andrade (1890–1954), author of the manifesto *Pau-Brasil* (*Brazil Wood*) of 1924 and the "Manifesto Antropófago" ("Cannibal Manifesto") of 1928; poet, novelist, art historian, and critic Mário de Andrade (1893–1945), who published the seminal novel *Macunaíma* in 1928; the painters Anita Malfatti (1889–1964), considered to be the first Brazilian artist to introduce modern pictorial ideas from abroad, and Tarsila do Amaral (1886–1973); and the poet and painter Paulo Menotti Del Picchia (1892–1988). All were active in the publishing world either as authors,

book designers, or illustrators, and their books were landmarks of modern design in Latin America. In his *Pau-Brasil* manifesto and the "Manifesto Antropófago", Oswald de Andrade characterized Brazilian modernism by its ability to cannibalize European culture for its own ends. With this argument, he and others associated with the Brazilian modern movement were asserting simultaneously their desire to be modern and their refusal to adopt European precedents.

The art critic P. M. Bardi has noted that the new visual ideas that were introduced in the Modern Art Week exhibition soon began to penetrate the world of book and magazine publishing and consequently had a considerable effect on popular graphic styles. Following the event, some of the organizers including Mário de Andrade launched a cultural review, which they called *Klaxon* to signal their intent to noisily proclaim the advent of a new culture. The review, which lasted for only nine issues, radically introduced the visual rhetoric of the Soviet avant-garde, particularly the design of the first cover with its large "A" that ran the length of the page and its limit to black, white, and red, both of which seem to be indirect quotations from El Lissitzky's avant-garde books of the same period (Fig. 29.15). Similarly, the way the cover design incorporated a single letter in multiple words recalled Lissitzky's idea of visual economy.

Klaxon published articles and poetry in various languages and brought numerous examples of European avant-garde writing to the attention of its Brazilian readers. However, the editors, among whom Mário de Andrade was a central figure, were adamant in separating themselves from any particular avant-garde movements. "Klaxon," they declared, "is klaxonist." The review's advertising was also innovative and even included a parody ad for a factory that produced sonnets, madrigals, ballads, and *quadrinhas*, a poetic form with four stanzas. Thus, the Constructivist rhetoric of the cover was mingled with a Dada spirit that was evident as well in the occasional page with an eclectic mix of types.

Fig. 29.15: *Klaxon*, cover, 1922. Biblioteca Brasiliana Guita e José Mindlin Universidade de São Paulo.

Klaxon and another avant-garde review that followed it in 1925, *Terra Roxa e Outras Terras* (*Purple World and Other Worlds*), were the two publications of the 1920s that best represented an interest in avant-garde typography. Both were printed by the Typografía Paulista in Sao Paulo, which otherwise specialized in publications dedicated to the Italian community. Other avant-garde publications that Modern Art Week participants produced include Oswald de Andrade's 1925 book of poems, *Pau-Brasil*, which was illustrated by Tarsila do Amaral who also designed the ironic cover that featured a vertical Brazilian flag with the name "Pau-Brasil" inside the flag's blue globe (Plate

53). In 1928, the first issue of the *Revista de Antropofagia* (*Cannibalism Review*) appeared, featuring de Andrade's "Manifesto Antropófago". In its first phase the review lasted for ten issues, after which it became a tabloid and was circulated for a brief period on a weekly basis by the *Diário de Sao Paulo*. In this form, the editors also experimented with the typography, featuring isolated quotes in large bold type as well as a mix of typefaces within the orderly two-column layout. With the coming to power of Getúlio Vargas in 1930, the climate for intellectual cosmopolitanism and political irreverence changed and the avant-garde impulse to create a modern expression of "Brasilidade" or Brazilianness subsided.

Printers and typographers

Both Rio de Janeiro and Sao Paulo were centers of publishing in the 19th and early 20th centuries and each had its share of printing establishments. Most of these, particularly in Sao Paulo, were founded by immigrants who also published books, magazines, and ephemeral materials including posters in their own languages as well as in Portuguese. Among the oldest of them was a print shop that was founded by Henrique Gröbel in 1887. It printed one of the most interesting illustrated magazines of the 1920s, *A Garoa* (*The Girl*). The Typografia Paulista, founded by an Italian, José Napoli, in 1904, published periodicals for the Italian community but as already mentioned also printed two of the leading avant-garde reviews, *Klaxon* and *Terra Roxa e Outras Terras*. Weiszflog and Company, established around 1908, published a monthly magazine called *O Imigrante* (*The Immigrant*) in multiple languages and was associated with the designer Mauricio Bünhaeds (dates unconfirmed) in the design and printing of commercial packaging. Other firms included Duprat and Company, Typografia Moderna, and Typografia Ideal. The latter specialized in printing playing cards. In the 1920s, the print shop founded by Elvino Pocai dedicated itself to high-quality limited edition books.

One of the large printing establishments was run as part of the earlier mentioned Liceu de Artes e Ofícios de Sao Paulo (Sao Paulo School of Arts and Trades). It had a well-equipped graphic studio and print shop, where students and their teachers produced work of the highest quality. Despite the plethora of printing enterprises in Brazil, however, there was an absence of type foundries. Type was imported from abroad, mainly from France but also from Germany. Even experimental publications like *Klaxon* had to depend on whichever imported fonts were available in a particular print shop.

Book publishing and design

At the end of World War I, the book trade in Brazil was still not well developed. In fact, some books by Brazilian authors were published in Europe and then distributed at home. There were few bookshops or other outlets for selling books and this made distribution difficult. Art Nouveau and occasionally the Arts and Crafts aesthetic of William Morris were strong influences on the design of book covers and some layouts. This was evident in the cover and layout that Fernando Correia Dias created for *Nos* (*Us*), a book of poems by Guilherme d'Almeida, in 1917. The cover, which recalls the work of the American Arts and Crafts designer Will Bradley as well as the drawing style of Aubrey Beardsley, featured the title in red decorative letters, a stark black and white drawing of a woman in a tragic posture, and the author's name in stylized medieval letters. The text layout had wide spacing between the lines of type, considerable white space, and decorative initials such as might be found in the Kelmscott Press books of William Morris. Correia Dias's cover and illustrations for this book were among the many he did for books and magazines in the ensuing years. His versatility was typical of numerous Brazilian artists and illustrators who moved easily back and forth between fine art, book publishing, and the world of magazine design. The Beardsley influence was more directly evident in Emiliano de Cavalcanti's early work, particularly his title page for Oscar Wilde's *Ballad of Reading Gaol* of 1919 and his illustrations for the same author's partially completed play, *A Florentine Tragedy*, of 1924.

The man who is often credited with launching modern Brazilian publishing is José Bento Monteiro Lobato (1882–1948), an author and journalist who was also a staunch nationalist. In 1918, Monteiro Lobato published a highly successful collection of stories, *Urupês* (*White Fungus*), about life in the Brazilian interior. The book served as a rallying cry for the emerging nationalist movement. It had a cover, which depicted typical Brazilian vegetation, and illustrations by the painter José Wasth Rodrigues (1891–1957). At the time *Urupês* was published, Monteiro Lobato bought the journal *Revista do Brasil* for which he established a new layout, cover design, and the use of vignettes as decorative elements. His design sense was significantly different from the modernists, however, and in 1917 he achieved great notoriety by writing a harsh review of the artist Anita Malfatti's first exhibition after her return from abroad, claiming that her visual distortions were the result of mental disturbances.

Monteiro Lobato began to develop a publishing enterprise, which he revolutionized in a number of ways. One was to focus more attention on his books' cover designs, which at the time were mainly reproductions of their title pages on gray or yellow paper. Monteiro Lobato also modernized the layouts of his books along with the *Revista do Brasil*, changing from crowded page designs to cleanly designed typographic spreads. He employed Juvenal Prado (1895–1980) to transform the mundane lettering on the cover of *Revista do Brasil* to a more ornate and decorative design. Prado also created a number of decorative tailpieces for the magazine. Though he specialized in lettering and ornamental design, he produced narrative covers and illustrations as well.

Monteiro Lobato commissioned leading artists, caricaturists, and illustrators to design his book covers. Most were best known at the time as contributors to Brazil's popular magazines. They included Antônio Paim Viera (1895–1988), Mick Carnicelli (1893–1967), and Benedito Carneiro Bastos Barreto (1896–1947), known as Belmonte. Within several years, Monteiro

Lobato had made extensive investments in printing equipment and around 1926 joined with a partner to form the Companhia Editora Nacional, which published a broad selection of books in many fields. As his list expanded, so did Monteiro broaden the range of artists whom he commissioned to design book covers. To the list of those to whom he had already given commissions, he added the decorative artist and interior designer John Graz, along with Juvenal Prado and Fernando Correia Dias.

Around 1930, the design and printing of Brazilian books had reached a low ebb with the exception of Monteiro Lobato's Companhia Editora Nacional, which he had founded after the failure of his first publishing enterprise, Companhia Editora Monteiro Lobato. Among the few other publishers who appreciated Monteiro Lobato's commitment to design was José Olympio, whose Livraria José Olympio Editora published a wide range of political and literary works in the 1930s and 1940s. The reputation of Olympio's press for handsome books was due to Tomás Santa Rosa (1909–1956). An aspiring artist, Santa Rosa had moved to Rio de Janeiro from the north-east of Brazil and began designing books to earn a living. His first books were for Ariel Editora, which also published a literary review. Two of the books were novels by Jorge Amado, who was also from the north-east. For Amado's novel *Cacáu* (*Cocoa*), Santa Rosa created a cover that integrated the bold expressive lettering of the title with a lively illustration and the author's name underneath (Plate 54). He also designed the layout, which revealed his attention to the total integration of typography, margins, line spacing, and the placement of illustrations. While Monteiro Lobato had a sense of the relation between a publication's cover and its interior, Santa Rosa brought a more modern and coherent sensibility to book design. He developed distinctive visual identities for the various Olympio series, which then contributed to the publisher's overall identity. José Olympio published a number of authors who were part of the socially oriented regionalist movement such as

Jorge Amado, José Lins do Rego, Rachel de Queiroz, and Graciliano Ramos, all of whom wrote about the Brazilian north-east. For the cover of Ramos's seminal novel, *Vidas Secas* (*Barren Lives*), which chronicled the poverty of north-eastern Brazil, Santa Rosa featured a black and white illustration of a peasant sitting against a stark backdrop with a bare tree and a mountain range. The illustration was placed on a reddish brown surface, perhaps to represent the parched earth. Beneath it was the title in large italic letters. The format was part of a series whose covers featured comparable illustrations with text underneath. Santa Rosa remained with José Olympio until 1954, during which time he produced many memorable book designs both for covers and typographic layouts.

A number of notable book designs, particularly covers, were also created for writers associated with the Brazilian modernist movement, particularly Oswald and Mario de Andrade, the poet Raul Bopp, the critic and essayist Guilherme de Almeida, and Antônio de Alcântara Machado. While visually dramatic, for the most part they lacked the coherence between image, layout, and type that characterized the designs of Santa Rosa. One of the most intriguing of these more experimental books, however, was the cover and layout design that Antônio Paim Viera (dates unconfirmed) did for Antônio de Alcântara Machado's novel *Pathé-Baby* in 1926, perhaps the most original layout done during the 1920s, The title was taken from the name of a small home projector that Pathé Frères first marketed in 1922. It influenced the structure of the book, which was designed to recall the atmosphere of a movie theater. Paim Viera created a fold-out cinematic sequence of drawings that humoristically depicted a musical quartet who disappeared progressively as they accompanied a silent film.

Besides the few publishers in Rio de Janeiro and Sao Paulo who understood the value of well-designed books and covers, there were several in other parts of Brazil who also believed in the value of design. Prominent among them was Livraria do Globo in

Porto Alegre, a city located in the southern province of Rio Grande do Sul, where many Germans immigrants settled. Though founded in 1883, Livraria do Globo only began an active book-publishing program in the late 1920s. In 1929, the firm also started to publish a journal, *Revista do Globo*, which featured high-quality graphic design. A number of the covers were done in a variety of styles from Art Deco to realism by Sotero Cosme (1905–1978), a talented artist, printmaker, and cartoonist.

Whereas Monteiro Lobato and José Olympio emphasized Brazilian authors, Livraria do Globo was better known for its translations, particularly of English and American writers but also of German, French, and Russian authors as well. One of their featured Brazilian authors was the novelist Érico Veríssimo, who was also in charge of Livraria do Globo's translations from English to Portuguese. The publisher developed a special relationship with Getúlio Vargas, who was also from Rio Grande do Sul, and published didactic materials for the government's education program.

Livraria do Globo's major designer was Ernst Zeuner (1895–1967), a German who emigrated to Brazil in 1922. As a student in Germany, Zeuner attended the Leipzig Hochschule für Graphische Kunst und Buchgewerbe (Leipzig Academy of Graphic Arts and Book Design), where he preceded the young Jan Tschichold by several years. Both men were strongly influenced by Walter Tiemann, who taught lettering and type design at the Leipzig Academy. Besides studying in Leipzig, Zeuner worked there as a calligrapher and illustrator and was exposed to the latest developments in printing technology.

When he arrived at Livraria do Globo, Zeuner found a traditional approach to book design that he was able to modernize. With his multiple talents in illustration, layout, and typography, he created book covers and illustrations for novels as well as vignettes and other graphic elements as exemplified by his cover for Érico Veríssimo's *Fantoches*. To handle the broad range of graphic design projects that Livraria do Globo

was becoming engaged with, management created a Design Department and put Zeuner in charge. Few Brazilian artists were trained in the range of activities that the department undertook, and Zeuner served as a mentor to numerous young artists, many from Porto Alegre, who came to work for the company. By the end of the 1930s, the quality of work that the Design Department produced was of a high level. Under Zeuner's guidance, which derived from his experience in Leipzig, the book covers of Livraria do Globo always displayed an appropriate balance of expressive lettering and striking illustrations.

Among the designers who joined the Design Department were João Fahrion (1898–1970), who had studied painting in Europe and who did covers and illustrations for children's books; Edgar Koetz (1913–1969), who created book covers and illustrations; and Nelson Boeira Faedrich (1912–1994), who illustrated more than 100 books for Livraria do Globo and did numerous covers as well. Besides designing books, the Design Department produced the monthly *Revista do Globo*, whose covers often adopted an Art Deco style similar to other Brazilian magazines of the period.

Magazines

Illustrated magazines have a long history in Brazil and are connected as elsewhere in Latin America with the rise of urbane metropolitan populations. The major illustrated magazines in the late 19th century were the *Revista Illustrada* (*Illustrated Review*), which the Italian cartoonist Ângelo Agostini launched in Rio 1876, and the *Semana Illustrada*, published in Sao Paulo by Henrique Fleuiss (see Chapter 15). These magazines were strongly influenced by the layouts and caricature styles of French publications of the period.

The relation to French graphic styles continued in a different form after the turn of the century when Art Nouveau decoration, particularly in lettering design, made a strong impact on new cultural magazines like *Kosmos*, which was founded in 1904 and continued until 1909. Although Art Nouveau had waned in

Europe by about 1905, it continued to influence the look of some Brazilian publications, particularly book covers and layouts, as already mentioned, rather than magazines, for years to come.

Among the first illustrated magazines of the new century were *O Malho* (*The Mallet*), founded in 1902, and the children's magazine *O Tico-Tico*, which appeared three years later, as well as *Fon-Fon!*, and *A Careta* (*The Grimace*), both of which were first published in 1908. Rather than relying on fine artists, these magazines, which strove to depict modern urban life, counted heavily on a new generation of caricaturists who drew covers, illustrations, and cartoons. Prominent among them was J. Carlos (1884–1950), whose full name was

Fig. 29.16: J. Carlos, *Para Todos*, cover, 1929. Biblioteca Brasiliana Guita e José Mindlin Universidade de São Paulo.

José Carlos de Brito e Cunha. His style eschewed the complicated textures of the 19th-century French carica-turists, who worked primarily in black and white and achieved their effects through intricate linear patterns. J. Carlos had an eye for exaggerating the features of a subject and did so with a comic touch. His line was fluid and instead of textural shading, he relied on flat areas of color. Not all his drawings were cartoon-like, however. He could also draw in a French Deco style.

J. Carlos was a regular contributor to *O Malho, Fon-Fon!*, and *A Careta*, serving as the principal illus-trator for *A Careta* from 1908 to 1921, when he left to become the art director as well as an illustrator for *O Malho*. S.A., a company in Rio de Janeiro that published some of the major illustrated magazines—*Para Todos* (*For All*), *Ilustração Brasileira* (*Brazilian Illustration*), and *O Tico-Tico* (Fig. 29.16). For *O Tico-Tico*, Carlos created not only covers but also vignettes for story titles and several comic strips. He was one of a group of cartoonists who began to publish in the illustrated magazines in Rio early in the century. The other major figures were Calixto Cordeiro (1877–1957), who signed his work K.lixto and was art director of *O Malho* and *Fon-Fon!* for a period, and Raul Paranhos Pederneiras (1874–1953), known simply as Raul. According to art historian Rafael Denis, these two and J. Carlos formed the "golden trio" of Brazilian caricature.

A new generation of magazines was published in the 1920s. Some continued the style of the preceding period, while others adopted aspects of the Art Deco style, then popular in Paris and New York. Antonio Paim Viera, designer of the aforementioned book *Pathé-Baby*, founded *A Garoa* (*The Drizzle*) in 1921. At the time, Paim, as he was known, was already contributing to various magazines and was designing book covers and illustrating books. The art editor was Juvenal Prado, who, like Paim, was also active as a book illustrator and decorator as well as a designer of book covers.

A Maçã (*The Apple*), which first appeared in 1922, rapidly became Rio's most popular weekly, although

Fig. 29.17: *A Maçã*, cover, 1922. Biblioteca Brasiliana Guita e José Mindlin Universidade de São Paulo.

it lasted only seven years. It was a satirical magazine, which was published by the well-known author of critical essays and satirical tales, Humberto de Campos (1886–1934). Its popularity was due at least in part to its lively design, which adopted elements from the French fashion publications but included original elements as well. The initial art director was Manlius Mello (dates unconfirmed), who worked under the pseudonym Ivan.

More than most other magazines, the covers of *A Maçã* usually featured a risqué scene or at least an attractive young modern woman with bobbed hair, sometimes in undergarments or even nude (Fig. 29.17).

The drawing styles of the covers were extremely diverse and the masthead changed several times, beginning with a serpent entwined with the letters of the title for which were later substituted various forms of lettering. None of these were particularly satisfying. Among the artists associated with *A Maçã* were the caricaturists K.lixto along with the Uruguayan Andrés Guevara (1904–1963), whose harsh graphic style became a stronger influence on younger cartoonists than the more gentle humorous approach of J. Carlos. Guevara's mordant political caricatures and anti-Nazi cartoons later appeared in such publications as *Crítica* and *Fôlha Carioca* (*Rio Sheet*). The most impressive graphic quality of the magazine, however, was the lively page layouts, which ranged from line drawings that framed the columns of type to title pages that integrated the printed copy into symmetrical ornamental designs.

By the late 1920s, some of the popular magazines used photography extensively. Notable among them were *Para Todos* and *O Cruzeiro* (*The Cross*). Inaugurated in 1928, *O Cruzeiro* featured a mixture of articles that covered many aspects of modern living from contemporary interior design to ceramics and art. Layouts for the photographic articles included titles with diverse lettering styles. In an article on indigenous culture that highlighted several drawings of Brazilian Indians by Henrique Cavalleiro (1892–1975), the artist included a script based on Indian ornaments that was specially designed for the magazine. *O Cruzeiro* also published stories that were illustrated by prominent artists including Osvaldo Teixeira (1905–1974), the Surrealist Ismael Neri (1900–1934), Orózio Belém (1903–1985), and the modernist Gilberto Gaetano Fabregat (dates unconfirmed). The eclectic covers ranged from portraits of modern women inspired by Art Deco to more humorous illustrations by J. Carlos. Numerous artists also drew covers for another popular magazine, *A Cigarra* (*The Cicada*). They included two women, Noemia Mourão Moacyr (1912–1992) and Hilde Weber (1913–1994), a German émigré, along with the painter and designer Diógenes de Campos Ayres, known as Diógenes (1881–1944).

Many of the illustrated magazines such as *O Malho* and *A Careta* that appeared before or after World War I continued publication during the 1930s despite the heavy censorship of the Vargas administration. Some cartoonists like J. Carlos even published caricatures of Vargas himself. The regime had its own propaganda magazines, however, and as in architecture, supported the most advanced modernist aesthetics. In the case of the monthly large-format propaganda publication *S. Paulo*, this meant photo essays and photomontage. *S. Paulo* presented the city as a dynamic modern metropolis that was undergoing rapid modernization and was ripe for foreign investment. In a spread that presented a montage of tall buildings to convey a sense of intense construction, the editors melded the images together behind a photograph of a newsboy hawking papers. The boastful rhetoric as well as the actual montage techniques and visually rich rotogravure printing strongly recalled a comparable

publication, *USSR in Construction*, published in the Soviet Union during the same period.

Advertising, packaging, and propaganda

Both French and American advertising were initial influences on advertising in Brazil—French for the Art Nouveau style of expressive lines and dreamy women, and American for the practical depictions of products. Principal venues for advertising were the pages of the many illustrated magazines, which published black and white ads with illustrations and occasional lettering drawn by artists whom the companies hired for specific jobs. Typical of these artists was the Italian Umberto della Latta (1883–1961), whose drawing skills were applied to advertisements as well as to numerous magazine covers. He did a series of ads for Falchi Chocolates that employed exotic settings. One depicted an Oriental princess in historic garb holding a saber in one hand and a tray with the chocolate in the other,

Fig. 29.18: Tatuzinho cachaça label. Photo: Edson Rontani Jr.

while another portrayed a colonial setting with a bewigged servant bringing chocolates on a tray to an aristocratic patron. By the 1920s, however, publicity agencies had begun to take over more product advertising and the idiosyncratic and decorative imagery of the prior years declined.

Complementing the early newspaper advertisements were various types of lithographed materials in color, ranging from posters to ornate labels for beer, cigarettes, and the typical Brazilian drink, cachaça, made from fermented sugar cane juice and sugar. The designs of cachaça labels numbered in the hundreds. Among the best known was the armadillo icon for the Tatuzinho distillery, which was founded in 1909 (Fig. 29.18). Other cachaça icons range from pinups and Indians to native birds and gauchos, each expressing some aspect of a regional identity.

One of the early packaging designers was Maurício Bünhaeds, who arrived in Brazil from Vienna in 1889 and worked in Sao Paulo, where he was associated with the previously mentioned Weiszflog printing establishment. In Rio de Janeiro, the Estamparía Colombo, founded by the entrepreneur Raymundo Ottoni de Castro Maya, created lithographed labels and packaging for a large number of enterprises including the iconic can for Castro Maya's own Carioca coconut fat. Among the distinctive packages of this period were those for the different brands of cigarettes produced by the Souza Cruz Cigarette Company. The company not only considered the packaging but also the brand name and may have been the first to name a cigarette brand after a woman. The lithographed package for Dalila cigarettes featured a supine woman in a diaphanous garment lounging languorously on a chair with a cigarette in one hand. Following the success of the Dalila brand, the company launched others with women's names—Salomé, Marly, Odette, Selma, Diana, and Yolanda, which was probably the most successful of these. Other well-known packages, some with characteristic trademark figures, were designed for Fiat Lux matches, Duchen biscuits, Minancora ointment, and Leite Moça condensed milk.

The first Brazilian advertising agencies included Eclética and Moderna, founded in 1919, and the Agência de Publicidade Pettinatti, established in 1920. In 1929, Armando D'Almeida, an experienced advertising executive who had worked in General Electric's advertising department, decided to establish his own agency. That same year, J. Walter Thompson opened an office in Brazil and introduced high-powered American methods to Brazilian advertising. An early client of theirs was General Motors for whom the agency undertook a national advertising campaign to promote GM's Chevrolet, the first such campaign in Brazil. In 1931, N. W. Ayer from Philadelphia established a Brazilian office, and McCann-Erikson, which had offices elsewhere in Latin America, came to Brazil in 1935. Competitors included Standard Propaganda, founded in 1933, and the Empresa de Propaganda Época, founded by the German poster and book cover designer Baron Geza von Puttkammer (dates unconfirmed) in 1933.

A specialized agency was the Companhia dos Annuncios em Bondes (Tramway Advertising Company), established in Rio in 1917, which produced advertising posters for streetcars. In 1927 the company hired as its art director Henrique Mirgalowsky (dates unconfirmed). He supervised a talented group of artists whom the company had brought together. Mirgalowsky, a Polish artist who had emigrated to Brazil, was important for the creation of a modern Brazilian poster style. Others who contributed to this style in the 1920s and 1930s included the Brazilian Ary Fagundes (1903–d.o.d unconfirmed) and a number of immigrant designers—Geraldo Orthof (1903– d.o.d unconfirmed), Theo Gygas (dates unconfirmed), and Fulvio Pennacchi (1905–1992), who was primarily a painter but like Orthof became a pioneer in the development of outdoor advertising in Brazil.

Posters also played a more political role after Vargas came to power in 1930. In 1932, the writer Plínio Salgado founded a nationalist political movement known as *Integralismo*, which was modeled to some degree on the Fascist Party in Italy. Instead of black shirts and hats, however, the Integralists wore green shirts and peaked caps. Similar to the Nazis, they attacked Marxism and liberalism and some in the movement were also anti-Semitic. In 1938, the year after Vargas attained absolute government power after a coup, he cracked down on the Integralists and the movement disintegrated. While in its active recruiting phase, however, the Integralists distributed posters, some modeled on the famous World War I recruiting posters that foregrounded Lord Kitchener and Uncle Sam. One featured a uniformed Integralist with the movement's flag, most likely modeled on the Nazi flag except that it had the movement's symbol—a sigma instead of a swastika—pointing his finger at the viewer. The slogan at the top read, "Brazil needs you," a paraphrase of "Uncle Sam Wants You," on James Montgomery Flagg's World War I poster.

In 1939 the Vargas regime created its own propaganda agency, the first in Latin America: the Departamento de Imprensa e Propaganda (Department of Press and Propaganda) or DIP, which had been preceded by several other organizations. Headed by Lourival Fontes (1899–1967), the DIP had broad powers of censorship and media control, which it used to promote the vision of a strong cohesive nation under the leadership of Vargas. The regime used various graphic means to this end including posters by Ary Fagundes and other artists. Fagundes, whose work might be considered in relation to modern European and American poster designers like A. M. Cassandre, Joseph Binder, and E. McKnight Kauffer, designed a number of posters for events such as the Brazilian Congress of Urbanism, actions to support Brazil's involvement in World War II, and a call to laborers to participate in the nation's industrialization. Posters were also commissioned by private organizations such as the Centro Carioca, which sponsored an annual Congresso de Brasilidade (Congress of Brazilianness), announcing the event with patriotic propaganda imagery. Propaganda that promoted the regime would prevail until Vargas was overthrown by a military coup in 1945.

Bibliography
Bibliographic essay

With few exceptions, the literature on product design and graphic design in Latin America is in Spanish or Portuguese. Various volumes of *The Cambridge History of Latin America*, among other books, provide social, economic, and political background. A few books on industrial development such as Lloyd Hughlett, *Industrialization of Latin America*; Warren Dean, *The Industrialization of São Paulo, 1880–1945*; Wilson Suzigan, *Indústria Brasileira: Origem e Desenvolvimento*; and Sanford Mosk, *Industrial Revolution in Mexico* also contain some material on the development of products. Maria Cecilia Loschavio dos Santos, *Móvel Moderno no Brasil* is the rare volume that focuses exclusively on an aspect of Latin American product or furniture design.

There has been extensive writing on aspects of graphic design in Latin America—posters, magazines and book design, and advertising. Helpful books on graphic design include two by Rafael Cardoso Denis on Brazilian design—his edited volume *O Design Brasileiro antes do Design. Aspectos da História Gráfica, 1870–1960* and his introductory design history text, *Uma Introdução à História do Design.* Chico Homem de Melo, *Linha do Tempo do Design Gráfico no Brasil* is a broad and detailed survey of Brazilian design history. On Cuba, Vicki Gold Levi and Steven Heller, *Cuba Style: Graphics from the Golden Age of Design* has a lot of useful images with brief introductory texts. There is extensive documentation on graphic design in Mexico during this period. Julieta Ortiz Gaitán, *Imágenes del Deseo: Arte y Publicidad en la Prensa Ilustrada Mexicana (1894–1939)* is an authoritative account of Mexican advertising, magazine publishing, and illustration from the 1890s to World War II and I have relied heavily on it. Cuauhtémoc Medina *Diseño antes del Diseño: Diseño Gráfico en México, 1920–1960* is the catalog of an exhibition that has an excellent introductory text and many illustrations. I have also profited from two voluminous histories of Mexican graphic design:

Luz del Carmen Vilchis Esquivel, *Historia del Diseño Gráfico en México, 1910–2010* and Giovanni Troconi, *Diseño Gráfico en México; 100 Años, 1900–2000.* The Taller de Gráfica Popular has been covered in numerous volumes. Besides these and other books, I have also found invaluable information on many websites in Spanish, Portuguese, and English.

Books

General: Arts

Ades, Dawn. *Art in Latin America: The Modern Era, 1820–1980.* Contributions by Guy Brett, Stanton Loomis Catlin, and Rosemary O'Neill. New Haven and London: Yale University Press, 1989.

Art Déco na América Latina. 1º Seminário Internacional. Centro de Arquitetura e Urbanismo do Rio de Janeiro. Rio de Janeiro, Prefeitura da Cidade do Rio de Janeiro/SMU, Solar Grandjean de Montigny – PUR/RJ, 1997.

Castedo, Leopoldo. *A History of Latin American Art and Architecture from Pre-Columbian Times to the Present.* Translated and edited by Phyllis Freeman. New York and Washington: Frederick A. Praeger, 1969.

Catlin, Stanton Loomis and Terence Grieder. *Art of Latin America since Independence.* New York: October House, 1966.

Collazos, Óscar, *Los Vanguardismos en la América Latina.* Barcelona: Ediciones Península, 1977.

Craven, David. *Art and Revolution in Latin America, 1910–1990.* New Haven and London: Yale University Press, 2002.

de Moraes Belluzzo, Ana Maria, ed. *Modernidade: Vanguardas Artísticas na América Latina.* São Paulo: Fundação Memorial da América Latina, 1990.

de Usabel, Gaizka S. *The High Noon of American Films in Latin America.* Ann Arbor: UMI Research Press, 1982.

Franco, Jean. *An Introduction to Spanish-American Literature.* London and New York: Cambridge University Press, 1969.

Gabara, Esther. *Errant Modernism: The Ethos of Photography in Mexico and Brazil.* Durham and London: Duke University Press, 2008.

Henríquez Ureña, Max. *Breve Historia del Modernismo.* México and Buenos Aires: Fondo de Cultura Económica, 1954.

Henríquez-Ureña, Pedro. *Literary Currents in Hispanic America.* Cambridge, MA: Harvard University Press, 1945.

Lejeune, Jean-François, ed. *Cruelty & Utopia: Cities and Landscapes of Latin America.* New York: Princeton Architectural Press, 2003.

Lynes, Russell. *Good Old Modern: An Intimate Portrait of the Museum of Modern Art.* New York: Atheneum, 1973.

Noyes, Eliot F. *Organic Design in Home Furnishings.* New York: The Museum of Modern Art, 1969 (c. 1941).

Segre, Roberto, ed. *Latin America in its Architecture.* Fernando Kusnetzoff, editor of the English edition. Translated from the Spanish by Edith Grossman. New York and London: Holmes & Meier, 1981.

Sosnoski, Saul, ed. *La Cultura de un Siglo. América Latina en sus Revistas.* Madrid and Buenos Aires: Alianza Editorial, 1999.

Sullivan, Edward J., ed. *Latin American Art in the Twentieth Century.* London: Phaidon, 1996.

Traba, Marta. *Art of Latin America 1900–1980.* Washington, DC: Inter-American Development Bank, 1994. Distributed by the Johns Hopkins University Press.

Turner, Jane, ed. *Encyclopedia of Latin American & Carribean Art.* London: Macmillan, and New York: Grove's Dictionaries, 2000.

Unruh, Vicky. *Latin American Vanguards: The Art of Contentious Encounters.* Berkeley, Los Angeles, and London: University of California Press, 1994.

General: Economics, History, Development

Arciniegas, Germán. *Latin America: A Cultural History.*

Translated from the Spanish by Joan MacLean. New York: Alfred A. Knopf, 1970.

Bethell, Leslie, ed. *The Cambridge History of Latin America, Volume 4, c. 1870–1930*. Cambridge and New York: Cambridge University Press, 1986.

—ed. *The Cambridge History of Latin America, Volume 5, c. 1879–1930*. Cambridge and New York: Cambridge University Press, 1994.

—ed. *The Cambridge History of Latin America, Volume 6, pt. 1. Latin America Since 1930: Economy and Society*. Cambridge and New York: Cambridge University Press, 1994.

—ed. *The Cambridge History of Latin America, Volume 8, Latin America Since 1930: Spanish South America*. Cambridge and New York: Cambridge University Press, 1994.

—ed. *The Cambridge History of Latin America, Volume 9, Brazil since 1930*. Cambridge and New York: Cambridge University Press, 2008.

—ed. *Latin America: Economy and Society since 1930*. Cambridge and New York: Cambridge University Press, 1998.

Bulmer-Thomas, Victor. *The Economic History of Latin America since Independence*, 2nd ed. Cambridge Latin American Studies 77. Cambridge and New York: Cambridge University Press, 2003.

Bulmer-Thomas, Victor, John H. Coatsworth, and Roberto Cortés Conde, eds. *The Cambridge Economic History of Latin America, Volume 2: The Long Twentieth Century*. Cambridge and New York: Cambridge University Press, 2006.

Cardenas, Enrique, José Antonio Ocampo, and Rosemary Thorp, eds. *An Economic History of Twentieth-Century Latin America, Vol. 1: The Export Age: The Latin American Economies in Late Nineteenth and Early Twentieth Centuries*. Houndmills and New York: Palgrave, 2000.

—eds. *An Economic History of Twentieth-Century Latin America, Vol. 3: Industrialization and the State in Latin America: The Postwar Years*. Houndmills and New York: Palgrave, 2000.

Coerver, Don M. and Linda B. Hall. *Tangled Destinies: Latin America & The United States*. Albuquerque: University of New Mexico Press, 1999.

Connell-Smith, Gordon. *The United States and Latin America: An Historical Analysis of Inter-American Relations*. London: Heinemann Educational Books, 1974.

Davies, R. E. G. *Airlines of Latin America since 1919*. Washington, DC: Smithsonian Institution Press, 1984.

Herring, Hubert. *A History of Latin America from the Beginnings to the Present*, 2nd ed., rev. New York: Alfred A. Knopf, 1967.

Hughlett, Lloyd J., ed. *Industrialization of Latin America*. Westport: Greenwood Press, 1946.

New York World's Fair 1939. Official Guide Book, 2nd ed. New York: Exposition Publications, 1939.

Phelps, Dudley Maynard. *Migration of Industry to South America*. The Evolution of International Business 1800–1945, Vol. 7. New York and London: McGraw-Hill, 1936.

Skidmore, Thomas E. and Peter H. Smith. *Modern Latin America*, 2nd ed. New York and Oxford: Oxford University Press, 1989.

Thorp, Rosemary. *Progress, Poverty and Exclusion: An Economic History of Latin America in the 20th Century*. Washington DC: Inter-American Development Bank, 1998. Distributed by the Johns Hopkins University Press.

—ed. *Latin America in the 1930s: The Role of the Periphery in World Crisis*. London: Macmillan, 1984.

—ed. *An Economic History of Twentieth-Century Latin America, Vol. 2: Latin America in the 1930s: The Role of the Periphery in World Crisis*. Houndmills and New York: Palgrave, 2000.

Cuba

Alonso, Alejandro G., Pedro Contreras, and Martino Fagiuoli. *Havana Deco*. New York and London: W.W. Norton, 2007 (c. 2003).

Bethell, Leslie, ed. *Cuba: A Short History*.

Cambridge and New York: Cambridge University Press, 1993.

Bondil, Nathalie, ed. *Cuba: Art and History from 1868 to Today.* Montreal: Montreal Museum of Fine Arts, 2008.

Gott, Richard. *Cuba: A New History.* New Haven and London: Yale University Press, 2004.

Levi, Vicki Gold and Steven Heller. *Cuba Style: Graphics from the Golden Age of Design.* New York: Princeton Architectural Press, 2002.

Massaguer; Su Vida y Su Obra, Autobiografia, Historia Grafica, Anecdotario. Havana: Cinuentenario Massagueriano, 1957.

Pérez Jr., Louis. *On Becoming Cuban: Identity, Nationality & Culture.* New York: The Ecco Press, 1999.

Schwarz, Rosalie. *Pleasure Island: Tourism and Temptation in Cuba.* Lincoln and London: University of Nebraska Press, 1999.

Mexico

60 Años: Taller Gráfica Popular. México D.F.: Consejo Nacional para la Cultura y las Artes, Instituto Nacional de Bellas Artes, 1997.

Agrsánchez Jr., Rogelio. *Cine Mexico: Posters from the Golden Age, 1936–1956.* Introduction by Charles Ramírez Berg. San Francisco: Chronicle Books, 2001.

Apuntes para la Historia y Crítica de la Arquitectura Mexicana del Siglo XX: 1900–1980, Vol. 1. Mexico D.F.: Secretaria de Educacion Publica, instituto Nacional de Bellas Artes, 1982, nos. 20–21.

Art Déco: Un País Nacionalista, Un México Cosmopolita. México D.F.: Museo Nacional de Arte, 1997.

Beezley, William H. *Judas at the Jockey Club and Other Episodes of Porfirian Mexico,* 2nd ed. Lincoln and London: University of Nebraska Press, 1989.

Blanco, Jorge Ayala. *La Aventura del Cine Mexicano en la Época de Oro y Después.* México D.F.: Editorial Grijalbo, 1993.

Burian, Edward R. *Modernity and the Architecture of*

Mexico. Foreword by Ricardo Legorreta. Austin: University of Texas Press, 2007.

Caplow, Deborah. *Leopoldo Méndez: Revolutionary Art and the Mexican Print.* Austin: University of Texas Press, 2007.

Costa, Gina. *Para la Gente: Art, Politics, and Cultural Identity of the Taller de Gráfica Popular. Selected Works from the Charles S. Hayes Collection of Twentieth-Century Mexican Graphics.* South Bend, IN: Snite Museum of Art, University of Notre Dame, 2009.

Covarrubias, Miguel; Homenaje. México D.F.: Centro Cultural Arte Contemporaneo, 1987.

Cronos y Cromos. México D.F.: Central Cultural Arte Contemporaneo, 1994.

Debroise, Olivier. *Mexican Suite: A History of Photography in Mexico.* Austin: University of Texas Press, 2001.

De la Torre Villar, Ernesto. *Ilustradores de Libros: Guión Biobibliográfico.* Mexico D.F.: Universidad Nacional Autónoma de México, 1999.

Del Carmen Vilchis Esquivel, Luz. *Historia del Diseño Gráfico en México, 1910–2010.* Mexico D.F.: Instituto Nacional de Bellas Artes/Conaculta, 2010.

De los Reyes, Aurelio. *Cine y Sociedad en México, 1896–1930: Vivir de Sueños, Vol. 1 (1896–1920).* México D.F.: Universidad Nacional Autónoma de México, 1983.

El Diseño de Clara Porset: Inventando un México Moderno/ Clara Porset's Design: Creating a Modern Mexico. México D.F.: Museo Franz Mayer/Universidad Nacional Autónoma de México/Turner, 1983.

Gaitán, Julieta Ortiz, *Imágenes del Deseo: Arte y Publicidad en la Prensa Ilustrada Mexicana (1894–1939).* Mexico D.F.: Universidad Nacional Autónoma de México, 2003.

Gallo, Rubén. *Mexican Modernity: The Avant-Garde and the Technological Revolution.* Cambridge, MA, and London: MIT Press, 2005.

Hannes Meyer: Architekt Urbanist Lehrer, 1889–1954. Frankfurt: Ernst & Sohn, 1989.

Heinzelman, Kurt, ed. *The Covarrubias Circle: Nikola*

Muray's Collection of Twentieth-Century Mexican Art. Austin: University of Texas Press, 2004.

Ittmann, John, ed. *Mexico and Modern Printmaking: A Revolution in the Graphic Arts, 1920–1950.* With contributions by Innis Howe Shoemaker, James M. Wechsler, and Lyle W. Williams. New Haven and London: Yale University Press, 2007.

Kirkwood, Burton. *The History of Mexico.* Westport and London: Greenwood Press, 2000.

La Patria Portátil: 100 Years of Mexican Chromo Art Calendars. México D.F.: Museo Soumaya, 1999.

Medina, Cuauhtémoc. *Diseño antes del Diseño: Diseño Gráfico en México, 1920–1960.* Mexico D.F.: Museo de Arte Alvar y Carmen T. de Carillo Gil, 1991.

Mosk, Sanford. *Industrial Revolution in Mexico.* New York: Russell & Russell, 1950.

Salinas Flores, Oscar. *Clara Porset: Una Vida Inquieta, Una Obra sin Igual.* México D.F.: Universidad Nacional Autónoma de México, 2001.

Stewart, Virginia. *45 Contemporary Mexican Artists: A Twentieth-Century Renaissance.* Stanford: Stanford University Press, 1951.

Taller de Gráfica Popular: 4 Decadas del Grabado en Mexico. Catalog, n.d.

Taller de Gráfica Popular: Plakate und Flugblätter su Arbeiterbewegung und Gewerkschaften in Mexiko, 1937–1986. Berlin: Ibero-Amerikanisches Institut – Preussischer Kulturbesitz, 2002.

Tenorio-Trillo, Mauricio. *Mexico at the World's Fairs: Crafting a Modern Nation.* Berkeley, Los Angeles, and London: University of California Press, 1996.

Tibol, Raquel. *Gráficas y Neográficas en Mexico.* Mexico D.F.: Secretaría de Educación Pública and Universidad Nacional Autónoma de México, 1987.

Troconi, Giovanni. *Diseño Gráfico en México; 100 Años, 1900–2000.* Mexico D.F.: Artes de Mexico, 2010.

Villalba, Angela: *Mexican Calendar Girls.* Foreword by Carlos Monsiváis. San Francisco: Chronicle Books, 2006.

Williams, Adriana. *Covarrubias.* Edited by Doris Ober. Austin: University of Texas Press, 1994.

Brazil

Amaral, Aracy. *Artes Plásticas na Semana de 22.* São Paulo: Editôra Perspectiva, 1970.

Bardi, P. M. *História da Arte Brasileira: Pintura, Escultura, Arquitetura, Outras Artes.* São Paulo: Edições Melhoramentos, 1975.

—*O Modernismo no Brasil.* São Paulo: Sudameris – Banco Francêsm e Italiano para a América do Sul S/A, 1978.

Batista, Marta Rossetti, Telé Porto, Ancona Lopez, and Yone Soares de Lima, eds. *Brasil: 1º Tempo Modernista – 1917/29 Documentação.* São Paulo: Instituto de Estudos Brasileiros, 1972.

Burns, E. Bradford. *A History of Brazil.* New York and London: Columbia University Press, 1970.

Cavalcanti, Lauro. *When Brazil Was Modern: Guide to Architecture 1928–1960.* Translated by John Tolman. New York: Princeton Architectural Press, 2003.

Cunha Lima, Guilherme. *O Gráfico Amador: As Origens da Moderna Tipografia Brasileira.* Rio de Janeiro: Editora UFRJ, 1997.

Dean, Warren. *The Industrialization of São Paulo, 1880–1945.* Austin and London: University of Texas Press, 1969. Published for the Institute of Latin American Studies.

de Azevedo, Fernando. *Brazilian Culture: An Introduction to the Study of Culture in Brazil.* New York: Macmillan, 1950.

de Castro Lopes, Sonia. *Lourival Fontes: As Duas Faces do Poder.* Rio de Janeiro: Litteris Editora, 1999.

de Lima, Yone Soares. *A Ilustração na Produção Literária São Paulo – Décade de Vinte.* São Paulo: Instituto de Estudos Brasileiros, 1985.

Denis, Rafael Cardoso. *Uma Introdução à História do Design.* São Paulo: Editôra Edgard Blücher, 1999.

Denis, Rafael Cardoso, ed. *O Design Brasileiro antes do Design. Aspectos da História Gráfica, 1870–1960.* São Paulo: Cosac Naify, 2005.

Ferreira, Márcia Christina. *Santa Rosa e a Invenção do Livro Modernista.* Projeto Conclusão: PUC Rio de Janeiro, 1997.

Goodwin, Philip L. *Brazil Builds: Architecture New and Old 1652–1942.* New York: The Museum of Modern Art, 1943

Gráfica Arte e Indústria no Brasil: 180 Anos de História. São Paulo: Bendeirante S.A. Gráfica e Editora, 1991.

Hallewell, L. *Books in Brazil; A History of the Publishing Trade.* Metuchen, NJ, and London: The Scarecrow Press, 1982.

Homem de Melo, Chico. *Linha do Tempo do Design Gráfico no Brasil.* São Paulo: Cosanaify, 2011.

Johnson, Randal. *The Film Industry in Brazil: Culture and the State.* Pittsburgh: University of Pittsburgh Press, 1987.

Lima, Herman. *História da Caricatura no Brazil, Vol. 1.* Rio de Janeiro: Livraria José Olympio Editôra, 1963.

Loschavio dos Santos, Maria Cecilia. *Móvel Moderno no Brasil.* São Paulo: Livros Studio Nobel, Editora de Universidade de São Paulo, 1995.

Pontual, Roberto. *Dicionário das Artes Plásticas no Brasil.* Rio de Janeiro: Editôra Civilização Brasileira, 1969.

Sobral, Julieta. *O Desenhista Invisibel.* Rio de Janeiro: Folha Seca, 2007.

Suzigan, Wilson. *Indüstria Brasileira: Origem e Desenvolvimento.* São Paulo: Editôra Brasiliense, 1986.

Viégas, João Alexandre. *Vencendo o Azul: História da Indústria e Tecnologia Aeronáuticas no Brasil.* São Paulo: Livraria Duas Cidades, 1989.

Williams, Daryle. *Culture Wars in Brazil: The First Vargas Regime, 1930–1945.* Durham and London: Duke University Press, 2001.

Chapters in books

Cardoso, Rafael, "Ambiguously Modern: Art Deco in Latin America," in Charlotte Benton, Tim Benton, and Ghislaine Wood, eds. *Art Deco 1910–1939.* Boston, New York, and London: Bulfinch Press, 2003.

Johnson, Randal, "Regarding the Philanthropic Ogre: Cultural Policy in Brazil, 1930–45/1964–90," in Daniel H. Levine, ed. *Constructing Culture and Power in Latin America.* Ann Arbor: University of Michigan Press, 1993.

Articles

"Diseño antes del Diseño," *Mexico en el Diseño* 2, no. 8 (Febrero–Marzo 1992).

Encinas, Rosario, "José Vasconcelos (1882–1959)," *Prospects* 24, nos. 3–4 (1994).

The Journal of Decorative and Propaganda Arts 22 (1996) Cuba theme issue.

The Journal of Decorative and Propaganda Arts 26 (2010) Mexico theme issue.

The Journal of Decorative and Propaganda Arts 21 (1995) Brazil theme issue.

López, Bruno. "Trayectoria del Cartel en el Cine Mexicano," *DX* 2–3 (2000).

México en el Tiempo: Revista de Historia y Conservación 32. El Cartel en México Special Issue.

Rivadulla Jr., Eladio, "The Film Poster in Cuba (1940–1959)," *Design Issues* 16, no. 2 (Summer 2000).

Tenorio Trillio, Maurice, "1910 Mexico City: Space and Nation in the City of the Centenario," *Journal of Latin American Studies* 28, no. 1 (February 1996).

Internet

Design Gráfico Brasileiro, http://designgraficobrasileiro.wordpress.com/category/diogenes/ (accessed October 2, 2014).

Gaitán, Julieta Ortiz, "Francisco Eppens y Los Mensajeros del México Moderno," Revista Electrónica Imagines, instituto de Investigaciones Estéticas, http://www.esteticas.unam.mx/revista_imagenes/dearchivos/dearch_ortizgaitan02.html (accessed October 2, 2014).

Herkenhoff, Paolo (1993), "Brasil Marajoara – A Modernidade das Artes Decorativas," FAU-UFPA, http://fauufpa.wordpress.com/2011/07/01/brasil-marajoara-a-modernidade-das-artes-decorativas/ (accessed October 2, 2014).

"O Malho" Revista Internética João do Rio, http://www.joaodorio.com/site/index.php?option=com_content&task=view&id=422&Itemid=117 (accessed October 2, 2014).

Simioni, Ana Paula Cavalcanti, "Regina Gomide Graz: Modernismo, Arte Têxtil e Relações de Gênero no Brasil," Revista do Instituto de Estudos Brasileiros, http://www.revistasusp.sibi.usp.br/scielo.php?script=sci_arttext&pid=S0020-38742007000900006 (accessed October 2, 2014).

Chapter 30: Latin America: Chile, Argentina, Colombia, Venezuela, and Uruguay 1900–1939

Chile

The 20th century began in Chile with the nation's commitment to parliamentary democracy. It was evident in the formation of new political parties that represented the middle class as well as those formed by working-class activists. In the late 19th century, Chile had developed nitrate mines in the border territory that had once belonged to Peru and Bolivia and the miners there became the bedrock of the country's new working class. The first national labor organization, the Federación Obrera de Chile (Workers' Federation of Chile) (FOCh) was established in 1909. It was followed by a political party, the Partido Obrero Socialista (Socialist Workers' Party) (POS), founded three years later by a typesetter and political activist Luis Emilio Recabarren (1876–1924). Initially the Socialist Workers' Party aspired to create a single working class that would share equally in the fruits of production. In 1922, it was transformed into the new Chilean Communist Party (CPCh), whose founder was also Recabarren. A new Partido Socialista de Chile (Socialist Party of Chile) was founded in 1933. Whereas the leftists gained considerable strength in the cities, the parties of the right, however, had much greater control of the rural areas.

The Chilean economy was relatively successful in the years preceding World War I. Britain and Germany were both large investors and Chile had developed a national transportation infrastructure, especially to move raw materials from the mines to the ports. Before the war, the country depended heavily on exports, notably nitrate, and had imported a large portion of its goods for domestic consumption. Similar to other Latin American countries, Chile began to put more emphasis on import substitution when the war ended as relations with its traditional trading partners, Britain and Germany, were disrupted. From the 1920s, the United States replaced both of those countries as the major foreign economic presence in Chile.

Until the late 1920s, Chile was a parliamentary democracy, although a series of undistinguished presidents did little to improve the conditions of the working and peasant classes. In 1925, the parliament passed a new constitution that embodied a number of important changes including the separation of Church and state and the recognition of workers' right to organize, but in 1927, declining economic conditions enabled a military figure, Carlos Ibáñez, to become president as the result of a rigged election. Sometimes referred to as the Chilean Mussolini, Ibáñez asserted dictatorial powers, exercising repressive measures against union members, journalists, and the left political parties. As an economic policy, he promoted industry and public works, which had a positive effect on the economy for several years until the Great Depression. In mid-1931, Ibáñez fled the country to Argentina as a result of widespread dissatisfaction with his repressive political measures and his inability to resolve the country's severe economic difficulties.

Chile returned to electoral democracy in 1932 when Arturo Alessandri, who had been president in the early 1920s, was re-elected. Like Ibáñez before him, he reduced unemployment by promoting industry and government projects but he also neglected the social needs of the working class and threatened the left by forming a sizeable civilian paramilitary force. During Alessandri's regime, the leftist political parties joined together with some moderates to form a Popular Front, which rallied the middle and working classes around the goals of democracy, social welfare, and industrialization. It also adopted a strong oppositional stance against the fascist movements in Europe.

In 1938, the Popular Front was strong enough to elect as president Pedro Aguirre Cerda, a member of the Radical Party, which represented the center rather than the left. Aguirre Cerda continued the emphasis of Ibáñez and Alessandri on industry, but he made a greater commitment to state capitalism when he created the Corporación de Fomento de la Producción (Chilean Economic Development Agency) (CORFO) in 1939. CORFO took an active role in the country's economic development by providing loans and other support to Chilean enterprises. The Popular Front, which included the Communists and Socialists, supported Aguirre Cerda because they recognized the need to strengthen Chile's domestic industries; hence they deferred their original calls for a total revolution and adopted a pragmatic economic position.

There was also good reason for leftists and centrists to unite politically to combat the local fascist movements that sprang up in Chile in the 1930s. First among them was the Movimiento Nacional-Socialista de Chile (National Socialist Movement of Chile) (MNS), which was founded in 1932 by the lawyer Jorge González von Marées and the economist Carlos Keller. Known as *nacistas,* their ideology was drawn from the German Nazi Party as well as the Italian Fascists with some local concerns added. Like their counterparts in Europe, they adopted uniforms and similar tactics of promoting their ideas through street demonstrations and their own publications including the daily newspaper *Trabajo* (*Work*). The MNS also had its own flag, which was based on the original Chilean flag and featured a lightning bolt that was positioned diagonally across the stripes. By the late 1930s, the militancy of the MNS had softened somewhat as the group's leaders sought to claim a place in the national political debate. In 1938, another group, the Partido Nacional Facista (National Fascist Party) (PNF), which took its name directly from that of the Italian Fascist Party, emerged with a program that rivaled the original one of the MNS with a strong anti-Semitic component added. The PNF too had its own publication, *La Patria* (*The*

Fatherland), but the party never gained more than a small number of adherents before it collapsed several years after it started. A third party, the Movimiento Nacional Socialista (National Socialist Movement), emerged in 1940 but, like its predecessor the PNF, it did not gain many members nor did it last very long.

New elections were held after the death of Cerda in 1941. His successor was Juan Antonio Ríos, who continued the development of state capitalism through the Chilean Economic Development Agency. This resulted in the establishment of three national companies, the Empresa Nacional de Electricidad (National Power Company) (Endesa) in 1943, the Empresa Nacional de Petróleos (National Oil Company) (ENAP) in 1945, and a year later the Compañía de Aceros del Pacífico (Pacific Steel Company) (CAP), which began operations with the huge Huachipato steelworks adjacent to the port of Talcahuano. Though Rios was not a particularly strong president, his support for the government's involvement with industrial development positioned the Chilean economy after World War II as one of the strongest in Latin America.

The emergence of private enterprise

A major impetus to industrialization in the late 19th century was the War of the Pacific, which Chile fought between 1879 and 1883 with Peru and Bolivia over the control of territory with rich mineral deposits. Chile was victorious but the cost was large as the government faced the necessity to arm, equip, and support its military forces. This required clothing, footwear, leather goods, pharmaceuticals, guns, cannons, boilers for ships' engines, and other materiel. Foundries and metal workshops were under heavy pressure to fill government orders, which required them to establish efficient production methods. A major producer of weapons was the huge army factory, Fábricas y Maestranzas del Ejército de Chile (Factories and Arsenals of the Chilean Army) (FAMAE), which was established in 1811.

The war may also have stimulated the formation of the Sociedad de Fomento Fabril (Society for

Industrial Promotion) (SFF), an organization of industrialists that was founded in 1883. Among the SFF's early activities were the creation of numerous industrial training schools, the promotion of Chilean participation in international exhibitions, and the advocacy of high import tariffs to prevent foreign competition. In the early 1900s, the SFF opened a special office to foster the immigration of foreign technicians.

To a certain degree, the SFF might be compared to the Deutscher Werkbund, except there were no applied artists involved since the applied arts had not developed in Chile to the degree they had in Germany. In 1904, the SFF sponsored an exhibition of industry and agriculture that featured Chilean goods of high quality in a number of sectors—food and beverages, clothing, knitwear, leather goods, footwear, printing and paper goods, wooden products and furniture, chemical products, and a range of products made in foundries, machine shops, and metalworking establishments. As Henry Kirsch points out, these levels of excellence were achieved despite an insufficient pool of skilled labor and a lack of qualified technical personnel. The promotion of Chilean goods continued during the Centenary of Independence, held in Santiago in 1910, where national industrial and agricultural products were also on display.

Starting in the late 19th century, Chilean manufacturers traveled regularly to Europe and the United States to look for new products that might appeal to the domestic middle-class market, investigate new machinery, and, when possible, bring skilled workers back to Chile. Among the early factories that made consumer products was the Valparaíso metalworking firm V, Momus, Breynat & Cía, founded in 1894, which specialized in household iron goods. In 1905, the company changed its name to the Fábrica Nacional de Envases y Enlozados (National Factory for Containers and Enamel Ware). Four years later, the management purchased a glazed-ironware factory, which enabled an expansion of the company's product line for industry and the home.

In 1912, Oscar Smits Longton fused several small manufacturers of beds into the Compañía Industrial de Catres (Industrial Bed Company) (CIC). By the end of World War I, the CIC had gained a sizeable share of the furniture market. Capitalizing on its expertise in producing metal furniture, the company broadened its product line by the end of the 1930s to include refrigerators, bicycles, and motorbikes. These less expensive domestically-made products can be contrasted with the luxury goods such as silver dinnerware that were imported by Casa Muzard, a French family company that was set up in 1865.

One of the few Latin American countries to produce railroad locomotives, Chile manufactured its first one in 1886 at the state-owned foundry in Santiago. After that, however, private firms made subsequent locomotives. In 1887, the Sociedad Fundición de Chile, the principal private manufacturer of bridges and locomotives, produced Locomotive No. 126, the *José Manuel Balmaceda*, which was named after the current president. It was said to be the first made in South America by a private company.

Compared to the locomotive factories in Britain or the United States, the number of locomotives produced in Chile was miniscule. Most of those in use were imported from Europe or the United States, but the local manufacture of even a few locomotives was an important contribution to the formation of a Chilean heavy goods industry. Unfortunately, the government did not give the local foundries consistent orders, making it impossible for them to set up regular assembly-line production. Consequently, most foundries that had produced locomotives for the state railroads in the past went out of business.

By 1915, Chile had 7,800 factories, although most were quite small. Nonetheless they produced about 80 percent of domestic consumer needs and this percentage jumped considerably during the next several years. Domestic products ranged from metal goods and furniture to pottery, glass utensils, food and beverages, soap, and tobacco. Many of the entrepreneurs were immigrants, as no comparable spirit of entrepreneurship existed among the Chilean elite, whose values remained those of a traditional rural society where wealth was generated by the possession of land and the production of agricultural goods. There were, of course, enterprising Chileans such as Carlos Cousiño and Augustín Edwards Mac-Clure whose holdings ranged from newspapers and magazines to breweries, lumber mills, cement factories, and coal mines. The Sociedad de Fomento Fabril also continued its efforts to promote local industry and by 1924 it had councils or affiliates in cities throughout Chile.

Beginning in the 1920s, private industrial development on a large scale was led by American companies. Unlike European manufacturers who preferred to sell Chilean customers the patent rights to their manufacturing processes, the American firms established foreign branches of their factories or else built on existing businesses. Among those active in Chile between 1920 and 1932 were the automobile manufacturers Ford and General Motors; the Singer Sewing Machine Company; and RCA Victor, which produced radios and phonographs. These companies had plants to assemble their products, which were made primarily with parts imported from the United States. The factories also produced some parts locally for variants of standard products that would appeal to local consumers. After Ford and General Motors, the most ambitious assembly plant was operated by the airplane manufacturer Curtiss-Wright, which established a branch factory, Fabrica Chilena de Aviones Curtiss-Wright (Chilean Curtiss-Wright Airplane Factory), where workers assembled airplanes but also made some parts. Similar to the factories that produced locomotives in Chile, the Curtiss-Wright factory was one of the few in Latin America where airplanes were made rather than imported.

Although American investment in Chile was welcomed after World War I, there was nonetheless a strain of economic nationalism that resisted domination by outsiders and called for Chile to develop its own

industrial potential. This was evident as early as 1912 in the work of historian and political theorist Francisco Antonio Encina (1874–1965), who wrote in his seminal book *Nuestra Inferioridad Economica, Sus Causas, Sus Consequencias* (*Our Economic inferiority, Its Causes, Its Consequences*) of 1912 that if Chile wished to be a modern nation, it would have to develop its own technical skills and entrepreneurial spirit for which it relied on foreigners at the time. Despite the country's steady industrial growth, due largely to mining and small businesses, this lesson was not well learned until the late 1930s, when the government embarked on its most ambitious plan ever to stimulate domestic industrial development.

Government support of industry

In 1887, the Chilean government established a Ministry of Industry and Public Works, an initial step towards greater state involvement in national industrial development. However, the state did not attend significantly to issues of industrialization until the mid-1920s when it provided funding to FAMAE, the military arsenal, for the distribution of plows, agricultural equipment, and other goods on the open market in competition with private companies. In 1927, after Carlos Ibáñez became president, the government established a Ministry of Development, which was responsible for industry and public works as well as transportation and agriculture. Within the ministry, special consideration was given to manufacturing through the creation of the Dirección General de Industrias Fabriles (General Directorate of Manufacturing Industries). To favor domestic products, Ibáñez also worked closely, especially on tariff issues, with the Society for Industrial Promotion, which gained considerable power during his tenure.

To promote Chilean industry abroad, the Ibáñez regime commissioned a pavilion for the 1929 Ibero-American Exposition in Seville, Spain. Designed by the architect José Martinez (dates unconfirmed), it was a conservative three-storey building in a Neo-Colonial style that emphasized Chile's local architectural tradition. The pavilion housed displays of the country's extractive industries, notably replicas of a nitrate mine and a copper plant, along with a selection of arts and crafts made by the Mapuche Indian tribe.

The Mapuche exhibit, indicative of the government's belief that Chile, like other countries in Latin America, had to reclaim its indigenous heritage as part of its national identity, was expanded into a broader ethnographic display for the Chilean Pavilion at the 1939 World's Fair in New York. This pavilion, designed by a New York architect, Theodore Smith-Miller (dates unconfirmed), also featured a mining exhibit as was the case in Seville, but unlike the Seville pavilion, it included a section that promoted tourism, a developing industry in Chile during the 1930s. The decoration of the pavilion was supervised by the painter and poster artist Camilo Mori (1896–1973), who also created a large mural for the interior.

In an attempt to combat the effect of the Great Depression on Chile's economy, Ibáñez inaugurated a campaign called "Choose Chilean Products," which was accompanied by identifying labels such as "Chilean Product" and "Made in Chile." Unfortunately, the campaign did not to do enough to stave off the economic devastation the Depression wrought and which helped to cause Ibáñez's abdication of the presidency in mid-1931.

The boldest government initiative to support industry was President Pedro Aguirre Cerda's experiment in state capitalism, the previously mentioned Chilean Economic Development Agency or CORFO. The agency was originally founded to offer relief to victims of an earthquake that year but soon began to make loans to companies in all sectors of the economy. Significant funding came from the Export-Import Bank, which the United States government had set up. Although much of CORFO's emphasis was on heavy industry, it also loaned money to companies that produced domestic consumer goods. Prominent among them was Manufacturas de Metales (Metal Manufactures) (MADESMA), a producer of home

appliances and many other products made with local metals. Another beneficiary was Manufacturas de Cobre (Copper Manufactures) (MADECO), which produced metal fixtures, among its various products. CORFO made loans as well to other companies that created consumer goods such as electrical appliances, radios, and automobile tires. If Chile had made considerable progress by 1914 towards becoming self-sufficient in the production of goods for domestic consumption, CORFO advanced the process of import substitution even further, including the promotion of consumer goods and the creation of heavy industries as well.

Education for the trades and applied arts

Like a number of other countries in Latin America during the 19th century, Chile recognized the need for industrial education and in 1849 the government established the Escuela de Artes y Oficios (School of Arts and Trades) in Santiago. The plan was to create such schools throughout the country, something that had been done in Uruguay and elsewhere in Latin America. The program at the school included a course of several years to train industrial workers and tradesmen who were knowledgeable about casting, metal construction, boilermaking, carpentry, and electrical work and then to add a certificate for technicians who would have more advanced knowledge of electricity, mechanics, or chemistry. In 1905, some professors from the school, along with a group of architects, engineers, and businessmen, founded a monthly magazine, *El Arte Industrial* (*Industrial Art*), in which they published examples of labels, lettering, and other advertising graphics that could be adapted for advertising purposes.

In 1927, as part of the extensive educational reform that the Ibáñez regime undertook, the curriculum of the School of Arts and Trades was revised and a third level, designed to prepare industrial engineers, was introduced. The addition, as with the changes that the Ministry of Education would legislate for the applied arts, was intended to train workers for a more developed industrial economy.

Chile did not have a School of Applied Arts until 1928. The nation's first art school, the Academy of Fine Arts, was founded in 1849, the same year as the School of Arts and Trades. In 1879 it was integrated into the University of Chile as the School of Fine Arts. In 1904, the school found itself in the middle of a debate about how art could be turned towards productive ends. That year the government proposed to create a School of Decorative Arts, whose graduates would be useful to industry. The new school was envisioned as one that would raise the general level of culture, while also improving the quality of Chile's industrial production.

With the support of the School of Fine Arts' director, the sculptor Virginio Arias (1855–1941), who had studied at the École des Arts Décoratifs in Paris, a new School of Decorative Arts opened in Santiago in 1907. As Eduardo Castillo Espinoza had noted, its courses were based on French examples. They included ornamental and decorative sculpture applied to architecture, modeling in stone or marble, woodworking, metalwork, and the history of ornamental drawing and decorative painting. The thrust of the curriculum was towards the production of decorative objects and interiors rather than the preparation of applied artists for industrial production.

In 1928, the painter and composer Carlos Isamitt (1887–1974), then Director of the School of Fine Arts, decided to close the School of Decorative Arts and replace it with a new School of Applied Arts, whose curriculum would be more closely allied to the needs of the Chilean economy. Isamitt differentiated the new curriculum from its predecessor by emphasizing the various industries that he believed had not realized their potential. He had visited the Exposition Internationale des Arts Décoratifs in Paris as well as some of the applied arts schools in Germany and Austria, preferring their approach to the more traditional one of France's École des Arts Décoratifs. As a Chilean, however, he was concerned with the issue of national identity. He took a strong interest in the

indigenous culture of the Mapuche Indians and in Chile's popular folklore, introducing these topics into discussions about contemporary education in the fine and applied arts, where he called for a new culture that was in accord with what he considered to be the necessities of the nation's race, its land, and its daily life. The year that Isamitt created the new School of Applied Arts, the Ministry of Education closed the School of Fine Arts for a period of several years in order to rethink its objectives. The Ibáñez government sent a group of professors and students to various countries in Europe to strengthen their knowledge of the fine and applied arts so they could return to Chile and introduce new programs and courses as university teachers.

The School of Fine Arts closed at the end of 1928, but the new School of Applied Arts remained open, even during the most difficult economic trials of the early 1930s. The curriculum was quite broad, but not all the studios were in operation during the early years. The range of programs included ceramics, glass, weaving,

Fig. 30.01: Abel Gutiérrez. *Dibujos Indígenas de Chile*, alphabet, 1931. Private Collection.

Fig. 30.02: *Escuela de Artes Plasticas, Seccion Artes Aplicadas*, catalog cover, 1934. Private Collection.

Gutiérrez's students for carpets, stained glass, and architectural detailing that were stimulated by them. On the back cover was an alphabet that was similarly inspired (Fig. 30.01).

In 1929, José Perotti (1893–1956), a painter and sculptor as well as a craftsman who specialized in enamelwork and ceramics, became Director of the School of Applied Arts, and remained in that position for more than 20 years (Fig. 30.02). Early in the 1920s, Perotti had joined the Grupo Montparnasse (Montparnasse Group), whose members—painters and sculptors—challenged the traditional values of Chilean art, promoting instead the paintings of Cézanne and other French modernists including Picasso, Gris, and Léger.

Historian Pedro Álvarez Caselli has raised the question of whether the school under Perotti's direction squarely addressed the technological and functional aspects of products or whether the emphasis remained primarily on their aesthetic form. Álvarez Caselli also notes an Arts and Crafts mentality among some faculty who imagined that the objects they were teaching their students to make were restoring the dignity of everyday artifacts that mechanization had taken away. Perotti himself espoused a view that elevated the craftsman. Like William Morris, he believed that art was for everyone. According to him, there was no separation between the fine and applied arts, as both were united by the quest for beauty, which the artist or the craftsman could equally provide. As a consequence, according to some critics, graduates of the School of Applied Arts did not have a major effect on Chilean industry with the exception of the poster artists, who created a school of Chilean poster design that was perhaps the strongest in Latin America during the interwar years.

Graphic design

Printing and typography

With a relatively high rate of literacy at the end of the 19th century, there were approximately 200 printers

metalwork, goldsmithing, woodworking, ornamental sculpture, graphic arts, and scenography. More than the earlier School of Decorative Arts, the new school strove to create a professional orientation for its students. However, Isamitt continued to emphasize the problem of how professors and students could draw on their national heritage to create products with a local identity rather than one derived from Europe or the United States.

In 1931, Abel Gutiérrez (dates unconfirmed), an architect and professor at the University of Chile, where the School of Applied Arts was located, published a book entitled *Dibujos Indígenas de Chile* (*Indigenous Drawings of Chile*), which contained a collection of motifs from native pottery that could be applied as decoration for industrial products or architecture. Besides drawings of the motifs themselves, the book also included examples of projects by Professor in Chile, albeit many were quite small and possessed limited amounts of type. The three largest printing establishments were the Imprenta Cervantes and the Imprenta y Litografía Barcelona in Santiago and the Sociedad Imprenta y Litografía Universo in Valparaíso. Types and vignettes came mainly from England and France. In the 1930s, modern decorative typefaces such as Morris Fuller Benton's Broadway from the American Typefounders were popular as was a style of Art Deco lettering that was influenced by French precedents. Two journals, *Revista Tipográfica* and *Noticias Gráficas*, each of which was founded in 1892, were dedicated to the study of the graphic arts. The editor of both was the Spanish émigré Manuel Ramos Ochotorena (dates unconfirmed), who published articles on printing history as well as new technologies such as photoengraving, which was introduced to Chile around 1892. Gradually, photoengraving began to replace lithography, which resulted in the publication of more photographs in the popular magazines.

As a result of the strong labor movement that had originated in the nitrate mines during the 19th century, printers and typesetters formed their own labor organizations. *El Tipógrafo* (*The Typographer*), a publication founded in 1878, was perhaps the first to promote the workers in the printing industry. In 1892 the Liga General del Arte de la Imprenta en Chile (General League of the Chilean Printing Art) was created to defend the rights of workers in the printing plants. After a series of strikes and the formation of several other organizations, the Federación Obrera de la Imprenta de Chile (FOICH} (Federation of Chilean Printing Workers) was founded in 1921 and became a national organization with branches in numerous cities.

Periodicals and books

Pedro Álvarez Caselli has noted that by 1910 Chile had more than 400 magazines and newspapers, a number that jumped to well over 700 by 1923. The first illustrated magazine to be printed by photoengraving was *El Payaso* (*The Clown*), which appeared in 1897

but folded the following year. Its art director was the prominent architect Josué Smith Solar (1867–1938), who had studied in the United States and traveled in Europe. Like *La Revista Cómica* (*The Comic Review*), the first illustrated magazine to be published in Chile, *El Payaso* enhanced its graphic effects with the use of color printing. Other illustrated magazines of the late 1890s, many inspired by the *Illustrated London News*, were *La Revista Ilustrada* (*The Illustrated Review*) and *La Revista de Santiago* (*The Santiago Review*).

The leading artists who created covers for these and other publications such as *Chile Ilustrada* (*Chile Illustrated*) were Alejandro Fauré (1865–1912) and Luis Fernando Rojas (1857–1942). The two can probably be considered as Chile's first commercial artists since their work ranged from magazine illustrations and covers to advertising posters. Fauré, a skilled draftsman, initially became active as a commercial artist in the 1890s. Within a decade, he was drawing covers for all the major illustrated magazines and served as art director for two of them, *La Lira Chilena* (*The Chilean Lyre*) and *Noticias Graficas*. Fauré had great talent as a draftsman but most of his drawings and lettering were derived from European sources, notably the Symbolist-inspired drawings and decorative ornament of Art Nouveau, as well as the posters of Jules Chéret and the ceremonial iconography of Victorian England (Fig. 30.03).

Beginning around 1875, Rojas began to make his mark as an illustrator in the popular press. He produced numerous illustrations, many portraits of famous Chileans, and became a specialist in portrayals of military figures and battle scenes. He also collaborated on several large pictorial albums such as the *Álbum de las Glorias de Chile* (*Album of Chilean Glories*) and the *Historia General de Chile* (*General History of Chile*). In 1895, he co-founded the aforementioned *La Revista Cómica*, while contributing illustrations to various other publications. Although he occasionally drew on Art Nouveau iconography, Rojas was primarily a 19th-century realist who specialized in art for lithographic production. Other magazine art directors of the

Fig. 30.03: *La Lira Chilena*, cover, c. 1905. Private Collection.

period include Emilio Dupré (dates unconfirmed), the Italian émigré José Foradori (dates unconfirmed), and the Spaniard Juan Martín (dates unconfirmed).

In 1905, the Chilean businessman Agustín Edwards Mac-Clure founded the Editorial Zig-Zag in Santiago. Within a few years, it became a large publishing conglomerate with numerous magazines and newspapers. Edwards Mac-Clure's previous publishing involvement was with the newspaper *El Mercurio de Santiago,* which he founded in 1900. One of his aims in establishing the Editorial Zig-Zag was to compete with the Imprenta Universo in Valparaíso, publisher

of *Sucesos,* an illustrated magazine of contemporary life that had been founded in 1902.

Before launching the magazine *Zig-Zag,* Edwards Mac-Clure traveled to the United States to buy the most advanced printing equipment and brought back an American manager, William Phillips, to run it. The publication was entirely in color and sold for a very low price. *Zig-Zag*'s first cover depicted a baby—representing the new magazine—stepping out of an eggshell held by a figure in a winged helmet who may be the Greek god Hermes. Its designer was the French artist Paul Dufresne (dates unconfirmed), whom Edwards Mac-Clure had hired from Paris to be the magazine's art director (Plate 55). Among the first illustrators were José Foradori and Carlos Zorzi (dates unconfirmed), both émigrés from Italy who designed posters as well; the French engraver León Bazin (dates unconfirmed); and the Spanish artist and art director Juan Martín. Besides illustrations, Julio Bozo (1879–1942), known by the name Moustache, was a leading cartoonist as was José Délano (dates unconfirmed), whose pen name was Coke. Coke became one of Chile's most important satirical artists and in 1931 he founded his own weekly magazine, *Topaze,* which conveyed a sense of the times through a number of fictional characters he created such as the peasant Juan Verdejo. Other artists who drew for *Zig-Zag* included Pedro Subercaseaux (1880–1956), known as Lustig, and Edmundo Searle (1894–1982). Subercaseaux drew a comic strip whose main characters were Don Federico Von Pilsner and his friend Don Otto, both German caricatures, and Von Pilsner's dachshund, Dudelsackpfeifergeselle. Searle specialized in cartoons that depicted the foibles of the Chilean aristocracy. Besides *Zig-Zag,* he drew for other publications in Chile and spent considerable time abroad, where he produced cartoons for major newspapers and magazines.

Nathaniel Cox Méndez (date unconfirmed), considered to be Chile's leading caricaturist of the time, specialized in portraits that were almost realistic except for slight deformations that accentuated the subject's personality. Other political caricaturists from *Zig-Zag's* early years were Lamberto Caro (dates unconfirmed), Emilio Álvarez (dates unconfirmed), Santiago Pulgar (dates unconfirmed), and Juan Oliver (dates unconfirmed). Oliver emigrated to the United States, where he had a successful career as an advertising artist.

It was a major achievement of Edwards Mac-Clure to attract so many and such diverse artists to his publishing ventures. Within several years of launching *Zig-Zag*, he introduced a number of other magazines including *El Peneca* (*The Youth*), a children's magazine, and *Corre-Viela* in 1908; *Selecta*, an art review, and *Familia* (*Family*), a women's publication, in 1909; and *Pacífico Magazine* in 1913. In 1919, Edwards moved on to other ventures and sold the Editorial Zig-Zag to his rival, Gustavo Helfmann, owner of the Imprenta Universo.

Many of the *Zig-Zag* artists also drew for other publications in the editorial group but some new artists were hired as the publishing empire founded by Edwards Mac-Clure expanded. For *El Peneca*, Walter Barbier (dates unconfirmed) drew several comic strips including *The Adventures of Huauhuau* and *The Levacorta Family*. In 1932, the illustrator Mario Silva Ossa (1913–1950), who published his drawings under the name Coré, joined the art staff of *El Peneca*. He drew many covers as well as the graphic series *Quintín the Adventurer*. Filled with stories, poems, drawings, and photographs, *El Peneca* circulated widely in Latin America, and Coré's drawings gained considerable notoriety throughout the continent.

The European influence was evident on the covers of some magazines outside the Editorial Zig-Zag group. In the 1920s, covers by Julio Arévale (dates unconfirmed) for *Para Todos*, a magazine with the same name as its Brazilian counterpart, recalled the Jazz Age cartoons of American publications and the French fashion illustrations of the *Gazette du Bon Ton*. Later, in the 1930s, Art Deco motifs were evident on covers of publications such as the film magazine *Ecran*.

Although Santiago and Valparaíso were the principal centers for magazine publishing, Pedro Álvarez Caselli has noted that a number of illustrated magazines also appeared in some of Chile's smaller cities. The review *El Polar* was first published in Punta Arenas in 1905. A weekly magazine of commerce and literature, it featured rough woodcuts or linoleum cuts as cover illustrations with an undistinguished masthead that harkened back to the 19th century. *Austral,* first published in Valdiva in 1913, adopted a graphic approach similar to the most successful of the Editorial Zig-Zag publications. In Iquique, capital of Chile's northernmost region, a Chilean version of the Argentine weekly illustrated magazine *Caras y Caritas* appeared, following a similar editorial and artistic direction as its progenitor in Buenos Aires.

Besides the growing number of magazines, book production expanded considerably in the 1920s and 1930s. Earlier, the large printing establishments like Imprenta Cervantes, Imprenta Universo, and Imprenta y Lithografía Barcelona, which were publishers as well as printers, ceded part of the literary market to the new expanding publishing houses like Editorial Zig-Zag, which produced books as well as magazines, and Editorial Ercilla, a book publisher with its own illustrated magazine that competed with *Zig-Zag*. Other large book publishers included Editorial Osiris, Editorial Nascimento, and Editorial Cultura. However, as Bernard Subercaseux writes, most publishers did not emphasize the design of their books or their covers. They focused on the practical matters of printing and distribution rather than the visual aspects. One exception was the Editorial Nascimento, which devoted considerable attention to its typography and layouts.

Large numbers of books were published. By the end of 1936, for example, Editorial Ercilla had approximately 800 titles in its catalog. The covers of books by the major publishers frequently featured simple typography and decorative borders. Lettering could vary between traditional and modern forms, as could the ornamental designs. Once students began to graduate from the School of Applied Arts in the 1930s, a few received commissions for more modern covers with illustrations and contemporary Deco lettering.

In the mid-1930s, the painter and graphic artist Gustavo Carrasco (1907–1999), who had studied at the School of Fine Arts in Santiago with the Russian émigré artist Boris Grigoriev (1886–1939), and also took courses at the School of Applied Arts in Berlin, began to work for Editorial Zig-Zag and in 1937 he designed a series of attractive covers for their Library of Chilean Writers. In 1940, Editorial Zig-Zag hired as its art director Mauricio Amster, a Pole who had emigrated to Spain in 1930 and then to Chile in 1939. Amster had already gained a considerable reputation as a book designer in Spain, where he also created posters for the anti-fascist movement (see Chapter 24). At Editorial Zig-Zag, Amster worked with illustrators like Coré and sometimes designed as many as three or four books a day. He was also a co-founder of a small press, Editorial Cruz del Sur, which published a number of books by prominent Chilean authors. In 1944, he was a founder of the cultural review *Babel*, which he also designed.

Advertising, logotypes, posters

By 1900, Chile had a developed advertising culture, due to a thriving domestic consumer market. The first advertising agency, La Sudamérica, opened in 1906. It offered a number of services including placing ads in newspapers and magazines, painting large lettered signs, and distributing small notices in public places. In 1928, Carlos Bofill (1887–d.o.d. unconfirmed) opened an advertising office that functioned like a modern publicity agency. At first he concentrated on calendars and outdoor advertising, though he also sought to provide integrated services for his clients. Among the difficulties he faced was finding commercial artists who could do original drawings rather than copy ads from foreign magazines. It was also hard to find professional layout artists as well as an adequate selection of typefaces. In 1935, Bofill merged his office with that

of Arturo Edwards to form Bofill, Edwards y Cía. Before the merger, Edwards had worked extensively with Argentine commercial artists to create campaigns whose drawings were central in calling attention to the products. Competitors of Bofill, Edwards included Propaganda Fonck, founded in 1931 by a German immigrant, Oscar Fonck, and two companies established in 1936, the agency of Pablo Petrowitsch, who also worked with Argentine professionals, and Lucho Arón Publicidad. Early advertisements that were inserted in newspapers and magazines usually included a small black and white drawing accompanied by extensive copy.

Prominent artists for advertising campaigns were often the well-known illustrators and caricaturists who worked for the mass magazines. Among them was Moustache, who was responsible for numerous campaigns, notably one for Tisphorine, a tonic that suppressed the appetite. Magazine ads before World War I were often in color and frequently featured elaborate lettering with illustrations and occasional Art Nouveau ornaments added. As photography became more popular, it replaced illustrations, although hand lettering and decorative borders were often combined with photographic images. After 1920, when the United States became Chile's major economic partner, American popular magazines arrived in abundance and local artists and advertisers could see the sophisticated color ads with their "reason why" copy. However, American advertising was only one influence in the post-war years. French and Italian posters and illustration were also important sources; in fact Chilean illustrators and commercial artists had a long tradition of looking to France rather than the United States for images of modernity.

Trademarks also became popular in the 1920s and 1930s and a number of marks were created that have endured for years. Similar to French designer Charles Loupot's two waiters who serve as the trademark for St. Raphael Quinine, the trademark for Viña Santa Carolina (Santa Carolina Vineyard)—a waiter striding forward with a bottle of wine on a tray in one hand and a tray with three glasses in the other—is attributed to the cartoonist Edmundo Searle. Other durable marks include the Dutch girl who personified Klenzo detergent—a reminder of the American Dutch Maid mark, Los Andes matches, and the lettering for Gath y Chaves, the exclusive department store with a large advertising budget.

From the 1930s, advertising created abroad for American products was widespread and competed with locally produced advertising. As in Cuba, where American products dominated the economy, American product ads were mostly created by advertising agencies in New York and introduced in Latin America with Spanish texts.

Though newspaper and magazine advertising was extensive, given the large number of daily, weekly, and monthly publications, posters remained a popular publicity medium. They were central to the intense competition between two tea companies, Té Ratampuro and Té Demonio, around 1906. Luis Fernando Rojas designed lithographic posters for both companies. His poster for Té Ratampuro was typical of late 19th-century advertising in Europe and the United States. It featured an image that had nothing to do with the product, in this case a clown holding a teapot and a box of tea, flanked by two dancing girls. The lettering consisted mainly of three-dimensional forms that comprised a trite slogan, "Ratampuro is the better tea" (Plate 56).

At the beginning of the century, the Imprenta Barcelona held a series of poster competitions that brought to public attention the highly developed European graphic styles, notably Art Nouveau, that impressed Chilean artists at the time. When the magazine *Zig-Zag* was launched in 1905, the principal medium to disseminate news of its publication was the poster. The one chosen to promote the journal was simply an enlarged version of the aforementioned cover by Paul Dufresne. The publisher had 100,000 copies printed in New York and then distributed them

throughout Chile. Even after the magazine was sold in 1919, the new publisher Gustavo Helfmann continued to promote special issues with posters.

A significant date for the development of the poster in Chile is 1916, when the artist Otto Georgi (1890–1969), a former painting student at the School of Fine Arts in Santiago, won first prize in a poster competition sponsored by the Federation of Students, a university group. The poster commemorated an annual event known as the Spring Festival or Day of the Students. Georgi portrayed three figures, a clown and two masked women, set against a background of revelry. The flatness of the composition and the stylized figures distinguish the design from the earlier posters of Fauré and Rojas, which continued the 19th-century realist tradition.

For the next three years, the students' poster competition was won by another artist, Isaías Cabezón (1891–1963), who, like Georgi, had studied painting at the School of Fine Arts. There are vague references in Cabezón's posters to the carefree gestures of Jules Chéret's Belle Epoque figures, although Cabezón's energetic dancers display a wild energy that is lacking in the Chéret's posters.

With money gained from the poster competitions, Cabezón traveled in Europe, where he studied painting in Paris, participated in several salons, and became acquainted with modern tendencies in European art including Fauvism and Expressionism. When he returned to Santiago, he joined the Montparnasse Group, continued painting, and worked as a set designer and illustrator. Early in 1928, Carlos Isamitt, director of the School of Fine Arts, invited him to head a studio for decorative composition and poster design, the first of its kind in Chile. There Cabezón developed a series of exercises that engaged his students with studies of color, composition, and lettering that derived from European modern art. The studio was short-lived, however, since the Ministry of Education closed the School of Fine Arts that year.

As a consequence, Cabezón received funding to

supervise the studies of a group of students, known as the "Generation of 28," who were sent to Europe for five years to further their studies of the fine and applied arts so they could return to create an improved arts curriculum in Chile. He was joined in his supervisory duties by the painter Camilo Mori (1896–1973), a founding member of the Grupo Montparnasse, who had recently been named director of the National Museum of Fine Arts.

In the early 1930s, the School of Applied Arts at the University of Chile introduced a new course in poster design, headed by the painter Ana Cortés (1895–1998), the first woman to teach in a Chilean school of art or applied arts. In 1925, Cortés had gone to Paris, where she studied with the Cubist artist André Lhote. She became a strong advocate for modern art when she returned to Chile in 1928. In her course, Cortés introduced a methodology that emphasized the basic elements of composition and the fact that a poster was first and foremost a design and not an illustration. As a professor of drawing in the university's School of Architecture, Camilo Mori was also a strong influence on students interested in poster design.

A number of students who graduated from the School of Applied Arts became leading poster designers during the 1930s, a time when the poster flourished in Chile. These graduates included Arturo Adriazola (dates unconfirmed), Luis Troncoso (dates unconfirmed), Fernando Ibarra (dates unconfirmed), Nicolas Martínez (dates unconfirmed), Santiago Nattino (1921–1985), Lupercio Arancibia (dates unconfirmed), Héctor Cáceres (dates unconfirmed), and Luis Oviedo (dates unconfirmed). Besides them, Mori was extremely active, perhaps the most active, as a poster designer in the 1930s and early 1940s. For the most part, Mori's posters were conceptual rather than illustrative, but not all clients were comfortable leaving illustration behind. Mori tried to find a balance in a series of posters he created for the magazine *Zig-Zag* to announce a number of special issues. Other posters he designed for cultural or political events usually featured a strong graphic image that conveyed the message. Although there was an impetus among Chilean poster designers to distance themselves from the influence of Cassandre, Loupot, and Carlu in France, Mori's posters had a directness that was comparable to Cassandre's. This was evident in his poster for an exhibition of Chilean contemporary art, which featured a palette with colors on it, arranged to signify the Chilean flag. Mori was a highly sought after poster designer, whose clients ranged from government agencies and commercial enterprises to theaters and museums, publishers, and political parties.

The poster culture in Chile was enhanced in the late 1930s by the arrival of several émigré designers from Europe, notably Kitty Goldmann (dates unconfirmed) from Austria, and Francisco Otta (1908–1999) from Czechoslovakia. Both contributed to the creation of a modern style. Goldmann was from a comfortable Viennese family that moved in that city's intellectual and artistic circles. She arrived in Chile around 1939 and worked for a variety of clients, doing posters for government and political events as well as commercial concerns. Francisco Otta, who reached Chile in 1940, had a broad background in linguistics, law, art history, and painting. Like Goldmann, he designed posters for numerous organizations and causes. A major commercial client was Shell Oil, for whom he did a series of posters that featured stylized automobiles and other images combined with simple copy lines.

The burgeoning of the poster movement in the late 1930s was supported by commissions from a number of civic organizations and causes as well as municipalities and the federal government, which had a strong involvement with the economy and numerous social programs. The government commissioned posters for the national census, a literacy campaign, rail travel, and tourism, while the city of Santiago relied on the poster to announce its 4th Centenary, art museums publicized exhibitions, political groups urged solidarity with occupied countries in Europe, and companies like Shell and Bayer and the Chilean Steamship Line advertised their products and services. Chile's nitrate producers had a long tradition of promoting their product through various publicity materials and over time commissioned a number of posters for this purpose.

Motivated perhaps by the strong labor organization in the printing trades, a group of poster designers decided in 1942 to form the Unión Cartelistas de Chile (Chilean Poster Designers' Union). Its president was Camilo Mori, a political activist with a left-wing orientation, and its members included most of the prominent Chilean poster designers as well as several of the émigré artists. The group planned to hold annual salons, publish a technical bulletin, and mount a large retrospective of Chilean posters. While none of these events came to pass, the group did organize an exhibit of contemporary posters in 1944.

Graphics on the left

Graphics of the political left in Chile from the turn of the century to the end of the 1930s followed conventional 19th-century forms, notably publications to inform and persuade and propaganda for social causes. Numerous publications—newsletters, bulletins, and journals—were designed for workers in the typographic industry such as the members of the Sociedad Unión de los Tipografos (Typographers' Union Society), who had their own bulletin with an illustrated cover. After World War II, the émigré book designer Mauricio Amster created a strong cover for the bulletin that featured a griffin outlined in black with bold red letters underneath. The leftist political groups, notably the Socialist Party, the Socialist Workers' Party, the Federation of Socialist Youth, and the Communist Party of Chile also had their own publications including *El Socialista* (*The Socialist*), *Consigna* (*Order*), *Rumbos* (*Directions*), *Barricada* (*Barricade*), *El Despertar del Pueblo* (*The People Wake Up*), *El Siglo* (*The Century*), and *Bandera Roja* (*Red Flag*).

Posters played an important role among the left. Most of the artists who created posters for the Socialist

or Communist Party were graduates of the School of Applied Arts, where Eduardo Castillo Espinoza has described the atmosphere as being extremely open politically. The school was hospitable to students from working-class backgrounds and many studied in its evening classes as well as its daytime programs.

Fernando Marcos (dates unconfirmed), a graduate of the school, was an active designer for the Federation of Socialist Youth. He worked on the youth federation's magazine *Rumbos*, where he collaborated with the artist Mario Corvalán (dates unconfirmed), who signed his design work KOR. Marcos also designed posters for the youth federation, drawing his visual references from the posters of the Russian Revolution as well as the graphics that followed the revolution in Mexico. Posters of the Spanish Civil War were also an influence on Marcos, as they were on other designers on the left. Marcos's poster for a conference of socialist youth shows three militant figures—two men and a woman—marching forward Soviet-style. A factory in the background represents industrial production and the youth federation's flag with its red star logo serves as a background for the marching youth (Fig. 30.04). As well, Marcos designed a poster for the Socialist Party that promoted land reform, presenting an imposing peasant holding a strip of land with a small house and furrowed field on it.

Poster designers who were members of the Communist Party included Camilo Mori, Carlos Sagredo (dates unconfirmed), Santiago Nattino, and Luis Oviedo. Compared to Marcos's adoption of militant imagery that recalled the Russian Revolution or the Spanish Civil War, Mori remained committed to a modernist European style that was conceptual rather than tendentious. For a 1940 poster that announced the relaunch of the Communist Party's newspaper *El Siglo*, he chose a profiled head and an open hand to represent a statement being shouted out and he juxtaposed these with a page that bore the masthead of the newspaper. Mori linked the new publication to the national interest by distributing the parts of the Chilean flag among the

Fig. 30.04: Fernando Marcos, II National Days of Socialist Youth, poster, 1936. Private Collection.

poster's iconic elements. Another of the party members, Luis Oviedo, founded Estudios Norte (North Studios), where he produced posters using the inexpensive silkscreen technique.

Argentina

By the turn of the century, Argentina had the largest and most articulate middle class in Latin America, due in part to the success of its export activities but also due to its sizeable immigrant population, which arrived with valuable skills and the initiative to succeed. Some brought financial capital as well. Many in this class gravitated to professions rather than to industry and consequently industrial development moved slowly

before World War I. Nonetheless, by 1914, two-thirds of Argentina's industrial enterprises belonged to foreign-born owners.

Motivation to build domestic industries may have been diminished by the strong involvement of Britain in Argentina's economy. British firms had built the railroads, urban tramways, and other civic projects, while also playing a role in the meat packing industry. It was even a British firm that opened one of the first department stores in Buenos Aires, a branch of the London emporium Harrods, which began doing business there in 1912. Like its counterparts, Gath & Chávez, which opened in 1905, Bazar La Luna, and Bazar París, Harrods offered all the latest imported goods for an urban population that could afford to live comfortably. By the 1920s, the middle-class standard of living in Argentine cities was comparable to that in the United States and Europe.

One enterprise started by an immigrant entrepreneur was Alpargatas S.A., a shoe company that a Basque, Juan Etchegaray (dates unconfirmed) founded in 1883 with a Scottish partner, Douglas Fraser. The company originally manufactured cheap shoes with canvas tops and soles of jute rope or twine. Peasants and laborers in Spain traditionally wore them. In 1907, Alpargatas S.A. expanded to Brazil, where it added oilcloth and canvas tarpaulins to its product line. Owners of coffee plantations valued the shoes because of their light soles, which meant that workers did not damage the coffee beans when they walked on them. In 1933, the company began to produce shoes with vulcanized rubber soles instead of hemp ones.

Industry was also featured at the Exposición International del Centenario (The National Centenary Exposition), held in Buenos Aires in 1910 to celebrate Argentina's May Revolution of a century earlier. Although agriculture and cattle raising, two of Argentina's largest export enterprises, were highlighted in a prominent pavilion, there was a separate pavilion for industry where industrial machinery was on display. The exhibition included a number of foreign pavilions, in this instance those from Italy, Spain, and Germany—all of which had large immigrant populations in Argentina—as well as Britain with its major industrial commitments in the country, and several other nations. Many of the buildings were designed in the Art Nouveau style, which was subsequently perpetuated in Buenos Aires by some of the Italian architects including Francisco Gianotti (1881–1967) and Virginio Colombo (1885–1927). Between them, they designed several pavilions for the exhibition including Gianotti's completion of the Pavilion of Italy and they continued to work in Argentina after the exhibition.

As in Europe, villas in the Art Nouveau style were commissioned by the wealthy. Buenos Aires had its own counterparts to the urban villas of Guimard in Paris and Horta in Brussels. Two hallmarks of these buildings were stained-glass window panels and ornate ironwork for balconies, doors, and gates. They were evident in the design of some commercial buildings as well. Occasionally the image in a stained-glass window of a commercial building would be an advertisement for a company's product. French foundries that made decorative ironwork had representatives in Buenos Aires to secure commissions, while other foundries such as Pedro Vasena & Sons were local. Vasena's catalog displayed objects that ranged from gates and balconies to bandstands and storefronts.

Industry developed gradually during the 1920s, fostered in part by groups like the Unión Industrial Argentina, which organized exhibitions and undertook other activities to promote industrial growth. General Motors began to export Chevrolet Double Phaeton models to Argentina in 1924 and these met with great success. The following year, GM decided to reduce its costs by setting up an assembly line, where it produced a truck chassis and several automobile models including a version of the Double Phaeton, known as the *Especial Argentino*, which was designed particularly for the Argentine market. Following an increase in sales, GM added Oldsmobiles, Oaklands, and Pontiacs to their line.

In 1928, the chassis of the Chevrolet Double Phaeton was used for a new locally designed public transport vehicle, known as a *colectivo* (collective), whose form was redesigned several times before World War II. These were sold to private owners and were produced in the thousands. They were used for urban transport and provided stiff competition to the outmoded British street railway system of Buenos Aires. The city's residents patronized them as acts of resistance to the domination of the British trams. As they did in India, the British manufactured the tramcars in England and exported them to Argentina rather than build up an Argentine industry that could both train and employ local workers. However, the Germans and the Americans acted similarly to provide vehicles manufactured in their respective countries for the tramlines they owned in other Argentine cities.

The American stock market crash of 1929 severely affected Argentine exports, and the following year a military coup in Argentina brought an end to constitutional government. The new authoritarian regime was subsequently run until the end of World War II by a succession of military men including General Augustín Justo (1932–1938), with occasional civilian puppets. Military rule was continued after the war when Juan Perón was elected president in 1946.

Small businesses continued to dominate the industrial economy during the 1930s, but a number of large firms also succeeded. Most produced beer, cigarettes, matches, or processed foods, but Torcuato Di Tella's Sociedad Industrial Americana de Maquinarias (American Industrial Machinery Society) manufactured a variety of appliances under license from American companies. Beginning in 1940, the American firm Frigidaire began to manufacture refrigerators in a large Buenos Aires factory where General Motors, its parent company, produced automobiles.

A few architects were involved with furniture design, primarily as integral components of building projects. Notable among them was Alejandro Bustillo (1889–1982), who completed the Llao-Llao Hotel in

San Carlos de Bariloche in 1939. Originally a wooden structure, it burned down the year it was completed and was rebuilt the following year in concrete. While the Llao-Llao Hotel was designed in a rustic chalet style, Bustillo also designed modernist residences and worked extensively in a French Neo-Classical style, which he adopted for other hotels as well as the National Bank. For these buildings, he designed furniture—chaise longues for the hotels, and office furniture for the bank—that derived from Neo-Classical models. He collaborated on these projects with a team of architects who called themselves the Comte group.

Bustillo worked with the group, on the Llao-Llao Hotel interior as well. They adopted Louis XVI designs, which they stripped of details and to which they added elements from traditional Argentine furniture. They chose a mix of dark and light woods and upholstered the furniture with brightly colored hand-made fabrics. The result was a repertoire of forms that the Comte group used in other projects throughout the region until the end of World War II.

The group's reputation was enhanced in 1939 when the French furniture and interior designer, Jean-Michel Frank (1895–1941), who was prominent among the Parisian Art Deco designers, joined their staff. During his brief stay in Argentina before he left for New York, Frank designed several variants of an easy chair for the Llao-Llao Hotel lounge. Due to its bulk, it was known as the "elephant" chair, and to reinforce the hotel's rustic atmosphere, the chairs were covered with expensive animal hides.

The Russian architect Wladimiro Acosta (1900–1967) came to Argentina in 1929, having previously studied architecture and engineering in Italy and Germany. He was strongly influenced by the German and Swiss rationalist planners and architects like Ernst May, chief architect of the Neue Frankfurt, and Hannes Meyer, who joined the Bauhaus faculty in 1927 and remained at the school until 1930. Acosta, who found limited opportunities to apply his modernist architectural and planning ideas in Argentina, designed a tubular steel cantilevered chair, which was rare among modern furniture designs in Latin America. He had a major influence on students in Argentina's architectural schools and became an impetus to thinking about teaching design at the university level in conjunction with architecture.

Among modern furniture by architects in Argentina, the one piece that achieved international recognition was designed in 1938–1939 by Grupo Austral, a partnership of three architects: Antoni Bonet (1913–1989), who had recently immigrated from Spain because of the Spanish Civil War, and two Argentinians, Jorge Ferrari-Hardoy (1914–1977) and Juan Kurchan (1913–1975). All had worked in Le Corbusier's Paris office and Bonet had been a member of the Catalan group of modernist architects and designers, GATPAC. Known as the BKF chair, or more popularly the Hardoy chair or "Butterfly Chair" because of its shape, the piece originally consisted of an iron frame over which was stretched a suspended leather sling (Fig. 30.05). Given the prevalence of cattle in Argentina, the leather sling made economic sense, but in later years when the chair was widely reproduced, an inexpensive canvas sling replaced the leather one.

Fig. 30.05: Grupo Austral, BKF chair, 1938. © 2014. Digital image, The Museum of Modern Art, New York/Scala, Florence.

Furniture design was also central to the low-cost housing that the Hogar Obrero Cooperativa (Workers' Housing Cooperative) built. The cooperative, which was founded in 1905 by members of the Argentine Socialist Party including Juan B. Justo (1865–1928) and Nicolás Repetto (1871–1965), built thousands of low-cost homes for working-class consumers. As part of a continuous process of design improvement, the cooperative held an exhibition dedicated to the ideal home in Buenos Aires in 1934. Among the topics that were examined was the rational use of furniture.

Besides building homes, the Hogar Obrero Cooperativa created a network of cooperative super-markets throughout Argentina called Supercoops. The cooperative's broad approach to housing and working-class needs bears some similarity to the program of the Neue Frankfurt in Germany, the difference being that the Neue Frankfurt was confined to housing develop-ments in a single city and served far fewer people than the Hogar Obrero Cooperativa.

As the Argentine government became more repressive during the 1930s, the Hogar Obrero Cooperativa, with its emphasis on class solidarity and cooperative living, was one form of resistance to the dictatorship of General Justo and those who followed him. Under Justo, the government also began the planning and design of the Argentine Pavilion for the 1939 World's Fair in New York, which was designed jointly by Armando d'Ans (dates unconfirmed) and the American architect Aymar Embury (1880–1966). Intended to convey the image of a modern industrial nation, the pavilion featured four monumental pylons in front, along with sizeable illuminated letters that spelled out "Argentina." The walls of the large entrance hall were composed of glass showcases that featured major products along with dioramas of Argentine life. In the pavilion's theater, films were shown that presented examples of Argentine scenery and industrial activity. With less emphasis on the past and more on the country's present and future, the pavilion and exhibition design successfully positioned Argentina as an industrial leader among the Latin American nations, a fact that was corroborated by the steady pace of industrialization the country maintained during the 1920s and 1930s.

Commercial art, advertising, and publishing

Illustrated magazines and newspapers
Though Buenos Aires has a long history as a provincial city, it only became the capital of Argentina in 1880, a factor that stimulated the city's cultural life. The first illustrated magazine to be published in the new capital was *Don Quijote*, which appeared in 1884 and continued until 1905. Drawing on the rich heritage of French political satire and caricature as well as the humorous writing and illustrations of Britain's *Punch*, *Don Quijote* and the illustrated magazines that followed it nonetheless created their own tradition of political and cultural journalism.

The magazine that set the strongest precedent for other Argentine illustrated magazines was *Caras y Caretas* (*Faces and Masks*), which first appeared in Montevideo, Uruguay, in 1890. It was founded by a Spaniard, Eustaquio Pellicer (1859–1937), who relaunched the magazine as a weekly in Buenos Aires in 1898 along with a fellow Spaniard, the artist Manuel Mayol (1865–1929), who had earlier published drawings in *Don Quijote* under the pseudonym Heraclitus and who played a strong role in developing the magazine's artistic side.

Caras y Caretas built a sizeable audience with its broad coverage of art, literature, and current events. It was heavily illustrated and successfully combined humor with serious journalism. The art directors of *Caras y Caretas* and other illustrated magazines selected the artists to illustrate the covers, articles, and stories and supervised the layouts of the spreads and the design of the lettering. Among them was Eduardo Álvarez (1892–1967), a painter, caricaturist, and illustrator who had also worked for the magazine as a retoucher, layout artist, and letterer. Included among the weekly's comic illustrations were the forerunners of Argentina's *historietas* or comic strips. The first *historieta* to be published in *Caras y Caretas* was *Viruta y Chicharrón*, which originally appeared in 1912.

The multicolored covers featured humorous drawings or caricatures, while the layouts varied greatly from full-page comic drawings to more somber illustrations of articles and fiction. The drawing quality ranged widely from sophisticated to somewhat awkward, as did the layouts, which sometimes mimicked Art Nouveau lettering and had borders that consisted of whiplash lines. Some artists employed a drawing style adopted from Art Nouveau, which was known in Buenos Aires as *arte moderno* or modern art.

During the years of its publication between 1898 and 1941, *Caras y Caretas* attracted many outstanding caricaturists, artists, illustrators, and journalists from Argentina as well as other countries including Spain, Italy, Uruguay, Bolivia, and Peru. These included the Uruguayan artists Aurelio Giménez (1877–1910), who was also a co-founder of another weekly, *La Vida Moderna* (*Modern Life*); Alejandro Roux (1902–1960), a prolific artist who worked for numerous magazines besides *Caras y Caretas*; and the Peruvian artist and caricaturist Julio Málaga Grenet (1886–1963), who later became art director of the newspaper *La Nación* and is considered to be of one of Argentina's first advertising artists. Among the most prominent of the *Caras y Caretas* artists was José María Cao (1862–1918), who arrived in Buenos Aires as a young man from Galicia in north-east Spain. Cao specialized in political caricature and early in his career he was briefly jailed for one of his drawings of a leading Argentine political figure.

Besides Cao, another Spanish artist, Alejandro Sirio (1890–1953), got a start with *Caras y Caretas*. Though capable of comic drawings and caricature, Sirio aspired to a more delicate and refined technique, which he developed through black and white line drawings that combined a graceful linear style with intricate textures and occasional strong contrasts with black massed areas. Sirio was perhaps Argentina's first all-round commercial artist who could draw for the weekly magazines and daily newspapers, create film posters, or illustrate books. For the magazines, he contributed besides illustrations small ornate vignettes and calligraphic lettering in a variety of decorative styles. His most memorable work is the series of dense dramatic illustrations he drew for Enrique Laretta's historic novel *La Gloria de Don Ramiro* of 1908 (Fig. 30.06). It would not be difficult to think of Sirio as an Argentine Aubrey Beardsley but besides his debt to the English artist he drew from many other sources to finally forge a style of his own.

The large community of caricaturists, illustrators, and commercial artists as well as popular authors and journalists resident in Buenos Aires from the late 1890s on made possible a spate of other weekly and monthly magazines as well as newspapers that both complemented and competed with *Caras y Caretas*. In 1915, *Caras y Caretas* inaugurated a monthly magazine called *Plus Ultra*, which had high graphic standards and was directed particularly to the Spanish immigrant community. A direct competitor with *Caras y Caretas* was *Fray Mocho*, which adopted as its title the nickname of *Caras y Caretas*'s first editor.

Just a few years after *Caras y Caretas* started, an Englishman, Don Alberto Haynes, inaugurated a magazine for families, which he called *El Hogar* (*The Home*). Compared to *Caras y Caretas*, it became a general interest magazine for an audience less attuned to political satire, although Haynes hired many of the artists who worked for *Caras y Caretas* to illustrate articles in *El Hogar*. One of his principal collaborators was Alejandro Sirio. Haynes began to build a publishing empire with other illustrated magazines, notably *El Mundo Argentino* (*Argentine World*), and more specialized publications such as *Mundo Deportivo* (*Sports World*), *Mundo Agrario* (*Agrarian World*), and *Mundo Infantil* (*Children's World*). The newspaper Haynes founded, *El Mundo*, competed with Buenos Aires' two oldest papers, *La Prensa* (*The Press*) and *La Nación* (*The Nation*), which owned both

Fig. 30.06: Alejandro Sirio, *La Gloria de Don Ramiro*, illustration, 1908. Private Collection.

Caras y Caretas and *Plus Ultra*. Alejandro Sirio had collaborated extensively with those two publications and for many years he also served as a staff artist for *La Nación*, having replaced José María Cao.

Advertising

Due to the large number of daily, weekly, and monthly publications in Buenos Aires, advertising flourished and many artists who did editorial illustration also illustrated advertisements. Argentina produced little in the way of hard goods, so many of the ads were for food and drink, cigarettes, clothing, health and hygiene products, and cosmetics. Most were from domestic manufacturers, but some foreign companies like Lux Soap advertised extensively. Hard goods from abroad such as sewing machines and automobiles were also promoted through advertising. The ads appeared mainly in the illustrated magazines and daily press, although posters on outdoor hoardings were used sporadically, both for products and for films.

Similar to the development of advertising in other parts of the world during the period from the turn of the century to World War II, techniques and styles matured rapidly. Early ads in the illustrated magazines continued the 19th-century strategy of anecdotal illustration with occasional elaborate hand lettering. Art Nouveau was also an influence, sometimes to the point where artists lifted components directly from earlier European examples such as the ad for the famous Buenos Aires cafe La Brasileña, which recalls details of the posters for Rajah coffee by the Belgian artist Privat Livemont. Comic characters and comedic situations were also depicted in various ads.

Media scholars Oscar Steimberg and Oscar Traversa have defined a trajectory of transitions in Argentine advertising of this period that moves from 19th-century anecdotal illustration to Art Nouveau and then to Art Deco and realistic drawings and paintings in the American style of the 1920s and 1930s. Art Deco was introduced to Argentina in the late 1920s and was evident in advertising illustration from then until the 1930s. The delicate line drawings of French fashion illustrators like Erté strongly influenced advertisements for cosmetics and other products for women, but by the late 1930s the pragmatic American approach, which incorporated realistic illustrations into "reason why" copy that provided a hard sell to consumers, had become relatively widespread. By this time photography was also used extensively instead of illustration.

One person who worked outside the trajectory of styles proposed by Steimberg and Traversa was the poster artist Achille Mauzan. Though French, Mauzan had lived in Italy and was among Italy's most prominent poster artists in the early years of the 20th century along with Adolfo Hohenstein and Leopoldo Metlicovitz (see Chapter 17). He was steeped in the culture of European poster advertising and brought this knowledge to Buenos Aires. The sophistication of Mauzan's posters far surpassed anything that was being produced in Argentina at the time.

Mauzan arrived in Buenos Aires in 1927 and

remained there until 1932. He established a studio, Editorial Affiches Mauzan, where he was joined for a short period by the Italian poster artist Gino Boccasile (1901–1952), a former student of his who had worked in his studio in Milan. Boccasile was a supporter of Mussolini and was known in Italy for his posters of handsome men and women enjoying various contemporary products.

Mauzan quickly developed a clientele that included a number of international and Argentine companies such as Bayer Aspirin, Crosley radios, Craven cigarettes, Carpano vermouth, Hupmobile, Geniol pain relievers, and Alpargatas sandals (Plate 57). For Geniol, Mauzan created variations on the theme of the product's capacity for pain reduction. Not only did he design a humorous poster that showed a smiling man withstanding the pain of nails and pins stuck in his head, but he also devised a similar three-dimensional figure for pharmacies and other shops where Geniol was sold. Due to Mauzan, Geniol's advertising became extremely popular.

The posters Mauzan created introduced an entirely new visual vocabulary to Argentine clients. First was the rich variegated color that resulted from masterful lithographic printing. Second was the beautifully drawn lettering that was unique for each client. Third was Mauzan's ability to switch from whimsy to deeper emotional imagery, depending on the job. Fourth was his understanding of how to generate customer surprise by creating posters with variations that would be released sequentially. Fifth and last was his superb draftsmanship and integration of lettering and images. Mauzan's posters were also displayed elsewhere in Latin America including Brazil, where some were printed with Portuguese texts.

Posters, along with filmcards, were used as well to advertise Argentine films, but none evinced the visual sophistication and quality of Mauzan's product advertising. The first films by the Lumière brothers were shown in Buenos Aires in 1896 shortly after they were previewed in Paris, and Argentina produced its first silent film, a brief documentary, in 1899. One of the early film producers was Max Glücksmann, who promoted his films heavily with posters and newspaper advertisements. For the most part, the early posters were undistinguished, consisting mainly of one or more photographs of the film's stars framed by black linear borders and accompanied by the film's title in large letters and other information in smaller type. In later years, there was more variety in the posters, whose techniques ranged from cartoon drawings to photomontage, but no major poster artists emerged in this genre.

The design of books

By 1936, Argentina had become the largest publisher of Spanish-language books anywhere. A considerable number of intellectuals, artists, and even printers had emigrated to Argentina from Europe and elsewhere in Latin America. Numerous Spaniards came to escape the oppressive regime of General Francisco Franco that had resulted from the Spanish Civil War. Most immigrants settled in Buenos Aires, which had the country's greatest concentration of printing establishments as well as binderies, paper suppliers, and all the other services that a publishing enterprise required. Many of those who arrived were well educated and joined an Argentine middle class that supported the sale of books, magazines, and newspapers.

With the Spanish émigrés came many new ideas about socialism, anarchism, and the visual heritage of the avant-garde movements such as Constructivism. The majority of the print shop workers were anarchists and most participated in different anarchist unions.

One of the first literary magazines in Argentina was *Nosotros* (*Us*), published between 1907 and 1943, which represented the literary tendencies of the time but had become by the 1920s the publication that vanguard writers like Jorge Luis Borges would react against. Borges was part of the Florida group of writers who experimented with avant-garde techniques. They were associated with the journal *Martín Fierro*, which was published between 1923 and 1927. Other experimental journals were *Prisma* (1921–1922), *Proa* (1924–1926), and *Sur* (1931–1970). Opposing the Florida writers were members of the Boedo group, who were associated with the publisher Editorial Claridad. In contrast to the Florida writers' interest in literary experiment, the Boedo group favored realistic writing whose purpose was social change.

Editorial Claridad was founded in 1922 by Antonio Zamora (1896–1976), a Spanish immigrant with a socialist bent. Its first venture was a continuing series of inexpensive small books, *Los Pensadores* (*The Thinkers*), that were translations of writing by socially progressive writers, both Argentine and foreign. The series ceased publication in 1924 but Zamora published numerous other books, including fiction and non-fiction. At first he relied on outside printers but eventually purchased his own linotype machine so that he could print and also design his books in-house.

In 1926, Zamora began to publish a magazine, *Claridad*, which was a vehicle for writers on the left. The cover of each issue featured a large image, whether a photograph or else a drawing with a politically provocative theme. The lettering for the first masthead, all capital letters, followed the design of *Claridad*'s French predecessor, the bi-weekly paper *Clarté*, which was edited by the left-wing intellectual Henri Barbusse. However, over time, the masthead was changed to a script version, which was cleaned up and clarified from its first to its final version.

Among the other prominent publishing houses in the interwar years was Editorial Losada, which was established in 1938. One of its founders was the Italian painter and graphic designer Attilio Rossi. In 1933, Rossi had helped to establish and then co-edited *Campo Grafico*, the first Italian magazine dedicated to modern graphic design. Rossi moved to Buenos Aires in 1935 to escape Mussolini and the Italian Fascists and was active in the circle of Argentine writers that included Jorge Luis Borges. He brought knowledge of modern European design to his job as artistic director of

Editorial Losada, where he attempted for the first time to improve the quality of the mass-produced books that were being published in Buenos Aires. One of the distinctive books of Losada's for which Rossi designed the cover and drew the illustrations was the popular children's book *Platero y Yo* by the Spanish poet Juan Ramón Jimenez.

Other émigré graphic designers who made a strong impact on book design in Buenos Aires were the German Jacobo Hermelin (dates unconfirmed) and the Spanish artist and printmaker Luis Seoane (1910–1979). Seoane designed important book series for Emecé Editores, beginning in 1939. He continued the design of well-known series for Editorial Nova, which he founded in 1943. That same year, he also co-founded the literary review *Correo Literario*, whose layout during the years of publication (1943–1945) drew considerable attention.

Colombia
Initial efforts to industrialize

Colombia ushered in the 20th century in the midst of the Thousand Days War between the Conservative and Liberal Parties. Lasting from 1899 to 1902, the war resulted in the defeat of the Liberals and a considerable number of deaths. In early 1903, the Colombian congress turned down an offer from the United States to build a canal across the Isthmus of Panama, which borders on Colombia, causing the Panamanians to revolt against Colombia and negotiate a treaty with the United States themselves for the construction of the canal.

At the beginning of the 20th century, coffee dominated Colombia's economy and the country supplied about 3 percent of the world's coffee exports. When Rafael Reyes Prieto became president in 1904, he put a new emphasis on industrial development to which he gave major support during the six years of his presidency until he was overthrown in 1909. Reyes had served as Minister of Promotion and Commerce under President Rafael Núñez in the early 1890s and believed

PANAMA HATS ON THEIR WAY

THROUGH THE GAILLARD CUT TO MADURO'S SOUVENIR STORE

Fig. 30.07: Panama hats, postcard, 1919. © Universal Images Group (Lake County Discovery Museum)/Alamy.

that industrial capability was a strong component of a nation's modernity.

His task was made difficult by the fact that the Columbian economy consisted largely of thousands of small workshops, where goods were mainly produced by hand. A major product of these workshops was the Panama hat, which was made with local fibers, largely by women artisans (Fig. 30.07). In 1892, about 320,000 of these hats were exported to different parts of the world.

At least half of the workshops were in the province of Antioquia, which became one of Colombia's leading industrial areas. Several schools were established to train workers to produce Panama hats, although these schools tended to preserve traditional craft methods rather than explore more efficient mechanized techniques. Complementing the production of Panama hats in Antioquia in the early 1890s were more than 1,600 small weaving workshops in the province of Santander, where women worked at wooden handlooms, producing bolts of cloth as well as blankets, bedspreads, ponchos, and hammocks.

In contrast to the rural enterprises, which centered on woven goods, small workshops in urban areas like Bogotá and Medellín, the capitol of Antioquia, consisted of carpenters, furniture makers, locksmiths, shoemakers, tailors, and ironworkers, including blacksmiths, who primarily did manual work. For the most part, these workshops were comprised of family members and generally had no more than four or five workers. They could produce refined or inexpensive furniture, as well as clothing and other custom-made goods

By the late 1880s, a handful of workshops had begun to use imported machines and a few were making machines themselves, some of which were copies of those imported from abroad. Machine production was geared to the most stable industries, notably coffee growing, mining, and agriculture. Historian Alberto Mayor Mora likens the inventors of these machines to the entrepreneur-inventors of the early Industrial Revolution in Europe.

Coltejer, a textile factory, inaugurated in Medellín in 1907, was among a number of enterprises that developed in the period between 1902 and 1909, supported by President Reyes, who established a system of high tariffs to protect the local industries from foreign imports. Others industries included the Bello Textile Factory and Olano Fósforos, a factory that produced matches. What made these factories possible, however, was the introduction of electricity, which was essential for their machinery. Besides all the imported machines, there were occasional local inventions such as one by an engineer from Antioquia that separated the fibers of sisal, a local plant.

The centenary of Independence 1910

To commemorate Colombia's independence from Spain and to promote a vision of the country as a modern industrializing nation, President Reyes established a committee in 1907 to organize a centenary celebration, which would be joined by an exhibition dedicated to industry and agriculture. Expositions of this type were inaugurated in the 19th century, as exemplified by the Exposición Agroindustrial, which opened in the harbor city of Baranquilla in 1871. Precedents for such exhibitions elsewhere in Latin America included fairs held in Mexico in 1900 and Brazil in 1908.

After Reyes was deposed in 1909, the efforts to organize the centenary exhibition were sustained by the next president, Ramón González Valencia. The committee's intent was to celebrate the national past as well as to make visible more recent accomplishments in agriculture and industry. To achieve this latter aim, the committee members settled on a group of pavilions dedicated to the industrial and agricultural development of the country's different regions as well as several pavilions to promote Colombia's progress as an emerging civilized nation. It was also President González's hope that the centenary would

create an atmosphere of peace after the destruction of the Thousand Days War.

Two pavilions were built for the Exposition of Industry and Agriculture—one dedicated to industrial products and the other to machines. The latter was no doubt modeled on Dutert's and Contamin's Galerie des Machines at the Paris exhibition of 1889. The industrial pavilion, whose principal architect was Mariano Sanz de Sanatmaría (1857–1915), designer of the Municipal Theater, an eclectic pastiche of European compositional elements, which was typical of Colombian architecture of this period. Its references looked back to Art Nouveau rather than forward to the modern age.

The two pavilions displayed a miscellaneous array of products. Among them, textiles held a prominent place and examples of woven cloth, upholstery, and various fabrics were shown. The different galleries also housed glass, electric clocks, coffee grinders, horseshoes, cosmetics, fertilizer, polishers, machines for making noodles, and numerous other products whose aggregate display was intended to impress viewers by its sheer volume.

Further industrialization

The number of factories continued to grow in the years following the 1910 exhibitions. The majority were textile factories, though one of the most mechanized was the Compañía Colombiana de Tabaco (Colombian Tobacco Company) in Medellín. Nonetheless, industrialization was spotty and was concentrated mainly in the largest cities, notably Bogotá and Medellín. As the number of factories increased, the artisan class declined and was replaced by factory workers. Industrialists took a particular interest in American and French writings that promoted efficiency such as Frederick Winslow Taylor's *Principles of Scientific Management* and Henri Fayol's work on industrial administration.

Industrialization was particularly intense during the period 1925–1930, when Colombia and other Latin American countries had great difficulties bringing in goods from abroad and had to adopt import substitution. The intensity was due in part to a new generation of entrepreneurs such as Jorge Echavarría and Pedro Nel Ospina, both from the province of Antioquia. They realized that the most advanced techniques of production were required if Colombian industry was to compete successfully with products made in Europe and the United States.

As previously mentioned, Medellín and the province of Antioquia generally were two of Colombia's principal industrial centers. Among the enterprises that were established there in the 1920s were companies that made beer, cement, textiles, and cigarettes. During the 1930s, these industries continued to grow, and as a consequence of their success, the number of artisans declined drastically. As in other Latin American countries, Colombia was most successful in the production of consumables such as foodstuffs, beer, and cigarettes. The textile industry remained relatively strong, though it introduced fewer innovations than its competition abroad. Industrial engineers were highly regarded by the major industries and their knowledge of manufacturing efficiency and how production lines could be organized contributed to the success of numerous firms in Colombia.

The training of artisans

As early as the 1870s, there was an official movement to create a system of technical education in Colombia. A number of Escuelas de Artes y Oficios (Schools of Arts and Trades) were established, but given the lack of industrial development at the time, these schools oscillated between teaching traditional crafts such as ironwork, carpentry, and tailoring and more modern trades like mechanics, construction, ironwork, and pottery. Artistic crafts such as jewelry making, silverwork, leatherwork, and woodcarving were also added to the curricula in some schools.

Then, in 1904, President Reyes established in Bogotá the Escuela Profesional de Artes Decorativas e Industriales (Professional School of Decorative and Industrial Arts), whose curriculum was organized along the traditional lines of European decorative arts schools. Courses were offered in silverwork, ceramics, metalwork, woodcarving, and stonecutting. The school's founder and first director was the painter Andrés de Santa Maria (1860–1945), who had studied art for many years in France, where he was strongly influenced by the Impressionists. Santa Maria continued as director of the school until 1911 when he returned to Europe for good. Special schools were also established to prepare women for work in the home.

Graphic design

Most of the early graphic designers, advertising artists, caricaturists, and illustrators in Colombia were originally trained as painters. A number studied at the Institute of Fine Arts in Medellín, which was founded in 1910. They included Ricardo Rendón (1894–1931), Pepe Mexía (1895–1978), José Posada Echeverri (1906–1952) and Eladio Vélez (1897–1967). Rendón and Mexía were among the founders of Los Panidas, a group, named after the god Pan, which embraced the latest ideas in art, literature, and philosophy. The group was short-lived, reaching its apogee in 1915 with the publication of the *Revista las Panidas* (*Las Panidas Review*), but it nonetheless strongly influenced the development of new tendencies in Colombian art and literature. Other commercial artists studied at the School of Fine Arts in Bogotá, which opened its doors in 1886.

In 1910, *El Grafico* (*The Graphic*) was founded in Bogotá as a weekly publication. Among its aims was to promote the use of advertising. Early advertisements were published in the metropolitan newspapers, especially *El Tiempo*, a Bogotá paper that first began publication in 1911. Ads also appeared in an early illustrated magazine, *Cromos*, which was founded in 1916. For its covers, the editors of *Cromos* normally reproduced paintings by Colombian and European artists, the first ones being done by Coriolano Leudo (1866–1957), a prominent Bogotá painter who was one of the first professors at the Bogotá School of Fine Arts. Leudo was also an illustrator whose projects included the illustrations for a widely used government textbook that denounced alcohol consumption. The Italian artist Rinaldo Scandroglio (dates unconfirmed), who arrived in Bogotá from Italy in 1926, created a large number of illustrations for *Cromos*, many drawing on Cubist and Futurist precedents.

Advertisements became more artistic in the 1920s, as did the logos and packaging for Colombian enterprises. This was a period that saw the first advertising agencies in Colombia. Among the leading advertising artists were Ricardo Rendón and Pepe Mexía, both of whom had moved to Bogotá from Medellín by this time. In 1924, the cigarette company Coltabaco in that city, previously known as the Compañía Colombiana de Tabaco, created an advertising department, which was directed by the painter, illustrator, and caricaturist José Posada Echeverri was appointed art director. He remained in that position for more than 40 years, while also producing illustrations for many publications such as *El Grafico*, *Claridad* (*Clarity*), *Cromos*, *El Bodegón* (*The Still Life*), and *Pan*. Posada Echevarri worked in the style of Erté, Georges Lepape, and others who drew for the French fashion magazines, though he sometimes added a mystical element to his drawings that was reminiscent of Symbolism and Art Nouveau.

In 1925, Coltabaco hired Ricardo Rendón to design the package for a new cigarette brand, Pielroja (Redskin). Rendón drew the profile of an American Indian wearing a war bonnet, an image that was also widely used for other product brands, particularly in the United States. More important than Rendón's work as an advertising artist, however, was his career as Colombia's most trenchant political caricaturist during the 1920s, a period when he chronicled the political and social life of the country.

Also in 1925, another Medellín company, Postobón, which made soft drinks, hired Pepe Mexía to create advertisements for a new product, Freskola. Mexía created a whimsical ad that featured two men, both represented by line drawings, seated at café tables on one of which were four bottles of the new beverage.

Joined to the ad was a comic copy line that touted Freskola as a refreshing drink to imbibe after the excesses of alcohol.

According to art historian Álvaro Medina, the work of Mexía presented a new modern style while Ricardo Rendón prolonged a traditional technique of illustration. Mexía's Freskola ad is consequently something of a landmark in early Colombian advertising, not to be equaled even by the ads of the 1930s including those that adopted Art Deco lettering and occasional abstract ornamentation. A number of these were featured in *Pan*, a cultural magazine that began publication in 1935.

During the 1930s, other companies such as the textile firm Coltejer, the beer company Bavaria, and the Compañía Nacional de Chocolates followed the lead of Coltabaco by hiring artists to design logotypes and other corporate advertising. Some companies started their own art departments. Among the artists who worked on corporate commissions besides José Posada Echeverri, Ricardo Rendón, and Pepe Mexía were the Medellín painters Luis Eduardo Vieco (1882–1955) and Humberto Chávez (1891–1971).

The poster as an advertising medium was not well developed in Colombia during the years between the Thousand Days War and World War II. However, in 1938, Colombia hosted the first edition of the Juegos Deportivos Bolivarianos (Bolivarian Games), a regional sporting event for the countries in the northern part of South America but including Panama as well. The games also coincided with the 400th anniversary of the founding of Bogotá.

The artist chosen to do a series of posters that simultaneously commemorated the games and the founding of Bogotá was Sergio Trujillo Magnenat (1911–1999), a former painting student at the School of Fine Arts in Bogotá and later director of the decorative arts curriculum at the school. Trujillo Magnenat's series of posters depicted muscular male and female athletes actively engaged in various sporting events. Their stylistic references ranged from Ludwig Hohlwein to French fashion illustration. They were distinctive, however, for the strength of their painting style and their attempt to integrate the images of the athletes with bold lettering that announced both the games and the Bogotá anniversary.

Trujillo Magnenat was Bogotá's leading graphic designer, not only because of the variety of illustrative and lettering styles he employed but also due to the range of projects in which he was engaged. Beginning in 1931, he was an illustrator for the Sunday supplement of *El Tiempo*, and was also art director of a cultural magazine *Revista de las Indias*, which the Ministry of Education published between 1936 and 1938. For this publication, he designed a sober typographic cover as well as the interior pages, particularly those that featured poetry. Trujillo Magnenat took an especially strong interest in modern lettering, which he featured prominently in his layouts. He was as well the art director, illustrator, and designer of a children's magazine, *Rin Rin*, which was also published by the Ministry of Education. Like *Revista de las Indias*, it was short-lived, appearing between 1936 and 1938, but Álvaro Medina considers it to have been the best children's magazine of the period.

Another prominent art director and illustrator was Santiago Martínez Delgado (1906–1954), who was also known for his watercolors, paintings, and woodcarvings. Martínez Delgado was that rare Latin American artist who studied in the United States rather than Europe. He attended the Chicago Academy of Fine Arts and was a student of Frank Lloyd Wright at Taliesin. In Chicago, he created illustrations for *Esquire* magazine and worked in the Federal Art Project. The latter experience prepared him to become a prominent muralist in the 1940s after he returned to Colombia.

Martínez Delgado had contributed illustrations to *El Grafico* before he left for Chicago and following his return he became the art director of *Vida* (*Life*), a cultural publication of the Compañía Colombiana de Seguros (Colombian Insurance Company). As Álvaro Medina notes, Martínez Delgado's drawing style was eclectic. He was a master of the fine line, but his illustrations for *Vida* varied from highly decorative images to more contemporary drawings inspired by Art Deco.

While many magazines in Colombia continued to feature illustration, *Estampa* specialized in photography. Among the photographers who did reportage for the weekly publication was Gonzalo Ariza (1912–1995), a man better known as a painter but whose carefully composed photographs embodied the tenets of the German New Photography. Sergio Trujillo Magnenat, who was recognized for his photographs as well as his painting, illustration, and graphic design, contributed layouts to the magazine.

Ariza and Trujillo Magnenat worked for *Estampa* during the 1930s, a period that witnessed a return to liberal politics after a long period of conservatism. The decade also saw an improvement in the design of book covers. Among the leading cover designers were Adolfo Samper (1905–1991), a contributor to *El Grafico*, *Cromo*, and other publications; Alberto Arango Uribe (1897–1941), who became Bogotá's leading political caricaturist after the untimely death of Ricardo Rendón in 1931; and Pepe Gómez (1892–1936), former art director of the weekly illustrated magazine *Bogotá Cómico* (*Comic Bogota*) and its successor, *Semana Cómica* (*Comic Week*). All had versatile careers that included caricature and illustration.

Venezuela
Political and economic development

For much of the 19th century, Venezuela was ruled by *caudillos* or military strongmen. This was extended into the 20th century when General Cipriano Castro brought his provincial army from the Andean state of Táchira to Caracas and took over the government in 1899. Castro thus established a stronghold for other *caudillos* from Táchira, who ruled Venezuela for much of the next 59 years. In 1909, Castro was succeeded by General Juan Vicente Gómez, who seized power from the ailing president and subsequently controlled Venezuela with an iron hand until his death in 1935.

Prior to Gómez's exploitation of Venezuela's rich oil reserves in the 1920s, Venezuela was predominantly an agrarian country, which exported coffee and cacao. The economy was strengthened under Castro, but unlike Colombia where President Reyes strongly encouraged the country's industrial development, Castro did not promote industry in any way. Nor did Gómez, except to foster industries such as refining that were related to the discovery of oil. Beginning with Castro, the country did not have a successful history with foreign investors, except those who invested in the oil fields. Among them were the Big Three American oil companies—Standard Oil, Shell, and Gulf—to whom Gómez sold almost all the country's concessions. Consequently there was little incentive to encourage other enterprises.

Venezuela also had far fewer immigrants than either Argentina or Brazil and thus lacked the industrial innovation that immigrants brought to some other Latin American countries. Local goods were produced—primarily foodstuffs, beverages, cigarettes, and related small items—but the rapid expansion of oil revenues facilitated the purchase of foreign goods and reduced the incentive for developing local industries further. By the 1930s, Venezuela had become the wealthiest country in Latin America and the world's largest oil exporter, second only to the United States in total oil production. The boundary between public and private revenue was blurred and Gómez appropriated considerable oil revenues for himself. He brooked no dissent and continually censored the press and jailed or exiled those who criticized him.

After Gómez's death, Eleazar López Contreras, another *caudillo* from Táchira, became president and allowed a year of liberal reforms before adopting a more dictatorial stance, although freedom of the press and public debate remained relatively open. López Contreras founded a number of new economic and social institutions, which included the reform of the traditional Academy of Art. Supported by the Ministry of Education, the Academia de Bellas Artes was reorganized and renamed the Escuela de Artes Plásticas y Artes Applicadas de Caracas (School of Plastic and Applied Arts of Caracas). Its new director was Antonio Edmundo Monsanto (1890–1948), who believed that art could not stand alone, but had to relate to society. Consequently, he introduced a Section of Applied Arts, which included studios for graphic arts, stained glass, technical drawing, textiles, fresco painting, ceramics, and carving in stone and wood. The reorganization of the art academy came from the recognition that Venezuela needed to prepare applied artists for industry. As a consequence, the school became the principal training ground for many of the country's most important designers in the post-war years.

Another indication that López Contreras recognized the importance of developing a diversified economy was his introduction in 1938 of the Triennial Plan, which included government support for industry. He also sponsored a pavilion for the 1939 World's Fair in New York. Though the Venezuelan economy was still underdeveloped, with the exception of the oil fields, the government commissioned the American architects Skidmore & Owings and John Morse to design a pavilion that would project the image of Venezuela as a modern nation with a diverse flourishing economy. They incorporated the most contemporary techniques of modern architecture including glass curtain walls and a cantilevered roof. As a structure, the pavilion was impressive, but just as the country's oil riches encouraged the continual importing of foreign goods, so was the pavilion another example of importation; in this case it represented a modernist sensibility that was in many ways at odds with the repressive ways that Gómez and then López Contreras had governed Venezuela since 1908. The interior of the pavilion, whose set pieces were several large murals and a group of large sculpted figures representing Venezuelan products, was organized by Luis Alfredo López Méndez (1901–1996), a landscape painter who had spent many years abroad. Clearly López Contreras had the ambition to make Venezuela into a modern nation with appropriate economic and social institutions, a goal that Gómez lacked. In some ways, the vision of López Contreras might be related to what Getulio Vargas was trying to accomplish in Brazil during the same years. However, Vargas fostered far more industrial development than López Contreras was able to do and he could rely as well on a substratum of modernist culture that enabled Brazil to project an image of modernity to the world with its own cultural resources.

In 1941, yet another Táchira general, Isaias Mediana Angarita, succeeded López Contreras and he remained in power until the end of World War II. More than the generals who preceded him, Medina Angarita permitted the free activity of political parties and promoted a number of constitutional reforms, which included granting women the right to vote.

Graphic design

Magazines, newspapers, and books

Although the majority of the Venezuelan population was illiterate in the late 19th century, the country's cosmopolitan class supported various newspapers and illustrated magazines similar to comparable social groups in other Latin American countries. The leading magazine was *El Cojo Ilustrado* (*The Illustrated Cripple*), which was published in Caracas. It was actually a promotional publication of the Fábrica de Tabacos "El Cojo" (El Cojo Tobacco Factory). From the time it began in 1892 to when it ceased publication in 1915, *El Cojo Ilustrado* published Venezuela's best writers and exemplified an extremely high quality of printing. It had a three-column layout and its covers featured reproductions of fine art as well as imported illustrations. Besides Caracas, the city of Maracaibo, capital of the state of Zulia, also had a rich publishing history, which included the magazine *El Zulia Ilustrado* (*Zulia Illustrated*) (1888–1891) and the daily newspaper *El Fonógrafo* (*The Phonograph*), which was published between 1879 and 1917.

The leading printing establishment of the period was Litografía y Típografía del Comercio (Commercial Lithography and Typography). It was founded by a German immigrant, Pius Schlageter (dates unconfirmed), whose son Eduardo (1893–1974), a painter, also worked in the business and became one of Venezuela's leading poster artists in the 1930s. Litografía y Típografía del Comercio printed the first four-color magazine covers in Venezuela, introducing advanced techniques of lithographic printing that had been developed in Germany. Among the firm's clients was the magazine *El Farol* (*The Streetlamp*), whose covers it printed for many years.

Pius Schlageter's enterprise was a precedent for Tipografía Vargas, which Juan de Guruceaga (1897–1974) established in 1919. Tipografía Vargas was a multifaceted organization that consisted of a print shop; a publishing house, Editorial Elite; and some of the leading newspapers and magazines that were published in Venezuela during the 1920s and 1930s. In 1925, de Guruceaga launched *Elite*, a weekly illustrated publication that became the major cultural magazine of that period. The best writers and illustrators in Caracas wrote and drew for it and photography was also a feature.

Two years later, de Guruceaga introduced a daily newspaper, *Mundial*, and in 1930 the children's magazine *Kakadu*, which lasted only two years. *Kakadu* was followed by another publication for children, *Juan Bimbita*, in 1940. In 1935, Tipografía Vargas began to publish a second daily newspaper, *Ahora* (*Now*). Profiting from the more open publishing climate that followed the death of Juan Vicente Gómez, *Ahora* became the country's principal journal of opinion through its promotion of a new democratic culture. Among its leading contributors was the caricaturist Mariano Medina Febres (1912–d.o.d. unconfirmed), known as Medo, whose sharp political caricatures helped to raise hopes for a more open political system. Medo also created occasional book covers for Editorial Elite and in another vein invented the cartoon character Juan Bimba, a young boy from the countryside who for a time became a national Venezuelan icon.

During the 1920s and 1930s, Tipografía Vargas collaborated with many writers, graphic artists, and illustrators, particularly those who opposed the regimes of Gómez and López Contreras. Prominent among the graphic artists who worked with the firm were two men with many talents: Leoncio Martínez (1888–1941), a humorist, journalist, commercial artist, and caricaturist whose nom de plume was Leo; and Rafael Rivero Oramas (1904–1992), an artist, art director, illustrator, film director, and writer.

In 1912, Martínez published a newspaper article that urged a renewal in the arts. It served as a call to a group of artists and writers who founded the Círculo de Bellas Artes, an organization intended to counter the conservative policies of the Academia de Bellas Artes. Artist members explored European artistic trends, although they were most attracted to Impressionism rather than to any of the subsequent progressive and avant-garde movements. The writers in the group included essayists, novelists, and poets, many of whom became Venezuela's most prominent literary and journalistic figures in the ensuing years.

In 1923, Martínez and Francisco Pimentel (Job Pim) (1889–1942), an author of humorous verse, founded a weekly magazine titled *Fantoches* (*Masks*), which Martínez edited and for which he drew covers and provided interior illustrations. *Fantoches* became a platform for much of Leo's criticism of Juan Vicente Gómez and Eleazar López Contreras. As a consequence, both dictators put him in prison at various times. Martínez was also one of the leading commercial artists in Caracas, providing advertising illustrations for many clients, while continuing to collaborate as a journalist and illustrator for various publications.

With Juan de Guruceaga, Rafael Rivero Oramas was the co-founder of *Kakadu*, for which he served as editor, illustrator, and designer. Later he edited, designed, and illustrated two other children's magazines, both published by the Ministry of Education, beginning in 1938—*Onza, Tigre, Léon* (*Snow Leopard, Tiger, Lion*), and *Tricolor*, which followed it. Rivero Oramas also created the graphic look for *Elite*. He designed covers, provided illustrations, designed the various iterations of the title letters, drew initials, and laid out articles. In addition, he designed many book covers for Editorial Elite, including covers for the novels of major authors such as Arturo Uslar Pietri, Julián Padron, and Rómulo Gallegos. Rivero Oramas' cover for Gallegos' seminal novel *Doña Bárbara* (1929) represents the confrontation between civilization and the harshness of Venezuela's rural plains as a clash of abstract elements. Other book covers he did for Editorial Elite also averted illustrative conventions in favor of strong abstract or semi-abstract designs. Writing many years later about Rivero Oramas, the artist and graphic designer Carlos Cruz-Diez considered him to have been the first Venezuelan graphic designer. Rivero Oramas talked about layout and not design, Cruz-Diez wrote, noting as well that he could do anything from lettering to illustrating, making engravings, and even printing.

Advertising

Due to the sharp difference of literacy and cultural activity between urban and rural areas, advertising was directed at urban dwellers. By the beginning of the 20th century, advertisements with illustrations were appearing regularly in Venezuela's newspapers and illustrated magazines. Ads varied in their design from purely typographic ones that drew on a wide variety of display faces to those that combined illustrations with separate texts or integrated the lettering directly into the illustration.

Domestic and foreign products that were featured included foodstuffs, cosmetics and perfumes, cigarettes, and clothing. Among the foreign companies that advertised in Venezuela during this period were RCA Victor, Burroughs, Colgate, Michelin, and Bayer. While most of the early ads were mundane both in copy and illustrations, Bayer introduced a sophisticated series for its pharmaceutical products featuring lengthy narrative texts and illustrations in varied styles including delicate drawings that recalled Art Nouveau.

Whereas the artists who drew the first advertising illustrations are mainly anonymous, by the 1920s a number of recognized artists and caricaturists were starting to do advertising work. In 1921, the painter Raúl Santana (1883–1966), who had studied in the United States, opened the first advertising studio in Venezuela. He helped to raise the level of advertising design, particularly for fashion products and perfumes such as Guerlain from Paris. In addition to his advertising work, Santana published caricatures during the 1930s in *Elite* under his nom de plume, Santico.

Ads with a more local sensibility and a greater sense of humor were created by Leoncio Martínez, whose drawings were complemented by the copy lines of the poet Job Pim. Alejandro Alfonzo Larrain (1908–d.o.d. unconfirmed), known as Alfa, was also doing advertising illustrations during the 1920s. In 1924, Alfa and Rivero Oramas, both of whom had worked with Raúl Santana, created their own studio for advertising illustration called Gráfica Sum. Unfortunately, it closed quickly due to a lack of clients willing to purchase illustrations. Subsequently Larrain established another firm, Publicidad Alfa (Alfa Advertising), which became a precursor of later advertising agencies.

Beginning in 1925 Vepaco (Venezuelan Public Advertising Company) pioneered the introduction of outdoor advertising. Billboards they constructed in urban areas as well as along the roadsides advertised the products of a new type of corporate client exemplified by Shell Oil as well as Bandera Roja (Red Flag) cigarettes, whose campaigns featured occasional illustrations by Rafael Rivero Oramas. Besides the Santana studio and Vepaco, the most important agency before World War II was ARS Publicidad, which was founded in 1938 by Carlos Eduardo Frías (1906–1986), the author and journalist who was also a co-founder of the aforementioned newspaper *Ahora*, published by Tipografía Vargas. Originally Frías joined with Edgar Anzola, who came from the world of broadcasting, to form Anzola & Frías, a name that was soon changed to Publicitas

and finally to ARS Publicidad. The founders understood advertising as a modern practice and developed the capacity for integrated campaigns, following the American model. They created separate departments for radio, film, posters, and the press. Frías considered advertising to be a cultural activity and involved some of Venezuela's and even Latin America's leading writers in his campaigns.

Uruguay

Like its neighbor, Argentina, Uruguay experienced extensive immigration from Europe at the beginning of the 20th century, largely from Italy and Spain. Some immigrants bought land and others gravitated towards the capital city, Montevideo, where they entered professions and started small businesses as well as some industrial enterprises. Much of Uruguay's wealth came from the export of beef, leather hides, and wool. With a population of less than one million in 1900 and just over two million at the end of World War II, Uruguay had difficulty developing an internal market for its own manufactured goods and like other Latin American countries relied heavily on imports until World War I, when the country began to manufacture more products of its own. Small businesses, located primarily in Montevideo, created a range of goods including clothing, wine, and tobacco. Skilled artisans, many from Italy, supported the building industry with workshops that produced furniture, decorative ironwork, stained glass, and tiles.

José Batlle y Ordóñez, who was president from 1903 to 1907 and again from 1911 to 1915 but nonetheless dominated Uruguayan politics until his death in 1929, instituted a number of economic, social, and political reforms including a constitutional amendment that divided power between the president and a national administrative council. Unlike many other leaders in Latin America, Batlle y Ordóñez was strongly committed to the industrial development of his country, one consequence of which was an extensive program of industrial arts education.

Circulo de Bellas Artes

In 1905, two years after Battle y Ordóñez became president, a group of businessmen, intellectuals, and artists met in Montevideo to establish the Circulo de Bellas Artes (Fine Arts Circle). The group was interested in the education of painters and sculptors but also in providing training for the industrial and graphic arts. They believed that the industrial arts were important for the nation's economic development and studios were established in the new school for working in plaster and for ironwork, carpentry, and ornament applied to architecture. Students could also study the graphic arts to prepare for work in advertising. The first director, the painter Carlos María Herrera (1875–1914), ran the school from its founding until his death nine years later.

Many of Uruguay's best artists graduated from the Circulo, and a number of them returned to teach there. Government grants were obtained for some of the students to study in Europe and consequently they and the faculty were aware of various European trends and developments in the arts. Students tended to study with academic painters when they went abroad and neither they nor their professors promoted the avant-garde movements or schools such as the Bauhaus. Circulo graduates, however, formed the core of Uruguay's modern art movement, known as *planismo*, because it derived from Cézanne's technique of building up an image with planes.

Until the Circulo ceased to offer its decorative arts courses in 1923 in order to concentrate exclusively on fine art, these courses were taught by artists with no experience in industry. They featured drawing skills, as instructors did earlier in Britain's Schools of Design, and students learned to render natural forms such as leaves and flowers as well as birds, animals, and insects. Among the artists who studied or taught at the Circulo and had some involvement in the decorative or graphic arts either as teachers of designers were Carmelo de Arzadun (1888–1968), Guillermo Laborde (1886–1940), Domingo Bazurro (dates unconfirmed), Humberto Causa (1890–1925), Guillermo Rodríguez

(1889–d.o.d. unconfirmed), and Vicente Puig (dates unconfirmed),

Regionalism and its opposition

Besides the decorative arts courses at the Circulo de Bellas Artes, other schools began to provide instruction in these subjects as well. At the Faculty of Architecture, which was founded in 1915, courses in decorative arts as related to building and construction were introduced as part of the students' "artistic preparation." Such courses were developed more fully, however, at the Escuela Nacional de Artes y Oficios (National School of Arts and Trades) where the lawyer and artist Pedro Figari (1861–1938) served as director between 1915 and 1917. Figari was a controversial figure because he introduced the study of indigenous design into the curriculum, arguing for the importance of creating a national identity by incorporating visual motifs and forms that originated in Uruguay's Indian culture. Figari espoused a synthesis of iconographies drawn from nature as well as cultural sources. This was evident in the furniture, wicker objects, ceramics, stained glass, and woven fabrics that were on display at the Exposition de Arte Regionale (Exhibition of Regional Art), which the Escuela Nacional de Artes y Oficios sponsored in 1916.

Critics from the Faculty of Architecture, who espoused a rationalism derived from French classicism, accused Figari and his students of imitating the customs of cave dwellers by resorting to primitive methods of production and ignoring the tenets of science and progress. Due to the controversy that Figari created with his curriculum, his teaching career ended in 1917 and he subsequently devoted much of his energy to painting, becoming well known for his depictions of regional and indigenous themes.

Figari was not alone in his espousal of regionalism, however. This theme was reinforced by the architect Román Berro (1889–d.o.d. unconfirmed), who proposed to the First Pan American Congress of Architects, when it met in Montevideo in 1920, that architects should seek to create an architecture of the Americas through regional ornament that in each region would express the soul of the race. This fusion of regionalism and nationalism, and especially the assertion of racial identity, would play out in the decorative arts and architecture of Uruguay and other nations as well during the interwar years, especially in Brazil, Mexico, and Chile.

An example of how indigenous themes could be adapted to architecture as Román Berro had called for was the interior that the painter Milo Beretta (1875–1935), a collaborator of Figari's, designed for the house of philosopher Carlos Vaz Ferreira around 1920. Beretta's integrated design recalled the Art Nouveau villas of Hector Guimard, Victor Horta, and Josef Hoffmann. Beretta studied painting in Paris in the 1890s and would certainly have been aware of such examples. He designed a ceiling for Vaz Ferreira's study that integrated richly colored indigenous motifs into the design and he repeated such motifs as decoration on pieces of oak furniture. He also designed a number of lamps for the house, though in a modern style. The Casa Vas Ferreira exemplified the collaboration with architects that various proponents of the decorative arts had been calling for and it demonstrated that indigenous motifs could be successfully applied to the decoration of a modern dwelling.

Industrial schools

In 1916, the government mounted a vigorous campaign to expand training in the industrial arts. A law passed that year mandated the formation of a Higher Council of Industrial Education. Initially it was headed by Figari, who was subsequently succeeded by the artist Pedro Blanes Viale (1879–1926). Viale supervised the creation of three industrial schools in Montevideo: one for the building industries, one for the decorative arts, and one for "feminine industries," the Escuela Industria Feminina (Women's Industrial School). Evening courses for workers were introduced as were industrial courses in other cities and towns around the country.

The aim of the schools as indicated in the official literature was to train students to create forms and decoration for industrial products. In fact, their graduates were sought by architects, furniture firms, decorative arts studios, textile factories, and the graphic arts industries. The Higher Council of Industrial Education published a magazine, Trabajo (Work), in which student projects were documented. It circulated widely and did much to promote the students' accomplishments.

Courses were taught by well-known artists, many from the Circulo de Bellas Artes. Some artists such as Guillermo Laborde taught classes in the Circulo as well as the Industrial School of Decorative Arts. Laborde was primarily a painter, but was a man of many talents who played an important role in disseminating the spirit of Art Deco in Uruguay. Known for his murals as well as his paintings, he also occasionally designed posters, winning several prizes in a contest to create sports posters for Uruguay's Centenary celebration. He was also a designer of costumes and sets for theatrical productions and in addition did the reliefs for the wooden doors of a private villa.

In his studio for decorative painting in the Industrial School, Laborde had his students design tapestries, curtains, cushions, friezes, and other decorative objects, applying to them a repertory of decorative motifs similar to those of the best French Art Deco designers. As in the designs of Paul Poiret's École Martine, for example, Laborde's students adopted a repertory of stylized flowers, foliage, birds, and other natural forms.

National industries were promoted at the Exposición de las Industrias Nacionales (Exposition of National Industries) of 1928 and then in the Semana Uruguaya (Uruguay Week) of 1931. With the successful spread of industrial arts courses throughout the country, the government founded a new institution in 1942, the Universidad del Trabajo (University of Work). The driving force behind it was Dr. José F. Arias (dates unconfirmed), who had proposed such a university as early as 1925. Arias, a government official, had long sought to enhance the prestige of technical education and combat the tendency to look down on the Industrial Schools. The university was able to consolidate and expand the earlier initiatives in industrial education and mounted a curriculum that ranged from programs in mechanics, construction, and naval industries to decorative arts, graphic design, and evening courses for workers. Also included was a Museum of Technology.

The impact of the University of Work was of course limited by the degree of Uruguay's industrial development, which was modest compared to Europe and North America, but its programs confirmed and extended the earlier vision of Battle y Ordóñez that government support could help educate the architects, designers, graphic artists, and technical experts who were essential to industrial development.

The Uruguayan middle class supported the construction of comfortable homes that required specialists in the design of furniture, ironwork, stained glass, and other industrial arts, and in the 1920s and 1930s graduates of the various industrial and decorative arts programs were more likely to find employment in industries related to building than hard goods or transportation. The two leading furniture companies in this period, Mueblería Caviglia and Giorello y Cordano, were both founded by Italian immigrants. They maintained high standards of workmanship based on long traditions of woodworking that extended back to Europe. Mueblería Caviglia's services ranged from custom carpentry to total environments. The company could also provide sculptures and wall hangings as well as carpets, lighting, and various other decorative objects. Besides private homes, Mueblería Caviglia furnished various commercial spaces such as private clubs, retail establishments, and hotels. Italian immigrants were also the principal practitioners of artistic ironwork that included gates, fences, and window grills.

Graphic design

Advertising

During the interwar years a flourishing advertising industry developed in Montevideo, abetted in part by students trained in commercial art courses at the Circulo de Bellas Artes and the Escuelas Industriales. While there was little to promote in the way of domestic hard goods, Uruguay was a heavy importer of automobiles and other products from abroad. Domestic enterprises included cigarettes, beer, cosmetics, and foodstuffs. A leading brand of cigarettes was called Montevideo, a brand of matches was known as Victoria, and other brand names for cigarettes such as La Paz and Don Pepe were taken from episodes in Uruguayan history.

Theories of marketing from abroad were well known and local entrepreneurs adopted them. Ads were published regularly in the city's newspapers and magazines and posters were used as well. Among the poster artists was the painter Milo Beretta (1881–1935), whose posters promoted Baco wines. The tobacconist José Borro (dates unconfirmed) designed the logo, advertisements, and posters for his own enterprise. Vicente Acarino (dates unconfirmed), founder of an advertising agency in the late 1920s, announced to potential clients that they should embrace advertising so as not to appear antiquarian.

Magazines

One of Latin America's oldest illustrated weeklies, *Caras y Caretas*, was founded in Montevideo in 1890 before moving in 1898 to Buenos Aires. In 1916, *Anales Mundanos* (*Worldly Annals*), a magazine dedicated to Uruguay's wealthy class appeared. Known simply as *Anales*, its aim was broad, including in its coverage social life, art, literature, and sports. The graphic quality was excellent and the editor drew on artists such as Carlos Alberto Castellanos (1881–1945), a modernist painter whose logo for the magazine adhered to the French style of decoration and lettering.

Anales was followed by *Mundo Uruguayo* (*Uruguayan World*) in 1919. Modeled closely on *Mundo*

Argentino in Buenos Aires, it became Uruguay's leading illustrated magazine during the 1920s, featuring photography rather than illustration. *Mundo Uruguayo*, which was published by the Capurro advertising agency, hired Montevideo's leading photographers such as Anselmo Carbone (dates unconfirmed) and Horacio (dates unconfirmed) and Alfredo Canto (dates unconfirmed). The covers frequently featured photographs, but artists did many of them. At times, the visual references were too close to the *Saturday Evening Post*, particularly the covers of Norman Rockwell or James Leyendecker, but other covers made reference to French fashion illustration in a less derivative way. As with its counterparts abroad, *Mundo Uruguayo* purveyed images of modern life—automobiles, women with short hair and the latest Paris fashions, and dancing Negros whose depictions suffered from excessive caricature.

Books and literary journals

Uruguay had its share of literary journals, but the engagement of its writers with the avant-garde movements abroad was considerably less than in Argentina, Brazil, or Chile. One influence on Uruguayan poetry was the Spanish literary movement known as *ultraísmo* (ultraism), which encouraged experimentation with poetic language, particularly by including references to the modern world and technology. Among the Uruguayan poets influenced by the movement was Alfredo Mario Ferreiro, whose book of poems *El hombre que se comió un autobús: Poemas con olor a nafta* (*The Man Who Ate a Bus: Poems with the Odor of Naphtha*) appeared in 1927. The cover—most likely a linoleum cut—by the artist Melchior Méndez Magariños (1885–1945) is perhaps indicative of how far Uruguay was outside the mainstream of avant-garde movements (Plate 58). The artist sought to break up the title visually, just as poets did with their texts, but the breaks are awkward, the lettering lacks legibility, and the swirls and spikes of the background ornamentation make no reference to the text nor do they constitute a coherent decorative design. Cover designs

for *La Pluma* (*The Plume*), Uruguay's leading literary journal published between 1927 and 1931, were no more effective in adopting sophisticated international publication graphics to the Uruguayan milieu.

One exception was the artist Joaquin Torres-Garcia (1874–1949), who had studied in Europe and worked there extensively. A co-founder of the Cercle et Carré (Circle and Square) group of abstract artists in Paris, he returned to Montevideo in 1934 and there founded the Asociacíon de Arte Constructivo (Association of Constructive Art), which published numerous books of his lectures and theories about Constructivism. Torres-Garcia designed the books himself, featuring hand lettering and drawings on some of the covers and bold san serif type on others. He also lettered some of his texts himself instead of using type. In 1944, he set up a workshop to introduce students to his ideas and he founded a new constructivist journal, *Removedor*, for which he did the design.

Bibliography
Bibliographic essay

In addition to the books on Latin American history, industrialization, and art mentioned in the bibliography of Chapter 28, a number of books related to design in the countries discussed in this chapter have been helpful. Henry Hirsch, *Industrial Development in a Traditional Society: The Conflict of Entrepreneurship and Modernization in Chile* contains valuable material on Chilean industrialization. Eduardo Castillo Espinoza has written extensively on the School of Applied Arts at the University of Chile in a book he edited, *Artesanos, Artistas, Artífices: La Escuela de Artes Aplicadas de la Universidad de Chile, 1928–1968,* and in an English language article, "The School of Applied Arts, University of Chile (1928–1968)," *Design Issues* 25, no. 2 (Spring 2009). My principal source for design in Uruguay is the exhibition catalog *Los Veinte: El Projecto Uruguayo: Art y Diseño de un Imaginario, 1916–1934.*

Graphic design in Chile has been extremely well documented in Pedro Álvarez Caselli's thorough

Historia del Diseño Gráfico en Chile and his voluminous *Chile: Marca Registrada: Historia General de las Marcas Comerciales y el Imaginario del Consumo en Chile*, while political graphics have been covered by Eduardo Espinosa in *Puño y Letra: Movimiento Social y Comunicación Gráfica en Chile*. Alejandro Godoy's *Historia del Afiche Chileno* is short on text but has many images of posters. The catalog *Claridad: La Vanguardia en Lucha* provides valuable material about this important Argentine journal. Álvaro Medina has included some material about Colombian graphic design in his book *El Arte Colombiano de los Años Veinte y Trenta*. Alfredo Armas Alonso's *Diseño Grafico en Venezuela* is mostly about graphic design after World War II but also includes information on the years before the war.

Books

Chile

Basis, L. Isidoro. *100 Años de la Publicidad en Chile*. Santiago: Ediciones PubliMark, 2000.

Caselli, Pedro Álvarez, *Historia del Diseño Gráfico en Chile*. Santiago: Gobierno de Chile Consejo Nacional del Libro y la Lectura, Escuela de Diseño, Pontifica Universidad Católica de Chile, 2003.

—*Chile: Marca Registrada. Historia General de las Marcas Comerciales y el Imaginario del Consumo en Chile*. Santiago: Ocho Libros Editores/Universidad del Pacífico, 2008.

Castillo Espinosa, Eduardo, ed. *Artesanos, Artistas, Artífices: La Escuela de Artes Aplicadas de la Universidad de Chile, 1928–1968*. Santiago: Ocho Libros, 2010.

—*Puño y Letra: Movimiento Social y Comunicación Gráfica en Chile*. Santiago: Ocho Libros Editores, 2006.

Collier, Simon and William F. Sater. *A History of Chile, 1808–1994*. Cambridge: Cambridge University Press, 1996.

Godoy, Alejandro. *Historia del Afiche Chileno*. Santiago: Universidad ARCIS, 1992.

Gutierrez, Abel. *Dibujos Indigenas de Chile*. Santiago: Imprenta Universitaria, 1931.

Hauer, Mariana Muñoz and M. Fernanda Villalobos. *Alejandro Fauré: Obra Grafica*. Santiago: Ocho Libros, 2009.

Kirsch, Henry W. *Industrial Development in a Traditional Society: The Conflict of Entrepreneurship and Modernization in Chile*. Gainesville: University Press of Florida, 1977.

Pike, Frederick B. *Chile and the United States, 1880–1962: The Emergence of Chile's Social Crisis and the Challenge to United States Diplomacy*. South Bend IN: University of Notre Dame Press, 1963.

Sarabia, Rosa. *La Poética Visual de Vicente Huidobro*. Madrid: Ediciones de Iberoamericana, 2007.

Argentina

Amengual, Lorenzo Jaime. *Alejandro Sirio: El Ilustrador Olvidado*. Buenos Aires: Ediciones de Antorcha, 2007.

Bauer, Sergio, ed. *Claridad: La Vanguardia en Lucha*. Buenos Aires: Museo Nacional de Bella Artes, 2012.

Brughetti, Romualdo. *Historia del Arte en Argentina*. Mexico D.F.: Editorial Pormaca, 1965.

Finkielman, Jorge. *The Film Industry in Argentina: An Illustrated Cultural History*. Jefferson, NC, and London: McFarland & Co., 2004.

Fraser, Howard M. *Magazines and Masks: Caras y Caretas as a Reflection of Buenos Aires, 1898–1908*. Tempe: Arizona State University, 1987 (Center for Latin American Studies).

Sarlo, Beatriz. *Una Modernidad Periférica: Buenos Aires 1920 y 1930*. Buenos Aires: Ediciones Nueva Visión, 1999.

Steimberg, Oscar and Oscar Traversa. *Estilo de Época y Comunicación Mediática*, Tomo 1. Buenos Aires: Atuel, 1997. Coleccion del Circulo.

Traversa, Oscar. *Cuerpos de Papel: Figuraciones del Cuerpo en la Prensa, 1918–1940*. Barcelona: Editorial Gedisa, 1997.

Vásquez Lucio, Oscar E. *Historia del Humor Grafico y Escrito en la Argentina Tomo 1: 1880–1939*. Buenos Aires: Editorial Universitaria de Buenos Aires, 1985.

Colombia

Jaramillo Uribe, Jaime, Alvaro Tirado Mejia, Jorge Orlando Melo, and Jesús Antonio Bejarano. *Nueva Historia de Colombia.* Bogota: Planeta, 1989.

Medina, Álvaro. *El Arte Colombiano de los Años Veinte y Trenta.* Bogota: Colcultura, 1995.

Venezuela

Alfonso, Alfredo Armas. *Diseño Grafico en Venezuela.* Caracas, Maraven: Filial de Petróleos de Venezuela, 1985.

—*Juan de Guruceaga: La Sangre de la Imprenta.* Caracas: Monte Avila Editores, 1987.

Ewell, Judith. *Venezuela: A Century of Change.* Stanford: Stanford University Press, 1984.

Olivieri, Antonio. *Apuntes para la Historia de la Publicidad en Venezuela.* Caracas: Ediciones Fundación Neumann, 1992.

Uruguay

Los Veinte: El Projecto Uruguayo: Art y Diseño de un Imaginario, 1916–1934. Montevideo: Museo Municipal de Bellas Artes Juan Manuel Blanes, 2004.

Articles

Castillo Espinosa, Eduardo, "The School of Applied Arts, University of Chile (1928–1968)," *Design Issues* 25, no. 2 (Spring 2009).

The Journal of Decorative and Propaganda Arts 18 (1992), Argentine theme issue.

Klein, Marcus, "The New Voices of Chilean Fascism and the Popular Front, 1938–1942," *Journal of Latin American Studies* 33, no. 2 (May 2001).

Subercaseaux, Bernardo, "Editoriales y Círculos Intelectuales en Chile, 1930–1960," *Revista Chilena de Literatura* 72 (April 2008).

Chapter 31: Commonwealth Countries: Canada, Australia, and New Zealand 1900–1939

Introduction

In 1917, the British Commonwealth of Nations came into being, recognizing some members of the union as countries rather than colonies. The 1931 Statute of Westminster ended British parliamentary control over all the Commonwealth parliaments and made them sovereign states that nonetheless shared allegiance to the British Crown. Canada and New Zealand acknowledged this status readily but Australia did not ratify the statute until 1942. Although the three nations had somewhat different histories of economic development, they did share some common factors, notably the English language and similar access to events in Europe and the United States. By virtue of Canada's close geographical relation to America, the two countries developed closer ties than did Australia and New Zealand with the United States, even though American manufacturers actively sought to build markets for their goods in those countries as well. French Canadians established ties with France and had a relation with that country that was unique among the three nations.

Canada

Wilfrid Laurier, Canada's Prime Minister between 1896 and 1911, was a staunch nationalist who sought to create a single political entity from various provinces and territories. By 1905 the job was completed. Laurier wished to separate Canadian policies from Britain's and to establish Canada as a separate nation within the British Empire. A test came when Britain asked Canada to send soldiers to fight on its side in the Anglo-Boer War of 1899. Canada compromised by sending volunteers to serve under the British command.

The French nationalist movement, led by Henri Bourassa, was fiercely opposed to British collaboration and sought autonomy for Canada. In 1903, Bourassa founded the Ligue Nationaliste (Nationalist League) to encourage a broad Canadian spirit in the French-speaking population, and members of his movement established a newspaper, *Le Devoir* (*Duty*), in 1910 to espouse their views.

During World War I, when Laurier was no longer Prime Minister, the Canadian government instituted compulsory military service in the British Army, but the policy divided the country, particularly strengthening French Canadian opposition to British requests for military support. While Canada was loosening its political ties with Britain, it was strengthening its economic ties with the United States. The 20th century witnessed a new relationship between the two countries, as the United States became Canada's largest trading partner. However, Canada remained primarily a producer of raw materials that were generated from mining and agriculture, while also becoming a leading producer of pulp and paper.

World War I strengthened Canada's capacity for mass production as factories turned out a range of war materiel from packing crates to training aircraft, but, unlike the United States, these enterprises, with rare exceptions, did not coalesce into an industrial system with a highly developed infrastructure that grew on the basis of continuous invention and vertical integration of companies into large manufacturing conglomerates. With a few exceptions, Canadian entrepreneurs were more inclined to license American patents than to develop their own culture of product development. The largest enterprises were in the field of textiles, transport, and farm equipment, with only modest manufacturing of other goods such as appliances. Canada did have its own furniture industry, although manufacturers tended to follow styles from abroad rather than create their own.

During the interwar years, Quebec espoused an independent policy of economic development that strongly promoted crafts and small-scale production rather than mass manufacturing. Consequently, Quebecois entrepreneurs had considerably less to do with American companies seeking to establish subsidiaries or sell patents than did their counterparts in Ontario and elsewhere in Anglophone Canada. But industry and raw material production throughout the country suffered during the Great Depression and the economy barely recovered by 1939.

Furniture and domestic goods

Modern furniture design was slow to find a reception in Canada. With the exception of Quebec's relation to France, Canadians were relatively isolated from European cultural movements in the years before World War II. For the most part, major furniture companies continued to specialize in copies of historic styles. From the 1880s, western Ontario, which had attracted a large number of skilled tradespeople as immigrants, was the center of Canada's furniture industry just as Grand Rapids, Michigan, was in the United States. Canadian furniture companies included Andrew Malcolm, the Adams Furniture Company, the Knechtel Furniture Company, and J. W. Kilgour, which, unlike the others, was in Quebec.

The Globe Furniture Company specialized in furniture for schools and churches, while the Imperial Rattan Company and the Toronto Rattan Company made furniture of cane and rattan. Most of the latter followed conventional precedents for such pieces, but designers of the Toronto Rattan Company's Art-Reed Furniture strove for a contemporary look, combining rattan frames with geometric designs and cushions covered with fabric that had colorful abstract patterns.

As historian Virginia Wright points out, the earliest modern furniture in Canada, made of metal or molded plywood, was produced for institutions—schools, hospitals, assembly halls, or cafeterias. The Metal Craft Company of Toronto was a leading manufacturer of metal furniture for clinics, hospitals, and doctors' offices, producing a line of tables, chairs, and cabinets made of sheet steel or steel tubing. Chrome-plated steel stools could be found at lunch counters and cafes such as the one in the basement of Simpson's Department Store in Toronto.

Wright also notes that Canadian furniture tended to be based on examples that were either popular abroad or else were created by foreign designers. The Standard Tube Company, a manufacturer of hospital equipment, produced the first Canadian cantilever chairs, which were inexpensive copies of Mies van der Rohe's MR20 tubular steel armchair of 1927 with the difference that the Canadian chairs substituted patterned fabric for Mies's canvas or leather seats and backs. Both the Andrew Malcolm Furniture Company and McLagan Furniture introduced wooden furniture lines that were drawn from the work of Gilbert Rohde, design director for the Herman Miller Company in Michigan. Snyder's, a furniture manufacturer in Waterloo, Ontario, commissioned the American designer Russel Wright to create a line of living room, dining room, and dinette furniture called "Modern Maple," which consisted of pieces with gently rounded corners and contained a living room couch and armchairs with curved armrests. The pieces were modern in their simplicity and absence of historic references but still cozy and without the austerity of form or materials that characterized pieces designed by Mies or Le Corbusier's studio. Even the Knechtel Furniture Company, which specialized in period styles, produced a line of dining room furniture that it called "modernistic," although the designs were pastiched elements taken from different sources.

Beginning in the mid-1920s, modern furniture was also produced by a small Toronto company, Metalsmiths Co. Ltd, whose principal was an architect, Kenneth Noxon (1900–1979). Metalsmiths Co. Ltd specialized in custom metalwork for the home, not only producing furniture but also porch and interior stair railings, fire screens and andirons, plant stands, and many other items. Noxon's furniture did not have a single style. Chairs, for example, with painted wrought iron frames, might have designs drawn from modern or historic sources or they might be completely fanciful. The chairs could be made entirely of iron or else iron frames could support cushions. Besides wrought iron, Noxon also worked in cane and glass. At various times, he operated his own retail stores where pieces could be purchased or ordered.

The large department stores, notably Eaton's and Simpson's, both based in Toronto, were influential in shaping public taste for furniture. Like their counterparts in Paris, they promoted new styles through the exhibition of model rooms and they occasionally manufactured their own furniture or commissioned designs from outside designers for original pieces or sets. The T. Eaton Company, owners of Eaton's, and other retailers purchased French furniture and fixtures in the *art moderne* style in Paris during or shortly after the Exposition des Arts Décoratifs in 1925. They either sold it or manufactured copies, also importing "French" furniture in the *moderne* style from factories in Grand Rapids, Michigan. Eaton's hired a French architect, René Cera (1895–1992), to design furniture and room displays for their stores as well as interiors for their clients' homes. For their store in Montreal, a city where a familiarity with French styles and trends was greater than elsewhere in Canada, the T. Eaton Company hired a French decorator in 1928, Jeannette Meunier (dates unconfirmed), a graduate of the École des Beaux Arts in Paris. With a mandate to look broadly at modern home furnishing styles, not just French ones, she headed up a new department, l'Intérieur Moderne, which displayed local and imported furniture, fabrics, wallpaper, and accessories. In 1937, Eaton's in Montreal introduced a small section of furniture in the Swedish Modern and American styles.

Canada also had a burgeoning radio industry in which a number of manufacturers were participating by the 1920s. Early sets ran on batteries, but Ted Rogers (1900–1939) made a breakthrough when he developed a tube that could run on household current. Consequently the Rogers Batteryless Radio Receiving Sets gained a large share of the Canadian radio market. Early battery-driven sets were essentially boxes of polished wood with the dials on the front, but after Rogers obtained a patent for his AC tube in 1927, he began to market a floor console made of walnut with a receiver housed in a box that sat on four cabriole legs.

Regardless of product type, Canadian manufacturers made little or no use of industrial designers, a profession that did not emerge in Canada until after World War II. As Virginia Wright notes, furniture manufacturers relied on in-house staff, including the sales department, to determine new product lines. Sales managers consulted with store buyers to learn about competitors' products that might help to determine what their own companies should produce. Appliance firms such as Ted Rogers' simply copied prevailing designs without attempting to create new ones. Clearly, the modern streamlined forms that American industrial designers created had little influence on Canadian manufacturers during these years.

The Royal Canadian Academy of Arts tried to promote industrial design in a 1938 exhibit, Canadian Industrial Arts, which was held at the Art Gallery of Ontario. One of its purposes was to entice Canadian artists to design for manufacturing based on their sensitivity to beauty, while another was to arouse public demand for better design quality in Canadian products. However, the exhibition was far from inspirational, since it consisted of furniture, tableware, packaging, and a few appliances of which few gave evidence of any original design. One step forward was the inclusion of a section for Industrial Arts and Crafts in the new Federation of Canadian Artists that was formed in 1942.

Quebec: furniture, decorative arts, and crafts

Jean-Marie Gauvreau and the École du Meuble

In a seminal book of 1929, *Nos Intérieurs de Demain* (*Our Interiors of Tomorrow*), the Quebecois furniture and interior designer Jean-Marie Gauvreau (1903–1970) expressed his frustration with the state of the decorative arts in Quebec. In 1922, Gauvreau had graduated with a diploma in cabinetry from Montreal's École Technique, which was constructed between 1910 and 1911. The school originally specialized in carpentry, electrical work, ironwork, and smelting, with cabinetry a later addition.

After further study and some work experience, Gauvreau headed for Paris in 1926. There he became the first Canadian to study at the École Boulle, the renowned school of furniture and interior design, from which he graduated in 1929. In Paris, Gauvreau absorbed the modern spirit of decorative art that had been generated by the 1925 Exposition des Arts Décoratifs and he became familiar with the work of leading decorators such as Émile-Jacques Ruhlmann, Louis Sognot, and Leon Caillet (see Chapter 22).

Gauvreau believed that the French decorative arts movement could inspire designers in Quebec to produce decorative arts, especially furniture, of high quality. Strongly opposed to the mass production methods of American furniture makers, Gauvreau espoused original craftsmanship that made use of local materials, especially wood, which was abundant in Quebec.

Gauvreau's book, *Nos Intérieurs de Demain*, published after his return from France, served as a manifesto for the multifarious activities he would engage in to promote the decorative arts and crafts in Quebec during the ensuing years. Returning to Montreal in 1929, he became a professor of cabinetry at the École Technique in 1930. That year he and Louis Athanase-David (1882–1953), the Provincial Secretary, established the École du Meuble (School of Furniture), which began with three students as a department of the École Technique. Both Gauvreau and Athanase-David envisioned the school within a larger project of developing Quebec industry. It received government support because it was intended to satisfy a number of objectives—help create a market for domestic products, rectify a prior provincial neglect of the trades, provide new jobs for craftsmen, and revive a dying tradition of Quebec craftsmanship. An important predecessor of the École du Meuble was the École du Conseil des Arts et Manufactures (School of the Council of Arts and Manufactures), which had been established in the 1880s, following a report by the Council of Arts and Manufactures that assessed the state of applied arts education in Quebec. This school, with branches in different cities for artisans and apprentices, provided courses in drawing, architecture, decorative painting, and lithography, along with shoemaking and dressmaking.

By 1935 the École du Meuble had become independent and was made official by a provincial law of 1937. It expanded rapidly throughout the 1930s. To supplement the cabinetry course, Gauvreau initiated a program in interior decoration and applied art, the only one in Canada at the time. Modeled after a comparable program at the École Boulle, it was initiated in 1935 and was headed from 1936 to 1945 by the Montreal architect Marcel Parizeau (1898–1945), who, like Gauvreau, had also studied in Paris. As both architect and interior decorator, Parizeau created individualized furniture and interiors for the homes he designed in an *art moderne* style. Like the decorators in Paris, he worked for the luxury market in Montreal. His furniture, however, made with the help of his students, tended towards the more simplified designs of Le Corbusier and Mallet Stevens, although his pieces were bolder and more expressive than the typical École du Meuble pieces.

Among the other teachers at the school during the interwar years, besides Parizeau and Gauvreau himself, was Alphonse Saint-Jacques (dates unconfirmed), a mainstay of the program, who taught furniture design, assisted by two experienced cabinet-makers, using a shop manual that was the same one used at the École Boulle. Elzéar Soucy (1876–1970), a highly regarded sculptor with civic, ecclesiastical, and private clients, taught wood sculpture and woodcarving as they related to cabinetmaking and interior design. A specialist in liturgical sculpture, which had been traditionally widely practiced in Quebec, Soucy kept alive a skill that was gradually dying out, as were other craft skills in the province. Paul-Émile Borduas (1905–1960) taught drawing between 1935 and 1937, emphasizing the skills needed to make visual presentations of furniture and ornament designs. Borduas was a painter who became a leader of Quebec's vigorous school of abstract art after World War II.

Gauvreau placed considerable emphasis on traditional techniques of solid wood construction. Many of the designs followed those of the modern French decorators. Gauvreau disliked standardized manufacturing and the use of industrial materials, thus he rejected the pedagogy adopted by Bauhaus designers in the 1920s and refused as well the American streamlined aesthetic. Based on French models, the furniture produced at the school possessed a spare formal quality. Many pieces had elaborate inlaid marquetry designs and some included components of wrought iron or hammered metal.

Besides the professors at the École du Meuble, a few independent craftsmen also contributed to the development of Quebec's artisan industries. Prominent among them was Paul Beau (1871–1949), a metalsmith who refused to rely on machines, preferring to work by hand as did his European predecessors. He produced a wide range of objects and was known for combining metals of contrasting colors such as brass and red copper. He was fond of ornament, whether Greek geometric patterns on a classical urn or naturalistic leaves on a letterbox. He also undertook numerous architectural commissions, producing electric fixtures, fireplace accessories, door handles, wrought-iron grilles, and even the occasional weathervane.

The Quebec handicraft revival

The founding of the École du Meuble in 1930 was related to a larger plan that the provincial government initiated the same year to revive the handicrafts in Quebec. In 1929, provincial officials launched a study to consider the condition of Quebec's home industries, discovering in almost all cases that old techniques had been lost and taste had declined. In 1930, responding to the study, Quebec's Department of Agriculture created the École Provinciale des Arts Domestiques (Provincial School of Domestic Arts) in Quebec City to train nuns and other women to produce handicrafts and teach handicraft production that could serve as the basis of commercially viable industries. Many trainees were teachers from various schools known as Écoles Ménagères Régionales (Regional Household Science Schools). Most of the staff were handicraft experts hired from Europe and the United States. The emphasis was on weaving, although courses on tanning were added. Ellen McLeod notes that the school sought standardized methods to replace individual techniques, although all artists were urged to use patterns and designs from Quebec. By 1933, more than 2,000 women had registered for courses at the school or for courses taught by teachers who trained there. Concomitant with this movement, the journalist Françoise Gaudet-Smet (1902–1986) advocated a role for rural women as artisans in her magazine *Paysana*, founded in 1938.

The École du Meuble and the handicraft revival had several objectives in common. Both were part of a larger ambition to improve the economic competitiveness of Quebec. Neither favored mass production and both were based on the belief that craft production, whether for expensive furniture or tourist rugs, was more compatible with the Quebecois way of life than industrial culture.

Whereas the handicraft revival drew on Quebec's indigenous craft traditions, the École du Meuble sought its design sources in the highly developed aesthetic atmosphere of Paris. Throughout the 1930s, Gauvreau continued to be a strong voice for developing the handicrafts as an instrument of Quebec's economic development. In his 1929 book, *Nos Intérieurs de Demain*, he had called for artists, industrialists, and educators to work together just as the founders of the Deutscher Werkbund had done in 1907. In 1939, Gauvreau suggested to the provincial government that it create a center to produce carpets and hooked rugs, and subsequently he encouraged the painter Georges-Edouard Tremblay (1902–1987) to open a studio where he could make hooked rugs based on his paintings.

The following year, Gauvreau published another book, *Artisans du Quebec* (*Artisans of Quebec*), in which he presented a survey of Quebec crafts ranging from crocheted tapestries by rural women to the design of canoes. What united all these projects was his advocacy of small craft-based enterprises as the basis of Quebec's provincial development. He envisioned regional specialization as a viable strategy for Canada's national economy and outlined new markets such as tourism for Quebec crafts. Gauvreau espoused the creation of a ceramics industry and questioned why Quebec craftsman didn't make their own pottery to compete with imports from Italy, Mexico, or Japan. In 1943, he saw part of his vision realized when the provincial Ministry of Trade and Commerce organized an Office Provincial de l'Artisanat et de la Petite Industries (Provincial Office of Craft and Small Industries), over which he presided.

While the École du Meuble was a crucial training ground for Quebec designers of furniture and later industrial designers, Gauvreau's role as a promoter of design and handicrafts along with small businesses as important components of Quebec's economic strategy is equally important. During the 1920s and 1930s, Quebec relied heavily on French sources for the development of its decorative arts and architecture, but there was less interest in the American model of production for mass consumption.

Although the province had strong industries—pulp and paper mills and chemical processing plants among them—these provided natural resources rather than finished goods for the market. One exception was Joseph-Armand Bombardier's design and production of snowmobiles, which developed into an enterprise of considerable size during World War II and expanded rapidly after that. Nonetheless, the government's interest in small business development and its espousal of craftsmanship as important for the province's economic development resulted in most industrialized enterprises such as railroad, automobile, and airplane manufacturing emerging in other parts of Canada, where the proclivity to create an industrial economy was more strongly espoused.

The national handicraft movement

The writings and work of William Morris were known among academics, artists, and art patrons in Toronto and Montreal. In Toronto, the architect Eden Smith (1858–1949), who had emigrated to Canada from England in the late 1880s, designed many buildings—primarily private residences but also several churches—in the Arts and Crafts style. George A. Reid (1860–1947), an academic narrative painter and muralist who became the first principal of the Ontario College of Art in 1912, also espoused Morris's philosophy, particularly his aim to unite the fine and applied arts. In 1903, Reid and others founded the Arts and Crafts Society of Canada. The society held its first applied arts exhibition in 1904. Changing its name the following year to the Canadian Society of Applied Art, it held a few more exhibitions until its demise around 1912, by which time the principal members had gone on to other activities. The society's definition of applied art centered on the crafts, ranging widely from metalwork, pottery, furniture and woodcarving to leatherwork, bookbinding, weaving and basketry.

Although not directly inspired by the Arts and Crafts movement, the Guild of All Arts, founded by Herbert Spencer Clark (1903–1986), an electrical engineer and social democrat, and his wife Rose Clark (dates unconfirmed) in the early 1930s, sought to become a craft community along the lines of Charles

Robert Ashbee's Guild of Handicraft, where craftsmen not only worked together but also shared a communal life. A directly acknowledged model was Roycroft, an Arts and Crafts community in East Aurora, NY, that Elbert Hubbard founded in 1895 (see Chapter 13). The Clarks were also influenced by the ideas of Americans Arthur Nash and his pupil William Hapgood, both advocates of worker ownership and shared management. On property owned by Rose Clark's family, the Clarks started workshops that produced handloom weaving, printed fabric, wrought iron, pewter, cabinetry, furniture, and other wooden objects. They brought over most of their master craftsmen from Europe. In 1934, the Guild of All Arts opened a craft shop on the premises and three years later another in downtown Toronto. By the time the community ceased to function around 1947, the Clarks had built up a sizeable business of manufacturing and selling handlooms for which they had obtained the patent in Britain. They also maintained their woodworking enterprise after the war, although they moved on to other projects that had nothing to do with their ambitions of the 1930s.

The organization that most actively promoted Canadian handicrafts for many years was the Canadian Handicrafts Guild that two women in Montreal, Alice Peck (dates unconfirmed) and Mary Phillips (1856–1937), founded in 1905. An early advocate of arts and crafts education for women, Phillips was co-principal in 1892 of the Victoria School of Art in Montreal, where women and children were taught design, china painting, and ceramics. Three years later she became head of her own School of Applied Art and Design, whose curriculum was intended to train students to work as designers for architects and manufacturers. It was active for just under a decade.

Phillips and most likely Alice Peck were founding members of the Montreal branch of the Women's Art Association of Canada (WAAC) in 1894. From its inception, the WAAC put considerable emphasis on crafts and applied design through workshops and lectures including talks on the British Aesthetic Movement and Arts and Crafts artists—Dante Gabriel Rosetti, Edward Burne-Jones, William Morris, and Walter Crane. It also initiated a series of exhibitions, and opened a sales venue, called simply Our Handicraft Shop.

After its founding, the Canadian Handicraft Guild, which began as and remained a women's organization, took over the shop and ran it for many years. The guild also launched an annual exhibition, which was held regularly in Montreal. Through the energetic promotion of Peck and Phillips, the Canadian Craft Guild played a central role in the fostering, exhibition, and marketing of crafts in Canada. Guild women sought pieces from craftspersons around the country and promoted them through the organization's exhibitions and sales gallery.

The guild's strong social agenda influenced its attitude towards craft production, emphasizing its multicultural aspects and recognizing the work of isolated, disabled, and immigrant groups. Of special interest were the crafts of Canada's Indian population. The guild also supported independent craftsmen such as snowshoe makers, blacksmiths, and chair caners. Besides the annual exhibitions, guild members organized many other exhibits of an educational nature, all of which recognized and promoted the crafts and craftspeople.

The guild played its part in World War I by launching a "Made in Canada" campaign in 1915. It held several competitions for Canadian toys to offset the absence of toys from Germany due to the war. The guild also promoted Canadian crafts abroad, receiving a Certificate of Honor for its exhibit at the 1924 British Empire Exhibition at Wembley. Surprisingly, Quebec officials did not include the guild in their plans for a handicraft revival at the end of the 1920s, perhaps due to male chauvinism or else a desire to maintain their initiative as a Francophone project.

Besides the active crafts promotion of the Canadian Craft Guild, numerous Canadian provinces recognized the crafts as a means to create jobs and generate wealth. This occurred largely in provinces where industry had not developed or was slow to take hold, especially the Maritime Provinces—New Brunswick, Nova Scotia, and Prince Edward Island—along with Newfoundland and Labrador. In 1907, the Grenfell Mission—founded by Dr. William Grenfell, a physician dedicated to improving the lives of people in Newfoundland and Labrador—established an industrial department to develop cottage industries, among them the production of fur coats and boots and rugs. In the early 1930s, the mission constructed a large industrial center to train local people in specific craft techniques, an activity that helped to offset the seasonal work of fishing, hunting, and lumbering. Another organization that promoted craft production in the region was the Newfoundland Outport Nursing and Industrial Association (NONIA), which was supported by the wife of the Governor of Newfoundland. Among its projects was a plan that would enable women in fishing communities to knit and weave in their homes and then sell their products at a retail store in St. John's. Over time, the women developed a variety of hand-knitted garments, many of which were woven on looms that the fishermen made.

In 1943, the Nova Scotia Department of Trade and Industry inaugurated a handicrafts program, providing government instructors to teach weaving, spinning, leather tooling, woodcarving, and jewelry making. A Handicraft Center was built, though the government did not purchase the final products, attempting instead to connect the craftsmen with potential customers. One form of promotion was the publication of *Handicrafts*, a bulletin that discussed handicrafts on all levels from local to international.

During the Depression, handicrafts became a means of survival for thousands of families in Nova Scotia. One industry that had roots in the late 19th century was the design and production of pressed glassware—drinking glasses, containers, and also household utensils. Of the numerous glass factories

founded in the 19th century, the most successful was the Humphrey Glass Company, which specialized in whiskey flasks, medicine bottles, lamps, glass rolling pins, and fruit jars. In 1908, the factory was turning out 25,000 pieces of glass a day. As the company expanded, it brought in glass blowers from Europe and the United States and began to produce more artistic objects such as pressed glass plates. The factory ceased operations in 1920 when the rates of natural gas, on which it depended, rose.

In New Brunswick, the Department of Education set up a youth training project in 1937 to introduce courses for young people in crafts that had been declining. Courses including carpentry, weaving, crocheting, needlepoint, and rug making were taught in numerous communities. During a two-year period, more than 2,000 girls participated, while many boys were trained in furniture making, using local birch and maple wood.

Handicraft guilds and programs were also instituted in other provinces, but the economic consequences of such activities seemed particularly dramatic in the north-east, where harsh weather conditions, remote locations, and existing seasonal work deterred the establishment of industrial enterprises.

Most craftspeople in Canada during the interwar years were not widely known, but a few of them established enterprises that brought them recognition. A number were immigrants from Scandinavia, where there was a long tradition of craft production. Håkon Rudolph "Rudy" Renzius (1899–1968) was a Swedish metalsmith who trained with his father in Malmö and came to Toronto in 1930. He set up a studio and showroom, working primarily in pewter rather than silver. He designed various products for the home—mirrors, candlesticks and candelabra, coffee and tea sets, cocktail shakers and cups, trays, vases—and jewelry as well. Although he trained several metalsmiths whose designs were influenced by modern forms, his own designs had traditional elements such as ornate handles and curved shapes. In 1936, Renzius began teaching manual crafts at Pickering College near the town of Newmarket. Among the younger metalsmiths whose careers he influenced were Andrew Fussell (dates unconfirmed), who came to Toronto from Britain in 1926, Douglas Boyd (1901–1972), and Harold Stacey (1911–1979).

In New Brunswick, two Danish immigrants, Kjeld (1900–1963) and Erica Deichmann (dates unconfirmed), set up the Dykelands Pottery in 1934. Both trained in Denmark and drew on a Scandinavian sensibility for their designs. They used a mix of local clay from Nova Scotia and New Brunswick, while experimenting with novel shapes, subtle glazes, unusual textures, and joyful surface painting. Their forms were simple, reflecting the modern tendency to avoid decoration, and the objects were practical—plates, jugs, vases, bowls, lamp bases, and the like—although they produced some ceramic sculptures and small figurines as well. The Deichmanns were pioneers among studio potters in Canada. Though they initially sold their products from their own studio in New Brunswick, by 1940 they were sending their ceramics to shops outside the province.

Another Danish immigrant, Karen Bulow (1899–1982), settled in Montreal in 1929 and soon developed a large clientele for the woven objects she created at different scales ranging from scarves, bags, and men's ties—which were extremely popular—to rugs and hangings for individual homes, and larger commissions for public spaces such as the Bank of Nova Scotia headquarters in Montreal. Bulow was known for her vibrant color sense, which characterized all of her designs. She was the founder of Canada Homespuns, considered by some to have been the first professional weaving studio in Canada, employing up to 70 weavers, some of whom worked from home. Products included drapery fabric, which was extremely popular with interior decorators in Montreal and Toronto, ties and other small items, woven rugs, and wall hangings. Bulow collaborated with leading interior decorators such as Marcel Parizeau in Montreal and

also directed a weaving school, where some of Canada's top weavers were trained. Although she worked in Montreal, Bulow did not share either the Quebec government's or Jean-Marie Gauvreau's nationalistic view of the crafts as worthy of recognition because they were inherent in a region's cultural tradition. She referenced the craft philosophy of Scandinavia rather than the work of French decorators or Quebec farmwomen and appeared to differ from the Canadian Crafts Guild in her espousal of craft as a cultivated cultural practice rather than an activity for amateurs.

Farm equipment

Three companies came to dominate the farm implement market in the period before World War II: Massey-Harris, International Harvester, and the Cockshutt Plow Company. Following the establishment of its Canadian subsidiary in 1903, International Harvester, a leading American farm implement firm, became a serious competitor with Massey-Harris. In 1911 it purchased the Clatham Wagon Plant, where it began to manufacture wagons to supplement its line of farm implements, but a decade later it started to use the plant for the manufacture of trucks, which became one of its major products.

The Cockshutt Plow Company was small, and originally sold most of its plows to Massey-Harris until the larger firm acquired the Verity Plow Company and began to produce plows of its own. Cockshutt expanded its product line and made an arrangement with an American company that produced harvesting equipment to sell that company's products in Canada. Cockshutt subsequently acquired two Canadian carriage companies, thus enabling it to sell a full line of products to farmers in western Canada, where it experienced a large increase in business that was complemented by expanded sales abroad. Nonetheless, the company failed to produce a range of products that derived from the trend towards mechanization in agriculture—particularly gas-powered equipment— although it retained a strong position in the production and refinement of equipment for tilling, particularly its Tiller Combine, which featured a single operation for breaking the soil and planting the seeds.

Canadian farm implement companies were unprepared for the revolution that Henry Ford created with the introduction of his Fordson tractor in 1917. It was mass-produced on an assembly line, just as the Model T was, and it resulted from the same economy of scale as Ford's automobile. The Fordson was central to a major transformation in agriculture from animal and steam power to the more efficient means of powering equipment with gasoline engines. American companies led the field in tractor production, requiring Canadian firms to make arrangements to either import tractors from the United States or manufacture machines with American designs. Massey-Harris tried to produce its own general-purpose tractor with four-wheel-drive, but sales were weak and the vehicle was discontinued.

In the 1930s, Massey-Harris was successful, however, with two other products—an advanced version of its reaper-thresher that weighed about 3,000 pounds less than the previous model, and the self-propelled combine. The company had consistently led Canadian manufacturers in the development of combines to harvest and thresh grain, beginning with its reaper-thresher No. 1 in 1910. Number 5 had a gasoline engine to power the moving parts, although the machine still had to be pulled by a team of horses. Later versions were designed in the Massey-Harris Engineering Department for use with tractors. In 1936, most likely influenced by American streamlining, Massey-Harris introduced a modern aesthetic to its products, which had previously been designed with function as the primary aim.

A team led by mechanical engineer Tom Carroll (1888–1968), an Australian who had joined the company years earlier, created the Massey-Harris self-propelled combine, known as the No. 20, in 1937. Though not the first of these implements, the Massey-Harris version, due to its innovative design features, eventually gained a large share of the combine market.

With the motor and all the performance functions combined in one machine, it required only a single operator, who could reap, thresh, and generate a stream of grain from its raised delivery spout in a continuous automatic operation, thus drastically reducing the time involved for the entire process. Diminishing its weight and lowering its price improved the initial combine, resulting in the No. 21, which went into mass production in 1940, in time to address an acute shortage of rural labor due to World War II. By that time, Canadian farm implement companies were no longer heavily dependent on American designs and patents. They were developing their own products, some of which, like the No. 21 self-propelled combine, became world leaders in the field.

Transportation

In the 19th century, Canada had established itself as a manufacturer of ships, railroad engines, rolling stock, and farm equipment. In the 20th century, shipbuilding declined, but an active automobile industry developed. By World War I, the country was also producing military aircraft and later other planes.

The manufacture of railroad engines and rolling stock was well developed in the 19th century. Canadian companies and inventors introduced numerous design innovations for both locomotives and passenger cars. The intense railroad construction resulted in a railway network that stretched from one coast to the other. Led by the Canadian Pacific, a privately financed rail line, it was supplemented by the consolidated lines of the Canadian National Railroad. This network made possible the movement of raw materials and goods across the country and to ports and connecting railroad lines where they could be shipped to Europe or the United States.

Building on that background, the Canadian National Railroad inaugurated its 6100 series of locomotives in 1927. These were the last of the coal-burning engines. In 1928 the CNR built its first diesel locomotive, the 9000, which was followed by the 9001 (Fig. 31.01).

Fig. 31.01: Canadian National Railroad, 9000 diesel locomotive, 1931. Libraries and Archives Canada. PA-047876.

These diesel locomotives were jointly designed by the Canadian Locomotive Company in Kingston, Ontario, which built the car bodies; the Commonwealth Steel Company; Canadian Westinghouse; and the American Baldwin Locomotive Works. At the time the 9000 was the largest diesel electric locomotive in the world. It was also North America's first diesel passenger locomotive. The Canadian Pacific Railroad also introduced a diesel locomotive in 1937. Because of the Depression, the CNR only manufactured a few of the diesels, consequently missing an opportunity to develop a strong innovative product for export during the 1930s.

Perhaps the major Canadian contributions to rolling stock designs were the numerous types of freight cars and devices for unloading them that Canadian inventors patented for hauling grain. Most were designed in the 20th century, responding to the enormous grain production of the Canadian West. Prominent among them is the Dominion-Howe grain unloader. Its basic concept was developed by

an American engineer, C. D. Howe (1886–1960), who had emigrated to Canada as a young man. He worked with a young Canadian engineer, Fred Newell (dates unconfirmed), who collaborated on the patent. Howe was a partner in C. D. Howe and Company, a firm that constructed grain elevators and came to dominate this business in western Canada. The firm's elevators were better designed and more efficient and cheaper to produce than those of its competitors. The grain unloader, which could empty a grain car in eight minutes compared to an hour with other machines and required only two operators rather than a crew of 20, arose from Howe's interest in a system of efficient grain transport and storage rather than as an isolated phenomenon.

As in the United States and Europe, single inventors created the first automobile designs in Canada. In 1895, Tom Montgomery (dates unconfirmed) designed a three-wheeled vehicle propelled by a huge spring that had to be hand-wound, thrusting the vehicle no farther than a city block. George Foote Foss (1876–1968), a mechanic, blacksmith, and bicycle repairman, is said to have invented the first Canadian gasoline-powered car, later dubbed the Fossmobile, in 1897. He placed his engine at the car's front rather than beneath the seat as many other designers did, thus making maintenance easier. He also mounted the gears directly on the steering column, a design decision that was ahead of its time. Though Foss had an opportunity to produce the cars on an assembly line, he turned it down. There were, however, several other early Canadian cars such as the LeRoy that Milton (dates unconfirmed) and Nelson Good (dates unconfirmed) built in 1899. The LeRoy did go into production for a time but did not last. A number of additional manufacturers also attempted to produce automobiles. These included the Russel, built in Toronto from 1906 to 1915; the Gray-Dort, built in Chatham from 1916 to 1923; the Reo, produced in St. Catherine's; and the Brooks Steamer, built at Stratford, in 1924. Despite this activity, the failure rate for Canadian automobile companies was high and American cars came to dominate the Canadian automobile industry.

The first American firm to be established was Ford Canada in 1904. That year the new company built 117 Model C vehicles. By 1907, Ford was making four different cars: the Model B, Model C, Model R, and Model S. The Model T replaced them all in 1908, although there were slight differences from the American design, due to the use of some Canadian components. Throughout the decades that preceded World War II, Ford produced many Canadian models that duplicated those in the United States, although there were fewer of them. There were also some differences; for example, rumble seat models were available in more varieties for Canadians and a Special Deluxe car was produced in 1936.

The Buick got its start in Canada in 1908 when members of the McLaughlin family, which had previously run the McLaughlin Carriage Company, made an arrangement with the American Buick Company to produce a car with Buick technology called the McLaughlin, later rechristened the McLaughlin-Buick. After Buick became part of the newly formed General Motors, the Canadian company began to produce Chevrolets, tailored, however, to one of the McLaughlin brothers' designs. By 1938, General Motors of Canada, formed from the company that the McLaughlins had sold to American GM management, had produced more than three million vehicles. Studebaker of Canada was established in 1910 and Chrysler Canada became the successor to the Canadian Maxwell-Chalmers Motor Company in 1925. Given a high level of production, the number of automobiles purchased in Canada throughout the 1920s was second only to the United States.

Because of the large amounts of snow in parts of Canada, there was a need for off-road vehicles that could move easily on a snowy surface or a rough terrain. A successful one was invented by a self-taught Quebec mechanical engineer, Joseph-Armand Bombardier (1907–1964), in 1937. Bombardier originally operated a garage, where he gained experience fixing cars. For a number of years he sought to perfect a motorized vehicle that could travel on snow, and in 1937 he built a mechanized snowmobile, which he called the B7 (Fig. 31.02). It had an enclosed body, steerable skis in the front, and sprocketed Caterpillar tracks in back. Bombardier sold a small number of these in 1941 and that year he also introduced the larger B12, which could hold 12 passengers comfortably. In 1942, he established a company, l'Auto-Neige Bombardier Limitée, to manufacture the vehicles in larger numbers. Due to war needs, Bombardier was unable to manufacture large numbers of the B12 for civilian use; hence he adapted the vehicle for the military and produced a considerable number that were used to transport troops in countries with snowy climates such as Norway. He also devised an armored half-track vehicle for military use.

The two pioneers of the Canadian aircraft industry are Wallace Rupert Turnbull (1870–1954), a Canadian who studied mechanical engineering in the

Fig. 31.02: Joseph-Armand Bombardier, B-7 snowmobile, 1937. © Museum of Ingenuity J. Armand Bombardier.

United States, and Alexander Graham Bell (1847–1922), the American inventor of the telephone, who set up a research lab on Cape Breton Island to investigate the possibilities of manned flight. Whereas Turnbull was a lone inventor, Bell gathered together a group of experts with complementary knowledge in aeronautics. He called the group the Aerial Experiment Association (AEA).

Turnbull is credited with the invention of the variable-pitch propeller, which made it possible to adapt the blades to differing thrust levels and air speeds by adjusting their pitch. This enabled an airplane to take off with and carry larger payloads. Turnbull tested a successful system in 1927 and then licensed it to the American company Curtiss-Wright, which eventually incorporated the propeller into the aircraft it produced for the U.S. Navy and Army Air Force.

The AEA experimented with a number of planes before it achieved its greatest success, the Silver Dart, which was the first airplane to fly in Canada, or the British Empire for that matter. The plane derived its name from the silver Japanese silk that covered the wings. The frame and structure were made of steel tubing, combined with bamboo, wire, and wood. The

American Glenn Curtiss supplied the motor. Curtiss was a member of the AEA before he returned to the United States where he founded the Curtiss Airplane and Motor Company, later to become part of the Curtiss-Wright firm (see Chapter 28).

Following the pioneering flight of the Silver Dart, several members of the AEA formed the Canadian Aerodrome Company, with support from Alexander Graham Bell, to create an indigenous Canadian aircraft industry. The first plane they produced was the Baddeck 1, an improved version of the Silver Dart. Plans were also drawn up for a second aircraft, the Baddeck 2. A number of improvements to the Silver Dart were made, but neither version of the Baddeck was ever mass-produced.

There was little other aircraft design activity in Canada before World War I. Glenn Curtiss had set up a Canadian subsidiary, Curtiss Canada, which produced the Curtiss H-4, later renamed the Curtiss-Canada. It was the first twin-engine aircraft to be built and flown in the country. Curtiss's Canadian subsidiary also modified a "Curtiss Model H flying boat" to become a landplane, the C-1. It had its first successful flight in 1915.

A major breakthrough in airplane production occurred in 1917, when the Canadian government took over a few small aircraft plants and set up a company, Canadian Aeroplanes Ltd, which produced a military training aircraft for the Canadian Air Force before World War I ended. Known as the Canuck, it was inspired by the American training biplane, the Curtiss JN-3, though developed independently of it. It had a metal rudder and redesigned fins, while also becoming the first production plane in the United States or Canada to feature a stick control. At least 1,260 planes were completed, making the Canuck the first mass-produced airplane in Canada.

During the 1920s, the British aviation company Vickers established Canadian Vickers, which was responsible for producing a large number of airplanes before World War II. In 1923, the Canadian firm won a contract to provide Vickers Viking flying boats to the Canadian Air Force. The company produced some planes of its own design and built others under license. Canadian Vickers was also interested in small "bush planes" and produced one, the Vickers Vedette, that went into production in 1926.

In 1938, Canada Car and Foundry hired Elsie McGill (1905–1980) as its Chief Aeronautical Engineer. She was the first woman anywhere to hold such a position. Her principal project was the Maple Leaf II, a new training aircraft that was recognized for its high-altitude performance. McGill adapted several elements from an earlier training aircraft that the company had produced, but created an essentially new design. Though the plane was not adopted by the Canadian Air Force, which sought a more challenging trainer, a number were produced in Mexico. There its special properties were appropriate for the many different airfields where it operated.

In 1937, the Canadian parliament created Trans-Canada Airlines, the country's first passenger airline. A subsidiary of Canadian National Railways, it was launched with two passenger planes. A strong supporter of the airline's formation was C. D. Howe, the grain elevator magnate whom Prime Minister William Mackenzie King had appointed Minister of Railways and Canals in 1935. Howe kept the airline in his ministerial portfolio and remained active in its expansion during the post-war years.

Exhibiting design

The principal domestic site for the display of new Canadian inventions and manufactured products such as furniture and appliances, as well as many other things, was the Canadian National Exhibition, whose annual displays in Toronto were initiated in 1879, when it was christened the Toronto Industrial Exhibition. The name was changed to its current one in 1912.

Canadian displays and pavilions in international exhibitions before World War II were undistinguished. As a British colony, Canada exhibited at the 1851

exhibition in London and at others in the 19th century. As a nation with strong political ties to Britain, Canada took part in the British Empire Exhibition at Wembley in 1924. The country did not participate in the 1925 Paris Exposition des Arts Décoratifs, but then as a sovereign state following the 1931 Statute of Westminster, it had its own pavilions at the 1937 World's Fair in Paris and the 1939 Fair in New York. At the Paris fair, the Canadian Pavilion, designed by the Canadian government Exhibition Commission in London, looked like a miniature version of a concrete grain elevator and was attached to the building that housed the United Kingdom's display. However, the furniture and applied arts sector had put its best forward to produce an exhibit of modern home furnishings that was displayed inside.

For the 1939 New York World's Fair, Canada had a more respectable building that was freestanding and contained a more aggressively designed presentation of Canadian life and resources. W. F. Williams (dates unconfirmed) designed the pavilion in a style that might tentatively be called modernist, retaining as it did four columns at the entrance and possessing a heavy rectilinear mass. The exhibits were supervised by James Crockart (1885–1974), who worked primarily as a commercial artist, painter, and etcher in Montreal. The focus was on a display of panoramas, animated maps, dioramas, and photomontages that were intended to attract American tourists and businessmen to Canada. Perhaps reflecting Crockart's background as an etcher, a large illuminated map painted on burnished copper depicted aviation routes, mounted police outposts, grain fields, and mining areas. There was little to show of manufactured products.

A secondary hall featured natural resources and primary industries—mining, agriculture, forestry, and the like. Critics complained that the exhibits were outdated and not adequately representative of contemporary Canada. Most significant is the fact that, despite an increasingly active manufacturing sector that had produced significant breakthroughs in farm implements, railroad engines, radios, and aircraft design, Canada, as it represented itself in New York, was still unable to project a national identity that emphasized its potential as a competitive manufacturing power, rather than a repository of primary resources.

Graphic Design

Advertising

By 1900, advertising agencies could find numerous clients for their services among the many Canadian companies that made packaged food, clothing, cigarettes, and beverages. Services such as insurance were promoted as well. Newspapers and magazines were the principal outlets for ads, although posters and billboards were used to some degree. Products from abroad such as chewing gum and appliances were also widely advertised, some with ads that advertising agencies in the United States produced. Anson McKim (1855–1917) founded Canada's first advertising agency in 1889. Initially known as A. McKim and Company, it was located in Montreal. More than 20 years later, François-Émile Fontaine (dates unconfirmed) founded the Canadian Advertising Agency Ltd in the same city.

Initially, ad layouts were left to newspaper compositors who had no experience with designing appealing ad copy. As a result, many ads were poorly done with too much type and too many typeface variations. Consequently advertising agencies began to insist on having the ads set independently and delivering them as electrotypes—metal plates that contained the entire ad. This made possible national campaigns with the same ads rather than different layouts created by local compositors. Following the electrotype was the stereotype, a papier mâché mold from which a printing plate could be cast.

Advertising agencies were active during World War I, helping with recruiting, promoting investments in war bonds, encouraging greater production, and providing guidance for citizen participation in the war effort. Commercial art studios and printing plants produced posters, sometimes on their own initiative and other times through commissions. The uneven quality of these efforts prompted the government to set up the War Poster Service, while existing federal agencies also created posters for different purposes.

Among the many posters for both English- and French-speaking audiences were a few that stood out for the quality of their artwork. One of the strongest was by a Montreal architect, Percy E. Nobbs (1875–1954). A recruiting poster, it depicted a Canadian soldier about to thrust a bayonet through a black eagle, which represented Germany. Another World War I poster artist was Arthur Hider (1879–1952), whose parents had brought him to Canada from England in the early 1870s. Hider was known as one of Canada's best realist painters who had earlier distinguished himself as a war artist with his drawings and paintings of the Boer War. Several of his recruiting posters for World War I, particularly one addressed to potential French-Canadian recruits, showed a high quality of draftsmanship although they lacked overall design. Other World War I poster artists included Arthur Keelor (dates unconfirmed) and Malcom Gibson (dates unconfirmed).

Following World War I, posters were used sparingly for product advertising, being supplanted by billboards that signified the growing influence of the automobile. Neither product posters nor billboards broke any new ground during the interwar years. Billboards for tobacco, biscuits, and beer represented the product with a package or bottle. These objects were inserted into conventional narrative scenes of people smoking, eating, or drinking. In this sense, the advertising followed the lead of American advertising agencies whose billboards lined that nation's highways. A billboard illustration by Arthur Hider for Black Horse Ale depicted several "connoisseurs" admiring a painting of a black horse, clearly intended as a surrogate for a bottle of the eponymous ale. Among the most iconic billboard images were American illustrator James C. Leyendecker's depictions of Arrow Collar men, transposed to a Canadian setting. A rare exception to the American illustrative style were the designs of Raoul Bonin (1904–1949), a French-Canadian designer who worked briefly with A. M. Cassandre in Paris in the early 1930s. Bonin was perhaps the first graphic designer in Canada to adopt a conceptual approach to poster design.

Commercial art and book design

The distinction between fine art and commercial art in 19th-century Canada was blurred as it continued to be in the years that followed. In Toronto, Canada's leading painters—members of the Group of Seven, which was active between 1920 and 1933, and whose members sought to replace the nation's tradition of academic landscape painting with a more expressive modern style—initially worked as commercial artists for Grip Ltd, a photoengraving house in Toronto that also functioned as a commercial art studio (see Chapter 14). The presence of so many painters on the staff was due to the art director A. H. Robson (dates unconfirmed), who believed that fine artists were particularly well qualified for commercial work. This was sensible, given that most of the jobs at the time involved drawing, whether illustration or lettering, or the technical skill of engraving.

One of the first artists to join Grip Ltd was J. E. H. MacDonald (1873–1932), subsequently a Group of Seven painter, who arrived in 1895, having previously worked for the Toronto Lithographing Company. MacDonald, who had earlier studied at the Central Ontario School of Art, remained with Grip Ltd until 1903, when he went to London. There he worked for the Carlton Studio, a commercial art firm and advertising agency that was started in 1902 by several Canadian artists. Four years later he returned to Toronto, where he rejoined Grip Ltd as supervisor of the design department. He stayed until 1911, when he left to become a freelance designer and to concentrate on his painting.

Other members of the Group of Seven who worked for Grip Ltd were Franz Johnston (1888–1949),

Franklin Carmichael (1890–1945), Frederick Varley (1881–1969), and Arthur Lismer (1885–1969). Lismer had his own publicity studio in Sheffield, England, before he emigrated to Canada. The painters Tom Thompson (1877–1917), Tom McLean (1881–1951), who went on to head the art department at Brigdens Ltd in Winnipeg, William Broadhead (1888–1960), and Neil McKechnie (dates unconfirmed) also worked for Grip Ltd at various times.

In 1912, A. H. Robson, Grip Ltd's art director, left to work for a competitor, Rous and Mann, a printing firm that valued high-quality production and had been established only three years earlier.

Following Robson to Rous and Mann were four of the Grip Ltd artists, Franklin Carmichael, Tom Thomson, Arthur Lismer, and Fred Varley. They were joined by Alfred Casson (1898–1992), who became a Group of Seven artist when Franz Johnston left in 1921. In 1927, Casson left Rous and Mann to become the art director of Sampson Matthews, a printing firm that introduced serigraphy or screen-printing to Canada.

Tom McLean (1881–1951) went on to head the art department at Brigden's Ltd in Winnipeg, which opened in 1913. A branch of the established Toronto engraving firm that bore the same name, it was similar in many ways to Grip Ltd. Brigden's also employed artists including Charles Comfort (1900–1994), who later founded a successful commercial art studio with Will Ogilvie (dates unconfirmed) in Toronto during the 1930s; Philip Surrey (1910–1990); William Winter (1909–1995), who subsequently became a partner in a small Toronto publicity agency and a well-known illustrator; Fritz Brandtner (1896–1969), a German émigré who worked as a designer and lettering artist for Brigden's; and Eric Bergman (1893–1958), a wood engraver who also emigrated from Germany. At Brigden's, Bergman did the wood engravings for the Eaton's Department Store catalogs. The difference between the artists who worked for Brigden's and those on the staff at Grip Ltd was that the Brigden's artists were interested in a more cosmopolitan modernism than the Group of Seven artists in Toronto, whose emphasis was on painting nationalistic landscapes.

Not only did some of the Grip Ltd artists develop into major Canadian painters, but a number of them also went on to become prominent art educators. Before the Group of Seven formed, Arthur Lismer had served as principal of the Victoria School of Art and Design in Halifax between 1916 and 1919. Between 1920 and 1924, Franz Johnston was head of the Winnipeg School of Art and Art Gallery, leading a school that had been founded only seven years earlier, while Fred Varley went to the new Vancouver School of Decorative and Applied Arts in 1926, remaining there for ten years as Head of Drawing, Painting, and Composition.

J. E. H. MacDonald, the senior member of the Group of Seven artists, joined the Department of Design and Applied Art at the Ontario College of Art in 1921, subsequently becoming head of the department, then principal of the school in 1929, a position he held until his death in 1932. He became involved with commercial art education in 1909 when he designed the first of a series of booklets for students enrolled in the Commercial Design course at the Shaw Correspondence School in Toronto. He was made supervisor of the Shaw school's Department of Commercial Design the following year and continued in the position for some years after that.

Besides painting and teaching, MacDonald was active as a freelance commercial artist from the time he left Grip Ltd until he died. He was adept as an illustrator, calligrapher, and layout artist. The range of his clients was extensive and his work included booklets, brochures, programs, book title pages and jackets, lettering, vignettes, bookplates, magazine covers, borders and headpieces, newspaper ads, letterheads, and the occasional poster, along with memorial tablets and plaques, and hand-lettered certificates.

MacDonald worked in a figurative illustrative style and his lettering was based primarily on traditional serif and script faces. He designed book title pages for the Toronto publishers McClelland and Stewart and

the Ryerson Press, mainly in the Arts and Crafts manner, with decorated borders, hand lettering, and line drawings. Among the national magazines for which he worked were *Maclean's*, the *Canadian Magazine,* the *Canadian Forum,* and the *Canadian Courier.* For the latter publication, he designed numerous vignettes, section mastheads, and decorative borders.

MacDonald's son, Thoreau (1905–1989), was also a commercial artist, who specialized in book design and illustration. Color blind, he was noted for his black and white pen and ink drawings. Like his father, he was skilled at lettering as well as drawing and he admired earlier and contemporary British and American lettering artists and typographers such as Edward Johnston, Eric Gill, William Addison Dwiggins, and Fred Goudy.

Thoreau MacDonald was perhaps Canada's leading book designer and illustrator during the period from the 1920s to the 1940s. Like his father, he designed covers and title pages and did illustrations for the Toronto publishers McClelland and Stewart and the Ryerson Press, as well as other firms such as J. M. Dent and Macmillan. The editor of the Ryerson Press, Lorne Pearce (1890–1961), championed Canadian writers and had high standards for book design, which were exemplified by Thoreau MacDonald's title pages with their elegant lettering and illustrative black and white vignettes. He is well known for his illustrations of Louis Hémon's *Maria Chapdelaine*, a popular novel about French-Canadian farm life.

In 1933, Thoreau MacDonald launched his own imprint, the Woodchuck Press, whose books were important examples of the Canadian private press movement. Besides his work in book publishing, he also designed numerous exhibition catalogs and was affiliated with the *Canadian Forum*, a progressive political and cultural magazine that was founded in 1920. He was an early contributor of drawings and linocuts to the magazine before serving as its art director throughout most of the 1920s and the early 1930s, during which time he illustrated most of the covers as well as continuing to provide other artwork.

Railway publicity campaigns

When William Van Horne retired as president of the Canadian Pacific Railroad in 1899, he was succeeded by Thomas Shaughnessy, whom Van Horne had initially brought with him from the United States. Whereas Van Horne was a visionary who was willing to move mountains to lay down the track for a new route, Shaughnessy was a careful administrator who, nonetheless, presided over the greatest expansion in the railroad's history thus far.

In 1911, Shaughnessy created a separate publicity branch that was headquartered in Montreal, maintaining as its head George Ham (dates unconfirmed), whom Van Horne had previously appointed to that position. One function of the branch was the preparation of exhibits. Ham was assisted in this by John Murray Gibbon (1875–1952), a Scottish writer who joined the CPR in London. To the Canadian Pacific Pavilion designed for London's White City exhibition, which was topped by four moose guarding a globe, Gibbon added the slogan, "Canadian Pacific Spans the World." He was also instrumental in arranging the railroad's pavilion at San Francisco's Pan-Pacific Exhibition in 1915. Designed by Beaux Arts-trained American architect Frances Swales (1878–1962), who had also done the White City pavilion, it was a pastiche of elements from different historic periods.

In 1913, Gibbon came to Canada and replaced Ham as the head of advertising to which was added the responsibility for pubic relations. One of his first actions was to include French-language material in the company's advertising program; consequently brochures, pamphlets, and posters that had previously been published only in English were now translated into French as well. Gibbon also had a strong interest in folk art and literature and was responsible for the many folk festivals such as the Highland Gathering, Banff Indian Days, and the Great West Canadian Festivals of folksong, folk dance, and handicrafts that were held at Canadian Pacific hotels and became destinations for railroad travelers.

During the 1920s, Gibbon greatly expanded the number of artists who created posters and other publicity material for the CPR. He brought Alfred Crocker Leighton (1901–1965), a young but already prominent English artist, to Canada and invited him to sketch and paint at sites along the CPR line. Leighton was taken with the majesty of Canada's mountains and produced a number of paintings that were adopted for posters and brochures. During several subsequent visits, he painted sites in other parts of Canada before deciding to settle there. For a brief period, Leighton served as head of the Alberta College of Art, and also established a visual arts program at the Banff School of Fine Arts. By 1938 he had resigned his teaching positions to dedicate himself full-time to painting.

From the time the CPR began offering round-the-world and transpacific cruises in the 1890s, it had developed a separate advertising strategy for its maritime passenger and shipping services. Besides the cruises, the company also promoted ship travel for emigrants to Canada, helping them to acquire farms in the bargain. During World War I, the CPR amalgamated two shipping lines it owned into one, which it called Canadian Pacific Ocean Services (CPOS), a name that was changed to Canadian Pacific Steamships Ltd in 1921.

During the 1920s, C. W. Stokes (dates unconfirmed), the CPR's London director of publicity, recruited a number of British painters to create posters for the steamship division. These included Bernard Gribble (1873–1962), Odin Rosenvinge (1880–1957), Leonard Richmond (1889–1965), Kenneth Shoesmith (1890–1939), Harry Hudson Rodmell (1896–1984), and Norman Wilkinson (1878–1971). Shoesmith, Rodmell, and Wilkinson were also established commercial artists. Rodmell designed posters for various shipping lines, while Wilkinson's poster clients included some of Britain's regional railroads. C. W. Stokes also commissioned designs from British graphic designer Tom Purvis (1888–1959), whose posters for the London and North Eastern Railway (LNER) and the London tailor

Austin Reed did much to create modern images for those organizations.

Purvis notwithstanding, most artists hired by the CPR specialized in marine art and were commissioned to provide paintings of Canadian Pacific ships that could be adapted for lithographic posters with some uninspiring text added. These may be contrasted with the dramatic designerly icons that A. M. Cassandre and other modern poster designers created for rival steamship companies in Europe. In addition to posters, the CPR published lavish pamphlets with no expense spared to promote its cruises during the 1920s. Gold and silver leaf enriched the multi-hued pamphlets whose scenes of exotic destinations were depicted by talented illustrators.

By contrast with the CPR posters produced in London during the 1920s, only a small number of lithographic posters were created in Canada during that decade. Most of the artists remain unknown, although one can mention Canadian painters Gordon Fraser Gillespie (1891–1965), Hal Ross Perrigard (1891–1960), and Charles J. Greenwood (1893–1965), along with the American painter and graphic artist Reinhold H. Palenske (1884–1954). Some of these artists illustrated promotional materials as well.

A new phase of CPR poster production began in 1932 when the company opened a silkscreen printing shop in Montreal's Windsor Station. Among the reasons for adopting silkscreen were its low cost and the rapidity of production. The art director of the studio was Ernest W. Scraggier (dates unconfirmed), who was also assistant director of the Exhibits Branch, which supervised the poster production. Compared to the extensive use of British artists in the prior decade, the artists who created posters for the CPR in the 1930s were for the most part Canadian. The visual emphasis was on modern design rather than traditional painting, and themes shifted from the primacy of landscapes and scenic views to images of active men and women enjoying the outdoors. Suave couples were also depicted as guests at the CPR's luxury hotels or on its cruise ships. Vigorous skiers were shown racing down Quebec's snowy slopes. The overall style of the silk-screened posters was more designerly than the earlier lithographed ones. The most active artist during the 1930s was Norman Fraser (dates unconfirmed), who also created numerous designs that consisted entirely of type and lettering. Fraser is especially well known for his poster that promoted travel on the Canadian Pacific to the 1933 Century of Progress exhibition in Chicago.

The stylistic emphasis was on flat colors and dramatic compositions that featured human activity. Notable exceptions were the posters by Tom Hall (1885–d.o.d. unconfirmed), a wildlife painter and commercial artist, whose images promoted big game hunting featuring moose, deer, and grizzly bears. Two CPR poster artists who were strongly influenced by modern European advertising posters were Peter Ewart (1918–2001) and Roger Couillard (1910–1999), possibly the only French-Canadian to work for the CPR in those years. Ewart had been exposed to the work of A. M. Cassandre, Josef Binder, E. McKnight Kauffer, and Tom Purvis while studying at the Commercial Illustration Studio in New York. Not only did his posters emphasize the flat color of serigraphy, but he also eliminated unnecessary detail in order to create engaging compositions as is evident in a poster that promoted skiing in the Canadian Rockies (Plate 59).

Couillard had his own Montreal design office, Studio Coutrey, where he not only produced posters for the CPR but also for the city of Montreal and the province of Quebec. Unlike Ewart, Couillard created occasional posters that eschewed illustration for more conceptual images as Cassandre had done in many of his designs. Possibly he encountered this approach in the posters of his fellow Quebecois Raoul Bonin. Couillard's poster *See Europe Next*, which featured a map of Western Europe inside a life preserver with a curved red arrow pointing to the map, initially won a poster competition before the CPR published it in 1939. Others who designed modern posters for the CPR during the 1930s were James Crockart, the

Australian-American John Vickery, (1906–1983), and the aforementioned prolific British designer Tom Purvis.

Advertising for the Canadian Pacific Railroad far surpassed that of its rival, the Canadian National Railways (CNR), which did not complete its consolidation of various trunk railroads until 1922. During the interwar years, the CNR failed to mount a publicity program that could in any way rival that of the Canadian Pacific, which had been at it since the 1880s. One artist who did design some posters to promote tourism in Quebec and Ontario was J. E. Sampson (dates unconfirmed), who had gained recognition as a commercial artist for the posters he did during World War I for the Canadian Food Board and to promote the purchase of Victory Bonds.

Australia

The Commonwealth of Australia was created in 1901. At the time, the first Prime Minister, Edmund Barton, stated his intention to create a high court, a uniform railway gauge between the major cities in the east, and to provide various social services. He also promoted a White Australia policy to protect the country from an influx of Asian workers. As a consequence, the Immigration Restriction Act of 1901 was among the first laws the new parliament passed. The second Prime Minister, Alfred Deakin, inaugurated an ambitious program of policy and legislation that contributed to shaping Australia as a modern nation. Among Deakin's accomplishments were the establishment of a currency, the creation of the first independent navy in the British Empire, and the founding of a Bureau of Census and Statistics.

Early in World War I, Australian troops joined soldiers from New Zealand to form the Australia and New Zealand Army Corps (ANZAC), which joined the British forces. However, the term Anzac came to take on a nationalist connotation in Australia, signifying a soldier who had the resourcefulness and pioneer mentality of the settlers. Later the term "digger"

was adopted to characterize civilians with the same qualities.

Australia was offered independent status as a sovereign nation following passage of the 1931 Statute of Westminster in Britain, although the government did not ratify the statute until 1942. Like other countries throughout the world, Australia experienced considerable economic difficulties during the Great Depression of the 1930s. Recovery was a slow process, in part because the federal government had less power to stimulate the economy than did its counterparts in Britain or the United States.

During the interwar years, the policy towards Aborigines shifted from segregation to assimilation. Previously many had been removed to isolated reserves where they were kept in a state of dependence, but even as government officials spoke of granting citizenship to Aborigines, those who lived outside the reserves experienced harsh discrimination and the denial of their rights to housing, education, and employment. Advocacy groups such as the Australian Aborigines' League, founded in 1932, and the Aborigines Progressive Association, created in 1937, sought to redress the injustices done to their people, but progress was slow.

Government promotion of industry

At the time of federation, Australia was primarily exporting wool and metals, while importing many of the goods needed for daily life. The Associated Chambers of Manufacturers of Australia, which brought together the separate manufacturers' chambers that had formed in the colonies before federation, along with the publication of a *Manufacturer's Journal* between 1910 and 1925, helped to promote a manufacturing culture. The federation of Australia's six colonies created a new national market, which gave a strong impulse to industrialization. By 1918, the population was over 5 million, having grown rapidly from 3.8 million in 1901.

In 1918, Prime Minister William Hughes established a Bureau of Commerce and Industry whose director, however, envisioned Britain as a central factory with Australia as one of its branches. His idea, though, was that Australian industries could supply local markets as well as those of nearby countries and colonies. Concomitant with this impulse was the foundation of the Australian Made Preference League (AMPL) in 1924 to promote locally made products and foster import substitution. In the mid-1920s, the league created the Great White Train, an exhibition on wheels that supported the consumption of such products. In 1925 and 1926, the train made two lengthy tours in New South Wales, stopping at many small towns, where residents could view the exhibits and listen to speakers. Advocates of high tariffs, members of the AMPL expressed their views through their journal, the *Australasian Manufacturer*, in which they stated a strong belief in small businesses. Their position supported the idea of industrialization as import replacement, whereby the high tariffs would enable local companies to grow with less competition from abroad.

The regime that followed that of Hughes was more favorable to exports and abolished the Bureau of Commerce and Industry when it came to power in 1923. In 1926, the government headed by S. M. Bruce and Earle Page established a Council of Scientific and Industrial Research, which was initially directed to rural agricultural production. The government also committed itself to advertising and marketing abroad for local producers, forming numerous boards to promote separate agricultural products. Their migration campaign of the 1920s brought close to 300,000 Britons to Australia, although the intention to settle them in rural areas did not succeed. The 1920s also witnessed considerable foreign investment, which boosted manufacturing in sectors such as automobiles and electrical products. Nonetheless, a principal feature of Australian trade in the 1930s was reducing dependence on goods from abroad.

Industrial products

In the years just after World War I, the use of domestic electric appliances was limited. Although electrification

had begun earlier, the supply of electricity was unreliable and expensive and the cost of appliances was high. By 1925, this had changed and the use of such appliances was more widespread. As Colin Forster points out, however, electrical goods such as floor polishers, hair dryers, fans, dishwashing machines, or washing machines were not produced in significant numbers. At the end of the 1920s, the manufacture of refrigerators began in a small way as competition to the American refrigerators that had been imported since around 1912. The only Australian company to produce a significant number of them was the Electricity Meter Manufacturing Company, which had achieved a reasonable output in 1928 and then almost tripled its production the following year. Most firms, however, confined themselves to making cabinets for imported electrical units. In 1934, however, William Queale secured the production and distribution rights to Kelvinator electric refrigerators, which he began to manufacture around that time, changing the name of his company that sold engineering supplies to Kelvinator Australia Ltd.

Local manufacturers, however, were more successful in the production of electrical heating and cooking appliances. A major manufacturer of such appliances, located in Melbourne, was Hecla Electric Pty Ltd, which by the late 1920s had produced thousands of electric heaters and tea kettles, along with large numbers of radiators, electric foot warmers, electric frying pans, urns, coffee percolators, toasters, stoves, and commercial heating appliances for cafés, hospitals, and offices.

The founder of the company was C. W. Marriott (dates unconfirmed), a metalworker who designed and manufactured Australia's first carbon filament radiators in 1899. After extensive experiments, Marriott began manufacturing a range of heaters with a new nickel chromium heating element in 1916, and three years later he adopted the brand name Hecla, taken from Mount Heckla in Iceland, which erupted in 1919. For Marriott, Hecla was associated with heat and power, the two qualities that characterized his products. By late 1924, he had sold more than 80,000 electric heaters throughout Australia and eventually expanded his market to New Zealand, South Africa, and the South Pacific. In 1930, the American firm General Electric acquired a controlling interest in the company, although Hecla retained its local management and identity. During World War II, Hecla was a major producer of military equipment such as steel ammunition boxes, baking ovens for naval ships, and parts for airplanes.

Alex N. Cooke and Co. Pty Ltd was a prominent manufacturer of irons for clothing, beginning in 1918, although foreign competition reduced their output considerably after several years. A major competitor was the Australian General Electric Co., which produced the Hotpoint iron it had formerly introduced in the United States. A few companies such as Rotarex were making vacuum cleaners in the early 1920s with a significant drop in price by 1927. By 1934, R. H. Mytton & Co. was marketing a line of standard kitchen equipment known as Sunshine Units, which were designed as modular elements to fit any room. Mytton stated in its advertising that its intention was to overcome ill-designed and badly-fitted kitchens with equipment that could be flexibly arranged according to the customer's choice. The company's sophisticated marketing approach was evident in their Melbourne showroom where various combinations of kitchen units were on display.

Although electrical appliances had become widespread by the 1930s, telephones had not. As late as 1937, there were only 87 telephones per 1,000 people. The telephones and related equipment were imported for the most part. The main local manufacturer was L. P. R. Bean of Sydney, which was already producing a range of equipment such as phone jacks and cable boxes by 1926. The manufacture of electric lighting globes was handled by foreign companies. Due to competition between the Australian General Electric Company, Philips from the Netherlands,

and Thomson-Houston from Britain, the three came together to form a new jointly owned company to produce lighting globes.

Radios became popular after the development of public broadcasting in the 1920s. The simple technology enabled small companies to enter the field and produce both the electronic components and the handcrafted wooden cabinets that housed them. These were followed by machine-made Bakelite housings, which were often designed by engineers rather than artists. As Colin Forster has shown, the number of radios in Australia jumped exponentially from 430 in 1923 to more than 311,500 in 1930. Initially, Australian firms assembled radios with imported parts, sharing the market with British and American competitors.

By the end of the 1920s, the number of Australian radio companies had increased considerably. The major manufacturer was Amalgamated Wireless Australasia (AWA), which had been started in 1910 by British and German interests. The company's production capabilities had grown during World War I, when it produced wireless telegraph equipment for naval ships. Following the war, AWA expanded its capabilities by designing, manufacturing, and erecting broadcasting stations in several large cities. Their main radio receiver for home use was the Radiola, whose sales increased steadily. A popular model was the Radiola R52, known as the "Empire State" model because the shape of its Art Deco plastic housing was suggested by the eponymous New York skyscraper (Fig. 31.03). Historian Michael Boggle writes that AWA was one of the earliest Australian firms to use product designers. The company set up a small design department that specialized in radio cabinets and equipment. Headed by Lionel Neate (1909–1977), its initial focus was on the requirements for the Radiola. Among the designers AWA hired was R. Haughton James (1906–1985), who had arrived from Britain in 1939.

High tariffs in the 1930s enabled AWA and other radio manufacturers to develop with little competition from manufacturers abroad. Consequently, a number

Fig. 31.03: Radiola R52 "Empire State" model, 1936. Courtesy Leonard Joel http://leonardjoel.com.au/

of Australian firms became successful radio manufacturers. These include Airzone, which produced a range of models, both table-top and console; A. G. Healing, originally a bicycle manufacturer; Astor, whose receivers came in many different colors; Essanay; Kriesler; and Zenith, among whose radios was a battery-powered set that appealed to farmers who lacked access to the municipal electricity of city dwellers. Some companies combined radios and phonographs, as exemplified by the Centurion All-Electric Phono-Radio, which was housed in a cabinet designed to match a three-piece suite of Jacobean furniture.

Australian companies continued to develop farm equipment in order to serve the large rural market. H. V. McKay, whose Sunshine Harvester was a successful implement of the 19th century, continued to expand his company. In 1904, McKay purchased the Braybrook Implement Company, which made seed drills and castings. Around 1916, he bought the patent rights to a machine invented by a self-taught farm equipment designer, Headlie Shipard Taylor (1863–1957). Taylor

had taken out his first patent in 1910 for an improved stripper harvester and then designed a subsequent version that could harvest storm-damaged crops better than any other machine. It featured a comb with long fingers combined with a reciprocating knife and two spirals to convey the crop from the comb to the elevators. McKay put Taylor in charge of producing the machine whose numbers rose from six in 1916 to 325 two years later. Production rose again during 1920, when crops were damaged by widespread storms.

Taylor was dedicated to the design of farm equipment and subsequently created a number of other products for McKay: a crop lifter in 1917; pick-up attachments that enabled the header, as his improved stripper harvester was known, to harvest field peas in 1919; and then a series of improved headers and harvesters continuing into the 1950s. During World War II, he designed three machines that met the demand for equipment to harvest flax. Less successful than the string of products that Taylor invented was the "Sunshine" tractor that McKay introduced in 1916 and abandoned three years later, having found no market for it.

McKay became Australia's largest supplier of farm equipment, which it supported with repair services and other forms of assistance. In 1930 the company joined with the large Canadian firm Massey-Harris to become McKay-Massey-Harris, which brought a new line of tractors to Australia and made the new corporation one of the world's largest farm equipment producers.

Another important innovation was the traction wheel invented by Frank Bottrill (1871–1953), which made possible plowing on rough terrain. Bottrill fitted his traction wheels onto an existing tractor to fulfill a commission from the South Australian government and then went on to design a large tractor, known as "Big Lizzie," which could carry a sizeable load over any kind of terrain. Trained as a blacksmith, Bottrill managed the metalsmithing part of the tractor's construction but then received help from A. H. McDonald & Co. for the other components. Although he accomplished

Fig. 31.04: Frank Bottrill, "Big Lizzie" tractor, c. 1927. State Library of South Australia B 60757.

a number of jobs with his giant tractor, Bottrill ceased using it in 1928 and thus it remained a one-off machine for which no process of mass production was devised (Fig. 31.04).

A more successful implement was the rotary hoe, invented by Cliff Howard (1893–1971), who began experimenting with rotary tillers in 1912. Working through a succession of designs, Howard arrived at an L-shaped blade mounted on flanges that were fixed to a small rotor. After World War I, he patented a design with five rotary hoe cultivator blades and an internal combustion engine. In 1922, Howard formed a company, Austral Auto Cultivators Pty. Ltd, which was later known as Howard Auto Cultivators. To meet a growing worldwide demand for the rotary hoe, he founded a company in Britain, Rotary Hoes Ltd, and eventually established branches throughout the world.

During the interwar years, industrial design in Australia was done without professional designers. Engineers, independent inventors, or persons with mechanical abilities who worked for manufacturers designed most products. An awareness of industrial design began to grow in the 1930s, stimulated by the publication of books such as Herbert Read's *Art and Industry* and the return of several Australian designers from abroad. An early professional group in Australia was the Women's Industrial Art Society, which was established in 1935. It was followed four years later by the Design and Industries Association, one of whose founding members, R. Haughton James, published an article the same year in which he called on the professional design associations to lead the way in educating the public about design. Another supporter of industrial design was the publisher Sydney Ure Smith (1887–1949). He promoted Australian industrialization and the contribution of designers in his magazine *Australia: National Journal*, whose first issue appeared in 1939. That year, R. Haughton James, along with Geoff (1905–d.o.d. unconfirmed) and Dahl Collings (1909–1988), who had spent several years in London working in the design office of László Moholy-Nagy, formed the Design Centre, one of Australia's earliest design firms.

In 1940, the Australian Commercial and Industrial Artists' Association was founded and a year later, the Australian Broadcasting Commission aired a series of talks entitled *Design in Everyday Things*. As historian Michael Boggle notes, these talks, which were modeled on an earlier series of BBC broadcasts in London, addressed the issue of design quality in architecture, clothing, interiors, transportation, and urban planning, and identified a group of Australian products including Crown Crystal cookware, an AWA radio that R. Haughton James designed, and a Victorian Government Railways' streamlined locomotive as exemplary products. The combination of professional societies, design promotion in the press, and the national ABC broadcasts helped to introduce the idea of industrial design to the Australian public. Much was accomplished by self-styled inventors and engineers, but it was only after World War II that industrial design began to develop as a distinct profession.

Transportation

As Simon Jackson has shown, the first Australian car, the kerosene-fueled Pioneer, appeared in 1897, only a year after the initial internal combustion automobile, the Daimler-Benz, was invented in Germany. Before Australia produced its own Holden in 1948, there were no fewer than 100 attempts to design and manufacture a local Australian automobile. The Caldwell Vale of 1913, said to be the world's first touring car with four-wheel drive, was manufactured by the Caldwell Vale Truck and Bus Company, which operated from 1907 to 1913. With a patent for a four-wheel drive system, obtained before 1910, the company also manufactured trucks, tractors, and other vehicles.

Jackson also notes that many of the Australian cars had names that drew on national pride such as Australis, Austral, Australian Six, Auscar, and Southern Cross. Some took their inspiration from the outback,

as exemplified by the names Shearer, Roo, and Bullock. The prototype of the Southern Cross, designed by two aviators, Sir Charles Kingford Smith (1897–1935) and Jim Marks (dates unconfirmed), along with Marks' father, had a streamlined design, which preceded the Chrysler Airflow of 1934 by several years.

Due to import restrictions on foreign automobiles, an active industry of automobile body design developed. Foreign chassis were exempted so they could be imported and sold with bodies designed in Australia. It was not until the 1920s, however, that a market for automobiles developed. At the end of World War I, the automobile was only adopted by a privileged few, but within a decade its use was widespread. A consequence of its popularity was the decline of the horse-drawn carriage, which was almost extinct by the end of the 1920s.

Initially the coachbuilders featured customized bodies that were mounted on imported chassis but gradually production changed from the custom-built body to those that were standardized and built in factories. A leader in the production of standardized bodies was Holden's Motor Body Builders, one of the few large-scale producers along with T. J. Richards and Sons, Allied Motor Interests, Smith and Waddington, and Garrett's Ltd. These were joined by Ford of Canada, which entered the Australian market in 1925.

Holden was the first to adopt the American method of mass production, transforming the job of a skilled coachbuilder into an unskilled line position. In 1924, Holden made an agreement with General Motors to supply bodies for the Chevrolets and Buicks that General Motors Australia made, although the firm continued to design bodies for other companies such as Dodge, Chrysler, Hupmobile, Essex, and Durant. Seven years after its initial agreement with GM, Holden was absorbed by its American partner due to its financial difficulties at the outset of the Great Depression. After 1925, Ford and General Motors, both of which had established efficient assembly plants based on the American system of standardized production, came to dominate the Australian automobile market. Among the contributions by Australian designers were the Ford Coupe Utility, which combined the comfort of a coupe with the carrying capacity of a pick-up truck (Fig. 31.05). It was purportedly conceived by Ford's principal Australian designer, Lewis Bandt (1910–1987), who had started his career as a designer of customized automobile bodies. Later, Ford and General Motors produced versions for sale in the United States. Besides Ford, Holden also introduced an original car, the Sloper Coupe, which was adapted to the range of General Motors automobiles. It was characterized by a lowered front window and a sloping back that gave the vehicle a smoothly rounded rather than a boxy look

In 1929, Ford inaugurated a project to work with local artists to create color schemes for their new roadster and sedan. The company asked the artist and art publisher Sydney Ure Smith, and the artists Thea Proctor (1879–1966) and George Lambert (1873–1930), all associated with Smith's magazines *Art in Australia*

and *The Home*, to make color selections for the cars. In its advertising for the vehicles, Ford stated that color styling was a job that trained artists could do much better than the layman.

The Victorian State Railways continued to be a leader in the design of railway locomotives, with steam locomotives rather than diesel in use throughout the interwar period. In 1928 the railroad introduced the S class locomotive, designed under the supervision of the railroad's Chief Mechanical Engineer, Alfred E. Smith (dates unconfirmed), who was inspired by the pioneering modern designs of British locomotive engineer Nigel Gresley. The S class engines, which were the railroad's first three-cylinder locomotives, also showed some influence from American designs. Until 1937 these locomotives retained a conventional form, but that year several were streamlined and a "Royal Blue" color scheme was adopted, following a similar one on an American Baltimore & Ohio train. Dubbed the Edward Henty locomotive after one of Victoria's

Fig. 31.05: Ford Coupe Utility, 1934. State Library of South Australia, B 54446.

pioneer settlers, it pulled the Victoria Railways new streamlined train, the *Sprit of Progress*, which introduced a standard of speed and comfort that had not been seen in Australia before (Plate 60). Besides its streamlined design, the *Spirit of Progress* was fitted in an Art Deco style. It featured a dining car with a galley kitchen modeled after the most current hospital kitchens. Bringing up its rear was a round-ended parlor car that featured panoramic views of the Victorian landscape.

The plane that is generally considered to have launched the Australian aircraft industry is the Wirraway, a general-purpose trainer aircraft that was adapted from the North American NA-16, which had been selected by the Royal Australian Air Force after a survey of planes in a number of countries. It was made under license between 1936 and 1945 by the privately owned Commonwealth Aircraft Corporation (CAC). A succession of models was built. The basic model was the CA-3, followed by similar ones until the CA-16, which had major design changes, notably wing modifications to support a heavier bomb load and dive brakes for dive-bombing.

Lawrence Wackett (1896–1982), who chose the NA-16 as a model for the Wirraway, was a wing commander in the RAAF. In 1924, he was put in charge of the RAAF's newly established Experimental Aircraft Section, where he obtained funds to design a small flying boat. Known as the Widgeon, it was a biplane with a wooden hull, and preceded a larger amphibious version known as the Widgeon II. The section also produced the two-seat biplane Warrigal 1 in 1929, and in 1930 the Warrigal II, which was Australia's first all metal plane. The Experimental Aircraft Station was closed in 1931, presumably due to pressure from British manufacturers who saw the emerging aircraft production as a threat to their monopoly on aircraft sales in Australia. Wackett continued as a designer, moving to the Cockatoo Island Naval Dockyard, where he was involved with the design of watercraft as well as designs for several passenger aircraft of which only one,

the Codock, was built. His boat designs included the Cettien, a small motorboat, and the racing hydroplane, Century Tire II, as well as larger vessels that carried passengers.

Wackett and some of his staff joined Tugan Aircraft, a private company, in 1934. After he was chosen to lead the mission that selected the NA-16, Wackett returned to Tugan, where he designed a small passenger plane, the LJW7 Gannet, that entered series production. Shortly after its establishment, the Commonwealth Aircraft Corporation purchased Tugan Aircraft and Wackett became General Manager of the new company, where he oversaw the development of the Wirraway as the first mass-produced aircraft in Australia. Although the Wirraway was used for military purposes, commercial aviation was also developing, though with airplanes manufactured elsewhere. By the late 1930s, the main commercial airline was Australian National Airways (ANA), which imported the Douglas DC2 in 1936 and the DC3 in 1937.

Design for domestic space

Arts and crafts

The Arts and Crafts movement continued to influence Australian domestic design long after it had waned in Great Britain. A number of Australian architects had designed houses with integrated interiors in the late 19th century, following Arts and Crafts models, and this tendency continued into the 20th. The Tasmanian Arts and Crafts Society was formed in 1903, and others followed: New South Wales in 1906, Victoria in 1908, and Brisbane around 1912. These societies were extremely active before World War I, having established clubrooms, libraries, and classes. As Grace Cochrane points out, architects usually played prominent roles in the societies, as did teachers of applied arts. In New South Wales and Queensland, the membership consisted almost exclusively of women. In Tasmania, J. R. Tranthim-Fryer (1860–c. 1931) and Lucien Dechaineaux (1869–1957) sought to establish a movement that followed the principles that John

Ruskin and William Morris espoused, although many members of the Arts and Crafts societies tended to be skilled amateurs who were less interested in the aims of the movement's British founders than in opportunities to exhibit and sell their craft work.

An exhibition of 1907 in Melbourne, the Australian Exhibition of Women's Work, was not explicitly devoted to the arts and crafts but to the broader creative work of women, which included drawing, sculpture, and photography as well as crafts such as pottery, needlework, leatherwork, and weaving (Fig. 31.06). The exhibiton came just a few years after federation and attracted work from 31 countries. The aim of the exhibition's organizers was to establish a place for women's production within the emerging culture of the new state. There were 16,000 exhibits including 5,000 in the section on fine and applied arts. A number of exhibits showed most of the trades in which women and girls were employed, while some demonstrated actual manufacturing processes. Women's inventions were also on display as were exhibits that women ran. One of the exhibition's organizers was Eirene Mort (1879–1977), who had studied at the Royal College of Art and the Royal School of Needlework in London. She had returned to Sydney in 1906, and with Nora K. Weston (dates unconfirmed) set up a studio that was influenced by Pre-Raphaelite philosophy and the ideas of William Morris. The two women produced work related to numerous branches of applied art including printed textiles, embroidery, ceramics, brass, wood, and leather. Following Lucian Henry, Mort proposed a national school of design that would train students to produce designs with Australian motifs. After a 1909 return visit to England, she concentrated more on art education, etching, and book illustration.

Also in Melbourne, a large arts and crafts

Fig. 31.06: First Australian Exhibition of Women's Work, poster, 1907. Castlemaine Art Gallery, Victoria, Australia/Bridgeman Images.

exhibition was held in 1908. It showcased work by some of the leading craftspersons among the Australian enthusiasts such as Mabel Young (dates unconfirmed), who collaborated with her husband, the artist Blamire Young. Other craftspersons who, like the Youngs, designed furniture, moldings, and murals for domestic interiors included Rodney Howard Alsop (1881–1932), an architect and metalworker, and his sisters Edith (1871–1958) and Ruth (dates unconfirmed) as well as the husband and wife team Robin (1868–1920), an architect, and Mary Dods (1867–1951). The Dods also designed and produced textiles.

The writings of William Morris and Mackay Hugh Baillie Scott influenced some Australian furniture makers by urging simplicity of design. Besides the custom-made pieces, department stores such as David Jones in Sydney manufactured Arts and Crafts-style furniture in their own workshops, a trend that some larger commercial furniture companies followed. The latter included Craftsman-style furniture by John Hicks and Beard Watson & Co. for the Brisbane and Sydney markets respectively. Historian Harriet Edquist considers these initiatives to have produced the first modern furniture in Australia.

The Arts and Crafts emphasis on collaborative work could be seen in various public commissions such as the children's ward at the Melbourne Homeopathic Hospital, which had mural panels by a number of artists; the grand lounge that architect Harold Desbrowe-Annear (1865–1933), founder of the short-lived T Square Club, designed for Melbourne's Menzies Hotel; and the Café Australia in Melbourne, designed in 1916 by the American architects Walter Burley Griffin (1876–1937) and Marion Mahony Griffin (1871–1961), both of whom had worked for Frank Lloyd Wright. The café included decorative abstract and figurative plasterwork on columns, walls, and ceilings, stained glass, and tables and chairs, some of wood designed by themselves and some of cane. The plain furniture with curved lines for the Café Australia was developed further the next year in their project for Newman College, which was affiliated with University of Melbourne. Walter created distinctive chairs, tables, and bookshelves for the dining room and furniture for the bedrooms. The clean lines, unadorned surfaces, and simple upholstery reinforced the idea of simplicity in domestic furnishings, helping to shift Australian taste in a small way from the ornate Jacobean and other period styles that were dominant in the domestic interiors of middle- and upper-class home owners until that time.

Design for domestic use

During the interwar years, a few major manufacturers produced furniture in a range of styles. Department stores also created their own lines, while magazines such as *The Home* played a leading role in promoting modern design, identifying numerous Australians such as Hera Roberts, Thea Proctor, Michael O'Connell (dates unconfirmed), Roy de Maistre (1894–1968), Raymond McGrath, and A. N. Baldwinson (1908–1969) who were designing furniture, textiles, and interiors in a modern vein. *The Home* put a special emphasis on European modern design, particularly French examples. It covered the Exposition des Arts Décoratifs in Paris but also featured an article on the Bauhaus in the late 1920s. Le Corbusier was featured as well, as were excerpts from his book *Towards a New Architecture*.

The Sydney department store David Jones employed Molly Grey (dates unconfirmed), who had worked with several decorating firms in Europe and the United States before returning to Australia in 1934. Grey, considered to be one of Sydney's first commercial modern designers, originally arranged photo publicity for David Jones but subsequently designed furniture for the store in diverse styles that included Art Deco and pared down modern. Thea Proctor and Roy de Maistre (1894–1968) also worked for several Sydney department stores including Grace Bros, developing decor for retail furniture displays. Proctor, who had lived in Britain for almost 20 years, taught design at the art school of Julian Ashton when she returned to Sydney, and worked in many design fields ranging from interior decoration to graphic design and illustration. Her cousin Hera Roberts, though primarily a commercial artist and art director, designed a desk for the Stuart-Low Furniture Studio, which for the most part specialized in period styles.

Roy de Maistre was primarily a painter, but he also designed furniture and interiors. He was a principal organizer of an important furniture exhibition that was held at Burdekin House in Sydney in 1929. Juxtaposed with several large rooms of antique furniture were rooms of modern furnishings designed by six artists, designers, scholars, and architects among whom were de Maistre himself, Thea Proctor, and Hera Roberts (1892–1969). Other rooms were by Lindsay Sandler (dates unconfirmed), a professor of Asian studies, whose interiors displayed a strong Japanese influence; the painter Adrien Feint (1894–1971); Leon Gellert (1892–1977), poet and editor of *The Home*, who designed a man's study; Henry Peynor (dates unconfirmed); and Frank Weitzel (1905–1932), whose austere interior featured furniture that recalled some Bauhaus designs. Hera Roberts designed angular chairs, tables, and sideboards in an Art Deco mode that was complemented by carpets with colorful geometric designs. The furniture for the exhibition was made by prominent retailers such as Anthony Horden and Son, Beard Watson & Company, and William Grant & Company, most likely in the hope that the new style would catch on with the public. However, the exhibition had little commercial effect and the pieces it included were for the most part, one of a kind. The Art Deco style did influence some commercial furniture designs, if only in a modest way.

Furniture design in the international style was rare in Australia during the interwar years. In 1933, A. J. Healing Limited began producing chromed steel cantilevered chairs designed several years earlier by Marcel Breuer, then a Bauhaus teacher. The leading Australian designer of modern furniture was Frederick Ward (1900–1990), who, according to Robin Boyd,

began making plain wooden furniture in the late 1920s. Ward had an appreciation for the natural grains and colors of wood, preferring not to stain it, and he made extensive use of Australian woods that furniture makers had not used before. In the early 1930s the design department of Myer Emporium, Melbourne's most modern department store, engaged him to develop a unit line of modern wooden furniture. There he designed prototypes for a wide range of pieces that incorporated various details such as slanted drawers without handles. Ward designed for other companies as well, and in 1932 he opened his own studio. Also in Melbourne, the Melbourne Chair Company produced the "Kangaroo" chair, which had a wooden back slat adorned with kangaroos and wildflowers known as banksia. The company also made versions with emus and lyrebirds. After 1908, thousands were produced until the company's demise 30 years later.

The market for glassware in the 1920s, as Grace Cochrane notes, was dominated by cheap imported glass from abroad. The Australian Glass Manufacturers Co. (AGM) had gained a monopoly in Australia by purchasing other companies and opening branches throughout the country. Adopting a nationalist spirit of design, the company featured glassware with images of local fauna such as the kangaroo, emu, and kookaburra, and flora including the waratah and flannel flower. The company also produced some Art Deco forms with frosted surfaces that recalled the glassware of the French designer René Lalique. Distinctive also was Carnival Glass, which was notable for its shimmering colors. It was made from about 1918 to 1926 by Australian Crystal Glass Ltd, which was joined with AGM's Crown Glass Works to become the Crown Crystal Glass Company, which introduced cut crystal in the 1930s to complement its pressed glassware.

Pottery manufacturers such as the Hoffman's and Premier Potteries in Melbourne, along with Bakeman's and Mashman Bros. in Sydney, produced a range of domestic wares that adopted Art Deco motifs. The latter's Mashman Regal Artware featured vases and bowls of various shapes with drip glazes in different colors. Though originally influenced by English design, Mashman Bros. later incorporated nationalist motifs of Australian flora and fauna with the intent of appealing to local markets.

Where the appropriation of Aboriginal imagery in the 19th century was generally done without regard to the integrity of Aboriginal culture and frequently featured caricatures that lacked respect, discussions about the place of that culture within a national artistic identity became more serious in the years after federation. In 1925, the artist Margaret Preston (1875–1963) published a seminal article, "The Indigenous Art of Australia," in which she identified Aboriginal art as exemplary of authentic Australian culture. In a telling passage, however, Preston likened the Australian adoption of motifs from Aboriginal art to France's appropriation of imagery from the native arts of that nation's colonies.

Aboriginal motifs were used in the interwar years by china painters, textile designers, and potters, not to mention graphic designers. Preston idealistically believed that Aboriginal art might serve as the foundation for a unified Australian visual culture, although her idealism was severely undermined by the assimilationist policies of the Australian government during the 1930s that led to the kidnapping of thousands of Aboriginal children from their parents and their being sent to live with white families in order to learn the ways of the dominant Australian world.

Other artists who adopted Aboriginal motifs in their work include Frances Derham (1894–1987), a pioneering educator, and Frances Burke (1907–1994), a textile printer who produced her first collection of fabrics in 1937 and established her own textile workshop the following year (Fig. 31.07).

Margaret Preston's cultural assimilationist argument was elaborated in the exhibition Australian Aboriginal Art and Its Application, which the Australian Museum mounted in 1941. Held in the auditorium of the David Jones department store in Sydney, its intent was to demonstrate that Aboriginal art was a rich source of inspiration for Australian designers. The organizers displayed original source material from the museum's collection, which it compared with the work of craftspersons, commercial artists, and architects who had made use Aboriginal art in their own designs. The range of work included mural designs, interior decor,

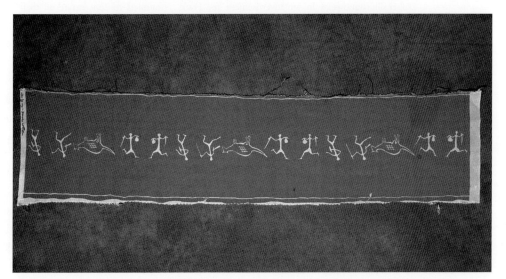

Fig. 31.07: Frances Burke, "The Hunt" fabric design, c. 1940. Collection: Museum of Applied Arts & Sciences, Sydney. Photographer unknown/Courtesy of RMIT Design Archives.

and other architectural applications along with an array of ceramicware, cigarette boxes, ash trays, table mats, textiles, and beach tiles that one might well argue extracted the motifs from their original cultural context and turned them into commercial icons.

Graphic design

Advertising

Harry Weston (dates unconfirmed), who started the Weston Company, an advertising studio, in 1901, was a jack-of-all-trades. He painted in oils and watercolors, made prints, created posters, and drew cartoons. His intent in opening his studio was to furnish artwork for clients as well as to sell advertising space. He came to Sydney from Tasmania and then Melbourne, where he had joined the cooperative poster studio formed by Blamire Young. His early clients included Dunlop Rubber and Boomerang Brandy.

After he found a business partner in 1904, Weston devoted himself entirely to graphic art, producing large numbers of posters and advertisements as well as magazine covers and book illustrations. He did not have a distinctive stylistic approach. Some ads consisted of anecdotal cartoons, while others featured more sober illustrations as in an advertisement for Franz Josef Lager of 1911, which depicted a wealthy young sportsman accepting a bottle of the lager from an older waiter in formal serving attire. Though intended to denote an Australian setting, the image recalls posters by Ludwig Hohlwein in Germany and the American J. C. Leyendecker, who by this time had already done numerous advertisements for various men's clothing companies that showed self-assured wealthy young men.

In Melbourne, Hugh Paton (1871–1951), who referred to himself as an "advertect," opened the Paton Advertising Service in 1904. At the time, businesses tended to create their own advertisements, which were generally dull and consisted primarily of text. Paton adopted the system that had already been established in Britain and the United States of preparing ads for clients and then placing them in publications. His ads featured illustrations, which he produced initially with woodblocks but then with photography as soon as process engraving made printing photographs possible. Paton's agency expanded and he led the way in creating trade associations like the Victorian Institute of Advertising to legitimize his profession.

Paton may be remembered more for developing and defining the role and function of advertising agencies than for any particular projects or campaigns. The agency that more than any other created memorable artistic ads in the early years of Australian advertising was Smith & Julius Studios, which Sydney Ure Smith (1887–1949) and Harry Julius (1885–1938) founded in 1906. Both men had studied at the art school set up by the prominent artist and teacher Julian Ashton in Sydney. There, Ashton taught both commercial and fine art.

Smith and Julius were excellent draftsmen and consequently much of their studio's early work consisted of black and white drawings, either illustrations for articles and stories in newspapers or advertisements for large department stores. By 1912, the firm had taken on a partner to manage the business, enabling the two founders to concentrate on their art. Over time, the agency was not only known for the quality of its work but also for the use of the most advanced printing technology.

By 1917, Smith and Julius had built a talented staff of trained artists whose commercial work, they believed, would also leave them time for their own endeavors. A number of the artists had also studied with Julian Ashton and went on to become major figures in the art world. There was, in fact, a close connection between the Julian Ashton School of Art, Smith & Julius Studios, and the Society of Artists in which both Ashton and Smith were active.

Smith & Julius clients included furniture companies, department stores, and some other large businesses, among them the Australian General Electric Company and Barnes Linseed Oil. Many of the advertisements the agency did for these clients appeared after 1916 in the magazine *Art in Australia*, which Sydney Ure Smith founded. Due to his interest in printing technology, the firm was able to print many of its ads in four colors.

The agency's ads followed a strict division between the image and the text, with the restrained layouts deriving more from book design than bold advertising rhetoric. For several ads the studio created to promote its own services, the decorative floral borders around the images and their placement in relation to the columns of text suggest a strong influence of the Arts and Crafts movement.

Among the major artists on the Smith & Julius staff were Lloyd Rees (1895–1988), who built a reputation as a landscape painter; Roland Wakelin (1887–1971), a founder of Sydney's modern art movement; and Percy Leason (1889–1959), a skilled draftsman who was a designer of posters and a book illustrator before he became Smith & Julius's chief designer. Subsequently, Leason contributed cartoons to several humor magazines, notably his drawings of Wiregrass, a mythical Australian town.

Other artists who worked for Smith and Julius included J. B. Godson (1882–1957), George Lawrence (c. 1901–1981), Rema Becke (dates unconfirmed), James Muir Auld (1879–1942), Adrian Feint, John Passmore (1904–1984), Albert Collins (dates unconfirmed), and Alek Sass (1877–1922). The firm also had a separate typography department with several employees including the typographers Perce Green (1889–1972), who did the layouts for most of the advertisements, and Percy Pickles (dates unconfirmed), a specialist in the design of decorative borders. They were later joined by a lettering man, W. E. Roberts (dates unconfirmed), who was considered the best in Sydney.

By 1924, Sydney Smith had ceased involvement with the advertising studio in order to focus on a number of publishing ventures he had initiated. Harry Julius and the artist Albert Collins then ran the business until it merged in 1934 with the Catts Patterson Advertising Agency, which by 1920 had become the largest and most comprehensive agency in Australia. Julius later pursued a career in animation, having created the first Australian animated film in 1912, after which he established Australia's first studio for the production of animated advertising films.

A leading competitor with Smith & Julius in Sydney was Jones & Jardine, which was established in 1905, with the illustrator Walter Jardine (1884–1970) as one of its principals. Jardine was a talented artist, known for his line and brush drawings, who had spent years working for the *Australian Star*, where he achieved wide recognition for his black and white illustrations. Jones & Jardine had built up a staff of about 20 artists and apprentices before Jardine left for New York, where he became a successful illustrator and graphic designer. After he returned to Sydney in 1928, he opened a studio and secured work from a range of clients that included the Orient Steam Navigation Company, the Stamina Clothing Company, the Department of Defense, and the Agricultural Society of New South Wales.

Though artists such as Harry Winston and Blamire Young had created advertising posters in limited numbers before World War I, the successful adoption of posters to promote Australia's involvement in the war gave evidence that the poster could be used as a powerful advertising medium. During the war, James Northfield (1887–1973) was a leading poster designer, creating posters for recruitment, the purchase of Peace Bonds, and other purposes. Northfield was originally apprenticed with several printing companies before the war, which led to a mastery of color lithography. After the war, he opened his own agency, Northfield Studios, in Melbourne. His clients included many companies, the Victoria Railways, and the Australian National Travel Association (ANTA). For the latter two, he did many posters to promote Australian tourism.

Northfield's designs for posters as well as for his billboards were illustrative and narrative, adopting rhetorical strategies of advertising such as emphasizing trade mark figures as he did in his posters for Jacko

Boot Polish and Roxy Baby Powder, or creating pithy narrative scenes as he did for Glen Valley Tea and Golden Fleece Underwear, where he depicted an entire family clad in the company's long johns, except for the mother who wore more delicate though hardly revealing garments.

Noteworthy among Northfield's advertising posters were those he did for Pelaco, a shirt manufacturer that had adopted for its trademark the image of a real Aboriginal man known as Mulga Fred. Instead of showing him as a near naked primitive, however, the owners depicted him wearing their formal dress

Fig. 31.08: James Northfield, Pelaco shirts, poster, 1930s. © James Northfield Heritage Art Trust.

shirt accompanied by copy lines that combined pidgin English with standard speech such as "Mine tink it, they fit." While some Pelaco advertisements portrayed Mulga Fred wearing only a shirt, a straw hat, and no pants, others showed him fully dressed. In one billboard depiction he was portrayed in full cricket attire, thus socialized into the white man's world, and in one of Northfield's posters he rises above the factory building in a fierce pose, ready to hurl a boomerang with one hand while holding several more in the other (Fig. 31.08).

Pelaco's choice of Mulga Fred, known in the ads as Pelaco Bill, comes closest to the American trademarks that featured black social types such as Aunt Jemimah and Uncle Ben. Years after Mulga Fred's image was widely publicized on posters, billboards, point of purchase displays, and in press advertisements, he was replaced by a well-known white female model named Patricia Tuckwell, who was known as Bambi Shmith, and the pidgin English was exchanged for an updated copy line in standard prose.

Aspiring commercial artists studied at the Sydney Art School, which featured a design course taught by Thea Proctor; the Art Training Institute in Melbourne, where James Northfield taught for many years and became Chief Director of Studies; and the Leyshon White Commercial Art School in the same city, which the painter and commercial artist Leyshon White (1894–1962) ran from around 1925 to 1935. As Geoff Caban notes, the early advertising studios in Australia such as James Northfield's usually consisted of one or two people who did everything, but the experiences of a few others such as the Weston Company, Paton Advertising Service, Jones & Jardine, and especially Smith & Julius with its range of different talents, pointed towards a different, more modern, model of a multi-service advertising agency with functions divided among specialized staff.

Trademarks and packaging

Trademarks in the interwar years did not change

considerably from the 19th-century tendency to adopt icons of nature or culture that represented aspects of Australian identity. One new icon was the map of Australia, formed from the six provinces that amalgamated into the new Commonwealth of Australia in 1901. Used as a trademark for myriad products, the map usually formed a frame within which there might be anything from the company's name to a product image. Local mammals and birds such as the kangaroo and kookaburra remained popular, as did other mammals less seen as 19th-century trademarks such as the koala. A contradiction to this tendency was William Ramsay's adoption of the flightless New Zealand bird, the Kiwi, as the brand name and image for a shoe polish he began to market with a partner in 1906 (Fig. 31.09). Ramsay did so to honor his wife, who was from New Zealand. The manufacturer of a rival product, Jacko Shoe Polish, substituted an Australian bird for the Kiwi in order to appeal to the customer's patriotic instinct. Nonetheless, Kiwi was a superior brand that eventually became the world's leading shoe polish.

Another type of nationalist trademark was the outback type who represented the Commonwealth's pioneering spirit. This might be a digger panning for gold; a stockman or stock rider, who herded cattle;

Fig. 31.09: Kiwi shoe polish can, date unconfirmed. © Lynne Sutherland/Alamy.

a drover, who moved animals over long distances; or simply an itinerant worker or swagman. These figures were associated with products ranging from veterinary ointment to eucalyptus oil, farm equipment or foodstuffs.

Aboriginal images such as that of Mulga Fred were used blatantly and in a derogatory manner. A paint company that called itself Abo featured a photograph of an Aboriginal man as its trademark, while Whacco Pty Ltd, which sold self-rising flour, created a trademark with its name emblazoned within a boomerang that framed an Aboriginal man with another boomerang ready to throw. By the 1940s, this trademark was streamlined, but the representation of the Aborigine, called "The Abo," remained the same.

Tourist graphics

Appointed as Chairman of the Commissioners of Victorian Railways in 1920, Harold Clapp (1875–1952) involved himself with all aspects of the railway's operation including its advertising. Likely inspired by the advertising program that Frank Pick introduced to publicize the London Underground, Clapp initiated a campaign to promote Victoria as a tourist destination. Posters were commissioned from leading commercial artists: James Northfield, Gert Sellheim (1901–1970), and Percy Trompf (1902–1964). Northfield, as already mentioned, specialized in advertising posters and billboards. Percy Trompf joined the commercial art firm of Giles and Richards in Melbourne in 1923 and later opened his own studio, where he specialized in advertising and poster design. Sellheim was an Estonian-born German who emigrated to Australia in 1926. He established an architecture and design practice in Melbourne in 1930 and began to design posters the following year. During World War II, he was interned briefly, and subsequently settled in Sydney.

The posters that Northfield and Trompf designed for the Victorian Railways were more conservative than many that Frank Pick commissioned for the London Underground. Instead, they were closer to the travel genre that had been established in Britain by Tom Purvis and others who created posters for the British railroads. Both Northfield and Trompf depicted handsome affluent visitors enjoying the resources of Victoria's national parks, while also portraying some of the state's magnificent natural settings such as Mt. Buffalo National Park and the Grampian Mountains.

With the establishment of the Australian National Travel Association (ANTA) in 1929, which was initially chaired by Harold Clapp, the Australian government launched a serious initiative to promote tourism as a significant contributor to the national economy. Funding for the initiative, which included the design and production of posters, along with advertising in overseas journals, providing literature to travel agents, and creating various publications and films, came from the government as well as other organizations such as the Commonwealth Railway, hotels, and shipping businesses that stood to gain from an increased flow of visitors. The ANTA's extensive poster program followed that of the Victorian Railways, no doubt because of Harold Clapp's influence. Artists were hired to depict prominent national sites such as the Great Barrier Coral Reef in Queensland, the Blue Mountains in New South Wales, and the new capitol of Canberra.

Those who created posters for the ANTA included the three artists who had established the poster program for the Victorian Railways—James Northfield, Percy Trompf, and Gert Sellheim. Both Northfield and Trompf produced posters for the ANTA that were similar in style and technique to those they had done for Victorian Railways. Though Trompf was captivated by natural settings, he was equally adept at portraying well-off travelers visiting not only sites of great natural beauty but also the outback where they might encounter rugged sheepherders as well as Aborigines, who were depicted as exotic natives. One of his exemplary posters, however, was of a different sort. In vivid colors and a detailed drawing style, he

portrayed the rich marine life of the Great Barrier Reef (Fig. 31.10).

Sellheim was a designer rather than an illustrator, and his posters were always conceptual instead of narrative. In fact, he was one of the first commercial artists to break away from the illustrative style that had previously dominated Australian advertising. His compositions for the Victorian Railways and ANTA posters were always well ordered and he generally used flat shapes with no attempt at modeling his figures. His colors were bright and contributed to the overall formal composition. Posters for the Surf Club included repeated figures of stylized bathers who became part of the design. His use of such figures to form a pattern was also evident in his ANTA poster for an Aboriginal Corroboree or ceremonial meeting. In that poster as in others, Sellheim also showed himself to be adept at lettering, which was integrated into the composition.

Sellheim may have been the first or at least one of the first Australian designers to use photographs in his posters. This was evident in those he did for both the Victorian Railways and the ANTA. His incorporation of photographic images most likely preceded that of Douglas Annand (1903–1976), who adopted the technique for both magazine covers and posters in the 1930s. Annand, in fact, incorporated photographs in several posters he designed for the ANTA in the late 1930s. Along with Richard Beck (dates unconfirmed), Walter Jardine, and other artists, Annand also created posters in the new design style for the Orient Line Cruises. Other artists who did posters for the ANTA included Robert Curtis (1898–1966), John Goodchild (1898–1980), Fred Grey (1899–1957), John Telfer Gray (1911–1972), Harry Kelly (1896–1967), Charles Meere (1890–1961), Raphael Roussel (1883–1967), Ronald Skate (1913–d.o.d. unconfirmed), and the English poster designer Tom Purvis.

The ANTA also published an illustrated magazine, *Walkabout*, whose first issue appeared in 1934. A travel publication intended to promote

Australian tourism with articles that ranged from culture and geography to science, its stories were amply illustrated with numerous photographs and it became a prime vehicle for the development of photojournalism in Australia (Fig. 31.10). Among the photographers whose work the magazine published in its early years were Harold Cazneaux (1878–1953) and Max Dupain (1911–1992), both of whom also contributed to the magazines that Sydney Ure Smith published.

A strong influence on the magazine's content was Charles Holmes, a central figure in the ANTA for 30 years. He traveled the continent with a photographer to collect interesting images and stories for the magazine. A supporter of the "White Australia" policy, Holmes had a derogatory view of Aborigines, who were presented in *Walkabout* as exotic primitives. The primary representations of this view were Roy Dunstan's photographs of "Jimmy" (Gwoja Tjungurrayi), an older Aboriginal man who was shown naked except for a loin cloth as an example of Australia's archetypal native population.

Jillian Barnes has identified three ways that *Walkabout* under Holmes' guidance interpreted the Australian landscape for tourists. First, through the "imperial" gaze that celebrated British discovery of the continent and the mastery of a hostile terrain; second was the "pioneer" tourist gaze that allied central Australia with modern civilization and indigenous people who were ill suited to it; and third was the "anthropological" gaze, which involved the juxtaposition of pre-modern people with images of Western progress. Barnes notes that these three views supported Holmes' selection of authors, his choice of photographs, their juxtapositions in layouts, and their captions.

Magazines and books

The "black-and-white" drawing style that became popular in the late 19th century, particularly in the weekly *Bulletin,* continued to flourish in the early years of the 20th century, not only in *The Bulletin* but also in new magazines such as *The Lone Hand* and *Smith's Weekly.* A principal founder of *The Lone Hand,* which appeared from 1907 to 1921, was the journalist J. F. Archibald, who had previously co-founded the popular *Bulletin. The Lone Hand* was, in fact, published by the Bulletin Company as a monthly and was intended to complement its weekly forerunner. Like *The Bulletin,* it was amply illustrated and featured full color covers by established artists and illustrators. Though some of its articles addressed political topics, *The Lone Hand* was primarily a cultural magazine rather than a publication of regular political commentary; hence it did not have a political cartoonist.

One artist whose work was extensively published in *The Lone Hand* was Norman Lindsay (1879–1969), a staff cartoonist and illustrator for *The Bulletin* but also a painter, etcher, and book illustrator who became

Fig. 31.10: *Walkabout,* cover, 1935. State Library New South Wales.

one of Australia's most prominent artists (see Chapter 14). Lindsay came from an artistic family that included his brother Lionel (1874–1961) and sister Ruby née Lindsay (1885–1919), who signed her work Ruby Lind. Both Norman and Lionel had been part of the short-lived Melbourne poster cooperative that Blamire Young formed in 1899, while Lionel and Ruby both drew for *The Bulletin*. As well, Ruby was known for her posters, whose flat colors and ethereal women recalled the work of Louis Rhead, Will Bradley, and others in Europe and the United States who created artistic posters in the late 19th century.

Visually, *The Lone Hand* was more elaborate than any magazine published in Australia until the 1920s. Numerous artists drew the covers, and the interior layout shows an attempt to use small pictures, expressive lettering, novel arrangements of text, and photographs to enhance the appeal of the articles, stories, and poems. Illustrators who drew for the magazine included, besides Norman and Lionel Lindsay and Ruby Lind, George Lambert (1873–1930), David Souter (1862–1935), Frank Mahony (1862–1916), and Fred Leist (1878–1945), all of whom had been or were still contributors to *The Bulletin*. A distinctive feature of *The Lone Hand* was Norman Lindsay's many drawings of his koala bear character "Billy Bluegum", some in comic strip form.

Norman Lindsay drew the magazine's first cover in 1907, while many other artists contributed drawings or paintings for covers during the magazine's relatively brief tenure (Fig. 31.11). Among them was the comic artist and illustrator Ruby Winkler (dates unconfirmed)—the first woman to create a cover for *The Lone Hand*. Another female cover artist was May Gibbs (1877–1969), illustrator, cartoonist, children's book author, and comic strip artist, who was known for her gum nut babies, also called "bush babies" or "bush fairies," and also for her comic strip *Bib and Bub*. The gum nut babies—little cherubs clothed in flower costumes, acorn hats, or cloaked in leaves—were the subject of several of her children's books as well as other magazine covers.

Founded in 1860, the *Sydney Mail*, was published in a stodgy newspaper format until 1912, when the magazine underwent a total graphic transformation and an overhaul of its contents. Most significant was the decision to produce a new color cover each week. The magazine's predictable cover depictions of rural life, sport, and masculine activities were punctuated by May Gibbs' covers featuring her gum nut babies; depictions of children by Dorothy Fry (1891–c. 1953), who also drew cartoons for *The Bulletin*; and Sydney Ure Smith's gentler cover portrayals of women, notably in the Ideal Homes Number of 1914. During World War I, the artist G. H. Brown (dates unconfirmed) created numerous propagandistic covers that showed Australian soldiers in dramatic battle postures. After the war, Percy Leason, one of the Smith & Julius advertising artists, also drew occasional nostalgic covers in several different styles.

When *Smith's Weekly* began publication in 1919, its closest rival was *The Bulletin*, and not the *Sydney Mail* or *The Lone Hand*. Unlike the latter, it did not aspire to be a literary magazine but rather a general interest publication that relied heavily on its artists who drew in black and white to spoof various Australian types. As a national figure, it featured the digger, a caustic character who was presented as an Australian Everyman. The humor of *Smith's Weekly* satirized daily life in a raucous way, pulling no punches in its depiction of social mores. The artist Cecil "Cec" Hartt (1884–1930), the first to join the *Smith's Weekly* staff, specialized in digger cartoons, producing hundreds of them during his tenure with the magazine. Alek Sass—painter, printmaker, poster artist, illustrator, and cartoonist—became the magazine's art editor in 1920 after previously having been a member of Smith & Julius's art staff. Another prominent artist who worked for *Smith's Weekly* was Stan Cross (1888–1977), who was born in America and came to Australia as a young boy. Vane Lindesay, an expert on Australian comic art, considers Cross to have been the magazine's finest draftsman. The range of types he caricatured included

[Registered at the General Post Office, Sydney, for transmission by Post as a Newspaper.]

THE LONE HAND
THE AUSTRALIAN MONTHLY

DECEMBER 1st 1908. 1/-

Printed and published by William Macleod, of Musgrave Street, Mosman, for THE BULLETIN Newspaper Co., Ltd., at the office of the Co., 214 George Street North, Sydney, New South Wales, Australia.

Fig. 31.11: Norman Lindsay, *The Lone Hand*, cover, 1908. State Library New South Wales.

(1895–1987), an outstanding caricaturist; Charles Hallett (c. 1919–1950), who specialized in flapper gags; and Virgil Reilly (1892–1974), whose Virgil Girl was a regular pinup figure. As did *The Bulletin*, *Smith's Weekly* featured several women artists, notably Mollie Horseman (1911–1974) and Joan Morrison (1911–1969), both of whom attended Sydney Technical College in the late 1920s. While Horseman drew gag cartoons with an emphasis on line, Morrison created voluptuous women with a wash technique, comparable to the girlie pinups in men's magazines elsewhere.

Other publications preceded *Smith's Weekly* and were published concurrently with it. These included the *Comic Australian*, a short-lived weekly humor magazine published between 1911 and 1913; and *Aussie* (1918–1919), originally a comic publication that was dedicated to the Australian soldier, although it reinvented itself in 1920 as the *Cheerful Monthly*, which sought an audience of sophisticated men and women and included some of Australia's best writers and cartoonists during its years of publication between 1920 and 1932.

Magazines began to specialize in the early 1920s, a time that saw several dedicated to women. In 1924, *The Bulletin* launched a weekly magazine, *The Australian Woman's Mirror*, which was directed to the housewife. It featured articles on domestic sciences, recipes, advice on gardening and making clothes, and beauty tips. Fiction and poetry were also included. Layouts were text heavy and included small illustrations within the articles and as parts of titles. For a long period the covers featured a masthead with the magazine's name below. It included a stylized drawing on the left of a modern woman, sometimes derived from French fashion illustrations, and on the right some text that described the contents. These were framed either by ornament or a colored border. Later in the 1930s, the covers featured large color photographic portraits of women with modern hairstyles or hats.

A related magazine was *The Australian Women's Weekly*, which did not begin publication until 1933.

farmers, clerics, and Aborigines. Although there had been earlier forms of sequential drawings, Cross introduced the first regular comic strip in Australia, *You and Me*, which was followed by several others including the popular *Wally and the Major*.

Other artists who drew for *Smith's Weekly* included Frank Dunne (1898–1937), who specialized in drawings of soldiers; the expatriate Swede Joe Jonsson (1890–1963), known for his depictions of horses and racetrack touts; Syd Miller (1901–1983), who drew cartoons with sports themes; George Finey

Its design was more like a tabloid newspaper, and it emphasized news about personalities and events as well as publishing romantic serial stories with seductive illustrations along with articles on fashion, cooking, and related topics. *Woman's World* took a more artistic approach to its design, inviting the artist Margaret Preston to create a number of color woodcuts of flowers for their covers during the 1920s.

The Home, which Sydney Ure Smith founded in 1920, was a very different magazine aimed at women. It followed by four years the launch of Smith's first publication, *Art in Australia*, which established exceptionally high standards for its printing quality and art direction. Modeled to some degree on *Vogue* and *Harper's Bazaar*, *The Home* promulgated a modern lifestyle with articles related to interior decoration, fashion, architecture, and art as well as the arts of poetry and literature. Its unabashed modernism was more international than other Australian magazines and it brought to the attention of its readers—mainly upper middle-class housewives—some of the latest trends in architecture, design, and the arts that were occurring abroad. Like other magazines of its day, *The Home* put great store in its cover designs, although the artists it used tended to draw upon the Jazz Age techniques of French fashion illustration rather than traditional illustrative styles.

More than other journals before it, *The Home* featured women as cover artists. They included Mabel Leith (dates unconfirmed); Wanda Radford (dates unconfirmed); Olive Crane (1895–1936), an illustrator who studied with Albert Collins at the Julian Ashton Art School; Thea Proctor; and Hera Roberts. As an illustrator, Roberts' many covers for *The Home* featured stylized female figures—portrayed with strong colors and angular lines—making a reference to the French Art Deco fashion drawings of Georges LePape, Erté and others. Beginning in the mid-1930s, Dahl Collings (1909–1988) and Douglas Annand, both designers rather than illustrators, produced covers for *The Home* based on design concepts. Collings' and Annand's witty

collage figures, created with bits of string, rope, fabric, feathers, and other materials, introduced a new type of magazine cover, paving the way for designers to become active in the design of covers after World War II.

During the 1930s, *The Home* began to use more photography, both for its covers as well as for its interior spreads. Frequently an artist would collaborate with photographer Harold Cazneaux, Australia's leading pictorialist photographer, to pose women for experimental fashion portraits with odd props, sharp angles, and unusual lighting effects. *The Home* also featured the surrealistic photographs of Max Dupain.

John Fairfax and Sons acquired Ure Smith's two magazines, *Art in Australia* and *The Home*, in 1934, and by 1938 he had been eased out of his editorial role. Consequently he started a new magazine, *Australia: National Journal*, which began publication in 1939. For its graphic format, Ure Smith emphasized design rather than illustration, drawing on the talents of Douglas Annand, Dahl Collings, Hal Missingham (1906–1994), and Elaine Haxton (1909–1999). Where this magazine differed from his earlier ones was in its promotion of industry along with art, architecture, and design as a sign of Australian achievement.

Man, a magazine for men, began publication in 1936 and was almost a direct copy of the American *Esquire* even to the point of using as iconic figures E. Simms Campbell's little sultan and his Esky mascot, the aging roué, who became *Esquire*'s trademark. One difference between the two magazines was that Arnold Gingrich, editor of *Esquire*, sought out and published high-quality fiction while the writers for *Man* were poorly paid and contributed stories of disputable value. Magazines for children had to compete with the flood of publications for young boys and girls that arrived from Britain, a country with a long tradition of producing books and magazines for youth. Australian publications included *Pals*, *The Comet*, and *Crossroads*, all of which featured covers with action-oriented visual themes.

Compared to the magazine publishers' emphasis

on cover art, the book publishing industry was less noteworthy. Publishers such as Angus and Robertson in Sydney, Hawthorn Press in Melbourne, and the Hassell Press in Adelaide commissioned book covers from artists, but none stand out as having been particularly distinguished. Australia also had a small private press movement during the interwar years. The Green Press was started by Perce Green, who at the time of its founding, around 1920, worked in the typography department of the Smith & Julius studio. The studio owned the Green Press, and Sydney Ure Smith used it to print a catalog of his own etchings as well as books for the Australian Limited Editions Society of which he was an active member. Other private presses included the Legend Press, founded by the Sydney artist, art dealer, and gallery director John Brackenreg (1905–1986), and the Fanfrolico Press, that the artist Norman Lindsay started with several others around 1923. The Fanfrolico Press published a number of handsome limited edition books, most of which were illustrated by Lindsay, who was also involved with the design of the title pages, initial letters, and covers. Ursula Prunster has compared these books to *The Yellow Book*, *The Savoy*, and other fin-de-siècle British publications with Aubrey Beardsley's illustrations.

Graphic design emerges

The generation of commercial artists who worked for advertising agencies or clients such as department stores through the 1920s were for the most part fine artists who did commercial art to make a living. While they produced excellent work, their orientation was towards illustration rather than comprehensive layouts that featured typography and images as integral parts of a design. By the 1930s, a new generation of young designers had emerged. Their initial training was in art schools, followed by diverse experience working for advertising agencies, printers, and even department stores. Both Douglas Annand, who was a mural painter as well as a graphic designer, and Geoff Collings (1905–2000) studied commercial art at the Central Technical

College in Brisbane. Initially Annand had a number of different jobs including employment at several advertising agencies. In 1931 he set up a graphic design studio in Sydney and undertook a range of commissions for textiles, wrapping papers, advertisements, and magazine covers. Most likely through his earlier contact with Sydney Ure Smith, Annand was commissioned to paint a mural on the ceiling of the Australian Pavilion for the 1937 World's Fair in Paris and perhaps through his contacts with the ANTA he was tapped to head the design team for the landmark Australian Pavilion at the 1939 World's Fair in New York.

Geoff Collings began his career in a Brisbane advertising agency, which was followed by a position with a process engraving company. In 1930, Collings left for London, where he worked for the publisher W. H. Smith & Sons. Returning to Australia in 1933, he met his wife-to-be Dahl and they married that year. She had studied art and design at the Sydney Technical College and got her first design job at the Anthony Hordern & Sons department store, where she did illustrations for their house magazine and catalog. She also began to do freelance work for other department stores along with covers for Sydney Ure Smith's *The Home* magazine.

In 1935, the Collingses went to London, where Geoff worked as an art director for an American advertising agency, and Dahl started to build a career as a freelance designer, working on murals, exhibitions, and illustrations for leading fashion magazines. Eventually, Dahl was offered a job in the studio of László Moholy-Nagy, who had come to London as an émigré in 1935. Moholy-Nagy had the account for Simpson's department store, with responsibility for the store's total image from publicity to interior design. Working with Moholy-Nagy and Gyorgy Kepes, a fellow Hungarian who had started to collaborate with Moholy-Nagy in Berlin a few years earlier, Dahl was exposed to a designerly way of working, where everything was considered as part of a total plan. Dahl also recommended another Australian whom Moholy-Nagy hired—Alistair Morrison (1911–1998). He had studied art in Melbourne, begun to freelance as a graphic designer there and then in Sydney, and afterwards went to London, like the Collingses, to seek more experience. Following his time with Moholy-Nagy, Morrison worked for other British clients including the publisher Lund Humphries and Shell Oil, which was developing a high-profile advertising campaign under the art direction of Jack Beddington (see Chapter 23).

In mid-1938, the Collingses and Alistair Morrison had a show of their commercial art at the Lund Humphries galleries in London. It was highly praised by E. McKnight Kauffer, the prominent American graphic designer then working in London, who said that the exhibition showed a more intellectual side of Australia than had been previously imagined. The year before, the three Australian designers had been joined in London by Gordon Andrews (1914–2001), a friend from Sydney, who worked for the Stuart Advertising Agency. Like them, Andrews went back to Australia in 1939, due to the threat of war.

When the Collingses returned to Sydney, they formed a new studio with the British designer Richard Haughton James. They called it the Design Centre to designate a broad idea of design, as their intent was to practice different types of design from the creation of products to graphics. They did obtain one commission for a product—the design of a radio for AWA—but most of their work was art direction, graphics, illustration, and exhibition design. In 1939, the Collingses also organized an Exhibition of Modern Industrial Art and Documentary Photography at the gallery that belonged to the David Jones department store. This was an opportunity to introduce to the Sydney public some of the new design ideas they had absorbed in London and to argue for a generalist design practice that might embrace the design of graphics, industrial products, exhibitions, or even the production of documentary films.

Exhibition pavilions

At the 1924 British Empire Exhibition in Wembley, the Australian Pavilion with its Beaux Arts classicism conveyed a British image, as did the pavilions of Canada and New Zealand. The displays, which emphasized Australia's ability to supply Britain and Europe with raw materials, featured demonstrations of sheep shearing, a working gold mine, and a bakery that provided visitors with cakes made with Australian ingredients. Australia did not exhibit at the 1925 Exposition des Arts Décoratifs in Paris, nor did it participate in other exhibitions of the interwar period until 1937 when the art publisher and artist Sydney Ure Smith supervised the design of a pavilion for the 1937 Exposition Internationale des Arts et Techniques in Paris. Little was spent on the pavilion and its circular design was uninspiring. Although numerous critics expressed dismay at the impression it made, it did have some significant departures from earlier pavilions, notably the concept of an exhibition rather than simply a collection of things to display. Douglas Annand created a mural for the ceiling that located Australia on a map of the world, while a number of photographic murals depicted images intended to represent the Australian way of life. As Simon Jackson has noted, however, the photo mural emphasized rural scenery and bush life while there was also a noticeable absence of finished goods in the pavilion even though at this time Australian companies were manufacturing a considerable number of products, almost all of which were for domestic consumption. Despite the attention to a designed space, Jackson considers the 1937 pavilion to be the last of an older style of display.

Certainly the Australian Pavilion at the New York World's Fair in 1939, which was a project of the Australian National Travel Association, may be considered a high point of Australian pre-World War II design practice. Like the 1937 pavilion, Sydney Ure Smith was on the advisory committee that put the project team together. Its members were dedicated to modern design and consequently the pavilion became a comprehensive representation of Australian modernism. Stephenson & Turner were the architects and one of their staff, John Oldham (1907–1999), who had trained as an architectural draftsman and previously founded graphic design studios in Perth and Sydney, supervised the exhibition planning. Oldham, who had come into contact with Bauhaus design through magazines and architectural journals, was interested in the work of Moholy-Nagy. In 1930, he set up Poster Studios in Perth with Harold Krantz (dates unconfirmed) and the two developed a linocut technique for making posters that was cheaper than using metal plates. Two years later, Oldham moved to Sydney, where he established the Oldham Publishing Company to produce posters, brochures, and advertising materials. Back in Perth in 1934, he joined an architectural firm and worked with the Communist Party's Workers' Art Guild for which he designed theater posters and brochures.

Oldham's interest in Moholy-Nagy may have had some influence on the pavilion's design. Central to the layout was a series of large photomontage murals that recalled the visual rhetoric of El Lissitzky's Soviet Pavilion at the 1928 Pressa exhibition in Cologne. It also recalled the pavilion that Moholy-Nagy, Herbert Bayer, Marcel Breuer, and Walter Gropius designed for the Werkbund exhibition in Paris in 1930. The murals in the Australian Pavilion were organized into a visual flow by Douglas Annand. Visitors were moved along a route that began with images of agriculture, continued with industry, and concluded with tourism. In the travel section was a gigantic photograph of Sydney Harbor with a view across the newly constructed Harbor Bridge.

The visitor approached the large photographic mural by the modernist photographer Max Dupain as if arriving by air. The large head of a worker by photographer Russell Roberts (1904–1999) contributed to the Lissitzkian rhetoric (Fig. 31.12). The adoption of photomontage as the principal visual medium of the pavilion was a bold move, given that graphic designer Gert Sellheim had been criticized only two years earlier for the photomontage mural he designed for the Government Tourist Bureau in Melbourne.

Additional visual material for the 1939 pavilion was provided by Dahl and Geoff Collings, Adrian Feint, and the artist Margaret Preston, who contributed six large paintings of Australian wildflowers. The exhibit concluded with a mezzanine at the end of the pathway around the photographs. On it was an invention called an "Illuvision." Set in a wall like a television, it offered full-color views of Melbourne, the Great Barrier Reef, and other Australian sights in three dimensions that were created with a complicated system of lights, mirrors, and a revolving cylinder.

Annand continued to develop his ideas for exhibition design as Director of the Cultural Section of the Australian Pavilion at the 1939 New Zealand Centenary International Exhibition in Wellington. Here he worked again with the architectural firm of Stephenson & Turner as well as with various colleagues including the designers Adrian Feint, Dahl and Geoff Collings, and the photographer Russell Roberts, with many of whom he had collaborated on the groundbreaking design of the Australian Pavilion for the New York World's Fair.

New Zealand

Though New Zealand remained a self-governing British colony until 1907, party politics gained greater traction towards the end of the 19th century. The first identified political party to govern was the Liberal Party, whose second leader, Richard John Seddon, served as New Zealand's premier from 1893 to 1906. Seddon was a populist who initiated large public works and railway construction projects, while also promoting manual and technical training and laying the foundation for a modern welfare state. Women voted in the 1893 election, making New Zealand the first country in the world to institute women's suffrage.

The Liberals favored a strong government role in the country's development, but almost no attention was paid to industrial policy until the late 1930s. The Liberal

Fig. 31.12: John Oldham et al., Australian Pavilion, New York World's Fair, 1939. Photograph by Robert E. Coates. Collection: Museum of Applied Arts & Sciences, Sydney.

Party expanded the scale of government, establishing no fewer than 12 new departments in its 12 states. They also put forth a strong vision for the colony, which supported the decision not to join the newly established federative Commonwealth of Australia in 1901. In 1907, New Zealand's status was changed from a colony to a dominion, making it equal to Australia and Canada. Of all the then British colonies, New Zealand had sent the largest number of troops to support Britain in the Boer War, and its soldiers, including a Maori battalion, also fought alongside Britain during World War I.

From 1900 to World War II, the New Zealand economy was dominated by agriculture and extractive industries such as flax milling, kauri gum digging, timber milling, and mining for gold and coal. Due to technological advances in sheep shearing, dairy farming, and the refrigeration of meat, New Zealand was able to make the agricultural sector more efficient and capable

of competing internationally. After the Liberals were defeated in 1912, the Reform Party, which represented many of the country's farmers, came to power. W. A. Massey, the party's founder and then New Zealand's Prime Minister from 1912 to 1925, was especially sympathetic to the concerns of rural New Zealanders and less so to labor union interests. Historian Miles Fairburn notes that Reform Party rule, which lasted until the late 1920s, favored traditional ways of life and induced a climate that was not conducive to innovation.

Of economic value in this period was the government's introduction of marketing boards to represent different economic sectors such as dairy, wool, fruit, and timber. Another positive tendency during the Reform Party years was the large increase in home ownership, which the government promoted. From 36 percent ownership in 1916, the number of homeowners jumped to 50 percent of the population in 1926.

Not only did this provide considerable work for the construction industry, but it also created a large market for furniture and household goods. New Zealand suffered during the Great Depression just as other countries did and the economy did not begin to recover until the late 1930s.

By that time, the Maori had also become more active politically. Between 1900 and 1909, the Liberal government introduced a series of Maori Land Acts, which eventually made the sale and lease of Maori land a more just process. A group of Maori reformers, who for the most part were associated with Te Aute College, an Anglican Maori school established in 1854, founded the Young Maori Party, which had a major effect on Maori culture, in part by encouraging and affirming the renewal of traditional customs. Many Maori still lived in rural areas before World War II, although the number that moved to the cities increased rapidly after that.

From arts and crafts to proto-industry

Most New Zealand household goods in the early 20th century were imported from Britain. British manufacturers designed wallpapers, curtains, upholstery fabrics, and floor coverings, and consequently middle-class homeowners were dependent on British taste, having few options of their own to define a distinctly New Zealand domestic style. The local art schools were founded on British models, though, unlike England, where theories of ornament and craft skills could be applied in industry, there was little of such manufacturing in New Zealand to absorb the art school graduates' skills.

The British Arts and Crafts movement was influential in the art schools and also shaped the tastes of a select group of consumers. With few opportunities to put design influenced by the movement into production, even to the limited degree that William Morris or Charles Robert Ashbee did in England, the art school graduates, most of whom were middle-class women, depended on exhibitions, one-off commissions, and occasionally small shops to present their work to the public. Women also had to face a strong patriarchal bias against their participation in industrial production. This was coupled with a comparable assumption that women's role in society was as homemakers and mothers.

Craftspersons were encouraged to draw on two indigenous sources of decoration—native New Zealand flora and fauna as well as Maori carvings and decorative patterns. Inevitably, Maori designs were taken out of context just as Aboriginal motifs were in Australia. Douglas Lloyd Jenkins describes a chair carved by two Pakeha or Anglo women, Edith Fenton (dates unconfirmed) and Martha Buchanan (dates unconfirmed), that was laden with motifs inspired by Maori carvings in their families' collections. As with earlier 19th-century European and American designs in which historical motifs were grafted onto contemporary furniture forms, the chair by Fenton and Buchanan is a pastiche object that combines stylized carved Maori figures on either side of the backrest with a Maori warrior that is part of the carved piece below the seat. There is a certain irony in middle-class Pakeha women employing a Maori carving style, especially when it was applied to objects that were not part of the original Maori repertoire and were used in settings that were alien to Maori culture.

Another example of Maori carving adopted for a middle-class home is Thyra Beetham's (dates unconfirmed) "Maori Carved Mantlepiece" which she showed at an Academy of Fine Arts exhibition and subsequently installed in her Wellington home, where it was accompanied by floor railings that were also decorated with Maori patterns. Maori motifs were evident as well in other prominent households, carved on fireplaces, bed ends, or chairs by women such as Edith Fenton and Martha Buchanan, or occasionally by a Maori carver such Jacob Heberly (1849–1906) of the Te Ati Awa tribe, who was equally at home doing traditional Maori carving or decorating the homes of wealthy Pakeha clients.

The occasional British manufacturer who exported goods to New Zealand also used Maori motifs as marketing devices. Such examples were on display at the 1906–1907 New Zealand International Exhibition in Christchurch, which had in part been inspired by Premier Seddon's visit to the 1904 World's Fair in St. Louis. Doulton, the British ceramic manufacturer, showed tableware that reproduced Maori painted rafter patterns on a range of items including cups, saucers, plates, and teapots. Designated "Maori Ware" and "Maori Art," the Doulton chinaware, according to historian Christopher Thompson, probably represented the first use of Maori designs on industrially manufactured products. While the Doulton appropriations were relatively accurate, other uses of Maori imagery fell more into the category of parody. Such was the case with a ceramic tobacco jar produced in Temuka as a customer gift for the National Electric and Engineering Company (NEECO) in the 1930s. A bust of a Maori elder sits on the jar's lid while the body is embossed with ceramic versions of carved Maori figures (Fig. 31.13).

Most of what was produced for the New Zealand home, whether furniture, ceramics, or other goods, was without distinctive adornment. Large furniture companies employed elements of historic styles, which generally led to nondescript designs, although firms like Tonson Garlick were not averse to more contemporary decorative arts tendencies such as Arts and Crafts, Art Nouveau, or Gustav Stickley's Mission style. Turnbull and Jones, a commercial lighting manufacturer mass-produced lighting in the Arts and Crafts style, using sheets of steel on which the hammer marks were applied by machine. They advertised these widely in the press as "Art Light Fittings."

Departures from the conventions and techniques of mass production were made occasionally by architects and craftsmen who established small workshops to service a limited number of clients. One such workshop was run by James Walter Chapman-Taylor (1878–1958), the leading Arts and Crafts architect in New Zealand, whose work was best characterized by

Fig. 31.13: Temuka tobacco jar, date unconfirmed. Museum of New Zealand Te Papa Tongarewa, negative number GH011287.

the English cottage style. Like Frank Lloyd Wright, Chapman-Taylor built much of his furniture—cupboards, bookcases, wardrobes, and dressers—into his house designs, but he also designed freestanding pieces including refectory tables, Morris chairs, corner cupboards, and fire screens. The latter are recognized less for the distinction of their design than for the way they exemplify the British Arts and Crafts aesthetic. Also influenced by that aesthetic was the metalworker Reuben Watts (1869–1940), who made various objects of beaten copper and brass such as clocks, trays, and wall plaques. Watts also began to make exterior and interior lighting, but his own hand-made pieces faced heavy competition from the cheaper industrial fixtures of Turnbull and Jones.

By the 1930s, a few New Zealand architects were designing houses in a modern style, adapting the white boxy volumes of European modernists. One exception was the town of Napier, which was reconstructed in an Art Deco style following the 1931 earthquake. To complement the modern buildings, department stores throughout the country carried furniture in what was called a modernistic style. Both small firms and large companies such as Tonson Garlick and Scoullar and Chisholm produced such pieces.

Local manufacturers tended to copy foreign designs, while modern furniture was also imported from abroad. Frustrated with the paucity of modern furniture in New Zealand, a few architects designed their own. By the late 1930s, several local manufacturers such as George Walker and Eden Electroplaters began to make tubular steel furniture. Some copied foreign models but there were a few original designs as well. Given New Zealand's distance from Europe and the fact that it was not closely connected to the debates on modern architecture and design, it is not surprising that no modern furniture designs emerged that might have made an impact abroad.

The same was true with the ceramics industry, which, unlike the mass-market furniture companies, made no effort to adopt modern styles from Europe, preferring instead to continue with the production of traditional designs. According to Christopher Thompson, New Zealand ceramic designs of the 1930s hardly differed from those of the 19th century. Among the leading firms were McSkimming and Son at Benhar, New Zealand Potteries in Wellington, New Zealand Insulators at Temuka, and Ambrico in Auckland.

Besides furniture and objects for the home, a few isolated individuals invented other kind of objects. For the most part these were not developed further or produced in New Zealand due to the lack of a manufacturing infrastructure. Richard Pearse (1877–1953) was an aviation pioneer who is reputed to have flown a heaver-than-air machine of his own design about nine months before the Wright Brothers made their first flight. In 1902, Pearse mounted a two-cylinder engine on a tricycle undercarriage to which he had fixed a linen-covered wing structure with attached controls. Several attempts to fly enabled him to make short hops, but not to keep the vehicle airborne. He improved that capacity the following year, but not sufficiently to move his experiments towards the design of a functional aircraft. His original machine had a number of innovations including wing flaps and a tricycle-type landing gear that eliminated the need for a landing strip or ramp. Instead the plane could touch down on any decent road. After several more years of work, Pearce discontinued his experiments without having achieved any significant improvements in his aircraft. During the 1930s and 1940s, he worked on the design of a tilt-rotor flying machine for individual use. His design resembled a helicopter, but had a tilting rotor blade and monoplane wings. Along with the tail, the wings could fold, enabling the machine to be parked in an ordinary garage.

Other inventors besides Pearse included Robert J. Dickie (1876–1958) and Ernest Godward (1869–1936). Dickie created the first stamp vending machine in 1905 and one was installed in the General Post Office in Wellington that year. After experiments with Dickie's patented prototype in Britain, production series machines were introduced there in 1907. Subsequently Dickie licensed the rights to sell the machine around the world, competing with other companies such as British Electric Machines Ltd, which also made inroads into foreign markets.

Ernest Godward was born in London but emigrated to New Zealand in 1886 as a boy. In Dunedin he became a partner in Southland Cycle Works, a company that manufactured Sparrowhawk cycles and imported British models as well. He had some basic training in engineering and left the cycle partnership to become an independent inventor. Among his inventions was a spiral hairpin for which he obtained worldwide patents that brought him considerable wealth. His other patented inventions included a rubber hair-curler, a mechanical hedge clipper, a non-slip egg beater, a tank-filter, and a lid for cans.

Perhaps Godward's most successful device was an early version of the carbureator that converted gasoline into gas before ignition occurred. Given the paucity of automobiles in New Zealand, it is not surprising that Godward went to London to establish the Godward Carburettor Company, opening a factory in Kingston near London. By 1916 he had an office in New York and eventually relocated there. Ten years later, the United States Army adopted the Godward Vaporiser for use in trucks and three years later the device, said to increase horsepower by about 15 percent, was installed in almost 600 buses in Philadelphia. During his later American career, Godward was recognized as a world authority on internal combustion engines.

With so little incentive or opportunity to support a nascent manufacturing culture, New Zealand had little to show in the way of domestic products at the two major exhibitions that were held after World War I—the New Zealand and South Seas International Exhibition, mounted in Dunedin in 1925–1926, and the New Zealand Centennial Exhibition, held at Wellington in 1939–1940. The initiator of the Dunedin exhibition was most likely the architect Edmund Anscombe (1874–1948), who received the commission to design its buildings. Anscombe had traveled extensively abroad and in 1919 published a pamphlet, *Modern Industrial Development*, in which he advocated the construction of public housing and industrial parks, providing also a vision of commercial buildings with flat roofs that could be used for multiple purposes. To support his advocacy of industrial construction, he invented a system of cellular concrete blocks in 1920 and marketed the blocks as the OK Dry Wall System.

The set piece of Anscombe's forward-looking plan for the Dunedin exhibition was a Festival Hall crowned by a large dome. At the center of an axial plan, the hall was complemented by seven pavilions and colonnaded passages that led towards it. Although the New Zealand government mounted an ambitious exhibit that showcased the work of different government departments, the largest displays were those of Britain, whose exports continued to dominate the New Zealand consumer economy.

Shortly after the Labor Party came to power in 1935, it recognized the need for a national industrial policy to cover all aspects of the economy. In 1936, the government introduced the Industrial Efficiency Act,

aimed at promoting new industries and insuring greater efficacy in production. The Act provided for a Bureau of Industry that would advise the Minister of Commerce and Industry and help organize an industrial sector.

The one segment of the economy that welcomed industrialization without any major government encouragement was agriculture, where mechanized equipment for shearing sheep, separating cream, and refrigerating meat had been adopted in the 1880s. Mechanization of the dairy industry continued after the turn of the century. In 1920, New Zealand farms were mostly without electric motors, but their number had jumped to more than 60,000 by 1941. They were used primarily for milking machines, which had been developed in the early years of the 20th century, but initially the poor quality of the rubber parts and the lack of reliable motors hindered their adoption. By the end of World War I, however, about 50 percent of the country's cows were milked by machine, a number that jumped to 86 percent by 1942.

With the onset of World War II, New Zealand continued the policy of import substitution that began in the 1920s. This was abetted by the Bureau of Industry, which provided support where possible for selective domestic industries. One of the strongest to emerge was Ambrico, a ceramics firm that produced tableware. It was formed in 1939 by its parent organization, the Amalgamated Brick and Pipe Company of Auckland, at the request of the Department of Industries and Commerce. The two large markets for the new company, located in the parent firm's Fine Earthenware Division, were the American armed forces, whose soldiers were stationed in New Zealand between 1942 and 1944, and the New Zealand Railways department, which was no longer able to order crockery from its previous British supplier.

For the American soldiers, Ambrico produced simple mugs and cereal bowls and for the railway an earthenware cup and saucer. Both the mug and the cup and saucer became national icons. Initially, the firm made a straw-colored mug without a handle, a design intended to be as different from the British prototype as possible. The railroad's initials, NZR, were stamped on the mugs in large block letters, and a handle was added in 1943.

In the absence of imported ceramic tableware due to the constraints on British exports and to tight government import restrictions, the government encouraged Ambrico by way of subsidy, exemption from manpower regulations, and the offer of guaranteed contracts to expand its product line in 1942 to include plates, cups, and saucers for domestic use as well as jugs, casserole dishes, and other ceramic containers. A prominent item in their new line was a 36-piece earthenware dinner service, which was intended to imitate the look of Britain's utility ceramics. Though sold undecorated during wartime, the line continued after the war with colored glazes and transfer prints that were obtained from Britain.

The government also gave a boost to the nascent radio industry when it hired Collier & Beale, one of a handful of New Zealand companies that designed and manufactured radios, to design a wireless field radio for combat use. Collier & Beale started in Wellington in 1926 and in 1939 the company introduced a line of radios with wooden cabinets. The name it gave the radio was "Pacemaker." Supported by the Ministry of Supply, particularly in obtaining components, Collier & Beale produced a successful field radio, known as the ZC1. Based on a British wireless set, it achieved success in its third version, of which about 15,000 were produced. The design was basic, with little distinction attributed either to the formal qualities or the ergonomics of the dial arrangement. Nonetheless, the radio was considered superior to a Canadian counterpart due to its range, low battery drain, easy operation and servicing, light weight, and ease of installation in military vehicles.

Another radio company that produced a range of equipment for the military was the Akrad Radio Corporation, founded in 1932 by Keith Marsden (1913–1946), who began with a small radio sales and repair shop in the gold mining town of Waihi. Akrad made communication radios, buzzers, signal lamps, and sirens for local defense. As with Collier & Beale, the company's wartime work prepared it to play an active role in New Zealand's modest electronics industry after the war.

Despite the declaration of war on Germany in 1939, the Labor government pushed ahead with plans for a large exhibition to commemorate New Zealand's centennial in 1940. The buildings for the Centennial Exhibition, held in Wellington, were designed, as they were for the earlier Dunedin fair, by Edmund Anscombe. Central to the design was a large tower that symbolized New Zealand's progress and ambitions. More so than in Dunedin, Anscombe's buildings evinced a modern aesthetic, which was complemented by an extensive use of electric lights that illuminated the fair at night. After the fair, following Anscombe's ideas about the efficient reuse of buildings that he had first put forth in 1919, the exhibition buildings were used by the Royal New Zealand Air Force during World War II and for storing wool following that.

Behind the Centennial Exhibition's veneer of modernity, however, traditional values prevailed. Its theme emphasized the courage and hard work of the early European settlers, who were represented by two huge sculptures of a pioneer man and a pioneer woman that flanked the Centennial Tower. Compared to the 1936 Johannesburg British Empire Exhibition, whose narrative presented South Africa's black population in a subservient role, the Maori fared far better, but they were nonetheless excluded as prominent partners in the nation's construction. Likewise, women were represented through their arts and crafts, particularly needlework and weaving, while lectures that addressed women's issues were confined to how women might best manage the domestic sphere. Finally, Britain continued to play a central role in New Zealand's narrative of nationalism as exemplified by the pride of place that was given to the United Kingdom Court in the exhibition plan.

Graphic design

Magazines, newspapers, and book publishing

Most of the printing around 1900 was for newspapers and a few magazines such as the *New Zealand Graphic and Ladies Journal* and *The New Zealand Illustrated Magazine*, which was founded as a monthly in 1899 and lasted only until 1905. The *Illustrated* featured poetry, short stories, and articles by New Zealand's top writers, along with drawings by prominent artists and illustrators. A leading illustrator for the magazine was Trevor Lloyd (1863–1937), an artist whose illustrations and cartoons also appeared regularly in the *New Zealand Graphic*, *The New Zealand Herald* and *The Auckland Weekly News*. Lloyd worked as an illustrator, graphic artist, and cartoonist for the *Weekly News*. He is said to have drawn the first cartoon that used the kiwi bird to represent New Zealand. Most of his early work consisted of line and wash drawings, although he later contributed pen and ink sketches to the Saturday supplement of *The New Zealand Herald*. Lloyd had a special interest in Maori culture and often used Maori motifs as well as New Zealand flora and fauna in his decorative borders for the *Weekly News*.

Other illustrators for *The New Zealand Illustrated Magazine* include Frances Hodgkins (1869–1947), one of New Zealand's first modern painters, and Andrew Kennaway Henderson (1879–1960), who worked as a commercial and lithographic artist for *The Weekly Press*, beginning in 1904. Henderson had earlier written, illustrated, and published two issues of an illustrated humor magazine, *Fun*, which lasted for two years. In 1936, shortly after the Labor Party won the national election, he began to edit and manage a radical political and literary magazine, *Tomorrow*, which closed in 1940, a victim of censorship. Each issue featured one of his cartoons that criticized a different institution, whether the press, the military, the Church, or business interests.

Among commercial book publishers, Whitcombe and Tombs was without a rival until 1932 when A. H. and A. W. Reed founded a firm that bore their names.

However, the major advances in fine printing were not made by the commercial publishers but by a group of small private presses, whose books evinced the high typographic standards of their printers. A central figure among these printers was Robert Lowry (1912–1963), who first demonstrated his interest in fine printing as the printer/typographer for four issues of *Phoenix*, a literary magazine published at Auckland University College in 1932–1933. Lowry was joined at the university by Ron Holloway (1909–2003), who assisted him with improving the university's typographical standards. Among his projects, he worked with Lowry on *Phoenix* and another journal, *Kiwi*.

Subsequently both left the university and became partners in the Unicorn Press, which began to publish books of poetry, fiction, and essays by New Zealand's leading writers such as R. A. K. Mason, Frank Sargeson, and Roderick Finlayson. In 1938, the partnership ended. Holloway and his wife established a new venture, the Griffin Press, where they published writers from the same milieu. Lowry began to publish a series of experimental typographic books, foremost of which was *The sky is a limpet* by A. R. D. Fairburn. The design had some analogy to various Surrealist and Dada publications. Lowry mixed typefaces and interspersed small line illustrations with the text, whose wordplay recalls James Joyce's *Finnegan's Wake*.

There was comparable small press activity in Christchurch, where the poet Denis Glover (1912–1980) founded the Caxton Press. As a student at Canterbury College in the early 1930s, Glover organized a printing club, which he named the Caxton Club Press. The press was moved off campus due to a conflict with the university authorities and was renamed the Caxton Press. Glover, who ran the press with a partner, worked as a jobbing printer, while also publishing books by emerging and established New Zealand writers.

Glover was joined by the artist Leo Bensemann (1912–1986), who collaborated with him on the typography and production of the Caxton Press books. As a graphic artist, Bensemann designed numerous decorative elements such as initial letters, chapter headings, and tailpieces, while also creating strong illustrations that reflected his interest in myth, folklore, and the grotesque. Another private press that was formed during the 1930s was Noel Hoggard's Handcraft Press, which, like its counterparts, matched outstanding design and handset printing with high-quality literature.

Posters, advertising, and publicity campaigns

Lithographic posters appeared much later in New Zealand than they did in Europe or the United States. Posters were mainly typographic until occasional lithographic placards began to appear around 1905. In the major urban centers, printers such as the Caxton Printing Company in Dunedin, Clarke and Matheson in Auckland, Whitcombe and Tombs in Christchurch, and the Government Printer in Wellington started to introduce flatbed litho presses, giving them the capability for poster production.

Though more than 10 percent of New Zealand's population served overseas during World War I, posters related to the war were comparatively few and generally lacked strong graphic images. Their intent was largely to solicit funds for the war effort rather than recruit soldiers or warn citizens of danger. The first major impetus to poster design came from the New Zealand Railways, which established a publicity branch, the Railways Studios, in 1920. It is likely that the publicity campaigns of the London Underground, campaigns of British regional railroads such as the London and North Eastern Railway (LNER), and those of the Canadian Pacific Railroad were stimuli for this service.

Publicity from the Railways Studios not only included posters but also pamphlets, maps, and pictorial postage stamps. Besides promoting the services of the railroad, the Railways Studios also created publicity for many government and business clients that advertised on poster hoardings in the railway stations, inside the rail cars, and on platforms where passengers boarded the trains. Beginning with

ten people, the staff grew to more than 70 commercial artists, sign painters, photographers, and carpenters by 1924. In late 1927 the railroad created its own Outdoor Advertising Branch, following a trip abroad by the Minister of Railways who observed how effectively many of the world's leading railways used publicity. The Outdoor Advertising Branch worked closely with the Government Tourist Department, which had been founded in 1901 to encourage travel within the country. Besides broad encouragement to see New Zealand, the department promoted travel to particular destinations such as the Waitomo Caves, Mt. Cook, Lake Wanaka, and Fiordland.

Many artists who worked for the Railways Studios came from painting backgrounds, consequently a number of the posters featured colorful landscape scenes of different destinations accompanied by lettering that varied from one poster to another and was most likely added by the printer. By the late 1920s, however, several art schools—notably the Elam School of Art in Auckland—were giving some emphasis to commercial art, and more design influence became evident in some of the railway posters such as one that promoted travel to Napier, which, as mentioned previously, had been rebuilt in an Art Deco style after the 1931 earthquake. This poster not only featured the flat color that lithography made possible, but also lettering that was integrated into the total design.

The Supervising Artist of the Outdoor Advertising Branch until the late 1930s was Stanley Davis (1882–1938), who had a large hand in shaping its advertising program. Davis had emigrated to New Zealand from England after World War I and joined the Railways Studios in 1922. Among the artists who undertook commissions for the Outdoor Advertising Branch was Edgar Lovell-Smith (1875–1950), a lithographer, illustrator, and painter whose colorful wash illustrations depicted dramatic landscapes such as the Franz Josef Glacier or scenes of tourists at prominent sites like the Chateau Tongariro.

Before World War II, government agencies were

probably the most active consumers of commercial art, particularly agencies whose primary concern was tourism. The settler government was interested in attracting tourists even before New Zealand became a dominion in 1901. A Tourist Office within the government Railways Department was established in 1901—a precursor to the Railways Studios—and within several years this office evolved into a separate Department of Tourist and Health Resorts. Among the early tourist attractions were thermal springs, along with beautiful settings that were suitable for outdoor recreation and sports. In 1923, the government formed a Publicity Office that was attached to the Department of Internal Affairs. One of its activities was to make short travelogues to promote tourism locally and overseas. The office hired a private studio, Filmcraft Ltd, to process these films, but around 1930 it bought out Filmcraft's studio, which became the home of the National Film Unit, established in 1941 to document New Zealand's war effort. The National Film Unit had its own publicity department, which produced posters and other materials.

Two artists who designed posters for Filmcraft and then for the Tourist and Publicity Department, formerly the Government Tourist Department, were George Bridgeman (1897–1966) and Leonard Mitchell (1901–1971). Bridgeman, an Englishman, arrived in New Zealand in the mid-1920s. After stints with Filmcraft and the Tourist and Publicity Department, he became art director of the government's National Publicity Studios, which produced posters related to health and safety among other subjects. Bridgeman is known for several posters of the 1940s that promoted automobile safety by showing the disastrous consequences of reckless driving—a distraught driver holding a dead girl, and a car out of control. As a designer, he understood the importance of lettering and used it dramatically in his posters.

Leonard Mitchell began as an apprentice sign writer and decorator before he became a commercial artist. He was head artist for Filmcraft Ltd in the late 1920s and then designed posters and produced illustrations for the Tourist and Publicity Department in the 1930s. He was also active as a stamp designer. Mitchell's lithographed tourist posters were of several genres. One was landscapes that were drenched in color, such as his posters for Mt. Egmont, Mitre Peak at Milford Sound, and others that depicted tourists enjoying tourist sites such as the thermal springs in Rotorua and the heights of Mt. Cook (Plate 61). Another artist who designed travel posters was Marcus King (1891–1983), who had studied painting with the Swedish artist Edward Friström at the Elam School of Art in Auckland. King worked a great deal with silkscreen printing, which emphasized the flatness of the colors. He did occasional landscape posters as did Leonard Mitchell, but his color palette was much lighter. On some of his posters, King featured iconic symbols like the Alpine Parrot and the Rata Blossom and he depicted as well scenes that characterized New Zealand life such as sheep and cattle droving. The Forest Service had its own dedicated commercial artist, A. H. Messenger (1877–1962), a prior art editor for the *Auckland Weekly News* and an ardent environmentalist.

An additional purpose of government publicity, besides tourism and public service messages, was the promotion of goods produced by the various marketing boards that had been established in the 1920s. Joseph Moran (1874–1953) worked extensively for the Fruit Marketing Board, producing posters and labels for the many different fruits—apples, pears, grapefruit, and oranges—that New Zealand farmers grew. A commercial illustrator rather than a painter, his style was closer to American realistic illustration or occasionally French Art Deco than those of other New Zealand poster artists. Moran also designed posters for other clients and these tended to feature comic drawings. He understood the place of lettering in a poster design more so than other poster artists whose backgrounds were in painting.

Posters for commercial products also began to appear at the time lithography became popular early in the 20th century. Among the first to do such posters was Peter McIntyre (1862–1932), whose posters for Arrow Brand raincoats and Tiger Teas displayed the extravagant lettering that characterized many comparable posters in Europe and the United States. A founder of the Caxton Printing Company in Dunedin and one of New Zealand's pioneer lithographers, McIntyre understood the possibilities of lithography and exploited them in his posters that Caxton printed.

Best known of the early commercial art firms was E. F. Chandler & Co. in Auckland. The art director for a number of years was David Payne (1880–1959), an Englishman who had studied art in Birmingham, England, and came to New Zealand in 1906. Payne

Fig. 31.14: David Payne, Tiki Bacon & Ham, poster, 1930s. Sir George Grey Special Collections, Auckland Libraries, 7-C1836.

was also a painter and printmaker, but his posters for E. F. Chandler were shaped by an advertising agency approach, which combined copy lines, strong icons or trademarks, and bold lettering. The firm adopted Maori language (Te Reo) for product names such as Kia Ora Jams and employed a kitsch version of a Polynesian woodcarving for the trademark of Tiki Bacon (Fig. 31.14).

Bibliography
Bibliographic essay

A number of books and articles discuss Canadian industrialization, business, and invention after 1900. They include J. J. Brown, *Ideas in Exile: A History of Canadian Invention*; W. T. Easterbrook and Hugh G. J. Aitken, *Canadian Economic History*; William L. Marr and Donald G. Paterson, *Canada: An Economic History*; and Peter Wylie's article, "Technological Adaptation in Canadian Manufacturing, 1900–1929," *Journal of Economic History* 49, no. 3 (September 1989). No texts broadly cover the history of product design in pre-World War II Canada although several books document the design of farm and railroad equipment. These include Merrill Denison, *Harvest Triumphant: The Story of Massey-Harris*; E. P. Neufeld, *A Global Corporation: A History of the International Development of Massey-Ferguson Limited*; and W. G. Phillips, *The Agricultural Implement Industry in Canada: A Study of Competition*. On 20th-century Canadian railroad history, see G. R. Stevens, *History of the Canadian National Railways*. For information about Canadian domestic design and crafts, I have relied on Virginia Wright, *Modern Furniture in Canada 1920–1970*; Gail Crawford, *A Fine Line: Studio Crafts in Ontario from 1930 to the Present*; Henry Gordon Green, ed., *A Heritage of Canadian Handicrafts*; and Ellen Easton McLeod, *In Good Hands: The Women of the Canadian Handicrafts Guild*. Sources on design in Quebec include Johanne Lépine's MA thesis, *Historique et Étude du Design Industriel au Quebec*; Gloria Lesser, *École du Meuble 1930–1950: La Décoration Intérieure et* les Arts Décoratifs à Montréal/École du Meuble 1930–1950: Interior Design and Decorative Art in Montreal; and books by a leader of the Quebec design movement, Jean-Marie Gauvreau, Artisans du Québec and Nos Intérieurs de Demain. Further information on Gauvreau can be found in Cinzia Maurizia Giovine, "Jean-Marie Gavreau [sic]: Art, Handicrafts and National Culture in Quebec from the 1920s until the 1950s," Design Issues 10, no. 3 (Autumn 1994). Elspeth Cowell's article "The Canadian Pavilion at the 1939 New York World's Fair and the Development of Modernism in Canada," SSAC Bulletin 19, no. 1 (March 1994) is the principal source for that project. Although there are no books on Canadian graphic design during this period, Robert Stacey's, The Canadian Poster Book: 100 Years of the Poster in Canada has much helpful information. Other books on Canadian posters are Marc Choko, L'Affiche au Québec des Origines à Nos Jours and Choko's Posters of the Canadian Pacific. H. E. Stephenson and Carlton McNaught offer useful material on Canadian advertising in The Story of Advertising in Canada: A Chronicle of Fifty Years. There are several monographs on major Canadian graphic designers J. E. H. MacDonald and his son Thoreau MacDonald. These are E. R. Hunter, J.E.H. MacDonald: A Biography & Catalogue of His Work; Albert H. Robson, J.E.H. MacDonald R.C.A.; Margaret E. Edison, Thoreau McDonald: A Catalogue of Design and Illustration; and L. Bruce Pierce, Thoreau MacDonald: Illustrator, Designer, Observer of Nature. See also Robert Stacey's essay "Harmonizing 'Means and Purpose': The Influence of Morris, Ruskin, and Crane on J.E.H. Macdonald," in David Latham, ed., Scarlet Hunters: Pre-Raphaelitism in Canada.

For general background on industrialization in Australia, I relied on a number of books including Peter Cochrane, Industrialization and Dependence: Australia's Road to Economic Development, 1870–1939; Colin Forster, Industrial Development in Australia, 1920–1930; Cecil R. Hall, The Manufacturers: Australian Manufacturing Achievements to 1960; and Geoffrey Serle, From Deserts the Prophets Come: The Creative Spirit in Australia, 1788–1972. The history of specific products is covered in Peter Cuffley, Chandeliers and Billy Tea: A Catalogue of Australian Life 1880–1940; Frances Wheelhouse, Digging Stick to Rotary Hoe: Men and Machines in Rural Australia; and Stewart Wilson, Wirraway, Boomerang and the CA-15 in Australian Service. Michael Bogle's Design in Australia 1880–1970 is a key source of material on industrial design as are Bogle's edited volume, Designing Australia: Readings in the History of Design and Simon Jackson's doctoral dissertation, The Discipline Without a Name: A History of Industrial Design in Australia. Books on domestic and decorative arts include Robin Boyd, Australia's Home; Harriet Edquist, Pioneers of Modernism: The Arts and Crafts Movement in Australia; Terence Lane and Jessie Searle, Australians at Home: A Documentary History of the Australian Domestic Interiors from 1788 to 1914; Christopher Menz, Morris & Company: Pre-Raphaelites and the Arts and Crafts Movement in South Australia; Ann Stephen, with Philip Goad and Andrew McNamara, eds., Modern Times: The Untold Story of Modernism in Australia; and Peter Timms, Private Lives: Australians at Home Since Federation. Grace Cochrane's comprehensive study, The Crafts Movement in Australia: A History, also has considerable material on the domestic and decorative arts and design. On Australian graphic design during this period, Geoffrey Caban's A Fine Line: A History of Australian Commercial Art is indispensible as an overview. More specialized topics such as trademarks, design of posters and magazine covers, and the history of black and white magazine illustration are treated in Mimmo Cozzolino with G. Fysh Rutherford, Symbols of Australia; Brian Carroll, The Australian Poster Album; Roger Butler, Poster Art in Australia; Robert Holden, Cover Up: The Art of Magazine Covers in Australia; Vane Lindesay, The Way We Were: Australian Popular Magazines, 1856–1969, and Lindesay's The Inked-in Image: A Survey of Australian Comic Art. Monographs on individual designers include Michele Hetherington, James Northfield and the Art of Selling

Australia; Elizabeth Butel, *Margaret Preston: The Art of Constant Rearrangement*; Heather Johnson, *Roy De Maistre: The Australian Years, 1894–1930*; and Anne McDonald, *Douglas Annand: The Art of Life*.

Information on industrialization in New Zealand is scattered throughout various sources. On the crafts and domestic arts several books were helpful: Ann Calhoun, *The Arts and Crafts Movement in New Zealand, 1870–1940: Women Make Their Mark,* and Douglas Lloyd Jenkins, *At Home: A Century of New Zealand Design.* Christopher Thompson's MA thesis, *Confronting Design: Case Studies in the Design of Ceramics in New Zealand,* provided extensive information on interwar ceramics. On graphic design, Hamish Thompson's *Paste Up: A Century of New Zealand Poster Art* and Richard Wolfe's *Well Made New Zealand: A Century of Trademarks* were the basic sources.

Books

Canada

Bothwell, Robert, Ian Drummond, and John English. *Canada, 1900–1945.* Toronto, Buffalo, and London: University of Toronto Press, 1987.

Brown, J. J. *Ideas in Exile: A History of Canadian Invention.* Toronto and Montreal: McClelland and Stewart, 1967.

Choko, Marc H. *L'Affiche au Québec des Origines à Nos Jours.* Montreal: Les Éditions de l'Homme, 2001.

Choko, Marc H. and David L. Jones. *Posters of the Canadian Pacific.* Richmond Hill, ON: Firefly Books, 2004.

Colgate, William. *Canadian Art: Its Origin & Development.* With a foreword by C. W. Jeffreys. Toronto: The Ryerson Press, 1943.

Crawford, Gail. *A Fine Line: Studio Crafts in Ontario from 1930 to the Present.* Toronto and Oxford: Dundurn Press, 1998.

Denison, Merrill. *Harvest Triumphant: The Story of Massey-Harris.* New York: Dodd, Mead & Co., 1949.

Easterbrook, W. T. and Hugh G. J. Aitken, *Canadian Economic History.* Toronto, Buffalo, and London: University of Toronto Press, 1988.

Edison, Margaret E. *Thoreau McDonald: A Catalogue of Design and Illustration.* Toronto and Buffalo: University of Toronto Press, 1973.

Encyclopedia Canadiana: Toronto, Ottawa, and Montreal: Grolier of Canada, 1970.

Gauvreau, Jean-Marie. *Nos Intérieurs de Demain.* Montréal: Librairie d'Action Canadienne-Française, Limitée, 1929.

—*Artisans du Québec.* Trois-Rivières: Editions du Bien Public, Montréal: Editions Beauchemin, 1940.

Green, Henry Gordon, ed. *A Heritage of Canadian Handicrafts.* Toronto and Montreal: McClelland and Stewart Limited, 1967.

Harper, J. Russell. *Painting in Canada: A History.* Toronto: University of Toronto Press, 1966.

Houser, F. B. *A Canadian Art Movement: The Story of the Group of Seven.* Toronto: The Macmillan Company of Canada Limited, 1926.

Hunter, E. R. *J.E.H. MacDonald: A Biography & Catalogue of His Work.* Toronto: The Ryerson Press, 1940.

Lesser, Gloria. *École du Meuble 1930–1950: La Décoration Intérieure et les Arts Décoratifs à Montréal/École du Meuble 1930–1950:Interior Design and Decorative Art in Montreal.* Montréal: Musée des Arts Décoratifs de Montreal/Montreal Museum of Decorative Arts, 1989.

Mann, Susan. *The Dream of Nation: A Social and Intellectual History of Quebec.* Montreal, Kingston, London, and Ithaca: McGill-Queen's University Press, 1982.

Marr, William L. and Donald G. Paterson. *Canada: An Economic History.* Toronto: The Macmillan Company of Canada, 1980.

McLeod, Ellen Easton. *In Good Hands: The Women of the Canadian Handicrafts Guild.* Montreal, Kingston, London, and Ithaca: McGill-Queen's University Press, 1999.

Miner, Muriel Miller. *G.A. Reid: Canadian Artist.* Toronto: The Ryerson Press, 1946.

Naylor, R. T. *The History of Canadian Business, 1867–1914.* Montreal, Kingston, London, and Ithaca: McGill-Queen's University Press, 2006 (c. 1975) (Carleton Library Series 207).

Neufeld, E. P. *A Global Corporation: A History of the International Development of Massey-Ferguson Limited.* Toronto: University of Toronto Press, 1969.

Pierce, L. Bruce. *Thoreau MacDonald: Illustrator, Designer, Observer of Nature.* Toronto: Norflex, 1971.

Phillips, W. G. *The Agricultural Implement Industry in Canada: A Study of Competition.* Toronto: University of Toronto Press, 1956.

Reid, Dennis. *A Concise History of Canadian Painting,* 2nd ed. Toronto: Oxford University Press, 1988.

Robson, Albert H. *J.E.H. MacDonald R.C.A.* Toronto: The Ryerson Press, 1937.

Stacey, Robert. *The Canadian Poster Book: 100 Years of the Poster in Canada.* Toronto, New York, London, and Sydney: Methuen, 1979.

Stacey, Robert with research by Hunter Bishop. *J.E.H. MacDonald, Designer: An Anthology of Graphic Design, Illustration and Lettering.* n.p.: Archives of Canadian Art (An Imprint of Carleton University Press), 1996.

Stephenson, H. E. and Carlton McNaught. *The Story of Advertising in Canada: A Chronicle of Fifty Years.* Toronto: The Ryerson Press, 1940.

Stevens, G. R. *History of the Canadian National Railways.* New York: The Macmillan Company, London: Collier-Macmillan Publishers, 1973.

Wright, Virginia. *Modern Furniture in Canada 1920–1970.* Toronto, Buffalo, and London: University of Toronto Press, 1997.

Australia

Bogle, Michael. *Design in Australia 1880–1970.* Sydney: Craftsman House, 1998.

—ed. *Designing Australia: Readings in the History of Design.* Annandale, NSW: Pluto Press Australia, 2002.

Boyd, Robin. *Australia's Home.* Melbourne: Melbourne University Press, 1987.

Bradley, Anthony and Terry Smith. *Australian Art and Architecture: Essays Presented to Bernard Smith.* Melbourne, Oxford, Wellington, and New York: Oxford University Press, 1980.

Butel, Elizabeth. *Margaret Preston: The Art of Constant Rearrangement.* n.p.: Viking in association with the Art Gallery of New South Wales, 1986 (c. 1985).

Butler, Roger. *Poster Art in Australia.* Canberra: National Gallery of Australia, 1993.

Caban, Geoff. *A Fine Line: A History of Australian Commercial Art.* Sydney: Hale & Ironmonger, 1983.

Carroll, Brian. *The Australian Poster Album.* Melbourne: Macmillan, 1974.

Cochrane, Grace. *The Crafts Movement in Australia: A History.* Kensington, NSW: New South Wales University Press, 1992.

Cochrane, Peter. *Industrialization and Dependence: Australia's Road to Economic Development, 1870–1939.* St. Lucia, Queensland: Queensland University Press, 1980.

Cozzolino, Mimmo with G. Fysh Rutherford. *Symbols of Australia.* Introduced by Geoffrey Blainey and Phillip Adams. Victoria: Penguin Books, 1980.

Cuffley, Peter. *Chandeliers and Billy Tea: A Catalogue of Australian Life 1880–1940.* Hawthorne, Victoria: The Five Mile Press, 1984.

Edquist, Harriet. *Pioneers of Modernism: The Arts and Crafts Movement in Australia.* Melbourne: Miegunyah Press/Melbourne University Publishing, 2008.

Fitzpatrick, Brian. *The Australian People, 1788–1945.* Westport, CT: Greenwood Press, 1951 (c. 1946).

Forster, Colin. *Industrial Development in Australia, 1920–1930.* Canberra: The Australian National University, 1964.

Fry, Tony. *Design History Australia: A Source Text in*

Methods and Resources. Sydney: Hale & Ironmonger and The Power Institute of Fine Arts, 1988.

Goddard, Julian, David Bromfield, Melissa Harpley and Pippa Tandy. *Aspects of Perth Modernism, 1929–1942.* Perth: Centre for Fine Arts U.W.A., 1986.

Hall, Cecil. R. *The Manufacturers: Australian Manufacturing Achievements to 1960.* Sydney, London, Melbourne, and Singapore: Angus and Robertson, 1971.

Hetherington, Michelle. *James Northfield and the Art of Selling Australia.* Canberra: National Library of Australia, 2006.

Hoffenberg, Peter. *An Empire on Display: English, Indian, and Australian Exhibitions from the Crystal Palace to the Great War.* Berkeley, Los Angeles, and London: University of California Press, 2001.

Holden, Robert. *Cover Up: The Art of Magazine Covers in Australia.* Rydalmere, NSW: Hodder & Stoughton, 1995.

Johnson, Heather. *Roy De Maistre: The Australian Years, 1894–1930.* Roseville, NSW: Craftsman House, 1988.

Lane, Terence and Jessie Searle. *Australians at Home: A Documentary History of the Australian Domestic Interiors from 1788 to 1914.* Introduction by Jessie Searle. Melbourne, Oxford, Auckland, and New York: Oxford University Press, 1990.

Lindesay, Vane. *The Inked-in Image: A Survey of Australian Comic Art.* Melbourne: Heinemann, 1970.

—*The Way We Were: Australian Popular Magazines, 1856–1969.* Oxford, Auckland, New York, and Melbourne: Oxford University Press, 1983.

Macintyre, Stuart. *The Oxford History of Australia, Vol. 4: 1901–1942, The Succeeding Age.* Melbourne, Oxford, Auckland, and New York: Oxford University Press, 1986.

—*A Concise History of Australia*, 3rd ed. Cambridge: Cambridge University Press, 2009.

McDonald, Anne. *Douglas Annand: The Art of Life.* Canberra: The National Gallery of Australia, 2001.

Menz, Christopher. *Morris & Company: Pre-Raphaelites and the Arts and Crafts Movement in South Australia.*

Adelaide: Art Gallery Board of South Australia, 1994.

Robb, Gwenda and Elaine Smith. *Concise Dictionary of Australian Artists.* Edited by Robert Smith. Melbourne: Melbourne University Press, 1993.

Sayers, Andrew. *Australian Art.* New York: Oxford University Press, 2001 (Oxford History of Art).

Serle, Geoffrey. *From Deserts the Prophets Come: The Creative Spirit in Australia, 1788–1972.* Melbourne: William Heinemann Australia, 1973.

Shaw, John, ed. *Australian Encyclopedia.* Sydney: Williams Collins Pty Ltd in association with David Bateman Ltd, 1984.

Stephen, Ann with Philip Goad and Andrew McNamara, eds. *Modern Times: The Untold Story of Modernism in Australia.* Carlton, Victoria: The Miegunyah Press, Sydney: Powerhouse Publishing, 2008.

Timms, Peter. *Private Lives: Australians at Home Since Federation.* Carleton, Victoria: The Miegunyah Press, 2008.

Underhill, Nancy D. H. *Making Australian Art, 1916–49.* Oxford et al.: Oxford University Press Australia, 1991.

Ward, Russel. *The History of Australia; The Twentieth Century.* New York, Hagerstown, San Francisco, and London: Harper & Row, 1977.

Wheelhouse, Frances. *Digging Stick to Rotary Hoe: Men and Machines in Rural Australia.* Melbourne: Cassell Australia, 1966.

Wilson, Stewart. *Wirraway, Boomerang and the CA-15 in Australian Service.* Weston Creek, ACT: Aerospace Publications Pty Ltd, 1991.

New Zealand

Calhoun, Ann. *The Arts and Crafts Movement in New Zealand, 1870–1940: Women Make Their Mark.* Auckland: Auckland University Press, 2000.

Jenkins, Douglas Lloyd. *At Home: A Century of New Zealand Design.* Auckland: Random House New Zealand, 2004 (A Godwit Book).

King, Michael. *The Penguin History of New Zealand*. Auckland: Penguin Books, 2003.

McLaughlin, Gordon, ed. *New Zealand Encyclopedia*. Auckland: David Bateman, 1984.

McLeod, A. L. *The Pattern of New Zealand Culture*. Ithaca: Cornell University Press, 1968.

Rice, Geoffrey W., ed. *The Oxford History of New Zealand*, 2nd ed. Auckland, Melbourne, Oxford, and New York: Oxford University Press, 1992 (c. 1981).

Sinclair, Keith, ed. *The Oxford Illustrated History of New Zealand*. Auckland, Oxford, New York, and Melbourne: Oxford University Press, 1990.

Thompson, Hamish. *Paste Up: A Century of New Zealand Poster Art*. Auckland: Random House New Zealand, 2003 (A Godwit Book).

Wolfe, Richard. *Well Made New Zealand: A Century of Trademarks*. Auckland: Reed Methuen, 1987.

Chapters in books

Allen, Ngapine, "Maori Vision and the Imperialist Gaze," in Tim Barringer and Tom Flynn, eds. *Colonialism and the Object: Empire, Material Culture and the Museum*. London and New York: Routledge, 1998.

Barnes, Jillian E., "Resisting the Captured Image: How Gwoja Tjungurrayi, 'One Pound Jimmy', Escaped the 'stone Age'," in Ingereth Macfarlane and Mark Hannah, eds. *Transgressions: Critical Australian Indigenous Histories*. Australian National University: E Press, 2007 (Australian History Monographs).

Carney, Lora Senechal, "Modernists and Folk on the Lower St. Lawrence; The Problem of Folk Art," in Lynda Jessup, ed. *Antimodernism and Artistic Experience: Policing the Boundaries of Modernity*. Toronto, Buffalo, and London: University of Toronto Press, 2001.

Davis, Angela E. "Ruskin and the Art-Workmen: Frederick Brigden, Sr., Engraver," in David Latham, ed. *Scarlet Hunters: Pre-Raphaelitism in Canada*. Toronto: Archives of Canadian Art and Design, 1998.

Jessup, Linda, "Bushwackers in the Gallery; Antimodernism and the Group of Seven," in Lynda Jessup, ed. *Antimodernism and Artistic Experience: Policing the Boundaries of Modernity*. Toronto, Buffalo, and London: University of Toronto Press, 2001.

McKay, Ian, "Handicrafts and the Logic of 'Commercial Antimodernism': The Nova Scotia Case," in Lynda Jessup, ed. *Antimodernism and Artistic Experience: Policing the Boundaries of Modernity*. Toronto, Buffalo, and London: University of Toronto Press, 2001.

Menz, Christopher, "'A Growing Enthusiasm for Modernity': Art Deco in Australia," in Charlotte Benton, Tim Benton, and Gislaine Wood. *Art Deco 1910–1939*. Boston, New York, and London: Bulfinch Press, 2003.

Petersen, Ann K. C., "The European Use of Maori Art in New Zealand Homes c. 1890–1914," in Barbara Brookes, ed. *At Home in New Zealand: Houses, History, People*. Wellington: Bridget Williams Books, 2000.

Stacey, Robert, "Harmonizing 'Means and Purpose': The Influence of Morris, Ruskin, and Crane on J.E.H. Macdonald," in David Latham, ed. *Scarlet Hunters: Pre-Raphaelitism in Canada*. Toronto: Archives of Canadian Art and Design, 1998.

Articles and pamphlets

Bériau, Oscar, "The Handicraft Renaissance in Quebec," *Canadian Geographical Journal* 7, no. 3 (September 1933).

Canadian Pacific Poster Art, 1881–1955: An Exhibition of Posters by Canadian Pacific Corporate Archives/L'Art de l'Affiche au Canadien Pacifique de 1881 à 1955. Montreal: Canadian Pacific Corporate Archives, n.d.

Charland, Maurice, "Technological Nationalism," *Canadian Journal of Political and Social Theory* 10, nos. 1–2 (1986).

Cowell, Elspeth, "The Canadian Pavilion at the 1939 New York World's Fair and the Development of

Modernism in Canada," *SSAC Bulletin* 19, no. 1 (March 1994).

Giovine, Cinzia Maurizia, "Jean-Marie Gavreau [sic]: Art, Handicrafts and National Culture in Quebec from the 1920s until the 1950s," *Design Issues* 10, no. 3 (Autumn 1994).

Mackay, Alice, "French-Canadian Handicrafts," *Canadian Geographical Journal* 6, no. 1 (January 1933).

McNeil, Peter, "Designing Women: Gender, Sexuality and the Interior Decorator c. 1890–1940," *Art History* 17, no. 4 (December 1994).

Wylie, Peter, "Technological Adaptation in Canadian Manufacturing, 1900–1929," *Journal of Economic History* 49, no. 3 (September 1989).

Dissertations and theses

Jackson, Simon. *The Discipline Without a Name: A History of Industrial Design in Australia.* PhD dissertation, Monash University, 1998.

Lépine, Johanne. *Historique et Étude du Design Industriel au Québec.* MA Thesis, Département d'histoire de l'art, Faculté des Arts et des Sciences, Université de Montréal, 1986.

Thompson, Christopher. *Confronting Design: Case Studies in the Design of Ceramics in New Zealand,* MA thesis, Auckland University of Technology, 2003.

Chapter 32: The Near and Middle East 1900–1939

The Ottoman Empire

At the end of the 19th century, the Ottoman Empire encompassed much of the Near East and Middle East regions. Istanbul was the capital of the empire and other major cities were Baghdad, Damascus, Beirut, Cairo, and Jerusalem. During the Tanzimat period between 1839 and 1876, a time of reorganization, the empire underwent a series of modernizing reforms that resulted in a new constitution as well as changes in the military, along with banking, and manufacturing. However, the constitutional reforms were short-lived and their revocation, coupled with an atmosphere of rising nationalism throughout Europe, increased dissatisfaction with the ruling Ottoman oligarchy headed by Sultan Abdul Hamid II, who ruled from 1876 to 1909. The Young Turk Revolution of 1908 led to a restoration of the suspended constitution and parliament, while Arab demands for greater autonomy within the empire contributed to the unrest. In the years leading up to World War I, the empire lost some of its territory in regional conflicts, and by the end of the war, during which the Ottomans had allied with the Germans and the Austro-Hungarians, who were defeated, their empire had begun to unravel.

As a result of the Turkish War of Independence, fought between 1918 and 1923 and led by Mustafa Kemal Pasha, subsequently known as Kemal Ataturk, the Republic of Turkey was established. Other parts of the empire were placed under mandates by the League of Nations. In 1922, Britain was given governing authority over Iraq, Palestine, and Transjordan, while the French were awarded dominion over Syria and Lebanon. The British had occupied Egypt in 1882 to defend their interests in the Suez Canal. Though Egypt was still officially within the Ottoman Empire, it came under the British sphere of influence and was made a protectorate in 1914, gaining independence in 1922. After World War I, the Arabian Peninsula over which the Ottomans previously had partial control, divided into a number of autonomous regions that eventually became states. These included Saudi Arabia, Kuwait, and Yemen. The one country in the region that had remained outside the boundaries of the Ottoman Empire was Iran.

Ottoman culture in the late 19th century embraced a mix of Western and Eastern influences. The social elite was oriented towards Europe and imported most of their goods from abroad, while others consumed local products that were made by independent craftsmen or in artisanal workshops and a few factories. Telephones were introduced in 1881 and were in limited use before World War I. Although the road system was still rather inadequate, the Ottoman government allowed the importation of automobiles and a few were in use in Istanbul, Izmir, and other provinces. As early as 1885, Belgian and French companies introduced streetcars to Izmir, then to Istanbul in 1889, Salonika in 1892, and later to Damascus and Beirut. Initially these streetcars were horse-drawn, but electric vehicles soon replaced them.

The late 19th- and early 20th-century Ottoman economy was predominantly agricultural (see Chapter 15), although there were factories and shipyards that produced equipment for the military, which was one of the few to have its own air force during World War I, even though its planes were manufactured abroad. Among the leading handicraft industries was the manufacture of shoes, which were produced in a few hundred small workshops rather than a single large factory. Despite this dispersal of production, however, the workshops managed to provide most of the shoes that were sold domestically, thus becoming one of the few Ottoman retail sectors that did not rely on foreign imports.

In addition to carpets produced in small workshops, a few factories made carpets and some other goods primarily for export. Among the carpet factories was Oriental Carpet Manufacturers Ltd, founded in 1908 by British merchants in the Izmir region. Managed by a local family, the company centralized the spinning, dyeing, and knotting processes with the help of German and Austrian technicians and then consolidated the weaving in a number of workshops, where local women and girls produced the carpets on company looms. The manufacturer paid the women low wages as was the case in European factories, and the division of labor became a major factor in the deskilling of carpetmakers in Anatolia. The company's design office, however, was staffed with British and French designers, who conceived and adapted patterns they knew would appeal to the European Orientalist taste. These carpets, produced with partial industrial methods, were a less expensive alternative to the higher-quality rugs that were woven in Persia and in the Turkish region of the Ottoman Empire. By introducing Western techniques to the production, marketing, and distribution processes, even though the actual weaving was done by hand, Oriental Carpet Manufacturers bested their competitors and by 1913 controlled 75 percent of the carpet production in the region, handling as well a sizeable portion of carpet exports.

The import of inexpensive mass-produced foreign goods, coupled with a lack of entrepreneurial spirit in the Ottoman middle classes, were among the causes that made it difficult for industries to develop. The major industrial project initiated by the Ottoman sultans was the construction of railroads. The Hijaz Railway, inaugurated in 1900 and completed in 1908, was built by the Ottomans with advice from German engineers. Sultan Abdul Hamid II intended the train to carry religious pilgrims from Damascus to Medina, although it had a strategic purpose as well. The Baghdad Railway was initiated in 1903 but was not completed until 1940. German banks and companies initially funded it, while German engineers managed the early construction. After World War I, both financing and construction were taken over by other investors. Additional railways were built earlier and later by German and French firms that provided both capital and expertise.

Following the 1908 revolution of the Young Turks, however, the Ottoman government took stronger steps to encourage industry, passing laws to that effect in 1909 and 1913. As the economist Charles Issawi points out, it became easier to import machinery, which prompted considerable investment in new factories, although the range of products was limited. Papermaking, canning, and glassmaking were among the leading industries. In 1918, modernizing reformers maintained the rhetoric of industrialization in *Sanayi* (*Industry*), a magazine that continued after the Turkish republic was founded with a new title.

The dominant Ottoman languages were Turkish, Persian, and Arabic, all of which were written in Arabic script. Despite a well-developed literary culture among the elite, however, at the end of the 19th century, only 15 percent of the Ottomans could read. Nonetheless, numerous newspapers, mass-circulation magazines, and books were published and were mostly designed by staff members of the publishing concerns or even by printers.

Turkey
Initial steps of the 1920s

When Kemal Ataturk became Turkey's first president in 1923, he sought to modernize the country in every way. In this he differed from all other leaders in the region except Reza Shah in Persia who followed Ataturk's example after he came to power in 1925. A year before Turkey was declared a republic, the new National Assembly abolished the sultanate and two years later all members of the Ottoman dynasty were expelled from the country. Though the majority of Turkey's new citizens were Muslims, Ataturk was determined to make Turkey a modern secular nation whose policies and way of life were based on European precedents.

Ataturk and a group of Western-minded intellectuals created their own political party, the Revolutionary People's Party (RPP), which carried out Ataturk's revolution from the top down, enabling the RPP to initiate cultural, legal, and economic changes with no real opposition. Ataturk believed that the government needed to be involved in industrial development and initiated a series of bold gestures during the 1920s to advance his economic agenda. In 1924 he inaugurated the Iş Bankası (Business Bank), a privately owned and financed institution. Established to provide capital for the independent development of factories and businesses, the bank financed a few small enterprises, but its main thrust became the development of coal mines on the Black Sea. The following year the National Assembly established the government-owned Turkish Industrial and Mining Bank to foster the creation of state industries. This was the beginning of government involvement in the economy, although it was intended to support Ataturk's principal goal of developing the economy through private enterprise. The government also revived the Chambers of Trade and Commerce that had been started under Abdul Hamid II. They were given the authority to develop crafts and trades, train apprentices, upgrade artisans, and generally to improve the conditions of employment for craftsmen.

Also in 1925, the Turkish Airplane Association, which had been created to manufacture airplanes and engines, entered an agreement with the German airplane manufacturer Junkers to form a company, TOMTAS, that would build and maintain planes for the Turkish Air Force, which had developed from the Ottomans' earlier involvement with aeronautics. An airplane factory was constructed in Kayseri and a building for maintenance functions was put up in Eskişehir. The joint venture was also supposed to establish a new national Turkish airline, but disagreements between the parties involved resulted in TOMTAS shutting

down in 1928 after only three years of operation. In 1933, however, the government did start its own airline. Known as Devlet Hava Yollari (State Airline), its planes were purchased abroad and all its flights were domestic until after World War II.

The same year that TOMTAS folded, the Turkish government signed a contract with Ford to build an automobile assembly plant, which also closed after several years. More successful was the government takeover of the Ottoman railway system and the commitment to a significant expansion of routes during the 1930s and 1940s. In 1927, the State Railways of the Republic of Turkey (TCDD) was created. The small railway repair shop in Eskişehir, which had been founded in 1894, had expanded its capacity by 1923 to produce boilers and gears for steam locomotives as well as parts for railway bridges, switches, and tracks. The crew also maintained a number of locomotives and passenger and freight cars. It was the experience of making parts and servicing existing stock that eventually enabled the workshop to build Turkey's first steam locomotive, Karkurt, in 1961.

In 1927, the government introduced the Law for the Encouragement of Industry, which provided multiple incentives for new enterprises ranging from free land and tax rebates to reduced costs for transporting goods, along with subsidies pegged to a percentage of annual output. The law also mandated government agencies to purchase Turkish products whenever possible. Although this led to limited success in several industries, a survey conducted the same year the law was passed indicated that most local manufacturing still took place in small workshops without the aid of machines. Thus, the gap between Ataturk's aims to modernize Turkey and the infrastructure he inherited from the Ottomans was considerable and would continue to hamper his ambitions even after the government adopted statism as a full-fledged industrial policy in the 1930s. Nonetheless, Ataturk pursued various strategies for development that did not depend on a pre-existing culture of industrialization.

During the 1920s, Ataturk's emphasis was on projects that would enable Turkey to compete internationally as an industrial nation, consequently primitive farming techniques endured in the agricultural sector. Ataturk enacted no ambitious program of land reform as occurred in the Soviet Union or in Mexico. Consequently, there was little need for mechanized agricultural equipment since farming plots remained small. As the economist Charles Issawi notes, in 1927 Turkish farmers were using 1,187,000 wooden plows, compared to only 211,000 iron ones. During the 1930s,

however, the Agricultural Bank promoted the adoption of more modern equipment.

As part of his plan for Turkey's modernization, Ataturk initiated a broad array of cultural changes. He established Turkey as a secular state and encoded this in the constitution. He also instituted a radical program of dress reform, outlawing the traditional fez for men and discouraging women from wearing the veil. Both men and women were urged to dress in Western attire, which was reinforced in advertising and government propaganda. Polygamy was ended and women's marital rights were enhanced.

Perhaps the most significant change that Ataturk promoted was the conversion of the Turkish language from Arabic script to roman letters, although the Arabic language and Arabic orthography continued to be widely used elsewhere in the former Ottoman Empire. Though no one before Ataturk had been able to substitute a roman alphabet for the Arabic script, others had sought to make Arabic orthography, especially for writing Turkish, more efficient. Such reforms were proposed as early as 1851. After the Young Turk Revolution, modernizing intellectuals urged that Arabic letters be written and printed separately so that students and printers would no longer have to deal with three or more forms of the same letter, depending on its position in a word. During World War I, Enver Pasha (1881–1922), then Minister of War, introduced a simplified Arabic alphabet to increase literacy among the soldiers. It was used to print a few official military documents but it did not last.

Emboldened perhaps by the Soviet government's substitution of Russian Cyrillic letters for Arabic script in the Turkic republics of the Soviet Union, Ataturk declared in 1928 that henceforth Turkish would be written with roman letters. For him, this change represented the most efficient form of modernization, simultaneously introducing a system for writing Turkish that was identified with the new republic, while also reducing and eventually eliminating access to the literature of the Ottoman past that had been

Fig. 32.01: Kemal Ataturk teaching the roman alphabet in Istanbul, c. 1928. Getty Images.

written and printed in Arabic script. At the same time, Ataturk claimed that the roman alphabet, which was phonetic and whose orthography was simpler than Arabic, would make it easier for those who were illiterate to learn to read (Fig. 32.01). Most literate Turks, however, who comprised a narrow segment of the population, were already familiar with the roman alphabet through their knowledge of Western languages such as French, Italian, English, or German. Thus, the transition to romanized Turkish was not difficult for the educated class.

The Six Arrows of the 1930s

At the 1931 Congress of the Revolutionary People's Party, Ataturk introduced six principles that would provide the foundation for his governance of Turkey. Known as the *Altı Ok* or Six Arrows, they were represented in the party's logo shooting out in all directions from a sphere whose outline was suggested by a negative space. The Six Arrows logo was applied in various ways including RPP flags and was also embossed on commercial objects such as cigarette lighters. The six principles that the arrows represented defined a constitutional republic based on modern institutions whose purpose was to serve the national good. Central to their enforcement was a strong government with Ataturk at its center. Statism, one of the six principles, declared that the government would have the primary responsibility for Turkey's economic development. Although there was a place for individual entrepreneurs, the government would invest in large state enterprises. Ataturk would have preferred private enterprise to fuel Turkey's economic development, but this strategy did not succeed during the 1920s.

After statism became the official economic policy, the government established the Sumerbank (Sumerian Bank), whose responsibility was to oversee existing state factories and enterprises, establish new ones, and participate in ventures with individual entrepreneurs. Over time, the Sumerbank was involved with all areas of production, including both heavy industry

and consumer products. As well, it started vocational schools that were related to its major industries and offered scholarships for study in Turkey and abroad. The Sumerbank also opened a chain of department stores to sell the products of its factories such as shoes and textiles. As a government enterprise, these stores were able to feature national products and keep prices down by controlling a part of the market that was no longer accessible to importers of foreign goods.

Although Turkey became a major trading partner with Germany during the 1930s, Ataturk based Turkey's economic development on the Soviet Union's Five-Year Plan. The two plans that the Turkish government implemented in the 1930s emphasized industrial development rather than agriculture. Unlike the Soviet plans that gave primacy to heavy industry, however, the first Turkish Five-Year Plan featured consumer goods, although heavy industries were also considered. These were developed largely by the Etibank (Hittite Bank), which was active in mineral and petroleum exploration, electric-power facilities, and coal mining. The Second Five-Year Plan paid more attention to capital industries such as mining, electricity, ports, and heavy machinery.

Part of Ataturk's industrialization program was to encourage the public to participate in new forms of consumption. In 1929 the government launched the National Economy and Savings Society, which was established to promote national products and to urge people to live moderately. This indicated a shift to a model of consumption exemplified by the Western middle classes and away from the extravagance of the previous Ottoman elite. The society convened a Congress of Industry in 1930 to discuss ways of increasing national production and improving the quality of Turkish goods.

By 1933, the National Economy and Savings Society had 210 branches in cities and towns throughout Turkey. Its program included propaganda materials, producing brochures for the public and materials for schools, and organizing an annual Savings and National Products Week. The society also promoted Turkey's participation in domestic and foreign exhibitions such as the Budapest International Exhibition of 1931, where the modern architect Sedad Eldem (1908–1988) designed Turkey's Pavilion. Turkey had a pavilion as well at the 1936 Levant Fair in Palestine, where it was one of the few states in the region that participated.

At home, the National Economy and Savings Society organized a major Exhibition of National Economy in 1933 on the 10th anniversary of the founding of the Turkish Republic. On display was an array of Turkish industrial and agricultural products including textiles and carpets, both products of traditional industries, along with various foodstuffs and maps and charts that depicted railroad construction and electrification. The rhetoric of the organizers looked ahead to a technological future, but it also made reference to heroic events in the Turkish past. The joining of industrial ambition to nationalist rhetoric was characteristic of Ataturk's six principles within which enterprise, consumption, and personal values were joined together in the project of nation-building.

Other exhibitions followed, each continuing to develop presentation techniques that had been pioneered by designers outside Turkey such as El Lissitzky with his bombastic Pressa Exhibition of 1928. Other influential exhibitions of the early 1930s included the 1932 Mostra della Rivoluzione in Rome (see Chapter 27). A 1934 exhibit that celebrated Turkey's First Five-Year Plan incorporated many techniques of those earlier exhibits: large-scale photographs, photomontage, enlarged typography, and bold graphics to recount the history of Turkish industry, agriculture, and economy from the late Ottoman period to the present.

The republic's most ambitious exhibition project, however, was the Izmir International Fair, which grew out of a series of industrial exhibits that had been held annually since 1927. It was officially launched in 1933 and moved in 1936 to a new site, the Kulturpark (Culture Park), which had been specially designed to accommodate a large number of pavilions. The Turkish

pavilions were mainly modern, making the fair a showcase for the latest designs by the nation's architects. The 1936 fair had only three pavilions from abroad, including one from Egypt, but the fairs between 1937 and 1939 featured pavilions built by a number of foreign governments including Italy, Germany, Britain, and Iran. The closest counterpart to the Izmir International Fair in the region was the Levant Fair in Palestine, which was a showcase for the modern pavilions designed by Jewish architects just as the Izmir fair featured pavilions by architects from Turkey.

Although the well-developed program of industrial exhibitions in Turkey during the 1930s promoted images of a modern lifestyle that exceeded the nation's manufacturing ability at the time, they nonetheless created aspirations that Turkish industries sought to fulfill after World War II. In the meantime, a number of companies did import modern products such as consumer appliances from abroad. The largest of these was probably Bourla Brothers, which brought to Turkey American radios manufactured by RCA, and refrigerators made by Frigidaire, along with German radios that Telefunken produced.

Some of Turkey's modern architects, whose buildings were characterized with the rubric "cubic architecture," were frustrated by the lack of companies that could produce a full range of modern furniture and appliances they believed should fill the houses they designed. In various popular and professional magazines, architects published drawings of modern interiors with "cubic furniture," but the Turkish furniture industry was not making pieces in this style, nor was there a sufficient market to induce leading manufacturers outside Turkey like Thonet to open showrooms in Istanbul or Ankara. Though some modern furniture was most likely imported by individual entrepreneurs, the absence of interior or furniture designers with a modern sensibility led the artist and critic Celal Esat Arseven (1876–1972) to propose that the architect ought also to be a furniture designer in order to attend to the many needs that arose from living in a modern house.

This was actually the case in a number of residences that architects designed for important figures including Ataturk himself.

The kitchen was the one part of the house in which the government took a particular interest, recognizing it as a crucial environment for the Turkish housewife, who was to be modern in her efficiency and traditional in the acceptance of her role as wife and mother. To prepare women for the multiple tasks of married life, the Ministry of Education opened a number of Girls' Institutes, where urban middle-class girls were instructed in rational methods of cooking, housework, and child-rearing. Among the courses taught was the organization of domestic space, and contrasts were drawn between traditional homes with their poorly arranged kitchens and modern dwellings whose kitchens were rationally organized. Among those active in the creation of the Girls' Institutes was the Austrian architect Grete Schütte-Lihotzky, who had designed the ultra-efficient Frankfurt kitchen that became a staple of the apartments in Germany's Neue Frankfurt housing developments in the late 1920s. Schütte-Lihotzky came to Turkey in 1938 to escape the Nazis and remained until 1941.

Graphic design and the state

Until the adoption of the roman alphabet in 1928, Turkish posters and publications—whether magazines, books, or newspapers—were printed in Arabic script and thus maintained some visual continuity with the publications of the Ottoman Empire. Following the political changes that Ataturk initiated after 1923, however, there were major differences in the graphic imagery, notably, no more fezzes for men or veils for women; instead, both men and women were portrayed in modern dress. To put Ataturk's radical linguistic program into effect called for the massive acquisition of roman fonts, which required three additional letters to complete the Turkish alphabet. Typesetters and printers adapted layout techniques from Western publications and by the middle of 1929, everything was printed with roman type.

Ihap Hulusi Gorey, poster artist

Caricaturists, illustrators, and printers, along with developments in Western poster art, typography, and publication design made little impact on the Ottoman Empire before World War I. Consequently, there was a lack of commercial artists in the new Turkish republic who were trained in modern graphic techniques. The one exception was Ihap Hulusi Gorey (1898–1986), who was born in Cairo of Turkish parentage and spent his early years there before going to Munich, where he studied painting and commercial art for five years. In Munich, Hulusi was attracted to the work of Ludwig Hohlwein and developed an illustrative style that was similar to that of the Munich designer. As an Ottoman Turk studying in Munich, Hulusi learned to incorporate roman lettering into his designs, which made it easy for him to adapt to the new roman orthography that Ataturk had mandated for the Turkish language.

When he returned to Istanbul in 1925, Hulusi worked for the Ministry of Foreign Affairs to please his father and also contributed cartoons to the political humor magazine *Akbaba*, which was founded in 1922. He finally left the ministry and dedicated himself to commercial art, opening a studio in 1929. Hulusi was better trained than any other artist in Turkey to become a modern graphic designer. He had already established himself as a successful poster artist in Munich and was well prepared for the plethora of commissions from local and foreign enterprises along with the Turkish government that came his way. Over time, these included not only posters, but also packaging, and logotypes for products, companies, and government agencies.

One of Hulusi's earliest and most successful commissions was the design of a label for Kulup Rakısı (Club Rakisi), a well-known Turkish liquor called rakı. Using himself as a model (Fig. 32.02), Hulusi depicted two handsome gentlemen in evening attire, thus positioning the liquor as a drink for the wealthy class (Fig. 32.03). The figures on the original label had a

Fig. 32.02: Ihap Hulusy Gorey as a model for the first Kulup Rakisi label, c. 1930. Courtesy Sadik Karamustafa.

Fig. 32.03: İhap Hulusi Gorey, Kulup Rakisi, label, c. 1930. CPA Media Co. Ltd./Pictures From History.

sporting look, but Hulusi subsequently redesigned the label to give the two men an older more distinguished appearance (Fig. 32.04). Similar to Hohlwein, Hulusi most often featured human figures in his posters and his ads, thus relating the product, institution, or service that was advertised to a particular group of consumers. For the most part, these were members of the middle class whom Hulusi portrayed in modern dress, thereby reinforcing Ataturk's call to Turkish citizens to adopt

Western fashions. Domestic clients included producers of foodstuffs, liquor, coffee, and other non-industrial products that were made in local factories. Foreign manufacturers included Bayer, Pirelli, and Kodak. Hulusi also drew advertisements and posters for the American and German appliances that the Bourla Brothers distributed.

Much of Hulusi's work was done for Turkish government agencies and enterprises, and in fact it was Hulusi who created the overall graphic image for Ataturk's regime. One major client was the National Lottery. Posters for the Is Bankası or Commerce Bank, which strongly supported Ataturk's aim to encourage savings, depicted smartly dressed middle-class men and women, while a poster for the Ziraat Bankası or Agricultural Bank portrayed a seated farmer reclining reflectively, while smoking a cigarette. Hulusi also designed numerous posters for the Sumerbank and some of its enterprises. Several posters promoted the shoes and textiles made in the Sumerbank factories. In a poster that advertised the department stores the Sumerbank established to sell its products, Hulusi depicted a modern urban woman and a peasant from the countryside dressed in traditional clothes including a headscarf (Plate 62). The point of the poster was to bring city and country dwellers together through consumption at the Sumerbank stores, which sold products for both modern urban dwellers and rural peasants.

The contrast between figures in modern and traditional dress was actually a rhetorical trope that the Ataturk regime adopted to contrast the old and the new, positioning the old as a sign of outmoded tradition and the new as an image of Turkish moderni- zation. The contrast was evident in political posters of the Republican People's Party, which compared, for example, traditional clothing and polygamy with modern dress and marriage to a single spouse. It was also a technique that Hulusi sometimes adopted, either for the government or for private clients, as he contrasted people who represented old ways with

Fig. 32.04: İhap Hulusi Gorey, redesigned Kulüp Rakisi label, 1930s. Courtesy Sadik Karamustafa.

Fig. 32.05: İhap Hulusi Gorey, Citizens. Fight against disrespect in society, poster, c. 1930s. CPA Media Co. Ltd./Pictures From History.

modern men and women, who wore smart Western clothes and used contemporary products. In a poster for sewing machines, for example, Hulusi compared an elderly woman holding her hand knitting with a young woman who was using a sewing machine. For a poster that promoted a new brand of coffee, he used the comparison of old and new in a different way, depicting the value of tradition by juxtaposing a maid holding a tray of modern demitasse coffee cups with a woman in traditional clothing baring a comparable tray with coffee served in old-fashioned glasses. A poster that encouraged good citizenship featured a man in modern attire urging citizens to be wary of people who disobey rules, and cause nuisances. People were urged to fight against disrespect in society (Fig. 32.05).

Hulusi fully espoused a rhetoric of modernization in his poster for the new Turkish National Airline, which shows a plane with its nose pointed upwards flanked by several passengers who also look forward into the distance. He most likely devised the logotype for the airline, an abstract bird in flight, which was adapted almost directly from the logo of the German airline, Lufthansa. Hulusi also promoted automobile travel through the occasional poster he did for the Turkey Touring and Automobile Club (Fig. 32.06).

Due to the changeover from Arabic script to the roman alphabet, much attention was given to writing and designing school textbooks, which had to be illustrated as well as printed with the new romanized Turkish characters. In 1934, the government commissioned Hulusi to illustrate a textbook that would be widely used throughout the country for teaching the alphabet. Entitled *Alfabe* (*ABC Primer*), its cover featured a drawing of Ataturk teaching the roman letters to a young girl while the book itself consisted of many pleasing illustrations intended to make learning agreeable to the students.

Fig. 32.06: İhap Hulusi Gorey, Izmir, poster, c. 1940. CPA Media Co. Ltd./Pictures From History.

Magazines

Popular illustrated magazines such as *Resimli Ay* (*Illustrated Monthly*) were published in Arabic script during the first years of the Turkish republic, but a spate of new periodicals appeared during and after the conversion to roman orthography in 1928. Among the first of these was *Muhit* (*Neighborhood*), whose initial cover recalled the lettering and graphic style of the *Saturday Evening Post* (Fig. 32.07). Along with other illustrated periodicals such as *Ayda Bir* (*Once a Month*), *Yedigun* (*7 Days*), and *Modern Turkiye Mecmuasi* (*Modern Turkish Magazine*) that appeared around the same time or a bit later, *Muhit* was directed to middle-class families and espoused a modern Western lifestyle. What distinguished these periodicals from their counterparts in the West, as Sibel Bozdoğan

has shown, was their editorial policies, which emphasized a modern lifestyle as something to strive for rather than something that could be taken for granted. Consequently, they frequently featured editorials or articles that lauded Western progress and accompanied these with photographs of skyscrapers, factories, or technological objects. Similar to the contrast of old and new that was evident in some of Ihab Hulusi's posters, the magazines' editors also published photographic juxtapositions that contrasted traditional ways of living with modern ones. Magazines like *Yedigun* were strong advocates of modern domestic architecture. Not only did they publish renderings of modern interiors, but they also looked ahead to houses of the future that would be filled with modern electrical appliances.

More research is needed to determine who actually designed these magazines, provided the illustrations, and produced the photographs. Commercial photography was already highly developed in the Ottoman period, as were magazines illustrated with photographs. Some of the new illustrators no doubt were trained as artists at the Academy of Fine Arts, which had been established as the School of Fine Arts in 1877. One known magazine illustrator is Munip Fehim (dates unconfirmed), who was also active as a book cover artist. As in many countries, artists turned to commercial art in order to make a living. Cover designs, which frequently featured attractive women in Western dress, and layouts were easily copied from Western magazines, as were border ornaments and illustrations along with decorative lettering. The range of typefaces was limited, given that roman fonts could not be easily appropriated since it was necessary to create three new letters for each font that was used.

The most distinctive publication of the 1930s was not one of the family-oriented periodicals but rather a government propaganda magazine, *La Turquie Kamaliste* (*Kemalist Turkey*), which the Press Office in the Ministry of the Interior published between 1934 and 1948, although only four issues appeared after 1941 (Fig. 32.08). It was a photo magazine similar to *USSR*

Fig. 32.07: *Muhit*, cover, c. 1928. Middle East Department, University of Chicago Library.

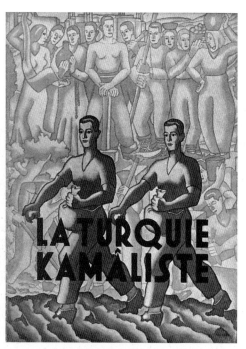

Fig. 32.08: *La Turquie Kamaliste*, cover, 1930s. Courtesy of Edhem Eldem.

Turkey's capital when the republic was founded in 1923, were shown frequently, notably in a special section called "Ankara Construit" ("Ankara Builds"). Also featured were photographs of mass gymnastics, female aviators, modern schools and nurseries, and military preparedness. As with other publications, the rhetorical contrast of old and new was frequently employed to demonstrate how Turkey as a modern nation was emerging from its allegedly primitive Ottoman past. Pferschy was adept at depicting his subjects in a heroic manner by using unusual angles, close-ups, and dramatic lighting.

Egypt

After several robust attempts at industrialization by Mohammad Ali and Ismael Pasha in the 19th century, Egypt was unable to freely pursue its economic interests during the British occupation that began in 1882. Even without the British presence, another effort to industrialize would have been difficult.

in Construction, which might have served as its model. Directed to a foreign audience, it featured short articles written either in French, German, or English.

La Turquie Kamaliste was edited by the artist and intellectual Vedat Nedim Tor (1897–1985), who may also have been responsible for its design. The photographs were taken by Othmar Pferschy (1898–1984), an Austrian photographer who worked for many years in Turkey.

The editorial purpose of *La Turquie Kamaliste* was to promote Turkey as a modern industrial nation. This was accomplished by presenting photographs of modern life and the new architecture. Examples of new construction in Ankara, which was designated

Few wealthy Egyptians who might otherwise have become entrepreneurs were drawn to industry, trade, or finance. Egypt also lacked an infrastructure for training engineers and technical experts. Foreigners had built Egypt's three major development projects of the 19th century—the railroad, the Suez Canal, and the Aswan Dam.

There was little stimulus from the British occupiers to encourage industrialization. Lord Cromer, the British Consul-General who was in Egypt from 1883 to 1907, had previously served in India where Britain strongly resisted Indian efforts to industrialize. In Egypt, Cromer was primarily opposed to protective tariffs for cotton mills, which in effect thwarted the development of a potentially major Egyptian industrial initiative. Although Cromer has been shown not to have been categorically opposed to industrial enterprise in Egypt, he nonetheless supported the British policy of placing its own economic interests first as a principle of colonial governance.

There were a few successful enterprises in Egypt such as an alcohol distillery, a Belgian cement factory, and a flourishing cigarette industry, but the nation's economy was primarily agricultural and its population barely literate. According to the 1907 census, male literacy was only 3 percent, while female literacy was 0.3 percent. In 1917, cotton was the principal export and only 5.9 percent of the labor force was involved in manufacturing. Most worked in small shops or plants refining agricultural products, making cement, ceramics, bricks, or soap, or were employed in small cigarette factories that produced "Egyptian" brands for export and local consumption. There were also a number of engineering workshops and foundries that made and repaired instruments that were used in large irrigation, dredging, and land-leveling projects.

As in India and elsewhere in the less developed world of the early 20th century, rural dwellers made many of the things they needed themselves or else purchased them from local craftsmen. These included rudimentary furniture, cooking utensils, and agricultural implements. In Egypt, farmers were still using plows and other tools that had not changed for centuries. By contrast, urban dwellers shopped at department stores that had been modeled on those in Europe. In the years preceding World War I, Cairo had a highly developed shopping culture with myriad department stores, each striving to outdo the other with dramatic buildings and elegant retail spaces. Most were owned by Jews, but the proprietors of one, Sednaoui, were Nazarenes from Syria. The Sednaoui Department Store was designed by the French architect George Parcq (1874–1939), who was responsible for much of Cairo's interwar Art Nouveau-inspired architecture including the Cairo Bourse.

All the department stores in Cairo and elsewhere in Egypt sold the latest merchandise from Paris, London, and other European capitals. For educated Egyptians, France was a mecca of culture and fashion, hence the architects of Sednaoui, Orsodi-Back (later to be known as Omar Effendi), Les Grands Magasins Cicurel & Oreco. and Tiring strove to create Cairene versions of the *grand magazins* such as Galeries Lafayette, Bon Marché, and Printemps. Originally patronized by Egypt's wealthy class, these department stores were increasingly destinations for the growing middle class for whom purchasing status-laden foreign goods was a convenient way to participate in Egypt's modernization process.

Due to the large domestic consumption of foreign goods, urban handicraft workers faced stiff competition and had great difficulties selling their wares. Foreigners, including, in fact, the department store patrons, dominated much of the Egyptian economy. Disillusioned with the traditional guild structure as well as the competition from abroad and motivated to participate in a slowly emerging nationalist movement against the British occupation, many artisans joined the Manual Trade Workers' Union, which was founded by the nationalist political party, the Waqf, in 1909. One consequence of this organizing effort was a nationalist uprising in 1919, a wave of strikes, and the formation of several new unions.

During World War I, when the flow of imported goods was disrupted, the need for industrial self-sufficiency became evident. Prompted in part by pressure from the Egyptian middle class as well as by an opportunity to create new possibilities for its own investors, the British government set up a Commission on Commerce and Industry in 1916. Its mandate was to recommend policies for strengthening industrial initiatives. As a result, the commission strongly criticized past attitudes that had privileged agriculture as the financial engine of the large Egyptian landholders as well as the basis of British colonial policy. Instead, it called for an industrial renaissance that would both revivify the artisan class and enhance Egypt's attempts at import substitution.

The report led to the establishment of a Department of Industry and Commerce after the war. Though foreign competition returned, the emerging elite espoused industrialization, which they equated with modernization and ultimately independence. Due to a lack of funds, government intervention in industrial development was minimal. Consequently, the private Misr Bank was established in 1920 with Egyptian capital. During the 1920s and 1930s, the Misr Bank set up almost 20 enterprises that dealt with goods and services as wide ranging as printing and publishing, transportation, fishing, weaving, mining, tourism, and even theater and film. Its lead enterprise was the Misr Spinning and Weaving Company, which was established in 1927. Its mechanized mill employed over 25,000 workers by the end of World War II, making it the largest industrial enterprise in the Middle East. Industrial development received a boost in 1930 when Egypt gained tariff autonomy and was able to protect its domestic industries from foreign competition. This encouraged a number of wealthy Egyptians to invest in industrial enterprises instead of real estate.

During the interwar period, Egypt thus became increasingly independent in quite a few industries that transformed raw materials into market commodities. Local factories produced alcohol and beer, cigarettes, matches, shoes, cement, lamp glass, and furniture. To promote its industries abroad, the Egyptian government sponsored pavilions for the Izmir International Fair in 1936 and the 1937 Paris Exposition Internationale.

Unlike Turkey, there was no movement to create modern interiors, thus furniture styles for the most part were based on traditional examples. As in Turkey, domestic appliances such as radios, refrigerators, and toasters were imported from abroad since Egypt had no factories to manufacture these products. One way that local taste for domestic furnishings was shaped was through home economics textbooks for middle-class and upper-class women. Books like Francis Mikhail's *Household Organization* and Antun al-Gamayyil's *The Girl and the Home*, as Mona Russell has noted, provided advice about home furnishings along with other topics. Mikhail's book was directed to a broad audience of young women while al-Gamayyil's was aimed at wealthy girls with servants. Mikhail recommended decorating the house with oriental crafts, antiques, and even the horns of animals. While Mikhail was quite specific in detailing the furniture and other items that each room required, al-Gamayyil was concerned that householders did not buy furniture that was beyond their means and that what they did purchase was in good taste, although he did not specify exactly what that taste was. These books may be compared with the proposals for "cubic furniture" that pervaded the family magazines in Turkey. Lacking an overarching ideology of lifestyle transformation that Ataturk sought to implement in Turkey and which Turkish architects transformed into images of modern interiors, there was no comparable impetus in Egypt to equate modern living with modern architecture. Rather, the emphasis in the home economics books was on cleanliness, efficiency, and order rather than on any specific style of furnishings or decor.

Living modern was not only an activity of domestic life; it also had its counterpart in public space, particularly with automobile ownership and use. Automobiles had been imported into Egypt since

1904. Initially they were mainly French. Among the manufacturers were Dion-Bouton, Peugeot, Renault, Panhard-Levassor, Clement-Bayard, and Darraq. Egypt's first taxi company was founded in Alexandria in 1907–1908 with a fleet of French Unic cabs, and the country's initial service station and garage, the Cairo Motor Company, opened around the same time. By the early 1920s, automobiles were being imported from Italy and the United States as well.

Ford had organized a company in 1932 to sell and service its automobiles in Egypt, using Alexandria as a base to expand its business elsewhere in the Middle East and North Africa. By the 1920s, Cairo and Alexandria had embarked on programs to create new thoroughfares and the government built roads to connect the large cities. Part of the motivation to create these roads was to enable busloads of tourists to visit sites of interest.

Tourism was also one of several motivations for an expansion of the railroads. Egypt's initial railroad, the first on the African continent, opened in 1856. Inaugurated by the Egyptian khedive Abbas I, it was constructed by Robert Stephenson (1803–1859), a British civil engineer and son of George Stephenson, who had built one of the first steam locomotives. By the end of the century, several different lines constructed by successive khedives had been completed. The State Railway Administration gradually absorbed the smaller lines and consolidated them into the Egyptian State Railways. Locomotives and rolling stock were manufactured abroad (Fig. 32.09). Rolling stock was manufactured by the Compagnie Internationale des Wagons-Lits (International Sleeping Car Company) in France, Ganz and Company in Hungary, and the Pullman Company in the United States. By the 1930s, luxury sleeping cars used for tourism and also to transport Egypt's wealthy class and royalty had electric lighting, air conditioning, and cold-water drinking fountains.

Among the major enterprises of the Misr Bank was the founding of a national airline in 1932. Originally known as Misr Airwork and then Misr Airlines, its name was eventually changed to Misr Egyptian Airlines and later to EgyptAir. The founding

Fig. 32.09: Egyptian National Railways, locomotive, date unconfirmed. SSPL via Getty Images.

of an airline was one manifestation of the nationalist spirit in Egypt during the 1930s. The Misr Bank management wanted to participate in the new world of aviation but was unable to establish its own facilities for aircraft production; thus it had to purchase its planes abroad, mainly from Britain. Initial routes were within Egypt with a few foreign destinations added, but by the late 1930s, Misr Airlines was flying to numerous countries and mandates in the Middle East and the Mediterranean including Syria, Iraq, Palestine, and Cyprus. The airline's logo was a cartouche containing Arabic script flanked by a pair of wings. Graphics for the company included timetables, brochures, baggage labels, and posters, all of which showed a company plane flying over pyramids, palm trees, or ruins, which were familiar Orientalist icons, not only in Egyptian tourist advertising but in most ads or posters intended to induce European or North American tourists to visit the region (Fig. 32.10).

Fig. 32.10: N. Strekalovsky, Misr Airwork, poster, c. 1930s. Private Collection/Photo © Christie's Images/Bridgeman Images.

Popular media and publicity

Calligraphy and typography

After the collapse of the Ottoman Empire, Egypt was the first former province to become an independent nation. With Turkey's adoption of the roman alphabet, it was left to Egypt, a center of printing and publishing in Arabic since the 19th century, to develop Arabic as a modern language in its spoken, written, and printed forms. In 1932 the Academy of Arabic Languages was formed under royal patronage. Administered by the Ministry of Education, it had several purposes. One was to adapt classical Arabic to modern usage. Another was to reduce widespread illiteracy in the Arab-speaking world. With the latter goal in mind, the academy launched a campaign in 1938 to make Arabic easier to read and write. The most extreme proposal for this was by Abdul Aziz Fahmi (dates unconfirmed), who urged replacement of the Arabic script with roman letters, as had happened a decade earlier in Turkey. Wilhelm Spitta, the German director of Egypt's National Library, had actually put forth such an idea in 1880, though coming from a European, it may easily have been interpreted as a proposal with strong colonial overtones. Elias Akkawi (dates unconfirmed) and several others emphasized ways of incorporating vowel marks into the letters and reducing the number of letterforms to a minimum. Akkawi published several versions of a proposed alphabet around 1943 and 1944 (Fig. 32.11). Despite various proposals, however, no major changes in the alphabet were made.

ﺍﻷﺑﺠﺪﻳﺔ ﻟﻔﺎﺭﻭﻕ

ﺃَﻟِﻔﺒَـــﺎﺀِ   ﻓَﺎﺭُﻭﻕ

Fig. 32.11: Elias Akkawi, 2nd proposal for a new Arabic alphabet, c. 1943. www.sakkal.com/articles/

Newspapers, magazines, books

Even under British rule, the Arab press flourished in Egypt since the British exercised little control over the many newspapers, magazines, journals, and books that were published. Among the leading publishers were Syrians, most of them Christians, who came to Egypt in considerable numbers. Their high literary standards, secular outlook, and refined business skills helped Egypt to become a thriving publishing center. As Ami Ayalon has noted, daily papers, rather than weeklies or monthlies, began to gain in importance in the late 1880s, and by 1900 they were the principal vehicles for news. The leading papers, all founded before 1900 by Syrians were *al-Ahram* (*The Pyramids*) and *al-Muqattam. Al-Mu'ayyad* (*The Supporter*) was founded at the end of 1889 by an Egyptian, Ali Yusuf (dates unconfirmed), who gathered a strong following for his Islamic and anti-British views. Ali Yusuf, who had formerly taught at al-Azhar University, may have been an example for Mustafa Kamil (1874–1908), another Egyptian who began to publish *al-Liwa* (*The Banner*), a paper that espoused strong nationalist views, in 1900. Between that year and 1914, approximately 250 new papers appeared in Egypt, mostly in Cairo. Despite this huge increase in newspapers, it must also be noted that Egypt was still a predominantly agricultural country with a very low level of literacy, and only a small group within Egyptian society was able to read the plethora of newspapers, magazines, and books that appeared.

However, this efflorescence of the Arab press was experienced throughout the Arab-speaking world, where Egyptian publications were widely distributed, thus contributing to a boom in printing establishments. Most Arabic typefaces were based on the cursive Naskh (Naqsh) calligraphy, which was used as a standard for type design. In 1911 the first Arabic type was created for casting on linotype machines, but the large number of characters extended the production time. Calligraphy historian Sheila Blair notes that the earliest Arab line-casting machine had 180 keys, a number eventually reduced to 90, but the consequence was a loss of typographic elegance. Types were designed by well-known calligraphers such as Nabih Jaroudi (dates unconfirmed).

Before the newspapers began to use photographs extensively in the 1920s, their layouts followed Western formats with mastheads, most likely drawn by calligraphers, at the top of the front page, headlines, and then columns of print. The papers also began to publish advertisements, comprised at first of print alone and then including illustrations. Ami Ayalon notes that Ali Yusuf was the first to replace the hand- or steam-powered press with an electric rotary press, which occurred in 1906. The larger papers eventually began to build staffs that specialized in writing articles, business management, and production and design.

The popularity of newspapers was accompanied by a lively array of weekly and monthly journals and magazines that discussed many aspects of daily life from politics to science and the arts. Early magazines included *al-Muqtataf* (*The Bulletin*), which was founded by Syrian Christians in Beirut in 1876 and then moved to Cairo eight years later, and *al-Hilal* (*The Crescent*), founded in 1892 by Jurji Zaidan (1861–1914), who had also come to Cairo from Beirut. Relli Schechter notes that *al-Hilal*, which became part of the

Dar al-Hilal publishing house that was run by Zaidan and his two sons, may have been the first of Egypt's popular illustrated magazines. It addressed political and social matters as did other publications, but in a less serious way.

Al-Hilal pioneered the additional broad coverage of fashion, sports, tourism, and cinema and presented its contents in attractive layouts with high-quality illustrations, cartoons, and photographs. The elevated printing standards and graphic presentations of *al-Hilal* and other illustrated magazines also offered new opportunities to advertisers, who could print advertisements with more visual content.

Another popular magazine published by Dar al-Hilal was *al-Musawar* (*The Illustrated*), a non-political weekly that first appeared in 1924. Its covers featured a bold calligraphic title combined with caricatures or large photographs of contemporary events such as King Fuad I appearing with foreign leaders. Other cover subjects included portraits of prominent statesmen such as Sa'ad Basha Zaghloul, leader of the nationalist Wafd Party (Fig. 32.12). In 1934, Dar al-Hilal published another weekly illustrated magazine, *al-Ithnayn* (*The Two*), which added generous doses of humor and popular culture to its coverage of modern life. The editor included short humorous pieces written in vernacular dialects along with parodies of Cairo's upper class. Layouts included unusual juxtapositions of photographs, many featuring popular Western and Egyptian movie stars and performing artists. The principal artist for *al-Ithnayn* was Juan Sintes (dates unconfirmed), a Spaniard who lived in Egypt for many years. Sintes was a master cartoonist and caricaturist who not only drew many covers for the magazine but also provided illustrations and vignettes to accompany the articles. At one point, *al-Ithnayn* began to feature full-page photographs, frequently of King Farouk I, on the front cover, joined by close-ups on the back cover of leading Egyptian and American film actresses such as Bahidja Hafez and Rosalind Russell (Fig. 32.13).

Fig. 32.12: *al-Musawar*, portrait of Sa'ad Basha Zaghloul, cover, 1924. Courtesy A. Bou Jawdeh.

Fig. 32.13: *al-Ithnayn*, King Farouk I, cover, 1947. Courtesy A. Bou Jawdeh.

Fig. 32.14: *Ruz al-Yusuf*, "The awakening of women," back cover. 1946. Courtesy A. Bou Jawdeh.

Sintes had earlier been associated with another satirical magazine, *al-Kashkul* (*Scrapbook*), which was launched in 1921 by Sulayman Fawzi. Unlike *al-Ithnayn*, however, its humor was directed more at the government than at cultural figures and famous personalities. Among the most popular weekly magazines of the interwar period, *al-Kashkul* condemned the corruption in the leading nationalist party, the Wafd, and critiqued the government's dealings with the British. A weekly publication, it featured in each issue four full-page color cartoons that frequently lampooned well-known political figures.

A principal rival of *al-Kashkul* was *Ruz al-Yusuf* (*Rose al-Yusuf*), a magazine of art and culture founded in 1928 by the popular actress Fatima al-Yusuf (Fig.

32.14). Under the editorship of Muhammad al-Tabi'i, *Ruz al-Yusuf* initially supported the Wafd but later fell out with the party. To create the covers, al-Tabi'i recruited an Armenian cartoonist and caricaturist Alexander Saroukhan (1898–1977), who came to Egypt in 1924 to escape persecution by the Turks. Saroukhan remained with *Ruz al-Yusuf* until 1934 when he left with al-Tabi'i to do the covers for a new satirical magazine, *Akhir Sa'a* (*The Final Hour*), that al-Tabi'i founded. Subsequently others took over the cartooning for *Ruz al-Yusuf.*

Saroukhan's cover for the first issue of *Akhir Sa'a* depicted him and al-Tabi'i holding a banner with the magazine's title and walking arm in arm with Saroukhan's widely known and beloved fictional character al-Misri Effendi (Mr. Average Egyptian), a caricature of a conservative middle-class Egyptian whom Saroukhan had launched in 1929. Other covers presented satirical images of daily Egyptian life (Fig. 32.15).

included *Zouzou and Foufou*, *The Peasants' Country*, and *The Red Girl*. The two-color illustrations featured on the covers and inside pages were innovative at the time.

Advertising

With the exception of film and tourist promotion, most domestic advertising appeared in the newspapers and popular magazines. Commercial advertising began in the 1890s with the appearance of the first mass-circulation newspapers. Initially, the ads included text only, but illustrations were added as printing techniques improved and newspapers and magazines expanded their readerships. Jurji Zaidan, founder of the magazine *al-Hilal*, was an early proponent of magazine advertising and published several articles that extolled its benefits. During the 1920s and 1930s, Dar al-Hilal, the publishing house run by his sons, was a leading promoter of advertising and included numerous ads in its many magazines.

The oldest advertising agency in Cairo was established in 1906: the Société Orientale de Publicité (Oriental Advertising Society) (SOP), which changed its name some years later to Société Egyptienne de Publicité (Egyptian Advertising Society) after it acquired a new partner, the newspaper *al-Misr*. By 1939, the SOP was involved in diverse businesses such as newspaper publishing—it owned several English and French language dailies—printing facilities, and outdoor advertising. Major publications such as the newspaper *al-Ahram* and the magazine *al-Hilal* also had their own advertising agencies.

Most of the initial advertised goods were imported, with cosmetics and patent medicines among the most popular. Other products included cigarettes, alcoholic beverages, clothing, and furniture as well as some professional services (Fig. 32.16). Many ads appeared in women's magazines, where ads for labor-saving appliances, which were heavily promoted in Turkey, for example, were less appealing to wealthy Egyptian women who could easily afford low-wage domestic help. However, some imported appliances

Fig. 32.15: *Akhir Sa'a*, cover, 1947. Courtesy A. Bou Jawdeh.

The booming market for newspapers and periodicals was also paralleled by book publishing. The achievement of independence in 1922 and the emergence of a middle class fostered a stimulating intellectual climate, with numerous intellectuals espousing liberal secular views in politics, science, and the arts. There was also a growing market for new writing in Arabic by Egyptian novelists, short story writers, and poets. More often than not, book covers featured a typographic title rather than an illustration, and the design of book texts tended to follow standard formats. The Dar al-Maarif publishing house brought out the first Arab picture books for children in 1912. Titles

روز اليوسف – العدد ٩٥٤ – ١٩

أسباب..

تجعل سجاير هوليوود أكثر السجاير رواجا فى مصر

١. دخانها الممتاز ذو النكهة الزكية والطعم اللذيذ
٢. طريقة توليفها المتقن تجعل تدخينها ممتعا ونفسها مريح
٣. تعبئتها المحكمة تحفظ السجاير طازجة فى كل آن وزمان

فى تدخين سجاير هوليوود لذة مستديمة ..

المزرعون: شركة إيسترن ش.م.م. س.ن. ٤٨٨٤ جنيه

Fig. 32.16: Hollywood Cigarettes, advertisement. Courtesy A. Bou Jawdeh.

generally shown wearing suits, some also wore fezzes, which were signs of Egyptian identity. Women were sometimes represented in traditional dress with head coverings and ankle-length robes or even with veils. Western manufacturers frequently adopted Pharaonic imagery, as did Palmolive with an ad that showed a modern women in Pharaonic dress with her elbow on a platform where two slaves were mixing olive and palm oils that were considered beauty aids at the time.

As in many countries, Egyptian advertising copy and illustrations frequently associated the products advertised with a modern lifestyle, which in many instances was Western. While ads for goods produced locally were far fewer, their rhetoric tended to differ. Egyptians were urged to buy local products as an act of patriotism, while advertisers also sought to relate the product's origin to the consumer's sense of national identity. This was evident in an ad for an Egyptian cigarette brand that depicted a man's militant raised arm holding a cigarette as if it were a rifle.

Advertising illustrations tended to be line drawings that were reproduced in black and white. Drawing techniques were not well developed and did not evince the individual styles that were evident in the cartoons and caricatures of Juan Sinte or Alexandre Saroukhan, for example. A number of commercial artists may have attended the Academy of Fine Arts, which was founded in 1908, while others were likely self-trained or perhaps they studied abroad.

Film posters

Besides being the leading Arab publishing center, Egypt was also the major producer of films that were widely distributed throughout the Arab world. The Lumière brothers screened a film of theirs in Alexandria in 1896, which led some foreign businessmen to import other films and open cinemas. Italians made the first local films, but subsequently a number were directed by Egyptians. The major breakthrough in the development of Egyptian cinema came in 1925 when the Misr Bank established the Misr Theater and Cinema Company.

such as radios, refrigerators, and fans were popular. Most of the advertisements promoted foreign products such as Lux and Palmolive Soap, Horlick's Malted Milk, and Kodak cameras. Unlike Turkey, where modern Western dress was strongly encouraged by the government and where the fez and veil were banned, men and women in Egyptian advertisements were depicted in varied types of Western or indigenous clothing. Cigarette ads tended to feature women with bobbed hair and Western garb; while men were

Four years later, Misr purchased a laboratory, which it equipped for developing, printing, and drying film. By the early 1930s, it was possible to produce sound films in Egypt and the industry developed various genres that included comedies, melodramas, musicals, and Bedouin fantasies that took advantage of dramatic desert locations. The Misr Theater and Cinema Company was the largest producer, having opened Studio Misr, a major production facility, in 1935.

Films were advertised with posters and lobby cards. The lobby cards, probably designed by local printers, featured photographic stills from the films surrounded by some text. These cards, produced by offset printing, could include hand lettering, which tended to be more extravagant than the advertising copy for newspapers and magazines that was produced with metal type. Initially, films were promoted with black-and-white handbills that featured roughly drawn illustrations similar to newspaper or magazine advertisements.

Gradually film advertising became more sophisticated and by the beginning of the 1940s, color posters printed by stone lithography were the standard means of promoting new films. The posters tended to highlight the actors rather than the story, emphasizing the actors' star quality rather than the film's narrative. A typical poster might depict the faces of the male and female leads, as was evident in posters for the many films such as *Bullet in the Heart* that featured the famed singing star Mohammad Abdel Wahab (Plate 63). Lettering generally followed conventional calligraphic examples, though it sometimes departed completely from any precedent.

Tourism promotion

Around 1911, the State Railway Administration consolidated the various trunk lines to become the Egyptian State Railways and developed an advertising campaign to make rail travel attractive to tourists. A series of posters featured paintings that depicted Bedouins and their camels, primitive sailboats, and views of the Pyramids with titles like *The Nile at Sunset* and *Egypt at Dusk*. These images appealed to the Orientalist imagination of the intended foreign audience by representing Egypt as a place whose tranquil way of life seemed to exist outside of time. What seemed to unite all these scenes was the mighty River Nile, which was present in every painting. Though romantic and nostalgic, the Orientalist view was less blatant than a poster published just a year earlier by the lithographic firm Riccordi in Milan. This poster, directed to a French audience, shows a close-up of a veiled woman astride a donkey led by a young Bedouin man. In the background is a pyramid, which was an essential component of Egyptian tourist iconography.

Fig. 32.17: F. H. Coventry, Ateliers Kalfa, Cairo, poster, 1935. © David Pollack/Corbis.

The potential of Egypt's past to attract tourists was heightened after the momentous discovery of King Tutankhamen's tomb in 1922. By the 1930s, the railway administration's graphic sensibility had become more sophisticated and modern. It commissioned several posters from the Turkish graphic designer Ihap Hulusi Gorey, which made reference to icons of the past but in a more contemporary idiom, even though one of his posters described Egypt as The Land of Mystery and Romance. A poster the railroad commissioned from Ateliers Kalfa in Cairo also dispensed with the hazy romantic imagery as Hulusi did and depicted instead a mosque, which appears to be the Grand Mosque, located in Cairo, a dynamic urban center (Fig. 32.17).

Iraq

During the 19th century, Iraq, then a part of the Ottoman Empire, underwent a process of selective modernization. Steamships on the Tigris and Euphrates rivers were in use as early as 1835 and the ensuing increase in trade led to the construction of port facilities at Al-Basrah in the 1860s along with the concomitant construction of telegraph lines to link Baghdad with Istanbul, the Ottoman capital. Roads were improved,

but railway construction came later than it did to other parts of the region.

The modernizing process received a boost in 1869 when Midhat Pasha (1822–1883) became the governor of Baghdad. He introduced rational city planning techniques, which included the construction of a water supply system, paved streets, and street lamps. He also constructed a tramway, established textile mills along with a hospital, and he built a bridge across the Tigris. Until his term ended in 1872, Midhat Pasha did much to develop the regional economy, promoting steamer services on the Tigris and Euphrates as well as shipping in the Persian Gulf. To strengthen the port facilities at Al-Basrah, he established ship-repair yards there. He also founded a press, where modern textbooks were printed. These served a limited number of students, however, as much of the population remained illiterate.

At the beginning of World War I, the British invaded Iraq and by the war's end, when the Ottoman Empire collapsed, they eventually gained control of the former Ottoman territory. The establishment of a monarchy in 1921, however, was the first step towards Iraqi independence, which was achieved in 1932. Despite the modernizing initiatives of Midhat Pasha, some writers believe that Ottoman rule in general inhibited Iraq from developing a modern economy.

Agriculture, remained Iraq's mainstay, complemented by numerous small workshops, where objects were made with traditional techniques to satisfy domestic demand. Adriano Lanzoni, writing in 1910, described many goods that were made in Baghdad, where the largest number of workshops were located. Items produced included traditional clothing such as *kufiya*—large kerchiefs embroidered with gold and silver—and the *awtar*—a long gown made of cotton; leather goods for the local inhabitants and Europeans; gold and silver handicrafts; copperwork of excellent quality; and ceramic vessels.

Before 1914, there were hardly any factories with power-driven machinery in Iraq and few were

Fig. 32.18: *Guffa*, 1932. Library of Congress, LC-DIG-matpc-13225.

constructed after that. Exceptions included two Ottoman military factories in Baghdad, which produced uniform cloth and flour respectively. More widespread were small establishments that relied on human or animal power. Several authors have described the intuitive skills of Iraqi craftsmen whose work ranged from the hulls of steamers for several shipping lines to the production of breech-loading rifles that were based on foreign models.

Boatbuilding was a specialty in Iraq, and workshops were spread out along the rivers. The *guffa* was a round boat of ancient origin that was made of wicker (Fig. 32.18). In Basra, Lanzoni noted an emphasis on the construction of sailboats for sea and river navigation. Boat makers also designed and built special vessels to navigate the marshes in the area. In Tikrit, they specialized in *kalaks*, timber rafts that were supported by inflated goatskins. These vessels could transport heavy loads that included men and animals. By the 1930s, the *kalak* industry collapsed, when modern vessels replaced these boats.

Perhaps the principal reason why industry did not develop further in Iraq during the interwar period was the discovery of oil and the beginning of its exploitation. In 1912, a group of parties representing British, Dutch, and German interests formed the Turkish Petroleum Company (TPC), which received government concessions to look for oil around Mosul and Baghdad. Oil was found in 1927 near Kirkuk and from that time it became Iraq's major export, thus mitigating the need to develop a manufacturing economy.

Transjordan

The territory that became Transjordan was originally part of the British mandate that included Palestine. For political reasons, the British divided the mandate and in 1921 handed over part to Emir Abdullah, whose brother Faisal became king of Iraq the same year. Transjordan began as a quasi-independent state in 1923 with British involvement in financial, military, and diplomatic matters continuing until full independence was achieved in 1946.

The country was essentially agricultural, with scarcely any industry. As in many parts of the region, some agricultural produce was exported, mostly in an unrefined state, and a limited number of manufactured goods were imported from abroad. Primitive equipment such as wooden olive presses continued to dominate the agricultural sector, while weaving occurred in small workshops. Bedouin garments known as *abayas* were produced along with some rugs and carpets, while Bedouin weavers made *iqals* or head dresses and plaited belts.

The government sought to stimulate craft production by establishing an Arts and Crafts School in Amman, where courses in theoretical and practical subjects were offered over a period of three to four years. Classes were provided in carpentry, furriery, cane work and upholstery. Graduates either opened their own workshops or found work in existing ones. The major hindrance to developing mechanized factories during this period, however, was the lack of electric power, which was available almost exclusively in Amman.

Palestine

Palestine was part of the Ottoman Empire until World War I. Though Palestinian deputies sat in the Ottoman parliaments, the Ottoman rulers considered the region marginal and devoted only modest resources to its development. A large commitment, however, was the construction of the Haifa branch line as part of the extensive Hijaz Railway. During the late 19th century, absentee Arab landlords, who lived in Cairo, Damascus, or Beirut, owned a considerable portion of the land. The economy was predominantly agricultural and large numbers of local Arabs leased land from distant owners. Leaders of modern agriculture were the German Templars, who were followed by the Jews.

A first wave of Jewish immigrants from Eastern Europe and Yemen came to Palestine in the 1880s. With savings they brought or with support from Jewish organizations in Europe, they purchased land and started their own farms. An eventual point of tension between Jews and Arabs was the Arab conviction that Jews were buying land that might have otherwise been available for them to farm. In order to build a Jewish community, Jewish farmers also tended to hire other Jews rather than Arabs.

Origins of the Bezalel School of Arts and Crafts

Many of the Jews who emigrated to Palestine in the 1880s left Eastern Europe to flee persecution. By 1897, an official movement, Zionism, had been founded by Theodore Herzl to promote a Jewish homeland in Palestine. The program drafted at the First Zionist Congress called for farmers, artisans, and manufacturers to settle there. In 1905, Boris Schatz (1867–1932), a Russian sculptor, brought a proposal to the Seventh Zionist Congress for a school of crafts that would be named after the biblical figure Bezalel ben Uri, who was the chief artisan of the Tabernacle, a dwelling place of God. Earlier, Prince Ferdinand of Bulgaria had invited Schatz to Sofia, where he founded the Royal Academy of Art.

Bezalel was not the first school of Jewish crafts to be established in Palestine. In 1882, the Alliance Israélite Universelle, an organization created in Paris in 1860 to defend Jewish rights around the world, founded a school in Jerusalem to prepare young Jewish men, particularly those from the lower or underprivileged classes, for practical trades. Among the subjects taught were carpentry, blacksmithing, locksmithing, coppersmithing, shoemaking, stone carving, metal founding, and woodcarving. The teachers were trained in Europe and the school shops were well furnished with the necessary equipment. A comparable school for poor Jewish girls was opened two years later with 15 departments, where trades then deemed suitable for women, such as tailoring, sewing, and embroidery, were taught. The Alliance schools had a practical orientation and were not concerned with introducing or perpetuating a particular ideology or aesthetic as Boris Schatz was.

With support from the Zionist movement, in 1906, Schatz, inspired by the theories of Walter Crane and John Ruskin as well as by his knowledge of the Arts and Crafts School in Sofia, opened the Bezalel School of Arts and Crafts in Jerusalem. From the beginning there was tension between Schatz and the school's board in Berlin. The board conceived the school as a commercial venture that would produce goods such as carpets that could be sold in Europe. They were less interested in Jewish themes than in designs that would be commercially attractive to the German middle class. Schatz, however, was an idealist who believed that Bezalel should be a vehicle for the creation of a new Jewish culture.

He divided the school into three parts: an art school for the most talented students; workshops and an evening school for various crafts; and a museum that would house Jewish art treasures, archeological artifacts, and flora and fauna of the region. By 1909, Bezalel had departments of silver filigree, wood and stone carving, carpentry, and a department that specialized in inlaid picture frames. These were followed by departments for Damascene work—a technique of incising designs in metal that originated in Damascus—cane furniture, metal repoussé, and lithography, while the number of workshops continued to increase.

Joining Schatz at the time the school was founded was the Russian artist Ephraim Moshe Lilien (1874–1925), who came to Palestine to teach art at Bezalel but did not remain long. Like him, other faculty arrived primarily from Poland or Russia. Among them were Ze'ev Raban (1890–1970), a Pole who had studied at the Munich Kunstgewerbeschule (Applied Arts School) and then headed Bezalel's metal repoussé department; Meir Gur-Arie (1891–1951), a Russian who was a Bezalel student before he taught ivory carving and painting; and Shmuel Persov (1885–1961) from Russia who studied silver filigree work in Damascus and then came to Jerusalem to direct the Silver Department at Bezalel. However, most of those who worked in the department were Jews from Yemen. Shmuel Ben-David

(1884–1927), a former student of Boris Schatz's at the Art Academy in Sofia, organized the carpet weaving workshop.

Schatz sought to create a "Hebrew style," which was to be realized through a distinct iconography that the workshops adopted for different objects. The icons, which art historian Nurith Shiloh Cohen has clearly delineated, were of three kinds: first were Jewish and Zionist symbols and images including the six-pointed Star of David, which had been adopted as the symbol of the First Zionist Congress, along with portraits of Theodore Herzl and other prominent Zionists; also in this category were images of Jewish pioneer life; second were images that derived from the Palestinian landscape and social life—local flora and fauna, depictions of different ethnic types, and scenes of historic sites, both sacred and secular; and third were the historic images—old coins, archeological artifacts, and biblical scenes. The three types of imagery were incorporated into the school's pedagogy, both as subject matter for training in drawing and sculpting, and as decorative motifs for objects that were produced in the workshops. Hebrew letters were also a source of iconography. Ya'akov Stark (d.o.b. unconfirmed—c. 1916) was a specialist in devising decorative motifs from these forms as well as creating ornamental Hebrew characters. His influences ranged from Islamic calligraphy to German *Jugendstil* designs (Fig. 32.19).

Bezalel emphasized the production of objects for export and more modestly priced goods for sale domestically, particularly as souvenirs. In addition to Jewish ceremonial objects such as menorahs, the workshops produced a variety of other things including inlaid wooden boxes, jewelry, desk sets, tiles, cane furniture, carpets, cigarette cases, and printed matter of all kinds (Fig. 32.20).

Besides his heavy promotion of Bezalel products in Jewish communities abroad at specially organized exhibitions of Bezalel crafts, Schatz sold Bezalel goods in a pavilion near the Jaffa Gate in the Old City, where the school competed with the nearby Arab craftsmen for a share of the tourist market. There was a long tradition in Jerusalem of making decorative or religious craft objects for tourists and pilgrims, and Jewish craftsmen had earlier gained a share of this enterprise.

Beginning in 1913, some faculty and staff at Bezalel began to set up independent workshops in Jerusalem, following a string of dismissals due to economic hardship. These workshops, which operated as branches or subsidiaries of Bezalel, were under the management of Schatz. They were called the United Bezalel Craft Shops, a name similar to the United Crafts, which the American Gustav Stickley founded in the United States at the end of the 19th century. The difference, however, is that these workshops did not collaborate on common

Fig. 32.19: Ya'akov Stark, Bezalel School of Arts and Crafts, c. 1910. Courtesy David Tartakover.

Fig. 32.20: Workshop at the Bezalel School of Arts and Crafts, 1909. By the courtesy of Kedem Auction House Ltd.

commissions as did Stickley's craftsmen or the craftsmen who were part of the Vienna Workshops.

The first of the Bezalel workshops was Zayit (Olive), which was concerned with inlaid wood and batik. Others that followed were Hatomer (Date Palm), which specialized in paintings on silk and velvet; Rimmon (Pomegranate), which featured paintings on fabric; Menorah (Lamp), whose products included household items and children's toys; Keter (Crown), which featured work in silver, gold, ivory, stone, shell, and repoussé; Shenav (Ivory), which produced ivory, wood, and stone carving; Nitzan (Bud), specializing in metalwork; Ayalah (Doe), producing copper etchings; and Marvadia (based on the Hebrew word for carpet, Marvad), featuring the production of carpets. One might think of these enterprises similarly to the manufacturing spin-offs at the Bauhaus, but the Jerusalem workshops remained based in craft culture with no intent to move towards mass production. This is not surprising since Shatz was a blatant anti-modernist who substituted a revival of Old Testament themes and imagery for John Ruskin's admiration of the Christian Middle Ages.

Though Schatz promoted Bezalel goods heavily to Jewish communities abroad, the school did not introduce any production techniques that were new to the region. Both Jews and Arabs in Palestine already had a rich craft tradition that extended back through multiple generations. Craftsmen specialized in carpet weaving, textile dyeing, pottery, glassmaking, leatherwork including shoemaking, forging agricultural implements, carpentry, and masonry. While some craftsmen made jewelry, pottery, and religious objects for sale to tourists in the Old City, others produced everyday goods that were required for daily life.

Palestine under the British mandate

In 1917, Britain established a military administration in Palestine. Without consulting the considerable Arab population, the Great Powers at the San Remo conference awarded Britain the mandate for Palestine, following which the British set up a civil administration there. They created a postal system, constructed roads and a telecommunications infrastructure, and built schools. English, Arabic, and Hebrew became the three official languages.

What complicated the British presence in the region was the Balfour Declaration, a policy document of 1917 that committed Britain to supporting a national home for the Jews without compromising the rights of the existing Arab community. This, however, became an impossible task and led to the conflict that continued to persist. Tensions were exacerbated by the rapid increase in Jewish immigration during the 1920s and 1930s, particularly after Hitler came to power in Germany. With the support of external funds, Jews purchased land for farming but also to create a new city, Tel Aviv, which was founded in 1909. There were Jews who arrived with sufficient capital to start their own businesses, others who exercised professional skills they had acquired in Europe, and some who engaged in the trades or continued the tradition of farming.

The British attempted to maintain an image of impartiality through various means, such as the postage stamps that the mandate issued in the 1920s. The stamp designs were the result of a competition, most likely among British artists. A set of four stamps that appeared in 1927 with the three languages, English,

Arabic, and Hebrew, depicted sites such as Rachel's Tomb, the Dome of the Rock, and the Citadel (Fig. 32.21). Together, these were intended to convey the possibility of the different groups in Palestine living together and even sharing a public iconography.

Economists are divided on whether to consider a single mandate economy that included both Arab and Jewish initiatives or to recognize two economies. While there was some interaction between Arabs and Jews, each group basically pursued its own economic interests. Jews created an independent educational system that included a modern high school; a technical institute that became the Technion, which was founded in 1912; and the Hebrew University, which was inaugurated in 1925. Where the later waves of Jewish immigrants from Europe brought with them the knowledge and will to create a modern industrial culture in Palestine, the Arabs, as elsewhere in the former Ottoman Empire, lacked experience with industrialization, having lived under the Ottoman rulers for centuries. Where industry did develop, it was predominantly to process agricultural products.

The British administration and Arab crafts

In 1918, the British Military Governor Sir Ronald Storrs brought Charles Robert Ashbee (1863–1942), a leading

Fig. 32.21: Mandate postage stamps depicting Rachel's Tomb, the Citadel, and the Dome of the Rock, 1927. Shutterstock.

figure of the British Arts and Crafts movement, to Jerusalem to serve as his Civic Advisor. Ashbee had previously been teaching English in Cairo, where he encouraged his students to wear traditional dress and where he first became interested in Arab crafts. Ashbee's charge in Jerusalem was to help rebuild the city after the neglect and devastation of the Ottomans. He prepared a report in which he made a thorough survey of the arts and crafts in the city, describing workshops as well as schools and religious organizations that taught craft techniques to students. His hope was to re-establish the arts and crafts as a means of social regeneration, thus fulfilling the Arts and Crafts ideal he held earlier when he founded the Guild of Handicrafts in the 1890s. His report also included a detailed plan for the rehabilitation of Jerusalem's neglected buildings and run down markets or *souks* and it laid out an expansive vision for the city's growth.

Storrs, whose title the British later changed to Civil Governor of Jerusalem and Judea, had spent years as a government administrator in Egypt. Considered Britain's leading Orientalist by T. E. Lawrence, he had a romantic vision of the Middle East. Fascinated with its rich past, he wished to preserve it rather than imagine a dynamic future for the region. His views aligned with Britain's economic policy, which considered all colonial territories as markets for British exports, while discouraging any industrial development that might compete with Britain's own manufacturing interests.

In Jerusalem, Storrs banned modern building materials and mandated the use of Jerusalem stone, forbade the construction of a tram line from Jerusalem to Bethlehem, prohibited the introduction of automobiles in the province of Judea, and confined outdoor advertising in Jerusalem to notice boards in specific areas. As an instrument to carry out his plans for the city, he established the Pro-Jerusalem Society and named Ashbee its secretary. Ashbee's brief included planning for the city's expansion as well as its preservation. His aim was to build in accordance with tradition, maintaining a vision of Jerusalem as a city of timeless tranquility.

The historian Noah Hysler-Rubin points out that Ashbee's greatest accomplishments during his brief tenure in Jerusalem between 1918 and 1922 were in the crafts rather than in town planning, where he was unable to realize the majority of the projects he originally envisioned. In his promotion of the crafts, Ashbee was cognizant of the Bezalel School of Arts and Crafts. He was sympathetic with its aim to oppose the industrial system, but he disliked its sectarianism and Jewish emphasis. He also believed that the Jews were more talented as planners than as craftsmen. Though half-Jewish himself, his sympathies, like those of most British colonials in Palestine, lay with the Arabs and he was opposed to the idea of a separate Jewish homeland. Nonetheless, Bezalel products were prominently displayed in the First Exhibition of Palestinian Crafts and Industries that Ashbee organized for the Pro-Jerusalem Society in 1921.

Ashbee established a weaving workshop, Jerusalem Looms, where a large number of apprentice weavers were trained using looms that had been donated by the Red Cross. He also sought to revive the glass-blowing industry in the ancient city of Hebron. He considered glass blowing to be one of the most beautiful, and in his words, characteristic, of the Palestinian crafts. He blamed the industry's decline on Western industrialism and advocated its revival as a reassertion of local craftsmanship in the face of what had been the debilitating effect of industrial competition. Ashbee's most ambitious attempt to revive the traditional crafts was the establishment of the Dome of the Rock Potteries to renovate the ceramic tiles of the Dome of the Rock on the Temple Mount, one of Jerusalem's most sacred buildings. The craftsmen, however, were not Palestinian Arabs but rather Armenians who were brought from Turkey at the behest of the Pro-Jerusalem Society. David Ohannessian (1884–1963), the potter Neshan Balian (1882–1964) and his wife Takuhi (1885–1961), and the painter Megerdish Karakashian (1895–1963) began their efforts to renovate the Dome of the Rock tiles. Due to technical and financial reasons, the project did not go forward at the time and consequently the Armenians established two workshops of their own, with Karakashian and Balian separating from Ohannessian, and calling their workshop Palestine Pottery. They concentrated on ceramic plates, tiles, and vessels, which they decorated with motifs derived from multiple sources including traditional Turkish ceramics from Iznik.

Ohannessian was commissioned to decorate houses, many belonging to wealthy Muslims, with tile pictures and inscriptions that covered door and window frames. As decorations he used arabesques and incorporated textual inscriptions chosen by the owners. His workshop also produced tiles and various ceramic vessels that were sold in the American Colony Hotel's shop, which exported them to all parts of the world, much as Boris Shatz was attempting to do with the goods produced in Bezalel's workshops.

Art historian Nurith Kenaan-Kedar has noted that Ohannessian's work in Jerusalem brought together

Fig. 32.22: David Ohannessian, trilingual street sign, Jerusalem, c. 1922. Shutterstock.

his knowledge of Muslim craft traditions that originated in Turkey, artistic concepts introduced by British officials such as Ashbee and Storrs, and ideas that derived from the special nature of Jerusalem itself. One project that Ashbee commissioned from the Ohannessian's Dome of the Rock Potteries was the production of tri-lingual ceramic street signs, which suited the desire of Storrs and Ashbee to maintain the traditional character of Jerusalem (Fig. 32.22).

Among the major projects Ohannessian completed during the 1920s and 1930s were four tile panels to cover the surface of an ancient lighting conductor in the Citadel or Tower of David, a group of panels for the American Colony Hotel, tile pictures for the fountain niche of the St. John's Hospital outpatient clinic, the niches and stone benches for the Scottish Church of St. Andrew, and the magnificent walls and roof for the fountain housing in the Rockefeller Archeological Museum. The religious and cultural diversity of these commissions is indicative of the cosmopolitan atmosphere in Jerusalem during the mandate years.

Besides abetting the development of craft workshops, Ashbee also undertook one major commission while in Jerusalem. In 1920, he supervised the redecorating of Government House, the residence of the mandate's High Commissioner. As art historian Kamal Boullata has noted, Ashbee used the commission to demonstrate the possibility of collaboration among craftsmen who belonged to Jerusalem's three major religions. Following the Arts and Crafts ideal of a unified interior that united the different crafts, Ashbee created an interior of four rooms whose layout was essentially Western but was inspired by an Islamic style that incorporated Byzantine elements as well. He designed the furniture, but hired local craftsman to make it. Craftsmen also did the woodwork, carved objects of marble and stone, and produced hand-painted ceramic tiles. Local weavers wove the wool for the wall hanging, while the glassblowers of Hebron, whose trade Ashbee sought to revive, created clusters of Hebron glass that formed part of the large chandelier that hung above the dining room table. Ashbee's cabinets had a neo-Ottoman style with their notched pinnacles that recalled the crenellated walls of Jerusalem's Tower of David. Ceramic panels with floral and geometric patterns were widely used in the rooms as wall coverings and backdrops to Ashbee's cabinets.

As Boullata observes, Ashbee's decoration of Government House was a pioneering project in the application of domestic crafts to architectural design, stimulating a number of wealthy Palestinian Arabs to decorate their own villas, particularly the exteriors, as described above in the discussion of David Ohannessian's work. With his commission for Government House, Ashbee gave a strong boost to the Hebron glassblowers, who were subsequently called upon for later commissions, and he helped the renewal of Arab crafts in general. Commendable as this was, however, it did little to equip the Palestinian Arabs for the modern era, as was the case in India where British art administrators like Ernest Binfield Havell (1861–1934) did much to sustain Indian crafts while refusing to recognize the tendencies within the country to create an industrial culture.

The image of Palestine as a timeless exotic land was prevalent in the Palestine Pavilion that the British mandate created for the British Empire Exhibition at Wembley in 1924. The pavilion, designed by the British architect Austen St. Barbe Harrison (1891–1976), strove for a typical representation of traditional Arab culture as represented by two domes at either end of the exhibition hall. The cost of the pavilion was shared by the mandate government and Jewish sources, hence the exhibition space dedicated to Palestine was divided to display Jewish agricultural produce and Bezalel crafts on one side and examples of Arab craft such as the shaped glass from Hebron on the other. Models of the Tabernacle and the Dome of the Rock were shown in a special annex.

As was evident in the Wembley pavilion, the motive to industrialize that had been brewing in India, particularly Bengal, was not evident within Palestinian Arab culture, consequently there were few initiatives to consider in terms of workshops that adopted machinery or other accoutrements of basic mass production. Instead, craft culture remained a model for Palestinian Arabs, which made it difficult for them to compete with the nascent Jewish industries in Tel Aviv or those of the German Templars that were the consequence of a different mentality, a European one that saw no conflict between factory production and life in a new desert environment.

One of the leading Arab craftsmen who established a distinct identity for his work was Jamal Badran (1909–1999). Badran came from a family of craftsmen. At a young age, he went to Cairo, then a center of training in the arts and crafts in the Middle East. There he studied at the School of Arts and Crafts. He remained in Egypt between 1920 and 1927, specializing in leatherwork as well as the arts of surface decoration in different media. After his return to Jerusalem, he began work on the restoration of the Al-Aqsa Mosque and the Dome of the Rock. Both projects were supported by the Supreme Muslim Council, which Sir Herbert Samuel, the High Commissioner for Palestine, set up in 1922 to manage the cultural, welfare, and community affairs of Palestine's Muslim population. The Council initiated work on Al-Aqsa and revived the restoration of the Dome of the Rock, following the failed attempt of Ashbee and Storrs several years earlier. Badran also showed his craftwork in the Palestine Pavilion at the First National Arab Fair, held in the Supreme Muslim Council's new building near Jerusalem's Jaffa Gate.

In 1934, the mandate government awarded Badran a scholarship to study at the Central School of Arts and Crafts in London, where he specialized in various arts and crafts including leatherwork, bookbinding, textile painting, ceramics, and sculpture. He graduated in 1937 and returned to Palestine, where he taught at several Arab schools. In the late 1930s,

Badran and members of his family opened Studio Badran for the Arts in Jerusalem with the aim of raising the standards of local craftsmanship and combining advances in technology with Islamic traditions. They were able to maintain the studio until 1948.

Other Arab craftsmen were trained at the Supreme Muslim Council's Islamic Orphanage in Jerusalem, which operated a vocational school to teach traditional crafts to Muslim orphans. Several years earlier, Ashbee had recommended such a school for craft training and it is entirely possible that the program at the Islamic Orphanage was based on his initial idea. The aim was to provide formal instruction in skills that had been handed down from father to son. These included bookbinding, weaving, furniture making, tailoring, shoemaking, metalwork, pottery, engraving and ornamentation, and Islamic calligraphy. Uri Kupferschmidt writes that by 1940 over 200 graduates of the orphanage's various departments had become successful at their occupations, some even emigrating to other countries. The Supreme Muslim Council was also instrumental in supporting the development of local crafts through its financing of the Al-Aqsa and Dome of the Rock renovation projects, which involved ironworkers, woodworkers, and experts in wickerwork, although the mosaic tiles that were used for these projects were imported from Turkey, where craftsmen in Kutahya made them.

Bezalel after World War I

Bezalel had a difficult time after World War I, and only survived with difficulty until it closed in 1929. Schatz had begun to think about departments that addressed the question of industrialization and sought to relate the school's programs to some of the industries founded by Jewish entrepreneurs that were emerging in the 1920s, although this effort did not yield significant results.

In 1921, Schatz published a major article in which he described about 30 trades that could be developed in Palestine. He expected Bezalel to play an important part in all of them. In the introduction

to the article, Schatz discussed the different options for industrial development, including cottage industry, factory work, and the formation of master craftsmen. He had a negative view of factory work similar to that of William Morris and thus recommended the creation of master craftsmen as the most viable economic strategy for the Jewish community.

His article is extremely detailed, describing a large number of crafts including silver and gold filigree work, carpet weaving, woodcarving, inlay work, embroidery, cane furniture, glass, and leatherwork. For each craft, Schatz considered the market, although his ideas centered heavily on specialty objects for tourists and foreign sales rather than the production of necessities for daily living in the local environment.

By the early 1920s, interest in Bezalel within the Zionist movement was waning as support shifted to the more industrial initiatives in Tel Aviv. Funding for the school continued to be a problem. Schatz pinned his hopes on a large exhibition of Bezalel products that he mounted in New York in 1926, but the exhibition failed to rally the funds needed to support the school and after several more years of struggle, Bezalel closed its doors. While the school had contributed much to the larger craft culture of Jerusalem, which involved Arabs, Armenians, and others as well as Jews, Schatz was unable to put Bezalel on a viable financial footing, partly because he was more concerned with building a school that embodied his idealistic vision of a traditional craft community in a Jewish homeland than with creating a viable school of arts and crafts that could serve the practical needs of the region.

Industry from the Ottoman period to the 1930s

Unlike Europe, where the Industrial Revolution began in the cities and was driven by the manufacture of consumer goods, in Palestine the earliest industrial development was in the agricultural sector. It came from American farmers and then from the German Templars, who founded their first settlement in 1868, as well as from Jews who began to farm in the region ten years after the Templars.

Initially, agricultural equipment was imported from Europe or the United States. The Templars brought in reapers, threshers, and light and heavy steel plows, including plows operated by horsepower and subsequently by steam locomobiles. In addition, they imported scythes, harvesting machines, drills, and mowing machines. A Jewish agricultural school at Miqwe Ysrael developed farming techniques using modern machinery, but most Jewish farmers used simple equipment since they could not afford the more expensive machines. The imported mechanical equipment was not suited to the local conditions and broke down frequently, which caused problems, as there were few skilled craftsmen in the region who could repair them.

Agricultural machinery was used principally by German and Jewish farmers, while Arab farming methods remained more traditional. Thomas Levy believes that Arab entrepreneurs generally refrained from investing in agricultural technology since they knew little about it and were more comfortable operating in other sectors of the economy where they had more experience.

Extremely important for advances in irrigation was the system of drilling for water. Originally, draft animals operated water-raising wheels but oil and coal gas engines imported from Europe soon replaced them. Two local firms were established in the late 1880s to handle the business of importing the necessary equipment for irrigation systems, assembling and adapting it for local use, stocking spare parts, and undertaking repairs. These firms were Wagner Brothers, established by a Templar family, and L. Stein and Company, that a Jewish proprietor, Leo Stein (dates unconfirmed) founded. Both firms were located in Jaffa, close to the future city of Tel Aviv, and were important in establishing that area as a center of industrial development.

Initially, Stein's workshop began to fabricate metal tools and repair equipment, and make axles and wheel rims for carts and wagons. After two Jaffa blacksmiths designed metal buckets to replace the wooden ones that had been previously used for irrigation systems, Stein followed suit. This required adding a foundry section to his workshop. The replacement of wooden screw presses with mechanized iron ones for pressing olive oil also created more business. Gradually, Stein shifted his workshop from the repair of imported equipment to the manufacture of diverse metal objects such as bases for flour mills and grain silos, and finally his firm manufactured complete flour mills, excluding the motors. As well, the workshop, which soon became a factory, produced various metal devices such as factory gates and machinery, and Stein began to manufacture the water pumps that he had previously imported. This pattern of development mirrors that in other countries such as China, where mechanized production in factories grew out of workshops that were originally set up to repair machinery.

By 1908, Stein's factory had 150 employees. Due to increased competition as well as management and financial problems, the momentum of L. Stein & Co. began to decline after that. During World War I, Stein invented a device that could turn small logs into coal from which gas for generators could be extracted. When the British occupied southern Palestine in 1917, they commandeered Stein's factory for military use. After World War I, problems continued to beset the company. Stein died in 1926 and the bank that took over the firm could not make a go of it. Consequently the factory closed in 1935.

Industries continued to develop as successive waves of Jewish immigrants, whose numbers increased dramatically in the interwar period, continued to arrive in Palestine, many fleeing the Nazis after Hitler came to power in 1933. A large number who came from cities in Europe were skilled in a variety of urban professions and trades. Many settled in the new urban center of Tel Aviv, whose name originated as the Hebrew title of Theodore Herzl's book *The Old-New Land*. Tel Aviv was founded in 1909 and the mandate government officially declared it a town in 1921. It was the principal center of industrial development until 1933, when Haifa became a major center, due to completion of the new port.

Among the products that Jewish industries were manufacturing by the early 1930s were bricks and tiles, cement, hosiery, fancy leather goods, bedsteads, tins and cans, foodstuffs of many kinds, matches, and cigarettes. At that time, according to Sir Harry Luke and Edward Keith-Roach, 5,300 factories and workshops were scattered across Palestine compared to 1,236 before World War I. Around 1924, Jewish immigrants from Łódź, Poland, a traditional center of textile production, began to arrive, bringing with them a knowledge of the textile trade, along with the requisite machinery to start factory production, which they did, calling their factory Lodzia.

From the mid-1920s, numerous factories that produced spare parts for machines, as well as metal utensils and other articles ranging from tools to bedsteads, were also founded. Though most were strictly utilitarian, one, Pal-Bell Co. Ltd, also known as Palbell, specialized in artsy bronze and brass items—decorative bowls, ewers, vessels, vases, pitchers, trivets, and ashtrays to name a few. Founded by the sculptor Maurice Ascalon (1913–2003), who was also the company's chief designer, Palbell introduced the Jewish metal craft industry to the use of a green patina, created by applying reactive chemicals to raw metal. This gave the objects an antique look, which became standard for the entire metal craft industry. Palbell also produced religious objects including a traditional olive branch menorah that Ascalon designed. He collaborated as well on the production of other Judaica items with the artist Ze'ev Raban, who had headed the repoussé workshop at Bezalel.

Other factories manufactured chemicals and electrical goods. There were even industries on the kibbutzim—collective settlements that were dedicated primarily to agriculture. In these settlements, small factories and workshops specialized in goods that primarily met their own needs: agricultural machinery and implements, furniture, toys, and food canning. A factory on a kibbutz that made boxes for agricultural produce became the largest manufacturer of plywood and wallboard in Palestine. Industry developed further in the public sector, which built transportation and power infrastructures. A Manufacturers' Association was formed in the early 1920s, as was the Jewish labor union, the Histadrut. An Association of Craftsmen and Small Industry complemented these organizations, while the Israel Industrial Bank was created in 1935.

It is no wonder that Bezalel struggled during the 1920s. The Orientalist vision of a bucolic future that Boris Schatz promulgated in his utopian novel *Jerusalem Rebuilt* of 1924 was out of step with the industrial drive of the European Jews who began to arrive in the mid-1920s. Schatz did try to participate in the construction of Tel Aviv by proposing to the mayor that Bezalel create ceramic street signs for the municipality similar to those that Ashbee had commissioned from David Ohannessian for Jerusalem, but his offer was not accepted. A few houses were decorated with ceramic tiles from Bezalel, but the architects who built Tel Aviv such as Richard Kaufmann and Arieh Sharon, were interested in European modernism, not the Ottoman revivalism that some architects had adopted in Tel Aviv in the 1920s.

In 1935, an incarnation of Bezalel, known as the New Bezalel Academy of Arts and Crafts, was founded in Jerusalem. Though its name was the same as the previous school, the two could not have been more different. The founders of the New Bezalel, who came from Germany as refugees from the Nazis, were steeped in that country's modernist culture of the 1920s and were committed to creating a school based on European modernist ideas. They had little interest in the biblical romanticism of Boris Schatz and sought instead to introduce technical discipline and aesthetic spareness to a new generation of students in Palestine.

Among the members of the school's executive committee was the architect Erich Mendelsohn

(1887–1953), who had built a strong reputation in Germany for his Expressionist sketches of industrial buildings and his completed works such as the Einstein Tower in Potsdam and the Schocken Department Store and Universum Cinema in Berlin. Mendelsohn was also among the idealistic Germans who went to the Soviet Union, where he designed the Red Flag Textile Factory in St. Petersburg in 1926. While in Palestine between 1935 and 1941, as a modern architect working in Jerusalem, Mendelsohn introduced a modern style that countered the romantic traditionalism of the former governor Sir Roland Storrs.

The first director of the New Bezalel was Joseph Budko (1880–1940), a German artist who participated in the revival of the woodcut. Combining Jewish tradition with modern artistic techniques, Budko helped to transform Jewish book illustration into a contemporary medium. Among those who taught at the New Bezalel besides Budko were Rudy Deutsch (1908–2004), who headed the Department of Graphics, where students studied commercial art and advertising. The school also

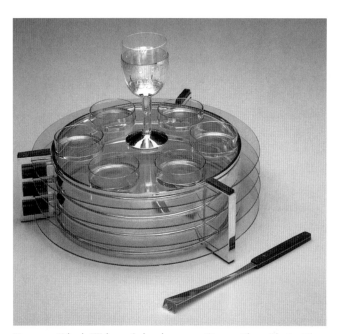

Fig. 32.23: Yehuda Wolpert, Seder plate, 1930. © 2014. Photo The Jewish Museum/Art Resource/Scala, Florence.

had a Department of Calligraphy, which was headed by Yerachmiel Schechter (1900–1989), considered to be the first teacher of Hebrew calligraphy in Palestine. Schechter was born in Poland and was self-taught. He moved to Palestine in 1934. Previously, he had been responsible for all the official writings of the Zionist Congresses from 1921 to 1927. Schechter developed a new version of the Hebrew calligraphic style, called "Yerushalmi," which stemmed from the inscriptions on the Second Temple and the earliest manuscripts of the Middle Ages.

Directing the Metal Workshop was Yehuda Wolpert (1900–1981), who had studied sculpture and metalwork at the Kunstgewerbeschule (Applied Arts School) in Frankfurt-am-Main. Though committed to modern forms, Wolpert specialized in Jewish ceremonial objects (Fig. 32.23). In 1940, the painter Mordechai Ardon (1896–1992) replaced Budko as director of the school after Budko's death. Ardon had taught at the New Bezalel since its beginning in 1935. Between 1920 and 1925 he was a student at the Bauhaus, where he studied with Itten, Klee, Kandinsky, and Feininger. He also taught painting at Itten's school in Berlin.

While the New Bezalel embraced an aesthetic of modernism and provided an effective counter to the Orientalist decorative arts and graphic design of the old Bezalel, it was still not a design school in the sense of preparing students to engage fully with industry, although the graphic design department under Deutsch trained commercial artists to work at a high level of professionalism. Wolpert, despite his commitment to a modern aesthetic, was still a craftsman who specialized in contemporary religious artifacts. The New Bezalel's location in Jerusalem also restricted the development of close relations with the plethora of industries that were burgeoning in Tel Aviv.

A principal means of promoting these new industries both within Palestine and abroad was a series of industrial fairs that began in the early 1920s. Their aim was to promulgate the growing local production and increase opportunities to market local products abroad. Instrumental in creating and promoting these fairs was an ardent Zionist, Alexander Ezer (1894–1973). He was born in the Ukraine and came to Palestine in 1921 by way of Shanghai. Through his company, Trade & Industry, Ezer had by 1929 expanded the fairs to an international scale. The first Levant Fair—the Levant being a term denoting the territory that now encompasses much of the Middle East and part of western Asia—was held in 1932.

The 1934 Levant Fair was a landmark event from a design perspective (Fig. 32.24). It encompassed 74

Fig. 32.24: Levant Fair, souvenir, 1934. Courtesy David Tartakover.

pavilions and was host to more than 600,000 visitors—six times the population of Tel Aviv. The site was located in a sandy area between the Yarkon River and the Mediterranean Sea, and the white predominantly rectangular buildings exuded a Mediterranean flavor. The fair was a sectarian event intended to promote Jewish products. Jewish architects did the planning and architectural design, and the Arab population had no part in its development. Consequently, they boycotted the fair, as did most Arabs in the region.

The idea to build a modern fairground stands in sharp contrast to Sir Roland Storrs' and Charles Ashbee's plan to preserve the traditional design of Jerusalem, which had been completed just over a decade earlier. The Levant Fair was a clear case of dynamic innovation compared to the conservative preservation of Jerusalem. Whereas Storrs and Ashbee had thought in terms of local craftsmen and architects building in a traditional style with local materials, the planners of the 1934 Levant Fair envisioned everything new, from the modernist layout and pavilion designs to the landscaping, interior exhibits, and graphics.

A Technical Bureau, headed by the artist and architect Arieh El-Hanani (1898–1985) and the engineer Willie Weltsch (1887–1978), supervised the design of the fair's every aspect. Multiple architects created the pavilions, which were built by some foreign countries as well as by Jewish organizations in Palestine. Architect members of the planning team included Richard Kaufmann (1887–1958), who emigrated to Palestine from Germany and who had been working in Palestine for a decade; Arieh Sharon (1900–1984), a former Bauhaus student who was born in Galicia and who designed many modernist buildings in Tel Aviv; and Genia Averbuch (1909–1977), a young architect who was a co-designer of the fair's round-shaped Cafe Galina.

Yaakov Nitzan (1900–2000), a pioneer landscape designer active in the development of a local gardening culture, created the landscaping for the entire fairground. Modern design was also evident in the interior displays of the pavilions, especially the Palestine Industries Pavilion, which contained exhibits from 200 Jewish industries; the National Institutes Pavilion; and the Histadrut (Labor Union) Pavilion. The photographer Moshe Vorobeichic (1904–1995), who later changed his name to Moshe Raviv, was recruited from Paris to design the Histadrut exhibit. Vorobeichic had studied with Klee, Kandinsky, and Albers at the Dessau Bauhaus before he went to Paris to study photography. Known in Paris as Moï-Ver, he was recognized for several outstanding photo books of the early 1930s, notably *Paris*, with its elaborate photomontage layouts that used each double-spread as a single plane. For the Histadrut pavilion he created a series of multilayered photomontages that promoted Zionist activity. Vorobeichic's photomontages also graced the fair's catalog as well as its advertising.

The fair's emblem was "The Flying Camel," which Arieh El-Hanani had previously designed for the 1932 Levant Fair (Plate 64). Representing traditional desert culture taking wings and flying into the future, it expressed a sense of dynamism. The emblem was used again for the 1936 Levant Fair, whose success was marred by the strikes and political protests of the Arab Revolt, which began in 1936 and continued until 1939 after turning violent. The revolt had numerous causes, including the massive influx of Jewish immigrants between 1933 and 1936, the murder of a national Arab religious leader by British forces, and widespread poverty and unemployment.

The Levant fairs complemented the Palestine pavilions that Alexander Ezer's Town & Industry organization created for two exhibitions in Paris, the Colonial Exhibition of 1931, and the World's Fair of 1937. Town & Country was also to be actively involved in the design of the Palestine Pavilion for the 1939 World's Fair in New York. The latter was a project initiated by American Zionists and organized by the American theatrical impresario and active Zionist, Meyer Weisgal. After rejecting a colleague's suggestion that Norman Bel Geddes design the pavilion, Weisgal settled on Arieh El-Hanani, the architect who headed the Technical Bureau for the Levant fairs.

The political stakes for the New York pavilion were higher than they had been for the Levant fairs, where the aim had been to showcase Jewish industrial achievements and promote the accomplishments of the Jewish settlers. In New York, Weisgal's objective was to depict the Jewish presence in Palestine as indicative of the right to nationhood. The pavilion's narrative thus concentrated on the Jewish story and excluded the Arabs, just as Herzl and other European Zionists had done in promoting their own visions of Palestine as a Jewish homeland.

The principal designer of the New York exhibits was Lee Simonson, a prominent American stage designer known for his dramatic lighting and expressive sets for such plays as Elmer Rice's *The Adding Machine*. The pavilion was replete with symbols that ranged from a granite cornerstone that had been excavated from an ancient synagogue to a giant menorah derived from an image on the Arch of Titus in Rome. Three giant copper repoussé relief figures representing The Scholar, The Laborer, and The Toiler of the Soil adorned the facade of the pavilion entrance (Fig. 32.25).

As in Norman Bel Geddes' Futurama Pavilion for General Motors, visitors undertook a voyage through the interior space. They ascended a staircase of rising immigration, encountering the statue of a pioneer at the top. The Hall of Transformation led into a series of connected galleries where the spirit of Jewish Palestine was depicted in a series of images. Other galleries presented examples of agriculture and resettlement, town planning and communication, industry, and a hall dedicated to labor and new social forms. A statue of Lot's wife symbolized the settlers' determination not to look backwards.

In an annex were several animated dioramas. One depicted the new city of Jerusalem beside the old, with the scene continuously altered by lights that simulated the movement of the sun. Other dioramas showed how Haifa, Tel Aviv, and Esdraelon morphed into modern cities and fertile valleys. Incorporating

Fig. 32.25: Sculptures by Maurice Ascalon on the Jewish Palestine Pavilion, New York World's Fair. The Scholar, The Laborer, and The Toiler of the Soil, 1939. © Maurice Ascalon.

state of the art lighting and stagecraft, they served as counterparts to the diorama of a modern metropolis divided by highways that Norman Bel Geddes constructed in the GM Futurama Pavilion at the same fair and to Henry Dreyfuss' diorama, Democracity. What the three exhibits had in common is that they were created by former American stage-set designers who were known for their dramatic lighting and mechanical innovations.

Ironically, the Jewish Palestine Pavilion, as it was designated in the Official Guide Book of the fair, opened while the Arab Revolt continued at home. Its purpose was to create the image of a seamless settlement in which energetic creative Jewish settlers transformed a vacant desert outpost into a thriving society. Just as the Arabs were absent from the pavilion's narrative, so

were they present in real life, making the narrative of settlement far more complex and contradictory than it originally seemed to Theodore Herzl or as it was depicted in the New York pavilion.

The Jewish industrial sector expanded rapidly at the onset of World War II as factories responded to the British need for war materiel. The British government had created a War Supplies Board (1941) and a Directorate of War Production in 1942. Between 1942 and 1944, factories that the Directorate supervised produced more than 3.6 million anti-tank mines, 8 million steel containers, and a range of other military goods—gas storage tanks, hydraulic jacks, and special bodies for particular types of military vehicles. Some of these factories were redirected in 1944 to produce consumer goods for the domestic market.

The list of new products for the civilian sector, which were mostly manufactured in Jewish factories, included industrial machinery and tools, spare parts for cars, electrical implements, kitchen utensils, and even false teeth. Most important is the fact that these factories as well as the British military received valuable support from Jewish scientific departments at the Hebrew University for the improvement of products and the efficient use of raw materials. The close relation between the Hebrew University and the manufacturing sector that developed during World War II created a culture of research and development that would be crucial for the state of Israel's economic development after its founding in 1948.

Graphic design

Any discussion of graphic design in Palestine during the Ottoman and mandate periods is complicated by the fact that there was no single stable language that was understood by everyone. During the time that Palestine was an Ottoman province, the language of the Ottomans (essentially Turkish with some Farsi and Arabic elements, but written in Arabic script) was spoken and read by officials and most likely by the local Palestinian elite, who may have spoken and read Arabic as well. After the collapse of the Ottoman Empire at the end of World War I, Arabic became the language of Palestine's Arab population. Until the turn of the century, Arab culture was predominantly oral rather than literate. By 1900, a print culture began to slowly emerge, especially through the publication of newspapers and journals and the printing of public notices. After the Ottoman collapse and the British occupation, school books that had been written in Ottoman Turkish had to be scrapped and new ones published in Arabic.

Hebrew was not a native language for the first Jewish settlers from Eastern Europe. In fact, it was a religious language that had to be reinvented for secular discourse. Yiddish, based on Middle High German, was the lingua franca of Jews in Eastern Europe, and many

such who were in the first wave of immigrants probably continued to speak it in Palestine. Immigrants had to be persuaded to learn and speak Hebrew, and modern lettering and typography for secular Hebrew also had to be designed. Hebrew became the "official" language of the settlers and street signs and public communication such as advertising, particularly in Tel Aviv, were in the Hebrew language.

Arab print culture

As the literary scholar Ami Ayalon has noted, the development of print culture in Palestine was short and intensive compared to the longer development elsewhere in the Arab-speaking world. Egypt, which had a lively and extensive literary tradition that extended back at least to the mid-19th century, was the publishing center for the region. Egyptian publishers and presses turned out hundreds of books, and many magazines and newspapers. Lebanon too had an active print culture, due largely to the presses of different religious orders that had been there for many years. Publications from Egypt and Lebanon circulated to other parts of the region and were well known among the literary elite in Palestine.

The number of newspapers in Palestine and elsewhere in the Ottoman Empire began to expand rapidly after the Young Turk Revolution of 1908, which greatly increased the freedom to publish. Ayalon describes the printing activity of a Greek-Orthodox Jerusalem citizen, Jurji Habib Hananya (1857–1920), who, following the revolution of the Young Turks, began to publish a semi-weekly Arabic newspaper, *al-Quds*, which was among 15 newspapers and journals in Arabic that appeared before the end of 1908. Other presses emerged around that time, and within several years they were publishing the papers *al-Insaf*, *al-Najah*, and *al-Nafir* (*Call to Arms*) in Jerusalem; *al-Akhbar* (*News*) and *Filastin* (*Palestine*) in Jaffa; and *al-Karmil* (*Carmel*) in Haifa. Generally, the visual quality was low, certainly when compared to the more sophisticated graphic standards of newspapers in Cairo or Beirut. The most popular of the local papers was *Filastin*. By the time it became a daily paper in the early 1930s, it was publishing photographs and had an attractive graphic layout.

The Arab newspaper presses in Palestine were mostly shoestring operations, and their owners, who were usually the editors of the papers, had to supplement their publishing with other jobs such as printing letterheads and envelopes, personal cards, and wedding invitations. The designs for these were more than likely done by the printers, as they were when printing first began in other countries. One of the more active presses in Palestine was the one that belonged to the Supreme Muslim Council's Islamic Orphanage. It printed all the Council's publications as well as the newspaper *al-Jami'ah al- 'Arabiyyah*, which began to appear in 1927 and which gained a decent-sized circulation. In addition, the press undertook printing commissions from all over the mandate.

With a limited number of authors and readers, few books appeared, especially compared to a country like Egypt. By the 1930s, no more than 20 books a year were published in Palestine. Not only were books by foreign authors imported, but also Palestinian authors often had their own books printed abroad. The books that were published in the greatest volume were school texts on such subjects as history, the Arabic language, and science. These were written in Arabic by Palestinian educators and printed in cheap editions for school use. Though literacy increased rapidly during the mandate, the plethora of newspapers, magazines, signs, and public proclamations still appeared within a community where literacy was not widespread; hence the continuation of public reading where a literate individual in a cafe or public square would read to an illiterate audience.

Noticeably absent from Arab public spaces during the Ottoman period were street signs. The few that existed were mainly in foreign languages and were for the benefit of tourists, primarily to direct them to hotels, banks, restaurants, shops, or doctors. The presence of foreigners did prompt a few local merchants

to put up signs in English or French to advertise their businesses. Signs in Arabic also began to appear, particularly to designate public buildings like libraries and administrative offices. After the British occupation and the beginning of the mandate, the British introduced written signs throughout the country. These named streets, identified public buildings, marked highway routes, and indicated Jewish and Arab settlements in Arabic, English, and Hebrew. Ayalon calls this process "textualizing" the public domain. Following the lead of the British, Jewish organizations and businesses also began adding Arabic to their public signs, and Palestinian Arabs soon followed with additional Arabic signs. Individual shop owners and professionals placed advertising boards above their shop doors or at the entrances to office buildings. These were most likely painted by the advertisers themselves, although there may also have been some professional sign painters to make them. For special events, including political rallies, cloth banners were stretched across city streets or hung on buildings. They were also carried during marches and demonstrations.

Ironically, it was the British who helped to create an active public sphere replete with political messages that were conveyed on posters, handbills, and leaflets. Besides the written signs they introduced to delineate the civic order, they also addressed the local population with leaflets, bulletin board announcements, and posters. When they entered Jerusalem in December of 1917, they proclaimed martial law with posters that were published in seven languages.

Palestinian political groups began to adopt similar methods. Sometimes their notices were handwritten and sometimes printed in multiple copies. Some were posted on public walls and surfaces of every kind, while others were handed out to passers-by or dropped on house doorsteps. A large number of these notices expressed Arab frustration with the growing Jewish immigration and issued demands for public action. One example was a notice issued in 1929 by a secret Arab organization, the Black Hand Society, which called for a general boycott of the Zionists. It featured a hand printed in black with the fingers spread out, one of the few images to appear on these political notices. Most notices consisted simply of text blocks similar to the layout of a printed page. By the early 1930s, writes Ayalon, such notices had become a standard feature of public life. Palestinian groups also printed occasional propaganda labels that were similar to postage stamps. In 1934, a label was printed to promote the Jerusalem Arab Fair and in 1938 a series of labels depicting the Dome of the Rock and the Church of the Holy Sepulcher in front of a map of Palestine appeared with the English and Arab text, "Palestine for the Arabs" (Fig. 32.26).

Arabic typefaces for all printed matter came from different sources. Some were imported from other Arabic-speaking countries like Egypt or Lebanon. Others came from European foundries that distributed Arabic fonts, and a few had already been imported

by religious orders that had their own presses and published books in Arabic. With the exception of the experimental typefaces that were created in Egypt in the 1930s and the rare fonts that were designed for the presses of religious orders in Lebanon, few new Arabic fonts were designed anywhere in the region during the interwar years, much less fonts that were compatible with linotype or monotype printing.

One exception was the Arabic typeface that Eric Gill designed at the behest of Sir Arthur Wauchope, who became the British High Commissioner for Palestine in 1931. The new face was to be used by the Government Printing Office in the city. Gill, who had designed a number of highly successful typefaces for the Monotype Corporation, had first come to Jerusalem in 1934 to carve some sculptures for the Rockefeller Museum. Following a meeting with Wauchope when he returned to Jerusalem in 1937, he was taken with

Fig. 32.26: Palestine for the Arabs, label, 1938. Courtesy Michael Hide.

the prospect of designing an Arabic typeface for the linotype and monotype machines at the GPO.

Others had confronted this challenge, which was made difficult by the large number of Arabic characters, given that each of the 28 has four forms, depending on its placement in a sentence. Gill also sought to counter the prejudice of most Arab calligraphers against Arabic typefaces that did not imitate the calligrapher's hand. He arrived at his forms by sketching the individual letterforms and then attempting to adjust them for typesetting. His inspiration, as he noted, was the monumental inscriptions on the interior perimeter of the Dome of the Rock.

Due to Wauchope's transfer from Jerusalem and the onset of events that led to World War II, Gill's Arabic typeface was never cut. Although there was no shortage of Arabic faces for hand setting, Gill was among the few typographers to design an Arabic typeface for linotype or monotype setting. Though most Arabic calligraphers and lettering experts who saw Gill's drawings disliked his typeface, it is nonetheless among the more successful attempts of its time to solve the problem of typesetting with Arabic letters.

Zionist graphics

The term "Zionist graphics" is not strictly confined to graphic design that was done to directly promote the Zionist movement. It refers in a broader sense to graphic design, lettering, and illustration that were done in the spirit of Zionist ideals, notably the envisioning of a Jewish homeland in Palestine. The visual images of Zionist graphics were varied. The initial tendency, which may be called a biblical style, was to represent biblical figures and landscapes and embellish the imagery with elaborate arabesques, which paraphrased and sometimes unintentionally parodied traditional Middle Eastern ornamental designs.

The first of the Zionist graphic artists to adopt the biblical style was Ephraim Moshe Lilien (1874–1925), who was from Galicia, then part of the Austro-Hungarian Empire. Lilien had worked as an illustrator for *Jugendstil* magazines in Munich, illustrated

Fig. 32.27: Ephraiam Moses Lilien, 5th Zionist Congress, announcement, 1901. Courtesy David Tartakover.

numerous books with Jewish themes, and contributed illustrations and layouts for Zionist publications and publicity material. He created graphic images for several of the annual Zionist congresses including his image for the 5th Zionist Congress of 1901 that depicts an old man with a bowed head behind whom is an angel, pointing a finger towards a new land where the sun is rising and a man is plowing a field (Fig. 32.27). The rising sun, which symbolized a new dawn for the Jewish people, became a motif in numerous announcements and book illustrations that Lilien did. His drawing style at times echoed the fine line of Aubrey Beardsley, while he mixed details from different historical periods in his depictions of historic themes and events.

Lilien came to Palestine to teach art at Bezalel but returned to Germany after only a short stay. He designed the graphic emblem for the school, which featured two nude figures embraced by wings, kneeling above two tablets, presumably the Ten Commandments (Fig. 32.28). Though Lilien did not remain long at

Bezalel, his graphic style strongly influenced that of the school, which produced a plethora of visual materials—announcements, diplomas, advertisements, posters, publications, and the like.

The leading proponent of the biblical style was the Bezalel teacher Ze'ev Raban, a former student at the Munich Kunstgewerbeschule (Applied Arts School) and the Royal Academy of Art in Brussels. In Munich, Raban had absorbed the tenets of the *Jugendstil* and was also influenced by the Symbolist ideas of his painting teachers in Brussels. He joined the Bezalel faculty in 1912 and remained until the school closed in 1929. He headed the department of metal repoussé, taught painting and sculpture, and also made posters and designed other graphics for the school. Raban designed two of the school's most important projects, the Holy Ark and Elijah's Chair, to which the various departments contributed. Both were shown in 1926 at the largest ever Bezalel exhibition in New York City. Over the years he designed myriad projects that carried the name of Bezalel or its workshops.

Like Lilien, Raban adopted biblical imagery for his posters and other graphics and chose biblical texts to complement the images. In a 1913 lithographic poster created with Ya'akov Stark for a Bezalel exhibition, he depicted a muscular craftsman, most likely Bezalel himself, holding a decorative menorah that he had presumably just crafted. The poster is filled with ornamental designs and the crenellated border at the top makes reference to the crenellation on the Bezalel school buildings in Jerusalem and possibly the Citadel in Jerusalem's Old City. The one modern element is the roman lettering, which has a strong *Jugendstil* flavor. In 1923, Raban joined with another Bezalel teacher, Meier Gur-Arie (1891–1951), to form the Industrial Art Studio, which was housed in the Bezalel building. This was the first multi-disciplinary design studio in Palestine. To suggest a diversity of activities, Raban's letterhead design featured an image of a bearded sculptor on the right and a female painter in biblical garb painter on the left (Fig. 32.29).

Fig. 32.28: Ephraiam Moses Lilien, Bezalel School of Arts and Crafts, emblem, c. 1905. Courtesy David Tartakover.

Fig. 32.29: Ze'ev Raban, Industrial Art Studio, letterhead, 1923. Courtesy David Tartakover.

Fig. 32.30: Ze'ev Raban, *Jerusalem Rebuilt*, title page, 1923. Courtesy David Tartakover.

The same year, Raban illustrated two books, *The Song of Songs* and *Aleph Beth*. *Song of Songs* had elaborate colored illustrations that were complemented by hand lettering, while in *Aleph Beth*, Raban dedicated a page to each letter of the Hebrew alphabet. Though biblical in theme, the richness of the illustrations and the lettering recalled some of the great Art Nouveau or *Jugendstil* books of the turn of the century.

Raban also designed and illustrated the title page for another book published by the school, Schatz's own utopian novel, *Jerusalem Rebuilt*. The title page depicted a strong figure in biblical costume beckoning a seated Schatz in contemporary dress towards a giant menorah. The two sit atop a structure with a crenellated wall, most likely on one of the Bezalel school buildings in Jerusalem (Fig. 32.30). Among the other books that Raban illustrated were a Passover Haggadah and a folk tale by the Hebrew poet Haim Nahman Bialik, one of the first Jewish poets to write in Hebrew. Raban's commercial graphics included product packaging, banknote design, and posters that promoted tourism and Jewish products such as Jaffa oranges. A 1925 poster that Raban did for Ruth cigarettes depicted an image of the biblical figure Ruth holding a sheaf of wheat. Flanked by a goat, she was depicted above a drawing of a cigarette with accompanying advertising copy. Notable in this poster as compared to Raban's book illustrations is the simple composition and modern san serif Hebrew lettering. Gur-Arie also did advertising posters although he was not fully committed to the biblical settings that were evident in much of Raban's work. His poster for the Third International Near East Fair of 1925, for example, portrayed a young fruit seller in a contemporary setting, though clad in traditional dress, calling people to the fair.

During the 1920s and 1930s, Raban was Palestine's

Fig. 32.31: Arieh El-Hanani, Palestine Produces Aromatic Tobacco, poster, 1925. Courtesy David Tartakover.

foremost designer. As a partner in the Industrial Design Studio, he created jewelry and large numbers of Jewish ceremonial objects as well as Jerusalem souvenirs. He also designed architectural decorative elements for Jerusalem buildings such as the King David Hotel and the Jerusalem YMCA and he created stained-glass windows for a synagogue in Kansas City and for the Great Synagogue in Tel Aviv. An exemplar of Zionist illustration and graphic design, his ability to work in different craft media recalls the diversity of William Morris. The interesting parallel is that Morris's imagery was also from the past, albeit an idealized medieval Christian past just as Raban recreated an idealized Jewish biblical past.

By the mid-1920s, a new tendency appeared in Zionist graphics. As the art historian Gideon Ofrat notes, differences began to develop in the 1920s between Jerusalem and Tel Aviv. Artists who came to Tel Aviv from Europe in those years were more interested in being modern and did not share the interest in biblical settings that animated Bezalel artists like Raban in Jerusalem. Though Raban was the most active and prominent Jewish graphic designer and illustrator in the 1920s, artistic tendencies of the Tel Aviv artists, notably their interest in Cubism and other contemporary developments in French art, broke not only with his biblical settings but also with the influences of Symbolism and the *Jugendstil* that he incorporated in his work.

Like artists elsewhere, some of the painters turned to commercial art to earn money. The shift away from the biblical style was evident in a series of posters that the artist and architect Arieh El-Hanani did in the mid to late 1920s. A major client of his was the Trade and Industry Department of the Palestine Zionist Executive, whose concern was to promote Jewish industrial production and Jewish goods. El-Hanani, like other artists, was fascinated by the desert landscape and depicted it in his posters. His emphasis, however, was not on the timeless past but on the new society that Jewish immigrants were building. Thus a poster for Palestine building industries mingled images of new towns that mixed modern and traditional architecture with a large electricity station in the center of the poster. Another poster that promoted tobacco grown by Jewish farmers portrayed a heroic farmer whom the artist foregrounded against a landscape of rolling fields, where industrious workers were tilling the soil and harvesting crops (Fig. 32.31).

Commercial graphic design in Tel Aviv

By the 1930s, commerce in Tel Aviv was extensive and expanding rapidly. Complementing the growing manufacture of goods from clothing and cement to cigarettes and foodstuffs was the development of a culture of advertising and promotion that involved advertising agencies, graphic designers, typographers, printers, and others concerned with commercial art. Street life in Tel Aviv was lively and the poster was a popular medium for advertising, though advertisements were designed for newspapers and magazines as well. In addition, some designers created covers, mastheads, and layouts for magazines and newspapers, along with covers and illustrations for books.

The major development in advertising and graphic design occurred during the period 1932–1939 as a consequence of the fifth wave or *aliyah* of Jewish emigrants who left Europe due to the rise of Nazism. Graphic designers and typographers who arrived in Palestine during this period already had extensive experience and in some cases substantial reputations in Europe. Many came from Germany, but some were from Austria, Hungary, and elsewhere. They were urban in orientation and adapted quickly to the bustling life of Tel Aviv as well as to modern Hebrew as the principal language of communication.

Among the most prominent designers who arrived were the Hungarian Pesach (István) Irshay; the Austrian Franz Krausz (1905–1998); Rudy Deutsch from Germany; and the Shamir Brothers, Gabriel (1909–1992) and Maxim (1910–1990), both Latvians. Other designers included Oskar Lachs (dates unconfirmed), Otte Wallish (1903–1977), Richard Levy (dates

Fig. 32.32: Pesach (István) Irshay, Pachter and Hoffman Iron Works, logotype, 1929. Courtesy David Tartakover.

unconfirmed), and Esther Yoel-Berlin (dates unconfirmed), all from Germany.

The first to arrive was Irshay, who came to Tel Aviv in 1925. He stayed until 1929, when he returned to Budapest where he continued to work for Palestinian clients. Irshay was the first graphic designer in Palestine, whose roots were in European modernism. It may be helpful to contrast his work with that of Ze'ev Raban, who undertook various commercial commissions during the same period but adhered to a 19th-century aesthetic, while Irshay's interests clearly lay with the European avant-garde. He may well have been familiar with the work of Russian and Polish Jewish avant-garde artists like the El Lissitzky and Henryk Berlewi. They and others experimented with the design and layout of Hebrew letters, although the publications they designed were in Yiddish, the German-based lingua franca of Jews in Europe, which was written with such letters.

During his first period in Palestine, Irshay was known for logotypes, magazine mastheads, book covers, posters, and miscellaneous advertising materials such as brochures. Among these projects were the logo, posters, and also scenography he designed for his friend Avigdor Hameiri's satirical theater, *The Teakettle*. Irshay's logotypes often integrated stylized letters and images, while his advertising materials displayed a sophisticated knowledge of formal design. His logo for the Pachter and Hoffmann Iron Works exemplifies this integration of image and letters (Fig. 32.32).

By the time the next group of commercial artists, which included Franz Krausz and Rudy Deutsch, arrived in Tel Aviv, Irshay had returned to Hungary. Krausz was an Austrian who had worked in Berlin as a book designer for the Friedrich Ernst Hübsch Verlag, some of whose brochures and catalogs in the 1920s were strongly influenced by Russian Constructivist graphics and the German New Typography. Krausz's own book cover and poster designs from Berlin show a familiarity with modern—though not avant-garde—layout and typography as well as a refined sense of design.

Krausz had been accustomed to German clients who understood the value of design, while in Palestine the level of design understanding among Jewish businessmen was not very high. He came to specialize in posters, although he also did other kinds of work. Krausz had absorbed the tenets of the German *plakatstil* or commercial poster style that Lucien Bernhard, Ludwig Hohlwein, and others had introduced. In fact, the Hohlwein influence on many of his posters, particularly those that featured human figures, was especially strong. He generally worked from photographs of his subjects that were taken by his wife.

Fig. 32.33: Franz Krausz, Daon Cigarettes, poster, 1939 Courtesy David Tartakover.

Krausz's clients were diverse, ranging from manufacturers of cigarettes, foodstuffs, and industrial products to breweries, as well as the Tourist Development Association. When he worked for clients such as Dubek cigarettes or the candy manufacturer Elite, he often designed the packaging as well as the advertising material. His Hebrew lettering was mainly san serif and he varied his lettering designs between rectilinear and curved forms.

Krausz was a Zionist, although he eschewed the traditional imagery of the desert culture. The figures

Fig. 32.34: Rudy Deutsch, Izhar Olive Oil, poster, 1930s. CPA Media Co. Ltd./Pictures From History.

he devised such as the pilot on a poster for Daon cigarettes were modern men and women who looked to the future (Fig. 32.33). Perhaps his best-known poster was for the Tourist Development Association of Palestine, a Jewish organization. Above a simple English text that said "Visit Palestine," Krausz presented an image of Jerusalem with the Dome of the Rock set against an orange landscape and a yellow sky. There are no humans in Krausz's poster and the buildings are depicted in a strong formal composition (Plate 65).

Rudy Deutsch, who also used the name Rudy Dayan, studied sculpture at the Munich Kunsthochschule (Munich Art Academy). He worked as a commercial artist in that city before coming to Palestine. Consequently the drawing style he adopted in Tel Aviv referred directly to European commercial art. Whereas Franz Krausz was best known for his posters, Deutsch designed a full range of logotypes, posters, packages, booklets, magazine covers, and layouts for commercial clients and also for Jewish organizations. His logotypes frequently incorporated Hebrew letters in the logo image similar to German designers like O. H. W. Hadank. Deutsch designed a map of Palestine for the Tourist Development Association and several publications for the village of Kfar Ussishkin, one of which featured the name of the village in Hebrew letters that was spelled out with an arrangement of village houses. Among his commercial clients was Izhar, a producer of olive oil. For this firm, Deutsch designed a logo that depicted an olive with oil dripping from it, packaging that featured the logo, and a witty poster that portrayed a camel with two cans of Izhar olive oil on its back instead of the traditional saddlebags (Fig. 32.34). Another of Deutsch's projects was the design of the magazine *Hadar* in Hebrew and English versions for the association of citrus growers. The *Hadar* cover featured bold letters similar to Alexander Rodchenko's earlier lettering for the Russian avant-garde magazine *Lef,* a column with small drawings of local desert imagery, and a white space that surrounded photographs of laborers in the citrus groves.

Shortly after Deutsch arrived in Tel Aviv, he employed an assistant, Eliyahu Koren (1907–2001), who subsequently founded his own publishing firm to produce a new edition of the Hebrew Bible for which he designed a special typeface. Before that, Koren worked from 1936 to 1957 as head of the graphics department at the Jewish National Fund, which was founded in 1901 to buy and develop land in Palestine. Earlier, the Fund had commissioned posters and other graphics in the biblical Zionist style from Ze'ev Raban and Meir Gur-Arieh.

Gabriel and Maxim Shamir both studied at the

Fig. 32.35: Gabriel and Maxim Shamir, The Worker, poster, 1937. CPA Media Co. Ltd./Pictures From History.

Kunstgewerbeschule (Applied Art School) in Berlin before they came to Palestine in the mid-1930s. Gabriel had worked in advertising agencies in Berlin and Stockholm and subsequently he and Maxim opened a graphic design studio in Riga in 1934, where they worked briefly before emigrating to Palestine.

They founded the Shamir Brothers Studio in Tel Aviv as soon as they arrived. Their work during the mandate years was less distinctive than that of Franz Krausz or Rudy Deutsch. They designed various newspaper ads for Jewish products such as Dafna Cigarettes and Katav pens as well as ads for Chevrolet. One of their more notable designs was a lithographic poster for the Levant Fair of 1936 that featured a large air-brushed modern building looming behind an existing structure to suggest the industrial potential of the fair. A principal client of theirs was the Histadrut, the national Jewish labor federation, for which they designed posters to promote various themes from celebrating the working class (Fig. 32.35) to supporting events sponsored by the Histadrut's sports organization, the Ha-Poel. When World War II began, the Shamir Brothers Studio was also active in recruiting Jews for the war effort through their illustrative posters for the Jewish Watchman Corps and the British Army.

Otte Wallish (1903–1977) immigrated in 1934 from Germany's Sudetenland and set up a design studio in Tel Aviv in 1936. Among his works were several Soviet-style posters and ads with heroic depictions of muscular agricultural workers as the "new men" of the Jewish settlements. Another poster from 1945 shows a man with a Jewish star on his chest leading a line of prisoners out of a crumbling building in the shape of a swastika. Wallish would distinguish himself after Israel's founding in 1948 as a prominent designer of postage stamps and coins for the new government. He also did the calligraphy and designed the scroll for Israel's Declaration of Independence.

Other designers from Germany included Oskar Lachs, who designed one of the Levant Fair posters in 1936, and in 1938 a poster for the short-lived Palestine

Fig. 32.36: Esther Yoel-Berlin, Zion. Won't You Ask How Your Immigrants are Faring? Freedom for Those Who Are Imprisoned, poster, c. 1946. Courtesy David Tartakover.

Fig. 32.37: Franz Krausz, *Commercial Art of Palestine*, booklet, 1938. Courtesy David Tartakover

Airways. Esther Yoel-Berlin was an artist who studied at the Kunsthochschule (Art Academy) in Hamburg and with the Expressionist painter Ludwig Meidner before emigrating to Palestine in 1925. Like other artists who arrived in the 1920s, she earned money as a commercial artist and was the first female graphic designer in Palestine. A 1933 ad for her design studio in Haifa announced that she could create advertisements, trademarks, catalogs, book covers, posters, packaging, labels, and other publicity materials. Her most prominent commission was the emblem for the City of Haifa, a project for which she won a competition in the mid-1930s. However, she also drew on the Expressionist woodcut technique as a means of creating posters (Fig. 32.36).

In these years the activity of graphic designers continued to expand. In 1935, a group of graphic designers led by Franz Krausz, Rudy Deutsch, and others founded the Association of Jewish Commercial Artists in Palestine. They held their first exhibition during the Levant Fair in 1936, and two years later published a booklet, *Commercial Art of Palestine*, that contained a review of their activities along with a list of members and photographs of their work, recommended prices for different commissions, and other professional information (Fig. 32.37). Joining forces with the Palestine Advertising Association, which was founded in 1937, they held an exhibition, Palestine: Commercial Art in Peace and Wartime, in 1943, together with the Industrialists' Association of Palestine.

FIlm posters in Tel Aviv

The first film theater in Tel Aviv was the Eden, which was built in 1914. While cinema eventually became an integral part of Tel Aviv culture, attitudes towards it among the early Zionists were mixed. Obviously, the enthusiastic entrepreneurs who built the earliest theaters, which included the Ophir, the Opera Mograbi, and the Rena Park believed they could create an audience for cinematic entertainment. Some Zionists, however, thought that film was a frivolous medium and preferred to support literature, poetry, theater, and art. For many years, film also had the handicap of being a medium that consisted of imports; thus the directors, actors, and actresses were not a part of the new culture that many Zionists were striving to create. At the same time, there was a craving for entertainment, and the cinemas did extremely well. Films were imported from the United States, Europe, and the Soviet Union. One

attraction of the foreign films in Tel Aviv, especially after the advent of sound, was the connection that many in the audience felt to the countries they had left behind.

The theaters depended on posters to announce each week's offerings. Initially these posters were printed with traditional Hebrew lettering and posted around Tel Aviv wherever there was an open spot. By the late 1920s, theaters had begun to feature images and print their posters in color. Little is known about the artists who did the artwork and lettering for these posters. Names like Eliezer Ettinger (dates unconfirmed), David Gilboa (1910–1976), Israel Hirsch (dates unconfirmed), Gertsovitz, Zaslevsky, and Zeitlin are recognized primarily for their poster designs and imaginative lettering, and the artists do not appear to have participated in the graphic design community. Their posters were printed by the linocut technique, which meant that the drawings were transferred to linoleum surfaces that the artist or a technician cut into, alternating the cutting with successive printings, to produce a multi-toned or multicolored image.

There is no evidence that the Tel Aviv film posters either influenced or were influenced by posters in Cairo, the other center of film activity in the region. There, artists were also creating posters for a sizeable film audience. One difference is that artists in Cairo were promoting Egyptian films rather than foreign ones and their depictions of local actors and actresses helped to create a cadre of domestic stars, while in Tel Aviv, the directors, actors, and actresses were all from abroad. However, artists in Cairo and Tel Aviv both resorted to sensationalism and romantic images to promote their respective films.

More than likely, posters from America and Europe, as well as posters by the Stenberg Brothers in the Soviet Union, influenced the Tel Aviv artists. In that sense, the iconography of Tel Aviv film posters can be sharply distinguished from the images of the "new Hebrews" whom Franz Krausz, Rudy Deutsch, Otte Wallish, and other graphic designers depicted

Fig. 32.38: *A Little Love for You*, poster, 1932. Courtesy David Tartakover.

on advertising and propaganda posters. The iconography fell into several standard categories: sensational scenes, single or combined portraits of leading actors or actresses, or love scenes. Several posters that Israel Hirsch did for *The Captain from Köpenick* and Pudovkin's *Storm Over Asia* are intense portraits intended to dramatize the films through the psychological depth of a single character. The richness of these portraits was rather unusual within the total oeuvre of Tel Aviv film posters, whose other examples tended to be more superficial though nonetheless dramatic. A poster for Max Neufield's film *Ein Bischen Liebe fur Dich* (*A Little Love*

for You) also featured portraits of the lead actors, while at the same time exemplifying the strong colors that the linocut printing process made possible (Fig. 32.38). By the late 1930s, color linocut posters were no longer printed. As designer and critic David Tartakover points out, the theater owners organized and standardized their advertising formats, replaced the images with text, reduced the poster size, and shifted to letterpress. Thus ended a distinctive era in Tel Aviv film advertising.

Hebrew typography

For centuries, Hebrew was the language of religious texts and chanted or sung liturgy. It was spoken in Jerusalem as a common language among Sephardic and Ashkenazi Jews in the early 19th century if not before, but its promotion as the language that would bind Jews in Palestine together did not begin until the late 19th century. Yiddish was the lingua franca of Jews in Eastern Europe, and many Eastern European Jews, who were in the first wave of immigrants, continued to speak it in Palestine. Some of the first Jewish immigrants to Palestine began to speak Hebrew and promote it as a secular written language, but its wider use was instigated in the late 19th century by Eliezer Ben Yehuda (1858–1922), an emigrant to Jerusalem from Lithuania. By 1914, typewriters with Hebrew characters were being sold in Germany by Wanderer-Werke, and by the 1930s, Remington, the American typewriter manufacturer, also had a Hebrew machine on the market.

Hebrew usage expanded during the second wave of Jewish immigration, when it was frequently adopted for public meetings and activities, and it received a further impetus after the founding of Tel Aviv, where all public signs and notices were in Hebrew and residents were strongly exhorted to speak the language. Following the British mandate, Hebrew was recognized as one of Palestine's three official languages, along with Arabic and English.

For centuries, the written Hebrew of religious texts bound the widely dispersed Jewish community together, although the Hebrew letterforms were initially

Fig. 32.39: Raphael Frank, Frank-Rühl typeface, 1908. Courtesy The Newberry Library, Chicago, z_250_5_h4_h4_1924.

influenced by local scribes and then by different type designers and punch cutters. In the 15th century, Hebrew script, known as the Ashkenazi style, was influenced by the gothic black letter, resulting in thick Hebrew characters (see Chapter 6). At the end of the 18th century, the Didot and Bodoni faces were models for the design of Hebrew, although neither was a suitable influence since their heavy horizontal and thin vertical strokes resulted in Hebrew type that was difficult to read. This kind of Hebrew letter prevailed throughout the 19th century.

An early example of typographic reform was Frank-Rühl, a typeface that Raphael Frank (dates unconfirmed) designed in 1908 for the Rühl Schriftgiesserei in Leipzig, which was purchased by the Berthold Foundry in 1918 (Fig. 32.39). Frank-Rühl corrected the extreme horizontal and vertical contrasts of the 19th-century Hebrew type and created more flowing letters with rounded serif strokes. Considered by some to have been influenced by the linear flow of Art Nouveau lettering, Frank-Rühl nonetheless escaped period stylization and became the most widely used Hebrew font in Germany, Palestine, and then Israel for many years.

The Berthold Foundry released a number of Hebrew fonts including Stam, which was a revival of the earlier Ashkenazi style and was designed by Francesca Baruch (1901–1989), who had studied graphic design and lettering at the Kunstgewerbeschule in Berlin and emigrated to Palestine in 1933. During the 1920s, Baruch worked in Berlin for the Schocken Verlag, a Jewish publisher that brought out some Hebrew texts and bilingual texts in German and Hebrew. For the publisher, she designed Schocken-Baruch, which was based on the Sephardic letters of early Italian printers rather than the Ashkenazic sources of Stam. The typefaces of Frank and Baruch represent one of two tendencies in modern Hebrew type design, namely the retention of serifs and the reference to traditional Hebrew letters. However, Frank-Rühl, which has been compared in significance to Stanley Morison's Times

Roman, was not derived directly from historic sources, as were the types that Francesca Baruch designed.

The second tendency is the design of san serif Hebrew alphabets that reject traditional forms. The first ones were based on the avant-garde alphabets of the 1920s such as those of *De Stijl* and the Bauhaus as well as types like Akzidenz Grotesk, the first popular san serif face, which the Berthold Foundry released in 1898, and later san serif faces of the 1920s such as Gill Sans and Futura.

Jewish avant-garde artists were experimenting with hand-drawn san serif Hebrew letters in the early 1920s as part of the Jewish Renaissance in Eastern Europe, but the publications they designed were in Yiddish. In Palestine, Pesach Irshay created square san serif letters for the title of Avigdor Hameiri's literary magazine, *Ha Mahar* (*Tomorrow*), around 1927. He used the letters as well for other projects. Although some religious leaders as well as the newspaper *Haaretz* attacked him for departing from the traditional calligraphic style, Irshay was also encouraged to continue with his san serif Hebrew lettering. He created the letters for a san serif Hebrew alphabet, which he called Haim after the poet Haim Nachman Bialik, but the drawings were never turned into a typeface.

In 1929 the Polish graphic artist Jan LeWitt (1907–1991) designed a typeface with similar san serif letters, which he also called Haim. LeWitt had visited Tel Aviv in 1927 and stayed for about a year and a half before returning to Warsaw. Thus he may well have known Irshay and would probably have been familiar with his lettering for *Ha Mahar* and other uses he made of san serif Hebrew letters. LeWitt's typeface consisted of even horizontal and vertical strokes for all the letters and a combination of angles (Fig. 32.40), thus distinguishing it from the more severe rectilinear *De Stijl* alphabet, which Theo van Doesburg designed.

For a time, Haim was the only Hebrew equivalent of Gill Sans or Futura and was widely used, particularly by commercial artists. It defined a new direction for modern Hebrew typography and led to

Fig. 32.40: Jan LeWitt, Haim typeface, 1929. Courtesy David Tartakover.

preserved the uniformity of Haim's horizontal and vertical strokes, but substituted soft curves for some of Haim's sharp angles. Consequently Aharoni was an unsuccessful hybrid whose thick uniform strokes and soft curves seemed mismatched.

Other modern serif and san serif Hebrew typefaces were designed in the 1930s, but none was as successful as Haim. The san serif faces included Miryam, designed by Raphael Frank, and a face by an anonymous designer, Sapir—a problematic face with uniform thin strokes and significant distortions of the original Hebrew letters to conform to a contemporary design that was driven by a formalism based on avant-garde experiments with roman letters. Eric Gill also designed a modern Hebrew serif face while he was in Jerusalem but it was only released in the 1950s by the Jerusalem Type Foundry.

Experiments with both serif and san serif letters were widely evident in advertising and poster design, especially film posters where the artists took extensive liberties with the Hebrew alphabet in order to produce visually compelling images. Modern Hebrew lettering was also used for shop signs and other public commercial graphics. Attempts were made as well to create standardized alphabets for street signs. In this sense, the visual forms of secular Hebrew evolved rapidly during the 1920s and 1930s, closely in sync with the modernization of Tel Aviv.

The most radical attempt to modernize Hebrew was the proposal to substitute Latin letters for Hebrew characters. The strongest advocate of this idea was Ittamar Ben-Avi (1882–1943), the son of Eliezer Ben-Yehuda, the proponent of spoken Hebrew. Ben-Avi published a Latinized Hebrew book, *Avi (My Father)*, in 1927, which included a list of the Hebrew characters and their romanized equivalents. There was considerable resistance in religious and cultural circles to Ben-Avi's attempts to romanize Hebrew, which did not deter him from further experiments, notably a weekly news supplement to the English language *Palestine Weekly*, which ceased after a short period,

the design of numerous other san serif faces during the mandate period and after the state of Israel was established. What made it a striking typeface were its strong angles, which linked it to the European avant-garde rather than the Hebrew calligraphic or typographic tradition.

Another popular san serif face that followed Haim was Aharoni, which the Polish artist Tuvia Aharoni (dates unconfirmed) completed in 1932. It was also widely used in advertising, notably by Franz Krausz for the cover of the 1938 booklet, *Commercial Art of Palestine*. Aharoni was a response to Haim. It and five years later *Deror* (*Liberty*), a newspaper whose Hebrew text was transliterated into roman characters. *Deror* contained four pages in Hebrew characters and four in Ben-Avi's romanized version. Like his earlier experiment, *Deror* lasted only a short time and failed to ignite a movement to romanize the Hebrew alphabet. Aside from considerable opposition, one obstacle to achieving the romanization was the difficulty that different proponents had in agreeing on a single pattern or transliteration.

Hugh J. Schonfield made another radical proposal to romanize Hebrew in his book *The New Hebrew Typography*, published in London in 1932. Schonfield claimed that conventional Hebrew was incapable of accommodating both upper- and lower-case letters, italics, and other variants that were characteristic of roman alphabets. Hence he redesigned the Hebrew alphabet, substituting some new letter shapes, believing that a redesigned alphabet ought to have the same flexibility as its roman counterparts. Therefore he envisioned alphabets such as Caslon Hebrew, Kabel Hebrew, and Ultra Bodoni Hebrew.

In an introduction to the book, the eminent British typographer Stanley Morison concurred with Schonfield's proposal, implying that the "Jew *qua* Jew has not yet come of age typographically." Touting the superiority of roman alphabets for printing purposes, Morison noted that historically Hebrew printers lacked typographic reformers of Francesco Griffo's stature and consequently their alphabets remained deficient for modern use. His most extreme statement, however, was that the roman alphabet was superior by "right of conquest" due to its "inherent flexibility and rationalism." By contrast, he stated that "There is no prospect for the future of Hebrew—in spite of all the prayers and propaganda—if none but the traditional signs are used."

Syria and Lebanon under the Ottomans and the French

At the beginning of the 20th century, Syria and Lebanon were part of the Ottoman Empire. Both provinces had large Muslim populations but also communities that were not Muslims, a small one in Syria and one of considerable size in Lebanon consisting of the Maronites, who were Christians, and the Druze. The diversity of communities in this region had two consequences: one was conflict and the other was a rich cultural development that derived from different languages and customs. Damascus and Beirut were major commercial centers with connections that extended to Egypt, other Mediterranean provinces and countries, and also to Europe. Beirut, for example, was influenced by *Al-Nahda* (*Renaissance*), the cultural awakening that began in Egypt in the late 19th century and then spread to other Arabic-speaking countries. Well before the 20th century, Western missionaries in both Syria and Lebanon established presses, schools, and colleges that contributed to the formation of an educated cosmopolitan class.

Following the collapse of the Ottoman Empire after World War I, the European powers pursued their own interests in the region. The San Remo conference, held in 1920 and attended by the four principal Allied powers in World War I—Britain, France, Italy, and Japan—divided part of the Ottoman Empire that had formerly encompassed Syria and Lebanon into two mandates, one for the British and one for the French. The British were given authority over the territory that was then partitioned into Palestine, Iraq, and Jordan, while the French received the newly constituted Syria and Lebanon. The same year, after King Faisal I assumed the kingship of Greater Syria, the French invaded Syria, intent on enforcing their own right to rule the region as established by the San Remo accord. Two years later, the newly created League of Nations formalized the British and French mandates.

The intent of the mandates was to prepare the regions under European supervision for self-rule, but neither Britain nor France felt the urgency to give up their control. Despite resistance to the French administration in both Syria and Lebanon, neither became independent until 1943, when the Free French forces invaded both mandates. While Germany occupied their own country, the Free French, supported by the British, proclaimed independence for the two territories.

Proto-industrialization and infrastructure

By the end of World War I, Syria and Lebanon had made limited progress towards industrialization. Under the Ottomans, they received scant encouragement to industrialize, although significant capital was invested in building up the ports in Damascus and Beirut, bringing in streetcars and electricity, and developing the waterworks. During the subsequent period of French rule, at a time when Turkey, Egypt, and Iran were strengthening their industrial development under strong national leaders, the French discouraged local initiatives to industrialize.

The strong merchant culture, however, required a developed banking system, and the Hejaz Railway, an Ottoman project, connected Damascus with Medina and many points in between, helping Syria to increase its agricultural production and foreign trade. One consequence of the French occupation of Syria and Lebanon was the improvement of the infrastructure, including the telegraph and postal system and roads, which led to a huge increase in motorized vehicles, all, however, imported from abroad.

In 1918, there were very few vehicles in the region, but this figure jumped to more than 11,000 cars, trucks, buses, and motorcycles by 1939. At the same time, the larger presence of Europeans in both territories increased the demand for consumer goods, housing construction, and overall modernization. During the 1930s, the adoption of telephones spread gradually, primarily to wealthy households and offices, but there were also a considerable number of telephone booths in public places.

Handicrafts and Industry

At the turn of the century, handicrafts played an important part in the Syrian economy, although they declined rapidly during World War I and made only a limited recovery in the interwar years. Practitioners of traditional crafts like leatherwork and metalwork, tile making, handloom weaving, and carpet production faced changing fashions and higher costs and had difficulty competing with mechanized manufacturing techniques.

During the 1920s, as the economists Roger Owen and Sevket Pamuk write, small factories in Syria and Lebanon produced cotton and silk, woven cloth, soap, leather goods, and tobacco products. However, few had any machinery. After the worldwide depression began in 1929, many failed while others were forced to introduce methods of mechanical production.

Attempts to modernize training for the trades was made in both Lebanon and Syria, with the establishment of the École Libanaise des Arts et Métiers (Lebanese School of Arts and Trades) in Beirut in 1925, the École des Métiers (School for Trades) in Damascus, and another school in Aleppo, Syria. There was also a trade school for girls in Damascus.

The training was geared to employment in factories rather than traditional handicrafts. Courses in Beirut, for example, included electro-mechanics, foundry work, machine assembly, and textile production. By contrast, farmers and landowners in Syria tended to resist the introduction of modern equipment, relying instead on traditional implements. A *Report on the Prospects of British Trade in Syria*, published in 1911, noted that more than 164 varieties of plows were used in the north and that farmers had strong prejudices against using plows from regions other than their own, much less purchasing equipment from abroad.

In the late 1920s, some larger plants began construction and more were built in the 1930s. Products they manufactured included foodstuffs, cement, textiles, soap, beer, cigarettes, and shoes—a range similar to that of other countries focused on import substitution. The beer industry for the region was centralized in Beirut, while Lebanese factories supplied about 70 percent of the region's matches. But large French monopolies controlled the railroads, urban tramways, gas and electricity, and the big banks. A major obstacle to modernizing local production was a shortage of capital and credit. However, some scholars believe that, despite French policies that discouraged industrialization, an important first step in that direction, fueled by local entrepreneurs, was nonetheless made during the interwar years.

Printing, publishing and advertising

The Ottoman period

Lebanon's long printing tradition began with several religious presses. At the beginning of the 18th century, the Patriarch of Aleppo founded a printing press in that city, and between 1706 and 1711 it issued

a number of religious publications for the Eastern Orthodox Church. About 20 years later, the Catholic convent of St. John the Baptist in Mount Lebanon inaugurated an Arabic press, which also specialized in religious works. The press published its first book in Arabic in 1735 with moveable type designed by the Catholic convert Abdallah Zakher (1684–1748), the press's founder.

By the mid-19th century, two important religious presses were established in Beirut: the American Mission Press of the Presbyterian Board of Foreign Missions, and L'Imprimerie Catholique des Pères Jésuites (The Catholic Press of the Jesuit Fathers). By 1860 these two presses had produced 360,000 copies of 30 different books. They published in Arabic, French, and English

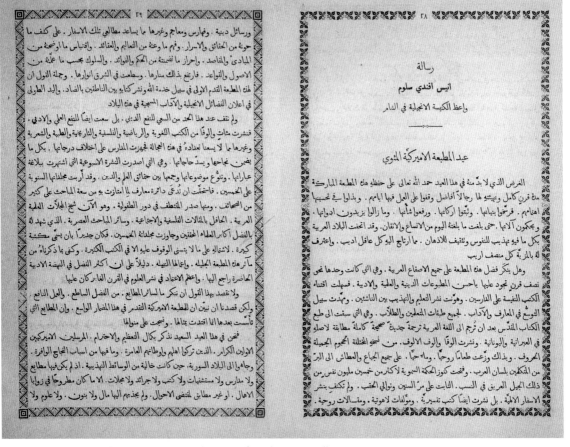

Fig. 32.41: *Americani* typeface, American Press, date unconfirmed. Private Collection.

with type that was imported from abroad. The most important volume of L'Imprimerie Catholique was the first Arabic edition of the Bible, which won a prize at the 1878 Exposition in Paris. The intense activity of the religious presses, which also published books on secular subjects, made Beirut a principal publishing center of the Arab world. Other presses also published both religious and secular books.

The American Press set up the first Lebanese type foundry in 1836. Its Arabic matrices, based on drawings by eminent Ottoman calligraphers, were cut in Leipzig. The fonts, known as *americani*, were produced in Beirut and then sold to other Lebanese publishers including L'Imprimerie Catholique (Fig.32.41). They were also exported to Syria, Palestine, Iraq, Persia, and the Maghreb in North Africa, as well as to countries in other parts of the world.

L'Imprimerie Catholique set up its own foundry in 1874, creating a typographic alphabet known as stambouli whose letters had the vocal accents attached. This foundry also engraved two fonts, one a geometric Kufic alphabet for linotype printing. In 1902, the foundry produced types for the Armenian, Syriac, and Coptic languages as well.

Besides its preeminence in printing and book publishing, Lebanon was also an important center of Arabic journalism in the late 19th century. Such figures as Butrus al-Bustani, a Maronite Christian, helped to create modern journalistic Arabic prose. Between 1880 and 1908, Lebanese publishers brought out 297 newspapers, although only 68 of them remained in Lebanon, since many were published in other countries. In Syria only a handful of papers appeared during the same period, but in both provinces Egyptian newspapers were widely read.

A sharp upturn in publishing occurred after the Young Turk Revolution of 1908. New publications adopted strident names like *al-Inquilab* (*Revolution*), *al-Hurriya* (*Liberty*), and *al-Wataniyya* (*Patriotism*). The Beirut daily paper *al-Watan* (*The Nation*) featured a bold masthead replete with signs of resistance and

revolution: a pen and arrow, a winged angel with a trumpet and the scales of justice, and an Ottoman flag unfurled above sailing ships and a speeding train, both icons of progress. Local artists most likely drew such images, which resembled those one would have seen in political cartoons of the period.

Criticism of the powerful, however, invoked harsh censorship, although the period after Sultan Abdul Hamid was deposed allowed for more openness than before. During Abdul Hamid's reign, members of a secret society in Beirut posted public notices, the precursors of posters, that called for the independence of Syria and Lebanon, an end to censorship, and the adoption of Arabic as the national language. Later protesters expressed political dissatisfaction by adopting a kind of calligraphic banner called a *yafta*. Statements and slogans were painted by hand on large swaths of cloth that were either fixed within a street or attached on both ends to wooden sticks and carried during a march. The calligraphy varied in style according to the message.

The mandate period

During the mandate period, the major presses of the 19th century, both religious and secular, continued to publish books in Arabic, French, and English, exporting their publications to the entire Arab world. The arrival in the region of many Armenians, who fled persecution by the Turks, led to a press that published books in the Armenian language. The French administrative bureau for the mandate set up its own press in Beirut, Imprimerie du Haut-Commissariat (Press of the High Command), which published official documents as well as maps of Syria and Lebanon.

A considerable number of newspapers and journals also appeared in Syria and Lebanon during the 1920s and 1930s. By the end of World War II, more than 40 newspapers were being published in the region. Those in Syria, according to Ami Ayalon, were considerably fewer and were largely crude in appearance and production. Many publications were

Fig. 32.42: *al-Dabbur*, cover, 1928. Courtesy A. Bou Jawdeh.

expense of women and in general maintained a patri-archal attitude. A popular mass-circulation magazine in Damascus was *al-Naqid* (*The Critic*). Its front cover featured a graphic masthead with the magazine's title in bold calligraphy and a drawing of a winged female figure with her hands beneath her chin as if she were an occult priestess. The back cover might feature a drawing or cartoon, along with a smaller version of the calligraphic masthead. Like its Beirut counterpart, *al-Dabbur*, *al-Naqid* also published cartoons that made fun of women, representing them according to various stereotypes such as the overbearing wife.

In contrast to the satirical weeklies, which were directed at a largely male audience, a few magazines that were started in the 1920s were aimed specifically at women, although their critique of Lebanese society and politics was quite broad. The first of these was Julia Dimashqiya's *al-Mar'a al'jadida* (*The New Woman*), which appeared in 1921, followed by Najla Abu al-Lam's *al-Fajr* (*The Dawn*), Nazik 'Abid's *Nur al-Fayha'* (*Light of Damascus*), and *al-Khidr* (*The Boudoir*), published by Afifa Fandi. None had distinctive graphics. *The New Woman* was published in a newspaper format. Its cover had two columns of text and a masthead with a calligraphic title and the image of a woman holding a sleeping child.

By 1945, more than 300 specialized magazines on myriad subjects from literature and political satire to women's issues and cinema had been inaugurated in Syria and Lebanon. Though many folded after a short time, a number did last. As in Egypt and Iran, some of these publications also featured advertising including ads for imported goods such as perfumes, electric appliances, and hair care products.

In the 1920s and 1930s, French railroads, airlines, and travel companies promoted Syria and Lebanon as prime tourist destinations. They appealed to potential travelers with colorful posters that depicted serene landscapes, lively port towns, or majestic ruins. During the interwar period, the PLM (the French Railroad—Paris to Lyon and the Mediterranean) commissioned

short-lived. Editors always had to contend with the censors, the problem of small audiences, and the combative positions of rival publications. Design was rarely an issue. For the most part, the editors themselves often laid out the papers according to conventional newspaper formats, although mastheads may have been drawn with expressive calligraphy.

As in Egypt, Lebanon had its satirical weeklies, including *al-Dabbur* (*The Wasp*), which the poet Yusuf Mukarzal founded in 1923; and *al-Sayyad* (*The Hunter*), inaugurated in 1943, the year of Lebanon's independence. *Al-Dabbur*, which hired freelance artists to draw covers and cartoons (Fig. 32.42) and which was addressed primarily to male readers, sometimes made jokes at the a set of lithographic posters from French painters and commercial artists. The idea for the series may have come from the set of travel posters featuring scenic landscapes that the Egyptian National Railway had created around 1911. The PLM posters were designed and printed in France and then shipped to Lebanon and Syria for distribution.

The poster artist Dabo (Geoffroy d'Aboville) (dates unconfirmed) portrayed a series of landscapes that were intensified by his rich color palette. His depiction of Palmyra, Syria, dramatized the archeological site by setting the Temple of Ba'alsamin against a dramatic orange sky (Plate 66). The PLM also commissioned posters from other French artists including André Frémond (1884–1965), whose poster for the Lebanese archeological site at Baalbek differed from Dabo's in that Dabo presented the Temple of Ba'alsamin itself in a striking setting while Frémond's depiction of Baalbek included small picturesque figures

in native dress including a man on a camel, thus adding Orientalist imagery to the scene by identifying the site with a primitive culture. Another PLM artist was Julien Lacaze (1886–1971), a painter who also created numerous posters for the railroad that depicted scenic views of European vacation spots. Though Lacaze did extensive commercial work, he was essentially a landscape artist who could portray a scene in a way that would appeal to tourists.

The Arabian Peninsula and Yemen

The Arabian Peninsula comprises more than one million square miles of land that is mostly desert. Sparsely populated, at the turn of the century it consisted predominantly of tribal regions. The Kingdom of Saudi Arabia brought together a number of separate units when it was established in 1932. Other areas were controlled by powerful families, many of which had treaties with Britain. Yemen had been under Ottoman

Fig. 32.43: A *sanbuq* from Yemen, date unconfirmed. Colonial Picture Archive, University Library of Frankfurt/ Main.

control until 1918 when Imam Yahya Muhammad established a proper kingdom after the Ottoman Empire ended.

Yemen was primarily agricultural, although it had a long tradition of shipbuilding. Boat builders specialized in dhows—small sailing ships with one or several masts. The different types of dhow were distinguished by their hull construction. Names such as *boum*, *sanbuq*, *zaruq*, and *baghlah* are associated with dhows that have distinctive stems and sterns (Fig. 32.43). All have similar triangular sails, although the number of sails varies with each ship. A British report of 1916 noted two kinds of dhows, one a small boat that transported cargo to larger ships and the other a more sizeable seagoing vessel.

Yemeni craftsmen were mainly Jews, who passed on their skills from one generation to another. The smith's occupation was considered most respectable within this community, and Yemeni silversmiths and goldsmiths were known for their ability to produce highly detailed jewelry and other craft objects. The majority of the silver and gold craftsmen who worked at the Bezalel School of Arts and Crafts in Jerusalem were, in fact, Jews from Yemen.

Elsewhere on the Arabian Peninsula, craftsmen in Bahrain were known for making sails, manufacturing mats from reeds, and building boats, while others produced basic utensils that were essential for a nomadic tribal culture. As in Iraq and Jordan, almost no industry developed in the region before World War II, the discovery of oil having spread to the peninsula, thus spawning a succession of oil states rather than manufacturing economies.

Persia (Iran since 1935)

The modernization of Persia began in the mid-19th century during the reign of the Qajar ruler Nasser al-Din Shah. The Qajar dynasty had ruled Persia since 1794 and would continue its reign until 1924. Nasser al-Din Shah supported Western science, technology, and educational methods and his Prime Minister

Amir Kabir founded Dar-al Fonoun, the first modern university in Persia. Kabir also opened a second school, the Majma'-e Dar-al-Sanayeh (the Polytechnic School of Crafts), where accomplished artists taught students various craft skills and techniques, both traditional and modern. Kabir also instituted a number of reforms and public works such as encouraging foreign trade and building Tehran's bazaar.

Nasser al-Din Shah was assassinated in 1896 and his son Mozaffar-e-din Shah proved to be an ineffective ruler. The country had no revenue and Mozaffar-e-din wasted two large loans from Russia on personal extravagance. Instead of marshaling local resources to develop the country, he sold concessions to European companies in exchange for generous payments to him and a cadre of public officials. In response to public dissatisfaction and protests, he agreed to the creation of a constitution in 1906 and the establishment of a parliament or Majles. However, events that followed—the attempt by Mozaffar-e-din's son and successor Mohammad Ali Shah to rescind the constitution and then the division of Persia into spheres of influence by the Russians and British—prevented the emergence of a constitutional democracy.

The occupation of Persia by foreign troops during World War I severely undermined the authority of then ruler Ahmad Shah, Mohammad Ali's son, and in 1921, Reza Khan, a Persian military officer, initiated a coup d'état that led to him becoming the new Shah in 1925. In 1941 he was forced into exile by British forces and was replaced by his son, Mohammad Reza Pahlavi.

Early industrialization attempts

In 1890, Lord Curzon, soon to become Viceroy of India, made a tour of Persia and wrote that factories, as the term was generally known, did not exist there nor were steam power or even waterpower in use. Instead, he observed, most towns had small cottage industries that specialized in particular products such as carpets, pottery, or cheap tiles. These were made for domestic consumption, but some products were also exported, primarily by British or Russian businessmen. Among the popular exports were carpets, shawls, and silk products. The economic historian Julian Bharier notes that working conditions in the handicraft industries were poor. Child labor was exploited and workers put in long hours, often laboring in shops that were badly lit and ventilated. There was an abundance of unskilled labor, while skilled craftsmen were few.

The rare attempts to introduce modern factories had failed by 1900. A Russian entrepreneur established a factory to produce matches in 1889, a Belgian company started a glass factory in 1891, and an Iranian opened a cotton-spinning plant in 1894. All faced high costs of materials due to an underdeveloped transportation system, along with an inexperienced workforce and stiff competition from cheaper foreign imports.

However, local craftsmen possessed diverse skills and produced a wide range of items for domestic consumption. Copper and brass workers made cooking pots and kettles, water decanters, trays, samovars, coffee urns, and small braziers for cooking. Foundry men produced a few consumer products but also made parts cast in copper, bronze, brass, or nickel silver that were used in a multitude of other goods. Carpenters built furniture for the home—beds, plain tables, chairs, chests, and large trunks to hold a woman's dowry. Among the more industrialized products were the large copper boilers that were used to heat water in the hamams or public baths. Some objects were embellished with ornament that craftsmen created with different techniques such as engraving or embossing.

Though craft skills were generally passed on from master to apprentice, there were also concerns that such skills could die out unless they were taught in a formal setting. Some time after the Constitutional Revolution of 1905–1906, the painter Mohammad Ghaffari (1848–1940), known as Kamal-al-Molk, founded the Kamal-al-Molk Art School, where students learned traditional crafts—carpet weaving, mosaic design, and woodwork—along with painting and sculpture. After

the death of Kamal-al-Molk, his school was renamed the School of Arts and Crafts and in 1940 it merged with the School of Architecture to become the Faculty of Fine Arts in the University of Tehran.

Despite the diversity of craftsmen, most people from the laboring class worked in agriculture, which accounted for more than 90 percent of the Persian economy in 1900. Until Reza Shah created a number of model farms in the 1930s and introduced modern mechanized agricultural equipment, farmers worked mainly with primitive tools. Craftsmen made wooden plows consisting of a yoke and harness to which was attached a wooden beam with a metal blade. The design of these plows differed somewhat from one region to another. Wooden harrows with spikes attached were used to turn over the soil, while various types of scythes and sickles were made for harvesting wheat and rice.

Though Ahmad Shah established a Ministry of Commerce and Public Utilities in 1900, he had little understanding of how to develop a productive economy and continued to regard the sale of concessions to foreigners as a principal source of revenue. In fact, the Ministry of Commerce and Public Utilities, which he established in 1900, had a miniscule budget and did little more than give out mining leases. Oil was discovered in 1908, and in 1913 Persia became the first country in the region to initiate commercial production, following the formation of the Anglo-Persian Oil Company. This organization built the world's largest oil refinery, which remained an isolated example of advanced industrial development within a country whose economy was dominated by small trades and local farmers.

A new industrialization policy

Attitudes to industrialization changed radically after the coup d'état of 1921. Even before Reza Khan became the Shah, government members began to consider questions of industrial development and exports. In an attempt to encourage native textile industries and combat the plethora of inexpensive imports, government employees and army personnel were required to wear clothing that was made locally.

In 1921, the government sponsored an exhibition of Persian crafts and industries in Tehran with the intent to increase exports and enhance manufacturing capability. A second exhibition of foreign machinery was held to encourage craftsmen to adopt modern technology. The latter exhibition led to a demand for new spinning and weaving machines and helped to promote a few large-scale factories to bolster the textile industry. It also led to the construction of several plants to produce paper and beverages. A few factories that made other goods followed.

The government provided support for these factories, notably the elimination of customs duties on imported machinery, on the condition that their founders would build them within a year and then employ a mainly local workforce. To improve the abilities of these new workers, the government founded a Technical Institute in 1924, where foreign experts trained a cadre of Persian students. Though such efforts were few compared to the vast number of craftsmen and farmers who continued to work in traditional ways, they constituted the beginning of an industrial economy that required skilled workers who understood techniques of mass production.

Reza Shah Pahlavi had ambitious plans for the modernization of Persia. He sought to create a secular society and diminish the influence of the Muslim clerics. Like Kemal Ataturk, he discouraged men from wearing traditional clothing, while a 1936 state decree eliminated the veil for women. He was a ruthless leader who admired the authoritarian states of Germany and Italy. During the 1930s, the Shah maintained close economic and political relations with the Nazi regime, adopting German models for mass education campaigns and giving German experts and advisors major roles in the country's financial and industrial institutions. He glorified Persia's past and Aryan origins and in 1935, prompted by his ambassador to Berlin, he changed the country's name from Persia to Iran to emphasize its role as the birthplace of the Aryan race.

The Shah strongly supported the industrialization of his country. Like Ataturk in Turkey, he wanted Iran to be economically self-sufficient, and early in his reign he pursued a policy of import substitution to reduce Iran's dependence on foreign goods. In 1927, he established the Bank Melli (National Bank) in Tehran, whose purpose was to foster industrial development. A German architect designed the monumental building in the style of the powerful Achaemenid Empire (550–330 BCE), whose culture provided images of his country's former glory.

With the advanced technical operations of the Anglo-Persian oil refinery as a precedent, Reza Shah launched the construction of the Anglo-Iranian Railroad in 1927. Although it was built entirely by foreign experts, the railroad was financed with local resources derived primarily from taxes on imported tea and sugar. The project responsibilities were apportioned to experts from different countries to reduce dependence on a single one. Initially, an international syndicate, Ulen and Company, led by American and German firms, managed the work. In 1933, the construction contract was transferred to a Danish company, Kampsax, which sub-contracted parts of the project out to firms from more than 12 countries, including Iran itself. The line opened in 1939, having been completed ahead of schedule and under budget. Its 230 tunnels, 4,100 bridges, and many stone buttresses that were built along a precipitous terrain made the Anglo-Iranian Railroad an astonishing technological feat.

In 1927, the government also arranged with the German aircraft company Junkers to establish a commercial airline, Company Havapeimai Yunkers dar Iran (Junkers Airline Company of Iran). Junkers set up a number of routes to carry passengers as well as mail, but this venture was less successful than the construction of the railroad. For unknown reasons Junkers' relationship with the government ended in 1932 and a gap in domestic air travel existed until 1938, when the Ministry of Post and Telegraph purchased several British planes, trained pilots to fly them, and started Iranian State Airlines. Though primarily intended to deliver mail, the planes also transported a few passengers.

In late 1930, Reza Shah referred to the Majles as his "Economic Parliament." However, the government realized that it lacked the infrastructure to achieve its ambitious industrialization goals. At the beginning of the 1930s, Iranian industry was represented primarily by a few factories that made carpets and silks. The national transport system was still inadequate to move goods and materials easily across the country, the banking system needed further development, and the country lacked trained managers, engineers, economists, and skilled personnel at all levels.

Intensive development occurred during the 1930s, when a considerable number of factories were built, some by German firms. Mainly owned by the regime, they manufactured various goods including processed foods, soaps, cigarettes, cigar and pipe tobacco, bricks, cement, and various steel products. Traditional techniques of spinning and weaving were also industrialized, a process that had begun some years earlier.

An exhibition of industrial and agricultural products, held in Tehran in 1934, could already demonstrate that Persian factories had achieved some success. The exhibition was put on again in 1937 and in subsequent years, while similar exhibitions were held in a number of provincial towns. An observer from the British Embassy attested to the good quality of the products on display and noted that it improved each year.

While Reza Shah did not achieve complete import substitution, the new factories managed to produce much of what local consumers needed. Craftsmen maintained their traditional production techniques, with very few expanding the number of employees in their workshops or purchasing machines to increase their production. One exception was the carpet industry. The government supervised carpet production, successfully managing the marketing as well as the modernization of manufacturing.

As a military man, the Shah had a particular interest in the manufacture of armaments and other military equipment. In fact, a third of his budget was dedicated to providing equipment, uniforms, and transportation for the army. He established a machine gun factory in Tehran and built an aircraft factory at Shahbaz. A Swedish engineer, N. H. Larsson (dates unconfirmed), was hired in 1933 to plan and organize the factory, which was completed in 1936. Its manager was British, though many of the other employees were local. The first planes they built were five de Havilland Tiger Moths, followed by five Audaxes, which were also small British biplanes. The factory did not originate its own aircraft, but instead constructed planes for which designs and parts already existed.

Despite Germany's strong economic presence, Iran remained neutral when World War II began. By that time the British had forced the Shah to abdicate, and his son Mohammad Reza Pahlavi replaced him. In 1943, Iran declared war on Germany and was recognized to have been on the side of the Allies when the war ended.

Printing, publications, and advertising

The Qajar monarchs

The Persian language, known as Farsi, has been written in Arabic since the Arab conquest of Persia in the 7th century. Traditionally Nastaliq, a cursive calligraphic style that is more fluid than the Naskh script, was used for writing letters and official documents, while Naskh became the standard for Arabic typeface design (Fig. 32.44).

In the 19th century the Qajar monarch Naser al-Din Shah allowed Catholic and Protestant missionaries to set up printing presses in Tabriz, Tehran, Isfahan, and other cities. He also established the Government Printing Office, which published books on a wide variety of subjects—military manuals, biographies of

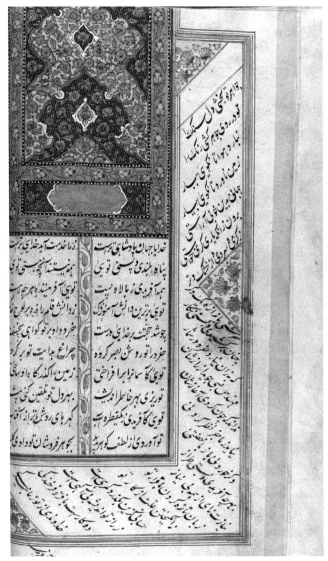

Fig. 32.44: Example of Naskh script, date unconfirmed. Beinecke Rare Book and Manuscript Library, Yale University.

illustrations in 1860, most of which featured the king, male government officials, court ceremonies, or public buildings.

The first Persian paper money was printed in Persia after 1888, when the British-owned New Oriental Bank began to operate in a number of Persian cities. This was the first modern bank in the country. A year later, Naser al-Din granted to the Imperial Bank of Persia, which became the nation's official bank though it was chartered by Queen Elizabeth, the exclusive concession to issue banknotes that were known as *eskenas*. Printed by an English company, the notes were elaborately engraved, featuring rich ornamentation and cartouches with portraits of Naser al-Din and the lion and sword—the symbol of imperial Persia (Fig. 32.45). After the Bank Melli was established in 1927, however, it took over the issuance of banknotes, replacing early designs with notes that contained portraits of Reza Shah.

Engraving was used for other purposes such as stamps and business certificates, which might also have elaborate ornamental designs along with the imperial lion and sword. The Post Office printed postcards, envelopes, and newspaper wrappings that were mostly contracted out to Enschedé & Zonen printers in the Netherlands. In addition, the Post Office issued official postcards with pictures of Naser al-Din Shah on them.

The Constitutional Revolution of 1905–1906 provoked an expansion of the periodical press and fostered the appearance of ideological left-wing papers like *Sur-e Esrafil* (*Esrafil's Trumpet*) and *Iran-e Now* (*New Iran*), both of which began in 1909. The first women's magazines also appeared during these years: *Danesh* (*Knowledge*), published in 1909, and *Shokufeh* (*Blossom*), which appeared in 1915. There were various other publications in the brief period before the coup d'état. *Alam-e Nesvan* (*Women's World*), first appeared in 1913, and *Kaveh*, a journal that espoused Iranian renewal after World War I, was published in 1916. *Zaban-e Zanan* (*Women's Voice*) was shut down by the Qajar authorities because of its strong political views.

Muslim leaders, translations of European literature, and even his own account of a European tour. In addition, the government produced numerous leaflets, letters, and official announcements. Such documents might be decorated with pictures of the crown, a lion, the sun, or Naser al-Din himself. The official gazette of the Qajar monarchy was *Vaqaye'-e Ettefaqiyeh* (*Chronicle of Events*), which was founded in 1851. It began to publish

Fig. 32.45: Persian banknote with portraits of Nasser al-Din and the lion and sword. Image Courtesy of Spink & Son, London.

Fig. 32.46: *Iran-e Emruz*, spread, 1930s. Middle East Department, University of Chicago Library.

The regime of Reza Shah Pahlavi

The periodical press expanded under Reza Shah even though it was more susceptible than ever to censorship. The leading daily newspaper was *Ettela'at* (*Information*). Founded in 1926, it managed to maintain a comfortable relationship with Reza Shah's regime. It began as a four-page paper with a small circulation and by World War II it had doubled in size and attained a readership of 60,000. A more precarious publication was *Khalq* (*The People*), which experienced a number of government shutdowns and one fire. The paper was originally published under a different name beginning in 1921, and its name changed several times before it ceased publication in 1933. Among the black-and-white cartoons that *Khalq* printed were some that compared backward conditions in Persia with modern life in Europe.

Prior to the 1930s, illustrations, whether editorial or for advertising, were primarily black-and-white drawings. By the 1930s, however, mass circulation magazines were using photographs, just as their counterparts in other countries were. Photographs were prevalent in magazines such as *Mehregan*, whose intended audience was teen and young adult readers. *Mehregan* published articles on film stars, beauty culture, and current fashion trends. Covers frequently featured pictures of Hollywood movie stars or European beauties, while photographs of modern women were also widely displayed in the magazine's interior spreads. Such photographs in *Mehregan* or other magazines would not have been possible before Reza Shah sought to remove women's veils and launch the Women's Awakening Project, which lasted from 1936 until his exile in 1941. Before this project, newspapers and magazines rarely published pictures of women and never Iranian women. Depictions of women in advertising were a bit more liberal, and after 1936 even a bit daring on occasion.

Photographs were also prevalent in several propaganda magazines. *Iran-e Bastan* (*Ancient Iran*) was edited by a Nazi supporter, Sayf Azad. Founded in 1933, the year Hitler came to power, it was suppressed by

Reza Shah's regime two years later. The masthead on the cover included expressive nastaliq lettering combined with drawings that extolled the glory of Iran's ancient past, but the imagery and the title were misleading. The magazine purported to introduce Iran to foreigners, but instead it devoted much of its content to photographic portrayals of life in the Third Reich.

Though it was shut down by the government, *Iran-e Bastan* may have served as the model for Reza Shah's own magazine, *Iran-e Emruz* (*Today's Iran*), which began publication in 1939. Its editor was Muhammad Hejazi, a novelist who served as the head of the press committee in the Bureau for Public Enlightenment that Reza Shah had established the year before. *Iran-e Emruz*, like *la Turquie Kamaliste* in Turkey, sought to project a strong image of Iranian modernity (Plate 67). Among its special features were articles about women who were defying traditional roles by excelling in athletics, working in factories, participating in the arts, and even flying airplanes. Central to the publication were the layouts in which images were often creatively displayed (Fig. 32.46).

Bibliography
Bibliographic essay

There is little written on design in any of the countries in the Near East and Middle East regions and I have consequently relied on books about economic and industrial development to provide information about handicrafts and other enterprises in these countries. Among the most useful general histories are Kurt Grunwald and Joachim O. Ronall, *Industrialization in the Middle East*; Charles Issawi, ed., *The Economic History of the Middle East, 1800–1914*; Roger Owen and Sevket Pamuk, *A History of Middle East Economies in the Twentieth Century*; and Roger Owen, *The Middle East in the World Economy 1800–1914*. Essential to understanding the history of Arab newspapers and magazines during this period is Ami Ayalon's *The Press in the Arab Middle East: A History*. On Arabic calligraphy and typography, key publications are Sheila

Blair, *Islamic Calligraphy*, and Huda Smitshuijzen AbiFarès, *Arabic Typography: A Comprehensive Sourcebook.*

For Turkey, Sibel Bozdoğan's book *Modernism and Nation Building: Turkish Architectural Culture in the Early Republic* was helpful for its discussion of Turkish middle-class consumer culture as well as its information about various exhibitions. For Egypt, Kristin Koptiuch's *A Poetics of Political Economy in Egypt* offered a useful way to think about Egyptian industrial policy and industrialization, Beth Baron wrote about the iconography of Egyptian nationalism in "Nationalist Iconography: Egypt as a Woman" in James Jankowski and Israel Gershoni, eds., *Rethinking Nationalism in the Arab Middle East*; and Donald M. Reid addressed a similar issue in his essay "Nationalizing the Pharaonic Past: Egyptology, Imperialism, and Egyptian Nationalism, 1922–1932," published in the same volume. Mona Russell's *Creating the New Egyptian Woman: Consumerism, Education, and National Identity, 1863–1922* contains much difficult to find information about Egyptian advertising and popular media as does Relli Shechter's article, "Reading Advertisements in a Colonial/Development Context: Cigarette Advertising and Identity Politics in Egypt, c. 1919–1939," *Journal of Social History* 39, no. 2 (Winter 2005).

Hans Wulff's *The Traditional Crafts of Persia: Their Development, Technology, and Influence on Eastern and Western Civilizations* has considerable detailed material about Persian crafts, while Camron Michael Amin's article, "Importing 'Beauty Culture' into Iran in the 1920s and 1930s: Mass Marketing Individualism in an Age of Anti-Imperialist Sacrifice," *Comparative Studies of South Asia, Africa and the Middle East* 24, no. 1 (2004) has much helpful material about advertising in Persia and Iran as it was later called.

The most extensive documentation for any country or area in the region is for Palestine, much of it related to the Jewish experience. An outstanding source for material on the broad topic of Jewish activity in Palestine is the massive catalog *Die Neuen*

Hebräer: 100 Jahre Kunst in Israel, edited by Doreet LeVitte Harten and Yigal Zalmona. The principal source for the Bezalel School of Arts and Crafts is Nurit Shilo-Cohen's comprehensive exhibition catalog *Bezalel 1906–1929*. Others who have written on Bezalel include Inka Bartz, Margaret Olin, and Dalia Manor. The Levant Fairs came to my attention through the book chapter by Sigal David Kunda and Robert Oxman, "The Flight of the Camel: The Levant Fair of 1934 and the Creation of a Situated Modernism," in Haim Jacobi, ed., *Constructing a Sense of Place: Architecture and the Zionist Discourse*, and I relied on the work of Barbara Kirshenblatt-Gimblett, "Performing the State: The Jewish Palestine Pavilion at the New York World's Fair, 1939/40," in Barbara Kirshenblatt-Gimblett and Jonathan Karp, eds. *The Art of Being Jewish in Modern Times* and James L. Gelvin, "Zionism and the Representation of 'Jewish Palestine' at the New York World's Fair," *The International History Review* 22, no. 1 (March 2000) for information on that topic. Charles Robert Ashbee's role with the Pro-Jerusalem Society is discussed in Inbal Ben-Asher Gitler, "C.R. Ashbee's Jerusalem Years: Arts and Crafts, Orientalism and British Regionalism," *Assaph* 5 (2000); Noah Hysler-Rubin, "Arts & Crafts and the Great City: Charles Robert Ashbee in Jerusalem," *Planning Perspectives* 21 (October 2006); and in Alan Crawford, *C.R. Ashbee: Architect, Designer & Romantic Socialist*. Further information on Arab crafts is contained in Kamal Boulatta, *Palestinian Art: From 1850 to the Present*. The authoritative work on the Armenian ceramicists in Jerusalem is Nurith Kenaan-Kedar, *The Armenian Ceramics of Jerusalem: Three Generations 1919–2003*. Rashid Khalidi, *Palestinian Identity: The Construction of Modern National Consciousness* provides helpful background material on the Arab situation in Palestine during the mandate years, while Ami Ayalon's extensive writings on Palestinian publishing and political media were my principal source of information on this subject. See his essay "Inscribing the Public Domain: Arabic Placards, Proclamations and Handbills," in Philip Sadgrove, ed.,

Printing and Publishing in the Middle East: Papers from the Second Symposium on the History of Printing and Publishing in the Languages and Countries of the Middle East and his book *Reading Palestine: Printing and Literacy 1900–1948*. Various catalogs have information about modern Jewish graphic designers in Tel Aviv. These include *Franz Krausz: Pioneer of Advertising Art in Israel*; *Hebrew Graphics: Shamir Brothers Studio*; and *Tel Aviv Film Posters of the 1930s*. Two valuable essays on modern Hebrew typography are Adi Stern, "Archaismus und Neuerung. Hebräische Schriftgestaltung in ersten Jahrzehnt nach der Staatsgründung," in the *Neuen Hebräer* catalog and Philipp Messner, "Tel Aviv und die Revolution des Hebräischen Schriftbilds," *Pardes: Zeitschrift der Vereinigung für Judische Studien* 15 (2009). In *The New Hebrew Typography*, Hugh J. Schonfield proposes a redesign of the Hebrew letters so that they will conform more easily to roman alphabets. For the entire chapter, all of these sources have been supplemented by exhaustive Internet searches and communication with knowledgeable colleagues.

Books

General

Ayalon, Ami. *The Press in the Arab Middle East: A History*. New York and Oxford: Oxford University Press, 1995.

Blair, Sheila S. *Islamic Calligraphy*. Edinburgh: Edinburgh University Press, 2006.

Fisher, Sidney Netleton. *The Middle East: A History*, 3rd ed. New York: Alfred A. Knopf, 1979 (c. 1959).

Grunwald, Kurt and Joachim O. Ronall. *Industrialization in the Middle East*. New York: Council for Middle Eastern Affairs Press, 1960.

Isenstadt, Sandy and Kishwar Rizvi, eds. *Modernism and the Middle East: Architecture and Politics in the Twentieth Century*. Seattle and London: University of Washington Press, 2008.

Issawi, Charles, ed. and with introductions. *The Economic History of the Middle East, 1800–1914*. Chicago and London: University of Chicago Press, 1966.

Longrigg, Stephen Hemsley. *Syria and Lebanon under French Mandate*. Oxford: Oxford University Press, 1958.

Monroe, Elizabeth. *Britain's Moment in the Middle East, 1914–1971*. New and revised edition. Baltimore: Johns Hopkins University Press, 1981.

Owen, Roger. *The Middle East in the World Economy 1800–1914*. London and New York: Methuen, 1981.

Owen, Roger and Sevket Pamuk. *A History of Middle East Economies in the Twentieth Century*. Cambridge, MA: Harvard University Press, 1998.

Smitshuijzen AbiFarès Huda. *Arabic Typography: A Comprehensive Sourcebook*. London: Saqi Books, 2001.

Turkey

Bozdoğan, Sibel. *Modernism and Nation Building: Turkish Architectural Culture in the Early Republic*. Seattle and London: University of Washington Press, 2001.

Bozdoğan, Sibel and Reşat Kasaba, eds. *Rethinking Modernity and National Identity in Turkey*. Seattle and London: University of Washington Press, 1997.

Hale, William. *The Political and Economic Development of Modern Turkey*. New York: St. Martin's Press, 1981.

Issawi, Charles. *The Economic History of Turkey 1800–1914*. Chicago and London: University of Chicago Press, 1980 (Publications of the Center for Middle Eastern Studies no. 13).

Landau, Jacob. M., ed. *Atatürk and the Modernization of Turkey*. Boulder: Westview Press, and Leiden: E. J. Brill, 1984.

Merter, Ender. *80. Yilinda Cumhuriyet'i Afişleyen Adam: İhap Hulusi Görey*. Istanbul: Literatür Yayincilik, 2003.

Quataert, Donald, ed. *Manufacturing in the Ottoman Empire and Turkey, 1500–1950*. Albany: State University of New York Press, 1994 (SUNY Series in the Social and Economic History of the Middle East).

Shaw, Stanford J. and Ezel Kural Shaw. *History of the Ottoman Empire and Modern Turkey, Vol. 2, Reform,*

Revolution, and Republic. Cambridge, London, New York, and Melbourne: Cambridge University Press, 1977.

Zürcher, Erik J. *Turkey: A Modern History.* London and New York: I. B. Tauris, 2001 (c. 1993).

Egypt

Crouchley, A. E. *The Economic Development of Modern Egypt.* London, New York, and Toronto: Longmans, Green and Co., 1938.

Gershoni, Israel and James P. Jankowski. *Redefining the Egyptian Nation, 1930–1945.* Cambridge: Cambridge University Press, 1995 (Cambridge Middle East Studies 2).

Jankowski, James P. *Egypt: A Short History.* Oxford: Oneworld Publications, 2000.

Khan, M. *An Introduction to the Egyptian Cinema.* London: Informatics, 1969.

Koptiuch, Kristin. *A Poetics of Political Economy in Egypt.* Minneapolis and London: University of Minnesota Press, 1999.

Mabro, Robert and Samir Radwan. *The Industrialization of Egypt 1939–1973: Policy and Performance.* Oxford: Clarendon Press, 1976.

Russell, Mona L. *Creating the New Egyptian Woman: Consumerism, Education, and National Identity, 1863–1922.* New York and Houndsmills: Palgrave Macmillan, 2004.

Wilkins, Mira and Frank Ernest Hill. Introduction by Allan Nevins. *American Business Abroad: Ford on Six Continents.* Detroit: Wayne State University Press, 1964.

Iraq

Tripp, Charles. *A History of Iraq.* Cambridge: Cambridge University Press, 2000.

Transjordan

Konikoff, A. *Transjordan: An Economic Survey.* Jerusalem: Economic Research Institute of the Jewish Agency for Palestine, 1946.

Palestine

Artists of Israel: 1920–1980. Exhibition curator Susan Tumarkin Goodman. Essays by Moshe Brasch, Yona Fischer, and Ygal Zalmona. New York: The Jewish Museum, 1981.

Ashbee, Charles Robert. *A Palestine Notebook, 1918–1923.* London: William Heinemann Ltd, 1923.

—ed. *Jerusalem 1920–1922: Being the Records of the Pro-Jerusalem Council during the First Two Years of the Civil Administration.* London: John Murray, 1921.

—ed. *Jerusalem 1918–1920: Being the Records of the Pro-Jerusalem Council during the Period of the British Military Administration.* London: John Murray, 1924.

Ayalon, Ami, *Reading Palestine: Printing and Literacy 1900–1948.* Austin: University of Texas Press, 2004.

Berkowitz, Michael. *Zionist Culture and West European Jewry Before the First World War.* Cambridge: Cambridge University Press, 1993.

Boulatta, Kamal. *Palestinian Art: From 1850 to the Present.* Preface by John Berger. London and San Francisco: Saqi, 2009.

Crawford, Alan. *C.R. Ashbee: Architect, Designer & Romantic Socialist.* New Haven and London: Yale University Press, 1985.

Eisenhut, Günter. *Franz Krausz: Pioneer of Advertising Art in Israel.* Graz-Wien: Hausner & Hausner Verlag, 2005.

Franz Kraus Posters. Tel Aviv: The Tel Aviv Museum, 1981.

Gilbar, Gad, ed. *Ottoman Palestine, 1800–1914: Studies in Economic and Social History.* Leiden: E. J. Brill, 1990.

Gross, Nachum. *The Economic Policy of the Mandatory Government in Palestine.* Jerusalem: The Maurice Falk Institute for Economic Research in Israel, 1982 (Discussion Paper no. 816, revised).

Harten, Doreet LeVitte and Yigal Zalmona, eds. *Die Neuen Hebräer: 100 Jahre Kunst in Israel.* Berlin: Nicolai, 2005.

Hebrew Graphics: Shamir Brothers Studio. Tel Aviv: Tel Aviv Museum of Art, 1999.

Kenaan-Kedar, Nurith. *The Armenian Ceramics of Jerusalem: Three Generations 1919–2003*. Jerusalem: Yad Izhak Ben-Zvi, and Tel Aviv: Eretz Israel Museum, 2003.

Khalidi, Rashid. *Palestinian Identity: The Construction of Modern National Consciousness*. New York: Columbia University Press, 1997.

Kirshenblatt-Gimblett, Barbara. *Destination Culture: Tourisms, Museums, Heritage*. Berkeley, Los Angeles, and London: University of California Press, 1998.

Kupferschmidt, Uri M. *The Supreme Muslim Council: Islam Under the British Mandate for Palestine*. Leiden and New York: E. J. Brill, 1987.

Levy, Thomas E., ed. *The Archeology of Society in the Holy Land*. New York: Facts on File, c. 1995.

Made in Israel No. 2: An Exhibition of Rare Historical Israeli Posters. Co-sponsored by the Farkash Gallery and the Great Neck Arts Center. Great Neck: Great Neck Arts Center, 2006.

Manor, Dalia. *Art in Zion: the Genesis of Modern National Art in Jewish Palestine*. London and New York: RoutledgeCurzon, 2005 (RoutledgeCurzon Jewish Studies Series).

Metzer, Jacob. *The Divided Economy of Mandatory Palestine*. Cambridge: Cambridge University Press, 1998 (Cambridge Middle East Studies 11).

Ofrat, Gideon. *One Hundred Years of Art in Israel*. Translated by Peretz Kidron. Boulder: Westview Press, 1998.

Schlör, Joachim. *Tel Aviv: From Dream to City*. Translated by Helen Atkins. London: Reaktion Books, 1996.

Schonfield, Hugh J. *The New Hebrew Typography*. Foreword by Stanley Morison. London: D. Archer, 1932.

Schreuder, Saskia and Claude Weber in conjunction with Silke Schaeper and Frank Grunert. *Der Schocken Verlag/Berlin: Jüdische Selbstbehauptung in Deutschland 1931–1938*. Berlin: Akademie Verlag, 1994.

Schwarz, Karl. *Jewish Artists of the 19th and 20th Centuries*. Freeport, NY: Books for Libraries Press, 1949.

Shilo-Cohen, Nurit, ed. *Bezalel 1906–1929*. Jerusalem: Israel Museum, 1983.

Tartakover, David, ed. *Tel Aviv Film Posters of the 1930s*. Jerusalem: The Israeli Film Archive, 1995.

Wasserstein, Bernard. *The British in Palestine: The Mandatory Government and the Arab–Jewish Conflict 1917–1939*, 2nd ed. Oxford: Basil Blackwell, 1991 (c. 1978).

Weisgal, Meyer. *Meyer Weisgal … So Far: An Autobiography*. New York: Random House, 1971.

Syria and Lebanon

Gates, Carolyn. *The Merchant Republic of Lebanon; Rise of an Open Economy*. London and New York: The Centre for Lebanese Studies in association with I. B. Tauris Publishers, 1998.

Thompson, Elizabeth. *Colonial Citizens: Republican Rights, Paternal Privilege, and Gender in French Syria and Lebanon*. New York: Columbia University Press, 2000.

Persia (Iran since 1935)

Banani, Amin. *The Modernization of Iran, 1921–1941*. Stanford: Stanford University Press, 1961.

Bharier, Julian. *Economic Development in Iran 1900–1970*. London, New York, and Toronto: Oxford University Press, 1971.

Floor, Willem. *Industrialization in Iran, 1900–1941*. Durham (England): University of Durham, 1984 (Occasional Papers Series No. 23).

Ghods, M. Reza. *Iran in the Twentieth Century: A Political History*. Boulder: Lynne Reinner Publishers, and London: Adamantine Press Ltd, 1989.

Lenczowski, George. *Russia and the West in Iran, 1918–1948: A Study in Big-Power Rivalry*. Ithaca: Cornell University Press, 1949.

Millspaugh, Arthur. *Americans in Persia*. Washington, DC: The Brookings Institution, 1946.

Wulff, Hans. *The Traditional Crafts of Persia: Their Development, Technology, and Influence on Eastern and Western Civilizations*. Cambridge, MA, and London: MIT Press, 1966.

Chapters in books

Akcan, Esra, "Civilizing Housewives vs. Participatory Users: Margarete Schütte-Lihotzky in the Employ of the Turkish Nation State," in Ruth Oldenziel and Karin Zachmann, eds. *Cold War Kitchen: Americanization, Technology, and European Users*. Cambridge, MA: MIT Press, 2009.

Ayalon, Ami, "The Beginning of Publishing in pre-1948 Palestine," in Philip Sadgrove, ed. *Printing and Publishing in the Middle East*. Oxford: Oxford University Press, 2008 (Journal of Semitic Studies Supplement 15).

—"Inscribing the Public Domain: Arabic Placards, Proclamations and Handbills," in Philip Sadgrove, ed. *Printing and Publishing in the Middle East: Papers from the Second Symposium on the History of Printing and Publishing in the Languages and Countries of the Middle East, Bibliothèque Nationale de France, Paris, 2–4 November 2005*. Oxford: Oxford University Press, 2008 (Journal of Semitic Studies Supplement 24).

Baron, Beth, "Nationalist Iconography: Egypt as a Woman," in James Jankowski and Israel Gershoni, eds. *Rethinking Nationalism in the Arab Middle East*. New York: Columbia University Press, 1997.

Bartz, Inka, "Trouble at Bezalel: Conflicting Visions of Zionism and Art," in Michael Berkowitz, ed. *Nationalism, Zionism and Ethnic Mobilization of the Jews in 1900 and Beyond*. Leiden and Boston: E. J. Brill, 2004.

Cole, Juan R. I., "Printing and Urban Islam in the Mediterranean World, 1890–1920," in Leila Tarazi Fawaz and C. A. Bayley with the collaboration of Robert Ilbert, eds. *Modernity and Culture: From the Mediterranean to the Indian Ocean*. New York: Columbia University Press, 2002.

Dougherty, Roberta L., "Badi'a Masabni, Artiste and Modernist: The Egyptian Print Media's Carnival of National Identity," in Walter Armbrust, ed. *Mass Mediations: New Approaches to Popular Culture in the Middle East and Beyond*. Berkeley: University of California Press, 2000.

Kirshenblatt-Gimblett, Barbara, "Performing the State: The Jewish Palestine Pavilion at the New York World's Fair, 1939/40," in Barbara Kirshenblatt-Gimblett and Jonathan Karp, eds. *The Art of Being Jewish in Modern Times*. Philadelphia: University of Pennsylvania Press, 2007.

Kunda, Sigal David and Robert Oxman, "The Flight of the Camel: The Levant Fair of 1934 and the Creation of a Situated Modernism," in Haim Jacobi, ed. *Constructing a Sense of Place: Architecture and the Zionist Discourse*. Aldershot: Ashgate, 2004.

Olin, Margaret, "Bezalel in Palestine," in Margaret Olin. *The Nation without Art: Examining Modern Discourses on Jewish Art*. Lincoln, NE, and London: University of Nebraska Press, 2001.

Owen, Roger, "Economic Development in Mandatory Palestine; 1918–1948," in George T. Abed, ed. *The Palestinian Economy: Studies in Development under Prolonged Occupation*. London and New York: Routledge, 1988.

Reid, Donald M., "Nationalizing the Pharaonic Past: Egyptology, Imperialism, and Egyptian Nationalism, 1922–1932," in James Jankowski and Israel Gershoni, eds. *Rethinking Nationalism in the Arab Middle East*. New York: Columbia University Press, 1997.

Smitshuijzen AbiFarès, Huda, "Arabic Type as Cultural Identity," in Philip Sadgrove, ed. *Printing and Publishing in the Middle East: Papers from the Second Symposium on the History of Printing and Publishing in the Languages and Countries of the Middle East, Bibliothèque Nationale de France, Paris, 2–4 November 2005*. Oxford: Oxford University Press, 2008 (Journal of Semitic Studies Supplement 24).

Articles

Amin, Camron Michael, "Importing 'Beauty Culture' into Iran in the 1920s and 1930s: Mass Marketing Individualism in an Age of Anti-Imperialist Sacrifice," *Comparative Studies of South Asia, Africa and the Middle East* 24, no. 1 (2004).

Aytürk, Ilker, "Script Charisma in Hebrew and Turkish: A Comparative Framework for Explaining Success and Failure of Romanization," *Journal of World History* 21, no. 1 (March 2010).

Ben-Asher Gitler, Inbal, "C.R. Ashbee's Jerusalem Years: Arts and Crafts, Orientalism and British Regionalism," *Assaph* 5 (2000).

Fuchs, Ron and Gilbert Herbert, "Representing Mandatory Palestine: Austen St. Barbe Harrison and the Representational Buildings of the British Mandate in Palestine, 1922–1937," *Architectural History* 43 (2000).

Gelvin, James L. "Zionism and the Representation of 'Jewish Palestine' at the New York World's Fair," *The International History Review* 22, no. 1 (March 2000).

Graalfs, Gregory, "Gill Sands," *Print* 52, no. 3 (May/June 1998).

Heller, Steven, "Berthold's 1924 Hebrew Type Catalogue: Renaissance Before the Fall," *Baseline* 50 (2006).

Hysler-Rubin, Noah, "Arts & Crafts and the Great City: Charles Robert Ashbee in Jerusalem," *Planning Perspectives* 21 (October 2006).

Messner, Philipp, "Tel Aviv und die Revolution des Hebräischen Schriftbilds," *Pardes: Zeitschrift der Vereinigung für Judische Studien* 15 (2009).

Shechter, Relli, "Reading Advertisements in a Colonial/Development Context: Cigarette Advertising and Identity Politics in Egypt, c. 1919–1939," *Journal of Social History* 39, no. 2 (Winter 2005).

Shiffman, J. "Palestine, The Levant Fair, Tel Aviv," *Town Planning Review* 16, no. 2 (December 1934).

Shilo-Cohen, Nurit, "The 'Hebrew Style' of Bezalel, 1906–1929," *The Journal of Decorative and Propaganda Arts* 20 (1994).

Chapter 33: Colonies: Africa 1900–1945

Introduction

Between 1880 and World War I, a group of European powers consolidated their control over most of Africa. Through military conquest and other means, they instituted a system of colonies, protectorates, and mandates that gave them the right to determine the conditions of life in their new African possessions. Portugal was the first European nation to establish a colony in Africa—Angola—in the 16th century, while Britain and France, the two nations that eventually controlled the largest part of the continent, did not actively begin to claim African territory until the late 19th century.

Some basic rules for dividing the continent were established at the Berlin Conference that the German Chancellor Otto von Bismarck convened in 1884. As a consequence of this meeting, Britain came to possess much of southern Africa, most of the east, and some of the west, while France dominated Sub-Saharan West Africa as well as the Maghreb, which comprised Algeria, Tunisia, and Morocco. Britain occupied Egypt and the Sudan in the early 1880s, but for the purposes of this volume, Egypt has been included in the chapter on the Middle and Near East, due to its closer economic and cultural ties to that region.

Portugal's principal colonies were Angola and Mozambique. Italy conquered portions of north and east Africa that had remained independent until 1936—Eritrea, Libya, Somaliland, and later Ethiopia. Germany claimed several scattered territories in southern Africa, but these were subsequently divided among some of the other colonial powers, following the Germans' defeat in World War I. In 1885, King Leopold of Belgium established the Congo Free State in central Africa as his private preserve, although it became a Belgian colony in 1908. Initially, Liberia was the only territory besides Ethiopia that remained independent. South Africa joined the British Commonwealth as a republic in 1910 following a merger of four separate territories—two British colonies and two former Boer provinces.

Colonialism had mixed consequences. On the one hand, the European powers occupied territories that belonged to Africans and imposed alien political and economic conditions on them. On the other hand, colonial practices resulted in demarcated territorial boundaries that later became the borders of new nation states. As a result of colonial economic policies, a growing number of Africans came to participate in the international market economy, though largely as providers of raw materials or as laborers in foreign enterprises such as mines.

The predominant colonial practice was to import raw materials from Africa and export European manufactured goods in return. As a result, increasing portions of the previous indigenous economies were brought within the orbit of colonial interests. The colonial governments were not inclined to promote manufacturing in Africa, given that the colonies had become markets for European products and sources of raw materials; hence relatively few factories were established during the colonial period.

In Britain, the Colonial Development Act was passed in 1929, but almost none of its funding was directed towards local industries. As late as 1935, the governors of several East African colonies stated at a conference in London that industrialization would be unwise in their colonies as it would jeopardize the production of agricultural products on which Britain depended. Earlier, William Ormsby-Gore, the Colonial Secretary, declared in Parliament that neither the peoples nor the financial conditions in the colonies lent themselves to factory conditions. By 1939, only 2 percent of the cash from the Colonial

Development Fund had been allocated for manufacturing industry. Many French companies that feared competition from indigenous producers also opposed African industrialization.

One consequence of colonialism that affected labor practices positively was the colonial powers' opposition to slavery. The historical process whereby Africans sold slaves internally and to foreign traders did not end immediately with the beginning of colonial occupation, but it did decline over time. The colonial powers, however, adopted coercive labor practices, particularly to meet the needs of large-scale mining and agricultural enterprises and the construction of railroads. They also imposed burdensome taxes on their colonial subjects.

It may be of value to compare the impact of colonialism in Africa with that of the Industrial Revolution in Europe, while recognizing that there were significant differences between the two continents. Both had in common the building of infrastructure, notably, roads, ports, and railroads and the introduction of motorized transport for moving goods. Between the 1870s and the 1930s, thousands of miles of railroad track were laid in Africa. The principal purpose was to ensure the transport of raw materials from remote locations to ports from whence the materials could be shipped to Europe. Consequently the routes favored the development of an export market rather than one that featured internal trade.

Europeans owned and ran the railroads, though some Africans were trained to work as mechanics in the maintenance workshops. Rolling stock was imported from abroad. Cars, trucks, and buses were also brought from overseas, although African entrepreneurs ran a number of the transport services at this scale. Gasoline was provided by foreign oil companies such as Shell, which began to install gas pumps during the late 1920s.

What did not happen in Africa was the growth of a factory system. Since European manufacturers preferred to sell their own goods to African consumers, there was little incentive to create such a system.

Extensive industrialization did occur in the Belgian Congo, due to the generous concessions that King Leopold offered to foreign manufacturers. There and elsewhere, foreign-owned processing plants for palm oil and other products were built, thus enhancing the efficiency of transforming indigenous raw materials into useful commodities.

Unlike Europe, neither an entrepreneurial class nor a widespread middle class emerged as a consequence of the limited manufacturing in Africa. There was no mass consumption, although the opening of mines, the establishment of plantations, and the introduction of other European enterprises did create an incipient working class, but it was not one with much money to spend. Southern Africa is perhaps the only region where an African factory system did lead to mass production and middle-class consumers, but these were all white people since South Africa's and Southern Rhodesia's large black populations remained socially and economically subjugated.

The economist Samir Amin has introduced the term "peripheral capitalism" to characterize the colonial economic system in Africa. He considers it one that had a high degree of integration into the world capitalist market but a low degree of internal development. A major difference from the Industrial Revolution in Europe is that agriculture continued to predominate, given that agricultural products comprised Africa's principal export commodities.

Colonialism did, nonetheless, lead to greater urbanization. At the end of the 19th century most Africans lived in small villages or towns. A limited number inhabited larger communities, some of which had grown from earlier tribal capitals or had become centers of trade or agriculture. This remained the case throughout the 1920s and 1930s, even as economic activity stimulated growth. However, the new urban areas did not grow organically. They housed considerable numbers of European administrators who were in Africa for limited periods, while also providing lodging for large groups of laborers who had left their villages to work in colonial enterprises. In the Belgian Congo and Northern Rhodesia, towns formed around mining businesses and more closely represented the traditional company towns in Europe. In Senegal, on the other hand, Dakar, where about half the total industry of French West Africa was concentrated before 1939, became a center of diverse enterprises and activities, while urban centers elsewhere like Lagos, Accra, Abidjan, Mombasa, and Nairobi grew into small cities that accommodated a greater range of living situations than did the company towns or the *nouvelles villes* in the Maghreb whose primary purpose was to house the families of French administrators and entrepreneurs. By the 1930s, Johannesburg in South Africa had become Africa's largest and most cosmopolitan city, with the exception of Cairo.

East and West Africa: From Craft Production to Manufacturing
The practice of crafts

Craft production was central to the diverse economies that characterized the multitude of tribal cultures in pre-colonial East and West Africa. It continued as well during the colonial period. Many craftsmen created goods primarily for local markets. Working within tight kinship networks, they produced for family members and exchanged crafted household items for necessities with others. In tribal centers, patronage might come from a chief for whom craftsmen would make more elaborate functional or ritual objects. Crafted artifacts were frequently decorated with patterns that were unique to a tribe or region.

In subsistence economies, trade had little impact on the larger economic system but some craftsmen also participated in the trading economy, producing surplus items that could be sold in distant markets located along the various trade routes. Here too the trade between Africans involved articles of everyday use, while European traders by contrast tended to be interested in craft objects that reinforced colonial images of primitive life; hence the lively trade in African masks,

shields, spears, and other ritual items. This was the principal means by which African crafts entered international markets, as there was no European demand for more utilitarian objects such as farm tools, containers, or woven mats, which were the mainstays of many African artisans.

In his book *Black Byzantium*, the anthropologist S. F. Nadel provides a description of how the Nupe people in Nigeria supported craft production in their community as late as the 1940s. Production was divided between the work organized by guilds and that of individual craftsmen. The guilds ranged across a number of different crafts including blacksmithing, brass- and silversmithing, weaving, glassmaking, beadwork, woodwork, and carpentry. Individual crafts included tailoring and embroidery, leatherwork, straw-hat making, indigo dyeing, mat making, and basket weaving. Most craftsmen were located in Bida, the principal Nupe town, but some also worked in surrounding villages. Within the guilds, Nadel distinguished two types of cooperation: that among guild members as a group and that among individuals working together in particular workshops. Family members usually worked under a senior relative who headed the workshop, and training occurred through a lengthy apprentice system.

Production was intended to satisfy the needs of daily life, which also included luxury items. Blacksmiths, for example, made the tools for farming, especially hoes for which they created the iron blades that were attached to wooden handles. When they found themselves with surplus goods, other family members were sent to surrounding towns and villages to try to sell them. Brass smiths made luxury items of adornment but also created a wealth of other objects—sword hilts and daggers, horse-trappings, bowls, jugs, trays, ladles, and various receptacles made of beaten brass and copper. By the early 1940s, the Nupe brass smiths were concentrating on export items, while also creating some pieces specifically for tourists. Individual objects had distinctive shapes and were also decorated with ornamental patterns.

Bida glassmakers, who specialized in bangles and beads, sold their products throughout Nigeria. They had their own market where they bought glass bottles, which they melted down for reuse, and where they sold their finished goods to traders and local consumers. Among other guild craftsman, weavers and beadmakers followed similar patterns. What Nadel demonstrated was that craft activity was embedded in a complex system of production and consumption that involved family members as well as traders and buyers from both neighboring and distant towns.

Besides the guild craftsmen, individual craftspersons were also part of the system. Pottery was largely made by women. In Bida, besides clay pots for cooking and storage, potters made clay lamps and small pitchers that Muslims used for their ablutions. Pots were also produced as components of systems such as the stacks of vessels that men and women used for storing clothing. One technique that some Nupe potters used was considered a secret and was handed down exclusively from mothers to daughters. Other womens' crafts included dyeing and weaving.

What is significant about the structure of Nupe crafts as Nadel described it, is that the actual work was embedded in a social system that involved numerous factors and had specific consequences. First, the standards of quality were shared by the craftsmen and the consumers. When craft producers were solicited to produce for the international market economy, the likelihood of lower standards increased as middlemen demanded volume production without a concomitant concern for quality. This was the case when indigenous craftspersons began to create objects for tourists. Removed from established networks of production and consumption, they started to produce what the anthropologist Nelson Graburn has called "tourist art."

Second, the craftsmen had close family or social ties to local consumers and personal relations with the traders who carried their wares to more distant markets. This reinforced the incentive for quality, while also embedding the objects within powerful systems of social exchange. Third, traditional ways of working were strong and change was resisted. Thus craftspersons were reluctant to modernize their practices to make them more efficient or increase their output, given that work methods were an integral part of their social identity. One exception was the enthusiastic adoption of the sewing machine, especially among young Nupe men. This mechanization of sewing was early evidence for Nadel of the modern industrial system in which the purchase of a sewing machine and its maintenance had to be factored into the cost of production.

Competition with African craftsmen came from the skilled Indians who began emigrating to East Africa, especially Kenya, before the colonial period. They brought with them long family traditions of working in tin, glass, wood, iron, and other materials. As Kenneth King notes, these families introduced an intermediate level of technology between the traditional crafts of the Africans and the mechanized techniques of the large foreign enterprises. They tended to improvise with tools rather than perpetuate codified traditional methods. They also had financial resources that enabled them to purchase necessary equipment and expand their workshops, and they were free to seek advantageous locations for their businesses without the obligation to remain within a kinship network. Consequently, they tended to settle in urban areas, where they could develop clients and markets for their products.

The Indian craftsmen hired Africans as apprentices and over time trained them in the techniques of their crafts. The Africans then set up businesses of their own, sometimes remaining in cities like Nairobi or Mombasa and sometimes returning to their villages. Among the more widespread industries were tinsmithing and blacksmithing. Indians originally made a number of different tin products in their workshops, most of which were intended for their own community. Among these were tin lamps and candle holders.

Despite the continued activity of craftsmen in communities throughout East and West Africa in the

1920s and 1930s, competition from European imports was nonetheless a strong factor in transforming that activity. Commerce with Europe intensified by the 1860s, due in part to the growing number of steamships that traveled back and forth between Britain and African ports. British shipbuilders learned to construct shallow-draught boats whose keels were close to the water line, enabling them to navigate the Niger River and similar waterways. In the late 19th century, British trading firms such as the Royal Niger Company received government charters to engage in import and export activity in West Africa. Eventually large trading companies bought up the smaller ones and by 1930 three major firms dominated West African trade with Europe—the United Africa Company, the Compagnie Française de l'Afrique Occidentale, and the Société Commerciale de l'Ouest Africain.

Their principal role was to distribute European consumer goods to African markets and to ensure that exports from Africa were sold in the industrial countries. They competed with African traders and showed little interest in training Africans in the techniques of modern business management. These companies also owned shares in European firms that provided products such as oil palm casks that Africans might have made themselves.

Adeline Apena notes the growing sophistication and variety of goods imported in Nigeria and describes how local people came to rely more on them, even though many of the imported products could easily have been produced at home had there been sufficient financial, educational, and technical support for the creation of local enterprises. Such products included kitchen utensils, radios, bicycles, and sewing machines. Poor quality was an issue with some imported goods, particularly the cheap cloth produced in British mills.

Imports were distributed through a complicated system that moved goods from middlemen to shopkeepers and petty traders in local markets. Distribution sites varied from a small European-owned department store in Nairobi to shops run mainly by Middle Eastern or Indian immigrants. The Compagnie Française de l'Afrique Occidentale, one of the three large trading companies, had its own network of *factoreries* or trading posts, where it sold imported goods. These posts stocked a wide range of products and aimed to serve the diverse interests of their local clientele. Very few Africans could obtain the credit to manage shops of their own, and most were reduced to selling through small roadside market stands, which were called *tabliers* in French Africa.

One European merchandising enterprise that failed was soap manufacturer William Lever's attempt to establish an equivalent of the British Woolworth stores. Around 1922, Lever opened a store in Lagos, Nigeria, where merchandise was displayed in open trays on counter tops. Prices were fixed and a cashier sat at the exit to take payment for the goods. However, African consumers did not respond favorably and Lever's store closed, unable to compete with the traditional market stalls.

Scholars are divided on the extent to which European-imported goods destroyed traditional crafts. Anthony Hopkins, among others, refutes the assertion that crafts were eliminated in wholesale fashion. He concedes that the proportion of goods supplied by local craft industries declined, but he offers several reasons for the survival of craft practices. First, he notes that it was impractical to import goods from abroad that indigenous craftsmen could more efficiently supply to local markets. One can cite the manufacture of furniture as an example. In fact, the presence of so many foreigners—colonial administrators, entrepreneurs, technical experts, and so forth—helped to create new markets for furniture, even without the decorative styles marketed by European manufacturers. Second, Hopkins points out that some African products were highly valued for their special qualities and competed well against imports of lesser quality. Here, one can mention iron pots, whose durability was greater than the cheaper imported ones. Hopkins also mentions products that established special niches and one can cite as examples the wooden headrests or ceremonial stools that were integral to numerous African tribal cultures. Finally, Hopkins observes that some crafts survived through the adoption of new techniques or equipment such as the sewing machine. He states as well that consumers did not uniformly substitute imported goods for local ones. Instead, they diversified their consumption, combining imports with locally made products. Hence the landscape of African production and consumption during the interwar period was more complicated than it appeared, given the multitude of different villages, towns, and cities where craftsmen worked and consumers traded or shopped.

One craft that did experience a noticeable transformation due to imports was blacksmithing. Traditionally, the production of ironware such as pots and tools involved smelting the iron ore as well as making the artifacts. Both were part of the blacksmith's trade. Smiths constructed blast furnaces, which varied greatly in design. Furnaces differed in size, depending on the amount of ore to be smelted. The furnace heat was controlled by bellows of several types that were made with wooden sticks or frames and goatskins. Smiths would take the molten iron direct from the forge and hammer it into the rough shape of an article. With the import of iron bars and implements, the need for smelting was significantly reduced because blacksmiths used the imported bars or melted down abandoned railroad ties or other types of scrap metal such as old cars.

Blacksmiths also faced stiff competition from imported hoes. Some found new sources of income making spare parts for cars and parts for looms. Kenneth King notes that blacksmiths in Kenya carried on a wide range of activities in the 1920s and 1930s including work in sheet metal. He cites one workshop's shift from making hoes and plows to building bodies for trucks and lorries. By contrast, creating containers of various sorts from the calabash, a type of gourd, was cheap and involved minimal labor; hence these containers more successfully survived the competition from European ceramic and enamel vessels than did the

iron goods of the blacksmiths. Because of their light weight, calabash containers were particularly valued by nomadic tribes. Calabashes of various sizes and shapes could be used for many types of vessels such as bowls, drinking cups, water jugs, and large containers for carrying produce on one's head. Calabash decoration was a distinct profession and calabashes were decorated with geometric motifs that varied from one village to another (Fig. 33.01). Pottery and basketmaking, both enterprises that women practiced, also continued despite competition from abroad.

Like other crafts, boatmaking has a long tradition in East and West Africa and was widely practiced during the 1920s and 1930s. Writing in 1933, Robert Forbes observed native canoes or pirogues everywhere on the rivers and lakes of the region's interior. When a waterway was close to forest country, the canoes were dug out of single logs and transported from the forest to the coast. Elsewhere, they were made from boards that were joined together or constructed from a patchwork of small pieces of wood. Louise Jefferson made a distinction among boatmakers in the Gold Coast between the carpenters who shaped the canoes in the forests and the patternmakers who decorated the boats when they reached the coast.

The boats were propelled with poles in shallow water, and paddles where the water was deeper. Jefferson also described the elaborate ornamentation on boat paddles and fishing spears, particularly the motif of the python, which is a water spirit. While the wooden canoes remained effective for fishermen in the Gold Coast, other types of mechanized boats such as steamboats and barges that the trading companies introduced began to replace the locally crafted vessels, thus contributing to some reduction of the boatbuilding industry. The growing use of the new types of boats demonstrated a need for faster and more efficient river transportation to accommodate the increasing level of economic activity in the region.

Change occurred more slowly in agriculture, where farmers were especially opposed to it. They

Fig. 33.01: Decorated calabash used for milk by Fulani women, Nigeria. Hausaland UIG via Getty Images.

continued to rely on the hoe, resisting the introduction of the plow, which would have required maintaining animals to pull it. Ralph Austen notes that plows proved unsuitable to the terrains of most of West and West Central Africa and East Africa as well. He also points out the problems of incorporating draft animals into the existing system of agriculture and notes that tractors were far too expensive for the typical farmer and would have been particularly difficult to manage since there was no developed infrastructure to provide gasoline, repairs, or spare parts.

The resistance to new methods of cultivation was frustrating to colonial agricultural specialists who did not have the authority to transform the agricultural sectors of their respective colonies. Nonetheless, Austen mentions some modest small-scale tools that were imported from Europe. These include light plows, small hulling devices, hand-operated oil presses, and pesticide sprayers, all specifically designed for African conditions. He states that colonial administrators put considerable effort into introducing these tools to farmers even though they were not readily adopted.

Schools for craftsmen

Apprenticeship training in the craft traditions of village economies as well as the improvised enterprises that grew out of urban migration can be contrasted with the efforts to train craftsmen that began with the Christian missionaries in the 19th century and were continued by the colonial governments thereafter. In the 1850s, a Catholic order, the Fathers of the Holy Spirit, taught crafts to a small group of students in Dakar, and in the early 20th century the French government, as part of its civilizing mission, established a technical school in that city, the École Pinet-Laprade, where students were to learn manual trades. Like Senegal, Gabon relied initially on Catholic missionaries, the Holy Ghost Fathers, to train carpenters, woodworkers, blacksmiths, masons, and farmers. In the Belgian Congo, Jesuit missionaries taught the native children carpentry, building, and other trades, notably those that would be useful to maintain the facilities of the mission itself.

The Basel Mission in the Gold Coast instructed African children in many branches of industry and opened several industrial establishments that provided work for joiners, wheelwrights, blacksmiths, and workers trained in other mechanical arts. The point of all these early missionary programs was not to foster industrial development but to further the aims of the missions themselves, either by providing employment for the young Christians who were no longer integral to tribal economies or else training workers for the maintenance and development of mission enterprises.

French and British educational policies as they related to craft education served colonial needs just as the Christian schools served the aims of the various denominations that sponsored them. Since France and Britain had little interest in the industrial development of their colonies, there was no need to prepare young Africans for careers in advanced technological fields like engineering or industrial management. It was preferable that they worked at lower level positions either as clerks in the colonial administrative apparatus; mechanics who helped maintain the railroads, imported vehicles, and the few industrial plants that existed; or else were able to work in the construction industry as carpenters, builders, furniture makers, and metalworkers. There was a need as well for other maintenance functions such as the repair of bicycles and imported appliances.

British government schools in Nigeria trained students to make furniture, office fittings, shoes, and some tools. Bookbinding was taught as well. In rural areas, artisans and mechanics were employed in workshops run by the government that included the railroads, public works offices, and printing departments. Africans also became skilled in handling mechanical equipment and eventually replaced many European workers. France, for the most part, left the development of technical education to the administrators of particular colonies. At Bamako in French Sudan, the government opened the Maison Artisanat, a training center for local craftsmen, in the early 1930s.

Government education programs followed conventional practices and for the most part broke no new ground in preparing Africans for work in the crafts and mechanical arts. Two exceptions were Makerere College, which was founded in Uganda in 1921, originally to train carpenters and mechanics, and Achimota College, founded by Dr. Kwegyir Aggrey and Rev. A. G. Fraser in the Gold Coast, near Accra, in 1924 with the support of the then governor-general of the colony, Sir Frederick Gordon Guggisberg.

Shortly after its establishment, Makerere College expanded to include courses in other fields and in 1939 an Art School was opened there. Its principal instructor was Margaret Trowell (d.o.b. unconfirmed–1984), a British London-trained art teacher who went to Kenya in 1929 with her husband, a doctor, and came to Uganda in 1935. Inspired by such thinkers as the Arts and Crafts architect William Lethaby, she forged a philosophy of art that emphasized its continuity in all aspects of daily life and she espoused the belief that art must arise from within the individual rather than from copying outside models.

In 1937, Trowell published an important book, *African Arts and Crafts: Their Development in the School,* in which she provided guidelines for teaching art to African students. Besides the study of painting and printing, she emphasized the crafts, which she believed displayed a strong sense of design. Trowell recommended that local practitioners teach the crafts according to the apprentice system so that, in her words, the village spirit would be kept alive. This radical proposal strongly countered the British policy of sending art experts from the metropole to train the natives in European techniques.

Trowell put some of her ideas into practice in an experimental art class she began to teach at Makerere College around 1937, and then developed them further after she started teaching in Makerere's newly founded School of Art in 1939. Her influence grew after World War II as she continued to teach in Makerere's expanded art program and published a number of books on African crafts.

Achimota College, which commenced instruction in 1927, three years after it's founding, was a school for the Gold Coast's African elite. Its aim was to instill Western intellectual attitudes in its students, while also urging them to preserve their own traditions. Funded by the colonial government and staffed extensively with British teachers, Achimota also combined qualities of the traditional Christian mission schools. African culture was taught within the curriculum and also introduced through extracurricular activities that gave it a value but only as it made sense within the colonial agenda.

African craftsmen taught students to carve swords, ceremonial stools, soup ladles, and other objects that were traditionally part of everyday life, but in the Achimota context were removed from situations of practical use and recognized simply as signs of Africanness. Other craft courses included weaving, bookbinding, metalwork, and silversmithing.

Initially, these courses supplemented the academic curriculum, but this changed in 1937 when H. V. Meyerowitz (1900–1945) was hired as arts and crafts supervisor. Meyerowitz, a German who had studied woodcarving at the Berlin Applied Arts School, created a new Arts and Crafts Department where he worked to replace the Western-style art classes with courses based on local skills and traditional techniques.

Meyerowitz was also interested in developing enterprises based on craft skills. Shortly after his arrival he conceived a plan for an Institute of West African Arts, Industries, and Social Sciences, which was to combine traditional craft skills with modern technology to create small-scale enterprises. Among the activities considered for the Institute were printing, carpentry, metalwork, glass manufacture, and the use of forest products.

Before it received its initial funding from the Gold Coast government in 1943, Meyerowitz took a number of steps to get it started. Shortly after he arrived he hired the British potter Harry Davis (1910–1986), who had worked with the Japanese-inspired Bernard Leach in England. Part of Davis's mandate was to research the possibilities of manufacturing various ceramic products. By the time he returned to England in 1942, Davis, with the help of apprentices, had built up enterprises for making bricks, tiles, glazed pottery, and ceramic water coolers. The tiles replaced makeshift corrugated iron as a roofing material, while the water coolers competed successfully against those imported from Germany. Davis was followed by another British potter, Michael Cardew (1901–1983), who expanded the pottery's output to include glazed ceramic bowls to collect latex that the Nigerian rubber industry had ordered, as well as electric insulators and terracotta pots for one of the Gold Coast's Cocoa Research Stations. By the end of World War II, however, the institute had suffered considerable losses, resulting in the closure of the pottery. The institute itself was closed down in 1945, due largely to the suicide of Meyerowitz, who had been its most ardent champion.

Manufacturing efforts

The attempt to create local craft enterprises at Achimota College was part of a larger effort, though not widespread, to start indigenous businesses that were independent of colonial support. A few Indian businessmen in East Africa such as Allidina Visram (1863–1916) became successful entrepreneurs, beginning in the first years of the 20th century. Visram opened a number of shops to provide meals and other necessities to the builders of the Uganda Railway, which linked Kenya to Uganda. Beginning in Kenya, he extended his entrepreneurial interests to numerous cities and towns in Uganda, opening many shops and starting other businesses such as a leather tannery, sawmills, cotton ginneries, a soap factory, and furniture workshops. While none of these enterprises produced objects that were distinctive, they did provide opportunities for workers to gain experience with mechanized production and machine repairs and for craftsmen to make products for local consumers.

In Nigeria, economic difficulties caused by World War I induced the British to create a few factories to produce goods that were otherwise difficult to import. One example was the sawmills that turned logs into cheap lumber, which was used for furniture. A carpentry workshop was established in Lagos to make furniture for all the government offices and a number of other carpentry shops, fitted with imported power-driven machinery, used local lumber to produce wooden casks, doors, window frames, and furniture, all of which were previously shipped to Nigeria from Britain.

The Nigerian textile industry also flourished, producing durable hand-made cotton Kano cloth that was woven either with plain white or colored threads. The quality was high and many European expatriates bought it for tropical suits, riding breeches, and women's dresses. As an export, Nigerian cloth would have competed favorably in Britain with cloth made there, which was one reason why the colonial government did not support its manufacture as an industrial enterprise.

In 1912, W. Essuman Gwira (dates unconfirmed), an employee in the Government Agricultural Service in the Gold Coast, as Ghana was then known, invented a machine for small-scale palm oil processing. Cheap, easily manufactured, and simple to operate, it could have enabled more Africans to become involved in this enterprise. The Aborigines' Rights Protection Society, which was established in 1897 to press for the interests of Gold Coast natives, pressured the British government to invest in refining the machine for African use. The government refused, instead supporting processing concessions to the Lever Brothers, based on the claim that the local people were not yet capable of processing the oil themselves.

Threatened by more efficient palm-oil production in the Belgian Congo and Southeast Asia, the British government began to experiment with mechanizing its extraction. After 1922, various types of hand presses were investigated and the government eventually settled on the Duchscher press that was made by a firm in Luxembourg. Recognized for its low cost and large capacity, it was deemed superior to competing British brands. However, the number of presses in use, never more than several hundred, was not significant, considering the large number of palm-oil producers. Consequently the Duchscher press had only a modest effect on improving the output of the palm-oil industry.

Since the British government refused to fund the development of Gwira's invention, there is no way to know whether it would have competed successfully with the Duchscher press or perhaps surpassed its sales. As a locally designed and produced device, it would have demonstrated the ability of Africans to create new machines and might well have spurred related inventions that could have resulted in cheaper products and provided new entrepreneurial opportunities for Africans that would otherwise not have existed.

In Nigeria, the United Africa Company, which controlled more than 40 percent of the colony's export-import trade after 1929, commissioned its Engineering Department to create an inexpensive hand press. In 1939, the department produced the Miller Hand Press,

based on the principle of an old cylinder press. Given the government's concern that the impending war might cut off its supply of Duchscher presses, it adopted the Miller Hand Press. Further research by the UAC's Engineering Department led to a larger extracting machine that was known as the Pioneer Oil Mill. It was intended as an intermediary between the hand processes and the highly mechanized machines adopted by large companies like Lever.

Though a number of these motor-driven mills eventually came into use, their initial trial posed a number of problems. First, the oil extraction technique involved the loss of the palm kernels whose processing at least in Nigeria had always been the work of women. Hence, it cut women out of the process. The need to locate the mills near dense clusters of palm trees also placed them at a distance from many small producers. Motor transport was not available, nor could most producers afford bicycles. Thus trekking and head portage remained their only option. Operating the mills also required a high degree of technical skill, which none of the producers possessed.

It was not until after World War II that a small number of the mills were set up. Initially there was strong opposition to them, but a considerable number were in use by 1960. As Susan Martin notes, however, the mills created new jobs but significantly reduced the number of those who participated in the Nigerian palm oil trade as farmers and processors. Furthermore, the mills were dogged by the same problems as their predecessors: operating inefficiency, the high cost of spare parts, and a lack of skilled personnel to run and maintain them. In the end, they served to undermine smallholder participation in the palm oil industry.

The introduction of mills and other mechanized processing plants created opportunities for some craftsmen who migrated to centers where the mills and plants were located. There was work as well for mechanics to support the growing number of imported cars and buses and to repair the even larger number of imported bicycles. Old cars, broken machines, and other industrial waste also created opportunities for craftsmen to invent new forms of bricolage to make useful objects out of scrap materials.

Despite the French and British governments' reluctance to support indigenous manufacturing enterprises in East or West Africa, calls for economic development became part of the African rhetoric of political freedom. Given the difficulty of obtaining funds from banks in Africa, some would-be entrepreneurs looked to Americans, both black and white, for financial support, A number of African leaders, especially in British East and West Africa, were drawn to the ideas of Marcus Garvey, a Jamaican who had moved to New York in 1917 and founded the first American branch of his Universal Negro Improvement Association. The core of Garvey's argument was that racial greatness was predicated on starting enterprises, fostering trade, and becoming what he called a commercial and industrial people. He admired Booker T. Washington, who had founded the Tuskegee Institute in Alabama to teach artisanal and mechanical trades to young blacks. However, Garvey went farther than Washington, emphasizing entrepreneurship instead, which he believed was the path to black independence.

Garvey inaugurated a shipping enterprise, the Black Star Line, to move people and goods between the United States and Africa. He managed to acquire several ships but because of poor business practices the enterprise failed. Among other businesses he started were the Universal Printing House, the Negro Factories Corporation, and *Negro World*, his successful newspaper. The Negro Factories Corporation aimed to build factories in major American cities, provide jobs for African-Americans, and manufacture goods for an exclusive black consumer market. It did manage to run several successful businesses for a brief period but, like the Black Star Line, poor management and unrealistic goals brought about its demise. One African who sought to follow Garvey's example was Chief Alfred C. Sam (c. 1881–c. 1930s), a Gold Coast resident, who went to Oklahoma in 1913 to sell stock in his Akim

Trading Company. Sam, like Garvey, purchased a ship, purportedly to transport American blacks to Africa, but, similar to Garvey, his enterprise was plagued by problems and it failed.

At the first session of the National Congress of British West Africa, which met in the Gold Coast in 1920, a call for economic self-determination was initiated. A British West African Co-operative Association was proposed, and banks and shipping facilities were promoted, as were the establishment of Cooperative Stores and buying centers. The man most responsible for attempting to move the congress program forward was Winifried Tete-Ansa (1889–1941), a businessman who was instrumental in founding several enterprises including a bank, the West African Cooperative Producers, and a corporation in the United States to buy cocoa and export manufactured goods to Africa that could be sold at affordable prices. These enterprises along with others such as the Nigeria Mercantile Bank, of which Crispin Adeniyi-Jones (1876–1957) was the president, were part of a program to improve opportunities for Africans in the British colonies. Though none of them achieved lasting success, they were significant as the inspiration for later ventures.

Other African leaders who called for economic liberation included J. B. Danquah (1895–1965), a lawyer and newspaper editor in the Gold Coast, who published a pamphlet in 1943 called *Self-Help and Expansion* in which he strongly argued that Africans in the Gold Coast had to manufacture and buy their own goods. "We must industrialise our country," he claimed, which for him also meant taking over the importing and selling of foreign products. Danquah called for cooperative societies of producers and consumers in order to keep the profits from commercial activities from going abroad.

Danquah, Tete-Ansa, Adeniyi-Jones, and other strong advocates for African economic independence had large ambitions but lacked sufficient capital and expertise to realize them. Their strategy to organize cooperatives made sense in that shared resources might have provided more leverage for small producers on the one hand and offered capital for new enterprises on the other. As in other parts of the developing world in the interwar period, import substitution was slow to develop, even slower in Africa because of a shortage of investment capital. Thus early indigenous enterprises such as small palm oil processing plants and factories that produced foodstuffs, beer and soft drinks, cigarettes, shoes, clothing, and furniture were mostly owned by Europeans. Technological products like radios, electrical appliances, and automobiles were imported until well after World War II and some until the present.

French North Africa: Crafts and Commerce

In 1830, France occupied Algeria, a former province of the Ottoman Empire, followed by Tunisia, which had the same status. Tunisia became a French protectorate in 1881 as did Morocco in 1912. Unlike Britain, which fostered a policy of considerable autonomy for its colonies, France sought to align its colonial subjects with French values, assigning them set places within the hierarchy of the colonial empire.

Whereas Britain did not place a high priority on the development of the crafts in its East and West African colonies, French colonial administrators valued craft production, although they were intent on wresting it from the autonomous control of the local guild systems and integrating it into a program of training and production that was guided explicitly by French interests.

In Algeria and Morocco, as Roger Benjamin and Hamid Irbouh have shown, early craft policies were prominent in the larger strategies of colonial governance. In 1900, Charles-Celéstin Jonnart assumed the post of Governor-General in Algeria. He developed a plan for the craft industries, which exemplified his concern for preserving Algeria's native heritage. Shortly after he took office, Jonnart commissioned Marius

Vachon (1850–1928), a specialist in decorative arts reform, to survey the arts industries in Algeria. Vachon returned a positive assessment, countering those who predicted the demise of local handicrafts due to mechanization and competition from foreign products such as the counterfeit metalwork from Germany and the contraband carpets smuggled into Algeria from Tunisia and Morocco.

Jonnart also commissioned a second inquiry into the native arts from Arsène Alexandre (1859–1937), a prominent Parisian art critic who reinforced the importance of strengthening local handicrafts. However, Alexandre thought that traditional apprenticeships were less effective than academic instruction in drawing, a practice that would pull craft training out of its indigenous locations in the workshops of the Arab medinas and relocate it to schools where students would be taught with French methods of instruction.

Jonnart sponsored a team to collect pattern books for carpets and embroidery and traditional recipes for textile dyes. The intent was to distribute these to various workshop schools for young boys and girls, where they would serve as the basis for new creations. In 1908, Jonnart established an Office of Indigenous Arts, and Prosper Ricard (1874–1952), an expert on North African architecture and decorative arts, was hired to run the office's Cabinet de Dessin. Its task was to document with photographs and drawings traditional craftwork from around Algeria, especially architectural details and quality handicrafts. The documentation was then distributed to workshops whose students were instructed in ways to produce decorative art based on the models they were shown.

Jonnart also initiated vocational craft schools where student apprentices worked with master craftsmen. In 1924, the government inaugurated the Oeuvre d'Artisinat, which helped indigenous craftsmen throughout Algeria to become self-employed.

Following the Algerian example, French officials in Tunisia also launched a number of vocational schools for women. Early schools revived a dying tradition of local embroidery. As in Algeria and later in Morocco, Prosper Ricard served as an advisor to the government. In 1914, the government founded an Institute of Arts and Crafts in order to modernize the craft industries, and in 1929 it created a fund to financially assist local craft cooperatives.

Jonnart's attempts to preserve the decorative arts in Algeria by codifying models for students to copy served as a precedent for Louis-Hubert Lyautey, who was Governor-General of Morocco from 1912 to 1925. Lyautey, similar to Jonnart, believed in preserving the traditional native crafts. He also adhered, as Jonnart did, to the associationist theory of colonial rule, whereby local "subjects" were encouraged to maintain their own way of life within a French administrative structure but without the privilege of attaining the full rights of French citizenship. Hence, Lyautey supported the preservation of Moroccan crafts, but sought to integrate them into a French system of production that would ensure a steady stream of craft goods that could be sold abroad.

As did Jonnart, Lyautey also commissioned a report on the traditional arts. One conclusion of the report was that Moroccan craftsmen had experienced declining levels of production due to competition from European imports, many of which were of cheaper quality such as the machine-made carpets from Britain. With the aim of opening the Moroccan market to French products and absorbing Moroccan industries into the French economic system, Lyautey organized the Casablanca Franco-Moroccan Fair in 1915. The fair presented products of local industries in separate pavilions that represented the medinas in different regions. The artifacts on display included carpets and blankets, inlaid wood, sculpted and painted wooden furniture, and silver jewelry. An exhibition of drawings by Moroccan children convinced the French authorities that they could establish schools to teach young people to become high quality craftsmen.

With the aim of developing products for foreign markets, the French government set up offices in Rabat and Fez to improve the quality of different indigenous crafts. Under the guidance of Prosper Ricard, museums were established in several cities to display replicas of older objects. Government craft inspectors commissioned works from the best artisans and also set up state workshops, where expert craftsmen were given salaries and were provided with materials. Inspectors also sought out examples of the best older carpets that could serve as models for future production. This proved to be an effective strategy, which resulted in carpets that were much admired at several exhibitions in Paris.

Prosper Ricard supervised the production of a massive catalog of Moroccan rugs, which was published as a set of four volumes between 1923 and 1934. Roger Benjamin notes that the books were intended to promote a high quality of carpet production within limits that conformed to French industrial policy for the colonies. He states that the reorganization of the carpet industry boosted sales but marginalized the more quirky rugs of irregular design, which could not obtain the official government seal to qualify them for export.

In 1918, as Hamid Irbouh writes, Lyautey established an Office of Native Craft Industry, which was intended to centralize all activities related to the production of Moroccan crafts for sale abroad. Ricard and a team of assistants traveled throughout Morocco encouraging artisans to participate in the renovation of their industries by urging them to copy examples that had been judged most appropriate for commercialization. The Office of Native Crafts also created workshops and exhibited the results in local galleries.

In the early 1920s, the French administration created the Casablanca School of Fine Arts to train Moroccan high school graduates for careers in the applied arts. Courses were dictated by the construction needs for the *villes nouvelles* (new towns) that were being built for French and European settlers. Consequently, while European students studied fine art in preparation for taking the exam for the École de Beaux Arts in Paris, the Moroccans were channeled into craft courses, where they were trained in carpentry, metalsmithing, and masonry. They were taught to assist French architects as draftsmen and to build architectural models. Some students also prepared to become commercial artists.

By 1930, the French had established 14 vocational schools in Morocco. Ten emphasized metalworking and woodworking, both of which had a direct relation to European industries. The other four, located in major craft centers, concentrated on cabinetmaking, maroquinery (the creation of leather goods for tourists), and ceramics. The intent of the schools was to prepare students to earn a decent living, which, as one critic has pointed out, would ensure that they did not become discontented subjects or rebels. Officials in Morocco defended the vocational schools as meeting the immediate needs of the students, as opposed to a more theoretical education that would, as they claimed, be of no value to them. Graduates were encouraged to join existing Moroccan workshops or small or medium-sized French industries, thus diffusing them into a variety of different work settings. This contrasted with an earlier policy in Tunisia whereby a Central Cooperative of Crafts and Trades grouped vocational school graduates into cooperatives, a practice that was later viewed as a mistake because it increased the craftsmen's political power.

After Lyautey left Morocco in 1925, the government programs he had put in place continued but without the vision of such a strong advocate. Though a small number of craftsmen prospered as a result of Lyautey's reforms, the international financial crisis of 1929, along with competition from cheap Japanese mass-produced goods and a shrinking domestic market, which had absorbed most of the craft production, contributed to the difficulties of the craft industries as a whole.

Encouraged by the success that Moroccan crafts achieved at the 1931 Colonial Exhibition in Paris, a Craft Committee met to seek ways of strengthening these industries. Through bank loans and the identification of new markets abroad, some industries benefited significantly as they exported to a growing number of countries. One strategy the committee adopted was to direct craftsmen from older industries like saddlemaking, for which there was a declining internal market, to newer industries that could employ similar skills such as the production of leather wallets, belts, and handbags for tourists. World War II created a further demand for new products, notably army supplies for French and Moroccan troops, including uniforms, shoes, belts, and rifle slings.

Although the French government provided considerable support for the crafts in Morocco, its ultimate aim was to integrate them into export markets by ensuring that craftsmen produced what foreign consumers were willing buy. To do so, they urged craftsmen to copy exemplars they selected, thus ignoring their identities as artists who might generate something original, and reinventing their work as skilled labor whose output was defined by anticipation of market success.

Italian North Africa: Colonizers and Colonized

Striving to compete with other European powers in the scramble for African colonies in the late 19th century, Italy invaded Eritrea, which became an Italian colony in 1890. Occupying Eritrea was the first of a succession of Italian forays into North Africa. It was followed by the invasion of Somalia in 1905, the occupation of Tripolitania and Cyrenaica in 1911, and after the Fascists came to power in 1922, the invasion of Ethiopia in 1935. A year later, Mussolini united these colonies in a short-lived empire, Africa Orientale Italiana (Italian East Africa), which only lasted until 1941, when it collapsed following the British invasion. From the time of Victor Emanuel II, following the occupation of Eritrea, Italy sent thousands of its own citizens to the colonies, where they were encouraged to build a better life than they had at home. Most engaged in farming.

Beginning in the 1890s, Italian architects designed signature buildings to house colonial offices, hotels, markets, banks, and theaters. In the Eritrean town of Asmara and in Tripolitania, the 1930s saw a spate of Art Deco and other modernist buildings that were intended to distinguish the colonizer's European aesthetic from the Moorish or indigenous building styles of the local populations. Mussolini selected Addis Ababa in Ethiopia as the capital city of the new Italian colonial empire. Though the plan for the city was never fully realized, it accentuated sharp differences between the Europeans, whose section featured monumental official buildings and comfortable homes, and the native Ethiopians, whose dwellings for the most part were comprised of concrete huts.

The emphatic distinction between colonizer and colonized was evident in the design of the Tripoli Trade Fair, which was held annually between 1927 and 1939. The fair arose from the ambitious program of economic development in Tripolitania and Cyrenaica that Giuseppe Volpi launched during his tenure as governor between 1921 and 1925. The fair had a significant propaganda function, which was evident in its layout, the design of its pavilions, and in the graphic

material that accompanied it. For Italians at home and for foreign audiences, the fair, as Brian McLaren notes, was intended to demonstrate Italy's potential as a colonial power. The aim was to increase trade between Italian and indigenous colonial industries, fostering the development of the indigenous industries, while creating a market for Italian goods.

The layout of the first fair followed the precedent of the annual trade fair in Milan. Displays of Italian products were organized by industry and also by region. The most prominent pavilion represented the city of Rome (Fig. 33.02). Designed by the architect Felice Nori (dates unconfirmed), it served as the symbolic entrance to the exhibition. The two huge sculptures of reclining figures that flanked the entryway conveyed a sense of *Romanità*, or Romanness. The return to the grandeur of Rome was central to Mussolini's Fascist propaganda and was extended to the colonies as well, notably in the heavy emphasis on the earlier Roman occupation of North Africa.

The first Tripoli Trade Fair emphasized Italian products, but by 1930 the fair was being billed as the

Fig. 33.02: Felice Nori, Tripoli Trade Fair, Roman pavilion, 1927. © 2006 Alinari/TopFoto.

Fig. 33.03: Fiera di Tripoli, poster, 1930. CPA Media Co. Ltd./Pictures From History.

"Great International Exhibition in Africa" (Fig. 33.03). Participation was expanded to include African colonies, protectorates, and mandates, along with South Africa. Several European countries that were interested in increasing their African trade, particularly Belgium and France, exhibited there as well. Smaller local trade fairs had been held previously in French North Africa, but the Tripoli fair was the first in Africa to claim continental participation. The Centennial Exhibition in Johannesburg followed it in 1936.

One of Giuseppe Volpi's initiatives to expand local industry, which consisted primarily of agriculture, was the establishment of the Ufficio Governativo delle Arte Applicate Indigene (Government Office of Indigenous Applied Arts) to strengthen local applied arts, notably jewelry making, metalworking, and carpet weaving. At the first of the Tripoli Trade Fairs in 1927, local crafts were presented in a Colonial Village, where products from the various regions of Tripolitania were shown. The emphasis on native crafts as emblematic of "authentic" life in Tripolitania became a leitmotiv in the expansion of tourism from the late 1920s through the 1930s.

In developing their policies towards the indigenous crafts, the Italians followed the precedents of the French in North Africa. They recognized the value of keeping the local population active with low-level jobs that were labor-intensive; not only for the sake of the economy but also to avoid the rebellious factions that were more likely to arise from more advanced education.

The Government Office of Indigenous Applied Arts organized exhibitions and displays, especially at the annual Tripoli Trade Fairs. The 1936 fair featured a Pavilion of Libyan Artistry (Tripolitania and Cyrenaica had joined together in 1935 to form the colony of Libya). There were also craft pavilions at Italian trade fairs in cities such as Milan and Naples. At the Turin International Exhibition of 1928, the government organized the Tripoli Village, which featured an indigenous market where vendors sold their craft products as they might at home.

In 1929, the Government Office of Indigenous Applied Arts became the School of Arts and Crafts, which was to increase its involvement in applied arts instruction along with promotional activities. Following the examples of Jonnart in Algeria and Lyautey in Morocco, Marshal Pietro Badoglio, then Governor-General of Tripolitania and Cyrenaica, commissioned a study of indigenous arts. When published in 1932, it described decay in the applied arts due partially to insufficient government intervention. As a result of the report, Badoglio increased his efforts to improve the local industries, an initiative that was to be continued under Italo Balbo, the flying ace, after he became Governor-General of Tripolitania and Cyrenaica when Badoglio left in 1933.

In 1935, Balbo created the Muslim School of Indigenous Arts and Crafts, which had a separate women's section where young girls were trained in various decorative arts. Among its projects, the school produced tiles for the Artisanal Quarter in Tripoli's Suq al-Mushir, which Balbo had set up to create an "authentic" experience for the hundreds of tourists whom the Libyan Tourism and Hotel Association was wooing to Libya from Italy. The Muslim School of Indigenous Arts and Crafts was also part of a larger effort to restructure Libyan craft production according to a Fascist corporatist model whereby the colonial government could control the labor force by requiring permits for each company and a license for each worker.

More important than the role of indigenous craftsmen in providing for the daily needs of the local population, was their role as exemplars of "authentic" native culture. To this end, the government supported the Muslim School of Indigenous Arts and Crafts, sponsored exhibitions and pavilions at trade fairs, and created shops in tourist venues like the Suq al-Mushir and in the network of hotels that the Libyan Tourism and Hotel Association constructed throughout the colony. The Tourism and Hotel Association also sold indigenous crafts at shops in Italy, where they served as evidence of the exotic culture that awaited tourists in Libya.

The characterization of indigenous crafts as emblematic of the native culture was sharply contrasted with the modern architecture and design that were intended to signify the Italian colonial presence in the colonies. The main proponent of the discourse on colonial modernity was Carlo Enrico Rava (1903–1986), a founding member of the group of young Rationalist architects, Gruppo Sette, that formed in 1927. In his early writing on colonial architecture, Rava, whose father was a colonial administrator, espoused a Mediterranean architectural aesthetic that was essentially modern but which appropriated compatible elements from the local building traditions. He sought to define a style of sophisticated colonial living that reinforced the difference between the Italian colonizers and the local denizens.

Rava's proposals for design for the colonies were on display at the 7th Triennale of architecture and design, held in Milan in 1940. For that event, Rava organized an Exhibition of Colonial Equipment in which he showed a wide range of prototypes that he and a group of architectural colleagues including Luigi Piccinato (1899–1983) and Giovanni Pellegrini (dates unconfirmed)—author of a 1936 "Manifesto of Colonial Architecture"—created for the Triennale. These were manufactured mainly by Italian firms, although some were produced by Libyan craftsman, following designs of the Italian architects. The potential users of these objects were not the poorer Italians who were encouraged to go to the colonies to farm but rather administrators and businessmen of a higher class.

Rava divided the objects on display into categories that included furniture, household goods, and equipment for traveling. The exhibit was an experiment on several counts. First was the design of new object typologies for colonial conditions. These included a camping bed with a mosquito net, hammocks with lightweight metal frames, and small leather folding seats, all designed for a life of "nomadism," which Rava saw as characteristic of the colonial experience. Second was the attention to materials. Furniture ranged from wicker designs and metal pieces for offices to experimental pieces in plastic that Rava wanted to test in new climatic conditions. Central to this category was a bedroom set that could be dismantled and shipped or stored in specially designed containers. Made of chipboard, it could be assembled without the use of nails, screws, or tools.

Rava supported a revival of the crafts but was opposed to the perpetuation of folkloric motifs that were exemplary of traditional Libyan culture. Instead, he displayed woven fabrics, ceramic dinner services, and numerous rugs, all designed by his colleagues and made by Libyan craftsmen. As in his program for colonial architecture, Rava espoused a *mediterraneanità*—a quality that combined traces of Mediterranean culture, particularly as the conquering Romans had shaped it earlier with a strong modern sensibility. Had the Fascists' North African empire not collapsed in 1941, some of the objects on display in Rava's pavilion might have gone into production. Instead, his ambitious attempt to design a good life for Italian colonials was undermined by the reality of Italy's inability to defend its territory against the Allied invasion of North Africa.

Southern Africa

Both South Africa and Southern Rhodesia created successful manufacturing cultures in the period between 1900 and World War II. South Africa achieved national independence in 1910, while Southern Rhodesia became a self-governing British colony in 1923. For both, the autonomy to develop as they chose and the large number of skilled European settlers were major factors in their development. Southern Africa was strictly segregated and blacks were severely constrained from entrepreneurial activity. In 1912, the South African Native National Congress (SANNC)—which became the African National Congress in 1923—was founded to combat racism and represent the interests of blacks. Though unable to reverse the laws that enabled whites to maintain economic superiority, it remained a point of resistance to white power.

The first president of the SANNC, John Langalibalele Dube (1871–1946), a Zulu who had become a Christian, was also the founder of the Zulu Christian Industrial School, later renamed the Ohlange Institute, in 1901. Ten years earlier, Dube had written a short book, *A Talk Upon My Native Land*, in which he promoted agricultural and industrial reforms for his fellow indigenous Africans. He subsequently made several trips to the United States, where he encountered Booker T. Washington's philosophy of black

self-sufficiency. The Zulu Christian Industrial School was modeled on Washington's Tuskegee Institute. Among the trades taught there were shoemaking, dressmaking, carpentry, motor mechanics, agriculture, and journalism. With its combination of manual training and academic courses, Dube's school pushed the boundaries of the white government's resistance to advanced education for black Africans.

Though much of the tribal life in South Africa was destroyed by the white settlers' occupation and their creation of an industrial culture, pockets did continue, notably among the Zulu, whose craft traditions enabled them to provide for all their daily life needs from the thatched beehive huts to woven sleeping mats, baskets, and spoon bags. Woodcarvers made utensils, low stools that served for sitting or head rests at night, and bowls of various kinds. Potters, a job reserved for women, built up their pots from thin coils of clay, eschewing the potter's wheel. Traditional decorations on the pottery featured linear patterns with small clay pellets known as *amasumpa* attached to the surface of some objects. Zulu beadwork involved elaborate social codes conveyed through patterns of beads woven into objects of adornment.

As in other parts of Africa, South African education specialists encouraged African craft students to adopt Western motifs. The so-called modern tribal artists were a product of the Native Training Schools, which became increasingly controversial as liberal educators argued against the value of handicraft training in an industrial culture and the reduction or denial of training in more academic subjects. The hybrid objects produced in the training schools were rarely displayed at international exhibitions, however, as the preference was for traditional crafts that became the new tourist souvenirs and helped perpetuate a myth of South Africa's primitive past that was successfully overcome by the introduction of Western ways. This myth was reinforced by the Color Bar Act of 1926, which prevented Africans from entering the skilled trades to compete with white workers.

Beginning in the early 18th century, craftsmen in Cape Town had developed distinctive styles of wooden furniture based on a sober aesthetic that resonated with the Calvinist past of many Dutch settlers. The furniture was without appended ornament although otherwise plain chairs, tables, and desks had legs with varied shapes. Chairs and benches might have wooden, cane, or upholstered seating, with cane being widely used. Though some chairs had backs that were cut in decorative patterns, others were as plain as the furniture of the Shakers. Cupboards and chests tended to be massive, with occasional simple inlay.

Nineteenth-century Cape metalsmiths made a variety of functional objects of brass, iron, and copper. These included coffee urns and coffee pots, chafing dishes, jugs, boiling pots, mugs, and laundry irons. Particularly distinctive were the coffee urns, which varied in shape and decoration. Handles could be

Fig. 33.04: Covered wagon, Great Trek, South Africa. © Mary Evans Picture Library/Alamy.

In the 19th century, the discovery of gold and diamonds helped to generate sufficient wealth to create a white consumer class that could support a lifestyle equivalent to that of middle-class Europeans. South Africa had a particular incentive to manufacture its own goods where possible. It was far from Europe, and imports tended to be expensive. Among the first industries were food processing, clothing, furniture, boatbuilding, tanning, construction, building materials, and wagon making. The ox-drawn wagon, built of different kinds of wood with iron-covered wheel rims, was associated with the Great Trek that the Boers made from the Cape Colony to the interior beginning in 1835. The driver sat on an open wooden seat behind which was a load-carrying area with a canvas cover draped over wooden arches (Fig. 33.04).

Fig. 33.05: Thomas Christopher Falck, coffee urn. Stephan Welz & Company (Pty) Limited.

ornate, as on the coffee urn by Thomas Christopher Falck (dates unconfirmed) (Fig. 33.05). Ornamentation was also created by cutting small decorative shapes out of the metal bases.

In the late 19th century, Cape furniture styles began to change. The population increased rapidly after the Boer War, which ended in 1902, and this led to a growing demand for home furnishings. The Cape manufacturer D. Isaacs and Company, established in 1874, announced in 1896 that it had constructed a steam-powered plant with labor-saving equipment that could produce furniture of better quality and lesser cost than imported pieces. Bell, Webb, and Bell was another company that entered the Cape Town market around this time, bringing with it new manufacturing technology from Europe.

At the beginning of the 20th century, Cape Town and the area around it was still South Africa's leading furniture manufacturing region, due largely to the long tradition of Cape cabinetmaking, as well as the city's easy access to local timber and an abundant supply of skilled labor. Cape manufacturers, comparable to the American companies in Grand Rapids, Michigan, produced furniture for homes as well as schools, churches, and offices. Most of it was known as "cottage furniture," due to its plainness. It was sold outside South Africa as well as domestically. In Johannesburg, Jocelyne's of Johannesburg had its own design staff, which produced plain wooden furniture—sideboards, easy chairs, dressing tables, and tea caddies—for a middle-class market.

Some time after the 1925 Exposition des Arts Décoratifs in Paris, Duros, a company that had been founded in Cape Town by a Jewish immigrant, Hyman Ospovat (dates unconfirmed), in 1903, began to produce a line of Art Deco furniture. However, unlike its Parisian exemplars, it was mass-produced and offered at modest prices. The range of pieces was wide—lounge suites, tea trolleys, side tables, dining room ensembles, sideboards, bedroom suites, cocktail cabinets, and lighting fixtures. The designs were derived or adapted from Parisian sources, although they were changed considerably for the South African market, which favored heavier pieces. Consequently, the Duros line is less notable for its formal innovation than as evidence of South Africa's striving to be modern on a mass scale.

A more original adaptation of the Art Deco style was evident in the work of the Ceramic Studio in the Transvaal, founded by Marjorie Johnstone (dates unconfirmed) and Gladys Short (dates unconfirmed) in 1925. Both had studied in Durban with John Adams (dates unconfirmed), who trained at the Royal College of Art in London. The Ceramic Studio produced tiles, architectural faience, monumental sculpture, vases, and tableware. Deep green was a favored color. As Dipti Bhagat notes, it was not easy for the Ceramic Studio since the ceramists had to compete with the foreign luxury goods that most wealthy South Africans preferred. The studio was active until 1942, when it was sold, due to a loss of staff and the difficulty of obtaining imported clays and glazes.

Though Johannesburg was not founded until 1886, it grew quickly, due in part to the discovery of gold in the nearby Witwatersrand. By 1939, the concentration of mines and factories in the region around Johannesburg was comparable to the industrial regions in Europe and the United States. The city's lack of tradition was perhaps the impetus for its striving for modernity. American skyscrapers and European Art Deco inspsired its architects, and the early 1930s saw a spate of new buildings that characterized Johannesburg as the most modern city in Africa.

Its modernity was celebrated at the Empire Exhibition of 1936, which commemorated Johannesburg's first 50 years. Intended to recognize South African advances in art, industry, and culture, the exhibition featured an array of Art Deco pavilions designed to promote Johannesburg to a world audience.

The signature icon of the exhibition was the Tower of Light, a striking illuminated column that could be seen for miles around. A number of the

Deco-inspired pavilions featured large blank surfaces, which were combined with various shapes such as towers and fins. The three-dimensional san serif lettering that identified the nations and colonies of the British Empire recalled the typographic architecture of the Italian Futurist Fortunato Depero.

As Jennifer Robinson notes, the exhibits themselves tended to adhere to conventional juxtapositions of the old and new—ox-wagons and automobiles, traditional crafts and modern industry, Johannesburg's original shanty towns and skyscrapers. In the pavilion of the Iron and Steel Corporation (ISCOR), a group of native ironsmiths from the Transvaal was put on display to provide a contrast to the government's program of industrial modernization.

Robinson also states that the historical narratives within the exhibition, as displayed in some of the regional pavilions and in the mammoth Pageant of South Africa, privileged the white settlers, both Afrikaners and English, and represented the Africans as marginal to the nation's development. They became part of South Africa's exotic past, which nonetheless still held an interest for tourists who were eager for an authentic African experience. In that sense, the Empire Exhibition shared much with the European colonial exhibitions, the difference being that the blacks in South Africa were not colonial subjects who lived far from the metropole—rather, they were the majority residents of South Africa who had been denied their rights as citizens by the nation's white minority.

Blacks were also marginalized from the economy in Southern Rhodesia. Manufacturing began there at the end of the 19th century with the inauguration of a lager beer brewery. At the same time, several small engineering firms started operations as suppliers of parts and equipment to the gold-mining companies. Railway workshops were also opened in Salisbury and Bulawayo, both of which had sufficient engineering capability to produce armored trains for use during the Boer War (Fig. 33.06).

The British South Africa Company was instrumental in promoting a number of enterprises in food processing, cement manufacturing, and flour milling, although the bulk of its investments were directed

Fig. 33.06: British armored train, Boer War, c. 1900. © Classic Image/Alamy.

towards mining, farming, and the lumber industry. During World War I, Southern Rhodesia made great headway in import substitution, with factories that produced footwear, clothing, soap, and cigarettes along with foodstuffs. Responding to military demand, factories began to manufacture smoke bombs, airplane parts, and a range of light-engineering products. Large-scale European immigration after the war created an impetus for further industrialization, particularly in housing construction. Sawmills produced lumber and furniture manufacturing flourished, although no distinctive designs emerged. Factories also fabricated metal doors and windows, along with other housing components.

A 1938 census of manufacturing recorded approximately 300 enterprises, though most were still on a small scale. Prior to 1940, the government had remained neutral towards industry, allowing private enterprise to fuel industrial development. However, wartime shortages induced the prime minister to take a stronger role, and an Industrial Development Advisory Committee was established in 1940. By 1942, the government began to promote state enterprise as the principal means of industrialization, resulting in the nationalization of various industries and the decision to make semi-finished products that could then be sold at low prices to private companies for finishing, so that they could compete more successfully with imported goods. By the end of the colonial period, South Africa had one of the largest industrial sectors in Africa.

Graphic design

During the early 20th century, African cultures were still predominantly oral, hence printing and publishing were limited, though they continued to expand in the interwar years. Africans were involved with the transcription of oral languages, which included the creation of syllabaries, while African design was centered on a few newspapers and the occasional magazine. By contrast, European graphic design that involved Africa took three forms. First was design directed at Africans, such as packaging and some newspaper advertising. Second was design directed at Europeans, especially travel posters, brochures, and other literature related to African tourism. Third was packaging and advertising directed at Europeans that used African imagery.

These three forms displayed varying degrees of positive or negative images. Design directed to Africans such as labels for cotton bales had generally positive depictions, although Africans were seen in positions that were subordinate to whites. In travel advertising, Africans were initially portrayed as exotic and sometimes primitive, although in later North African advertising posters they were depicted more sympathetically. Finally, images of Africans in European advertising were often derogatory and outright racist.

Scripts and syllabaries

The production of texts, first by hand and then by mechanical means, has a long history in Africa, despite the multitude of oral languages spoken by tribal groups across the continent. Through the spread of Islam over many centuries, numerous Africans, particularly across the Sahara and in West Africa, learned to read and write Arabic. When the French occupied North Africa they encountered a highly developed Arabic print culture. In other parts of Africa, local languages were sometimes written in Arabic script. In Ethiopia, Amharic existed as a vernacular language for centuries before the ancient Ge'ez script was adopted as its written form (Fig. 33.07).

Presses were established for various purposes. The dominant purpose was to spread Christian doctrine, which was done by various missionary societies and associations. A few missionaries went to Africa in the 15th century, but missionary activity became more intense in the late 18th century and continued through the 19th and into the 20th. Other groups who set up presses were foreign enterprises as well as colonial governments. The Sierra Leone Company, which traded in agricultural products, imported a press as early as 1794. Among the titles that such commercial

Fig. 33.07: Ge'ez Bible, 18th century. © Robert Preston/Alamy.

enterprises published were the Angolan periodical *O Comercio de Loanda* (1867), and in Mozambique and in South Africa, the *South African Commercial Advertiser*. These publications, however, represented foreign commercial interests and did not arise from the local cultures around them.

Portugal was perhaps the first colonial government to establish official printing presses in its colonies. The aim was to make it easier for local administrators to publish their own laws and official papers instead of having them printed in Lisbon. In 1836, the Portuguese government issued a decree stating that local presses should be set up in the colonies in order to publish *Boletins Oficiais* (*Official Bulletins*) as well as other documents. The decree was not fulfilled until 1842, when the first press was established in Cape Verde, followed by one in Angola in 1845 and another in Mozambique in 1854.

The spread of European languages came from various sources, particularly colonial administrations that needed low-level clerks to staff their offices and for whom teaching the language of the colonizer was a way of integrating the native into the colonial system. With little tolerance for native languages, for example, French colonial administrators put great emphasis on teaching French in colonial schools. Consequently, early literary efforts by African writers such as Ahmadou Mapaté Diagne, who published *Les trois volontés de Malic* (*The Three Wishes of Malic*) in 1920, were in French. Diagne's novel was perhaps the first in that language by a black African.

Mission presses emphasized the publication of books, tracts, pamphlets, and periodicals in native idioms. In Southern Africa, the Wesleyan Methodists and the Congregationalists introduced printing presses at mission stations among the Tswana in the interior, and Xhosa speakers in the Cape Colony, while the Anglicans brought presses to several stations in the 1860s and 1870s. The Methodists produced the earliest known Southern African newspaper, *Umshumayeli Wendaba* (*Publisher of the News*), between 1837 and 1841. *Ikhwezi* (*Star of Morning*), a Bantu journal, appeared in 1844.

In the later part of the 19th century, two major centers were important for the promotion of indigenous South African mission publishing: Lovedale in the Cape Colony, where the Presbyterians established the Lovedale Mission Press in 1861; and Morija in Basutoland, where the Paris Evangelical Missionary Society inaugurated the Morija Printing Works in 1874. While the Lovedale Mission Press printed materials mainly in English and Xhosa, the missionaries at Morija published books, pamphlets, and periodicals in as many as 45 languages for colonies throughout Sub-Saharan Africa. Although the primary purpose of the early native-language publications was to propagate Christian doctrine, as George Ayiki Alao notes, they also prepared the way for the development of an indigenous secular African literature, as exemplified by Thomas Mfolo's novel in the Sotho language, *Chaka*, which the Paris Evangelical Missionary Society published in 1925. In Nigeria, a Yoruba publication, *Iwe Irohim* (*The Journal*), came out in 1859, only a few years after the Yoruba language was given a written form in roman script by a freed slave, Samuel Crowther (1809–1891), in order to translate the Bible.

Although the first printing press was brought to Ethiopia in 1863, it was the establishment of a government press by Emperor Menalik II in 1911 that provided a major impetus for the development of printing there. Menalik's inauguration of a state printing press was just one part of his broad project of modernization that included the construction of bridges and modern roads, the erection of telegraph lines, the creation of a national bank and postal system, and the opening of a hospital, a Western-style school, and a hotel. Menelik's intent was to use the press for printing official documents as well as books that would contribute to Ethiopia's development.

Menelik II died in 1913, and subsequently Haile Selassie served as regent from 1916 to 1930, at which time he became Ethiopia's emperor. In 1923 he founded his own press on the palace grounds. Known at the time as the Regent's Press, its name was later changed to Berhanena Salam (Light and Peace). Selassie intended the press for the publication of newspapers and books. It also included a lithographic department for the production of printing blocks. The press brought out numerous religious books in both Ge'ez and Amharic, along with documents for public and private organizations as well as newspapers. The staff of 30 consisted entirely of Ethiopians. At the time of the Italian invasion in 1935, there were seven printing presses in Addis Ababa, the Ethiopian capital. These included the government press founded by Menelik II; Berhanena Salam, which had been established by Haile Selassie; and five other presses that were privately owned.

In general, the books, pamphlets, newspapers, and other publications that were printed in Africa before World War II displayed little or no sense of design. Illustrated works were rare and printers tended to handle the page layouts according to the most conservative typesetting conventions. Type was imported from abroad and there was a limited range of fonts to choose from. Paper also tended to generally be of low quality.

Besides the translations of oral languages into roman scripts, such as the project of Samuel Crowther, or translations into the Arabic alphabet, there were also projects that Africans initiated to create syllabaries consisting of phonetic symbols. Saki Mafundikwa has described a number of these. The Bantu syllabary in South Africa contains symbols that are both phonetic and pictographic, including representations of family members, warriors, chiefs, and planters, as well as abstract concepts like gossip, war, or passion. In 1921, a Somali scholar Yaasiin Cismaan Kenadiid (1919–1988) created a syllabary for the Somali language, although it was never widely used. Other syllabaries were invented by individuals such as Kisimi Kamara (1890–1962), a Muslim tailor in Sierra Leone who created one with 195 characters for the Mende language in 1921; Woyo Couloubayi (dates unconfirmed), who is credited with the invention of a syllabary for the Bambara language in 1930; Wido Zobo (dates unconfirmed), who invented one for Loma in Liberia in the 1930s; and Chief Gbili (dates unconfirmed), who created another for Kpelle in Liberia, also during the 1930s. One of the older written scripts called Vah belongs to the Bassa people in Liberia, who developed a written syllabary that was originally used to elude slave traders. After a decline, it was revived around 1900 by Thomas Gbianvoodeh Lewis (dates unconfirmed), a Liberian chemist, who set up schools to teach it.

Perhaps the most extensive publishing program that made use of a syllabary was created in the Bamum Kingdom in Cameroon, originally a German colony, at the end of the 19th century. King Ibrahim Njoya (dates unconfirmed) and his councilors not only invented a writing system, but used it to produce a large number of manuscripts in which the king recorded the history of his people. He also created a calendar, maintained administrative records, and wrote a book that Saki Mafundikwa compares to the Kama Sutra, all using the system of writing known as Shü-mom. The king was assisted in his endeavors by a group of talented artists who created images to complement his texts, recalling the manuscript tradition of the European Middle Ages. When the French took over Cameroon from the Germans after World War I, they destroyed the printing press that King Njoya had invented, decimated his libraries, and burned many of the books he had written.

Newspapers and magazines

Compared to the size of the African population, newspapers published in the 19th and early 20th centuries reached comparatively few readers. Prominent publishers were the missionary societies for whom editing newspapers in native languages was an important part of their effort to reach the local people. Their publishing activities, which included the aforementioned books and pamphlets as well as newspapers, went hand in hand with the schools they established to teach literacy along with other subjects.

In South Africa, missionary societies were the first to publish newspapers in African languages and thereby became the progenitors of a native African press. *Umshumayeli Wendaba* (*Publisher of the News*), printed at the Wesleyan Missionary Society between 1837 and 1841, was the first newspaper to be published for black readers. It spawned numerous others that were independent of the missionary societies. In 1884, John Tengo Jabavu (1869–1921), a prominent politician and educator, founded *Imvo Zabantsundu* (*African Opinion*), a newspaper written in the Xhosa language and the first to be controlled and written by blacks. Jabavu's paper, however, was established with white backing, and although he demanded equal rights for the black population and became a proponent of women's rights and public education, his critique of white rule was consequently rather mild.

Other pioneering black newspaper editors included Solomon Tshekisho Plaatje (1876–1932) and John Langalibalele Dube. Fluent in at least seven languages, Plaatje wrote in English but was also concerned with the preservation of the Setswana language, compiling its first phonetic reader. He was also part owner and editor of *Koranta ea Becoana* (*Bechuana Gazette*).

To publish the paper, Plaatje established the Bechuana Printing Works, which involved purchasing a press and hiring printers. After the *Gazette* foundered, he became owner and editor of two other papers, *Tsala ea Becoana* (*Friend of Bechuana*) and *Tsala ea Batho* (*Friend of the People*), which also lasted for limited periods. Plaatje, like other black editors, participated actively in the struggle of blacks in South Africa against injustice, particularly opposing segregation and unfair land distribution. He was elected the first

Secretary General of the South African Native National Congress, which was renamed the African National Congress in 1923.

In 1903, John Langalibalele Dube co-founded the first Zulu newspaper, *Illanga Lase Natal* (*The Natal Sun*), which he later edited. As mentioned previously, Dube was a great admirer of Booker T. Washington, the American black leader, and like Plaatje, he was a founder of the South African Native National Congress and became its first president. As Les Switzer notes, the early black papers faced extreme difficulties and rarely lasted for extended periods. They did not have adequate printing equipment, had to draw on a modest pool of skilled black printers, and lacked the more extensive distribution networks of the white press. Nonetheless, they survived for various lengths of time and prepared the way for the more militant black papers that were to appear in later years.

The readership of the early black press was largely middle class, the same audience that was targeted by the publishers of *Bantu World*, a weekly paper that first appeared in 1932. Modeled on the British tabloids, *Bantu World* was founded by a white man, Bertram Paver, who owned the paper along with some black investors for a year until a white-owned publishing conglomerate, the Argus Printing Company, took it over. Controlled by the mining industry, Argus dominated most of the black press in South Africa through its ownership of ten weekly papers.

Shortly after its founding, *Bantu World* introduced a woman's page, which featured an ongoing debate about the characteristics and qualities of the modern African girl. The paper ran beauty competitions and published photographs of the leading contenders. It was one of the first newspapers in South Africa, or in Africa for that matter, to incorporate photographic images. Besides news, *Bantu World* published poetry, short stories, and plays, as well as drawings by African artists. Whereas the earlier black papers had been run by one or two people, *Bantu World*, which had national distribution, maintained its own editorial, advertising, and printing departments, where many blacks gained professional training as printers, typists, clerks, salesmen, and also journalists.

Among the more radical papers was *Workers' Herald*, an irregular publication that appeared in four languages. It was launched in 1923 by the Industrial and Commercial Workers' Union, which had become the most important black political organization by the late 1920s.

There were as well numerous papers published for white South Africans in English and Afrikaans. Most of them, such as the *Rand Daily Mail* and the *Sunday Times*, which were first published at the beginning of the 20th century, were connected with the mining industry. They appeared almost 100 years after South Africa's first newspaper, the *Cape Town Gazette and African Advertiser*, which was owned by two slave dealers and first came out in 1800.

Few of these papers broke new ground in their layouts or typography. Besides *Bantu World*, several other papers were beginning to experiment with pictorial journalism by 1930s. Among them was *Umlindi we Nyanga* (*Monthly Watchman*), a Xhosa-English monthly that first appeared in 1934. It was published by a company in London that manufactured goods for the South African market. Though initially an advertising vehicle for the company's products, it was revived after World War II as a pictorial magazine that featured news photographs, drawings, and cartoons.

In the British colonies of East and West Africa, black entrepreneurs had more opportunities than in South Africa to start their own newspapers. Among the colonies where newspaper publishing prospered were the Gold Coast, Sierra Leone, Uganda, and Nigeria. Many editors of these papers were supporters of pan-African nationalism and a number were inspired by Booker T. Washington, W. E. B. Du Bois, Edward Blyden, or Marcus Garvey, especially Garvey's newspaper, *Negro World*. In the Gold Coast, Joseph Casely-Hayford co-founded the *Gold Coast Leader*, which was published between 1902 and the

1930s. In Sierra Leone, J. Claudius May owned the well-produced *Sierra Leone Weekly*, Ernest Beoku Betts established *Aurora*, and Isaac Wallace-Johnson, the radical labor activist, founded *The Sentinel*. In Nigeria, 51 newspapers were launched between 1880 and 1937. Among the first was John Payne Jackson's *Lagos Weekly Record*, which early on took an anti-imperialist stand. An important contemporary publication was the *Lagos Standard*, founded by George Alfred Williams, who had learned the art of printing as a young boy. Like Jackson, Williams also took a strong anti-imperialist position and was likewise influenced by Edward Blyden's pan-Africanism. Some years later, in 1937, Dr. Nnamdi Azikewe, also a strong proponent of pan-African ideas, founded another Nigerian paper, the *West African Pilot*. Other papers such as the *Nyasaland Times* and the *Uganda Argus* were owned by Europeans and reflected the voices of the white settlers in East Africa. In 1916, the Niger Company along with other European trading firms invested in the West African Publishing Company, which brought out a periodical journal, *West Africa*.

Few indigenous newspapers were published in the French colonies, as the French government maintained tighter control of the local press than did the British. Publications in native languages were also discouraged, hence the few newspapers that were published in these colonies tended to be in French. Among them was *La Démocratie du Sénégal*, founded in 1913. In North Africa, where Arabic was widely spoken and written, several papers appeared. In 1907, a reformist group known as the Young Tunisians began to publish a political newspaper, *Le Tunisien* (*The Tunisian*), in French. Two years later, an Arabic edition was started. In Fez, Morocco, *L'Action du Peuple* (*Action of the People*) was founded in 1933. The spread of communist activity to North Africa inspired a number of publications such as the Algerian journal *La Lutte Sociale* (*Social Struggle*) and communist propaganda published by Robert Louzon's Tunisian printing press, which included some material in Arabic that

attempted to demonstrate points of agreement between communism and Islam.

In Ethiopia, newspapers were published in several languages. Those in French included *Le Courrier d'Ethiopie* (*Ethiopian Courier*) and *L'Ethiopie Commerciale* (*Commercial Ethiopia*). There was also an Italian paper, *Il Notizario* (*The Bulletin*), that was established in 1933 and espoused a Fascist line, and four newspapers in Amharic including the weekly *Berhanena Salam*, a quasi-official paper that supported the views of Emperor Haile Selassie.

In the Portuguese colony of Mozambique, João dos Santos Albasani (1876–1922) was a founder in 1908 of *O Africano: Almanach Humorístico e Ilustrado* (*The African: A Humorous and Illustrated Almanac*), a weekly newspaper that was aligned with the political association Grêmio Africano. *O Africano* published articles that were critical of the Portuguese government, along with literary pieces and political cartoons. The inclusion of cartoons distinguished this paper from most others in Africa. It lasted until 1918, at which time Albasani started a new publication, *O Brado Africano* (*African Voice*), which published many of Mozambique's young writers. Elsewhere in the Portuguese colonies, the literary magazine *Claridade* (*Light*) first appeared in Cape Verde in 1936. It was a modernist publication that was part of a movement for cultural and political emancipation on the island. The founders Manuel Lopes, Baltasar Lopes da Silva, and Jorge Barbosa established high literary and linguistic standards, intending to free writers in Cape Verde from the weight of Portugal's literary tradition. The magazine was indicative of the political unrest that existed in Cape Verde during the regime of the Portuguese dictator António Salazar in the 1930s. It was one of the few publications in all of Africa during the interwar period to assimilate the typographic experiments of the Western avant-garde. The cover of the first issue displayed a hierarchy of type sizes and weights, with the title, consisting of hand-drawn expressive letters, placed at the bottom and the titles of three poems indicated in bold type that contrasted with the rest of the cover text. While the graphic image of their magazine was not as experimental as its counterpart publications in Europe, the editors nonetheless recognized that an innovative visual design was consistent with their attempts to forge a modern Cape Verdean literature. Nine issues appeared between 1936 and 1960, but only three were published before World War II.

Advertising, logotypes, and packaging

African artists created few graphic images during the period before World War II. As described in an earlier section, indigenous art education was limited and few Africans went abroad to study art. One exception to the lack of local advertising art was South Africa, which was the rare nation or colony on the continent to create a modern consumer economy. As in Europe and the United States, early South African pictorial newspaper advertisements featured stock woodcuts or simple line drawings, as well as ads with a mix of display types. Photographs began to replace line drawings in the 1920s. Advertisements in the white-run newspapers and magazines depicted white people as consumers, even if blacks also purchased some of the products advertised. One exception to the depiction of white men and women in product ads was the advertising for Bon Ami cleanser. Directed at white consumers, it was exemplified by an ad that portrayed a smiling black servant cleaning a bathtub.

Publications that blacks edited also incorporated advertising. Initial ads in *Bantu World* for the Apex Hair Company, an American firm that marketed cosmetics to black consumers, featured a light-skinned black woman, most likely drawn by an American illustrator, while later ads produced by the company incorporated photographs of South African women. *Bantu World* also depicted black men favorably in ads for skin creams and face powder (where the men were expected to buy the products for their lady friends). These products were manufactured by a white-owned company that sold cosmetics made especially for blacks.

Although there was a considerable number of advertising agencies in South Africa by the 1930s, advertising copy and illustration tended to be derivative of what was being produced in Great Britain and the United States. There were some local artists and photographers, but it is likely that European or American advertising illustrators created many of the drawings included in advertising for products, particularly those that were imported from abroad such as Singer sewing machines, Telefunken radios, and Gecophone record players.

European artists were responsible for other types of advertising in Africa before World War II, notably the trademarks and logotypes that the trading companies adopted, either to characterize their own identities or to brand the goods they imported. Trading companies chose visual icons that most often had some African reference. Their intent was to become part of the system of symbolic representation in which African chiefs participated. As Frederick Pedlar notes, animals identified many African tribes, while kings also had their own signs such as the Ashanti gold stool and the pot with holes that was the emblem of King Gezo in Dahomey. To express solidarity with his African trading partners, John Walkden adopted King Gezo's emblem for his own Lagos Stores, thus reinterpreting the original meaning that Dahomey could not survive unless its children worked together, each one stopping up a hole. As the emblem could be read according to Walken's appropriation of it, the European trading company was purported to be an integral part of Dahomey's survival.

Other emblems or symbols that European trading companies adopted included the lion's head, associated with the firm of Richard and William King; the unicorn, first selected by F. and A. Swanzy and then by G. B. Ollivant, a company that eventually settled on a horseman and rider; and the boar's head, adopted by W. B. MacIver in southern Nigeria. Several firms appropriated indigenous African symbols as their marks. Jurgen Colonial Products, for example, adopted the *anta,* an African charm, which was sometimes used alone or arranged with several others in a formal design. To appeal to Muslim consumers in Nigeria, Lagos Stores Ltd employed several marks, which were in use as early as 1893. One was a comb and crescent and the other was a slate—the traditional reading board in Islamic schools—with writing on it in Arabic that declared, "Patience conquers the world."

Companies frequently attached their trademarks to products such as bales of cotton cloth that they exported. Some labels were more elaborate than simple logos. The different designs on the cloth, which seem to have been based on traditional African patterns, had names such as Chaka Print, Bantu Print, or Rainbow Print. Their labels, drawn by British artists, featured the name of the print along with an illustration that characterized it. Compared to the negative stereotypes

of black Africans that were often used on products sold in Europe to Europeans, the images on these labels were complimentary, although they reinforced a traditional quality of native life which ensured that the African would remain subordinate to the white colonial European.

A label for a cloth called "Umfaan" depicted an African man in bush gear—a khaki shirt, shorts, and high socks—standing in front of a round Zulu house, while labels for Bantu Print and one called Fancy Blue portrayed women in village settings wearing dresses made of imported cloth. A label for Star Toto Print showed a small naked boy as the embodiment of primitive African culture (Plate 68). A different approach was evident in a label for Chaka Print, which depicted the Zulu warrior Chaka, a mythic figure considered to be a progenitor of the Zulu tribe, with a shield whose design was based on a motif derived from imported British cloth (Fig. 33.08).

Tourism graphics

During colonial rule, tourism became a means to accomplish various purposes for the ruling powers. Most important, it validated the colonial enterprise itself. Citizens visiting the colonies could find justification for the colonial project in their travels. They could observe industrial enterprises, witness the construction of railways, roads, and new buildings, and gain confirmation of colonial beneficence through their encounters with the native populace as service providers. Tourism also provided the impetus for new business ventures that involved the construction of hotels, the organization of transport, the planning of programs such as safaris and guided tours, and the production of art, crafts, and souvenirs for tourists.

Posters played an important role in promoting travel to the colonies. Within the French colonial administration and among French enterprises, posters were paramount. Well-established fine artists as well as prominent graphic designers produced them. Leading agencies and enterprises that commissioned travel

Fig. 33.08: Chaka Print cotton bale label, c. 1920s. © Mary Evans Picture Library/Alamy.

posters for the French colonies were Agence de Colonies, an agency in the French government's Ministère des Colonies; P. L. M., the Compagnie des Chemins de Fer de Paris à Lyon et à la Méditerranée (Railroad Company of Paris, Lyon, and the Mediterranean); and steamship companies that included the C. G. T. —the Compagnie Générale Transatlantique (General Transatlantic Company)—Messageries Maritime, and Compagnie de Navigation Paquet. Posters were also created by the colonial railroads such as the Chemins de Fer Tunisiens (Tunisian Railroad) and the multiple local tourist bureaus that were set up, especially in Morocco, where there was a well-organized association of such offices representing a number of cities and regions within the protectorate.

With the beginning of air travel in 1919, when the Compagnie Latécoère, later to become the Compagnie Générale Aérospatiale, provided the first regular air service to Morocco, airlines such as Air Afrique, Air Atlas, Air Bleu, Aeropostale, Imperial Airways, Sabena, and South African Airways also created posters that encouraged travelers to patronize their newly-established routes.

Early tourist posters in the late 19th century, notably those encouraging tourism in North Africa, were created by painters who worked in the Orientalist tradition. These artists depicted the Orient, whether the Middle East or North Africa, as a place of exoticism that was populated by sensuous women in harems, heroic soldiers on horseback, men riding camels through the desert, or bustling markets where people in long robes exchanged goods. Orientalism has a long tradition in French art. Its roots can be traced at least as far back as Napoleon's successful Egyptian campaign of 1798–1799, which was documented with thousands of illustrations including many copperplate engravings. Among the prominent Orientalist painters was Eugène Delacroix, whose paintings of Algerian harem women and Moroccan warriors from the 1830s prepared the way for lesser artists such as Jean-Léon Gérôme to display their Orientalist fantasies at the annual Paris Salons.

As early as the 1890s, companies like the P. L. M. Railway commissioned Orientalist painters, some of whom were then living in North Africa, to create paintings for their travel posters. The paintings were then adapted for lithographic printing, and lettering was added to the images. One feature of the posters that did not derive directly from Orientalist paintings was an emphasis on the scenery, whether it was palm trees, a bay, or some of the many historic sites that were promoted as tourist attractions. In an early travel poster that the P. L. M. and the C. G. T. shipping line produced jointly, artist Hugo d'Alesi ((1849–1906), best known for his European travel posters, did a poster for the C. G. T. that depicted several women covered almost completely in burquas strolling in the sand near the Bay of Algiers (Fig. 33.09). In an earlier poster by d'Alesi for the C. G. T., a woman in Oriental garb, though not a burqua, was depicted standing on a balcony with a beautiful scenic view of a bay behind her.

Other artists who created posters in this early Orientalist style were Gilbert Galland (1870–1956), who also did paintings depicting North African scenes for the Tunisian and Algerian rooms in the P. L. M.'s Train Bleu restaurant at the Gare de Lyon in Paris; Ernst-Louis Lessieux (1848–1925), who portrayed an Arab horseman holding a banner astride a rearing steed; Alexander Lunois (1863–1916), considered the inventor of the litho tint technique; and Maurice Romberg (1862–1943), whose poster of the Sultan of Morocco on his way to a mosque in Fez advertised travel to Morocco via Marseille. Romberg's poster recalls Delacroix's earlier painting *The Sultan of Morocco and His Entourage* of 1845. In a second poster that portrayed the Sultan and his followers, Romberg included a deluxe tourist vehicle with several well-attired tourists standing beside it, one with a camera. In this instance, the poster promoted the multiple services for tourists that the C. G. T. had developed—hotels, deluxe touring cars, and planned itineraries with anticipated spectacles such as the Sultan on horseback with his minions.

Fig. 33.09: Hugo d'Alési, Compagnie Générale Transatlantique and P. L. M., poster, c. 1900. © Swim Ink 2, LLC/CORBIS/Getty Images.

Gustave-Henri Jossot (1866–1951), a painter, illustrator, caricaturist, and poster artist who moved to Tunisia in 1911 and converted to Islam; Léon Carré (1878–1942), whose posters for Tlemcen, the sacred town in the west of Algeria, featured the rich color of the landscape while also depicting religious buildings and scenes of daily life; Joseph de la Nézière (1873–1944), an artist who was active in promoting the indigenous arts in Morocco under Maréchal Lyautey; Edouard Herzig (1860–1926), who spent many years in Algeria and showed his work with the Union Artistique de l'Afrique du Nord (Artistic Union of North Africa); Leon Cauvy (1874–1933), an artist who studied in Algeria in 1907 and subsequently became director of the École de Beaux Arts in Algiers; and Matteo Brondy (1866–1954), who followed General Lyautey to Morocco, settled in Meknes in 1918, and did a number of posters to support the local Meknes travel bureau.

There were several women among these artists, notably Odette Bruneau (1891–1984), a former student of Jacques Majorelle, and Jeanne Thil (1887–1968), a former student at the École de Beaux Arts in Algiers. A poster of Thil's for the Transatlantique shows a desert scene with close-ups of male and female figures, along with their animals drawn with heavy expressive outlines. Unlike the earlier Orientalist paintings, which created atmospheric scenes that drew the viewer in, this poster emphasizes the trace of the artist's hand and her distinctive composition (Plate 69).

One of the most prolific poster artists of this group was Georges Taboureau (1879–1960), who adopted the pseudonym Sandy Hook. Known as an artist who painted maritime scenes, Taboureau did posters for the major shipping lines that went to North Africa as well as the lines that headed to other parts of the world. Images of steamships were not present in all his posters, but they were depicted in most of them.

There were also a few professional poster designers and decorative artists who produced travel posters for North Africa. Among the decorative artists was J. H. Derche (dates unconfirmed), one of the first

In the 1920s, another generation of French artists began to create travel posters to promote North African tourism. Like the generation before them, they also depicted scenes of traditional North African life, but they did so with less romanticism and more emphasis on painterly or designerly values than their predecessors. Some adapted their images to techniques that featured flatness and bright colors, which was more suitable to the emerging modern poster format. These artists included Jacques Majorelle (1886–1962), a long-time resident of Marrakech and son of the Art Nouveau furniture designer Louis Majorelle;

to settle in Morocco, where he helped organize an exhibition of French artist-decorators in 1932. Work by specialists in poster design tended to be more conceptual or visually stylized than those of artists, as in the poster *Visit Morocco* that Francis Bernard (1853–1928), a regular designer of posters for the annual Salon des Arts Ménagers in Paris, created for the Compagnie de Navigation Paquet. It featured a stylized building with a minaret as the central image with a small ship in the background and large san serif letters integrated into the design. Roger Broders (1883–1953), perhaps the premier designer of French travel posters

in the interwar years, worked regularly for the P. L. M., not just for their North African tours but to promote their multiple destinations in France—Alsace Lorraine, Vichy, Jura, and the French Alps among them. Broders was particularly known for posters that depicted the colorful resorts of the Côte d'Azur. He strongly emphasized narrative scenes rather than the more conceptual designs of A. M. Cassandre, Paul Colin, or Jean Carlu. His poster for the golf course in La Soukra, a suburb of Tunis, is one of the very few that did not feature nativist imagery, except for the fez that the young caddy in the foreground wore.

In general, the North African travel posters were without humor, but Broders' poster promoting the auto tours that the C. G. T. sponsored along with the specially designed Renault cars they used was an exception. It featured the Michelin Man, Bibendum, signifying the company, whose tires were also promoted in the poster (Fig. 33.10). Clad in Arab garb—a burnoose on his head, a white cape, and babouches (local slippers) on his feet—he may well have offended local Arabs. The elongated touring car depicted in the poster was an earlier version of a Renault Routier, which had been specially designed for desert driving. With its six wheels and tank-like chassis, it was not only able to traverse the Sahara but also to cross the African continent from end to end, beginning in Colomb-Béchar in Algeria and terminating in Cape Town in South Africa. Its competitor for desert driving was the Citroën K1, with its half-track, similar to a tank tread, that had been invented by a French military engineer Adolphe Kégresse (1879–1943), who worked for Citroën during the 1920s and 1930s. Supposedly it was one of these Citroën vehicles that first crossed the Sahara in early 1923

Where private companies in France took the lead in developing tourism in France's North African colonies, the case was different in Libya, where the Italian Fascist government, as part of its corporatist policy, controlled the construction of hotels, the creation of tourist itineraries, and other elements that contributed to a "tourist system." Its principal

Fig. 33.10: Roger Broders, Auto-Circuits Nord-Africains, poster, 1917. akg-images. © ADAGP, Paris and DACS, London 2017.

vehicle was the Libyan Tourism and Hotel Association (ETAL), which was established in 1935. This organization replaced a prior system in which government agencies oversaw the initiatives of a group of private tourism companies.

Within the General Administration of the ETAL was a Publicity and Propaganda Service that managed all the organization's promotional campaigns. These included publications such as brochures, guidebooks, and postcards, billboards and films, and displays at exhibitions and fairs in Italy and elsewhere. Photographs were used extensively in the publicity materials as in a brochure depicting Libyan itineraries, published in 1935. Brian McLaren notes how photographic montages employed in this brochure characterized the tourist experience in Libya as a negotiation between the demands of comfort and the intent to provide an authentic encounter with the native culture. In a brochure of 1936, *La Libya*, photographs were used in a more straightforward manner whereby photos of different sizes were laid out on a modern two-column grid. In 1937, the ETAL began publication of its own monthly illustrated magazine, *Libya*, which featured articles on social and political development as well as tourism. Its layout was modern, as were its covers that were commissioned from established graphic designers like Bruno Santi (dates unconfirmed). Other publications included guidebooks like *Itinerario Tripoli-Gadames* (*Tripoli-Gadames Itinerary*), which offered detailed descriptions of the routes that the comfortable motor coaches covered. Modern graphic design techniques were also evident in some of the ETAL advertising, such as the promotional material for the new Hotel Derma, which featured an image of the hotel overlaid on a background that included repetitions of the hotel name in a modern san serif type accompanied by alternating colored stripes. Among the smaller design details that the ETAL was concerned with were the hotel baggage stickers, which were somewhat standardized typographically but differed in the illustrations that referred to the hotels and

their adjacent tourist sites. The modernity of ETAL's publicity material, however, was far less significant than the designs of the hotels where the tourists stayed. Guided by the ETAL's Hotel Service, they were created for the most part in a grandiose modernist style that reflected the principles of the Italian Rationalists, combined with references to Roman precedents.

The promotion of travel in other parts of the continent was less extensive than it was in either the French or Italian North African colonies. The Agence de Colonies of the Ministère de Colonies in France encouraged travel to French West Africa, reinforcing the colonial hegemony by portraying the Africans as living more primitively than Europeans. On one of its posters, produced by designer Michel Bouchaud (1898–d.o.d. unconfirmed), two African women are shown with bare shoulders and baskets on their heads, representing the life of native villagers. Britain's Imperial Airways adopted a similar approach for a generic poster that advertised African travel. As its representative image, the airline featured a group of smiling native women, one bare-breasted and several with children on their backs. The plane above conveys travelers from Europe, coming to glimpse exotic scenes of African life.

The Imperial Airways poster reinforces the colonial relationship less blatantly than several posters for the French airline Air Afrique, a strong competitor with Air France at the time. One Air Afrique poster strongly emphasized the colonial relationship between France and its colonies by showing a colonial administrator in a pith helmet and white tropical suit looking down at the landscape below as he reclines in his airplane seat. In another poster for the same airline, produced by the French artist and poster designer Charles-Jean Hallo, known as Alo (1882–1969), a group of black Africans in Bamako, Mali, look up as a plane approaches overhead. The main figure dressed in ritual garb opens his arms in a gesture of welcome as if a god or some other powerful figure is to descend from the sky (Plate 70).

African imagery in European advertising

Images of Africans were adopted for product advertising in all the European countries that possessed colonies on the continent. Such imagery mainly portrayed blacks, but Arab images were used as well. In France, as Dana S. Hale has shown, the black head was a standard advertising symbol between 1886 and 1913. Frequently prominent physical characteristics such as lips, teeth, or hair would be accentuated or caricatured. A smiling black head with thick lips, for example, was the trademark of the Société Générale de Huiles et Fournitures Industrielles (General Society of Industrial Oils and Supplies) for more than 20 years.

Another familiar trope was the black African child, who was generally depicted nude or else wearing a skimpy loincloth. This was the case with a German trademark for Tetzer ink, which portrayed an African boy with his feet in chains and a ring in his nose, bearing a large bottle of the company's ink on his back. A more benign though equally patronizing image was the Moretto, or little moor, whom the Italian poster artist Gino Boccasile drew frequently for Ettore Moretti, a manufacturer of waterproof fabrics, raincoats, and weather resistant camping equipment. One image by Boccasile depicted two white adults in colonial pith helmets peering into a Moretti tent, where four black waifs were cowering. Besides advertising camping gear, the image also served as a metaphor for Italian colonial power, represented by the white adults hovering over native Africans, who were portrayed as frightened children.

African children were also depicted in ads for products of African origin such as cocoa and soap, which was made from palm oil. In Britain, Cadbury's, Epps, and Fry's, all cocoa manufacturers, portrayed young Africans in varying poses ranging from ads that showed an African boy and a white English girl sitting together to a postcard for Fry's Cocoa that depicted a grinning black plantation worker pointing to a large cocoa bean and saying to a white man portrayed as John Bull, whom he called "Massa" or master, that the large bean was for him. The discrepancy in size between the two men ensured that the audience would see the considerably larger John Bull figure as a sign of authority. This relationship of an authoritarian white figure to a subservient black worker was typical of a number of advertisements in different countries.

In general, blacks in product advertisements were shown with little clothing on. An ad for Sunlight Soap of 1906 sought to make a joke of this by showing two African boys pointing to a clothesline on which they had hung scanty body coverings. The ad plays on irony through their mouthing the copy line, "We wash all our clothes with Sunlight Soap" (Fig. 33.11). Likewise, African women were frequently depicted with bare breasts, as in the Italian artist Seneca's poster for Perugina Cacao. An exception to these images was a German poster for Riquet Sudana Chocolate by Ludwig Hohlwein that featured a reflective watercolor painting depicting the head of a young African woman wearing a headscarf and large earrings.

The most egregious ads attacked blackness itself, especially in advertisements for soaps or body cleansers that showed Africans being washed white. This is evident in a Swiss poster by established poster artist Édouard-Louis Baud (1878–1948), for a washing compound that portrayed a black man becoming white as he dipped his hands in the compound, while a group of peasants appeared pleased with the results. This image of turning the black person white became an all too familiar trope for soap advertisements early in the 20th century.

One of the most enduring associations of a product with a black person is that of an African soldier with a chocolate drink made from cocoa, banana flour, sugar, and several other ingredients. As the story is told, a French journalist, Pierre Lardet, discovered a recipe for the drink when he was in Nicaragua in 1909. Returning to France, he began to market it commercially in 1912 with a smiling young Antillean woman, depicted by the poster artist Charles Tichon (dates unconfirmed), as his trademark. Perhaps to give the product, which he had named Banania,

Fig. 33.11: Sunlight Soap, advertisement, 1906. © Illustrated London News Ltd/Mary Evans.

the head and hands remained. While it is evident that the *tirailleur* is a product of the colonial mentality with his patois and cheerful mien despite his second-class status, he was nonetheless an improvement over the overtly racist and derogatory images of black subjects that pervaded most French advertising. By the 1950s, however, the figure had become cartoon-like, due to the designer Hervé Morvan (1917–1980), and more of a negative caricature.

In contrast to the depiction of black Africans, which was more often than not derogatory, the use of North African Arab imagery for product advertisements, notably in France, was far more positive. As Dana S. Hale points out, North African men were generally depicted on trademarks as either devout Muslims or Saharan warriors, the latter being similar to the images in paintings by Delacroix and other Orientalist artists. Arab women too were the subject of product advertising. Early advertising posters depicted them as seductive odalisques in an Orientalist manner—though fully clothed, unlike the odalisques of Ingres and Manet. By the 1920s and 1930s this image of Arab women had changed to more realistic portrayals. Some products such as Fatiha, a beauty powder marketed by the Pinaud perfume company, featured trademarks depicting a fully veiled woman, as did the products of several other companies. Unveiled peasant girls wearing scarves graced the trademarks of companies that sold grain, flour, fruit, and canned food. One explanation for the more sympathetic portrayal in French advertising of Arab men and women as opposed to black Africans might be that some of the goods were most likely sold in North Africa as well as in France. Such products included soaps, coffee, grains, and paradoxically liqueur, whose advertising with Arab imagery ignored the Muslim prohibition of alcohol consumption. Another explanation for the positive images is that they reinforced the agricultural abundance of the North African colonies, which French businessmen aggressively exploited.

more of a French identity, in 1915 he adopted the image of a Senegalese *tirailleur* as the drink's trademark figure. The *tirailleurs* were African soldiers who had fought for the French since the 1850s and continued to do so during World War I. The original poster by Alexandre De Andreis depicts the seated black *tirailleur*, his rifle by his side, consuming a portion of Banania with a big smile (Plate 71). As a copy line, Lardet adopted the slogan "y'a bon," African patois for "it's good." Over the years, the image of the *tirailleur* was changed numerous times. By 1920, the lower part of the body was eliminated and the face was featured. Within a decade, the chest and shoulders were erased and only

Bibliography

Bibliographic essay

There is ample background literature on the many aspects of colonialism in Africa but almost nothing has been published on the subject of design; hence material on the topic, where it is treated as craft, technology, or industrialization, appears in numerous publications with no direct relation to the existing design history literature. General economic histories have been particularly helpful, notably Ralph Austen, *African Economic History: Internal Development and External Dependency*; A. G. Hopkins, *An Economic History of West Africa*; J. Forbes Munro, *Africa and the International Economy, 1800–1960*; and Charles Wilson, *The History of Unilever: A Study in Economic Growth and Social Change*, Volume 1. Among the more specialized studies of African economies during this period are Adeline Apena, *Colonization, Commerce, and Entrepreneurship in Nigeria: The Western Delta, 1914–1960*; E. A. Brett, *Colonialism and Underdevelopment in East Africa: The Politics of Economic Change, 1919–1939*; Rhoda Howard, *Colonialism and Underdevelopment in Ghana*; Frederick Pedlar, *The Lion and the Unicorn in Africa: A History of the Origins of the United Africa Company 1787–1931*; R. M. A. Van Zwanenberg with Anne King, *An Economic History of Kenya and Uganda, 1800–1970*; Jean Suret-Canale, *French Colonialism in Tropical Africa, 1900–1945*; Zbigniew A. Konczacki, Jane L. Parpart, and Timothy M. Shaw, *Studies in the Economic History of Southern Africa*, 2 vols; and A. A. Lawal's essay, "Industrialisation as Tokenism," in Toyin Falola, ed., *Britain and Nigeria: Exploitation or Development?*

Books and articles on African technology contain much useful material. Those that were particularly helpful include Thomas R. De Gregori, *Technology and the Economic Development of the Tropical African Frontier*; Daniel R. Headrick, *The Tentacles of Progress: Technology Transfer in the Age of Imperialism, 1850–1940*; Ralph A. Austen and Daniel Headrick, "The Role of Technology in the African Past," *African Studies Review* 26, nos. 3–4 (September–December 1983); and Robert

H. Forbes "The Black Man's Industries," *Geographical Review* 23, no. 2 (April 1933). There are far more books on African arts and crafts than on African technology, a sign that many scholars still view African production in terms of pre-industrial practices rather than a more modern means of making things. One problem with the books on crafts, well documented as they are, is that they do not generally provide names of craftsmen or dates to accompany the images, thus suggesting that such production is always anonymous and naturally endures unchanged over time instead of being affected by historical forces just as all other human activity is. The best of these books that document African crafts include René Gardi, *African Crafts and Craftsmen*; Louise E. Jefferson, *The Decorative Arts of Africa*; Laure Meyer, *Art and Craft in Africa*; Roy Sieber, *African Furniture & Household Objects*; and Margaret Trowell, *African Design*. Books on the crafts of specific tribes or regions include the volume edited by Margaret Trowell and K. P. Wachsmann, *Tribal Crafts of Uganda*; H. Ellert, *The Material Culture of Zimbabwe*; and J. W. Grossert, *Zulu Crafts*. S. F. Nadel's *A Black Byzantium: The Kingdom of Nupe in Nigeria* is an anthropological study that discusses crafts within the context of Nupe social organization, an approach that helps to explain how craft practices are framed by social values and practices. Tanya Harrod's "'The Breath of Reality': Michael Cardew and the Development of Studio Pottery in the 1930s and 1940s," *Journal of Design History* 2, nos 2 & 3 (1989) is an excellent study of craft education in British Africa, focusing on its development at Achimota College in the Gold Coast.

Books and articles by historians of art, architecture, and the decorative arts have also been helpful. Roger Benjamin, *Orientalist Aesthetics: Art, Colonialism, and French North Africa, 1880–1930* and Hamid Irbouh, *Art in the Service of Colonialism: French Art Education in Morocco, 1912–1956* were my primary sources on French policies related to the crafts and decorative arts in North Africa, while I also relied extensively on Brian McLaren, *Architecture and Tourism in Italian Colonial*

Libya: An Ambivalent Modernism for discussions of craft policy and tourist promotion in that country. Dipti Baghat's essay "Art Deco in South Africa" which appeared in the catalog *Art Deco 1910–1939* was extremely helpful as were other books, catalogs, and articles on South Africa's architecture, design, and exhibitions—Clive Chipkin, *Johannesburg Style: Architecture and Society 1880s–1960s*; Deon Viljoen and Piér Rabe, *Cape Furniture and Metalware*; and Jennifer Robinson, "Johannesburg's 1936 Empire Exhibition: Interaction, Segregation and Modernity in a South African City," *Journal of South African Studies* 29, no. 3 (September 2003).

Not a lot has been written on African graphics. For information on African scripts and syllabaries, I have relied almost exclusively on the seminal book by Saki Mafundikwa, *Afrikan Alphabets: The Story of Writing in Afrika*. Abderrahman Slaoui, *The Orientalist Poster: A Century of Advertising through the Slaoui Foundation Collection* is an indispensible resource for visual documentation and background text on French travel posters in North Africa as well as related subjects. Lynn M. Thomas, "The Modern Girl and Racial Respectability in 1930s South Africa," *The Journal of African History* 47, no. 3 (2006) and "Skin Lighteners in South Africa: Transnational Entanglements and Technologies of the Self," in Evelyn Nakano Glenn, ed., *Shades of Difference: Why Skin Color Matters* are rare studies of African advertising. Much valuable information on the history of South African newspapers can be found in Les Switzer, ed., *South Africa's Alternative Press: Voices of Protest and Resistance, 1880s–1960s* and a related volume, Keyan Tomaselli and P. Eric Louw, eds., *The Alternative Press in South Africa*. There is also an extensive literature on the representation of Africans and other colonial subjects in Europe through exhibitions, advertising, and other means. Relevant books and essays include Thomas G. August, *The Selling of the Empire: British and French Imperialist Propaganda, 1890–1940*; Michael Scholz-Hänsel, *Das Exotische Plakat*; Anandi Ramamurthy,

Imperial Persuaders: Images of Africa and Asia in British Advertising; Dana S. Hale, *Races on Display: French Representations of Colonized Peoples, 1886–1940*; Karen Pincus, *Bodily Regimes: Italian Advertising under Fascism*; Raymond Bachellot, Jean-Barthélmi Debost, Anne-Claude Lelieur, and Marie-Christine Peyrière, *NégriPub: L'Image des Noirs dans la Publicité*; and Anne McClintock, "Soft-soaping Empire: Commodity Racism and Imperial Advertising," in George Robertson, Melinda Mash, Lisa Tickner, Jon Bird, Barry Curtis, and Tim Putnam, eds., *Traveller's Tales: Narratives of Home and Displacement*.

Books

General

Adu Boahen, A., ed. *General History of Africa (abridged edition). Volume 7: Africa Under Colonial Domination 1880–1935*. Paris: Unesco, and London: James Currey, 1900 (c. 1985).

Alao, George Ayiki. *La Press Littéraire Africaine: Deux Examples Contemporains, Xiphefo (Mozambique) et Prométhée (Bénin)*. Villeneuve d'Ascq: Presses Universitaires du Septentrion, 1996.

August, Thomas G. *The Selling of the Empire: British and French Imperialist Propaganda, 1890–1940*. Westport, CT, and London: Greenwood Press, 1985 (Contributions in Comparative Colonial Studies 19).

Austen, Ralph. *African Economic History: Internal Development and External Dependency*. London: James Currey, and Portsmouth, NH: Heinemann, 1987.

Bachellot, Raymond, Jean-Barthélemi Debost, Anne-Claude Lelieur, and Marie-Christine Peyrière. *Négripub: L'Image des Noirs dans la Publicité*. Paris: Somogy, 1994.

Crowder, Michael. *West Africa Under Colonial Rule*. London: Hutchinson, 1968.

De Gregori, Thomas R. *Technology and the Economic Development of the Tropical African Frontier*. Cleveland and London: Case Western Reserve University Press, 1969.

Derrick, Jonathan. *Africa's "Agitators": Militant Anti-Colonialism in Africa and the West, 1918–1939*. New York: Columbia University Press, 2008.

Duignan, Peter and L. H. Gann, eds. *Colonialism in Africa, 1870–1960: Vol. 4: The Economics of Colonialism*. Cambridge: Cambridge University Press, 1975.

Fieldhouse, D. K. *Colonialism 1870–1945: An Introduction*. London: Weidenfeld and Nicolson, 1981.

Freund, Bill. *The African City: A History*. Cambridge: Cambridge University Press, 2007.

Gann, L. H. and Peter Duignan, eds. *Colonialism in Africa, 1870–1960 Vol. 1: The History and Politics of Colonialism 1870–1914*. Cambridge and New York: Cambridge University Press, 1969.

—eds. *Colonialism in Africa, 1870–1960 Vol. 2: The History and Politics of Colonialism 1914–1960*. Cambridge and New York: Cambridge University Press, 1970.

Gardi, René. *African Crafts and Craftsmen*. English translation by Sigrid MacRae. New York: Van Nostrand Reinhold, 1969.

Headrick, Daniel R. *The Tentacles of Progress: Technology Transfer in the Age of Imperialism, 1850–1940*. New York and Oxford: Oxford University Press, 1988.

Herskovits, Melville J. and Mitchell Harwitz, eds. *Economic Transition in Africa*. Evanston, IL: Northwestern University Press, 1964 (Northwestern University African Studies 12).

Hopkins, A. G. *An Economic History of West Africa*. New York: Columbia University Press, 1973 (The Columbia Economic History of the Modern World).

Jefferson, Louise E. *The Decorative Arts of Africa*. New York: The Viking Press, 1973.

Kasfir, Sidney Littlefield. *African Art and the Colonial Encounter: Inventing a Global Commodity*. Bloomington and Indianapolis: Indiana University Press, 2007.

Klein, Leonard S., ed. *African Literatures in the 20th Century: A Guide*. New York: Ungar Publishing Company, 1986.

Lewis, David Levering. *W.E.B. Du Bois: The Fight for Equality and American Century, 1919–1963*. New York: Henry Holt & Co., 2000.

Mafundikwa, Saki. *Afrikan Alphabets: The Story of Writing in Afrika*. West New York: Mark Batty, 2004.

Meyer, Laure. *Art and Craft in Africa*. Paris: Éditions Terrail/Édigroup, 2007.

Oliver, Roland and Anthony Atmore. *Africa Since 1800*. Cambridge et al.: Cambridge University Press, 2005 (c. 1967).

Oliver, Roland and J. D. Fage. *A Short History of Africa*. Baltimore: Penguin Books, 1962 (Penguin African Library).

Oliver, Roland and Michael Crowder, eds. *The Cambridge Encyclopedia of Africa*. Cambridge: Cambridge University Press, 1981.

Pieterse, Jan Nederveen. *White on Black: Images of Africa and Blacks in Western Popular Culture*. New Haven and London: Yale University Press, 1992.

Ramamurthy, Anandi. *Imperial Persuaders: Images of Africa and Asia in British Advertising*. Manchester and New York: Manchester University Press, 2003.

Roberts, A. D., ed. *The Cambridge History of Africa, Vol. 7: From 1905 to 1940*. Cambridge: Cambridge University Press, 1986.

Scholz-Hänsel, Michael. *Das Exotische Plakat*. Stuttgart: Institut für Auslandsbeziehungen, Staatsgalerie Stuttgart, Edition Cantz, 1987.

Sieber, Roy. *African Furniture & Household Objects*. New York: American Federation of Arts, and Bloomington and London: Indiana University Press, 1980.

Simelane, Hamilton Sipho. *Colonialism and Economic Change in Swaziland, 1940–1960*. Kampala and Manzini: Janyeko Publishing Center, 2003.

Slaoui, Abderrahman. *The Orientalist Poster: A Century of Advertising through the Slaoui Foundation Collection*. Casablanca: Malika Editions, 1997.

Stein, Judith. *The World of Marcus Garvey: Race and Class in Modern Society*. Baton Rouge: Louisiana State University Press, 1986.

Trowell, Margaret. *African Design*. New York and Washington: Frederick A. Praeger, 1960.

Wickins, Peter. *Africa 1880–1980: An Economic History*. Cape Town: Oxford University Press, 1986.

Wieschhoff, H. A. *Colonial Policies in Africa*. Westport, CT: Negro Universities Press, 1972 (c. 1944).

Wilson, Charles. *The History of Unilever: A Study in Economic Growth and Social Change*, 2 vols. London: Cassell & Company, 1954.

British Africa

Apena, Adeline. *Colonization, Commerce, and Entrepreneurship in Nigeria: The Western Delta, 1914–1960*. New York: Peter Lang, 1997 (Society and Politics in Africa, Vol. 2).

Brett, E. A. *Colonialism and Underdevelopment in East Africa: The Politics of Economic Change, 1919–1939*. New York, London, and Lagos: NOK Publishers, 1973 (Studies in East African Society and History).

Constantine, Stephen. *Buy and Build: The Advertising Posters of the Empire Marketing Board*. London: Her Majesty's Stationery Office, 1986.

Danquah, J. B. *Self-Help and Expansion*. Achimota: Achimota Press, 1943.

Ellert, H. *The Material Culture of Zimbabwe*. Harare: Longman Zimbabwe and Sam Gozo Ltd, 1984.

Howard, Rhoda. *Colonialism and Underdevelopment in Ghana*. New York: Africana, 1978.

King, Kenneth. *The African Artisan: Education and the Informal Sector in Kenya*. London et al.: Heinemann, and New York: Teachers College Press, 1977.

Martin, Susan M. *Palm Oil and Protest: An Economic History of the Ngwa Region, South-Eastern Nigeria, 1800–1980*. Cambridge and New York: Cambridge University Press, 1988.

Munro, J. Forbes. *Africa and the International Economy, 1800–1960*. London: J. M. Dent & Sons, and Totowa, NJ: Rowman and Littlefield, 1976.

—*Britain in Tropical Africa, 1880–1960: Economic Relationships and Impact*. London: Macmillan, 1984 (Studies in Economic and Social Theory).

Nadel, S. F. *A Black Byzantium: The Kingdom of Nupe in Nigeria*. Foreword by Lord Lugard. London, New York, and Toronto: Oxford University Press, 1965 (c. 1942).

Nyong'o, P. Anyang. *The Possibilities and Historical Limitations of Import Substitution Industrialization in Kenya*. Trenton, NJ: Africa Research and Publications Project, n.d.

Pedlar, Frederick. *The Lion and the Unicorn in Africa: A History of the Origins of the United Africa Company 1787–1931*. London: Heinemann, 1974.

Trowell, Margaret and K. P. Wachsmann, eds. *Tribal Crafts of Uganda*. With a foreword by H. J. Braunholtz. London, New York, and Toronto: Oxford University Press, 1953.

Van Zwanenberg, R. M. A. with Anne King. *An Economic History of Kenya and Uganda, 1800–1970*. London and Basingstoke: Macmillan, 1975.

French Africa

Benjamin, Roger. *Orientalist Aesthetics: Art, Colonialism, and French North Africa, 1880–1930*. Berkeley, Los Angeles, and London: University of California Press, 2003.

Berliner, Brett. *Ambivalent Desire: The Exotic Black Other in Jazz Age France*. Amherst, MA: University of Massachusetts Press, 2002.

Bonin, Hubert. *C.F.A.O.: Cent Ans de Compétition*. Paris: Economica, 1987.

Boone, Catherine. *Merchant Capital and the Roots of State Power in Senegal, 1930–1985*. Cambridge: Cambridge University Press, 1992 (Cambridge Studies in Comparative Politics).

Hale, Dana S. *Races on Display: French Representations of Colonized Peoples, 1886–1940*. Bloomington and Indianapolis: Indiana University Press, 2008.

Irbouh, Hamid. *Art in the Service of Colonialism: French*

Art Education in Morocco, 1912–1956. London and New York: Tauris Academic Studies, 2005.

Suret-Canale, Jean. *French Colonialism in Tropical Africa, 1900–1945*. Translated from the French by Till Gottheiner. New York: Pica Press, 1964.

Italian Africa

Fuller, Mia. *Moderns Abroad: Architecture, Cities and Italian Imperialism*. London and New York: Routledge, 2007.

McLaren, Brian L. *Architecture and Tourism in Italian Colonial Libya: An Ambivalent Modernism*. Seattle and London: University of Washington Press, 2006.

Palumbo, Patrizia, ed. *A Place in the Sun: Africa in Italian Colonial Culture from Post-Unification to the Present*. Berkeley, Los Angeles, and London: University of California Press, 2003.

Pincus, Karen. *Bodily Regimes: Italian Advertising under Fascism*. Minneapolis and London: University of Minnesota Press, 1995.

Sbacchi, Alberto. *Ethiopia under Mussolini: Fascism and the Colonial Experience*. London: Zed Books, 1985.

Segrè, Claudio G. *Fourth Shore: The Italian Colonization of Libya*. Chicago and London: University of Chicago Press, 1974 (Studies in Imperialism).

Vandewalle, Dirk. *A History of Modern Libya*. Cambridge: Cambridge University Press, 2006.

Portuguese Africa

Newitt, Malyn. *Portugal in Africa: The Last Hundred Years*. Harlow: Longman, 1981.

South Africa

Chipkin, Clive. *Johannesburg Style: Architecture and Society 1880s–1960s*. Cape Town: David Philip, 1993.

Grossert, J. W. *Zulu Crafts*. Pietermaritzburg: Shuter & Shooter, 1978.

Konczacki, Zbigniew A., Jane L. Parpart, and Timothy M. Shaw. *Studies in the Economic History of Southern Africa*, 2 vols. London: Frank Cass, 1991.

McGillivray, Kenneth I. *Introducing South African*

Art Deco Furniture. Claremont, South Africa: BeauSéjour, 2003.

Nelson, Don. *A Pictorial History of Advertising in South Africa*. Cape Town: Don Nelson Publishers, 1990.

Switzer, Les, ed. *South Africa's Alternative Press: Voices of Protest and Resistance, 1880s–1960s*. Cambridge: Cambridge University Press, 1997 (Cambridge Studies in the History of Mass Communication).

Tomaselli, Keyan and P. Eric Louw, eds. *The Alternative Press in South Africa*. Belleville, South Africa: Anthropos, and London: James Currey, 1991 (Studies on the South African Media).

Viljoen, Deon and Piér Rabe. *Cape Furniture and Metalware*. Cape Town: Deon Viljoen and Piér Rabe, 2001.

Chapters in books

Bhagat, Dipti, "Art Deco in South Africa," in Charlotte Benton, Tim Benton, and Ghislaine Wood, eds. *Art Deco 1910–1939*. Boston, New York, and London: Bulfinch Press, 2003.

Ciarlo, David, "Advertising and the Optics of Colonial Power at the Fin de Siècle," in Volker M. Langbehn, ed. *German Colonialism, Visual Culture, and Modern Memory*. New York and London: Routledge, 2010.

Davies, P. N., "The Africa Steam Ship Company," in J. R. Harris, ed. *Liverpool and Merseyside: Essays in the Economic and Social History of the Port and Its Hinterland*. London: Frank Cass & Co., 1969.

Fuller, Mia, "Building Power: Italian Architecture and Urbanism in Libya and Ethiopia," in Nezar Al Sayyad, ed. *Forms of Dominance: On the Architecture and Urbanism of the Colonial Enterprise*. Aldershot: Avebury, 1992.

Johnson, Marion, "Technology, Competition, and African Crafts," in Clive Dewey and A. G. Hopkins, eds. *The Imperial Impact: Studies in the Economic History of Africa and India*. London: The Athlone Press, 1978.

Lamprakos, Michele, "Le Corbusier and Algiers: The

Plan Obus as Colonial Urbanism," in Nezar Al Sayyad, ed. *Forms of Dominance: On the Architecture and Urbanism of the Colonial Enterprise.* Aldershot: Avebury, 1992.

Lawal, A. A. "Industrialisation as Tokenism," in Toyin Falola, ed. *Britain and Nigeria: Exploitation or Development?* London and New Jersey: Zed Books, 1987.

McClintock, Anne. "Soft-soaping Empire: Commodity Racism and Imperial Advertising," in George Robertson, Melinda Mash, Lisa Tickner, Jon Bird, Barry Curtis, and Tim Putnam, eds. *Traveller's Tales: Narratives of Home and Displacement.* London and New York: Routledge, 1994.

Perkins, Kenneth J. "The Compagnie Générale Transatlantique and the Development of Saharan Tourism in North Africa," in Philip Scranton and Janet F. Davidson, eds. *The Business of Tourism: Place, Faith, and History.* Philadelphia: University of Pennsylvania Press, 2007 (Hagley Perspectives on Business and Culture).

Thomas, Lynn M., "Skin Lighteners in South Africa: Transnational Entanglements and Technologies of the Self," in Evelyn Nakano Glenn, ed. *Shades of Difference: Why Skin Color Matters.* Stanford: Stanford University Press, 2009.

Articles

Austen, Ralph A. and Daniel Headrick, "The Role of Technology in the African Past," *African Studies Review* 26, nos. 3–4 (September–December 1983).

Forbes, Robert H., "The Black Man's Industries," *Geographical Review* 23, no. 2 (April 1933).

Harrod, Tanya, "'The Breath of Reality': Michael Cardew and the Development of Studio Pottery in the 1930s and 1940s," *Journal of Design History* 2, nos 2 & 3 (1989).

Hopkins, Anthony, "Economic Aspects of Political Movements in Nigeria and the Gold Coast, 1918–1939," *Journal of African History* 7, no. 1 (1966).

Martin, Marilyn, "Art Deco Architecture in South Africa," *The Journal of Decorative and Propaganda Arts* 20 (1994).

Massing, Jean Michel, "From Greek Proverb to Soap Advert: Washing the Ethiopian," *Journal of the Warburg and Courtauld Institutes* 58 (1995).

McLaren, Brian L. "The Tripoli Trade Fair and the Representation of Italy's African Colonies," *The Journal of Decorative and Propaganda Arts* 24 (2002).

Okonkwo, R. L. "The Garvey Movement in British West Africa," *The Journal of African History* 21, no. 1 (1980).

Robinson, Jennifer, "Johannesburg's 1936 Empire Exhibition: Interaction, Segregation and Modernity in a South African City," *Journal of South African Studies* 29, no. 3 (September 2003).

Sieber, Roy, "African Furniture and Household Goods," *African Arts* 12, no. 4 (August 1979).

Smith, Robert, "The Canoe in West African History," *The Journal of African History* 11, no. 4 (1970).

Thomas, Lynn M., "The Modern Girl and Racial Respectability in 1930s South Africa," *The Journal of African History* 47, no. 3 (2006).

Chapter 34: Colonies: India, Hong Kong, and Burma 1900–1945

Introduction

Though India, Hong Kong, and Burma were all British colonies, each embodied a very different set of conditions for the development of crafts, manufacturing, and design. At the beginning of the 20th century, promoters of industrialization in India faced uncountable odds—Indian resistance in the British colony, lack of capital and personnel, and especially the absence of a market for mass-produced products. The resistance effort was further complicated by the extensive Indian debates that ranged from all-out support for industrial development on a Western model to Gandhi's extreme exhortation for a simple life of self-sufficiency. The short-lived *swadeshi* movement in Bengal extended the 19th-century desire to be free of British goods and prepared the way for Gandhi's call for *Swaraj* that combined *swadeshi* practices of economic self-sufficiency with a political strategy of resisting the British on a much wider front. Industrialists were frustrated with Gandhi's antagonism to machines and his espousal of a simple rural life, but they benefited from his ability to galvanize masses of people to struggle for independence. E. B. Havell's and Ananda Coomaraswamy's craft romanticism and Alfred Chatterton's advocacy of small-scale enterprises each had merit but did not provide economic solutions for the rural masses on the one hand or support for ambitious industrialists on the other. Consequently, the period in India from the turn of the century to the end of World War II was a complicated mix of competing strategies for economic betterment, all of which remained useful after independence when the new Indian government had more leeway to consider approaches to economic development that were not encumbered by the need to overcome Britain's inclination to impede them.

As with India, Britain did not encourage industrialization in the Southeast Asian region, preferring instead to extract raw materials and sell their own mass-produced goods. Hong Kong was an exception, due to its long history of entrepreneurial activity, which continued actively under British rule.

It was not just the Western countries that sold their products in Southeast Asia and Hong Kong, however. The region was a huge market for Japanese and Chinese goods. Calendar posters created in China were distributed to Chinese communities in Hong Kong and throughout Southeast Asia to advertise these products. Among those who profited from the Chinese networks was Aw Boon Haw, the entrepreneur in Burma who invented Tiger Balm.

India
The role of the crafts

One way that Britain exercised its imperial power over its largest colony was to flood the Indian market with British mass-produced goods. In the second half of the 19th century, the introduction of these goods, particularly cheap cotton cloth from Manchester, as well as the establishment of British factories within the country, severely weakened a number of India's indigenous craft industries. However, there were still craftsmen, both in the cities and the rural areas, who were able to resist this phenomenon for various reasons. The economist Tirthankar Roy believes that the principal challenge to local craftsman from abroad was in the textile industry, which was, however, one among many that also included metalwork, glass, pottery, leather, and woodworking.

Due to the sizeable rural population and the dominance of agriculture in the Indian economy, one of the largest markets was for agricultural tools. These were provided mainly by blacksmiths and carpenters, who were also skilled at repairing them. With the advent of the iron plow and cane-crushing press, carpenters were affected, as the market for wooden equivalents declined.

Although villages had their local smiths and woodworkers, many of whom also worked part-time in agriculture, a large number without obligations in the villages moved to urban areas, which ranged from small towns to large cities. D. R. Gadjil notes that among village craftsmen, potters were particularly hard hit due to competition from larger Indian potteries, domestic brass and copperware suppliers, and imported enamelware.

The need for cooking utensils supported the brass, copper, and bell-metal industries. As demand increased for other metal products such as cutlery, tools, and machine parts, small factories sprang up, especially in or near cities, to produce these goods.

The urban furniture industry also attracted carpenters who had previously made traditional furniture for a rural market. They created new designs for a rising urban clientele, many of whom had been influenced by British taste. The small rural furniture workshops were replaced by larger ones, some of which introduced limited machinery to the production process. Other products made by these small or medium-scale workshops included trunks, safes, locks, and various electroplated products. Among the workshops was the Godrej and Boyce Manufacturing Co., a manufacturer of locks and then safes, which was founded in 1897 by the nationalist Ardeshir Godrej (1868–1936), a lawyer and inventor who intended his company to compete with foreign brands and help India become economically independent.

One product unique to India was the trolley on wheels used by vendors at railway stations to hawk

SWEETMEAT VENDOR, POONA STATION BUILDING PLATFORM.

Fig. 34.01: Railway station trolley, c. 1920s. SSPL via Getty Images.

sweets, cigars, and tobacco. These trolleys consisted of a wood framed box with glass panels that sat on a frame which supported the wheels (Fig. 34.01). Such objects, which combined wood and metalwork as well as glass cutting, could be easily manufactured in small workshops that employed craftsmen with diverse skills.

Craft practices in the villages remained almost unchanged. Local craftsmen accepted raw materials from their customers and charged them for the labor to create a product. By contrast, the growing number of small and medium-sized workshops in the urban areas adopted a more entrepreneurial approach, whereby they sought to market finished goods rather than simply charge for their labor. One factor that urban craftsmen had to face, however, was the decline in demand for high-quality work. This was particularly noticeable in crafts such as wood and ivory carving and working in metal. The decline was due to diminishing commissions from the royal courts and an increase in demand for cheaper goods from the growing urban populations.

Gadjil defines four stages in the development of urban craft workshops. Instrumental to this process was a new type of entrepreneur, who could provide artisans with capital or materials as needed. In the first stage, the entrepreneur furnished the necessary resources but did not buy the finished goods. In the second, he supplied resources, then bought the finished products and marketed them. In the next stage, the businessman provided the raw materials and paid the artisan on a piece-work basis for the finished goods. In the final phase, he brought the artisans together in a small factory and managed both the production and sale of the products they made.

When one considers the many forces that affected the status of the traditional crafts, whether at the village level or among the highly skilled craftsmen who worked for the luxury market, it is evident that competition from British mass-produced goods was only one of many factors that caused the traditional crafts to decline. Another was the shift from rural craft practices to small and medium-scale urban workshops, which introduced new forms of entrepreneurship that addressed a market rather than an individual customer. However, what inhibited the majority of these smaller workshops from developing into larger factories was the absence of existing markets, due to widespread poverty on the one hand and a lack of technical expertise and capital on the other. The development of factories was not in the best interest of the colonial administration, hence economics became conjoined with politics as Indian activists took steps to improve the conditions required for industrialization while also fostering a movement of self-sufficiency to produce goods locally and resist foreign ones.

The swadeshi movement

A number of factors made the process of industrialization far more difficult in India than it had been in Europe or the United States. Most significant was the competition from British manufacturers, who preferred that India remain a market for their goods rather than become an economic competitor. This attitude was reinforced by the British Raj, which at times half-heartedly promoted industrialization but managed in ways both subtle and obvious to subvert it.

There was little capital within India to finance large-scale enterprises. The majority of wealthy Indian princes, who retained their opulent lifestyles even under British rule, were not interested in industrial development. Instead, they funded enormous palaces with luxurious interiors, many of which British firms and designers created. Numerous educated Indians with upper-class backgrounds but lesser means believed that business was beneath their station and they were likewise not inclined to engage in entrepreneurial activity. Familiarity with how industrialization had altered the landscape in Britain also contributed to ambivalence about introducing the factory system to India. Thus, support for industrialization had to compete with the belief that a resurgence of native crafts would more effectively lead to economic independence. Even R. C. Dutt, an early proponent of industrialization and a prominent economic historian, stated in his impressive *Economic History of India* of 1902–1904 that he believed Indians to be ultimately better off working in their own fields or at their own looms than laboring for a landlord or as wage-earners in large factories.

By 1903, *swadeshi*, or self-reliance, a movement that had first emerged in the late 19th century, had begun to spread, particularly in the state of Bengal, where it was fueled by the British decision to partition the region into two sectors in 1905. This prompted a call to boycott British goods and led to a large number of initiatives to create and market indigenous products. The *swadeshi* message was actively promoted by the ardent nationalist Satish Chandra Mukherjee (1865–1945) through his journal *Dawn*, which he founded in 1897 and edited until 1913, and the Dawn Society, which held classes and seminars between 1902 and 1907.

Swadeshi activists did not adopt one strategy only. Some thought in terms of starting new industries, while others favored strengthening local craftspeople. Beginning in the 1890s, efforts were made to promote indigenous goods through exhibitions and shops such as the Swadeshi Emporium, which had been set up in 1891, and the Indian Stores, founded a year later. By 1905, the year of partition, the number of *swadeshi* shops in Calcutta had increased considerably.

Among the *swadeshi* products that sold well in the shops were cutlery, porcelain, and some items of clothing. The medium-sized Calcutta Pottery Works was one of the few successful Bengali enterprises. With imported machinery and a skilled ceramist who had studied in Japan, the factory advertised *swadeshi* teacups, saucers, and teapots as well as additional items. Other competitors were less successful due to undercapitalization and a lack of skilled workmen. Several entrepreneurs announced plans to manufacture bicycles but could not attract the resources to begin production and resorted instead to importing and repairing them. The most successful

swadeshi efforts were several cotton mills, although they barely scraped by due to a shortage of capital.

By 1908, Bengali entrepreneurs, discouraged by a paucity of manufacturing success stories, shifted their interest towards services such as banking and insurance, although these businesses too had trouble raising operating funds. In general, the *swadeshi* movement in Bengal failed to produce the economic renaissance that its leaders had initially hoped for. Part of the problem was that the educated Bengalis were not able to mobilize the massive village population to support the movement. But *swadeshi* did condition many Bengalis to think in terms of economic independence and helped prepare the way for Mahatma Gandhi's powerful campaign beginning in the 1920s to resist the British Raj by weaving *khadi* cloth instead of buying British cotton.

The Orientalists and craft romanticism

Like his fellow arts administrators, John Lockyard Kipling and George Birdwood, E. B. Havell (1861–1934) also stressed the value of Indian design and craftsmanship when he was Superintendent of the Art School in Madras between 1884 and 1891. At the school, he championed the revival of traditional handicrafts and introduced practical courses to improve them. When he was named Principal of the Calcutta Art School in 1896, he took a more radical position, initiating reform of the curriculum that eradicated the distinction between the fine arts and the crafts and made Indian art the basis of instruction. As keeper of the Calcutta Art Gallery, Havell removed most works of European art and replaced them with Indian examples.

To quicken the development of the cotton industry in Bengal, Havell began promoting the fly-shuttle loom around 1902. Invented by the Englishman John Kay (1704–c.1779) in 1733 and a major force in the Industrial Revolution, this loom enabled the craftsman to speed up the weaving process and significantly increase production. Nationalist leaders embraced the new looms and set up a number of schools to train youth from Bengal's elite social class to use them. Havell too established a training center, the Central Weaving College, thus marking a moment where his own romantic view of Indian crafts intersected with the Indian nationalists' attempt to produce their own goods instead of patronizing British merchants. By 1908, however, the attempt to introduce fly-shuttle looms had achieved little success, as the upper-class Indian youth lost interest in weaving and native weavers found the looms to be too expensive.

Due to health reasons, Havell returned to England in 1906 but continued to promote and write about Indian arts after his return. In 1912 he published a book, *The Basis for Artistic and Industrial Revival in India*, in which he put forth a patronizing view of *swadeshi*, arguing vigorously against indigenous cotton mills and factories, celebrating village craftsmen, and denigrating mill owners, factory workers, and shopkeepers. Like other British arts administrators who promoted craft education, he believed that industrialization had brought moral and physical depravity and degradation to the large commercial cities of Europe. As one antidote, he cited a Dutch industry that was producing handkerchiefs, neckties, and related items that were made with the traditional lost-wax process that had been imported from Java.

Havell's vision of an India free of industrialization's horrific effects relegated Indians to a life without technology, neither telephones nor automobiles nor the "Swadeshi gramophones" that would signal the doom of Indian civilization should there be factories to make them. To be fair, Havell did not espouse a repressive view of Indian economic development, but he refused to consider a future for India that might require relinquishing the spiritual ideals he believed to be part of the nation's heritage in favor of an industrial process that would wreak havoc on the heritage of indigenous artisanry he so much admired.

Havell's anti-industrial views were shared by Ananda Kentish Coomaraswamy (1877–1947), an Anglo-Ceylonese scholar of south Asian art and a friend of Charles Ashbee and others connected to the Arts and Crafts movement. In 1907, Coomaraswamy moved to Chipping Campden, where Ashbee had founded the Guild of Handicraft, an Arts and Crafts workshop, five years earlier. During the time he spent there before traveling to India in 1910, Coomaraswamy and Ashbee shared many discussions about the negative consequences of industrialization.

One result of this friendship was Coomaraswamy's 1909 book *The Indian Craftsman*, for which Ashbee wrote the introduction. Projecting onto India all the ideals he felt Europe had lost, Ashbee foresaw the eventual disintegration of what he called "the great city of mechanical industry" and claimed that India possessed a fundamental and enduring order that was far more admirable. Like others who imagined a nation of peaceful villages populated by craftsmen who were fulfilled in their work, Ashbee ignored the colonial context in which Indians lived, as did Coomaraswamy, a patrician himself, who condoned the caste system, which ensured the continuity of distinct craft traditions even as it perpetuated wide disparities of privilege. Coomaraswamy further romanticized Indian craftsmanship by claiming that craft expertise originated in the divine skill of an Indian god, Visvakarma. In his assertion that the Indian craftsman was blissfully free of the struggle for existence that oppressed the working man in Britain, Coomaraswamy ignored the dynamic structure of the Indian craft economy, which had resulted in a significant move by craftsmen from villages to towns and cities as well as the activity of small entrepreneurial workshops which had become necessary for the craftsman's survival.

Following his arrival in India, where he remained from 1910 to 1913, Coomaraswamy began to engage more directly with the realities of Indian social and political life. In *Art and Swadeshi*, a collection of essays he published in 1911, he criticized the goods he found in *swadeshi* shops, noting their deterioration from earlier aesthetic standards as well as their poor quality and high price. Like William Morris, he equated beauty with morality and lamented that India was bereft of both. He echoed the Arts and Crafts reluctance to use machinery except in the most basic way, relegating the craftsman to production in small workshops rather than envisioning that same person as a designer for mass production. Coomaraswamy echoed Havell in his call for Indian tradition to replace Western methods in the art schools and he adopted some of the nationalist rhetoric in his call for Indians to take charge of their own cultural development and rediscover their cultural traditions, notably in the crafts and various arts that he believed had once made the country great. Politically, he avoided the question of resisting British goods and lamented the passing of the Indian courts that were once great patrons of Indian craftsmanship. Graduates from the schools of art demeaned their talent, he said, by making cheap goods for tourists or creating teapots laden with cheap ornament for Anglo-Indian bungalows.

There is much in the critiques of both Havell and Coomaraswamy that makes sense. Both feared the worst effects of industrialization that they observed in Britain and both mourned the loss of an authentic and spiritual Indian craft tradition. Coomaraswamy added to this a concern that Indian craftsmen were cheapening their skills by catering to tourist markets and producing bowdlerized imitations of British taste for what he called Anglo-Indians. Neither Coomaraswamy nor Havell, however, addressed the actual dynamic of the Indian economy, where British interests continued to dominate, nor did they support industrialization as a necessary strategy for national development. As a consequence, they inadvertently condoned imperial policies, which, in their worldviews, might just as well exist so long as they did not prevent the moral superiority and spiritual serenity that pre-industrial Indians were more likely to achieve than their industrialized British counterparts.

Foreign designers and Indian consumers

The very "Anglo-Indians" whom Coomaraswamy criticized for their attraction to cheap imitations of European designs were the intended clientele for the many foreign companies that either sold goods to Indian customers through local agents or else opened their own showrooms in India. British firms that produced luxury goods had paid attention to the Indian market since the 18th century. Many were located in Calcutta, one of the world's largest ports, and also the capital of British India since 1776. Among these were producers of lighting, furniture, and other domestic objects such as clocks and glassware. In addition, architects and interior designers also sought business from Indian clients.

Customers for British goods and services ranged from the inordinately rich maharajas and princes to university-educated Anglophile clerks and other professionals. Hunting was a favorite sport of some maharajas, who purchased elaborately decorated rifles by Holland and Holland, Remington, and other weapons manufacturers. Leading European firms and department stores like Louis Vuitton, Hermès, and Harrods created custom-designed luggage, wardrobes, picnic baskets, and gift boxes. These were for the most part produced by their staffs in Europe. Larger items included specially modified automobiles with lavish interiors, applications of rare metals and gems to exterior designs, and unique features such as sliding roofs, cow guards, and extra storage compartments.

The maharajas' taste in palaces ranged from adaptations of traditional Indian forms to historic European styles, or else to the Indo-Saracenic or Indo-Gothic style, which was a pastiche of native Indian or Islamic forms and motifs and English Gothic Revival or Victorian elements. British furniture companies and decorators such as Waring & Gillow and Maples & Co. had showrooms and agents in India, where they competed for the commissions to furnish these palaces. Several maharajas showed a marked preference for a modern Art Deco style. Among them was Umaid Singh of Jodhpur, whose Umaid Bhawan Palace combined Art Deco with ancient Hindu temple forms. The Deco interior was created by the Polish designer Stefan

Norblin, who came to India because of the worsening political situation in Europe. Norblin made sketches for the maharaja's luxurious furniture, which was fabricated by local artisans. He also produced a number of large murals, glass paintings, and mosaics for both public and private spaces within the palace.

The most remarkable appropriation of European modern design for a maharaja's palace, however, was Manik Bagh, the residence of Maharaja Yeshwant Rao Holkar II of Indore and his wife. As their architect, they hired the German Eckart Muthesius (1904–1989), son of Hermann Muthesius, a founder of the Deutscher Werkbund. Among other palaces of the time, Manik Bagh was perhaps unique in its owners' commitment to modern European architecture and furnishings in the Art Deco style. The exterior consisted of clean white walls that were punctuated by awnings over the windows, while the interior furnishings and lighting

by leading French and German designers and architects featured custom-designed pieces by Muthesius, Jacques-Émile Ruhlmann, Louis Sognot, Georges Djo-Bourgeois, and Michel Dufet, along with well-known iconic furniture such as Eileen Gray's Transat armchair and Le Corbusier and Perriand's chaise longue. Carpets with geometric designs were by French furniture and carpet designer Ivan Da Silva Bruhns (1881–1980) (Fig. 34.02).

Besides the palace, Muthesius also designed for the Maharaja a railway car, a hunting caravan, an airplane interior, and the model for a houseboat residence. The railway car featured air conditioning, electric utilities, and mirrored sliding doors with specially designed cutlery, porcelain, and bed linens. The caravan consisted of four trucks whose rear ends, when the trucks were in a cross formation, each functioned—whether as a dining room, bathroom,

Fig. 34.02: Eckart Muthesius, Manik Bagh, entrance hall, c. 1931. Wikimedia.

bedroom, or study—as part of a temporary dwelling. The modern houseboat design had a modified streamlined form with rounded rooms at either end, an exterior deck around the living space, and a lavish distribution of windows.

Following World War I, there was a middle class of sufficient numbers—though still a significant minority of the population—to form a market for less expensive mass-produced goods such as furniture and lighting. At the end of the 1920s, Bombay witnessed a rise in modern apartment buildings, many in the Art Deco style. British furniture companies resident in India such as John Roberts & Co., McKenzie's, and William Jacks & Co. promoted Art Deco furnishings for these new dwellings, noting that their staffs consisted of well-trained European decorators who could help their clients purchase furniture that was reflective of contemporary trends. In 1937, modern furniture was also featured in Bombay's Ideal Home Exhibition, which was modeled on similar events in England. The Indian Institute of Architects organized the exhibition to promote modern architecture and interior design.

Gandhi and the politics of khadi

Before Mohandas Gandhi (1869–1948) returned to India from South Africa in 1915, resistance to British rule had not gained sufficient momentum to become a full-scale opposition movement. Gandhi had previously been a lawyer and political activist in South Africa, where his life was transformed by reading *Unto This Last*, John Ruskin's critique of modern civilization. It is ironic that Gandhi, who would play such a central role in the struggle for Indian independence, would have been influenced so profoundly by an author with an admittedly low opinion of Indians. What Gandhi took from Ruskin, however, was a valorization of the simple life that was unfettered by material accoutrements. In 1904, while in South Africa, he started the Phoenix Settlement, an attempt to build a self-sustaining community, but he was called away to

political work and was unable to continue living there. He first articulated a credo for Indian independence in *Hind Swaraj* (*Indian Self Rule*), a series of articles which he published as a book in 1908. Following Ruskin, he took a dim view of materialism and the dependence on technology that characterized modern life. His antagonism to machines was particularly extreme. Not only did he state an abhorrence of machine-made goods and the factories where they were produced, but he also declared that he would have liked to do away with the railroads if that had been possible.

Gandhi was able to put some of his views into practice in 1910 when he and a group of family and friends established Tolstoy Farm, not far from Johannesburg. Gandhi named the farm after the Russian writer Leo Tolstoy to show his sympathy for Tolstoy's spiritual and moral beliefs, which he believed were close to his own. The residents of the farm built their own houses, baked their own bread, and even began to make their own sandals. It was this experience with the simple life that Gandhi brought back to India and which he made a hallmark of his political program.

By 1921, Gandhi had persuaded the Indian National Congress to adopt *Swaraj* or self-rule as a principal objective and had come to recognize *swadeshi* as a valuable political strategy. But he developed his own extreme form of *swadeshi*, which centered on the production of homespun *khadi* cloth. To make the cloth, Gandhi introduced the *charkha*, a simple wooden spinning wheel, which became a national symbol (Fig. 34.03). He would spin for about half an hour each day, testifying to his followers that resistance to the British could take a productive and non-violent form. But spinning was more than a symbolic act for Gandhi. He saw it as a way to instill discipline and bring financial assistance to the poor. In 1925, he established the All-India Spinners Association, which he hoped to make an instrument of economic reform by fostering the development of hand spinning. Although the organization did manage to organize weaving in

Fig. 34.03: Margaret Bourke-White, Gandhi spinning *khadi* cloth, 1946. Time & Life Pictures/Getty Images.

many villages by collecting and distributing yarn and to open a number of stores that sold *khadi*, it was ultimately a modest effort, given the vastness of rural India, which would have taken a far more ambitious and better funded program to transform.

Once Gandhi had rejected British society as a viable model for a free India, he ceased to wear European clothes and adopted Indian garments made of *khadi* including a *dhoti*—a piece of cloth that was wound around the body—and occasionally a white "Gandhi cap," made from several pieces of *khadi* that were sewn together.

For many Indians, particularly educated ones, *khadi* came to symbolize resistance. By 1921, all members of the Indian National Congress dressed in *khadi* garments, becoming what Jawaharlal Nehru, who was to serve as India's first prime minister after independence, called "the livery of freedom."

As the design scholar S. Balaram has shown,

Gandhi was a master at endowing things around him, including *khadi*, with symbolic significance. For example, Balaram likens Gandhi's spinning in the midst of political turmoil to Lord Krishna's singing the Bhagavad-Gita, a portion of the great Mahabharata epic, while war ranged around him. He also attributes Gandhi's ability to influence millions of people to his use of symbols and rhetorical devices.

To follow Balaram's argument, we can note that Gandhi was less successful in converting the Indian economy to one of self-sufficiency through spinning *khadi* cloth than he was in using spinning as a symbol of self-reliance that encouraged masses of people to actively struggle against British rule. Ironically, Gandhi shared with the 19th- and 20th-century art school reformers and craft idealists like Kipling, Birdwood, Havell, and Coomaraswamy a critique of European industrial civilization—in fact, his antagonism to the machine was far greater than any of theirs. However, he differed from them in his recognition that an idyllic society of serene village artisans could not exist unless the British departed and India became an independent nation.

Industrialization: the British policy

Lord Curzon, Viceroy of India between 1899 and 1905, who considered himself a promoter of Indian industrialization, established a Department of Commerce and Industry in 1905, though he was also known for his statement that the vast majority of Indians were only trained for agriculture and would never be fit for anything else. This contradiction typified the position of the British Raj towards industrialization in India and exemplified its preference for a colony that consumed British goods rather than made its own, much less marketed them abroad in competition with Britain's national interests. In fact, Curzon's short-lived department was of primary benefit to an elite group of British entrepreneurs as well as Indians who were favorable to the Raj.

Although colonial administrators like E. B. Havell instituted reforms in Indian art schools and promoted revivals of local craftsmanship, the various agencies of the Raj that required professional design and engineering services consistently favored British personnel. The government ordnance factories that made weapons hired mechanics and artisans from England, thus reducing the opportunities for Indians to gain comparable training, while a principal problem in developing a cadre of local engineers capable of handling complex projects was that large government engineering contracts were rarely offered to Indians and therefore few entered the profession.

Mention has already been made of the government's sparse patronage of Indian firms that manufactured railroad locomotives and carriages. Similarly, the government met most of its other material needs—supplies for the Indian and British police; water, gas, and sewage systems; hospital equipment; and even stationery for administrative offices—by purchasing the required goods in Britain and shipping them to India. Through its policies of giving preferential treatment to British goods and services, the Raj maintained the message that these were superior, even when there were clearly Indian professionals and entrepreneurs who could have provided local equivalents, and at a considerably lower cost.

Alfred Chatterton (1866–1958), a young British engineer who came to India in 1888 to teach in the College of Engineering at the University of Madras, was one of the rare British colonials who promoted Indian industrialization, even though he did so at the level of small and medium enterprises. Chatterton worked with the provincial government of Madras, becoming the Director of Industrial and Technical Inquiries when the Madras government established a full-fledged Department of Industries in 1906.

With a government grant, Chatterton began a program in 1898 at the Madras School of Art, where E. B. Havell had once been the principal, to design and manufacture household vessels of aluminum, then a relatively new material for industrial use. The program was a success and prepared the way for private enterprise in Madras. It led to the establishment of the Indian Aluminum Company by Eardley Norton, a strong supporter of the Indian National Congress, and stimulated the creation of other enterprises that were based on existing craft skills, including a tannery where water buckets, shoes, and sandals were manufactured using the industrial technique of chrome tanning, which involved treating the skins chemically. Based on Chatterton's employment of chrome tanning, it was widely adopted in India. Chatterton also helped to establish the Salem Weaving Factory, which produced shawls, cotton goods, and silk cloths.

Although Indians in the region welcomed the Madras Department of Industries, it raised alarm among British businessmen who saw the emerging enterprises as unwarranted competition. As a result of their protests, Lord Morley, then Secretary of State for India, closed down the department in 1910 and discouraged the establishment of any pioneering industries supported by the Madras government. Chatterton subsequently left Madras and became an advisor to the government of Mysore.

In 1912, he published in Madras a collection of essays entitled *Industrial Evolution in India.* His espousal of industrialization based on craft skills was a foil to Havell's and Coomaraswamy's romantic adulation of the individual craftsman. Like them, Chatterton recognized the harmful effects of the factory system in Europe and proposed a different direction for India. Instead of large factories, he supported the development of small and medium-scale firms that would adopt what he called a judicious combination of men and machines.

Chatterton believed that Indian artisans should have access to all the instruments of success—capital, organizational skill, and appropriate tools. While his espousal of Indian entrepreneurship, even on a small scale, went against the grain of the typical British businessman in India, he was nonetheless a staunch proponent of British rule, skeptical of *swadeshi* politics, and convinced that Indians would always need the British to set high standards of service.

There was considerable Indian opposition to Lord Morley's decision to abolish the Madras Department of Industries, and consequently the Raj backtracked to some degree. By 1914, Madras had established a new department, as had Bengal and several other provinces. When World War I began, India was cut off from foreign imports and a surge in demand arose for products that were produced domestically. This stimulated a number of industries including cotton production, leather tanning, and shipbuilding. As a response to the situation, particularly the need to strengthen Indian production capacities, the British government established an Indian Industrial Commission in 1916. Its mandate was to explore the possibilities for further industrial development in India and lay the groundwork for a permanent industrial policy. After extensive research, the commission

produced a final report in 1918, concluding that the British government should play a more active role in the country's industrial development.

Among the specific recommendations were the establishment of provincial Departments of Industry that would be coordinated by an Imperial Industrial Service; improving technical education; and providing technical and financial aid to demonstration factories in emerging industries. However, the British did not sustain a national position on industrialization and, despite some successful initiatives, provincial governments were not given sufficient resources or incentives to pursue the ambitious program that had been outlined in the commission's report. Failing to forcefully implement the commission's recommendations, which would have significantly increased state support for new and struggling local enterprises, the government fell back on its earlier policy of economic *laissez-faire*, which favored more experienced British enterprises and reinforced the difficulties of newly-established Indian businesses to compete with them.

In a 1929 book, *The Economic Development of India*, the British economist Vera Anstey argued that despite some isolated industrial successes, India had not achieved anything that might be called an industrial revolution even though a potential to develop new industries existed. Arguing that India still suffered serious financial, technical, and labor deficiencies, she called for a British industrial policy that would have included financial aid, technical training, and intensive promotion of improved production methods, but such a policy did not come to be. Consequently, the few major industrial achievements of Indian entrepreneurs during the interwar years were due primarily to their courage and perseverance, which defied the British government's proclivity to protect its own interests first and foremost.

Industrialization: the Indian response

At its annual meeting in 1901, the Indian National Congress concluded that the decline of indigenous crafts, caused by the incursion of British industry, was at the root of Indian poverty. Nonetheless, by that time most Indian nationalists had determined that India would need to build its own industrial system. This was easier said than done given the numerous obstacles that faced the country. Unlike the industrialized countries, no infrastructure was in place to foster industrial development. Not only did India lack a culture of technological invention such as existed in Britain or the United States, but there was also a severe shortage of capital as well as skilled professionals to perform design, production, and managerial tasks. In fact, the abundance of human labor reduced incentives to replace workers with machines. Besides, neither machines, the electrical energy to power them, nor the repair facilities and replacement parts were as readily available in India as they were abroad.

In 1900, the Indian National Congress created an Industrial Committee and the following year began to include an Industrial Exhibition as a part of each meeting. An important stimulus to industrial enterprise was the Association for the Advancement of Scientific and Industrial Education, which was founded in 1904. Its principal mission was to raise funds to send Indian students abroad for technical education. It did manage to provide a number of scholarships and some of the students started enterprises when they returned. In opposition to the educational policies of E. B. Havell and other British art educators, nationalists also criticized the art school emphasis on elevating the cratsman's skills. They claimed that India already had enough trained artisans, and they called instead for more technical education to foster the establishment of large-scale factories that would employ designers and engineers to produce domestic products that could compete with British imports.

In 1905, as the activities of the earlier Indian Industrial Association waned, a new organization, the Indian Industrial Conference took over the association's mission to promote industrialization within India.

With the economic historian and activist R. C. Dutt as its first president, the members presented papers at an annual meeting in conjunction with the Indian National Congress. Dominated by Western-oriented Indian businessmen, however, it sidestepped the more militant *swadeshi* activism that pervaded Bengal during the first years.

Despite the lack of trained Indian industrial designers and engineers, a number of small to medium-sized enterprises were established in the interwar years to produce goods that were based more on mechanical than artisanal processes. Though most such enterprises lasted only a short time, a few did become successful. India Steel & Wire Products Ltd made wire nails, barbed wire, and related merchandise. The first major factory for glassware, the Paisa Fund Glass Works, was established around 1908 in the city of Talegaon, located in the province of Maharashtra. It exemplified perfectly a strategy of resistance by amassing small investments from local farmers and employing an Indian chemical engineer who had studied in the United States at MIT. Due to the attention it paid to training its workers, the Paisa Fund Glass Works spawned a number of other factories that were founded by former employees. These included the United Provinces Glass Works, which was India's largest by 1936, and the Ogale and Bombay Glass Works, both located in the Bombay area. A budding glass industry also developed in Firozabad, a city in the province of Uttar Pradesh, where 15 factories were set up between 1925 and 1931 to manufacture glass beads and bangles. Some progress was also made elsewhere in the manufacture of lamps.

Due to the impact of the *swadeshi* movement, the province of Bengal had a considerable number of such enterprises. Though extremely popular in India, sewing machines were mainly imported from abroad. In fact, Gandhi, who opposed most industrial products, praised the Singer sewing machine. In 1935, the Jay Engineering Works, a small firm founded in Calcutta that year, began to experiment with the production of its own sewing machine, which it planned to market under the brand name Usha. In 1938, the industrialist Lala Shri Ram (1884–1963) took over the company. Four years earlier he had acquired the Bengal Pottery Works, an enterprise initiated by the Maharaja of Kasimbazar in 1907, which had been languishing until Shri Ram made it profitable. Other Bengali enterprises included the Bengal Waterproof Works Ltd, set up in 1920 to manufacture rubberized "Duckback" products; the Bengal Electric Lamp Works, founded in 1932; the Calcutta Fan Works, created in the 1930s; and the India Flashlight Manufacturing Company, which was established in 1933.

Due to difficulties already outlined, few companies were inaugurated on a large scale. Of these, the Tata Iron and Steel Company (TISCO) was by far the most successful. Although it was a producer of steel rather than finished products, TISCO acquired and developed a number of subsidiaries that did produce industrial goods made of steel or which included steel in their manufacture. Within the history of mass production in India, TISCO is highly significant because for many years it was the rare Indian company that adopted the business model of vertical integration demonstrated by American manufacturers like Westinghouse, John Deere, and Ford. Thus, TISCO was able to produce finished products based on material that it manufactured itself.

The Parsi businessman Jamshetji Nusserwanji Tata (1839–1904) started planning the company in 1899, although TISCO did not begin manufacturing steel until 1907, three years after his death. Tata sought funding unsuccessfully from British sources and consequently raised all the operating capital in India from a combination of family investments and modest sums acquired from a large number of supporters. The machinery came from Germany and the initial group of experts was American. At first, TISCO was managed by Tata's oldest son, who oversaw the establishment of a planned company town, Jamshedpur, where the factory, worker housing, and other facilities were located. In 1921, TISCO management opened

the Jamshedpur Technical Institute, which trained Indian students for both managerial and high-level technical jobs. This facilitated the gradual elimination of foreign personnel and the eventual staffing of most positions with Indians. In 1927, the company started an Apprentice School, which trained personnel for the line jobs as welders, machinists, blacksmiths, pattern makers, and so forth. TISCO's ability to staff almost all its positions with Indians within two decades of its founding was a stinging rebuke to all the stereotypes held by British administrators regarding the unsuitability of Indians for industrial ventures.

Similar to large corporations abroad, TISCO developed or acquired a group of companies that were intended to produce goods made of steel, though few of these achieved notable success. The aforementioned India Steel & Wire Products Ltd, which began in the 1930s, was the successor to a company that had collapsed in the prior decade. The Peninsular Locomotive Company was unsuccessful until World War II, when it began to manufacture armored vehicles with steel plates. The Agricultural Implements Company (Agrico), which TISCO acquired, had originally been created to produce hand tools primarily for the extensive agricultural market, but despite the solid design of its products, it never became very successful because it had to compete with the myriad local blacksmiths and small enterprises that manufactured rival implements more cheaply with scrap metal. Most successful was the Tinplate Company that was formed in 1922 jointly with a Scottish firm, Burmah Oil, to produce the tin sheets for the firm's oil containers as well as tins for tea and biscuits. While TISCO did not train industrial designers as such, all of its manufacturing companies required design, which was most likely done by engineers or other employees assigned to such tasks.

Despite the less than impressive showing of TISCO's subsidiaries, the overall success of the steel mill inspired other Indian entrepreneurs to think about enterprises on a large scale. In 1935, a group of industrialists met in Bombay to discuss the establishment of an automobile factory. Following an initial wave of enthusiasm, a 1936 report by an Automobile Factory Committee expressed doubts, which were reinforced by the Raj's reluctance to provide any support. However, several projects were initiated independently of the committee, one led by the industrialist Seth Walchand Hirachand (1992–1953) and another by Ghanshyamdas Birla (1894–1983). In 1942, the Birla group established Hindustan Motors Ltd in Calcutta, while Walchand formed Premier Automobiles Ltd in Bombay two years later. Because of the war, neither could begin production until peace was declared when, due to lack of expertise, each had to find a foreign partner with whom to collaborate, despite their mutual ambition to inaugurate a home-grown automobile industry as a sign of India's industrial progress.

Not one to think small, in 1940 Walchand also founded Hindustan Aircraft with assistance from Mirza Ismail, a high-ranking official who represented the King of Mysore. Walchand's aim was to manufacture airplanes for the Indian Air Force. The undertaking was short of capital, thus he sold his stake. The Kingdom of Mysore refused to follow suit, although due to a lack of experience, it decided to yield management control to the British. After independence, the new Indian government nationalized the company and it played an important role in modernizing the Indian Air Force. Eventually, it became one of the largest aerospace companies in Asia.

Tata, Walchand, and Birla were all bold entrepreneurs who acted on the belief that India would need to compete with the already industrialized nations once it gained independence. In a speech of 1943, Walchand expressed his longing for the day when India would have its own automobiles, airplanes, buses, locomotives and railway coaches, ships, and all the products of an advanced industrial culture that the country still had to import. For him, India's ability to design and manufacture its own products would ensure the alleviation of poverty and the arrival of prosperity for everyone. While inordinately hopeful, Walchand

nonetheless equated industrialization and the capacity for mass production with social improvement, a connection that envisioned Indian capitalism as social betterment for all rather than the accumulation of riches for the few.

Typography, publications, and advertising

At the beginning of the 20th century, literacy was still restricted to a limited segment of the Indian population. With the establishment in the 1920s and 1930s of S. S. Brijbasi, a publisher of lithographic prints in Karachi, and other publishers, the print culture inaugurated by the Calcutta Art Studio, the Ravi Varma Studio, and others in the 19th century was greatly expanded, thus ensuring the continued traffic in cheap printed chromolithographs of mythological figures.

Besides the popularity of these images, however, the publication of reading matter also expanded. Type fonts were available in most if not all indigenous languages, and presses existed throughout the country, producing a wide range of materials from official documents to newspapers, books, and magazines. India's linguistic diversity was extensive, despite the large number of Hindi speakers and the prevalence of the Devanagari script. Artists invented new forms of lettering for posters and other printed matter, but India in these years was not a sufficiently developed commercial culture to warrant more extensive activity in type design. The Linotype company introduced a typesetting machine for Bengali in 1935, but did not make machines for other Indian scripts until after World War II.

The printing historian B. S. Kesavan estimates that more than 500 newspapers and journals were being published at the beginning of the 20th century. Among these was the illustrated journal *Modern Review* that the Bengali Ramananda Chatterjee (1865–1943) published, beginning in 1907. *Modern Review*, which appeared in English, promoted nationalist views and quickly attracted a nationwide readership. It featured lithographic illustrations, but these were replaced by half-tones as soon as the technology was available. The magazine's illustrations influenced publishers throughout India, and by the 1920s and 1930s a number of other illustrated magazines had appeared. As Kajri Jain notes, these magazines reached a plurality of publics from the non-literate to the literate. *Kalyan*, published first in Hindi and then in an English edition for overseas Indians, disseminated religious imagery, which, Jain states, helped to address some of the dilemmas of daily life. The educated class also read English-language pictorial magazines such as the *Illustrated Weekly of India*, which had started as the *Times of India Weekly Edition* in 1880 but was renamed in 1923.

Fig. 34.04: Calcutta Art Studio, Kali Cigarettes, calendar, 1908. The Granger Collection/TopFoto.

Advertising

What distinguishes the Indian mass public's engagement with print culture is that prints were the visual embodiment of deeply held religious or even political beliefs and not simply pictures dedicated primarily to aesthetic pleasure. This quality was exploited by businessmen, both British and Indian, who sought to link their products to mythological narratives, a practice that had started in the 19th century when several companies adopted paintings by Ravi Varma for advertising purposes.

Spirituality and politics came together in a well-known lithographic calendar poster of 1908 for Kali Cigarettes, which depicted the goddess Kali in her most destructive aspect, waving a bloody scimitar (Fig. 34.04). Produced by the Calcutta Art Studio, the calendar featured a small crouched lion in the upper-left corner—a symbol for Britain—and a decapitated soldier in the lower right corner, both of which provoked British officials to read the poster as a sign of political rebellion. The likelihood of this interpretation was supported by the text, which characterized the East India Cigarette Manufacturing Enterprise as a *swadeshi* business whose support would aid India's poor workers.

By the end of World War I, there was a sufficient consumer-oriented Indian middle class to entice some of the large companies from abroad to establish manufacturing facilities in India or else begin serious marketing operations there. Among British firms, Lever and Associated Biscuit Manufacturers sought to sell soap and biscuits respectively. The Czech firm Bata intended to compete with indigenous tanning factories and market shoes, while Dunlop promoted tires, and General Electric and Philips sold light bulbs. Kodak also set up operations in India to sell cameras to the rising middle class.

The advertising strategies of these companies shifted from one to another, but also depended on which audiences the companies were trying to reach. These varied. First was the Indian consumer who might be from a range of economic strata, although, given the products on offer, the likely market was the middle class. Then there were the foreigners living in India, including British colonials but not limited exclusively to them. And for some services, like the Indian State Railways, the market was in Britain. For each group of consumers there were particular advertising strategies and representations of Indian culture.

The strategy of associating a product with a spiritual figure or narrative was evident in a 1932 calendar for Woodward's Gripe Water, a remedy for babies. The image by the Indian painter Mahadev Vishwanath Dhurandhar (1867–1944) played on the story of Lord Krishna's proclivity to steal butter from female cow herders. The advertising concept is that eating butter can make a child sick and Woodward's Gripe Water provides the cure. In the story, Krishna is rebuked by his mother who, in the calendar painting, is depicted as a middle-class housewife. Kajri Jain points out that this mingling of mythic and contemporary narratives was a strategy to reach both Indian and British audiences simultaneously. A related strategy was adopted by the manufacturer of Sunlight Soap, which featured the Hindu god Vishnu with two consorts on one of its posters (Plate 72). The depiction of gods and goddesses was evident as well on some of the matchboxes that were produced in the thriving match factories throughout the country (Fig. 34.05).

Dhurandhar was a serious painter and watercolor artist who worked extensively in advertising for British and Indian companies including the South Indian Railway. An illustrator of textbooks, literary works, and magazines, he was a former student at the J. J. School of Art in Bombay, where he later became a teacher, principal, and then the first Indian director. The school was known for its realistic painting style, which Dhurandhar exemplified in his commercial work. As a teacher and administrator, he no doubt influenced a number of students who later became prominent poster artists and advertising pamphlet designers for the emerging Bombay film industry. In the absence

Fig. 34.05: Flying Rani, matchbox cover. Photo © Luca Tettoni/Bridgeman Images.

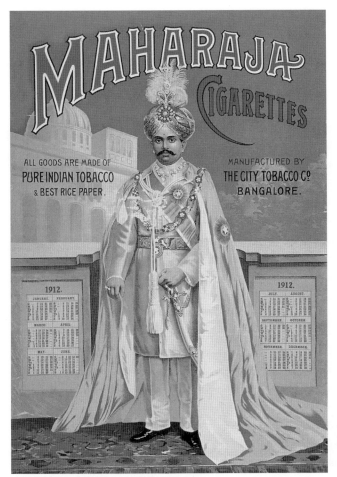

Fig. 34.06: Raja Ravi Varma, Maharaja Cigarettes, calendar poster, 1912. Private Collection.

of specific training for graphic designers, it was thus artists, either self-trained or graduates of the art schools, who were prepared to do the commercial work.

Ravi Varma was perhaps the first Indian painter to earn money from commercial art, and even after his death in 1906 his paintings were still popular for advertising purposes. Though his pictures of mythological subjects were most frequently sought, there was also interest in his other genres such as portraiture. His painting of the Maharaja of Mysore was adopted for a calendar to advertise Maharaja Cigarettes, manufactured by the City Tobacco Company of Bangalore (Fig. 34.06). In this case, the audience was likely to have been

educated Indians for whom the aristocratic maharaja may have had some moderate nationalist appeal, given his commitment to the social needs of his people.

Kodak took a different approach in a 1931 brochure, where the company associated its camera with modernity rather than tradition. The brochure image depicts an Anglicized Indian woman with a Kodak camera standing before a snake charmer. Behind her, other women are walking away with pots on their heads. Like the snake charmer, they are exoticized representations of Indianness with which the modern woman holding the camera is contrasted (Fig. 34.07).

The Indian State Railways, which were owned and managed by the Raj, also used exotic imagery in an extensive advertising campaign during the 1930s to encourage tourists from Britain to see India by rail. Similar to the poster campaign of the London Underground and those of the British railroads that were influenced by it, the Indian State Railways posters

Fig. 34.07: Kodak, brochure, 1931. SSPL via Getty Images.

featured scenic destinations, including a number of temple sites. As fodder for the tourist gaze, Indians were always included as part of the scenery. In some posters they were dwarfed by the impressive monuments, while in others, such as posters that depicted the Khyber Pass or the holy city of Benares, their activity was an essential part of the narrative. The poster artists were all British and included Austin Cooper and Fred Taylor, who had both done posters for the London Underground and the London and North Eastern Railway (LNER), along with William Spencer Bagdatopolos (1888–1965) and Victor Veevers (1885–1968) among others. Cooper's poster for Amber, a city in Rajasthan, depicts a maharaja sitting atop an elephant parading through the city as part of a public spectacle that was calculated to attract tourists (Plate 73).

Indian film posters

The first film advertisement appeared in the *Times of India* in 1896 to promote the *cinématographe*, which the French Lumière Brothers had introduced in Paris only a few months before. Seventeen years later, in 1913, D. G. Phalke produced, directed, and edited the first Indian feature film, *Raja Harishchandra*, a mythological drama whose visual style Phalke adopted from Ravi Varma. He came to know Varma's paintings when he worked in the artist's print studio in 1905. Phalke founded the Hindustan Film Company in 1917 and it was soon followed by others—Dhiren Ganguley's Lotus Film Company, Baburao Painter's Maharasthra Film Company, the Prabhat Film Company, Bombay Talkies, and Wadia Movietone. The largest number of studios was in Bombay, which became the center of the Hindi film industry, but there were other studios in south India, notably in Madras, which developed as the center for films made in the Tamil language.

Early film advertising included painted banners, cut-outs, and posters. Printed handbills were also distributed from decorated bullock carts that were drawn around the towns and villages where the films were shown. Initially the handbills consisted of simple

typefaces, but more decorative fonts along with illustrations were introduced as printing technology improved. Beginning in the 1920s, posters and handbills were supplemented by a new form of advertising, the film booklet, which contained pictures as well as a summary of the film. The cover images and those inside became particularly important aspects of the promotional strategy, as they represented to the distributors and the public the film's content and visual style.

One of the earliest printed film posters and among the first to depart from the Ravi Varma aesthetic was Baburao Painter's *Kalyan Khajina* (*The Treasures of Kalyan*) of 1924. Painter (1890–1954), who was the film's director as well as its poster designer, adopted a pictorial strategy, already widely used for 19th-century theater posters, of featuring a crucial moment in the drama. In the case of *Kalyan Khajina*, it is the moment when the emperor Shivaji discovers some crates of treasure and encounters a woman instead of the anticipated coins (Fig. 34.08). Painter sought to imitate the realistic style of Bombay's J. J. School of Art, where so many artists who did advertising posters had trained. But he was an untrained artist whose style was not as refined as the art school poster designers such as Bide Viswanathan (dates unconfirmed), who came to prominence in the post-war years. Given the J. J. School of Art's proximity to the new film studios, it is not surprising that so many of the industry's poster designers studied there.

Though many studios tended to produce cheap posters without regard for visual quality, artists who learned to paint in the J. J. School of Art's realistic style helped to improve the aesthetic level of film publicity. Those who came into the industry with no art school training learned on the job by painting lettering for the advertising hoardings and absorbing other skills. D. G. Pradhan (dates unconfirmed) designed publicity for Wadia Movietone, which was founded in 1933 after the introduction of sound films two years earlier. To compensate for his lack of formal art training, Pradhan studied informally with a J. J. School of Art student, M. R. Acharekar (1907–1979), who later became deputy

Fig. 34.08: Baburao Painter, *Kalyan Khajina*, poster, 1924. Image Courtesy of The Advertising Archives.

director of the school. Hired by Pradhan, Acharekar supplemented his income doing film posters for Wadia. In the 1930s, he collaborated frequently with one of his students, Mirajkar, and began to incorporate photography, which he combined with painting to create collage compositions.

Art Deco graphics entered India by way of film posters, whose designers adopted the style as a sign of modernity. By the 1930s, the themes of Indian films had expanded beyond the original mythological and historical dramas to include modern situations as well. In his booklet cover for *Dr. Madhurhika or Modern Wife* and others he did for Sagar Movitone Productions, J. Mistry (dates unconfirmed) adopted stylized Art Deco lettering, not only for the English text but for the Devanagari script as well. He also adopted the Deco airbrush style and depicted a piece of glass equipment as if it were a streamlined train. As in the West, the stylized Art Deco graphics were associated with the 1930s and were rarely used anywhere in the post-war years. Their significance in India, however, was to create hybrid graphic forms that mingled traditional Indian scripts with modern Western lettering styles. This tendency would continue after the war as Indian film companies moved towards a brash blockbuster graphic style that was already evident in some of the posters of the 1930s.

Hong Kong

At the beginning of the 20th century, Hong Kong had an extensive manufacturing culture, which had been developing for a considerable period. Products—many made for export in small factories—included clocks, dishes, handstoves, furniture, valises, and leather goods. A few of these product types were on display at the first Hong Kong Arts and Crafts Exhibition in 1906. It was conceived by the governor, Sir Matthew Nathan, who promoted it less for commercial purposes than to display a range of attractive locally made objects that he believed had not been adequately appreciated. Though much on exhibit fell into the category of minor arts such as embroidery or lacemaking, there were nonetheless some impressive pieces of furniture, though many were made by British firms.

Hong Kong factories were small to mid-sized and produced a wide range of objects, whose design concepts were for the most part derived from foreign sources, whether Japanese, Chinese, or Western. There were a number of furniture manufacturers, for example the You On Company, a producer of wooden furniture; the Kowloon Rattan Ware Company, specializing in rattan; and the Tai Ying Steel Window Manufactory Company, which made furniture of steel. The Ottawa Agreement of 1932, which initially allowed Hong Kong manufacturers to export their products to other British colonies and later to Commonwealth countries, opened up new markets and stimulated additional manufacturing. Following the agreement, Hong Kong companies were successfully exporting their "Empire Made" products to Malaya, India, and a number of British colonies in Africa. As a sign of Hong Kong's growing industrial capacity, the Chinese Manufacturers Association was founded in 1934 and shortly thereafter held its first industrial products exhibition. By the time of the second exhibition in 1939, the association had developed a broad concept of industrial design that embraced modern production, patterning, style, and marketing.

This concept was evident in various products that were created in the late 1920s and the 1930s, such as the flashlight made by the Ling Nam Hardware Manufacturing Company. In the 1930s, after Japan occupied Manchuria and then following its invasion of China in 1937, a number of Shanghai companies relocated to Hong Kong, thus strengthening the colony as a manufacturing base. Successful products of the late 1930s included locally produced radios that could operate more successfully than foreign imports in the colony's high humidity, and the diesel trucks made by South China Iron Works.

The colony's developing manufacturing capabilities were matched by the growth of a graphic design community that created the advertising and packaging for new industrial products as well as for the large number of Chinese medicines that were produced in Hong Kong. Among the designers, Kwan Wai Nung (1880–1956) was the leading figure. Due to the many calendar paintings of Chinese women he created, he was known as the "King of Calendar Art." Born into a family of artists and a master of both Chinese and Western painting, Kwan left Hong Kong in 1912 for Shanghai, where he worked with the Gao brothers on the *True Record* until its demise the following year. Returning to Hong Kong, he took up his former position as art director of the English language daily *South China Morning Post*, leaving it in 1915 to start his own company, the Asiatic Litho Printing Press.

His company was a leader in using chromolithography and also employed other printing techniques that made it a leading printing house of the time. As he became more successful, Kwan opened branch offices in Singapore and in the Chinese cities of Guangzhou and Shanghai. At its peak in the 1930s, his company could produce a new calendar poster every four or five days. One of Kwan's oldest clients was the Kwong Sang Hong cosmetics company, whose trademark of two girls may well have been inspired by the American trademark for Smith Brothers cough drops, although one story has it that the firm's founder created the mark after seeing a vision of two angels. Kwan produced his first poster for the company in 1913, depicting the girls in conventional Chinese dress in a traditional landscape. He updated that image considerably for a poster of 1932 in which he showed them in modern dress with contemporary hairstyles and Western high heels.

Besides numerous calendar posters, Kwan's company also did a considerable amount of Chinese medicine packaging like other designers in Hong Kong. The preparation of Chinese medicines has a long tradition and was spread among many companies in the colony by the time of World War I. Packaging was one way for these companies to compete, either by incorporating a photograph of the company's founder into the design to indicate authenticity or by adding a catchy slogan or a striking logo. Packaging ranged from metal tins with images and text screened onto them to cardboard boxes, glass vessels, or paper packets, while trademark images varied from animals known through folk tales to deities or religious figures.

A factor that designers had to consider was ensuring that the consumer knew how to use the medicine. To abet this process, some manufacturers adopted simple illustrations comparable to those in children's schoolbooks. The illustrations might depict

Fig. 34.09: Aw Boon Haw, trademark and packaging for Tiger Balm, c. 1909. Haw Par Corporation Limited.

situations in which the medicines would be used or else they would portray a body part or body with acupuncture points indicated to help with the proper medical application. Some packages included a guarantee coupon with an intricate hard-to-copy design to prevent imitators

Burma

Most Chinese throughout Southeast Asia were engaged in small-scale local trade, but a few profited from widespread ethnic networks to become regional entrepreneurs. Such was the case of Aw Boon Haw (1882–1954) in Burma. Beginning with a small shop that sold traditional Chinese medicines in the city of Rangoon, which Aw Boon Haw and his brother inherited from their father, Aw built a marketing and media empire that centered on a muscle salve he called Tiger Balm. Modeling his marketing campaign on the packaging, posters, and advertisements of Western businesses that he observed on his travels in Asia, he chose a springing tiger as his trademark and, as Sherman Cochran has shown, he made it the core of his advertising campaign (Fig. 34.09). Initially Aw designed the Tiger Balm posters himself, but subsequently he recruited leading commercial artists to create his publicity, among them the prominent Hong Kong calendar poster designer Kwan Wai Nung. Aw was a master at tailoring his advertising campaigns to different cultural groups, using any language— whether Chinese, English, Burmese, or Thai—that was prevalent in a local market. What remained consistent in all of his publicity was the image of the tiger. The packages ranged from tins with colorful images screened onto them to paper boxes and what became a classic container, the hexagonal jar with an embossed metal lid. Tiger Balm became one of the first locally created regional products in Asia as a result of Aw Boon Haw's aggressive marketing strategy, which followed and frequently surpassed the sales techniques of foreign firms such as the British American Tobacco Company.

Bibliography
Bibliographic essay

Substantial material on Indian industrialization can be found in a number of economic histories by Indian scholars including D. R. Gadgil, *The Industrial Evolution of India in Recent Times, 1860–1939*; Rajat Kanta Ray, ed., *Entrepreneurship and Industry in India, 1800–1947* and Ray's own *Industrialization in India: Growth and Conflict in the Private Corporate Sector, 1914–47*; Sumit Sarkar, *The Swadeshi Movement in Bengal, 1903–1908*; and Sunil Kumar Sen, *Studies in Economic Policy and*

Development of India (1848–1939). Vera Anstey, *The Economic Development of India*, written in 1929, contains helpful information but looks at India's economic history from a colonial point of view. Judith Brown, *Gandhi: Prisoner of Hope* is a thorough biography of the Indian leader. S. Balaram's article "Product Symbolism of Gandhi and Its Connection with Indian Mythology," *Design Issues* 5, no. 2 (Spring 1989) offers an explanation of how Gandhi manipulated symbols for political ends, while Susan S. Bean, "Gandhi and Khadi, the Fabric of Indian Independence," in Annette B. Weiner and Jane Schneider, eds., *Cloth and Human Experience* addresses Gandhi's connection to this material. Information on E. B. Havell and Ananda Coomaraswamy can be found in various sources including Debashish Banerji, "The Orientalism of E.B. Havell," *Third Text* 16, no. 1 (March 2002); Roger Lipsey, *Coomaraswamy: His Life and Work*; and Vishwanath S. Naravene, *Ananda K. Coomaraswamy*. Their own books, particularly Havell's *The Basis for Artistic and Industrial Revival in India* and Coomaraswamy's *The Indian Craftsman* and *Art and Swadeshi* reveal much about the two men's attitudes towards Indian crafts and their resistance to industrialization. Similarly, Alfred Chatterton, *Industrial Evolution in India* offers an extensive explication of his views. Amin Jaffer, *Made for Maharajas: A Design Diary of Princely India* contains ample documentation in words and images of the maharajas' involvement with architecture and design. Jaffer also wrote an article on "Indo-Deco" in Charlotte Benton, Tim Benton, and Ghislaine Wood, eds., *Art Deco 1910–1939*, the catalog of the Art Deco exhibition at the Victoria and Albert Museum.

Information on Indian graphic design has to be pieced together from various sources. Christopher Pinney is an expert on Indian print culture and has written a number of valuable books and articles on the subject including *"Photos of the Gods": The Printed Image and Political Struggle in India* and the article, "The Nation (Un)Pictured? Chromolithography and 'Popular' Politics in India, 1878-1995," *Critical Inquiry*

23, no. 4 (Summer 1997). See also Anindita Ghosh, *Power in Print: Popular Publishing and the Politics of Language and Culture in a Colonial Society, 1778–1905*. Kajri Jain's *Gods in the Bazaar: The Economies of Indian Calendar Art* has some useful material on commercial art but like Pinney she writes mainly about prints. Rachel Dwyer's and Divia Patel's *Cinema India: The Visual Culture of Hindi Film* has an excellent section on the first Indian film posters. Books about Indian art in this period also have material related to commercial print culture. See Tapati Guha-Thakurta, *The Making of a New "Indian" Art: Artists, Aesthetics and Nationalism in Bengal, c. 1850–1920*; Partha Mitter, *Art and Nationalism in Colonial India, 1850–1922:Occidental Orientations* and *Much Maligned Monsters: History of European Reactions to Indian Art*; and Pushpa Sindar, *Patrons and Philistines: Arts and the State in British India, 1773–1947*. Also useful are the catalogs of Indian visual culture that Neville Tuli edited for Ossian's: *A Historical Epic. India in the Making. 1757–1950: From Surrender to Revolt, Swaraj to Responsibility*; *A Historical Mela: The ABC of India. The Art, Book and Cinema*; and *India: A Historical Lila. Auctions of Indian Modern & Contemporary Paintings, Drawings and Graphic Art*.

The exhibition catalog *Made in Hong Kong: A History of Export Design in Hong Kong, 1900–1960* is a good source of information on Hong Kong design and manufacturing, while Simon Go's *Hong Kong Apothecary: A Visual History of Chinese Medicine Packaging* has helpful material on medicine package design. Sherman Cochran's *Chinese Medicine Men: Consumer Culture in China and Southeast Asia* is the best account of Aw Boon Haw and other regional entrepreneurs.

Books
General

Clark, John. *Modern Asian Art*. Honolulu: University of Hawaii Press, 1998.

Cochran, Sherman. *Chinese Medicine Men: Consumer Culture in China and Southeast Asi*a.

Cambridge, MA, and London: Harvard University Press, 2006.

Davenport-Hines, R. P. T. and Geoffrey Jones, *British Business in Asia since 1860*. Cambridge: Cambridge University Press, 1989.

Nock, O. S. *Railways of Asia and the Far East*. London: Adam and Charles Black, 1978.

India

Anstey, Vera. *The Economic Development of India*. London, New York, and Toronto: Longmans, Green & Co., 1952 (c. 1929).

Barnouw, Erik and S. Krishnaswamy. *Indian Film*, 2nd ed. New York, Oxford, and New Delhi: Oxford University Press, 1980.

Bayley, C. A., ed. *The Raj: India and the British, 1600–1947*. London: National Portrait Gallery Publications, 1990.

Brown, Judith M. *Gandhi: Prisoner of Hope*. New Haven and London: Yale University Press, 1989.

Chandra, Bipan. *The Rise and Growth of Economic Nationalism in India: Economic Policies of Indian National Leadership, 1880–1905*. New Delhi: People's Publishing House, 1966.

Chatterton, Alfred. *Industrial Evolution in India*. Madras: The "Hindu" Office, 1912.

Coomaraswamy, Ananda K. *The Indian Craftsman*. With a Foreword by C. R. Ashbee. London: Probsthain & Co., 1909.

—*The Arts & Crafts of India & Ceylon*. New York: Farrar, Straus and Company, 1964.

—*Essays in National Idealism*. New Delhi: Munshiram Manoharlal, 1981.

—*Art and Swadeshi*. Madras: Ganesh, n.d.

de Schweinitz Jr., Karl. *The Rise and Fall of British India; Imperialism as Inequality*. London and New York: Methuen, 1983.

Dotz, Warren. *Light of India: A Conflagration of Indian Matchbook Art*. Berkeley and Toronto: Ten Speed Press, 2007.

Dwyer, Rachel and Divia Patel. *Cinema India: The Visual Culture of Hindi Film*. London: Reaktion Books, 2002.

Gadgil, D. R. *The Industrial Evolution of India in Recent Times, 1860–1939*. Bombay: Oxford University Press, 1971.

Gandhi, Mohandas K. *Gandhi, An Autobiography: The Story of My Experiments with Truth*. Translated from Gujarati by Mahadev Desai. Foreword by Sissela Bok. Boston: Beacon Press, 1993.

Ghosh, Anindita. *Power in Print: Popular Publishing and the Politics of Language and Culture in a Colonial Society, 1778–1905*. Delhi: Oxford University Press, 2006.

Guha-Thakurta, Tapati. *The Making of a New "Indian" Art: Artists, Aesthetics and Nationalism in Bengal, c. 1850–1920*. Cambridge and New York: Cambridge University Press, 1992.

Havell, E. B. *The Basis for Artistic and Industrial Revival in India*. New Delhi: Usha Publications, 1986 (c. 1912).

Iyer, Raghavan. *The Moral and Political Thought of Mahatma Gandhi*. n.p. Concord Grove Press, 1983.

Jaffer, Amin. *Made for Maharajas: A Design Diary of Princely India*. New York: The Vendome Press, 2006.

Jain, Kajri. *Gods in the Bazaar: The Economies of Indian Calendar Art*. Durham and London: Duke University Press, 2007.

Kesavan, B. S. *History of Printing and Publishing in India: A Story of Cultural Awakening, Vol. 1: South Indian Origins of Printing and Its Efflorescence in Bengal*. India: National Book Trust, 1985.

Kumar, Dharma and Tapan Raychaudhuri, eds. *The Cambridge Economic History of India, Vol. 2: c. 1757–c. 1970*. With the editorial assistance of Meghnad Desai. London: Cambridge University Press, 1983.

Lipsey, Roger. *Coomaraswamy: His Life and Work, 3*. Princeton NJ: Princeton University Press, 1977 (Bollingen Series LXXXIX).

MacCarthy, Fiona. *The Simple Life: C.R. Ashbee in the Cotswolds*. Berkeley and Los Angeles: University of California Press, 1981.

Mathur, Saloni. *India by Design: Colonial History and Cultural Display.* Berkeley, Los Angeles, and London: University of California Press, 2007.

Mitter, Partha. *Much Maligned Monsters: History of European Reactions to Indian Art.* Oxford: Clarendon Press, 1977.

—*Art and Nationalism in Colonial India, 1850–1922: Occidental Orientations.* Cambridge: Cambridge University Press, 1994.

Naravene, Vishwanath S. *Ananda K. Coomaraswamy.* Boston: Twayne Publishers, 1977.

Pinney, Christopher. *"Photos of the Gods": The Printed Image and Political Struggle in India.* London: Reaktion Books, 2004.

Ray, Rajat Kanta. *Industrialization in India: Growth and Conflict in the Private Corporate Sector, 1914–47.* Delhi: Oxford University Press, 1979.

—ed. *Entrepreneurship and Industry in India, 1800–1947.* Delhi: Oxford University Press, 1992.

Roy, Tirthankar. *The Economic History of India, 1857–1947.* New Delhi.: Oxford University Press, 2000.

Ruskin, John. *Unto This Last and Other Writings.* Edited with an introduction, commentary and notes by Clive Wilmer. Harmondsworth: Penguin Books, 1985.

Sarkar, Sumit. *The Swadeshi Movement in Bengal, 1903–1908.* New Delhi: People's Publishing House, 1973.

—*Modern India, 1885–1947.* Delhi: Macmillan, 2002 (c. 1983).

Sen, Sunil Kumar. *Studies in Economic Policy and Development of India (1848–1939).* Calcutta: Progressive Publishers, 1972.

Sindar, Pushpa. *Patrons and Philistines: Arts and the State in British India, 1773–1947.* Delhi: Oxford University Press, 1995.

Tomlinson, B. R. *The Economy of Modern India 1860–1970.* Cambridge: Cambridge University Press, 1993 (*The New Cambridge History of India, Vol. 3 pt. 3*).

Tuli, Neville, curator and text. *India: A Historical Lila. Auctions of Indian Modern & Contemporary Paintings, Drawings and Graphic Art.* Mumbai: Ossian's, 2001.

—ed. *A Historical Epic. India in the Making. 1757–1950: From Surrender to Revolt, Swaraj to Responsibility.* Mumbai: Ossian's, 2002.

—ed. *A Historical Mela: The ABC of India. The Art, Book and Cinema.* Mumbai, Ossian's, 2002.

Hong Kong

Go, Simon. *Hong Kong Apothecary: A Visual History of Chinese Medicine Packaging.* New York: Princeton Architectural Press, 2003.

Made in Hong Kong: A History of Export Design in Hong Kong, 1900–1960. Hong Kong: Hong Kong Museum of History, 1988.

Wong, Wendy Sui. *Hong Kong Comics: A History of Manhua.* New York: Princeton Architectural Press, 2002.

Chapters in books

Bagghi, Amiya Kumar, "European and Indian Entrepreneurship in India, 1900–1930," in Edmund Leach and S. N. Mukherjee, eds. *Elites in South Asia.* Cambridge: Cambridge University Press, 1970.

Bean, Susan S., "Gandhi and Khadi, the Fabric of Indian Independence," in Annette B. Weiner and Jane Schneider, eds. *Cloth and Human Experience.* Washington and London: Smithsonian Institution Press, 1989.

Jackson, Anna, "Art Deco in East Asia," in Charlotte Benton, Tim Benton, and Ghislaine Wood, eds. *Art Deco 1910–1939.* Boston, New York, and London: Bulfinch Press, 2003.

—"Inspiration from the East," in Charlotte Benton, Tim Benton, and Ghislaine Wood, eds. *Art Deco 1910–1939.* Boston, New York, and London: Bulfinch Press, 2003.

Jaffer, Amin, "Indo-Deco," in Charlotte Benton, Tim Benton, and Ghislaine Wood, eds. *Art Deco*

1910—1939. Boston, New York, and London: Bulfinch Press, 2003.

Articles

Ahlawat, Deepika, "Empire of Glass: F. & C. Osler in India, 1840–1930," *Journal of Design History* 21, no. 2 (2008).

Balaram, S., "Product Symbolism of Gandhi and Its Connection with Indian Mythology," *Design Issues* 5, no. 2 (Spring 1989).

Banerji, Debashish, "The Orientalism of E.B. Havell," *Third Text* 16, no. 1 (March 2002).

Basu, Aparna, "Technical Education in India, 1900–1920," *Indian Economic Social History Review* (1967).

Lai, Edwin K., "The Hong Kong Arts and Crafts Exhibition of 1910," *Besides: A Journal of Art History and Criticism* (1997).

Pinney, Christopher, "The Nation (Un)Pictured? Chromolithography and 'Popular' Politics in India, 1878–1995," *Critical Inquiry* 23, no. 4 (Summer 1997).

Raina, Dhruv and S. Irfan Habib, "The Unfolding of an Engagement: 'The Dawn' on Science, Technical Education and Industrialization: India, 1896–1912," *Studies in History* 9, no. 1 (1993).

Trivedi, Lisa N., "Visually Mapping the 'Nation': Swadeshi Politics in Nationalist India, 1920–1930," *The Journal of Asian Studies* 62, no. 1 (February 2003).

Dissertations and theses

Huppatz, D. J. *Hong Kong Design: Culture Meets Commerce*. PhD Thesis, Monash University 2003.

Chapter 35: Asia: China and Siam 1900–1939

Introduction

Industrialization in China during the period between the fall of the Qing dynasty in 1911 and the Japanese invasion in 1937 proceeded slowly. The foreign companies that operated in the treaty ports were exceptions to the slow development in the vast rural areas that were dedicated primarily to farming. Of the numerous treaty ports, Shanghai was the one where modernity took hold in its most blatant form. It was not only evident in the city's sizeable manufacturing base but also in its widespread openness to Western influences.

The collapse of the Qing dynasty, due to impatience with the Manchu rulers' resistance to reform, was spurred by the rise of a revolutionary movement led by Sun Yat-sen. He served briefly as president of a new democratic Republic of China before the military leader Yuan Shikai, who had been prime minister in the Qing government, replaced him. Sun Yat-sen then became the leader of a new political party, the Guomindang (National Party), which played a major role in the political struggles of the ensuing years.

In 1914, Japan declared war on Germany and seized Kiaochow, a German colonial territory in China's Shandong province. The following year Japan presented China with Twenty-one Demands that included the right to occupy Kiaochow and to colonize Manchuria and Mongolia and a claim to considerable control over China's military and economic affairs. The Chinese government accepted a negotiated version of the demands, although the ensuing treaties were never ratified.

When Yuan Shikai died in mid-1916 shortly after having declared himself emperor, a political vacuum ensued, leading to a period of civil war between the Guomindang and the Chinese warlords, who were themselves competing for power. Meanwhile, the Versailles Treaty at the end of World War I affirmed Japan's right to Kiaochow, which led to protests in China that were known as the May Fourth Movement of 1919. It was spearheaded by students and intellectuals who decried China's slowness to modernize. Hundreds of new publications attacked Chinese traditions and extolled foreign ideas about social and cultural matters. In 1921, members of the movement's extreme left wing founded the Chinese Communist Party.

In 1921–1922, a group of foreign powers convened the Washington Conference, where they signed a treaty that rejected Japan's claim to Kiaochow and affirmed the historic Open Door Policy that had granted them considerable freedom to operate in China's treaty ports. This ensured that foreign companies and entrepreneurs would continue to play an important role in the development of the Chinese economy.

Failing to gain support from the Western countries, Sun Yat-sen made an alliance between the Guomindang and the Communists, accepting help from Russian advisors in reorganizing his party along Soviet lines. At its first party congress in 1924, the Guomindang adopted Sun Yat-sen's Three Principles of the People: nationalism, democracy, and livelihood.

Sun died in 1925 and the party leadership was taken over by Chiang Kai-shek, a military leader who gained control of most of south and central China by waging a campaign known as the Northern Expedition. He reversed Sun's policy of cooperating with the Communists and executed many of their leaders, an act that initiated a long-running civil war with them. Chiang chose the southern city of Nanjing as the capital of a new government, which gained international recognition, and he governed there between 1927 and 1937, a period known as the Nanjing Decade. In opposition to the Guomindang, the Communists set up a government in Jiangxi, but Chiang's continued military campaigns forced them to abandon the province in 1934 and begin a long march to the north-west, during which Mao Zedong became the party's leader. The Communists established a base in Yan'an, where they continued to struggle against the Guomindang. The same year that the long march began, Chiang introduced the New Life Movement, a set of dicta intended to enforce personal discipline, build character, and counter excess and corruption. Guomindang organizations sought to maintain its tenets through propaganda campaigns and harassment of those who did not toe the line.

Taking advantage of the ongoing conflict between the Guomindang and the Communists, the Japanese invaded Manchuria in 1931 and established a puppet state, Manchukuo, in 1932. Five years later, Japan mounted a full-scale invasion of China, provoking a struggle with a Chinese united front. The invasion quickly became part of Japan's larger ambition to dominate Asia in a Greater East Asia Co-Prosperity Sphere, which was challenged by the Allied forces that fought Japan in the Pacific theater during World War II.

In Southeast Asia, the entire region was under colonial rule in the period before World War II, with the exception of Siam, which was permanently renamed Thailand in 1949. Laos, Cambodia, and Vietnam were part of French Indochina. The Dutch East Indies, now Indonesia, belonged to the Netherlands and Britain controlled Burma, Malaya, Hong Kong, and Singapore. While under United States dominion, the Philippines underwent a series of steps towards independence. Though Siam remained independent and espoused a rhetoric of economic self-sufficiency, the country still depended primarily on exports of teak and tin, while manufacturing few finished goods of its own. Local handicraft production continued in the region's villages as it did in India, while cities supported some small industries like metal, tile, and furniture workshops, printing presses, and heavy equipment maintenance. For the most part, colonial officials treated native crafts as an art form to be shown off at exhibitions in Europe.

China
Crafts, early industrialization, and proto-design

Western industry made its initial impact in China through the treaty ports, which were established following the Treaty of Nanjing in 1842 and had been open to foreign investment since 1895. They were centers of intensive industrial activity, and the machine-made goods that were produced in treaty port factories competed against domestic handicraft products just as British-made products did in India.

As Albert Feuerwerker notes, handicraft remained the dominant mode of production throughout the republican period, accounting for almost 70 percent of industrial output as late as 1933. Rural people, who constituted the majority of the population, relied mainly on their own craft skills rather than industrially-made goods. They frequently combined farming with household craft production, though much was produced in small workshops by urban or semi-urban craftsmen including those who created luxury goods for wealthy clients. Larger workshops or "manufactories," located mainly in urban areas, adopted industrial models of production, although they operated without power machinery.

To compete with the mass-produced treaty-port goods and other goods from abroad, Chinese entrepreneurs concentrated on products that did not require complicated technology or sizeable financial investments, namely textiles, which were unfortunately shoddily made during China's initial stage of industrialization. In general, Chinese businessmen in the early years of the republic bore the consequences of the Qing tradition that held technology in low esteem; hence they had little expertise to draw on as they sought to compete with foreign firms.

Initially, many small workshops were established to undertake machinery repairs and in time some of these evolved into businesses that manufactured products as well. The owners had often gained experience working for foreign firms or through studying abroad. Even during the Qing period, however, many technicians had learned their trade in the railway factories and arsenals that were administered by the government ministries.

Exemplary among the early workshops is the Ta-lung Machinery Works. It was established in Shanghai in 1902 by several men including Yan Yutang (dates unconfirmed), who bought out his partners around 1906. The firm began by repairing steamships, largely with Chinese workmen recruited from foreign companies, and then started to service the machinery of several large textile mills. Growing experience with technical machinery enabled the Ta-lung factory to begin manufacturing its own textile machines in the 1920s. The new design department, which was staffed by engineers and technicians, began by adapting British textile machinery to Chinese requirements. This led to the company's establishment of seven textile plants that used Ta-lung machines. Owning its own textile factories helped immensely in the company's campaign to expand the market for its machines beyond its own plants. At the time of the Sino-Japanese War in 1937, Ta-lung had a staff of 1,300, which included a team of engineers who made continual innovations to the manufacturing process and then oversaw the development of new products such as stoves, engines, and agricultural equipment.

Though few other enterprises were as successful as Ta-lung, there did develop, as Thomas Rawski notes, a budding engineering sector that was located primarily in Shanghai. Companies besides Ta-lung turned out machinery for cotton-spinning and match factories as well as pumps, machine tools, and related products.

By 1933, more than 300 Shanghai machine plants were in operation. There was also a considerable expansion of machine shops in some of China's

secondary industrial centers like Wusih, Hangchow, and Chunking. Gradually the production of Chinese machines began to replace foreign competition in a number of industries. According to Rawski, Chinese machines were generally of lesser quality than those from abroad, but they gained market advantage because of their lower price.

Due to the small market for consumer goods, Chinese entrepreneurs focused heavily on the machine sector with the exception of textile production. A number of Chinese factories, however, produced modest consumer products such as foodstuffs, cigarettes, matches, pencils, soap, toothpaste, medicines, and cosmetics. Among the comparably few manufacturers of durable goods, one can cite several examples including the Wada Enamel Factory, which made enamelware. It was started by a Japanese group and subsequently came under Chinese ownership. Other Chinese durables were based on European or American models. The prototype for an early Chinese bicycle, manufactured in Shanghai in the mid-1930s, was an English Raleigh from around 1903. As a foreign observer noted in 1935, bicycles were cheap and had already become mass products in China. Around the same time, a Chinese factory produced the first domestic sewing machine, which was based on the Singer sewing machine from America. Early manufacturers of fountain pens also modeled their designs on American ones. The bicycle and sewing machine, along with a watch, were considered to be the *san-chuan* or "three things that go round," that some girls demanded of their fiancés before getting married.

Following the death of Yuan Shikai in 1916 and the collapse of his government, there was a great demand for weapons among the feuding warlords, who began to build their own arsenals to manufacture guns and ammunition. By the early 1920s, most provincial capitals had arsenals that were equipped to produce personal weapons and light artillery in small amounts, while those warlords without an arsenal would employ local blacksmiths to make their weapons. The provincial arsenals were the beginning of an armaments industry that had

Fig. 35.01: Rickshaw with metal spoked wheels, date unconfirmed. Getty Images.

The development of modern forms of transport occurred slowly during the republican period. The vehicle most widely used in the cities at the beginning of the century was the rickshaw. The first ones in China had been imported in the 1880s from Japan, where the rickshaw originated, but Chinese designers and craftsmen later improved the original model by replacing the iron frame with a lighter one and adding metal spoked wheels (Fig. 35.01). Rickshaws also became easier to pull when paved streets were introduced to cities, where there had previously been rough dirt roads. The vehicles provided work for rickshaw men—more than 20,000 in Beijing in 1915—who would ferry their passengers around the cities in the absence of motorized transport. In 1924, the Beijing Streetcar Company introduced French-made streetcars to Beijing, thus reducing the number of rickshaws and rickshaw pullers but not eliminating them by any means.

taken on considerable proportions by the 1930s. Besides arms and artillery, the larger arsenals could produce armored trains and even aircraft and like the mechanized factories, they could also manufacture machinery for their own use and for sale to others.

Most inland river transport was handled by Chinese-made junks, which were sailing ships with several masts, or *sampans*—flat-bottomed boats that

Fig. 35.02: Chinese *sampans*. Library of Congress, LC-USZ62-118501.

were usually propelled by a boatman with a pole (Fig. 35.02). These vessels were made primarily from traditional designs in small to medium-sized workshops. By 1911, small steamships and steam launches also transported goods along Chinese waterways, but they were far outnumbered by the junks and sampans that carried most of the nation's inland trade.

Art education and the 1925 Exposition Internationale des Arts Décoratifs

During the Qing dynasty, manufacturing occurred primarily in the arsenals and little thought was given to training designers for a consumer market. In the republican period, more attention was paid to consumer goods, but the goods turned out by most Chinese factories were copies of foreign models. While design training was not a priority for the leaders of the new republic, it was nonetheless included in the movement to modernize art education that began after Sun Yat-sen took power in 1911.

An early pioneer in this movement was Cai Yuanpei (1868–1940), who served briefly as Minister of Education under Sun Yat-sen and Yuan Shikai. While in this position, Cai began to actively promote art training and declared aesthetic education to be one of his five principles of pedagogy. As chancellor of Peking University, beginning in 1917, he proposed that aesthetics replace religion as an expression of spiritual and emotional value. Cai was very much involved in the New Culture Movement of 1917–1923, which adopted a critical stance towards traditional Confucian values and urged a different culture that incorporated Western political, artistic, and scientific ideas.

While living in Paris in 1924, Cai was honorary chairman of an exhibition of Chinese art, calligraphy, and crafts, which was held in Strasbourg. For him, the exhibition was an opportunity to promote the new engagement of young Chinese artists with Western culture, but it had little impact on European audiences; nor did China's exhibit at the Exposition des Arts Décoratifs the following year. Along with the United States, China was one of two invited countries that declined to participate officially, which, in China's case, was due to its unsettled political situation. However, two associations of Chinese artists in Paris did organize a display for the exhibition, which consisted mainly of traditional Chinese decorative art that had been gathered from a number of antique dealers and import-export houses.

By 1928, after his return to China, Cai had again become an important educational leader within the Guomindang, and in 1928 he founded China's first national art academy, along with Lin Fengmian (1900–1991), a Chinese painter with a Western orientation. Located in Hangzhou, far from Peking where the expression of liberal ideas on culture and politics had become dangerous, the National Academy of Art offered classes in design as well as Western and Chinese painting and sculpture.

Lin Fengmian, the school's first director, shared Cai Yuanpei's view that aesthetic experience was central to modern life. He was exposed to the latest currents in modern art when he lived in France and Germany. In France, he had been one of the organizers of the Chinese exhibit at the Paris expo in 1925. He continued to promote modern forms of expression at Hangzhou, while also educating students in traditional Chinese art practices. Several professors in the design department had studied in France and consequently they introduced the Art Deco style to the curriculum. It was evident in some student decorations for lacquerware as well as in lettering designs and advertising illustrations that were published in several popular Shanghai magazines.

In Shanghai, the painter Liu Haisu (1896–1994), who, like Lin Fengmian, was oriented to Western art, opened a small art school in 1912, and by 1921 it had expanded to become the Shanghai Academy of Art. The school, which was the largest in the city, offered programs in handicrafts and commercial art along with courses in Chinese and Western painting among other subjects. Its design department was headed by

Hong Qing (1913–1979), an architect who had studied in Paris and who had a special interest in architectural decoration. The Shanghai Academy was a major source of graphic designers for the city's many advertising agencies, magazines, and publishing houses as its orientation to Western methods of drawing and painting facilitated the students' adaptation to commercial art. Other schools in Shanghai that produced commercial artists included the Dongfang and Shinhua Art Academies, both of which incorporated Art Deco styling into their curricula. In Guangzhou, a southern stronghold of the Guomindang after it regrouped in 1917, Sun Yat-sen appointed the painter Gao Jianfu (1879–1951) to the Industrial Art Commission of Guandong province and made him head of the Industrial Art School.

Fig. 35.03: Zhang Guangyu, furniture designs, 1930s. Baiyaxuan collection.

Shanghai modern

Dubbed "The Paris of the East," Shanghai was China's most modern city. The largest of the treaty ports, it was the country's center for trade, finance, manufacturing, publishing, and a number of other activities. Shanghai was also the principal gateway for Western goods to enter the country. Though China had no automobile industry of its own, Shanghai had more imported cars than any other Chinese city. The consumer-oriented lifestyle of the Chinese middle class and the considerable number of foreigners who lived in Shanghai also demanded large amounts of electrical energy, which officials bragged was the cheapest in the world.

Shanghai was as well the center of debates about the role of design in a modern China. Articles in mass circulation magazines, as historian Carrie Warra points out, championed *gongyi meishu* or "industrial arts" as a way to build a strong national identity and respond to foreign competition. One of the magazines, *Meishu Shenghuo* (*Art and Life*), featured a few products in the Art Deco style that were made by small Shanghai manufacturers—a thermos, cup and saucer, and tumblers from the Shanghai Bakelite Products Company, and decorative mirrors and cosmetics cases from the Zhongxing Celluloid factory. The Art Deco style was visible everywhere in Shanghai. Many of the wealthiest class adopted it for home furnishings and fashions. Strongly influenced by French styles, local Deco furniture featured traditional Chinese elements combined with foreign influences. Among those who designed modern furniture was Zhang Guangyu (dates unconfirmed), a commercial artist (Fig. 35.03). He published a book in 1932 entitled *Modern Applied Arts*, in which he identified Berlin, Paris, and Vienna as sources of new styles in the applied arts. The style was also evident in the mass media such as advertising. Calendar posters portrayed attractive women in Art Deco interiors, while the dresses of some film actresses were made of material that had modern geometric Deco patterns

The producers of traditional Chinese decorative arts were criticized for not responding to the new conditions of modern life, while the art academies were taken to task for not developing more courses in the applied arts. Although Chinese manufacturers for the most part were not yet prepared to produce appealing consumer products, the shops and

Fig. 35.04: Wing On department store, date unconfirmed. Private Collection.

department stores on Shanghai's Nanjing Road, which initially marketed foreign goods primarily, developed a thriving consumer culture by appropriating the most advanced Western techniques of merchandising including window displays, outdoor advertising, and customer service. Chinese businessmen financed the four biggest department stores—Sincere, Wing On, Sun Sun, and Dah Sun. Their buildings included the latest technology such as escalators, and architects sought to incorporate distinctive elements into the designs. The Sun Sun department store, designed by the Hungarian architect C. H. Gonda (dates unconfirmed), was known as "The Store with the Needle Tower," while Wing On and Sincere, which had been built earlier, had highly decorated facades (Fig. 35.04). There were also dance halls, bars, restaurants, and playgrounds in the buildings, thus defining shopping as a form of entertainment. Sun Sun operated a radio station where famous singers performed live.

The stores carried a dazzling array of products. On its opening day, Sincere, the first to be built, offered more than 10,000 different items, almost all of which had been made abroad (Fig. 35.05). Smaller emporia also featured foreign goods. Among them was the showroom that the Sanyou company created, called Peach Blossom Stream, which was named after an earlier poetic image of paradise. Furnished like a modern urban home, it contained multiple rooms that displayed furniture in arrangements that departed from conventional Chinese norms. The mingling of traditional Chinese imagery and modern marketing supports Sherman Cochran's contention that importing Western goods and lifestyles was not simply done as a form of imitation but rather as an attempt to invent a new Chinese identity. The blend of foreign and Chinese influences was also evident in Shanghai fashion, notably the design of the *qipao*, a tight-fitting dress with a high collar and short sleeves. In the 1930s, the *qipao* was

Fig. 35.05: Sincere department store, furniture department, date unconfirmed. Private Collection.

promoted by film stars and through images of modern women on the omnipresent calendar posters.

The National Products Movement

The adoption of the *qipao* by Chinese women who were striving to be modern was one example of the larger National Products Movement so aptly described by the historian Karl Gerth. The movement had its roots in the boycotts of American and Japanese goods before and during World War I. Coincidental with the founding of the Chinese republic, the National Products Protection Association (NPPA) was formed in 1911 to spread the idea that the survival of the new republic depended on the protection of China's own industries.

Boycotts of Japanese products in response to Japan's Twenty-One Demands fueled the expansion of the NPPA and related organizations. A principal issue

was to determine exactly what a national product was. This was complicated by the fact that some so-called Chinese products used foreign materials and techniques while foreign manufacturers sometimes imitated Chinese techniques and disguised their products as national ones.

The movement was strengthened following the 1927 establishment of the Guomindang government in Nanjing. In 1928, a set of National Products Standards was created to resolve the problem of defining a Chinese product. These standards were widely disseminated and reinforced through a series of what Karl Gerth calls "national commodity spectacles," where national products were exhibited. Under the direction of the Ministry of Trade and Commerce, the Shanghai Municipal National Products Museum opened in 1928 to display Chinese products and promote their use. Similar museums followed in other cities.

The National Products Movement also affected the Shanghai department stores and shops, which had to adjust to the Buy China demands. By 1930, the Wing On department store had signed up about 70 domestic suppliers and helped them to produce quality goods by providing them with examples of current fashions from abroad and sending their own technicians to be of service as needed.

In 1928, the Guomindang's Ministry of Trade and Commerce sponsored a large National Products Exhibition in Shanghai, where Chiang Kai-shek gave a speech that linked the existence of such exhibits to the Guomindang's reunification of China and also codified a relationship between good citizenship and the consumption of national products. The exhibition's success encouraged exhibits elsewhere in China as well as the organization of a traveling exhibit that the Ministry of Trade and Commerce designed to encourage Chinese living abroad in Southeast Asia to buy national goods.

Pressure to "Buy Chinese" was also allied with Chiang's New Life Movement, which fostered a highly disciplined and regimented lifestyle as a civic duty. By 1934, when this movement was inaugurated, the National Products Movement had gained strong local and national government support and its aims had become allied with the citizen's highest duty to the nation. Some of its slogans, such as "Wasting money buying foreign products is the most immoral act," even began to sound like the simplistic declaratives that Mao Zedong published in his Little Red Book in the early 1960s.

Graphic design

As China's leading commercial city, Shanghai was also the country's center of commercial art. Like New York, London, Paris, or Tokyo, Shanghai housed an array of printers, publishers, advertising agencies, and art schools, all of which supported a flourishing commodity culture. In advertising graphics as well as book design, magazine layouts, and packaging, a negotiation between Chinese tradition and Western modernism was evident. Calendar posters, for example, made frequent references to earlier Chinese visual culture even as they were produced with Western drawing techniques. A predominant visual style of other commercial graphics was Art Deco, which influenced drawing technique as well as lettering design. The woodcut societies that arose after the May Fourth Movement returned to a more indigenous Chinese reproduction technique but were influenced by revolutionary graphics in Germany and the Soviet Union.

Advertising

The calendar poster, known as *yuefenpai*, was the principal advertising medium of the republican period, mirroring in its depiction of female beauties the period's changing values from perpetuating tradition to embracing modernity. Initially, cigarette companies sponsored these posters, but they were quickly adopted to promote other consumer products such as cosmetics as well as medicines and home remedies. A foreign company, British American Tobacco (BAT), was the first to employ calendar posters for mass advertising, although producing them was only one of its many advertising activities.

BAT founded an art department in 1915. After the failure of its advertising campaigns that Westerners designed, the company added Chinese artists to its staff. Assignments in the art department ranged from drawing black-and-white newspaper ads to designing packaging, creating inscriptions in Chinese and foreign languages, and designing cigarette packages and tins. Ellen Laing notes that these tasks were extremely specialized and even the design of calendar posters was divided among different experts who drew the figures, backgrounds, borders, and lettering. In 1917, BAT established its own school to develop its art and printing staff.

BAT was producing calendar posters before it founded its advertising department. The artist Zhou

Muqiao (1868–1922) had begun to create calendar art for the company as early as 1908. His original drawings from which final chromolithographs were reproduced were outlined in black ink and colored by hand.

Considered by some scholars as the first calendar artist to be recognized for his own style, Zhou had been working commercially since the 1890s, when he created illustrations of attractive women in modern settings for Wu Youru's pictorial magazine *Feiyingge huabao* (*Fleeting Shadow Pavilion Pictorial*). In his posters for BAT and other commercial clients such as

Fig. 35.06: Zheng Mantuo, calendar for Reinsurance "Rossia." Gao Jianzhong Collection.

Standard Oil of New York, Zhou portrayed women in new styles of Chinese dress, although he placed them in the foreground of conventional landscapes. He also flanked them with elaborate borders and drawings of product packages or logos as in his 1914 poster for the Xiehe Trading Company (Plate 74).

Cigarette manufacturing was one economic sector in which Chinese companies competed most easily with foreign firms, since manufacturing cigarettes was much cheaper than producing durable goods or mechanical equipment. The plethora of Chinese cigarettes with brand names like Golden Horse and Patriot also contributed to the success of the National Products Movement, which continued to benefit from the increasingly bold marketing of the Chinese companies.

BAT's biggest rival was the Nanyang Brothers Tobacco Company. Founded in Hong Kong in the early 20th century, Nanyang Brothers moved to Shanghai in 1913. Like BAT, the company had its own art department, in which Pan Dawei (1881–1929), an artist and journalist who had participated in the overthrow of the Qing dynasty, was a central figure. Working for Nanyang Brothers, Pan continued his political activity by promoting the company's cigarettes as indigenous products and recruiting poster artists as part of the National Products Movement. Another Nanyang Brothers artist was Zhou Bosheng (1887–1955), known for his newspaper and periodical drawings of women in contemporary dress.

Zhou Bosheng was influenced by Zheng Mantuo (1888–1961), who transformed the design, production, and subject matter of calendar posters beginning around 1914. Zheng introduced to poster art the traditional "rub-and-paint" technique, which entailed laying down a base of carbon powder that was used for shadows and then applying watercolors over it. This made possible subtle gradations of tone that Zheng's competitor Zhou Muqiao could not attain with line drawings and it did much to further the decline of Zhou's influence as a calendar artist.

Besides adopting the "rub-and-paint" technique, Zheng added new subjects to the calendar poster repertoire. His depiction of half-length figures, which was already widespread in advertising posters abroad, was a decisive break with the tradition of Chinese painting to which Zhou Muqiao adhered. Zheng also portrayed women engaged in modern activities such as using the telephone and he introduced a new erotic element to attract consumers. Zheng portrayed women putting on their make-up or he showed them fully clothed in suggestive positions. More daringly, he emphasized the semi-nude female body as in his poster of 1919 for the

Dachang Tobacco Company, where he depicted Yang Guifei, a Tang dynasty concubine, emerging from her bath. Attended by two fully clad maids, she wears a diaphanous garment that has fallen off one shoulder, exposing her bare breast.

Until the 1930s, when Zheng returned to painting, his calendar posters for Nanyang Brothers and numerous other clients chronicled the increasing acceptance of Western dress and lifestyles in Shanghai (Fig. 35.06). By the 1920s, many Shanghai women bobbed their hair and wore flapper dresses and high heels. Instead of Western clothing, some chose tight-fitting *quipaos* with short sleeves and hemlines (Fig. 35.07). A calendar poster by Zheng from around 1927 for the Wuxi Maolun Silk and Satin Factory depicts two women in silk *quipaos* and high heels dancing the tango together—a liberating image compared to Zhou Muqiao's more conservative posters of a few years earlier.

Fig. 35.07: Zheng Mantuo, Shanghai Huiming Electric Flashlight and Battery Company, calendar poster. Private Collection.

Another important producer of calendar posters and other advertising was Shanghai's Commercial Press. Founded in 1897, the press controlled a vast array of publishing activities that ranged from textbooks and technical manuals to short-story magazines and special interest periodicals. With its advanced printing technology, it also served commercial needs by selling business cards, account books, and standardized formats for advertisements. Under the influence of Xu Yongqing (1880–1953), who started at the press as a textbook illustrator, the company's management began to look beyond illustration and to support commercial art on a broad scale.

Around 1911, they started to offer generic colored calendar posters on which any company could print its own name. In 1918, the press established an advertising agency, the China Publicity Company, that provided art and copywriting services. The Commercial Press also had its own art department, which serviced its publishing activities as well as the advertising agency. The department became an important training ground for many Shanghai commercial artists, a number of

Fig. 35.08: Zhiying Studio, Kwong Sang Hong cosmetic company, calendar poster, 1937. Private Collection.

work on separate commissions. Hang Zhiying headed the studio, assisted by Li Mubai (1913–1991) and Jin Xuechen (1904–1997). Seven or eight other artists worked under them, aided by unpaid apprentices. The Zhiying Studio was one of the first commercial art studios in Shanghai, if not the first. Besides creating about 80 calendar posters a year, the studio undertook many other commissions for commercial clients in Shanghai. These included designs for cigarette cards, packaging, and advertisements, and pictures of stylish women for magazine covers.

Though Hang Zhiying was initially influenced by Zhou Mantuo, he made his own contributions to the calendar poster style. Whereas Zhou and other artists had departed from full-figure depictions of women to show them as half-figures, Hang went farther. In some of his paintings, he depicted only women's heads. Hang also departed from the conventional portrayal of minimal facial expressions to show women with broad smiles, as they were portrayed in Western advertisements with which he was familiar (Fig. 35.08). Following Western examples, he painted women in seductive positions that showed off their breasts and curvaceous figures.

A calendar painting for the Great Eastern Dispensary Ltd depicted a woman sitting in a canoe with her top pulled down to expose one of her breasts (Plate 75). It exemplifies a technique that Hang Zhiying adopted from Zhou Mantuo's earlier calendar painting of Yang Guifei leaving her bath. Like Zhou in his later posters, Hang and his staff also portrayed women in Western clothing as well as tight-fitting *quipaos*. The Zhiying Studio's portrayals of women accented their modernity by showing them associated with or engaged in outdoor activities such as boating and archery in addition to posing in dance halls or drawing rooms.

The Zhiying Studio's poster for the Great Eastern Dispensary Ltd was commissioned by the dispensary's owner, Huang Chiuju, a leading manufacturer of medicines and home remedies. In creating his

whom were students in its art school, which Xu Yongqing headed until he left the press in 1915.

The man who surpassed Zhou Mantuo as Shanghai's most important calendar artist was Hang Zhiying (1900–1947). He began to work in the Commercial Press's art department as a teenager and left around 1922 to found his own studio. Whereas calendar artists who were not employed by in-house art departments generally worked alone, supplying paintings to various clients, the Zhiying Studio had a staff of artists who were organized into teams of specialists to pharmaceutical company, Huang had been influenced by a Japanese firm that made a product called Jintan or Humane Elixir. In the 1910s, it was the most widely advertised product in China. As Sherman Cochran notes, Jintan was initially promoted on billboards that were erected throughout the country. These featured the product trademark—the head and shoulders of a man with a handlebar moustache and an admiral's hat—who framed two simple Chinese characters. The combination of the trademark and the simple characters fulfilled one of advertising's first tenets: creating a product image that is easy to remember.

Following Japan's presentation of the Twenty-One Demands in 1915, there were widespread exhortations to boycott Japanese products. Huang Chiuju took advantage of the situation to promote his own version of Jintan, which he called Human Elixir instead of the original Humane Elixir. Presenting Human Elixir as a national product, Huang played on the Chinese antagonism to Japanese goods. He patriotically named his firm the Dragon and Tiger Company, adopting his imagery from Chinese legends and folk art. Both the dragon and the tiger were part of his trademark, which also included the characters for "Chinese National Goods."

Huang Chiuju spent a sizeable portion of his budget on advertising and established an advertising department where he and his staff planned and designed the company's promotional campaigns. He commissioned some of Shanghai's top calendar poster artists including Zheng Mantuo and Hang Zhiying to create calendars for his products and his dispensary.

Huang also understood the importance of design for successful retailing and he formulated a set of guidelines for new stores, which included large plate-glass windows to showcase his products and an absence of steps so the frail and elderly could enter the stores without difficulty. In 1917, he opened a building, which he called Great World, in Shanghai's French Concession. It was an amusement hall for popular entertainment whose walls he covered with large advertisements for his medicines. He advertised as well on billboards that he attached to the building's exterior. Huang Chiuju was exceptional in his recognition of advertising's potential to sell goods and in his own active involvement with publicity campaigns for his company.

While large firms like his had their own publicity departments, smaller firms relied on outside agencies to devise their advertising. Chinese headed most agencies, but foreigners ran some of them. The Commercial Press promoted advertising techniques in various books that it published, including translations of the American publication *How to Advertise* and a seminal book by the American psychologist and advertising theorist Walter Dill Scott, *Psychology of Advertising*.

Ellen Laing suggests that the first advertising company in Shanghai may have been the Weiluo Advertising Agency that Wang Zilian (dates unconfirmed) founded in 1909. In 1918, an American, Carl Crow (1884–1945), inaugurated Carl Crow Inc., an advertising firm that grew out of his earlier translation business through which he built an initial client base. Crow served numerous American companies such as Buick, Colgate, and Pond's who were trying to develop a Chinese market for their products. He introduced many services that American agencies had pioneered—organizing direct mail campaigns and buying advertising space in newspapers and magazines among them. His company also produced artwork and copy and managed what was perhaps the largest billboard operation in China.

Crow's strategy was to blend American marketing know-how with Chinese visual and linguistic conventions. His art department, close to being Shanghai's largest, employed many Chinese artists, most of whom worked on a freelance basis. The department specialized in black-and-white newspaper advertisements and billboards rather than calendar posters, hence it employed a considerable number of illustrators and cartoonists. However, Crow advertised that he could also produce calendar posters if requested.

Among the cartoonists who worked for Crow was Georgi Sapojnikov (d.o.b. unconfirmed–1949), a Russian whose nom de plume was Sapajou. He was a refugee from the Bolshevik Revolution who was best known in Shanghai as a cartoonist for the *North-China Daily News*. He also drew cartoons for other Shanghai papers and did commercial art for various companies. Sapajou illustrated books by Crow and occasionally other authors including himself.

Carl Crow's principal Chinese artist was Xie Zhiguang (1900–1976), known as well by his romanized name, T. K. Zia. Xie most likely developed his skill in line drawing while an apprentice to Zhou Muqiao for a brief period. He also worked for the Huacheng Tobacco Company and Nanyang Brothers Tobacco. As a creator of newspaper advertisements, Xie adopted the American visual strategy introduced by Crow, which featured the picture rather than the copy and emphasized a strong connection between a product and the person who used it. Xie's newspaper ad of 1921 for Shanghai Xiangya Gongsi, a company that made cold cream and toilet water, showed a woman in modern Chinese dress dabbing toilet water behind her ear. The design departs from Chinese pictorial conventions by minimizing the text, eliminating the background, incorporating ample white space, and featuring the toilet water bottle. This composition differs markedly from the calendar posters, which always privileged the human figure and treated the product package as a subordinate element.

A master of Chinese and Western painting techniques as well as line drawing, Xie Zhiguang also produced paintings for calendar posters and did paintings for magazine ads. Like Zhen Mantuo and Hang Ziying, he was known for his erotic images, but he pushed traditional conventions farther than most Chinese artists with his painting of a seductive nude woman lying on her back smoking. It was part of a 1934 advertisement for My Dear cigarettes.

Publishing

Not only was Shanghai the hub of China's advertising industry, but it was also the country's publishing center. From the fall of the Qing dynasty to the first years of the Nationalist government in Nanjing, publishing activity in the city increased sixfold. Largest of the publishers was the Commercial Press, whose many divisions spanned the entire publishing process from casting type to editing, designing, and printing numerous books and periodicals. Its principal rivals were several other large publishers—Zonghua Books, World Books, and the Great Eastern Book Company. These were complemented by many smaller presses as well as bookstores that published no more than a single magazine or journal.

Magazines and journals

Throughout the republican period, publishers experimented with the visual formats of journals and popular magazines. Initially, these consisted mainly of text, which might have been complemented by occasional drawings, but during the 1920s, single photographs and photographic spreads were frequently adopted. By the 1930s, a few popular magazines were comprised almost entirely of photographs.

Dongfang zazhi (*Eastern Miscellany*), one of the first journals intended for the urban middle class, was introduced by the Commercial Press in 1904. A combination of political articles, cultural commentaries, translations, and scholarly essays, it was not noted initially for its appearance. *The True Record*, a thrice-monthly Shanghai journal that began publication in 1912, emphasized visual elements more strongly than its predecessor and, in fact, is the starting point for the development of pictorial magazines in the 1920s and 1930s (Fig. 35.09). Edited by Gao Qifeng (1889–1933), one of the founders with his brother Gao Jianfu (1879–1951), it featured articles on politics and culture as did *The Eastern Miscellany*, but it also strongly criticized the government of Yuan Shikai, perhaps due to support it may have received from the recently ousted president,

The True Record's hard-hitting political cartoons, probably the first to appear in the republican period, set a precedent for the plethora of cartoons that satirical magazines like *Shanghai Sketch* would publish in the late 1920s. The design and art direction of *The True Record*, which was the first to use photographs, were innovative in many ways and influenced subsequent pictorial magazines. It was shut down after only one year because of its criticism of Yuan Shikei.

Liangyou huabao (*The Young Companion*), unlike *The True Record*, was a lifestyle magazine rather than a political journal. Founded in 1925 by Wu Liande, who had once worked for the Commercial Press, it depicted contemporary life in Shanghai, largely through photography. Each cover featured a photograph of a beautiful woman, many of whom were movie stars or students, although images of "fantasy" women, as Leo Ou-fan Lee calls them, appeared from 1927 on. What the real and the fantasy women had in common was their embodiment of modernity through their poses, hairstyles, and fashions. Initially black-and-white photographs of them were colored by hand, but as printing technology developed, the magazine adopted color photographs. The editors' intent to embody modernity in all aspects of the magazine's art direction was also evident in the design of the Chinese masthead, whose characters were derived from modern Western lettering rather than traditional Chinese calligraphy.

While many of the articles and themes in *Liangyou huabao* were of particular interest to women, the magazine was not directed specifically to them. However, it no doubt stimulated the publication of others that were, such as *The Ladies' Journal*, *Violet*, and *The Woman's Pictorial*. Though some of these featured photographs of women on their covers, others depicted them in diverse media that ranged from the calendar poster figures of the Zhiyang Studio to Art Deco drawings that seemed to come straight from the pages of the *Gazette du Bon Ton* in Paris.

The editorial policy and layout of *Liangyou huabao* owed much to the picture magazines in Europe,

Fig. 35.09: Gao Qifeng, *The True Record*, cover, 1912. Shanghai Library collection. Photographer: Zhang Fumei.

Sun Yat-sen. The colorful lithographed covers, many based on Gao Qifeng's paintings, featured a mix of Chinese and Western pictorial styles. As historian Carrie Warra notes, the magazine's claim to reveal the truth was central to its identity and was reinforced visually in different ways. The English title was printed in a nondescript roman type, while Chinese characters for "Truth" appeared on a number of covers in a gestural calligraphic style. The cover of the third issue, for example, depicts a man in formal dress, drawing a curtain to reveal "Truth," which is metaphorically represented by the appropriate Chinese characters.

particularly in Germany. Although the editors were not as adept at arranging photographic spreads as their European counterparts, during the 1930s they did employ montage to convey the sense of simultaneity that had become central to the modernist vision. For example, one spread was laid out to invoke a sense of vibrant urban life by combining such disparate images as a seated woman, a skyscraper, a horse race, and a jazz band under the rubric, "Intoxicated Shanghai."

But there was also another side to the portrayal of the city. With the growing power of Chiang Kai-shek's National Party in the early 1930s, the expansive Western-influenced lifestyle that was evident in Shanghai during the prior decade came into question. In the same aforementioned spread, *Liangyou huabao* also raised questions about the merits of this lifestyle, adding comments to the pictures suggesting that metropolitan excitement disrupted the inclination for a normal life and asking whether or not Shanghai's appellation as the "Paris of the East" was really a good thing. This was an unusual inversion of the earlier adoption of montage in the European pictorial press to convey an exuberant image of modernity.

The incipient signs of ambivalence towards the West in *Liangyou huabao* were also evident in a different kind of pictorial magazine that emerged in the 1930s, one that adopted a more overtly nationalist stance. Chiang Kai-shek's New Life Movement, which sought to promote national reunification through activities that required physical and mental discipline, was introduced in early 1934 and this surely influenced the editorial programs and policies of most popular magazines, although they ranged from *Meishu shenghuo* (*Art and Life*), which published artistic photographs of nude women, to the *Central China Monthly*, whose emphasis was on articles related to social and political life. *Meishu shenghuo* was published by a small printing company that wanted to showcase its advanced capabilities. The magazine strongly promoted the virtues of art, and also purveyed modern views on technology, industrial design, physical culture, and urban planning,

while simultaneously encouraging women to adopt traditional social roles. Publishing photographs of nudes by Lang Jinshan (1892–1945), one of China's pioneering modern photographers, might seem to contradict its conservative view of women's place in society, but the editors presented the photographs as examples of edifying art rather than prurient images.

By the 1930s, some designers and photographers had become interested in Russian Constructivist graphic design as well as the photographs of Alexander Rodchenko and others who were working for Soviet illustrated periodicals like *USSR in Construction*. *Pictorial Weekly*, published by the Chinese Photography Association, paid homage to the Russians both in its Constructivist layout and its photographs shot from above and below. Similar design and photographic strategies were evident in the *Central China Monthly* and *Ladies' Life*, among other publications.

Perhaps the most graphically interesting of these nationalist publications was *The Ark*, which first appeared in 1934 and ceased publication in 1937, when the Japanese invaded China. It was published in Tianjin, a treaty port that had long absorbed foreign influences. The masthead design was unusual in its adoption of thin black lines for the characters—the equivalent of the German New Typography—rather than traditional calligraphic strokes on the one hand or thick Art Deco or Constructivist forms on the other.

Drawings derived from French fashion advertising appeared on some covers of *The Ark* in its first year, probably produced by the Shanghai designer Liu Xiamo (dates unconfirmed), but by 1935 the design had changed drastically to reflect work being done in the Soviet Union, the Netherlands, and Switzerland. Photographs were central to *The Ark*'s new design strategy, but these were used in varying ways—sometimes in montages of faces or placed against decorative patterns, or in compositions that combined photos at various scales and with different colored overlays (Plate 76).

Publishing and the May Fourth Movement

The dramatic rise of publishing as a consequence of the May Fourth Movement brought about new opportunities for graphic designers, particularly the chance to create covers for the myriad books and journals that appeared. Many of these publications also resulted from the New Culture Movement, which was initiated by the journal *Hsin ching-nien* (*New Youth*), an influential periodical that began publication in 1915. Although *New Youth* was founded to promote broad philosophical ideas about science and progress, it initially served as a vehicle to oppose the politics of Yuan Shikai and the warlords who followed him. Influenced by the Russian Revolution, *New Youth* began to promote Marxism as part of its philosophy and from 1920 it supported the fledgling Chinese Communist Party. The magazine was shut down in 1926.

The movements for political and cultural change after the establishment of the republic made a great impact on literature and consequently on the physical appearance of books. Central to the literary reformers was the substitution of vernacular speech, known as *pai-hua*, for the stilted classical prose of Qing dynasty writers. There was a renewed interest in popular culture including folk tales and folk songs as well as visual patterns from traditional textiles and forms derived from stone sculptures. The cultural nationalism inherent in some of the new writing was also evident in the design of book and journal covers.

The best-selling popular literature, known as the "Mandarin Duck and Butterfly School," may be contrasted with the more serious attempts of the New Culture writers to create fiction that characterized China as an emerging modern nation. The New Culture authors often combined a romantic temperament with a desire to ground their stories in realistic situations. Unlike Japan, avant-garde literary theories, whether Expressionist, Futurist, or derived from Dada, were of little interest to Chinese authors who were more concerned with their own subjective experience than with the pure aesthetics of literary form.

A number of the new writers originally joined together in groups to promote their ideas. Two of the most influential groups were the Literary Association, formed in 1920, and the Creation Society, founded a year later. In 1921, the Literary Association arranged with the Commercial Press to edit one of its publications, the *Short Story Magazine*, which the literary scholar C. T. Hsia notes was the primary journal for the development of modern Chinese literature until the early 1930s. The *Short Story Magazine* featured striking graphic covers as did *Creation Monthly*, the rival publication of the Creation Society.

It was through *Creation Monthly* that the fin-de-siècle artist Aubrey Beardsley, whose sexually provocative drawings had shocked Victorian England, was first presented to China's literati. Beardsley's decorative style was adopted in China by a younger member of the Creation Society, Ye Lingfeng (1905–1975), who became known as "China's Beardsley." Ye's interpretation of Beardsley aroused the ire of Lu Xun (1881–1936), China's most influential writer during the republican era. Lu had a strong interest in English book illustration and appreciated Beardsley's intricate drawing style. However, he disliked Ye's imitation of it.

Cai Junpei had put Lu Xun in charge of cultural affairs when he headed Sun Yat-sen's Ministry of Education in 1911. Lu was energized by the New Culture Movement and began to publish short stories, which were the first to be written in a Western style. As much a scholar as a writer, Lu developed an extensive knowledge of traditional Chinese culture, both visual and literary. He was also an avid collector of ancient seals and inscriptions, stone rubbings, and early books with woodcut illustrations.

Active as a short-story writer, poet, essayist, and translator, Lu Xun published numerous books. In 1909 he designed the cover for an early collection of his own short stories, combining a small line drawing that was reminiscent of Art Nouveau illustration with simple characters for the title that were commissioned from a professional calligrapher. The cover provided an early indication of Lu's synthetic interests in European and Chinese culture, although later book covers by him would not reflect this synthesis so blatantly. In fact, his design of 1923 for *Peach Colored Cloud*, a translation of fairy tales, showed no trace of Western influence. It featured a decorative motif from the ancient Han dynasty, which Lu tastefully combined with his own calligraphy.

For many of the books that Lu wrote, edited, or translated, he invited artists to design covers of their own or to collaborate with him. Among these artists were two leading designers of book and periodical covers in the republican period: Tao Yuanqing (1893–1929) and Chen Zhifo (1896–1929). Tao was a painter who began to collaborate with Lu Xun in 1924, providing a sketchy calligraphic drawing of a nude woman surrounded by flowers for Lu's translated work, *Symbols of Depression*. Tao, who taught design at the National Academy of Art in Hangzhou, was interested in ancient Chinese patterns and motifs as well as modern Western art. His covers draw on many sources from prehistoric carvings and stone rubbings to traditional Chinese scroll painting and Western watercolor techniques. Some scholars consider his best design to be the cover for Lu Xun's 1926 short story collection, *Wandering*. It is comprised of flat shapes that depict three abstract seated figures beneath a radiant sun on a reddish brown ground. A black line divides the image from the modest calligraphy of the title.

Chen Zhifo began as a weaver and textile designer. He trained in China and in Japan, where, beginning in 1919, he was the first foreign student to study design at the Tokyo Academy of Arts. In 1923, he settled in Shanghai, where he started a company to train fabric designers, but this enterprise ran into difficulties and instead he became one of Shanghai's leading graphic artists. The Commercial Press hired him to design covers for the *Eastern Miscellany*, which he did for six years. Another assignment for the Press was a series of covers for the *Short Story Magazine*. Though Chen's cover designs of the early 1930s express his

interest in patterns, prior work such as his 1927 cover for an issue of the *Short Story Magazine* was strongly influenced by Art Nouveau and French fashion illustration just as the designs of numerous other Shanghai graphic artists were. His later covers, particularly those for the journal *Modern Student* in 1931, contain traces of European illustration, but these are integrated with complicated overlays of decorative motifs. As a working commercial artist, Chen had to create images that suited his clients, hence his stylized depictions of women and his virtuoso execution of ornamental forms. He could also rely more directly on traditional Chinese patterns as he did for several book covers on which he collaborated with Lu Xun in the early 1930s. For a collection of Lu's writings published in 1933, Chen created a stark rectilinear formal composition, based on the design of a traditional Chinese temple, which provided a space for Lu to draw his own calligraphic title. For another collaboration with Lu, Chen devised an overall pattern of complex fretwork to which Lu added his own calligraphy. Chen also taught commercial art in Shanghai and Guangzhou and published several books on basic design including a popular textbook, *Tuan Goucheng (ABC of Design Method)*, which first appeared in 1930 and went through multiple editions.

Unlike Tao Yuanqing and Chen Zhifo, Qian Juntao (1906–1998) started his career as a graphic designer. He studied at the Shanghai Arts Normal School, where one of his teachers, the cartoonist Feng Zikai (1898–1975), had a particularly strong influence on him. Feng had been a student of Li Shutong (1880–1942), who studied Western oil painting at the Tokyo School of Fine Arts with Kuroda Seiki. Li then established a comparable course in Hangzhou when he returned to China in 1912. Among his many innovations, Li introduced graphic illustrations to Chinese newspapers, which at the time carried only pictorial advertisements. He was also an early advocate for adding commercial art to the traditional art curriculum.

After his studies, Qian Juntao was hired in 1925 by the Kaiming Book Company, a major Shanghai press, where Feng Zikai was on the board of directors. There Qian became a prominent member of the design staff. Working for Kaiming and for other clients, he designed covers for journals and books in various styles, depending on what was required for a particular commission. There is little evidence in Qian's work of the traditional Chinese motifs or themes that one finds in the designs of Tao Yuanqing or Chen Zhifo. Qian's designs for book and journal covers of the late 1920s and early 1930s include stylized images of leaves and other natural forms as well as narrative elements for the covers of novels such as part of a woman's nude body in a Cubist-inspired composition for *Another Wife*, or a man and a nude woman facing each other for *A Great Love*. The journals for which Qian designed covers include *Student*, *Modern Woman*, *Ahead of the Times*, and the *Short Story Magazine*.

Around 1930, Qian turned to Russian Constructivism and especially the book and journal covers of Alexander Rodchenko, El Lissitzky, and Liubov Popova, whose bold geometric lettering was an integral part of their cover compositions. To these precedents he added nothing particularly new except to adapt the expressive Constructivist lettering style to the design of Chinese characters and to apply the geometric compositions of the Russians to the design of Chinese book and journal covers. This was evident in his design for the cover of *Literature Monthly*, whose first issue appeared in 1935 (Plate 77). Of the major graphic designers in the republican era, Qian worked in the broadest range of styles and had the strongest sense of the modern book or journal cover as a unified composition whose lettering was successfully integrated with other design elements.

Among Chinese graphic designers, Art Deco was by far the most popular foreign style or graphic language. It was widely adopted for colorful book and journal covers, although it was frequently joined with Chinese elements such as traditional pattern fragments or even images. This hybrid mix, known as the Shanghai Style or *haipai*, was not only evident in graphic design but also in other art forms.

Typography and lettering

Missionary presses developed the most widely used Chinese typefaces in the 19th century. During the republican period, the type trade came to be dominated by three large Shanghai publishers: the Commercial Press, Zhonghua Books, and World Books. The missionary types, particularly the Song/Meihua fonts that the Englishman William Gamble (1830–1866) developed, were adequate but could not fulfill the demands of some educated Chinese who had an appreciation for calligraphy. Efforts by Chinese typographers working for the Commercial Press and other presses were made to expand the range of available typefaces, with frequently limited success, while the original missionary Song typefaces underwent revisions, often based on Japanese improvements. The Song font dominated in its various Chinese and Japanese reincarnations. Of the fonts trying to imitate early Song printing, Fangsong (1916), created independently but purchased by Zhonghua Books, was the most important (Fig. 35.10). Successful calligraphic styles had to wait for the later development of other typefaces.

By comparison with the Western countries and even Japan, the number of Chinese fonts was limited, thus accentuating the contrast between the printed texts of books and journals and their far more flamboyant covers that frequently featured hand-drawn characters in a modern style. These characters could take diverse forms. Some were highly decorative and mirrored the intricate complexity of traditional Chinese fabric designs or fretwork patterns, while others were created as equivalents of Western san serif letters. Known as *Hei ti* or "black types," these consisted of either thin or thick lines or a combination of the two. The types also varied between those that retained the forms of traditional *kai shu* characters, and those whose geometric structures were derived from Constructivist or *De Stijl* precedents. Although few fonts were actually cast during the republican era, experimental lettering was in great demand, not only for book titles and magazine mastheads but also for

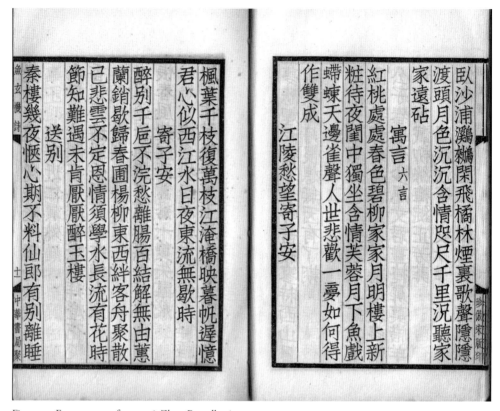

Fig. 35.10: Fangsong typeface, 1916. Zhou Bo collection.

advertisements, signs, and other visual expressions of modernity.

Manhua and the satirical journals

The Chinese term *manhua* was borrowed from the Japanese *manga,* which refers to comics or cartoons. The scholar Zheng Zhenduo first used it in 1925 to describe the comic drawings of Feng Zikai, which he published in the *Literature Weekly* that year. Feng's simple ink drawings, which commented on daily life with gentle humor, became very popular and led to the publication of a collection, *Zikai manhua* (*Comics by Zikai*) in 1926.

Though Feng is considered a founder of Chinese comics, others preceded him, particularly the political cartoonists who appeared in *The True Record* beginning in 1912. But Feng had a more direct influence on

the group of young cartoonists who established the Shanghai Sketch Society in 1927. Among them were Ye Qianyu (1907–1995), Zhang Guangyu (1900–1964) and Lu Shaofei (1903–1995). Ye and Zhang edited the society's weekly satirical magazine, *Shanghai manhua* (*Shanghai Sketch*), between 1928 and its demise in 1930.

Ye Qianyu was primarily a cartoonist and illustrator although he had studied painting, while Zhang Guangyu had previously built a successful career as a commercial artist, painting covers for romance fiction magazines and producing calendar poster pictures for the Nanyang Brothers Tobacco Company. From Nanyang Brothers, Zhang moved to the art department of the British American Tobacco Company, where he worked while he was editing *Shanghai manhua* and where he remained for a time after it folded. Another of the *Shanghai manhua* staff members was Ye Lingfeng

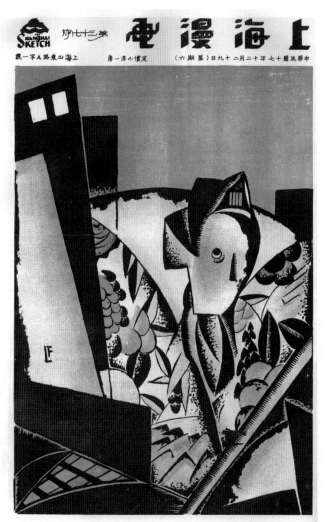

Fig. 35.11: Ye Lingfeng, *Shanghai manhua*, cover, 1928. Private Collection.

(1904–1975), a writer and artist whose drawings were subject to several Western influences. One was Cubism and the other was Aubrey Beardsley, although his own drawings omit the lewd quality of many Beardsley drawings (Fig. 35.11).

Published in the form of a tabloid newspaper, *Shanghai manhua* included four pages of comics in each issue as well as photographs, paintings, and essays. Like the pictorial magazine *Liangyou huabao*, the journal additionally featured work by contemporary photographers such as Lang Jinshan and Hu Boxiang

(dates unconfirmed). It also published one of China's first comic strips, *Mr. Wu*, which was drawn by Ye Qianyu. While the magazine included several political cartoons in each issue and did not shy away from political commentary, its broader editorial policy was to chronicle the mores of Shanghai life. Drawing styles for cover art varied, as did the cover themes. Cartoonists and caricaturists could depict modern Shanghai women or criticize Chiang Kai-shek and the Nationalist Party. One cover featured a cartoon drawing of a Nationalist soldier with a bloody bayonet, most likely a reference to the army's massacre of Communists in Shanghai in 1927. Another showed Chiang Kai-shek in civilian dress with a small head and a huge clenched fist, indicating his willingness to wield power in an authoritarian way.

Shanghai manhua spawned other satirical periodicals, which numbered almost 20 by the mid-1930s. Among them were *Modern Sketch*, *World Knowledge*, *Manhua Shenghuo* (*Comics and Life*), and *Zhongguo manhua* (*China Sketch*). Of these, *Modern Sketch* was perhaps the most noteworthy. It was edited by the illustrator and cartoonist Lu Shaofei, a founder of *Shanghai manhua*. Like its predecessor, *Modern Sketch* published numerous cartoons and satirical drawings by members of the Shanghai Sketch Society. After Japan attacked China in 1931, established the puppet government of Manchukuo in Manchuria in 1932, and bombed Shanghai the same year, many artists began to speak out against these acts of aggression. Some also criticized the Nationalist Party's increasing censorship, its drive for social control, and its support for leaders of totalitarian regimes such as Mussolini and Hitler.

Zhang Guangyu's drawing on the cover of *Modern Sketch*'s first issue announced the combative posture the magazine would adopt. Zhang drew an inkbottle as a warrior seated on a horse with a body of paper, pencils for legs, a brush for a tail, and an eraser for a head. The magazine maintained this posture until it ceased publication in 1937, when the Japanese declared war on China. During its brief tenure, *Modern Sketch* published the work of more than 100 cartoonists, a number of whom joined the militant anti-Japanese propaganda organizations and brigades that sprang up after the Japanese invasion.

The woodcut movement and propaganda graphics
With financial support from the Ministry of Education that Cai Yuanpei obtained for him in 1927, Lu Xun began to amass a collection of European, American, and Russian prints. In late 1928 he published five volumes of foreign woodcuts, one of which was devoted entirely to Soviet examples. Through several exhibitions and the founding of a woodcut workshop for young Chinese artists, Lu championed the woodcut as the ideal

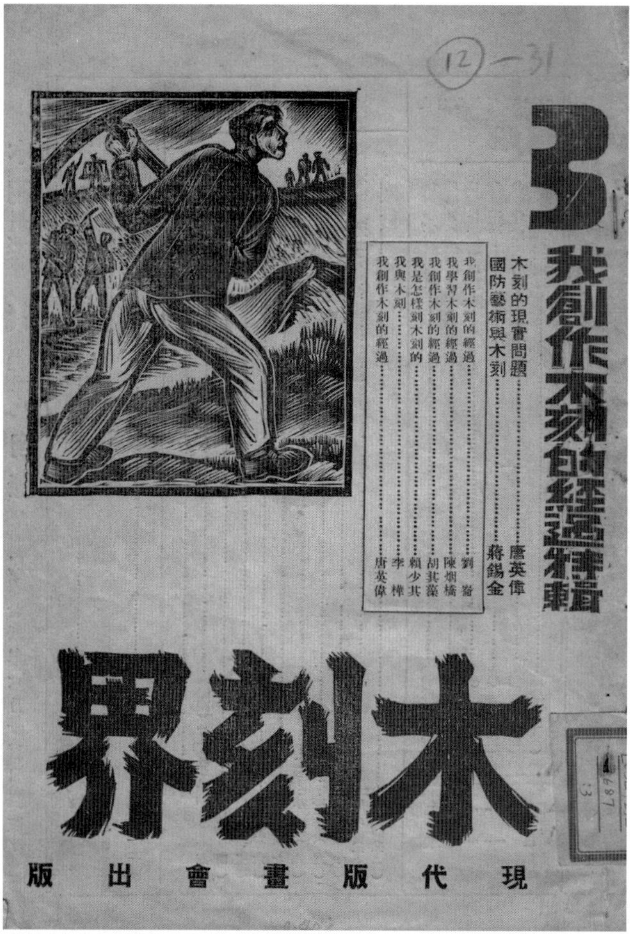

Fig. 35.12: Tang Yingwei, *Woodcut World*, cover, 1936. Central Academy of Fine Arts Library collection. Photographer: Zhou Bo.

medium for portraying social life and conveying political themes. It was actually Li Shutong (dates unconfirmed), however, who first developed the woodcut as a modern art form almost 20 years earlier, although he did not think of it as a political medium as Lu did.

In 1930, Lu helped to organize an exhibition of Soviet prints, cartoons, and posters in Shanghai. He also supported the radical League of Left-Wing Writers and in the summer of 1930 he gave a lecture to its artist's section, where he extolled the beauty of French artist Jean-François Millet's 19th-century realist painting, *The Gleaners*, and contrasted it with what he considered to be the ugliness of a typical Shanghai calendar picture.

Inspired by Lu Xun, various societies of woodcut artists sprang up, but the Nationalist government, which opposed their leftist imagery, persecuted them. Many of the artists were influenced by the writer Kuo Mojo who declared that art was first and foremost an instrument of propaganda. Their sources ranged from Käthe Kollwitz's German woodcuts of malnourished women and children to the militant Socialist Realism of Soviet artists.

Guangzhou was a center of woodcut production, where several groups were active. In 1934, Li Hua (1907–1994), a forceful woodcut artist in his own right, organized the Modern Woodcut Society, which published the magazine *Modern Woodcut* between 1934 and 1936. The magazine featured original prints that were pasted onto blank pages, while a signature print was also attached to each cover. In 1936, the Modern Woodcut Society inaugurated a new magazine, *Woodcut World*, which was edited by the young artist Tang Yingwei (1915–d.o.d. unconfirmed) (Fig. 35.12). Tang had fully embraced Kuo Mojo's call for a propagandistic art. His woodcut for the cover of the fourth issue of the magazine features a group of militant men and women marching forward under a banner emblazoned with the word "Liberation." After war broke out, the magazine ceased publication and the Modern Woodcut Society disbanded. Some artists made their way to the Communist stronghold in Yan'an, where the Lu Xun Academy of Literature and Art had been established. Its fine arts department included courses in propaganda painting, caricature, and print making, and the school spawned a number of mobile woodcut groups that traveled through the countryside documenting the disastrous actions of the Japanese military and eventually depicting the struggle of the peasants to overcome their feudal past. Woodblock prints were made quickly and distributed freely as a primary means of disseminating Communist Party propaganda. Although the school was named after Lu Xun, he never joined the party, holding out instead for a socially conscious art that was grounded in humanism rather than political ideology.

Siam
Crafts and the economy

Modernization began in Siam in the 19th century under King Chulalongkorn, who reigned until 1910. Through skillful diplomacy, he was able to protect the country, whose name permanently became Thailand in 1949, from colonization, while also reforming its administrative structure and education system. When his son King Vajiravudh succeeded him, he found that Siam's arts and crafts had been profoundly neglected and he lamented the Western-oriented elite's preference for thermos flasks and cheap cigarette cases rather than locally made bowls and mother-of-pearl boxes.

To reinvigorate the arts and crafts, King Vajiravudh created a Department of Fine Arts in 1912 and the following year he initiated plans for a School of Arts and Crafts, which was dedicated on the one hand to preserving traditional practices but on the other to introducing new techniques from abroad. Continuing his father's efforts to modernize Siam and to further his own promotion of Siamese nationalism, King Vajiravudh encouraged economic self-sufficiency, though he had no good strategy for industrialization. In an essay of 1915 entitled "Wake Up, Siam," he opposed the importation of goods from abroad and called for a return to a time when the country could produce for its

own needs. Refusing the Meiji model in Japan, where the Japanese government and military played a strong role in the industrialization process, the king exhorted Siamese businessmen and laborers to take more responsibility and not expect the government to be the leader.

Nonetheless, King Vajiravudh engaged in various activities to improve and promote his country's products. Beginning in 1913, he fostered a series of annual Arts and Crafts Fairs and he used these as bully pulpits to champion the arts and encourage the purchase of work by local artists and craftsmen. By 1920, furniture, baskets, and silver and ivory work were among the examples of domestic artisanry on display at these fairs. The king also promoted Siam's participation in foreign exhibitions, supporting pavilions to display Siamese arts and crafts at the Turin Exhibition of 1911, the Leipzig International Exhibition of 1914, and San Francisco's Panama Pacific International Exhibition of 1915. For Turin and San Francisco, the pavilions were constructed in traditional Siamese style. The country's presence at these exhibitions was significant, given that no other nation in Asia with the exception of Japan had a comparable sense of participation. All of Siam's neighbors were colonies and were represented abroad, if at all, as European possessions.

King Vajiravudh's greatest effort to strengthen the local economy was his plan for a grand Siamese Kingdom Exhibition that was to open in 1925. His intention was to invite countries around the world to present products such as farm machinery that could aid the economy and to also provide a forum where local entrepreneurs could display their own goods to an international audience. Work on the exhibition was well underway in late 1925 when the king died, but the project was terminated as a cost-cutting measure by his successor King Prajadhipok.

Prajadhipok reigned until 1935, although Siam changed from an absolute to a constitutional monarchy following a coup in 1932. The Ministry of Education, which was established after the coup, set up a new School of Fine Arts in 1933. The school reduced the emphasis on tradition that had existed in the earlier School of Arts and Crafts, focusing instead on more Western-oriented techniques. Such preparation enabled some of the graduates to pursue successful careers as commercial artists.

Graphic Design

As a kingdom rather than a colony, Siam was responsible for designing all of its own official documents, currency, and postage stamps. The country issued its first stamps in 1883, when the postal service was established. The text was in Siamese but the name Siam in English was added once the country joined the Universal Postal Union two years later and letters were mailed abroad. The stamp designs featured portraits of the king and his successors surrounded by ornate borders.

Much printed matter was produced for the royal household, and this included everything from menus for state dinners to invitation cards, seals, and stationery. Businesses required letterheads, bills and receipts, whose most interesting graphic characteristic was the range of Siamese letterforms they adopted, and commercial graphics also included medicine and cigarette packages and cigarette cards. Much of the cigarette advertising was designed for the local market by the British American Tobacco Company, more than likely in their Shanghai office.

Reflecting his strong nationalist feelings, King Vajiravudh, a prolific author of novels, plays, and essays, put forth several radical schemes to reform the transliteration of Siamese characters into roman letters and to change the Siamese writing system. The latter entailed a return to an earlier system of writing and was intended to make the language easier for foreigners to read. It never caught on, however, and was eventually abandoned. The king also took an interest in book production, and many of his own writings were issued in volumes designed and illustrated by leading Siamese artists including Prince Naris (1863–1947), a half-brother of King Chulalongkorn, who was active as a painter and sculptor, craftsman, architect, and

composer as well as an illustrator. At the request of the king, he also drew up an official state coat of arms that enclosed in a circle three figures of Hindu and Buddhist mythology, Garuda, Naga, and Vishnu, which the king preferred to an earlier coat of arms he had devised in a Western heraldic style. However, after a brief period he requested Prince Naris to remove Naga and Vishnu, thus leaving the mythical Garuda bird as Siam's principle icon.

As part of an earlier interest in Western culture, a number of popular Western novels by authors such as H. Rider Haggard and Sir Arthur Conan Doyle were translated into the Siamese language at the beginning of the century. By the 1920s, a plethora of books by local authors also appeared. Primarily romantic novels and ghost tales, they were published in soft cover versions with colorful covers that enticed the reader with dramatic portrayals of the characters. Cover artists tended to depict men and women in modern Westernized dress and with Western hairstyles and facial features. The most prominent among the artists was Hem Wetchakon (1903–1969), who did thousands of illustrations for books and magazines. Around 1924, he illustrated a number of textbooks for the Ministry of Defense and by the late 1920s he had become a prolific illustrator of fiction covers. After the constitutional monarchy was established in 1932, interest in reading spread and various hardback non-fiction titles as well as more serious fiction books were published. Though some of their covers continued the sensationalist imagery of the popular novels, others reflected a more serious attempt to represent the contents graphically.

In addition, women's magazines proliferated during the reign of King Prajadhipok and after. Like the books of popular fiction, they were also attractive vehicles for commercial artists. A leading illustrator of magazine covers was Saneh Khlaikhlu'an (dates unconfirmed), whose covers for *Nat Nari* were largely derived from Western examples or Chinese calendar posters. They depicted modern women with bobbed hair, modern clothes, and Westernized physical features.

Both Saneh Khlaikhlu'an and Hem Wetchakon were also active as advertising artists. However, Thai advertising during this period broke no new ground. Largely, ads copied Western precedents, though Thai iconography would occasionally be included. The most distinctive logo from the period is the red lion that identifies Singha Beer, a product of the Boon Rawd Brewery, whose early posters highlighted the bottle in different settings. Chinese calendar posters with texts in both Chinese and Siamese also circulated widely to promote various "China Made" products such as cigarettes, medicine, or cosmetics to Siam's sizeable Chinese population.

Bibliography
Bibliographic essay

Books and articles rarely address the topic of industrial design in China during the Republican period. Shou Zhi Wang, "Chinese Modern Design: A Retrospective," *Design Issues* 6, no. 1 (Fall 1989) does have some material on the interwar years even though it concentrates on the period after World War II. An extensive literature on industrialization in China exists including a number of studies by Albert Feuerwerker; Victor D. Lippit, *The Economic Development of China*; Dwight H. Perkins, ed., *China's Modern Economy in Historical Perspective*; and Thomas Rawski, *Economic Growth in Prewar China* and *China's Transition to Industrialism: Producer Goods and Economic Development in the Twentieth Century*. Karl Gerth, *China Made: Consumer Culture and the Creation of the Nation* is the principal source for the National Product Movement.

There are a number of books on modernism in China and especially its manifestations in Shanghai. See Jo-Anne Birnie Danzker, Ken Lum, and Zheng Shengtian, eds., *Shanghai Modern, 1919–1945*; Edward Denison and Guang Yu Ren, *Modernism in China: Architectural Visions and Revolutions*; Lynn Pan, *Shanghai Style: Art and Design Between the Wars*; Anna Jackson's essay, "Art Deco in East Asia," in Charlotte Benton, Tim Benton, and Ghislaine Wood, eds.,

Art Deco 1910–1939; and Wen-hsin Yeh, "Shanghai Modernity: Commerce and Culture in a Republican City," *The China Quarterly*, no. 150 (June 1997). Shanghai commerce is discussed in Sherman Cochran, ed., *Inventing Nanjing Road: Commercial Culture in Shanghai, 1900–1945*.

For graphic design, Ellen Laing has written the authoritative book on calendar posters, *Selling Happiness: Calendar Posters and Visual Culture in Early-Twentieth-Century Shanghai* and an excellent online essay about the journal *Shanghai Sketch*, "*Shanghai Manhua*, the Neo-Sensationalist School of Literature, and Scenes of Urban Life." Scott Minick and Jiao Ping, *Chinese Graphic Design in the Twentieth Century* is a good starting point for graphic design in the Republican era as well as afterwards. Julia Andrews' essay on "Commercial Art and China's Modernization," in the catalog of a Guggenheim Museum exhibition, *A Century in Crisis: Modernity and Tradition in the Art of Twentieth-Century China*; Carrie Waara's article "The Bare Truth: Nudes, Sex, and the Modernization Project in Shanghai Pictorials," in Jason Kuo's edited volume, *Visual Culture in Shanghai, 1850s–1930s*; and Leo Ou-fan Lee, *Shanghai Modern: The Flowering of a New Urban Culture in China, 1930–1945* all have useful information on the design of Chinese books and magazines. Kuiyi Shen's essay "Lianhuanhua and Manhua – Picture Books and Comics in Old Shanghai," in John A. Lent's edited volume *Illustrating Asia: Comics, Humor Magazines, and Picture Books* is an excellent study of Shanghai's satirical journals. On Chinese typography, see Christopher A. Reed, *Gutenberg in Shanghai: Chinese Print Capitalism, 1876–1937*. Paul French's biography *Carl Crow – A Tough Old China Hand: The Life, Times, and Adventures of an American in Shanghai* has excellent material about early advertising developments in Shanghai.

Michael Sullivan, *Art and Artists of Twentieth-Century China* and his *Modern Chinese Artists: A Biographical Dictionary* both have a good deal of information related to Republican-era graphic design and designers. Material on revolutionary publications can be found in Ralph Crozier, *Art and Revolution in Modern China: The Lingnan (Cantonese) School of Painting, 1906–1951*, while Christoph Harbsmeier, *The Cartoonist Feng Zikai: Social Realism with a Buddhist Face* describes a leading cartoonist of the revolutionary movement.

For background material on Thailand, see *The Cambridge History of Southeast Asia Volume 2, pt. 1: From c. 1800 to the 1930s*, which contains an excellent overview of the region. Walter F. Vella's *Chaiyo! King Vajiravudh and the Development of Thai Nationalism* describes the king's involvement with the kingdom's arts and crafts, while Helen Michaelsen, "State Building and Thai Painting and Sculpture in the 1930s and 1940s," in John Clark, ed., *Modernity in Asian Art* discusses Thai art education. Anake Nawigamune's *A Century of Thai Graphic Design* is the principal source on this subject.

Books

General

Clark, John. *Modern Asian Art*. Honolulu: University of Hawaii Press, 1998.

Davenport-Hines, R. P. T. and Geoffrey Jones. *British Business in Asia since 1860*. Cambridge: Cambridge University Press, 1989.

China

Adshead, S. A. M. *China in World History*, 3rd ed. Houndmills: Macmillan, and New York: St. Martin's, 2000.

Andrews, Julia F. and Kuiyi Shen. *A Century in Crisis: Modernity and Tradition in the Art of Twentieth-Century China*. With essays by Jonathan Spence, Shan Guolin, Christina Chu, Xue Yongnian, and Mayching Kao. New York: Guggenheim Museum, 1998.

The Cambridge History of China Vol. 12, pt. 1. John K. Fairbank, ed. *Republican China, 1912–1949*. Cambridge: Cambridge University Press, 1983.

The Cambridge History of China Vol. 12, pt. 2. John K.

Fairbank and Albert Feuerwerker, eds. *Republican China, 1912–1949*. Cambridge: Cambridge University Press, 1986.

Chen, Chaonan and Yiyou Feng. *Old Advertisements and Popular Culture: Posters, Calendars and Cigarettes, 1900–1950*. San Francisco: Long River Press, 2004.

Cochran, Sherman. *Encountering Chinese Networks: Western, Japanese, and Chinese Corporations in China, 1880–1937*. Berkeley, Los Angeles, and London: University of California Press, 2000.

—*Chinese Medicine Men: Consumer Culture in China and Southeast Asia*. Cambridge, MA, and London: Harvard University Press, 2006.

—ed. *Inventing Nanjing Road: Commercial Culture in Shanghai, 1900–1945*. Cornell: East Asia Program, Cornell University, 1999.

Crozier, Ralph. *Art and Revolution in Modern China: The Lingnan (Cantonese) School of Painting, 1906–1951*. Berkeley, Los Angeles, and London: University of California Press, 1988.

Danzker, Jo-Anne Birnie, Ken Lum, and Zheng Shengtian, eds. *Shanghai Modern, 1919–1945*. Ostfildern-Ruit: Hatje Cantz, 2004.

Denison, Edward and Guang Yu Ren. *Modernism in China: Architectural Visions and Revolutions*. Chichester: John Wiley & Sons, 2008.

Duus, Peter, Ramon H. Myers, and Mark R. Peattie, eds. *The Japanese Informal Empire in China, 1895–1937*. Princeton NJ: Princeton University Press, 1989.

Fairbank, John King. *China: A New History*. Cambridge, MA, and London: The Belknap Press of Harvard University Press, 1992.

Feuerwerker, Albert. *The Chinese Economy, 1912–1949*. Ann Arbor: University of Michigan Center for Chinese Studies, 1968.

—*The Chinese Economy, ca. 1870–1911*. Ann Arbor: University of Michigan Center for Chinese Studies, 1969.

—*The Chinese Economy, 1870-1949*. Ann Arbor:

University of Michigan Center for Chinese Studies, 1995.

French, Paul. *Carl Crow – A Tough Old China Hand: The Life, Times, and Adventures of an American in Shanghai.* Hong Kong: Hong Kong University Press, 2006.

Gerth, Karl. *China Made: Consumer Culture and the Creation of the Nation.* Cambridge, MA: Harvard University Asia Center. Distributed by the Harvard University Press, 2003.

Goldman, Merle and Leo Ou-Fan Lee, eds. *An Intellectual History of Modern China.* Cambridge and New York: Cambridge University Press, 2002.

Harbsmeier, Christoph. *The Cartoonist Feng Zikai: Social Realism with a Buddhist Face.* Oslo and Bergen: Universitetsforlaget, 1984.

Hsia, C. T. *A History of Modern Chinese Fiction*, 3rd ed. With an introduction by David Der-wei Wang. Bloomington and Indianapolis: Indiana University Press, 1999 (c. 1961).

Judge, Joan. *"shibao" and the Culture of Reform in Late Qing China.* Stanford: Stanford University Press, 1996.

Kuo, Jason, ed. and with an introduction. *Visual Culture in Shanghai, 1850s–1930s.* Washington, DC: New Academia Publishing, 2007.

Laing, Ellen Johnston. *Selling Happiness: Calendar Posters and Visual Culture in Early-Twentieth-Century Shanghai.* Honolulu: University of Hawaii Press, 2004.

Lee, Leo Ou-Fan. *Shanghai Modern: The Flowering of a New Urban Culture in China, 1930–1945.* Cambridge, MA, and London: Harvard University Press, 1999.

Lent, John A. *Illustrating Asia: Comics, Humor Magazines, and Picture Books.* Honolulu: University of Hawaii Press, 2001.

Link, E. Perry Jr. *Mandarin Ducks and Butterflies: Popular Fiction in Early Twentieth-Century Chinese Cities.* Berkeley, Los Angeles, and London: University of California Press, 1981.

Lippit, Victor D. *The Economic Development of China.* Armonk, NY, and London: M. E. Sharpe, 1987.

Mair, Victor H. *The Columbia History of Chinese Literature.* New York: Columbia University Press, 2001.

Minick, Scott and Jiao Ping. *Chinese Graphic Design in the Twentieth Century.* New York: Van Nostrand Reinhold, 2010 (c. 1990).

Modern Metropolis: Material Culture of Shanghai and Hong Kong. Hong Kong: Hong Kong Museum of History, and Shanghai: Shanghai History Museum, 2009.

Pan, Lynn. *Shanghai Style: Art and Design Between the Wars.* San Francisco: Long River Press, 2008.

Perkins, Dwight H., ed. *China's Modern Economy in Historical Perspective.* Stanford: Stanford University Press, 1975.

Rawski, Thomas G. *China's Transition to Industrialism: Producer Goods and Economic Development in the Twentieth Century.* Ann Arbor: University of Michigan Press, 1980.

—*Economic Growth in Prewar China.* Berkeley, Los Angeles, and Oxford: University of California Press, 1989.

Reed, Christopher A. *Gutenberg in Shanghai: Chinese Print Capitalism, 1876–1937.* Vancouver: University of British Columbia Press, 2004.

Shih, Shu-mai. *The Lure of the Modern: Writing Modernism in Semicolonial China, 1917–1937.* Berkeley, Los Angeles, and London: University of California Press, 2001.

Spence, Jonathan. *The Search for Modern China*, 2nd ed. New York and London: W. W. Norton & Co., 1999.

Strand, David. *Rickshaw Beijing: City People and Politics in the 1920s.* Berkeley, Los Angeles, and London: University of California Press, 1989.

Sullivan, Michael. *Chinese Art in the Twentieth Century.* With a foreword by Sir Herbert Read. Berkeley and Los Angeles: University of California Press, 1959.

—*Art and Artists of Twentieth-Century China.* Berkeley,

Los Angeles, and London: University of California Press, 1996.

—*Modern Chinese Artists: A Biographical Dictionary.* Berkeley, Los Angeles, and London: University of California Press, 2006.

Wright, Tim. *The Chinese Economy in the Early Twentieth Century: Early Chinese Studies.* Houndmills: The Macmillan Press Ltd, 1992.

Zanasi, Margherita. *Saving the Nation: Economic Modernity in Republican China.* Chicago and London: University of Chicago Press, 2006.

Siam and Southeast Asia

Anake, Nawigamune. *A Century of Thai Graphic Design.* Bangkok: River Books, 2000.

Tarling, Nicholas, ed. *The Cambridge History of Southeast Asia, Vol. 2pt. 1: From c. 1800 to the 1930s.* Cambridge: Cambridge University Press, 1999 (c. 1992).

Vella, Walter F. assisted by Dorothy B. Vella. *Chaiyo! King Vajiravudh and the Development of Thai Nationalism.* Honolulu: University Press of Hawaii, 1978.

Chapters in books

Jackson, Anna, "Art Deco in East Asia," in Charlotte Benton, Tim Benton, and Ghislaine Wood, eds. *Art Deco 1910–1939.* Boston, New York, and London: Bulfinch Press, 2003.

—"Inspiration from the East," in Charlotte Benton, Tim Benton, and Ghislaine Wood, eds. *Art Deco 1910–1939.* Boston, New York, and London: Bulfinch Press, 2003.

Michaelsen, Helen, "State Building and Thai Painting and Sculpture in the 1930s and 1940s," in John Clark, ed. *Modernity in Asian Art.* Broadway, NSW: Wild Peony, 1993 (University of Sydney East Asian Series No. 7).

Waara, Carrie, "The Bare Truth; Nudes, Sex, and the Modernization Project in Shanghai Pictorials," in Jason C. Kuo, ed. and with an introduction. *Visual Culture in Shanghai,* 1850s–1930s. Washington D.C.: New Academia Publishing, 2007.

Articles

Wang, Shou Zhi, "Chinese Modern Design: A Retrospective," *Design Issues* 6, no. 1 (Fall 1989).

Yeh, Wen-hsin, "Shanghai Modernity: Commerce and Culture in a Republican City," *The China Quarterly,* no. 150 (June 1997).

Internet

Ellen Johnston Laing, "*Shanghai Manhua,* the Neo-Sensationalist School of Literature, and Scenes of Urban Life," MCIC Resource Center, http://mclc.osu.edu/rc/pubs/laing.htm (accessed October 2, 2014).

Chapter 36: Asia: Japan, its Colonies, and its Territories 1900–1937

Introduction

Japan began its rise as a major economic and military power in Asia during the course of the Meiji era, which lasted from 1868 to the death of the Meiji emperor in 1912. During this period, the country embarked on an ambitious course of industrial development that prompted the rapid growth of heavy industry and resulted in resounding military victories over the Chinese and Russians in the Sino-Japanese War of 1894–1895 and the Russo-Japanese War of 1904–1905. Japan supported the Allies in World War I and as a result it gained control of German concessions in China after the war.

Until the end of World War II and even beyond, Japan was the only Asian country that had a national industrialization policy. With much of the region colonized by the British, French, and Dutch, there was little competition with the exception of China, a country much slower to industrialize due in part to a more diffuse political situation and a weaker economic infrastructure. The Taisho era in Japan, which lasted from 1912 to 1926, was a period of relative political openness and a time when the nation sought to create its own version of modernity. Young men who embraced the modern spirit were called *mobo* (modern boy) and their girlfriends were known as *moga* (modern girl). In 1923, Japan was beset by a great tragedy, the Kanto earthquake, which destroyed much of Tokyo, although it led to a reconstruction plan that included a modern network of roads, transport, parks, and new dwellings. Politically, the Japanese government became more open

in the Taisho years, although extreme positions were not tolerated. The Bolshevik Revolution of 1917 stimulated the formation of a Japanese Communist Party in 1922, but it was dissolved two years later. Several socialist organizations were also banned.

The Taisho era witnessed the emergence of a new middle class in the cities, but the greatest economic power rested with a handful of wealthy businessmen who headed the family-owned *zaibatsu* or conglomerates that controlled diverse companies in many different fields including banking, shipbuilding, iron making, mining, and chemicals. The initial "Big Four" *zaibatsu* were Mitsui, Mitsubishi, Sumitomo, and Yasuda, which, like large American or European corporations, sought to build organizations whose varied enterprises were integrated vertically as much as possible. These were followed by a second wave of "New *Zaibatsu*," created primarily by a breed of ambitious young entrepreneurs, many of whom were educated at engineering colleges. When Japan began to militarize in the 1930s, both the old and new *zaibatsu* collaborated closely with the military. Outside of the *zaibatsu* most Japanese manufacturers had fewer than 100 employees and many had less than ten.

While the *zaibatsu* concentrated on heavy industry and military technology, consumer goods for domestic consumption were largely produced by smaller firms—unlike the United States and Europe, for example, where big corporations such as General Electric, Westinghouse, Siemens, and the AEG pioneered the production of electric appliances for a large consumer market. In fact, the Japanese consumer class was considerably smaller than that in the United States or Europe and the Japanese economy consisted as well of a large rural population whose standard of living was far below that of the city dwellers.

The Showa era, which followed the inauguration of Emperor Hirohito at the end of 1926, initially continued the liberal Taisho climate of reform and Westernization, but soon factions espousing ultra nationalism and militarism came to dominate the country. In 1915, Japan had presented China with its Twenty-One Demands, which called for China's recognition of Japan's special interests in particular parts of the country. In 1931, the Japanese Army created the Manchurian Incident, when it moved aggressively to gain control of Manchuria, a name given to the territory in north-east China. The following year, Japan established the puppet state of Manchukuo, while continuing to exploit Manchuria for its resources and as an additional market for Japanese goods as well as a place to send settlers from its own poor agricultural regions. In 1937, Japan started a full-scale war with China and this conflict continued until the end of World War II, even as the Japanese military widened the conflict by launching the Greater East Asia Co-Prosperity Sphere in 1940 and attacking the United States at Pearl Harbor in December 1941.

Developing a design policy

As part of its move to become an industrial nation during the Meiji era, Japan was concerned with the quality of its exports. Its greatest industrial success, however, was not in the creation of mass-produced consumer goods, which it did not believe to be essential for its economic development, but rather in heavy industry and the production of military equipment. Nonetheless, the Ministry of Agriculture and Commerce, which was founded in 1881, was interested in improving international trade. Initially, the most successful strategy was making traditional objects for Western consumption. Such objects seemed a breath of fresh air to British designers like E. W. Godwin and Christopher Dresser who found in Japanese export wares a welcome alternative to the stifling ornamentation of European revival styles. Consequently, Japanese pavilions at Chicago's Century of Progress Exhibition in 1893 and the 1900 Exposition Universelle in Paris were designed in a traditional style to perpetuate an Orientalist image of Japan, even as the nation was actively industrializing. Shortly after the turn of the century, the market for traditional Japanese crafts such as lacquer and porcelain began

to decline and the Meiji government, which needed a means to obtain foreign currency, had to rethink its export strategy.

In 1911 the Minister of Agriculture and Commerce, Makino Nobuaki (1861–1949), requested a proposal to improve the marketability of Japanese crafts and promote their export. Submitted by two professors from the Tokyo Higher School of Industrial Art, the proposal contained a series of recommendations: setting up an official crafts bureau in the ministry; establishing craft exhibitions and prizes for outstanding designs that could then be produced for export; and creating a crafts museum that would display crafts from Japan and other parts of the world. At the beginning of the Taisho era in 1913, the Ministry of Agriculture and Commerce created an annual exhibition, known by its shortened form Noten, to display new craft designs that might be produced for export. Although the exhibition changed its name several times, it remained in existence until 1939, and the annual displays became a valuable support for craftsmen. It is important to recognize that the discourse of designing consumer products for mass production, which had animated European and American design thinking since the 1830s, garnered less attention in Japan than that related to craft production, which for many officials and businessmen, particularly managers of small and medium-sized enterprises, substituted for design. This was due in large part to the government's lack of interest in creating a strong domestic market for mass-produced goods.

By contrast, the question of what to export was as central to Taisho officials as it had been to officials in the Meiji era. In the early part of the century, Meiji administrators emphasized the establishment of heavy industry and the creation of products that would be useful to the military, striving continually to reduce their dependence on foreign experts. Their main aim was to catch up with the West, particularly in areas of high technology. Consequently, far less attention was paid to creating new products, whether technological or aesthetic, that could be successful in Western markets.

Throughout the 1920s and 1930s, the challenge of improving the quality of export goods remained on the agenda of the Ministry of Agriculture and Commerce and one of its successors, the Ministry of Commerce and Industry. At the same time, an emerging middle class was exploring the potential of a new lifestyle that might draw from both Western and Japanese cultures, while selected groups of designers and manufacturers, particularly in the sectors of furniture, appliances, household goods, and fashion, were creating new prototypes and products that signified major changes in cultural practices.

French influences

In the late 19th century, some Japanese artists and craftsmen became interested in Western painting and decorative arts. Among Japanese craftsman, Itaya Hazan (1872–1963) adopted some Art Nouveau themes based on photographs he saw in the British design magazine *The Studio*, and in 1902 the critic, editor, and design educator Fukuchi Mataichi (1862–1909), who had studied art in Paris, organized the first Japanese exhibition of Art Nouveau objects. Art Nouveau ceramics, textiles, and graphics were also prominently displayed at the Fifth National Industrial Exhibition in Osaka in 1903.

In Paris during the 1920s, a master lacquer craftsman, Sugawara Seizo, who had emigrated there from Japan around 1906, taught Eileen Gray and Jean Dunand how to apply lacquer techniques to the production of French *moderne* furniture and copper urns. Sugawara, however, was working outside the exotic image that the Japanese government continued to convey in the products it sent abroad.

The Japanese Pavilion for the 1925 Exposition des Arts Décoratifs, an exhibition replete with design in the new Parisian *moderne* style, was a traditional wooden dwelling filled with artisanal objects including historic dress and bamboo and lacquer furnishings. Japanese artists living in Paris, who were seeking to become part of the international modernist community, criticized the vernacular character of the pavilion. Tsuda Shinobu (1875–1946), a professor of metalwork at the Tokyo Bijutsu Gakko (Tokyo School of Fine Arts), was in Paris at the time of the exhibition and was invited to serve on the exhibition's international jury. When he returned to Japan, Tsuda promoted the *moderne* style, which was taken up by some younger craftsmen, who formed a group they called Mukei (Formless) in 1926. Group members were interested in European Deco not simply as a formal style but as evidence of individual creativity, which they opposed to the reproduction of traditional forms. In their manifesto, they espoused "[freshness], vividness, vitality," while rejecting "nostalgia … silence, conservatism." Though comprised mainly of metalworkers, the group included other craftsmen as well. A principal member was Takamura Toyochika (1890–1972), a former student of Tsuda's, who was joined by others including the metalworker Naito Haruji (1895–1979), and the lacquer artists Yamazaki Kakutaro (1899–1984) and Matsuda Gonroku (1896–1986). What characterized the work of the Mukei craftsmen was the combination of modern forms and patterns that originated in the West with techniques of Japanese craftsmanship. A wooden box by Yamazaki from 1934 displays a deep knowledge of lacquer technique, but its design emphasizes stylized leaf motifs and woods of different colors. Yamazaki had actually studied European design in Paris, where he became acquainted with Jean Dunand and other French decorative artists. He was adamant about making the new forms and motifs integral to the objects he produced and in an essay of 1929 he criticized those craftsmen who simply incorporated superficial details derived from European styles. Yamazaki's concern for integral form was evident in Takamura Toyochika's metal vase, which the artist titled "Construction for Flower Arrangement." It joined together geometric forms—cylinders, rectilinear shapes, and a sphere—in a vase form that might just as well refer to Russian Constructivism as to French Deco, while Naito Haruji's cast bronze wall clock of

1927 strongly resisted a functional approach by its eclectic combination of diverse shapes that surrounded the face. Meanwhile, Matsuda Gonroku found new forms for his lacquer work including a suite of modern furniture and decorations for the verandah doors of two large ocean liners operated by the NYK Line, the *Terukuni-maru* and the *Yasukuni-maru*. Unlike some of the European avant-garde groups, the objects that the Mukei designers produced were extremely diverse, and by 1933, without a firm program, the members of the group had dispersed.

While still affiliated with the Mukei group, Matsuda Gonroku became the artistic director for the Namiki Manufacturing Company, which developed a line of fountain pens with lacquer cases that were distributed throughout the world. The company was established in 1918 by Ryosuke Namiki (1998–1954), an engineer who developed a fountain pen with a nib made of gold and an iridium alloy that was specially adapted to writing Japanese characters and script. Namiki replaced the conventional pen body made of ebonite, a vulcanized sulphur and rubber compound, with a new material comprised of ebonite and raw lacquer. What distinguished his pens from their competitors was his introduction of traditional lacquer decoration that used the *maki-e* technique. This consisted of building up layers of lacquer on the pen base and then creating a design by sprinkling flakes or powders of gold or other metals onto the wet surfaces of the layers before they dried. The designs on Namiki's pens varied from historical scenes and the daily life of pre-modern Japan to legends and mythical beasts. Some also had a hint of Art Deco detail.

Matsuda, who advised the Namiki company for many years, produced the designs and samples that were copied by the artists he trained to do the extraordinarily minute execution. Craftsmen painted delicate designs on the lacquer using brushes that often had a single hair. It might take weeks or months to complete one pen, and only 400 were produced between 1926 and 1949. In 1929, Namiki signed an agreement with Alfred Dunhill Ltd of London to distribute its products under the Dunhill Namiki name. These came to include pencils, clocks, desk sets and lighters as well as pens. In 1938, Namiki changed the firm's name to the Pilot Pen Company, most likely to avoid the Japanese association following Japan's declaration of war on China. The collaboration with Dunhill was an unusual example of how a Japanese traditional craft technique might be adapted to a product for the Western market. Recognizing this possibility, Ryosuke Namiki was rare among Japanese small businessmen, who had difficulty discovering a niche market that lay between the technological products in whose manufacture the West excelled and traditional Japanese crafts whose market potential had declined severely after 1900.

Within Japan, the Art Deco style, known as French *moderne*, was taken up by the department stores, particularly Mitsukoshi, where the Furansu Bijutsu Tenrankai (French Art Exhibition) was held in 1928. The exhibition included pieces that the French government, eager to promote the style abroad, sent to Tokyo. These included furniture by Jacques-Émile Ruhlmann, Jules Leleu, René Prou, and others, which served as a source of ideas for local manufacturers. Among the furniture groups that Mitsukoshi produced for the emerging middle class that was experimenting with a new Western life style was an Art Deco set that became one of its best sellers. Although the French Deco style was not particularly popular among Japanese modernist architects, an issue of the *Nippon Architect* from 1928 included a photograph of a desk and chair that the designer Kajita Megumi (1890–1948) derived from French Deco sources.

The Rationalization Movement

In March 1925, the Ministry of Agriculture and Commerce was split in two. All matters pertaining to agriculture, which had dominated the older ministry, were transferred to the newly formed Ministry of Agriculture and Forestry, while everything related to commerce became the province of a new Ministry of

Commerce and Industry (MCI). The separation was strongly motivated by some officials within the original ministry who felt that economic and trade issues were being overshadowed by an emphasis on agriculture. During the early 1920s, Yoshino Shinji (1888–1971), a section chief within the Industrial Affairs Bureau of the Ministry of Agriculture and Commerce, began to pay attention to medium and small enterprises, which employed the majority of Japan's workers. He noted that the smaller enterprises dedicated much of their production to goods for sale abroad, but were nonetheless failing, due to numerous factors including an overabundance of small firms, an excess of cheap labor, and poor channels for distributing marketing information. As a result, the small firms were dumping cheap goods abroad at low prices.

Once the new Ministry of Commerce and Industry was formed, Yoshino continued to focus on issues of international trade. In 1926, the ministry created a Committee for the Promotion of Domestic Products, which was intended to reduce the trade deficit by encouraging import substitution—the production of goods domestically—instead of bringing them from abroad. The following year, Yoshino was influential in creating a Trade Bureau, although it was not funded until 1930, and he was also instrumental the same year in establishing a Commerce and Industry Deliberation Council to take a broad look at Japan's economic problems and consider what the Ministry of Commerce and Industry might do about them. An important achievement of the council was introducing to Japanese industry the concept of *sangyo gorika* (industrial rationalization) an amalgam of efficiency strategies derived from the Americans Frederick Winslow Taylor and Henry Ford and from the trusts and cartels in Germany that were set up to improve industrial performance.

In March 1928 the Ministry of Commerce and Industry, again with the strong support of Yoshino Shinji, set up the Kogei Shidosho (Industrial Arts Research Institute) (IARI) whose principal purpose was to improve the quality of goods for export in order to help improve Japan's balance of payments. At the time, a large proportion of Japanese manufactured goods went to less industrialized regions in Asia, including its colonies and Manchuria, where Japan was developing economic interests. Japanese firms tended to produce goods that were cheaper and simpler than Western prototypes, often learning how to design them through reverse engineering or taking apart the original models to find out how they were put together.

The IARI was initially located in the northern city of Sendai, although it moved to Tokyo in the 1930s. The purpose for the original location was to focus attention on activities in various regional centers rather than the more cosmopolitan cities. Sendai was also in a region of forests with a large potential for developing wood products to export. At the time, Japanese economic policy did not support the development of a strong manufacturing base for the production of industrial products such as electrical appliances or automobiles—products that would become major exports in the post-war years—hence the institute focused on crafts to whose design and production it hoped to apply more rationalized processes. According to director Kunii Kitaro (1883–1967), the institute's research efforts would result in a new hybrid, which he called *sangyo kogei* (industrial crafts) instead of *bijutsu kogei* (art crafts). The Institute worked with numerous materials including wood, metal, bamboo, ceramic and textiles—all related to products for household use— and its initial activities included evaluating existing products and devising manufacturing techniques and prototypes for new ones. The Industrial Arts Research Institute disseminated its results to schools, enterprises, chambers of commerce, and professional organizations throughout the country by sponsoring juried exhibitions, holding training workshops for artisans, and sending its staff engineers and designers around the country to advise on craft manufacture. It also published a monthly journal originally titled *Kogei Shido* (*Industrial Art Direction)* whose name was changed to *Kogei Nyusu* (*Industrial Art News*) in 1932.

The new publication became an important source of information on design activities overseas as well as research on new products that was being conducted at home. A related magazine, *Teikoku Kogei* (*Imperial Craft*) was published by another organization, the Teikoku Kogeikai (Imperial Society of Industrial Arts), which sought like the Ministry of Commerce and Industry to promote exports by revitalizing industrial production, modeling itself to some degree on the Deutscher Werkbund.

In contrast to the Industrial Arts Research Institute's regional location, its staff designers were primarily from schools in Tokyo. Most had studied at the government-sponsored Tokyo Koto Kogei Gakko (Tokyo Higher School of Arts and Technology), which was founded in 1922. Among the staff were Toyoguchi Kappei (Katsuhei) (1905–1991), Kenmochi Isamu (1912–1971), Riki Watanabe (1911–2013), Kosugi Jiro (1915–1981), Koike Iwataro (1913–1992), and Mosuke Yoshitake (1909–1993), all of whom became prominent designers or design educators after World War II.

In 1933, the Industrial Arts Research Institute hired the eminent German architect Bruno Taut as a design consultant for a few months. After a brief stint in the Soviet Union, Taut sought refuge from the Nazis in Japan, where he remained until 1936, when he left to become a professor of architecture in Istanbul. Though Taut designed some of the most important *siedlungen* or housing projects in Weimar Germany, he began his career as a utopian who espoused close-knit rural communities in the mountains as he described them in his book *Alpine Architecture* of 1919. In a later book he published on Japanese architecture in 1937, *Houses and People of Japan*, Taut reinforced his dislike of cities and celebrated the 17th-century Katsura Detached Palace as the epitome of Japanese design sensibility.

Taut came to the attention of Kunii Kitaro, director of the Industrial Arts Research Institute, when he critiqued an exhibition of the institute's prototypes at the Mitsukoshi Department Store in Tokyo. According to Taut, there were relatively few items of good quality. Most, he said, were poor imitations of European and American products. As a consultant to the institute in 1933–1934, Taut cogently recommended that Japan should "exploit its own unique spirit and unique technology" and cease its imitation of Western goods. Yuko Kikuchi and others have argued that as an advisor to the Industrial Arts Research Institute, Taut adopted a "Modernist Orientalist" view of Japanese crafts as evidenced by a series of proposals for the creation of a new style, Japanese Modern. Though based on Taut's enthusiasm for traditional Japanese crafts, Japanese Modern was meant to replace export kitsch with objects of quality that represented strong Japanese formal principles of simplicity and sensitivity to materials. For Taut, there was no contradiction between creating modern objects that were also "quintessentially Japanese." In a large number of products that he designed while in Japan, primarily for the workshop of Inoue Fusaichiro (1898–1993) at Takasaki in the Gumma Prefecture, Taut adopted bamboo as the material that best exemplified Japanese Modern. Among the objects he designed was a table lamp that closely replicated the glass, plastic, and chrome model Wilhelm Wagenfeld and Karl Jucker produced in Moholy-Nagy's Bauhaus Metal Workshop in 1924. His other products and prototypes included furniture and numerous small objects such as umbrella handles, paper knives, and napkin holders. Beginning in 1935, Inoue sold some of these at the Miratesu craft shop in Tokyo.

Despite Taut's revulsion against cheap imitations of Western products and his concomitant dislike of stereotypical Japanese kitsch, his view of Japanese design was nonetheless Orientalist. This was exemplified by his prejudice against the elements of Western modernity that had been more enthusiastically embraced by a number of Japanese applied artists.

Well before Taut arrived in Japan, two professors at the Tokyo Higher School of Arts and Technology, Kogure Joichi (1882–1943) and Moriya Nobuo (1893–1927), became active in the movement to promote a Western lifestyle in Japan through the design of

Western furniture and interiors. In a number of publications such as *Design and Manufacture of Furniture*, Kogure, who was head of the school's woodworking department, promoted the reformation of furniture, particularly the introduction of chairs, and modern furniture fabrication. He subsequently pushed his ideas forward as a member of the housing committee that the Alliance for Lifestyle Improvement commissioned to recommend reforms in housing and interior design. In several other books written between 1927 and 1930, Kogure continued to extol Western home furnishings but not as stylistic innovations the way the department stores promoted them. Rather, he saw home furnishings as components of a more rational and democratic lifestyle in which housework would be shared by others besides the wife and would be done more efficiently, as the American reformer Christine Frederick had advocated.

From 1920 to 1922, Moriya Nobuo, a trained designer, traveled in Europe and the United States as a fellow of the Ministry of Education. While abroad, he studied drafting and methods of making furniture, learning as well about manufacturing, design, education, and craft museums. Following his return, he began as previously mentioned to teach interior design and woodworking along with Kogure Joichi at the Tokyo Higher School of Arts and Technology, which was attracting other faculty members interested in designing for a new Western lifestyle.

However, as Sarah Teasley has shown, Moriya was not primarily a rationalist and in fact he responded more strongly to German Expressionism than to Bauhaus or Corbusian Functionalism. This was evident in the three model rooms he designed for the 1925 National Art Exhibition, where he featured chairs and beds as did other Western lifestyle designers he added more expressive ornaments to the pieces and mixed traditional Japanese motifs with references to European historic styles and also Chinese styles. Although Moriya's rooms embodied the essence of bourgeois comfort, he felt strongly that well designed

furnishings should be accessible to the working class, and in 1927 he joined with three partners to found Kinome-sha, a studio whose aim was to create mass-produced furniture at a moderate price. The designers quickly produced a line of prototypes including dining tables, chair and desk sets, wardrobes, and bookshelves, as well as a bed. Before they could find a manufacturer for their prototypes, however, Moriya passed away and Kinome-sha ceased its activities.

In October 1928, just a few months after the establishment of the Industrial Arts Research Institute, a new design group, Keiji Kobo (Ideal Form Studio), was created by, Kurata Chikada (1895–1966), a professor of interior design at the Tokyo Higher School of Arts and Technology, and a number of his students including Toyoguchi Kappei (Katsuhei) , who was also employed by the Industrial Arts Research Institute; Kobayashi Noboru (dates unconfirmed); and Matsumoto Masao (dates unconfirmed). Until the dissolution of Keiji Kobo around 1940, its designers concentrated on furniture and publicized their prototypes through exhibitions and lectures. They also published information about their designs in architectural magazines and sought to increase their audience beyond the cognoscenti by promoting mail-order sales of standardized furniture in the mass-circulation women's magazines such as *Shufu no tomo* (*The Housewife's Companion*). The chair designs tended to be based on simple linear construction with wooden frames that were combined with seats and sometimes backs of cane or woven hemp. The hemp seat on a 1934 prototype by Toyoguchi suggests an affinity with Scandinavian Modern furniture, particularly the Eva chair of Swedish designer Bruno Matthson from the same year. Due in large part to the lack of distribution systems, markets, and places for use, the prototypes of Keiji Kobo's designers did not go into mass production but nonetheless remained as representations of a Japanese modernist sensibility and production techniques that would become important for the nation's designers after World War II.

European modern design was a strong inspiration for Keiji Kobo, but there is no clear evidence of a specific Bauhaus influence on the group's activities. The Bauhaus was first introduced in Japan in 1924 through a series of articles in the art journal *Mizue* by the artist and critic Nakata Sadanosuke (1888–1970), who was one of the few Japanese to visit the school in Weimar. Only three Japanese students attended the Bauhaus, all in Dessau—the architect Mizutani Takehito (1902–1969), who was there from 1927 to 1929, and the husband and wife Yamawaki Iwao (1898–1987), an architect and student of Mizutani, and Yamawaki Michiko (1910–2000), a textile designer, who entered the program in 1930 and remained until 1933 (Fig. 36.01).

Fig. 36.01: Yamawaki Iwao, End of the Dessau Bauhaus, photomontage, 1932. Bauhaus-Archiv Berlin; © Yamawaki Iwao & Michiko Archives.

In 1931, Kawakita Renshichiro (1902–1975), also an architect, opened a short-lived private school in Tokyo, the Shin-kenchiku-Kogei-Gakuin (the School of New Architecture and Industrial Arts), which was based on Bauhaus principles. The curriculum included at various times courses in architecture, painting, stage design, dressmaking, and weaving. The school faced a host of problems including a lack of sponsorship by the Ministry of Education, and unfortunately it only lasted until 1936. When the Yamawakis returned to Japan, they contributed materials to the school's pedagogical program and taught there briefly. Among the relatively small number of students who studied at the school were Kamekura Yusaku (1915–1997), who became one of Japan's leading graphic designers after World War II, and the dress designer Kuwasawa Yoko (1910–1977), a student of Yamawaki Michiko, who became a design journalist after she graduated and in 1954 founded the influential Kuwasawa Design School, also based on the Bauhaus model.

In 1934, Kawakita Renshichiro and Takei Katsuo (dates unconfirmed), an elementary school educator, published a book on art and design education, *Kosei kyoku taikei* (*Basic Design Education*) that described the Bauhaus program in some detail and included translated writings by Kandinsky and material on Johannes Itten's pedagogy. Takei and other educators subsequently introduced some of the ideas of basic art education the book espoused into Japan's elementary school curriculum.

By 1937, the Japanese government had understood the value of presenting the image of a modern nation to the international community and commissioned the architect Sakakura Junzo (1901–1969) to design its pavilion for the Exposition des Arts et Techniques dans la Vie Moderne that was held in Paris in 1937. Sakakura, who had absorbed the techniques of modern building design while working as an assistant in Le Corbusier's Paris studio from 1931 to 1936, was an appropriate choice for the commission. His pavilion adopted much from Le Corbusier's formal vocabulary—notably the rectilinear volumes, glass facades, walkways, and pilotis or support columns—and conjoined them with aesthetic elements from traditional Japanese architecture and design, particularly exposed linear construction and the gridded windows that looked like *shoji* screens.

Lifestyle Improvement and Western-Style Goods

Beginning in the Meiji era, the adoption of Western customs and material forms of Western culture became an important issue for the Japanese. During the Taisho period, which corresponded to the emergence of a new middle class in Japan's cities, aspects of Western lifestyles were promoted through multiple channels including department stores, mass media periodicals, school textbooks, and social organizations. Women were the principal targets of these efforts based on the government's promotion of the home as the woman's domain.

Among department stores, Tokyo's Mitsukoshi was the oldest, having been founded in 1673 as a retailer of kimonos. Its development into a full-scale department store was strongly influenced by Western models including pioneering stores like the Bon Marché in Paris, which mingled cultural activities with commerce in order to promote their merchandise.

According to Jordan Sand, Mitsukoshi was the first department store to establish a position for an interior decorator when it hired Hayashi Kohei (dates unconfirmed) in 1906. Although Hayashi's first commission for the store was the interior of the Japanese Embassy in Paris, which he designed in a Japanese style, domestically he created Mitsukoshi displays of furniture in traditional Western styles such as Louis XV, Jacobean, and English Cottage. His strategy as a decorator, as Sand notes, was to add ornament to Western furniture in order to diminish what he calls its "Westernness." Hayashi's adoptions of Western styles were expensive and their display in Mitsukoshi's exhibitions functioned primarily, as Sand indicates, to educate a new consumer class, initially the wealthy bourgeoisie and then the broader emerging middle class.

In 1910, Mitsukoshi began to manufacture its own furniture. Though it also sold items for the traditional Japanese household, it promoted Western-style pieces—chairs, tables, and beds—as signs of a new lifestyle, as did other department stores like Takashimaya. Mitsukoshi offered these pieces in multiple styles. Around 1910, a Secession style based on Austrian and German examples was particularly popular among young designers, although a furniture competition the department store organized in 1914, where a number of pieces in that style were featured, also indicated that the designers had little practical knowledge of designing for mass production.

One of Mitsukoshi's more popular pieces was an inexpensive rattan chair, which combined a cumbersome Western-style design with an indigenous material. For many consumers, these chairs were the first they ever acquired. Besides chairs, the Mitsukoshi workshop turned out other relatively inexpensive mass-produced furniture—lamps, tables, desks, tea shelves, and plant stands. Unlike Hayashi's ornate hybrid pieces, which were aimed at an elite market, these mass-produced pieces had simple designs that sometimes embodied decorative elements derived from Secession or Art Nouveau sources. Even though they cost less than the custom-made pieces, their prices were still beyond what many Japanese consumers could afford.

Before World War I, the Tokyo Electric Light Company, which had an affiliation with General Electric in the United States, produced most of the nation's household lamps. When General Electric's patent on the tungsten filament for light bulbs expired in 1927, new Japanese companies entered the field to profit from the extension of electric power to the home. By 1931, the Tokyo Electric Light Company had a number of large self-contained factories that could manufacture everything related to the lamps from the components for the light bulb to the packaging.

Besides this one large company, however, a group of mid-sized firms as well as numerous small factories and workshops also produced house lamps, ranging from fancy styles to cheap exemplars. In general, these lamps did not benefit from a designer's involvement and the majority were made according to the most expedient methods of production.

Concomitant with the cultural reforms embodied in the Western furniture that was intended to replace Japanese customs such as sitting, eating, and sleeping on the floor, was the reform in kitchen design that centered on two features: the introduction of more efficient techniques for food preparation and the substitution of new gas-burning appliances for the traditional *shichirin*, a small coal-burning equivalent of the hot plate.

As early as 1904, the Tokyo Gas Company began to market a gas-burning rice cooker as well as a single-burner gas stove. A selling point for the new appliances was that they could replace a servant, due to their increased efficiency. The adoption of these smaller appliances was all that most families could afford. Western-style ovens as well as refrigerators were also on the market, but few people bought them because of the price as well as lack of space and their unfamiliarity with those products.

Similar to the household efficiency movement that Christine Frederick spearheaded in the United States around 1915, Japan had its own female efficiency advocates. Prominent among them was Hani Motoko (1873–1957), publisher of the widely-read women's magazine *Fujin no tomo* (*Ladies' Companion*). A principal concern for Hani was to make a change from working on the floor in a crouching or sitting position to working standing up. By 1913, the mail-order division of *Ladies' Companion* was offering a worktable that combined a raised work surface with drawers, compartments, and shelves for storing cooking utensils and food.

In its "Efficiency" issue of 1917, *Ladies' Companion* published plans for two entire kitchens that were designed for efficient work. The difference between them and those that Christine Frederick espoused is that the Frederick kitchen incorporated a number of electrical appliances, while the Japanese version, with limited appliances such as a clock and gas burner, put more emphasis on body positions and movements. The low number of appliances in Japanese households continued throughout the 1920s and 1930s. Although Japan became a world leader in household electrification, by 1937 less than 1 percent of Japan's households had a refrigerator and about 0.2 percent had washing machines compared, for example, to more than 50 percent of American households, which had electric refrigerators and washing machines at the beginning of the 1940s.

One appliance that did become popular was the radio. The first ones on the market were crystal sets that Hayakawa Tokuji (1894–1980) produced to correspond with Japan's first radio broadcasts in 1925. Within a year, Hayakawa was marketing his radios, which he sold in nondescript wooden housings, under the name "Sharp Dyne." Soon thereafter, "Sharp" became the brand name for all his products. In 1928, he replaced the crystal sets with vacuum-tube radios, and by 1929, Sharp was Japan's leading radio manufacturer. Hayakawa continued to make improvements in his new models. The Sharp Dyne Type 31 of 1930 had a horn speaker perched on a wooden box, and the Sharp Dyne Fuji Type 33 of 1932, by which time there were more than one million radio listeners in Japan, was perhaps the first of Hayakawa's products to have a more artistic appearance. The housing had angled corners and a shaped frame around the mesh that covered the vacuum tubes. The speaker, which sat on top of the housing, was shaped like a hexagon and had an ornamental wooden decorative form on its façade. Sharp was one of the earliest Japanese companies outside the automobile manufacturers to install a conveyor belt on its production line, thereby reducing the time spent on the assembly of a radio to less than a minute.

Beginning in 1933, Hayakawa began to open new markets for his radios throughout Southeast Asia, thus becoming one of Japan's few medium-sized enterprises to create a successful mass-produced product for export. Although the radio did not figure directly within the various plans and programs for Japan's lifestyle improvement, it was nonetheless an important component of the country's modernization process.

As historian Kashiwagi Hiroshi has emphasized, reform movements originated both in the private sector as well as the government. The Ministry of Education was a leader in the government's effort to encourage rationalization and the adoption of Western practices and products. In 1919, the ministry sponsored the Seikatsu Kaizen-ten (Lifestyle Improvement Exhibition), and the same year it established the Seikatsu Kaizen Domeikai (Alliance for Lifestyle Improvement), which occupied itself with all areas of life from housing and clothing to food and even social interactions. Among its many committees was one to improve housing on which design educator Kogure Joichi served. In 1924, the committee's report, *The Reform of Domestic Furniture*, considered six themes including sitting on chairs rather than the floor, shunning decoration in domestic structural facilities, and redesigning floor plans to emphasize family needs rather than those of visitors. The report called for furniture that was simple and strong to accord with the general reforms that were recommended. The call for change had a particular urgency, which resulted from the enormous number of homes in Tokyo that the Kanto Earthquake had destroyed the previous year. Although the Alliance for Lifestyle Improvement did not have the power to mandate social change, it strongly advocated a new lifestyle, disseminating its program through its journal and other means.

Mingei and New Mingei

In contrast to the efforts to promote a Western lifestyle in Japan, *mingei* theory, as developed by Yanagi Soetsu (1889–1961) and others, celebrated Japan's native craft traditions. The term *mingei* (folk-craft) was actually a compound of two Chinese characters as well as a contraction of a Japanese phrase that means "popular crafts." Addressed to collectors rather than those who made everyday objects for the market, Yanagi's strict definition of *mingei* referred to common household objects that were made by anonymous craftsmen. He saw these as examples of *getemono* or low crafts made for common people. Yanagi's interest in *mingei* corresponded to a certain degree with William Morris's interest in the lesser arts, which he, like Yanagi, hoped to elevate to a higher status. Both Morris and John Ruskin were a strong influence on Yanagi as they were on others in Japan, but Yanagi combined the ideas and values he absorbed from the British thinkers with a strong interest in Buddhism.

Mingei also had a particular role within the discourse on Japanese modernity. For Yanagi, who first developed his theory through a study of traditional crafts in Korea, it was a way to retain a sense of Japanese identity within a process of modernization that originated in the West and that was strongly encouraged during the Taisho era. Like William Morris, Yanagi accepted the limited use of machines but fiercely resisted the idea of a machine age. He also espoused socialism as the Arts and Crafts writers did, believing, as historian Kim Brandt notes, that it would bring about what he called the "Kingdom of Beauty," in which the masses would adopt a pre-industrial craft aesthetic as Morris had described in his utopian novel, *News from Nowhere*.

Others who were active in the initial promotion of *mingei* were the Japanese potters Tomimoto Kenkichi (1886–1963), Hamada Shoji (1894–1978), and Kawai Kanjiro (1890–1966), and the British potter Bernard Leach (1887–1979). Though Morris's writings had been translated into Japanese as early as 1891, Tomimoto published the first biographical article on Morris in 1912 and is credited with introducing him to the Japanese public as a designer rather than a political figure. In 1914, Tomimoto launched his own design office in Tokyo, following the model of William Morris & Co. He offered a range of services including the design of wallpaper, interiors, furniture, pottery, textiles, metalwork, lacquer ware, stage sets, books, and advertising, but unlike Morris & Co., which existed for many years, even after Morris's death, Tomimoto's office remained open for only a few months.

The public became more familiar with *mingei* theory through a series of articles that Yanagi began to publish in 1927 and which were collected in a book, *Kogei no michi* (*The Way of Crafts*), the following year. *Mingei*'s physical form was publicized at the same time in the *Mingeikan* or *mingei* model house that Yanagi designed for the Imperial Exposition for the Promotion of Domestic Industry, held in Tokyo's Ueno Park in 1928. As Yuko Kikuchi has noted, the pavilion was a hybrid that combined elements of different Japanese buildings from a teahouse and townhouse to a farmhouse, all mixed with a hint of English Tudor half-timbered design. A small group of craftsmen who were inspired by Yanagi's writings created much of the furniture. They formed a guild in Kyoto—the Kamigamo Mingei Kyodan (Kamigamo Mingei Guild)—that was similar to Ashbee's Guild of Handicraft or Ruskin's Guild of St. George. As an introduction to *mingei* theory, the house and its furnishings represented a compromise with Yanagi's original definition of *mingei* as consisting of anonymous household objects for common people. On display in the distinctly middle-class parlor were tables and chairs by guild member Kuroda Tatsuaki (1904–1982). The parlor also included a fireplace with surrounding tiles by Hamada Shoji, which, as Kikuchi notes, may well have been inspired by the one in Morris's Red House. The wife's room, by contrast, featured a tatami mat, futon, and a traditional lacquered chest.

Yanagi published an article towards the end of the exposition in which he supported the manufacture of tables, chairs, and other types of Western furniture, although he argued that such pieces had to embody Japanese form rather than serve as copies of Western

designs. This argument was actually close to that of various lifestyle reformers and furniture designers like Moriya Nobuo, who would have been less likely to agree with Yanagi's strong interest in Japanese crafts, particularly his espousal of inexpensive common objects by anonymous craftsmen. Concluding his article, Yanagi urged that *mingei* embody an "Orientalist spirit" which he associated with a larger Asian identity, a position that the Japanese military would appropriate a few years later.

By early 1931, Yanagi was promoting the idea of new *mingei* or newly manufactured handicrafts that possessed the qualities of the vernacular objects he admired. Frequently guided by entrepreneurs and activists from the cities, craftsmen in rural workshops produced goods destined for sale in the metropolitan centers. Among the venues where new *mingei* was sold were urban shops such as Takumi, Misuzawa, and Minatoya in Tokyo and later some of the large department stores.

Kim Brandt has called attention to the class and gender base of new *mingei* objects. Though Yanagi envisioned *mingei* in every home, it was in fact the comfortable urban middle class that became its principal consumers. Hand woven neckties, canes, dress shirts of homespun cloth, and banded Panama hats were clearly directed to the well-to-do man about town, while other objects for the home such as wooden stands to display ceramic plates and literary accessories like bookends and ink stands were also meant for masculine pursuits. Objects intended to evoke the interest of women, who were presumed to purchase most items for the home, included napkins, tablecloths, lampshades, hand towels, curtains, and cushions. New *mingei* was marketed in the upscale lifestyle magazines, which primarily women read, as a signifier of high fashion, both in home decor and also as fabric for kimonos or dresses. By 1937, however, *mingei*'s social role had shifted. Instead of marking a new urban lifestyle for a privileged class, it was called upon to reinforce national unity once the military declared war on China and then sought to create a unified Asian region or Greater East Asia Co-Prosperity Sphere that would be guided and managed according to Japanese interests.

Heavy Industry and Transportation

If Japanese small and medium-scale industries seemed slower than their Western counterparts to develop modern techniques of mass production, the larger companies in heavy industries such as steel and chemical production absorbed Western techniques quickly during the late Meiji period and by the beginning of the 20th century were able to reduce their dependence on foreign experts considerably. In fields that involved design, notably all areas of transport, engineers learned to manage large-scale projects that involved complex applications of technology. They were trained primarily at the University of Tokyo, but the Japanese government also sent large numbers of students abroad, many following their basic engineering studies in Japan. Although Japan was considerably less developed than Western Europe and the United States in numerous technological areas, the country produced a generation of courageous entrepreneurs who inaugurated large projects without trepidation and eventually made them successful.

Japan's rapid progress in developing shipyards, railroad rolling stock, motorized vehicles, and aircraft was due in large part to government patronage, especially that of the army and navy, which financed many projects to create armaments and other materiel. In the Sino-Japanese War of 1894–1895, the Japanese Navy destroyed the technically larger Chinese fleet in one day, while in the Russo-Japanese conflict of 1904–1905, Japan again demonstrated its superiority in naval technology, particularly through its design of large high-speed ships that were the most heavily armed of any cruisers built up to that time.

Japan's learning process, whether in shipbuilding, railroad rolling stock construction, airplane design, or automobile manufacturing was generally to purchase one or more foreign examples, engage in extensive testing procedures including in some cases reverse engineering, make improvements where feasible, and then arrange for production either with a government or military facility or with a company in the private sector. Foreign experts were often hired in the early years of this process, as was the case of Sir Edward Reed (1830–1906), Britain's most prestigious naval architect, who supervised the construction of Japan's first warship. As Christopher Howe notes, when the Japanese commissioned ships to be built in British shipyards, their specifications were frequently higher than those of the British Navy.

By 1907, Japan had its own shipyards, notably the Naval Shipyard in Kure and the Nagasaki Shipyard, owned by Mitsubishi, one of Japan's four *zaibatsu*. The start of World War I greatly increased the production of ships, largely as a response to the needs of Japanese shipping companies, which were cut off from access to Western vessels. By 1914, Japan had become the world's third largest shipbuilder after Great Britain and the United States, and by the time World War II began, the technological level of ship design in Japan had more or less caught up with the West.

As early as 1896, the NYK (Nippon Yusen Kaisha) Line, which had formed in 1885 through a merger of two existing lines and become a state monopoly that operated the majority of Japan's ocean liners, tankers, and merchant ships, opened the first regular passenger ship service from Japan to the west coast of the United States. By 1901, NYK Lines ranked as the seventh largest shipping company in the world. In the late 1920s the company undertook the ambitious project of designing and building two world-class ocean liners: the *Asama Maru*, which entered service in 1929, and the *Tatsuta Maru*, launched a year later. Both ships, created at the Mitsubishi Shipyard, embodied the epitome of luxury ocean travel—lavishly decorated public rooms, comfortable cabins, and swimming pools on the decks.

The interior decoration was done in a European style, though not an innovative one. Waring & Gillow, the London furniture maker, designed the first-class dining and reading rooms on the *Asama Maru* in a traditional British gentry style, while the Japanese textile firm Kawashima Orimono, known for the elaborate hangings it created for exhibitions during the Meiji period, was involved in designing the first-class cabins.

By the 1930s, the NYK Line came to rely less on foreign firms for their interior design and more on Japanese architects, whom they invited to create a modern indigenous style. Perhaps following the example of the *Normandie* in France, the NYK Line employed the architect Nakamura Junpei (1887–1977), an early exponent of the Secessionist style in Japan who subsequently studied at the École des Beaux Arts in Paris, to design modern Art Deco luxury interiors for another of its passenger ships, the *Nishiki Maru*, which was launched in 1934. Nakamura combined traditional and modern materials including Japanese lacquer and mother-of-pearl with metal, glass, and resin. Similar to Matsuda Gonroku's designs for Namiki pens, his mingling of Japanese and Western materials and craft techniques produced a hybrid style that could be characterized as one example of Japanese modernity.

Like the shipping industry, the railroads were also controlled by a state monopoly. In 1906 the Railway Nationalization Act brought most of Japan's private railroads under the supervision of a new national body, the Railway Agency, which became the Japanese Government Railways. Limited railway service began in Japan with imported equipment in 1872, and by 1893 the first steam locomotive of Japanese manufacture, though completely British in appearance, was designed and produced at the government's Kobe works. Construction was supervised by Richard Francis Trevithick (1850–1931), who came to Japan from Britain in 1888 to manage rolling stock production. Trevithick—the grandson of Richard Trevithick, the British mechanic who built the world's first steam locomotive—trained many Japanese engineers who went on to become leaders in locomotive design.

Japanese firms also built railway coaches and strove to keep up with the innovations of the Pullman Company in the United States and other foreign coach manufacturers. Japanese coaches incorporated interior electric lighting in 1898, while Sanyo Railways introduced the first dining cars the same year and inaugurated the first sleeping cars two years later.

By the early 1920s, Japanese steam locomotives had developed a distinctive character, although their design was still more heavily determined by technological factors than styling. One of the most widely employed engines was the C51 "Pacific," of which more than 300 were built between 1919 and 1928. Designed to pull express passenger trains, the C51 had an elongated boiler topped by a well-shaped iron chimney, which was sheathed on either side by large panels. A number of improvements were made on this engine and subsequent models in the C50 series were produced until the mid-1930s.

Although they chose streamlining for the modern Asia Express train that operated in Manchuria, railroad executives in Japan were far more cautious about adopting streamlining at home. In 1935, locomotive designers sheathed a C53 "Pacific" engine in a metal housing, but the design was not particularly inspiring and the reduced fuel costs from the lower air resistance were not sufficient to offset the higher maintenance expenses. The following year a second attempt was made with an engine of the C55 class, but despite an improved design, the results were no better and the decision was made not to streamline any other engines. Regardless of the attitude toward streamlining, however, Japan built an extremely efficient rail system throughout the 1920s and 1930s. Both passenger and freight engines were continually improved and the engineering staff kept abreast of the latest technology and designs in the railway industry.

There was, however, initially less support in Japan for producing automobiles. Unlike the shipping industry and the railroad, both of which were effectively nationalized, no such process occurred with automobile manufacturing, and strong government support for the automobile industry did not emerge until after World War II.

The Locomobile Company of America first introduced automobiles to Japan in 1901 when it opened a sales showroom in Tokyo. In 1907, Uchiyama Komanosuke (dates unconfirmed), who originally worked as a bicycle technician and had designed his first automobile in 1902 with a motor imported from the United States, created the Takuri, generally considered to be Japan's first gasoline-powered automobile. Its bodywork, including comfortable leather seats, followed the model of various European luxury cars. While Uchiyama managed to approximate the formal design of the European models, the Tokyo Automobile Works, which intended to manufacture the Takuri, was only able to produce about ten of them.

The inability to manufacture automobiles in quantity plagued other entrepreneurs who were interested in producing cars but who had little or no knowledge of them. In 1913–1914, Hashimoto Masujiro (1875–1944), who had gained experience working with engineering firms in the United States, designed a car with a two-cylinder engine and called it the DAT, a name he derived from the initials of his three major investors. By 1916, Hashimoto had upgraded the DAT's engine to four cylinders but had been unable to produce more than a few cars. In 1918, he and others in the budding automobile industry received a boost from the government's Military Motor Vehicle Subsidy Law, whose intention was to subsidize the production of buses and trucks for the army. It was through this program that several companies such as Hashimoto's learned to mass-produce military vehicles, a skill that they were later able to transfer to the manufacture of automobiles for the general market.

An important figure in the development of the Japanese automobile industry was William R. Gorham (1888–1949), an American mechanical engineer who went to Japan in 1918 to promote an aircraft engine he had designed. Failing to find support for it, he devised a three-wheel two-passenger vehicle that was powered by a Harley Davidson engine. This led to his joining a company headed by Kubota Gonshiro (1871–d.o.d. unconfirmed) that merged with Hashimoto's firm. The new company produced his subsequent design of a small car called the Datson, or son of DAT, to indicate its smaller size in relation to its larger counterpart. The Datson was introduced to the Japanese market in 1931, although its impact was relatively minor at the time.

Throughout the 1920s, Japanese auto manufacturers had a difficult time competing with the two large American companies, Ford and GM, which had established their own subsidiaries, Japan Ford and Japan GM, in 1925. While these companies were strong competition for the local manufacturers, they also brought important innovations to Japan that were later to be of great benefit to the Japanese auto industry. First were the conveyor belt and the mass production assembly line that Ford introduced to Japan for the first time. Second, the presence of these companies induced the Japanese government to promote an industry of parts suppliers. Japan Ford and Japan GM helped immensely to raise the quality of those products, which included batteries, wheels, glass, tires, and various other rubber goods. They also established quality control, which the Japanese would excel at in the post-World War II years, and they established chains of dealerships that were required to maintain repair and service shops and to stock replacement parts. As well, the two American companies introduced monthly payment plans. In effect, the American firms brought to Japan an entire system of production, financing, and maintenance without which it would have been impossible to develop a domestic automobile industry. Until the early 1930s, the American firms were producing roughly between 2,000 and 5,000 cars annually while the Japanese companies turned out fewer than 500 per year. These figures reversed after the reorganization of the Japanese auto industry in the early 1930s.

In 1931 the Survey Committee for the Establishment of the Automobile Industry, which the Ministry of Commerce and Industry set up, recommended that the smaller firms consolidate and concentrate on the mass production of trucks and mid-sized cars so as not to compete with the larger vehicles that the American companies manufactured. As a result, three major companies—Isuzu, Nissan, and Toyota—emerged as the leaders in the field. Isuzu was primarily a producer of trucks, while Nissan was formed in 1933 as a result of further consolidation between the manufacturer of the Datson and another company. The Datson's name was changed to Datsun in 1932 because the former name had a negative connotation in Japanese. Gorham remained a consultant to Nissan whose objective was to compete with Japan Ford and Japan GM in the mass production of passenger cars. He brought in several more engineers from the United States and helped Nissan institute a manufacturing process that was more like an American assembly line than that of any other Japanese automobile company.

The 1932 Datsun, an improved version of its 1931 predecessor, was a small car with an enclosed cab, shaped fenders, and a running board. It resembled the Austin 7, which might have been an unofficial impetus to its design. In 1936, Nissan concluded an agreement with the American company Graham-Paige to introduce a Japanese version of its economy car, the Crusader. This vehicle, larger than the Datsun, was produced in Japan as the Nissan 70. It differed considerably from the Datsun in its design, due to its rounded corners, curved grill, fuller fenders, and more sculptural form. It was only produced for one year, however, since Nissan stopped making passenger cars in 1938 in order to support the war effort with the production of military vehicles.

The Toyota company resulted from the efforts of Kiichiro Toyoda (1894–1952), who had a passion for automobiles and established an automobile section in 1933 in his father's successful textile machine firm, Toyoda Automatic Loom. His first prototype was the Toyota A-1, which was modeled closely on the Chrysler

Airflow. Only three were built, but the car served as a model for the Toyota AA, the company's first automobile produced for the mass market in 1936. It came in two versions—sedan and phaeton—and about 1,400 were built before it ceased production in 1943. The automobile division was separated from the larger firm in 1937 and christened Toyota Motor Co., a title thought to have a stronger market appeal than the family name.

Japanese automobile companies survived the competition from the more experienced American firms because of two factors. One was the enthusiasm and willingness to take risks that characterized Japan's pioneering auto entrepreneurs like Hashimoto Masujiro and Kubota Gonshiro, the merger of whose companies led to the formation of Nissan; Aikawa Yoshisuke, who spearheaded Nissan in its early years; and Toyoda Kiichiro, the founder of Toyota. Second was the protection afforded these companies by the Japanese government, which not only awarded them contracts to produce military vehicles but also passed the Automobile Manufacturing Enterprise Law in 1936, which mandated that automobile companies turning out more than 3,000 cars a year had to have majority Japanese ownership. As a result, both Japan Ford and Japan GM closed down their operations and left the country in 1939. Due to the war and the post-war turmoil, however, the Japanese auto industry did not develop sufficiently to compete successfully in international markets until the early 1960s.

Besides the role it played in supporting fledgling Japanese automobile manufacturers through large orders for trucks and other vehicles, the military was crucial to the development of aviation in Japan. The first attempt to design an airplane was by a civilian, Ninomiya Chuhachi (1866–1936), who devised plans and a model for a flying machine with a propeller and landing gear in 1893. Unable to interest the army in his idea when he left the military after the Sino-Japanese War, he set up a factory to build a full-scale motorized aircraft with three engines. However, the Wright

Brothers designed their own plane before he was able to finish his and he subsequently retired from the field.

The army took a greater interest in aircraft after the historic flight of the Wright Brothers' *Kitty Hawk*, and established a study group to conduct research. The first plane made in Japan had an engine that was reverse engineered from a French model and an imported Farman frame, also from France. During World War I, the military used aircraft for the first time when it fought against the Germans in China, a factor that spurred its interest after the war in developing an aviation industry. In 1918, the University of Tokyo established an Aviation Laboratory, which began to supply a steady stream of aviation engineers. At first they worked under foreign experts who had been hired by the various companies, but later they became chief engineers who were given the responsibility to develop new aircraft or engines of their own.

Between 1917 and 1925, a number of private companies began to produce aircraft. As Christopher Howe notes, these companies were of two types. One was the established shipyards with their broad engineering skills, extensive experience, and profits accumulated from World War I. They were exemplified by Mitsubishi Heavy Industries, a company that belonged to the Mitsubishi *zaibatsu*.

The other type was a group of new companies founded by ambitious aeronautical engineers or else firms whose initial purpose had been to work with different technologies. These included the Nakajima Hikoki (Nakajima Aviation Company) and the Aichi Kokuki (Aichi Aircraft Company). Initially Aichi manufactured clocks and gramophones, but was persuaded by the navy to begin producing seaplanes. To help these companies, the army and navy brought in foreign advisors, imported examples of the important monoplanes, biplanes, and seaplanes, and also purchased licenses for the local manufacture of the most widely accepted foreign airplane engines. The military's impetus to become independent of foreign experts and technology increased after it invaded Manchuria in 1931

and established Manchukuo as a puppet government in 1932. That year, the navy inaugurated the Yokosuka Naval Air Technical Arsenal to conduct research and also design new planes. The increased emphasis on research not only led to technological independence but also to significant design innovations in areas such as instrumentation, glass cockpits, autopilot systems, split wing-flap devices, and radio communications systems. With designs like Mitsubishi's A5M Claude fighter of 1935 and the same company's G3M Nell long-range bomber, which entered production in 1936, many within the Japanese aircraft industry felt that they had not only held their own against world standards in aircraft design but had, in fact, surpassed them. In August 1937, a force of G3Ms based in Taipei flew more than 1,200 miles to bomb targets in China, thus carrying out what some believe was the first transoceanic air attack in history.

Given that the army and navy promoted most of Japan's aircraft development, the greatest design advances were made for military rather than civilian purposes. The first commercial air service, the Japanese Air Transport Institute, in fact, used a fleet of sea planes that it purchased from the navy. Other small airlines followed, and in 1928 several of these were consolidated into a new company, the Japan Air Transport Corporation which the government intended to become Japan's national airline in accord with its ambitious plans for expansion in Asia. The airline used a variety of planes, first from the Japanese military and then from foreign manufacturers such as Fokker, whose planes were also manufactured under license by the Nakajima Aviation Company.

In late 1934, Japan Air Transport began to import Douglas DC2s from the United States for commercial air travel, and Nakashima set about manufacturing them under license to the Douglas Aircraft Company. In 1936, the Japanese company put into service Nakashima's design for a smaller twin-engine version of the DC2. Known as the AT-2, it was initially intended for civilian aviation, but in response to a growing demand for transport after the military declared war on China in 1937, the army adapted the AT-2 for military use by fitting it with more powerful engines. Around 30 were produced for civilian purposes, not only for Japan's national airline but also for the quasi-governmental Manchurian Air Transport Company that had been established in Manchuria in 1932. By comparison, more than 300 of the AT-2s were built for military use.

By the time Japan declared war on China in 1937, the country had intensified its imperial expansion throughout Asia. Japan Air Transport had its own airline with routes to Manchukuo as well as Japan's older colonies, and when the airline was reconstituted in 1938 as Dai Nippon Koku (International Air Transportation Company), it had no trouble increasing its routes throughout Asia as part of Japan's Greater East Asia Co-Prosperity Sphere.

Graphic Design

From the beginning of the 20th century, graphic design in Japan was strongly influenced by the many new art and design movements in Europe, but these were adapted to an existing Japanese visual culture that was already highly developed by the 19th century. Relief printing flourished during the Tokugawa period (1603–1868), and in the 18th century, colored woodblock prints, known as *ukiyo-e*, were derived from multiple impressions. By the late 19th century, various techniques were used for printing book illustrations, advertisements, and packaging. The latter ranged from matchbook covers and labels for beer, wine, and soy sauce to cigarette and cosmetic boxes. Photographic printing for newspapers from metal relief plates began around 1888, the time when color lithography using imported American machines was introduced to print tobacco labels. The first chromolithographic poster, which advertised Kirin beer, was printed in 1903.

In 1905 the illustrated humor magazine *Tokyo Puck* began publication. Named after its American predecessor and featuring political cartoons as well as comic strips, it became a vehicle for a number of Japanese illustrators.

It was also one of the first mass-circulation publications to take advantage of Japan's advances in color printing. Besides the Japanese edition, the magazine also circulated widely in English and Chinese.

Tokyo Puck was founded by Kitazawa Rakuten (1876–1955), one of Japan's earliest professional cartoonists, also considered by many to be a founding father of Japanese *manga*, or comics. Kitazawa was trained as a painter but learned editorial cartooning from the Australian artist Frank Nankivell (1869–1959), who came to Japan around 1891 and began to draw cartoons for the English-language magazine *Box of Curios*. Nankivell was instrumental in Kitagawa's joining the *Box of Curios* staff as its first Japanese employee. In 1902, Kitazawa, inspired by *The Yellow Kid* and other American comic strips, created Japan's first serialized strip, *Mokube Sightseeing in Tokyo*.

Within a decade of *Tokyo Puck's* appearance, other important printing milestones occurred. In 1914 offset lithography—invented in the United States in 1906—was introduced to Japan, the same year as rotogravure printing. Offset lithography, used for printing artwork, employs the same principle as printing from lithographic stones except that the images are photographically transferred to metal printing plates. Rotogravure, by contrast, is an intaglio process whereby an image is engraved onto a metal cylinder. These new techniques, adopted in Japan within a few years of their introduction in United States and Europe, greatly improved the quality of color reproductions in Japanese mass-circulation publications.

Typography and lettering

There were also innovations in typographic design, which were adopted for the three Japanese writing systems—*kanji*, *hiragana*, and *katakana* (see Chapter 5). The conventional way of representing them in print is known as *mincho*, a style that originated in the calligraphy of the Chinese Ming dynasty in the 14th century. As with roman faces, many variants of *mincho* have been created including bold, italic, extended, condensed, and outline forms. An alternative to *mincho* was created around 1916. Known as *goshikku*, it is a style of typography and lettering without horizontal strokes or serif equivalents. The name derives from the English word gothic, which originated in the 19th century to designate san serif letters. Besides the lack of serif-like strokes, *goshikku* characters tend to be more consistently even than their *mincho* counterparts.

The modernization of traditional *mincho* forms and the invention of *goshikku* were both stimulated by Japanese designers interested in creating their own versions of modern advertising. In 1926, Yajima Shuichi (dates unconfirmed) published the *Zuan moji taikan* (*Typographic Handbook*) in which he introduced designs for many different forms of modern display lettering in both *mincho* and *goshikku* styles. Because the total number of *kanji*, *hiragana*, and *katakana* runs to several thousand elements, Yajima was only able to suggest lettering styles that might then be creatively developed for posters, book covers, advertisements, and other graphic forms. The architect Takeda Goichi (1872–1938), then head of the graphic arts program at the Kyoto College of Technology, wrote the book's introduction. Takeda had visited Europe 20 years earlier and was a great admirer of Charles Rennie Mackintosh and the designers of the Vienna Secession. In his introduction, he reinforced the function of typography and lettering as signs of modernity and highlighted their contribution to attractive advertising.

In 1929 the inventor Sugimoto Kyota (1882–1972) patented a typewriter with 2,400 *kanji* characters. They were arranged by frequency of use on a cylindrical carriage that could move forward and backward as well as to the right and left. That same year, a Japanese typesetting machine was introduced. Typesetting technology improved during the 1930s, which resulted in its wider use. Traditionally, Japanese was written or printed in vertical lines, but by the 1920s, as part of a larger modernization process, typesetters were sometimes requested to print horizontal texts as was done in the West. This created some inconsistency,

which was compounded by the fact that there was no rule for reading horizontal lines from left to right or right to left. As Richard Thornton points out, this problem was not settled until after World War II, when the government adopted a rule that horizontal lines of text should be read from left to right.

The emergence of graphic design

Leading exemplars of a new graphic design style at the beginning of the century were the little magazines such as *Myojo* (*The Morning Star*) and *Shirakaba* (*White Birch*), which published articles about new tendencies in Western literature and art as well as Japanese culture that was influenced by these tendencies. These journals did not have innovative layouts, but their covers tended to feature designs by painters and printmakers who drew heavily on the visual techniques of Art Nouveau, Expressionism, and other Western movements. Covers by the artist Fujishima Takeji (1867–1943) for *Myojo*, which was founded in 1900 and lasted until 1908, showed the artist's debt to Alphonse Mucha as well as to other Western artists, and in fact *Myojo* published an article on Mucha in 1904. Mucha's influence was also evident in a lithographic poster by the painter and printmaker Tsunetomi Kitano (1880–1947) for an Exhibition of Export Articles in Kobe. He portrayed a Mucha-like Japanese woman in a gossamer gown floating above an image of the Kobe port that is ringed by an ornamental border (Plate 78). Artists who designed covers for *Shirakaba*, which began publication in 1910, included the British potter Bernard Leach, whose graphic work suggested an Arts and Crafts aesthetic rather than that of Art Nouveau. Nonetheless, Art Nouveau remained a source of design for postcards and other popular media (Fig. 36.02).

Before Fujishima Takeji left for Europe in 1905 to continue his art studies, he was active as a designer of book covers, especially for the female poet Yosano Akiko. His 1901 cover for a book of sensuous poems by Yosano, *Tangled Hair*, featured a heart containing a woman's face and flowing hair, which was pierced by an arrow

Fig. 36.02: Art Nouveau postcard (Muse and Musical Score in Commemoration of the Goni Fair), 1906. The Wolfsonian–Florida International University, Miami Beach, Florida, The Mitchell Wolfson, Jr. Collection, XC1996.332.2. Photo: David Almeida.

(Fig. 36.03). This image, which Fujishima intended to express the passion in Yosano's poetry, contributed to the strong impact the book made on the Japanese literary world. Other artists of the period who designed book or magazine covers that drew on European paintings and posters include Asai Chu (1856–1907), Wada Eisaku (1874–1959), and Nakazawa Hiromitsu

(1874–1964), all of whom had studied Western art either at the Tokyo School of Fine Arts or in Europe. Yumeji Takehisa (1884–1934) was a self-taught artist who created commercial illustrations for newspapers, magazines, postcards, and sheet music (Fig. 36.04). In addition, he was known as a designer of *furoshiki* (wrapping cloths) and patterned papers. Considered by some to be the "modern Utamaro" or even the Japanese Toulouse-Lautrec, Takehisa's depictions of women in a

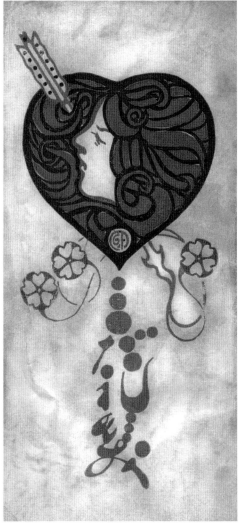

Fig. 36.03: Fujishima Takeji, *Tangled Hair*, cover, 1901. CPA Media Co. Ltd./Pictures From History.

Fig. 36.04: Yumeji Takehisa, *Please Love Me*, sheet music cover. The Wolfsonian–Florida International University, Miami Beach, Florida, The Mitchell Wolfson, Jr. Collection, XC1993.325.1. Photo: David Almeida.

modern version of the *nihonga* or Japanese traditional painting style were widely popular with the public. He is also considered to have been an influence on Yamana Ayao, the well-known designer of graphics for the Shiseido cosmetics company.

One designer who sought to bridge the separation between text and images in Japanese book design was Onchi Koshiro (1891–1955), a founder of the Japanese modern print movement, *sosaku hanga*. A former student at the Tokyo School of Fine Arts,

although he never completed the requirements for his diploma, Onchi was also interested in abstract art. He began to design and illustrate books around 1913, and by the late 1930s he had become Japan's leading book designer. During his long career, Onchi is said to have designed over 1,000 books and devised a similar number of lettering styles, each developed individually for the books he designed.

As an innovative printmaker, Onchi frequently made color woodcuts for his covers and illustrations, although he focused on the relation of the images to the text and to the choice of typography and paper. His high standards of design were evident in his books for the specialty publisher Arusu, which was dedicated to publishing deluxe editions. The books Onchi designed for Arusu were frequently Japanese translations of European literature, but also included new work by Japanese poets. Taking as his examples European collectors' editions illustrated by well-known artists such as Raoul Dufy and André Derain, Onchi often featured covers with abstract images that were printed in three or four colors, and he created novel layouts as well as woodblock illustrations.

He continued to design books for other publishers as well. In 1932, he created several for a small press that specialized in photography and two years later he published his own photographic book, *Hiko kano* (*Sense of Flight*), with an abstract cover and original *goshikku* text. The book recalled Moholy-Nagy's *Painting, Photography, Film*, as well as experimental books by El Lissitzky and Alexander Rodchenko. In 1935, Onchi and Shimori Taro (dates unconfirmed) inaugurated a new monthly journal dedicated primarily to book design. Entitled *Shoso* (*Window on Books*), the journal featured articles on book formats and layouts, typography, and illustration. It became a forum for discussion as well as a purveyor of information about book design abroad, and continued publication until 1943.

Bijin-ga posters

The term *bijin-ga* means "beautiful woman." Originally it described the stylized depictions of courtesans in the 18th-century woodblock prints of the Edo period, but it was later applied to any images of Japanese women in traditional dress, whether these were done as prints, lithographs, or paintings. At the beginning of the 20th century, *bijin-ga* images were adopted for advertising posters, resulting in an indigenous Japanese commercial art form. The association of attractive women with products was already an established technique of Western advertising by the late 19th century, but in Japan it attained a new level of elegance, given the richness of the women's garments and their often subtle facial expressions.

The Mitsukoshi Department Store in Tokyo pioneered the use of *bijin-ga* posters to advertise its kimonos. In 1907, Mitsukoshi reproduced a painting by Okada Saburosuke (1869–1939), *Portrait of a Lady*, as a color lithographic poster with its *monsho* or crest and the store name added. Okada, an artist who worked in the *yoga* or Western style of painting, taught at the Tokyo School of Fine Arts, where a department of Western painting had been established in 1897. Sensing the value of *bijin-ga* images for advertising, Mitsukoshi held a competition for a *bijin-ga* poster in 1911. From more than 300 entrants, the winner was Hashiguchi Goyo (1880–1921), who had studied both Japanese and Western painting at the Tokyo School of Fine Arts before beginning to work as a book designer and illustrator. Hashiguchi first gained recognition in 1905 for the layout and illustrations he did for Natsume Soseki's satirical novel, *I Am a Cat*. He had a special interest in the *ukiyo-e* tradition which involved printing multiple layers of flat colors in woodblock prints, and his Mitsukoshi poster, which was printed as a color lithograph, required 35 separate runs to produce the rich color (Plate 79).

Hashiguchi's *bijin-ga* poster differed considerably from Okada's painting. The woman whom Okada depicted had a pensive look that she directed away from the picture frame, but Hashiguchi's seated woman looked directly outwards, inviting a relation with the viewer. Hashiguchi also created a rich texture of flat colors that combined traditional Japanese flower patterns with Art Nouveau ornament. The woman is holding a book that depicts women of the past in kimonos, which the viewer is invited to compare with the modern kimono that Mitsukoshi was advertising. Hashiguchi might have become a successful poster designer but instead he turned his attention to printmaking, subsequently creating a modest number of exquisite woodblock prints in the new modern style.

The success of Hashiguchi's *bijin-ga* poster led Mitsukoshi to commission others. Hiraoka Gompachiro (dates unconfirmed) adopted Hashiguchi's approach for a 1913 poster of a woman clad in a richly patterned kimono holding a traditional Japanese stringed instrument, the *biwa*. Sugiura Hisui (1876–1965) also used the same approach the following year for a poster that promoted both kimonos and furniture. Sugiura portrayed a woman in a distinctly modern Mitsukoshi kimono seated on a chair covered in a fabric inspired by Art Nouveau. Next to her are a chair and table in the Secession style that Mitsukoshi was then promoting, along with an Art Nouveau vase and a European print on the wall to suggest the department store's cosmopolitan approach to household furnishings and décor. The woman in Sugiura's poster also holds a Mitsukoshi catalog that features his design on the cover. Unlike Hashiguchi or Hiraoka, who were independent artists, Sugiura joined the Mitsukoshi art department, which had been established in 1909, as chief designer in 1910 and, despite numerous outside activities, remained there until 1934.

During the Taisho period, many other artists created *bijin-ga* posters that advertised everything from clothing and cosmetics to soft drinks and beer. Beer companies, in fact, were particularly avid users of *bijin-ga* imagery. The pictorial conventions for most *bijin-ga* posters were similar. A seated woman clad in

Fig. 36.05: Tada Hokuu, Kirin Beer, poster, 1937. CPA Media Co. Ltd./ Pictures From History.

(1889–1948), whose posters were particularly identified with Kirin beer. Though most of Tada's posters showed a woman either in traditional or modern dress, a 1937 poster of his adopted a more modern advertising technique, which was prevalent in the United States at the time: the depiction of either a man or woman in a social situation where their relation to the product has a positive effect. Tada's poster shows a modern young woman or *moga* holding a glass of Kirin beer while surrounded by a bevy of men, suggesting that her association with Kirin has made her more popular (Fig. 36.05). In 1922, Tada founded his own design office, Sun Studio, where he trained a host of students and young associates over a period of 20 years. For some posters, he adopted, perhaps too readily, the styles of leading European poster artists such as Sepo in Italy and Jean Carlu in France.

In 1922 the liquor producer Kotobukiya, which had been founded as Torii Shoten in 1899, introduced a photographic *bijin-ga* poster that depicted a woman whose upper torso was exposed (Fig. 36.06). Although it was purportedly the first poster to reveal a woman's body to that extent, Japanese artists had nonetheless been painting female nudes since they began to study Western art in the late 19th century. However, the poster, which advertised the company's Akadama Port Wine, did rupture prior *bijin-ga* conventions. It was art directed by Kataoka Toshiro (1882–1946), designed by Inoue Mokuda (dates unconfirmed), and photographed by the Kawaguchi Photo Studio. What made it an early icon of Japanese modernity was not only the suggestive image of the woman, who holds a glass of port wine and looks invitingly at the viewer. It was also the first poster in Japan to be printed by photogravure, a technique that had already been exploited by Alfred Stieglitz and photographers abroad to enhance a photograph's depth and richness of tone.

This poster most likely increased displays of sensuality in subsequent *bijin-ga* posters, but for the most part the visual conventions for such posters remained conservative. Their popularity began to wane

kimono with an elaborate hair arrangement was shown either holding or touching a product or looking at it. Her gaze, however, might be direct or indirect.

During the Taisho period, *bijin-ga* posters were also affected by the widespread aspirations to be modern. By 1920, some of the women in these posters were portrayed with Western hairstyles, although still clad in kimonos, and subsequently some were also shown in Western dress. Several leading *bijin-ga* poster specialists were Machida Ryuyo (dates unconfirmed), whose designs depicted women dressed either in kimono or modern Western clothing, and Tada Hokuu

美味 滋養 葡萄酒
赤玉ポートワイン

Fig. 36.06: Kataoka Toshiro (art director) and Inoue Mokuda (designer), Akadama Port Wine, poster, 1922. CPA Media Co. Ltd./Pictures From History.

by the end of the 1920s once photography came into widespread use for advertising in the 1930s, but besides photography, new techniques and styles of graphic design also provided competition.

Bijin-ga posters did employ a range of lettering styles for their texts, but the posters were essentially illustrative, and lettering played only a minor part in their designs. While the posters did reflect a modernizing impulse in depicting the dress and hairstyles of Japanese women as these changed from traditional Japanese to Western modern, their pictorial conventions remained relatively stable even as they were adopted for the new photographic posters beginning

in the 1930s and continued through World War II and into the post-war period.

Graphic design matures

In the late 1920s, graphic design became a recognized profession in Japan due largely to the leadership of two men, the designer Sugiura Hisui and the theorist Hamada Masuji (1892–1938). Though Sugiura remained with Mitsukoshi for 24 years, he designed posters for numerous other clients, radically changing his style from *bijin-ga* to posters that were influenced by modern European art movements. As a designer, he remained eclectic, drawing from the London Underground posters as easily as from the more stylized and sensuous drawings of Paul Colin and French fashion illustrators. His placard for a poster exhibition at the Mitsukoshi Department Store in 1928 featured a sensuous nude woman whose face bears an expression of ecstasy and whose body is covered by a vertical line of thin *goshikku* lettering. A seminal poster of 1927, which commemorated the opening of Tokyo's first subway line, became an icon of Taisho modernity. It featured an image of the train, seen in fixed-point perspective, and a platform filled with people mainly dressed in Western clothing. Sugiura had gained knowledge of Western art as a student at the Tokyo School of Fine Arts, where he studied with the painter Kuroda Seiki (1866–1924), as did many early poster artists.

In 1926, Sugiura formed a designers' association, which he called Shichininsha (Group of Seven). He intended it to be a group that studied and documented what was happening in graphic design rather than one whose purpose was to further the members' professional interests. Between 1927 and 1930, the Group of Seven published a magazine, *Affiches* (*Posters*), which featured the work of Japanese as well as foreign designers and for which Sugiura did a number of the covers. In addition, the group held annual exhibitions of Japanese and foreign posters.

Sugiura also collaborated with Hamada Masuji, a painter and commercial artist as well as a theorist who had formed Shogyo Bijutsuka Kyokai (Association of Commercial Artists) the same year that Sugiura founded the Group of Seven. Like Sugiura's group, members of the Association of Commercial Artists also organized annual exhibitions and in 1930 they began to publish one of Japan's first graphic design magazines, *Shogyo bijutsu* (*Commercial Art*). In 1932, Hamada opened the Shogyo Bijutsu Kosei Juku, his own Institute of Commercial Art, where he conducted a three-year program that certified students as commercial artists.

As art historian Gennifer Weisenfeld has stated, Hamada made his greatest impact on the development of Japanese graphic design with the publication of a 24-volume collection of commercial art entitled *Gendai shogyo bijutsu zenshu* (*The Complete Commercial Artist*), which featured visual examples of shop windows, signs, typography, posters, and other printed print material from many countries. For the first 15 volumes, Hamada worked with an editorial committee that included Sugiura Hisui, and he then served as chief editor for the final nine. The volumes were purchased by commercial retailers and large manufacturers as well as advertising agencies, newspapers, and others who used graphic design.

Hamada's compendium of design examples served several purposes. First and foremost it was a visual anthology from which Japanese graphic designers could draw. Second, it acquainted both designers and clients with what was being done outside Japan so they could situate their own work in relation to these new trends. And third, it stimulated designers to create their own modern designs that were indigenous to Japanese culture.

Another important promoter of modern graphic design in Japan was Murota Kurazo (dates unconfirmed), editor of the magazine *Kokokukai* (*Advertising World*), which he published between 1924 and 1941 and for which he designed many of the modern covers. Like Hamada, Murota also published a series of portfolios entitled *Shoten zuan senshu* (*A Selection of Designs for Shops*), which featured examples of modern graphic design that might be adapted for commercial use.

Various companies that mounted exemplary advertising campaigns in the 1920s and 1930s took up Sugiura's, Hamada's, and Murota's promotion of modern graphic design. They were primarily in consumer-oriented sectors, notably beauty and hygiene products, cigarettes, sweets, and beer. Jintan, a producer of patent medicines, Club cosmetics, the Morinaga Confectionary Company, and Sapporo, Kabuto, and Kirin beer were among the leaders.

One manufacturer who fully embraced modern design was Shiseido, a leading cosmetics manufacturer, who adopted an artistic advertising strategy that was rooted in French fashion publicity and illustration. The company was founded in 1872 as Japan's first Western-style pharmacy, but had become a leading manufacturer of cosmetics by 1915, when it began to shift away from pharmaceuticals and concentrate on beauty products. During this period, the president was Fukuhara Shinzo (1883–1948), a son of the founder, who had lived in France and photographed there following his pharmaceutical training in the United States. An artist as well as a businessman, Fukuhara designed the Shiseido logo in 1915. It featured two camellias in a frame that recalled a traditional Japanese *monsho* or crest. Fukuhara emphasized Shiseido's connection to France by adopting stylized roman letters for the company name and adding a visual flourish by stretching out the S like a wave. In 1916, he established the company's first design department to create packaging, newspaper and magazine advertising, and window displays. Shiseido also inaugurated an in-house magazine in 1924 called *Shiseido Geppo* (*Shiseido Monthly*), which was renamed *Shiseido Gurafu* (*Shiseido Graph*) in 1933. Although Shiseido advertising derived largely from French fashion culture and relied more on illustration than photography, photographs by Fukuhara Shinzo and his brother Roso (1892–1946) were featured on *Shiseido Monthly* covers. Shiseido publications such as *The Home Calendar* of 1930 also contain some of Japan's earliest photomontages.

Fig. 36.07: Yamana Ayao, Shiseido, advertisement. Shiseido Corporate Museum.

The first designer Fukuhara hired was the artist Yabe Sue (dates unconfirmed), who joined the company in 1917 and remained there until 1925. One of Yabe's early projects was a patterned wrapping paper that was widely recognized and helped to define Shiseido's corporate image. He also created a series of posters for Shiseido products that featured drawings of slightly Asianized women in the style of Georges Le Pape's fashion illustrations from the *Gazette du Bon Ton*. Other early members of the design department were Sawa Reika (1896–1970), the chief designer in the

late 1920s, and Maeda Mitsugu (1903–1967). Like Yabe, Sawa created slightly modified versions of Le Pape's elongated French women, whom he memorialized in a series of posters. Maeda's posters also derived from French precedents, although he is better known for his collaboration with Shiseido's photographer Ibuka Akira (dates unconfirmed).

Shiseido advertising became less derivative of Parisian fashion illustration after the company hired Yamana Ayao (1897–1980) in 1929. Yamana, who had studied Western painting in Osaka and worked for the Platon Company, a publisher of popular Western-oriented magazines, was the first to create a distinctive Shiseido look. He admired Aubrey Beardsley, although his own mores were considerably more restrained than the English artist's. What he took from Beardsley, however, was an elegant line, which he adopted for his advertisements and posters. Many of Yamana's figures were childlike and considerably different from the Le Pape imitations that preceded them (Fig. 36.07). He could also draw in an elegant French style, which he adopted for numerous ads, although some of his images became more realistic beginning in the late 1930s. During a long career at Shiseido, which lasted until his death in 1980, Yamana left the company several times to work for others. This included his affiliation with the Nippon Kobo studio where he served as art director for the pictorial magazine *Nippon* from 1934 to 1936. Another Shiseido designer who moved away from French fashion precedents in the 1930s was Yamamoto Takeo (1910–d.o.d. unconfirmed), a superb draftsman who specialized in softly modeled and beautifully painted heads of women that exuded an ethereal quality. Yamamoto's compositions were also clean and spare, heralding some of the Japanese fashion industry's layouts of later years.

The advertising for Shiseido circulated widely in Japan and helped to establish a climate for modern design, as did new magazines such as *Advertising World* and *Commercial Art*, the designers' associations, and the books and portfolios of examples that were available to potential clients. Besides the design studios that the big companies and department stores set up, and the big advertising agencies like Dentsu and Hakuhodo, graphic designers founded their own studios and worked with diverse clients. These designers did not follow a single style and their approaches were extremely diverse.

In 1931, Okuyama Gihachiro (1907–1981), a printmaker who was active in the modern print movement, opened a commercial art studio, which he called the Tokyo Advertising Art Association, a name that he later changed to the Tokyo Advertising Creator's

Fig. 36.08: Okuyama Gihachiro, Nikke Wool Goods, poster, 1937. CPA Media Co. Ltd./Pictures From History.

Club. Clients included the Japan Wool Company and Nikka Whiskey, but the one that brought him the most attention was Nikke, a clothing company that commissioned a series of inventive posters beginning in the early 1930s. Unlike Tada, Sugiura, or Yamana, Okuyama was strongly attracted to the graphic style of *ukiyo-e* printmakers like Hiroshige and Harunobu. This was especially evident in several posters he designed for Nikke Bathing Suits, but in other posters for the company such as one for Nikke Wool Goods, he adopted a more eclectic and playful visual style (Fig. 36.08). Okuyama also incorporated *goshikku* lettering into his designs, and in the Wool Goods poster, he enlarged the letters so that they became equal in visual presence to the woodblock image. In other posters he considered the text elements as graphic forms and treated them with considerable wit. As a graphic designer, he was not part of any larger movement and he designed his posters as if they were personal prints. In fact, he did not remain in commercial art and became widely known as a printmaker after World War II.

Besides the large and small companies, another group of advertising clients were the film studios, located mainly in Tokyo and Kyoto. The first Japanese film was produced around 1898, and silent films prevailed well into the 1930s, considerably later than in the United States and Europe. The largest Japanese studios in the 1920s were Shochiku Kinema and Nikkatsu, with Toho becoming a major competitor after sound films were introduced in the 1930s. The studios specialized in two major genres—*jidi-geki* (period stories) and *gendai-geki* (contemporary dramas). They competed with the large American film companies—among them Paramount, Fox, United Artists, and Columbia. Major directors included Ozu Yasujiro, Mizoguchi Kenji, and Naruse Mikio.

In the 1920s, film was the most popular entertainment form in Japan. The large studios were vertically integrated companies that controlled both production and distribution. They had their own stables of actors and directors and owned the theaters where they showed their films. They employed artists to produce newspaper advertisements and posters as well as to design film sets and sets for the theater companies they also owned. Shochiku, originally a theatrical company, first began producing films in 1920, and by 1921, Yamada Shinkichi (1904–c. 1982) was designing posters for its productions. The posters that Yamada designed throughout the 1920s changed radically and quickly in their style from Symbolist imagery and modernist formalism in the early to mid-1920s to a gritty realism, featuring large images of the lead actors, in the late 1920s. Although Shochiku was a major production studio for domestic films by directors like Ozu Yasujiro, it was also a leading importer of American and European films which it showed with Japanese subtitles and whose style it adapted for its own actors and directors. Yamada's posters were heavy with bold lettering in both *monsho* and *goshikku* styles, some of which appeared to be derived from Russian Constructivism.

In 1929, Shochiku hired Kono Takashi (1906–1999), a graduate of the Tokyo School of Fine Arts, and put him in charge of its design department, which included designing sets for plays, dance perfor-mances, and films as well as creating advertisements and film posters. Kono's poster designs for Shochiku revolutionized the film poster medium, which was characterized by illustrative images and dense, often chaotic, lettering. They also pointed the way to a more conceptual and iconic graphic style that would characterize Japanese design modernism in the 1950s and 1960s. In fact, Kono's work had a major impact on post-war designers such as Yokoo Tadanori and Tanaka Ikko.

Kono's designerly approach is evident in the poster he created for Ozu Yasujiro's 1931 film, *The Lady and the Beard*. In the 1930s, Ozu was to become known for his subtly photographed family dramas, but his early films for Shochiku were in a light comedy genre known as *nansensu* (nonsense). In *The Lady and the Beard*, Ozu tells the story of a scruffy bearded man who shaves off his beard and has to cope with the advances of several women. Instead of a literal narrative, Kono reduced the poster imagery to cartoon-like depictions of the bearded man and a woman he tries to seduce. He drew the woman's face with the dual perspective of a Picasso painting and integrated the bold lettering and drawings into a strong balanced composition within a field of empty space (Plate 80). Though it made modest reference to European art and graphic precedents, Kono's poster introduced a modernist style that refer-enced European precedents without being derivative of them, thus serving as an early and influential example of modern Japanese graphic design. In this sense, the poster might be compared with Yamana Ayao's posters and advertisements for Shiseido.

Other major clients for posters included the Japanese Government Railways, which produced a series of travel posters for distribution overseas. Highly derivative of earlier examples for the British LNER and the French National Railroad, they were handsomely printed lithographs but broke no new conceptual ground. The same could be said for the posters by Ito Junzo (dates unconfirmed) and others for the South Manchuria Railway. Like the posters of the Japan Tourist Bureau, the railway posters presented more stereotypical imagery in their appeal to potential European travelers.

The avant-garde and proletarian graphics

During the 1920s and 1930s, Japanese artists actively engaged with European avant-garde movements from Cubism in France and Futurism in Italy to Expressionism and Dada in Germany and Constructivism in the Soviet Union. As in Europe, the avant-garde created some of the most experimental Japanese poster designs, book layouts, and periodical covers. A figure who was central to this activity was the multifaceted artist Murayama Tomoyoshi (1901–1977), who discovered the European avant-garde while in Berlin from 1921 to 1923. After his return to Tokyo, Murayama founded the Mavo group, which included the artists Yanase Masamu (1900–1945), Ogata Kamenosuke (1900–1942), Oura Shuzo (1890–1928), and Okada Tatsuo (1900–1937), and the poet Hagiwara Kyojiro (1899–1938). "Mavo" was a made-up word that also served as the title of the group's short-lived journal, which was published between 1923 and 1925.

Murayama's theory of "conscious constructivism," which *Mavo* represented, entailed broadening the definition of art to include all of life. Besides publishing and designing the journal, as Gennifer Weisenfeld notes, other activities of the Mavo group included the design of books and posters, as well as art exhibitions, theater and dance performances, and

Fig. 36.09: *Mavo* 1, cover, 1924. Spencer Collection, The New York Public Library, Astor, Lenox and Tilden Foundations.

architectural projects. The layout of the group's journal involved various Dada and Constructivist devices—upside down words, partitioned sections framed by heavy black rules, collage, and photomontage, and the incorporation of newspaper sheets as pages. The roman letters of the title as displayed on the first four covers were bold and idiosyncratic, featuring strange pointed flourishes at the ends of letters instead of serifs. Besides being featured in roman letters, the word Mavo was also spelled out in heavy Japanese *katakana* syllables, which formed an integral part of the cover's composition (Fig. 36.09). The first four cover designs recalled the strong Constructivist rhetoric of the Polish journal *Blok* (1924–1926), while the last three, with their emphasis on the first two letters of the title, made reference to Lajos Kássak's Hungarian journal *MA* (1916–1926).

Among the Mavo book projects was the collective design of anarchist and neo-Dada poet Hagiwara Kyojiro's book of poems, *Shikei senkoku* (*Death Sentence*), in 1925. Like F. T. Marinetti, Hagiwara (1899–1938) expressed his emotions through typography. Characters were printed in different styles or sizes, many poems featured onomatopoeia—characters and syllables that conveyed expressive sounds—and characters without meaning, or groups of dots and triangles sometimes replaced words. The graphic layouts of Hagiwara's poems were complemented by numerous abstract linocut prints by Mavo members along with several photographic reproductions of Mavo works that had been previously published in the group's journal.

Okada Tatsuo, a printmaker who shared Hagiwara's belief in anarchism, designed the cover of *Death Sentence*. By contrast with his beliefs, however, it was actually quite orderly. Published with more than one color scheme, it consisted of two heavy ladder-like shapes that framed a circle in the center and a gridded box at the bottom with some of the boxes filled in to suggest roman letters. Colored bands covered the author's name and the book's title, which consisted of characters arranged in a bold pattern.

Mavo posters and announcements for avant-garde art exhibitions and theater performances featured equally complex compositions of lettering and abstract elements. Posters for exhibitions by the artists' group known as Sanka, as well as experimental theater pieces, were intended to convey a sense of experiment that characterized the events they advertised. Murayama's poster for a 1925 Sanka exhibition, for example, incorporated iconographic elements, abstract forms, and tightly composed lettering in a composition that recalls designs by Russian Constructivist artists. Yanase Masamu combined Dada and Constructivist elements in a 1924 poster for the Senku-za theater group in which he also mixed roman letters and numbers with Japanese lettering and abstract typographic elements to create a composition that was every bit as intricate as Theo Van Doesburg's poster for several Dada performances of 1923 or El Lissitzky's 1924 poster for two Merz events in Hanover. Posters with a Dada or Constructivist rhetoric by Japanese avant-garde artists, in fact, were not derivatives of Western examples but were instead incorporated into Japanese visual culture in an entirely original way.

Besides doing work for their own and other avant-garde organizations, Mavo members were active as commercial artists. Early in his career, Murayama drew illustrations for children's magazines and worked as well for *Ladies' Companion*, the popular magazine for which he created decorations for page margins that often employed Western letters and numbers arranged in abstract patterns. Oura Shuzo, another of the original Mavo members, worked as an advertising artist and window display designer for the prominent Tokyo publisher Maruzen, which also owned a book store and operated a manufacturing division whose products included safety razors and inks.

Yanase Masamu was one of Japan's most prolific modernist graphic designers and also the most politically radical. When he first came to Tokyo in 1920, he designed books for the socially progressive journalist and publisher Hasegawa Nyozekan, who also co-founded a political journal, *Warera* (*We, Ourselves*), for which Yanase provided illustrations. In 1925, the year Murayama left Mavo, Yanase renounced fine art and with Murayama helped to spearhead the emerging proletarian arts movement.

The Taisho period, during which Mavo and its activities flourished and in which the proletarian arts movement began, was relatively liberal. It was followed by the Showa era, which in its early years ushered in increasing militarism and authoritarian rule that was antagonistic to political dissent. The Japanese Social Democratic Party, which had been established in 1901, suffered a continuing series of setbacks in its early years, but was reanimated by the Russian Revolution of 1917. Japan's Communist Party was outlawed almost immediately after its founding in 1922, but the party became an underground organization and members continued to operate clandestinely.

The proletarian arts movement was thus a bold political initiative that entailed considerable risks. When the Proletarian Literature and Art League was founded in 1925, Murayama and Yanase were among the first members of its art section. In November 1928 the First Proletarian Art Exhibition was held in Tokyo and the work exhibited revealed the considerable influence of the Socialist Realist tendencies in the Soviet Union. While Murayama became involved with radical theater productions, Yanase was the principal graphic designer for the events and publications of the new movement.

Soviet Constructivist graphics continued as a source for Yanase and others who did design work for the movement, such as the artist Okamoto Toki (1903–1986). But Socialist Realism became the strongest influence and Yanase adopted an aggressive pictorial style that recalled the first posters for the Russian Revolution by Dmitri Moor, Viktor Deni, and Boris Kustodiev. For a 1926 poster that promoted the recently established *Musansha Shimbun* (*Proletarian Newspaper*), Yanase painted a huge red hand on a page of newsprint that invited the public to join 50,000 other readers of the newspaper, while he foregrounded a worker in silhouette holding a red flag on a poster for the Japan Cooperative Education Association that announced a new cooperative school for farm and city workers. Yanase also illustrated a number of covers for the revolutionary journal *Senki* (*Fighting Flag*), which was published between 1928 and 1931. As with his posters, Yanase's magazine covers featured figures and narratives derived from Soviet models such as a smiling Japanese worker with bulging muscles standing in front of a huge industrial plant, or a heroic fighter piercing the metaphorical fortress walls of capitalism with a pointed pole bearing an unfurled red flag.

Following a crackdown on Communist Party members in 1928 and the strengthening of a law that prohibited opposition to the prevailing political system, Murayama was arrested in 1930 and briefly imprisoned

for publishing a tract on proletarian art, while Yanase, who had joined the Communist Party in 1932, was also arrested that year and tortured in prison, although a stringent sentence was commuted the following year and he was released. Due to the increasing militarization in the 1930s, opposition to the government was impossible except by covert means. Yanase had acted courageously and after his release from prison had to resort to politically benign activities such as drawing *manga* illustrations and caricatures for various publications and working briefly as a travel photographer.

Photography in advertising and publications

The German New Photography, which challenged traditional photographic pictorialism with its emphasis on sharply focused images, unusual angles, and urban

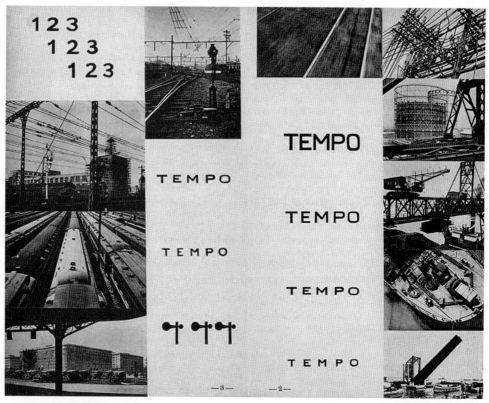

Fig. 36.10: Horino Masao, "The Character of Greater Tokyo," spread, *Central Review*, 1932. CPA Media Co. Ltd./ Pictures From History.

imagery, found eager adherents in Japan, as did the photo reportage of the pictorial weeklies like the *Berliner Illustrirte Zeitung* and the *Münchner Illustrierte Presse* along with the photographic spreads in more specialized lifestyle magazines like *Die Neue Linie* and *Die Dame*.

Articles on leading German photographers as well as modern photographers elsewhere appeared in *Photo Times*, a popular Japanese photography magazine that was founded in 1924. *Photo Times* was a strong promoter of work by László Moholy-Nagy, a key figure in the German New Photography movement, particularly his theory of *typofoto*, which addressed the relation of text and image. One photographer who was strongly influenced by Moholy-Nagy's theory was Horino Masao (1907–2000), who published his own version of Moholy-Nagy's 1925 typofoto essay "Dynamic of the Metropolis" as "The Character of Greater Tokyo" in the magazine *Chuo koron* (*Central Review*) in 1931 (Fig. 36.10). The following year, Horino produced a book, *Kamera, Me x Tetsu/Kosei* (*Camera, Eye x Steel: Composition*), which featured photographs of objects made of steel—ships, bridges, tanks, towers, and buildings—that were shot from unusual angles. Another photo book that was heavily indebted to Moholy-Nagy as well as to the Surrealists was *Shoka shinkei* (*Early Summer Nerves*) of 1933, a collection of photographs by Kiyoshi Koishi (1908–1957). The book's cover was made of metal, as was the spiral binding, while the ten photograms and photographs used images of metal coils, gears, and other industrial objects to poetically explore the relation between humans and machines.

By the mid-1920s, photography had begun to compete with graphics and illustration in advertisements. In 1926, the photographer Kanamaru Shigene (1900–1977), who had been a member of Sugiura Kohei's Group of Seven, co-founded Kinreisha, Japan's first commercial photography studio. Kinreisha struggled during its early years but became more successful after Kanamaru took it over himself in 1929. He adopted many of the advertising techniques that had been successful in Germany—photomontage, product close-ups, unusual angles, and dramatic lighting. Among his clients were the Morinaga Candy Company, Yamasa Soy Sauce, and Kao Soap.

In 1930, two important events occurred: a group of photographers formed the Shogyo Shashinka Kyokai (Association of Advertising Photography), and the inaugural International Advertising Photography Exhibition was held in Tokyo. A Japanese photographer, Nakayama Iwata (1895–1949), who had worked abroad for ten years in New York, Paris, and Berlin, won first prize in the exhibition, and a Japanese won the prize again in 1931, when Koishi Kiyoshi was recognized for his Club soap advertisements. That year, Japanese photographers had a chance to experience the European New Photography at first hand when a reduced version of the Deutscher Werkbund's 1929 Film und Foto exhibition came to Tokyo and Osaka. Included in the exhibition were examples of work by Moholy-Nagy and Albert Renger-Patzsch as well as the Dutch designer/photographers Piet Zwart and Paul Schuitema.

Among the first companies to build its advertising campaign around photography was Kao Soap. Nagase Tomiro established the company in 1890, and by 1910 the soap had become a national brand at a time when few other Japanese products had either brand name or national recognition. The logo was a crescent moon, which was chosen when the company was founded and it was updated periodically until 1925.

In 1931, Kao Soap introduced an ambitious advertising campaign to market a "new and improved Kao." It was directed by the Christian Socialist Ota Hideshige (1892–1982), considered to be one of the first professional art directors in Japan. Ota headed a new design division that was housed in Kao's advertising section and he was responsible for all the company's visual imagery as well as its advertising copy. A major component of the "new and improved Kao" campaign, as Gennifer Weisenfeld has noted, was the shift to national direct marketing, which required a more aggressive advertising and brand identification approach.

Ota was a pioneer in the use of photography in advertising. Shortly after he took charge of the new campaign, he hired Kanamaru Shigene, who produced a striking newspaper advertisement that showed a crowd of Kao employees shot from above. It was one of the earliest examples of full-page newspaper advertising in Japan. Ota also hired Kimura Ihee (1901–1974), with whose gritty documentary photographs of Tokyo he had become familiar.

Kimura produced a series of newspaper ads for Ota that identified Kao Soap with industrial workers and common people struggling to survive. A well-known ad of 1931 in this series showed a makeshift shanty on an empty lot with a woman washing clothes outside and clothing hanging on a line. Possibly she was a survivor of Tokyo's Kanto earthquake who had not been resettled. While Kimura's ads sought to demonstrate that Kao Soap was popular with a wide section of the populace, they also performed a progressive social function by bringing to public attention the range of circumstances in which people lived. The photographic ads that Ota ran, which adopted photomontage as a strategy in some instances, were among the most conceptually advanced of any in Japan at the time. They were complemented by innovative shop window displays that perfectly exemplified Hamada Masuji's call for "art with a purpose."

In 1932, as one result of the Film und Foto exhibition, a group of photographers and critics founded *Koga*, a photography journal that advanced the tenets of the Japanese New Photography through its articles as well as the photographic portfolios it published. The founders were Nojima Yasuzo (1889–1964), an avid promoter of modern photography; Nakayama Iwata; Kimura Ihee; and the critic Ina Nobuo (1898–1978). Ina's manifesto, "Return to Photography," published in the first issue, urged photographers to abandon art photography and engage with social life.

Though *Koga* only endured for a brief period, it strongly influenced a new generation of graphic designers for whom photography was a central component of their work. Foremost among them was Hara Hiromu (1903–1986), a great admirer of Moholy-Nagy, Herbert Bayer, Jan Tschichold, and El Lissitzky. In 1931, Hara published a pamphlet on modern typography in which he urged Japanese designers not to copy the European modernists but instead to develop typographic practices that were especially suited to the Japanese language. He also stressed the importance of photography and its relation to type. These views were evident in his poster designs as well as the photography displays he created for the Japanese pavilions at the 1937 World's Fair in Paris and the 1939 World's Fair in New York.

A poster of 1935 that he designed for an exhibition of mannequins in Sapporo featured a photograph of a mannequin by Kimura Ihee set against a white background with English and Japanese lettering

Fig. 36.11: Hara Hiromu, Exhibition of Mannequins, poster, 1935. CPA Media Co. Ltd./Pictures From History.

incorporated into the composition. Although Hara admired Tschichold's new typography, he was not a strict Functionalist and he introduced a poetic element in the Sapporo poster by placing several hand-drawn colored scarves around the mannequin's neck (Fig. 36.11). Though photography was widely accepted in advertising by the mid-1930s, it was rarely used as effectively as Hara employed it. Many companies continued the *bijin-ga* approach, featuring photographs of attractive women in modern dress for their posters and newspaper advertisements. Sometimes designers copied European precedents, as did Takahashi Kinkichi (1911–1980), who simply adapted Herbert Matter's Swiss travel poster designs for a Japanese ski manufacturer.

In 1933, the photojournalist Natori Yonosuke (1910–1962) founded a multipurpose design group, Nippon Kobo (Japanese Studio) that would make photography central to its creation of advertisements, exhibitions, and publications. Natori had studied commercial and applied arts and photojournalism in Germany between 1928 and 1932, and while there he worked for the Ullstein Verlag, which published the *Berliner Illustrirte Zeitung* and other periodicals, an experience that gave him a firm understanding of the German periodical press.

Nippon Kobo pioneered new techniques that blurred the boundaries between avant-garde art, photojournalism, advertising design, and national propaganda. The initial members of the studio included Hara Hiromu, the filmmaker Okada Sozo (1903–1983), and two former founders of the photo magazine *Koga*, Kimura Ihee and Ina Nobuo. Within a year, Hara, Kimura, and Ina had left Nippon Kobo, and in 1934, Natori reconstituted the studio. Over the next several years he brought in the graphic designers Yamana Ayao; Kono Takashi, who had worked for the Shochiku Film Studio; and Kamekura Yusaku, a former student at the Bauhaus-inspired New Academy of Architecture and Industrial Arts, who had also worked for Kao Soap under the guidance of art director Ota Hideshige.

The studio undertook numerous advertising commissions but much of its energy was dedicated to the publication of a pictorial propaganda magazine, *Nippon*, which first appeared in 1934. Published quarterly for a decade, *Nippon* was intended for foreigners. Its purpose was to promote Japan as a tourist destination, hence its content invoked all the clichés of Japanese culture such as photographs of temples, cherry blossoms, and demure women in kimonos and geta, the traditional Japanese wooden shoes. These images, however, were carefully balanced with those of modern life, particularly Japan's industrial achievements. *Nippon* was preceded by other Japanese photo magazines that were based on German examples. Foremost among these was *Asahi Gurafu (Asahi Graph)*, a weekly magazine that the *Asahi Shimbun*, a national daily newspaper, launched in 1923.

By the time *Nippon* appeared in 1934, Japan had occupied Manchuria and established the puppet regime of Manchukuo. The Japanese had also provoked a military confrontation with China in Shanghai. Japan had become a militaristic state and *Nippon*'s editorial policy was firmly rooted within the state's propaganda program. To present the magazine's content, however, Natori and his staff adopted avant-garde techniques including innovative layouts as well as an extensive use of photomontage.

Nippon was multilingual and, like its Soviet counterpart, *USSR in Construction*, was available in a number of countries. Natori was the editor and Yamana Ayao, who left Shiseido to join Nippon Kobo, where he remained for several years before returning to the cosmetics company, was the first art director. Besides supervising the layout, Yamana also designed a number of the covers, including the one for the first issue (Plate 81). Among the photographers Natori hired to shoot stories for *Nippon* were Domon Ken (1909–1990), Horino Masao, Kimura Ihee, Watanabe Yoshio (1907–2000), and Furukawa Narutoshi (1900–1996). Photographers and graphic designers also collaborated on advertising projects for Nippon Kobo such as the photomontage poster that Kamekura Yusaku designed with photographs by Domon Ken for the Shibaura Motor Company in 1938.

Once Japan declared war on China in 1937, Natori went on to found other propaganda magazines to support the government's expansionist policies, notably the English-language graphic magazine *Shanghai* in 1938 and the following year *Commerce Japan*, as well as *Manchukuo* and *Kanton*. In a short span of time, Natori had built an advertising and publishing empire that became central to Japan's campaign to establish the Greater East Asia Co-Prosperity Sphere and promote its legitimacy abroad.

The Japanese Abroad

With the annexation of Hokkaido in 1869 and that of the Ryuku islands ten years later, Japan began to create the foundation of an overseas empire that grew modestly but never rivaled those of the European powers in size. After Japan defeated China in the Sino-Japanese War of 1895, the Chinese ceded Taiwan to Japan under the terms of the Treaty of Shimonoseki. Also contained in the treaty was a provision for China to recognize the independence of Korea, thus preparing the way for Japan to colonize that country 15 years later.

Following the Russo-Japanese War, of 1904–1905, when Russia was defeated, Japan took a strong economic interest in Manchuria, a region in north-east China, The Japanese gained control of the South Manchuria Railway in 1906 and built it into a large corporation known as Mantetsu, which encouraged Japanese tourism and settlement. They occupied Manchuria in 1931 and the next year they established a puppet state they named Manchukuo.

This combination of annexed territories and colonies served as the basis for the brief existence of Japan's dream of empire, the Greater East Asia Co-prosperity Sphere, which included Manchukuo and during World War II the occupation of colonies in Asia that had been previously held by the European powers. With Japan's defeat in the war, its ambitious plans for an Asian empire collapsed.

Fig. 36.12: South Manchuria Railway, *Asia Express*, 1934–1943. Wikipedia.

Manchuria

Japan's activity in Manchuria rivaled the aggressive production of foreign factories in the Chinese treaty ports and China's own industrialization efforts. Until the 1930s, Japan considered Manchuria primarily as a market for its own exports, but after Manchukuo was established, the Japanese redefined the region as ripe for full industrial development. Consequently, a large planning initiative was undertaken and this attracted a number of Japanese firms. In late 1936, Nissan, one of Japan's nascent automobile companies, established the Manshu Heavy Industries Development Company, a holding enterprise that managed a range of subsidiaries. While the aim of most subsidiaries was to exploit natural resources, there were also several manufacturing firms including Dalian Ceramics, South Manchurian Glass, and Dowa Automobile Manufacturing.

Mantetsu constructed hotels for Japanese tourists along the railway stops and established schools, hospitals, and other facilities for settlers. To encourage tourists from Japan and elsewhere to visit Manchuria, Mantetsu adopted up-to-date Art Deco graphics, which emphasized the speed and comfort of its streamlined train, the *Asia Express*. Streamlining was first adopted for the two large "Pacific" locomotives that the South Manchuria Railway built in Japan for the ultra-modern high-speed train that was inaugurated in Manchuria in 1934 (Fig. 36.12). Whereas Japanese railroad engines had previously been entirely black, the streamlined engines of the *Asia Express* were painted sky blue with thin red coupling rods to provide contrast. The South Manchurian Railway also chose Art Deco as the style for the luxury interiors as part of its campaign to market the *Asia Express* to Western tourists. With its streamlined engines and modern interior design, the train was perhaps Japan's most salient sign of modernity, showing to the rest of the world that it could hold its own with the Western powers, particularly as a seemingly beneficent colonizer of the Chinese in that region. The Japanese also promoted Manchuria's modernity to tourists through graphic means such as postcards that featured images of local women dressed in modern styles, a propaganda adaptation of the traditional *ukiyo-e* prints that depicted female beauties of their day (Plate 82).

Taiwan

After it occupied Taiwan, Japan went to great lengths to make it a "model colony." This was demonstrated through an occupation that can be divided into three periods. The first is the period between the Japanese arrival in 1895 and the Tapani Incident, a large armed uprising against Japanese rule that occurred in 1915 and during which many Taiwanese were killed. In this first period of rule, the Japanese followed the philosophy of the colony's Governor-General, Count Kodama Gentaro, who believed that the Taiwanese could not be assimilated and consequently Japan would have to adopt the British approach and establish an entirely new set of laws to administer the colony's affairs. This policy was rejected in 1918 after Hara Takashi became the Japanese prime minister. Hara believed that the Taiwanese and the Koreans were similar enough to the Japanese to be governed by the same legal and administrative approaches that were used in Japan.

During the second period between the Tapani Incident and the Marco Polo Bridge Incident in China—generally considered to have launched the Second Sino-Japanese War in 1937—the Japanese government pursued a policy of *Doka* or assimilation. Based on the understanding that the Taiwanese would be taught the roles and responsibilities of Japanese subjects, the policy was formally announced in 1919 and continued for the next 20 years. Nonetheless, many indigenous movements arose and these led to numerous social and cultural undertakings.

Following the eruption of the Second Sino-Japanese War, the Japanese government introduced the *kominka* movement to instill Japanese spirit in the Taiwanese and incorporate them into the growing war effort. This entailed encouraging local people to speak the Japanese language, take Japanese names, wear Japanese clothing, and convert to the Shinto religion.

The Taiwanese were also encouraged to volunteer for the Japanese Army once World War II began.

A notable feature of Japanese rule was the introduction of social change from the top down, much of which was driven by administrators in the colonial government. One example was the education system, which the Japanese believed to be a means to assimilate the Taiwanese people. Japanese was made the formal school language and a pragmatic curriculum was introduced, including mechanical drawing and handicraft training. This training, as Tsun-Hsiung Yao, Chu-Yu Sun, and Pin-Chang Lin note, became a foundation for those who would later become leaders in the Taiwanese design field.

The Taiwanese economy for the most part was directed to serve Japan's advantage. The Japanese government initially relied on Taiwan's existing industries, but instituted a policy of intensive industrialization after 1930. Large public works projects were introduced, a railway system was constructed, and telecommunications were implemented.

One technology that the Japanese introduced was the push car railways, which were in general service during the course of the occupation. The push cars— passenger and freight cars that were powered by human labor—complemented the developing system of steam locomotives. The push car was simply a platform attached to railway wheels that operated on narrow gauge railway tracks. There were two raised poles behind the platform that laborers could grasp in order to push the cars. The platforms could seat up to four people, while freight push cars could carry as much a 450 pounds of goods (Fig. 36.13). The push-car line, which the Japanese began to build shortly after they arrived, ran across the western coastal area of Taiwan from Taipei to Kaohsiung. It reached a peak during the late 1920s and early 1930s, when modern road systems for cars and buses gradually replaced it.

Similar to the British in India, the Japanese took a great interest in the development of their colonies' folk crafts. As early as 1903 at Japan's Fifth National Industrial Exhibition, which was held in Osaka, the

Fig. 36.13: Taiwanese push car, c. 1920s. taipics.com.

Taiwanese Pavilion featured craft examples from its aboriginal population including the "savage textiles" of the Atayal tribe, who were patronizingly described as the most developed and elaborate of all the tribes. The Japanese aestheticizing of art that native people made was similar to the aesthetic adulation of African tribal masks that occurred in Europe around the same time.

After the occupation of Taiwan, the Colonial Government Museum, established there in 1908, began to create taxonomies for a range of tribal arts that its staff collected. The official interest in folk art corresponded to the *mingei* movement in Japan, founded by Yanagi Soetsu, which celebrated the beauty of everyday Japanese objects that were made by ordinary people. Yanagi, in fact, visited Taiwan for a month in 1943 to study local folk crafts. When he returned to Japan, he participated in an exhibition of "Savage Textiles" in the Japanese Folk Art Museum. Under Yanagi's guidance, the *mingei* movement in Taiwan was initiated by Kanaseki Takeo (1897–1983), a professor of medicine who founded *Minzoku Taiwan* (*Folkways Taiwan*), a monthly journal of Taiwanese folklore and crafts that was published between 1941 and 1945; the Japanese artist Tateishi Tetsuomi (1905–1980); and Yan Shui-long (1903–1997), a Taiwanese painter and designer.

Tateishi, an admirer of traditional Taiwanese folk culture, was a prolific illustrator who recorded the folklore and culture of Taiwan through his woodcuts. Yan Shui-long studied art in Japan and France before returning to Taiwan in 1937, where he carried out field research on Taiwanese crafts under the sponsorship of the colonial government. He designed numerous products for the Southern Asia Handicraft Association, which he founded. These included shopping bags, slippers, hats, and doormats. As Yuko Kikuchi notes, Yan made a substantial profit selling these goods overseas in Japan and China. One consequence of his activity was some revitalization of the rural Taiwanese economy.

Yamamoto Kanae (1882–1946), a Japanese painter and woodblock print artist, visited Taiwan in 1924 to advise the government on how to develop the Taiwanese craft industry. An admirer of aboriginal crafts, which he judged second best in the world after the crafts of Scandinavia, Yamamoto suggested that they should form the basis of a new Taiwanese craft industry, which would be developed through an agency called Banchi Sangyo Kogei (Aboriginal Industrial Crafts). Urging an emphasis on "local color," Yamamoto sought both to preserve local culture while also generating an income for aboriginal people. As Yuko Kikuchi points out, he had two strategies: one to make reproductions of the best examples of aboriginal crafts and sell them as souvenirs; and the other to create new products with aboriginal designs, while also adding designs from nearby South Asian countries. Though originating in a colonial mentality, Yamamoto's ideas were quite similar to those proposed by American designers who were sent to Asia in the 1950s to assist with a similar aim of developing local crafts into products that could circulate in modern international markets.

During World War II, the Japanese government developed a strong interest in "substitute products" that could replace those made of metals vital for national defense. Bamboo was a principal material for such products. Since the 1910s, the Japanese had funded bamboo pulp centers and bamboo craft training centers to create products for export, while bamboo crafts had come to represent for the journal *Minzoku Taiwan* the colony's most remarkable folk objects. After the war started, a large exhibition entitled Shinko Daiyohin (Newly Invented Substitute Products) featured objects that Taiwanese companies created. Organized by the Chamber of Commerce of Taiwan, it traveled around the colony, displaying such products as buckets and suitcases that were made from local materials.

Graphic design in Taiwan received an impetus from Japanese artists who came to teach there. They showed their work at the annual Taiwan Fine Arts Exhibition or Taiten, where they displayed it in one of the two categories: Oriental or Western painting, both of which had an influence on Taiwanese art students. Among the most prominent Japanese artists were Gohara Koto (1887–1965) and Shiotsuki Toho (1885–1954), both graduates of the Tokyo School of Fine Arts; Ishikawa Kinichiro (1871–1945); and Tateishi Tetsuomi, who had a close connection to the novelist Nishiwaka Mitsuru, a Japanese writer who introduced a Western style to modern Taiwanese literature. Tateishi was responsible as an illustrator or cover designer for more than 150 books and is considered by some to have been Taiwan's greatest book artist during the colonial period.

Japanese businesses in Taiwan began using modern marketing techniques for advertising, packaging, retail displays, and show windows. The rise of marketing was paralleled by the spread of newspapers, magazines, books, and posters. Advertising in the magazines, similar to China and Japan, was strongly influenced by Western graphic styles.

Taipei, the capital of Taiwan, was the center for much of the island's commercial activity. The graphic designers were primarily trained in the fine arts. Through the active advocacy of the Japanese administrators and artists, the modern style prevalent in Japan was widely imitated. Many Taiwanese shops strove to emulate Western product advertising, sometimes plagiarizing it directly. This was the case, for example, with a poster for a local wine that directly copied Cassandre's famous poster for the French wine company Dubonnet.

To improve the quality of Taiwanese products, the colonial government organized many industrial design exhibitions. These had several purposes. They were intended to demonstrate the beneficence of colonial rule that was bringing prosperity to Taiwan, while also promoting accelerated industrial development by showing exemplary products from abroad. In 1931, for example, a display in the Taichung Product Exhibition Hall entitled Nationwide Canned Product Exhibition featured attractively packaged canned goods from Japan. Following the second colonial period, as Tsun-Hsiung Yao, Chu-Yu Sun, and Pin-Chang Lin point out, the Office of the Governor-General sought to elevate product and graphic design by holding competitions in different cities. It also organized exhibitions of posters from abroad. A City Logo Exhibition, for example, displayed an array of city logos collected from Japan, Korea, and Taiwan.

One of the largest of these exhibitions in Taiwan during the colonial period was the Commercial Art Exhibition that was held in 1932. On display were design examples from Europe, the United States, Japan, and Taiwan. These included posters, advertising, propaganda fliers, packaging, and products. Following this exhibition were others that displayed and promoted modern design, thus enabling modern ideas and techniques of graphic design in particular to become widely known in Taiwan's design community.

The most important exhibition to be held during the colonial period was the Taiwan Exhibition that the Governor-General hosted to commemorate 40 years of Japanese rule. Staged in 1935 and lasting for two months, its purpose was to celebrate the achievements of the Japanese government during its occupation as well as to promote a new political agenda, the Nanshin-ron (Southern Expansion Doctrine). The exhibition, which sought to emulate some of the large celebratory exhibitions that had been held abroad, featured numerous pavilions in a broad range of styles. It had four major venues. The first displayed developments in the colonies—Taiwan and Korea and in the puppet state of Manchukuo. The second was devoted to achievements in different categories such as industrial products. The third included displays related to social customs as well as exhibits from other places in Southeast Asia. The final venue introduced a number of tourist attractions. Within the exhibition were more than 40 pavilions devoted both to places such as Korea, Manchuria, or Kyoto and to particular topics such as industries, transportation, and forests.

The exhibition was promoted with a range of graphic formats including posters, street signs, and other types of publicity. Two of the posters were designed by the Japanese artist Tsukamoto Kakuji (dates unconfirmed), who featured on one of them a large dove of peace hovering over the exhibition buildings. Advertising was widespread as companies created publicity for themselves in urban venues such as benches, streetlights, and trashcans. In scope and sophistication, the exhibition, though smaller than the major world expos, more than held its own with many other more local exhibitions that were held in different parts of the world during the same period. It was effective in announcing to the world that Taiwan had become a "model colony" that had willingly cooperated with the Japanese to alleviate its backward ways and become a thriving modern society.

Korea

In the late 19th century, Korea profited greatly from foreign trade, which resulted in Hanyang (later Seoul), its capital, becoming the first city in East Asia to have electricity, streetcars, and telegraph systems (Fig. 36.14). This was the consequence of joint Korean-American enterprises that included the Hansong Electric Company and the Hansong Electric Trolley Company. Aside from these innovations, however, Korea was a predominantly agricultural country when the Japanese annexed it in 1910 and made it their second colony.

The Japanese pursued a policy of what has been called "colonial mercantilism," which entailed heavy investment in infrastructure—roads, port facilities, and a railroad system—primarily to facilitate transportation for the export of raw materials such as timber, foodstuffs, coal, and iron ore. Initially, the colonial administration's main priority was an increase in agricultural production to meet a growing domestic need for rice. Among the enterprises that were dedicated to the export of rice were the rice mills that were built by Japanese migrants who hoped to sell milled rice back to their homeland. The migrants were supported in this endeavor by the Governor-General who provided financial and infrastructure support.

During the late 1920s and into the 1930s, the

Fig. 36.14: Streetcar in Hanyang (Seoul), early 1900s. Library of Congress, LC-USZ62-86831.

Japanese made a concentrated effort to build up Korea's industrial base, particularly in heavy industries such as chemical plants, steel mills, and munitions production. After World War I, the Japanese government encouraged some of the nation's large companies with huge financial surpluses to invest in enterprises overseas. Consequently, leading *zaibatsus* like Mitsui, Mitsubishi, and Noguchi built factories in Korea, many of which were related to war industries. The Choson Hydroelectric Power Company and the Choson Nitrogenous Fertilizer Company were other examples of large enterprises founded by Japanese companies. Industrialization accelerated during the 1930s, impelled by a new demand for war materiel, especially after the Japanese annexed Manchuria in 1931.

The economist Atul Kohli believes that Japan's extended promotion of industrial development in Korea was almost unique in colonial history and he cites the average annual rate of growth during the 1910–1940 period as nearly 10 percent. Japanese owned the heavy industries that required large amounts of capital outlay, but a class of Korean entrepreneurs also developed in the 1920s, although they were primarily involved with goods for the retail market. These entrepreneurs were preceded by a group of Koreans who had taken an interest in modern industry at the end of the 19th century, believing they could compete successfully with the Japanese. Of major interest to them was the manufacture of textiles, which formed a precedent for the new industries of the 1920s. An Kyong-su founded the Choson Textile Company in 1897. The Chongno Textile Company was established in 1900 and the Kim Tok-chang Textile Company opened in 1902 in a modernized building that had previously been an antiquated factory. Other factories dedicated to ceramics, rice-cleaning, and tobacco products were also started around this time.

Under the Japanese occupation, most Korean entrepreneurs were operating small to medium-sized "household industries," which the colonial administration tolerated. These continued to expand in response to a rising consumer demand that resulted from growing Korean incomes, the influx of Japanese colonial officials, and the inability of the Japanese to supply goods to meet all of Korea's consumer needs.

Financed by local capital, Korean entrepreneurs in the 1920s evinced a strong dedication to nationalist causes to combat the Japanese colonial presence and the influx of Japanese goods. The commitment to a nationalist agenda followed the March First Movement of 1919, when as many as two million Koreans took to the streets to protest against the Japanese occupation. Many people were killed and a considerable number were arrested during the myriad demonstrations. As a result, the colonial administration replaced the military police with a civilian police force and permitted a lenient degree of press freedom. At the time of the Second Sino-Japanese War and World War II, the leniency was reversed and pressure on the Koreans to become more like the Japanese increased.

In the 1920s, however, there were opportunities to participate in nationalist causes, which many Korean entrepreneurs did. The Paeksan Trading Company, which dealt with a range of products, contributed considerable funds to the Korean independence cause, while also engaging actively in Korean education and the Korean cooperative movement. Kim Song-su's Kyongsong Textile Company, established in 1919, manufactured a durable, heavy cloth that appealed particularly to the rural population. Kim Song-su established a middle school for Korean youth and was a founder of the *Tong-ah Ilbo* newspaper, which was a vehicle for the expression of Korean public opinion. Other examples of Korean capital investment are the knitwear and rubber goods factories of Pyongyang, which began to blossom after 1920. The factories produced mainly socks and stockings in a Western style. Some of the factory owners such as Yi Chin-sun of Kongsin Hosiery and Son Chang-yun of Samsong Hosiery began as struggling small merchants, accumulating capital to build their own factories by hard work and frugality. A product that appealed to local markets was the rubber shoe that was styled after traditional Korean footwear. Its designer was Yi Pyong-du, who became the plant supervisor of the Chongchang Rubber Goods Company. Another firm that produced rubber goods was the Mokpo Rubber Company. Other industries in which Korean entrepreneurs were involved included metals, dyeing, papermaking, ceramics, sake, and soy sauce.

In Kyongsong (the Japanese name for Korea's capital city that became Seoul after 1945), the Hwasin Department Store acquired a privileged place among Koreans because it was the only one in the city during the 1920s and 1930s that was owned by a Korean, Pak Hung-sik. With its appealing display of commercial products, the Hwasin Department Store must have played a similar role in Seoul as the department stores on Nanjing Road played in Shanghai during the same period, both signifying the aim to adopt modern methods of merchandising that originated in the West.

As a form of soft resistance to the influx of Japanese goods, a Korean consumer cooperative movement started in the 1920s in association with the Buy Korean Products Campaign of that period. The campaign's leader was Lee Chan-gap (1904–1974), who was also involved in community development in Hongsong in the south, where he established a school, a consumer co-op, and a credit union.

Hangul and publishing

The Hangul script in which the Korean language is written was created in the 15th century (see Chapter 7). As a result of Korean nationalism and a push by Western missionaries, it was first adopted in Korea for official documents in 1894 and introduced in elementary school texts the following year. Nonetheless the literary elites maintained their long tradition of writing with Chinese or Hanja characters, while a majority of Koreans in the late 19th century were illiterate. Japanese became Korea's official language in 1910 when the occupation began, but Hangul continued to be taught in schools that Koreans established, though it was written in a mixed script of Hanja and Hangul characters. The Japanese tolerated Hangul until 1938, when the Korean language was banned from the schools. Koreans were forced to speak and write Japanese and were strongly encouraged to adopt Japanese names as an act of assimilation. Korean publications were forbidden in 1941.

Given the disparate policies that governed the use of Hangul in Korea, it is not possible to trace a simple lineage of publications such as newspapers, magazines, and books. Alan Altman writes that the Japanese published the first modern newspaper in Korea, the *Choson Shinbo* (*Choson News*) in 1881. It contained separate articles in Chinese and Japanese. In the Chinese section, the Japanese emphasized their economic and political aspirations for Korea, while the articles in Japanese were more closely tied to the daily lives of Japanese traders, although a number of items expressed stereotypes of Koreans and generalizations about them.

The country's first Korean language newspaper was the thrice-monthly *Hansong sunbo* (*Hansong News*), launched in 1883 by the government's Office of Culture and Information through the efforts of the Progressive Party. It was printed in the Hanja script and featured a layout with a mix of characters in different sizes to create a visual hierarchy. The paper was printed at the government printing office with equipment brought from Japan and operated by a Japanese technician. A government publication, it covered news within Korea and from abroad, introducing new ideas that came from the West. The *Hansong sunbo* only lasted for a year and was shut down following a failed coup by one of its founders. It reemerged in 1886 as the *Hansong chubo* (*Hansong Weekly*), a paper that was printed with a mixture of Hangul and Hanja types. The content featured editorials, news, and commentary as well as advertisements. A newspaper established in 1896, *Tongnip Sinmun* (*Independent Gazette*), was printed in both Hangul and English and featured impartial news stories while at the same time serving as a strong advocate for citizens' rights. A related paper, *Hwangsong*

Sinmun (*Capitol Gazette*), appeared in 1898. Published with a mix of Hanja and Hangul types, it sought to appeal to the middle and upper classes, who were proficient in Chinese. The *Gazette* was in the forefront of resistance to the Japanese and protested strongly against Japan's aggression. Another paper that appeared the same year as the *Gazette* was the *Cheguk Sinmun* (*Imperial Gazette*), which appealed to the middle and lower classes, though with a less political agenda.

To combat the Japanese censorship that occurred even though Japan had not yet officially colonized Korea, an English journalist, Ernest T. Bethell, joined with a Korean colleague to publish the bilingual *Korea Daily News* in 1905. Originally published with mixed Hanja and Hangul characters, it later appeared exclusively in Hangul to reach a broader audience, while an English language edition for foreign readers was published as well. Several other papers that followed the *Korea Daily News* also helped to raise the political awareness of the Korean population.

After Korea's annexation in 1910, the *Korea Daily News* was one of the few surviving newspapers, though it was converted into a mouthpiece for the Japanese Governor-General under the abridged name *Daily News*. Thus for a period, the Korean people did not have a press that spoke to their concerns and issues. After the March First Movement, several papers were launched to express the voice of the Korean populace. These included *Choson Ilbo* (*Choson Daily*) and *Tong-ah Ilbo* (*Tong-ah Daily*), which was funded by the Korean owner of the Kyongsong Textile Company, Kim Song-su. A number of magazines were also published in the period following the March First Movement. *Sin yoja* (*New Woman*) *and Sin yosong* (*New Woman*) were both women's magazines, the first adopting a feminist position and the second also addressing womens' issues but from a wider perspective. Literary magazines were numerous and became the vehicles for the emergence of a modern Korean literature. A starting point was *Changjo* (*Creation*), which was founded in 1919. It was followed by a spate of others—*Pyeho* (*The Ruins*)

in 1920, *Changmichon* (*Rose Village*) in 1921, *Paekcho* (*White Tide*) in 1922, and *Kumsong* (*Gold Star*) the following year. *Paekcho* was known for literature in the romantic tradition and sometimes featured drawings that derived from the themes and styles of late 19th-century European romantic illustrators.

Modern book publishing was strongly influenced by Christian missionaries. In 1885, a missionary Bible with both Korean and English type was published and three years later a French priest transferred a Bible printing office from Japan to Korea, introducing some new printing technology by working with three kinds of Hangul letters. The first complete Korean edition of the Bible was printed in 1910. With the exception of the Bible, the design of Korean books was originally highly derivative of Chinese volumes. Sometimes Chinese and Korean books were so similar in format, language, and writing style that it was difficult to tell them apart. A number of modern Korean novels appeared in the first decades after the March First Movement, but by 1940 the Japanese had ordered the literary magazines to cease publication and forbade the publication of books in the Korean language.

Bibliography
Bibliographic essay

An excellent introduction to Japanese history during the 1900–1939 period is Peter Duus, ed., *The Cambridge History of Japan, Volume 6. The Twentieth Century,* while a more focused volume is Louise Young, *Japan's Total Empire: Manchuria and the Culture of Wartime Imperialism.* An excellent concise introduction to the period is Mikiso Hane, *Japan: A Short History.* Most of the research on Japanese industrial design has concentrated on the post-war period and little has been written on the period from 1900 to World War II. Principal sources are Kazuko Sato's, essay "Japan: From Anonymous Craftsmanship to the Western Model," in *History of Industrial Design, Vol. 3. 1919–1990: The Domain of Design* and Hiroshi Kashiwagi, "On Rationalization and the National Lifestyle: Japanese

Design in the 1920s and 1930s," in Elise Tipton and John Clark, eds., *Being Modern in Japan: Culture and Society from the 1910s to the 1930s*. Limited material on this period of Japanese industrial design can also be found in Penny Sparke's *Modern Japanese Design,* while Sarah Teasley has looked at one designer of furniture in her article "Furnishing the Modern Metropolitan: Moriya Nobuo's Designs for Domestic Interiors 1922–1927," *Design Issues* 19, no. 4 (Autumn 2003). Iwao Yamawaki provided a brief account of the time he spent at the Dessau Bauhaus in "Reminiscences of Dessau," *Design Issues* 2, no. 2 (Fall 1985). Haruhiko Fujita adds further material on Japanese furniture design in his unpublished paper "Meaning of Dual Life: Japanese Furniture and Interior Design in the Ages of Westernization and Internationalization," which was presented at the 3rd International Conference on Design History and Design Studies, Istanbul, July 2002.

By contrast with the limited material on Japanese industrial design, there is a considerable body of literature on Japanese industrialization. Books on this topic include Johannes Hirschmeier and Tsunehiko Yui, *The Development of Japanese Business, 1600–1973*; Christopher Howe, *The Origins of Japanese Trade Supremacy: Development and Technology in Asia from 1540 to the Pacific War*; Michio Morishima, *Why Has Japan 'succeeded'? Western Technology and the Japanese Ethos*; Tessa Morris-Suzuki, *The Technological Transformation of Japan: From the Seventeenth to the Twenty-first Century*; Harold G. Moulton, with the collaboration of Junichi Ko, *Japan: An Economic and Financial Appraisal*; Hiroyuki Odagiri and Akira Goto, *Technology and Industrial Development in Japan: Building Capabilities by Learning, Innovation, and Public Policy*; and E. B. Schumpeter, ed., *The Industrialization of Japan and Manchukuo, 1930–1940. Japanese Economic History 1930–1960*. Books and articles that focus on the design of automobiles or railroad rolling stock are Michael Cusumano, *The Japanese Automobile Industry*; Phyllis A. Genther, *A History of Japan's Government–Business Relationship: The Passenger Car Industry*;

Marco Ruiz, *Japanese Car*; Hirofumi Yamamoto, ed., *Technological Innovation and the Development of Transportation in Japan*; O. S. Nock, *Railways of Asia and the Far East;* and R. E. G. Davies, *Airlines of Asia since 1920*. A number of books and articles discuss design within Japanese culture and embed its discussions in issues of modernism. General books on the subject include Ian Buruma, *Inventing Japan 1853–1964*; Reed Darmon, *Made in Japan*; Amar Lahiri, *Japanese Modernism*; Jackie Menzies, ed., *Modern Boy, Modern Girl: Modernity in Japanese Art, 1910–1935*, the catalog of an exhibition at the Art Gallery of New South Wales; Jordan Sand, *House and Home in Modern Japan: Architecture, Domestic Space, and Bourgeois Culture, 1880–1980* and his chapter "The Cultured Life as Contested Space: Dwelling and Discourse in the 1920s," in Elise Tipton and John Clark, eds., *Being Modern in Japan: Culture and Society from the 1910s to the 1930s*; Miriam Silverberg, *Erotic Grotesque Nonsense: The Mass Culture of Japanese Modern Times*; *Taishō Chic: Japanese Modernity, Nostalgia, and Deco*; Peter McNeil, "Myths of Modernism: Japanese Architecture, Interior Design and the West, c. 1920–1940," *Journal of Design History* 5, no. 4 (1992); and Julia Sapin, "Merchandising Art and Identity in Meiji Japan: Kiyoto *Nihonga* Artists' Designs for Takashimaya Department Store 1868–1912," *Journal of Design History* 17, no. 4 (2004). Related works on the subject of Japanese style include the exhibition catalog *Art Nouveau in Japan 1900–1923: The New Age of Crafts and Design* and on Art Deco the two essays by Anna Jackson, "Inspiration from the East" and "Art Deco in East Asia," both in the exhibition catalog from the Victoria & Albert exhibition, *Art Deco 1910–1939*. On the production of lacquer ware, see Jan Dees's PhD dissertation, *Facing Modern Times: The Revival of Japanese Lacquer Art, 1890–1950*.

There is a growing literature on *mingei* theory exemplified by two excellent books, Kim Brandt, *Kingdom of Beauty: Mingei and the Politics of Folk Art in Imperial Japan* and Yuko Kikuchi, *Japanese Modernisation and Mingei Theory: Cultural Nationalism and Oriental Orientalism*. Kikuchi has published several additional articles on the subject: "The Myth of Yanagi's Originality: The Formation of *Mingei* Theory in its Social and Historical Context," *Journal of Design History* 7, no. 4 (1994) and "Hybridity and the Oriental Orientalism of *Mingei* Theory," *Journal of Design History* 10, no. 4 (1997). These books and articles on *mingei* theory are complemented by Brian Moeran's article, "Bernard Leach and the Japanese Folk Craft Movement: The Formative Years, *Journal of Design History* 2, nos. 2–3 (1989).

On graphic design Richard Thornton's *The Graphic Spirit of Japan* is an essential overview. There is material on the Japanese avant-garde and graphic design in the Centre Pompidou exhibition catalog, *Japon des Avant Gardes, 1910–1970*. A related work is the monograph by Elizabeth de Sabato Swinton, *The Graphic Art of Onchi Koshiro: Innovation and Tradition*. Gennifer Weisenfeld has written a valuable book on the Japanese avant-garde group Mavo entitled *Mavo: Japanese Artists and the Avant-Garde, 1905–1931* and has published a number of articles, book chapters, and Internet essays on Japanese graphic design in the 1920s and 1930s that have been indispensible for this chapter. See her chapter, "Japanese Modernism and Consumerism: Forging the New Artistic Field of 'shôgyô Bijutsu' (Commercial Art)," in Elise Tipton, and John Clark, eds., *Being Modern in Japan: Culture and Society from the 1910s to the 1930s* and her articles "Touring 'Japan as Museum': NIPPON and Other Japanese Imperialist Travelogues," *Positions: East Asia Cultures Critique* 8, no. 3 (Winter 2000); "'From Baby's First Bath': Kao Soap and Modern Japanese Commercial Design," *The Art Bulletin* 86, no. 3 (September 2004); "Publicity and Propaganda in 1930s Japan: Modernism as Method," *Design Issues* 25, no. 4 (Fall, 2009); and the website "Selling Shiseido: Cosmetics Advertising & Design in Early 20th-Century Japan," which is part of the MIT Visualizing Cultures project. James Fraser, Steven Heller, and Seymour Chwast, *Japanese Modern: Graphic Design Between the Wars* is most

valuable as a compendium of visual material. The brief texts are mainly drawn from other sources but there is some helpful material not available elsewhere. Books on Japanese posters and packaging include *Posters Japan, 1800s–1980s* and *Packaging in Japan, 1858–1956*. John Clark has written two useful essays on printing, "Changes in Popular Reprographic Representation" and "Appendix: Chronology. Japanese Printing, Publishing and Prints 1860s–1930s," both published in the book he co-edited with Elise Tipton, *Being Modern in Japan: Culture and Society from the 1910s to the 1930s*. Books on the history of Japanese art and photography have also provided material relevant to this chapter's section on graphic design. These include John Clark, *Modern Asian Art* and his edited volume *Modernity in Asian Art*; Ann Tucker, *The History of Japanese Photography*; *A History of Japanese Photography* that the Japan Photographers' Association produced; and Penelope Mason's *History of Japanese Art*.

The literature in Western languages on design, manufacturing, or publishing in Japan's colonies, Taiwan and Korea, is limited. Yuko Kikuchi's discussion of *mingei* theory in Taiwan in her book *Japanese Modernisation and Mingei Theory: Cultural Nationalism and Oriental Orientalism* was especially helpful for an account of Taiwanese crafts. See also Shui-long Yen, *Shui-long Yen: The Public Spirit: Beauty in the Making*. There is little written in Western languages about design or crafts in Korea so I relied instead on literature related to entrepreneurship and manufacturing. Ki-Baik Ye's *A New History of Korea* was an excellent source for such material as it was for information about early newspaper and magazine publishing. On Korean industrialization during the Japanese period, I relied a lot on Atul Kohli's article "Where do High Growth Political Economies Come From? The Japanese Lineage of Korea's 'Developmental State,'" *World Development* 22, no. 9 (1994).

Books

Japan

Art Directors' Club of Tokyo. *Packaging in Japan, 1858–1956.* Tokyo: Bijutsu Shuppan-sha, 1968.

Art Nouveau in Japan 1900–1923: The New Age of Crafts and Design. Tokyo: The National Museum of Modern Art, 2005.

Brandt, Kim. *Kingdom of Beauty: Mingei and the Politics of Folk Art in Imperial Japan.* Durham and London: Duke University Press, 2007.

Buruma, Ian. *Inventing Japan 1853–1964.* New York: The Modern Library, 2003.

Clark, John. *Modern Asian Art.* Honolulu: University of Hawaii Press, 1998.

—ed. *Modernity in Asian Art.* Broadway, NSW: Wild Peony, 1993 (University of Sydney East Asian Series no. 7).

Cusumano, Michael. *The Japanese Automobile Industry.* Cambridge, MA: Harvard University Press, 1985 (Harvard East Asian Monographs 122).

Darmon, Reed. *Made in Japan.* San Francisco: Chronicle Books, 2006.

Davies, R. E. G. *Airlines of Asia since 1920.* London: Putnam Aeronautical Books, 1997.

Fraser, James, Steven Heller, and Seymour Chwast. *Japanese Modern: Graphic Design Between the Wars.* San Francisco: Chronicle Books, 1996.

Genther, Phyllis A. *A History of Japan's Government–Business Relationship: The Passenger Car Industry.* Ann Arbor: Center for Japanese Studies, University of Michigan, 1990.

Hall, John W., Marius B. Jansen, Madoka Kanai, and Denis Twitchett, general eds. *The Cambridge History of Japan, Vol. 6. The Twentieth Century*, Peter Duus, ed. Cambridge and New York: Cambridge University Press, 1988.

Hane, Mikiso. *Japan: A Short History.* Oxford: One World Publications, 2000.

Hirschmeier, Johannes and Tsunehiko Yui. *The Development of Japanese Business, 1600–1973.* Cambridge, MA: Harvard University Press, 1975.

Howe, Christopher. *The Origins of Japanese Trade Supremacy: Development and Technology in Asia from 1540 to the Pacific War.* Chicago: University of Chicago Press, 1996.

Japan Photographers' Association. *A History of Japanese Photography.* Introduction by John W. Dower. New York: Pantheon Books, 1980.

Japon des Avant Gardes, 1910–1970. Paris: Editions du Centre Pompidou, 1986.

Keene, Donald. *Dawn to the West: Japanese Literature of the Modern Era: Poetry, Drama, Criticism.* New York: Holt, Rinehart and Winston, 1984.

Kikuchi, Yuko. *Japanese Modernisation and Mingei Theory: Cultural Nationalism and Oriental Orientalism.* London and New York: Routledge Curzon, 2004.

Lahiri, Amar. *Japanese Modernism.* Tokyo: The Hokuseido Press, 1939.

Mason, Penelope. *History of Japanese Art.* New York: Prentice-Hall and Harry N. Abrams, 1993.

Menzies, Jackie, ed. *Modern Boy, Modern Girl: Modernity in Japanese Art, 1910–1935.* Sydney: Art Gallery of New South Wales, 1998.

Morishima, Michio. *Why Has Japan 'Succeeded'? Western Technology and the Japanese Ethos.* Cambridge and New York: Cambridge University Press, 1982.

Morris-Suzuki, Tessa. *The Technological Transformation of Japan: From the Seventeenth to the Twenty-first Century.* Cambridge: Cambridge University Press, 1994.

Moulton, Harold G. with the collaboration of Junichi Ko. *Japan: An Economic and Financial Appraisal.* Washington, DC: The Brookings Institution, 1931.

Nock, O. S. *Railways of Asia and the Far East.* London: Adam and Charles Black, 1978.

Odagiri, Hiroyuki and Akira Goto. *Technology and Industrial Development in Japan: Building Capabilities by Learning, Innovation, and Public Policy.* With a Foreword by Richard R. Nelson. Oxford: Clarendon Press, 1996.

Posters Japan, 1800s–1980s. Nagoya: Bank of Nagoya, 1989.

Ruiz, Marco. *Japanese Car*. New York: Portland House, 1986.

Sand, Jordan. *House and Home in Modern Japan: Architecture, Domestic Space, and Bourgeois Culture, 1880–1980*. Cambridge, MA, and London: Harvard University Asia Center, 2003.

Schumpeter, E. B., ed. *The Industrialization of Japan and Manchukuo, 1930–1940. Japanese Economic History 1930–1960*. Selected and with a new introduction by Janet Hunter. London and New York: Routledge, 2000 (c. 1940).

Silverberg, Miriam. *Erotic Grotesque Nonsense: The Mass Culture of Japanese Modern Times*. Berkeley, Los Angeles, and London: University of California Press, 2006.

Sparke, Penny. *Modern Japanese Design*. New York: E.P. Dutton, 1987.

Swinton, Elizabeth de Sabato. *The Graphic Art of Onchi Koshiro: Innovation and Tradition*. New York and London: Garland, 1986.

Taishō Chic: Japanese Modernity, Nostalgia, and Deco. Essays by Kendall H. Brown and Sharon A. Minichiello. Honolulu: Honolulu Academy of Arts, 2001.

Taut, Bruno. *Houses and People of Japan*, 2nd ed. Tokyo: Sanseido, 1958 (c. 1937).

Thornton, Richard S. *The Graphic Spirit of Japan*. New York: Van Nostrand Reinhold, 1991.

Tipton, Elise and John Clark, eds. *Being Modern in Japan: Culture and Society from the 1910s to the 1930s*. Honolulu: University of Hawaii Press, 2000.

Tucker, Anne. *The History of Japanese Photography*. New Haven and London: Yale University Press, 2003.

Weisenfeld, Gennifer. *Mavo: Japanese Artists and the Avant-Garde, 1905–1931*. Berkeley, Los Angeles, and London: University of California Press, 2002.

Yamamoto, Hirofumi, ed. *Technological Innovation and the Development of Transportation in Japan*. Tokyo: United Nations University Press, 1993.

Young, Louise. *Japan's Total Empire: Manchuria and the Culture of Wartime Imperialism*. Berkeley, Los Angeles, and London: University of California Press, 1998

Taiwan

Yao, Tsun-Hsiung. *A Graphic Understanding of Taiwan: The Packaging Design of Popular Taiwanese Commodities during the Japanese Colonial Period*. Taichung: Moring Start Publisher, 2013.

Yen, Shui-long. *Shui-long Yen: The Public Spirit: Beauty in the Making*. Taipei: Taipei Fine Arts Museum, 2011.

Korea

Ye, Ki-Baik, *A New History of Korea*. Translated by Edward W. Wagner with Edward J. Schultz. Cambridge, MA: Harvard University Press, 1984.

Chapters in books

Jackson, Anna, "Art Deco in East Asia," in Charlotte Benton, Tim Benton, and Ghislaine Wood, eds. *Art Deco 1910–1939*. Boston, New York, and London: Bulfinch Press, 2003.

—"Inspiration from the East," in Charlotte Benton, Tim Benton, and Ghislaine Wood, eds. *Art Deco 1910—1939*. Boston, New York, and London: Bulfinch Press, 2003.

Kashiwagi, Hiroshi, "On Rationalization and the National Lifestyle: Japanese Design in the 1920s and 1930s," in Elise Tipton and John Clark, eds. *Being Modern in Japan: Culture and Society from the 1910s to the 1930s*. Honolulu: University of Hawaii Press, 2000.

Kikuchi, Yuko, "Shui-Long Yen and Vernacularism in the Development of Modern Taiwanese Crafts," in *Shui-Long Yen: The Public Spirit: Beauty in the Making*. Taipei: Taipei Fine Arts Museum, 2012.

Sand, Jordan, "The Cultured Life as Contested Space: Dwelling and Discourse in the 1920s," in Elise Tipton and John Clark, eds. *Being Modern in Japan: Culture and Society from the 1910s to the 1930s*. Honolulu: University of Hawaii Press, 2000.

Sato, Kazuko, "Japan: From Anonymous Craftsmanship to the Western Model," in *History of Industrial Design, Vol. 3. 1919–1990: The Domain of Design*. Milan: Electa, 1991.

Articles and conference papers

Altman, Albert A., "Korea's First Newspaper: The Japanese Chōsen shinpō," *The Journal of Asian Studies* 43, no. 4 (August 1984).

Čapková, Helena, "Transnational Networkers – Iwao and Michiko Yamawaki and the Formation of Japanese Modernist Design," *Journal of Design History* 27, no. 4 (2014).

Fujita, Haruhiko, "Meaning of Dual Life: Japanese Furniture and Interior Design in the Ages of Westernization and Internationalization," paper presented at the 3rd International Conference on Design History and Design Studies, Istanbul, July 2002.

Kikuchi, Yuko, "The Myth of Yanagi's Originality: The Formation of *Mingei* Theory in its Social and Historical Context," *Journal of Design History* 7, no. 4 (1994).

—"Hybridity and the Oriental Orientalism of *Mingei* Theory," *Journal of Design History* 10, no. 4 (1997).

Kohli, Atul, "Where do High Growth Political Economies Come From? The Japanese Lineage of Korea's 'Developmental State,'" *World Development* 22, no. 9 (1994).

Masuda, Kingo, "A Historical Overview of Art Education in Japan," *The Journal of Aesthetic Education* 37, no. 4 (Winter 2003).

McNeil, Peter, "Myths of Modernism: Japanese Architecture, Interior Design and the West, c. 1920–1940," *Journal of Design History* 5, no. 4 (1992).

Moeran, Brian, "Bernard Leach and the Japanese Folk Craft Movement: The Formative Years," *Journal of Design History* 2, nos. 2–3 (1989).

Sapin, Julia, "Merchandising Art and Identity in

Meiji Japan: Kyoto *Nihonga* Artists' Designs for Takashimaya Department Store 1868–1912," *Journal of Design History* 17, no. 4 (2004).

Teasley, Sarah, "Furnishing the Modern Metropolitan: Moriya Nobuo's Designs for Domestic Interiors 1922–1927," *Design Issues* 19, no. 4 (Autumn 2003).

Weisenfeld, Gennifer, "Touring 'Japan as Museum': NIPPON and Other Japanese Imperialist Travelogues," *Positions: East Asia Cultures Critique* 8, no. 3 (Winter 2000).

—"'From Baby's First Bath': Kao Soap and Modern Japanese Commercial Design," *The Art Bulletin* 86, no. 3 (September 2004).

—"Publicity and Propaganda in 1930s Japan: Modernism as Method," *Design Issues* 25, no. 4 (Fall 2009).

Yamawaki, Iwao, "Reminiscences of Dessau." Introduction and translation by Mary Chow. *Design Issues* 2, no. 2 (Fall 1985).

Yao, Tsun-Hsiung, Chu-Yu Sun, and Pin-Chang Lin, "The Enlightenment of Taiwan Modern Design during the Japanese Colonial Period (1895–1945)," *Design Issues* 29, no. 3 (Summer 2013).

Dissertations and theses

Dees, Jan., *Facing Modern Times: The Revival of Japanese Lacquer Art, 1890–1950*, PhD dissertation, University of Leiden, 2007. http://openaccess.leidenuniv.nl/bitstream/1887/11458/6/Jan%2BDees%2BBBW%2Bcompleet-1.pdf - (accessed October 2, 2014).

Internet

Allen, Joseph R., "Exhibiting the Colony, Suggesting the Nation: The Taiwan Exhibition, 1935, http://www.cwru.edu/affil/sce/Texts_2005/Allen%20MLA%202005%20w%20illustrations.pdf (accessed July 12, 2013).

Greimer, Andrea, "Visual Propaganda in Wartime East Asia – The Case of Natori Yonosuke," *The Asia-Pacific Journal; Japan Focus*, http://www.

japanfocus.org/-Andrea-Germer/3530   (accessed October 2, 2014).

Mori, Hitoshi, "Japanese and American Design Through Russel Wright," www.livingwithgooddesign.org/essay_3/html (accessed October 2, 2014).

"Taiwan's Most Prominent Exhibition," Digital Taiwan – Culture & Nature, http://culture.teldap.tw/culture (accessed April 6, 2012).

Weisenfeld, Gennifer, "Selling Shiseido: Cosmetics Advertising & Design in Early 20th-Century Japan," MIT Visualizing Cultures, http://ocw.mit.edu/ans7870/21f/21f.027/shiseido_01/sh_essay03.html (accessed October 2, 2014).

Chapter 37: World War II 1939–1945

Introduction

World War II served as a powerful stimulus for design, especially the design of weaponry, although many of the new discoveries in science and engineering that were prompted by the war also had valuable applications for peacetime products when the war ended. From the moment German armored tank divisions rolled into Poland in 1939, it was clear that technology would be a driving force in determining how the war was fought. Forbidden to rearm after defeat in World War I, Germany nonetheless began to secretly develop tanks, planes, and other weapons in the 1920s and 1930s

Meanwhile, the French and British armies as well as the United States military were slow to introduce new weapons. By 1939, for example, the British Army lacked armored vehicles, while the Germans had amassed a tank corps that was unequaled anywhere in the world. The German panzer divisions, as the tank divisions were known, worked together with mechanized infantry, foot soldiers, and dive-bombers to assault the Allies on multiple fronts. The mechanization of warfare was, in fact, central to the German strategy of "blitzkrieg" or lightning war, which was evident in the early years of World War II. In 1939, the German Luftwaffe or Air Force was the strongest airborne fighting unit anywhere.

Once Germany and Great Britain declared war on each other and Germany declared war on the United States, Great Britain and the United States began to mobilize rapidly. Though the Soviet Union signed a treaty of non-aggression with Germany in August 1939, its military continued to produce new weapons enabling the country to successfully engage the Germans after Hitler attacked the Soviet Union in June 1941. Japan had begun an aggressive military build-up in the 1920s, which prepared the country to occupy Manchuria in 1931 and then attack Shanghai in 1937, thus initiating an invasion that soon became part of a wider war.

Although the United States had begun its military mobilization before the Japanese bombed Pearl Harbor in December 1941, that event and the subsequent American declaration of war on Japan the day after the attack spurred the rapid deployment of American resources that led to the near miraculous volume of war materiel that the United States produced between 1942 and 1945. Numerous new inventions accompanied the production of tanks, planes, and ships, due to the close collaboration between the American scientific community and the military. It was during this period, in fact, when many civilian business executives became involved in weapons manufacturing, that the military-industrial complex about which President Dwight Eisenhower warned in a speech of 1961 began.

Given the technical demands that accompanied the design of much military equipment, the idea of design expanded during World War II. Physicists, chemists, mathematicians and other scientists, along with engineers from all engineering disciplines, worked on projects for new types of aircraft, tanks, amphibious vehicles, and rockets. Collaboration was essential to address the complex challenges of new weapons. Not all countries were able to successfully organize the relationship between science, engineering, design, and production, but those that did created weapons whose physical and technical complexity far exceeded anything that had been designed previously. Weaponry developed rapidly as teams of experts made continual refinements to the planes, ships, and other weapons they designed. In some cases, improved versions were manufactured annually or even more rapidly. New mass-production methods were also introduced to vastly increase the volume of weapons that factories turned out.

Though all countries engaged in the war had centralized organizations that were responsible for war materiel, they didn't function with equal efficiency. Rivalries between military services or between such services and civilian organizations were impediments, as were disagreements about what weapons to produce. Besides the ordinary weaponry that every country manufactured, there were also the super weapons that were introduced late in the war—the V1 and V2 rockets in Germany, and the atomic bomb in the United States. The use of these weapons permanently altered the terms of military engagement.

New propaganda techniques were also pioneered in World War II. Radio played a central role, providing not only news of how the war was progressing but inspirational speeches from national leaders. Radio broadcasts from Britain also reached the occupied countries of Europe, where listeners picked them up on clandestine receivers. Posters continued to play an important role as a means to motivate or encourage more production, the purchase of war bonds, or hatred of the enemy. They were widely employed on the home fronts, while leaflets, dropped from planes over enemy territory, were instrumental in swaying opinion and especially in encouraging the surrender of enemy troops.

Germany

Within several years, the weapons advantage that Germany had accrued due to its early rearmament efforts was superseded by Great Britain and the United States, following their respective mobilizations after Germany's declarations of war. In 1936, Germany had inaugurated a Four-Year Plan, ostensibly to strengthen the German economy but most likely to also develop resources for a further weapons build-up. That year Hitler established a Hauptamt für Technik (Central Office for Technics), headed by the engineer Fritz Todt (1891–1942). Two years later, Todt founded the

eponymous Organization Todt, which joined together government and private companies for large-scale infrastructure projects. In 1940, when Germany was officially at war, Todt became Reich Minister for Armaments and Munitions. Following an inspection tour of the Eastern Front after Germany had invaded the Soviet Union, Todt recommended to Hitler that he end the war in the East because German equipment and supplies were inadequate. Hitler ignored his recommendation and the German Army continued to fight until it was forced to retreat after the Battle of Stalingrad. In early 1942, Todt died in a plane crash and was replaced as Minister for Armaments and Munitions by the architect Albert Speer.

Speer had great difficulty coordinating his ministry's plans for arms production, which included army weapons, along with production for the navy and air force. In an attempt to overcome organizational rivalries, he established the Central Planning Board, which gave the three services responsibility for the design, planning, and contracting of all their own weapons and equipment, a policy that led to heavy competition for raw materials allocations. Speer decentralized his own responsibilities by creating a system of committees and "rings," whereby he put a number of other managers, especially industrialists, in charge of specific areas of production. He was interested in reducing the number of product types, using the rationale that fewer weapons would require fewer parts. The idea was generally opposed by the various industrialists who collaborated with him on the grounds that retooling for the production of new types would not alleviate the need to continue producing parts for old ones. As it turned out, one example of retooling, the Opel three-ton truck, turned out to be a costly mistake.

The Germans did adopt the "Einheit" (standard) for what they called "E" vehicles. There were several classes of such vehicles, each with manufacturers who built them to set specifications. Unfortunately, many of these vehicles had mechanical problems and could not be mass-produced in the required numbers. Therefore they were supplemented with civilian models. The military also adopted additional vehicles in the countries it occupied, resulting in 1,500 types of unarmored vehicles at the time the Russian campaign began.

Other difficulties Germany faced in developing a coherent armaments program included Hitler's sometimes erratic decisions about new weapons and his occasional interference with the decisions of others. High officials in the Nazi Party were also reluctant to make the best use of Germany's scientists and engineers. These officials lacked scientific backgrounds themselves and consequently made decisions based more on intuition and the protection of fiefdoms than on broader strategic visions that required extensive scientific knowledge and cooperation between organizations. Germany also lost many talented Jewish scientists who emigrated to Great Britain, the United States, and elsewhere to escape Nazi persecution.

For the reasons cited above and others, Germany soon squandered the advantage in weapons accumulation it had achieved before the war began. By 1941,

for example, the Germans had not developed a tank that was a match for the Soviet's T-34. To compete with the Soviets, the Germans started manufacturing the first version of the Panther in 1943. Rushed into production without adequate trials, many of the tanks had mechanical failures, although the problems were remedied and they were used successfully on all the fronts. In fact, their robust firepower forced the Soviets to strengthen that of the T-34. However, relatively few Panthers were produced, due to the Allied bombing of German factories.

As Robert M. Citino notes, Germany, more than other nations, embraced the idea of "miracle tanks." Two versions of the Tiger heavy tank were designed, one by the Henschel aircraft company and another by the Porsche design office. Although the Tiger had a powerful gun and strong armor, its design was too complicated and it was therefore difficult to produce. It was followed by a heavier model, designed again by Henschel and Porsche. Known to the Germans as the King Tiger, it did not see action on either the

Fig. 37.01: King Tiger tank, c. 1944. © dpa picture alliance/Alamy.

Eastern or Western front until mid-1944 (Fig. 37.01). It was nonetheless a powerful weapon. Its own armor was almost impenetrable and its main gun, more than 20 feet long, could pierce the armor of other vehicles from a considerable distance. Its drawbacks, however, included a smaller engine than it required and consequently its bulk slowed it down on the battlefield. This resulted in frequent breakdowns. Many King Tigers were in fact abandoned or destroyed by their crews when they ran out of fuel.

The largest manufacturers of military aircraft were the Junkers Flugzeug und Motorenwerke (Junkers Aircraft and Motor Works), Dorner Flugzeugwerke (Dorner Aircraft Works), the Heinkel Flugzeugwerke (Heinkel Aircraft Works), Henschel & Sohn (Henschel & Son), and Messerschmitt AG, the latter named after the company's chief aircraft designer, Willy Messerschmitt (1898–1978). By 1943, airplane production had fallen to 20 percent of that of Germany's enemies. At that time, some historians claim, Germany had declined from an armaments powerhouse to a nation that lacked the technical means to win the war.

One of the Luftwaffe's most successful aircraft was Junkers Ju 88. A versatile plane, it was known for its prowess as a dive-bomber but was also adaptable for other functions—night fighting, dropping torpedoes, and reconnaissance. Though heavier than other bombers in the German fleet, it was also faster. Fewer Ju 88 planes were lost due to their ability to dive at high speed to evade contact with British fighters.

Bombing successes of the Luftwaffe were enhanced by the radar devices invented by Johannes Plendl (1900–1992), an engineer who worked originally for Telefunken. His initial work was on radio communication that civilian aircraft and the Hindenburg zeppelin used, but Göring discovered him and put him in charge of the Luftwaffe's long-range bombing and high-frequency research. A key radar device in the early stage of the war was the Knickbein or "crooked leg" aerial, which responded to radio waves from transmitters that enabled more accurate night bombing.

Another radar device the Luftwaffe employed, though not designed by Plendl, was the Y- Gerät (Y- device), which used a single narrow beam from the ground, enabling the plane to be guided to its target by ground controllers. After a few raids, the Luftwaffe abandoned the system, recognizing that the British capacity to intercept its signals was too advanced and would probably remain so should the Luftwaffe attempt to develop other radio navigation systems. However, Luftwaffe planes were among the first to incorporate night navigation devices, now standard in all commercial airliners.

One aircraft project that exemplified the poor planning on more than one occasion behind German weapons development was the Messerschmitt Me-262, considered to be the world's first jet-powered fighter aircraft. As Edward Filbert describes its development, the Air Ministry had requested the Messerschmitt firm to design such an aircraft in 1938, but a successful model was not produced until 1944. Designs for the airframe had been completed by mid-1940, but engine problems caused a delay. Weak support and indecisiveness from the Air Ministry resulted in considerable postponement of a plane that might have played a much stronger role in Germany's air defense.

There were several other missed opportunities. One was the navy's failure to develop the Schnorchel, as the Germans called the piping system they found on three captured Dutch submarines. It enabled a submarine with a periscope to operate its diesels underwater, something the navy did not see as a priority until the Allies sank numerous U-boats. Operational U-boats did not start to use the Schnorchel until early 1944 and even then it was only installed on a limited number of boats.

Another mistake was the failure to commit seriously to computer technology when, in fact, several German scientists were pioneers in the field. Principal among them was Konrad Zuse (1910–1995), who is generally credited with the first computing machine that could be automatically programmed to do sequences of calculations. This was in 1941, some two years before anyone else. Zuse's first machine was known as the Z1. A collaborator on this project as well as on a successor machine was the electrical engineer Helmut Schreyer (1912–1984), who made an important contribution by suggesting the use of discarded 35mm movie film for programming instead of the harder to obtain paper.

Zuse approached the German Research Center for Aviation with the proposal to build a larger computer and did receive some support, resulting in a machine known as the Z3. Due to its limited memory, however, the Z3 was not successful at performing routine functions. Zuse began work on a new computer, the Z4, whose construction was impeded by Allied bombing raids in 1944. He also built another relay machine, the S1, which replaced 35 women calculators at Henschel & Son, where a flying bomb was developed.

Civilian manufacturing, generally, remained under the Ministry of Economics, which had its own examples of poor planning. A different example of inefficient production, although one related to the concept of the weapon itself rather than to design or development difficulties, was the Krupp factory's "Fat Gustav," the biggest gun ever made. It was designed to pierce five-feet-thick armor plating and 11-feet-thick concrete from a distance of 25 miles.

Work on it began in 1935 under the leadership of Dr. Erich Mueller (1892–1963), Krupp's chief gun designer. The gun barrel was 130 feet long and the gun was moved along a railway track. It did not arrive in the Soviet Union in time for the Siege of Leningrad for which it was intended, but it was used to considerable effect at the Battle of Sebastapol in June 1942. However, it was far too cumbersome to be used again and was returned to Germany where it lay in Krupp's Essen factory until Allied soldiers dismantled and destroyed it in 1945. Aside from "Fat Gustav," however, Krupp was a principal manufacturer of guns, tanks, and U-boats for the Nazis. By the end of 1943, the firm employed over 115,000 people in shipyards, gun shops, tool factories, and armor-plating works. Krupp went out of its way to use slave labor, and by late 1944 had more than 70,000 such workers.

Several factories that contributed to the German war effort were subsidiaries of American firms. Opel was a General Motors subsidiary that produced among other things components for the Ju 88 aircraft. The Opel factory manufactured fuselage panels, cabin canopies, hydraulic devices, and landing gear for the Junkers plane. It also produced torpedo detonators, aircraft motor gears, and army munitions. General Motors executives remained directly involved in the company until late 1940 and even though it was then turned over to Germans, GM claimed the wartime profits after the German surrender and then began to manufacture Opel automobiles again in 1948.

IBM was more directly involved with the Nazi war effort through its subsidiary, Dehomag, an acronym for Deutsche Hollerith-Maschinen Gesellschaft (German Hollerith Machine Society). Dehomag was created in 1910 to sell the tabulating machines that Herman Hollerith designed. In 1923, an American firm, the Computing Tabulating Recording Corporation, which was renamed IBM in 1924, acquired majority ownership of Dehomag. IBM then supported Dehomag's leasing of tabulating equipment to the Nazi Party, which adopted it for numerous purposes including the census. Beginning in 1933, the party, using Dehomag equipment and IBM punch cards, was able to collect bloodline data on Jews and by 1935 introduced a series of harsh racial laws. Dehomag employees worked with Nazi officials to custom-design punch cards for various projects besides the census. These eventually included managing slave labor, shipping prisoners to concentration camps, and keeping track of them once there. Nearly every concentration camp had a Hollerith Department.

The Hollerith machines were also central to organizing the affairs of the occupied countries. For all applications, punch cards were routinely shipped from IBM in the United States to sources the Nazis controlled in Europe until Dehomag set up its own plant to print the cards. Though IBM had to distance itself from Dehomag at a certain point just as General Motors distanced itself from Opel, the subsidiary continued to support the needs of the German Reich and, like General Motors, IBM claimed the wartime profits after the German surrender.

In addition to Opel, other automobile manufacturers joined the war effort. Daimler-Benz produced trucks and aircraft engines as well as parts for products that the three military services commissioned. Like other German companies, Daimler-Benz made use of forced labor. Volkswagen built military vehicles using the Volkswagen chassis. The Austrian Ferdinand Porsche designed the first prototypes of the people's car in 1936 and construction began on a factory in 1938 (see Chapter 27). The plan was to start producing the cars for the public as soon as the factory was completed,

but when Hitler began his expansion eastward the demand for military equipment superseded the plan to produce a car for the popular market. Between 1941 and 1944, about 630 cars, which Hitler had renamed the KdF Wagen, were produced as wartime transport vehicles for Nazi functionaries. The military commissioned several alternative vehicles that were built on Volkswagen chassis. One was the Kübelwagen Type 82, a light military vehicle that might be loosely compared to the American Jeep. Designed by the Porsche office, it had square-rigged high-sided coachwork, which was built by Ambi-Budd in Berlin (Fig. 37.02). Proving its usefulness on varied terrains including the desert, the Kübelwagen Type 82 was much in demand by the military, although only a limited number had been produced by the war's end.

Porsche also designed a second vehicle for the military, built like the Kübelwagen on the basic Volkswagen chassis. Known as the Schwimmwagen

Fig. 37.02: Ferdinand Porsche office, Kübelwagen Type 82, c. 1940. © Ladi Kirn/Alamy.

(swimming car) Type 166, it was designed in response to a call by the SS for a vehicle that could replace the motorcycle and sidecar. The Schwimmwagen combined four-wheel drive with a retractable rear propeller to ensure its versatility on land and in water. Porsche also designed other wartime vehicles that could be built on a Volkswagen chassis including the Kommandowagen (command car), conceived to transport an officer, a driver, and an aide. The officer was seated behind the driver, while the aide sat in the front seat with a map and a foldout writing desk. Wooden slats were adopted for the floors so the cars could be used in the Russian mud. Other vehicles included the Schneeraupe (snow caterpillar), fitted for conditions on the Russian front—although this vehicle was never produced due to its cost—and another car with flanged steel wheels that could be driven on railroad tracks.

Germany's most ambitious weapons development was the design of the V1 and V2 rockets, which were developed by a team of scientists at Peenemunde, a remote island near the Baltic Sea. Goebbels called these rockets revenge weapons and placed great hopes in their ability to help defeat Britain. This did not occur and ironically the United States recruited many of the leading Nazi scientists to work on the post-war missile defense and NASA space programs.

Italy

When Italy signed the Pact of Friendship and Alliance, known as the Pact of Steel, with Germany in May 1939, the Italians stipulated that neither country would make war without the other earlier than 1943. In fact, the Italian Under-Secretary for War Production Carlo Favagrossa, a former diplomat and military officer, declared that his country could not be ready for such a war until October 1942 at the earliest. Though Italy, like Germany, had the opportunity to build up its military during the 1930s, it did not do so to anywhere near the degree that Germany did. Italy's industrial sector was relatively weak compared to other major powers in Europe. Its production of automobiles, for

example, lagged far behind Great Britain and France, thus making it difficult to gear up for a mechanized military force.

The Regio Esercito (Royal Army) was somewhat depleted when World War II began. Its tanks were of poor quality and most of its artillery dated from World War I. The principal fighter plane of the Regio Aeronautica (Italian Air Force) was the CR-42, a biplane with an open cockpit that had seen service in World War I. Though its design was advanced for its time, it was obsolete compared to the more recently designed monoplane fighters of other nations. The Regia Marina (Royal Navy) had only a few modern battleships and no aircraft carriers. To remedy this situation, the government sought to spend a high percentage of its 1939 budget on armaments, but as in Germany, Italy lacked an effective process of armaments development.

Though much of Italy's wartime materiel remained obsolete, some weapons were at least on a par with those of other combatant nations, and one or two were superior. The Autoblinda 41 armored vehicle fitted with Breda anti-aircraft cannons and machine guns was used extensively by reconnaissance patrols in North Africa. A kit that was available to convert the car for use on railroad tracks included railway wheels along with additional lighting and signal devices as well as a searchlight that could be mounted on the turret.

Design of the P40 tank, known by its Italian designation Carro Armato (armored car) P40, began in 1940, but only a few had been built by the time Italy signed an armistice with the Allies in September 1943. One cause of delay was the lack of a sufficiently powerful engine, although it is not clear why the companies that monopolized the production of Italian tanks, Fiat and Ansaldo, did not consider aircraft engines the way manufacturers of British and American tanks had done. After an encounter with Russian T-34 tanks on the Eastern Front, the design of the P40, which was roughly equivalent to the American M4 Sherman and the German Panzer IV, was changed. The armor plates were given a greater slope and a larger gun was added. A heavier version of the P40, dubbed the P43, was planned but the design never advanced beyond several wooden scale models.

Among Italy's most formidable weapons were its self-propelled guns—large artillery pieces that were mounted on tank chassis. Of these, the Semovente 75/18s were used extensively in the North African campaign and during the defense of Sicily against the Allied invasion. Successive versions were developed that had longer and more powerful barrels. The Ansaldo company manufactured the prototype for such a barrel, the Semovente 149/40, which was mounted on a tank chassis without a turret. Before production could begin, however, the Italians surrendered and only a promising prototype remained.

Leading manufacturers of military aircraft were the Società Italiana Caproni and its subsidiary, Officine Meccaniche Reggiane; Savoia-Marchetti; Macchi Aeronautica; Fiat; and the Società Italiana Ernesto Breda. One of Italy's major military aircraft designers was Mario Castoldi (1888–1968), who worked for several different companies. Although the Italian Air Force began later than others to create a monoplane fleet, it eventually adopted several designs including the Savoia-Marchetti SM 79 Sparviero (Sparrrowhawk), a successful torpedo bomber that had been originally designed as a passenger aircraft, and the SM 93, a single-engine dive-bomber for a two-person crew. However, the air force lacked a coherent strategy for the development of a range of planes, while it also had problems with organization and production. Mass-production methods were never adopted, and Italian aircraft, like many Italian products, were still skillfully crafted by hand, which meant that manufacturing was slow and production minimal. Among the mistakes made was

Fig. 37.03: Antonio Parano and Giuseppe Panzeri, Breda Ba.88 Lince, c. 1936. © CORBIS/Getty Images.

the production of three similar monoplane fighters at the same time. Due to successful experience with other forms of transport design, Italian airplane frames, whether built of wood or metal, were of high quality, but the airplane engines were not and consequently Italian aircraft designers were handicapped until the rights to a German engine were acquired in 1940. One of the more promising planes was the Breda Ba.88 Lince (Lynx) that Antonio Parano (dates unconfirmed) and Giuseppe Panzeri (dates unconfirmed) designed in 1936. It was a monoplane with a framework of steel tubes and a sleek futuristic all-metal shoulder wing (Fig. 37.03). Designed to fulfill an air force requirement for a heavy fighter-bomber, it established several world speed and distance records, but its downfall was the addition of military equipment, whose weight resulted in a loss of performance that made it inoperable for combat purposes.

Great Britain

Britain had begun preparing for a military conflict before declaring war on Germany in September 1939, following Germany's refusal to withdraw its troops from Poland. As an island nation, Britain had less to fear from a land invasion than from air strikes and naval battles. The British more than held their own against the Germans at sea and developed a sophisticated air defense system to aid the Royal Air Force in countering German air attacks. Though Britain was heavily damaged by German bombs and the V1 and V2 rockets that were launched late in the war, its advanced technologies and an air force that eventually outpaced the Germans in size and capability enabled the country to ultimately defend itself against German air power. British troops fought on the European continent and Britain engaged German land forces in North Africa, but Britain's strategic emphasis was on air power and a strong air defense system, which was supplemented by sophisticated methods of breaking enemy codes.

The management of Britain's military efforts, both preceding and during the war, was complicated.

The Admiralty, War Office, and Royal Air Force developed conventional weapons but also supported a considerable number of small covert units, many unbeknownst to the others, that did research on new weapons and systems, developed prototypes, and prepared some of the designs for production. Design in different forms was thus widespread though not necessarily coordinated within the different organizations, factories, and research units that were charged with supporting the war effort. Weapons production was enhanced by a new method that British scientists pioneered—operations research—which was extremely effective in improving combat strategies and the efficacy of new weapons.

Preparations for war had several foci. One was the design and production of conventional weaponry and advanced telecommunications; another was the creation of more experimental designs; and the third was the support of covert operations in Europe—secret agents, underground cells, and resistance movements. Much of the weaponry that derived from these foci was developed within the military services themselves: the Admiralty, which supported the Royal Navy; the War Office to which the army was attached; and the Royal Air Force. The Ministry of Supply (MOS) was formed in 1939 to coordinate the provision of equipment to all three services. The MOS managed the Royal Ordnance Factories, which produced explosives, propellants, and ammunition as well as guns and rifles. It was also responsible for the supply of tanks and other armored vehicles, although these were mostly built by private companies such as Vickers, the aircraft and shipbuilding firm.

In 1936, the government appointed a Minister for Coordination of Defense, Sir Thomas Inskip, whose function was to oversee and manage Britain's rearmament program. Neither Inskip nor his successor was able to successfully get the three services to work together and the position was wound down when Winston Churchill, who had been First Lord of the Admiralty, became Prime Minister in May 1940. At that time Churchill also assumed the position of Minister of Defense, and was especially aggressive in promoting the development of new weapons as well as increasing the production of existing ones.

During World War I, the first time Churchill served as Lord of the Admiralty, he was responsible for establishing the Royal Navy's Landships Committee, which produced the world's first tanks. Another project that interested him was the design of an armored vehicle that could dig its own trench as it advanced towards the enemy. Such a trench was to be wide and deep enough to protect the vehicle as well as other vehicles and infantry that followed it. Unable to bring the project to fruition during World War I, Churchill revived it during his second tenure in the Admiralty. This time he hoped to build an entire fleet of such vehicles despite the War Department's lack of enthusiasm. To develop the vehicle, he set up a top secret Department of Naval Land Equipment within the Ministry of Supply.

The initial design included a huge plow combined with a rotating cylinder that together would cut through the earth at two levels, creating a trench five feet deep and almost eight feet wide. The vehicle itself—a cumbersome machine almost 80 feet long and 100 tons in weight—was to advance on tank treads (Fig. 37.04). During the design process, a similar project for a trench-forming machine was being developed elsewhere in the government, but an attempt to integrate the two designs failed. A full-scale prototype of Cultivator No. 6, as the trench digger came to be called, was produced for field trials, but its potential usefulness was undermined by the German occupation of France, where it was to have been deployed. Though work on the project continued after the occupation, it was finally cancelled in 1943.

Also within the Admiralty was the Directorate of Miscellaneous Weapons Development (DMWD), known colloquially as the Wheezers and Dodgers, which was established in 1940. As with other such units, its purpose was to develop unconventional weapons. The director was the Canadian chemist Charles F. Goodeve (1904–1980), whose initial interest was in defusing mines. This led to a method for reducing the magnetic field around ships that triggered the mines. As director of the DMWD, Goodeve emphasized antisubmarine

Fig. 37.04: Winston Churchill with Cultivator No. 6, c. 1941. © IWM.

warfare, producing a range of successful products as well as some failures. The head of engineering was the aeronautical engineer Nevil Shute Norway (1899–1960), who wrote novels under the pen name Nevil Shute.

DMWD undertook a wide range of projects. Among its successes was the Hedgehog, an antisubmarine mortar that was deployed on escort warships. It consisted of a group of small spigot mortar bombs that exploded on contact after release, thus achieving a higher sinking rate against enemy submarines than depth charges did. By 1943, the Hedgehog was replaced by the more effective Squid mortar, which was also designed in the DMWD. Among the other projects were flamethrowers, gliders, and rockets as well as the Harvey Projector, a special mount for firing anti-aircraft rockets. It was made for ships that could not support conventional anti-aircraft guns. Nevil Shute Norway had a leading role in the development of an Acoustic Warning Device, which had highly sensitive microphones to be placed atop ship masts to detect approaching aircraft. Though used briefly, the device was taken out of service, as more ships were equipped with radar.

The unit's greatest failure was without a doubt the highly experimental Panjandrum, a machine consisting of two large wheels and an axel that was to be packed with explosives and propelled by rockets towards enemy fortifications (Fig. 37.05). It was to blow up upon impact, thus leaving room for tanks to penetrate the structure. The problem was stabilizing the machine, which would veer off to one side whenever the rockets were fired up. This was the case during the final demonstration for top military personnel who decided not to include it in the D-Day arsenal.

The War Office had its own covert weapons development units. The Military Intelligence Research Branch (MIR) was established in 1938 as the research section of the General Staff. It was concerned with weapons of irregular warfare and among its activities was research on sabotage devices, conducted by a

Fig. 37.05: Nevil Shute Norway and DMWD engineers, Panjandrum, c. 1943. © IWM.

military engineer, Millis Jefferis. The work of MIR overlapped with that of a related unit, Section D, which was also located within the War Office.

After Churchill became Prime Minister, he encouraged the merger of MIR and Section D into a new organization, the Special Operations Executive (SOE), a unit that was to support the conduct of guerilla warfare and provide aid to local resistance movements against the Axis powers by developing weapons and special equipment for espionage, sabotage, and reconnaissance activities. The unit was created in July 1940 by Hugh Dalton (1887–1962), Minister of Economic Warfare, who was to be promoted two years later to President of the Board of Trade, where he oversaw the Utility Furniture and Utility Clothing Schemes.

The new unit collaborated closely during the middle years of the war with the Combined Operations Headquarters in the War Office, which was set up to harass the Germans with commando raids that included both army and navy forces. Similar to Churchill's promotion of the trench digger, Geoffrey Pyke (1893–1948), who had developed ideas for several military inventions, spearheaded Project Habbakuk, a proposal to create giant aircraft carriers made of ice that was laced with wood fibers. Churchill was enthusiastic and urged the project's rapid development. One result of the research was a new material, pykrete, a mixture of water and wood pulp that melted more slowly than ice and could withstand a powerful ballistic impact. A small prototype of the aircraft carrier was constructed in Canada, but numerous technical problems impeded the ship's successful completion. Meanwhile, advances in aircraft design and deployment undercut the project's value, and development was halted in 1943. Pyke, however, continued to conceive new inventions, one a less ambitious use of pykrete ships to support an amphibious landing assault and the other a plan for moving combat personnel from ship to shore or across terrains where conventional transport was difficult through large pipes, a system that he called "Power-Driven Rivers." However, neither project was pursued.

The Special Operations Executive also had a top-secret laboratory known as Station IX, whose purpose was to develop specialized military equipment. Formed in July 1940, it was headed by John Dolphin (1905–1973), a British engineer and inventor who designed several land and sea vehicles during his tenure as director. Under the Executive's Chief of Scientific Research, Station IX's projects included military vehicles and equipment, explosives, camouflage, and devices related to biological and chemical warfare. The laboratories and workshops were located near the town of Welwyn, hence all projects began with the prefix Wel.

Together with Harry Lester (dates unconfirmed), a former racing bike engineer, Dolphin developed a small motorbike for paratroopers that could be folded up and dropped in a parachute airdrop container. Codenamed the Welbike, it was the smallest motorcycle ever designed for the British armed services. Rapid assembly on the ground was easy and almost 4,000 were built and widely used by members of various forces (Fig. 37.06). Two drawbacks were the low power and small wheels that caused difficulty on rough battlefield roads, leading to bikes being abandoned in some instances. Other projects of Dolphin's were the Welman and the Welfreighter. The Welman was a miniature submarine without a periscope, requiring the sole person inside to look through armored glass segments in a small tower. It was designed to attach explosive charges to its targets with magnetic clips, but these could not be made to work properly. The first trial, an attempted attack on the Floating Dock in Bergen, Norway, failed when the Welman became entangled in an antisubmarine net, thus ending further trials and leading the navy to concentrate on the X class and XE class midget submarines. Following the success of the former, Dolphin led a team that designed another midget vessel, the Welfreighter, that was intended to land and pick up secret agents behind enemy lines. After three prototypes, resulting in increased underwater endurance and the capacity to carry more passengers and cargo, a limited number

Fig. 37.06: Harry Lester and John Dolphin, Welbike, c. 1942. © Motoring Picture Library/Alamy.

were put into production. The Welfreighter looked like a conventional motorboat, and a dummy mast and sail could be attached to disguise it as a fishing vessel. The production timing was unfortunate as the first ones were completed just as the secret war in Europe was ending. Several were shipped to Asia but were not considered useful there, hence the Welfreighter was not put into service on either front.

At the time MIR and Section D merged into the Special Operations Executive, one section within MIR was not included. Instead, it formed the basis of a new covert weapons research and development laboratory, Ministry of Defense 1 (MD1), which was also known as Winston Churchill's Toyshop due to the Prime Minister's strong interest in it. It was headed by military engineer Millis Jefferis (1899–1963) and the inventor Stuart Macrae (dates unconfirmed), who edited the magazine *Armchair Science* before he joined MD1. During its period of operation, MD1 produced 26 different devices, among them the sticky bomb— designed by Macrae and Jefferis—the limpet land

mine, an anti-tank weapon known as PIAT, and the pencil detonator. The sticky bomb was a hand grenade that could adhere to a tank, while the PIAT was an anti-tank weapon that consisted of a steel tube, trigger mechanism, and a firing spring. Its value was in its capacity to launch bombs with a spring mechanism rather than a propellant. The limpet land mine was attached to a target by magnets, and the pencil detonator, which featured a time delay before it ignited an explosive, was used extensively by resistance groups.

Due to Britain's strategic emphasis on air defense, less attention was paid to conventional weapons for ground combat. A staple of the 1930s, the Vickers Light Tank, which was widely used for imperial policing duties in India and elsewhere in the empire, proved useless during the early campaigns of World War II, due in large part to the thinness of its armor. More successful was the Cruiser MK VIII Cromwell, which entered service in 1943, and several others such as the heavier armored Churchill tank, which was used as the basis for a number of other tanks that were modified for the

Normandy invasion in 1944. Named Hobart's Funnies after the armored warfare expert Percy Hobart, these invasion tanks were fitted with additional equipment for special purposes. The Crocodile had a flamethrower instead of a machine gun, while the AVRE (Armored Vehicle, Royal Engineers), lacking a machine gun, had a mortar intended to destroy roadblocks and bunkers. The ARK (Armored Ramp Carrier), which had extendable ramps instead of a turret, was used by other vehicles to drive over and avoid obstacles, while the Crab had a mine flail that exploded landmines in its path. The Armored Bulldozer, a conventional Caterpillar bulldozer fitted with armor, was designed to clear obstacles from invasion beaches and create accessible roads by clearing away rubble and filling in bomb craters. Finally, the Rhino Tank was retrofitted with rotating angled iron pieces from Czechoslovakia to form hedge clippers in order to clear the growth in the Normandy forests. Called hedgehogs, they were originally used as anti-tank roadblocks.

One of the most widely adopted land vehicles was the Universal Carrier, which Vickers created in 1934. These varied in design depending on their use. Complementing the different models that were fitted with machine guns, flame throwers, mortal platforms, medi-vac and gun tractors, was a version on which a light machine gun, known as a Bren Gun, was mounted. Adopted in the 1930s, the Bren Gun was a modified version of a Czech weapon (in fact its name was derived from Brno where it was originally designed), which had a curved box magazine, quick-change barrel, and a bipod mount. In 1940, production was focused on a single model of the Universal Carrier of which more than 200,000 were produced. It saw action in every theater of the war and was considered to be one of the most widely used of the many armored fighting vehicles.

Car manufacturers Ford, Morris, and Humber produced light vehicles for the army. The Humber FFW (Fitted for Wireless) had seating for two wireless operators and a detachable body that could be used on the ground as a wireless center or command station. The Humber Lorry used the chassis of a 1939 saloon car, incorporating a wireless set, map table, and equipment required for field operations. Batteries for the wireless set could be recharged from a generator connected to the main engine.

To address Winston Churchill's call in mid-1940 for an amphibious vessel that could land at least three heavy tanks on a beach, the Inter-Service Training and Development Center developed the LCT (Landing Craft Tank) Mark 1. It was somewhat effective during the British evacuation from Greece and Crete in 1941, but left considerable room for improvement. Engineers were prompted to work on further versions and subsequently they developed seven others. Research was driven by increases in size and the number of tanks that could be transported. A variant of the LCT was the Landing Ship, Docks (LSD), a floating dock that could transport landing craft, amphibious vehicles, and troops. At a landing area, it also functioned as a repair dock for damaged ships. Besides their use by the Royal Navy, a number of these were built for the U.S. Navy as well.

Following the evacuation from Dunkirk, the British lost many weapons and needed to produce a new machine gun quickly and in quantity. With the German MP38 as a model, Major R. V. Shepherd (dates unconfirmed) and H. J. Turpin (dates unconfirmed), a civilian, both working at the Enfield Lock Small Arms Factory, designed the Sten Mk 1 for cheap and quick production. It was made up of steel tubes and easily manufactured parts that were joined together with welds, pins, and bolts. Its form was ugly but it functioned well and the design was deemed successful. About 100,000 were produced within months and these were followed by successive versions that simplified the mechanical function and improved the physical appearance.

After World War I, the Royal Air Force had undertaken an extensive program of reorganization. Air Marshal Hugh Montague Trenchard created a comprehensive and far-reaching plan for the development of a strong air force that was independent of the other services. Under his leadership between 1919 and 1929, the Royal Air Force (RAF) demonstrated its effectiveness in a number of conflicts, notably within Britain's colonial empire. In the 1930s, the RAF began to develop a series of combat aircraft that included fighters, bombers, and long-range reconnaissance planes. Two of the most effective fighter aircraft, both designed in the 1930s, were the Supermarine Spitfire and the Hawker Hurricane. The aeronautical engineer R. J. Mitchell (1895–1937) designed the Spitfire. As Chief Designer of the Supermarine Aviation Works, where he had conceived 24 aircraft between 1920 and 1936, Mitchell began work on the Spitfire in 1933. It was a monoplane, made entirely of metal with thin elliptical wings. Many of its components had been designed by others and Mitchell's role was to bring them together in a new design. A prototype first flew in 1936 and the Spitfire entered service in 1938. It played a key role against the Luftwaffe during the Battle of Britain and was used effectively in other conflicts as well (Fig. 37.07).

The Hawker Hurricane, also a monoplane, was designed by Sydney Camm (1893–1966), who joined Hawker Aircraft Ltd as a senior draftsman in 1923 and was promoted to Chief Designer two years later. Besides the Hurricane, Camm and his design team created a number of other planes for the RAF in the interwar years including the Hawker Typhoon and Hawker Tempest. Both the Spitfire and the Hurricane featured sleek fuselages with pointed nose cones. The Hurricane had a humpbacked silhouette due to the cockpit that was mounted high on the fuselage to increase the pilot's visibility. Unlike the all-metal structure of the Spitfire, the Hurricane had a wood frame covered with sealed linen, though an all-metal duralumin wing was introduced in 1939. The advantages of the Hurricane, which entered military service in late 1938, included its ease of maintenance and handling. The Hawker Hurricane

Fig. 37.07: R. J. Mitchell, RAF Spitfires, c. 1940. Library of Congress, LC-USW33-022632-C.

was highly effective in the Battle of Britain, accounting for 60 percent of Britain's air victories and, like the Spitfire, it was also deployed in all the major theaters of the war. Both planes benefitted from research done at the Royal Air Force Establishment (RAE), which had produced numerous aircraft at the Royal Aircraft Factory up to and during World War I. After the war, the design and development of aircraft ended. The RAE then became a research center where, during World War II, the aeronautical engineer Beatrice Shilling (1909–1990) found a solution to a carburetor problem in the engine that powered the Hurricane, Spitfire, and other RAF planes. Other results of the RAE research included the Mark XIV bombsight, intended for area bombing. It was the first bombsight that was stabilized by a gyroscope, thus enabling heavy bombers to follow an irregular flight path without losing aim. Among the scientists who worked on this project was P. M. S. Blackett, who was instrumental in promoting the widespread application of a new method of problem analysis, operations research, within the different services during the war.

Private aircraft companies that contracted directly with the RAF produced both the Spitfire and the Hurricane. In 1940, after Winston Churchill became Prime Minister, he formed the Ministry of Aircraft Production, a specialized supply ministry set up to support the war effort, notably to address the production challenges related to the Battle of Britain. Under the Canadian publishing mogul, Lord Beaverbrook, the ministry sought priority over all other types of armament production, an effort eventually countered with a quota system that allocated fixed amounts of raw materials to each ministry that required them. Beaverbrook, however, introduced an unorthodox campaign called "Saucepans to Spitfires," which encouraged citizens to donate old aluminum pots, pans, and utensils to the Air Ministry so they could be melted down and used for manufacturing airplanes.

The Ministry of Aircraft Production was highly effective in increasing the number of aircraft that were produced in the early months of 1940 and was responsible for Britain surpassing Germany's rate of aircraft production by more than two and a half times. As a consequence, Britain was better prepared than Germany for the crucial Battle of Britain—the intense air war fought in the summer and fall of 1940—and was ultimately able to defeat the Germans.

The big breakthrough in British military aviation during the war was the Gloster Meteor, Britain's and the Allies' first jet fighter, which followed the Italian Caproni N.1 and the German Messerschmitt Me262. Designed by the engineer George Carter (1889–1969), the Meteor was manufactured by the Gloster Aircraft Company. Eight prototypes were produced before the majority of the design problems were overcome. The Meteor, which had twin turbojet engines that Frank Whittle designed, first flew in 1943 and saw initial action in July 1944. One of its most effective uses was to shoot down German V1 rockets.

Besides the development of new aircraft, the RAF was active in various kinds of experimental research, as were the Admiralty and the War Office. A primary focus of the RAF was the development of radar, although scientists and engineers considered its use in different ways, which included its integration into early warning systems. Research on radar began with the Committee for the Scientific Survey of Air Defense, also named the Tizard Committee after its chairman, Sir Henry Tizard, Rector of the Imperial College in London. Established by the Air Ministry in late 1934, the committee's mission was to explore new technologies the RAF might use to defend Britain against bomber attacks.

In 1936, the Tizard group moved to the RAF's Bawdsey Research Station, which had been set up to study how radar could be used to intercept enemy aircraft. The station Superintendent was Robert Watson-Watt (1892–1973), a pioneer in radar's development. At the Bawdsey Research Station, a ring of coastal radio towers was developed to track German planes. Known by the code name of Chain Home, these towers could determine the distance and direction of incoming aircraft formations. Despite their limitations due to obstacles caused by local geography, operators became skilled at estimating the size of the detected formations based on display data. This method of aircraft detection later came to be called radar, a condensation of the term Radio Direction and Ranging, which replaced its original code name, RDF, an acronym coined by A. P. Rowe, who became head of the Bawdsey Research Center after Watson-Watt.

One of the RAF's most effective weapons was not an airplane but its integrated Air Defense System. Conceived by Hugh Dowding (1882–1970), head of the RAF's Fighter Command during the Battle of Britain, it was considered to be the world's first. The Dowding system, as it was called, enabled the early warning of Luftwaffe raids, which was vital to the British victory in the Battle of Britain. A strong believer in research, Dowding had previously pushed for the development of the Spitfire and the Hurricane as well as radar, while subsequently promoting the need to obtain information of impending enemy attacks. His integrated system linked together various units from different services—the RAF Fighter Command, the army's Anti-Aircraft Command, the Chain Home radar system, and others.

The Dowding system was an organized set of elements that foresaw the idea of systems design, which developed within the British design methods movement in the 1960s. Located in an underground RAF command center known as the Battle of Britain Bunker, its function was to coordinate incoming data about German aircraft movements with a range of British responses that included the numbers and formations of British planes to dispatch and the use of anti-aircraft guns. At the system's core was a visual display that included a map table on which were placed numbered blocks that signified the location of enemy and friendly aircraft formations. Also part of the display was a tote board with a series of lights that indicated the current activities of the air

squadrons in the No. 11 Group. In addition, colored discs indicated weather conditions, while the passage of time was shown with a coordinated display of clock and colored indicators. Information was received from Fighter Command headquarters or the sector stations by telephone before conversion into the visual displays. Though it operated with basic visual display techniques, the Dowding system presaged the early warning systems of the post-war era that used progressively advanced technology.

In 1940, the Tizard group, which had started its work at the Bawdsey Research Station, moved to a new location in the village of Worth Matravers and its name was changed to the Telecommunications Research Establishment (TRE). Its director was A. P. Rowe (1898–1976), who continued to push research on radar and related technologies after he arrived at TRE from Bawdsey. Similar to other wartime laboratories, numerous results were achieved. The GEE radio navigation system that R. J. Dippy (dates unconfirmed) developed was used in British bombers to improve bombing accuracy and bring planes safely back to their bases. The system involved sending precisely timed signals from a series of transmitters, which the plane's navigator observed on an oscilloscope. When a signal from two stations arrived at the same time, the navigator could determine a line of position, making it easier to successfully choose a return route from a bombing mission.

A TRE team, headed by Robert Cockburn (1909–1994), devised a method to jam German radios by releasing thin metal foil strips into the air to interfere with the radio beams. These strips caused a radar echo that thwarted German pilots from finding their targets. The British radio company EKCO manufactured parts for the jamming equipment and the sets were likely assembled at TRE headquarters.

In collaboration with the Royal Aircraft Establishment, Frank Jones (1914–1988) and Alec Reeves (1902–1971) developed a navigation system called "Oboe," which could pinpoint bombing accuracy within 50 yards. The most precise bombing system used during World War II, it had the added virtue of not being susceptible to enemy jamming as was the GEE system.

Other devices designed at TRE included the Automatic Gun-Laying Turret (AGLT), and the electronic flight simulator. The AGLT system enabled an aircraft gunner to track and fire on a target in total darkness. Designed under the aegis of the physiologist Alan Hodgkin (1914–1998), the system was made up of a transmitter/receiver that operated through a scanning aerial attached to a standard gun turret. Signals sent back to the turret were displayed on a CRT screen and projected onto the gun sight. The gunner had only to turn the gun so that the "blip" was in the center of the gun sight and then to fire since the wind and bullet drop had already been calculated.

Although TRE scientists were not the first to devise calculations for a flight simulator, they were the first to design and build one. This occurred in 1941 as a training device for radar operators. The simulator was a computing machine based on the ideas of F. C. Williams (1911–1977). He was a key figure at TRE who made important contributions to a number of projects including the IFF (Identifying Friend or Foe) systems that enabled radar operators to make a distinction between friendly and enemy aircraft; the onboard AI (Airborne Interception) systems that helped operators track and intercept other aircraft; and the "velodyne" system, a more advanced version of the AI technology.

Several of Britain's biggest technological breakthroughs during the war occurred at the Government Code and Cypher School (GCCS), which was housed within the Foreign Office. The GCCS had been established after World War I as a consolidation of intelligence services run by the army and navy. Before World War II, it was moved to Bletchley Park outside London, where a staff had been assembled to break the German Enigma code and work on additional decoding projects as well. Among the staff was Alan Turing (1912–1954), who invented the Turing machine,

which was influential in the development of the modern computer. As head of the unit at Bletchley Park that was concerned with breaking German naval codes, Turing developed the bombe, a machine that enabled the decryption of messages in Enigma. The engineering design was by Harold Keen (1894–1973), the leading British innovator of punched-card technology, and the construction was by the British Tabulating Machine Company. The bombe was designed to discover some of the daily settings in the Enigma machines, which it did by replicating certain mechanical features of the German device such as the rotors with letters on them that were spun to create the encryption.

Decoding was further enabled by the Colossus, Britain's first electronic computing machine that was designed by the engineer Tommy Flowers (1905–1998), who was responding to a request by Turing to build a decoder for the bombe machine. Although that project was abandoned, Flowers moved ahead with plans for a machine that could contribute calculations to the decoding process in a way that was impossible by hand. He obtained some backing from the Post Office Research Station in London and in 1943 he and his staff produced the world's first programmable electronic computer. Dubbed Colossus Mark I, it began operation in February 1944. The Mark 1 was five times faster than Bletchley Park's then current code-breaking equipment, which was being used to crack German coded messages that were generated by the Lorenz cipher machine. It was followed by the Mark 2, a machine first used at the beginning of June 1944, in time to provide crucial information for the D-Day landings in Normandy, which occurred five days later.

Operations research

Operations research (OR) began as a method to analyze the use of radar to identify and counter enemy air attacks, which quickly resulted in broader efforts to improve Britain's entire early warning system and defense strategy. Though initially employed by the RAF, OR methods quickly spread to the other services. By the end of the war, numerous design decisions related to a broad range of military actions had resulted from the recommendations of operations research analysts, who were primarily scientists, engineers, and mathematicians. Though operations research was never considered a science, researchers applied scientific methods to analyze and manage large-scale projects.

Operations research methods were considered to have been employed for the first time at Biggin Hill Airfield, where experiments were conducted in 1936 to establish effective communication between pilots and ground controllers. At the Bawdsey Research Station, A. P. Rowe, then Assistant Superintendent, continued the Biggin Hill momentum in 1937 by assigning several staff to study the control room and tower operations of the Chain Home system. Their assignment is considered to have been the first to which the term "operations research," purportedly coined by Rowe, was applied. When war broke out in 1939, Rowe assigned additional staff, headed by Harold Lardner (dates unconfirmed), to Fighter Command Headquarters at Stanmore so that OR analysis could be applied to a widening set of problems. The work of this group was highly influential and eventually the members came to head OR sections in other commands throughout the military establishment. Though some RAF senior staff did not initially see the value of ground control, their skepticism was overcome once the Chain Home system was shown to be effective

When the Battle of Britain was at its peak, the army's Anti-Aircraft Command also sought to apply OR analysis, bringing in the physicist P. M. S. Blackett (1897–1974), who had earlier been a member of the Tizard Committee. Blackett recruited a multidisciplinary team of scientists that came to be called Blackett's Circus. They analyzed air defense as a system that included the flow of data from radar and sound equipment through the devices that communicated altitude, range, and course of enemy aircraft to operators of anti-aircraft guns and searchlights. Their analyses showed that the distribution of gun batteries,

previously thought able to protect London, was inadequate, which led to combining smaller batteries into larger ones so they could benefit from the few radar sets available, although as more sets were procured this consolidation was no longer necessary. Studies by others showed, for example, that fewer men than previously required could operate available anti-tank weapons.

Blackett was the first to write about OR as a research tool that had broad implications for many types of design and strategy problems. In a seminal paper of 1941, "A Note on Certain Aspects of the Methodology of Operational Research," he argued for operations research as a method that required scientifically trained individuals to work at the highest operational level of the military establishment to analyze problems and serve as a link between those who developed weaponry and the operating commands that authorized its deployment. His intent was to replace emotion with rational analysis, claiming as well that scientists had concentrated too heavily on creating new equipment and had given little consideration to how it could most effectively be used. During the course of the war, Blackett brought OR methods to all three services. From the army's Anti-Aircraft Command, he moved to Coastal Command and then to the Admiralty, where he became Director of Naval Operational Research.

The problems that OR analysts addressed and the solutions they proposed were numerous. OR specialists advised designers on the technical efficiencies of equipment, consulted with manufacturers on reliability problems, and above all addressed questions of how best to deploy equipment and personnel. Their emphasis on the user experience with equipment and systems was an early application of a practice that subsequently permeated the commercial world of product development.

Within Fighter Command, OR staff created a radar-based system for offensive fighter guidance and control, which differed markedly from the defensive system employed in the Battle of Britain. Their analyses proved invaluable in the RAF attacks on enemy communication lines preceding the invasion of northern France in 1944. For Coastal Command, operations research was employed to make airborne radar aids effective. Design decisions included the recommendation that RAF night bombers, previously painted black, be painted with light colors on their bottom and side surfaces for daytime raids in order to reduce visibility. OR researchers in Coastal Command employed what they called density methods to identify deficiencies in strategy and equipment. Consequently they recommended better courses of action that included improved training, equipment changes, and different tactics. Under P. M. S. Blackett, for example, the improved capacity to destroy submarines in the Bay of Biscay came from modifying a radar device so that German submarine commanders could not easily detect it. Changes were also made to Coastal Command's formation of airplane squadrons for

offensive and defensive missions. Previously based on the availability of aircraft rather than on an analysis of a particular mission, OR studies showed that missions could be flown with fewer serviceable planes and a more efficient use of service personnel on the ground. These findings led to the expanded application of planned flying and maintenance among the various Commands of the RAF. The Operations Research Section of Bomber Command identified fuel tanks as a cause of bomber losses due to fire and proposed a new system to reduce the likelihood of explosion or fire as fuel was consumed.

One of the most valuable strategic recommendations that Blackett's staff made during his involvement with naval operations research concerned losses incurred by ship convoys that crossed the Atlantic in 1941 and 1942. The recommendation that larger convoys be deployed eventually reduced the number of ships that were destroyed.

Fig. 37.08: John Baker, Morrison shelter, 1940. © War Archive/Alamy.

Besides its application to military problems, operations research was also applied to civil defense. In May 1939, the Ministry of Home Security established a Civil Defense Research Committee. One of its members, John Baker (dates unconfirmed), who joined the Research and Experiments Branch of the ministry when war broke out, set up a Design and Development Section to gather information on how buildings were affected by bombing. His interest in what happened when structures collapsed led to his design of the Morrison shelter. Named after the Home Secretary, Herbert Morrison, it was conceived to withstand the pressures of a collapsing building (Fig. 37.08). The shelter was designed to protect people during air raids and was large enough for several individuals to sleep in if necessary. Produced with Churchill's support, it saved many lives during the blitz and the ensuing bombardment of V1 rockets.

Baker's shelter followed by two years the Anderson shelter that William Patterson (dates unconfirmed) and Karl Kerrison (dates unconfirmed) designed in response to a request from the Home Office. It was a small curved structure of corrugated steel panels that was erected outside the home. One and a half million were distributed between February 1939 and the outbreak of war and a further two million were erected after the war began. Besides the design and construction of air raid shelters, the Ministry of Home Security also distributed gas masks, provided ambulances, and trained five million civilians as firewatchers and fire fighters. By September 1939, 38 million people had been issued gas masks, which they were asked to carry with them at all times in case of an attack. Beginning in 1939, 12 regional War Rooms and a single national War Room were set up to coordinate these efforts.

Utility schemes and other designs for the home

The Utility Furniture Scheme that Hugh Dalton, President of the Board of Trade, inaugurated in 1942, had two purposes. One, stated officially in a set of rules and regulations, was to provide inexpensive furniture to people who had lost theirs due to bombing, and to newlyweds who were setting up a home for the first time. The other, stated less formally by Board of Trade officials, was to direct popular taste towards simple unadorned furniture designs that might also be manufactured for post-war homes.

The Board of Trade's second objective echoed one stated in a 1937 report, *The Working Class Home, its Furnishings and Equipment*, which had been issued by the Council for Art and Industry. The council was set up in 1934 with funding from the Board of Trade to enhance the public understanding of design and thereby improve the quality of British goods and raise public taste (see Chapter 23). A number of the ideas for the Utility scheme, in fact, were taken from this earlier council report.

Confronted with a shortage of materials, the Ministry of Supply introduced a rationing system in 1939 that included the control of timber, leather, and other materials affecting the furniture industry. Early in 1941, the Board of Trade introduced a program to produce Standard Emergency Furniture, which was undistinguished in either design or construction. When the Utility Furniture Scheme was launched the following year, more attention was paid to design and manufacturing quality. Dalton, a socialist to whom government regulation of manufacturing made sense, appointed a distinguished Advisory Committee on Utility Furniture, which included the well-known furniture designer Gordon Russell, a leading proponent of simple unadorned designs; Elizabeth Denby (1894–1965), the low-cost housing advocate who had helped to prepare the 1937 report on furniture in the working-class home; and John Gloag, a prominent design critic and commentator.

The committee approached nine designers and chose drawings by Edwin Clinch (dates unconfirmed) and Herbert Cutler (dates unconfirmed), both veterans of the companies in High Wycombe that produced furniture for the mass market. Their brief was to use as little material as possible and design pieces to be manufactured by the simplest and most economical processes. Utility furniture was first shown to the public in an exhibition of prototypes held in late 1942 and it became available when the first catalog was published in January 1943. As shown in the catalog, the furniture was divided into five sections—living room, bedroom, kitchen, nursery furniture, and items such as bookcases that might be used in different rooms. The pieces were made of hardwood oak or mahogany, while all panels were covered with thin strips of oak veneer. Pieces were designed to function as parts of suites as well as to stand alone. Besides chairs, tables, and beds, there were also chests, cabinets, and sideboards (Plate 83). About 700 firms throughout Britain manufactured all this furniture. Consequently, the production values varied considerably despite the Board of Trade's aspirations for high quality at a low price.

To complement the Utility furniture, Dalton introduced another Board of Trade commodity, pottery. To address a shortage, he conceived a plan for the production of inexpensive ceramics. Known as Victory Ware, the pieces were created by the Wedgwood firm, which had been making mass-produced pottery since the 18th century. As with Utility furniture, Dalton specified simplicity of form and he limited the colors to white, cream, or brown.

The numerous Wedgwood pieces were designed by the firm's art director, Victor Skellern (1909–1966), who introduced some techniques and devices that improved the ease of manufacture, storage, and cleaning, and strengthened the pottery's durability. His innovations included stackable cups and beakers, plate rims that stopped condiments from running off, and serving dishes with tab handles.

For Gordon Russell, the simple design of Utility furniture conformed to his long-held ideas of good taste. To develop the initial Utility designs further, Russell wrote to Dalton, proposing a Design Panel that would make further recommendations for new furniture designs. Dalton agreed and invited Russell to

chair it. The panel, consisting primarily of architects and designers, first met in June 1944. It may well have been the inspiration for the more wide-ranging Council of Industrial Design that Dalton set up six months later to promote the improvement of design in British industry.

Once established, Russell's Design Panel met regularly, devoting most of its attention to the next phase of Utility furniture that would be manufactured when the war ended. Among the panel's members was the textile designer Enid Marx, who designed a number of fabrics for later Utility pieces. By the time Allied victory was declared in May 1945, the Design Panel had created some new furniture prototypes that were displayed at an exhibition entitled Design for the Home, which addressed the question of what domestic life in post-war Britain might be like.

Another contributor to the topic of post-war housing needs was Jane Drew (1911–1996), a modernist architect and town planner who was a leading proponent of the European modern movement in the interwar years. During and after the war she was active in the design of social housing including housing for the 1951 Festival of Britain. From 1941 to 1943 she was a consultant to the British Commercial Gas Association and in 1944 she published jointly with the Association a small book entitled *Kitchen Planning*, with an introductory photomontage by John Heartfield.

The publication was intended to provide examples of rationally designed kitchens that would serve as alternatives to the poor organization of existing spaces. Following the tradition of American efficiency experts Catherine Beecher and Christine Frederick and the designer of the Frankfurt kitchen, the Austrian Greta Schütte-Lihotsky, Drew proposed a number of different models ranging from a prefabricated "package kitchen," which would combine all the essential equipment in a minimal space, to a larger work space that was separated from a family dining room by a low divider. *Kitchen Planning* also addressed the design and placement of gas water heaters, which were the principal concern of the publication's sponsor.

Hugh Dalton's socialist vision of a world in which standardized products would reduce the disparity between classes, while also making manufacturing less expensive and consequently goods more affordable, was evident as well in the scheme for a National Motor Vehicle (NMV) that the inventor and entrepreneur Leslie Hounsfield (1877–1957) had proposed. Beginning as a designer of pumps, Hounsfield produced a prototype for a small economical automobile as early as 1913. In 1920, he started a company, Trojan Ltd, that created a few small vehicles, which he named Trojan Utility Cars. After some initial interest in them, sales waned and the company survived for a period by manufacturing delivery vans.

In 1942, Hounsfield proposed to the British government that it support a utilitarian National Motor Vehicle, which he would build to standard government-approved designs that paralleled the programs for Utility furniture and clothing. Hounsfield did not intend the car for the motoring enthusiast but rather for the individual who only made occasional use of a vehicle, and then usually for relatively short trips. The body design Hounsfield envisaged was to be as normal as possible. In that sense, his idea for a small non-stylized car was not so different from Ferdinand Porsche's design for the Volkswagen or even the design of the Fiat 500. Although the Board of Trade did not take up the NMV scheme, Hounsfield's proposal nonetheless contributed to the vision of a post-war Britain where equal access to low-cost standardized housing and products would ensure a modicum of wellbeing for everyone.

The Utility Clothing Scheme and wartime clothing

Throughout the war, the regulation of material for clothing was a major concern for the Board of Trade, as was the design of clothing with available resources. In fact, the Board had a Director-General of Civilian Clothing, Sir Thomas "Tommy" Barlow (1883–1964), from 1941 to 1945. In 1941, the Board introduced the Utility Clothing Scheme, with the aim of producing clothes with significantly reduced resources and labor. Among the Board's numerous programs to provide clothing for everyone was the Couturier Scheme, whereby eight fashion designers who were members of the Incorporated Society of London Fashion Designers were asked to submit designs for four basic women's garments—a topcoat, a suit, an afternoon dress, and a more widely usable cotton dress. All the garments had to conform to Board regulations, be made with Utility fabrics, and bear the Civilian Clothing label, dubbed as two "cheeses" because of the letters' similarity to cheese wheels. From the designs submitted, a few were selected and were available in stores the following year. The designs received praise from *Vogue* magazine, but some criticized the scheme for going outside the fashion trade for designs from high-profile couturiers.

Another government design scheme was carried out in 1941 by the Design and Style Center of the Cotton Board, which commissioned textile designs from prominent artists including Duncan Grant, Ben Nicholson, and Graham Sutherland. More popular than these artistic fabrics, however, were the propaganda prints that used slogans and wartime imagery to boost patriotism and sales abroad. A large number were produced by Jacqmar, a London company founded in the 1930s. Originally it supplied fine silks to French couture houses, but the directors realized that the company could make a profit by using the offcut pieces for scarves. Jacqmar's principal designer was Arnold Lever (dates unconfirmed), whose wartime propaganda prints were extremely popular. Some of Lever's scarf designs were turned into items of clothing such as blouses, aprons, and waistcoats by the fashion designer Bianca Mosca (d.o.b. unconfirmed–1950), who also participated in the Board of Trade's Couturier Scheme.

Soviet Union

The Soviet Union was surprised by Germany's invasion in June 1941, which ruptured the non-aggression pact the two countries had signed only two years earlier. In the interwar years, Russia did not aggressively build up its military capabilities, although some efforts were made that enabled the country to rearm rapidly once the invasion had occurred.

At the end of 1936, a People's Commissariat of Defense Industry was formed to supervise the design and production of tanks, planes, firearms, and other military equipment. Six months before the Germans attacked, the Presidium of the Supreme Soviet issued a decree that divided the Defense Industry Commissariat into four departments or separate commissariats, which dealt with aviation, shipbuilding, arms or general weaponry, and munitions.

Each commissariat oversaw a number of design offices and factories. As a consequence of Stalin's concentration on heavy industry in the Five-Year Plans that began in 1928, the Soviet Union had a number of factories capable of producing tanks, aircraft, and light vehicles as well as shipyards where large vessels could be built. A week after the German invasion, the Soviet Union's ruling bodies formed the State Defense Committee as a command and control center for the new wartime economy. Stalin was the chairman and had the power to approve or reject designs and prototypes for new weapons, which he did on more than one occasion. Some military assistance in the form of weapons came from the United States between 1941 and 1945 through the Lend-Lease program, but these contributions could only supplement Soviet production. However, support from Western allies enabled the Russians to concentrate on a few weapons including the T-34 medium tank, the GAZ R-1 light vehicle, and the Ilyushin II 2 jet fighter. At one point, Stalin used the phrase "war of motors," to indicate his belief that superiority in military technology would determine military victory. Given Stalin's power and temperament, military designers were always in danger of being sent to prison for designs that did not measure up to prevailing criteria and expectations and this did happen to some of them.

Weapons research and design actually began

well before the creation of the Defense Industry Commissariat. In 1928, the year the First Five-Year Plan was inaugurated, a Tank Design Team was established in the Kharkov Locomotive Factory (KhPZ). Founded in 1895, the factory had produced about 20 percent of the Russian Empire's railway engines before the Bolshevik Revolution. After the Communists took power, it turned out tractors and then began to make tanks. In the 1930s, the Tank Design Team became the T2K Tank Design Bureau, which began to work on a light armored vehicle, the BT tank. Produced in large numbers between 1932 and 1941, the BT was known as the "convertible tank," because its tracks could be easily removed and replaced by a chain drive attached to the rear wheels on both sides, enabling it to travel on roads at high speeds. This feature had been designed by the American engineer and inventor J. Walter Christie (1865–1944) and incorporated into the Russian tank based on two prototypes of Christie's own M1931 tank chassis that his company had illicitly shipped to the Soviet Union.

In 1937, following the establishment of the People's Commissariat of the Defense Industry, a new design bureau was created at the Kharkov factory to build a replacement for the BT light tank, which lacked firepower and armor, thus making it unsuitable as a main battle vehicle. The bureau was headed by the engineer Mikhail Koshkin (1898–1940), who oversaw the design of the T-34, considered to be the most effective medium tank of the entire war. In 1940, Koshkin died of pneumonia while driving prototypes of the T-34 on a grueling route from Kharkov to Moscow. Alexander Morozov (1904–1979), who was named Chief Designer of the T-34 Main Design Bureau, replaced him. Morozov had contributed to the design of the successful BT fast tanks and developed the drive-train design for the T-34 while working under Koshkin between 1937 and 1940. As head of the T-34 Design Bureau, he presided over the factory's evacuation to the Ural Mountains and supervised the redesign of components for the T-34 to make production more efficient. Another important tank design bureau was the Experimental Design Mechanical Department, known by its Russian acronym OMKO. Located at the Leningrad "Bolshevik" Factory, it oversaw design changes in the British Vickers light infantry tank, called the T-26, and it conducted design studies for heavy tanks beginning in 1930. Several versions of an amphibious tank were also designed at the Leningrad factory.

When the war began, there were few T-34s but an all out effort by the military resulted in rapidly increasing numbers of them, which were produced at several different factories including the Stalingrad Tractor Factory. Morozov also led the development of the more heavily armored T-44, the T-34's successor, which began production in late 1944 but was not used operationally before the war ended. After the war, Morozov guided the development of other versions, the T-54 and T-64, which became staples of the post-war Soviet tank forces.

In March 1941, the Gorky Automobile Factory, which produced the GAZ line of automobiles and trucks before the war, introduced a utility vehicle for the Red Army. Initially called the GAZ R-1 and then the GAZ-64, its design was based on the American Bantam BRC, an early version of the American Jeep. Vitaly Grachev (dates unconfirmed), a young engineer, directed the design team, which produced the prototype in less than two months. The GAZ-64 was in competition with another vehicle, the NATI "AR," designed at the NATI Research Institute. Though some considered the AR to be a more modern design, Stalin nonetheless chose the GAZ-64 for the army. An improved version, the GAZ-67, whose design was based on the American Willys Jeep, went into production in 1943 and remained in use for a decade.

The People's Commissariat of Aviation Industry was particularly active in fostering research and promoting production, building on an infrastructure of research and manufacturing that had begun in the late 19th century. The Soviet Union's most prominent aircraft designer in the early 1930s was Andrei Tupolev

(1888–1972), who created the gigantic but short-lived eight-engine Maxim Gorky plane in 1935 (see Chapter 27). Beginning in 1929, Tupolev was a leading designer at the Central Aerohydrodynamic Institute (TsAGI), where aviation research was conducted and major aircraft were designed. The Central Design Bureau there produced a number of bombers and some civilian airliners. A number of young aircraft designers including Pavel Sukhoi (1895–1975), Vladimir Petlyakov (1891–1942), Mikhail Gurevich (1893–1976), and Sergei Ilyushin (1894–1877) worked under Tupolev. Among the planes they helped design were the heavy bombers TB-1 and TB-3 as well as the Petlyakov Pe-8, created under Vladimir Petlyakov's leadership. Made primarily of duralumin, it was the only four-engine bomber built during the war.

In 1938, Sukhoi replaced Tupolev as head of the department of design, although he left the following year to head his own engineering and design office, OKB Sukhoi (Sukhoi Experimental Design Bureau). There he began work on the Su-6, a single-seat armored fighter aircraft. He completed two prototypes but the Su-6 did not go into production. Despite its excellent flight tests, Stalin selected its rival, the Ilyushin Il-2, as the military's principal ground attack airplane and consequently it was manufactured in record numbers. Sergei Ilyushin and his team designed the Ilyushin Il-2 after Ilyushin formed his own studio, OKB Ilyushin (Ilyushin Experimental Design Bureau) in 1935.

Another studio, OKB Lavochkin (Lavochkin Experimental Design Bureau) was created in 1937 by the aircraft designer Sergei Lavochkin (1900–1960), who played a principal role in the design of one of the Soviet Air Force's stronger fighter planes, the La-5, later improved as the La-7. Though considered inferior to German fighters at high altitudes, the La-5 was more successful in combat closer to the ground. Lavochkin actually worked on the plan with two other designers, Vladimir Gorbunov (dates unconfirmed) and Mikhail Gudkov (dates unconfirmed), who together headed a new experimental design bureau that was established in 1939. A significant factor in the design of the La-5 was Gorbunov's plan that the plane have an all-wood structure to counter the lack of aluminum and facilitate increased output. In the La-7, some of the wooden parts were replaced with alloy components.

Later iterations of another fighter plane, the MIG, gained prominence after World War II, but the first of this series, the MIG-1 and MIG-3, saw service during the war. The MIG-1 originated in the experimental design bureau of Nikolai Polikarpov (1892–1944), a pioneer designer of Soviet fighter planes. Though Artiom Mikoyan (1905–1970) and Mikhail Gurevich, both of whom had worked in Polikarpov's studio, are credited as the designers of the MIG, other engineers contributed as well. Mikoyan was put in charge of the project at Aviakhim plant No. 1, where an experimental studio was set up. Although the original prototype had a number of flaws, it was nonetheless rushed into production and most of the few that were manufactured before the German invasion of the Soviet Union were destroyed in the initial battles of Operation Barbarossa. The MIG-3 remained a demanding aircraft for pilots even after substantial modifications of the MIG-1 were made. It was different from the older fighters and few pilots were sufficiently trained to fly it. The plane was more effective at higher altitudes than lower ones, where it frequently had to engage the Germans, although performance improved when the MIG-1s were reassigned to other engagements where low altitude combat was less important.

The Experimental Design Bureaus that Sukhoi, Ilyushin, Lavochkin, Polikarpov, and other aircraft designers set up were part of a system of small state-funded design offices that the People's Commissariat of Aviation Industry established. The directors of these bureaus worked on the conception and prototyping of advanced technological projects and the prototypes selected by the government would then be assigned to factories for mass-production.

Designers were also arrested for producing failed designs, sometimes due to unrealistic Five-Year Plan expectations. They were either sent to Moscow's Butyrka Prison, where they worked in a Special Design Bureau operated by the Secret Police, or to one of the gulags, or Soviet labor camps, which housed secret research and development laboratories known as *sharashkas*. Scientists and engineers who worked in the *sharaskas* were selected from various camps and prisons and assigned to work on scientific or technical problems for the state. Among the *sharashka* scientists were the previously mentioned aviation engineers Andrei Tupolev, Vladmir Petlyakov, and Nikolai Polikarpov, as well as others who were prominent in their respective fields.

Japan

Participation in the Allies' victory in World War I empowered the Japanese to expand their sphere of Asian influence, particularly in China. Following the war, Japanese leaders began to define a multi-pronged agenda to prepare for the possibility of future conflicts. Among the government's considerations was securing an adequate supply of natural resources, which Japan, a small island nation, was lacking. Other considerations included strengthening the nation's military capabilities, motivating the populace to support state goals, and devising a plan to mobilize industry, the military, and the economy if necessary.

Japan began an aggressive military engagement in Asia in 1931, when its army independently attacked Chinese troops in Manchuria. The establishment of Manchukuo as a puppet state, following China's defeat, empowered the army at home. Six years later, in July 1937, it started a full-scale war with China without the support of the parliament, which did not challenge the action but instead began to prepare the country for a possibly wider conflict. The need for modernizing the military arsenal was made clear when the Russians routed the army at a battle on the border between Manchuria and Mongolia in 1939.

In 1938, Prince Kono Fumimaro, who had headed the parliament since 1937 and had gone along with the army's attack on China, introduced the *Shin Taisei* or New Order, which embodied a major transformation of daily life culture (*seikatsu bunka*) as part of a mobilization for war. To carry out its goals, the prince established the Taisei Yokusankai (Imperial Rule Assistance Association) (IRAA) in 1940 as a centrally controlled political party intended to replace the parliamentary system. Its aim was to foster a collective culture as a means to enforce popular support for the nation's militaristic goals.

Concomitant with his creation of the IRAA, Kono introduced the Greater East Asia Co-Prosperity Sphere, a concept to justify Japan's quest for political and economic hegemony of the entire Pacific region. Under the guise of liberating Europe's Asian colonies, Japan envisioned a new political order that would unite under its leadership Manchukuo, China, Japan's own colonies—Korea and Okinawa—and the former European colonies in Asia. To prepare for such a future, the Colonial Ministry was abolished in 1942 and replaced by a more ideologically driven Greater East Asia Ministry. As if establishing domination over all of East Asia were not sufficiently ambitious, Japan bombed Pearl Harbor in December, 1941, thus starting a war with the United States, which ended in defeat four years later, sadly because the United States dropped atomic bombs on Hiroshima and Nagasaki.

Military equipment

The Emperor of Japan was nominally the supreme commander of the Imperial Japanese Army and Imperial Japanese Navy and both were accountable to him alone rather than to the civilian government. This gave the two services exceptional power in conducting war, manufacturing armaments, and mobilizing a fighting force from among the population. The army and navy were rivals of sorts and developed much of their respective weaponry themselves. The lack of a unified procurement process was a liability for the military, as was Japan's disadvantage as a more recently industrialized nation. The cost of continuing the military campaigns in Manchuria and China also proved a hindrance to full-scale research, design, and production of new weapons.

The navy had four large arsenals or shipyards, where its myriad battle vessels were constructed and refitted. The army's principal manufacturing plant was the Osaka Arsenal, which the Meiji government had established in 1870 and which supplied weapons and munitions during World War II. The army's primary center for the development of new weapons, however, was the Army Technical Bureau. After the appointment of a leading rifle designer, General Arisaka Nariakira (1852–1915) as director in 1903, the bureau's focus was on the improvement of rifles and the design of small arms. Chief among its projects was the bolt-action Type 38 or Arisaka Rifle that was designed by the general himself. These were in use until the end of World War II. The bureau also worked on large-caliber siege weapons and fortress guns.

Working under Arisaka was the prolific small-arms designer Nambu Kijiro (1869–1949), who is credited with the design of the Nambu pistol, a semi-automatic handgun that bore some relation to the German Luger but differed in the plan of its spring action (Fig. 37.09). It was widely used by the army and the navy during World War I and World War II. After his retirement from military service in 1924, Nambu founded the Nambu Arms Manufacturing Company, which fulfilled many contracts from the army and navy for side arms as well as light and heavy machine guns.

Japan came late to the development of tanks in part because it did not have a tradition of horse cavalry that tanks were intended to replace. The army's focus had also been on equipment of a lighter-weight tank, due to its estimates of enemy capability, the need for ease of transport, and the type of terrain on which it had traditionally fought. Weight limitations resulted in vehicles that were poorly protected compared to those of the Western armies.

After acquiring several British and French tanks, the army decided in 1925 to develop one of its own.

Fig. 37.09: Nambu Kijiro, Nambu pistol, c. 1902. Courtesy of Rock Island Auction Company.

Engineers in the Army Technical Bureau finished a prototype for a medium tank in 1926. This was a new experience for them since they had previously designed trucks and tractors. One member of the design team was Hara Tomio (dates unconfirmed), who was to emerge within the next decade as Japan's leading tank designer.

The prototype, called Type 87 but also known as Experimental Tank No. 1, was sent to the Osaka Arsenal, where it was put into production in 1927. Designed for a crew of five, it had a water-cooled gasoline engine due to the expectations of use in a hot climate. Other models followed. By 1932, the gasoline engines were replaced with an air-cooled diesel engine that Mitsubishi Heavy Industries had developed, largely at the insistence of Hara. Development stabilized with the design of another medium tank, Type 89, in 1929 and then with Type 95, a lighter model that Hara had proposed. Mitsubishi Heavy Industries completed prototypes of the latter in 1934 and subsequently produced more than 1,100 vehicles. Compared to numerous other tanks, the Type 95 had a comparatively short gun barrel. Quarters were cramped and the tank commander had to aim, load, and fire the gun as well as carry out other duties. A heavier model, the Type 97 Chi-Ha, whose lead designer was again Hara

Tomio, followed the Type 95. Built by Mitsubishi, the Type 97 featured a longer gun barrel and quarters for a larger crew. The Type 97 Chi-Ha was successful against the Chinese in the late 1930s, less so against the Russians at the Battle of Nomonhan in 1939, and was then employed extensively in various battles during the Pacific War.

The increasing engagement with American tanks in the Pacific theater prompted the army to commission engineers in the Army Technical Bureau to design a piece of self-propelled (SP) artillery that could counter them. The plan to mount obsolete artillery on an obsolete tank chassis was executed by placing a howitzer that had been developed before World War I on a Type 97 Chi-Ha tank chassis, calling the new weapon the SP Ho-Ro. Very few were produced as they had to be assembled by hand and most of those that did see action were destroyed, thus indicating the difficulty that Japanese industry had late in the war keeping up with the greater numbers and technical superiority of enemy weapons.

A similar situation existed with the production of aircraft. The Japanese design of airplanes for civil aviation was less developed than in the Western countries, thus posing a disadvantage for the manufacture of military aircraft. The army and navy developed their own planes, sometimes working with the same manufacturers. Both services provided briefs that commercial factories used to create prototypes.

Japan's most common fighter plane was the navy's Mitsubishi A6M, known as the "Zero." Design work began in 1937 at Mitsubishi Heavy Industries with a team led by the company's chief designer Horikoshi Jiro (1903–1982), who was involved in the design of many other fighter planes that Mitsubishi manufactured. To meet the navy's requirements, the plane had to be as light as possible. Consequently, Horikoshi was able to use a new top-secret aluminum alloy called Extra Super Duralumin (ESD). Though lighter and stronger than other alloys, it was also more brittle. There was no armor for the pilot or engine, thus making the plane more agile but also increasing the likelihood that it could catch fire and explode when hit by enemy fire. The Zero was a monoplane with a cantilever wing layout, retractable landing gear, and an enclosed cockpit, and its easy maneuverability enabled it to outrun any Allied fighters at the time. It made its operational debut in the war with China in 1939. Several improved versions were produced until 1943 by which time the Zero was frequently bested by the greater firepower, armor, and speed of enemy aircraft.

Besides Mitsubishi, other companies that turned out aircraft for the army and navy included the Nakajima Aircraft Company, which had been founded in 1919, and Kawasaki Aircraft Industries, established the year before, which developed numerous fighters and bombers for the army and navy during the 1930s and 1940s. These included the Kawasaki Ki-45 Toryu night fighter and the Kawasaki Ki-48 light bomber that was intended to counter the Soviet Tupolev SB-2. The navy also had its own aircraft design center, the Yokosuka Naval Air Technical Arsenal, where a number of planes were designed.

Commercial companies manufactured the arsenal designs. Prominent among them was the Aichi Aircraft Company, which had been established in 1898 to make watches and electrical products but began turning out airplanes in 1920. The company had a particular advantage in that it received covert technical assistance from Heinkel, the German airplane manufacturer, which had otherwise been forbidden to do military research as a consequence of Germany losing World War I.

The most unusual plane developed at the arsenal was the Yokosuka MXY-7 Ohka (cherry blossom). Nicknamed "Baka" (Idiot) by American sailors, it was a rocket-powered glider a junior naval officer, Ohta Mitsuo (dates unconfirmed), conceived along with students at the University of Tokyo's Aeronautical Research Institute, although engineers at the Air Technical Arsenal created the working drawings (Fig. 37.10). The Ohkas first saw service in 1945, towards the end of the war. They were designed for *kamikaze* or suicide pilots who would guide them towards a target with a full payload of explosives and then blow themselves up with their targets. The gliders were fastened to mother planes and then launched when

Fig. 37.10: Ohta Mitsuo, MXY-7 Suicide Attacker, 1944. © PF-(sdasm3)/Alamy.

the targets were within striking range. Later versions were designed for launching from coastal airbases or submarines equipped with catapults, although this never occurred. Damage that the Ohkas might have inflicted on American ships was mitigated by the fact that American fighter aircraft destroyed most of the mother planes, although a few gliders did hit their targets, causing considerable destruction.

Daily life goods at home and abroad

Policies for the production of daily life goods had several purposes. First was the Ministry of Commerce and Industry's interest in developing export markets for Japanese products. This dovetailed with the Kono cabinet's New Order that was to initially organize domestic life but to eventually regulate the life of everyone living in a future East Asia under Japanese dominance. The introduction of new daily life practices was coordinated by the imperial Rule Assistance Association (IRRA), which had been formed to carry out the tenets of the New Order. A leading figure in the daily life movement was Miki Kiyoshi (1897–1945), who proposed the formation of the IRAA's Culture Section, which was responsible for daily life concerns. However, the idea of daily life culture was somewhat vague and extremely broad in that it included, besides the design and production of consumer goods, activities ranging from art exhibitions to day care centers and cooperative cooking.

Conformity to shared social norms was a central concern for the Imperial Rule Assistance Association, and one proposal to enforce this was embodied in the idea of national dress, which various ministries had been interested in since the early 1930s. In early 1940, a committee organized by the Ministry of Welfare and the army produced several designs for men. Such clothing was adopted widely—over 10 percent of Japanese men were wearing it in the early 1940s—unlike the standard dress designs that the Ministry of Welfare produced for women. One purpose of both national and standard dress was to save cloth and another was to create a sense of public uniformity, but the army had an additional agenda, which was to break down the distinction between military and civilian clothing.

Also central to the concerns of the Imperial Rule Assistance Association were the goods that were part of daily life. In this regard, Yanagi Soetsu, founder of the *mingei* movement and also head of the Japan Folk Crafts Association, sought to ally the aesthetics and culture of *mingei* with the wartime needs that the New Order promulgated. A vital part of Yanagi's goal was the argument that inexpensive mass-produced handicrafts possessed other virtues besides practical ones. He emphasized the idea of "proper beauty," which he believed should be inherent in all that Japan produced so the world could see where the nation's true values lay. Among his suggestions for improving daily life objects was the revival of Japan's rural economy through the development of craft enterprises or *shin mingei* (*new mingei*), a topic of great interest to New Order officials. To cultivate regional handicrafts, Yanagi proposed a Local Handicrafts Promotion Association that would be supported by various ministries.

The Japanese Folk Arts Association was just one of the organizations concerned with the development of a new daily life culture. Another was the previously mentioned Industrial Arts Research Institute, which was part of the Ministry of Commerce and Industry. To support the New Order's demand for *daiyohin* or substitute products made of bamboo and other materials—wood, paper, and clay—that would replace metal, which was needed to support the war effort, the institute organized a series of exhibits that included a public competition of 1941 for what it called simple and healthy products. The results were displayed at Tokyo's Takashimaya Department Store in an exhibition entitled Exhibition of Household Products for the Nation. The goods on display included furniture, toys, trays, bowls, and other household items, mostly made of wood or bamboo. As Yuko Kikuchi notes, these goods were to embody four basic qualities: simplicity and functionality, rational design, appropriate use of materials, and affordability. Although the Industrial Arts Research Institute and Yanagi's Japanese Folk Arts Association were compatible in a number of ways, where they differed was in the former's promotion of modernity rather than tradition as the basis for design. In the 1941 exhibition, however, the differences were somewhat conflated, given that simplicity in Japan was a valued quality of both traditional and modern products and that the objects on display had to use substitute materials, which included wood and bamboo, rather than metal—normally a sign of modernity in product design.

Besides its practical application, bamboo also took on the symbolic representation of simplicity, health, and thriftiness, qualities that were seen as virtues of a nation at war. Kawai Kanjiro (1890–1966), a well-known potter and activist in the *mingei* crafts movement, was interested in bamboo and started a business in Kyoto called the Japanese Bamboo Bed Manufacturing Company. It was staffed by Taiwanese craftsmen—specialists in bamboo products, who made bamboo beds of local wood. Supported by this company, Kawai designed his own bamboo furniture for domestic use. Like the beds, Kawai's furniture was also made by Taiwanese.

Taiwan was Japan's first overseas colony and during the 1930s it was subject to a policy of *kominka*, a series of reforms intended to integrate the Taiwanese into a greater Japanese empire (see Chapter 36). The same policy was introduced in Korea. Consequently, Japan took an interest in both craft production and the potential for industry in the two colonies. Officials especially interested in bamboo goods that they could promote for export, while others products such as dolls for the traditional puppet theater were left to languish.

Bamboo was also central to the contribution that French designer Charlotte Perriand made to Japanese design. Perriand had previously worked in Le Corbusier's office, where she collaborated with him and his cousin Pierre Jeanneret on a line of tubular steel and leather furniture in the late 1920s (see Chapter 22).

In early 1940, the Japanese Ministry of Commerce and Culture invited her to Japan to assist with the design of goods for export. The invitation came through the architect Sakakura Junzo, who had known Perriand when he worked for Le Corbusier in Paris and who designed the modernist Japanese Pavilion for the 1937 Paris World's Fair. Surely, Perriand knew that Japan had invaded China and was at war there but it is not clear whether she was aware of the discourse around the New Order and the growing militarization that was then at the core of Japanese domestic politics. Like Bruno Taut, who spent several years in Japan in the early 1930s, Perriand was critical of Japanese attempts to imitate Western designs. Thus she, like Taut, adopted an Orientalist view that romanticized traditional Japanese culture and crafts. This conformed to the *mingei* philosophy of Yanagi Soetsu, who was her guide as she traveled around Japan during the first part of her stay, visiting museums, factories, shops, and other sites.

Her conclusions and recommendations were summarized in an exhibit, Tradition, Sélection, Création, which she curated in spring 1941 at the Takashimaya department stores in Tokyo and Osaka before she departed. The exhibit included three categories of products that she deemed worthy of export. First were the simple artifacts of craftsmen, which she believed could be easily adapted for Western use and modernist taste. Next, she identified materials and techniques such as traditional weaving methods that could be adopted for new uses. And finally there were the furniture pieces she designed herself, some completely new and others based on already existing designs. Bamboo was her preferred material and its application included a bamboo and wood version of the tubular steel chaise longue she had helped design in Le Corbusier's office (Fig. 37.11). This and several other pieces she designed including a bed frame and a bamboo table that supported a tray of the same material were made into prototypes for the exhibition but were never produced. Perriand shared an interest in folk crafts

Fig. 37.11: Charlotte Perriand, bamboo *chaise longue*, 1940. © Les Arts Décoratifs, Paris/Laurent Sully Jaulmes/akg-images. © ADAGP, Paris and DACS, London 2017.

with Yanagi and was inspired by *mingei* theory, while at the same time, ironically, she was criticized by some of the young modernists in the Industrial Arts Research Institute such as the design theorist Katsumi Masaru (dates unconfirmed) and the designers Yamawaki Iwao and Kenmochi Isamu, who had been much influenced by Bruno Taut. In a round table discussion with Perriand that was held after her exhibition opened, Yamawaki stated that her interest in folk crafts was anachronistic, while her sensibility was too far removed from the majority of urban Japanese. Others characterized her designs as examples of foreign Orientalism. Perriand defended her choices, but her situation was complicated by the interest of these and other young Japanese designers in Western products that could inspire their own version of Japanese modernism, which ran counter to her infatuation with traditional Japanese objects, techniques, and materials. After the war, it was the young designers from the Industrial Arts Research Institute who led Japan's economic revival rather than the traditionalists whose views were welcomed for ideological and practical reasons during wartime but were of no relevance to those who led Japan's post-war reindustrialization.

United States
Planning for production

During World War II, the United States created an elaborate system for marshaling resources, designing and manufacturing weapons, and then getting them to the battlegrounds where they were needed. It involved an extensive network of organizations and agencies, some of which had existed before the war and others that were created specifically for wartime. The network handled different aspects of planning, research, financing, design, and the production of weaponry. Concerns included converting existing factories to wartime production, constructing new ones, allocating and distributing raw materials, and adopting techniques to improve design quality such as operations research, ergonomics, and systems theory. Unskilled and semi-skilled workers had to be trained to produce war materiel and then military personnel had to learn how to use it, thus fostering a vast training operation with new methods of instruction.

In addition, planning for the production of weaponry had to be integrated with military strategy. Thus, coordination was required between military planners, the organizations that did research on new weapons, and the factories or shipyards that produced them. Research often led to innovative weapons that did not fit conventional strategic formulations but nonetheless had to be incorporated into new strategic plans. For the first time, scientists worked alongside engineers and designers, resulting in an enormous number of new devices, machines, and even systems for developing technology and managing production.

The key to American mobilization was coordinated effort. Military services, research laboratories, and industrial enterprises worked together in ways that were less evident in Germany, Italy, Japan, or even Britain. Cooperation from the public was also required to maintain an austerity economy since extensive resources were allocated to the war effort. To compensate for the austerity, numerous companies, as well as the government, promised that research done in wartime would result in new products for a better post-war world, and in fact this was the case.

Military organization was divided between the Navy Department, which included the Marine Corps and the Coast Guard, and the War Department, which housed the Army and the Army Air Force. Following recommendations by army Chief of Staff George C. Marshall, the War Department was reorganized in March 1942 into three autonomous units: the Army Ground Forces, the Army Air Forces—which soon became virtually independent—and the Services of Supply, which were renamed the Army Service Forces in 1943. Within the navy, three units, the Bureau of Ships, the Bureau of Aeronautics, and the Bureau of Ordnance, were concerned with the production of war materiel. The Bureau of Ships, established in 1940, supervised the design, construction, and maintenance of naval vessels, while the Bureau of Aeronautics was responsible for naval aircraft. The navy had its own facility for aircraft design and manufacturing – the Naval Aircraft Factory in Philadelphia. New planes were built and tested there, although the facility engendered controversy because it competed with federal funding against civilian industry. It closed in 1945. Guns, ammunition, bombs, torpedoes, and related materiel were the purview of the navy's Bureau of Ordnance.

In the War Department, the development of weapons for land and air warfare was divided between the Army Ground Forces and the Army Air Forces, while the Service Forces were responsible for the complex job of ensuring their production and delivery. Within the Service Forces, the Ordnance Department and the Quartermaster Corps had the primary responsibility for procurement. In April 1941, the Ordnance Department created 25 advisory committees that included engineers, industrialists, and military personnel to review all aspects of demand including the design, specification, and production of new weapons. The Ordnance Department also oversaw the construction of 49 plants to produce arms and ammunition.

Heading the army's Services of Supply, as the Service Forces were originally called, was General Brehon B. Somervell (1892–1955), who sought to unify the dispersed procurement activities of both the army and navy. He established the integrated Army Supply Program (ASP), a management system that was to control the process of procurement from contracts and production schedules to the delivery and distribution of supplies to the field. Over time, the ASP covered not only army requirements but also those of the navy, the Lend-Lease program, and other special programs. Aircraft requirements were handled by a separate agency, the Joint Air Force Resources Control Office.

To manage the complexity of the procurement process, the ASP introduced a Supply Control System in early 1944. Although not considered to have been an outcome of design thinking at the time, this system was a forerunner of later ones that are now considered to be within design's purview, such as that devised to handle large projects like the missile production of the 1950s and the Apollo Program of the late 1960s and early 1970s. Central to the army's Supply Control System was an elaborate set of forms and records to enable the gathering and recording of up-to-date information on all phases of ASP's operations. The number of primary items to be managed had risen to 1,900 in August 1944. The number of secondary items such as spare parts was approximately 900,000, although they constituted only a small percentage of total expenditures. Central to the control of the primary items was a newly designed Long Form that contained spaces for nearly 500 statistical entries. For the first time, the form brought together all the necessary procurement information for each item. By July 1945, the Supply Control System was providing a wealth of detail and a frequency of reporting that far exceeded the capabilities of ASP itself. A month later, wartime procurement ceased when the United States declared victory over Japan.

The procurement system that operated during World War II resulted in large part from planning efforts that began early in the 1930s, when, at the prompting of Bernard Baruch, a financier who had advised President Wilson on economic matters during World War I and after, the War Department initiated a series of Industrial Mobilization Plans that argued for a close relation between military preparedness and the capacity of the national economy, which meant a strengthened relation between the Navy Department, the War Department, and American business. By 1939, those involved with the mobilization plans believed that preparation for a future war should begin before an actual outbreak occurred. U.S. mobilization accelerated after the German Army's blitzkrieg against Western Europe in 1940. The Lend-Lease program of 1941, which was established to provide equipment to those nations that were already at war with the Axis powers, stimulated American arms production and became the impetus for creating a coordinated manufacturing effort. In early 1942, President Roosevelt called for the production of 60,000 airplanes during that year, 125,000 additional aircraft in 1943, and 120,000 tanks within the same two-year period. By the end of the war, American industry had produced 300,000 warplanes, 124,000 ships, 100,000 tanks and armored cars, and 2,400,000 military trucks.

In January 1942, the year that would witness the greatest expansion of military production thus far, the President established the War Production Board (WPB) to oversee the conversion to a wartime economy by enabling industries to meet wartime needs, allocating scarce materials to war production, and prohibiting the production of non-essential goods. The Board also instituted the rationing of vital materials such as gasoline, metal, rubber, paper, and plastic. Shortly after its founding, the WPB issued orders to curtail the production of automobiles, refrigerators, and other items made of vital materials, and by early May, 1942, a sweeping order stopped the production of more than 400 civilian products. Two years later, the Office of Civilian Requirements within the WPB had prepared a program to reinstate a number of items that did not interfere with military production.

Although Americans experienced the deprivation of normal consumer goods, it was nowhere near as severe as in Britain.

The crisis of war brought diverse industries together to meet the military's weapons needs. Donald Nelson, who headed the WPB, has described the extraordinary cooperation between companies that were manufacturing war materiel. As one example, successful efforts were made among 29 companies that were producing 60 different types of military vehicles to standardize equipment as much as possible. Engineers, production managers, and others involved in the manufacturing process drastically reduced the number of battery types, spark plugs, generators, and fan belts required for the equipment, while also agreeing to manufacture one door handle for all the vehicles rather than eight separate ones. Different firms working on the same vehicle also arranged to use similar equipment and the same subcontractors.

One major company involved in military production was the Chrysler Corporation, which produced more than 35 different types of vehicles and weapons including tanks and tank equipment, anti-aircraft guns, gyrocompasses, range finders, and devices for the manufacture of atomic bombs. Other automobile companies involved in the war effort were General Motors, Studebaker, and Ford. Civilian aircraft companies included Northrup, Boeing, Lockheed, Grumman, and Douglas, while firms that normally manufactured consumer goods such as Frigidaire, Nash Kelvinator, and Remington Rand made propellers, engines, and other weapons components.

To turn out weaponry in the quantity required for the war effort, mass-production was essential. For several categories of production—notably aircraft and cargo ships—mass-production techniques replaced processes that previously had a large if not total craft component. Besides aircraft companies, airplane production was also handled by automobile factories that modified their assembly lines. This was not done without considerable adjustment, prompted by the large number of parts an airplane required as well as the considerable space needed for its assembly. The factories were also working with designs for aircraft types that had not been produced before. One exception to the conversion process was the Willow Run plant—the nation's largest producer of airplanes—that Henry Ford built specifically to manufacture B-24 bombers. At its peak, the plant was turning out one plane per hour.

A similar shift to mass-production occurred in shipbuilding where Henry Kaiser, whose engineering company was a prime contractor in the construction of the Hoover Dam, introduced mass-production techniques to the manufacture of Liberty ships. Central to this shift was the replacement of riveting, always considered a shipbuilding craft, by welding large sections together. These sections were prefabricated at dispersed sites and then brought to the Kaiser shipyards, where they were joined. The work was done largely by men and women with no prior welding or shipbuilding experience who had to be trained quickly.

The mass-production process that Kaiser introduced drastically cut the time required to build a ship from around 230 days to an average of 42 days, thus resulting in a record number of Liberty vessels that

Fig. 37.12: Willys-Overland Jeep, 1942. Library of Congress, LC-USW33-027846-ZC.

were produced. There were problems with the welding technique, especially hull and deck cracks, although some of these were accounted for by the use of a cheap grade of steel that could not easily withstand extremely cold water temperatures. The problems were addressed, however, and for the most part the Liberty ships served their purpose.

Jeeps, Tanks, and Landing Craft

These ships were examples of the vast number of weapons that the United States produced for the war. Some were initiated before the war began, while others resulted from strategic needs that were determined once combat had started. As in other countries, a percentage of the weapons was based on earlier models, while other weapons, drawing on wartime research, were completely new. Such was the Willys Jeep, a four-wheel-drive light reconnaissance vehicle that General George C. Marshall considered America's greatest contribution to the war effort.

The army solicited prototypes for the Jeep in mid-1940 from the Bantam Car Company and Willys-Overland Motors. Only Bantam created one within the allotted time. An automotive engineer, Karl Probst (1883–1963), designed it. Given the short time span for development, much of the vehicle was put together with off-the-shelf parts. Designed for two persons, it had a canvas top, which reduced its weight, as well as open sides to facilitate getting in and out (Fig. 37.12). The army was satisfied with the prototype design, except for the engine. For that reason and the concern that Bantam could not meet its production requirements, contracts for further prototypes were awarded to Willys-Overland and Ford, each of which built their own model based on the original Bantam design. The Willys model, which featured a more powerful engine, was selected for production, and between Willys and Ford, some 640,000 Jeeps were produced before the war ended.

The most widely used of the army's mechanized combat vehicles was the M4 Medium Tank, known as the Sherman M4, following the British practice of naming their American-built Lend-Lease tanks after Civil War generals. Two earlier versions, the M2 and M3, were designed to match the firepower of Germany's medium tank, the Panzer IV. At the time of the Germans' successful blitzkrieg in 1940, the United States had only 18 M2 medium tanks, all of which had guns with less firepower than the Panzers. To build the M3 tank, engineers added a more powerful gun on the tank's side to supplement the gun in the turret. The side gun also featured a gyrostabilizer, made by the Sperry Corporation, which improved firing accuracy while the tank was in motion. Although imperfect, the M3 helped the British halt the advance of the Panzers in North Africa.

The M4 featured a bigger gun in the turret and was made in two versions, one with a welded hull and the other with a single-piece cast hull, which was more difficult to manufacture. The army's reliance for the most part on at least seven variations of the M4 rather than the continuous development of new versions reduced the amount of time spent on retooling and made the most of mass-production techniques. More than 40,000 Sherman tanks were produced by the end of the war and while the quality did not did not exceed their German counterparts, their numbers considerably overwhelmed the German tank corps.

Landing craft that transported soldiers, light vehicles, and tanks were crucial for the amphibious assaults conducted on the beaches of Normandy and many Pacific islands. The boats had flat bottoms and many featured flat fronts that could be lowered to form ramps. Although various landing craft were developed in Britain before they were in the United States, one vessel used extensively in the Normandy invasion of June 1944 was a homegrown version that preceded other models produced in the United States. Known as the "Higgins boat," it was designed by Andrew Jackson Higgins (1866–1952). The earliest versions of the boat with flat bottoms and rounded hulls were intended for oil drillers and trappers operating in shallow swamps and marshes along the Gulf Coast. Later versions,

refined over a number of years, came to the attention of the navy and Marine Corps, which opted for a design that included a ramp instead of the original rounded bow. In military parlance, the boat was known by the acronym LCVP (Landing Craft, Vehicle, Personnel). It was produced in large numbers by Higgins Industries, the shipbuilding firm that Andrew Higgins founded in 1930, while production was supplemented by other companies under license to Higgins (Fig. 37.13). A variant known as the LCPL (Landing Craft, Personnel, Large) was manufactured as well. It had an enclosed cockpit but lacked a loading ramp. Higgins Industries also produced PT Boats, or small motorized torpedo vessels, for the navy and made the first American airborne lifeboat, the A-1, a powered boat that could be parachuted from a plane into water for a rescue mission.

Aircraft design

By 1939, the United States was a world leader in civil aviation with a well-developed aircraft industry, although it lagged behind Germany, Great Britain, and Japan in the design and production of military airplanes. Once the United States entered the war, however, the development gap was closed,. In the early part of World War II, the F4F Wildcat that Grumman Aircraft produced was the principal fighter plane available for combat in the Pacific theater, but it was outpaced by the more nimble Mitsubishi Zero, which prompted Grumman to develop an improved version, the F6F Hellcat, a bigger plane that could carry more fuel and ammunition. The new Hellcat was also faster than the Zero and achieved considerable success in combat with the enemy plane.

America's engagement in the Pacific theater required aircraft with a capacity to transport troops and equipment over long distances and bombers large enough to traverse similar routes with heavy payloads. The Curtiss-Wright C-46 Commando was a transport plane originally conceived as a civil aircraft, the Curtiss CW-20, by George A. Page Jr. (1892–1983),

Fig. 37.13: LCVP (Landing Craft, Vehicle, Personnel), 1942–1945. © Photos 12/Alamy.

Curtiss-Wright's chief engineer, who designed more than 60 different aircraft for the firm. Though intended as an advanced passenger carrier with a new standard in pressurized cabins, it attracted the attention of General Henry "Hap" Arnold, who was interested in its potential as a military transport.

The modified design featured enlarged double cargo doors, a floor that could support a strengthened load, a cargo winch that was hydraulically operated, and a cabin that could be easily converted to carry supplies or troops. A related transport aircraft was the Douglas C-47 Skytrain, best known by its nickname, the "Gooney Bird." A modified version of the stream-lined DC-3, which set a high standard for civil aircraft in the 1930s, the C-47 was considered by General Dwight Eisenhower to be one of America's four "Tools of Victory," along with the bazooka, the Jeep, and the atomic bomb. It was used to transport troops and

supplies, tow gliders, and in a slightly modified version, to drop paratroopers.

In the mid-1930s, the Army Air Corps began to develop a sequence of heavy bombers that played a key strategic role in the air war. The first of these was the B-17. Its design was completed in 1935 and it entered service several years later. Its multiple gun installations and capacity for transporting heavy bomb loads over long distances earned it the appellation "Flying Fortress." The B-17 went through a number of iterations before and during the war, with one of its notable improvements being a nose cone made of clear Plexiglas, a durable acrylic material that was first brought to market in 1933 by an American company, Rohm and Haas.

The B-17, known for dropping more bombs than any other American plane during World War II, was supplemented by two other bombers: the B-24

Liberator and the B-29 Superfortress. As mentioned earlier, the B-24 was initially manufactured at Henry Ford's Willow Run plant, using the most advanced mass-production capabilities. More than 18,400 were produced, the largest number of any single American military aircraft in World War II. The B-24 was faster than the B-17 and could carry more bombs, although its lightweight construction, which was designed to extend its range and make assembly-line production more efficient, also made it more vulnerable to enemy fire. One significant innovation was the bomb doors that retracted into the fuselage like a roll-top desk, minimizing aerodynamic drag and enabling the plane to maintain a high speed over a ground target.

The B-29, America's largest heavy bomber, is the plane that dropped the atomic bombs on Japan. Designed as a response to the Army Air Corps' call for a "superbomber," it was intended specifically for use in the Pacific theater, and was especially designed to carry heavier bomb loads over longer distances than either the B-17 or B-24 (Fig. 37.14). It included a number of advanced features such as a pressurized cabin, an electronic fire-control system, and remote-controlled gun turrets sighted by periscopes. The B-29 also incorporated five different radar systems. Particularly noteworthy was the complexity of its production, which involved four principal assembly plants and

a few thousand subcontractors, all of whose work had to be tightly coordinated. Design changes were frequent and special modification centers were required to service the planes after they left the factories and before they were ready to fly.

Small weapons and devices

Besides the large vehicles, ships, and planes, a number of smaller weapons and devices contributed to the success of the war effort. The bazooka was a portable anti-tank rocket launcher that derived from a design by the pioneer rocket scientist Dr. Robert H. Goddard (1882–1945). Its further development occurred during World War II when Edward Uhl (1918–2010), an Army Ordnance Officer, encased the rocket in a metal tube with a wooden handgrip that could rest on a soldier's shoulder (Fig. 37.15). A battery in the wooden shoulder rest ignited when the trigger was pulled and launched the rocket grenade, although problems with the battery led to its replacement with a more efficient sparker system. The bazooka was generally operated by a two-man team, one to aim and the other to load the rockets. The second improved version had enough power to destroy an enemy tank, while other tasks included knocking out pillboxes and blasting holes in barbed wire. During the fighting in North Africa, the Germans captured several bazookas and then reverse engineered their own version.

Ground communication was made more effective with the invention of two portable two-way radios, both produced for the Army Signal Corps by the Galvin Manufacturing Company, which became Motorola in 1947. The SCR-536, an AM radio, known as the "handie-talkie," was a hand-held set that first became operational in 1941. It was developed by a team at Galvin that the firm's chief engineer Donald Mitchell (dates unconfirmed) headed. The second radio, the SCR-300 or "walkie-talkie," was a backpack sender and receiver that was widely deployed in 1944, when it became invaluable for communication among foot soldiers under mobile conditions, while also facilitating

Fig. 37.14: B-29 Superfortress, 1944. © Everett Collection Historical/Alamy.

communication between infantry and tank crews. The SCR-300 was a low-powered FM radio that could be operated over short ranges of a few miles (Fig. 37.16). Used during the Allied invasion of Italy and in the Pacific theater, it was also especially valuable in the Battle of the Bulge, a major conflict of the European theater late in 1944.

One of the simplest though most widely used pieces of equipment was the inflatable life vest, known as the Mae West because of the user's buxom appearance when wearing it. The prolific inventor Andrew Toti (1915–2005) created the vest in 1936 when he was only 16 years old. It could be inflated either by blowing air into a tube or pulling cords that filled both of the vest's chambers with carbon dioxide. Sold to the War Department for several thousand dollars, it saved many pilots and sailors from drowning.

The role of designers

Much of the design for wartime was done by engineers and scientists but designers also played a part. One iconic design object was the plywood splint that Charles and Ray Eames designed for the navy. As Cranbrook students, Charles Eames and Eero Saarinen had gained attention in 1940 for the plywood furniture they submitted to the Organic Design in Home Furnishings competition at New York's Museum of Modern Art. In 1942, after Charles and his wife Ray had moved from Cranbrook to California, they opened a workshop to produce lightweight molded-plywood splints for the navy. These replaced the uncomfortable padded metal splints then in use. The Eameses' splint had a light shallow wooden trough at the bottom and a molded section above that encased the calf and thigh (Fig. 37.17). After a modest initial production run, the Eameses' company joined the larger Evans Products Company as its Molded Plywood Products Division, which made it possible to respond to a sizeable order for several hundred thousand splints. The Eameses and their team also developed a prototype for a plywood stretcher, produced nose cones for aircraft with a

Fig. 37.15: Bazooka, 1942. Library of Congress, LC-USZ62-135435.

Fig. 37.16: Galvin Manufacturing Company, walkie-talkie, 1943. Library of Congress, LC-USW3-023044-C.

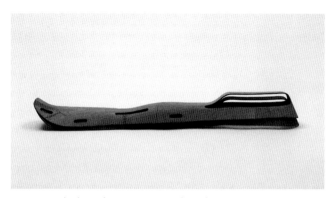

Fig. 37.17: Charles and Ray Eames, wooden splint, 1943. © 2014. Digital image, The Museum of Modern Art, New York/Scala, Florence.

specially designed machine, and experimented with plywood pilot seats and fuel tanks. It wasn't only Charles Eames who gained an understanding of how to bend plywood from the projects he submitted to the MoMA exhibition—so did Eliot Noyes, the director of MoMA's Department of Industrial Design and the organizer of the exhibit. Noyes had learned about plywood gliders through an interest in sailplanes while a student at Harvard and put this knowledge to use in the Army Air Force, trying to persuade Air Force officers to create a glider fleet.

Other designers also served the war effort with the navy hiring quite a number of them. Walter Dorwin Teague's office undertook numerous projects for the Bureau of Ordnance including the design of naval artillery controls, while Viktor Shreckengost, who had previously taught industrial design at the Cleveland Institute of Art, served as director of the Naval Research Center, where he addressed the problem of fitting amputees with artificial limbs by developing a system of muscular movements that could guide this process. Henry Dreyfuss worked on military contracts for Bell Labs, continuing a relation that he had established a few years earlier when he and his office redesigned the Bell telephone. Dreyfuss also undertook a project for the Army Ordnance Division to redesign an aircraft gun carriage. Reorganizing the components reduced the deployment and set-up time from 15 to three and

a half minutes. Other projects that industrial designers undertook included camouflage, color coding, and the construction of simulation models. Norman Bel Geddes, for example, simulated a shoreline near Tunis, which was used to brief landing forces. Designers were also hired for projects that were not related to combat situations. Don Wallance (1909–1990), for example, was commissioned by the Army Quartermaster Corps to design furniture for officers' residences in humid regions. His solution to the problem of wood warping was to substitute aluminum frames for dressers and cabinets.

Perhaps the highest-profile project that involved industrial designers was the creation of a Situation Room for monitoring combat operations. It was originally the idea of Bill Donovan, recently named head of the new American intelligence agency, the Office of Strategic Services. Donovan envisioned a room with the most advanced presentation technology that could keep the President as well as the Joint Chiefs of Staff informed about the state of the war. Prior to the Pearl Harbor attack, he contacted the offices of several prominent industrial designers—Walter Dorwin Teague, Henry Dreyfuss, and Raymond Loewy—and secured their involvement in the project. Joining the planning effort were the engineer Buckminster Fuller, architects Louis Kahn and Bertrand Goldberg, and the stage designer Lee Simonson, along with Walt Disney. Teague, Dreyfuss, and Loewy produced a scale model of a separate building, but outside factors intervened and despite its plethora of advanced presentation technology, the Situation Room was never built.

However, the value of visual presentation was recognized within the Office of Strategic Services, which established a Visual Presentation Branch with a Graphic Section headed by Donal McLaughlin (1907–2009), who had previously worked with Walter Dorwin Teague on exhibits and dioramas for the 1939 World's Fair. As Barry Katz notes, McLaughlin managed a team of artists, editors, illustrators, industrial designers, and social scientists who produced film reports, charts, graphs, and maps to simplify complex information. There was also a Special Exhibits Division, responsible for three-dimensional projects. The architect Eero Saarinen (1910–1961) headed it, while a Design Section was run by the stage designer Jo Mielziner (1901–1976). Among the major projects that the Visual Presentation Branch undertook was creating a full range of graphic services for the San Francisco conference where the United Nations was first discussed as well as the architectural arrangements for the Nuremberg War Crimes Trials.

The Office of Scientific Research and Development

In June 1940, President Roosevelt established the National Defense Research Committee (NDRC), whose purpose was to conduct scientific research related to weapons of war. The committee was proposed to him by Vannevar Bush (1890–1974), then President of the Carnegie Corporation and previously an eminent engineer at MIT. Bush, in fact, had directed a laboratory that produced the Differential Analyzer, an early mechanical device for mathematical calculations. During its first year of operation, the NDRC put in place a research structure that would continue with some changes throughout the war, but there were also problems with converting scientific research into military technology. Bush believed these could be alleviated by making the NDRC an advisory body to a new agency, the Office of Scientific Research and Development (OSRD), and this occurred when that agency was created in June 1941. The OSRD was divided into an expanded number of divisions that produced many useful inventions. Among its major accomplishments were the further development of radar, advanced methods of fire control for anti-aircraft guns, and the creation of the atomic bomb.

The NDRC and OSRD worked with approximately 300 research and industrial laboratories around the United States, contracted for more than 2,000 projects, and produced more than 200 new devices.

Among the university laboratories, three at MIT were prominent. The MIT Radiation Laboratory devised a system that enabled aircraft to detect the location of other objects using electromagnetic waves. The first success with such a device in the United States, the SCR-720 Airborne Radar, was installed in British and American planes and proved invaluable for night fighting as well as for the basic British air defense as previously described. An improved system, SCR-584, the first automatic microwave tracking system that directed anti-aircraft guns, enabled British gunners to shoot down about 85 percent of the German V1 rockets that were fired at London in 1944. Included with the system was a proximity fuse developed by the NDRC that detonated an explosive device when it came close to a target. Besides the SCR-584, the lab's activities expanded to produce more advanced radar systems and other products. In 1942, Ivan Getting (1912–2003), one of the engineers who developed the SCR-584, became the head of a new Systems Division in the Radiation Laboratory.

Opposing the tendency to break the problem of fire control into separate parts with multiple contractors, Getting proposed an integrated systems approach whereby all the parts—radar, computers, and fire control devices—would be designed together, putting issues of technical compatibility before the creation of individual components. The challenge was to connect radar with fire control mechanisms, which Getting met by designating the Radiation Laboratory as a "system integrator." The product that resulted from his new approach was the Mark 56 gun fire control system, which required two operators above deck to locate targets and direct a radar antenna, while calculations, managed by two additional operators, occurred in computers below. Despite the advanced design methods, however, the Mark 56 did not make it into production in time for wartime use.

Earlier work on systems design had been carried out by another MIT engineer, Harold Hazen (1901–1980), whose emphasis was on human–machine interaction in a system rather than on the conditions for designing a system's technological components. Hazen thought it essential to design equipment that suited human capabilities rather than try to adapt humans to existing devices. He wrote a seminal memo on the subject in May 1941, where he argued that the capacity of the operator was a necessary determinant for the design of a system's mechanical parts, and he called for simulated models that could represent human performance when a system was being designed.

The Servomechanisms Laboratory, or Servo Lab, directed by an electrical engineer, Gordon S. Brown (1907–1996), a pioneer in research on servo controls, was also concerned with system design. It specialized in automatic aiming and fire control systems that were designed to help a gun operator hit a target. The lab's work began with the navy's interest in servomechanisms—sensors that can correct the performance of a mechanism through a feedback process. Early research in the lab included the operation of servomechanisms for the remote control of anti-aircraft guns. This was necessitated by increased aircraft speed, which required higher rates of gun movement. The lab also managed Project Whirlwind, a navy-funded project headed by Jay Forester (b. 1918), who would later lead the team that created the Limits to Growth model for the Club of Rome in 1972. The aim of Project Whirlwind was to produce a flight simulator to replicate flight motion, with an instrument panel that would be updated continually by an analog computer. Such a computer, the first that was entirely digital, was built but did not work accurately and could not be made more effective without a considerably larger machine that lab scientists were unable to build at the time.

The Instrumentation Laboratory, headed by mechanical engineer Charles Stark Draper (1901–1987), worked on guidance and control systems. Draper began teaching aircraft instrumentation at MIT in the late 1920s and became a leading expert in the field. A key invention of Draper's lab, the Mark 14 Gunsight, was a small optical device designed in collaboration with the Servo Lab that used a gyro mechanism to improve the accuracy of anti-aircraft guns.

OSRD's largest program was the Manhattan Project, which produced the atom bomb. It was essentially a research effort by scientists who were concerned with problems of detonation and explosive force rather than weaponry that required human operators. Besides the Manhattan Project, however, OSRD's research was essentially directed to devices that required human operation. Many were installed on ships, planes, or tanks. Considerable research was dedicated to fire control, whose purpose was to enable a gun to hit a fast-moving target, and this work resulted in many useful devices. OSRD's Division 7 produced a number of gunsights while Division 14 specialized in radar range finders. Such finders increased a turret gunner's tracking ability fourfold by alleviating the need to estimate the firing range.

The NDRC also contracted with the Hazeltine Service Company to produce a mine detector called the SCR-625, which became standard equipment for ground troops. Another device for infantry soldiers was a portable flamethrower, an improvement on the cumbersome models that were used in World War I. The OSRD cooperated as well with the Joint Aircraft Committee and the Joint Radio Board, which set up objectives for the design of headphones, headsets, and an improved microphone that was quickly put into production.

OSRD's Division of Aviation Medicine studied the causes of aircraft accidents and recommended the redesign of airplane seats, control panels, safety harnesses, and escape hatches. Complementing that research were other efforts to understand the relation between the design of aircraft equipment and those who used it. A major center for such research was the Army Air Force's Aero Medical Lab in Dayton, Ohio. One problem it addressed was the design of the B-17's control panel, where pilots sometimes confused the switches that controlled the flaps and landing gear because of their proximity and similarity of shape. This resulted in a number of runway crashes. A psychologist in the lab, Alphonse Chapanis (1917–1902), who became a pioneer in the field of ergonomics or human factors engineering, devised a solution—shape coding—whereby a circular shape was attached to the end of the landing gear control and a triangular shape to the flaps control so the two could be easily distinguished by touch alone. This eliminated the pilot's confusion and put a stop to the crashes. Another psychologist who worked on ergonomic issues for the Army Air Force was Paul Fitts (1912–1965), who, like Chapanis, became a leader in the human factors movement after the war.

While most of what NDRC and OSRD developed was either technical systems or devices of modest scale, OSRD was responsible for a major combat vehicle, the DUKW, a landing craft that could operate both in the water and on land (Fig. 37.18). Known colloquially as the "duck," it was conceived by a yacht designer, Rod Stephens Jr. (1909–1995);

Dennis Puleston (1905–2001), a British sailor; and Frank W. Speir (dates unconfirmed). The DUKW was a six-wheel-drive truck that was used primarily for carrying goods and troops and for amphibious attacks. Designed in partnership with General Motors, the DUKW concept began with the modification of a GM military truck known as the "deuce." To it were added a modified chassis and a propeller, with the final production design completed by engineers in GM's truck division. A novel element was a device that enabled the driver to vary the tire pressure from hard to soft, depending on whether the DUKW was on a road or a softer surface such as a beach.

Operations research

A British delegation introduced operations research to the United States in September 1940 as part of a mission to share British military technology so the United States could contribute to its development for the benefit of both countries. The same mission brought

Fig. 37.18: Rod Stephens Jr., Dennis Puleston, and Frank W. Speir, DUKW, 1942. © Military Images/Alamy.

the technology that led to the further advances in radar. Vannevar Bush regarded operations research with some hesitation, as he believed that the close cooperation with military commanders that it entailed was incompatible with his own management strategy for OSRD, which sought to insulate civilian scientific research from military or government interference. Consequently OSRD had little involvement with the applications of operations research in the service branches. The navy's Bureau of Ordnance was the first to apply operations research's techniques of analysis, focusing on the study of anti-submarine warfare. An Anti-submarine Warfare Operations Research Group (ASWORG) was formed to improve the efficacy of attacks on enemy submarines in the North Atlantic. The group quickly published a search and attack manual and addressed two other areas—the placement of depth charge explosions and the creation of barrier patrols to better detect submarines moving from Japan to Germany. The success of AWORG led to the formation of the navy's Operational Research Group, which included subgroups related to submarines, aircraft, anti-aircraft, amphibious operations, and strategies to counter kamikaze attacks.

The Army Air Force initially employed operations research to improve the bombing accuracy of the Eighth Air Force, which was stationed in England. Operational Research Sections (OAS) were also attached to other air force commands. They operated loosely in relation to the needs of each command rather than within a single group, as was the case in the navy. The OAS in Libya developed a major concept in defensive aerial gunnery, called leading toward the tail, which meant that the gunner would aim to hit the back of an enemy aircraft rather than its front. Operations research sections also helped the Army Signal Corps with radio direction finding and radar. While used effectively in the American military, operations research did not play the crucial role it did in Britain, where it was central to intense aerial combat with Germany as it also was to the development and refinement of Britain's air defense system.

The first computers

Interest in the computer as a machine to manage large numbers of calculations began well before World War II, but the wartime need to handle complex calculations accelerated its development. A major impetus was the requirement for firing tables that enabled a gunner firing at a target miles away to achieve a reasonable degree of accuracy. Firing tables provided the gunner with appropriate angle settings and indicated the firing range for a given piece of artillery. Such tables, which were tailored to particular types of guns and projectiles, could also determine the velocity of a projectile when it hit its target.

Vannevar Bush's Differential Analyzer reduced the time for making calculations, but it lacked speed. Progress was made with the Automatic Sequence Controlled Calculator (ASCC), known as the Mark I, which was both larger than previous machines and was also the first computer to be unveiled to the general public. Many scholars consider it to have heralded the beginning of the computing age. It was conceived by Howard Aiken (1900–1973), who began to explore mechanical computing devices while a doctoral student at Harvard. Aiken interested IBM in a calculating machine, and the company's president, Thomas Watson, agreed to provide IBM engineers for its design, although most of the funding came from the navy.

Aiken operated as a consultant to the engineers, sketching out desired functions and leaving them to develop the hardware, which incorporated the punch card technology that was an IBM specialty. While Aiken concentrated on the machine's computational functions, Watson determined its appearance. He insisted that the machine, which was more than 51 feet long and 8 feet high, be encased in polished steel and glass, thus establishing a visual rhetoric for future computers of that scale. The Mark 1 was the largest machine of its kind ever constructed and was able to perform a series of programmed operations without error. After it was finished in early 1943 it was moved to Harvard, where it began doing calculations for the navy's Bureau of Ships in early 1944, several months before its public dedication. It was also used to perform calculations for the construction of the atomic bomb.

Although IBM made a strong commitment to the Mark 1, Watson viewed it more as a military effort than a product for commercial exploitation. Related research was also underway elsewhere. Engineers at Bell Telephone Labs developed a series of computing machines that used metallic devices or relays, which assumed an open or closed position to control an electric current. The catalyst there was George R. Stibitz (1904–1995), a mathematician who built a computing device in 1937 that could perform mathematical functions with relay technology. Company executives agreed to finance a larger model and in 1940 the Complex Number Calculator (CNC) was completed. It marked a significant advance in computing, since commands could be sent to the computer over telephone lines from a teletype machine, which functioned as the first computer terminal. Completed calculations could be returned to the machine via the same phone lines. The system could accommodate several terminals although only one could be used at a time. Despite this success, however, Bell Labs was not interested in building general-purpose computers and concentrated instead on wartime projects such as the M-9 Gun Director, which helped a gunner track a moving target. Stibitz became a member of the National Defense Research Committee and continued his research on computers, developing several improved versions of the CNC, which were helpful in calculating weapons trajectories.

Despite Stibitz's work for the NDRC, neither that organization nor the OSRD fully recognized the future potential of computing machines, hence the development of the machine that inaugurated the computer revolution occurred outside the principal wartime research organization. The need for more efficient means of preparing artillery firing tables was the impetus for the design of ENIAC (Electronic Numerical Integrator and Computer), an electronic digital computer that is generally considered to have

ushered in the era of high-speed electronic computing. It was many times faster than its predecessors and capable of being reprogrammed to solve a wider range of problems. Whereas the navy funded most of Mark 1's design and development, ENIAC was financed by the Army Ordnance Department, which planned to use the computers in its Ballistic Research Laboratory.

Design and production took place at the University of Pennsylvania's Moore School of Engineering, which had an established relation with the Ballistic Research Lab. The Moore School had previously trained several hundred women to do trajectory computations for the Lab with desk calculators. They were known as "computers" before the name was applied to machines, However, their efforts could not keep up with the need for firing tables, and the Ballistics Lab became interested in the project for an electronic digital computer that was developed by John Mauchly (1907–1980), a physics professor, and J. Presper Eckert (1919–1995), an electrical engineer. It was ultimately built at the Moore School with the involvement of many others besides Mauchly and Eckert. Construction began in July 1943 and ENIAC ran its first programs in December 1945. Its calculation speed was more than 1,000 times faster than previous electro-mechanical machines such as the Mark 1. The final form consisted of several different types of units that were connected to each other by wires and arranged in a horseshoe shape around a large room. Though men designed ENIAC, its programmers were all women, who had to master the machine's mathematical complexities and its temperamental operation.

The home front

The 1942 order of the War Production Board to drastically reduce the number of consumer products that American companies manufactured contributed to the feeling of sacrifice that the government was asking of all Americans. No automobiles were produced until the war ended nor were the abundant consumer goods from the 1930s such as washing machines and dryers, dishwashers, and other home appliances. Metals like aluminum, tin, and steel were required for military production, leaving substitute materials such as plastic for domestic goods. The demand for austerity was not as severe as it was in Britain, but nonetheless, people had to radically alter their consumption habits. There were some interesting new materials such as Saran and Cellophane, both thin plastic sheets that were perfect for wrapping, while plastics of different grades were adopted for as many products as possible. It was regarded as unpatriotic to promote consumption, hence corporate advertising emphasized what companies were doing to help the war effort.

Given the required austerity of the war years, it is no surprise that the government and commercial manufacturers encouraged the public to look ahead to a better time after the war. In a speech of 1942, President Roosevelt told Americans that the country was fighting for a brighter future, which he did not explicitly delineate but which certainly implied a life of material comfort. Industrial designers, especially the prominent designers of the 1930s, played an important part in promoting a post-war future of high consumption. Both Walter Dorwin Teague and Raymond Loewy agreed with the National Association of Manufacturers, who opposed the New Deal, and Teague espoused corporate planning as a better way to stimulate consumption than any government program. He even went so far as to claim that government planning was an impediment to social evolution.

Designers also sought work from companies they hoped to aid with designs for the post-war world. Brook Stevens, for example, prepared drawings that showed how a Willys Jeep could be redesigned as a civilian vehicle, while also proposing a streamlined bubble car that looked like a vehicle from a Buck Rogers film. There were proposals for flying cars and predictions of streamlined personal commuter aircraft as one could see in Du Pont's promotional booklet, *Glimpses into the Wonder World of Tomorrow.*

One topic that provoked considerable discussion

was the House of Tomorrow, which electronics manufacturers foresaw as a container for appliances to alleviate the drudgery of housework. Among these wondrous new artifacts-to-be was the 1942 "Day After Tomorrow's Kitchen," a prototype designed by H. Creston Doner (1903–1991), Director of the Design Department at the Libby-Owens-Ford Glass Company. The company's promotional kitchen featured an open plan, high-tech appliances, streamlined fixtures, and an abundant use of glass. Several full-scale models were sent around the country to major department stores, where customers had a chance to vote on the features they would most like to see in a future kitchen of their own. In truth, American taste was considerably more conservative than the L-O-F futuristic kitchen would have suggested. Although new appliances were popular in post-war America, the same preferences for traditional home and furniture styles that dominated the 1920s and 1930s were still very much in evidence when the war ended and people began spending again.

Propaganda

Printed propaganda, whether posters, leaflets, pamphlets, newspapers, or magazines, received considerable competition during World War II from new media such as radio and sound film. Advances in aircraft technology also made possible a much more intensive use of propaganda leaflets dropped over enemy territory than was possible in World War I. The power of radio to put audiences in direct contact with their leaders and the capacity of film to incorporate sound and image to bring viewers a sense of immediacy were ably demonstrated in the interwar years by Germany and Italy, both of which formed propaganda ministries after their authoritarian leaders Benito Mussolini and Adolf Hitler came to power in 1922 and 1933 respectively. By the time the two Axis powers were at war with Britain, Russia, and the United States, they had finely-honed propaganda apparatuses that functioned smoothly until they began to face the possibility of defeat.

The British and American governments wound

down their propaganda efforts after World War I and had to begin anew to face the Axis powers. The United States created propaganda to abet its engagement in the Pacific theater as well as in Europe. In the end, however, propaganda was only as good as the facts that backed it up, and once countered by military defeat, as was the case with Germany, Italy, and Japan, it lost its edge. However, black propaganda, which was widely used by all combatants, throve on misinformation and techniques of psychological warfare.

Although radio and sound film were powerful media, print continued to play an important role in World War II. Every nation used posters extensively, while newspapers and magazines remained vital means of persuasion as well. The leaflet war was particularly intense, especially as a way to induce enemy troops to surrender. Leaflets were used in every place that could be reached by an airplane and were also fired at the enemy in specially designed artillery shells.

Germany

By the time Britain and France declared war on Germany after the Germans invaded Poland on September 1, 1939, Joseph Goebbels had already established a powerful Ministry of Propaganda and Popular Enlightenment that could make use of any medium or art form to promote the Third Reich's objectives. Goebbels started preparing the German people for war immediately after Hitler came to power in 1933 by complaining about the unjust punishment that the victors of World War I meted out to Germany through the Versailles Treaty. He then began to proclaim the need for Lebensraum or "living space," which justified Hitler's plan to annex all of Eastern and Western Europe. After the blitzkrieg of 1940 that led to the conquest of France, the Netherlands, Belgium and other European countries, the Nazis began to espouse their philosophy of the New Order, which would unite these countries under German rule. It was to be an order free of Jews, Bolsheviks, and other undesirables whom the Germans planned to eradicate. To fortify this New

Order against an Allied invasion, the Nazis unfurled the doctrine of *Festung Europa* (*Fortress Europe*), which was their plan to protect Europe against an Allied invasion. As the war progressed, however, German propaganda changed from the confidence of the initial period to desperation after the army's defeat at Stalingrad, which was expressed in a fervent speech by Goebbels, who called for the nation to rise up and unleash a "total war." This theme continued with his naming of the V1 and V2 rockets as "Wonder Weapons" that would miraculously turn defeat into victory.

The Germans targeted their propaganda to four different audiences: the populace at home, the enemy in countries under attack, the Allied forces they fought in Europe after the Normandy invasion of 1944, and the citizens of the countries they occupied in Western Europe. Propaganda emanated from several sources, notably the Nazi Party's own Reichspropagandaleitung (Reich Propaganda Office) in Munich and the Propaganda Ministry, known colloquially as Promi, in Berlin. Joseph Goebbels headed both organizations. A rival propaganda apparatus was maintained by the Oberkommando Wehrmacht (Military High Command), whose Propaganda Companies engaged in their own independent activities on the battlefield and in the occupied countries. It was, in fact, Wehrmacht propagandists who created the sexually explicit leaflets that were dropped on Allied soldiers in the last phase of the war.

The Nazi Party had its own publishing house, which brought out various textbooks and manuals on propaganda technique. In 1938, the party published a specially commissioned book on poster strategy, *Das Politische Plakat: Eine Psychologische Betrachtung* (*The Political Poster: A Psychological Reflection*). Written by Dr. Erwin Schockel, the amply illustrated study contained detailed analyses of posters from Allied and Axis countries, concluding, first, that posters had to be part of a larger propaganda campaign, and, second, that powerful imagery and simplicity were required for positive effects.

In the spring of 1939, the Reich Propaganda Office launched a series of Party Wall Newspapers, each of which featured a weekly message or motto. They were intended for homes and offices and were aimed especially at justifying Germany's aggressive military action, relying on techniques such as demonizing the enemy and lying about the causes of current events. Besides drawn imagery, the designers used photographs in conjunction with short statements that were frequently written with bold gestural letters to convey strong emotion. A particularly egregious poster blamed the British Prime Minister Neville Chamberlain for the deaths of Polish citizens that resulted from the German invasion of Poland. A line-up of dead Poles was depicted

in a photograph over which red lettering conveyed the claim that this was "Chamberlain's Work." The letters appear to have been scrawled in blood, which was dripping on the dead bodies.

Within the Propaganda Ministry, Goebbels established the Propaganda-Atelier (Propaganda Studio), where he brought together a group of highly talented artists and copywriters to undertake special assignments. With access to the best technical equipment and large budgets, they were able to work full-time on propaganda campaigns, most likely guided by the findings of such research as Schockel's book. Themes ranged from posters illustrating specific commands to black-out lights at home and the depiction of more general slogans such as "One People, One Nation, One Leader;" "Victory or Bolshevism;" or "Adolf Hitler is Victory." The poster bearing the latter slogan coupled it with a stately portrait of Hitler by the academic painter and graphic artist Rudolf Gerhard Zill (1913–d.o.d. unconfirmed) (Fig. 37.19). This poster, published in 1943, was indicative of a technique that the Propaganda Ministry employed to amalgamate qualities of national strength and pride in the image of Hitler. Not only Zill's poster, but also numerous others featured portrayals of the Fuehrer as the embodiment of a belief in German unity and the confidence that Germany would win the war. However, Zill's poster was withdrawn from circulation after Germany's defeat at Stalingrad.

A major campaign addressed the issue of careless talk. During World War I, the phrase "Careful. The enemy is listening" was adopted. It was carried over to World War II in a slightly changed version, "Pst! The Enemy is Listening," or simply "The Enemy is Listening." Copywriters in the Propaganda Ministry shortened the former to "Pst!", although posters with all three slogans were produced. What united them was a shadowy shape who lurked behind the portrayals of people talking, suggesting that one party in the conversation was working for the enemy. Artists in the German Propaganda Studio who worked on this campaign included the commercial poster designer

Fig. 37.19: Rudolf Gerhard Zill, Adolf Hitler is Victory, poster, 1943. © ArtPix/Alamy.

Erich L. Stahl (1886–1943) and the painter Franz O. Schiffers (dates unconfirmed).

A central theme of German propaganda was the demonization of Jews. This occurred not only on posters but in the cinema as well. One of the major anti-Semitic films was Viet Harlan's *Jew Süss*, released in 1940. The film promulgated the stereotype of the Jew as a despicable moneylender. It was reinforced by the poster, which featured the large head of a bearded man with shifty eyes and a greenish visage (Plate 84).

Following the German defeat at Stalingrad, propaganda became more desperate and the public was both threatened with retribution for disloyalty and fervently exhorted to resist the enemy. A 1944 poster, for example, depicted a man with his ear to a radio, listening to an enemy broadcast. It contained only one word, *Traitor*. Fear tactics were used to unite the nations of Europe against the specter of Bolshevism that threatened to engulf them. One poster showed a menacing hand reaching out to clutch the map of Europe. The hand was resisted by the European populace, which was personified by the letters *Europa* that had bayonets protruding from them. As beleaguered German troops were preoccupied with battling the Allied forces, the Volksturm (People's Storm) or national militia was called upon to defend the fatherland. They were depicted in posters as a courageous cadre of young and old men as well as women who were prepared to resist the enemy.

Among the numerous artists whose posters contributed to the wartime propaganda effort, three stand out—Hans Schweitzer (1901–1981), whose nom de plume was Mjölnir, the name for Thor's hammer in Teutonic mythology; Theo Matejko (1893–1946); and Ludwig Hohlwein. Mjölnir began to collaborate with the Nazi Party around 1926 and became the graphic artist most identified with it throughout its brief history. In the 1920s and 1930s, he did drawings for various party newspapers and created posters for early Nazi political campaigns (see Chapter 27). During the war, Mjölnir employed his gritty graphic style to envision the horrors

of Bolshevik occupation, create stereotypes of Jews, and heroicize members of the Volksturm.

Theo Matejko was an Austrian artist who produced magazine illustrations, film posters, and book illustrations. Around 1933, he began to work for the Nazi Party for whom he created numerous posters. A number of them illustrated atrocities such as the deaths in Poland as a result of the German invasion, European destruction caused by British bombing, and the Katyn massacre, where the Soviet Secret police murdered more than 20,000 Polish prisoners. Matejko's atrocity posters were aimed at foreign audiences, although he also designed placards for display inside Germany.

Ludwig Hohlwein was Germany's most successful advertising poster artist from around 1908 through the 1930s. For the Nazis he specialized in depictions of handsome blond Aryan youth. He created posters for the Hitler Jugend (Hitler Youth) and for other student organizations. He also designed posters to promote the 1936 Olympics. Additional designers of posters for the Nazis included the commercial artist Willi Petzold (1885–1978), Otto Flechtner (1881–1952), the team of Werner (1848–1949) and Maria Axter-Heudtlass (dates unconfirmed), and the painter Herman Witte (dates unconfirmed), an artist employed by a Hamburg printer, whose party clients included the Strength through Joy organization and the Arbeitsdienst or Labor Service.

Besides posters, other means of propaganda were adopted to gain support for the war at home. One successful technique of the 1930s was the exhibition. Goebbels had fostered large exhibitions that demonized Jews and Bolsheviks—The Eternal Jew and Bolshevism—and these served as models for wartime efforts. The earlier anti-Bolshevik exhibit had preceded the Molotov-Ribbentrop Pact of August 1939, which the Nazis broke when they invaded Russia less than two years later. To justify the invasion, the Ministry of Propaganda mounted a large exhibit in 1942 that was ironically titled Soviet Paradise. Dedicated to the horrors of Bolshevism and the valor of the German invasion, it featured an historical narrative of Jewish-Bolshevik scheming to take over the world. Among the topics it depicted were the grimness of daily life in the Soviet Union, harsh working conditions, and the pervasive role of the secret police. Overall, the exhibit sought to justify the Nazis' military engagement with the Russians as a crusade to liberate Europe from the potential of Soviet oppression.

Illustrated magazines also played an important role in domestic and foreign propaganda. At home, *NS-Frauen-Warte* (*NS-Women's Watchtower*), published by the National Socialist Women's League between 1935 and 1945, encouraged its readers to take a hand in the war effort. With its wide circulation, the magazine was a prime vehicle for spreading propaganda to women. It was primarily a photographic publication, but its covers fluctuated between black-and-white or tinted photographs, and hand-drawn illustrations. Another popular illustrated magazine, this one directed to the entire family, was the bi-weekly *Der Rundblick* (*The Panorama*). The Nazi Party's illustrated weekly was the *Illustrierter Beobachter* (*Illustrated Observer*). It began in 1926 and ceased publication in 1943 around the time of the Nazi defeat in the Soviet Union. The Luftwaffe or air force had its own illustrated publication, *Der Adler* (*The Eagle*), which featured photographic covers like other magazines but also creative layouts that made use of photographs in varied scales and combinations.

The leading propaganda magazine distributed outside Germany was *Signal*, a publication of the Wehrmacht's propaganda division. It appeared between April 1940 and March 1945. Promoted by Hasso von Wedel (1893–1945), chief of the division, the magazine was read throughout occupied Europe as well as in neutral countries and appeared in as many as 30 languages. Its covers consisted of black-and-white photographs with the title in striking red letters accompanied by a red vertical strip that flanked each photograph. The Soviet Union's *USSR in Construction* may have been a model for *Signal*, which featured high-quality black-and-white photographs on its pages

as well as double-page photographic center spreads. The photographs, taken by Germany's best combat photographers, emphasized the battle conditions that German soldiers and their allies faced on all fronts. These images reinforced *Signal*'s principal theme—the New Order—with its emphasis on Europe's common struggle against Bolshevism.

The layout of *Signal* and other illustrated magazines was affected by a shift in official policy on typography that occurred in 1941. When Hitler came to power in 1933, he decreed that all typefaces should be in the gothic or Fraktur style, also known as black letter. By 1935, he was concerned that such types did not express the clarity he then believed was synonymous with being German, but it was not until January 1941 that Hitler's aide Martin Bormann issued a directive on the Fuehrer's behalf forbidding the further use of gothic types. Bormann referred to them as Schwabacher-Jewish because, he claimed, Jews had controlled the printing establishments in Germany when Fraktur type was first introduced around the end of the 15th century. Bormann's directive stated that type featuring roman letters, known as Antiqua-Schrift, would henceforth be the Normal-Schrift or normal typeface. The first magazines and newspapers to change over to the roman faces were designated as those intended for circulation abroad, so that foreign readers would not be deterred by type that was difficult to read. Within Germany, some publications did make the change while others, including a number of party publications, continued with the Fraktur faces, at least for their mastheads if not for their interior texts.

Occupied Europe

After Germany annexed Austria in March 1938, German troops invaded Czechoslovakia one year later and then occupied Poland in September 1939. The German show of force in the East preceded a comparable aggressive campaign in Western Europe, beginning in early 1940, when the Wehrmacht conquered Norway and Denmark and then overran France, the Netherlands,

Luxembourg, and Belgium in rapid order. In all the occupied countries the Nazis took over factories and in several cases put in puppet rulers. Everywhere they mounted vicious campaigns against Jews that resulted in mass deportations to death camps. In some cases, especially that of Poland, citizens were sent to Germany as forced labor to work in factories and on farms.

Propaganda was created by four different groups—German Propaganda Offices within the occupied countries; outside groups that opposed the occupations; collaborationist groups inside the occupied countries; and resistance groups, also under the occupation. German propaganda came from the Propaganda Abteilungen or Propaganda Offices that

Fig. 37.20: Anon, People of the Netherlands, the Waffen-SS calls you!, poster, c. 1943. akg-images/ullstein bild.

were established in a number of countries. These offices controlled all media from newspapers and magazines to film, radio, and theater. Shared operations were generally negotiated between the Oberkommando Wehrmacht and Goebbels' Propaganda Ministry in Berlin. Besides exercising the power of censorship, each Propaganda Abteilung generated its own materials. One propaganda objective of the German occupation in Western Europe was to recruit young men for the Waffen SS, a multinational military force that served as an armed wing of the Nazi Party (Fig. 37.20). Another objective was to recruit foreign workers for German factories. To these ends, poster campaigns were mounted for the occupied countries. In the Netherlands, for example, a series of Waffen SS recruiting posters combined heroic images of SS soldiers with portraits of national leaders, suggesting continuity between patriotism and service to Germany. The purpose of Waffen SS recruitment was to build up the German fighting force on the Eastern Front to help defend Europe against Bolshevism, a recurrent theme in occupied Europe after the Germans invaded the Soviet Union in June 1941. Recruiting posters for workers suggested a positive experience that was contradicted by the harsh conditions that faced them in German factories.

German propaganda also sought to gain support for the occupying army and to turn citizens of occupied countries against the Allies. Posters to the latter end were frequently circulated to different countries with a common image and texts in local languages. A poster by Theo Matejko, for example, depicted the destruction that British bombs wrought on a European city, blaming the RAF for the death of a child shown in the arms of an old woman.

A propaganda battle that the Germans least expected to be involved in was the V for Victory campaign that began in 1941 when the BBC in London encouraged listeners in the occupied countries to write or paint the letter V (which stood for "victory" in several European languages) on walls or other surfaces, particularly on existing propaganda posters, as a sign

Fig. 37.21: V sign on the Eiffel Tower, 1944. Getty Images.

occupation, gain sympathy for the occupied nations, and promote groups that were fighting for the liberation of their homelands. The Free French, headed by General De Gaulle in London, publicized the organization France Forever with an image of Joan of Arc, while another poster for the same group, created by the well-known French designer, Jean Carlu, featured two raised hands pulling a pair of handcuffs apart. Similar posters were produced for other countries—Belgium, Denmark, Czechoslovakia, Yugoslavia, and Greece—some by well-known designers such as E. McKnight Kauffer and others by lesser-known ones.

The volume of propaganda that collaborators created within an occupied country varied. It was particularly abundant in France, primarily because part of the country remained quasi-independent of Germany for several years. The German Army had immediately occupied northern France and left the south to the French. There Marshal Philippe Pétain headed the Vichy regime, which operated independently though in conformity with German laws and objectives. Even after the Germans occupied the south in November 1942, however, the regime remained in place until August 1944.

In Vichy, the use of language played an important role in establishing new values. First, the appellation "French republic" was abolished and replaced by "French state." Then the republican motto, "Liberty, equality, fraternity," was supplanted by the more conservative, "Work, family, and country." As in Germany, where Hitler's image appeared extensively on posters, so in Vichy was Pétain, the aging World War I hero, celebrated. As Michel Wlasikoff notes, the leaders of the older generation of poster artists from the interwar period either left France, as did Jean Carlu, or withdrew from commercial design, as did Cassandre, Colin, and Leupot.

Consequently, younger artists as well as others who had reputations from the interwar period established relations with the Vichy regime, carrying forward the modern advertising style that had characterized

of resistance. Its success was such that the Germans had to devise their own V campaign, equating V with "Victoria," the Latin word for victory. They painted the white V on walls and used it on posters, but their boldest response was to mount a huge V on the Eiffel Tower, where it was accompanied by a banner stating that Germany would be victorious on all fronts (Fig. 37.21). Symbolically, this not only gave the German V a prominent place in the Parisian landscape, but its placement on the Eiffel Tower also testified metaphorically to Germany's dominance of France.

Several occupied countries had governments in exile or support organizations abroad that created posters and other propaganda to oppose the German

French posters in the 1920s and 1930s. Designers who worked for the regime included Jean Adrian Mercier (1899–1995), a successful creator of film and advertising posters; René Péron (1904–1972), also an accomplished film poster designer; Max Ponty (1904–1972), known for his advertising and travel posters and as the future designer of the seminal post-war Gitane cigarette packaging; Roland Hugon (1911–d.o.d. unconfirmed), a recognized designer of advertising and travel posters; Edgar Derouet (1910–2010), a commercial artist who had done a series of lively posters for the National Lottery; Éric Castel (dates unconfirmed); Bernard Villemot, a student of Paul Colin and widely recognized as the designer of post-war advertising posters for Orangina and Bally; and the Equipe Alain Fournier, which consisted of five young artists, all based in Lyon.

Villemot created three posters for the Vichy regime that illustrated the themes expressed in its new motto. The first featured photographic images of craftsmen and farmers at work, while the second portrayed the family theme with photographs of an elderly rural couple set against a backdrop that depicted a houseful of children with a young mother around a dinner table. The third featured a photographic bust of Pétain backed by an image of a small town (Plate 85). Together, the three posters convey a mystical vision of France as a traditional nation of craftsmen and farmers with Marshal Pétain at its head to inspire the eternal endurance of the French state.

The Equipe Alain Fournier, named after the French author of the classic novel *The Wanderer*, was founded in 1940 by two young designers—Jean Demachy (dates unconfirmed) and Géraud de la Garde (dates unconfirmed)—who added several others including Phillipe Noyer (1917–1985) and P. Prud'hon (dates unconfirmed). The group supported the values of work, family, and country that Pétain espoused and produced more than 60 posters to represent them. A few posters promoted good hygiene, for example, while one of the group's strongest designs, done by Noyer, warned citizens not to participate in the black market.

More militant posters were produced by various militia and groups such as La Légion Français de Combattants (The French Legion of Combatants) and La Milice Française (The French Militia), the Parti Populaire Français (French Popular Party), and Le Mouvement Française (Francist Movement), a Fascist and anti-Semitic group. Such posters depicted marching legions in uniforms, hands holding raised swords, or in one instance a uniformed militiaman struggling with a rapacious wolf that represented communism. Other groups devised less militant but nonetheless political imagery. La Corporation Paysanne (Peasant Corporation), for example, which sought to organize farm workers throughout the country, created posters with images of smiling farmers and village or rural scenes. The fiercest posters were the anti-Semitic and anti-Bolshevik ones that Michel Jacquot (dates unconfirmed) created for the Comité d'Action Antibolchevique (Committee for Antibolshevik Action) and l'Institut d'Études de Questions Juives (Institute for the Study of Jewish Questions) (Fig. 37.22). Central to the anti-Semitic propaganda of the occupation was the large exhibition, Le Juif et la France, held in 1941 and for which Jacquot designed the poster. It was followed by a second exhibition in 1942, Le Bolchevisme contre l'Europe (Bolshevism against Europe), which reiterated a central Nazi theme that without resistance under their leadership, the Bolsheviks would overrun all of Europe.

In sharp contrast to Jacquot, who actually went to Germany to work for the Nazi Party, Maximillian Vox, a leading typographer and editor in the interwar years, worked with the Vichy Ministry of Information, designing propaganda material to promote Pétain's National Revolution. He was art director of the ministry's photographic album, *La France Nouvelle Travail* (*France New Work*), and wrote the section on graphic design for its catalog, *Nouveaux Destins de l'Intelligence Française* (*New Destinies of French Intelligence*). Vox had suggested to Pétain a typographic policy for the new French state, and to this end an Office of Typographic Rationalism was created to coordinate the design of

Fig. 37.22: Michel Jacquot, Out of Here, poster. © Photos 12/Alamy.

had offered the possibility of a renewed nation with different values that did not occur in other countries where the German occupation was total. In the Netherlands, Nazi sympathizers were united in the NSB or Nationaal Socialistische Bewegung (National Socialist Movement), a party that was founded in 1933 under the leadership of Anton Mussert. NSB posters, including one that depicted young men with black shirts whose hands were raised in the Nazi salute, appeared throughout the late 1930s and into the occupation when the NSB collaborated actively with the Nazis. As in France, other collaborationist posters warned against careless talk, discouraged participation in the black market, and demonized Bolsheviks and Jews. A leading creator of collaborationist propaganda was the Studio Arend Meijer, whose head with the same name was a dedicated supporter of the NSB. Other collaborators included Jan Lavies (1902–2005), a commercial artist who had worked for a number of years in The Dutch East Indies, and Marinus Adrianus Koekkoek (1873–1944), an artist known for his bird paintings, who created propagandist posters for the collaborationist youth organization, the Nationale Jeugdstorm.

In Belgium, chief Nazi supporters were the Rexist movement on the French side and the Vlaamsch National Verband (VNV) on the Flemish side. The leader of the Rexist movement, Léon Degrelle, created the Legion Wallonie (Waloon Legion), a militia to fight against Bolshevism. The legion not only issued posters but was also able to create postage stamps to promote its cause. Nazi sympathizers in Flemish Belgium were recruited for the SS Langemarck Brigade.

Actually, the most feared posters in the occupied countries were the simplest. They were the broadsides, usually bilingual, that announced an execution or a harsh restriction against a particular individual or group. These posters generally had the German text on the left and the local language on the right, with both surrounded by a black border and divided by a thick black rule. In many cases the designer added a

all the documents the Vichy regime was publishing. Vox, a firm advocate of a Latin typography that was opposed to the modernist German style, redesigned the typographic standards of the French National Railroads (SNCF) in 1942, although his program was not fully applied at the time nor was the Office of Typographic Rationalism able to accomplish much. Shortly after Vox completed the typographic standard for the SNCF, he joined the French resistance just as some of the poster artists such as Mercier and Ponty stopped working for the Vichy regime after the Germans occupied the southern zone at the end of 1942.

Similar propaganda campaigns to those in France were carried out in other occupied countries, although the establishment of the Vichy regime drawing of a German eagle perched atop a wreathed swastika.

Resistance movements occurred throughout occupied Europe, East and West. Besides armed opposition, a principal activity was the publication of newspapers, journals, books, fliers, pamphlets, leaflets, and even stickers. In Belgium, more than 500 clandestine papers and journals were published, while considerable numbers of both appeared in other countries as well. Printing presses, with a few exceptions, were small and ranged from hand presses to mimeograph machines, but there were also larger presses that could turn out newspapers in the tens of

Fig. 37.23: H. N. Werkman, *Der Blauwe Schuit*, c. 1942. Koninklijke Bibliotheek/National Library of the Netherlands.

thousands. Publications consisted mostly of text only, but some also included photographs and drawings.

In the Netherlands, more than 1,000 clandestine books were published. One of the most active clandestine presses was De Bezige Bij (The Busy Bee) in Amsterdam, while the Vijf Ponden Pers (Five Pounds Press), run by the Amsterdam book dealer A. A. Balkema—with cooperation from the eminent typographer Jan van Krimpen and the designer Dick Elffers—was known for its books with high-quality design. As Alston Purvis notes, many established graphic designers such as Willem Sandberg and Otto Treumann (1919–2001) devoted considerable energy to making false identity and ration cards as well as passport stamps. For a few designers like Sandberg and H. N. Werkman, clandestine publishing also provided an opportunity for graphic experimentation. Sandberg designed 19 booklets, which he titled *experimenta typografica*, although only five were ever published. Werkman, the experimental printer, produced 40 issues of *Der Blauwe Schuit* (*The Blue Barge*), which were printed in his own shop. Distributed within a small circle, they were booklets or portfolios in various formats whose contents included poems, Christian sermons, and legends from Hassidic Judaism (Fig. 37.23).

Italy

Benito Mussolini declared war on Britain and France in June 1940, following the alliance he made with Nazi Germany the year before. In October 1940 he declared war on Greece, but after fighting there for some months, his attempt to conquer the Greek people was unsuccessful. Similarly in North Africa, Italy could not defeat the British, despite an army that was many times larger. When the Allies invaded Sicily in 1943 and then began moving north on the mainland, the Italian Army was unable to stop them. The war continued to go badly for the Italians and in July 1943, King Victor Emmanuel dismissed Mussolini as Prime Minister. Several months later, Italy surrendered to the Allied forces. The Germans continued to fight against the

Allies as well as against the Italian partisans until the European war ended in 1945.

During the war, the Ministry of Popular Culture continued to create propaganda as it had previously done. *Cronache della Guerra* (*Chronicles of War*), one of its publications, was a general interest large-format photographic magazine that was filled with articles about the conflict. Propaganda was also disseminated by means of wall newspapers such as *Notizie da Roma* (*News from Rome*), which foregrounded quotes by Mussolini that were joined with illustrations or caricatures of enemy figures and provocative texts. It was published by the Federazione Fascista dell'Urbe.

Posters were a principal means of propaganda, as they had been during the 1920s and 1930s. In fact, the Fascist Party's continuous propaganda during those years prepared the public for more of the same during wartime. The difference was that propaganda before the war strongly supported Fascist organizations, but as Italy continued to suffer losses and began to face defeat, the government had to compensate by continuous calls of support for the army, the Fascist blackshirts, and the workforce. Early in the war, a 1941 poster showing hands raised in the Fascist salute could promise victory, or propaganda postcards by the illustrator Aurelio Bertiglia (1891–1973) could show Axis troops as children trampling the British in London, bearding the British lion, or kicking British troops out of Africa, Europe, and Asia.

Before the Italians engaged in heavy combat with the British and Americans, Italian propagandists could mock their enemy's military capabilities and attack them on other grounds. They could also demonize Jews and Bolsheviks. Italy's most prominent wartime poster artist, Gino Boccasile, whose role as a poster designer for the Fascists was similar to that of Mjölnir or Matejko for the Nazis in Germany, was a master of such themes. Boccasile had been a prominent designer of advertising posters before the war, specializing in finely rendered depictions of curvaceous women that sometimes bordered on the pornographic (see

Chapter 27). An anti-Semitic poster he created in 1942 conveyed a crude image of a Jew, while his ugly caricature of a black American serviceman with his arm around the Venus de Milo pitted American barbarism against European high culture (Plate 86). Another of Boccasile's anti-American posters depicted an American as a gangster with a machine gun standing over a young boy whom he had just killed. Boccasile also drew heroic portraits of muscular Italian soldiers, in one case depicting a young man in the uniform of the Italian SS. He also portrayed a German soldier on a poster that sought to persuade Italians that the Germans were their friends. One of his best-known images was a British soldier with a cocked ear, illustrating the slogan "Quiet. The enemy is listening."

By 1943, Italian propaganda had become desperate. Posters urged women to make sacrifices for the fighting men, and as Italy's fortunes declined, the image of Mussolini was supplanted by others such as an Italian matriarch wearing a traditional black head covering who exhorted young men to save the country by joining the army. A related poster recalled Italy's past glory in order to inspire resistance against the Germans and Americans. It depicted the 19th-century Italian hero Goffredo Mameli leading a nationalist insurrection with an unfurled Italian flag in one hand and a raised sword in another.

The Italians also supported propaganda produced by the Germans, paralleling themes that were evident in the countries the Germans occupied. A patronizing poster for the German Todt Organization, known for its harsh treatment of forced labor, depicted a kindly member of the organization dandling an Italian baby on his knee and offering the baby a loaf of bread. In this poster, the German was portrayed as a strong adult offering succor to a helpless child, who represented Italy. Other posters encouraged Italians to come to work in Germany,

In opposition to the official propaganda, the partisans in the resistance movement created posters, pamphlets, and leaflets. One established graphic designer in the resistance was Albe Steiner (1913–1974), who joined the Communist Party in 1939 along with his wife Lica. In 1940, they founded a studio in Milan, Graphica Foto, where their work incorporated photography and ideas from Russian Constructivism, the Bauhaus, and other modern movements. Among the designs that Steiner did for the partisans were several anti-Fascist posters, one displaying the hammer and sickle above the dead bodies of Hitler and Mussolini and another making use of photomontage to juxtapose a photograph of Mussolini against a burial site with numerous crosses marking the graves.

Britain and the British Commonwealth

In World War I, Britain employed propaganda more successfully than any other country. In fact, Adolf Hitler praised the British techniques in his book *Mein Kampf* and adopted them as a model for his own Propaganda Ministry. When the war ended, however, the British had little inclination to maintain such efforts, which had been ably led by the press magnate Lord Northcliffe. The government did establish a Ministry of Information in 1918, but closed it within a year. Planning for a new propaganda organization began secretly in 1935 in response to the threat of another war, but no official steps were taken until war actually broke out in 1939. Immediately, two new propaganda agencies were founded: the Ministry of Information (MOI), which was charged with domestic propaganda; and the Department of Propaganda to Enemy Countries, which became the Political Warfare Executive (PWE) shortly thereafter. Among the responsibilities of the latter was the leaflet campaigns directed at the enemy as well as the black propaganda that was based on false information, including fake postage stamps.

The MOI was responsible for propaganda at home as well as in Allied and neutral countries. Special divisions created materials for the United States and the empire, while the Home Publicity Division undertook three types of campaigns for the British public—those that promoted its own causes, those for other government departments, and specific campaigns in the 12 defense regions. The General Production Division (GPD) was responsible for the design of posters, publications—through a Publications Division—and other materials. The Art Director and Studio Manager of GPD was Edwin Embleton (1907–2000), a commercial designer who had been Studio Manager of the Oldham Press before moving over to the Ministry of Information when the war began. At the MOI, Embleton had a large staff of painters, designers, illustrators, typographers, layout artists, cartoonists, retouchers, letterers, and calligraphers who were responsible for all official government literature as well as posters and other visual material for domestic and overseas audiences. Besides the MOI, other government ministries and organizations produced posters. These included the Ministries of Food, Health, Labor and National Service, and Fuel and Power, as well as the War Office, the General Post Office, and the Railway Executive Board. London Transport, which had for years issued posters by Britain's best designers, was also a major contributor to the wartime propaganda campaigns.

Besides printed materials, the MOI created exhibitions and hired industrial designer Misha Black as the Principal Exhibitions Officer. Working along with Milner Gray, F. H. K. Henrion, and others, Black oversaw the design of numerous exhibits including The Battle for France, Tanks, and The British Army. Among the exhibition sites was London's Charring Cross Underground station, where MOI mounted The Unconquerable Soul, whose theme was resistance in the occupied countries.

In January 1943, Misha Black, Milner Gray, the critic and historian Herbert Read, and several others set up the Design Research Unit (DRU), which they intended to be an independent multidisciplinary design agency that could undertake commissions in almost any design field. Gray and Black had previously been partners in the Industrial Design Partnership, which was founded in 1935. With only a few projects before the

Fig. 37.24: Frank Newbould, Your Britain. Fight for it Now, poster, 1942. © IWM.

war ended, the DRU became a major force in British design after the Germans and Japanese surrendered.

British propagandists wasted little effort on demonizing the enemy since the continual shelling and bombing by the Germans were sufficient to arouse patriotic feelings and the desire for retribution. Motivation to defend Britain emphasized the preservation of traditional values rather than promoting fear of a menacing adversary. This was evident in a series of four posters the War Office issued entitled, "Your Britain: Fight for it Now" (Fig. 37.24). They were designed by Frank Newbould (1887–1951)**,** known previously for his travel posters, especially those with romantic portrayals of the British countryside. London Transport issued a related series of six posters in 1944, with *The Proud City* as its theme. Illustrated with paintings by the artist Walter Spradbery (1889–1969), who had depicted tranquil country landscapes on Southern Railway posters before the war, the posters conveyed the theme of endurance through images of cities that had survived the German bombings.

Several more aggressive campaigns, intended for factory workers, were built around the slogans, "Back Them Up" and "The Attack Begins in the Factory." The posters consisted of dramatic paintings by various artists that showed British fighting forces in the midst of battle contrasted with the campaign slogans in bold black letters. The point of both series was to reinforce the courage and efficacy of all branches of the armed forces and to emphasize that the factory workers who supplied them with arms and ammunition were crucial to Britain's military success.

Much effort was spent on campaigns to conserve valuable resources, which were at a premium, and to promote habits that would enhance personal and collective health and safety. Thus, people were asked to work hard to support the fighting forces, use less fuel, create victory gardens, mend their old clothes instead of buying new ones, and avoid unnecessary travel. A particularly sensitive theme was the admonition to avoid careless talk, which was conveyed through several major poster campaigns. One, featuring the slogan "Careless Talk Costs Lives," depicted a series of scenes in which military men were talking with women who were in some cases wives and in others attractive companions.

More than in the propaganda of any other country, humor was an effective tool of persuasion in Britain, despite the hardships and danger that the population endured. As the uncertainties of daily life were difficult enough, humor was a way to boost the public's spirits in the face of adversity. A popular campaign on the careless talk theme was created for the Ministry of Information by the cartoonist Cyril Kenneth Bird (1887–1965), who drew under the name Fougasse, a word for an improvised landmine. Fougasse was art editor of the British humor magazine *Punch* at the time he did eight posters that depicted people chatting in different situations where they might be overheard. One showed two women on a tram with Goering and another Nazi officer sitting behind them (Plate 87), while another depicted a man and woman talking in a restaurant while Hitler was under their table listening. Besides the careless talk posters, Fougasse designed other visual propaganda including books, pamphlets, and press advertisements, working for almost every ministry and for many groups such as the Women's Voluntary Service. Other cartoonists and caricaturists who were active wartime poster designers included Bruce Bairnsfather (1888–1959), whose cartoon character "Ole Bill," a brash Cockney with a thick moustache, became a poster favorite; Bert Thomas (1883–1966), who had published cartoons in many of London's newspapers and popular magazines; and H. M. Bateman (1887–1970), known for a series of popular cartoons in *The Tatler*. For the Railway Executive Board, Thomas did a series of posters on the theme "Is Your Journey Really Necessary?" A popular icon of British propaganda that the illustrator Phillip Boydell (1896–1984) developed was the Squander Bug, an impish creature whose ironic role in a campaign of advertisements and posters was to urge people to spend money rather than save. Later iterations showed the Squander Bug with a visage and haircut that recalled Adolf Hitler and a body with swastikas spread over it.

Britain's favorite cartoonist was David Low (1891–1963), a New Zealander who had worked in Sydney for the popular Australian illustrated magazine *The Bulletin* before coming to England. In 1927, Low went to work for Lord Beaverbrook's conservative newspaper, the *Evening Standard*, with the understanding that he could freely express his own left-oriented political views. Low opposed Chamberlain's policy of appeasement and well before the war began, he was drawing cartoons that ridiculed Hitler and Mussolini, a practice he continued after war was declared.

The Ministry of Information was far from conservative in its choice of poster designers, giving commissions to many who had begun to develop a modernist approach including Jan Lewitt and George Him, Hans Schleger, F. H. K. Henrion, Tom Eckersley, James Fitton, and Reginald Mount (1906–1979). These artists worked for other ministries and agencies as well. Their styles could range from light-hearted to Surrealistic and none of them employed the overtly harsh imagery of German or Russian poster artists or the more illustrative approach of many American designers.

Posters by Pat Keely and Abram Games, who were also associated with pre-war modernist graphics, tended to be more somber. Keely had previously worked for London Transport, the Southern Railway, and the General Post Office, where his seminal "Night Mail" poster adopted abstract imagery and a dark background to convey a sense of a mail train speeding through the night. He employed minimal imagery and a polished airbrush technique to produce strong images such as a black cat with glowing yellow eyes peering out of a black background, which illustrated the admonition to "Look Out in the Blackout." He also designed posters for the Ministry of Labor and National Service and the Royal Society for the Prevention of Accidents, among other organizations.

Abram Games created the most visually powerful propaganda posters of any nation engaged in World

War II. He worked in the War Office from 1941 to 1946, having been promoted to Official War Office Poster Designer in 1942. Frank Newbould assisted him in that role. A large number of Games's posters were done for Britain's fighting forces rather than civilians. Much was at stake in communicating with soldiers about weapons safety, careless talk, and other activities related to national security, thus Games's images were particularly cogent. His posters, which gave evidence of his expertise with an airbrush, were always conceptual, never illustrative. Surrealism, with its fluid transformations of images and magical depictions of objects was

Fig. 37.25: Abram Games, Your Talk May Kill Your Comrades, poster, 1942. Estate of Abram Games.

a strong influence on him, as was photography. The central image on his poster urging soldiers to grow their own food was a tabletop with a plate of food floating above a garden of the same shape. The supports for the table were a shovel and pitchfork, which became a knife and fork as they penetrated the tabletop.

Another example of Games's fluid imagery is the poster "*Your Talk May Kill Your Comrades*", where the sound waves emanating from a soldier's mouth change into a bayonet blade that pierces three of his fellow combatants (Fig. 37.25). The Surrealistic and photographic influences were especially evident in Games's series of posters that discouraged soldiers from tampering with their weapons. One showed a coffin-shaped flat board floating in space, supporting two skeletal hands that were dismantling a projectile, while the central image in another was a coffin with a dead child in it that became an arrow pointing to a hand grenade on the ground.

Games's Surrealistic technique was also evident in his own version of the theme "Your Britain: Fight for it Now." Instead of the nostalgic country landscapes that Frank Newbould depicted, Games, in a series of three dramatic posters, pointed to the future by portraying walls with images of modern buildings that masked the rubble of bombed out cities. One of the posters included a boy with rickets in the rubble, an image that offended Winston Churchill who demanded that the poster be taken out of circulation. Reconstruction was also the subject of 12 book covers that Games designed with photographic image fragments and abstract shapes for a series entitled *Target for Tomorrow*, which addressed varied themes from health and education to town planning and food.

Such themes were also discussed in *Picture Post*, Britain's leading photojournalistic magazine, which first appeared in 1938 (Fig. 37.26). It was co-founded and then edited by the Hungarian émigré Stefan Lorant, who had pioneered the use of photographic layouts as art editor of the *Münchner Illustrierte* in the late 1920s. Although *Picture Post* has been compared to *Life*

Fig. 37.26: *Picture Post*, cover, 1940. Zoltan Glass/Picture Post/Hulton Archive/Getty Images.

1940, he was replaced as editor by Tom Hopkinson (1905–1990), who continued the magazine's emphasis on picture stories and played a strong role in creating a sense of national identity amidst the hardships of wartime. In 1941, the magazine published a socially progressive "Plan for Britain," which helped to define the debate that led to the British welfare state after the war. Hopkinson also took over the editorship of another magazine that Lorant had founded in 1937 prior to *Picture Post*. Entitled *Lilliput*, it was a small-format monthly publication that featured humor, short stories, photographs, and writing on the arts.

One of the Ministry of Information's mandates was to create propaganda for the Commonwealth countries and the colonies on which Britain depended for military support. An MOI poster series with the theme *Our Allies, the Colonies* featured portraits of soldiers from different colonial fighting units such as the Ceylon Garrison Artillery and the King's African Rifles. The theme of unity was also expressed in a poster that portrayed soldiers from numerous colonies and dominions, including India and those in Africa, marching behind the British flag. The Egyptian cartoonist Kimon Evan Marengo (1904–1988), who adopted the nom de plume Kem, was a ministry employee who contributed propaganda for Arabic speaking audiences. He drew several thousand political cartoons that were published in newspapers, though many were also reproduced as postcards and posters.

The Commonwealth nations—Canada, Australia, New Zealand, and South Africa—produced numerous posters to support the war effort. Recruiting posters were a priority, as were posters for government war loans. In December 1939, the Canadian government created a Bureau of Public Information to inform citizens about the progress of the war, and the following year it established a Ministry of National War Services. Poster production was centralized in the Bureau of Public Information, which was integrated into an organization with broader responsibilities, the War Information Board (WIB) in 1942. Guided by the WIB, ministries and

magazine and did adopt *Life*'s graphic format for its cover, its roots were actually in the illustrated magazines of the Weimar Republic (see Chapter 27).

Picture Post's first two photographers were German émigrés, Felix Man (1893–1985) and Karl Hutton (1893–1960), both of whom worked previously for the illustrated press in Germany. *Picture Post* had a wide readership, reaching a weekly circulation of almost two million readers by 1943. Its politics were liberal and anti-Fascist. From the beginning it campaigned against the persecution of the Jews in Germany and regularly ran stories that denigrated Hitler and the Nazi leadership. When Laurent left for the United States in agencies of the government such as the Canadian Food Board, the Ministry of Labor, and the Ministry of Munitions and Supply produced more than 700 propaganda posters. A number of the government posters were commissioned by the painter and commercial artist Albert Cloutier (1902–1965), who worked for the War Information Board. He called upon Canadian graphic artists such as Henry Eveleigh (1909–1999), Eric Aldwinckle (1909–1980), and Roger Couillard. Cloutier also relied heavily on the large advertising agencies that were based mainly in Toronto. Several seminal posters produced in bilingual editions under Cloutier's direction were Eveleigh's *Allons-y Canadiens!* (*Lets Go Canada!*), which depicted a soldier with his gun and bayonet thrust forward, and one by Eric Aldwinckle and Cloutier, *Notre Armée a Besoin de Bons Canadiens* (*Our Army Needs Good Canadians*), which depicted a contemporary soldier pulling up the front wheel of his motorcycle as if he were a medieval knight on horseback.

Another source of posters was the National Film Board of Canada, which was established in 1939 based on a recommendation by the Scottish documentary film pioneer, John Grierson (1898–1972). When Canada entered the war in 1939, Grierson headed the Film Board, whose principal focus was propaganda films, many of them directed by Grierson himself. In 1940, the Film Board launched a series of theatrical propaganda shorts, *Canada Carries On*, which was followed by *The World in Action*, a series that was strongly influenced by the American *March of Time* newsreels. Harry Mayerovitch (1910–2004), who created his posters under the pen name Mayo, headed the National Film Board's Graphic Arts Division, which not only produced posters for films but also for a broad range of other causes. Mayerovitch did many of the posters for the *Canada Carries On* and *The World in Action* series. Sympathetic to left-wing causes, he was influenced by the heroic realism of 1920s and 1930s leftist painters. This was evident in his 1943 poster for the film *Coal Face*, which depicts a miner with huge hands holding a drill. To print his posters, Mayerovitch employed serigraphy, an inexpensive medium but also one that highlighted his gestural graphic style.

Leading wartime poster designers in Australia included Percy Trompf and James Northfield, both well-known travel poster and advertising artists, as well as Norman Lindsay, who had worked previously in almost every visual medium. In New Zealand, advertising artist Albert James O'Dea (1918–1986) did an airbrush poster in 1944 for the Victory Loan. With its prominent soldier's head that recalled similar images by Abram Games, it was one of the country's strongest war posters. The Victory Loan poster was part of a series that O'Dea produced to raise money through the Liberty and Victory Loan programs. His styles and themes varied from the gritty close-up visage of a fatigued soldier to the metaphorical image of a swastika and Japanese flag being pierced by an Allied bayonet. Other New Zealand commercial artists who contributed to the war effort were Marcus King, known for his travel posters in the 1930s, and B. E. Pike (dates unconfirmed). In South Africa, more than 400 propaganda posters were produced for recruitment, national security, war production, and arousing opposition to the enemy.

Soviet Union

Immediately after Germany launched Operation Barbarossa, its surprise attack on the Soviet Union, on June 22, 1941, Soviet propagandists went to work. The day after the attack, artists Mikhail Cheremnykh (1890–1962), Vladimir Denisovsky (1901–1981), and Pavel Sokolov-Skalia (1899–1961) proposed to Alexander Gerasimov, head of the Soviet Artists' Union, that a propaganda poster studio be formed. They envisioned it as similar to the ROSTA news agency studio that so effectively produced stenciled posters in support of the Red Army during the Russian Civil War (see Chapter 20). Cheremnykh had been an active artist in that studio and was also a founder of the satirical magazine *Krokodil* in 1922.

With approval from the Communist Party's Department of Agitation and Propaganda, the Tass

Studio was set up under the auspices of the Tass News Agency. Denisovsky headed it and Sokolov-Skalia was the Artistic Director. The original Literary Editor was A. Kulagin, who was followed by Osip Brik, a close collaborator with Alexander Rodchenko and Vladimir Mayakovsky in the avant-garde LEF group in the 1920s. Initially, the Tass Studio produced single paintings for display along with stenciled posters but the paintings were soon discontinued in favor of the wider distribution the posters enabled.

The studio adopted two styles, one of serious painting that derived from Socialist Realism, and the other a satirical style that had its roots in the long tradition of Russian cartoons and caricatures in the popular press. Both styles were evident in the earlier ROSTA posters as well. Regardless of the style, each poster was a collaboration between an artist and a poet, who together produced a sketch of the image with a related caption. The proposal had to be approved by a representative of the People's Commissariat of Education before work could begin on the poster. Themes were initially drawn from political directives or official reports, but soon Stalin's speeches became a prime source of material. Once a sketch was approved, the stencils, which could range in number from 12 to as many as 65, were cut and the posters were painted by hand.

Subject matter ranged from depictions of Nazi plundering and brutality to images of Soviet soldiers and people from the different Soviet republics heroically beating back the Germans. The posters of Nazi brutality would have been especially effective since many Soviet citizens, unlike the British, had experienced it at first-hand. Artists who created posters in the realist style tended to have backgrounds as painters rather than poster designers. They included Denisovsky and Sokolov-Skalia as well as Victor Ivanov (1909–1968); Yuri Pimenov (1903–1977), a member of the liberal OST group of artists in the 1920s and 1930s; Georgy Savitsky (1887–1949), who belonged to the AKhRR group of realist painters; and Mikhail Soloviev

(1905–1990), another AKhRR painter who had been a student of Sokolov-Skalia's.

Among the satirical artists, the most prominent were the Kukriniksy, a group of three artists—Porfiry Krylov (1902–1990), Mikhail Kuprianov (1903–1991), and Nikolai Sokolov (1903–2000)—who worked together as a collective. They met when they were students at the Soviet art and design school Vkhutemas in the 1920s. Although experts at caricature, the Kukriniksy's drawings and posters frequently mingled comic and serious elements. Besides their posters, they also published cartoons in Soviet newspapers. These tended to be humorous caricatures of Hitler, Goebbels, or other Nazi leaders. In one drawing, they portrayed Hitler as a gunner with Goebbels as a machine gun spewing out propaganda and in another, called "Lie-Locator", they showed Goebbels speaking into two microphones that replaced the ears of a donkey who was writing down what Goebbels said with its tail. A particularly strong drawing, which was also made into a Tass poster, showed Hitler ordering rows of troops to march across the Russian steppes as they progressively turned into swastikas and then crosses that marked their graves. The Kukriniksy's persistent ridicule of Hitler is also evident in a poster from 1944, when the Russians were routing the Germans after their triumph at Stalingrad the year before. A general reporting to Hitler for further orders is greeted by Hitler whose head is on his chair with his buttocks facing the general as if they were his face. Other artists who created posters in a satirical style include Mikhail Cheremnykh and Victor Deni; Boris Efimov, a cartoonist for *Krokodil* and other satirical magazines who drew the famous caricature of Goebbels as Mickey Mouse; and Peter Sarkisian (1922–1970), an active designer who created more than 70 posters for the Tass Studio.

The Tass Studio's chief rival in poster production was the state publishing house, Iskusstvo, which published fewer posters—880 compared to the Tass Studio's 1,240—but whose total in distribution was far more since all the Iskusstvo posters were mechanically produced by offset lithography. Iskusstvo employed some of the same artists that worked for the Tass Studios, but also many who did not. The latter included Alexei Kokorekin (1906–1959), among whose posters were several that depicted angry workers calling for more production; Dementy Shmarinov (1907–1999), a painter who also illustrated Russian literary classics such as *Crime and Punishment* and *War and Peace*; Victor Koretsky (1909–1998); and Irakly Toidze (1902–1985). Victor Ivanov created posters of his own for Iskusstvo, while also collaborating with Olga Burova (1911–d.o.d. unconfimred). A significant difference between the Tass Studio posters and others is that the former were always developed together with a short poetic text, thus the images possessed a narrative quality not necessarily present in the Iskusstvo designs.

Though images of Stalin were pervasive in Socialist Realist paintings of the 1930s and beyond, the Russian leader was relatively infrequently portrayed in wartime propaganda posters and far less than Hitler was in Germany. Whereas German propagandists persisted in adopting Hitler's portrait as a national metaphor that represented Germany itself, in the Soviet Union, Stalin urged Russians to protect the Soviet motherland, setting the tone for this theme in a seminal speech of late 1941 when he called upon the Soviet people to defend "holy Russia." His focus on the motherland generated a key theme of Soviet propaganda—the parallel between heroic battles of the past and those of the current war. Several posters included images of great fighters of Russian history such as Alexander Suvorov, an 18th-century general; Vasily Chapayev, a hero of the Russian Civil War; and General Mikhail Kutuzov, who drove Napoleon's army from Moscow in 1812. A 1942 poster by Ivanov and Burova showed Russian soldiers hunkered down behind their cannons and machine guns with the specter of Kutuzov behind them.

In 1930s Socialist Realist paintings, women were normally painted as strong contributors to the Soviet state. Artists showed them driving tractors, pitching

hay, and cheering Stalin at public events. During the war, the image of the strong woman as seen in posters by Ivanov and Burova and Toidze's "The Motherland Calls", with its female allegorical figure, were complemented by others that showed women as weak or suffering. A poster by Ivanov depicted a grateful young woman hugging a smiling soldier, while another by Ivanov and Burova portrayed an anguished girl behind a barbed wire fence waiting to be shot by a Nazi gunman.

During the 1930s, Socialist Realist paintings had for the most part replaced avant-garde visual techniques such as photomontage, and the prevalence of Socialist Realism persisted in World War II propaganda posters, except for those of the satirists. Among several exceptions was El Lissitzky's "Produce More Tanks", done with the assistance of Nikolai Troshin, and published by Iskusstvo. It employed photomontage to show a male and female worker along with photographs of a bomber, a tank, and a factory interior. Not only was the photomontage an exception to the prevailing graphic techniques of Soviet propaganda posters, but it also conjoined more images than was typical in such posters (Plate 88).

Japan

In September 1940, Japan signed a Tripartite Pact with Germany and Italy, thus allocating to it a sphere of influence in Greater East Asia and leaving Germany and Italy to establish a New Order in Europe. Consequently, Japanese propaganda strongly promoted the ambition to create a Greater East Asia Co-Prosperity Sphere. Propagandists had also begun to demonize America and Britain in the late 1930s and continued after Japan bombed Pearl Harbor in December 1941. Such demonizing propaganda included the Australian and New Zealand military forces, which the Japanese were also fighting in the Pacific theater. Japan was additionally engaged in a propaganda war with China, which it had attacked in 1937, and the Japanese subsequently experienced a strong resistance movement from

Chinese propagandists who relied heavily on cartoons to rally support against their occupiers.

In 1936, the Home Ministry created an Information and Propaganda Committee, which issued official press statements and worked on censorship issues. The following year the committee was upgraded to a department and with its new power it began applying censorship guidelines to all Japanese media. In 1940 the department became the Cabinet Information Bureau, which consolidated separate propaganda departments from the army, navy, and Foreign Ministry, giving it total control over all news, advertising, and public events. This bureau dealt only with civilian affairs, leaving war bulletins to the press departments of the army and navy. Due to paper shortages, the government suppressed many magazines and newspapers, leaving only a few survivors by the end of the war.

Most visual propaganda was produced outside the Home Ministry. In 1938 an exhibition of commercial art from Japan, Germany, and Italy introduced new visual styles from abroad and in 1940 the Cabinet Information Bureau began to work with a civilian group, the Hodo Gijutsu Kenkyukai (Society for the Study of Media Technology), known also by its abbreviated name, Hoken. Its members included some of Japan's leading art directors and graphic designers—Yamana Ayao; Arai Seiichiro (1907–d.o.d. unconfirmed), an art director for the Morinaga confectionary company; Tada Hokuu (1889–1948); and Kiichi Akabane (1910–d.o.d. unconfirmed), a finalist in the poster competition for the 1940 Japanese summer Olympic Games, which were ultimately canceled. Together, they and their colleagues produced posters and exhibition panels for different ministries and organizations. Among the group's themes were civilian activities such as the conservation of electricity and the encouragement of calisthenics. A strong theme was the warnings against careless talk, which was expressed in a particularly cogent poster that depicted only a pair of lips and a brief text: "Prevent Espionage".

Advertising agencies were also a primary source of war posters, with many commissioned by the Imperial Rule Assistance Association. Themes included encouraging civil defense, promoting bond drives, boosting war production, and recruiting young men for military service. Styles and techniques varied from realistic painting to modern conceptual graphics. Airbrush use was prevalent in a number of posters, and photography was also occasionally adopted. The Japanese characters that conveyed the texts were frequently bold and blocky, reflecting the influence of the Russian Constructivists that was first seen in Japanese avant-garde graphics of the 1920s and 1930s.

Like Germany and to a lesser extent the United States, Japan was creating propaganda for multiple audiences: citizens at home; people abroad; the former European colonies and its own colonies that were being brought under the umbrella of the Co-Prosperity Sphere; and enemy combatants.

Photojournalism was a strong element of propaganda directed to home audiences and to those abroad. In February 1938 the Cabinet Information Bureau began to publish a photographic propaganda magazine, *Shashin shuho* (*Pictorial Weekly*). Its editorial policy mixed a glorification of the armed forces with lifestyle stories ranging from coverage of a swim team to a photo essay on the men who worked on a fishing trawler. As it was an official publication that was circulated by neighborhood associations, it reached a wide audience. Its photographers included the best documentarians of the 1930s such as Domon Ken and Kimura Ihee, whose photographs graced the covers and contributed to the content of the magazine. Domon and Kimura had previously worked for *Nippon*, the pictorial magazine that was founded in 1934 (see Chapter 36). Though *Life* magazine, which had begun publication only a short time after that, was surely a model for *Shashin shuho*, it is more than likely that the propagandistic tone of the photo essays derived from other publications such as *USSR in Construction. Shashin shuho* was an important vehicle of domestic propaganda for the Cabinet Information Bureau, which continued to publish it until July 1945, just a month before the United States dropped an atomic bomb on Hiroshima.

The influence of the new Japanese documentary photography of the 1930s was also evident in another pictorial magazine, *Front*, a large-format publication that began in 1942, just after the Pacific War started. *Front* was edited and published by Tohosha (Far East Company), a creative group of civilians that the Intelligence Bureau of the Army General Staff Office brought together a year earlier. Like *USSR in Construction*, *Front*'s most obvious predecessor, the magazine's purpose was to present Japan as a nation that was militarily powerful as well as socially cohesive. Each issue was dedicated to a separate theme such as the army, the navy, or parachuting, which its writers and photographers explored in depth.

Initially published in 15 languages, *Front* was directed to Japan's enemies and to the colonies that the nation sought to incorporate in the Greater East Asia Co-Prosperity Sphere. Chairman of the Tohosha board was Okada Sozo (1903–1983), who was to found the documentary film company Tokyo Cinema in the 1950s. Sozo brought in the literary critic Hayashi Tatsuo (1896–1984) along with Hara Hiromu as the graphic designer and Kimura Ihee as head of the photography department. *Front* emulated *USSR in Construction* in numerous ways. A number of its themes derived directly from its Soviet predecessor, as did its tabloid size and use of multicolor rotogravure printing. Photomontage was widely adopted, as was a style of photo essay in which individual photographs were combined as elements of larger thematic compositions. Besides Kimura, *Front* employed other documentary photographers including Hamaya Hiroshi (1915–1999), Hayashi Shigeo (1918–2002), Kikuchi Shunkichi (1916–1990), Sonobe Kiyoshi (1921–1996), and Hayashi Shigeru (1918–1990).

Cartoons also played a role in Japanese propaganda. By the time World War II began, Japan already had a long history of cartoon magazines, which started with the British-influenced *Japan Punch* in 1862. In November 1940, the New Cartoonists Association, a group that supported the New Order, began to publish *Manga*, a monthly magazine of cartoons, comic strips, and articles. It had the support of the Government Information Bureau and by mid-1941 had also received the imprimatur of the Propaganda Division of the Imperial Rule Assistance Association. *Manga*'s editor was the cartoonist Kondo Hidezo (1908–1979), who had previously published his cartoons in *Tokyo Puck* and the *Yomiuri Shimbun*. For *Manga*, Kondo drew most of the covers and many of the two-page color spreads. Cartoons in the magazine attacked and ridiculed the enemy, especially enemy political leaders, Roosevelt, Churchill, and Chiang Kai-shek. As the war progressed, and particularly as Japan began to experience the force of enemy attacks, these leaders were portrayed in progressively demonized images, sometimes even as animals with human heads. Cartoonists also created some of the propaganda leaflets that the Japanese dropped on enemy soldiers, especially the Australians, whom they taunted with drawings of British and American soldiers making time with their women while they were at the front.

China

Cartoons were additionally used as a weapon against the Japanese. Provoked by Japan's invasion of their country, Chinese cartoonists declared "cartoon warfare" (*manhua zhan*), a term coined by the cartoonist Wang Dunqing (1899–1990), a key figure in the early Chinese cartoon movement. In July 1937, a group of cartoonists formed the National Salvation Cartoon Association, which created a propaganda team, the Cartoon Propaganda Corps, led by Ye Qianyu (1907–1995), author of the famous Shanghai comic strip, *Mr. Wang*. As they moved from town to town, the eight members of the Propaganda Corps conceived their mission as encouraging all citizens to resist the Japanese as well as raising the morale of Chinese soldiers at the front. They created cartoon street shows, recording Japanese brutality in cartoons they painted on huge white pieces of cloth. They also staged anti-Japanese cartoon exhibitions that drew large crowds. These activities were coupled with a magazine they edited called *Resistance Cartoons*. In 1940 the Propaganda Corps disbanded and its members scattered to different cities. Other teams were also formed and engaged in similar activities. Guangzhou was a cartoon center, but when it fell to the Japanese in 1938, Hong Kong took its place.

As many as 800 Chinese cartoonists were at work during the war, producing the hundreds of cartoon images that appeared on posters and in newspapers, pamphlets, and leaflets. Cartoonists drew quickly and tried to keep up with current events. A new genre, the "woodcut cartoon" (*muke manhua*), emerged when it became difficult to obtain zinc printing plates. Another new form of presentation, "picture storytelling" (*jiehua*), was devised to explain the cartoons that were painted on the cloth banners. The drawing style was relatively crude, but the images were graphic and addressed the immediate effects of the war. An exemplar of this approach is Feng Zikai, also a painter and writer, whose simple lines and brush strokes reduced his drawings to bare essentials. Some cartoonists developed a serial technique, presenting a sequence of drawings to tell a story.

Many Chinese wartime cartoonists were intent on shifting the audience for cartoons from the middle class, who encountered them in popular magazines, to the peasants, whom they engaged with cartoon shows and events in their villages. Another tendency was to go directly to the battlefront to document the actual fighting. Shen Yiqian (1908–1944) was the first to do this. After his initial encounters, he formed a team of artists who traveled from one battlefield to another to record the struggle of the Chinese soldiers. Another leader among the traveling cartoonists was Zhao Wangyun (1906–1977), who did not specialize in battlefield drawings but instead forcefully portrayed the spirit and determination of rural peasants in their fight against the Japanese.

United States

President Roosevelt established the Office of War Information in June 1942. His intention was to consolidate the efforts of various other agencies that he had previously sanctioned to disseminate information about the war. In March 1941, he had created the Division of Information of the Office of Emergency Management (OEM) as the principal source of news about government defense activities, but he did not give it adequate support. However, the OEM turned its attention to other activities, namely the formation of the Office of Civil Defense. Founded in May 1941, that office's purpose was to facilitate participation of all persons in civilian defense activities and protect the population in case of war.

In July 1941, President Roosevelt appointed William Donovan to head a new Office of the Coordinator of Information, whose responsibility was to counter Axis propaganda abroad. Donovan aroused the ire of many officials with his secretive methods and use of espionage to collect vital intelligence. He also had to deal with the Foreign Information Service, an agency that was set up a month later. Initially located within Donovan's office, its intention as stated by its director, the playwright Robert Sherwood, was to explain to the world outside the United States the American government's aims and purposes. One of its important achievements was creating the Voice of America, which broadcast radio programs about the United States to people around the world.

Also in July, Roosevelt established the Office of the Coordinator of Inter-American Affairs (OIAA) within the State Department, which had not been prepared to respond to the anti-American propaganda that the Axis powers were disseminating in Latin America. As Coordinator, Roosevelt chose Nelson Rockefeller, the New York businessman who was then President of the Museum of Modern Art. Rockefeller's job was to manage a program of cooperation with the Latin American nations and to counter Axis influence in the region.

In October 1941, the President approved yet another agency, the Office of Facts and Figures (OFF), which was to operate within the United States. Its role was to identify topics on which the public ought to be better informed and then to create plans for action that could be delegated to various agencies. Its director, the poet and dramatist Archibald MacLeish, who was Librarian of Congress at the time, had strong views about the war against fascism and set out to make use of truthful statements to convince the public of fascism's threat. This agency too had difficulties, in part because many journalists opposed its role and partly because the President often went around it to issue news bulletins directly to the press. Finally, the Office of War Information, headed by the journalist Elmer Davis, consolidated most activities of the prior offices and agencies, although Rockefeller convinced the President to leave the Office of the Coordinator of Inter-American Affairs out of OWI. Donovan retained control of clandestine activities as head of a new Office of Strategic Services, which became the Central Intelligence Agency after the war.

The OWI had a Domestic Branch, an Overseas Branch—the former Foreign Information Service—and a Psychological Warfare Branch, which was located in London. At home, the OWI had separate divisions for different media. These included the Bureau of Motion Pictures, the Domestic Radio Bureau, the Bureau of Campaigns, and the Bureau of Publications and Graphics. Tensions arose within the agency between two groups, those with advertising backgrounds and the writers and artists. Advertising professionals in the Domestic Branch, which was headed by Gardner Cowles Jr., the publisher of *Look* magazine, thought the agency should persuade people by any means to participate in broad campaigns such as collecting scrap metal and conserving fuel, while the writers and artists believed the OWI's mission was to build its programs on the public's basic belief in democracy's preservation as the impetus to act.

The growing influence of the advertising specialists within the Domestic Branch affected the poster artists as well as the writers. As a result, Francis Brennan (d.o.b. unconfirmed–1992), a former art director of *Fortune* magazine who headed the Graphics Bureau, resigned in early 1943. Brennan had sought to produce posters that combined the visual sophistication of modern art with the promotion of war aims, just as he had espoused modern art as a basis for *Fortune*'s covers. He was opposed by officials from the advertising world who wanted posters to look more like ads. This conflict helps to explain why so few of the hundreds of posters published by OWI had any graphic distinction. It also explains why most of the OWI posters were produced by artists and illustrators rather than graphic designers, whose approach to the various themes would have been more conceptual. Posters were also published by other government agencies and departments including the War Production Board, the War Department, the Department of the Navy, the Department of Agriculture, and the Office of Emergency Management. The corporations that were turning out military hardware also produced large numbers of posters.

A few themes were dominant. Exemplary of the posters that heralded America's military might was artist and illustrator Bernard Perlin's (1918–2014) "Avenge December 7", which depicted an American sailor brandishing a huge fist that the artist contrasted with the explosion of the USS *Arizona*, a ship that was destroyed when the Japanese bombed Pearl Harbor (Fig. 37.27). A related theme was the comparison of factory workers to soldiers, suggesting that attributes of military success such as endurance and valor were also required to produce weaponry. The theme was evident in a poster by illustrator David Stone Martin (1913–1992) that showed three hands raised, two with tools and one with a rifle. It was evident as well on James Montgomery Flagg's poster "Jap … You're Next", which depicted a muscular Uncle Sam brandishing a wrench as if it were a weapon.

A dominant propaganda theme, as in all countries, was the admonition against careless talk.

Fig. 37.27: Bernard Perlin, Avenge December 7, poster, 1942. © Image Asset Management Ltd/Alamy.

It was epitomized in an illustrative poster by John Atherton (1900–1952) featuring a cross with a helmet and cartridge belt hung from it along side the slogan *A careless word … another cross*. The artist and illustrator Stevan Dohanos (1907–1994) expressed the idea more aggressively in his poster "Award for Careless Talk", which depicted a hand with a Nazi ring holding an Iron Cross, ostensibly for someone who has given away a military secret.

The theme of which American propagandists can be least proud is the demonization of the Japanese. A sad story of the war is the internment of thousands of innocent Japanese-Americans, an egregious act that was reinforced by the harsh racial stereotypes of Japanese soldiers that appeared on posters intended to scare Americans into producing more weapons and ammunition (Fig. 37.28). Scare tactics were also evident in a poster that depicted a bombed home and car accompanied by the slogan "It Can Happen Here! Unless We Keep 'Em Firing".

A socially significant poster, though not one whose visual technique broke any new ground, featured the image of a female factory worker drawn by illustrator J. Howard Miller (1918–2004), one of a series he did for the Westinghouse Company's War Production Coordinating Committee. The poster was not widely known during the war since it was done for the company's internal use, nor was the woman originally called Rosie the Riveter as she was later, but her combination of masculine muscle flexing, painted fingernails and bright red lipstick, joined with the slogan *We Can Do It!*, not only made the point that women could do men's work but also emphasized that they could do so without sacrificing their female attributes (Fig.

Fig. 37.28: Go ahead, Take Day Off, poster, c. 1943 National Archives.

Fig. 37.29: J. Howard Miller, We Can Do It!, poster, 1942. National Archives.

37.29). Another socially groundbreaking theme was evident on an OWI poster that that showed black and white welders working together at an integrated aircraft plant. The poster's slogan, *United We Win*, had a double meaning: first, united workers of all ethnicities could defeat the enemy, and second, winning suggested the value of overcoming segregation.

A relatively small number of the posters that the OWI produced are visually exceptional, but a few stand out above the rest. The artist Ben Shahn (1898–1969) did two of them. One warned Americans of Nazi cruelty in occupied France and the other publicized the Nazi massacre of men and children in the Czech town of Lidice. Shahn represented the murdered Czech civilians by a man in chains with an

executioner's hood covering his head. Behind him is a high brick wall that prevents escape and stripped across the poster under the slogan "This is Nazi Brutality" is a description of the massacre whose urgency is conveyed as the text of a telegram (Plate 89). The stark drama of Shahn's Lidice poster can be contrasted with Norman Rockwell's illustrative paintings of the Four Freedoms that President Roosevelt enunciated in his 1941 State of the Union address. These were originally published in the *Saturday Evening Post* and proved so popular that the Office of War Information later produced them as posters in conjunction with one of the government war bond drives.

In addition to the posters for the home front that the OWI's Domestic Branch produced, its Overseas Branch in New York created a number of magazines that were directed both at the enemy and those under enemy rule. Among the experienced graphic designers who worked for the Overseas Branch was Bradbury Thompson (1911–1995), Associate Chief of the Branch's Art Section from 1942 to 1945. Collaborating closely with Tobias Moss (dates unconfirmed), who had come to the OWI from *Life* magazine, Thompson designed two publications for overseas distribution: *Victory* and *USA*. *Victory* was a lavishly illustrated magazine with ample color photography. The first issue came under fire from some Republicans in Congress, not because of its design but because they saw it as a vehicle for promoting Roosevelt's New Deal. However, OWI chief Elmer Davis defended it, and its publication continued. Another experienced designer, William Golden (1911–1959), who had been working in the promotion department at CBS, joined the OWI in 1941 but enlisted in the U.S. Army shortly thereafter and went to Europe, where he served as art director of army training manuals. Other graphic designers such as Will Burtin (1908–1972), who emigrated to the United States from Germany in 1939 and became a leader in post-war information design, also designed training materials. Burtin used photography and diagramming techniques to teach young Army Air Force recruits how to become aerial gunners or to take a rifle apart and reassemble it.

Besides the magazines that the OWI's Overseas Branch was producing for foreign consumption, another team of writers and artists in New York was putting together *Yank*, a weekly magazine published by the army and eventually circulated in 21 editions around the world. Staffed entirely by servicemen and based on an idea of Egbert White (1894–1976), who had an important role in establishing newspapers for soldiers that were written and edited by them, *Yank*, which was directed exclusively to a readership of servicemen,

Fig. 37.30: Antonio Arias Bernal, United for Victory, poster, c. 1942. Library of Congress.

appeared between 1942 and 1945 and achieved a readership of several million. To some extent it was modeled on *Life* magazine. Its cover format mimicked *Life* to a great degree, although the images were as often art as they were photographs. *Yank* employed numerous sketch artists such as Jack Coggins (1911–2006), known for the illustrations he did for *Life* and the *Saturday Evening Post*; Robert Greenhalgh (dates unconfirmed), previously an illustrator for the *Chicago Tribune* and *Esquire*; and Howard Brodie (1915–2010), who had formerly worked for the *San Francisco Chronicle*. *Yank* also published the *G.I. Joe* cartoons of David Breger (1908–1970) and the well-known cartoon *Sad Sack* created by George Baker (1915–1975). Besides sketches from the different battlefronts, the magazine featured the work of combat photographers such as Slim Aarons (1916–2006) and David Conover (1919–1983), who is credited with publishing in *Yank*'s renowned pinup section the first photographs of Marilyn Monroe, then known as Norma Jean Dougherty.

The Office of the Coordinator of Inter-American Affairs (OCIA), which created propaganda for Latin America that opposed the Axis powers, made better use of modern designers for its graphics than did the OWI. At least three of its posters were produced by E. McKnight Kauffer, who had earlier established a reputation with his work for the London Underground in the early 1920s. Kauffer's posters for the OCIA usually featured a single image such as the menacing head of a Nazi officer or an abstracted profile of Lady Liberty set against a solid colored background. Given Rockefeller's involvement with the Museum of Modern Art, it is not surprising that he would have been more inclined to commission modern designers to do his posters. Others were created by Herbert Bayer, and the Mexican caricaturist and film poster artist Antonio Arias Bernal, who did several posters with caricatured figures (Fig. 37.30) and a powerful one, "Like a Single Man", that depicted a towering soldier with a rifle whose feet were planted in the two continents of North and South America. The OCIA also hired graphic designer Lester

Beall to design a large-format Spanish language book, "Hacia La Victoria" ("Towards Victory"), that featured photographs by Edward Steichen, whom Rockefeller would have known as the curator of the Museum of Modern Art's important exhibition, Road to Victory. Carl Sandburg, author of the text for the MoMA exhibition, wrote the book's copy.

Modern graphic design was also evident in the Office of Emergency Management (OEM), where Charles Coiner was appointed art consultant to its Division of Information in 1940. There he was able to do for modern graphics what Frances Brennan could not do in the Graphics Bureau of the OWI. Coiner's reputation as an art director for N. W. Ayer in the 1930s was based on his use of modern art in the agency's advertising campaigns. He continued this policy at the Office of Emergency Management through publishing posters by such modern designers as Herbert Matter, Leo Lionni (1910–1999), Lester Beall, and Jean Carlu. Matter

was a recognized Swiss poster designer who arrived in America in 1936. Lionni had done advertising design in Italy before moving to the United States in 1939, while Carlu, one of the important French poster designers of the 1920s and 1930s along with A. M. Cassandre, Paul Colin, and Charles Leupot, had come to America in 1939 to organize the French Pavilion for the World's Fair, was stranded because of the war, and did not return to France until 1953. His poster for the OEM, "America's answer! Production", which depicted a gloved hand tightening a bolt that was also the letter O in "Production," was based on a conceptual idea that was in sharp contrast to the illustrative posters of workers that normally hung on wartime factory walls (Fig. 37.31). Coiner also art directed another poster with a more abstract idea, "He's Watching You", by illustrator Glenn Grohe (1912–1956), which featured the helmeted head of a man whom viewers had difficulty identifying as a German.

In 1941, Coiner developed an identity program

Fig. 37.31: Jean Carlu, America's answer! Production, poster, 1942. Library of Congress.

for the OEM's Office of Civil Defense, assisted by Colonel Walter B. Burn. The program's basic symbol consisted of the red letters CD, which formed a circle inside a white triangle that was enclosed by a blue disk. Coiner then developed a related visual system with separate icons to identify the different auxiliary workers of the Citizen's Defense Corps such as firemen, nurses, rescue workers, and air raid wardens. He also did an identity program for the National War Fund in 1943. For that program he used a variation of the blue eagle that he had devised as a symbol for the National Recovery Administration ten years earlier, but in the updated version he bracketed the eagle with two horizontal red bars, each containing several stars. The symbol was conceived for flexible use in various statewide campaigns, with or without the lettering, "National War Fund. For our Own—For Our Allies".

Coiner had a hand as well in the ground-breaking series of wartime advertisements that Chicago's Container Corporation of America (CCA) produced for *Fortune* magazine in order to publicize the wartime use of its paperboard products. As an art director at Container's Philadelphia advertising agency, N. W. Ayer, Coiner was in a position to hire designers for the CCA campaign. Instead of playing on sentiments of patriotism as many companies did, the CCA ads were informative and conceptually challenging in the way they explained to viewers how CCA paperboard products were aiding the war effort. Some were produced by American designers and illustrators such as Matthew Liebowitz (1918–1974), and Paul Nonnast (1918–d.o.d. unconfirmed), as well as Container's corporate art director Egbert Jacobson, while many were by émigré modernists to whom Coiner had been particularly helpful. They included not only graphic designers—Herbert Bayer, Herbert Matter, and Jean Carlu—but also artists such as Fernand Léger. Coiner also hired the American avant-garde photographer Man Ray, who had previously done a striking poster for the London Underground.

Among American museums, the Museum of

Modern Art played a particularly important role in the war effort by mounting war-related exhibitions and sponsoring poster competitions. Its first competition, Posters for National Defense, took place in April 1941. The two themes were the U.S. Army Air Corps and National Defense Savings Bonds and Stamps. The respective winners were Joseph Binder, the prominent Austrian advertising poster designer who had emigrated to the United States in 1934, and the painter and illustrator John Atherton. MoMA's second involvement with posters was the 1942 National War Poster Competition, which it co-sponsored with Artists for Victory and the Council for Democracy. Prizes were offered in eight different categories including Production, Sacrifice, Loose Talk, and The Nature of the Enemy. Perhaps the best-known poster from that competition was in the category This is the Enemy—Karl Koehler's and Victor Ancona's depiction of a stern Prussian-like Nazi general in whose monocle a hanging man was reflected. Though it garnered the support of the judges, who included Charles Coiner and Frances Brennan, it was not reproduced for wide distribution, nor is it likely to have been effective since the portrayal of the general was too serenely depicted to arouse fear in the public. Another well-known poster from the competition was Austrian émigré Henry Koerner's "Someone Talked". It showed a large hand made up of a crumpled newspaper with a finger pointing to a small man who was supposedly responsible for a ship that was sunk by an enemy submarine, as indicated in a headline embedded in the hand. More than 2,200 posters were entered in the competition and of these about 200 were exhibited at the Museum of Modern Art and then at the National Gallery of Art in Washington. It is not clear whether government agencies actually printed and distributed any of these posters despite the publicity they received from the museums. Also in 1942, MoMA mounted a third poster exhibition, A Hemisphere United, consisting of designs that forged links between the Americas. Aligned with the objectives of Nelson Rockefeller's Office of the Coordinator of

Inter-American Affairs, the exhibition featured entries by artists and graphic designers from both the United States and Latin America.

MoMA also presented two thematic propaganda exhibits—Road to Victory and Airways to Peace—which represented the most advanced techniques of exhibit design to date. Both were designed by Herbert Bayer, who had done MoMA's important Bauhaus exhibit in 1938. Road to Victory, mounted in 1942, was curated by the photographer Edward Steichen with texts by the poet Carl Sandburg. It was a paean to America and its power to fight against fascism. Bayer created a pathway through the display of large photos that moved the viewer from images of Native Americans through scenes of farming, then industry, and on to a large blow-up of the bombing of Pearl Harbor. It concluded with sizeable photographs of American troops in action interspersed with scenes that depicted America's hopes for the future. The designer created dramatic lighting and arranged the photographs at different scales and angles to enhance their impact on the viewer.

A year later, Bayer designed Airways to Peace, which Monroe Wheeler of the museum's staff organized. For this exhibit he devised an immersive display that featured a large walk-in globe to house the maps, globes, charts, and other paraphernalia that told the story of how air travel had changed the world for both good and the ills of war. Besides the propaganda exhibits at MoMA, there were also large exhibits with photomurals, dioramas, and innovative display techniques in the Rockefeller Center that the Office of War Information organized on such themes as This is Our War and The Nature of the Enemy.

Mexico

The United States was spending considerable funds through its Office of the Coordinator of Inter-American Affairs in the State Department to foster opposition to the Axis powers in Latin America. One aspect of the U.S. message, however, was that the Latin American countries and the United States shared not only a hatred of fascism but also a favorable view of democracy as it was practiced in the United States. The pro-Americanism that the State Department encouraged was not part of the anti-fascist efforts of radical Latin American artists such as the members of Mexico's Taller de Gráfica Popular. While these artists opposed the Nazis, many were Communists. Influenced by the Mexican mural painters of the 1920s, their anti-fascist imagery was graphic and visceral, akin to the posters of the Russian Revolution or the radical political graphics of John Heartfield.

Members of the Taller de Gráfica Popular did illustrations for the anti-fascist press, created backdrops for rallies, produced posters, and organized exhibitions against fascism. Collaborating with the Liga Pro-Cultura Alemana, a group of fiercely anti-fascist German expatriates, they created 18 large lithographed posters to advertise a series of anti-fascist lectures in 1938 (Fig. 37.32). Posters by Leopoldo Méndez, Pablo O'Higgins, Alfredo Zalce, and others conveyed tough graphic images to illustrate the horror of Nazism. O'Higgins, for example, depicted a man chained to a Nazi swastika, paraphrasing an earlier photomontage of John Heartfield's, while Leopoldo Méndez showed a figure on another poster with a megaphone for a head holding a Molotov cocktail and blaring Nazi propaganda across Mexico. The Taller artists also produced posters in support of the Red Army, and at the war's end, Ángel Bracho designed one entitled Victoria (Victory), whose dominant icon was a large flag with a red star, waving above the crumbling symbols of fascism.

Links to the German émigrés were also fostered by Hannes Meyer, the left-wing architect and former Bauhaus director who had come to Mexico in 1939. Meyer had begun to work with an exile organization, Alemania Libre (Free Germany), which had a small press, El Libro Libre (The Free Book), that he used to bring out a remarkable publication, El Libro Negro del Terror Nazi en Europa (The Black Book of Nazi

Fig. 37.32: El Nazismo, poster, 1938. CONADICOV archives.

Terror in Europe). It consisted of texts, photogaphs, drawings, and prints that portrayed the tragic effects of Nazi actions in Europe. Writers included major German authors in exile, along with others from Russia, Mexico, and other countries. Also included was work by an international group of visual artists, primarily recognized leftists. Besides the reproduction of numerous prints by artists from the Taller Gráfica Popular, the book featured art by Kathe Kollwitz, John Heartfield, Frans Masereel, and William Gropper. Images included some of the savage atrocities that the Nazis committed, especially the deportation of Jews to the death camps and torture methods of the Gestapo. Since the book was published in Spanish, its influence and the important information it included were limited to the Spanish language community. Perhaps due to the considerable number of leftist writers and artists who

contributed, the American ambassador to Mexico took no interest in it and no efforts were made to translate it into English.

The Mexican government also sponsored the production of anti-Nazi posters. Besides the artists of the Taller de Grafica Popular, poster designers in another group, the Artistas Libre de Mexico (Free Artists of Mexico), created patriotic posters that were widely displayed on walls, buses, and also in shops. Artists in this group included the painters Julio Prieto (1912–1977), Santos Balmori (1899–1992), Gabriel Fernández Ledesma and the painter and printmaker José Chávez Machado (dates unconfirmed). Their posters supported the government of President Manuel Ávila Camacho, while also attacking Nazi Germany.

Bibliography
Bibliographic essay

Books on different subjects were sources of information for this chapter. Considerable literature on World War II weapons exists. *The Encyclopedia of Weapons of World War II* edited by Chris Bishop was indispensible as it provided separate entries for several hundred weapons of all types that Allied and Axis forces used. On warfare, Robert Citino, *Armored Forces: History and Sourcebook* and *The Encyclopedia of Twentieth Century Warfare* edited by Dr. Noble Frankland were helpful.

Edward R. Zilbert, *Albert Speer and the Nazi Ministry of Arms: Economic Institutions and Industrial Production in the German War Economy* is a thorough account of how weapons production was organized in Germany. For material on how the United States organized for wartime manufacturing see the following: Paul A. Koistinen, *Arsenal of World War II: The Political Economy of American Warfare, 1940–1945* and *The Military-industrial Complex: A Historical Perspective*; Gerald D. Nash, *World War II and the West: Reshaping the Economy*; Donald M. Nelson, *Arsenal of Democracy: The Story of American War Production*; and R. Elberton Smith, *The Army and Economic Mobilization*. Three books that discuss the cooperation of American businesses with Germany are Edwin Black, *IBM and the Holocaust: The Strategic Alliance between Nazi Germany and America's Most Powerful Corporation*; Henry Ashby Turner Jr., *General Motors and the Nazis: The Struggle for Control of Opel, Europe's Biggest Carmaker*; and Mira Wilkins and Frank Ernest Hill, *American Business Abroad: Ford on Six Continents*. Arthur Pulos, *The American Design Adventure, 1940–1975* describes the contributions of American industrial designers to the war effort as do Pat Kirkham, *Charles and Ray Eames: Designers of the Twentieth Century* and monographs on Henry Dreyfuss and Brooks Stevens.

Books on the history of computers, control engineering, ergonomics, and operations research include Michael Williams, *A History of Computing Technology*, 2nd ed.; Paul E. Ceruzzi, *Reckoners: The Prehistory of the Digital Computer, From Relays to the Stored Program Concept, 1935–1945*; Stuart Bennett, *A History of Control Engineering, 1930–1955*; David A Mindell, *Between Human and Machine: Feedback, Control, and Computing before Cybernetics*; David Meister, *The History of Human Factors and Ergonomics*; Saul I. Gass and Assad A. Arjang, *An Annotated Timeline of Operations Research: An Informal History*; and Raúl Rojas and Ulf Hashagen, *The First Computers – History and Architectures*. Joseph McCloskey's articles on the beginnings of operations research in Great Britain and the United States were invaluable. See "The Beginnings of Operations Research: 1934–1941," *Operations Research* 35, no. 1 (January–February 1987); "British Operational Research in World War II," *Operations Research* 35, no. 3 (May–June 1987); and "U.S. Operations Research in World War II," *Operations Research* 35, no. 6 (November–December 1987). James Phinney Baxter, *Scientists Against Time* describes the Office of Scientific Research and Development, the agency where much of American weapons research was conducted.

Design for the American home front is covered in Cynthia Lee Henthorn, *From Submarines to Suburbs: Selling a Better America, 1939–1959* and to some degree in John Morton Blum's definitive *V was for Victory: Politics and American Culture during World War II*. British Utility schemes are discussed in Judy Attfield, ed., *Utility Reassessed: The Role of Ethics in the Practice of Design*; Harriet Dover, *Home Front Furniture: British Utility Design, 1941–1951* and the exhibition catalog *Utility Furniture and Fashion, 1941–1951*. The exhibition catalog *Charlotte Perriand* and Charlotte Benton's article "From Tubular Steel to Bamboo: Charlotte Perriand, the Migrating *Chaise-longue* and Japan," *Journal of Design History* 11, no. 1 (1998) describe Charlotte Perriand's wartime activity in Japan.

There is ample literature on World War II propaganda, especially on poster design. Anthony Rhodes' *Propaganda: The Art of Persuasion, WWII*, edited by Victor Margolin, is a broad survey of the topic. Books about the posters of all nations include

Joseph Darracott and Belinda Loftus, *Second World War Posters*; Mario De Micheli, *Manifesti della Seconda Guerra Mondiale*; Denis Judd, *Posters of World War Two*; Peter Paret, Beth Irwin Lewis, and Paul Paret, *Persuasive Images: Posters of War and Revolution from the Hoover Institution Archives*; *What Did You Do in the War Daddy?: A Visual History of Propaganda Posters*; and, Zbyněk Zeman, *Selling the War: Art and Propaganda in World War II*. The definitive book on Soviet Tass posters is Peter Kort Zegers and Douglas Druick, eds., *Windows on the War: Soviet Tass Posters at Home and Abroad, 1941–1945*. Victoria Bonnell's *Iconography of Power: Soviet Political Posters under Lenin and Stalin* has a section on World War II as does Klaus Waschik and Nina Baburina, *Werben für die Utopie: Russische Plakatkunst des 20. Jahrhunderts*. Aristotle A. Kallis, *Nazi Propaganda and the Second World War* describes the policies and politics of German propaganda, while *State of Deception: The Power of Nazi Propaganda* puts more emphasis on the visual representation of specific themes. See also Andreas Fleischer and Frank Kämpfer, "The Political Poster in the Third Reich," in Brandon Taylor and Wilfried van der Will, eds., *The Nazification of Art: Art, Design, Music, Architecture & Film in the Third Reich*. Erwin Schockel, *Das Politische Plakat: Eine Psychologische Betrachtung* is a study of propaganda posters that the Nazi Party published.

British posters are specifically discussed in John D. Cantwell, *Images of War: British Posters, 1939–1945* and Oliver Green, *Underground Art: London Transport Posters, 1908 to the Present*, 2nd. ed. Naomi Games, Catherine Moriarty, and June Rose, *Abram Games: His Life and Work* has an extensive section on Games's WWII posters. Three books with ample information on wartime propaganda in occupied France are Stéphane Marchetti, *Images d'une Certaine France: Affiches, 1939–1945*; Laurent Gervereau and Denis Peschanski, *La Propagande sous Vichy, 1940–1944*; and *Signes de la Collaboration et de la Résistance* with essays by Michel Wlassikoff and Philippe Delangle. On Japan,

Barak Kushner's *The Thought War: Japanese Imperial Propaganda* has an excellent section on advertising, art direction, and graphic design in wartime, while Gennifer Weisenfeld makes some mention of this subject in her article "Publicity and Propaganda in 1930s Japan: Modernism as Method," *Design Issues* 25, no. 5 (Autumn 2009). Rei Okamoto's chapter "Images of the Enemy in the Wartime *Manga* Magazine, 1941–1945," published in John Lent, ed., *Illustrating Asia: Comics, Humor Magazines, and Picture Books* was the source for my discussion of Japanese wartime cartoons. Chang-Tai Hung, *War and Popular Culture: Resistance in Modern China, 1937–1945* provides a detailed account of China's anti-Japanese poster movement.

Alan M. Winkler, *The Politics of Propaganda: The Office of War Information, 1942–1945* describes the founding and operation of America's propaganda agency, while discussions of American posters are dispersed through all the general books on World War II posters and propaganda. Contributions of individual graphic designers can be found in monographs on Herbert Bayer and Lester Beall as well as in Roger Remington and Barbara Hodik, *Nine Pioneers in American Graphic Design* and Remington's *American Modernism; Graphic Design, 1920 to 1960*. Leo Margolin, *Paper Bullets: A Brief History of Psychological Warfare in World War II* contains a discussion of how propaganda leaflets were used by all sides.

Books
General

Atkins, Jacqueline M., ed. *Wearing Propaganda: Textiles on the Home Front in Japan, Britain, and the United States, 1931–1945*. New Haven and London: Yale University Press, 2007. Published for the Bard Graduate Center for Studies in the Decorative Arts, Design, and Culture.

Balfour, Michael. *Propaganda in War, 1939–1945: Organizations, Policies and Publics in Britain and Germany*. London, Boston, and Henley: Routledge and Kegan Paul, 1979.

Bennett, Stuart. *A History of Control Engineering, 1930–1955*. Stevenage: Peter Peregrinus Ltd, 1993.

Bishop, Chris, ed. *The Encyclopedia of Weapons of World War II*. New York: Metro Books, 1998.

Ceruzzi, Paul E. *Reckoners: The Prehistory of the Digital Computer, From Relays to the Stored Program Concept, 1935–1945*. Westport, CT, and London: Greenwood Press, 1983.

Citino, Robert M. *Armored Forces: History and Sourcebook*. Westport, CT, and London: Greenwood Press, 1994.

Crawford, Anthony, ed. *Posters of World War I and World War II in the George C. Marshall Research Foundation*. With an introduction by O. W. Riegel. Charlottesville: University of Virginia Press, 1979 (A George C. Marshall Research Foundation Publication).

Darracott, Joseph and Belinda Loftus. *Second World War Posters*. London: Imperial War Museum, 1972.

De Micheli, Mario. *Manifesti della Seconda Guerra Mondiale*. Milano: Fratelli Fabbri Editori, 1972.

Eskilson, Stephen J. *Graphic Design: A New History*. London: Lawrence King Publishing, 2007.

European Resistance Movements, 1939–1945. New York, Oxford, London, and Paris: Pergamon Press, 1960.

Frankland, Dr. Noble, ed. *The Encyclopedia of Twentieth Century Warfare*. New York: Crown Publishers, 1989.

Gass, Saul I. and Arjang A. Assad. *An Annotated Timeline of Operations Research: An Informal History*. New York: Kluwer Academic Publishers, 2007.

Guidot, Raymond. *Histoire du Design, 1940–1990*. Paris: Éditions Hazan, 1994.

Heller, Steven. *Iron Fists: Branding the 20th Century Totalitarian State*. London and New York: Phaidon, 2008.

Heppenheimer, T. A. *A Brief History of Flight: From Balloons to Mach 3 and Beyond*. New York: John Wiley & Sons, 2001.

Jubert, Roxane. *Typography and Graphic Design: From Antiquity to the Present*. Forewords by Ellen Lupton and Serge Lemoine. Paris: Flammarion, 2006.

Judd, Denis. *Posters of World War Two*. New York: St. Martin's Press, 1973.

Margolin, Leo. *Paper Bullets: A Brief History of Psychological Warfare in World War II*. New York: Froben Press, 1946.

Matricardi, Paolo. *The Concise History of Aviation*. New York: Crescent Books, 1984.

Meister, David. *The History of Human Factors and Ergonomics*. Mahwah, NJ, and London: Lawrence Erlbaum Associates, 1999.

Paret, Peter, Beth Irwin Lewis, and Paul Paret. *Persuasive Images: Posters of War and Revolution from the Hoover Institution Archives*. Princeton, NJ: Princeton University Press, 1992.

Parker, Geoffrey, ed. *The Cambridge History of Warfare*. Cambridge: Cambridge University Press, 2005.

Raizman, David. *History of Modern Design: Graphics and Products since the Industrial Revolution*. London: Lawrence King Publishing, 2003.

Rhodes, Anthony. *Propaganda: The Art of Persuasion, WWII*. Edited by Victor Margolin. New York: Chelsea House, 1976.

Rojas, Raúl and Ulf Hashagen. *The First Computers – History and Architectures*. Cambridge, MA, and London: MIT Press, 2000.

Smil, Vaclav. *Transforming the Twentieth Century: Technical Innovations and Their Consequences*. Oxford and New York: Oxford University Press, 2006.

War, Revolution and Peace: Propaganda Posters From the Hoover Institution Archives, 1914–1945. An Exhibition Organized by Paula Harper and Marcia Cohn Growdon. Palo Alto: Stanford University Art Department, c. 1970.

Weill, Alain. *The Poster: A Worldwide Survey and History*. Boston: G. K. Hall & Co., 1985.

What Did You Do in the War Daddy? A Visual History of Propaganda Posters. Introduction by Peter Stanley. A selection from the Australian War Memorial. Melbourne, Oxford, and New York: Oxford University Press, 1983.

Williams, Michael R. *A History of Computing Technology*,

2nd ed. Los Alamitos, CA: IEEE Computer Society Press, 1997.

Zeman, Zbyněk. *Selling the War: Art and Propaganda in World War II*. New York: Exeter Books, 1978.

Germany

Batty, Peter. *The House of Krupp; The Steel Dynasty That Armed the Nazis*. With a New Afterword by the Author. New York: Cooper Square Press, 2001 (c. 1966).

Burke, Christopher. *Paul Renner: the Art of Typography*. New York: Princeton Architectural Press, 1998.

Herf, Jeffrey. *Reactionary Modernism: Technology, Culture, and Politics in Weimar and the Third Reich*. Cambridge: Cambridge University Press, 1984.

Kallis, Aristotle A. *Nazi Propaganda and the Second World War*. Houndmills: Palgrave Macmillan, 2005.

Ludvigsen, Karl. *Battle for the Beetle*. Foreword by Ivan Hirst. Cambridge, MA: Bentley Publishers, 2000.

Nelson, Walter Henry. *Small Wonder: The Amazing Story of the Volkswagen*. Boston and Toronto: Little, Brown and Co., 1967 (c. 1965).

Rutz, Rainer. *Signal: Eine Deutsche Auslandsillustrierte als Propagandainstrument im Zweiten Weltkrieg*. Essen: Klartextverlag, 2007.

Schockel, Erwin. *Das Politische Plakat: Eine Psychologische Betrachtung*, 2nd ed. Munich: Zentral Verlag der NSDAP, 1939.

State of Deception: The Power of Nazi Propaganda. Washington, DC: United States Holocaust Memorial Museum, 2009.

Zilbert, Edward R. *Albert Speer and the Nazi Ministry of Arms: Economic Institutions and Industrial Production in the German War Economy*. Rutherford: Fairleigh Dickinson University Press, and London: Associated University Presses, 1981.

Great Britain and the Commonwealth Nations

Attfield, Judy, ed. *Utility Reassessed: The Role of Ethics in the Practice of Design*. Manchester and New York: Manchester University Press, 1999.

Blake, Avril. *Misha Black*. London: The Design Council, 1984.

Cantwell, John D. *Images of War: British Posters, 1939–1945*. London: HMSO, 1989.

Dover, Harriet. *Home Front Furniture: British Utility Design, 1941–1951*. Aldershot: Scolar Press, 1991.

Drew, Jane. *Kitchen Planning: A Brochure of New Plans and Suggestions for Labour-Saving Kitchens*. London: The Gas Industry, 1944.

Games, Naomi, Catherine Moriarty, and June Rose. *Abram Games: His Life and Work*. New York: Princeton Architectural Press, 2003.

Green, Oliver. *Underground Art: London Transport Posters, 1908 to the Present*, 2nd. ed. London: Laurence King, 2001.

MacCarthy, Fiona. *A History of British Design, 1830–1970*. London, Boston, and Sydney: George Allen & Unwin Ltd, 1972.

Russell, Gordon. *Designer's Trade: Autobiography of Gordon Russell*. London: George Allen & Unwin Ltd, 1968.

Utility Furniture and Fashion, 1941–1951. London: Greater London Educational Authority, 1974.

Soviet Union

Bonnell, Victoria E. *Iconography of Power: Soviet Political Posters under Lenin and Stalin*. Berkeley, Los Angeles, and London: University of California Press, 1997.

Logan, Robert A., ed. *The Great Patriotic War: A Collection of World War II Soviet Propaganda Posters*. Guelph: University of Guelph Library, 1984.

Waschik, Klaus and Nina Baburina. *Werben für die Utopie: Russische Plakatkunst des 20. Jahrhunderts*. Bietigheim-Bissingen: Edition Tertium, 2003.

Zegers, Peter Kort and Douglas Druick, eds. *Windows on the War: Soviet Tass Posters at Home and Abroad, 1941–1945*. Chicago: The Art Institute of Chicago, and New Haven and London: Yale University Press, 2011.

Japan

Brandt, Kim. *Kingdom of Beauty: Mingei and the Politics of Folk Art in Imperial Japan*. Durham and London: Duke University Press, 2007.

Charlotte Perriand. Paris: Centre Pompidou, 2005.

Dower, John. *War Without Mercy: Race and Power in the Pacific War*. New York: Pantheon Books, 1986.

Duus, Peter, Ramon H. Myers, and Mark R. Peattie, eds. *The Japanese Wartime Empire, 1931–1945*. Princeton, NJ: Princeton University Press, 1996.

Hane, Mikiso. *Japan; A Short History*. Oxford: One World, 2000.

Kikuchi, Yuko. *Japanese Modernisation and Mingei Theory: Cultural Nationalism and Oriental Orientalism*. London and New York: Routledge Curzon, 2004.

Kushner, Barak. *The Thought War: Japanese Imperial Propaganda*. Honolulu:University of Hawaii Press, 2006.

Posters – Japan, 1800's–1980's. Nagoya: Bank of Nagoya Ltd, 1989.

Thornton, Richard S. *The Graphic Spirit of Japan*. New York: Van Nostrand Reinhold, 1991.

Tucker, Anne Wilkes, Kotaro Lizawa, and Naoyuki Kinoshita. *The History of Japanese Photography*. New Haven and London: Yale University Press in association with the Museum of Fine Arts, Houston, 2003.

Young, Louise. *Japan's Total Empire: Manchuria and the Culture of Wartime Imperialism*. Berkeley, Los Angeles, and London: University of California Press, 1998.

United States

Adamson, Glenn. *Industrial Strength Design: How Brooks Stevens Shaped Your World*. Milwaukee: Milwaukee Art Museum, and Cambridge, MA, and London: MIT Press, 2003.

Albrecht, Donald, ed. *World War II and the American Dream: How Wartime Building Changed a Nation*. Washington, DC: National Building Museum, and Cambridge, MA, and London: MIT Press, 1995.

Baxter, James Phinney 3rd ed. *Scientists Against Time*. Boston: Little, Brown & Co., 1946.

Black, Edwin. *IBM and the Holocaust: The Strategic Alliance between Nazi Germany and America's Most Powerful Corporation*. New York: Crown Publishers, 2001.

Blum, John Morton. *V was for Victory: Politics and American Culture during World War II*. San Diego, New York, and London: Harcourt, Brace, Jovanovich, 1976.

Bruce, Gordon. *Eliot Noyes: A Pioneer of Design and Architecture in the Age of American Modernism*. London and New York: Phaidon, 2006.

Chanzit, Gwen Finkel. *Herbert Bayer and Modernist Design in America*. Ann Arbor and London: UMI Research Press, 1987.

Cohen, Arthur A. *Herbert Bayer: The Complete Work*. Cambridge, MA, and London: MIT Press, 1984.

Duis, Perry and Scott LaFrance. *We've Got a Job to Do: Chicagoans and World War II*. Chicago: Chicago Historical Society, 1992.

Henthorn, Cynthia Lee. *From Submarines to Suburbs: Selling a Better America, 1939–1959*. Athens: Ohio University Press, 2006.

Herbert Bayer: Painter, Designer, Architect. New York: Reinhold Publishing Corp., and London: Studio Vista Ltd, 1967.

Kirkham, Pat. *Charles and Ray Eames: Designers of the Twentieth Century*. Cambridge, MA, and London: MIT Press, 1995.

Koistinen, Paul A. C. *The Military-industrial Complex: A Historical Perspective*. Foreword by Les Aspin. New York: Praeger Publishers, 1980.

—*Arsenal of World War II: The Political Economy of American Warfare, 1940–1945*. Wichita: University Press of Kansas, 2004.

Lynes, Russell. *Good Old Modern: An Intimate Portrait of the Museum of Modern Art*. New York: Atheneum, 1973.

Miekle, Jeffrey L. *American Plastic: A Cultural History*. New Brunswick, NJ: Rutgers University Press, 1995.

Mindell, David A. *Between Human and Machine: Feedback, Control, and Computing before Cybernetics.* Baltimore and London: The Johns Hopkins University Press, 2002 (Johns Hopkins Studies in the History of Technology).

Mossman, S. T. I. and P. J. T. Morris, eds. *The Development of Plastics.* London: Royal Society of Chemistry, 1994.

Nash, Gerald D. *World War II and the West: Reshaping the Economy.* Lincoln and London: University of Nebraska Press, 1990.

Nelson, Donald M. *Arsenal of Democracy: The Story of American War Production.* New York: Harcourt, Brace and Co., 1946.

Pulos, Arthur J. *The American Design Adventure, 1940–1975.* Cambridge, MA, and London: MIT Press, 1988.

Remington, R. Roger. *Lester Beall: Trailblazer of American Graphic Design.* New York and London: W. W. Norton & Co., 1996.

—*American Modernism: Graphic Design, 1920 to 1960.* London: Lawrence King Publishing, 2003.

Remington, Roger and Barbara J. Hodik. *Nine Pioneers in American Graphic Design.* Cambridge, MA, and London: MIT Press, 1989.

Smith, R. Elberton. *The Army and Economic Mobilization.* Washington, DC: Office of the Chief of Military History, Department of the Army, 1959 (United States Army in World War II; the War Department).

Turner, Henry Ashby Jr. *General Motors and the Nazis: The Struggle for Control of Opel, Europe's Biggest Carmaker.* New Haven and London: Yale University Press, 2005.

Wilkins, Mira and Frank Ernest Hill. *American Business Abroad: Ford on Six Continents.* Introduction by Allan Nevins. Detroit: Wayne State University Press, 1964.

Winkler, Alan M. *The Politics of Propaganda: The Office of War Information, 1942–1945.* New Haven and London: Yale University Press, 1978.

—*Home Front U.S.A.: America during World War II.* Arlington Heights, IL: Harlan Davidson, 1986.

France

De la Broise, Tristan and Félix Torres. *Schneider: l'Histoire en Force.* Paris: Éditions Jean-Pierre de Monza, 1996.

Marchetti, Stéphane. *Images d'une Certaine France: Affiches, 1939–1945.* Préface de Alain Weill. Lausanne: Edita, 1982.

La Propagande sous Vichy, 1940–1944. Ouvrage publié sous la direction de Laurent Gervereau et Denis Peschanski. Paris: Musée de Histoire Contemporaine de la Bibliothèque de Documentation Internationale Contemporaine, 1990.

Signes de la Collaboration et de la Résistance. Textes de Michel Wlassikoff et Philippe Delangle. Paris: Éditions Autremont, 2000.

Wlasikoff, Michel. *The Story of Graphic Design in France.* Corte Maderia, CA: Gingko Press, 2005.

Netherlands

Broos, Kees, and Paul Hefting. *Grafische Formgebung in den Niederlanden 20. Jahrhundert.* Basel: Wiese Verlag, 1993.

Kok, René and Erik Somers. *V = Victorie: Oorlogsaffiches, 1940–1945.* Amsterdam: Nederlands Instituut voor Oorlogsdocumentatie, 2003.

Purvis, Alston W. *Dutch Graphic Design, 1918–1945.* New York: Van Nostrand Reinhold, 1992.

Mexico

Caplow, Deborah. *Leopoldo Méndez: Revolutionary Art and the Mexican Print.* Austin: University of Texas Press, 2007.

Miller, Michael Nelson. *Red, White, and Green: The Maturing of Mexicanidad, 1940–1946.* El Paso: Texas Western Press, 1998 (Southwestern Studies No. 107).

Taller de Gráfica Popular, Werkstatt für Grafische Volkskunst: Plakate und Flugblätter zu Arbeiterbewegung und Gewerkschaften in Mexico, 1937–1986. Berlin: Ibero-Americanisches Institut – Preussischer Kulturbesitz, 2002.

China

Hung, Chang-Tai. *War and Popular Culture: Resistance in Modern China, 1937–1945*. Berkeley, Los Angeles, and London: University of California Press, 1994.

Chapters in books

Fleischer, Andreas and Frank Kämpfer, "The Political Poster in the Third Reich," in Brandon Taylor and Wilfried van der Will, eds. *The Nazification of Art: Art, Design, Music, Architecture & Film in the Third Reich*. Winchester: The Winchester Press, 1990.

Friedman, Mildred, "From *Futurama* to *Motorama*," in Brooke Kamin Rapaport and Kevin L. Stayton, *Vital Forms: American Art and Design in the Atomic Age, 1940–1960*. New York: Brooklyn Museum of Art in association with Harry N. Abrams Inc., 2002.

Horrigan, Brian, "The Home of Tomorrow, 1927–1945," in Joseph J. Corn, ed. *Imagining Tomorrow: History, Technology, and the American Future*. Cambridge, MA, and London: MIT Press, 1986.

Katz, Barry, "The Arts of War: 'Visual Presentation' and National Intelligence," in Richard Buchanan, Dennis Doordan, and Victor Margolin, eds. *The Designed World: Images, Objects, Environments*. Oxford and New York: Berg, 2010.

Mindell, David A. "Automation's Finest Hour: Radar and System Integration in World War II," in Agatha C. Hughes and Thomas P. Hughes, eds. *Systems, Experts, and Computers: The Systems Approach in Management and Engineering. World War II and After*. Cambridge, MA, and London: MIT Press, 2000.

Okamoto, Rei, "Images of the Enemy in the Wartime *Manga* Magazine, 1941–1945," in John Lent, ed. *Illustrating Asia: Comics, Humor Magazines, and Picture Books*. Honolulu: University of Hawaii Press, 2001.

Peattie, Mark R., "Japanese Attitudes Toward Colonialism, 1895–1945," in Ramon H. Myers and Mark R. Peattie, *The Japanese Colonial Empire, 1895–1945*. Princeton, NJ: Princeton University Press, 1984.

Rau, Erik P., "The Adoption of Operations Research in the United States during World War II," in Agatha C. Hughes and Thomas P. Hughes, eds. *Systems, Experts, and Computers: The Systems Approach in Management and Engineering. World War II and After*. Cambridge, MA, and London: MIT Press, 2000.

Articles

Benton, Charlotte, "From Tubular Steel to Bamboo: Charlotte Perriand, the Migrating *Chaise-longue* and Japan," *Journal of Design History* 11, no. 1 (1998).

Johnson, Stephen B., "Three Approaches to Big Technology: Operations Research, Systems Engineering, and Project Management," *Technology and Culture* 38, no. 4 (October 1997).

Light, Jennifer, "When Computers Were Women," *Technology and Culture* 40, no. 3 (July 1999).

Llewelyn, Mark, "Designed by Women and Designing Women: Gender, Planning and the Geographies of the Kitchen in Britain, 1917–1946," *Cultural Geographies* 11, no. 1 (2004).

McCloskey, Joseph, "The Beginnings of Operations Research: 1934–1941," *Operations Research* 35, no. 1 (January–February 1987).

—"British Operational Research in World War II," *Operations Research* 35, no. 3 (May–June 1987).

—"U.S. Operations Research in World War II," *Operations Research* 35, no. 6 (November–December 1987).

Owens, Larry, "The Counterproductive Management of Science in the Second World War: Vannevar Bush and the Office of Scientific Research and Development," *The Business History Review* 68, no. 4 (Winter 1994).

Rabinach, Anson G., "The Aesthetics of Production in the Third Reich," *Journal of Contemporary History* 11, no. 4 (October 1976).

Weisenfeld, Gennifer, "Publicity and Propaganda in 1930s Japan: Modernism as Method," *Design Issues* 25, no. 4 (Autumn 2009).

Internet

Canadian War Museum, "Propaganda/Propagande:

Canadian Wartime Propaganda," http://www. civilization.ca/cwm/exhibitions/propaganda/ poster20_e (accessed November 17, 2014).

Schubert, Frank N., *Mobilization: The U.S. Army in World War II. The 50th Anniversary.* Washington: U.S. Army Center for Military History, 1994., http://www.history.army.mil/brochures/Mobilization/mobpam.htm (accessed July 27, 20011).

Index